An Introduction to the Study of **INSECTS**

An Introduction to the

Study of **INSECTS**

Sixth Edition

Donald J. Borror
Late of The Ohio State University

Charles A. Triplehorn
The Ohio State University

Norman F. Johnson
The Ohio State University

Saunders College Publishing
Harcourt Brace College Publishers
Fort Worth   Philadelphia   San Diego
New York   Orlando   Austin   San Antonio
Toronto   Montreal   London   Sydney   Tokyo

Text typeface: Trump Mediaeval

Compositor: Omegatype

Acquisitions Editor: Edward Murphy

Production Management: P. M. Gordon Associates

Art Director: Carol C. Bleistine

Art Assistant: Doris Bruey

Text Designer: Tracy Baldwin

Cover Designer: Lawrence R. Didona

Production Manager: Merry Post

Cover credit: Milkweed Long-Horned Beetle, Tetraopes
tetraophthalmus (Foster). Courtesy of Robert S. Copeland.

Printed in the United States of America

Library of Congress Catalog Card Number: 88–043541

ISBN 0–03–025397–7

901234 039   15 14 13 12 11 10

Dr. Dwight Moore DeLong, coauthor of this book through the first five editions, died on August 23, 1984, at the age of 92. Although his main interest was in the systematics of leafhoppers, the subject of most of his 450 publications, he possessed a broad knowledge of insects—their biology, morphology, ecology, and control. This is reflected in his overall contributions to this book.

During the course of his long and distinguished career, Dr. DeLong served as major professor for 98 M.S. and 49 Ph.D. degrees in Entomology at The Ohio State University and is remembered as a legendary teacher in General and Economic Entomology and Insect Ecology courses at the undergraduate level.

We, the authors of this sixth edition of our book, fondly dedicate it to the memory of our late friend and colleague with the hope that he would have approved of our efforts.

D.J.B.
C.A.T.
N.F.J.

Preface

The importance of the role played by insects in the world of living things is becoming more appreciated each year, not only because of the attention given to the species that act as pests, but also because of the increasing realization that many species are extremely valuable to humanity. The study of insects is an important part of the training of every agriculturalist, biology teacher, and student of nature.

Many books are already available to the student or teacher interested in insects. Some give special emphasis to the biological or economic aspects, and others emphasize the taxonomic phase of entomology, but few combine emphasis on both insect study—working with insects—and identification. This book is intended to serve as a text for a beginning college course in entomology and as a guide for teachers and others interested in the study of insects. It might also serve as a text for an advanced course in systematic entomology because it contains keys for the identification of all the families of insects occurring in North America north of Mexico and keys to some subfamilies.

The discussions of morphology and physiology in this book may not be as complete as in some other books. Our aim has been to present enough material on these phases of entomology to enable the student to use the keys and to understand something of the general biology of the insects encountered. An attempt has been made to make the keys as workable as possible by illustrating most of the key characters. No attempt has been made to present keys to immature forms.

Insects should be observed and studied in the field as well as in the classroom and laboratory, and this book is designed to serve as a text for entomology courses that involve both field- and laboratory work. We realize that fieldwork is difficult or impossible in some courses, because of the season in which the course is given, the location of the school, or other factors, but many insects can be maintained indoors in cages or aquaria, and the study of living material can be substituted for field observations.

In our treatment of the various orders, we have relied to a considerable extent on the advice of specialists in deciding on the classification to follow and in updating our account of the insects in the order. In a few cases (indicated in the chapters concerned), these specialists have largely or completely rewritten the chapters for us. The bibliographies at the ends of each chapter are far from comprehensive; rather than striving for completeness, we have tried to list references that can serve as a starting point for the student interested in going further.

There have been a number of changes in the sixth edition. The chapter on development and metamorphosis has been combined with the chapter on anatomy and physiology (now Chapter 3, "The Anatomy, Physiology, and Development of Insects"), and portions of this material have been rather extensively revised. The classification in some orders has been updated, with some changes in the number of families recognized from North America. Many of the keys have been revised (e.g., Phthiráptera, Díptera, and Siphonáptera), and there have been a few changes in the illustrations. General changes have been made throughout the book, in some cases by minor revisions in the wording, and in others by completely rewriting a section or changing its content.

Many people have made valuable suggestions or criticisms regarding particular parts of this book, and others have helped with taxonomic problems or in other ways, but we are particularly indebted to the following people for assistance in preparing this edition: R. D. Alexander, B. Barris, R. W. Baumann, G. W. Byers, Chen Cheng-ping, P. S. Cwikla, D. R. Davis, F. W. Fisk, G. A. P. Gibson, J. R. Gorham, M. R. Hamerski, J. B. Heppner, R. W. Hodges, K. M. Hoffman, James B. Johnson, Joan B. Johnson, K. C. Kim, K. Krishna, E. LaRue, Jr., R. E. Lewis, N. Miller, E. L. Mockford, J. C. Morse, G. R. Needham, L. B. O'Brien, N. D. Penny, R. D. Price, G. T. Riegel, E. S. Ross, J. A. Slater, R. J. Snider, R. Taylor, B. W. Triplehorn, J. B. Whitfield, and L. Yocum.

During the preparation of the manuscript for this sixth edition of *An Introduction to the Study of Insects*, Dr. Donald J. Borror, the senior author, died on April 28, 1988. Dr. Borror's knowledge of classical languages, his keen interest in the preparation of analytical keys, and his extraordinary ability to synthesize vast amounts of information and to organize it into a logical and workable format have been the hallmark of this book since the first edition in 1952. We hope that what we have produced on these pages would meet with Dr. Borror's high standards of excellence.

C. A. Triplehorn
N. F. Johnson

Acknowledgments

Throughout previous editions a great many people have made valuable suggestions and criticisms regarding specific portions of this book or have helped solve problems of taxonomy in various orders. We would like to acknowledge their help in the past.

First Edition

J. Gordon Edwards, T. H. Hubbell, Maurice T. James, Clarence H. Kennedy, Josef N. Knull, Karl V. Krombein, John E. Lane, A. W. Lindsey, Harlow B. Mills, C. F. W. Muesebeck, Alvah Peterson, E. S. Ross, H. H. Ross, Marion R. Smith, Kathryn M. Sommerman, Louis J. Stannard, Edward S. Thomas, and E. M. Walker.

The majority of the original drawings in this book were made by or under the direction of Donald Borror. The following persons have assisted in the preparation of these drawings: Richard D. Alexander, Calvin E. Beckelheimer, Arthur C. Borror, G. Mallory Boush, William C. Costello, Edward W. Huffman, John E. Lane, Paul D. Ludwig, George W. Murphy, Robert F. Ruppel, and Celeste W. Taft. The original photographs were made principally by D. M. DeLong, assisted by Oscar Metze.

Many entomologists and a few editors have assisted with the loan of illustrations or permission to use certain illustrations previously printed in their publications. In each case where a borrowed illustration is used, its source is indicated. Special credit, we believe, should be given the following persons: James S. Ayars, Stanley F. Bailey, Richard M. Bohart, Hazel E. Branch, A. W. A. Brown, H. E. Burke, Barnard D. Burks, R. W. Burrell, C. P. Clausen, Ralph H. Davidson, Donald DeLeon, Lafe R. Edmunds, Richard C. Froeschner, B. B. Fulton, Robert Glenn, Ashley B. Gurney, David G. Hall, Philip

H. Harden, M. J. Hayell, William R. Horsfall, H. B. Hungerford, Maurice T. James, B. J. Kaston, George F. Knowlton, J. N. Knull, J. W. Leonard, Philip Luginbill, E. A. McGregor, Luis F. Martorell, John Moser, Claud R. Neiswander, Harry L. Parker, Alvah Peterson, Edward S. Ross, Herbert H. Ross, John G. Shaw, Herbert H. Smith, Kathryn M. Sommerman, R. W. Strandtmann, George R. Struble, Edwin Way Teale, C. A. Triplehorn, G. Stuart Walley, E. M. Walker, and Mrs. Blanche P. Young. To all organizations and individuals who have loaned illustrations, we wish to express our sincere thanks for permission to use their material.

Second Edition

Richard D. Alexander, Ross H. Arnett, Jr., Arthur C. Borror, Osmond P. Breland, Theodore J. Cohn, Paul H. Freytag, Theodore H. Hubbell, F. P. Ide, D. E. Johnston, Josef N. Knull, Michael Kosztarab, Alan Stone, Charles A. Triplehorn, Barry Valentine, and Richard E. White. The following have assisted with the loan of illustrations or permission to use illustrations previously printed in their publications: Richard D. Alexander, Arthur C. Borror, Adrien Robert, Charles A. Triplehorn, and Richard E. White.

Third Edition

Richard D. Alexander, Donald M. Anderson, Ross H. Arnett, Jr. (particularly for the loan of a number of illustrations of beetles), M. Wilson Britt, Barnard D. Burks, George W. Byers, Donald R. Davis, W. Donald Duckworth, J. Gordon Edwards, Frank W. Fisk, Oliver S. Flint, Richard H. Foote, Raymond J. Gagné, Robert C. Graves, Ashley B. Gurney, Robert W. Hamilton, Ronald W. Hodges, F. P. Ide, Donald E. Johnston, Josef N. Knull, L. V. Knutson, Karl V. Krombein, John D. Lattin, Paul M. Marsh, Frank W. Mead, Frank J. Moore, Thomas E. Moore, C. F. W. Muesebeck, Lois B. O'Brien, Kellie O'Neill, Vincent D. Roth, Louise M. Russell, Curtis W. Sabrosky, Howard A. Schneiderman, F. Elizabeth Sims, David R. Smith, Thomas E. Snyder, Paul J. Spangler, Ted J. Spilman, George C. Steyskal, Alan Stone, William H. Telfer, Charles A. Triplehorn, Barry D. Valentine, Luella M. Walkley, Richard E. White, Willis W. Wirth, J. Porter Woodring, and David A. Young.

Fourth Edition

Dwight Bennett, Glen Berkey, N. Wilson Britt, Harley P. Brown, Leland R. Brown, Horace R. Burke, Donald S. Chandler, Frank W. Fisk, Donald F. J. Hilton, Roger Hoopingarner, C. Dennis Hynes, Albin T. Khouw, Alice B. Kolbe, Robert J. Lavigne, John F. Lawrence, Kingston L. H. Leong, William F. Lyon, Carl R. Mappes, Frank W. Mead, Arnold Menke, Carl Mohr, Ian Moore, Martin H. Muma, Milledge Murphy, Joseph C. Schaffner, Charles L. Selman, Robbin W. Thorp, J. R. Vockeroth, Tsing Cheng Wang, and Richard E. White.

Fifth Edition

Carl W. Albrecht, Richard D. Alexander, Harold J. Ball, Richard M. Baranowski, Theodore L. Bissell, N. Wilson Britt, Horace R. Burke, J. M. Campbell, Donald S. Chandler, Joan B. Chapin, Rod L. Crawford, W. A. Drew, John S. Edwards, Wilbur R. Enns, John C. Franclemont, Paul H. Freytag, Saul I. Frommer, Lisa Gassin, J. Richard Gorham, Richard C. Hall, John B. Heppner, Ronald W. Hodges, Richard Kaae, K. C. Kim, Kingston L. H. Leong, Herbert W. Levi, Candace Martinson, Frank W. Mead, John R. Meyer, Edward L. Mockford, Carl Mohr, Lowell R. Nault, Lois B. O'Brien, J. A. Rudinsky, Lee C. Ryker, James A. Slater, Robbin W. Thorp, Robert E. Treece, Barry D. Valentine, Larry E. Watrous, Joseph E. Weaver, Quentin D. Wheeler, Richard E. White, Pedro Wygodzinsky, Kenneth V. Yeargan, and Eric Yensen.

Contents

Chapter 1   **Insects and Their Ways**

Insects are the dominant group of animals on the earth today. They far surpass all other terrestrial animals in numbers, and they occur practically everywhere. Several hundred thousand different kinds have been described—three times as many as there are in the rest of the animal kingdom—and some authorities believe that the total number of different kinds may approach 30 million. More than a thousand kinds may occur in a fair-sized backyard, and their populations often number many millions per acre.

A great many insects are extremely valuable to humans, and society could not exist in its present form without them. By their pollinating activities they make possible the production of many agricultural crops, including many orchard fruits, nuts, clovers, vegetables, cotton, and tobacco; they provide us with honey, beeswax, silk, and other products of commercial value; they serve as food for many birds, fish, and other beneficial animals; they perform valuable services as scavengers; they help keep harmful animals and plants in check; they have been useful in medicine and in scientific research; and they are looked upon as interesting animals by people in all walks of life. A few insects are harmful and cause enormous losses each year in agricultural crops and stored products, and they may transmit diseases that seriously affect the health of humans and other animals.

Insects have lived on the earth for about 350 million years, compared with less than 2 million for humans. During this time they have evolved in many directions to become adapted to life in almost every type of habitat (with the notable and puzzling exception of the sea) and have developed many unusual, picturesque, and even amazing features.

Compared with humans, insects are peculiarly constructed animals. They might be said to be inside out because their skeleton is on the outside, or upside down because their nerve cord extends along the lower side of the body and the heart lies above the alimentary canal. They have no lungs, but breathe through a number of tiny holes in the body wall—all behind the head—and the air entering these holes is distributed over the body and directly to the tissues through a multitude of tiny branching tubes. The heart and blood are unimportant in the transport of oxygen to the tissues. Insects smell with their antennae; some taste with their feet; and some hear with special organs in the abdomen, front legs, or antennae.

In an animal whose skeleton is on the outside of the body, the mechanics of support and growth are such that the animal is limited to a relatively small size. Most insects *are* relatively small; probably three-fourths or more are less than 6 mm in length. Their small size enables them to live in places that would not be available to larger animals.

1

Insects range in size from about 0.25 to 330 mm in length and from about 0.5 to 300 mm in wingspread; one fossil dragonfly had a wingspread of over 760 mm! Some of the longest insects are very slender (the 330 mm insect is a walking stick occurring in Borneo), but some beetles have a body nearly as large as one's fist. The largest insects in North America are some of the moths, with a wingspread of about 150 mm, and the walking sticks, with a body length of about 150 mm.

The insects are the only invertebrates with wings, and these wings have had an evolutionary origin different from that of the vertebrates. The wings of flying vertebrates (birds, bats, and others) are modifications of the forelimbs; those of insects are structures *in addition to* the paired "limbs" and might be likened to the wings of the mythical Pegasus. With wings, insects can leave a habitat when it becomes unsuitable; adult aquatic insects, for example, have wings, and if their habitat dries up they can fly to another habitat. Fish and other aquatic forms usually perish under similar adverse conditions.

Insects range in color from very drab to brilliant; no other animals on earth are more brilliantly colored than some of the insects. Some insects are glittering and iridescent, like living jewels. Their colors and shapes have inspired artists.

Some insects have structures that are amazing when we compare them to vertebrates. The bees and wasps and some of the ants have their ovipositor, or egg-laying organ, developed into a poison dagger (sting) that serves as an excellent means of offense and defense. Some ichneumonids have a hairlike ovipositor 100 mm long that can penetrate solid wood. Some snout beetles have the front of the head drawn out into a slender structure longer than the rest of the body, with tiny jaws at the end. Some flies have their eyes situated at the ends of long slender stalks, which in one South American species are as long as the wings. Some of the stag beetles have jaws half as long as their bodies and branched like the antlers of a stag. Certain individuals in some of the honey ants become so engorged with food that their abdomens become greatly distended. These ants serve as living storehouses of food, which they regurgitate "on demand" to other ants in the colony.

Insects are cold-blooded creatures. When the environmental temperature drops, their body temperature also drops, and their physiological processes slow down. Many insects can withstand short periods of freezing temperatures, but some can withstand long periods of freezing or subfreezing temperatures. Some insects survive these low temperatures by storing in their tissues ethylene glycol,

the same chemical that we pour into our car radiators to protect them from freezing during the winter.

Insect sense organs often seem peculiar compared with those of man and other vertebrates. Many insects have two kinds of eyes—two or three simple eyes located on the upper part of the face and a pair of compound eyes on the sides of the head. The compound eyes are often very large, occupying most of the head, and may consist of thousands of individual "eyes." Some insects hear by means of eardrums, while others hear by means of very sensitive hairs on the antennae or elsewhere on the body. An insect possessing eardrums may have them on the sides of the body at the base of the abdomen (short-horned grasshoppers) or on the front legs below the "knee" (long-horned grasshoppers and crickets).

The reproductive powers of insects are often tremendous; most people do not realize just how great they are. The capacity of any animal to build up its numbers through reproduction depends on three characteristics: the number of fertile eggs laid by each female (which in insects may vary from one to many thousands), the length of a generation (which may vary from a few days to several years), and the proportion of each generation that is female and will produce the next generation (in some insects there are no males).

An example that might be cited to illustrate insects' reproductive powers is *Drosóphila*, the fruit fly that has been studied by so many geneticists. These flies develop rapidly and under ideal conditions may produce 25 generations in a year. Each female will lay up to 100 eggs, of which about half will develop into males and half into females. Suppose we start with a pair of these flies and allow them to increase under ideal conditions, with no checks on increase, for a single year—with the original female laying 100 eggs before she dies and each egg hatching, growing to maturity, and reproducing again, at a 50:50 sex ratio. With 2 flies in the first generation, there would be 100 in the second, 5000 in the third, and so on, with the 25th generation consisting of about 1.192×10^{41} flies. If this many flies were packed tightly together, 1000 to a cubic inch, they would form a ball of flies *96,372,988 miles in diameter*—or a ball extending approximately from the earth to the sun!

Throughout the animal kingdom an egg usually develops into a single individual. In man and some other animals one egg occasionally develops into two individuals (i.e., identical twins) or, on rare occasions, three or four. Some insects carry this phenomenon of polyembryony (more than one young from a single egg) much further; some platygastrid wasps have as many as 18, some dryinid wasps have as many as 60, and some encyrtid wasps have *more than 1000* young developing from a single egg. A few insects have another unusual method of reproduction: paedogenesis (reproduction by larvae). This occurs in the gall gnat genus *Miástor* and the beetle genera *Micromálthus, Phengòdes,* and *Thylódrias.*

In the nature of their development and life cycle, insects run the gamut from very simple to complex and even amazing. Many insects undergo very little change as they develop, with the young and adults having similar habits and differing principally in size. Most insects, on the other hand, undergo in their development rather remarkable changes, both in appearance and in habits. Most people are familiar with the metamorphosis of insects and possibly think of it as commonplace, which, as a matter of fact, it is. Consider the development of a butterfly: an egg hatches into a wormlike caterpillar; this caterpillar eats ravenously and every week or two sheds its skin; after a time it becomes a pupa, hanging from a leaf or branch; and finally a beautiful winged butterfly emerges. Most insects have a life cycle like that of a butterfly; the eggs hatch into wormlike larvae, which grow by periodically shedding their outer skin (together with the linings of the foregut, hindgut, and breathing tubes), finally transforming into an inactive pupal stage from which the winged adult emerges. A fly grows from a maggot; a beetle grows from a grub; and a bee, wasp, or ant grows from a maggotlike larval stage. When these insects become adult they stop growing; a little fly (in the winged stage) does not grow into a bigger one.

An insect with this sort of development (complete metamorphosis) may live as a larva in a very different type of place from that in which it lives as an adult. One common household fly spends its larval life in garbage or some other filth; another very similar fly may spend its larval life eating the insides out of a grub or caterpillar. The junebug that beats against the screens at night spends its larval life in the ground, and the long-horned beetle seen on flowers spends its larval life in the wood of a tree or log.

Many insects have unusual features of structure, physiology, or life cycle, but probably the most interesting things about insects are what they do. In many instances the behavior of an insect seems to surpass in intelligence the behavior of man. Some insects give the appearance of an amazing foresight, especially as regards laying eggs with a view to the future needs of the young. Insects have very varied food habits; they have some interesting means of defense; many have what might be considered fantastic strength (compared with that of vertebrates); and many have "invented" things that we may think of as strictly human accomplishments. Complex and fascinating social behavior has been developed in some groups of insects.

Insects feed on an almost endless variety of foods, and they feed in many different ways. Thousands of species feed on plants, and practically every kind of plant (on land or in fresh water) is fed upon by some kind of insect. The plant feeders may feed on almost any part of the plant; caterpillars, leaf beetles, and leafhoppers feed on the leaves, aphids feed on the stems, white grubs feed on the roots, certain weevil and moth larvae feed on the fruits, and so on. These insects may feed on the outside of the plant, or they may burrow into it. Thousands of insects are carnivorous, feeding on other animals; some are predators, and some are parasites. Many insects that feed on vertebrates are blood sucking; some of these, such as mosquitoes, lice, fleas, and certain bugs, not only are annoying pests because of their bites, but may serve as disease vectors. Some insects feed on dead wood; others feed on stored foods of all types; some feed on various fabrics; and many feed on decaying materials.

The digger wasps have an interesting method of preserving food collected and stored for their young. These wasps dig burrows in the ground, provision them with a certain type of prey (usually other insects or spiders), and then lay their eggs (usually on the body of the prey animal). If the prey animals were killed before being put into the burrows, they would dry up and be of little value as food by the time the wasp eggs hatched. These prey animals are not killed; they are stung and paralyzed, and thus "preserved" in good condition for the young wasps when they hatch.

Insects often have interesting and effective means of defense against intruders and enemies. Many "play dead," either by dropping to the ground and remaining motionless or by "freezing" in a characteristic position. Others are masters of the art of camouflage, being so colored that they blend with the background and are very inconspicuous; some very closely resemble objects in their environment— dead leaves, twigs, thorns, or even bird droppings. Some insects become concealed by covering themselves with debris. Others that do not have any special means of defense closely resemble another that does, and presumably are afforded some protection because of this resemblance. Many moths have the hind wings (which at rest are generally concealed beneath the front wings) brightly or strikingly colored—sometimes with spots resembling the eyes of a larger animal (for example, giant silkworm moths; see Figure 34–76)—and when disturbed display these hind wings; the effect may sometimes be enough to scare off a potential intruder. Some of the sound-producing insects (for example, cicadas, some beetles, and others) will produce a characteristic sound when attacked, and this sound often scares off the attacker.

Many insects utilize a "chemical warfare" type of defense. Some secrete foul-smelling substances when disturbed; stink bugs, broad-headed bugs, lacewings, and some beetles might well be called the skunks of the insect world because they have a very unpleasant odor. A few of the insects utilizing such defensive mechanisms are able to eject the substance as a spray, in some cases even aiming it at an intruder. Some insects, such as the milkweed butterflies, ladybird beetles, and net-winged beetles, apparently have distasteful or mildly toxic body fluids and are avoided by predators.

Many insects will inflict a painful bite when handled. The bite may be simply a severe pinch by powerful jaws, but the bites of mosquitoes, fleas, black flies, assassin bugs, and many others are much like hypodermic injections; the irritation is caused by the saliva injected at the time of the bite.

Other means of defense include the stinging hairs possessed by some caterpillars (for example, the saddleback caterpillar and the larva of the io moth), body fluids that are irritating (for example, blister beetles), death feigning (many beetles and some insects in other orders), and warning displays, such as eyespots on the wings (many moths and mantids) or other bizarre or grotesque structures or patterns.

One of the most effective means of defense possessed by insects is a sting, which is developed in the wasps, bees, and some ants. The sting is a modified egg-laying organ; hence only females sting. It is located at the posterior end of the body, so the "business" end of a stinging insect is the rear.

Insects often perform feats of strength that seem nearly impossible compared with those of human beings. It is not unusual for an insect to be able to lift 50 or more times its own weight, and some beetles rigged with a special harness have been found able to lift more than 800 times their own weight. In comparison with such beetles, a man could lift some 60 tons, and an elephant could lift a fair-sized building! When it comes to jumping, many insects put our best Olympic athletes to shame. Many grasshoppers can easily jump a distance of 1 meter, which would be comparable to a man long-jumping the length of a football field, and a flea jumping several inches up in the air would be comparable to a man jumping over a 30-story building.

Many insects do things that we might consider strictly an activity of civilized humans or a product of our modern technology. Caddisfly larvae were probably the first organisms to use nets to capture aquatic organisms. Dragonfly nymphs, in their intake and expulsion of water to aerate the gills in the rectum, were among the first to use jet propulsion. Honey bees were air-conditioning their hives long before humans even appeared on earth. The hornets were the first animals to make paper from wood pulp. Long before people began making crude shelters many insects were constructing shelters of clay, stone, or "logs" (Figure 33–7), and some even induce plants to make shelters (galls) for them. Long before the appearance of man on earth the insects had "invented" cold light and chemical warfare and had solved many complex problems of aerodynamics and celestial navigation. Many insects have elaborate communication systems, involving chemicals (sex, alarm, trail-following, and other pheromones), sound (cicadas, many Orthóptera, and others), behavior (for example, honey bee dance "language"), light (fireflies), and possibly other mechanisms.

These are only a few of the ways in which insects have become adapted to life in the world about us. Some of the detailed stories about these animals are fantastic and almost incredible. In the following chapters we have tried to point out many of the interesting and often unique features of insect biology—methods of reproduction, ways of obtaining food, techniques for depositing eggs, methods of rearing the young, and features of life history—as well as the more technical phases that deal with morphology and taxonomy.

Chapter 2

The Relation of Insects to Humans

People benefit from insects in many ways; without them, human society could not exist in its present form. Without the pollinating services of bees and other insects, we would have few vegetables, few fruits, little or no clover (and hence much less beef, mutton, and wool), no coffee, no tobacco, few flowers—in fact, we would not have many of the things that are an integral part of our domestic economy and civilization. Insects provide us with honey, beeswax, silk, and many other useful products. Many species are parasitic or predaceous and are important in keeping the pest species under control; others help in the control of noxious weeds; and still others clean up refuse and make the world a little more pleasant. Insects are the sole or major item of food of many birds, fish, and other animals (including humans in some parts of the world). Some species have been used in the treatment of certain diseases. The study of insects has helped scientists solve many problems in heredity, evolution, sociology, stream pollution, and other fields. Insects also have aesthetic value: artists, milliners, and designers have made use of their beauty, and many people derive a great deal of pleasure from the study of insects as a hobby.

On the other hand, many insects are obnoxious or destructive. They attack various growing plants, including plants that are valuable to humankind, and feed on them, injuring or killing them or introducing disease into them. They attack human possessions, including homes, clothing, food stores, and destroy, damage, or contaminate them. They attack people and animals and are annoying because of their presence, odors, bites, or stings. Many are agents in the transmission of some of the most serious diseases that beset humans and animals.

Most people are much more aware of the injurious insects and their effects than they are of the beneficial insects, and the injurious species are probably better known than the beneficial ones. In spite of the excessive attention paid to injurious insects by the public in general and entomologists in particular, we believe that the good done by the beneficial insects outweighs the harm done by the injurious ones.

Beneficial Insects

It is difficult if not impossible to estimate the value of insects to human society in terms of dollars and cents. The pollinating services of insects are worth about $19 billion annually in the United States, and commercial products derived from insects are worth about $300 million more. No value can be put on the role insects play as entomophagous animals, as scavengers, and in research. It seems safe to say that insects are worth about $20 billion annually.

Insects and Pollination

Sexual reproduction in the higher plants is made possible by the process of pollination. This process consists of the transfer of pollen (the male germ cells) from the stamens to the stigma; from the stigma a pollen tube grows down the style to the female germ cell. This process must take place in practically every plant before the flower will bear seed. As the seed develops, the tissues around it swell and form the fruit.

A few of the higher plants are self-pollinating, but most are cross-pollinated; that is, the pollen of one flower must be transferred to the stigma of another. Pollen is transferred from one flower to another in two principal ways, by wind and by insects. Wind-pollinated plants produce a large amount of dry pollen that is blown far and wide; such plants manage to reproduce because a few of the millions of pollen grains produced happen to land on the stigma of the right flower. Insect-pollinated plants produce smaller amounts of pollen, which is usually sticky and adheres to the bodies of insects that visit the flower. This pollen is later rubbed off the insect onto the stigma of another flower, in most cases more or less by accident as far as the insect is concerned.

Figure 2–1. A honey bee collecting pollen. Note the large mass of pollen on the hind leg of this bee. (Courtesy of Teale.)

Many flowers have peculiar features of structure that help to ensure pollination. Some, such as the iris, are so constructed that an insect cannot get to the nectar without collecting pollen on its body and cannot enter the next flower of this same kind without leaving some of the pollen on the stigma of that flower. Milkweeds have special pollen masses, the pollinia, which are arranged in such a way that when an insect alights on the edge of the flower, its legs slip into fissures in the pollinia; the pollinia then become attached to the insect's leg and are carried to the next flower.

Some plants depend on a single species or type of insect for pollination. Some of the orchids are pollinated only by certain long-tongued hawk moths. The Smyrna fig is pollinated by the fig wasp, *Blastóphaga psènes* (see page 717), and yuccas are pollinated solely by yucca moths (*Tegetícula*) (see page 623).

The plants that are wind-pollinated and hence not dependent on insects include corn, wheat, rye, oats, timothy, and other grasses; trees such as the willows, oaks, hickories, elms, poplars, birches, and conifers; and many wild plants such as ragweed and pigweed. On the other hand, many plants depend on insects for pollination, including such orchard fruits as apples, pears, plums, cherries, citrus fruits, and nuts; strawberries, blackberries, cranberries, and blueberries; such vegetables as melons, cucumbers, pumpkins, squash, cabbage, onions, and carrots; such field crops as the clovers and tobacco; and many flowers.

The rosaceous plants (apple, pear, cherry, blackberry, strawberry) depend chiefly on honey bees for pollination; the clovers depend on various bees, chiefly honey bees and bumble bees. Many plants with strongly scented and conspicuous nocturnal flowers, such as honeysuckle, tobacco, and petunias, are pollinated not only by bees but also by moths. Umbelliferous plants like carrots and parsnips are pollinated chiefly by flies, bees, and wasps. Pond lilies, goldenrod, and some other flowers are pollinated by bees and certain beetles.

Clover is an important farm crop in many parts of the country and is used as hay and forage and to enrich the soil. The average annual crop of clover seed in Ohio (250,000 bushels) would plant some 3 million acres in clover; this acreage would yield about 4.5 million tons of hay (worth about $100 million) and add about 273 million pounds of nitrogen to the soil (worth about $60 million). Red and alsike clovers are entirely dependent on insects for pollination and seed production, and sweet clover and alfalfa, though somewhat self-pollinated, depend on insect pollination for profitable seed yields.

The job of pollinating clover is tremendous; an acre of red clover, for example, contains about 216 million individual flowers, and every one of these must be visited by an insect before it will produce seed. Under normal field conditions (at least in Ohio) about 82% of the pollinating of red clover is done by honey bees and 15% by bumble bees. The average seed yields of red clover and alsike in Ohio are about 1.0 and 1.6 bushels per acre, and with maximum insect pollination, they can be increased to 12 and 20 bushels per acre.

Sheep may be raised on grasses that are wind-pollinated, but a practical sheep raiser prefers clovers. Some years ago the sheep ranchers in New Zealand imported red clover seed to improve their pastures. The clover grew but produced no seed for the next year's crop because there were no suitable insects in New Zealand to pollinate the clover. After bumble bees were introduced there and had been established, thus making possible the pollination of clover, there was continuous good grazing for New Zealand sheep.

Orchard fruits, with the possible exception of sour cherries and most peaches, are largely or entirely insect-pollinated, and this job is done chiefly by bees. Experiments involving the use of cages over orchard trees have shown that if bees are excluded from the tree when it is in bloom, the set of fruit is usually less than 1% of the blooms. If a hive of bees is caged with a tree, the set of fruit is increased in some cases to as high as 44% of the blooms. Such experiments indicate that the fruit yields in orchards can be greatly increased by the use of bees. Although many factors complicate the problem of orchard pollination, a large number of growers obtain considerably increased yields of fruit by placing hives of bees in their orchards when the trees are in bloom.

By far the most important insect pollinator is the honey bee, *Àpis mellìfera*. Without this insect it would be almost impossible to produce commercially most pome fruits, stone fruits, cucurbits, melons, almonds, some citrus, and many seed crops. Other insects are capable of pollinating these crops, but with more and more urbanization in agricultural areas and the trend toward growing large stands of single crops, the habitats and hence the abundance of other insects (including possible pollinators) are being reduced. The honey bee becomes important because pollination of crops can be ensured by moving hives of bees into the fields and orchards at the time of pollination.

The economic value of the pollinating insects is enormous; the annual yields of insect-pollinated plants in the United States are valued at about $19 billion. Of all the insects that pollinate plants, the most important is the honey bee. This insect is highly prized for its honey and wax, but for every dollar's worth of honey and wax it produces, $14 to $20 worth of pollinating services is rendered to agriculture.

Commercial Products Derived from Insects

Honey and Beeswax.   The production of honey is a very old industry, dating back to the time of the pharaohs. Honey bees are not native to the United States, but were introduced about 1638. Several strains of this insect now occur in the United States. Honey is used extensively as a food and in the manufacture of many products. Beeswax is widely used by industry in making candles, sealing wax, polishes, certain types of inks, models of various kinds, dental impressions, cosmetics, and other products.

Beekeeping is a multimillion-dollar industry. The approximately 4 million colonies of bees in the United States in 1978 produced about 230 million pounds of honey and 3.7 million pounds of beeswax; at average retail prices ($0.97 per pound for honey and $1.67 per pound for beeswax), the 1978 crop of honey and wax in the United States was worth about $230 million. The annual consumption of honey in the United States is about 285 million pounds; the difference between this figure and U.S. production is made up by imports.

Silk.   The silk industry is an ancient one, extending as far back as 2500 B.C. The rearing of silkworms and the processing and weaving of silk are principally an oriental industry, but they are practiced to some extent in a number of other countries, especially Spain, France, and Italy. Several types of silkworms have been utilized for the production of commercial silk, but the most important is *Bómbyx mòri*, a domesticated species. Although silk is at the present time being replaced by various synthetic fibers, it is still a very important industry. The annual world production of silk is about 65–75 million pounds.

Shellac.   Shellac is produced from the secretions of the lac insect, *Láccifer lácca*, a type of scale insect occurring on fig, banyan, and other plants in India, Burma, Indochina, Taiwan, Sri Lanka, and the Philippine Islands. These insects form encrustations 6 to 13 mm thick on the twigs of the host plant. The twigs containing these encrustations are collected and ground; the "seed lac" so formed is melted and dried in sheets or flakes, which are shipped to a processing plant where the shellac is made. About $9 million worth is shellac is used annually in the United States.

Dyes and Other Materials.   Several insects have been used in the manufacture of dyes. The cochineal insect, *Dactylòpius cóccus*, a scale insect somewhat similar to mealybugs, is used for the production of cochineal dyes. These insects feed on *Opúntia* cacti (prickly pear) in the southwestern states and Mexico. The dye is now largely replaced by aniline dyes. Dyes have also been made from other types of scale insects and from certain cynipid galls. Some of the cynipid galls have also been used as a source of tannic acid, which is used in the manufacture of ink and for other purposes. Certain drugs have been made from insects, including cantharidin, which is made from the dried bodies of a European blister beetle, the Spanishfly, *Lýtta vesicatòria* L. Many insects, such as hellgrammites and crickets, are sold as fish bait.

Entomophagous Insects

Insects have a high reproductive capacity and are potentially able to build up tremendous populations, but they seldom do so, largely because of the many animals that feed on them. A considerable proportion of these entomophagous, or insect-eating, animals consists of insects. The check exerted upon insect pests by entomophagous insects is a very important factor in keeping down the populations of pest species. Probably no method that people can use to control insects will compare with the control exerted by entomophagous animals, yet the public has little knowledge or appreciation of this enormous benefit (see pages 75–77).

A classic example of the successful control of an insect pest by a predator is that of the cottony cushion scale, *Icérya púrchasi*, a serious pest of citrus in California, by a ladybird beetle. This scale was first found in California in 1868 and, in 15 years, threatened to destroy the citrus industry in southern California. In 1888–1889 a ladybird beetle, *Rodòlia cardinàlis*, was introduced from Australia (where it was thought the scale originated), and in less than two years the scale was under complete control.

Though here we have classified predaceous and parasitic insects as beneficial to humanity, it should be understood that their economic importance is determined by the insect they attack. If the species attacked is injurious, the entomophagous insect is considered beneficial, but if it attacks a beneficial species, it is considered injurious.

Insects as Scavengers

Insect scavengers are those that feed on decomposing plants or animals or on dung. Such insects assist in converting these materials into simpler substances that are returned to the soil, where they are available to plants; they also serve to remove unhealthful and obnoxious materials from our surroundings. Insects such as the wood-boring beetles, termites, carpenter ants, and other wood feeders are important agents in hastening the conversion of

Figure 2–2.   A damsel bug attacking an aphid. (Courtesy of Ohio Agricultural Research and Development Center.)

Figure 2–3. Parasitic chalcidoids attacking the larva of the alfalfa weevil. (Courtesy of Ohio Agricultural Research and Development Center.)

fallen trees and logs to soil. The galleries of these insects serve as avenues of entrance for fungi and other decay organisms that hasten the breakdown of the wood. Dung beetles (Scarabaèidae and others) hasten the decomposition of dung. Carrion-feeding insects such as blow flies, carrion beetles, skin beetles (Derméstidae and Trogìnae), and others are of considerable value in the removal of carrion from the landscape. Insect scavengers are essential to maintaining a balance in nature.

Some of the dung-feeding scarabs have been introduced into Australia and some western states to reduce fly populations in cattle areas. These beetles feed on cow dung, and they clean up the dung so quickly that the flies breeding in the dung do not have time to complete their development.

The Importance of Soil Insects

Many types of insects spend a part of or all their lives in the soil. The soil provides the insect a home or nest, protection, and often food. The soil is tunneled in such a way that it becomes more aerated, and it is enriched by the excretions and dead bodies of the insects. Soil insects improve the physical properties of the soil and add to its organic content.

Soil insects vary in feeding habits. Many feed on humus or decaying plant materials; some feed on the underground parts of growing plants (and may be injurious); many are scavengers. Many feed above ground and use the soil only as a nest site; some of these, such as ants, digger wasps, and bees, bring food into the soil in connection with feeding the young.

Soil insects are often very numerous. The population of springtails alone may be millions per acre. Ants are sometimes extremely abundant; they generally nest in the soil and feed above ground. Other important soil-inhabiting insects are the mole crickets, cicadas (nymphal stages), termites, various burrowing bees and wasps, many beetles and flies (usually in the larval stage only), and some aphids.

Insects as Destroyers of Undesirable Plants

A large proportion of the insects feeds on plants, but only a small number of these are considered pests. Many of the others may be beneficial because they destroy noxious weeds, cacti, or certain undesirable deciduous plants. It often happens that when a plant is introduced into a geographic area it thrives to such an extent that it becomes a pest. In some cases plant-feeding insects have been introduced to bring this plant under control.

Prickly pear cacti (*Opúntia* spp.) were at one time introduced into Australia and by 1925 had spread over some 25 million acres to form a dense, impenetrable growth. In 1925 a moth, *Cactoblástis cactòrum*, the larvae of which burrow in the cactus plants, was introduced into Australia from Argentina. As a result of the feeding of this moth, the dense cactus growth is now reduced to about 1% of the area it occupied in 1925.

A European species of Saint-John's-wort, *Hypéricum perforàtum* L., was introduced into northern California in about 1900. It became particularly abundant in the vicinity of the Klamath River and is commonly called Klamath weed or goatweed. By the mid-1940s it had spread over about 2.5 million acres of range land in California and over extensive acreage in other western states. This plant is considered a pest because it replaces desirable range plants and is poisonous to livestock. Attempts to control it by chemicals were expensive and not entirely effective. From 1944 to 1948 a few species of European beetles (chrysomelids and buprestids) were imported into California to control Klamath weed; one of the chrysomelids, *Chrysolìna quadrigémina* (Rossi), proved particularly effective. The Klamath weed has now been reduced to about 1% of its former abundance, and more desirable plants on the range have increased.

Alligatorweed, *Alternánthera philoxeròides* (Martius) Grisebach, is an aquatic plant native to South America that first appeared in the United States (in Florida) in 1894 and has subsequently spread throughout the Southeast and westward to Texas and California. It is a plant that forms dense mats near the water surface, impeding boat traffic, blocking drainage canals, killing fish and other wildlife by crowding out desirable food plants, providing habitats for mosquitoes, and contributing to water pollution. The area infested with this plant in 1970 was estimated to be some 70,000 acres. Herbicides have not been successful in controlling this plant, and studies of its insect enemies in South America indicated that three species might help to control the plant in the United States: a thrips, *Amỳnothrips ándersoni* O'Neill; a pyralid stem borer, *Vòtgtia málloi* Pastrana; and a flea beetle, *Agásicles* sp. These were brought to the United States and released, the first introduction being in 1964. The flea beetle and thrips have become established, and are most abundant in Florida. The beetle, particularly, appears to be providing good control of the alligatorweed.

Three species of ragweeds (*Ambròsia* spp.) have recently been introduced into Eurasia from their native North America. In the U.S.S.R. they are fast becoming abundant agricultural weeds in pastures and orchards and on cultivated lands, and (as in North America) are important sources of allergenic pollen. A noctuid moth, *Tarachídia candefácta* Hübner, was introduced from California into the U.S.S.R. and has since become established as far north as Leningrad. This is the first species intentionally introduced from North America into Europe for weed control.

It should be noted that weed-feeding insects are not always beneficial. In some cases an insect may feed on weeds early in the season and later invade cultivated crops. Sometimes weeds may provide food on which large populations may be built up, later to attack crop plants. In other cases an insect may change its host from a wild to a cultivated plant. The Colorado potato beetle, for example, originally fed on a wild species of *Solànum* (nightshade) and later changed to the potato.

Insects as Food of People and Animals

A great many animals utilize insects as food. Insectivorous animals may be important to humankind as food (for example, many fish, game birds, and mammals); they may have an aesthetic value (many birds and other vertebrates); or they may act as important agents in the control of insect pests. People are sometimes insectivorous themselves.

Many freshwater fish feed to a large extent on insects, particularly on such aquatic forms as mayflies, stoneflies, caddisflies, mosquito larvae, midge larvae, and larvae of aquatic beetles. Although most species of game fish prey upon smaller fish or on other aquatic animals, the insects are a basic item in the food chains leading to these game fish.

The birds that feed largely or entirely upon insects have an aesthetic value because of their interesting habits, and they often have a practical value because they act as important predators of insect pests. Birds that feed on insects consume large quantities of them; nestlings will often eat their weight in insects daily. Many examples might be cited of cases where birds have been instrumental in checking insect outbreaks. A particularly striking case is that of gulls checking a Mormon cricket outbreak in Utah in 1848, an event now commemorated by a monument in Salt Lake City.

Many other vertebrates are insectivorous, and some of these have been of value in controlling insect pests. Toads, frogs, lizards, bats, skunks, moles, and shrews feed largely or entirely on insects.

Insects are utilized as food by people in many parts of the world. The Arabs eat locusts (Acrídidae). In certain parts of Africa ants, termites, beetle grubs, caterpillars, and grasshoppers are eaten. Grasshoppers are frequently eaten in the Orient. In Mexico "gusanos de maguey" are considered a delicacy; these are the larvae of one of the giant skippers, which are collected from the fleshy leaves of the maguey plant. They are sold fresh in the market and are fried before eating; they may also be purchased in cans (Figure 2–4), already fried and ready to eat. The caterpillars are about 65 mm long when full grown. Cans of these and other edible insects are available in many places in the United States.

About the only insects knowingly eaten by people in the United States are the few that are canned and sold in gourmet food shops (such as those shown in Figure 2–4), and relatively few people eat even these. However, in Western society honey (which has been regurgitated by insects) and some close relatives of insects (lobsters, shrimps, and crabs) are eaten and considered excellent foods. For most westerners, eating insects is strictly "for the birds" and definitely not for humans. Any food containing the least trace of insects is considered contaminated and unfit for human consumption. Food-processing companies spend millions of dollars each year to keep insects out of their products. Nevertheless, for

Figure 2–4. "Gusanos de Maguey," edible caterpillars canned and sold in Mexico.

thousands of species of animals (including some primates) insects constitute the principal or sole items of their diet, and thus insects do have considerable food value.

Insects in Medicine and Surgery

For centuries people have used insects or their products as therapeutic agents. Cantharidin, an extract from the bodies of blister beetles, has been used in the treatment of certain conditions of the urogenital system. Bee venom has been used in the treatment of arthritis. Malaria has been induced in patients suffering from paresis, to produce high body temperatures.

One of the most striking roles of insects in medicine is the use of blow fly larvae in treating conditions involving decaying tissues. For centuries military surgeons had noticed that severe wounds that remained untreated for several days and became infested with maggots healed better when dressed than similar wounds that had not been infested. After World War I, this fact was investigated experimentally, and it was found that the fly larvae fed on the decaying tissues of such wounds and secreted something into the wound that promoted the healing process. From this experimental work, a technique was developed for treating diseases such as osteomyelitis with blow fly larvae. The larvae were reared under aseptic conditions, to avoid introducing additional infection, and were placed in the decaying tissues of the patient. There they were allowed to feed and, when full grown, were replaced by younger larvae. This treatment resulted in a less conspicuous scar afterward, and there were fewer recurrences than in the operative treatment formerly used. After further study of this process it was discovered that the excretion of the larvae that produced the curative effect was allantoin. At present, allantoin is used in the treatment of osteomyelitis and other deep-seated wounds in which there is decaying tissue. Thus, fly larvae have been instrumental in developing a modern medical treatment for a condition that was previously very difficult to cure.

The Use of Insects in Scientific Research

Basic physiological processes, as well as such biological phenomena as inheritance, population dynamics, variation, and evolution, are essentially similar in all animals—and since many insects have a short life cycle and are relatively easy to maintain in the laboratory, they are frequently used in scientific studies of these processes.

Studies of insect physiology have advanced our knowledge of physiology generally. Extensive studies of insect nutrition, neuromuscular physiology, and hormones have contributed to our knowledge of these functions in other animals as well. Cockroaches, hornworms, silkworms, triatomid bugs, and house flies are most frequently used in these studies.

The little fruit flies, *Drosóphila* spp., which are easily reared in large numbers and whose larvae have giant salivary gland chromosomes, have been used extensively in genetic studies. Much has been added to our knowledge of the basic principles of inheritance by the study of these flies.

Insects have often been used as the experimental animal in studies of behavior. Studies of social insects, for example, have provided much interesting and valuable information on social organization and behavior, thus increasing our understanding of human social behavior. Studies of the responses of insects to various environmental factors, such as temperature, moisture, and photoperiod, have increased our understanding of the action of these factors in other animals as well.

Insect populations are often used as an index of ecological conditions. In studies of stream or lake pollution, for example, the degree of pollution can be determined by the type and amount of insect life present. Insect populations may also serve as an index to successions; the length of time an animal has been dead can often be determined by its insect fauna.

The Aesthetic Value of Insects

Insects become fascinating animals when one begins to study them carefully. For many people insect study provides a stimulating hobby, one just as interesting as the study of birds, flowers, or other natural objects.

The beauty of insects has been utilized for patterns by artists, jewelers, and designers. Some of the butterflies, moths, and beetles have provided basic patterns in many types of art. A brilliantly colored tropical leafhopper, *Agrosòma pulchélla* (Guérin), has a black, white, and red pattern that is frequently used in Mexican and Central American art. Insects are used in jewelry, either by using all or part of actual specimens or by using them as designs. Bracelets, necklaces, necktie pins, and scatter pins are often made in the design of an insect. In some tropical countries necklaces are made of "ground pearls," the wax cysts of female scale insects of the genus *Margaròdes*. The wings of *Mórpho* butterflies, brilliant bluish butterflies occurring in the American tropics, are often mounted under glass and made into trays, pictures, and jewelry. Showy insects mounted in plastic or under glass are sometimes made into paperweights or bookends.

Injurious Insects

Human society suffers tremendous losses from the feeding and other activities of insects. Many insects feed on cultivated plants. Others feed on stored materials, clothing, or wood that have economic value. Still others feed directly on humans and other animals.

The annual losses in the United States resulting from insects have been estimated at about $5 billion, which is less than the amount representing the benefits derived from insects. Thus, we may say that the good done by insects outweighs the harm they do, though the good is often less evident than the harm.

Insects Attacking Cultivated Plants

Most types of plants, including all sorts of growing crops, are attacked and injured by insects. The injury is caused by the insects' feeding or ovipositing on the plant or serving as agents in the transmission of plant diseases. This injury may vary from a reduction in crop yields to the complete destruction of the plant. The damage to plants by insects has been estimated to amount to about $3 billion annually in the United States.

Plant Injury by Feeding.   Most of the plant damage by insects falls in the category of injury by feeding. The methods of feeding and types of damage done by insects feeding on plants are discussed later (under "Phytophagous Insects," pages 74-75). Such feeding produces injury of various types, and the severity of the injury may vary all the way from only very slight damage to the death of the plant.

Plant Injury by Oviposition.   A few insects injure plants when they lay their eggs, particularly when

A   B

Figure 2–5.   Plant injury by aphids. **A,** injury by an infestation of the rusty plum aphid, *Hysteroneùra setàriae* (Thomas); **B,** curling of the leaves of wild sunflower caused by *Àphis debilicòrnis* (Gillette and Palmer). (Courtesy of the Illinois Natural History Survey.)

they oviposit in stems or fruits. The periodical cicada, in laying its eggs in twigs, usually injures the twig so much that the terminal portion dies or weakens it so that it is easily broken at the point of oviposition. Tree crickets, treehoppers, and certain leafhoppers injure twigs in a similar manner. Insects that lay their eggs in fruits often cause the fruits to become misshapen.

Insects and Plant Disease. During recent years much has been learned of the role played by insects in the transmission of plant diseases. Some 200 plant diseases have been shown to have insect vectors. About three-fourths of these diseases are caused by viruses. A summary of the more important plant diseases transmitted by insects is given in Table 2–1.

There are three ways by which insects cause plant pathogens to enter the plant.

1. The pathogen may accidentally gain entrance through egg or feeding punctures or openings through which the insect has entered the plant tissue. Certain molds and rots enter in this fashion.
2. The pathogen may be transmitted on or in the body of the insect from one plant to another. Flies and bees pick up and spread the bacilli that cause fire blight in apple and pear. The fungus causing Dutch elm disease is transmitted in this fashion by the elm bark beetle.
3. The pathogen may remain in the body of the insect for a short time (nonpersistent or semipersistent) or for long periods (persistent or circulative) and be inoculated into the plant by the feeding of the insect. In some cases the pathogen passes a part of its life cycle in the insect

(text continued on page 15)

Table 2–1
Plant Diseases Transmitted by Insects and Other Arthropods[a]

A. Virus

Disease	Vectors	Host	Type of Virus and Transmission
Sugarcane mosaic	Aphids: *Rhopalosìphum màidis* (Fitch), *Hysteroneùra setàriae* (Thomas), *Schizàphis gráminum* (Rondani), and many others	Sugarcane, sorghum, corn	Flexous rod, nonpersistent
Cucumber mosaic	Aphids: *Mỳzus pérsicae* (Sulzer), *Àphis gossýpii* Glover, *Àphis fàbae* Scopoli, and many others	Cucumber, tobacco	Isometric, nonpersistent
Alfalfa mosaic	Aphids: *Mỳzus pérsicae, Acyrthosìphon pìsum* (Harris), and many others	Alfalfa, beans, tobacco	Rhabdovirus, nonpersistent
Sugar beet yellows	Aphid: *Mỳzus pérsicae*	Sugar beet, lettuce, spinach	Long flexous rods, semipersistent
Pea enation mosaic	Aphids: *Acyrthosìphon pìsum, Mỳzus pérsicae,* and others	Peas, beans, alfalfa, clover	Isometric, circulative
Lettuce necrotic yellows	Aphid: *Hyperomỳzus lactùcae* (L.)	Lettuce	Rhabdovirus, propagative
Maize chlorotic dwarf	Leafhopper: *Graminélla nìgrifrons* (Forbes)	Corn, sorghum, Johnson grass	Isometric, semipersistent
Sugar beet curly top	Leafhoppers: *Circùlifer tenéllus* (Baker), *C. opacipénnis* (Lethierry)	Sugar beet	Isometric, circulative
Wound tumor	Leafhoppers: *Agállia constrícta* Van Duzee, *Agalliópsis novélla* (Say)	Clover	Isometric, propagative
Potato yellow dwarf	Leafhoppers: *Aceratagállia lóngula* (Van Duzee), *A. sanguinolénta* (Provancher), *A. curvàta* Oman, *A. obscùra* Oman, *Agalliópsis novélla, Agállia constrícta, A. quadripunctàta* (Provancher)	Potato	Rhabdovirus, propagative
Maize mosaic	Planthopper: *Peregrìnus màidis* (Ashmead)	Corn, sorghum	Rhabdovirus, propagative
Bean golden yellow mosaic	Whitefly: *Bemísia tabàci* (Gennadius)	Soybeans	Isometric, circulative
Cowpea mosaic	Beetles: *Cerótoma variegàta* (Fabricius), *Diabrótica undecimpunctàta* Mannerheim, *Epiláchna varivéstis* Mulsant, and others	Beans	Isometric, circulative
Wheat streak mosaic	Eriophyid mite: *Eriophỳes tùlipae* Kiefer	Wheat, corn	Flexous rod, semipersistent

(continued)

Table 2–1 (*Continued*)

B. Mollicute Diseases

Disease	Vectors	Host	Type of Mollicute and Transmission
Aster yellows (North American western strain)	Leafhoppers: *Gyponàna angulàta* (Spang), *Scaphytòpius acùtus* (Say), *S. delóngi* Young, *S. irroràtus* (Van Duzee), *Acinópterus angulàtus* Lawson, *Macrósteles fáscifrons* (Stål), *Éndria inímica* (Say), *Chlorotéttix símilis* DeLong, *Colladònus flavocapitàtus* (Van Duzee), *C. hòlmesi* (Bliven), *C. intricàtus*, and others	Aster, celery, squash, cucumber, wheat, barley	Mycoplasma, propagative
Alfalfa witches' broom	Leafhopper: *Scaphytòpius acùtus cirrus* Musgrave	Alfalfa	Mycoplasma, propagative
Peach X-disease (western)	Leafhoppers: *Graphocéphala conflùens* (Uhler), *Scaphytòpius acùtus cirrus, Colladònus geminàtus* (Van Duzee), *C. montànus* (Van Duzee), *Fieberiélla flòrii* (Stål)	Peach	Mycoplasma, propagative
Clover phyllody	Leafhoppers: *Aphròdes álbifrons* (L.), *Scaphytòpius acùtus acùtus* (Say), *Macrósteles cristàta* (Ribaut), *M. fáscifrons, M. viridigríseus* (Edwards), *Eùscelis lineolàtus* (Brullé), *E. plébeja* (Fallén)	Clover	Mycoplasma, propagative
Corn stunt	Leafhoppers: *Dálbulus elimàtus* (Ball), *D. màidis* (DeLong and Wolcott), *Graminélla nígrifrons* (Forbes), and others	Corn	Spiroplasma, propagative
Citrus stubborn	Leafhoppers: *Scaphytòpius nitrìdus* DeLong, and others	Orange and other citrus, periwinkle	Spiroplasma, propagative

C. Bacterial Diseases

Disease	Vectors	Host	Type of Bacteria and Transmission
Pierce's disease of grape	Leafhoppers: *Cuérna costàlis* (Fabricius), *C. occidentàlis* Oman and Beamer, *C. yúccae* Oman and Beamer, *Homalodísca coagulàta* (Say), *H. laceràta* (Fowler), *Oncometòpia orbòna* (Fabricius), *Carneocéphala fláviceps* (Riley), *C. fúlgida* Nottingham, *C. triguttàta* Nottingham, *Draeculacéphala crassicòrnis* Van Duzee, *D. minérva* Ball, *D. noveboracénsis* (Fitch), *D. portòla portòla* Ball, *Graphocéphala cythùra* (Baker), *Helochàra comùnis* Fitch, and others	Grape	Rickettsia, circulative
Phony peach disease	Leafhoppers: *Oncometòpia nígricans* (Walker), *O. orbòna, Homalodísca insòlita* (Walker), *H. coagulàta, Cúerna costàlis, Draeculacéphala portòla, Graphocéphala versùta* (Say)	Peach	Rickettsia, circulative
Stewart's wilt	Corn flea beetle, *Chaetocnèma pulicària* Melsheimer; corn rootworms, *Diabrótica* spp.; seedcorn maggot, *Hylemỳa platùra* (Meigen)	Corn	*Erwínia stéwarti* Smith, circulative
Cucurbit wilt	Cucumber beetles: *Acalýmma vittàta* (Fabricius), *D. undecimpunctàta hówardi* Barber	Cucumber and other cucurbits	*Erwínia tracheíphila* (Erw. Smith), circulative
Fire blight	Various insects, especially flies, bees, and leafhoppers	Pear, apple, quince	*Erwínia amylóvora* (Burrill), carried externally

Table 2–1 (*Continued*)

D. Fungus Disease

Disease	Vectors	Host	Type of Fungus and Transmission
Dutch elm disease	Smaller European elm bark beetle, *Scólytus multistriàtus* (Marsham)	Elms	*Ceratocýstus úlmi* (Buisman) C. Moreau, carried externally

ªPrepared by Dr. Lowell R. Nault, Ohio Agricultural Research and Development Center, The Ohio State University.

and may reproduce there (propagative). Many of the viruses and mollicutes (mycoplasmas and spiroplasmas) multiply in their insect vectors and may even cause disease in the vector. For example, *Dálbulus elimàtus* (Ball) infected with corn stunt spiroplasma live only half as long as disease-free leafhoppers. Some of the propagative plant viruses (such as wound tumor virus) are passed on to the progeny through the eggs.

Many plant viruses or mollicutes are transmitted by only one or two insect or mite species. Others are transmitted by many species, but all vectors will belong to the same insect family. Several dozen species transmit sugarcane mosaic virus, but all are aphids. There are many vectors of the aster yellows mycoplasma, but all are leafhoppers.

The damage done by an insect feeding alone may not be severe, but a disease vector can inoculate a plant with a pathogen that may reduce its productivity or even kill it. Two sugar beet leafhoppers per beet plant cause little damage by their feeding, but if they are carrying the curly top virus, they may cause enormous losses.

Insects Attacking Stored Products

After materials produced by plants and animals have been stored as food or clothing or have been utilized in buildings or fabrics, they may be attacked and damaged by insects. The damage is done by the insects' feeding or tunneling in these materials or contaminating them, and the possibility of insect attack greatly increases the expense of packing and storage. The annual damage to stored products in the United States has been estimated to be about $1 billion.

Pests of Wood. All sorts of wooden structures, such as buildings, furniture, fence posts, utility poles, and materials such as pasteboard and paper are subject to attack by insects. One of the most widespread and destructive pests of wood and wood products is the termite. Termites eat out the interior portions of beams, sills, floors, and joists and often build tunnels over or through foundations to reach the wooden parts of buildings. Timbers attacked eventually collapse. Powderpost beetles and carpenter ants tunnel in posts and timbers and weaken them.

Pests of Fabrics and Clothing. Most materials made from animal fibers, such as furs, clothing, blankets, rugs, and upholstering, may be attacked and damaged by insects. The amount of material actually eaten may be small, but the value of the materials attacked may be greatly reduced. The most important fabric pests are dermestid beetles and clothes moths.

Pests of Stored Foods. Many types of stored foods, particularly meats, cheese, milk products, flour, meal, cereals, stored grain, nuts, and fruits, may be attacked by insects. Considerable damage may be done by the feeding or tunneling of the insects, or the actual damage may be slight and the effect of the insects mainly contamination. The important pests of this type are the Angoumois grain moth, Indian meal moth, Mediterranean flour moth, confused flour beetle, granary and rice weevils, Khapra beetle, saw-toothed grain beetle, and flour mites. Some of these attack whole grain, and others feed mainly on meal or flour. Bean and pea weevils tunnel in and may completely destroy stored beans and peas. Stored meats and cheese are attacked principally by the larder beetle, cheese skipper, and various mites. Drugstore beetles attack a variety of vegetable products, including chocolate, pepper, and tobacco.

Insects Attacking Humans and Animals

Insects affect human beings and animals directly in four principal ways: (1) They may be merely annoying; (2) they may inject venom by their bites or stings; (3) they may live in or on people or animals as parasites; or (4) they may serve as agents in the transmission of disease. These types of damage by insects have been estimated to cost about $670 million annually in the United States.

Annoyance of Insects. Everyone has been bothered by insects that buzz around or crawl over one's body. Such effects are mainly psychological, but in some cases the "nuisance value" of annoying insects may be considerable. Bot flies and face flies, though they neither bite nor sting, cause great annoyance to cattle (Figure 2–6). Many insects annoy by their odors or secretions; others may get into one's eyes or ears.

For some people, the mere presence of insects (or the thought of such presence) may evoke fear, and such entomophobia may sometimes be costly. Many homeowners have paid dearly to rid their homes of insects that were quite harmless, simply because of their fear of insects in general.

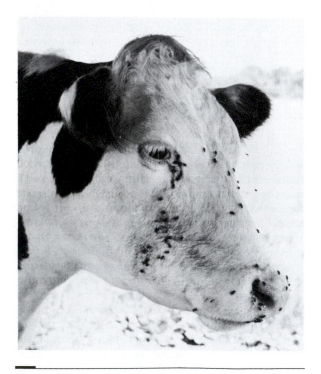

Figure 2–6.   Face flies, *Músca autumnális* DeGeer, on a cow. (Courtesy of Ohio Agricultural Research and Development Center.)

Venomous Insects. Many arthropods inject into humans and animals toxins that cause irritation, swelling, pain, and sometimes paralysis. Those that inject a venom by their bite include various biting flies, bugs, mites, ticks, centipedes, and spiders. The bites of some of these are very painful, often resulting in swelling or (for example, in the case of certain spiders) a necrotic ulcer, and in some cases may cause death. Some tick bites result in paralysis. Those that inject a venom by their sting include the bees, wasps, and scorpions. Such stings may be very painful and often cause considerable swelling; the sting of some scorpions may be fatal. Many people are particularly sensitive to bee or wasp stings and may suffer anaphylactic shock or even death as a result. More people in the United States are killed by wasp or bee stings than by the bites of venomous snakes. A few caterpillars, such as the saddleback, puss moth larvae, and larvae of the io moth, have stinging hairs that produce a type of dermatitis. Some of the blister beetles have body fluids that are irritating to the skin. A few insects, such as rose chafers, are toxic when swallowed.

Parasitic Insects. Many insects and other arthropods live in or on the bodies of people or animals as parasites and cause irritation, damage to tissues, and in some cases even death. The chewing lice are external parasites of birds and mammals, feeding on hair, feathers, dermal scales, and other external structures. They cause considerable irritation and a general run-down condition in the animal attacked. The sucking lice are external parasites of mammals and are bloodsucking. They cause irritation, and bad sores often result from the rubbing or scratching brought on by their bites. Fleas, bed bugs, and other biting forms cause similar irritation. The mange and scab mites, which burrow into the skin of people and animals, are often extremely irritating.

Many flies pass their larval stage as internal parasites of man and animals, causing a condition known as myiasis. These animals may cause serious damage, even death, to the animal affected. The larvae of the ox warble flies live under the skin of the host. They produce a general run-down condition in cattle, reduce milk production, and lower the value of the hides for leather. The sheep bot fly larva burrows in the nasal passages of its host. The screwworm fly lays its eggs in wounds and other exposed tissues of the host. The larvae of the horse bot flies develop in the alimentary tract of horses and cause irritation and damage to mucous membranes there.

Insects and Disease Transmission. The insects that attack people and animals do their greatest damage when they act as disease vectors. The bites and stings of venomous insects and the disturbance caused by parasitic insects may be severe, but are rarely fatal; many insect-borne diseases have a high mortality rate. Insects act as agents in the transmission of disease in two general ways: they may serve as mechanical vectors of the pathogen, or they may act as biological vectors. In the latter case the insect serves as a host in the life cycle of the pathogen. There are some diseases, known to be transmitted by insects or other arthropods, in which the exact role played by the vector is not completely understood.

The insects of chief importance in the mechanical transmission of pathogenic organisms are the filth-inhabiting flies such as house flies and blow flies. These insects pick up the pathogens on their tarsi or on other parts of their body when feeding on fecal material or other wastes, and they may ingest the pathogens. Later they contaminate food when they feed on it. The flies have the habit of regurgitating materials that were previously eaten, particularly on foods that are solid or semisolid, and some may contaminate human foods. Typhoid fever, cholera, and dysentery may be transmitted by flies in this way.

The arthropods that serve as a host of the pathogen as well as a vector are chiefly the bloodsucking forms. They pick up the pathogen when feeding on a diseased host and later infect another host. In such cases there is usually a period during which certain phases of the pathogen's life cycle are passed before the arthropod is capable of infecting another host. The host is usually infected either by the bite of the vector or by having the excretions or body fluids of the vector rubbed into the skin. In a few cases the vector must be swallowed before infection results.

Malaria. This disease is a typical example of those in which an insect serves as both vector and host of the pathogen. Millions of people throughout the world are affected by it. Malaria, which is characterized by rather regularly recurring paroxysms of chills and fever, is a disease in which the red blood cells are destroyed by the pathogen. It is caused by protists in the genus *Plasmòdium* and is transmitted by certain species of mosquitoes in the genus *Anópheles*. Three types of malaria are common in humans: benign tertian malaria, caused by *P. vìvax* (Grassi and Feletti), which has a wide distribution; malignant tertian malaria, caused by *P. falcíparum* (Welch), which is principally tropical and is the most dangerous type of malaria; and quartan malaria, caused by *P. malàriae* (Grassi and Feletti), which is the least common of the three types.

A person normally acquires malaria only through the bite of an infective female *Anópheles* mosquito that has previously obtained the plasmodia from a malaria victim. When such a mosquito bites a person, large numbers of tiny spindle-shaped bodies (the sporozoite stage of the *Plasmòdium*) are injected into the bloodstream with the mosquito's saliva (Figure 2–7). These leave the bloodstream within a period of 30 or 40 minutes and enter the parenchymal cells of the liver. After one or more generations (the number depending on the species of *Plasmòdium*) of asexual reproduction in the liver cells, they enter the red blood cells. In a red blood cell the *Plasmòdium* is an irregularly shaped stage called a trophozoite, which feeds on the blood cell. When the trophozoite matures, its nucleus begins to divide and the trophozoite becomes a schizont. By successive nuclear divisions of the schizont, some 10–24 daughter organisms are formed; these products of schizont division are called merozoites. The red blood cell soon ruptures, and the merozoites are released into the plasma. They enter other red blood cells, and the process of feeding and asexual reproduction (which is here called schizogony) continues. The asexual cycle of *Plasmòdium* in the bloodstream of man is repeated every 24–72 hours, the interval depending on the species of *Plasmòdium*. The release of the merozoites into the plasma coincides with the paroxysms of the disease.

After several generations of merozoites have been produced, sexual forms called gametocytes appear. Gametocytes are of two types, male and female. The gametocytes develop no further until they are ingested by a suitable *Anópheles* mosquito. If the *Anópheles* mosquito bites a malarial patient and does not pick up any gametocytes, it does not become infective. If it picks up gametocytes, the parasite continues its cycle of development in the mosquito. Once in the stomach of the mosquito, the gametocytes undergo certain changes: the male gametocyte throws off flagellated bodies, and the female gametocyte throws off some of its chromatin material. The fusion of a flagellated body with a modified female gametocyte constitutes fertilization and results in the formation of a zygote. The zygote soon becomes elongated and motile, burrows into the stomach wall, and forms a cystlike structure known as an oocyst. Successive nuclear divisions in the oocyst result in the formation of a large number of elongate spindle-shaped bodies, the sporozoites. After some 10–15 days, depending on the temperature, the oocyst ruptures and releases the sporozoites into the body cavity of the mosquito. The sporozoites (or at least some of them) travel to and enter the salivary glands of the mosquito. From this time on, until the

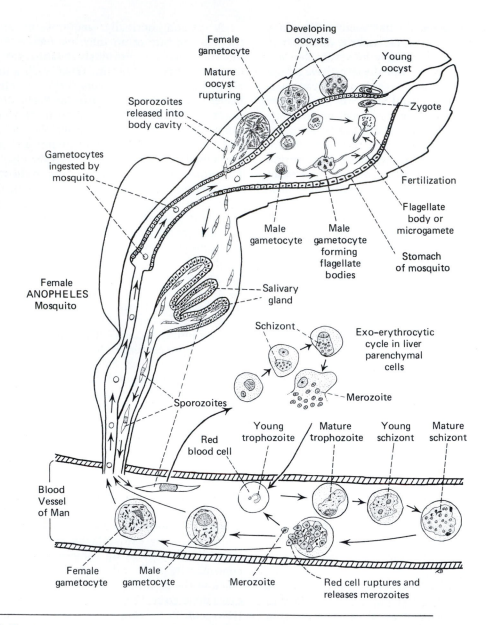

Figure 2–7. Life cycle (diagrammatic) of the malarial parasite, *Plasmòdium vìvax* (Grassi and Feletti). For explanation, see text.

mosquito dies or until it hibernates, it is capable of infecting a person with malaria.

Some of the most serious diseases of humans and animals are transmitted by insects and other arthropods, and the principal vectors are the biting flies, sucking lice, fleas, bugs, mites, and ticks. A summary of the more important diseases transmitted by arthropods is given in Table 2–2. The arthropods listed as "vectors" sometimes play a passive role in the transmission of the disease.

Insect Control

Humankind has competed with insects for food and fiber for a long time, and while many battles have been won, the war is far from over. A number of methods and strategies have been used for suppressing insect populations and reducing their damage, including mechanical, cultural, biological, and chemical methods. Each method has had particular success against certain pests, but studies are continuing on all phases of control, including such new approaches as the use of pheromones, juvenile hormones, and radioactively induced sterility.

From the middle 1940s to the late 1960s, the emphasis in insect control was focused on chemicals. Effective chemicals were readily available during this period and were relatively inexpensive. Effects on the environment—on nontarget organisms such as predators, parasites, and pollinators—and the matter of harmful residues on foods were in many cases not given much attention. Commercial producers and the general public were conditioned to the proposition that for every insect pest a spray or dust offered the best solution to the control problem.

One result of this dependence on chemicals was the development of resistance to the chemicals by many pests, requiring increasing amounts of the insecticide to achieve adequate control. Mechanisms of resistance are of many sorts, but the phenomenon (text continued on page 21)

Table 2–2
Animal Diseases Transmitted by Insects and Other Arthropods

A. Diseases Caused by Helminths (Roundworms and Flatworms)

Disease	Pathogen	Vector	Host	Distribution
Tapeworm	*Dipylídium canìnum* (L.)	Dog flea, *Ctenocephálides cànis* (Curtis)	Dog, man	Worldwide
Tapeworm	*Hymenólepis diminùta* (Rudolphi)	Rat flea, *Xenopsýlla cheòpis* (Rothschild)	Rat, man	Worldwide
Tapeworm	*Diphyllobóthrium látum* (L.)	Copepods, *Cỳclops* spp. (Crustàcea)	Man, animals	Worldwide
Lung fluke	*Paragònimus westermánni* (Kerbert)	Crabs, crayfish	Man	Far East, Africa, South and Central America, Mexico
Filariasis	*Wucheréria báncrofti* (Cobbold), *Brùgia màlayi* (Brug)	Mosquitoes, principally in the genera *Aèdes*, *Cùlex*, *Anópheles*, and *Mansònia*; some biting midges (*Culicòides*)	Man	Worldwide in the tropics and subtropics
Onchocerciasis	*Onchocérca vólvulus* (Leuckart), a roundworm	Black flies, *Simùlium* spp.	Man	Mexico, Central America, equatorial Africa
Loaiasis	*Lòa lòa* (Cobbold), a roundworm	Deer flies, *Chrỳsops* spp.	Man	Africa

B. Diseases Caused by Protista

Disease	Pathogen	Vector	Host	Distribution
Malaria	*Plasmòdium vìvax* (Grassi and Feletti), *P. falcíparum* (Welch), *P. maláriae* (Grassi and Feletti)	Mosquitoes in the genus *Anópheles*	Man	Worldwide in tropical, subtropical, and temperate regions
African sleeping sickness	*Trypanosòma gambiénse* Dutton, *T. rhodesiénse* Stephens and Fanthom	Tsetse flies, *Glossìna* spp.	Man, animals	Equatorial Africa
Nagana	*Trypanosòma brùcei* Plimmer and Bradford	Tsetse flies, *Glossìna* spp.	Wild and domestic animals	Equatorial Africa

(continued)

Table 2–2 (*Continued*)

B. Diseases Caused by Protista (*Continued*)

Disease	Pathogen	Vector	Host	Distribution
Chagas disease	*Trypanosòma crùzi* Chagas	Assassin bugs, principally in the genera *Triátoma* and *Rhódnius*	Man, armadillo, opossum, rodents	South and Central America, Mexico, Texas
Kala-azar	*Leishmánia dónovani* (Laveran and Mesnil)	Sand flies, *Phlebótomus* and *Lutzomỳia* spp.	Man	Mediterranean region, Asia, South America
Espundia	*Leishmánia braziliénsis* Vianna	Sand flies, *Lutzomỳia* spp.	Man	South and Central America, Mexico, North Africa, southern Asia
Oriental sore	*Leishmánia trópica* (Wright)	Sand flies, *Phlebótomus* and *Lutzomỳia* spp.	Man	Africa, Asia, South America
Texas cattle fever	*Babèsia bigémina* Smith and Kilbourne	Cattle tick, *Boóphilus annulàtus* (Say)	Cattle	Southern United States, Central and South America, South Africa, Philippines
Amoebic dysentery	*Endamoèba histolỳtica* (Schaudinn)	House fly, *Músca doméstica* L.; various blow flies and flesh flies	Man, animals	Worldwide

C. Diseases Caused by Bacteria

Disease	Pathogen	Vector	Host	Distribution
Bubonic plague	*Yersínia péstis* (Lehmann and Newmann)	Various fleas, especially the rat flea, *Xenopsýlla cheòpis*	Man, rodents	Worldwide
Tularemia	*Francisélla tularénsis* (McCoy and Chapin)	Deer flies (*Chrỳsops* spp.); ticks, principally *Dermacéntor* spp. and *Haemaphysàlis* spp.	Man, rodents	United States, Canada, Europe, the Orient
Anthrax	*Bacíllus anthràcis* Cohn	Horse flies, *Tabánus* spp.	Man, animals	Worldwide
Typhoid fever	*Eberthélla typhòsa* (Zopf)	House fly, *Músca doméstica*; various blow flies and flesh flies	Man	Worldwide
Bacillary dysentery	*Bacíllus* spp.	House fly, *Músca doméstica*; various blow flies and flesh flies	Man	Worldwide
Cholera	*Víbrio cómma* (Schroeter)	House fly, *Músca doméstica*; various blow flies and flesh flies	Man	Worldwide

D. Diseases Caused by Spirochaetes

Disease	Pathogen	Vector	Host	Distribution
Relapsing fever	*Borrèlia recurréntis* (Lebert), *B. dúttoni* (Breinl)	Ticks (*Ornithódoros* spp.); body louse, *Pedículus h. humànus* L.	Man, rodents.	Worldwide
Fowl spirochetosis	*Borrèlia anserìna* (Sakharoff)	Fowl tick, *Árgas pérsicus* (Oken)	Chicken, turkey, goose	North America, Brazil, India, Australia, Egypt
Lyme disease	*Borrèlia burgdórferi* Johnson *et al.*	*Ixòdes dámmini* Spielman *et al.*, *I. rícinus* (L.)	Man, deer, mice	United States, Canada, Europe

Table 2–2 (*Continued*)

E. Diseases Caused by Bartonella and Rickettsia Organisms

Disease	Pathogen	Vector	Host	Distribution
Verruga peruana or Oroya Fever	*Bartonélla bacillifórmis* (Strong *et al.*)	Sand flies, *Lutzomỳia* spp.	Man	Bolivia, Peru, Ecuador, Chile, Colombia
Epidemic typhus	*Rickéttsia prowazéki* da Rocha Lima	Body louse, *Pedículus h. humànus;* rat flea, *Xenopsýlla cheòpis;* rat mite, *Liponýssus bàcoti* (Hirst)	Man, rodents	Worldwide
Endemic or murine typhus	*Rickéttsia mooseri* Monteiro	Rat flea, *Xenopsýlla cheòpis;* various other fleas, lice, mites, and ticks on rodents	Man, rodents	Worldwide
Scrub typhus or tsutsugamushi disease	*Rickéttsia tsutsugamùshi* (Hayashi)	Harvest mites or chiggers, *Trombícula* spp.	Man, rodents	Japan, China, Taiwan, India, Australia, East Indies, some South Pacific islands
Spotted fever	*Rickéttsia rickéttsii* (Wolbach)	Various ticks, mainly *Dermacéntor andersòni* Stiles and *D. variábilis* (Say)	Man, rodents	North and South America
African tick fever, Q fever	*Rickéttsia* spp.	Various ticks (Ixódidae)	Man	South Africa, Australia, western United States

F. Diseases Caused by Viruses

Disease	Pathogen	Vector	Host	Distribution
Yellow fever	A virus	Various mosquitoes, especially *Aèdes aegýpti* (L.)	Man, monkeys	American and African tropics and subtropics
Dengue	A virus	Mosquitoes in the genus *Aèdes*, principally *A. aegýpti* and *A. albopíctus* Skuse	Man	Worldwide in tropics and subtropics
Encephalitis	Several virus strains	Various mosquitoes in the genera *Cùlex* and *Aèdes*	Man, horse	United States, Canada, South America, Europe, Asia
Pappataci fever	A virus	Sand fly, *Phlebótomus papatàsii* (Scopoli)	Man	Mediterranean region, India, Sri Lanka
Colorado tick fever	A virus	Various ticks	Man	Western United States

of resistance is basically the result of genetic selection: the survivors of repeated exposures to an insecticide pass on to their offspring their resistant traits (chemical, physical, behavioral, or whatever). Successive generations, when subjected to applications of the same insecticide, have more survivors, and resistant strains of the pest species are developed. Eventually, the only solution to this resistance is to increase the dosage or the number of applications or to change to another, perhaps more toxic chemical.

The ultimate result of a dependence on chemicals is that harmful residues remain in and are translocated through the soil, and eventually find their way into streams and lakes. Studies of food chains have shown that a number of pesticide residues, especially those of the chlorinated hydrocarbons (DDT, chlordane, heptachlor, and others), are concentrated by each link in the chain, so that very high levels of these toxicants may be present in the ultimate consumer in the food chain. Birds and other desirable organisms may be adversely affected by these residues. Beneficial naturally occurring predators and parasites are eliminated indiscriminately, so that previously innocuous insects may become important pests. Residues on foods have become of increasing concern, and new techniques have been developed to detect minute traces of harmful chemicals, so that pesticides with a zero tolerance on certain foods have had to be phased out. Finally, in the search for more and effective chemicals, the cost of treatment has greatly increased.

Agricultural and medical entomologists have concluded that all available methods must be used to keep insect damage below an economic threshold and at the same time satisfy the demands placed on the environment in accomplishing that goal.

Integrated pest management, to use the modern terminology, is really not new. It is a concept of employing the optimum combination of control methods to reduce a pest insect population to below an economic threshold, with as few harmful effects as possible on the environment and nontarget organisms, and is based on several considerations: (1) the amount of damage that is tolerable, (2) the cost of reducing the damage to this acceptable level, and (3) the effect on the environment. A number of such pest management programs have been initiated and have been particularly effective in the control of pests of apples, cotton, corn, soybeans, tobacco, and alfalfa.

Integrated pest management does not rule out or necessarily minimize the use of chemical control methods, but represents a move from preventive to as-needed applications of a chemical. Applications are made when there is potential damage and not according to a fixed schedule whether or not the insects are present. Such a program requires an intimate knowledge of the pest species and careful monitoring of populations on the crop. It is most effective and economical when conducted on a regional basis, with all growers cooperating.

References

Apple, J. L., and R. F. Smith. 1976. Integrated Pest Management. New York: Plenum Press, 200 pp.

Baker, E. W., T. M. Evans, D. J. Gould, W. B. Hull, and H. L Keegan. 1956. A Manual of Parasitic Mites of Medical and Economic Importance. New York: National Pest Control Assoc., 170 pp.

Beard, R. L. 1963. Insect toxins and venoms. Annu. Rev. Entomol. 8:1–18.

Bishopp, F. C., G. J. Haeussler, H. L. Haller, W. L. Popham, B. A. Porter, E. R. Sasscer, J. S. Wade, B. Schwarz, K. S. Quisenberry, E. R. McGovran, and A. Stefferud. 1952. Insects. USDA Yearbook, 780 pp.

Black, L. M. 1962. Some recent advances on leafhopper borne viruses. In Biological Transmission of Disease Agents, K. Maramorosch (Ed.). New York: Academic Press, pp. 1–9.

Brittain, W. H. 1933. Apple pollination studies. Can. Dept. Agr. Bull. 162; 198 pp.

Carter, W. 1973 (2nd ed.). Insects in Relation to Plant Diseases. New York: Wiley, 759 pp.

Chandler, A. C., and C. P. Read. 1961 (10th ed.). Introduction to Parasitology. New York: Wiley, 882 pp.

Coppel, H. G., and J. W. Martins. 1977. Biological Insect Pest Suppression. New York: Springer-Verlag, 314 pp.; illus.

Davidson, G. 1974. Genetic Control of Insect Pests. New York: Academic Press, 158 pp.

Davidson, R. H., and W. F. Lyon. 1979 (7th ed.). Insect Pests of Farm, Garden, and Orchard. New York: Wiley, 596 pp.

DeBach, P. 1974. Biological Control by Natural Enemies. New York: Cambridge Univ. Press, 325 pp.

Faust, E. C., P. C. Beaver, and R. C. Jung. 1962. Animal Agents and Vectors of Human Disease. Philadelphia: Lea and Febiger, 485 pp.; illus.

Free, J. B. 1970. Insect Pollination of Crops. London: Academic Press, 544 pp.

Furniss, R. L., and V. M. Carolin. 1977. Western Forest Insects. USDA Misc. Publ. 1339; 654 pp.; illus.

Gorham, J. R. 1976. Insects as food. Bull. Soc. Vector Ecol. 3:11–16.

Greenberg, B. 1973. Flies and Disease. 2 vol. Vol. 1: Ecology, Classification, and Biotic Associations, 856 pp. Vol. 2: Biology and Disease Transmission, 447 pp. Princeton, N.J.: Princeton Univ. Press.

Harris, K. F., and K. Maramorosch. 1977. Aphids as Virus Vectors. New York: Academic Press, 559 pp.; illus.

Horsfall, W. R. 1962. Medical Entomology: Arthropods and Human Disease. New York: Ronald Press, 467 pp.; illus.

Huffaker, C. B., and P. D. Messenger (Eds.). 1976. Theory and Practice of Biological Control. New York: Academic Press, 788 pp.; illus.

Hunter, G. W., III, W. W. Frye, and J. C. Swartzwelder. 1960 (3rd ed.). A Manual of Tropical Medicine. Philadelphia: W. B. Saunders, 892 pp.; illus.

James, M. T., and R. F. Harwood. 1969 (6th ed.). Herms's Medical Entomology. New York: Macmillan, 484 pp.; illus.

Jaycox, E. R. 1977 (rev. ed.). Beekeeping in the Midwest. Urbana: Univ. Illinois Press, 168 pp.; illus.

Maddox, D. M. 1973. *Amynothrips andersoni* (Thysanoptera: Phlaeothripidae), a thrips for the biological control of alligatorweed. I. Host specificity studies. Environ. Entomol. 2:30–37.

Maddox, D. M., L. A. Andres, R. D. Hennessey, R. D. Blackburn, and N. R. Spencer. 1971. Insects to control alligatorweed, an invader of aquatic ecosystems in the United States. BioScience 21:985–991.

Maddox, D. M., and A. Mayfield. 1979. Biology and life history of *Amynothrips andersoni*, a thrips for the biological control of alligatorweed. Ann. Entomol. Soc. Amer. 72:136–140; illus.

Maramorosch, K., and K. F. Harris (Eds.). 1979. Leafhopper Vectors and Plant Disease Agents. New York: Academic Press, 654 pp.; illus.

Markell, E. K., and M. Voge. 1958. Diagnostic Medical Parasitology. Philadelphia: W. B. Saunders, 276 pp.; illus.

Mattingly, P. F. 1969. The Biology of Mosquito-Borne Disease. New York: American Elsevier, 184 pp.; illus.

Metcalf, C. L., and W. P. Flint. 1962 (4th ed., revised by R. L. Metcalf). Destructive and Useful Insects. New York: McGraw-Hill, 1087 pp., illus.

Metcalf, R. L., and W. Luckman (Eds.). 1975. Introduction to Pest Management. New York: Wiley, 587 pp.

Morse, R. A. 1975. Bees and Beekeeping. Ithaca, N.Y.: Cornell Univ. Press, 296 pp.; illus.

Nielson, M. W. 1968. The leafhopper vectors of phytopathogenetic viruses (Homoptera, Cicadellidae): Taxonomy, biology, and virus transmission. USDA Tech. Bull. 1382, 386 pp.; illus.

Richards, A. J. (Ed.). 1978. The Pollination of Flowers by Insects. New York: Academic Press, 214 pp.; illus.

Smith, K. G. V. 1973. Insects and Other Arthropods of Medical Importance. London: British Museum (Natural History), 576 pp.; illus.

Snow, K. R. 1974. Insects and Disease. New York: Wiley, 208 pp.; illus.

Taylor, R. L. 1975. Butterflies in My Stomach, or, Insects in Human Nutrition. Santa Barbara, Calif.: Woodbridge Press, 224 pp.; illus.

Taylor, R. M. 1967. Catalogue of Arthropod-Borne Viruses of the World. Bethesda, Md.: National Institute of Allergy and Infectious Diseases, 898 pp.

Tinsley, T. W. 1977. Viruses and the biological control of insect pests. BioScience 27(10):659–661.

Watson, D. L., and A. W. A. Brown (Eds.). 1977. Pesticide Management and Insecticide Resistance. New York: Academic Press, 656 pp.

Watson, T. F., L. Moore, and G. W. Ware. 1976. Practical Pest Management. San Francisco: Freeman, 196 pp.

Williams, R. E., R. D. Hall, A. B. Broce, and P. J. Scholl (Eds.). 1985. Livestock Entomology. New York: Wiley, 335 pp.; illus.

Chapter 3

The Anatomy, Physiology, and Development of Insects

A knowledge of anatomy and physiology is essential to an understanding of insects. It is also necessary to have names for structures in order to be able to talk about them. The nomenclature of insect anatomy should be viewed as a language, a tool, that makes precise discussions about insects possible, and not as a barrier to understanding. In fact, many of the terms (for example, *femur, trochanter, mandible*) have analogous meanings in vertebrate anatomy. The terms that have special meanings in individual orders are discussed in the appropriate chapters. In addition, all terms used are defined in the glossary at the back of this book.

Insects are more or less elongate and cylindrical in form and are bilaterally symmetrical; that is, the right and left sides of the body are essentially alike. The body is divided into a series of segments, the metameres, and these are grouped into three distinct regions or *tagmata* (singular, *tagma*): the head, thorax, and abdomen (Figure 3–1). The primary functions of the head are sensory perception, neural integration, and food gathering. The thorax is a locomotory tagma and bears the legs and wings. The abdomen houses most of the visceral organs, including components of the digestive, excretory, and reproductive systems.

The Body Wall

The skeleton of an animal supports and protects the body, and transfers the forces generated by the contraction of muscles. One of the fundamental features of arthropods is the development of hardened plates, or *sclerites*, and their incorporation into the skeletal system of the animal. This is usually referred to as an *exoskeleton* because the sclerites are part of the outer body wall of the arthropod. In fact, however, arthropods also possess an extensive endoskeleton of supports, braces, and sites for the attachment of muscles. The characteristics of the body wall also influence the way in which substances such as water and oxygen move into and out of the animal.

The integument of an insect is composed of three principal layers (Figure 3–2): a cellular layer, the epidermis; a thin acellular layer below the epidermis (i.e., toward the inside of the animal), the basement membrane; and another acellular layer, outside of and secreted by the cells of the epidermis, the cuticle.

The cuticle is a chemically complex layer, not only differing in structure from one species to another, but even differing in its characteristics from one part of an insect to another. It is made up of

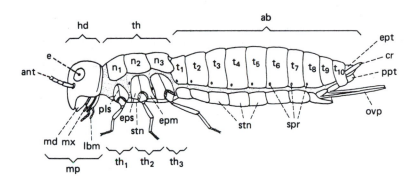

Figure 3–1. General structure of an insect. *ab*, abdomen; *ant*, antenna; *cr*, cercus; *e*, compound eye; *epm*, epimeron; *eps*, episternum; *ept*, epiproct; *hd*, head; *lbm*, labium; *md*, mandible; *mp*, mouthparts; *mx*, maxilla; *n*, nota of thorax; *ovp*, ovipositor; *pls*, pleural suture; *ppt*, paraproct; *spr*, spiracles; *stn*, sternum; t_{1-10}, terga; *th*, thorax; th_1, prothorax; th_2, mesothorax; th_3, metathorax. (Modified from Snodgrass, 1935, *Principles of Insect Morphology*, by permission of the McGraw-Hill Book Company, Inc.)

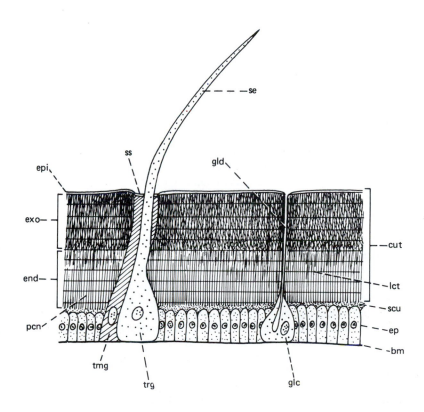

Figure 3–2. Structure of the body wall (diagrammatic). *bm*, basement membrane; *cut*, cuticle; *end*, endocuticle; *ep*, epidermis; *epi*, epicuticle; *exo*, exocuticle; *glc*, gland cell; *gld*, duct of gland cell; *lct*, layer of the cuticle; *pcn*, pore canal; *se*, seta; *ss*, setal socket; *tmg*, tormogen cell (which forms the setal socket); *trg*, trichogen cell (which forms the seta).

chains of a polysaccharide, chitin, embedded in a protein matrix. Chitin is primarily made up of monomers of the sugar N-acetylglucosamine (Figure 3–3). Individual chitin chains are intertwined to form microfibrils, and these microfibrils are often laid down in parallel in a layer called a lamina.

Chitin itself is a very resistant substance, but it does not make the cuticle hard. The hardness is derived from modifications of the protein matrix in which the microfibrils are embedded. The cuticle initially secreted by the epidermis, called procuticle, is soft, pliant, pale in color, and expandable to a

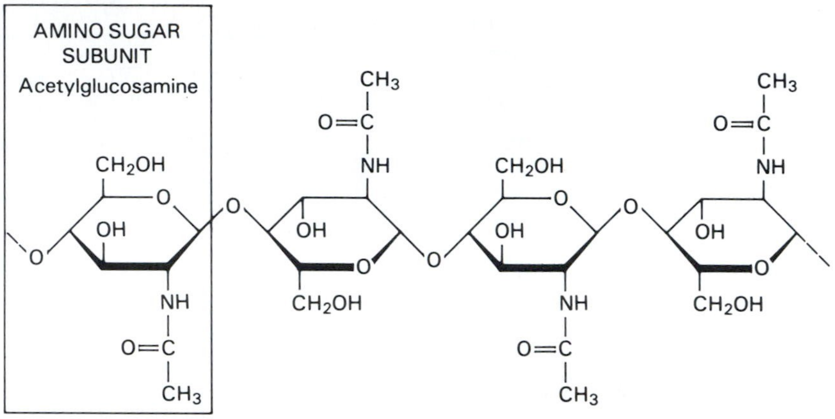

Figure 3–3. Chemical structure of chitin and its primary monomeric component, N-acetylglucosamine (from Arms and Camp).

limited extent. The formation of sclerites in this cuticle is the process of hardening and darkening, or sclerotization. This results from the formation of cross-bonds between protein chains in the outer portions of the procuticle. Such sclerotized cuticle is called exocuticle (Figure 3–2, *exo*). Below the exocuticle may be unsclerotized cuticle called endocuticle (Figure 3–2, *end*). This pliant endocuticle forms the "membranes" that connect sclerites and can be resorbed into the body before molting.

Atop the endo- and exocuticle is a very thin, acellular layer, the epicuticle (Figure 3–2, *epi*). This is itself composed of layers: those generally present are an inner epicuticle, outer epicuticle (or cuticulin), a wax layer, and a cement layer. The epicuticle contains no chitin. The wax layer is very important to terrestrial insects because it serves as the primary mechanism to limit the loss of water across the body wall (both exocuticle and endocuticle are permeable to water). As a solid decreases in size (as measured by volume, surface area, or some linear dimension) the surface-area-to-volume ratio, that is, the relative amount of surface area, increases. Therefore, the loss of water across the body surface is relatively much more important to a small creature than to a large one. Many small terrestrial animals are known that do not have such a protective wax layer, for example, snails and isopods, but these creatures are usually restricted to regions of high relative humidity, thus decreasing the rate at which water is lost from their body.

The sclerites of the body wall are often subdivided by grooves and crests, or may project into the body as internal struts. In general, an external groove marking an infolding of cuticle of the outer body wall is called a *sulcus* (plural, *sulci*) (Figure 3–4, *su*). The term *suture* is also very widely used and refers to a line of fusion between two formerly separated

sclerites. The distinction is a subtle one and often difficult or impossible to make simply by looking at the external structure of a specimen; therefore, in this book we will generally use these terms more or less synonymously. The lines of inflection seen externally usually correspond to internal ridges, or *costae* (Figure 3–4, *cos*). The internal costae may serve as strengthening braces or as the sites of muscle attachment. An external crest may be referred to as a costa or *carina* (or any number of common English names such as a keel). Internal projections of cuticle are also referred to as *apodemes* or *apophyses* (Figure 3–4, *apo*).

Abdomen

We begin our discussion of the three tagmata of insects with the abdomen because it, in comparison with the head and thorax, is relatively simple in structure. Arthropods, like vertebrates, are built upon a basic groundplan of repeated body segments, or metameres. These are most clearly visible in the abdomen. In general, the abdomen of an insect is made up of 11 metameres (Figure 3–1, *ab*). Each metamere typically has a dorsal sclerite, the *tergum* (plural, *terga*; Figure 3–1, t_1–t_{10}; Figure 3–5A, *t*); a ventral sclerite, the *sternum* (plural, *sterna*; Figure 3–1, *stn*; Figure 3–5A, *stn*); and a membranous lateral region, the *pleuron* (plural, *pleura*; Figure 3–5A, *plm*). The openings to the respiratory system, the spiracles (Figure 3-1, *spr*), typically are located in the pleuron. Terga and sterna may be subdivided; these parts are referred to as *tergites* and *sternites*. Sclerites in the pleural wall are called *pleurites*.

This segmentation of the abdomen differs from that found in other nonarthropod protostomes such as the segmented worms (Annélida). In these the

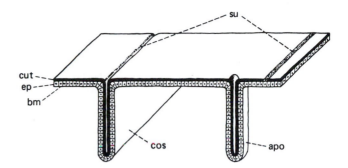

Figure 3–4. Diagram of external and internal features of the body wall. *apo*, apophysis; *bm*, basement membrane; *cos*, costa; *cut*, cuticle; *ep*, epidermis; *su*, sulcus or suture.

externally visible grooves in the body wall delimiting the metameres serve as the points of attachment for the dorsal and ventral longitudinal muscles. In arthropods, these muscles attach to internal costae, the *antecostae*, which are located near, but not at, the anterior margins of the terga and sterna (Figure 3–5B, *antc*). Externally, the position of the antecosta is indicated by a groove, the *antecostal suture* (Figure 3–5B, *ancs*). The region of the tergum anterior to the antecostal sulcus is the *acrotergite* (Figure 3–5B, *act*). The corresponding region of the sternum is the *acrosternite* (Figure 3–5B, *acs*). The main dorsal longitudinal muscles extend between the antecostae of successive segments. Contraction of these muscles results in a telescoping, or retraction, of the abdominal segments. This body plan, in which the segmentation that is externally apparent does not conform

to the attachment of the longitudinal muscles, is known as *secondary segmentation*.

The genitalia of insects are generally located on or about abdominal segments 8 and 9. These segments have a number of specializations associated with copulation and oviposition. Our discussion of them is therefore included in the section below on the reproductive systems. Segments 1–7, anterior to the genitalia, are the pregenital segments. In most adult winged insects these segments have no appendages. In the primitively wingless insects,[1] the orders Microcorýphia and Thysanùra, the ventral portion of a pregenital segment is generally com-

[1]As described in Chapter 7 we are distinguishing between the terms Hexápoda and Insécta, restricting the latter to refer to the Pterygòta, Thysanùra, and Microcorýphia.

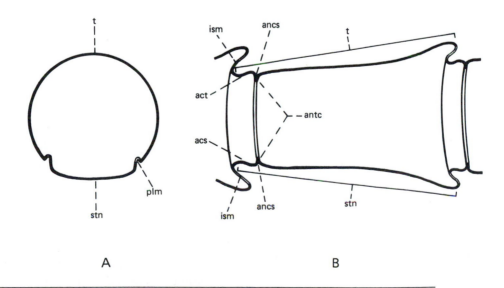

A   B

Figure 3–5. Structure of a typical abdominal segment (diagrammatic). **A,** cross section; **B,** sagittal section. *acs*, acrosternite; *act*, acrotergite; *ancs*, antecostal suture; *antc*, antecosta; *ism*, intersegmental membrane; *plm*, pleural membrane; *stn*, sternum; *t*, tergum.

posed of a small medial sternum and two large plates laterad of the sternum, the *coxopodites* (see Figure 9–1B, *cxp* and *stn*). The coxopodites are remnants of the bases of the abdominal legs and apically they bear a musculated *stylus* (Figure 9–1A,B, *sty*). The styli probably represent the apical portions of these legs (the telopods), but they are no longer segmented as are the thoracic legs. The styli generally function as sensory organs and also support the abdomen, much like the runners of a sled. Mesal to the styli are one or sometimes two pairs of eversible vesicles, which function in water absorption. They are everted from the body by hydrostatic pressure and retracted by muscles. In many cases the coxopodites and the sternum are fused into a single composite sclerite, the *coxosternum.*

Pregenital abdominal appendages are present in winged insects only in immature stages (with the exception of male Odonàta). In embryos the appendages of the first abdominal segment, known as *pleuropodia*, are present. These are glandular structures and are lost before the insect hatches from the egg. The larvae of some Neuróptera (Figure 27–6A–C) and Coleóptera (Figures 28–20A,B, 28–22A) bear lateral styluslike structures that have variously been interpreted as representing leg rudiments, styli, or secondarily developed gills. The nymphs of Ephemeróptera bear a series of platelike gills along the upper lateral portions of the body (Figure 10–2). Again, from just what structures these gills were derived and what their serial homologues may be on the thorax have been matters of considerable debate.

The immature stages of a number of orders possess structures known as prolegs on the pregenital segments. These are typically fleshy, short appendages that are important in walking or crawling (see, e.g., Figures 34–3, *prl*; 34–74, *ventral plg*; and 35–37). Hinton (1955) came to the conclusion that prolegs had evolved independently a number of times. Others, such as Kukalová-Peck (1983), interpret these structures as modified abdominal legs, both homologous between orders and serially homologous with the segmented thoracic legs.

The postgenital segments are typically reduced in insects. Among hexapods the Protùra are unique in that they have 12 well-developed segments in the abdomen (representing 11 metameres and an apical nonmetameric telson). In general, the only indication of an 11th segment among insects is a dorsal sclerite, the *epiproct*, and two lateral sclerites, the *paraprocts* (Figure 3–1, *ept, ppt*). Between them are inserted the appendages of the apical abdominal segment, the *cerci* (singular, *cercus*). Typically the cerci are sensory organs, but in some cases they are modified as organs of defense (as in the forceps of Der-

máptera, Figures 18–1 and 18–2) or may be specialized as accessory copulatory organs. Very often the apical abdominal segments are highly reduced or normally retracted within the body.

Thorax

The thorax is the locomotory tagma of the body, and it bears the legs and wings. It is made up of three segments, the anterior *prothorax, mesothorax*, and posterior *metathorax* (Figure 3–1, th_1–th_3). Among insects a maximum of two pairs of spiracles open on the thorax, one associated with the mesothorax, one with the metathorax. The mesothoracic spiracle serves not only that segment, but also the prothorax and head. The terga of the thorax are typically referred to as *nota* (singular, *notum*). Among present-day insects wings are borne at most on the mesothoracic and metathoracic segments; collectively these two segments are called the *pterothorax*. These have several modifications associated with flight that are not shared with the prothorax.

The prothorax is connected to the head by a membranous necklike region, the *cervix* (Figure 3–6, *cvx*). Dorsal longitudinal muscles extend from the mesothorax through the prothorax and insert upon the head; the pronotum has no antecosta. Movements of the head are coordinated with the rest of the body by means of one or two pairs of *cervical sclerites* (Figure 3–6, *cvs*) that articulate with the prothorax posteriorly and the head anteriorly.

The system of secondary segmentation described above in reference to the abdomen is modified in the pterothorax in order to accommodate the flight musculature. The dorsal longitudinal muscles of the meso- and metathorax are greatly enlarged and are involved in depression (downward movement) of the wings (Figure 3–7B, *dlm*). As a corollary, the sites of insertion of these muscles—that is, the antecostae of the mesothorax, metathorax, and first abdominal segments—are also greatly enlarged and project downward within the thorax. These enlarged antecostae are called the first, second, and third *phragmata* respectively (singular, *phragma*; Figure 3–7B, ph_1–ph_3). Externally, the mesonotum and metanotum are typically divided transversely by a sulcus that gives added flexibility. The sulcus divides each notum into an anterior *scutum* (Figure 3–6, sct_2, sct_3) and a posterior *scutellum* (Figure 3–6, scl_2, scl_3). In addition, the portions of the notum bearing the second and third phragma are often separated from the following scutum from which they are derived, and moved forward, sometimes even entirely fused with

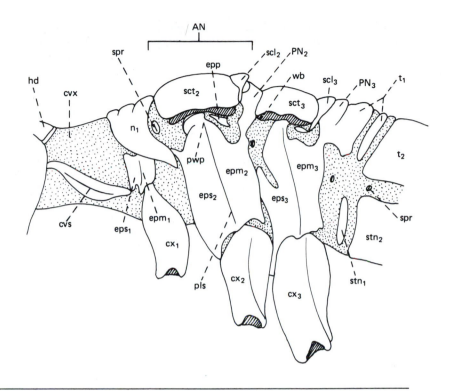

Figure 3–6.   Thorax of *Panórpa*, lateral view. *AN*, alinotum; *cvs*, cervical sclerite; *cvx*, cervix; *cx*, coxa; *epm*, epimeron; *epp*, epipleurite; *eps*, episternum; *hd*, head; n_1, pronotum; *pls*, pleural suture; *PN*, postnotum; *pwp*, pleural wing process; *scl*, scutellum; *sct*, scutum; *spr*, spiracle; *stn*, abdominal sternum; *t*, abdominal tergum; *wb*, base of wing. (Redrawn from Ferris and Rees.)

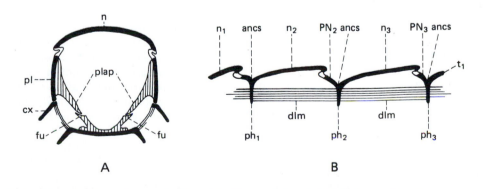

Figure 3–7.   Endoskeleton of the thorax (diagrammatic). **A,** cross section of a thoracic segment; **B,** longitudinal section of the thoracic dorsum. *ancs*, antecostal suture; *cx*, coxa; *dlm*, dorsal longitudinal muscles; *fu*, sternal apophyses or furca; *n*, notum; n_1, pronotum; n_2, mesonotum; n_3, metanotum; *ph*, phragmata; *pl*, pleuron; *plap*, pleural apophyses; PN_2, mesopostnotum; PN_3, metapostnotum; t_1, first abdominal tergum. (Redrawn from Snodgrass, by permission of the McGraw-Hill Book Company, Inc.)

the sclerites anterior to them. These sclerites bearing the second and third phragmata are called *post-nota* (Figures 3–6 and 3–7, PN_2, PN_3).

The lateral portion of the thorax in winged insects is very different from the abdomen in that typically it is strongly sclerotized and relatively rigid. The origin of these pleural sclerites has been the subject of considerable debate. Some workers have argued that these pleural sclerites evolved *de novo* and have no serial homologues in other parts of the body. Many others postulate that the pleural sclerites represent the incorporation of a basal leg segment, the *subcoxa*, into the body wall. Finally, others have suggested that, in essence, both are correct in that the thoracic pleurites are composite in origin. In any case, the sclerotized portion of the pleuron is divided by a suture that extends from the base of the leg to the base of the wing; this is the *pleural suture* (Figure 3–6, *pls*) and divides the pleuron into an anterior *episternum* (Figure 3–6, eps_1–eps_3) and a posterior *epimeron* (Figure 3–6, epm_1–epm_3). According to the subcoxal theory of the origin of pleural sclerites, the pleurites were originally composed of a pair of incomplete rings above the base of the leg: an upper *anapleurite* and a lower *catepleurite* (the latter also called katepleurite, catapleurite, or coxopleurite). These sclerites are visible in the primitively wingless hexapods and in a few pterygotes. The catepleurite articulates with the leg. Thus the combination of the pleural suture and the two rings of the subcoxa can theoretically define four regions of the pleuron: anepimeron, anepisternum, catepimeron, and catepisternum (for an example see terminology of McAlpine *et al.* for the dipteran thorax in Chapter 32). In addition to its dorsal articulation with the catepleurite, the leg articulates anteroventrally with a narrow sclerite (often entirely fused with the episternum), the *trochantin*. The wing rests upon the *pleural wing process* (Figure 3–6, *pwp*), which forms the dorsal apex of the pleural suture. Anterior to the pleural wing process is a small sclerite, the *basalare* (Figure 3–12A,B, *ba*); posterior to the pleural wing process is another sclerite, the *subalare* (Figure 3–12A, *sb*; occasionally two small sclerites are found here instead of one). These sclerites (sometimes collectively called epipleurites) are attached to the base of the wing and serve as means of controlling the attitude of the wings or may be directly involved in wing depression.

The external pleural suture corresponds to an internal costa, the pleural ridge. This ridge extends internally on either side as a pair of pleural apophyses (or pleural arms; Figure 3–7A, *plap*). These pleural apophyses are connected with a corresponding pair of apophyses arising from the sternum (Figure 3–7A, *fu*). The two may be connected by muscle or tendon, or in some cases they are fused together.

Legs

The thoracic legs of insects are sclerotized and subdivided into a number of segments. There are typically six segments (Figure 3–8): the *coxa* (*cx*), the basal segment; the *trochanter* (*tr*), a small segment (occasionally two segments) following the coxa; the femur (*fm*), usually the first long segment of the leg; the *tibia* (*tb*), the second long segment; the *tarsus* (*ts*), usually a series of small segments beyond the tibia; and the *pretarsus* (*ptar*), consisting of the claws and various padlike or setalike structures at the apex of the tarsus. A true *segment* of an appendage (including the six just described) is a subdivision with musculature inserted at its base. The subdivisions of the tarsus, though commonly called tarsal segments, are not true segments in this sense and are more properly called subsegments or tarsomeres. The pretarsus usually includes one or more padlike structures between or at the base of the claws. A pad or lobe between the claws is usually called an *arolium* (Figure 3–8A,B, *aro*), and pads located at the base of the claws are usually called *pulvilli* (Figure 3–8C, *pul*).

The movements of a leg depend on its musculature and the nature of the joints between its segments. These leg joints may be *dicondylic*, with two points of articulation, or *monocondylic*, with one point of articulation (Figure 3–9). The movement at a dicondylic joint is largely limited to the plane perpendicular to a line connecting the two points of articulation, while that of a monocondylic joint (which is like a ball-and-socket joint) can be more varied. The joints between the coxa and body may be monocondylic. If it is dicondylic, the axis of rotation is usually more or less vertical, and the leg moves forward and backward (promotion and remotion). The coxo-trochanteral, trochantero-femoral, and femoro-tibial joints are usually dicondylic. The movement between the coxa and trochanter and the femur and tibia is dorsal and ventral (elevation and depression of the leg). The tibio-tarsal joint is usually monocondylic, thus permitting more varied movements.

Wings

The wings of insects are outgrowths of the body wall located dorsolaterally between the nota and pleura. They arise as saclike outgrowths, but when fully developed are flattened and flaplike, and are

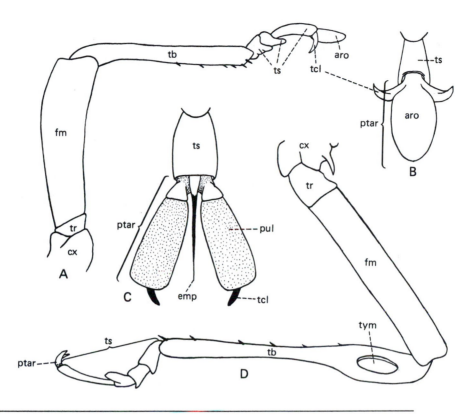

Figure 3–8. Leg structure in insects. **A,** middle leg of a short-horned grasshopper (*Melánoplus*); **B,** last tarsal segment and pretarsus of *Melánoplus*; **C,** last tarsal segment and pretarsus of a robber fly; **D,** front leg of a long-horned grasshopper (*Scuddèria*). *aro*, arolium; *cx*, coxa; *emp*, empodium; *fm*, femur; *ptar*, pretarsus; *pul*, pulvillus; *tb*, tibia; *tcl*, tarsal claw; *tr*, trochanter; *ts*, tarsus; *tym*, tympanum.

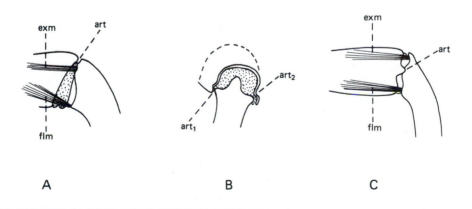

Figure 3–9. Articular mechanisms in insect legs. **A,** a monocondylic joint; **B** and **C,** end view and side view of a dicondylic joint. *art*, points of articulation; *exm*, extensor muscle; *flm*, flexor muscle. (Redrawn from Snodgrass, by permission of the McGraw-Hill Book Company, Inc.)

strengthened by a series of sclerotized *veins*. Among living insects, fully developed and functional wings are present only in the adult stage. The one exception is the presence of functional wings in the penultimate instar in Epheméroptera (the subimago). At most, two pairs of wings are found in living insects, located on the mesothoracic and metathoracic segments. Most of the muscles that move the wings are attached to sclerites in the thoracic wall rather than to the wings directly, and the wing movements are produced indirectly by changes in the shape of the thorax.

The wing veins are hollow structures that may contain nerves, tracheae, and hemolymph (blood). There is considerable variation in the pattern of venation among different groups of insects. Little is known about the functional significance of these differences, but the pattern of wing venation is very useful as a means of identification. Several venational terminologies have been developed, and the most widely used has been the Comstock (or Comstock-Needham) system (see Figure 3–10). This system basically recognizes a series of six major *longitudinal wing veins* (with their abbreviations in parentheses): *costa* (C), *subcosta* (Sc), *radius* (R), *media* (M), *cubitus* (Cu), and *anal veins* (A). Each of these veins, with the exception of the costa, may be branched. The subcosta may branch once. The branches of the longitudinal veins are numbered from anterior to posterior around the wing by means of subscript numerals: the two branches of the subcosta are designated Sc_1 and Sc_2. The radius first gives off a posterior branch, the *radial sector* (Rs), usually near the base of the wing; the anterior branch

of the radius is R_1; the radial sector may fork twice, with four branches reaching the wing margin. The media may fork twice, with four branches reaching the wing margin. The cubitus, according to the Comstock-Needham system, forks once, the two branches being Cu_1 and Cu_2; according to some other authorities, Cu_1 forks again distally, with the two branches being Cu_{1a} and Cu_{1b}. The anal veins are typically unbranched and are usually designated from anterior to posterior as the first anal vein (1A), second anal vein (2A), and so on.

Cross veins connect the major longitudinal veins and are usually named accordingly (for example, the medio-cubital cross vein, m-cu). Some cross veins have special names: two common examples are the *humeral cross vein* (h) and the *sectorial cross vein* (s).

The spaces in the wing between the veins are called *cells*. Cells may be *open* (extending to the wing margin) or *closed* (completely surrounded by veins). The cells are named according to the longitudinal vein on the anterior side of the cell; for example, the open cell between R_2 and R_3 is called the R_2 cell. Where two cells separated by a cross vein would ordinarily have the same name, they are individually designated by number; for example, the medial cross vein connects M_2 and M_3 and divides the M_2 cell into two cells; the basal one is designated the first M_2 cell and the distal one the second M_2 cell. Where a cell is bordered anteriorly by a fused vein (for example, R_{2+3}), it is named after the posterior component of that fused vein (cell R_3). In some insects certain cells may have special names, for example, the triangles of the dragonfly wing and the discal cell of the Lepidóptera.

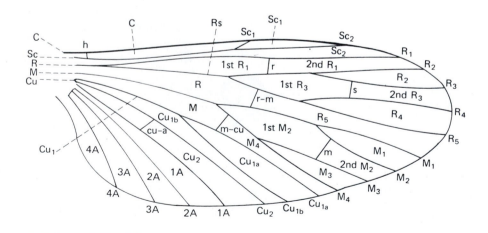

Figure 3–10.   Generalized wing venation, according to Comstock; for a key to the lettering, see accompanying text. In some orders the vein here labeled Cu_1 is called Cu by Comstock (and its branches Cu_1 and Cu_2), and the remaining veins anal veins.

The wings of insects are attached to the thorax at three points (see Figures 3–11 and 3–12): with the notum at the *anterior* and *posterior notal wing processes* (Figure 3–11, *awp, pnwp*), and ventrally at the pleural wing process (Figure 3–12A, *pwp*). In addition there are small sclerites, the *axillary sclerites* (or *pteralia*) at the base of the wing that are important in translating the movements of the thoracic sclerites into wing movements. In most living insects (the Neóptera) there are three axillary sclerites (Figure 3–11, axs_1–axs_3). Anteriorly the *first axillary* articulates with the anterior notal wing process, the subcostal vein, and the *second axillary.* The second axillary articulates with the first, the radial vein, the pleural wing process, and the *third axillary.* The third axillary articulates with the second, the anal veins, and the posterior notal wing process. In the Neóptera a muscle (*am*) inserted on the third axillary causes it to pivot about the posterior notal wing process and thereby to fold the wing over the back of the insect. (In some groups of Neóptera, such as butterflies, this ability to flex the wings over the back has been lost.) Two groups of winged insects, the Ephemeróptera and Odonàta, have not evolved this wing-flexing mechanism, and their axillary sclerites are arranged in a pattern different from that of the Neóptera; these two orders (together with a number of extinct orders) form the *Paleóptera.*

The Comstock-Needham system made great strides in recognizing the homology in wing veins among the orders and in reducing the number of names associated with them. Kukalová-Peck (1978, 1983, 1985) and Riek and Kukalová-Peck (1984) have proposed a reinterpretation of the origin and basic structure of insect wings. The veins are interpreted to consist of a series of *paired* blood channels, the anterior vein protruding from the dorsal surface (a convex vein) and the posterior vein protruding from the ventral surface (a concave vein). The fundamental venation in this interpretation consists of eight major longitudinal vein systems: the precosta, costa, subcosta, radius, media, cubitus, anal vein, and jugal vein. The "vein" in the costal margin of living insects is thus formed from the fusion of the precosta, costa, and sometimes portions of the subcosta. This interpretation has been applied to the orders Ephemeróptera and Odonàta, cases in which peculiarities in venation and axillary structure had led some to postulate that wings had evolved in insects more than once (see Chapters 10 and 11).

Flight

Many insects have powers of flight that exceed those of all other flying animals; they can steer accurately and quickly, hover, and go sideways or backward. Only the hummingbirds approach insects in their ability to maneuver on the wing.

Most insects have two pairs of wings, and the two wings on each side may be overlapped at the base or hooked together in some way so that they move together as one, or they may be capable of independent movement. In many Odonàta the front and hind wings move independently, and there is a phase difference in the movements of the two pairs; that is, when one pair is moving up, the other pair is moving down. In other Odonàta and in most Orthóptera there is a less pronounced phase difference, with the front wings moving a little ahead of the hind wings.

Figure 3–11. Diagram showing the articulation of the wing with the thoracic notum. *am*, axillary muscles; *awp*, anterior notal wing process; *axcr*, axillary cord; *axs*, axillary sclerites 1–3; *hp*, humeral plate; *jl*, jugal lobe; *mdp*, median plates; *pnwp*, posterior notal wing process; *tg*, tegula. The letters at the right side of the figure indicate the veins. (Redrawn from Snodgrass, by permission of the McGraw-Hill Book Company, Inc.)

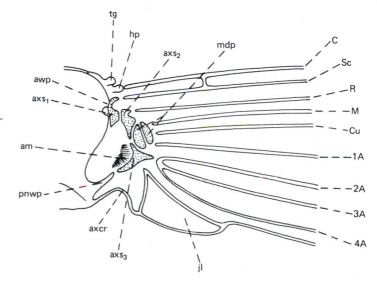

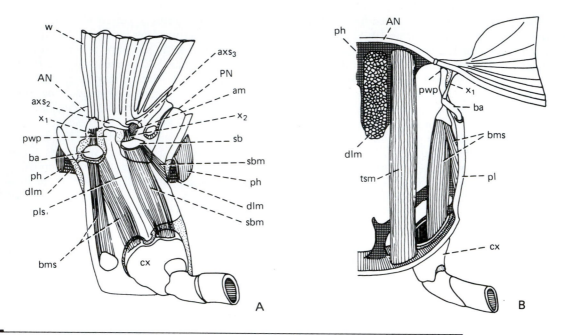

Figure 3–12.   Diagram of the wing muscles of an insect. **A,** lateral view; *B*, cross section of a wing-bearing segment. *am*, axillary muscles; *AN*, alinotum; *axs₂* and *axs₃*, second and third axillary sclerites; *ba*, basalare; *bms*, basalar muscles; *cx*, coxa; *dlm*, dorsal longitudinal muscles; *ph*, phragma; *pl*, pleuron; *pls*, pleural suture; *PN*, postnotum; *pwp*, pleural wing process; *sb*, subalare; *sbm*, subalar muscles; *tsm*, tergosternal muscles; *w*, wing; *x₁* and *x₂*, connections between basalare and subalare and wing base. (Redrawn from Snodgrass, by permission of the McGraw-Hill Book Company, Inc.)

The forces needed to fly—lift, thrust, and attitude control—are generated by the movement of the wings through the air. These movements, in turn, are generated by the thoracic muscles pulling either directly upon the base of the wing (*direct flight mechanism*) or causing changes in the shape of the thorax, which in turn are translated by the axillary sclerites into wing movements (*indirect flight mechanism*). In most insects the primary flight muscles are indirect: the *dorsal longitudinal muscles* (Figure 3–12A,B, *dlm*) cause the notum to bow, thereby raising the notal wing processes in relation to the pleural wing process, resulting in depression of the wing. The antagonistic movement is generated by contraction of the *tergosternal* (= dorsoventral or tergopleural) *muscles* (Figure 3–12B, *tsm*); these pull down on the notum, drawing the notal wing processes down in relation to the pleural wing process, thereby causing elevation of the wing. In addition, muscles inserted on the basalare (Figure 3–12, *bms*) the subalare (Figure 3–12A, *sbm*) can be involved in direct depression of the wing (by means of their connection to the wing margin at *x₁* and *x₂*) or may be important in controlling the angle at which the wing moves through the air.

Flight, however, is not a simple matter of flapping the wings up and down. In addition, the wings are brought forward (promotion) and backward (remotion), and twisted; that is, the leading edge is turned downward (pronation), or the trailing edge is turned downward (supination). The manner in which these wing movements are produced involves a complex integration of the anatomical details of the attachment of the wing to the thorax and the contraction of muscles. The details are not completely known for any species, and it is in only a few that we can begin to say that they are understood at all. In fact, it is clear that insects of different sizes and shapes fly in different ways. A minute parasitic wasp of about 1 mm in length moves its wings differently and has wings of a different shape from a house fly's, for example, and the aerodynamics of its flight are probably also quite different.

Head

The head of insects is composed of a series of metameric body segments, together specialized for food gathering and manipulation, sensory perception, and neural integration. Exactly how many segments

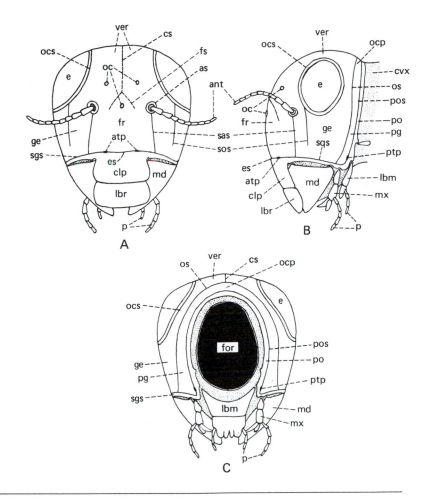

Figure 3–13. General structure of an insect head. **A,** anterior view; **B,** lateral view; **C,** posterior view. *ant,* antenna; *as,* antennal sulcus; *atp,* anterior tentorial pit; *clp,* clypeus; *cs,* coronal suture; *cvx,* cervix; *e,* compound eye; *es,* epistomal sulcus; *for,* foramen magnum; *fr,* frons; *fs,* frontal suture; *ge,* gena; *lbm,* labium; *lbr,* labrum; *md,* mandible; *mx,* maxilla; *oc,* ocelli; *ocp,* occiput; *ocs,* ocular sulcus; *os,* occipital sulcus; *p,* palps; *pg,* postgena; *po,* postocciput; *pos,* postoccipital suture; *ptp,* posterior tentorial pit; *sas,* subantennal sulcus; *sgs,* subgenal sulcus; *sgs,* subgenal sulcus; *sos,* subocular sulcus; *ver,* vertex. (Modified from Snodgrass, by permission of the McGraw-Hill Book Company, Inc.)

are in the head has long been a matter of contention among morphologists, with the postulated number ranging from 3 to 7. The head bears the eyes, antennae, and mouthparts. Its shape differs quite widely between groups of insects, but some landmarks are consistently visible to enable identification of its component parts.

The head is divided by grooves into a number of more or less distinct sclerites (Figure 3–13). Typically there is a transverse sulcus extending across the lower part of the face just above the base of the mouthparts; the medial or anterior part of this sulcus is the *epistomal sulcus* (*es*), and the lateral portions above the mandibles and maxillae are the

subgenal sulci (*sgs*). The anterior portion of the head capsule, above the epistomal sulcus and between the large compound eyes, is the *frons* (*fr*). The anterior area below the epistomal sulcus is the *clypeus* (*clp*). The area below the eye, on the side of the head, and above the subgenal sulcus is the *gena* (*ge*). The top of the head, between the eyes, is the *vertex* (*ver*). In many, if not most insects, the frons, vertex, and genae are general areas of the head, and their edges are not clearly defined by sulci.

The head is connected with the thorax by the membranous cervix (*cvx*). The opening on the posterior side of the head is the *occipital foramen* (or foramen magnum; *for*); through it run the ventral nerve cord, tracheae, the digestive system, muscles, sometimes the dorsal blood vessel, and so on. The most posterior line of inflection on the head capsule in front of the occipital foramen is generally the *postoccipital suture* (*pos*). This suture defines the limits of the posterior segment of the head, the labial segment, so named because it bears ventrally the most posterior set of mouthparts, the labium. The area behind the postoccipital suture is the *postocciput* (*po*); the area on the side of the head anterior to this suture is the *postgena* (*pg*); and the dorsal portion of the head anterior to the suture is the *occiput* (*ocp*). In some cases an *occipital sulcus* (*os*) is present that defines the anterior limits of the occiput and postgenae (separating them from the vertex and genae), but this is far from universally present.

The points on the head where the arms of the *tentorium* (a set of internal braces, see below) meet the head wall are usually marked by pits or slits visible externally. The *anterior tentorial pits* (*atp*) are at the lateral ends of the epistomal sulcus; the *posterior tentorial pits* (*ptp*) are at the lower ends of the postoccipital suture.

In different insect groups the sulci and sclerites just described may be absent, or they may be supplemented by others. The nomenclature usually makes use of the landmarks mentioned; for example, the frontogenal sulci are lines of inflection separating the genae from the frons. In many groups, however, the naming of these parts follows the traditions developed by taxonomists over the last century or more and may not be standardized.

The head is braced internally by a group of apophyses forming the tentorium (Figure 3–14). This structure is usually H-shaped, X-shaped, or shaped like the Greek letter π (pi) with the principal arms in a more or less horizontal plane and extending from the lower part of the rear of the head to the face. The points where the anterior arms of the tentorium (Figure 3–14, *ata*) meet the face are marked externally by the anterior tentorial pits (*atp*), which are located at either end of the epistomal sulcus between the frons and clypeus. The posterior arms of the tentorium meet the head wall at the posterior tentorial pits (*ptp*), which are located at the lower ends of the postoccipital sutures. These arms unite from side to side to form a *tentorial bridge* (Figure 3–14, *ttb*). Some insects have dorsal arms on the tentorium (*dta*) that extend to the upper part of the face near the antennal bases. The tentorium serves to brace the head capsule against the pull of the powerful mandibular muscles, as the point of attachment for muscles moving the head appendages, and as protection for the subesophageal ganglion and pharynx.

The head appendages of hexapods, starting posteriorly and moving forward, are (1) the *labium* (Fig-

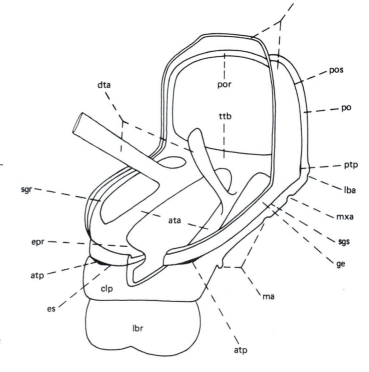

Figure 3–14. Head of an insect with a section of the head wall cut away to show the tentorium (diagrammatic). *ata*, anterior tentorial arms; *atp*, anterior tentorial pits; *clp*, clypeus; *dta*, dorsal tentorial arms; *epr*, epistomal ridge; *es*, epistomal sulcus; *ge*, gena; *lba*, labial articulation; *lbr*, labrum; *ma*, mandibular articulation; *mxa*, maxillary articulation; *ocp*, occiput; *po*, postocciput; *por*, postoccipital ridge; *pos*, postoccipital suture; *ptp*, posterior tentorial pit; *sgr*, subgenal ridge; *sgs*, subgenal sulcus; *ttb*, tentorial bridge. (Redrawn from Snodgrass, by permission of the McGraw-Hill Book Company, Inc.)

ure 3–13, *lbm*); (2) the maxillae (*mx*); (3) the mandibles (*md*); (4) the labrum (*lbr*); and (5) the antennae (*ant*). These are described in more detail below. These represent modified appendages, serially homologous to the thoracic walking legs. In the ancestral condition, the mouthparts are directed downward; such a head is called *hypognathous*. In many predatory and burrowing species the mouthparts are directed anteriorly, the *prognathous* condition. Finally, in some groups, especially the Homóptera, the mouthparts are directed posteriorly; this is the *opisthognathous* condition (or, when speaking of the beak of Homóptera, the *opisthorhynchous* condition).

The posterior surface of the head, between the foramen and the labium, is membranous in most insects, but in a few this region is sclerotized. This sclerotization may be the result of the hypostomal areas (areas below the subgenal sulci posterior to the mandibles) extending ventrally and toward the midline to form what is called a *hypostomal bridge*, or (particularly in prognathous insects) the result of the postoccipital sutures extending forward onto the ventral side of the head, with a sclerite developing between these sutures and the foramen. In the latter case the anterior extensions of the postoccipital sutures are called *gular sutures*, and the sclerite between them the *gula* (see Figure 28–4, *gu*). In some groups, the hypostomal bridge may be "overgrown" by extensions of the postgenae, thus creating a *postgenal bridge*.

The number of segments making up the head is not apparent in the adult insect, as the head sulci rarely coincide with the sutures between the original segments. Entomologists do not agree on the number of segments in the insect head; the one area of consensus is that the posterior three sets of mouthparts correspond to appendages (serially homologous with the thoracic legs) of three postoral (behind the mouth) segments. The area anterior to the mouth bears the compound eyes, ocelli, antennae, and labrum; the interpretation of this region is a matter of contention, and some of the hypotheses and the evidence in support of them are succinctly summarized by Rempel (1975).

Antennae

The antennae are paired segmented appendages located on the head, usually between or below the compound eyes. The basal segment is called the *scape* (Figure 3–15N, *scp*), the second segment the *pedicel* (*ped*), and the remainder the *flagellum* (*fl*). In insects (the Pterygòta and the apterous orders Thysanùra and Microcorýphia) the "segments" of the

flagellum lack intrinsic musculature and therefore are thought to represent subsegments of the apical, third true antennal segment. These are often called flagellomeres to distinguish them from true musculated segments (although this anatomical characteristic is widely recognized, these subsegments are still often called segments). This type of antenna is called an *annulated antenna*, referring to the subsegmentation of the flagellum. In the orders Diplùra and Collémbola more than the basal three antennal segments are musculated; these are called *segmented antennae*. An antenna arises from an antennal socket that is membranous but is surrounded by a ringlike antennal sclerite that often bears a small process, the *antennifer*, on which the scape pivots. The antennae are primarily sensory in function and act as tactile organs, organs of smell, and in some cases organs of hearing.

Insect antennae vary greatly in size and form and are important in identification. The following terms are used to describe their shapes.

Setaceous: Bristlelike, the segments becoming more slender distally; for example, dragonfly (Figure 3–15A), damselfly, leafhopper.

Filiform: Threadlike, the segments nearly uniform in size and usually cylindrical; for example, ground beetle (Figure 3–15B), tiger beetle.

Moniliform: Like a string of beads, the segments similar in size and more or less spherical in shape; for example, wrinkled bark beetle (Figure 3–15C).

Serrate: Sawlike, the segments, particularly those in the distal half or two-thirds of the antenna, more or less triangular; for example, click beetle (Figure 3–15G).

Pectinate: Comblike, most segments with long, slender, lateral processes; for example, fire-colored beetle (Figure 3–15H).

Clubbed: The segments increasing in diameter distally (Figures 3–15D–F,L,M). If the increase is gradual, the condition is termed *clavate* (Figure 3–15D,E). If the terminal segments are rather suddenly enlarged, the condition is termed *capitate* (Figure 3–15F). If the terminal segments are expanded laterally to form rounded or oval platelike lobes, the condition is termed *lamellate* (Figure 3–15M). Where the terminal segments have long, parallel-sided, sheetlike, or tonguelike lobes extending laterally, the condition is termed *flabellate* (Figure 3–15L).

Geniculate: Elbowed, with the first segment long and the following segments small and going off at an angle to the first; for example, stag beetle, ant, chalcid (Figure 3–15N).

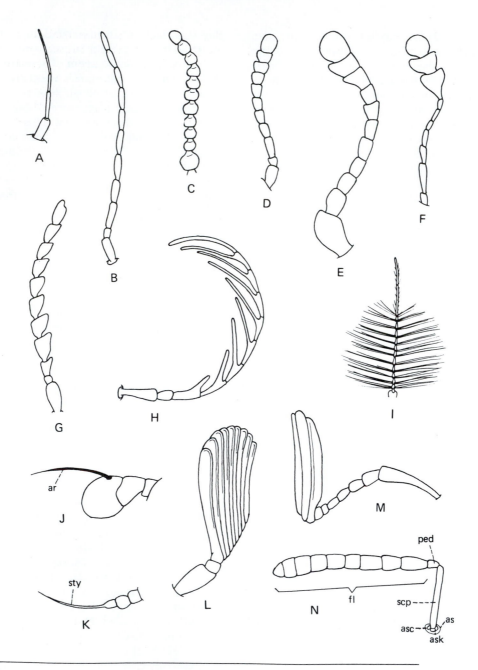

Figure 3–15.   Types of antennae. **A,** setaceous (dragonfly); **B,** filiform (ground beetle); **C,** moniliform (wrinkled bark beetle); **D,** clavate (darkling beetle); **E,** clavate (ladybird beetle); **F,** capitate (sap beetle); **G,** serrate (click beetle); **H,** pectinate (fire-colored beetle); **I,** plumose (male mosquito); **J,** aristate (syrphid fly); **K,** stylate (snipe fly); **L,** flabellate (cedar beetle); **M,** lamellate (June beetle); **N,** geniculate (chalcid). Antennae such as those in **D–F, L,** and **M** are also called clubbed. *ar,* arista; *as,* antennal sulcus; *asc,* antennal sclerite; *ask,* antennal socket; *fl,* flagellum; *ped,* pedicel; *scp,* scape; *sty,* style.

Plumose: Feathery, most segments with whorls of long hair; for example, male mosquito (Figure 3–15I).

Aristate: The last segment usually enlarged and bearing a conspicuous dorsal bristle, the arista; for example, house fly, syrphid fly (Figure 3–15J).

Stylate: The last segment bearing an elongate terminal stylelike or fingerlike process, the style; for example, robber fly, snipe fly (Figure 3–15K).

Mouthparts

Insect mouthparts typically consist of a *labrum*, a pair each of *mandibles* and *maxillae*, a *labium*, and a *hypopharynx*. These structures are modified, sometimes significantly, in different insect groups and are often used in classification and identification. The type of mouthparts an insect has determines how it feeds and (in the case of most injurious species) what sort of damage it does. We describe below the basic structure of the mouthparts, followed by a few of the significant modifications. Further information on the variations in mouthpart structure may be found in the discussion of individual insect orders.

Mandibulate Mouthparts.   The most generalized condition of the mouthparts is found in chewing insects, such as a cricket. These are said to be "chewing" or "mandibulate" mouthparts because of the heavily sclerotized mandibles that move transversely and are able to bite off and chew particles of food. The mouthparts are most easily seen and studied by removing them from a preserved specimen one at a time and examining them under a microscope.

The *labrum*, or upper lip (Figure 3–13, *lbr*; Figure 3–16E), is a broad flaplike lobe located below the clypeus on the anterior side of the head, in front of the other mouthparts. On the posterior or ventral side of the labrum may be a swollen area, the *epipharynx*.

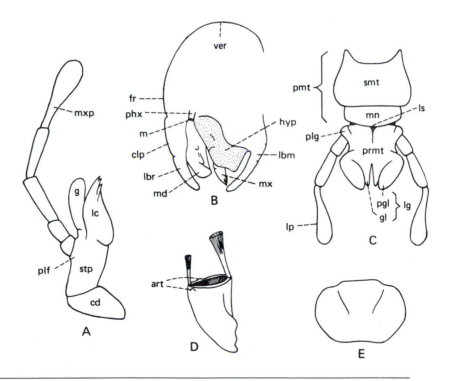

Figure 3–16.   Mouthparts of a cricket (*Grýllus*). **A,** maxilla; **B,** median vertical section of the head, showing relation of hypopharynx (*hyp*) to the other parts (somewhat diagrammatic); **C,** labium; **D,** mandible, showing muscle attachments and points of articulation; **E,** labrum. *art,* points of articulation of mandible; *cd,* cardo; *clp,* clypeus; *fr,* frons; *g,* galea; *gl,* glossa; *hyp,* hypopharynx; *lbm,* labium; *lbr,* labrum; *lc,* lacinia; *lg,* ligula; *lp,* labial palp; *ls,* labial suture; *m,* mouth; *md,* mandible; *mn,* mentum; *mx,* maxilla; *mxp,* maxillary palp; *pgl,* paraglossa; *phx,* pharynx; *plf,* palpifer; *plg,* palpiger; *pmt,* postmentum; *prmt,* prementum; *smt,* submentum; *stp,* stipes; *ver,* vertex.

The *mandibles* (Figure 3–13, *md*; Figure 3–16D) are the paired, heavily sclerotized, unsegmented jaws lying immediately behind the labrum. In the winged insects and the order Thysanùra they articulate with the head capsule at two points, one anterior and one posterior, and move transversely (and therefore these two taxa are classified together as the Dicondýlia). The mandibles of chewing insects may vary somewhat in structure; in some insects (including the cricket) they bear both cutting and grinding ridges, while in others (such as certain predaceous beetles) they are long and sicklelike.

The *maxillae* (Figure 3–13, *mx*; Figure 3–16A) are paired structures lying behind the mandibles; they are segmented, and each maxilla bears a feeler-like organ, the *maxillary palp* (*mxp*). The basal segment of the maxilla is the cardo (*cd*); the second segment is the stipes (*stp*). The palp is borne on a lobe of the stipes called the *palpifer* (*plf*). The stipes bears at its apex two processes: the lacinia (*lc*), an elongate jawlike structure; and the galea (*g*), a lobelike structure.

The *labium*, or lower lip (Figure 3–13, *lbm*; Figure 3–16C), is a single median structure (though it evolved from two maxilla-like mouthparts fusing along the midline) lying behind the maxillae. It is divided by a transverse sulcus into two portions: a basal *postmentum* (*pmt*) and a distal *prementum* (*prmt*). The postmentum may be divided into a basal *submentum* (*smt*) and a distal *mentum* (*mn*). The prementum bears a pair of *labial palps* (*lp*) and a group of apical lobes which constitute the *ligula* (*lg*). The labial palps are borne on lateral lobes of the prementum, called *palpigers* (*plg*). The ligula consists of a pair of mesal lobes, the *glossae* (*gl*), and a pair of lateral lobes, the *paraglossae* (*pgl*).

If the mandible and maxilla on one side of a specimen are removed, the *hypopharynx* (Figure 3–16B, *hyp*) becomes visible; this is a short tongue-like structure located immediately in front of or above the labium and between the maxillae. In most insects the ducts from the salivary glands open on or near the hypopharynx. Between the hypopharynx, mandibles, and labrum lies the preoral food cavity, the *cibarium*, which leads dorsally to the mouth.

Variations in Insect Mouthparts. Insect mouthparts can be classified into two general types, mandibulate (chewing) and haustellate (sucking). In mandibulate mouthparts the mandibles move transversely, that is, from side to side, and the insect is usually able to bite off and chew its food. Insects with haustellate mouthparts do not have mandibles of this type and cannot chew food. Their mouthparts are in the form of a somewhat elongated proboscis

or beak through which liquid food is sucked. The mandibles in haustellate mouthparts either are elongate and styletlike or are lacking.

The Mouthparts of Hemíptera and Homóptera. The beak in these orders (Figure 3–17) is elongate, usually segmented, and arises from the front (Hemíptera) or rear (Homóptera) of the head. The external segmented structure of the beak is the labium, which is sheathlike and encloses four piercing stylets: the two mandibles and the two maxillae. The labrum is a short lobe at the base of the beak on the anterior side, and the hypopharynx is a short lobe within the base of the beak. The labium does no piercing, but folds up as the stylets enter the tissue fed upon. The inner stylets in the beak, the maxillae, fit together in such a way as to form two channels, a food channel and a salivary channel. The palps are lacking.

The Mouthparts of the Díptera. The biting Díptera in the suborder Nematócera and the infraorder Tabanomórpha include the mosquitoes (Figure

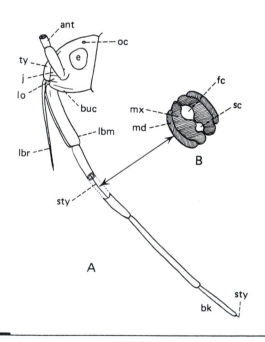

Figure 3–17. Mouthparts of the large milkweed bug, *Oncopéltus fasciàtus* (Dallas). **A,** lateral view of the head showing beak, with the labrum detached from front of beak; **B,** cross section of stylets (somewhat diagrammatic). *ant*, antenna; *bk*, beak; *buc*, buccula; *e*, compound eye; *fc*, food channel; *j*, jugum; *lbm*, labium; *lbr*, labrum; *lo*, lorum; *md*, mandible; *mx*, maxilla; *oc*, ocellus; *sc*, salivary channel; *sty*, stylets; *ty*, tylus.

3–18), sand flies, punkies, black flies, horse flies, and snipe flies. Females of these insects have six piercing stylets: the labrum, the mandibles, the maxillae, and the hypopharynx; the labium usually serves as a sheath for the stylets. The stylets may be very slender and needlelike (mosquitoes) or broader and knifelike (the other groups). The maxillary palps are well developed, but labial palps are lacking (some dipterists regard the labellar lobes as labial palps). The salivary channel is in the hypopharynx, and the food channel is located between the grooved labrum and the hypopharynx (for example, the mosquitoes) or between the labrum and the mandibles (for example, punkies and horse flies). The labium does no piercing and folds up or back as the stylets enter the tissue pierced.

In the Muscomórpha the mandibles are lacking, and the maxillae are represented by the palps (maxillary stylets are usually lacking). The proboscis consists of the labrum, hypopharynx, and labium. There are two modifications of the mouthparts in these flies: (a) a piercing type and (b) a sponging or lapping type.

The Muscomórpha with piercing mouthparts include the stable fly (Figure 3–19), tsetse fly, horn fly, and louse flies. The principal piercing structure in these flies is the labium; the labrum and hypopharynx are slender and styletlike and lie in a dorsal groove of the labium. The labium terminates in a pair of small hard plates, the labella, which are armed with teeth. The salivary channel is in the hypopharynx, and the food channel is between the labrum and hypopharynx. The proboscis in the louse flies (Hippobóscidae) is somewhat retracted into a pouch on the ventral side of the head when not in use.

The remaining Díptera with sponging or lapping mouthparts include the nonbiting species such as the house fly (Figure 3–20), blow flies, and fruit flies. The mouthpart structures are suspended from a conical membranous projection of the lower part of the head called the rostrum. The maxillary palps arise at the distal end of the rostrum, and the part of the proboscis beyond the palps is termed the haustellum. The labrum and hypopharynx are slender and lie in an interior groove of the labium, which forms the bulk of the haustellum. The salivary channel is in the hypopharynx, and the food channel lies between the labrum and the hypopharynx. At the apex of the labium are the labella, a pair of large, soft, oval lobes. The lower surface of these lobes bears numerous transverse grooves that serve as food channels. The proboscis can usually be folded up against the lower side of the head or into a cavity there. These flies lap up liquids; the food may be already in liquid form,

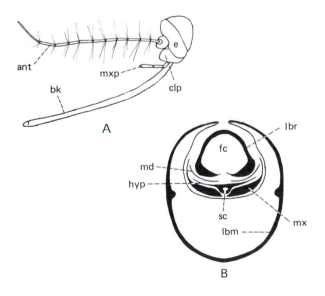

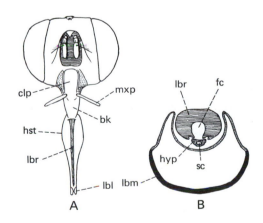

Figure 3–18. Mouthparts of a mosquito. **A,** head of *Aèdes*, lateral view; **B,** cross section of proboscis of *Anópheles. ant,* antenna; *bk,* proboscis; *clp,* clypeus; *e,* compound eye; *fc,* food channel; *hyp,* hypopharynx; *lbm,* labium; *lbr,* labrum; *md,* mandible; *mx,* maxilla; *mxp,* maxillary palp; *sc,* salivary channel. (**B** redrawn from Snodgrass, after Vogel.)

Figure 3–19. Mouthparts of the stable fly, *Stomóxys cálcitrans* (L.). **A,** anterior view of head; **B,** cross section through haustellum. *bk,* rostrum; *clp,* clypeus; *fc,* food channel; *hst,* haustellum; *hyp,* hypopharynx; *lbl,* labellum; *lbm,* labium; *lbr,* labrum; *mxp,* maxillary palp; *sc,* salivary channel. (Redrawn from various sources; somewhat diagrammatic.)

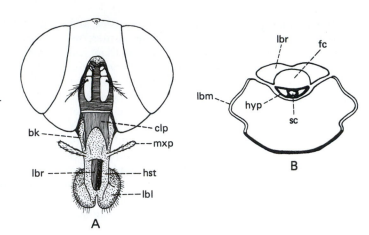

Figure 3–20. Mouthparts of the house fly, *Músca doméstica* L. **A,** anterior view of head; **B,** cross section through haustellum. *bk,* rostrum; *clp,* clypeus; *fc,* food channel; *hst,* haustellum; *hyp,* hypopharynx; *lbl,* labellum; *lbm,* labium; *lbr,* labrum; *mxp,* maxillary palp; *sc,* salivary channel. (Redrawn from Snodgrass, by permission of the McGraw-Hill Book Company, Inc.)

or it may first be liquified by salivary secretions of the fly.

The Mouthparts of Lepidóptera.

The proboscis of adult Lepidóptera (Figure 3–21) is usually long and coiled and is formed of the two galeae of the maxillae; the food channel is between the galeae. The labrum is reduced to a narrow transverse band across the lower margin of the face, and the mandibles and hypopharynx are lacking (except in the Micropterígidae). The maxillary palps are usually reduced or absent, but the labial palps are usually well developed. There is no special salivary channel. This type of mouthpart structure is sometimes called siphoning-sucking, for there is usually no piercing,

and the insect merely sucks or siphons liquids up through the proboscis. There are some moths in southeast Asia and northern Australia, however, that use the proboscis to pierce the skins of soft fruits and then siphon liquids from the tissues underneath. When used, the proboscis is uncoiled by blood pressure; it recoils by its own elasticity.

Insect Muscles

The muscular system of an insect consists of from several hundred to a few thousand individual muscles. All are composed of striated muscle cells, even those around the alimentary canal and the heart.

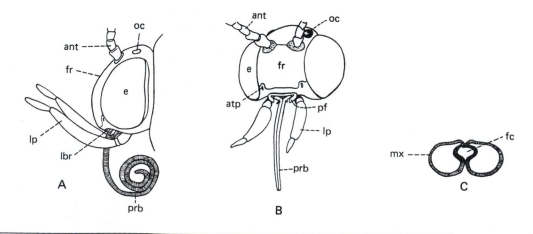

Figure 3–21. Mouthparts of a moth. **A,** lateral view of head; **B,** anterior view of head; **C,** cross section through proboscis. *ant,* antenna; *atp,* anterior tentorial pit; *e,* compound eye; *fc,* food channel; *fr,* frons; *lbr,* labrum; *lp,* labial palp; *mx,* maxilla (galea); *oc,* ocellus; *pf,* pilifer; *prb,* proboscis. (Redrawn from Snodgrass, by permission of the McGraw-Hill Book Company, Inc.)

The skeletal muscles, which attach to the body wall, move the various parts of the body, including the appendages. The cell membranes of the muscle and epidermis are interdigitated and interconnected by desmosomes. From the desmosomes, microtubules run to the outer epidermal cell membrane, and from there attachment fibers run through the cuticle to the epicuticle. The attachment fibers are not broken down between the times when the epidermis is separated from the old cuticle (apolysis) and the shedding of that cuticle (ecdysis; see section on molting below). Thus the muscles remain attached to the body wall, and the insect continues to be able to move during the period when a new cuticle is being formed. The locations of the points of attachment of the skeletal muscles are sometimes useful in determining the homologies of various body parts. The visceral muscles, which surround the heart, the alimentary canal, and the ducts of the reproductive system, produce the peristaltic movements that move materials along these tracts. They usually consist of longitudinal and circular muscle fibers.

The muscles moving the appendages are arranged segmentally, generally in antagonistic pairs. Some appendage parts (for example, the galea and lacinia of the maxillae and the pretarsus) have only flexor muscles. Extension of these structures is usually brought about by a combination of hemolymph pressure and the elasticity of the cuticle. Each segment of an appendage normally has its own muscles. The tarsal and flagellar "segments" do not have their own muscles and, therefore, are not true segments.

Insect muscles seem to us to be very strong; many insects can lift 20 or more times their body weight, and jumping insects can often jump distances equal to many times their own length. These feats appear very remarkable when compared to what humans can do; they are possible not because the muscles of insects are inherently stronger, but because of the smaller size of insects. The power of a muscle varies with the size of its cross-sectional area, or with the square of its width; what the muscle moves (the mass of the body) varies with the cube of the linear dimension. Thus as the body becomes smaller, the muscles become *relatively* more powerful.

Insect muscles are often capable of extremely rapid contraction. Wing stroke rates of a few hundred per second are fairly common in insects, and rates up to 1000 or more per second are known. In insects with relatively slow wing-stroke rates and in most other skeletal muscles, each muscle contraction is initiated by a nerve impulse. Such muscles are called synchronous or neurogenic muscles because of this one-to-one correspondence between action potentials and muscle contractions. In insects with higher wing-beat frequencies the muscles contract much more frequently than the rate at which neural impulses reach them. The rates of contraction in such asynchronous muscles (found principally in flight muscles, but sometimes in other oscillating systems) depend upon the characteristics of the muscles themselves and the associated sclerites. Nerve impulses are necessary to initiate contractions, but thereafter serve to generally maintain the rapid rate of contractions rather than to stimulate each one individually.

The fact that insect muscles may have such an extremely rapid contraction frequency, which is sometimes maintained for a prolonged period, attests to the efficiency of their metabolism. The large volumes of oxygen needed for such metabolic rates are provided by the tracheal system. In most insects the tracheoles (across whose walls gas exchange takes place) indent the cell membranes of the muscles, thus minimizing the distance across which diffusion of gases must take place. Insects use a variety of fuels for flight. Carbohydrates are important for many species; in others lipids are the primary fuels; in some flies (such as the tsetse) amino acids form the substrate for generating the energy necessary for flight. The high rate of carbohydrate metabolism in many flight muscles places a premium on the availability of NAD (nicotinamide adenine dinucleotide) as a reducing substrate in glycolysis. $NADH_2$ is rapidly oxidized by the conversion of dihydroxyacetone phosphate to α-glycerophosphate. This latter molecule enters the mitochondrion, where it is oxidized and transfers the hydrogen to the cytochrome chain. The pyruvate (the end product of glycolysis) and α-glycerophosphate are rapidly oxidized in the mitochondrion and do not accumulate. This α-glycerophosphate "shuttle" keeps the availability of NAD from becoming a limiting step in respiration in the flight muscles (Sacktor 1974, Chapman 1982).

Digestive System

Insects feed upon almost every organic substance found in nature, and their digestive systems exhibit considerable variation. The alimentary canal is a tube, usually somewhat coiled, which extends from the mouth to the anus (Figure 3–22). It is differentiated into three main regions: the *foregut*, or stomodaeum; the *midgut*, or mesenteron; and the *hindgut*, or proctodaeum. Both the foregut and hindgut are derived from ectodermal tissue and are lined internally by a thin layer of cuticle, the *intima*. This

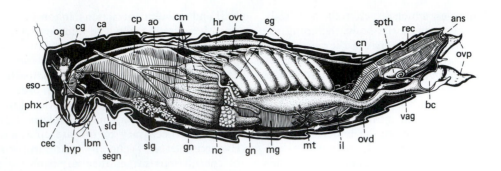

Figure 3–22.   Internal organs of a grasshopper, shown in longitudinal section (somewhat diagrammatic). *ans*, anus; *ao*, dorsal aorta; *bc*, bursa copulatrix; *ca*, corpus allatum; *cec*, circumesophageal connective; *cg*, cerebral ganglion (part of the brain); *cm*, gastric caeca; *cn*, colon; *cp*, crop; *eg*, eggs; *eso*, esophagus; *gn*, ganglia of ventral nerve cord; *hr*, heart; *hyp*, hypopharynx; *il*, ileum; *lbm*, labium; *lbr*, labrum; *mg*, midgut mesenteron; *mt*, Malpighian tubules; *nc*, ventral nerve cord; *og*, optic ganglion (part of the brain); *ovd*, oviduct; *ovp*, ovipositor; *ovt*, ovarian tubules; *phx*, pharynx; *rec*, rectum; *segn*, subesophageal ganglion; *slg*, salivary gland; *sld*, salivary duct; *spth*, spermatheca; *vag*, vagina. (Redrawn from Robert Matheson: *Entomology for Introductory Courses, Second Edition.* Copyright 1951 by Comstock Publishing Company, Inc. Used by permission of the publisher, Cornell University Press.)

cuticle is shed at each molt along with the outer exoskeleton.

Most insects possess a pair of glands lying below the anterior part of the alimentary canal (Figure 3–22, *slg*). The ducts from these glands extend forward and unite into a common duct that opens near the base of the labium or hypopharynx. These *labial glands* (so-named because they open at the base of the labium) generally function as salivary glands. There is often an enlargement of the duct from each gland that serves as a reservoir for the salivary secretion. The labial glands in the larvae of Lepidóptera, Trichóptera, and Hymenóptera secrete silk, which is used in making cocoons and shelters and in food gathering by net-spinning caddisflies.

The foregut is usually differentiated into a *pharynx* (*phx*, immediately beyond the mouth), *esophagus* (*eso*, a slender tube extending posteriorly from the pharynx), *crop* (*cp*, an enlargement of the posterior portion of the foregut), and *proventriculus*. At its posterior end is the *stomodaeal valve*, which regulates the passage of food between the foregut and midgut. In some groups, such as cockroaches and termites, the proventriculus may bear an armature of teeth internally; these are used to further crush the food before it enters the midgut. The intima is secreted by the foregut epithelium and is relatively impermeable. The intima and epithelium are often longitudinally folded. Outside of the epithelium is an inner layer of longitudinal muscles and an outer

layer of circular muscles. The longitudinal muscles sometimes have insertions on the intima. The anterior part of the foregut is provided with dilator muscles, which have their origins on the walls and apodemes of the head and thorax and their insertions on the stomodaeal muscle layers, the epithelium, or intima. These are best developed in the pharyngeal region in sucking insects, where they make the pharynx into a sucking pump. The crop is specialized for the temporary storage of food. It may be a simple enlargement of the foregut, or, as in mosquitoes and Lepidóptera, it may be a lateral diverticulum off the digestive tract. Little or no digestion of food takes place in the foregut.

The midgut (*mg*) is usually an elongate tube of rather uniform diameter, sometimes differentiated into two or more parts. It often bears diverticula, the *gastric caeca* (*cm*), near its anterior end. The midgut is not lined by cuticle. The epithelial layer of the midgut is involved both with the secretion of digestive enzymes into the lumen and in the absorption of the products of digestion into the body of the insect. Individual midgut epithelial cells are generally rather short-lived and are constantly being replaced. These dividing cells may be scattered throughout the midgut, or may be concentrated as pockets of growth. Such areas are sometimes visible from the lumen of the gut as invaginated crypts and from the outer side as bulges (called nidi). The midgut is the primary site of digestion and absorption in the alimentary canal. In many species the midgut epithelium and the food are separated by a peritrophic membrane—a nonliving, permeable network of chitin and protein that is secreted by the epithelium. The function of the peritrophic membrane is unclear. It may serve to limit abrasion to the epithelium, to inhibit the movement of pathogens from the food to the insect's tissues, or as a means of separating endo- and ectoperitrophic spaces within which digestive specialization can occur.

The hindgut extends from the *pyloric valve,* which lies between the midgut and hindgut, to the anus. Posteriorly it is supported by muscles extending to the abdominal wall. The hindgut is generally differentiated into at least two regions, the anterior *intestine* and the posterior *rectum* (*rec*). The anterior intestine may be a simple tube, or it may be subdivided into an anterior *ileum* (*il*) and a posterior *colon* (*cn*). The *Malpighian tubules* (*mt*), which are excretory organs (see below), arise at the anterior end of the hindgut, and their contents empty into it. The hindgut is the final site for resorption of water, salts, and any nutrients from the feces and urine. The rectum in several species has large thick rectal pads that are important in removing water from the feces.

The *filter chamber* is a modification of the alimentary canal in which two normally distant parts are held close together by connective tissue; it occurs in many of the Homóptera and varies somewhat in form in different members of the order. The midgut in these insects is differentiated into three regions: the first, second, and third ventriculi. The first and second ventriculi are saclike structures immediately posterior to the esophagus, and the third ventriculus is a slender tube. Typically, the third ventriculus turns forward and comes to lie close to the first ventriculus, often coiling about it, where it is held in place by connective tissue. This complex—the first ventriculus, the coiled third ventriculus, and the connective tissue—forms the filter chamber (Figure 3–23). Beyond the filter chamber the alimentary canal continues backward, usually as a slender tube, to enter the rectum. The Malpighian tubules emerge either from the filter chamber or just beyond it.

The Homóptera live on plant juices, which they usually ingest in large quantities. The filter chamber is believed to be a device that allows water from the ingested sap to pass directly from the anterior portion of the midgut to the hindgut, thus concentrating the sap prior to its digestion in the posterior part of the midgut. This excess fluid passes from the anus as honeydew. However, since honeydew is often rich in carbohydrates and amino acids, there is some doubt about the exact function of the filter chamber.

Digestion is the process of changing food chemically and physically so that it may be absorbed and nourish various parts of the body. This process may begin even before the food is ingested, but usually occurs as the ingested materials pass through the digestive tract. Solid foods are broken down by various mechanical means (chiefly the mouthparts and proventricular teeth), and all foods are subjected to a battery of enzymes as they pass through the digestive tract.

Insects feed on a great variety of living, dead, and decomposing animals, plants, and fungi and on their products. In some cases liquids such as blood or plant juices may constitute their entire food supply. The digestive system varies considerably with the different kinds of foods consumed. The food habits may even vary greatly in a single species. Larvae and adults usually have entirely different food habits and different types of digestive systems. Some adults do not feed at all.

Most insects take food into the body through the mouth. Some larvae that live endoparasitically in a host animal are able to absorb food through the surface of their bodies from host tissues. Many insects have chewing mandibles and maxillae that cut, crush, or macerate food materials and force them into the pharynx. In sucking insects the pharynx functions as a pump that brings liquid food through the beak into the esophagus. Food is moved along the alimentary canal by peristaltic action.

Saliva is usually added to the food, either as it enters the alimentary canal or before, as in the case of many sucking insects that inject it into the fluids they siphon up as foods. Saliva is generally produced by the labial glands. The labial glands of many insects produce amylase. In certain bees these glands secrete invertase, which is later taken into the body with nectar. In bloodsucking insects such as mosquitoes, the saliva generally contains no digestive enzymes but contains a substance that prevents coagulation of the blood and the consequent mechanical plugging of the food channel. It is this saliva that causes the irritation produced by the bite of a bloodsucking insect.

Many insects eject digestive enzymes upon food, and partial digestion may occur before the food is ingested. Flesh fly larvae discharge proteolytic enzymes onto their food, and aphids inject amylase into the plant tissues and thus digest starch in the food plant. Extraintestinal digestion also occurs in the prey of larvae of antlions and predaceous diving beetles and in bugs that feed on dry seeds.

Most chemical digestion of the food takes place within the midgut. Some of the midgut epithelial cells produce enzymes, and others absorb digested

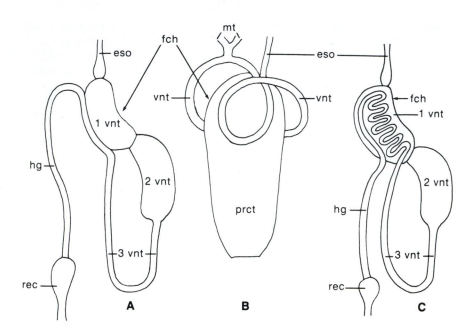

Figure 3–23. The filter chamber of Homóptera (diagrammatic). **A,** a simple type of filter chamber, in which the two ends of the midgut (the first and third ventriculi) are bound together; **B,** the filter chamber of a scale insect (*Lecànium*); **C,** a filter chamber in which the posterior part of the midgut (the third ventriculus) coils about the anterior part (the first ventriculus), with the hindgut emerging from the anterior end. In **A** and **B** the junction of the midgut and hindgut (where the Malpighian tubules, which are not shown, enter the alimentary tract) is in the filter chamber. *eso,* esophagus; *fch,* filter chamber; *hg,* anterior portion of the hindgut; *mt,* Malpighian tubules; *prct,* proctodaeum; *rec,* rectum; *vnt,* ventriculus (*1,* first; *2,* second; *3,* third).

food. Sometimes secretion and absorption are carried out by the same cells. Enzymes may be released into the lumen of the midgut by the disintegration of the secretory cells (holocrine secretion) or by the release of small amounts of enzymes across the cell membrane (merocrine secretion).

Only a few species of insects produce enzymes that digest cellulose, but some are able to use cellulose as food as a result of symbiotic microorganisms present in their digestive tracts. These microorganisms, usually bacteria or flagellated protists, can digest the cellulose, and the insects absorb the products of this digestion. Such microorganisms are present in termites and many wood-boring beetles and are often housed in special organs connected to the gut.

The fat body is a large, often somewhat amorphous organ housed in the abdomen and thorax. In many ways its function is analogous to that of the vertebrate liver. It serves as a food-storage reservoir and is an important site of intermediate metabolism. In some species it is also important in storing excretion (see page 47). The fat body is usually best developed in the late nymphal or larval instars. By the end of metamorphosis it is often depleted. Some adult insects that do not feed retain their fat body in adult life.

Excretory System

The primary excretory system of an insect consists of a group of hollow tubes, the Malpighian tubules, which arise as evaginations at the anterior end of the hindgut (Figure 3–22, *mt*). These tubules vary in number from one to more than several hundred, and their distal, free ends are closed. These tubules function in removing nitrogenous wastes and in regulating, together with the hindgut, the balance of water and various salts in the hemolymph. Ions are apparently actively transported across the outer membrane of the tubule, generating an osmotic flow of water into the lumen. Along with this water a number of small solutes—amino acids, sugars, and nitrogenous wastes—enter the tubule passively. This primary urine is therefore an isosmotic solution containing the small molecules present in the hemolymph. Some of these solutes and the water may be actively resorbed into the hemolymph in the basal portions of the Malpighian tubules or in the hindgut. The principal nitrogenous waste is usually *uric acid* (Figure 3–24), a chemical that is relatively nontoxic (and can therefore be tolerated in higher concentrations) and insoluble in water (again, recall the water balance problems inherent to a small terrestrial organism).

In some insects, most notably many beetle and moth larvae, the Malpighian tubules are bound very closely to the hindgut; these are called *cryptonephridia*. In species such as the mealworm, *Tenèbrio mólitor*, that live in conditions of high water stress, this arrangement of the tubules is apparently involved in the extraction of water from the fecal pellets. The mealworm, in fact, is able to extract water vapor from the air when the relative humidity exceeds 90%.

In addition to the Malpighian tubules, insects may have a variety of methods of removing wastes or toxic substances from the hemolymph. One method is to store chemicals, such as uric acid, more or less permanently within individual cells or tissues. This process is known as *storage excretion.* Cockroaches store uric acid in their fat body, and the white pigment in the scales of pierid butterflies is derived from uric acid stored within them. At the anterior end of the dorsal blood vessel may be a group of cells, the pericardial cells, that are important in absorbing and breaking down colloidal particles in the hemolymph. In other cases similar cells may be widely distributed throughout the hemocoel.

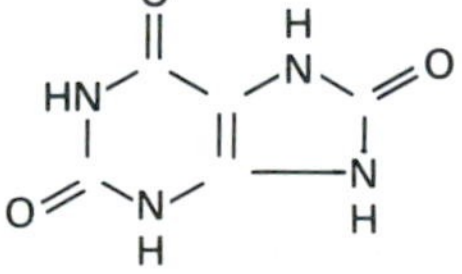

Figure 3–24. Structure of uric acid. (From Arms and Camp.)

Circulatory System

The principal function of the blood, or hemolymph, is the transport of materials—nutrients, hormones, wastes, etc. In most cases it plays a relatively minor role in the transport of oxygen and carbon dioxide. The hemolymph is also involved in osmoregulation, the balance of salts and water in the body; this function also involves other organs, particularly the Malpighian tubules and the rectum. The hemolymph has an important skeletal function—for example, in molting, in the expansion of the wings after the last molt, and in the protrusion of eversible structures such as eversible vesicles and genitalia. It may also function in the animal's internal defenses, in the phagocytic action of hemocytes against invading microorganisms, in plugging wounds, and in walling off certain foreign bodies such as endoparasites. Finally, the hemolymph is also a storage tissue, serving as a reservoir for water and such food materials as fats and carbohydrates.

The circulatory system of an insect is open. The main (and often only) blood vessel is located dorsal to the alimentary tract and extends through the thorax and abdomen (Figure 3–22). Elsewhere the hemolymph flows unrestricted through the body cavity (the hemocoel). The posterior part of the dorsal blood vessel, which is divided by valves into a series of chambers, is the *heart* (hr), and the slender anterior part is the *aorta* (ao). Extending from the lower surface of the heart to the lateral portions of the terga are pairs of sheetlike muscle bands. These constitute a dorsal diaphragm more or less separating the region around the heart (the pericardial sinus) from the main body cavity (or perivisceral sinus, sometimes further divided into a perivisceral sinus and a perineural sinus). The heart is provided with paired lateral openings called ostia, one pair per heart chamber, through which hemolymph enters the heart. The number of ostia varies in different insects. In some cases there may be as few as two pairs.

The hemolymph is usually a more or less clear fluid in which are suspended a number of cells (the hemocytes). It may be yellowish or greenish but is only rarely red (as in some aquatic midge larvae and some aquatic Hemíptera, owing to the exceptional presence of hemoglobin). It makes up from 5% to 40% of the body weight (usually about 25% or less).

The liquid part of the hemolymph (the plasma) contains a great many dissolved substances (salts, sugars, proteins, hormones, etc.). These vary considerably—in different insects and in the same insect at different times. The plasma contains very little oxygen; the transport of oxygen is the function of the respiratory system and is decoupled from the circulatory system.

The hemocytes vary considerably in number—from about 1000 to 100,000 per mm³—but average about 50,000 per mm³. These cells vary greatly in shape and function. Some circulate with the hemolymph, and some adhere to the surface of tissues. The functions of the various types of hemocytes are not well known, but many are capable of phagocytosis. They may ingest bacteria, and they play a role in removing dead cells and tissues during metamorphosis. The hemolymph of different insects differs in clotting ability; the hemocytes may migrate to wounds and form a plug. Hemocytes often congregate around foreign bodies such as parasites, forming a sheath around them and walling them off from the body tissues. Other than the action of these hemocytes, insects have no immune system comparable to the antibodies of vertebrates (thus facilitating transplantation experiments).

The movement of hemolymph is brought about by pulsations of the heart and is aided in other parts of the body, such as the base of the legs and wings, by accessory pulsatile organs. The heartbeat is a peristaltic wave that starts at the posterior end of the dorsal blood vessel and moves forward. Hemolymph enters the heart through the ostia, which are closed during the systolic phase of the heartbeat, and is pumped anteriorly. The rate of the heartbeat varies greatly: observed rates in different insects range from 14 to about 160 beats per minute. There is an increase in this rate during periods of increased activity. The pulsations of the heart may be initiated within the heart muscle (myogenic), or they may be under nervous control (neurogenic). A reversal of the direction of the peristaltic wave of contractions, thus moving the hemolymph backward instead of forward, is not unusual.

Very little pressure is developed in the general flow of hemolymph through the body. The hemolymph pressure may sometimes be less than atmospheric pressure. It can be increased by muscular contraction and compression of the body wall or by dilation of the alimentary canal (produced by swallowing air). It is by such means that pressure is developed to break out of the remainder of the old exoskeleton at the time of molting and to inflate the wings.

Respiratory System

Gas transport in insects is the function of the tracheal system. The circulatory system of insects, unlike that of vertebrates, usually plays only a minor role in this process.

The tracheal system (Figure 3–25) is a system of cuticular tubes (the *tracheae*) which externally open at the spiracles (*spr*) and internally branch and extend throughout the body. They terminate in very fine closed branches called *tracheoles* that permeate and actually penetrate the living tissues (indenting, but not actually breaking through the cell membranes). The tracheae are lined with a layer of cuticle, and in the larger branches this is thickened to form helical rings, called *taenidia*, that simultaneously give the tracheae strength (against collapse) and flexibility (to bend and twist). The tracheoles (also lined with cuticle) are minute intracellular tubes with thin walls, and they often contain fluid. It is across the walls of the tracheoles that gas exchange actually takes place.

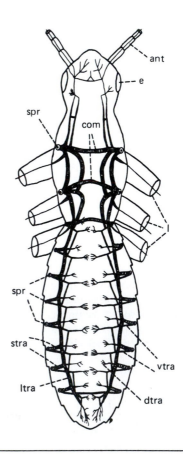

Figure 3–25. Diagram of a horizontal section of an insect showing the arrangement of the principal tracheae. *ant*, antenna; *com*, commissural trachea; *dtra*, dorsal trachea; *e*, compound eye; *l*, legs; *ltra*, main longitudinal tracheal trunk; *spr*, spiracles; *stra*, spiracular trachea; *vtra*, ventral tracheae.

The spiracles are located laterally in the pleural wall and vary in number from one to ten pairs (some species have no functional spiracles). There is typically a pair on the anterior margin of the meso- and metathorax, and a pair on each of the first eight (or fewer) abdominal segments. They vary in size and shape and are usually provided with some sort of valvelike closing device. These valves therefore play an important role in the retention of body water.

In insects with an open tracheal system (i.e., with functional spiracles), air enters the body through the spiracles, then passes through the tracheae to the tracheoles, and oxygen ultimately enters the cells of the body by diffusion. Carbon dioxide leaves the body in a similar fashion. The spiracles may be partly or completely closed for extended periods in some insects. Water loss through the spiracles may be minimized in this way.

Insects generally have longitudinal tracheal trunks (connectives, *ltra*) connecting the tracheae from adjacent spiracles on the same side of the body and transverse commissures (*com*) connecting the tracheae on opposite sides of the body, so that the entire system is interconnected. The movement of air through the tracheal system is by simple diffusion in many small insects, but in most larger insects this movement is augmented by active ventilation, chiefly by the abdominal muscles; the movements of the internal organs, or of the legs and wings, may also aid ventilation. Where ventilation occurs, air may move in and out of each spiracle, but generally enters through the anterior spiracles and leaves by the posterior ones. This flow of air through the tracheal system is effected by controlling which spiracles are open and when. Sections of the main tracheal trunks are often dilated to form air sacs, which may assist in ventilation.

Closed tracheal systems have the spiracles permanently closed, but have a network of tracheae just under the integument, distributed either widely over the body or particularly below certain surfaces (the gills). Closed systems are found in some aquatic and parasitic insects. In these species, gases enter and leave the body by diffusion across the body wall between the tracheae and the external environment, and the movement of gases through the tracheal system is effected by diffusion.

A great many insects live in water; these get their oxygen from one (rarely both) of two sources: the oxygen dissolved in the water or atmospheric oxygen. Gas exchange in many small, soft-bodied aquatic nymphs and larvae (and possibly some adults) occurs by diffusion through the body wall, usually into and out of a tracheal system. The body wall in some cases is unmodified except perhaps for having a fairly rich tracheal network just under the integument. In other cases there are special thin extensions of the body wall that have a rich tracheal supply and through which gas exchange occurs. These structures, called tracheal gills, come in a variety of shapes and may be located on different parts of the body. The gills in mayfly nymphs are in the form of leaflike structures on the sides of the first seven abdominal segments (Figure 10–2). In dragonfly nymphs they are folds in the rectum, and water is moved into and out of the rectum and over these folds. In damselfly nymphs the gills are in the form of three leaflike structures at the end of the abdomen as well as folds in the rectum (Figure 11–1). In stonefly nymphs the gills are fingerlike or branched structures located around the bases of the legs or on the basal abdominal segments (Figure 20–2B). Gas exchange may occur through the general body surface of these insects, and in some cases (e.g., damselfly nymphs) the exchange through the body surface may be more important than that through the tracheal gills.

Insects that live in water and get their oxygen from atmospheric air do this in one of three general ways: from the air spaces in the submerged parts of certain aquatic plants, through spiracles placed at the water surface (with the body of the insect submerged), or from a film of air held somewhere on the surface of the body while the insect is submerged. A few larvae (for example, those of the beetle genus *Donàcia* and the mosquito genus *Mansònia*) have their spiracles in spines at the posterior end of the body, and these spines are inserted into the air spaces of submerged aquatic plants. Many aquatic insects (for example, waterscorpions, rattailed maggots, and the larvae of culicine mosquitoes) have a breathing tube at the posterior end of the body, which is extended to the surface. Hydrophobic hairs around the end of this tube enable the insect to hang from the surface film, and they prevent water from entering the breathing tube. Other aquatic insects (for example, backswimmers and the larvae of anopheline mosquitoes) get air through posterior spiracles that are placed at the water surface. These insects do not have an extended breathing tube.

The insects that get their oxygen from atmospheric air at the water surface do not spend all their time at the surface. They can submerge and remain underwater for a considerable period, getting oxygen from an air store either inside or outside the body. The air stores in the tracheae of a mosquito larva, for example, enable the larva to remain underwater for a considerable period.

Many aquatic bugs and beetles carry a thin film of air somewhere on the surface of the body when they submerge. This film is usually under the wings or on the ventral side of the body. This air film acts like a physical gill, with dissolved oxygen in the water diffusing into the bubble when the partial pressure of oxygen in the film falls below that of the water. The insect may obtain several times as much oxygen from this temporary structure as was originally in it as a result of the gas exchanges between the air film and the surrounding water. A few insects (for example, elmid beetles) have a permanent layer of air around the body surface, held there by a body covering of thick fine hydrophobic hairs; such a layer is called a *plastron*. The air reservoirs of aquatic insects not only play a role in gas exchange, but also may have a hydrostatic function (like the swim bladder of fish). Two crescent-shaped air sacs in *Chaóborus* larvae (Figure 32–33A) are apparently used to regulate this insect's specific gravity: to hold it perfectly motionless or to enable it to migrate up or down in the water column.

Parasitic insects that live inside the body of their host get oxygen from the body fluids of the host by diffusion through their integument, or (for example, in tachinid fly larvae) their posterior spiracles may be extended to the body surface of the host or attach to one of the host's tracheal trunks.

Body Temperature

Insects are generally considered to be cold-blooded or poikilothermic; that is, their body temperature rises and falls with the environmental temperature. This is the case with most insects, particularly if they are not very active, but the action of the thoracic muscles in flight usually raises the insect's temperature above that of the environment. The cooling of a small object is fairly rapid, and the body temperature of a small insect in flight is very close to that of the environment. In insects such as butterflies and grasshoppers, the body temperature in flight may be 5 or 10°C above the environmental temperature, and in insects such as moths and bumble bees (which are insulated with scales or hair), the metabolism during flight may raise the temperature of the flight muscles 20 or 30°C above the environmental temperature.

With most flying insects, the temperature of the flight muscles must be maintained above a certain point in order to produce the power necessary for flight. Many larger insects may actively increase the temperature of their flight muscles prior to flight by a "shivering" or a vibration of the wing muscles.

Honey bees remain in the hive during the winter, but do not go into a state of dormancy at the onset of cold weather (as most other insects do). When the temperature gets down to about 14°C, they form a cluster in the hive and, by the activity of their thoracic muscles, maintain the temperature of the cluster well over 14°C (as high as 34–36°C when they are rearing brood).

Nervous System

The central nervous system of an insect consists of a brain located in the head above the esophagus, a *subesophageal ganglion* (Figure 3–26, *segn*) connected to the brain by two nerves (the circumesophageal connectives, *cec*) that extend around each side of the esophagus, and a ventral nerve cord extending posteriorly from the subesophageal ganglion. The brain consists of three pairs of lobes, the protocerebrum (br_1), deutocerebrum (br_2), and tritocerebrum (br_3). The protocerebrum innervates the compound eyes and ocelli; the deutocerebrum innervates the antennae; the tritocerebrum innervates the labrum and foregut. The two lobes of the tritocerebrum are separated by the esophagus and are connected by a commissure that passes under the esophagus (*comn*). The ventral nerve cord (Figure 3–22, *nc*) is typically double and has segmental ganglia (Figure 3–22, *gn*). Frequently some of these ganglia are fused, resulting in fewer visible ganglia than segments.

The functional units of the nervous system are the neurons or nerve cells, of which there are three principal types: sensory, internuncial, and motor. The cell bodies of sensory neurons generally lie close to the body surface, where they are arranged singly or grouped into sense organs. From each cell body a more or less elongate axon extends to a ganglion of the central nervous system. Motor neurons have the cell body in a ganglion and the axon extending to an effector organ (a muscle or gland). Internuncial cells, or interneurons, are cells through which incoming nerve impulses are channeled both into appropriate motor cells and to other internuncial cells.

The ganglia of the central nervous system (brain, subesophageal ganglion, and segmental ganglia of the ventral nerve cord) serve as the coordinating centers. Each of these has a certain amount of autonomy; that is, each may coordinate the impulses involved in activities in particular regions of the body. Activities involving the entire body may be coordinated by impulses from the brain, but many of these can occur with the brain absent.

Sense Organs

An insect receives information about its environment (including its own internal environment)

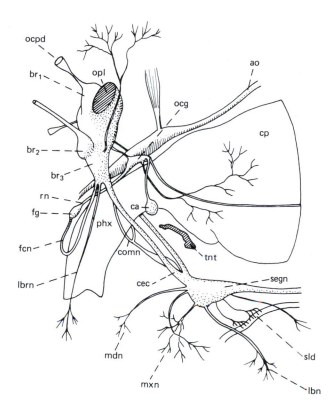

Figure 3–26. Anterior part of the nervous system of a grasshopper. *ao,* dorsal aorta; *br$_1$,* protocerebrum; *br$_2$,* deutocerebrum; *br$_3$,* tritocerebrum; *ca,* corpus allatum; *cec,* circumesophageal connective; *comn,* tritocerebral commissure; *cp,* crop; *fcn,* frontal ganglion connective; *fg,* frontal ganglion; *lbn,* labial nerve; *lbrn,* labral nerve; *mdn,* mandibular nerve; *mxn,* maxillary nerve; *ocg,* occipital ganglion; *ocpd,* ocellar pedicel; *opl,* optic lobe; *phx,* pharynx; *rn,* recurrent nerve; *segn,* subesophageal ganglion; *sld,* salivary duct; *tnt,* tentorium. (Redrawn from Snodgrass, by permission of the McGraw-Hill Book Company, Inc.)

through its sense organs. These organs are located mainly in the body wall, and most are microscopic in size. Each is usually excited only by a specific stimulus. Insects have sense organs receptive to chemical, mechanical, auditory, and visual stimuli, and possibly such stimuli as relative humidity and temperature.

Chemical Senses. Chemoreceptors—those involved in the senses of taste (gustation) and smell (olfaction)—are important parts of an insect's sensory system and are involved in many types of behavior. Feeding, mating, habitat selection, and parasite-host relationships, for example, are often directed by the insect's chemical senses.

Generally each sensillum consists of a group of sensory cells whose distal processes form a bundle extending to the body surface (Figure 3–27C). The endings of the sensory processes are usually in a thin-walled peglike structure (*scn*). The peglike process may be sunk in a pit, or the sensory processes may end in a thin cuticular plate set over a cavity in the cuticle. In some cases the endings of the sensory processes may lie in a pit in the body wall and not be covered by cuticle.

The organs of taste are located principally on the mouthparts, but some insects (for example, ants,

bees, and wasps) also have taste organs on the antennae, and many (for example, butterflies, moths, and flies) have taste organs on the tarsi.

The exact mechanism by which a particular substance initiates a nerve impulse in the sensory cells of a chemoreceptor is not known. The substance may penetrate to the sensory cells and stimulate them directly, or it may react with something in the receptor to produce one or more other substances that stimulate the sensory cells. In any event, an insect's sensitivity to different substances varies; two very similar chemicals (such as the dextro and levo forms of a particular sugar) may be quite different in their stimulating effect. Some scents (for example, the sex attractant produced by a female) can be detected by one sex (in this case, the male) but not by the other. The sensitivity of chemoreceptors to some substances is very high. Many insects can detect certain odors at very low concentrations up to a few miles from their source.

Mechanical Senses. Insect sense organs sensitive to mechanical stimuli react to touch, pressure, or vibration, and provide the insect with information that may guide orientation, general movements, feeding, flight from enemies, reproduction, and

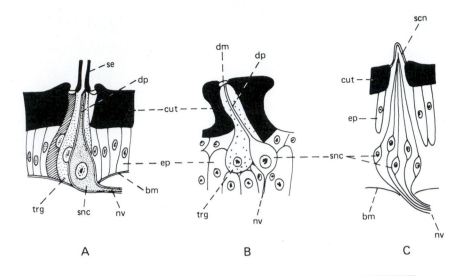

Figure 3–27.   Insect sensilla. **A,** hair sensillum; **B,** campaniform sensillum; **C,** chemoreceptor. *bm,* basement membrane; *cut,* cuticle; *dm,* domelike layer of cuticle over nerve ending; *dp,* distal process of sensory cell; *ep,* epidermis; *nv,* neuron; *scn,* sense cone; *se,* seta; *snc,* sensory cell; *trg,* trichogen cell. (**A, C,** redrawn from Snodgrass, by permission of the McGraw-Hill Book Company, Inc.)

other activities. These sense organs are of three principal types: hair sensilla, campaniform sensilla, and scolopophorous organs.

The simplest type of tactile receptor is a hair sensillum (Figures 3–27A and 3–28). A process from the sensory neuron extends to the base of the seta, and movements of the seta initiate impulses in the neuron. In a campaniform sensillum the neuron ending lies just under a domelike area of the cuticle (Figure 3–27B), and distortion of this dome elicits a neuronal response. Scolopophorous organs (also known as chordotonal organs) are more complex sensilla that consist of a bundle of sensory neurons whose dendrites are attached to the body wall; they are sensitive to movements of the body (including pressure and vibration). These organs, which are widely distributed over the body, include the subgenual organs (usually located at the proximal end of the tibiae), Johnston's organ (in the second antennal segment, sensitive to movements in the antennal flagellum), and the tympanal organs (involved in hearing). Mechanical stimuli act by displacement. The stimuli may come from outside the insect (for example, touch and hearing) or from inside it (stimuli resulting from position or movement). The mechanical stimuli initiate a series of nerve impulses, the character of which is determined by the stimulus. In some cases the nerve impulses may be transmitted at frequencies as high as several hundred per second.

The sense of touch in insects operates mainly through hair sensilla. The character of the nerve impulses initiated is determined by the rate and direction of the hair deflection. This sense is generally quite acute: very little hair deflection may be necessary to initiate a series of neuronal impulses.

Many insects show a response to gravity, for example, in the surfacing of aquatic insects and in the vertical constructions (burrows in the ground, combs in a beehive, and the like) some insects make. Insects generally do not have organs of equilibrium comparable to the statocysts of crustaceans, though air bubbles carried on the body surfaces by certain aquatic insects when they submerge may act in a similar manner. The forces of gravity and pressure generally are detected by other means.

Many joints in insects are provided with tactile setae that register any movements of the joint, thus providing the insect with information on the position of the joint (this is known as proprioception). Pressure on the body wall, whether produced by gravity or some other force, is usually detected by campaniform sensilla. Pressure on the legs may be detected by subgenual organs or by sensitive setae on the tarsi.

An insect detects movements of the surrounding medium (air or water currents) chiefly by tactile setae. It receives information on its movements both by mechanoreceptors and by visual cues. Movements of air or water past an insect (whether the insect is stationary and the medium is moving, or the insect is moving) are detected largely by the antennae or sensory setae on the body. The antennae appear to be the most important detectors of such movements in the Díptera and Hymenóptera. In other insects, sensory setae on the head or neck may be the most important receptors. The halteres of the Díptera play an important role in maintaining equilibrium in flight. They move through an arc of nearly 180° at rates of up to several hundred times per second. Any change in the direction of the insect produces a strain in the cuticle due to the gyroscopic property of the rapidly beating halteres and is presumably detected by the campaniform sensilla distributed on the base of the haltere.

Hearing.   The ability to detect sound (vibrations in the substrate or in the surrounding medium) is developed in many insects, and sound plays a role in many types of behavior. Insects detect airborne sounds by means of two types of sense organs, hair sensilla and tympanal organs. Vibrations in the substrate are detected by subgenual organs.

Many insects apparently can detect sound, but the particular sensilla involved are not always known. In some of the Díptera (for example, mosquitoes), however, it is known that the setae of the antennae are involved in hearing (the sensilla being Johnston's organ in the second antennal segment).

Tympanal organs are scolopophorous organs in which the sensory cells are attached to (or very near to) tympanic membranes. The number of sensory cells involved ranges from one or two (for example, in certain moths) up to several hundred. The tym-

panic membrane (or tympanum) is a very thin membrane with air on both sides of it. Tympanal organs are present in certain Orthóptera, Homóptera, and Lepidóptera. The tympana of short-horned grasshoppers (Acrídidae) are located on the sides of the first abdominal segment. Those of long-horned grasshoppers (Tettigonìidae) and crickets (Grýllidae), when present, are located at the proximal end of the front tibiae (Figure 3–8, *tym*). The tympana of cicadas are located on the first abdominal segment (Figure 25-11, *tym*). Moths may have tympana on the metathorax or the base of the abdomen.

Vibrations in the substrate may be initiated in the substrate directly or may be induced (through resonance) by airborne sound vibration. The detection of substrate vibration is mainly by subgenual organs. The frequency range to which these organs are sensitive varies in different insects, but is mainly between about 200 and 3000 Hz. Some insects (for example, bees) may be largely insensitive to airborne sound, but can detect sound vibrations reaching them through the substrate.

The sensory setae that detect airborne sound are generally sensitive only to relatively low frequencies (a few hundred hertz or less; rarely, a few thousand). Probably the most efficient auditory organs in insects are the tympanal organs. These are often sensitive to frequencies extending well into the ultrasonic range (up to 100,000 Hz or more),[2] but their discriminatory ability is to amplitude modulation

---

[2]The upper limit of hearing in man is generally about 15 kHz.

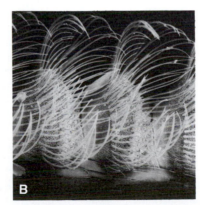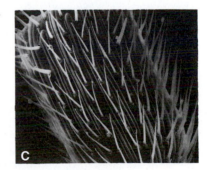

Figure 3–28.   Scanning electron microscope photographs of some insect sensilla. **A,** sensilla on the antenna of an aphid, 1750 ×; **B,** hair sensilla on the antenna of a clearwing moth, 95 ×; **C,** hair sensilla on the antenna of a braconid, 500 ×. (Courtesy of the Ohio Agricultural Research and Development Center.)

rather than to frequency modulation. An insect's response (its behavior and the nerve impulses initiated in the auditory nerves) is not affected by differences in the frequencies of the sound as long as these frequencies are within the detectable range; an insect thus does not detect differences (or changes) in the pitch of a sound, at least at the higher frequencies. On the other hand, tympanal organs are very sensitive to amplitude modulation, that is, the rhythmic features of the sound. These are the most important features of an insect's "song."

Vision. The primary visual organs of insects generally are of two types, the frontal *ocelli* and faceted *compound eyes.*

Ocelli have a single corneal lens that is somewhat elevated or domelike; beneath this lens are two cell layers, the corneagenous cells and the retina (Figure 3–29A). The corneagenous cells, which secrete the cornea, are transparent. The light-sensitive portion of insect photoreceptors is made up of closely packed microvilli on one side of the retinal cells called the rhabdom. In the ocelli the rhabdoms are in the outer part of the retina. The basal portions of the retinal cells are often pigmented. The frontal ocelli apparently do not form focused images (the light is focused below the retina). They seem to be organs sensitive mainly to differences in light intensity.

The most complex light receptors in insects are the compound or faceted eyes, which are composed of many (up to several thousand) individual units called *ommatidia* (Figure 3–29C,D). Each ommatidium is an elongate group of cells capped externally by a hexagonal corneal lens. The corneal lenses are usually convex externally, forming the facets of the eye. Beneath this corneal lens is usually a crystalline cone of four Semper cells (Figure 3–29D, *cc*) surrounded by two pigmented corneagenous cells (*pgc*), and beneath the crystalline cone is a group of elongate sensory cells, usually eight in number, surrounded by a sheath of epidermal pigment cells (*pgc*). The striated portions of the sensory cells form a central or axial rhabdom (*rh*) in the ommatidium.

The pigment surrounding an ommatidium (Figure 3–29D, *pgc*) generally extends far enough inward so that the light reaching a rhabdom comes through just the one ommatidium; the image the insects gets is thus a mosaic, and such an eye is spoken of as an apposition eye. If the pigment is located more distally in relation to the rhabdom, light from adjacent ommatidia may reach a given rhabdom; this is a superposition eye. In some insects that fly both day and night, such as moths, the migration of the pigment around an ommatidium operates somewhat like the iris of the human eye: in bright light the pigment migrates inward, surrounding the rhabdom so that the only light reaching the rhabdom is that

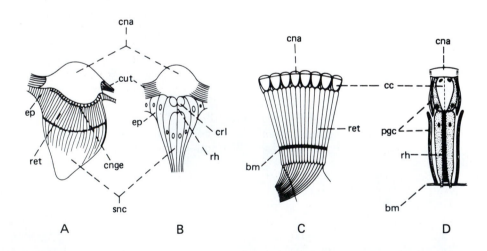

Figure 3–29. Eye structure in insects (diagrammatic). **A,** dorsal ocellus of an ant; **B,** lateral stemma of a caterpillar; **C,** vertical section of part of a compound eye; **D,** ommatidium of a compound eye. *bm,* basement membrane; *cc,* crystalline cone; *cna,* cornea; *cnge,* corneagenous cells; *crl,* crystalline lens; *cut,* cuticle; *ep,* epidermis; *pgc,* pigment cells; *ret,* retina; *rh,* rhabdom; *snc,* sensory cells of retina. (**B, C,** redrawn from Snodgrass, by permission of the McGraw-Hill Book Company Inc.; **D,** redrawn from Matheson, by permission of Cornell University Press.)

coming through that ommatidium (an apposition eye); in the dark the pigment moves outward, so that light from adjacent ommatidia may also reach the rhabdom (a superposition eye). The time required for this movement of the pigment varies in different species. For the codling moth, it is from 30 to 60 minutes.

In many immature insects (and some adults) compound eyes are absent, and in their place may be small groups of visual organs that are similar to ocelli in external appearance (Figure 3–29B). These are called stemmata (or sometimes lateral ocelli). These structures are quite varied in their structure, but all apparently represent highly modified compound eyes (see Paulus 1979).

The flicker-fusion frequency in insects (the rate of flicker at which the light appears continuous) is much higher than in man: 45–53 per second in man and up to 250 or more in insects. This higher rate means that insects can perceive form even when in rapid flight and that they are very sensitive to motion. In some insects (for example, dragonflies) the ommatidia of one eye are oriented so that their axes intersect with those of the other eye, allowing steroscopic vision. If a dragonfly nymph is blinded in one eye, the nymph is unable to judge the position of its prey very accurately.

The range in wavelength to which insect eyes are sensitive is from about 2540 to 6000 Å, compared with about 4500 to 7000 Å in humans. Insects' visual range is shifted to shorter wavelengths in comparison to that of vertebrates. Many insects appear to be color-blind, but some can distinguish colors, including ultraviolet. The honey bee, for example, can distinguish blue and yellow, but cannot see red. Just how an insect distinguishes different colors is not clear. There is evidence that it may result from different retinal cells being sensitive to light of different wavelengths. Some insects (for example, the honey bee) are able to analyze polarized light. From the pattern of polarization in a small patch of sky, they can determine the position of the sun. The head capsule of some weevils contains a region that transmits only far-red and near-infrared light. In the alfalfa weevil, *Hỳpera pòstica*, this extraocular cutoff filter apparently works in conjunction with the compound eyes, enabling the insect to use visual cues in locating and recognizing its host plant.

Other Sense Organs.   Insects usually have a well-developed temperature sense. The sense organs involved are distributed over the body but are more numerous on the antennae and legs. Some insects also have a well-developed humidity sense. The sen-silla involved in these senses are quite diverse in structure, and in many cases the relationship between the observed structure and function is not well understood (see Altner and Loftus 1985).

Endocrine System

Several organs in an insect are known to produce hormones, the principal functions of which are the control of the reproductive processes, molting, and metamorphosis. Chemicals similar to hormones of vertebrates, including androgens, estrogens, and insulin, have recently been detected in insects, but their function is yet unknown.

The neurosecretory cells in the brain are neurons that produce one or more hormones that play a role in growth, metamorphosis, and reproductive activities. One of these, commonly called the brain hormone or prothoracicotropic hormone (PTTH), plays an important role in molting by stimulating a pair of glands in the prothorax to produce the hormone ecdysone that causes apolysis. Other hormones produced by the brain may have other functions. For example, it is believed that a brain hormone plays a role in caste determination in termites and in breaking diapause in some insects.

Ecdysone (Figure 3–30A) initiates growth and development and causes apolysis. This hormone occurs in all insect groups that have been studied, in crustaceans, and in arachnids, and it is probably the molting hormone of all arthropods. It also plays a role in the differentiation of the ovarioles and accessory reproductive glands in females and in several steps in the process of egg production (oogenesis). Ecdysone, in fact, is also produced within the ovaries of insects.

The corpora allata (Figure 3–26, *ca*) produce a hormone called the juvenile hormone (JH, Figure 3–30B), the effect of which is the inhibition of metamorphosis. Various substances, particularly terpenes like farnesol, show considerable juvenile-hormone-like activity. JH also has effects on other processes besides the inhibition of metamorphosis. It is involved in vitellogenesis, accessory reproductive gland activity, pheromone production, and sexual behavior (see Raabe 1986).

Substances chemically related to ecdysone and juvenile hormone occur in certain plants and may protect the plants from feeding by insects. Chemical analogs of ecdysone and juvenile hormone are being studied to see whether they can function as new kinds of insecticides.

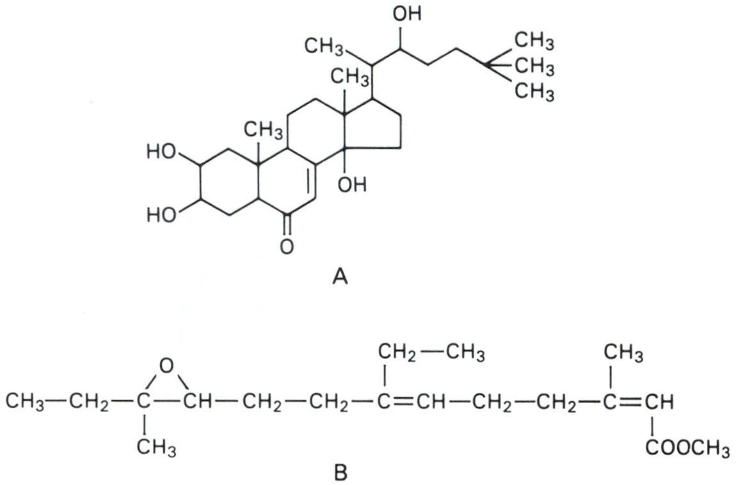

Figure 3–30.   Structure of two insect hormones. **A,** ecdysone; **B,** juvenile hormone. (From Arms and Camp.)

Reproductive Systems

Internal Reproductive Systems

The internal reproductive system of the female (Figure 3–31A) consists of a pair of ovaries (*ovy*), a system of ducts through which the eggs pass to the outside, and associated glands. Each ovary generally consists of a group of ovarioles (*ovl*). These lead into the lateral oviduct posteriorly (*ovd*) and unite anteriorly in a suspensory ligament (*sl*) that usually attaches to the body wall or to the dorsal diaphragm. The number of ovarioles per ovary varies from 1 to 200 or more, but it is usually in the range of 4–8. Oogonia (the primary germ cells) are located in the anterior apical portion of the ovariole, the germarium. The oogonia undergo mitosis, giving rise to the oocytes and trophocytes (or nurse cells; the mechanism by which it is determined which daughter cell becomes an oocyte and which become trophocytes is unknown). Ovarioles in which trophocytes are produced are called meroistic ovarioles; no trophocytes are produced in panoistic ovarioles. The oocytes pass down through the ovarioles, maturing as they go. Thus the temporal sequence of oocyte maturation is reflected in the spatial sequence in the ovariole. The trophocytes may be connected to the oocyte by cytoplasmic filaments, and may remain in the germarium (telotrophic ovarioles) or pass down the ovariole with each oocyte (in polytrophic ovarioles). The trophocytes are important in passing ribosomes and RNA to the oocyte. An oocyte, the surrounding epithelium, and trophocytes (in polytrophic ovarioles) together form a follicle. Yolk proteins (vitellogenins) are synthesized outside the ovariole and transported into the oocyte by the follicular epithelium. In this region of the ovariole (the vitellarium) the oocytes greatly increase in size owing to the deposition of yolk (the process of vitellogenesis). Yolk consists of protein bodies (largely derived from hemolymph proteins), lipid droplets, and glycogen. Many insects harbor microorganisms in their bodies, and in some cases these may get into the egg during its development, usually through the follicle cells. The maturation divisions of the oocyte may occur at about the end of vitellogenesis or even after insemination, resulting in eggs with the haploid number of chromosomes. In the lower portion of the ovariole a vitelline membrane is formed around the oocyte, and the follicular epithelium secretes the chorion (or eggshell) around the mature oocyte.

In many insects, all or most of the oocytes mature before any are laid, and the egg-swollen ovaries may occupy a large part of the body cavity and may even distend the abdomen. The two lateral oviducts usually unite posteriorly to form a single common (or median) oviduct, which enlarges posteriorly into a genital chamber or vagina. The vagina extends to the outside, the opening being called either the ovipore (in reference to the opening through which the eggs are laid) or vulva (the copulatory opening). Because the vagina usually also receives the male genitalia during copulation, it is sometimes known as the bursa copulatrix. Associated with the vagina are usually a saclike structure called the spermatheca, in which spermatozoa are stored, and often various accessory glands, which may secrete adhesive material to fasten the eggs to some object or provide material that covers the egg mass with a protective coating.

In many Lepidóptera (the Ditrỳsia) there are two openings to the reproductive tract of the female. The

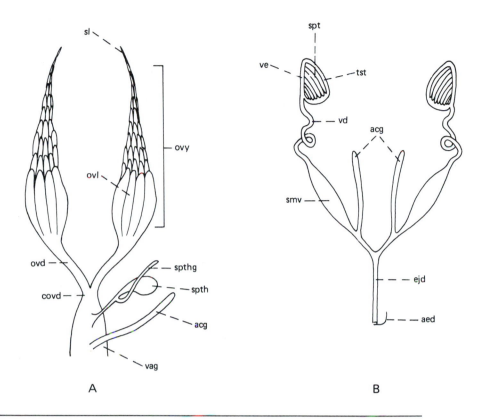

Figure 3–31. Reproductive systems of insects. **A,** female reproductive system; **B,** male reproductive system. *acg,* accessory gland; *aed,* aedeagus; *covd,* common oviduct; *ejd,* ejaculatory duct; *ovd,* oviduct; *ovl,* ovariole; *ovy,* ovary; *sl,* suspensory ligament; *smv,* seminal vesicle; *spt,* sperm tube; *spth,* spermatheca; *spthg,* spermathecal gland; *tst,* testis; *vag,* genital chamber or vagina; *vd,* vas deferens; *ve,* vas efferens. (Redrawn from Snodgrass, by permission of the McGraw-Hill Book Company, Inc.)

common oviduct leads to the vagina and the ovipore to the outside on segment 9. During copulation, however, the male places his genitalia and deposits the spermatophore in a separate opening, the vulva, on segment 8. The vulva leads to the bursa copulatrix, which is connected to the vagina and thence to the spermatheca by a sperm duct, through which the spermatozoa must move.

Egg development is usually complete about the time the adult stage is reached, but in some cases it is completed later. In those aphids in which the female gives birth to living young parthenogenetically, the eggs are matured and development begins before the adult stage is reached. In the beetle genus *Micromálthus* (see page 407) the eggs are matured and begin their development (without fertilization) in the ovaries of the larvae, and are passed to the outside (as either eggs or larvae) before the mother becomes an adult. In the cecidomyiid genus *Miástor* (see page 539), egg development is also completed in the larval stage, but in this case the young larvae (which have developed parthenogenetically) break out of the ovaries into the body cavity and develop there. They eventually rupture the cuticle of the mother larva and escape to the outside. Reproduction by a preadult stage is called paedogenesis.

Egg production appears to be controlled in many insects by one or more hormones from the corpora allata, including juvenile hormone (Figure 3–30B), that act by controlling the initial stages of oogenesis and yolk deposition. Removal of the corpora allata prevents normal egg formation, and their reimplantation (from either a male or a female) induces ovarian activity again. The corpora allata have nerve connections with the brain, and nerve impulses affect their activity. It is also believed that (at least in some cases) neurosecretory cells in the brain may produce a hormone that affects the activity of the corpora allata. Many external factors (for example, photoperiod and temperature) affect egg production, and these factors probably act through the corpora allata.

The reproductive system of the male (Figure 3–31B) is similar in general arrangement to that of the female. It consists of a pair of gonads, the testes, ducts to the outside, and accessory glands. Each testis (*tst*) consists of a group of sperm tubes (*spt*) or follicles surrounded by a peritoneal sheath. Each sperm follicle opens into a short connecting tube, the vas efferens (*ve*; plural, *vasa efferentia*), and these connect to a single vas deferens (*vd*; plural, *vasa deferentia*) on each side of the animal. The two vasa deferentia usually unite posteriorly to form a median ejaculatory duct (*ejd*), which opens to the outside on a penis or an aedeagus (*aed*). In some insects there is an enlargement of or a lateral diverticulum from each vas deferens in which spermatozoa are stored. These are called seminal vesicles (*smv*). The accessory glands (*acg*) secrete fluids that serve as a carrier for the spermatozoa or that harden about them to form a sperm-containing capsule, the spermatophore.

The sperm begin their development in the distal (anterior) ends of the sperm follicles of the testes and continue development as they pass toward the vas efferens. The processes of spermatogenesis (production of haploid germ cells from diploid spermatogonia) is usually completed by the time the insect reaches the adult stage or is completed very shortly thereafter.

The spermatozoa of insects come in an almost bewildering variety of shapes and sizes, often differing quite strikingly from the typical tadpole-shaped cells one thinks of (see Jamieson 1987). One notable characteristic is that the flagellum, or axoneme, is made up of the typical 9 + 2 arrangement of microtubules characteristic of flagella and cilia, but in addition has an outer ring of 9 single microtubules that are derived from the ring of 9 doublets. This 9 + 9 + 2 arrangement is characteristic of hexapods as a whole. In addition to the more familiar threadlike or tadpolelike cells, some hexapods have spermatozoa with two flagella instead of one, cells in which the axoneme is "encysted" so that they are immobile, and, in some Protúra, even simple diskshaped immobile cells. Among species of *Drosóphila* the spermatozoa range in length from about 55 μm to 15 mm (the total body length of the familiar *D. melánogaster* is less than 5 mm)!

External Genitalia

The external genitalia of most insects are generally believed to be derived from appendages of abdominal segments 8, 9, and possibly 10. The male genitalia are primarily organs involved with copulation and the transfer of sperm to the female. The female genitalia are involved in the deposition of the eggs on or in a suitable substrate. These structures are called external genitalia even though they may be retracted within the apical abdominal segments when not in use and are often (especially in the male) not visible without dissection.

The appendicular ovipositor of pterygote insects is believed to have evolved from a structure similar to that now found in the female genitalia in the Thysanùra (Figure 3–32A). This consists of an ovipositor, which is formed from the appendages (gonopods) of segments 8 and 9. The *first gonocoxa* (= *first valvifer*, from segment 8, gcx_1) articulates dorsally with tergum 8; the *second gonocoxa* (= *second valvifer*, from segment 9, gcx_2) articulates with tergum 9. Laterally, the gonocoxae bear styli, the *gonostyli*. These are presumably serial homologues of the styli on the pregenital segments and thus represent the derived telopods of the primitive abdominal appendages. Medially each gonocoxa bears an elongate process known as a *gonapophysis* (also called a *valvula*). The second gonapophyses (gap_2, segment 9) lie above the first gonapophyses (gap_1, segment 8), and together these form the shaft of the ovipositor. Coordination of the movement of these four elongate structures is achieved by two mechanisms. First, the two gonapophyses on each side are connected by a tongue-in-groove mechanism known as an *olistheter*. Additionally, there is a small sclerite on each side, the *gonangulum*, that articulates with the second gonocoxa (from which it is derived), the first gonapophysis, and tergum 9. Again, this interconnects the movements of the first and second gonapophyses on each side.

In the pterygote insects that retain an appendicular ovipositor the first gonostylus is lost, and the second gonocoxa is elongate (perhaps incorporating remnants of the second gonostylus) to form a sheathlike outer covering for the ovipositor shaft, the *gonoplacs* (also known as the third valvulae, Figure 3–32B, *gpl*). In most insects the gonoplacs serve both a protective and a sensory function and are not involved in penetrating the substrate in order to oviposit. In the Orthóptera, however, the gonoplacs are cutting or digging structures, taking over the function of the second gonapophyses, which become reduced and function as egg guides.

There are a number of modifications of this basic appendicular ovipositor structure within the pterygotes, but the most generalized condition is found in some Odonàta, Homóptera, Orthóptera, and Hymenóptera. In many Holometábola the appendicular components of the ovipositor are very highly re-

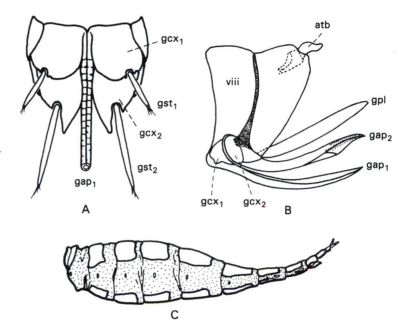

Figure 3–32. Ovipositor of insects. **A,** ovipositor of Thysanùra, ventral view; **B,** ovipositor of a leafhopper, lateral view with parts spread out; **C,** secondary ovipositor of Mecóptera, lateral view. *atb,* anal tube; *gcx₁,* first gonocoxa; *gcx₂,* second gonocoxa; *gap₁,* first gonapophysis; *gap₂,* second gonapophysis; *gpl,* gonoplac; *gst1,* first gonostylus; *gst₂,* second gonostylus. (**A** and **C** redrawn from Snodgrass, by permission of the McGraw-Hill Book Company, Inc.)

duced and are not involved in oviposition. Instead, the terminal abdominal segments form a telescoping tube, called the pseudovipositor or oviscapt, which the female extends when ovipositing (Figure 3–32C). In some cases, such as tephritid flies, this type of ovipositor bears apical cutting plates, thus enabling the female to place her eggs deep within a suitable substrate.

The external genitalia of male insects show such incredible diversity that it has been difficult to infer the primitive structures from which they evolved and to homologize the parts in different orders. The genitalia of the Thysanùra and Microcorýphia are generally similar to that of the females, but with an additional median penis derived from segment 10 (Figure 3–33A). However, the male genitalia of silverfish and bristletails are not involved with copulation. In these insects, as well as the entognathous hexapods, sperm transfer is indirect: the male places his spermatophore or a sperm droplet on the substrate, and the female actively places it in her gonopore. The penis of lepismatids is used to spin a silk web upon which the spermatophore is placed.

There is considerable debate concerning the origin of the male genitalia in pterygotes. Some authors contend that they are derived from the appendages of segment 9 alone, and some include both these appendages and the penis of segment 10 (as seen in machiloids and lepismatoids). Snodgrass (1957) claimed that the genitalia are derived from outgrowths of sternum 10. In very general terms the genitalia are composed of outer clasping organs and

a median intromittant organ (Figure 3–33B). The outer claspers, or *parameres* (*pmr*), may arise from a common base, the *gonobase* or basal ring (*gb*). The median intromittant organ is the *aedeagus* (*aed*). The opening of the aedeagus through which the spermatophore or the semen passes is the *phallotreme* (*phtr*). In many species the ejaculatory duct is everted through the phallotreme during copulation; this

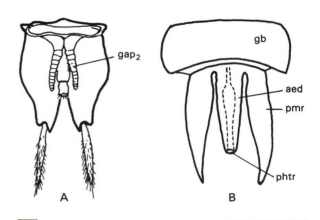

Figure 3–33. **A,** male genitalia of Machílidae, ventral view; **B,** external genitalia of pterygotes (diagrammatic). *aed,* aedeagus; *gap₂,* second gonapophysis; *gb,* gonobase; *pmr,* paramere; *phtr,* phallotreme. (**A,** redrawn from Snodgrass, by permission of the McGraw-Hill Book Company, Inc.; **B,** redrawn from Snodgrass.)

eversible lining is called the endophallus. Such diversity exists in the structure and nomenclature of the male genitalia that it is beyond the scope of this book to describe them in more detail (see Tuxen, 1970, for an order-by-order account of genitalic structure and the nomenclature used). This diversity of structure is very useful in identifying many groups of insects at the species level; such identification usually requires dissection and mounting of the genitalia for closer study.

Development and Metamorphosis

Sex Determination

The chromosomes of insects (as well as other animals) usually occur in pairs, but in one sex the members of one pair do not match or are represented by one chromosome only. The chromosomes of this odd pair are called sex chromosomes; those of the other pairs, autosomes. In most insects the male has just one X (sex) chromosome (and is called heterogametic) and the female has two (homogametic). The male condition is generally referred to as XO (if only one chromosome in this pair is present) or XY (the Y chromosome being different in size or shape from the X chromosome), and the female as XX (two X chromosomes). One major exception to this generalization is in the Lepidóptera: in most species in this order it is the female that is heterogametic, or XY.

The autosomes appear to contain genes for "maleness," while the X chromosomes contain genes for "femaleness." More accurately, it seems that the sex is determined by the balance between these two groups of genes. With two autosomes of each pair and only one X chromosome, the genes for maleness predominate and the animal becomes a male. With two autosomes of each pair and two X chromosomes, the genes for femaleness predominate and the animal becomes a female.

Sex is determined a little differently in the Hymenóptera and a few other insects. In these insects the males are generally haploid (only very rarely diploid), and the females are diploid. The males develop from unfertilized eggs and the females develop from fertilized eggs (a type of parthenogenesis called arrhenotoky). Just how a haploid condition produces a male and a diploid condition produces a female is less well understood, but it is believed that sex in these insects depends on a series of multiple alleles (Xa, Xb, Xc, etc.): haploids and homozygous diploids (Xa/Xa, Xb/Xb, Xc/Xc, etc.) are males, while heterozygous diploids (Xa/Xb, Xc/Xd, etc.) only are females.

Parthenogenetic development producing females occurs in many insects (this type is called thelytoky). In some of these species males are relatively rare or are unknown. These insects usually have the XO or XY male and XX female sex-determining mechanism, which means that either the eggs fail to undergo meiosis and are diploid or they do undergo meiosis and two cleavage nuclei fuse to restore the diploid condition. Some insects (for example, gall wasps and aphids) produce both males and females parthenogenetically (at certain seasons). The production of a male apparently involves the loss of an X chromosome, and the production of a female involves either a fusion of two cleavage nuclei to restore the diploid condition or diploid eggs arising from tetraploid germ tissue.

Individual insects sometimes develop with aberrant sex characters. Individuals having some male tissues and some female tissues are called gynandromorphs; such individuals sometimes occur in the Hymenóptera and Lepidóptera. In the Hymenóptera, where the sex-determining mechanism is haploidy = male and diploidy = female, a gynandromorph may develop from a binucleate egg in which only one of the nuclei is fertilized or when an extra sperm enters the egg and undergoes cleavage to produce haploid (male) tissue in an otherwise female individual. Individuals with a sexual condition intermediate between maleness and femaleness are called intersexes. These usually result from genetic imbalance, particularly in polyploids (for example, a triploid Drosóphila with an XXY sex chromosome content is an intersex and is sterile).

Eggs

The eggs of different insects vary greatly in appearance (Figures 3–34 through 3–36). Most eggs are spherical, oval, or elongate (Figure 3–34B,C,G), but some are barrel-shaped (Figure 3–35), some are disk-shaped, and so on. The egg is covered with a shell that varies in thickness, sculpturing, and color: many eggs are provided with characteristic ridges, spines, or other processes, and some are brightly colored.

Most insect eggs are laid in a situation where they are afforded some protection or where the young, on hatching, will have suitable conditions for development. Many insects enclose their eggs in some sort of protective material. Cockroaches, mantids, and other insects enclose their eggs in an egg case or capsule. The tent caterpillars cover their eggs with a shellaclike material. The gypsy moth lays its eggs in a mass of its body hairs. Grasshoppers, june beetles, and other insects lay their eggs in the

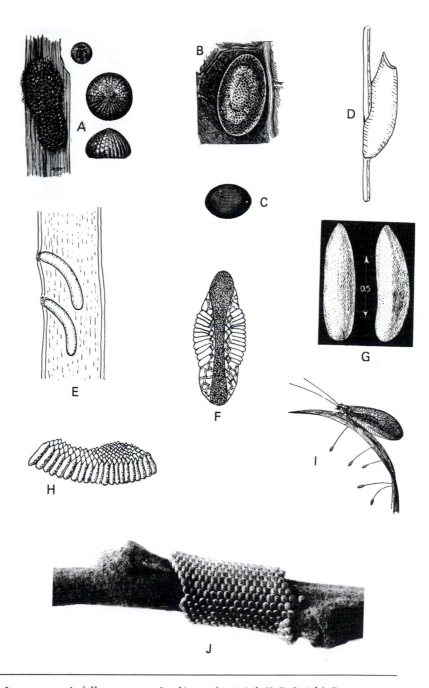

Figure 3–34.   Insect eggs. **A,** fall armyworm, *Spodóptera frugipérda* (J. E. Smith); **B,** grape leaffolder, *Désmia funeràlis* (Hübner); **C,** southern corn rootworm, *Diabrótica undecimpunctàta hówardi* Barber; **D,** horse bot fly, *Gasteróphilus intestinàlis* (De Geer); **E,** snowy tree cricket, *Oecánthus fúltoni* Walker; **F,** *Anópheles* mosquito; **G,** seedcorn maggot, *Hylemÿa platùra* (Meigen); **H,** *Cùlex* mosquito, egg raft; **I,** lacewing, *Chrysòpa* sp.; **J,** fall cankerworm, *Alsóphila pometària* (Harris). (**A–C** and **I,** courtesy of USDA; **J,** courtesy of the Ohio Agricultural Research and Development Center.)

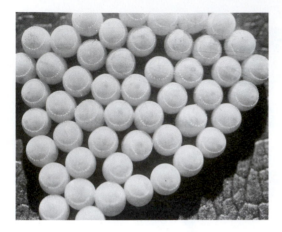

Figure 3–35. Eggs of a stink bug. (Courtesy of the Ohio Agricultural Research and Development Center.)

ground. Tree crickets insert their eggs in plant tissues (Figure 3–34E). Most plant-feeding insects lay their eggs on the food plant of the young. Insects whose immature stages are aquatic usually lay their eggs in water, often attaching them to objects in the water. Parasitic insects usually lay their eggs in or on the body of the host. Some insects deposit their eggs singly, while others lay their eggs in characteristic groups or masses (Figures 3–34H,J, and 3–35). The number laid varies from one in certain aphids to many thousands in some of the social insects, but most insects lay from 50 to a few hundred eggs.

Most insects are oviparous, that is, the young hatch from the eggs after they have been laid. In a few insects the eggs develop within the body of the female, and living young are deposited. The extreme in this case is seen in the sheep ked, for example: the female fly retains the egg and larva within her body for an extended period of time. When parturition ("birth") finally occurs, the larva almost immediately burrows in the ground and pupates. Thus the only active feeding stage is the adult parasitic fly.

Embryonic Development

The egg of an insect is a cell with two outer coverings, a thin vitelline membrane surrounding the cytoplasm and an outer chorion. The chorion, which is the hard outer shell of the egg, has a minute pore or set of pores (the micropyle) at one end, through which sperm enter the egg (Figure 3–37A). Just inside the vitelline membrane is a layer of cortical cytoplasm. The central portion of the egg, inside the cortical cytoplasm, is largely yolk.

Figure 3–36. Eggs of clearwing moths (Sesìidae). **A,** egg of *Podosèsia syríngae* (Harris), 50 ×; **B,** same, showing detail of egg surface, 290 ×. (Courtesy of the Ohio Agricultural Research and Development Center.)

Most insect eggs undergo what is termed superficial cleavage. The early cleavages involve only the nucleus, giving rise to daughter nuclei scattered through the cytoplasm (Figure 3–37B). Eventually these nuclei migrate to the periphery of the egg (to the layer of cortical cytoplasm). After nuclear migration the peripheral cytoplasm becomes subdivided into cells, usually each with one nucleus, forming a cell layer, the blastoderm (Figure 3–37C, *bl*). This is the blastula stage. Within the blastoderm, in the mass of yolk material, are a few cells that do not take part in the formation of the blastoderm; these consist mainly of yolk cells.

The blastoderm cells on the ventral side of the egg enlarge and thicken, forming a germ band or ventral plate that will eventually form the embryo. The remaining cells of the blastoderm become the serosa and (later) the amnion. The germ band becomes differentiated into a median area or middle plate and two lateral areas, the lateral plates (Figure 3–38A). The gastrula stage begins when the mesoderm is formed from the middle in one of three ways:

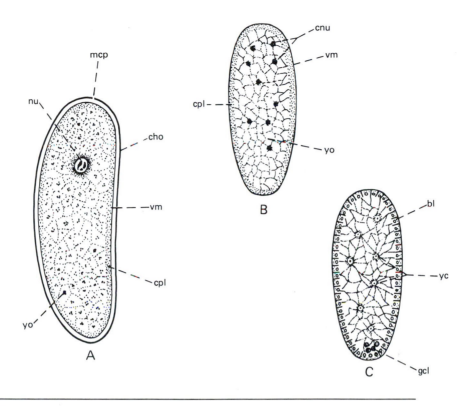

Figure 3–37. **A,** diagram of a typical insect egg; **B,** early cleavage; **C,** peripheral blastoderm layer formed. *bl*, blastoderm; *cho*, chorion; *cnu*, cleavage nuclei; *cpl*, cortical cytoplasm; *gcl*, germ cells; *mcp*, micropyle; *nu*, nucleus; *vm*, vitelline membrane; *yc*, yolk cells; *yo*, yolk. (Redrawn from Snodgrass, by permission of the McGraw-Hill Book Company, Inc.)

by an invagination of this plate (Figure 3–38B,C), by the lateral plates growing over it (Figure 3–38D,E), or by a proliferation of cells from its inner surface (Figure 3–38F). Cells proliferate from each end of the mesoderm and eventually grow around the yolk. These cells represent the beginnings of the endoderm, and they form the lining of what will be the midgut of the insect (Figure 3–39). From the three germ layers—ectoderm, mesoderm, and endoderm—the various organs and tissues of the insect develop: the ectoderm gives rise to the body wall, tracheal system, nervous system, Malpighian tubules, and anterior and posterior ends of the alimentary tract; the mesoderm gives rise to the muscular system, heart, and gonads; the endoderm develops into the midgut.[3]

The alimentary tract is formed by invaginations from each end of the embryo, which extend to and

unite with the primitive midgut (Figure 3–39). The anterior invagination becomes the foregut, the posterior invagination becomes the hindgut, and the central part (lined with endoderm) becomes the midgut. The cells lining the foregut and hindgut are ectodermal in origin and secrete cuticle.

Body segmentation becomes evident fairly early in embryonic development, appearing first in the anterior part of the body. It involves ectoderm and mesoderm, but not endoderm, and is reflected in the segmental arrangement of the structures developing from these germ layers (nervous system, heart, tracheal system, and appendages). The appendages appear soon after segmentation becomes evident. Typically, each segment begins to develop a pair of appendages, but most of these are resorbed and do not develop further.

At some time early in its development the embryo becomes surrounded by two membranes, an inner amnion and an outer serosa. Later it acquires a cuticular membrane secreted by the epidermis. The formation of the amnion and serosa sometimes

---

[3]Note that these embryonic tissues, in particular, the so-called endoderm, may not be homologous to that of deuterostomes.

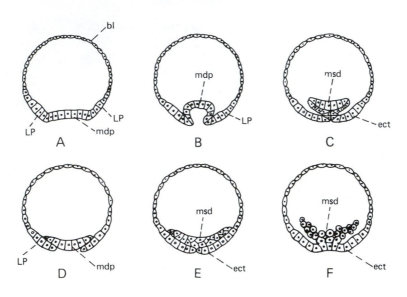

Figure 3–38. Cross-section diagrams showing mesoderm formation in insects. **A,** germ band differentiated into middle and lateral plates; **B** and **C,** stages in mesoderm formation by invagination of middle plate; **D** and **E,** stages in mesoderm formation by lateral plates growing over middle plate; **F,** mesoderm formation by internal proliferation from middle plate. *bl,* blastoderm; *ect,* ectoderm; *mdp,* middle plate; *LP,* lateral plate; *msd,* mesoderm. (Redrawn from Snodgrass, by permission of the McGraw-Hill Book Company, Inc.)

involves a reversal of position of the embryo in the egg; the embryo turns tail first into the yolk, away from the blastoderm. This turning carries part of the extraembryonic blastoderm into the yolk, and when the turning is complete, the opening into the embryonic cavity is closed. The extraembryonic blastoderm thus forms a lining (the amnion) around the embryonic cavity, and the outer part of the blastoderm, which surrounds the egg, becomes the serosa. The embryo later returns to its original position on the ventral side of the egg. In other cases the amnion and serosa are formed by folds of the blastoderm, which grow out from the edge of the germ band and unite beneath it. These membranes usually disappear before the embryo is ready to leave the egg. Cuticular coverings of the embryo (sometimes called pronymphal membranes) occur in insects with simple metamorphosis and in a few with complete metamorphosis. These are shed by a process akin to molting before or very shortly after hatching.

A young insect may escape from the egg in various ways. Most insects with mandibulate mouthparts chew their way out of the egg. Many insects possess what are called egg-bursters—spinelike, knifelike, or sawlike processes on the dorsal side of the head—which are used in breaking through the eggshell. The eggshell is sometimes broken along weakened lines, either by the wriggling of the insect within or by the insect taking in air and rupturing the shell by internal pressure. The hatching from the egg is called eclosion.

Polyembryony is the development of two or more embryos from a single egg. It occurs in some of the parasitic Hymenóptera. In the embryonic developments of such an insect, the dividing nucleus forms cell clusters, each of which develops into an embryo. The number of embryos that grow to maturity in a given host depends on the relative sizes of the parasite larvae and the host. In some cases there are more parasite larvae than the food supply (the body contents of the host) will support, and some of them die and may be eaten by the surviving larvae. The number of young from a single egg varies in *Macrocéntrus* (Bracónidae) from 16 to 24, but in *M. ancylívorus* Rohwer only one parasite larva leaves the host. In *Platygáster* (Platygástridae) from 2 to 18 larvae develop from a single egg, and in *Aphelòpus* (Dryínidae) from 40 to 60 develop from a single egg. In some of the Encýrtidae more than 1500 young develop from a single egg.

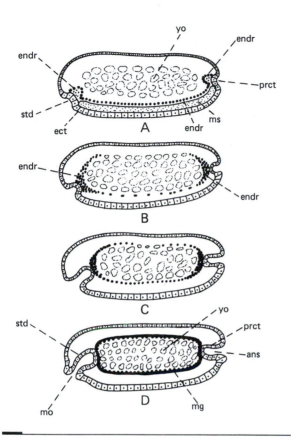

Figure 3–39. Diagrams showing the formation of the alimentary canal. **A,** early stage in which the endoderm is represented by rudiments; **B** and **C,** development of endoderm around yolk; **D,** completion of alimentary canal. *ans,* anus; *ect,* ectoderm; *endr,* endodermal rudiments; *mg,* midgut; *mo,* mouth; *ms,* mesoderm; *prct,* proctodaeum; *std,* stomodaeum or foregut; *yo,* yolk. (Redrawn from Snodgrass, by permission of the McGraw-Hill Book Company, Inc.)

Postembryonic Growth

The fact that an insect possesses an exoskeleton presents a problem as far as growth is concerned. To function as an exoskeleton, the insect's body wall must be relatively rigid, but if it is rigid, it cannot expand very much. Therefore, as the insect grows or increases in size, the exoskeleton must be periodically shed and replaced with a larger one. The process of digesting portions of the old cuticle and synthesizing the new cuticle is called molting, which culminates in the shedding of the old cuticle (ecdysis).

The molt involves not only the cuticle of the body wall, but also the cuticular linings of the tracheae, foregut, and hindgut and the endoskeletal structures. The tracheal linings usually remain attached to the body wall when it is shed. The linings of the foregut and hindgut break up, and the pieces are passed out through the anus. The tentorium usually breaks into four pieces, which are withdrawn through the tentorial pits during the molt. The cast skins, called exuviae, often retain the shape of the insects from which they were shed.

The initial stages in the molting cycle are triggered by the release of PTTH (brain hormone) from neurosecretory cells in the brain. This stimulates the prothoracic glands (also sometimes called the molting glands) to release ecdysone into the hemolymph. Ecdysone, in turn, stimulates the separation of the old cuticle from the underlying epidermis, a process known as apolysis. The epidermis undergoes mitosis and grows in size; after this the new cuticle is produced. Molting fluid secreted from the epidermal cells contains enzymes that digest the old endocuticle (but do not affect the epicuticle or exocuticle), and as a new cuticle is being deposited, the digestive products are resorbed into the body. Once this new exoskeleton is complete, the insect is ready to shed or break out of the old one. Ecdysis is triggered by a molting hormone, and begins with a splitting of the old cuticle along lines of weakness, usually in the midline of the dorsal side of the thorax. The rupturing force is pressure of the hemolymph (and sometimes air or water), forced into the thorax by contraction of the abdominal muscles. This split in the thorax grows, and the insect eventually wriggles its way out of the old cuticle.

When it first emerges from the old cuticle, the insect is pale in color, and its cuticle is soft. Within an hour or two the exocuticle begins to harden and darken. During this brief period the insect enlarges to the size of that instar, usually by taking in air or water. The wings (if present) are expanded by forcing hemolymph into their veins. The alimentary tract often serves as a reservoir of the air used in this expansion: if the crop of a cockroach, for example, is punctured with a needle, the insect does not expand but collapses; if the wing tips of an emerging dragonfly are cut off, hemolymph escapes from the cut end and the wings fail to expand. In addition to allowing the cuticle to expand, this period between ecdysis and hardening of the cuticle allows insects that pupate in the soil, for example, to crawl to the surface, there to expand the cuticle. In some species, a proteinaceous hormone, bursicon, has been identified that controls the process of sclerotization.

The number of molts varies among most insects from 4 to 8, but some of the Odonàta undergo 10 or

12 molts, and some of the Ephemeróptera may undergo as many as 28 molts. A few hexapods, such as the entognathous orders, silverfish, and bristletails, continue to molt after reaching the adult stage, but winged insects neither molt nor increase in size once the adult stage is reached. (Mayflies have a winged instar preceding the adult, the subimago, that molts.)

The stage of the insect between ecdyses is generally called an instar. The first instar is between hatching and the first larval or nymphal molt; the second instar is between the first and second molts; and so on. However, the full process of molting is not instantaneous. There is a period of time, usually short, but sometimes very long, between apolysis and ecdysis during which the next instar of the insect is "hidden" within the old cuticle. Hinton (1971) suggested that the term instar be used to refer to the period of time from one apolysis to the next, and he proposed the term pharate instar to refer to the insect during the time between apolysis and ecdysis. In many cases this time period is sufficiently short that little confusion arises concerning which event signals the end of one instar and the beginning of the next. However, in some, such as the cyclorrhaphous Díptera, the distinction is important. In these flies larval-pupal apolysis is *not* followed by an immediate ecdysis. Instead, the last larval cuticle is hardened to form a sort of cocoon within which is found the pharate pupa. Full development of the pupa is followed by the pupal-adult apolysis. The adult cuticle is then formed, and at that point ecdysis occurs with the adult fly shedding both the last larval and pupal cuticle at the same time.

The increase in size at each molt varies in different species and in different body parts, and can be influenced by a number of environmental conditions. In many insects, however, the increase generally follows a geometric progression. The increase in the width of the larval head capsule in Lepidóptera, for example, is often a factor of 1.2–1.4 at each molt (Dyar's rule). In species where the individual molts are not actually observed, Dyar's rule can sometimes be applied to head capsule measurements of a series of different-sized larvae to estimate the number of instars.

Metamorphosis

Most insects change in form during postembryonic development, and the different instars are not all alike. This change is called metamorphosis. Some insects undergo very little change in form, and the young and adults are very similar except for size (Figure 3–40). In other cases the young and adults are quite different, in habits as well as in form (Figure 3–42).

There is quite a bit of variation in the metamorphosis occurring in different insect groups, but these variations can be roughly grouped into two general types: simple metamorphosis and complete metamorphosis. In simple metamorphosis the wings (if any) develop externally during the immature stages, and there is ordinarily no quiescent stage preceding the last molt (Figures 3–40 and 3–41). In complete metamorphosis the wings (if any) develop internally during the immature stages, and there is a quiescent or pupal stage preceding the last molt (Figure 3–42). The pupal stage is quiescent in that the insect at this time ordinarily does not move around, but a very considerable amount of change (to the adult) is taking place in this stage.

The changes during metamorphosis are accomplished by two processes, histolysis and histogenesis. Histolysis is a process whereby larval structures are broken down into material that can be used in the development of adult structures. Histogenesis is the process of developing the adult structures from the products of histolysis. The chief sources of material for histogenesis are the hemolymph, fat body, and histolyzed tissues such as larval muscles. Ectodermal structures, such as wings and legs, develop beneath the larval cuticle as epidermal thickenings called imaginal discs. These tissues respond in a way quite different from that of other larval tissues to the hormonal milieu of the insect. In the late larval instars these tissues are elaborated to form the adult structures, and when the insect pupates, they are everted (hence one name for holometabolous insects, the Endopterygòta, referring to the development of the wings inside the body of the larva). Other organs may be retained from the larva to the adult or may be completely rebuilt from regenerative cells.

Simple Metamorphosis. The young of insects with this type of metamorphosis are called nymphs[4] and are usually very similar to the adults. Compound eyes are present in the nymph if they are present in the adult. If the adults are winged, the wings appear as budlike outgrowths in the early instars (Figure 3–41) and increase in size only slightly up to the last molt. After the last molt the wings expand to their full adult size. Simple metamorphosis occurs in the hexapod orders 1–22 (see list, Chapter 7).

---

[4]In the European literature the immature stages of all insects are generally referred to as larvae.

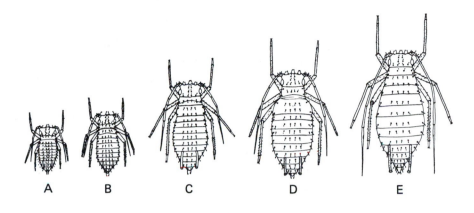

Figure 3–40.   Stages in the development of the strawberry aphid, *Chaètosiphon fragaefòlii* (Cockerell). **A,** first instar; **B,** second instar; **C,** third instar; **D,** fourth instar; **E,** adult female. (Courtesy of Baerg and Arkansas Agricultural Experiment Station.)

There are differences in the kind and amount of change occurring in the insects with simple metamorphosis, and some entomologists recognize three types of metamorphosis in these insects, ametabolous, paurometabolous, and hemimetabolous. Ametabolous insects (with "no" metamorphosis) are wingless as adults, and the only obvious difference between nymphs and adults is size. This type of development occurs in the apterygote orders (Protùra, Collémbola, Diplùra, Microcorýphia, and Thysanùra) and in most wingless members of the other orders with simple metamorphosis. In hemimetabolous metamorphosis (with "incomplete" metamorphosis) the nymphs are aquatic and gill-breathing and differ considerably from the adults in appearance. This type of development occurs in the Epheneróptera, Odonàta, and Plecóptera, and the young of these insects are sometimes called naiads. Paurometabolous insects (with "gradual" metamorphosis) include the remaining insects with simple metamorphosis. The adults are winged; the nymphs and adults live in the same habitat; and the principal changes during growth are in size, body proportions, the development of the ocelli, and occasionally the form of other structures.

Complete Metamorphosis.   The immature and adult stages of insects that undergo complete metamorphosis are usually quite different in form, often live in different habitats, and have very different

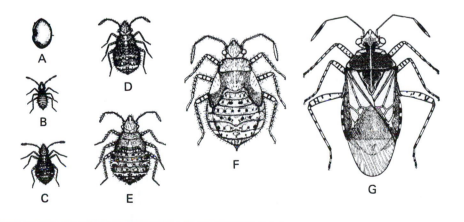

Figure 3–41.   Stages in the development of the grass bug, *Arhýssus sìdae* (Fabricius). **A,** egg; **B,** first instar; **C,** second instar; **D,** third instar; **E,** fourth instar; **F,** fifth instar; **G,** adult female. (Courtesy of Readio and the Entomological Society of America.)

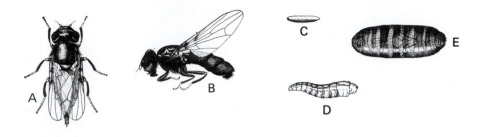

Figure 3–42.   Stages in the development of the sugarbeet root maggot, *Tétanops myopaefòrmis* (Röder). **A,** adult female; **B,** adult male; **C,** egg; **D,** larva; **E,** puparium (pupa inside). (Courtesy of Knowlton and the Utah Agricultural Experiment Station.)

habits. The early instars are often more or less wormlike, and the young in this stage are called larvae (Figures 3–42D and 3–43). The different larval instars are usually similar in form but differ in size. The wings, when they are present in the adult, develop internally during the larval stage and are not everted until the end of the last larval instar. Larvae generally have chewing mouthparts, even in those orders in which the adults have sucking mouthparts.

Following the last larval instar, the insect transforms into a stage called the pupa (Figure 3–44). The insect does not feed in this stage and is usually inactive. Pupae are often covered by a cocoon or some other protective material, and many insects pass the winter in the pupal stage. The final molt occurs at the end of the pupal stage, and the last stage is the adult. The adult is usually pale in color when it first emerges from the pupa, and its wings are short, soft,

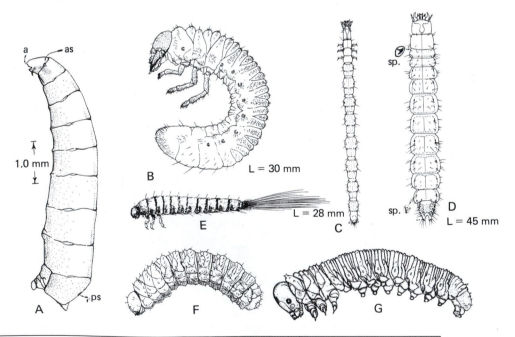

Figure 3–43.   Insect larvae. **A,** maggot or vermiform larva of *Hylemỳa platùra* (Meigen) (Díptera, Anthomyìidae); **B,** grub or scarabaeiform larva of *Phyllóphaga rugòsa* (Melsheimer) (Coleóptera, Scarabaèidae); **C,** elateriform larva of *Cardióphorus* sp. (Coleóptera, Elatéridae); **D,** elateriform larva of *Álaus oculàtus* (L.) (Coleóptera, Elatéridae); **E,** campodeiform larva of *Attagènus megàtoma* (Fabricius) (Coleóptera, Derméstidae); **F,** vermiform larva of *Cỳlas formicàrius elegántulus* (Summers) (Coleóptera, Apiónidae); **G,** eruciform larva of *Caliròa aèthiops* (Fabricius) (Hymenóptera, Tenthredínidae). *a,* antenna; *as,* anterior spiracle; *L,* length; *ps,* posterior spiracle; *sp,* spiracle. (**A** and **E–G,** courtesy of USDA; **B–D,** courtesy of Peterson, reprinted by permission.)

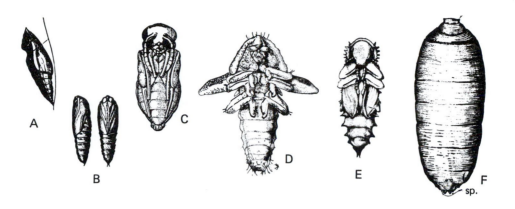

Figure 3–44. Insect pupae. **A,** chrysalis of the sulphur butterfly, *Còlias eurýtheme* Boisduval (Lepidóptera, Piéridae); **B,** fall armyworm, *Spodóptera frugipérda* (J. E. Smith) (Lepidóptera, Noctùidae); **C,** clover seed chalcid, *Bruchóphagus platýptera* (Walker) (Hymenóptera, Eurytómidae); **D,** sweetpotato weevil, *Cỳlas formicàrius elegántulus* (Summers) (Coleóptera, Apiónidae); **E,** sawtoothed grain beetle, *Oryzaéphilus surinaménsis* (L.) (Coleóptera, Cucùjidae); **F,** seedcorn maggot, *Hylemỳa platùra* (Meigen) (Díptera, Anthomyìidae). **A** and **B** are obect pupae, **C–E** are exarate pupae, and **F** is a coarctate pupa. (Courtesy of USDA.)

and wrinkled. In a short time, from a few minutes to several hours or more, depending on the species, the wings expand and harden, the pigmentation develops, and the insect is ready to go on its way. This type of metamorphosis occurs in orders 23–31 and is often called holometabolous (see list, Chapter 7), and these orders are classified together as the Holometábola.

Hypermetamorphosis is a type of complete metamorphosis in which the different larval instars are not of the same type. The first instar is active and usually campodeiform, and the subsequent larval instars are vermiform or scarabaeiform. Hypermetamorphosis occurs in parasitic insects; the first instar seeks out the host and, once in the host, molts into a less active type of larva. This type of complete metamorphosis occurs in the Melòidae (Figure 28–71) and Rhipiphóridae (Coleóptera), the Mantíspidae (Neuróptera), the Strepsíptera, and a few Díptera and Hymenóptera.

Intermediate Types of Metamorphosis. Not all insects have a type of metamorphosis that can be readily classified as simple or complete. Some have a metamorphosis that is somewhat intermediate between these two types. Such metamorphosis is found in thrips (Chapter 26), whiteflies (Chapter 25), and male scale insects (Chapter 25). In fact, these groups have gone far toward evolving complete metamorphosis independently of the orders just discussed.

The first two instars of thrips (Thysanóptera) are wingless and active and are usually called larvae. The next two instars (the next three in the suborder Tubulífera) are inactive, with external wings. The first of these (the first two in Tubulífera) is called a prepupa, and the last a pupa. The final instar is the adult. Apparently at least some of the wing development is internal during the first two instars. This metamorphosis resembles complete metamorphosis in that at least some of the wing development is internal, and an inactive, "pupal" stage precedes the adult. It is similar to simple metamorphosis in that the early instars have compound eyes, and external wing buds are present in more than one preadult instar.

Whiteflies have five instars, the last of which is the adult. The first instar is active and wingless, while the next three instars are inactive, sessile, and scalelike, with the wings developing internally. The fourth instar is called the pupa, and it has external wings. The first three instars are usually called larvae. The molt from the last larval instar to the pupa takes place inside the last larval skin, which forms the puparium. This metamorphosis is essentially complete, though most other members of this order (Homóptera) have simple metamorphosis.

The males of scale insects have a type of metamorphosis that is very similar to that in whiteflies. The first instar (Figure 25–29B), the "crawler," is active and wingless, but the remaining preadult instars are sessile and inactive. The last preadult instar, which has external wings, is called the pupa. The development of wings is at least partly internal.

Control of Metamorphosis.

The metamorphosis of insects is controlled by three hormones: PTTH (prothoracicotropic or brain hormone), ecdysone, and JH (juvenile hormone). PTTH is produced by neurosecretory cells in the brain and stimulates the prothoracic glands (also known as the molting glands) to produce ecdysone, which induces apolysis and promotes growth. JH is produced by cells in the corpora allata and inhibits metamorphosis, thereby promoting further larval or nymphal development. Removal of JH from a larva or nymph (by removing the corpora allata) will cause the larva to pupate and the nymph to develop into an adult when ecdysone is present. Injection of juvenile hormone into a pupa (in the presence of ecdysone) will cause the pupa to develop into a second pupa. Injection of JH into a last-instar nymph or larva will cause another nymphal or larval stage to be produced at the next molt. The corpora allata are active during the early instars and usually cease secreting JH in the last preadult instar. The absence of the hormone in this instar results in metamorphosis.

The changes from instar to instar in insects with simple metamorphosis are generally relatively slight and gradual, being most marked at the final molt to the adult, but in insects with complete metamorphosis there is considerable reorganization within the insect in the pupal stage. Some structures in the larva, such as the heart, nervous system, and tracheal system, change very little at metamorphosis. Other adult structures are present in a rudimentary form in the larva and remain so during successive larval instars. Then, more or less suddenly, they develop to their adult form in the pupal stage. Still other adult structures are not represented in the larva and must be developed at the time of metamorphosis.

Types of Larvae.

The larvae of insects that undergo complete metamorphosis differ considerably in form, and several types have been recognized.

Eruciform: Caterpillarlike (Figure 3–43G); body cylindrical, the head well developed but with very short antennae, and with both thoracic legs and abdominal prolegs. This type occurs in the Lepidóptera, Mecóptera, and some Hymenóptera (suborder Sýmphyta).

Scarabaeiform: Grublike (Figure 3–43B); usually curved, the head well developed, with thoracic legs but without abdominal prolegs, and relatively inactive and sluggish. This type occurs in certain Coleóptera (for example, Scarabaèidae).

Campodeiform: Resembling diplurans in the genus *Campòdea* (Figure 8–3A); body elongate and somewhat flattened, the cerci and antennae usually well developed, the thoracic legs well developed, and the larvae usually active. This type occurs in the Neuróptera, Trichóptera, and many Coleóptera.

Elateriform: Wirewormlike (Figure 3–43C,D); body elongate, cylindrical, and hard-shelled, the legs short, and the body bristles reduced. This type occurs in certain Coleóptera (for example, Elatéridae).

Vermiform: Maggotlike (Figure 3–43A,F); body elongate and wormlike, legless, and with or without a well-developed head. This type occurs in the Díptera, Siphonáptera, most Hymenóptera (suborder Apócrita), and some Coleóptera and Lepidóptera.

Types of Pupae.

The pupae of insects with complete metamorphosis vary, and five types may be recognized.

Obtect: With the appendages more or less glued to the body (Figure 3–44A,B). This type occurs in the Lepidóptera and some Díptera (suborder Nematócera). The pupa in many Lepidóptera is covered by a silken cocoon formed by the larva before it molts to the pupal stage.

Exarate: With the appendages free and not glued to the body (Figure 3–44C–E). Such a pupa looks much like a pale, mummified adult and is usually not covered by a cocoon. This type occurs in most insects with complete metamorphosis, except the Díptera and Lepidóptera.

Coarctate: Essentially like an exarate pupa, but remaining covered by the hardened cuticle of the last larval instar, which is called a puparium (Figure 3–44F). This type occurs in the Díptera (suborder Brachýcera).

Decticous: With the mandibles movably articulated with the head. This type is also always exarate and occurs in the Neuróptera, Trichóptera, and some Lepidóptera.

Adecticous: With the mandibles immovably attached to the head. This type of pupa is found in the remaining groups of holometabolous insects.

Variations in Life History

The length of a generation and the way it is fitted to the different seasons vary quite a bit in different insects. Most insects in temperate regions have what is called a heterodynamic life cycle; that is, the adults appear for a limited time during a particular season, and some life stage passes the winter in a state of dormancy. The overwintering stage may be the egg (for example, most Orthóptera and Homóptera), nymph (for example, most Odonàta and many Orthóptera), larva (for example, many Lepidóptera), or adult (for example, most Hemíptera and many Coleóptera and Hymenóptera). Many insects, particularly those living in the tropics, have a homodynamic life cycle; that is, development is continuous and there is no regular period of dormancy.

Most insects in the United States have a single generation a year. Some require two or more years to complete their life cycle, as is usually the case with large insects occurring in the northern part of the country. Some of the large beetles, dragonflies, and moths in the northern states and Canada require two or three years to complete their development. Perhaps the longest life cycle of any insect is that of some of the periodical cicadas (*Magicicàda* spp.), which lasts 17 years (see Chapter 25).

Many insects have more than one generation a year. In some cases the number of generations in a year is constant throughout the range of the species. In other cases the species may have more in the southern part of its range. A few insects, usually rather small species that can complete their life cycle in a few weeks, have many generations a year. Such insects continue to reproduce through the season as long as weather conditions are favorable. Insects of tropical origin, such as those of the household and those which attack stored products, may continue breeding throughout the entire 12 months.

In many insects development is arrested during a specific stage of the annual cycle. This period of genetically programmed (i.e., predetermined) dormancy is known as diapause, in contrast to periods of quiescence in response to adverse environmental conditions. A period of winter dormancy in temperate or arctic regions is often called hibernation, and a period of dormancy during high temperatures is called aestivation.

Diapause in insects is genetically controlled, and both onset and termination may be induced by environmental factors such as photoperiod or temperature. The chief factor initiating diapause seems to be photoperiod (day length). Studies of hornworm larvae (Sphíngidae) have shown that all individuals that enter the soil for pupation before a certain date will complete their development, emerge as moths, and reproduce, but individuals entering the soil after this date go into diapause and do not complete their development until the following spring. This factor of day length apparently operates similarly in the case of the codling moth. Individuals of the first generation pupate and emerge as adults in the summer, but individuals of the second generation (in autumn) do not. In some cases (for example, *Antheraèa*, family Saturnìidae), day length may also control emergence from diapause. The larvae of the second generation of the codling moth in Ohio will remain as diapausing larvae in silk-lined cells under the bark of apple trees unless subjected to a short period (some three weeks) of low temperatures (0°C or lower). When then returned to normal developmental temperatures, they pupate and complete their development. The effect of day length is usually direct, on the insect itself, but may occasionally be indirect by its effect on the food eaten by the insect. Photoperiod may also be an important cue for the initiation of diapause in tropical insects, even though changes in day length are much smaller than in temperate regions. Diapause in tropical insects may be associated with alternating wet and dry seasons, high temperatures, or the availability of appropriate food, instead of the avoidance of winter (Denlinger 1986).

References

Altner, H., and R. Loftus. 1985. Ultrastructure and function of insect thermo- and hygroreceptors. Annu. Rev. Entomol. 30:273–295; illus.

Anderson, D. T. 1973. Embryology and Phylogeny in Annelids and Arthropods. New York: Pergamon Press, 495 pp.; illus.

Chapman, R. F. 1982. The Insects: Structure and Function, 3rd ed. Cambridge, Mass.: Harvard University Press, 919 pp.; illus.

Commonwealth Scientific and Industrial Research Organization (CSIRO). 1970. The Insects of Australia. Carlton, Victoria: Melbourne University Press, 1029 pp.; illus.

Daly, H. V., J. T. Doyen, and P. R. Ehrlich. 1978. An Introduction to Insect Biology and Diversity. New York: McGraw-Hill, 564 pp.; illus.

Davey, K. G. 1965. Reproduction in the Insects. San Francisco: Freeman, 96 pp.; illus.

Denlinger, D. L. 1986. Dormancy in tropical insects. Annu. Rev. Entomol. 31:239–264.

Dethier, V. G. 1963. The Physiology of Insect Senses. New York: Wiley, 266 pp.; illus.

Dethier, V. G. 1976. The Hungry Fly: A Physiological Study of Behavior Associated with Feeding. Cambridge, Mass.: Harvard University Press, 489 pp.

Fox, R. M., and J. W. Fox. 1964. Introduction to Comparative Entomology. New York: Reinhold, 450 pp., illus.

Gilbert, L. I. 1976. The Juvenile Hormones. New York: Plenum Press, 572 pp.

Hepburn, H. R. (Ed.). 1976. The Insect Integument. New York: American Elsevier, 572 pp.; illus.

Hinton, H. E. 1955. On the structure, function, and distribution of the prolegs of the Panorpoidea, with a criticism of the Berlese-Imms theory. Trans. Roy. Entomol. Soc. Lond. 106:455–545; illus.

Hinton, H. E. 1971. Some neglected phases in metamorphosis. Proc. Roy. Entomol. Soc. Lond. (C) 35:55–64; illus.

Hinton, H. E. 1981. Biology of Insect Eggs. 3 vols. New York: Pergamon Press, 1125 pp.; illus.

Horn, D. J. 1976. Biology of Insects. Philadelphia: W. B. Saunders, 439 pp.; illus.

Horridge, G. A. (Ed.). 1975. The Compound Eye and Vision of Insects. New York: Clarendon Press, 595 pp.; illus.

Jacobson, M. 1972. Insect Sex Hormones. New York: Academic Press, 382 pp.; illus.

Jamieson, B. G. M. 1987. The Ultrastructure and Phylogeny of Insect Spermatozoa. Cambridge: Cambridge University Press, 320 pp.; illus.

Jones, J. C. 1977. The Circulatory System of Insects. Springfield, Ill.: C. C. Thomas, 255 pp.; illus.

Kerkut, G. A., and L. I. Gilbert (Eds.). 1985. Comprehensive Insect Physiology, Biochemistry and Pharmacology. 13 vols. Vol. 1: Embryogenesis and Reproduction; 482 pp. Vol. 2: Postembryonic Development; 505 pp. Vol. 3: Integument, Respiration and Circulation; 625 pp. Vol. 4: Regulation: Digestion, Nutrition, Excretion; 639 pp. Vol. 5: Nervous System: Structure and Motor Function; 646 pp. Vol. 6: Nervous System: Sensory; 710 pp. Vol. 7: Endocrinology I; 564 pp. Vol. 8: Endocrinology II; 595 pp. Vol. 9: Behaviour; 735 pp. Vol. 10: Biochemistry; 715 pp. Vol. 11: Pharmacology; 740 pp. Vol. 12: Insect Control; 849 pp. Vol. 13: Cumulative Indexes; 314 pp. New York: Pergamon Press.

Kukalová-Peck, J. 1978. Origin and evolution of insect wings and their relation to metamorphosis, as documented by the fossil record. J. Morphol. 156:53–126; illus.

Kukalová-Peck, J. 1983. Origin of the insect wing and wing articulation from the arthropodan leg. Can. J. Zool. 61:1618–1669; illus.

Kukalová-Peck, J. 1985. Ephemeroid wing venation based upon new gigantic Carboniferous mayflies and basic morphology, phylogeny, and metamorphosis of pterygote insects. Can J. Zool. 63:933–955; illus.

Manton, S. M. 1977. The Arthropoda, Habits, Functional Morphology, and Evolution. Oxford: Clarendon Press, 527 pp.; illus.

Matsuda, R. 1970. Morphology and evolution of the insect thorax. Mem. Entomol. Soc. Can. No. 76; 431 pp.; illus.

Matsuda, R. 1976. Morphology and Evolution of the Insect Abdomen, with Special Reference to Developmental Patterns and Their Bearing on Systematics. New York: Pergamon Press, 532 pp.; illus.

Menn, J. J., and M. Beroza (Eds.). 1972. Insect Juvenile Hormones, Chemistry and Action. New York: Academic Press, 341 pp.; illus.

Nachtigall, W. 1968. Insects in Flight (translated from German). New York: McGraw-Hill, 153 pp.; illus.

Neville, A. C. 1975. Biology of the Arthropod Cuticle. New York: Springer-Verlag, 450 pp.; illus.

Novak, V. J. A. 1975 (2nd ed.). Insect Hormones. New York: Halsted, 600 pp.; illus.

Paulus, H. F. 1979. Eye structure and the monophyly of Arthropoda. In: Arthropod Phylogeny, ed. A. P. Gupta, 299–383. New York: Van Nostrand Reinhold Company, 762 pp.; illus.

Payne, T. L., M. C. Birch, and C. E. J. Kennedy (Eds.). 1986. Mechanisms in Insect Olfaction. Oxford: Clarendon Press, 364 pp.; illus.

Peterson, A. 1948. Larvae of Insects. Part I. Lepidoptera and Hymenoptera. Ann Arbor, Mich.: Edwards Bros., 315 pp.; illus.

Peterson, A. 1951. Larvae of Insects. Part II. Coleoptera, Diptera, Neuroptera, Siphonaptera, Mecoptera, Trichoptera. Ann Arbor, Mich.: Edwards Bros., 416 pp.; illus.

Raabe, M. 1986. Insect reproduction: Regulation of successive steps. Adv. Ins. Physiol. 19:29–154; illus.

Rainey, R. C. (Ed.). 1976. Insect Flight: Proceedings of a Symposium. New York: Halsted, 288 pp.; illus.

Rempel, J. G. 1975. The evolution of the insect head: The endless dispute. Quaest. Entomol. 11:7–25; illus.

Riek, E. F., and J. Kukalová-Peck. 1984. A new interpretation of dragonfly wing venation based upon Early Upper Carboniferous fossils from Argentina (Insecta: Odonatoidea) and basic character states in pterygote wings. Can. J. Zool. 62:1150–1166; illus.

Rockstein, M. (Ed.). 1973–1974. The Physiology of Insecta. 6 vols., illus. Vol. 1: Physiology of Ontogeny—Biology, Development, and Aging, 512 pp. (1973). Vol. 2: The Insect and the External Environment. Part A. I. Environmental Aspects. Part B. II. Reaction and Interaction, 517 pp. (1974). Vol. 3: The Insect and the External Environment. Part A. II. Reaction and Interaction. Part B. III. Locomotion, 517 pp. (1974). Vol. 4: The Insect and the External Environment. Homoeostasis I, 488 pp. (1974). Vol. 5: The Insect and the External Environment. Homoeostasis II, 648 pp. (1974). Vol. 6: The Insect and the External Environment. Homoeostasis III, 548 pp. (1974). New York: Academic Press.

Rodriguez, J. G. (Ed.). 1972. Insect and Mite Nutrition. New York: American Elsevier, 701 pp.

Roeder, K. D. 1967 (rev. ed.). Nerve cells and insect behavior. Cambridge, Mass.: Harvard University Press, 238 pp.; illus.

Romoser, W. S. 1973. The Science of Entomology. New York: Macmillan, 499 pp.; illus.

Rothschild, M., Y. Schlein, and S. Ito. 1986. A Colour Atlas of Insect Tissues via the Flea. London: Wolfe, 184 pp.; illus.

Sacktor, B. 1974. Biological oxidations and energetics in insect mitochondria. In Physiology of Insecta, M. Rockstein, ed., vol. 4, 271–353. New York: Academic Press.

Schwalm, F. 1988. Insect Morphogenesis. Monographs in Developmental Biology, vol. 20. New York: Karger, 356 pp.; illus.

Scudder, G. G. E. 1971. Comparative morphology of insect genitalia. Annu. Rev. Entomol. 16:379–406.

Snodgrass, R. E. 1935. Principles of Insect Morphology. New York: McGraw-Hill, 667 pp.; illus.

Snodgrass, R. E. 1952. A Textbook of Arthropod Anatomy. Ithaca, N.Y.: Comstock, 363 pp.; illus.

Snodgrass, R. E. 1957. A revised interpretation of the external reproductive organs of male insects. Smithson. Misc. Coll. 135(6):1–60; illus.

Stehr, F. (Ed.). 1987. Immature Insects. Dubuque, Iowa: Kendall/Hunt, 754 pp.; illus.

Tuxen, S. L. (Ed.). 1970. Taxonomist's Glossary of Genitalia in Insects. Copenhagen: Munksgaard, 359 pp.; illus.

Usherwood, P. N. R. 1975. Insect Muscle. New York: Academic Press, 622 pp.; illus.

Wigglesworth, V. B. 1970. Insect Hormones. San Francisco: Freeman, 159 pp.; illus.

Wigglesworth, V. B. 1973 (7th ed.). The Principles of Insect Physiology. London: Metheun, 827 pp.; illus.

Wigglesworth, V. B. 1984 (8th ed.). Insect Physiology. New York: Chapman and Hall, 191 pp.; illus.

Wootton, R. J. 1979. Function, homology and terminology in insect wings. Syst. Entomol. 4:81–93; illus.

Chapter 4   **Behavior and Ecology**

The importance of insects is determined largely by what they do. Much is said in this book, in the accounts of the various insect groups, about the things insects do. In this chapter we discuss some general activities common to insects in different groups.

Feeding

All insects must eat or they will eventually starve. Much of the activity of many animals is concerned with feeding—finding food and eating it. Food is a very important factor in determining an animal's abundance and where it lives (hence its distribution). The feeding behavior of an insect, what it eats and how it feeds, generally determines that insect's economic importance.

The food of an insect consists of other organisms, plant or animal, living or dead (or plant or animal products, that is, organic material). Many insects are quite specific in their food preferences, and if particular foods are not available they either starve or move to another area. Others are less specific in their food preferences, and if a particular food is scarce or not available they will switch to another. The type and amount of food an insect eats may affect it in many ways—its growth, development, reproduction (certain insects require specific

types of food before they can lay eggs), behavior, and often various morphological characters (size, color, and so on).

It is convenient to classify insects by their feeding behavior into three categories—phytophagous, zoophagous, and saprophagous—but it should be understood that not all insects belong exclusively to one of these categories. Many insects are rather varied feeders and may feed on either living or dead plants or animals.

Phytophagous Insects

Phytophagous (or herbivorous) insects feed on plants and probably outnumber those feeding on other things. There are very few terrestrial or freshwater plants that are not fed upon by some insects, and these insects feed in different ways and on different parts of the plants. Phytophagous insects that feed on plants used by humans often cause considerable economic losses.

The feeding of chewing insects on foliage results in leaves that are skeletonized, riddled with holes, eaten around the edges, or entirely consumed. The smaller insects eat between the veins of the leaf and skeletonize it; the larger ones consume a part or all of the leaf. The principal insects that feed in this way are grasshoppers, the larvae of various butterflies, moths, and sawflies, and beetles. When abundant, such insects can completely defoliate large areas of crop or forest.

Other insects feed on plants by sucking sap from the leaves or other parts of the plant. Leaf feeding by sucking insects produces a characteristic spotting or browning of the leaves or a curling and wilting (Figure 2–5B); such feeding on stems or twigs may cause dwarfing or wilting. The damage to the plant is caused by the removal of the sap and by an actual injury to the plant tissues. The principal insects that feed in this way are scale insects, aphids, leafhoppers, froghoppers, and various bugs. Scale insects are usually quite minute, but may occur in such numbers as to encrust the bark of a tree or the twigs or stems of a plant. They are able to kill orchard or shade trees. Aphids produce a curling of the leaves and, when feeding on fruits, may leave the fruits stunted or misshapen.

Many types of insects feed inside plant tissues, as miners in the leaves, or as borers in the stems, roots, or fruits. Leaf miners tunnel and feed between the two surfaces of the leaf; their mines are of various sorts, but each leaf-mining species produces a characteristic type of mine in a particular species of plant. There are more than 750 leaf-mining species of insects in the United States, representing the orders Lepidóptera (about 400 species in 17 families), Díptera (300 species in 4 families), Hymenóptera (principally sawflies), and Coleóptera (about 50 species in the families Chrysomélidae, Bupréstidae, and Curculiónidae).

Many insects, chiefly the larvae of certain moths and beetles, bore into stems. Such stems are usually killed, resulting in a stunted or misshapen plant. Other insects, chiefly the larvae of various moths, flies, and beetles, burrow into fruits. Many insects bore into the wood or cambium of living trees, weakening, deforming, or sometimes killing the trees. The most important phloem and wood borers are various beetles (chiefly in the families Cerambýcidae, Bupréstidae, Scolýtidae, and Curculiónidae), certain moths (Cóssidae and Sesìidae), horntails, carpenter ants, and termites.

Many insects that feed on plants inject a chemical into the plant that causes it to grow abnormally and produce a gall. Galls may be produced on various parts of a plant, but each species of gall insect produces a characteristic gall on a certain part of a particular type of plant. Each gall may harbor one or many insects. The stimulus to the formation of the gall is usually provided by the feeding stage of the insect; in a few cases the ovipositing female provides the stimulus when she lays her eggs in the plant. A plant gall may have an opening to the outside (for example, the galls of Homóptera and mites), or they may be entirely closed (galls of larval insects). Five orders of insects contain gall-making species: Díptera (principally Cecidomyìidae, Tephrítidae, and Agromỳzidae), Hymenóptera (Cynípidae, some Chalcidòidea, and some Tenthredínidae), Coleóptera (certain Curculiónidae, Bupréstidae, and Cerambýcidae), Lepidóptera (for example, the goldenrod gall moth), and Homóptera (various aphids, psyllids, and coccids). Other plant galls are caused by mites, roundworms, or fungi.

Some insects that feed on plants live in the soil and feed on the underground parts of the plant. It is usually the larval or nymphal stage of the insect that feeds in this way. Root-feeding insects are principally wireworms (Elatéridae), white grubs (Scarabaèidae), some mealybugs, cicada nymphs, various aphids, and some fly larvae.

Perhaps the most interesting behavior found among the phytophagous insects is that of the few insects that grow their own plant food (a fungus). Such "fungus gardens" are produced and tended by certain ants, ambrosia beetles, and some termites. The fungus-growing ants in the United States belong to the genera *Átta* and *Trachymýrmex*; one species of *Átta, A. texána* (Buckley), occurs in the South and Southwest, and *Trachymýrmex* ants occur as far north as Canada. *Átta* ants nest in the ground, where they excavate a complex system of galleries and chambers. They cut circular pieces of leaves and carry them—like parasols—back to their nests; they are commonly called leaf-cutting or parasol ants. The leaves are taken to special chambers in the nest, chewed up, and "seeded" with a fungus. The resulting fungus garden is tended by certain workers, which weed out any foreign fungi that may be brought in with the leaves, and it is this fungus that serves as the food of the colony. Queens that start a new colony take with them a bit of this fungus (carrying it in their mouths) to start the fungus gardens in the new colony.

Zoophagous Insects

Zoophagous (or carnivorous) insects are those that feed on other animals. These other animals may be of various types, but the majority of the zoophagous insects feed on other insects, and hence might be termed entomophagous. Entomophagous insects play an important role in keeping down the populations of pest species.

Entomophagous insects are of two general sorts, predators and parasites. The distinction between these two is sometimes not very sharp, but in general, predators feed on smaller or weaker insects, usually using one or more for a single meal. They live apart from their prey and often seek insects in different places for different meals. Predators are usually active, powerful insects. Parasites live in or on the bodies of their hosts and live continually with their hosts during at least a part of their life cycle. They obtain successive meals from these hosts, and their feeding is at the expense of the hosts. Parasites are smaller than their hosts, and often more than one parasite may live in or on the same host individual.

A great many insects are predaceous on other insects. Dragonflies and damselflies are predaceous during both nymphal and adult stages. The nymphs feed on a variety of aquatic insects and other small aquatic animals, and the adults feed on mosquitoes, small moths, and other insects. The most important predators among the beetles are the ground and tiger beetles (which feed, as both adults and larvae, on a variety of insects) and the ladybird beetles (which are important predators of aphids). Most of the Neuróptera are predaceous. Lacewings (Chrysòpidae) are important predators of aphids. A number of groups of bugs (Hemíptera) are predaceous. For example, some of the stink bugs feed on caterpillars, and many of the aquatic bugs feed on mosquito larvae and other aquatic animals. The important predators among the flies (Díptera) are the robber flies, long-legged flies, dance flies, and syrphid flies (the latter only in the larval stage).

Different predators employ different strategies to obtain their prey. The majority forage for it, but some employ various "tricks" to catch or subdue their prey. Many insects, such as ambush bugs and mantids, lie in wait for their prey, and attack it when it comes within reach. Some insects construct snares of one sort or another, and feed on the animals caught in these snares. Spiders (though not insects) are perhaps the best-known makers of snares or webs, but some insects (e.g., caddisflies) also construct webs or nets. The larvae of some antlions (Myrmeleóntidae) and flies (Vermileónidae) construct pits, and feed on the insects caught in them. Wasps use their sting to immobilize prey, and some Neuróptera larvae (e.g., beaded lacewings and antlions) use a chemical to subdue their prey. In the case of the beaded lacewings this chemical (an allomone) is ejected from the anus. In the case of the antlions the chemical is injected by the bite (with mandibulate mouthparts) of the antlion larva. Most predaceous insects with sucking mouthparts (e.g., various bugs and flies) immobilize their prey by injecting saliva into it when they bite. A few predaceous insects (e.g., *Photùrus vérsicolor*, see below under Bioluminescence) attract prey by mimicking the sex-attracting light signals of another firefly species, then attack and feed on the animals attracted.

Insects parasitizing other insects often operate a little differently from those parasitizing larger animals such as vertebrates, and some authorities use the term "parasitoid" for these insects. A parasite of a larger animal usually does not kill its host or consume a large part of its tissues, but an entomophagous insect parasite (a parasitoid) consumes most or all of its host's tissues and eventually kills it.

A typical entomophagous insect parasite seeks out a host and lays one or more eggs in (or on) it, then goes on to repeat the process with more host individuals—showing no further concern for the host, or its own offspring, once it has oviposited. This oviposition usually has little or no effect on the host, which goes on about its normal activities and shows no sign of being parasitized until the parasite has done considerable damage to it. In some of the hymenopterous parasites, especially the stinging ones (for example, scolioid wasps and pompilids), oviposition in a host is accompanied by the injection of a toxin into the host that paralyzes it. In some cases (for example, in some of the Pompílidae) the female pays no further attention to its host or to its own offspring and goes on to attack other hosts, but in other cases it may take the paralyzed host to a sheltered place—or in still other cases may construct a nest or burrow for it. The latter procedure occurs with most of the solitary wasps (pompilids, vespoids, and sphecoids). The insect or other arthropod caught and stung by the female normally is not eaten by this female, but by its young. In some of the digger wasps (for example, some sphecids), the nest burrow is constructed and eggs are laid in it. *Then* the female goes out and captures insects (or spiders), stings and paralyzes them, and puts them into the nest. When the young wasps hatch, food is there awaiting them. In some sphecids (for example, bembicines), new food animals are brought to the nest as the young are growing. In the social vespids, the food animals caught by the female are eaten by this female and later regurgitated and fed to the young. Whether some of these wasps should be termed parasites, parasitoids, or predators is perhaps a matter of opinion. The victims, whether called hosts or prey, are eventually killed and eaten by the wasp young.

Most entomophagous insect parasites are parasitic only during the larval stage. The adult stage is usually active and free-living and generally locates the host and lays its eggs in, on, or near it. When the parasite eggs are laid entirely apart from the host, the host may be located and attacked by an active larval stage of the parasite; the larva may "hitch a ride" to the host on another animal (entomologists call this behavior *phoresy*); or the eggs may be eaten by the host. Parasitic insects may feed internally or externally on their host, depending on the species. They may pupate in the host, on the outside of it, or entirely apart from it.

Some entomophagous insects are hyperparasites; that is, they parasitize another parasite. In such cases the parasite of a nonparasitic species is termed a primary parasite, and the hyperparasite a secondary parasite. There are occasionally tertiary parasites, which attack another hyperparasite.

Most of the entomophagous insect parasites belong to the orders Díptera and Hymenóptera. Among the Díptera the most important parasites are the tachinid flies. Other families containing entomophagous parasites are the Sarcophágidae, Pyrgòtidae, Pipuncùlidae, Acrocéridae, and Bombylìidae. The principal parasitic Hymenóptera are the Ichneumonòidea, Chalcidòidea, Proctotrupòidea, and Scolìòidea. These groups contain hundreds of species that parasitize other insects. Only a few insects in other orders are entomophagous parasites, for example, the Strepsíptera, and the Melòidae and Rhipiphòridae among the beetles.

The term parasite is sometimes applied to insects that live in the nests of other species. The exact relationship between some of these and the members of the host species are not well understood, but many are treated as guests or inquilines, and some—which feed on the food stored by the host individuals for their own young—are called cleptoparasites.

Many insects live as parasites in or on the bodies of vertebrates, and some of these are serious pests of man or domestic animals. Most of them are external parasites, chiefly the lice and fleas. Some fly larvae (for example, bot fly larvae) are internal parasites of vertebrates, producing a condition called myiasis. Some insects and mites live as external parasites of other insects, at least during part of their life cycle, and do relatively little damage to their host. For example, some of the Ceratopogónidae live on the wings of dragonflies, many mites are ectoparasites of beetles, and water mites are ectoparasites of other insects during a part of their life cycle.

Saprophagous Insects

Saprophagous insects are those feeding on dead or decaying plant or animal materials, such as carrion, dung, leaf litter, dead logs, and the like. These materials often support large insect populations. Not all insects present in decaying material feed on it. Some, such as the flies that feed on decaying fruits, may feed principally on the microorganisms present rather than on the decaying fruits; and others, such as some of the rove beetles found around carrion, may feed on other insects there rather than on the carrion.

Saprophagous insects are found in many orders, but probably the most important are in the orders Blattària (cockroaches). Isóptera (termites), Coleóptera (many families), and Díptera (many families, chiefly muscoids). The most common carrion feeders are carrion beetles (Sílphidae), skin beetles (Derméstidae and Trogìnae), and the larvae of various flies (especially blow flies). The most common dung feeders are certain dung beetles (Scarabaèidae, Histéridae, and others) and the larvae of various flies (chiefly muscoids).

Food Webs and Trophic Levels

Organisms and their habitat interact to produce a system (the ecosystem, or community) in which exchanges of materials occur between parts of the system. The basic features of such a system are (1) the reception of energy, (2) the production of organic substances by producer organisms, (3) the consumption of materials by consumer organisms, and (4) the decomposition of organic compounds and their transformation into materials suitable for use by the producers. The ultimate source of energy for all organisms on this planet is the sun, whose energy reaches the earth in the form of light. The producer organisms are green plants that, through the process of photosynthesis, convert inorganic substances into organic substances. The consumers are of two basic types: herbivores, which feed on green plants, and carnivores, which feed on herbivores and other carnivores. The carnivores may be of two or more levels, as suggested by the jingle,

Great fleas have little fleas upon their backs to bite 'em,
And little fleas have lesser fleas, and so *ad infinitum.*

The decomposition of dead organisms and waste products is accomplished largely by microorganisms, principally bacteria.

Thus in any ecosystem there are *food webs:* one organism is eaten by another, which is in turn eaten by still another, and so on. In a farm pond, for example, the producers are the plants, chiefly algae. These may be eaten by small invertebrates (insects, crustaceans, and so on), which may in turn be eaten by such fish as bluegills, which may be eaten by bass, which may be eaten by people.

These steps in the food web involve energy transformations, and no energy transformations are 100% efficient; some energy is lost at each step. For example, some of the potential energy of the organic compounds produced by green plants through photosynthesis is radiated back into space as heat and does not get to the next link. Accordingly, in any ecosystem there are so-called *ecological pyramids*—of numbers, or organism size, and of biomass. The largest numbers of individuals and the greatest biomass are at the bottom trophic level—the producers (usually green plants). As one goes up through the trophic levels the numbers and biomass decrease. In carnivores the organism size tends to increase, while in parasites the size tends to decrease (and the numbers of individuals tend to increase). This is a very important feature of an ecosystem if we are concerned with its productivity, for example, how much organic material (such as food) can be produced in a given area. The closer we are to the base of the web (the green plants), the more material will be available. Quantitative figures on this point vary with the situation and organisms concerned, but it has been stated that it takes about 40 pounds of grass to produce 1 pound of beef. The essential point here is that a given area can produce a lot more material for herbivores than for carnivores.

Man's concern with ecosystems is largely with how they affect his welfare, as by providing food or other materials. For example, if his concern is a farm crop, he is only one of the potential users (consumers) of this crop, and if he wants to have as much of it as possible for himself, he must reduce the consumption of it by other consumers (such as insects). For maximum production of the crop, he must be concerned with all the factors affecting its growth. He has little control over many physical factors (such as climate), but he can increase the supply of some essential materials (by fertilizing) and reduce the amount removed by other consumers.

Defensive Strategies of Insects

Every species of animals is subject to attack by various enemies; and to survive, it must have some means of defense. Many types of defense are found among insects; some rely on their appearance or location to avoid attack, some attempt to escape, some attack the predator, and some rely on what amounts to chemical warfare.

Passive Means of Defense

Most insects will attempt to escape when attacked or threatened—by flying, running, jumping, swimming, or diving—and many are extremely quick. An insect collector, like a fisherman, may often speak of the "one that got away" because he didn't swing the net quite fast enough or because the insect could fly faster than the collector could run.

Many insects "play dead" when disturbed. Some beetles fold up their legs, fall to the ground, and remain motionless, often resembling a bit of dirt. Many caterpillars "freeze," often in a peculiar position. Some of the inchworms hold the body out like a twig, holding on by means of prolegs at the posterior end of the body. Some hawk moth larvae elevate the front part of the body and assume a sphinxlike position (it is because of this behavior that these moths are sometimes called sphinx moths). And larvae of the handmaid moths elevate both ends of the body, holding on with the prolegs in the middle of the body.

The Use of Shelters

A great many insects live in situations where enemies have difficulty attacking them. Many burrow into plant or animal tissues, under rocks, or into the soil, and others construct and live in cases or shelters. Such devices are often less effective against parasites than against predators. Many parasites (especially some of the Hymenóptera) have long ovipositors with which they can reach hosts in seemingly protected situations, and sometimes these parasites are able to thrust their ovipositors through material as hard as wood to reach a host.

Many insect larvae construct cases of one sort or another, which they carry about with them and in which they eventually pupate. The best known of these are the caddisflies, certain moth larvae, and a few beetle larvae. Caddisfly larvae construct their cases of bits of leaves, twigs, sand grains, pebbles, or other materials (Figure 33–7), which are fastened together with silk or cemented together. Each species builds a characteristic sort of case, and when a case is outgrown, another is built (in some instances the cases of young larvae are different from those made by older larvae). A common case-making caterpillar is the bagworm, whose cases are made of bits of leaves and twigs tied together with silk (Figure 34–37). The larvae of the case-making leaf beetles construct a case composed largely of the insects' excrement.

Many lepidopterous larvae, and a few insects in other orders (for example, leaf-rolling grasshoppers and sawflies), live in a shelter made of leaves tied together with silk. In some cases a single leaf is folded or rolled up to serve as a shelter, and in some cases two or more leaves are involved. Some of the gregarious caterpillars, such as the webworms, make a large shelter involving many leaves or even entire branches.

The adults of most wasps and bees construct nurseries for their young in protected nests of various sorts—in the soil, in stems, or in natural cavities. Most social insects (termites, ants, wasps, and bees) construct fairly elaborate nests, usually in the soil. The larvae of many insects with complete metamorphosis, after completing their feeding and growth, construct a cocoon or other type of case in which they pupate.

Camouflage

Many insects are colored so that they blend perfectly with their background. Many grasshoppers are colored like the ground on which they alight; many moths are colored like the bark of a tree; and many beetles, bugs, flies, and bees are colored like the flowers they visit. Many insects resemble objects in their environment, in both color and shape. Walking-sticks and inchworms resemble twigs, so much so that it sometimes takes a keen eye to detect them when they remain motionless. Certain treehoppers

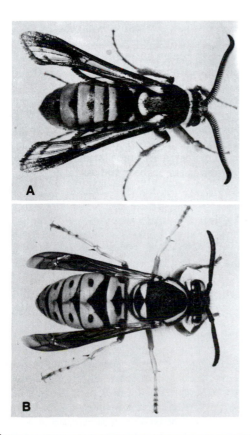

Figure 4-1. Mimicry of a yellowjacket (**B**) by a clearwing moth (*Parathène* sp.) (**A**). (Courtesy of the Ohio Agricultural Research and Development Center.)

resemble thorns. Some of the butterflies resemble dead leaves; some beetles resemble bits of bark; and some caterpillars resemble bird droppings.

Some insects are rendered inconspicuous by covering themselves with debris or excrement. The larvae of tortoise beetles (Figure 28–88A) attach bits of debris and excrement to a pair of spines at the posterior end of the body and hold this material over their body like a parasol. Many dragonfly nymphs become covered with silt and debris as they rest on the bottom of a pond. The masked hunter (an assassin bug) becomes covered with lint and looks like nothing more than a mass of fuzz. The larvae of some lacewings cover themselves with debris, which affords them concealment.

One of the most remarkable types of mimicry found in insects is Batesian mimicry, where an insect without a special means of defense resembles another that has a sting or some other effective defense mechanism. This resemblance may be in behavior as well as in size, shape, and color. Some of the robber flies, hawk moths, and syrphid flies mimic bumble bees, and many syrphid flies, thick-headed flies, clear-winged moths, and beetles mimic wasps. This mimicry is often very striking, and only a trained observer will notice that these insects are not wasps and will neither bite nor sting. Some butterflies have distasteful body fluids and are seldom attacked by predators. Other species, without such body fluids, may mimic them very closely. The mimicry of the monarch by the viceroy (Figure 4–2) is an example of Batesian mimicry.

A somewhat similar type of mimicry occurs in some Lepidóptera, where the larvae strongly resemble certain vertebrates and sometimes even *act* a little like the vertebrates they resemble. Some swallowtail larvae have the anterior end enlarged and marked with eyespots, and strongly resemble small snakes. If such a larva is touched, the scent gland (Figure 34–3, *osm*) is everted, giving a striking resemblance to a forked tongue of a snake. The combination of the eversion of what looks like a snake's tongue and the giving off of an unpleasant odor is likely to deter many potential predators.

Chemical Defenses

Chemical defenses may involve body fluids that are distasteful to predators, the use of repellent secretions, or the injection of poisons into an attacker. Most insects using such defenses are brightly or strikingly colored, advertising the fact that they are dangerous. One experience with such an insect, by another animal or a person, is usually sufficient to cause that type of insect to be avoided in the fu-

Figure 4–2.   An example of mimicry in butterflies. **A,** the viceroy, *Basilárchia archíppus* (Cramer); **B,** the monarch, *Dánaus plexíppus* (L.). (Courtesy of the Ohio Agricultural Research and Development Center.)

ture—and its bright coloration makes it easily recognized.

A few insects, such as the monarch butterfly and ladybird beetles, are seldom attacked by predators because they have distasteful body fluids. Some insects give off foul-smelling substances when disturbed. Stink bugs, broad-headed bugs, green lacewings, swallowtail larvae, and others might be called the skunks of the insect world, because some of them have a very unpleasant odor. A few of the insects utilizing such defensive mechanisms are able to eject the substance as a spray, in some cases even aiming it at an intruder. Bombardier beetles give off from the anus a liquid that quickly volatilizes and looks like a puff of smoke. Some ants eject a very irritating liquid (mostly formic acid) from the anus. And some earwigs can squirt a foul-smelling liquid from glands on the dorsal side of the abdomen. Most of these substances appear to act as repellents, though some may be mildly toxic.

The larvae of the monarch butterfly obtain certain substances from the milkweed plants on which they feed, and these substances become especially concentrated in the wings of the adults. Birds that feed on these butterflies do not die, but vomit vio-

lently, and soon learn to avoid monarchs (and any other butterfly that resembles them). The larvae of some pine sawflies (Dipriónidae), when disturbed, discharge from the mouth an oily material that is an effective deterrent to predators. This material is similar chemically to a resin of the host plant (pine), and during feeding it is stored in pouches in the insect's foregut. These represent cases of plant-feeding insects utilizing protective chemicals of the host plants.

While some insects have developed foul-smelling secretions that may repel their enemies, others have developed more potent means of chemical defense— the use of poisons that kill or injure the attacker. These may have an irritative effect on the skin of the attacker (for example, the exudations of some blister beetles), or they may be injected into the attacker by means of special poison hairs, by the bite of the insect, or by a sting. The effect of these poisons on a human depends primarily on that person's sensitivity to the poison and on the insects involved. Some people are more sensitive than others to these poisons, and some insects are much more toxic than others.

A few species of caterpillars have stinging hairs or spines that may cause severe skin irritation. The most common are the larvae of the io moth (Figure 34–74D), the saddleback caterpillar (Figure 34–51B), and the puss caterpillar. The io larva is a spiny greenish caterpillar, about 50 mm long when full grown, with a narrow lateral reddish stripe that is edged below with white. The saddleback caterpillar (Figure 34–51B) is smaller and is greenish with a brown saddlelike mark on the back. The puss caterpillar, *Megalopÿge operculàris* (J. E. Smith) (family Megalopÿgidae), is densely covered with soft brown hair, but beneath the hair are numerous poison spines that can cause severe skin irritation.

Many insects will bite when handled, and some will bite if given the opportunity, whether handled or not. The bite may simply be a severe pinch by means of powerful jaws, as in certain ants and beetles, or it may be a piercing by needlelike mouthparts. Bites by mandibulate insects do not ordinarily involve any injection of poison, but the bites of sucking insects are very much like hypodermic injections, and the irritation they cause is due to the saliva injected by the insect. The bites of some sucking insects (for example, mosquitoes and bed bugs) are not particularly painful but may cause considerable subsequent irritation. The bites of some others (for example, some of the assassin bugs and creeping water bugs) are quite painful. Centipedes, spiders, and ticks are other arthropods that inject venom when they bite.

Of all the chemical defenses used by insects, the use of a sting is probably the most effective: the effect is immediate and often severe. The only stinging insects are certain Hymenóptera (bees, wasps, and some ants), and since the sting is a modified egg-laying organ, only females sting. Some people are particularly sensitive to insect stings, and for such people a sting can be fatal. Indeed, more people are killed each year in the United States by insect bites and stings than by poisonous snakes.

Insect Migrations

The term "migration" usually brings to mind the spring and fall flights of birds, where most or all of the individuals of a species fly a considerable distance from nesting grounds to wintering grounds, or vice versa. Somewhat similar mass movements occur in some species of insects, but with insects the movements are nearly always only one-way; that is, the migrating individuals either do not make a return flight or make only a short one, and the return flight is made largely or entirely by a subsequent generation.

One of the best know of the migratory insects is the monarch butterfly, *Dánaus plexíppus* (L.), which occurs throughout most of the United States and southern Canada and in some other parts of the world as well. The movements of this species have been studied by tagging. The tag is a small piece of paper fastened to the front edge of the front wing, and each tag bears an identifying number and some information on whom to notify if the tag is recovered. Thousands of monarchs have been tagged, most of them by Dr. F. A. Urquhart, of the Royal Ontario Museum of Zoology and Paleontology, and his associates, and enough of them have been subsequently recovered to give an idea of their movements.

Monarchs in the North may have two or more generations there. As fall approaches, a combination of factors (probably decreasing day length and decreasing temperature) produces (through hormones) a generation that behaves differently from the preceding generations: gonadal development is suppressed, and these individuals fly south. The farther south they go, the more numerous they become, and in some parts of the country enormous aggregations of monarchs may be seen. In the far West, the monarchs overwinter in coastal areas from San Francisco to Los Angeles. One of the most famous overwintering colonies in California is at Pacific Grove. In the East the monarchs fly south and west. Some winter colonies exist in Florida, but most of these butterflies

continue to Mexico. The longest flight known for a tagged individual is 1870 miles (2896 km), from Ontario to San Luis Potosí, Mexico—from September 18, 1957, to January 25, 1958. A few years ago a wintering colony was discovered in northern Michoacán that covered nearly 4 acres and was estimated to contain 13.8 million butterflies. It is probable that many such overwintering colonies exist in Mexico.

As spring approaches, the gonads of the overwintering individuals mature, and these individuals move north. Most (if not all) of the individuals reaching the northern part of the breeding range are not the same ones that left there at the end of the previous summer. Even so, it is estimated that many monarchs may fly 1500 miles or more south in late summer and up to 1000 miles north the following spring—a very considerable flight for an animal that weighs little more than half a gram.

Another butterfly that undergoes rather spectacular migratory flights in some parts of the world is the painted lady, *Cýnthia cárdui* (L.), which is almost worldwide in distribution. In North America these butterflies apparently overwinter south of the Mexican border and, in the spring, fly northward over a broad front. They breed in the United States and Canada, the larvae feeding on thistles. There does not appear to be a mass migration south in late summer in North America, but such movements have been observed in the Old World.

A number of insects have a permanent breeding area in the southern part of the United States and undergo mass movements northward in the spring and early summer. The insects making these flights breed in the North but do not overwinter there and, in most cases, die out at the onset of cold weather. Such movements are known to occur in some of the noctuid moths and leafhoppers, for example, the black witch, *Érebus òdora* (L.); the cotton leafworm, *Alabáma argillàcea* (Hübner); the potato leafhopper, *Empoásca fàbae* (Harris); and the beet leafhopper, *Circùlifer tenéllus* (Baker). In the case of the beet leafhopper, when the food supply in the North becomes unfavorable in late summer, a mass movement south may occur (but not involving the same individuals that migrated north in the spring).

Mass migrations of short-horned grasshoppers have been known since biblical times, the migrating hordes often containing millions and millions of individuals and eating everything in sight during the stopovers in their flight. Uvarov (1977) lists some of the better documented estimates of swarm sizes. Swarms have covered up to 1000 km², and estimates of total numbers reach 50 billion insects and up to 260 grasshoppers per square meter. Such flights still occur in Africa and the Middle East, but are seldom seen in the United States anymore.

Acoustic Behavior

Some of the most interesting behavior in insects occurs in relation to sound. A great many insects (probably as many as all other animals combined) produce sound by means of special structures, but only a few, such as the crickets, grasshoppers, and cicadas, are heard by most people. The sounds produced by many insects are very soft or very high-pitched and are seldom, if ever, heard by humans. Sound in many insects plays an important role in behavior.

A serious problem encountered by early students of insect sounds was accurate description based on aural observations. The human ear is not a very good sound-analyzing instrument. Many features of insect sounds, including some of those most important to the insects themselves, cannot be detected by the human ear, and a given insect often sounds different to different people because of differences in their hearing ability. The advent of such electronic aids as the tape recorder and some sound-analyzing instruments has opened up the field of bioacoustics. With the tape recorder we can "capture" a sound for further study and can play it back to the insect (and observe the insect's reaction to it). Sound-analyzing instruments make it possible to determine characteristics of frequency (pitch) and rhythm with considerable accuracy. Instruments such as the sound spectrograph give a graph of the sound (for example, Figures 4–3, 14–3, 14–12, 25–10, 28–2), making possible an objective description. The minute details shown by these graphs enable us to detect features not apparent to the ear.

Sound-Producing Mechanisms

Insects produce sound in several ways: (1) by stridulation, (2) by the vibration of special membranes called tymbals, (3) by striking some part of the body against the substrate, (4) by forcibly ejecting air or liquid from some body opening, (5) by the vibration of their wings or other body parts, and (6) by such general activities as moving about or feeding. The sounds produced by the last two methods are similar in that they are incidental sounds produced by general activity. All these sounds, at least in some insects, may have communicative significance.

Stridulation involves the rubbing of one body part against another. One part is generally sharp-edged,

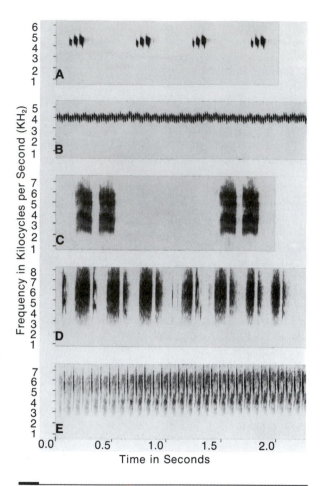

Figure 4–3.   Audiospectographs of some insect sounds. **A,** four chirps of the calling song of a field cricket, *Grýllus* sp.; **B,** a portion of the callingsong of the tree cricket, *Oecánthus nigricòrnis* Walker; **C,** two 2-pulse songs of the northern true katydid, *Pterophýlla camellifòlia* (Fabricius); **D,** stridulation sounds produced by the sawyer beetle, *Monochàmus notátus* (Drury) (the insect illustrated in Figure 28–79); **E,** a part of the calling song of the cicada *Tibìcen chloromèra* (Walker). Frequency is shown here in kilohertz (or kilocycles per second); 4 kHz is approximately the pitch of the top note of a piano.

and the other is more or less filelike. Stridulatory structures are developed in a great many insect orders and involve almost all parts of the body. Some of the best-known singers (males of the crickets and long-horned grasshoppers) stridulate with the two front wings (see page 208). Some of the short-horned grasshoppers rub the hind femora (which bear a row of peglike processes) over the front wings (see page 209 and Figure 14–4H). Some long-horned beetles

(*Priònus*) stridulate by rubbing the hind legs along the edges of the elytra. Other beetles stridulate by rubbing hardened tubercles on the dorsal side of the abdomen against the hind wings (Passálidae) or against filelike ridges on the underside of the elytra (some Curculiónidae). Many long-horned beetles stridulate by rubbing the rear edge of one thoracic segment (usually the pronotum) against the front edge of the segment behind it. In some Hymenóptera (ants, mutillid wasps) the edges of adjacent abdominal segments are rubbed together. Some aquatic bugs stridulate by rubbing the legs against the head. Stridulatory structures have been reported on various other body parts.

Sound production by the vibration of tymbals is best known in the cicadas (see page 322), but some of the leafhoppers also produce sound in this way. The tymbals are membranelike structures, usually located ventrally on the basal abdominal segment, that are moved by muscles—somewhat like moving the end of a tin can in and out. A few insects tap or drum on the substrate with their head (deathwatch beetles), their feet (some grasshoppers), or the tip of the abdomen (some stoneflies and cockroaches).

Sound production by the expulsion of air or liquid from some body opening is relatively rare in insects, though the expulsion of air to produce vocal sounds is the common method of sound production in mammals, birds, and some other vertebrates. The bombardier beetles produce a popping sound when they expel a glandular fluid from the anus (see page 409). The death's-head sphinx moth, *Acheróntia átropos* (L.), expels air forcibly from the pharynx to produce a whistling sound. And certain cockroaches (for example, *Gromphadorìna*) produce a hissing sound by expelling air from certain spiracles. These sounds are usually produced in response to disturbance.

The wing movements of most insects produce a humming or buzzing sound, but in some cases the thorax is also involved in this sound. A bumble bee held by the wings will still buzz (by vibrations of the thorax). Some insects, when they run about on certain types of surfaces, may produce an audible sound. Most feeding by insects produces such weak sounds that they are scarcely or not at all audible, but in some cases feeding sounds are easily audible. A large wood-boring beetle found feeding inside a log may sometimes produce a sound audible several feet away. These sounds produced by wing movements, running about, or feeding may play a role in communication—at least from the insect to humans—in indicating the insects' presence. The wing noise of certain flies is known to play a role in attracting a mate.

The Character of Insect Sounds

Most insect sounds are noiselike; that is, they contain many nonharmonically related frequencies and cannot be assigned a definite pitch. Relatively few are musical or capable of being assigned a definite pitch. The principal musical sounds are those produced by wing vibration (in which case the fundamental of the sound represents the wing-stroke rate) and those produced by cricket stridulation. The musical character of cricket sounds is the result of the membranous structure of the wings; the pitch appears to be determined by the tooth-strike rate. The pitch of most insect sounds (stridulating sounds, sounds produced by vibrating tymbals) is usually constant throughout the sound; in only a few cases are there pitch changes through the sound. Judging by the sensitivity of the auditory organs in these insects, it is unlikely that the insects detect any pitch changes that may occur.

The principal differences in the sounds produced by related species are in their rhythm. In the tree cricket genus *Oecánthus*, for example, the pulses of the sound (a "pulse" is the sound produced by one stroke of the scraper across the file) may be produced for relatively long periods (continuous trills), with the songs of different species differing in the pulse rate, or they may be produced in groups (bursts or chirps) (Figure 14-3D–F). The songs of different species having the pulses grouped may differ in the pulse rate in the groups or in the group length and rate. The insects themselves are very sensitive to these differences in rhythm. The discrimination occurs in the central nervous system.

Sound Production Behavior

Many insects, such as the crickets, grasshoppers, and cicadas, produce sounds more or less continuously through certain periods. Some insects "sing" only during the day (cicadas); some sing only at night (most long-horned grasshoppers and some tree crickets); and some sing both day and night (field crickets). These periods of song are probably determined largely by light intensity, temperature, and possibly other factors. In many species of singing insects, neighboring individuals synchronize their songs. When the first individual begins to sing, others nearby chime in very quickly, synchronizing their pulses or chirps. This synchronization occurs in spite of other species singing in the same area, indicating that the individuals involved must be able to recognize the song of their own species very quickly. The singing of crickets, grasshoppers, and cicadas is done almost entirely by the males.

The rhythmic features of insect songs are affected by temperature. Pulse rates, chirp rates, and the like rise or fall with temperature. The rate in one species may rise with temperature to a rate occurring in another species at a lower temperature, but it is still recognized by a female of this species if she is at the same temperature as the male. If she is at a different temperature, she may not respond to the male's song.

The Role of Sound in Behavior

Many insects respond to sound by flight or evasive behavior. Some moths have auditory organs capable of detecting the ultrasonic sounds emitted by bats. When they hear these sounds they go into a tumbling or erratic flight and head for the ground. Many insects produce what might be called a "disturbance" sound when disturbed, captured, or handled. These sounds are believed to have some survival value in possibly discouraging a predator. Song in the field cricket plays a role in the maintenance of territory. A male will remain on his territory and sing for long periods, thereby advertising the fact that it is *his* territory. When another male enters this territory, the song of the resident male changes to what might be termed an aggressive song (Figure 14–3A,B), which usually serves to drive off the intruding male. (If it doesn't, there may be a fight.)

The principal role played by sound in many insects is to bring the sexes together. The common song of the male attracts the female. In a few cases the singing of the male may cause the female to produce a sound that enables the male to locate her. In some species (for example, crickets) the male sings a somewhat different song (often called a "courtship" song) in the presence of a female (Figure 14–3C). Male mosquitoes are attracted to the female by the wing sounds she produces, and wing sounds act similarly in some other Díptera. While sound plays an important role in bringing together the sexes of many species, once they are in close proximity, then other stimuli (different sounds, odors, visual stimuli, and the like) may be involved in bringing about copulatory activity.

Because the songs of different species of singing insects are different, and because the females respond only to the songs of their own species, song plays a role in species isolation and evolution. It often provides good taxonomic characters, which in some cases (for example, in the cricket genus *Grýllus*) are more diagnostic than morphological characters.

Bioluminescence

Bioluminescence, the production of light, occurs in many different types of organisms: fungi, protists, various worms, mollusks, tunicates, fish, and some arthropods, including a few crustaceans, centipedes, and hexapods (in the orders Collémbola, Díptera, and Coleóptera). The early interest in bioluminescence was in how the light was produced. Current studies are also concerned with the function of the light. The light emitted by luminescent animals appears to serve one or more of three principal functions: illumination, attracting potential prey (and sometimes also predators), and mating behavior. In insects, bioluminescence has been most studied in the beetle family Lampýridae (fireflies).

Little is known about the luminescence of Collémbola, but apparently a few of the Podùridae are able to emit light. In some the glow is continuous, but others emit light only when stimulated (from the entire body surface, for a period of 5 to 10 seconds).

The only Díptera known to be luminescent are the larvae of certain fungus gnats (Mycetophílidae) in the genera *Keroplàtus*, *Orfèlia*, and *Arachnocámpa*. These larvae occur only in deeply shaded areas or caves, where they spin silken webs. Their luminescence attracts small insects, which are trapped in the webs and eaten by the mycetophilid larvae. The light produced by *Orfèlia fúltoni* (Fisher) (Figure 32–28) is continuous and light blueish. It is produced by organs in the anterior four or five segments and at the posterior end of the body, with the luminous bodies located along main tracheal trunks. The New Zealand species *Arachnocámpa luminòsa* (Skuse) spins webs on the ceilings of caves. The luminous organs are the enlarged tips of the Malpighian tubules, at the posterior end of the body. The light in this species can be turned on and off.

The best-known luminous insects are beetles in the families Elatéridae, Phengòdidae, and Lampýridae. In *Pyróphorus* (Elatéridae), which occurs in Florida and Texas and throughout tropical America, the luminescent organs are two spots on the hind corners of the pronotum (which emit a greenish light) and areas on the first abdominal segment (which emit an orange light). The light appears slowly, persists for a few seconds, and then fades out. The larvae of the Phengòdidae, often called glowworms, have pairs of luminous spots on several body segments, and when these are glowing the insect looks like a railroad car at night.

The Lampýridae (lightningbugs or fireflies) are the best known of the luminous insects. Many species have well-developed light-producing organs. These organs are located just under the body wall (which is transparent) on the ventral side of the terminal abdominal segments. They consist of a layer of light-producing cells or photocytes, backed by another cell layer that acts as a reflector. These organs have a rich tracheal supply and are supplied with nerves that generally follow the tracheae. The nerve endings are in the tracheolar cells. The light is produced by the oxidation of a substance called luciferin, catalyzed by the enzyme luciferinase, in the presence of ATP (adenosine triphosphate) and magnesium ions. The luciferinase presumably exists in an inhibited form. A nerve impulse reaching the organ releases acetylcholine, which in turn leads to the synthesis of pyrophosphate. This reacts with the inhibited luciferinase to give free luciferinase and ATP, and the free luciferinase reacts with the luciferin in the presence of oxygen to produce light (and some by-products). Practically 100% of the energy released in this reaction is light.

The light signals emitted by the Lampýridae serve primarily as a means of bringing the sexes together. Each species with luminescent organs has a characteristic flash code, which involves the length and rate of the flashes, and a specific period of delay before a flash is answered. When a male is seeking a mate he usually flies over an area and flashes. Stationary females located in the vegetation respond by flashing at a specific interval after the male flashes, and a male receiving a response will fly to the female. Light is the only cue involved in the recognition; neither sex recognizes the other without the appropriate flashing. These insects can be attracted to artificial lights if the lights are flashed at the proper rhythm.

In *Photìnus pýralis* (L.) the males fly about a meter above the ground, and each flash (of about 0.5-second duration) is emitted during an upward swoop. The flashes are repeated about every 7 seconds. Stationary females answer each flash with a 0.5-second flash of their own, about 3 seconds after the male flash.

The flash pattern of some fireflies may vary with the circumstances. In *Photìnus macdérmotti* Lloyd, for example, a searching male flashes at regular intervals. When a female responds and he approaches her through the vegetation, he shifts to a series of paired flashes (each pair being followed by a flash from the female). In some fireflies in the genus *Photùris*, the flash rate increases to a glow as the insect approaches the ground (at night) and ceases after the insect has landed. This sequence is followed mainly by the females, and its sole function appears to be illumination. The flash pattern in this landing is different from that used in mating and elicits no visible response from males nearby.

In the case of some fireflies in the genus *Pteróptyx*, which occur in southeast Asia, large numbers of males gather in trees and flash in unison (about twice per second), producing a signal that attracts individuals of both sexes from considerable distances. This phenomenon is comparable to that of some orthopterans (certain tree crickets and katydids) that synchronize their songs, thereby producing a more intense signal that is effective over greater distances.

In the case of *Photùris vérsicolor* (Fabricius), the female prior to mating answers the triple flash of the male with a characteristic flash, the two sexes eventually get together, and mating ensues. After mating the female becomes predatory and mimics the flash responses of the females of other species, attracting males of these other species, then pouncing on them and eating them (Lloyd 1965 called these *femmes fatales*!).

Pheromones

Pheromones are substances that serve as chemical signals between members of the same species. They are secreted to the outside of the body and cause specific reactions by other individuals of the species. Pheromones, which are sometimes called "social hormones," act in a group of individuals somewhat like hormones in an individual animal. Pheromones are the predominant medium of communication among insects (but rarely the sole method). Some species produce only a few pheromones, but others produce many with various functions. Pheromone systems are the most complex in some of the social insects.

Chemical communication differs from that by sight or sound in several ways. Transmission is relatively slow (the chemical signals are usually airborne), but the signal can be persistent (depending upon the volatility of the chemical) and is sometimes effective over a very long range. Localization of the signal is generally poorer than localization of a sound or visual stimulus and is usually effected by the animal moving upwind in response to the stimulus. The ability to modulate a chemical signal is limited, compared with communication by visual or acoustic means, but some pheromones may convey different meanings (and result in different behavioral or physiological responses) depending on their concentration or when presented in combination. This "limitation" is compensated by the elaboration of the number of exocrine glands that produce pheromones. Thus, some species, such as ants, are very articulate creatures, but their medium of communication is difficult to study and appreciate because of our own olfactory insensitivity and the technological difficulties in detecting and analyzing these pheromones.

Pheromones play numerous roles in the activities of insects. They may act as alarm substances, play a role in individual and group recognition, serve as attractants between the sexes, mediate the formation of aggregations, function as foraging trails, and be involved in caste determination. Alarm pheromones in ants are usually produced by mandibular or anal glands. Sex attractants are usually produced by the female and serve to attract the male (the reciprocal relationship is also found). Trail-marking chemicals are usually discharged from glands associated with the sting or anus. Pheromones involved in caste determination include the ''queen substance'' produced by queen honey bees and somewhat similarly acting substances produced by termites and ants. These generally must be ingested to be effective.

Alarm pheromones may serve as a means of defense in some species. Aphids, for example, are particularly vulnerable to predators because of their gregarious habits and sedentary nature. They are preyed upon by many types of insects, particularly ladybird beetles, lacewing larvae, and certain bugs. Some aphids are active enough to avoid approaching predators, but for most aphids the defense involves a secretion from the cornicles, which is produced when the aphid is attacked (Figure 4–4). Nearby aphids respond to the alarm pheromone in this secretion by moving away (Figure 4–5). The cornicle secretion may also have a mechanical protective function: if it gets on the predator's head, it gums the mouthparts and irritates the sense organs, often resulting in the release of the aphid prey. The receptors for this alarm pheromone are on the aphid's antennae (Figure 3–28A).

The chemical composition of many insect pheromones is known. Some are quite specific (that is, isomers are inactive), and some appear to be complex mixtures containing specific proportions of each chemical. Closely related species may use the same chemicals, but in different ratios or isomers. Numerous species in the moth family Tortrícidae have been studied because of their economic importance; 12- and 14-carbon alcohols, acetate esters, and aldehydes seem to predominate (see Roelofs and Brown 1982). Despite the seeming similarity between their pheromones, individual males respond only to the appropriate chemicals of the appropriate isomers in the relative concentrations for the sex attractant of their species.

Probably the most effective use of pheromones in insect control is to observe populations. The expansion of the range of the gypsy moth (*Lymántria díspar*) is monitored by use of sticky traps baited with the sex attractant. Males are extremely sensitive to this pheromone, and the presence of the gypsy moth in an area can be detected by the males captured in the traps. A number of schemes have been proposed that would make use of pheromones to control insects directly. It has been suggested that if an area is

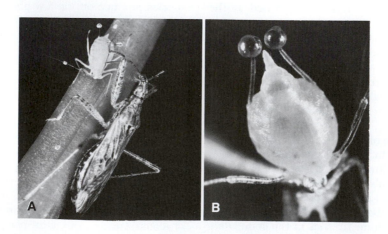

Figure 4–4. **A,** a damsel bug, *Nàbis americóferus* Carayon, attacking the aphid *Acyrthosìphon pìsum* (Harris), and the aphid secreting cornicle droplets in response to the attack; **B,** secreted droplets on the tips of the cornicles of the aphid *Acyrthosiphon sòlani* (Kaltenback). (Courtesy of L. R. Nault, Ohio Agricultural Research and Development Center.)

allomone is a chemical secreted by an individual of species A (the sender) that has an adverse effect on an individual of species B (the receiver). A *kairomone* is a chemical that has an adverse effect on the sender. For example, some ichneumonid wasps find their hosts by cueing in on the chemicals from the mandibular glands (salivary glands) of their lepidopteran hosts; some clerid beetles (predators) are attracted by the aggregation pheromone of bark beetles, thus locating a rich source of food in the larvae and adults burrowing beneath the bark of the tree. In the latter case it is clear that a given chemical signal may have both positive and negative effects on its sender, and the use of such terms as pheromone and kairomone depends on the context in which they are studied.

Gregarious and Social Behavior

Many insects occur in groups, and these groups differ in the factors responsible for bringing the individuals together and in the nature of the interactions between individuals.

Aggregations

Some insect groups are simply the result of a positive reaction by many individuals to the same stimulus, for example, the insects attracted to a light or to a dead animal. Others may result from the simultaneous emergence of many adults, for example, emerging mayflies. The larvae of many Lepidóptera, which hatch from a given egg mass, may remain together during most of their larval life as a result of their reaction to a common food supply or to each other. Other aggregations where some mutual attraction, as well as a common reaction to the same stimulus, is involved in keeping the aggregation together include hibernating aggregations (for example, ladybird beetles), sleeping aggregations (for example, monarch butterflies), and others.

Insect Societies

Ants, termites, and some of the bees and wasps live in more integrated groups called societies, and these groups have some features of special interest. The most complex insect societies are found among species in the orders Isóptera (termites) and Hymenóptera (among the ants, bees, and wasps). These *eusocial* colonies are characterized by (1) cooperation among their members in rearing young, (2) the presence of one or more nonreproductive, often sterile castes, and (3) an overlap of generations. All termites

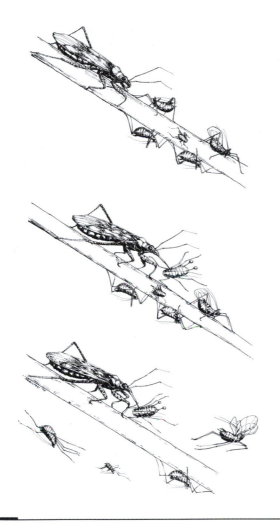

Figure 4–5. Sequence showing a damsel bug approaching a group of aphids (top), an aphid attacked and responding by secreting droplets from its cornicles (center), and nearby aphids responding to the alarm pheromone by moving away (bottom). (Courtesy of L. R. Nault, Ohio Agricultural Research and Development Center.)

"saturated" with a sex-attractant type of pheromone, the males will be less successful at finding females; therefore, fewer fertilized eggs will be laid, and populations will decrease. Attempts have also been made to lure bark beetles to specific trees (which are then destroyed) in order to reduce their populations so that they no longer pose a danger to other trees in the area. None of these direct control measures has yet been proven effective.

Chemicals also mediate a number of interspecific interactions, and a series of terms have been proposed to distinguish between their functions. An

and ants are eusocial (with the exception of some ant species that have evolved into social parasites of other ants). Presocial colonies or aggregations—that is, groups with only one or two of the characteristics of eusociality—are found in the Hymenóptera and a number of other orders, including Blattària, Hemíptera, Homóptera, and Coleóptera (see Michener 1974, Wilson 1971).

A distinctive feature of an insect society is the polymorphism (caste differentiation) of its members, which is accompanied by differences in behavior. There is thus a division of reproduction in the society. Only some individuals are involved in reproduction: the kings and queens of termite colonies, and the queens and males (drones) of hymenopteran societies. The individuals in nonreproductive castes (called workers) may be rather generalized, performing all the functions necessary for maintenance of the colony and rearing of the brood, or in some cases there is further morphological and behavioral specialization to perform the functions of defense (soldiers) or foraging and brood rearing (workers).

Social insects form new colonies in one of two ways: by swarming or by new reproductives (males and females) leaving the parental colony, mating, and starting a new colony. Swarming is the method used by the honey bee and some ants. The old queen, along with a group of workers, leaves and establishes a new colony somewhere else, and a new queen is reared in the group that did not leave. A queen ant, after mating, begins a new nest and raises a brood of workers; thereafter she generally does little except lay eggs, with the workers taking over other activities. In some cases (for example, certain wasps) the queen may do some foraging (in addition to egg laying) after the first group of workers appears.

Thus the queen generally starts the colony, raises the first brood, and thereafter is concerned principally or entirely with producing eggs. The males (or one of them) fertilize the queen. The workers carry on various activities, and the different things done by different workers may be associated with the workers' age or with the particular environmental factors to which they are exposed. In the honey bee, for example, the worker engages in cell cleaning the first 2 days after it emerges; from 3 to 6 days of age it feeds older larvae with honey and pollen; from about 6 to 12 days of age, when its pharyngeal glands are most active, it feeds the younger larvae with a mixture of honey and saliva; from about 12 to 18 days of age, when its wax glands are most active, it works in the hive, building combs and storing nectar, and may make some preliminary flights outside the hive; and thereafter it is concerned mainly with foraging outside the hive, gathering nectar and pollen. The workers in some ant colonies are of different sizes, and the activities of these different-sized workers may differ: the larger ones act as soldiers, fighting and protecting the colony, and are fed by other workers; the intermediate-sized workers do most of the foraging and regurgitate food to other workers; and the smaller workers are concerned chiefly with tending the brood, nest construction, and the like.

The coordination of different body parts in an individual insect is accomplished largely by the nervous and endocrine systems, which serve as a means of communication between different body parts. Social insects communicate, but such communication does not operate to the extent that the nervous system does for the individual. Observations of the nest-building activities of a group of ants, or of the activities of a group during a raid, might lead one to suspect that the coordination of the activities of different individuals is accomplished by "commands from a leader," but this is probably not the case; different individuals are simply responding to particular conditions as the situation changes. The chief means of communication in ants is by means of pheromones. A honey bee worker, upon returning to the hive after finding a nectar source, communicates information about this source to the other workers by means of a characteristic dance (see page 733).

Insect societies often have associated with them various other organisms: other insects, mites, other animals, and sometimes fungi. Some of these may be parasites or predators, attacking various members of the colony. Some may be commensals or scavengers, tolerated by the members of the society and feeding on refuse. Some may be "guests," not only tolerated but actually fed by the host insects. Many social insects cultivate fungi upon which they feed and might be called insect farmers. Many ants "tend" aphids and feed on the honeydew secreted by them (see page 338).

A characteristic activity in insect societies is the interchange of materials (food, secretions, and so on) between individuals (trophallaxis). Workers frequently lick one another, and many workers regurgitate food for another individual. This is apparently one of the important mechanisms by which pheromones are passed from one individual to another, and these interchanges are apparently important in colony coordination. Another feature common to insect societies is the ability to recognize members of one's own group and members of another group. This recognition involves nest odor: the particular characteristics of this odor apparently involve both genetic and environmental factors. An individual (even of the same species) with a different odor entering another nest is generally attacked.

There are some interesting differences between the societies of termites and those of Hymenóptera. Termites have a "child labor" society in that the young, from about the second instar on, must take care of themselves; the nymphs of both sexes are thus the workers and, except for those that become soldiers or reproductives, remain workers for the rest of their lives. In most species they live a shut-in existence in their nests and rarely leave. The hymenopteran society is one built on adult female labor; the relatively helpless young are protected from an adverse outside environment and cared for by the workers.

An insect society, though composed of many individual insects, operates as a unit and is in many ways comparable to a single individual: it grows, it carries on various life processes as a unit, and it reproduces itself. There are mechanisms by which the activities of different individuals (like the cells and tissues of an individual organism) are coordinated, and there are also mechanisms for keeping the individuals together. Unlike the cells or parts of an individual's body, the individuals in an insect society differ genetically and thus do not completely share one another's reproductive interests. This observation underlines a central problem in understanding insect societies: how can such systems evolve? Why do some individuals forgo reproduction and instead spend their lives rearing and protecting the offspring of another? The answers to these questions are yet to be found. The fact that eusociality has evolved once in the Isóptera but several times within the Hymenóptera suggests that the haplodiploid mechanism of sex determination in the latter order may be important. In general, it appears that the members of both eusocial and presocial insect colonies are generally related. Thus the workers are rearing the offspring of a relative and not of a completely unrelated individual.

References

Alcock, J. 1975. Animal Behavior: An Evolutionary Approach. Sunderland, Mass.: Sinauer Associates, 547 pp.; illus.

Alexander, R. D. 1967. Acoustical communication in arthropods. Annu. Rev. Entomol. 12:495–526.

Alexander, R. D. 1974. The evolution of social behavior. Annu. Rev. Ecol. Syst. 5:325–383.

Askew, R. R. 1971. Parasitic Insects. New York: American Elsevier, 316 pp.

Balduf, W. V. 1974. The Bionomics of Entomophagous Insects, Part 2 (a reprint of the 1939 ed.). Los Angeles: Entomological Reprint Specialists, 384 pp.; illus.

Brues, C. T. 1946. Insect Dietary. Cambridge, Mass.: Harvard Univ. Press, 466 pp., illus.

Carlson, A. D., and J. Copeland. 1978. Behavioral plasticity in the flash communication systems of fireflies. Amer. Sci. 66(3):340–356; illus.

Chapman, R. F. 1982 (3rd ed.). The Insects: Structure and Function. Cambridge, Mass.: Harvard Univ. Press, 919 pp.; illus.

Clausen, C. P. 1941. Entomophagous Insects. New York: McGraw-Hill, 688 pp., illus.

Commonwealth Scientific and Industrial Research Organization (CSIRO). 1970. The Insects of Australia. Carlton, Victoria: Melbourne University Press, 1029 pp.; illus.

Daly, H. V., J. T. Doyen, and P. R. Ehrlich. 1978. An Introduction to Insect Biology and Diversity. New York: McGraw-Hill, 564 pp.; illus.

DeLong, D. M. 1971. The bionomics of leafhoppers. Annu. Rev. Entomol. 16:179–210.

Dethier, V. G., and E. Stellar. 1964 (2nd ed.). Animal Behavior. Englewood Cliffs, N.J.: Prentice-Hall, 118 pp.; illus.

Dingle, H. (Ed.). 1978. Evolution of Insect Migration and Diapause. New York: Springer-Verlag, 284 pp., illus.

Eisner, T. E. 1970. Chemical defense against predators in arthropods. In Chemical Ecology, ed. E. Sondheimer and J. B. Simeone, 157–217. New York: Academic Press.

Eisner, T. E., and J. C. Meinwald. 1966. Defensive secretions of arthropods. Science 153:1341–1350.

Frisch, K. von. 1967. The Dance Language and Orientation of Bees. Cambridge, Mass.: Belknap Press, 566 pp.; illus.

Frisch, K. von. 1971 (rev. ed.). Bees, Their Vision, Chemical Senses, and Language. Ithaca, N.Y.: Cornell Univ. Press, 157 pp., illus.

Haskell, P. T. 1974. Sound production. In The Physiology of Insects (2nd ed.), ed. M. Rockstein, vol. 2, 353–410. New York: Academic Press.

Hutchins, R. E. 1966. Insects. Englewood Cliffs, N.J.: Prentice-Hall, 324 pp.; illus.

Johnsgard, P. A. 1967. Animal Behavior. Dubuque, Iowa: Wm. C. Brown, 156 pp., illus.

Lin, N., and C. D. Michener. 1972. Evolution of sociality in insects. Quart. Rev. Biol. 47:131–159.

Lloyd, J. E. 1965. Aggressive mimicry in Photuris: Firefly femmes fatales. Science 149:653–654.

Lloyd, J. E. 1966. Studies on the flash communication system in Photinus fireflies. Univ. Mich. Mus. Zool. Misc. Publ. No. 310; 96 pp.

Lloyd, J. E. 1977. Bioluminescence and communication. In How Animals Communicate, ed. T. A. Sebeok, 164–183. Bloomington: Indiana Univ. Press.

Lloyd, J. E. 1983. Bioluminescence and communication in insects. Annu. Rev. Entomol. 28:131–160.

Matthews, E. G. 1976. Insect Ecology. New York: Univ. of Queensland Press, 226 pp.; illus.

Matthews, R. W., and J. R. Matthews. 1978. Insect Behavior. New York: Wiley, 507 pp.; illus.

Michener, C. D. 1974. The Social Behavior of Bees: A Comparative Study. Cambridge, Mass.: Belknap Press, 404 pp.; illus.

Michener, C. D., and M. H. Michener. 1951. American Social Insects. New York: Van Nostrand, 267 pp., illus.

Papageorgis, C. 1975. Mimicry in neotropical butterflies. Amer. Sci. 63(5):522–532, illus.

Price, P. W. 1975. Insect Ecology. New York: Wiley, 514 pp.; illus.

Rettenmeyer, C. W. 1970. Insect mimicry. Annu. Rev. Entomol. 15:43–74.

Roelofs, W. L., and R. L. Brown. 1982. Pheromones and evolutionary relationships of Tortricidae. Annu. Rev. Ecol. Syst. 13: 395–422.

Romoser, W. S. 1973. The Science of Entomology. New York: Macmillan, 449 pp.; illus.

Uvarov, B. 1977. Grasshoppers and Locusts: A Handbook of General Acridology. Volume 2: Behaviour, Biogeography, Population Dynamics. London: Centre for Overseas Pest Research, 613 pp.

Van der Kloot, W. C. 1968. Behavior. New York: Holt, Rinehart and Winston, 166 pp.; illus.

Wallace, R. A. 1973. The Ecology and Evolution of Animal Behavior. Pacific Palisades, Calif.: Goodyear, 342 pp.; illus.

Wigglesworth, V. B. 1972. The Life of Insects. New York: Universe Books, 360 pp.; illus.

Williams, C. B. 1958. Insect Migration. London: Collins, 356 pp.; illus.

Wilson, E. O. 1971. The Insect Societies. Cambridge, Mass.: Harvard Univ. Press, 548 pp.; illus.

Chapter 5   **Classification, Nomenclature, and Identification**

The theme of diversity almost inevitably dominates any discussion of insects and their relatives. Not only are there a large number of individual insects (the biomass of ants in the tropics probably exceeds that of all vertebrates combined), but there is an almost overwhelming number of different kinds of insects. The study of the diversity of organisms and of the relationships between them is the scientific field of *systematics*. This discipline encompasses the study of the means of classifying organisms, the field of *taxonomy*. Systematics is clearly one of the oldest areas of biological enquiry. Aristotle developed principles of biological classification in the fourth century B.C. Indeed, the Bible states that one of the first acts of Adam in the Garden of Eden was to name the creatures that surrounded him. Systematics is fundamentally important because it forms the foundation upon which all other biological disciplines are based. The names of organisms provide a key to the published literature and enable workers to communicate with one another. Classifications serve both as information retrieval systems and, insofar as they reflect the relationships among organisms, provide means of prediction of the distribution of characteristics among organisms. The past 20–30 years, however, have been a period of foment for systematics, a time during which the fundamentals have been carefully reexamined and the foundations of such basic concepts as similarity and

relationship have been questioned. This period has been characterized by a search for more precise and repeatable methods for measuring and expressing such concepts.

The fundamental unit of systematics is the *species*. Our concepts of what a species is and how they originate are based largely on studies of vertebrates. Extrapolation beyond them to other animals, especially to fundamentally different organisms in other kingdoms, must be done with some care. Basically, most workers dealing with living animals define the species to be a group of individuals or populations in nature that (1) are capable of interbreeding and producing fertile offspring, and (2) under natural conditions are reproductively isolated from (that is, ordinarily not interbreeding with) other such groups. This is known as the biological species concept. Because these criteria involve characteristics of living organisms, they are difficult, sometimes perhaps impossible, to address directly. Therefore, usually the first steps in systematics involve attempts to infer the limits of a species (the extent of a reproductive community) by observation of the phenotypic expression of that gene pool—that is, to look for the smallest set of phenotypic homogeneity while acknowledging and incorporating known aspects of variability, such as sexual dimorphism, developmental stages, seasonal changes, geographic variation, and individual variability. Hence, one often must rely on morphological or other characters to determine specific limits; this determination must be made with some caution, since there are "good" species (groups reproductively isolated) that cannot be distinguished by morphological characters (known as sibling species), and conversely, within a single species there may be a number of different forms.

The subspecies category is sometimes used to refer to recognizable and geographically restricted subdivisions of a species. Because different subspecies of a given species are capable of interbreeding, the differences between them are usually not clear-cut but intergrading, particularly where adjacent subspecies come in contact. This category has been misused, especially in the early part of this century, to refer to any distinguishable variant, often a color variant.

In a formal biological classification species are grouped according to estimates of their similarity or relatedness. Such groups are called *taxa* (singular, *taxon*). These taxa are arranged in a hierarchical pattern. The most commonly used categories or levels in the system of zoological classification are the following (listed from most inclusive to least):

Phylum
  Subphylum
    Class
      Subclass
        Order
          Suborder
            Superfamily
              Family
                Subfamily
                  Tribe
                    Genus
                      Subgenus
                        Species
                          Subspecies

In this scheme, the animal kingdom is divided into a number of phyla (singular, *phylum*). Each phylum is divided into classes, classes into orders, orders into families, families into genera (singular, *genus*) and genera into species. The species is probably the only level that can be assessed by objective criteria. A genus is one or more species classified together; a family is one or more genera; and so on. Any scheme of classification that is developed for a group of animals will be affected by the particular characters used, the relative weight they are given, and how they are analyzed. If different people use different characters or a different "weighting" of a series of characters, they will arrive at different classifications.

The last two decades have witnessed a vocal debate over the principles and fundamentals of classification. The field of numerical phenetics (sometimes called numerical taxonomy) rose in opposition to traditional taxonomy and what was viewed as the idiosyncratic assignment of weight, or special importance, to certain characters and not to others in formulating classifications. The proponents of phenetics emphasized that all characters should be weighted equally and that large numbers of characters must be used to estimate the degree of similarity among organisms. Similarity, according to their position, could be thought of as a statistical measure of the number of observable features shared by organisms. Large numbers of characters are required to obtain an effective sample of the phenotype of an organism. The large data sets thus generated have required the use of computers to handle them. For a summary of this field see Sneath and Sokal (1973).

Numerical phenetics initially emphasized the objective assessment of similarity as the basis for producing classifications. It held that the phylogenetic history of organisms was unknowable and had no place in the formulation of classifications. The vast majority of systematists, however, are devoutly interested in the evolutionary history of their organisms. The field of phylogenetic systematics (also known as cladistics or numerical cladistics) explicitly addresses this question by providing methods for inferring relationships. In this context, *relationship* refers to the relative recency of common ancestry. For example, given three organisms—A, B, and C— A and B are more closely related to one another than to C if they share a more recent common ancestor than either does with C. Relationship, in turn, is inferred by distinguishing between characters that represent an ancestral condition for the organisms in question and those that represent the derived condition. Shared derived characters among organisms are evidence of common ancestry, the implication being that the derived state appeared first in the common ancestor and was passed on to its descendants. In this method of analysis, shared ancestral characters are meaningless. Groups of organisms that are inferred to have been derived from a common ancestor and to be more closely related among themselves than to any other species are called monophyletic (i.e., they represent an inclusive branch of the phylogenetic tree). This is a strict definition of monophyly, namely, that *all* descendants of a given ancestor are included within the taxon in question. In contrast, one or more species in a nonmonophyletic group share a more recent common ancestry with species outside the group than with those species in it. The distinction is sometimes made between paraphyly and polyphyly: a paraphyletic group is one based upon shared ancestral characters; a polyphyletic group is one based upon misinterpreted characters. A taxon uniting birds and bats on the basis of the shared possession of wings is, in one sense, polyphyletic, because the wings in these two groups evolved independently. In another sense it could be considered to be paraphyletic in that birds and bats share a number of characters that are ancestral for all tetrapods. In any case, such a taxon is clearly *not* monophyletic, in that birds are more closely related to crocodilians (among extant animals) and bats to other mammals. Because of the difficulties in interpreting characters as ancestral or derived and in distinguishing among truly homologous characters and character convergences, parallelisms, and reversals, phylogenetics often relies upon computer algorithms for assessing relationships (hence the term *numerical cladistics*).

Much of the dissatisfaction of more traditionally trained systematists is not with the methods of phylogenetic systematics as a means of inferring relationships, but with its applications to the more formal practice of classification. In a classification each taxon is given a formal name. Some extreme positions hold that *all* groupings found in a phylogenetic analysis not only can but must be given formal nomenclatorial status, and various schemes have been proposed to minimize the number of names that need to be coined for these. Another point of disagreement concerns whether paraphyletic groups are acceptable in a formal classification. The pages of the journal *Systematic Zoology* are filled with arguments on such questions. Unfortunately, in terms of the classification of insects and arthropods, surprisingly little is known of the relationships between the major groups. The classifications that we present throughout this book do not represent the final word. In many cases alternatives are available and stoutly defended. Our objective has been to present classifications that are widely accepted or that are consistent with the criterion of monophyly. It must be stressed that arthropod systematics is an active field of research, and our ideas of relationships will change through time.

Nomenclature

Animals have two types of names, scientific and common. Scientific names are used throughout the world, and every animal taxon has one that is unique to it. Common names are vernacular names, and they are often less precise than scientific names. (Some common names are used for more than one taxon, and a given animal taxon may have several of

them.) Many animals lack common names because they are small or seldom encountered.

Scientific Nomenclature

The scientific naming of animals follows certain rules, which are outlined in the *International Code of Zoological Nomenclature* (Ride *et al.* 1985). Scientific names are latinized, but they may be derived from any language or from the names of people or places. Most names are derived from Latin or Greek words and usually refer to some characteristic of the animal or group named.

The names of groups above genus are latinized nouns in the nominative plural. The names of genera and subgenera are latinized nouns in the nominative singular. Specific and subspecific names may be adjectives, present or past participles of verbs, or nouns. Adjectives and participles must agree in gender with the genus name, and nouns are in either the nominative or the genitive case.

The scientific name of a species is a binomial; that is, it consists of two words (the genus name and a specific name). That of a subspecies is a trinomial (the genus name, the specific name, and a subspecific name). These names are always printed in *italics* (if written or typewritten, italics are indicated by underlining). Names of species and subspecies are sometimes followed by the name of the author, the person who described the species or subspecies. Authors' names are not italicized. The appended author name is often important in dealing with the systematics of a species or in cases where the same name has been mistakenly applied to two different species (a case of homonymy). In most other cases it is simply superfluous and adds nothing more than a false sense of authority to the person citing the name. The names of genera and higher categories always begin with a capital letter; specific and subspecific names do not. If the author's name is in parentheses, it means that he described the species (or subspecies, in the case of a subspecies name) in some genus other than the one in which it is now placed. For example,

Papílio glaùcus Linnaeus[1]—the tiger swallowtail. The species *glaùcus* was described by Linnaeus in the genus *Papílio*.
Leptinotársa décemlineàta (Say)—the Colorado potato beetle. The species *décemlineàta* was described by Say in some genus other than *Leptinotársa*, and this species has since been transferred to the genus *Leptinotársa*.

---

[1]Throughout this book Linnaeus is abbreviated "L."

Árgia fumipénnis (Burmeister). The species *fumi-pénnis* was described by Burmeister in some genus other than *Árgia* and has subsequently been transferred to the genus *Árgia*. There are three subspecies of this species in the eastern United States: a northern subspecies (*violàcea*) with clear wings and considerable violet coloration, a southern subspecies (*fumipénnis*) with smoky wings and considerable violet coloration, and a subspecies in peninsular Florida (*átra*) with very dark wings and dark brownish (not violet) coloration. These three subspecies would be listed as *Árgia fumipénnis violàcea* (Hagen), *Árgia fumipénnis fumipénnis* (Burmeister), and *Árgia fumipénnis átra* Gloyd. Hagen's name in parentheses means that *violàcea* was described in a genus other than *Árgia*, but there is no way of knowing from this name whether *violàcea* was originally described as a species, as a subspecies of *fumipénnis*, or as a subspecies of some other species. Gloyd's name not in parentheses means that *átra* was originally described in the genus *Árgia*, but there is no way of knowing from this name whether *átra* was originally described as a species of *Árgia*, as a subspecies of *fumipénnis*, or as a subspecies of another species of *Árgia*. (Actually, Hagen originally described *violàcea* as a species of *Ágrion*, and Gloyd originally described *átra* as a subspecies of *Árgia fumipénnis*.)

Some entomologists have used trinomials for what they have called "varieties" (for example, *A-us*, *b-us*, var. *c-us*). Such names, if published before 1961, are assumed to be names of subspecies, in which case the "var." in the name is dropped, or if they are shown to designate an individual variant, they are considered "infra" categories, which are not covered by the Rules of Zoological Nomenclature. Such names published after 1960 are considered to designate individual variants ("infra" categories), not covered by the rules. The taxonomic categories listed on page 92 apply to *populations* and not to individual variants such as color forms, sexual forms, and seasonal forms.

A species referred to but not named is often designated simply by "sp." For example, "*Gómphus* sp." refers to a species of *Gómphus*. More than one species may be designated by "spp."; for example, "*Gómphus* spp." refers to two or more species of *Gómphus*.

The names of categories from tribe through superfamily have standard endings and hence can always be recognized as referring to a particular category. These can be illustrated by some taxa of bees, as follows:

Superfamily names end in *oidea*; for example, *Apòidea*, bees.

Family names end in *idae*; for example, *Àpidae*, euglossine bees, bumble bees, and honey bees.

Subfamily names end in *inae*; for example, *Apìnae*, honey bees.

Tribe names end in *ini*; for example, *Apìni*, honey bees.

Types.   Whenever a new taxon (from subspecies to superfamily) is described, the describer is supposed to designate a *type*, which is used as a reference if there is ever any question about what the taxon includes, and it serves to anchor the name. The type of a species or subspecies is a single specimen (the *type*, or *holotype*); the type of a genus or subgenus is a species (the *type species*); and the type of a taxon from tribe through superfamily is a genus (the *type genus*). Names of taxa from tribe through superfamily (see the previous examples) are formed by adding the appropriate ending to the root of the name of the type genus. (For the type genus *Àpis* in the previous examples, the stem is *Ap-*.) If a species is divided into subspecies, the particular subspecies that includes the holotype of the species has the same subspecific as specific name (for example, *Árgia fumipénnis fumipénnis*). Similarly, if a genus is divided into subgenera, the subgenus that includes the type species of the genus has the same subgenus name as genus name—for example, *Formìca* (*Formìca*) *rùfa* L. (The name in parentheses is the subgenus.) As concepts of the limits of species or other taxa are revised, it is absolutely necessary to refer to the available types (and ultimately the holotypes of the relevant species) to determine to which concepts the types of the systematist belong, and thus to determine which name or names are applicable to it. The significance of holotypes is nomenclatorial; they have nothing necessarily to do with representing a "typical" member of a species.

Priority.   The starting point of modern binomial zoological nomenclature was the publication of the tenth edition of Linnaeus' *Systema Naturae*; the date is taken as 1 January 1758. It often happens that a particular taxon is described independently by two or more people, and hence may have more than one name. In such cases the first name used from 1758 on (provided the describer has followed certain rules) is the correct name, and any other names become synonyms. A particular name will often be used for a long time before it is discovered that another name has priority over it.

Sometimes a person describing a new taxon will give it a name that has previously been used for another taxon; if the taxa involved are at the same taxonomic level, the names are termed homonyms, and all but the oldest must be discarded and the taxa renamed. There cannot be two (or more) species or subspecies with the same name in a given genus (except that the name of the type-containing subspecies has the same name as the specific name). There cannot be two (or more) genera or subgenera in the animal kingdom with the same name (except that the subgenus containing the type species of the genus has the same name as the genus). Nor can there be two (or more) taxa in the family group of categories (tribe through superfamily) with the same name (though the names of the typical subdivisions will be the same except for their endings). The fundamental rule is that every animal must have a unique name.

Because of the large number of animal taxa and the vast amount of zoological literature, errors in naming (homonyms and synonyms) are not easy to discover. As they are discovered, it becomes necessary to change names, not only of genera and species, but also of families and even orders. The problems of priority in scientific nomenclature are often very intricate, and it is sometimes difficult to determine just what name is the correct one. Name changes may also result from increased knowledge. This added knowledge may indicate that groups should be split or combined, resulting in name changes for some of the groups involved.

In cases where two or more names for a group have been in fairly wide use, we have listed first in this book what we believe to be the correct name and have listed other names in parentheses.

Pronunciation

The pronunciation of some of the technical names and terms used in entomology may be found in a good dictionary or glossary, but very few texts or references give the pronunciation of the bulk of scientific names. There *are* rules for the pronunciation of these names, but few entomologists are familiar with them and many names are pronounced differently by different people and in different countries. We have therefore listed some of the general rules for the pronunciation of the technical names and terms used in zoology and, throughout this book, have indicated the accent in and general pronunciation of scientific names by the use of a grave or acute accent over the vowel of the accented syllable.

We realize that not all entomologists will agree with our pronunciation of some names. There are two reasons for such disagreement: (1) a given pronunciation, whether it follows the rules or not, may become established through usage as the "correct" pronunciation, and we may be unaware of some of these; and (2) the correct pronunciation of many scientific names depends on the derivation of the name and the vowel sound in the source language, and it is difficult or impossible to determine the derivation of some names. Hence there will always be a question as to the correct pronunciation of some scientific names.

The principal rules for the pronunciation of scientific names and terms are outlined here.

Vowels. All vowels in scientific names are pronounced. Vowels are generally either long or short, and in the examples that follow (and elsewhere in this book), a long vowel sound is indicated by a grave accent (ì) and a short vowel sound by an acute accent (í); for example, *màte, mát, mète, mét, bìte, bít, ròpe, rót, cùte, cút, bỳ, sýmmetry.* A vowel at the end of a word has the long sound, except when it is an *a*; a final *a* has the *uh* sound, as in *idea.* The vowel in the final syllable of a word has the short sound, except *es,* which is pronounced *ease.*

Diphthongs. A diphthong consists of two vowels written together and pronounced as a single vowel. The diphthongs are *ae* (pronounced *è,* rarely *é*), *oe* (usually pronounced *è,* rarely *é*), *oi* (pronounced as in *oil*) *eu* (pronounced *ù*), *ei* (pronounced *ì*), *ai* (pronounced *à*), and *au* (pronounced as in *August*). The final *ae* in family and subfamily names is pronounced *è.*

Consonants. *Ch* has the *k* sound, except in words derived from a language other than Greek. When *c* is followed by *ae, e, oe, i,* or *y,* it has the soft (*s*) sound; when it is followed by *a, o, oi,* or *u,* it has the hard (*k*) sound. When *g* is followed by *ae, e, i, oe,* or *y,* it has the soft (*j*) sound; when it is followed by *a, o, oi,* or *u,* it has the hard sound (as in *go*). In words beginning with *ps, pt, ct, cn, gn,* or *mn,* the initial letter is not pronounced, but when these letters appear together in the middle of a word, the first letter is pronounced (for example, the *p* is not pronounced in the word *pteromorph,* but it is pronounced in the word *Orthoptera*). An *x* at the beginning of a word is pronounced as *z,* but as *ks* when it appears elsewhere in a word. When a double *c* is followed by *e, i,* or *y,* it is pronounced as *ks.*

Accent. The pronunciation of technical names and terms in this book is indicated by a grave or acute accent on the vowel of the accented syllable. When the accented syllable contains a diphthong, the accent mark is placed over the vowel that gives the diphthong its sound (for example, *aè, oè, eù, eì, ài*) or over the first vowel of the diphthong (for example, *òi, àu*). The accented syllable is either the penult or the antepenult (in very long words there may be a secondary accent on a syllable near the beginning of the word). The principal rules governing the syllable accented and the vowel sound (whether long or short) are as follows:

1. The accent is on the penult syllable in the following cases:
   a. When the name contains only two syllables; for example, *Àpis, Bómbus.*
   b. When the penult contains a diphthong; for example, *Culicòides, Hermileùca, Lygaèus.*
   c. When the vowel in the penult is followed by *x* or *z*; for example, *Coríxa, Prodóxus, Agromỳza, Triòza.*
   d. When the vowel of the penult is long. Whether the penult vowel is long or short often depends on the derivation of the word and the vowel sound in the source language. The vowel *e* in a word derived from the Greek is long if the vowel in the Greek word is eta (η), but short if it is epsilon (ϵ). For example, in words derived from the Greek μηροφ, meaning *thigh*, the *e* is long (*Diapheromèra, epimèron*), while in those derived from the Greek μεροσ, meaning *part*, the *e* is short (Heterómera). Similarly, the vowel *o* in a word derived from the Greek is long if the vowel in the Greek word is omega (ω), but short if it is omicron (*o*). For example, in words derived from the Greek σωμα, meaning *body*, the *o* is long (*Calosòma, Malacosòma*), while in those derived from the Greek στομα, meaning *mouth*, it is short (*Melanóstoma, Belóstoma, epístoma*). The penult vowel is long in subfamily names (for example, *Sphecìnae*) and tribe names (for example, *Sphecìni*); in tribe names, the final *i* is also long. The penult vowel is usually long in the following cases:
      (1) Words derived from the Latin past participle and ending in *-ata, -atus,* or *-atum*; for example, *maculàta.* (The penult vowel is short in such Greek plurals as *Echinodérmata.*)
      (2) Latin adjectives ending in *-alis* (masculine and feminine) or *-ale* (neuter); for example, *orientàlis, orientàle, verticàlis, verticàle.*
      (3) Words ending in *-ina*; for example, *carolìna, Ceratìna, Glossìna.*
      (4) Words ending in *-ica*; for example, *Formìca, Myrmìca.*
      (5) Words ending in *-ana, -anas,* or *-anum*; for example, *americàna, Tabànus, mexicànum.*
      (6) Words ending in *-ura*; for example, *Thysanùra, Xiphosùra.*
      (7) Words ending in *-odes*; for example, *Sabulòdes, Sphecòdes.*
      (8) Words ending in *-otes*; for example, *Epiròtes.*
      (9) Words ending in *-ates*; for example, *Aceràtes, Hippelàtes.*
      (10) Words ending in *-ales*; for example, the names of plant orders, such as *Graminàles.*
      (11) Words ending in *-osis*; for example, *pediculòsis, trichinòsis.* There are a few exceptions in modern usage; for example, *metamòrphosis.*
      (12) Words ending in *-soma*; for example, *Calosòma, Eriosòma.*
      (13) Words ending in *-pogon*; for example, *Heteropògon, Lasiopògon.*
      (14) Words ending in *-chlora*; for example, *Augochlòra.*
      (15) Words in which the vowel of the penult is *u*, except when the *u* is followed by *l*; for example, *Fenùsa, Ctenùcha* (exceptions, *Libéllula, Bétula*).
      (16) When the vowel is followed by *z*; for example, *Agromỳza, Triòza.*
   e. When the vowel of the penult is short and followed by two consonants, except a mute followed by *l* or *r*; for example, *Pseudocóccus, pulchélla, Pterophýlla, Vanéssa, Chlorotéttix, Latrodéctus, Enallágma, Gryllotálpa, Adélges, Hemerocámpa, Microbémbex, Philánthus, Monárthrum, Leptinotársa, Schistocérca, Sapérda, Polyérgus, Osmodérma, Panórpa, Pyromórpha, Chionáspis, Cordulegáster, Derméstes, Mantíspa, Prionoxýstus, Macrópsis.* When the vowel of the penult is followed by a mute (*b,* hard *c, d, g, k, p, q, t, ch, ph,* or *th*) and *l* or *r*, the accent is on the antepenult: for example, *Cutérebra, Geómetra, Ánabrus, Ránatra, Éphydra, Grýllacris, Melánoplus, Stenóbothrus, élytra.*

2. In other cases the antepenult is accented.
   a. The vowel of the antepenult is long in the following cases:
      (1) When it is followed by another vowel; for example, *Anthomỳia, Epèolus, Hepìalus, Llavèia, Sìalis.* This includes family names that have a vowel immediately preceding the *-idae: Danàidae, Canacèidae, Citheronìidae, Melòidae, Grùidae, Melandrỳidae.*
      (2) When it is *a, e, o,* or *u,* followed by a single consonant and two vowels, the first of which is *e, i,* or *y;* for example, *Aràneus, Callosàmia, Citherònia, Climàcia, Cordùlia, Lecànium, Làsius, Nemòbius, Orthèzia, Plòdia, Redùvius, Rhàgium, Tèlea, Xylòmya.*
      (3) When it is *u* followed by a single consonant; for example, *Libellùlidae, Linguatùlida.*
      (4) When it is *y* followed by *z;* for example, *Agromỳzidae, Anthomỳzidae.*
      (5) In family names when this vowel is long in the name of the type genus; for example, *Aleyròdidae, Asìlidae, Beròthidae, Chrysòpidae, Gyròpidae, Hèbridae, Isometòpidae, Nàbidae, Nèpidae, Phylloxèridae,* names ending in *-mỳzidae,* names ending in *-psòcidae,* names ending in *-sòmidae.*
   b. The vowel of the antepenult is short in other cases. This category includes all family names in which the antepenult vowel is followed by a consonant (except when the vowel is *u* followed by a single consonant or *y* followed by *z*); for example, *Belostomátidae, Elatéridae.* The following names, and others with similar endings, have the antepenult vowel short: *Heterócera, Geócoris, Conocéphalus, Tiphódytes, Chauliógnathus, Pantógrapha, Chirónomus, Mallóphaga, Drosóphila, Anthóphora, Orthóptera, Micrópteryx, Chilópoda, Triátoma.*

Common Names of Insects

Because there are so many species of insects, and because so many of them are very small and poorly known, relatively few have common names. Those that do are generally particularly showy insects or insects of economic importance. American entomologists recognize as "official" the common names in a list published every few years by the Entomological Society of America, but this list does not include all species of insects (and other arthropods) to which common names have been applied. The common names used in this book for individual species have been taken from this list or have been obtained from other sources.

Many common names of insects refer to groups such as subfamilies, families, suborders, or orders, rather than to individual species. The name "tortoise beetle," for example, refers to all species in the subfamily Cassidìnae (about 3000 world species and 24 in North America) of the family Chrysomélidae. The name "leaf beetle" applies to all species in the family Chrysomélidae (about 25,000 world species and nearly 1400 in North America). The name "beetle" applies to all species in the order Coleóptera (some 300,000 world species and about 30,000 in North America). The name "damselfly" applies to the entire suborder Zygóptera, of which there are hundreds of species.

Most common names of insects that consist of a single word refer to entire orders (for example, beetle, bug, caddisfly, cockroach, stonefly, and termite). Some (bee, damselfly, grasshopper, and lacewing) refer to suborders or groups of families. Only a few (such as ants) refer to families. Most common names applying to families consist of two or more words, the last being the name of the larger group, and the others descriptive (for example, brown lacewings, click beetle, soldier flies, and small winter stoneflies).

The members of a group are often referred to by an adjectival form of the group name. For example, insects in the order Hymenóptera might be called hymenopterans; the wasps in the superfamily Sphecòidea are called sphecoids; those in the Sphécidae are called sphecids; and those in the subfamily Nyssonìnae might be called nyssonines. It is standard practice to use an adjectival form of the family or subfamily name as a common name.

The names "fly" and "bug" are used for insects in more than one order, and the way the names of these insects are written may indicate the order to which the insect belongs. For example, when a fly belongs to the order Díptera, the "fly" of the name is written as a separate word (for example, black fly, horse fly, and blow fly); when it belongs to another order, the "fly" of the name is written together with the descriptive word (for example, dragonfly, butterfly, and sawfly). When a bug belongs to the order Hemíptera, the "bug" of the name is written as a separate word (for example, damsel bug, stink bug, and lace bug); when it belongs to another order, the "bug" of the name is written together with the descriptive word (for example, mealybug, ladybug, junebug, and sowbug).

The Identification of Insects

When one encounters an insect, one of the first questions that will be asked is, "What kind of insect is it?" One of the principal aims of the beginning student in any field of biology is to become able to identify the organisms he or she is studying. The identification of insects differs from the identification of other types of organisms only in that it is likely to be somewhat more difficult, for there are more kinds of insects than anything else.

Four things complicate the problem of insect identification. First, there are so many different kinds (species) of insects that the beginner may be discouraged about ever becoming proficient in insect identification. Second, most insects are small, and the identifying characters are often difficult to see. Third, many insects are poorly known, and when they are finally identified, the student may have only a technical name (which he may not understand) and little biological information. Fourth, many insects go through very different stages in their life history, and one may come to know insects in one stage of their life cycle and still know very little about those same insects in another stage.

There are about five ways in which a student may identify an unknown insect: (1) by having it identified for him by an expert, (2) by comparing it with labeled specimens in a collection, (3) by comparing it with pictures, (4) by comparing it with descriptions, and (5) by using an analytical key, or by a combination of two or more of these procedures. Of these, obviously the first is the simplest, but this method is not always available. Similarly, the second method may not always be available. In addition, the use of a collection is of limited value if one does not know the characteristics that distinguish the species in a particular group. In the absence of an expert or a labeled collection, the next best method is usually the use of a key. In the case of particularly striking or well-known insects, the identification can often be made by the third method mentioned, but in many groups this method is unsatisfactory. No book can illustrate all kinds of insects and still sell for a price a student can afford to pay. Where an unknown insect cannot be definitely identified by means of illustrations, the best procedure is to use an analytical key and then to check the identification by as many of the other methods mentioned as possible. Identification from pictures is often inaccurate, because there are many instances in the insect world in which one type of insect looks a great deal like another.

As a general rule in this book, identification will be carried only to family. To go further usually re-quires specialized knowledge and is beyond the scope of this book. Identifying insects only to family reduces the number of names from many thousand to several hundred, and of these probably only 200 or fewer are likely to be encountered by the average student. We reduce the problem still further by being concerned largely with *adults*. Thus, insect identification becomes less formidable.

The Keys in This Book

Analytical keys are devices used to identify all sorts of things, living as well as nonliving. Different keys may be arranged somewhat differently, but all involve the same general principles. One runs an insect (or other organism) through a key in steps. At each step he is faced with two (rarely more) alternatives, one of which should apply to the specimen at hand. In our keys there is either a number or a name following the alternative that best fits the specimen. If there is a number, the next step is the couplet with this number. Thus, each step leads to another step and its alternatives until a name is reached.

The couplets of alternatives in our keys are numbered 1 and 1', 2 and 2', and so on. In each couplet after the first is a number in parentheses. This is the number of the couplet from which that couplet is reached, and it enables the student to work backward in the key if a mistake is discovered. This method of numbering also serves as a check on the accuracy of the organization of the key. In a few large keys, certain couplets may be reached from more than one previous couplet; this fact is indicated by two or more numbers in parentheses.

The keys in this book have been prepared from three principal sources: other published keys, descriptions, and an examination of specimens of the groups concerned. Many are taken largely from previously published keys (generally with some changes in wording or organization), but some represent a new approach. Our aim with each key has been to prepare something that is *workable* for practically every species (or specimen) in the groups covered. Most of these keys have been tested by student use over a number of years. In many of the insect orders (particularly the larger ones), some groups key out in more than one place. This is the case in two types of situations: (1) where there is significant variation within the group, and (2) with borderline cases where the specimen might seem to fit both alternatives of a couplet. In the latter situation a specimen should key out correctly from either alternative. While we hope that these keys will work for every specimen, we realize that there are species or specimens in many groups that are erratic in their characters. An attempt has been made to include as many as possible of these atypical forms in our keys, but it is possible that a few may not key out correctly. We believe that our keys should work for 95% or more of the insects of the United States and Canada. We believe that the user of our keys is more likely to reach an impasse because of an inability to see or interpret a character than because of a discrepancy in the key.

When a determination is reached in the key, the student should check the specimen against any illustrations or descriptions available. If these do not fit the specimen, then either a mistake has been made somewhere or the specimen is one that will not work out correctly in the key. In the latter event, the specimen should be saved until it can be shown to an expert. It may be something rare or unusual.

One's success in running an insect through a key depends largely on an understanding of the characters used. In many cases in this book the key characters are illustrated. Often several characters are given in each alternative. In case one character cannot be seen or interpreted, the student can use the other characters. If at any point in the key the student cannot decide which way to go, try following up both alternatives and then check further with illustrations and descriptions when a name is reached.

A great many families of insects are very unlikely to be encountered by the general collector because they contain small or minute forms that may be overlooked, because they are quite rare, or because they have a very restricted geographic range. Such families are indicated in most of our keys by an asterisk, and couplets containing such groups can often be skipped by the beginning student.

Most measurements in this book are given in metric units. Tables for the conversion of these to English units appear on the inside back cover.

It should be understood that analytical keys are made for people who do not know the identity of a specimen they have. Once a specimen has been identified with a key, subsequent identifications of this same insect may often be based on such characters as general appearance, size, shape, and color, without reference to minute characters.

It will be apparent very early during the student's work in identifying insects that a good hand lens, and preferably a binocular microscope, is necessary to see many of the characters of the insect. Most insects, once the student knows what to look for, can be identified by means of a good hand lens (about $10 \times$).

The mere identification and naming of insects should not be the student's final objective in insect study. There is much more of interest in insects than just identifying them. The student should go further and learn something of the habits, distribution, and importance of insects.

Geographical Coverage of This Book

The taxonomic treatment in this book of the various insect orders and the other groups of arthropods applies to the fauna of North America north of Mexico. A few insects occurring in other parts of the world are mentioned, but the characters given for each group (and the keys) apply to North American species and may not apply to all other species occurring outside of North America. The terms "North America" and "North American" refer to that portion of the continent north of Mexico. Where the geographic range of a group in North America is more or less limited, information on this range is given. Groups for which there is no information on range are widely distributed in North America.

References

Blackwelder, R. E. 1967. Taxonomy, A Text and Reference Book. New York: Wiley, 698 pp.; illus.

Borror, D. J. 1960. Dictionary of Word Roots and Combining Forms. Palo Alto, Calif.: Mayfield, 134 pp.

Brown, R. W. 1978. Composition of Scientific Words. Washington, D. C.: Smithsonian Institution Press, 882 pp.

Chamberlin, W. J. 1946 (2nd ed.). Entomological Nomenclature and Literature. Ann Arbor, Mich.: J. W. Edwards, 135 pp.

Crowson, R. A. 1970. Classification and Biology. New York: Atherton Press, 350 pp.

Eldredge, N., and J. Cracraft. 1980. Phylogenetic Patterns and the Evolutionary Processes: Method and Theory in Comparative Biology. New York: Columbia University Press, 349 pp.

Hennig, W. 1965. Phylogenetic systematics. Annu. Rev. Entomol. 10:97–116; illus.

Hennig, W. 1966. Phylogenetic Systematics. Urbana: Univ. of Illinois Press.

Mayr, E. 1963. Animal Species and Evolution. Cambridge, Mass.: Belknap Press of Harvard University, 797 pp.

Mayr, E. 1969. Principles of Systematic Zoology. New York: McGraw-Hill, 428 pp.; illus.

Melander, A. L. 1940. Source Book of Biological Terms. New York: Department of Biology, City College of New York, 157 pp.

Ride, W. D. L., C. W. Sabrosky, G. Bernardi, and R. V. Melville. (Eds.) 1985 (3rd ed.). International Code of Zoological Nomenclature. Berkeley: Univ. of California Press, 338 pp.

Ross, H. H. 1973. Biological Systematics. Reading, Mass.: Addison-Wesley, 346 pp.; illus.

Schenk, E. T., and J. H. McMasters. 1956 (3rd ed.). Procedure in Taxonomy. Stanford, Calif.: Stanford Univ. Press, 119 pp.

Simpson, G. G. 1961. Principles of Animal Taxonomy. New York: Columbia Univ. Press, 247 pp.; illus.

Sneath, P. H. A., and R. R. Sokal. 1973. Numerical Taxonomy. San Francisco: Freeman, 574 pp.

Werner, F. G. 1982. Common names of insects and related organisms. College Park, Md.: Entomol. Soc. Amer. 132 pp. (This list is revised every few years.)

White, M. J. D. 1978. Modes of Speciation. San Francisco: Freeman, 455 pp.

Wiley, E. O. 1981. Phylogenetics: The Theory and Practice of Phylogenetic Systematics. New York: Wiley, 439 pp.

Chapter 6

Phylum Arthrópoda[1]
Arthropods

We are concerned in this book principally with insects, but it is appropriate to point out the place of the insects in the animal kingdom and to include at least a brief account of the animals most closely related to and sometimes confused with the insects.

The insects belong to the phylum Arthrópoda, the principal characters of which are as follows:

1. The body segmented, the segments usually grouped in two or three rather distinct regions
2. Paired segmented appendages (from which the phylum gets its name)
3. Bilateral symmetry
4. A chitinous exoskeleton, which is periodically shed and renewed as the animal grows
5. A tubular alimentary canal, with mouth and anus
6. An open circulatory system, the only blood vessel usually being a tubular structure dorsal to the alimentary canal with lateral openings in the abdominal region
7. The body cavity a blood cavity or hemocoel, the coelom reduced
8. The nervous system consisting of an anterior ganglion or brain located above the alimentary canal, a pair of connectives extending from the brain around the alimentary canal, and paired ganglionated nerve cords located below the alimentary canal
9. The skeletal muscles striated
10. Excretion usually by means of tubes (the Malpighian tubules) that empty into the alimentary canal, the excreted materials passing to the outside by way of the anus
11. Respiration by means of gills, or tracheae and spiracles
12. No cilia or nephridia
13. The sexes nearly always separate

The phyla most closely related to the Arthrópoda are the Annélida and the Onychóphora. The Annélida, which include the segmented worms (earthworms, marine worms, and leeches) differ from the arthropods in lacking segmented appendages, a chitinous exoskeleton, and a tracheal system. They have a closed circulatory system; the skeletal muscles are not striated; and excretion is by means of ciliated tubes called nephridia. Some insect larvae lack appendages and superficially resemble annelids. They can be recognized as insects by their internal organization (different types of circulatory and excretory systems and the presence of tracheae). The Onychóphora resemble the arthropods in the possession of (1) segmented antennae (the body is indistinctly segmented, the segmentation being indicated by the legs, which are unsegmented but bear claws at their

[1]Arthrópoda: *arthro*, joint or segment; *poda*, foot or appendage.

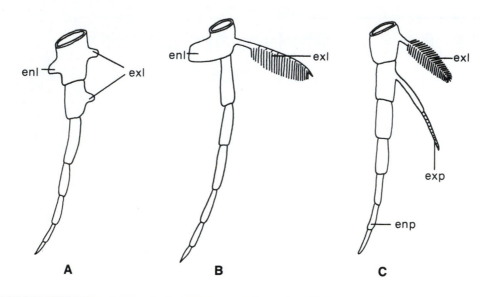

Figure 6–1. Some major variations in arthropod appendages. **A,** generalized; **B,** trilobite; **C,** crustacean. *enl,* endite lobe; *enp,* endopodite; *exl,* exite lobe; *exp,* exopodite.

apex), (2) a chitinous exoskeleton that is periodically shed and renewed, (3) a tracheal system, and (4) an open circulatory system. They resemble the annelids in the possession of nephridia, and in having the skeletal muscles not striated. The Onychóphora are wormlike or sluglike animals, varying in length up to several centimeters. They occur only in the southern hemisphere, where they live in moist situations.

Classification of the Arthrópoda

There are differences of opinion regarding the relationships of the various arthropod groups and the taxonomic level at which they should be recognized. A number of different taxonomic arrangements of these groups have been proposed. We follow here the classification of Barnes (1987) and recognize four major groups within the arthropods as subphyla; this arrangement is as follows (with synonyms in parentheses):

Phylum Arthrópoda—arthropods
  Subphylum Trilóbita—trilobites (fossils only)
  Subphylum Cheliceràta
    Class Merostomàta—horseshoe crabs (Xipho-
      sùra) and the fossil eurypterids
      (Euryptérida)
    Class Aráchnida—arachnids
    Class Pycnogónida—sea spiders

Subphylum Crustàcea—crustaceans
  Class Cephalocàrida
  Class Branchiópoda
  Class Ostrácoda
  Class Copépoda
  Class Mystacocàrida
  Class Remipèdia
  Class Tantulocàrida
  Class Branchiùra
  Class Cirripèdia
  Class Malacóstraca
Subphylum Ateloceràta
  Class Diplópoda—millipedes
  Class Chilópoda—centipedes
  Class Paurópoda—pauropods
  Class Sýmphyla—symphylans
  Class Hexápoda (Insécta)—HEXAPODS

Three phyla sometimes included in the Arthrópoda are the Onychóphora, Tardigràda, and Pentastómida (= Linguatùlida). The Onychóphora are somewhat intermediate between the Annélida and the Arthrópoda (as noted previously), but the other two groups are somewhat degenerate morphologically (e.g., they lack circulatory and excretory organs).

The preceding arrangement of the arthropod groups is based primarily on the character of the appendages (partially the jaws and legs) and the nature of the body regions. The trilobites, crustaceans, and Ateloceràta have a pair of antennae (usually two pairs in the crustaceans), while the chelicerates lack antennae. The endite lobes at the base of certain appendages function as jaws in the trilobites, chelicerates, and crustaceans, while (according to Manton, 1964, 1977) the Myriápoda and Hexápoda bite with the tips of the mandibles.

Arthropod appendages are subject to a great deal of variation, but are basically seven-segmented (Figure 6–1). The basal one or two segments sometimes bear mesal (endite) or lateral (exite) lobes or processes. These lobes or processes frequently have important functions and sometimes have special names. The endite lobes of certain appendages usually have a chewing function in the trilobites, chelicerates, and crustaceans, and an exite lobe of the basal segment often functions as a gill in the trilobites and crustaceans. In the crustaceans, the second segment usually bears a well-developed exite lobe, which is generally segmented and is sometimes as large as or larger than the rest of the appendage, thus giving the appendage a forked appearance. Such an appendage is spoken of as biramous. The exite lobe of the second segment is called the exopodite, and the rest of the appendage the endopodite (Figure 6–1C).

The homologies of the appendages in the major arthropod groups are outlined in Table 6–1. Heavy horizontal lines in this table separate body regions.

Subphylum Trilóbita[2]

The trilobites lived during the Paleozoic era (see Table 7–2, page 148), but were most abundant during the Cambrian and Ordovician periods. These animals were somewhat elongate and flattened, with three rather distinct longitudinal divisions of the body. (The lateral portions were extensions over the bases of the legs.) These animals had a pair of antennae, with the remaining appendages similar and leglike (Figure 6–1B). The anterior part of the body (the preoral region and the first three postoral segments) was covered with a carapace. The legs had an exite lobe or epipodite of the basal segment; this bore a series of lamellae and apparently functioned as a gill (these animals were marine). The endite lobes of the anterior legs apparently functioned as jaws.

Subphylum Cheliceràta[3]

Animals belonging to the subphylum Cheliceràta lack antennae and typically have six pairs of appendages. The first pair are chelicerae, and the rest are

---

[2]Trilóbita: *tri*, three; *lobita*, lobed (referring to the three longitudinal divisions of the body).

[3]Cheliceràta: with chelicerae.

Table 6–1
Homologies of the Appendages in the Major Arthropod Groups

| Segment | Cheliceràta | | Crustàcea | Ateloceràta | | |
	Xiphosùra	Aráchnida	Decápoda	Chilópoda	Diplópoda	Hexápoda
Preoral	—	—	Antennules	Antennae	Antennae	Antennae
1	Chelicerae	Chelicerae	Antennae	—	—	—
2	Legs	Pedipalps	Mandibles	Mandibles	Mandibles	Mandibles
3	Legs	Legs	1st maxillae	1st maxillae	Gnatho-chilarium	Maxillae
4	Legs	Legs	2nd maxillae	2nd maxillae	—	Labium
5	Legs	Legs	1st maxillipeds	Toxicognaths	1 pair legs	Legs
6	Legs	Legs	2nd maxillipeds		1 pair legs	Legs
7	Chilaria		3rd maxillipeds		1 pair legs	Legs
8		Abdominal segmenta-	1st legs (chelipeds)	Remaining segments, except	1–2 pair legs	Usually without append-
9	Platelike gills,	tion varia-	Legs	last 1 or 2, with	Remaining	ages in adult
10	last segment	ble, usually	Legs	1 pair of legs;	segments,	(except gon-
11	with spine-	without	Legs	last 1 or 2 seg-	except last,	opods on
12	like telson	paired	Legs	ments with	with 2 pairs	15–16)
13		appendages	Gonopods	short append-	of legs; last	
14			♂: Gonopods	ages (gonopods);	segment	
			♀: Swimmerets	last segment	with 1 pair	
15–17			Swimmerets	with a small	of legs	
18			Uropods and telson	lobelike telson		Epiproct, cerci, and paraproct

leglike. Endite lobes of the pedipalps (the second pair of appendages in the arachnids), or the leglike appendages in the horseshoe crabs, function as jaws. The body of a chelicerate usually has two distinct divisions: an anterior region called the prosoma (or cephalothorax) and a posterior region called the opisthosoma (or abdomen). The prosoma bears the chelicerae and the leglike appendages. The genital ducts open to the outside near the anterior end of the opisthosoma. Most chelicerates have an extra leg segment, the patella, between the femur and the tibia. The legs are generally uniramous, that is, there is no exite or exopodite.

Class Merostomàta[4]

Subclass Euryptérida[5]: The Euryptérida lived during the Paleozoic era, from the Cambrian to the Carboniferous periods. They were aquatic and somewhat similar to the present-day Xiphosùra, and some reached a length of more than 2 meters. The prosoma bore a pair of chelicerae, five pairs of leglike appendages, and a pair each of simple and compound eyes. The opisthosoma was 12-segmented, with platelike appendages concealing gills on the first 5 segments, and the telson was either spinelike or lobelike.

Subclass Xiphosùra[6]—Horseshoe Crabs or King Crabs: The horseshoe crabs are marine forms and are quite common along the Atlantic Coast from Maine to the Gulf of Mexico. They are found in the shallow water and along sandy or muddy shores where they spawn. They feed chiefly on marine worms. Horseshoe crabs are easily recognized by their characteristic oval shell and long spinelike tail (Figure 6–2).

Class Aráchnida—Arachnids[7]

The Aráchnida constitute by far the largest and most important class of the Cheliceràta (about 65,000 described species, with about 8,000 in North America), and a person studying insects will probably encounter more of them than of any other noninsect group of arthropods. Its members occur almost everywhere, often in considerable numbers.

Most authorities recognize 11 major groups of arachnids (all represented in our area), but not all agree on the names to be used for these groups or the taxonomic level they represent. We call these

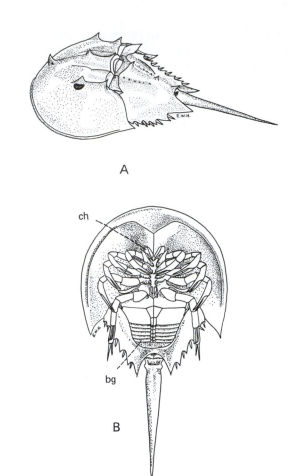

A

B

Figure 6–2. A horseshoe crab, *Límulus* sp. (subclass Xiphosùra). **A**, dorsolateral view; **B**, ventral view. *bg*, book gills; *ch*, chelicera.

groups orders (some would call them subclasses), and our arrangement is as follows (with other names and arrangements in parentheses):

Scorpiònes (Scorpiónides, Scorpiónida)—scorpions
Palpigràdi (Palpigràda, Palpigràdida, Microthelyphónida)—micro whipscorpions
Uropỳgi (Thelyphónida, Holopeltídia, Pedipálpida in part)—whipscorpions
Schizómida (Tartárides, Schizopéltida, Colopỳga, Pedipálpida in part)—short-tailed whipscorpions
Amblypỳgi (Amblypỳgida, Phrynìdes, Phrynèida, Phryníchida, Pedipálpida in part)—tailless whipscorpions, whipspiders
Aràneae (Aranèida)—spiders
Ricinùlei (Ricinulèida, Meridogástra, Podogonàta, Rhinogástra)—ricinuleids

---

[4]Merostomàta: *mero*, part; *stomata*, mouth.

[5]Euryptérida: *eury*, broad; *pterida*, wing or fin.

[6]Xiphosùra: *xipho*, sword; *ura*, tail.

[7]Aráchnida: from the Greek, meaning a spider.

Opiliònes (Phalángida, including Cyphophthálmi)—harvestmen
Àcari (Acarìna, Acàrida)—mites and ticks

Pseudoscorpiònes (Pseudoscorpiónida,Chernètes,
Chelonéthida)—pseudoscorpions
Solifùgae (Solpùgida)—windscorpions

Key to the Orders of Aráchnida

1.   Opisthosoma (abdomen) unsegmented or, if segmented, with spinnerets posteriorly on ventral side (Figures 6–5 and 6–8, *spn*) **2**

1'.   Opisthosoma distinctly segmented, without spinnerets **3**

2(1).   Opisthosoma petiolate (Figures 6–5 and 6–9 through 6–13) ....**Aràneae**   p. 108

2'.   Opisthosoma not petiolate, but broadly joined to prosoma (Figures 6–15 through 6–22)...**Àcari**   p. 124

3(1').   Opisthosoma with a taillike prolongation that is either thick and terminating in a sting (Figure 6–3) or slender and more or less whiplike (Figure 6–4A,B); mostly tropical **4**

3'.   Opisthosoma without a taillike prolongation or with a very short leaflike appendage **7**

4(3).   Opisthosoma ending in a sting (Figure 6–3); first pair of legs not greatly elongated; second ventral segment of opisthosoma with a pair of comblike organs ....**Scorpiònes**   p. 106

4'.   Opisthosoma not ending in a sting; first pair of legs longer than other pairs (Figure 6–4A,B); second ventral segment of opisthosoma without comblike organs **5**

5(4').   Pedipalps slender, similar to legs (Figure 6–4A); minute forms, 5 mm or less in length ....**Palpigràdi**   p. 106

5'.   Pedipalps usually much stouter than any of the legs (Figure 6–4B); mostly larger forms **6**

6(5').   With 2 median eyes on a tubercle anteriorly and a group of 3 eyes on each lateral margin; tail long, filiform, and many-segmented; pedipalps nearly straight or curved mesad, extending forward, and moving laterally (Figure 6–4B); body blackish, more than 50 mm in length ....**Uropỳgi**   p. 107

6'.   Eyes lacking, tail short, 1- to 4-segmented; pedipalps arching upward, forward, and downward and moving vertically; body yellowish or brownish, less than 8 mm in length ....**Schizómida**   p. 107

7(3').   Pedipalps chelate (pincerlike) (Figure 6–23); body more or less oval, flattened, usually less than 5 mm in length ....**Pseudoscorpiònes**   p. 129

7'.   Pedipalps raptorial or leglike, but not chelate; body not particularly flattened; size variable **8**

8(7').   Chelicerae very large, usually about as long as prosoma, and extending forward, and body slightly narrowed in middle (Figure 6–4C); color pale yellow to brownish; length 20–30 mm; mostly nocturnal desert forms occurring in western United States ....**Solifùgae**   p. 130

8'.   Without the above combination of characters **9**

9(8').   First pair of legs very long, with long tarsi; opisthosoma constricted at base; mainly tropical **10**

9'.   First legs similar to the others and (except in the Opiliònes) not usually long; opisthosoma not particularly constricted at base **11**

ORDER **Scorpiònes**[8]—Scorpions: The scorpions are well-known animals that occur in the southern and western parts of the United States. They are fair-sized arachnids, varying in length up to about 125 mm. The opisthosoma is broadly joined to the prosoma and is differentiated into two portions, a broad seven-segmented mesosoma and a much narrower five-segmented posterior metasoma that terminates in a sting (Figure 6–3). The prosoma bears a pair of eyes near the midline and two to five along the lateral margin on each side. The pedipalps are long and chelate. On the ventral side of the second opisthosomal segment is a pair of comblike structures, the pectines.

[8]Scorpiònes: from the Latin, meaning a scorpion.

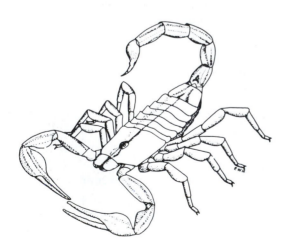

Scorpions are largely nocturnal and, during the day, remain concealed in protected places. When a scorpion runs, the pedipalps are held outstretched and forward, and the posterior end of the opisthosoma is usually curved upward. Scorpions feed on insects and spiders, which they catch with their pedipalps and sometimes sting. The young are born alive and, for a time after birth, are carried about on the back of the mother. Scorpions grow slowly, and some species require several years to reach maturity. The function of the pectines is not known, but they are believed to be tactile organs.

The effect of a scorpion sting depends primarily on the species of scorpion involved. The sting of most species is painful and usually accompanied by local swelling and discoloration, but it is not dangerous. Of the 40-odd species of scorpions in the United States, only one—*Centuròides sculpturàtus* Ewing—is very venomous, and its sting may be fatal. This species is slender and rarely exceeds 65 mm in length. It varies in color from almost entirely yellowish to yellowish-brown with two irregular black stripes down the back. There is a slight dorsal protuberance at the base of the sting. As far as known, this species occurs only in Arizona.

Scorpions do not ordinarily attack people, but will sting quickly if disturbed. In areas where scorpions occur, one should be careful in picking up boards, stones, and similar objects, and a scorpion found crawling on one's body should be brushed off rather than swatted.

ORDER **Palpigràdi**[9]—Micro Whipscorpions: These are tiny arachnids, 5 mm or less in length, that are

Figure 6–3.   A scorpion, 2×.

[9]Palpigràdi: *palpi*, palp or feeler; *gradi*, walk (referring to the leglike character of the pedipalps).

somewhat spiderlike in appearance but have a long segmented tail (Figure 6–4A). The pedipalps are leglike, and the first pair of legs is the longest. These animals are usually found under stones or in the soil. This group is represented in the United States by three species occurring in Texas and California.

ORDER **Uropỳgi**[10]—Whipscorpions: The whipscorpions are mainly tropical and, in the United States, occur only in the southern states. They are elongate and slightly flattened, with a slender segmented tail about as long as the body and powerful pedipalps (Figure 6–4B); the maximum body length is about 80 mm, and the total length including the tail may be 150 mm or more. They are somewhat scorpion-like in appearance, but the tail is very slender, and there is no sting. The first pair of legs is slender and used as feelers; only the three hind pairs of legs are used for walking. When disturbed, these animals emit (or spray, up to 0.5 meter) a substance with a vinegar-like odor from glands at the base of the tail, and hence they are often called vinegaroons (or vinegarones). Whipscorpions are nocturnal and predaceous. They are generally found under logs or burrowing in the sand. The eggs are carried in a membranous sac under the opisthosoma, and the young ride around on the back of the female for a time after they hatch. The whipscorpion most likely to be encountered in the southern states is *Mastigopróctus gigánteus* (Lucas), which occurs in Florida and the Southwest; it has a body length of 40 to 80 mm and is the largest species in the order.

ORDER **Schizómida**[11]—Short-tailed Whipscorpions: These animals are somewhat similar to the Uropỳgi but much smaller and more slender. In addition, the terminal appendage is not long and whiplike; the pedipalps arch upward and forward and move vertically; and there is a transverse suture on the prosoma. The first legs are slender and are not used for walking. The fourth legs are modified for jumping, and in the field these animals superficially resemble small crickets. There are no venom glands or eyes. The eight species of Schizómida in the United States occur in Florida and California. *Trithỳreus pentapéltis* (Cook), which occurs in California, is yellowish to reddish brown in color and 4.5–7.5 mm in length. It occurs under rocks and in leaf litter in the desert regions of southern California. A Florida species, *Schizòmus floridànus* Muma, is 3.0–3.3 mm in length and pale yellowish in color. It occurs in crevices in bark and in organic debris, from the Miami area south into the Keys.

ORDER **Amblypỳgi**[12]—Tailless Whipscorpions or Whipspiders: These arachnids are somewhat spiderlike in appearance, but the opisthosoma is distinctly segmented and, although narrowed at the base, is not petiolate. There are no spinnerets; the pedipalps are large, powerful, and spiny (and are used in capturing prey); and the first legs are very long and whiplike. The prosoma is wider than long and has rounded sides. There are no venom glands. The few North American species vary in length from about 10 to 55 mm and occur chiefly in the southern states. They

---

[10]Uropỳgi: *uro*, tail; *pygi*, rump (referring to the whiplike tail).

[11]Schizómida: *schizo*, split (referring to the transverse suture on the prosoma).

[12]Amblypỳgi: *ambly*, blunt; *pygi*, rump.

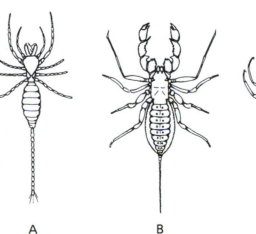
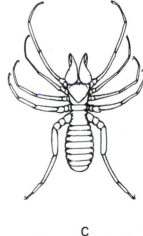

Figure 6–4. Arachnids. **A,** a micro whipscorpion (order Palpigràdi); **B,** a whipscorpion (order Uropỳgi); **C,** a windscorpion (order Solifùgae). (Courtesy of the Institute of Acarology.)

A   B   C

are found under bark or stones (usually scurrying sideways when disturbed) and sometimes enter houses.

ORDER **Aràneae**[13]—Spiders: The spiders are a large (about 2500 North American species), distinct, and widespread group. They occur in many types of habitats and are often very abundant. Many people have the idea that spiders are very venomous, but although nearly all have venom glands, they rarely bite humans. Only a few species in the United States are dangerously venomous.

The body of a spider is divided into two regions, the cephalothorax and the abdomen. The abdomen is unsegmented (in North American species) and attached to the cephalothorax by a slender pedicel (Figures 6–5A,B and 6–9 through 6–13). The cephalothorax bears the eyes, mouthparts, and legs, and the abdomen bears the genital structures, spiracles, anus, and spinnerets.

The cephalothorax is covered dorsally by the carapace and ventrally by the sternum. Anterior to the sternum is a small sclerite called the labium (Figure 6–5B, *lbm*). The eyes are simple and are located on the anterior end of the carapace (Figure 6–6). Most

spiders have eight eyes, but some have fewer. The number and arrangement of the eyes provide characters useful in distinguishing different families.[14] The area between the anterior row of eyes and the edge of the carapace is the clypeus.

The chelicerae are located at the anterior end of the cephalothorax, below the eyes, and are usually directed downward. They are two-segmented, with the basal segment stout and the distal segment fanglike. Spiders have poison glands, and the ducts from these glands open near the tips of the chelicerae. The fangs move laterally in most spiders (suborder Labidógnatha), but move vertically in the tarantulas and trapdoor spiders (suborder Orthógnatha). The basal segment of the chelicerae sometimes bears a small, rounded lateral prominence (the boss) at its base. Some spiders have a filelike ridge on the lateral surface of the chelicerae. Such spiders stridulate by stroking this ridge with the pedipalp to produce a soft sound.

The pedipalps, which are located behind the chelicerae and in front of the legs, are somewhat leglike

---

[13]Aràneae: from the Latin, meaning a spider.

[14]The anterior row of eyes is referred to in the key as the first row. An eye pattern described as 4–2–2 (for example, Figure 6–6C) would mean four eyes in the anterior row, two in the second row, and two in the posterior row.

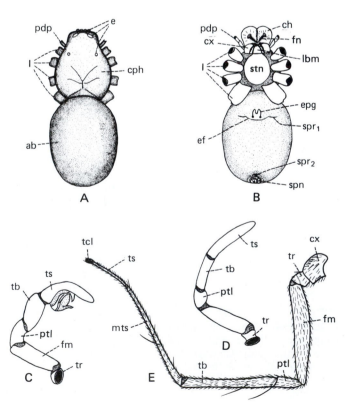

Figure 6–5. Structural characters of spiders. **A,** dorsal view (generalized); **B,** ventral view (generalized); **C,** male pedipalp; **D,** female pedipalp; **E,** leg. *ab,* opisthosoma or abdomen; *ch,* chelicera; *cph,* prosoma or cephalothorax; *cx,* coxa (the coxa of the pedipalp, shown in **B,** is expanded to form the endite); *e,* eyes; *ef,* epigastric furrow; *epg,* epigynum; *fm,* femur; *fn,* fang of chelicera; *l,* coxa of legs; *lbm,* labium; *mts,* metatarsus; *pdp,* pedipalp; *ptl,* patella; *spn,* spinnerets; *spr1,* book lung spiracle; *spr2,* tracheal spiracle; *stn,* sternum; *tb,* tibia; *tcl,* tarsal claw; *tr,* trochanter; *ts,* tarsus.

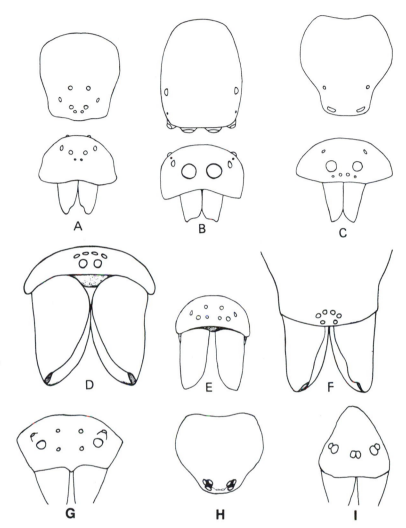

Figure 6–6. Chelicerae and eye patterns of spiders. In **A, B,** and **C** the upper figure is a dorsal view, and the lower figure is an anterior view. **A,** Oxyòpidae; **B,** Saltícidae; **C,** Lycòsidae; **D,** Dysdéridae (anterior view); **E,** Amaurobìidae (anterior view); **F,** Dysdéridae (dorsal view); **G,** Thomísidae (anterior view); **H,** Phólcidae (dorsal view); **I,** Loxoscélidae (anterior view).

or palplike. The basal segment, the endite (Figure 6–5B, *cx*), is enlarged and functions as a crushing jaw. The labium lies between the two endites. The pedipalps are clubbed in male spiders. The terminal segment is modified into a copulatory organ (Figure 6–5C).

The legs are seven-segmented (coxa, trochanter, femur, patella, tibia, metatarsus, and tarsus; Figure 6–5E) and usually bear two or three claws. Two are paired and the third is a median claw, which, when present, is usually small and difficult to see. The tip of the tarsus is usually provided with numerous hairs and bristles, which may obscure the claws. Bristles here that are thick, serrated, and somewhat clawlike are called spurious claws. Many spiders with only two claws have a dense tuft of hairs below the claws; this is the claw tuft (Figure 6–7D, *clt*). The legs are often provided with hairs or bristles

that are useful in separating families. The fine vertical hairs on the tarsi and metatarsi are called trichobothria (Figure 6–7B, *trb*). These hairs are probably sensory in function. Spiders with a cribellum (a structure on the abdomen; see the second paragraph following) also have on the metatarsi of the hind legs a close-set series of heavy bristles, the calamistrum (Figure 6–7B, *clm*). The calamistrum plays a part in the formation of the ribbonlike bands of silk spun by these spiders.

Near the anterior end of the abdomen on the ventral side is a transverse groove called the epigastric furrow (Figure 6–5B, *ef*). The openings of the book lungs (Figure 6–5B, spr_1) are located at the lateral ends of this furrow (book lungs are lacking in the Caponìidae), and the genital opening is located at the middle of the furrow. The book lungs are breathing organs consisting of saclike invaginations

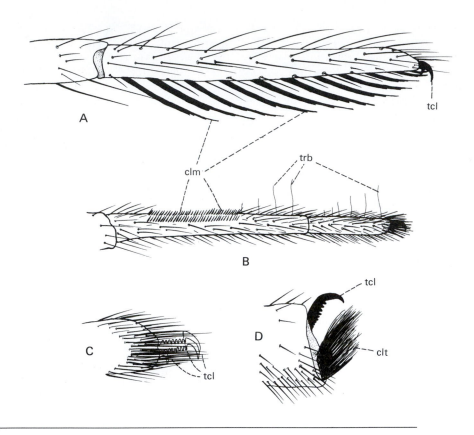

Figure 6–7. Leg characters of spiders. **A,** hind tarsus of *Theridion* (Theridìidae); **B,** hind tarsus of *Amauròbius* (Amaurobìidae); **C,** tip of tarsus of a lycosid; **D,** tip of a tarsus of a salticid. *clm,* calamistrum; *clt,* claw tuft; *tcl,* tarsal claws; *trb,* trichobothria.

containing a series of sheetlike leaves. A few spiders have a second pair of book lungs, the openings of which are located laterally behind the epigastric furrow. Spiders also have tracheae, and there is usually a single spiracle, located on the midventral line of the abdomen, anterior to the spinnerets (Figure 6–5B, spr_2). This spiracle is often difficult to see.

Most adult female spiders have a sclerotized structure, the epigynum, often somewhat conical in shape, at the genital opening (Figure 6–5B, *epg*). This structure varies considerably in different species and often provides good taxonomic characters. At the posterior end of the abdomen on the ventral side are six (rarely two or four) fingerlike structures, the spinnerets, from which the silk of the spider is spun (Figures 6–5B, *spn,* and 6–8B–E). At the apex of each spinneret are many (sometimes a hundred or more) spinning tubes from which the silk emerges. Above (posterior to) the spinnerets is a small, variously developed tubercle, the anal tubercle, in which the anus is located. A few families of spiders (those in the section Cribellàtae) have a sievelike structure,

called the cribellum, just anterior to the spinnerets (Figure 6–8B, *crb*); this is an accessory silk-spinning organ. A few spiders that lack a cribellum have a small conical appendage, the colulus, between the bases of the anterior spinnerets. The function of this structure is not known.

The two sexes of a spider often differ considerably in size, with the female being larger than the male. Mating is often preceded by a more or less elaborate courtship performance, which may involve a variety of body or pedipalp movements or stridulation, and in some cases the male may present the female with a fly or some other prey before mating. Males do not usually live long after mating, and in a few cases (for example, the widow spiders) the male may be killed and eaten by the female after mating.

Spider eggs are generally laid in a silken sac. These sacs vary in their construction and are deposited in all sorts of places. Some are attached to leaves or twigs or bark; some are placed in crevices; some are placed in or near the web; and some are carried about by the female. Some species make several egg sacs. The number of eggs in a sac varies in different species, but in some cases it may be as many as several hundred. The eggs usually hatch soon after they are laid, but if the eggs are laid in the fall the young spiders may remain in the sac until the following spring. The young spiders are sometimes cannibalistic, and fewer young may escape than there were eggs originally.

Spiders undergo very little metamorphosis during their development. When hatched, they usually look like miniature adults. If legs are lost during development, they can usually be regenerated. Spiders generally molt from 4 to 12 times during their growth to maturity. Female Orthógnatha continue to molt once or twice a year as long as they live. Most spiders live 1 to 2 years, but the Orthógnatha often take several years to mature, and some females may live as long as 20 years.

All spiders are predaceous and feed mainly on insects. Some of the larger spiders may occasionally feed on small vertebrates. The prey is usually killed by the poison injected into it by the bite of the spider. Different spiders capture their prey in different ways. The wolf spiders and jumping spiders forage for and pounce on their prey. Many crab spiders lie in wait for their prey on flowers, feeding on bees, flies, and other insects that frequent the flowers. The majority of spiders capture their prey in nets or webs.

A few spiders are commensals; that is, they live in the web of a larger spider and feed on small insects not eaten by the larger spider.

Various types of silk are spun by spiders. Many spin a strand of silk almost wherever they go, the strand serving as a dragline. Some silk is covered with minute drops of a very sticky material to which the spider's victims stick. In an orb web, the spiral strands are viscous, and the radiating strands are simple silk. Many spiders wrap up in silk the insects caught in their web. Some silk, such as that of the hackled-band spiders, consists of flattened strands.

The webs built by spiders are of several principal types. Each species of spider constructs a characteristic web that is often as distinctive as the spider itself. The house spider and others build irregular nets, with the strands of silk extending in almost every direction. The sheet-web spiders make a closely woven, sheetlike, and usually horizontal web. The web of the funnel-web spiders is somewhat sheetlike, but is shaped like a funnel. Many spiders build orb webs consisting of radiating and spiral strands. The trap-door spiders and some of the wolf spiders construct tunnels. Some spiders construct leaf nests. Many spiders have a retreat of some sort close to or adjoining the web. The spider spends most of its time in this retreat and comes out onto the web when it has caught something. The stimulus

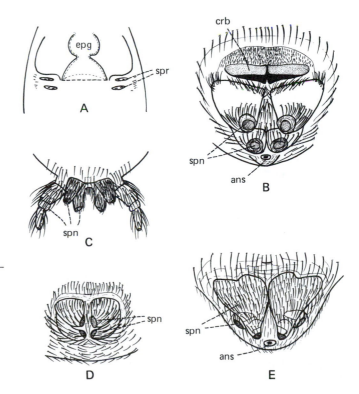

Figure 6–8. Abdominal characters of spiders. **A,** base of abdomen of *Dýsdera* (Dysdéridae), showing the two pairs of spiracles; **B–E,** spinnerets, ventral view; **B,** *Amauróbius* (Amaurobìidae); **C,** *Tegenària* (Agelènidae); **D,** *Lycòsa* (Lycòsidae); **E,** *Therídion* (Theridìidae). *ans,* anus; *crb,* cribellum; *epg,* epigynum; *spn,* spinnerets; *spr,* spiracle.

that brings out the spider is apparently the vibration of the web caused by the insect that is caught. A vibrating tuning fork held against the web will usually produce the same reaction by the spider.

Although spiders do not have wings, small ones often "fly." They get on top of a rock or post and spin out some silk. The wind catches the silk, and off "flies" the spider. If the wind is particularly strong, the silk may be torn off the spider. When many spiders are trying to fly on a windy day, large quantities of this silk ("gossamer") may be blown over the landscape. This flying of spiders is sometimes called "ballooning" or "parachuting," and it is usually young spiders that are involved.

Spiders play an important role in the general economy of nature, for they are quite numerous and their predatory habits serve to keep the numbers of many other animals, particularly insects, in check. They are in turn preyed upon by various other animals, particularly wasps. Spider silk was once used in the preparation of cross hairs in certain optical instruments. Many people dislike having spiders in the house because their webs are a nuisance (or simply because they dislike spiders), but spiders do not damage anything in the house and they may perform a service by destroying noxious insects. As we pointed out previously, the venomous nature of spiders is generally greatly exaggerated. Most spiders will not bite if handled carefully.

Classification of Spiders. North American spiders are divided into two suborders, the Orthógnatha and the Labidógnatha, primarily on the basis of the structure of the chelicerae. The order Labidógnatha is divided into two sections, the Cribellàtae and the Ecribellàtae. The Cribellàtae have a cribellum and calamistrum, which are lacking in the Ecribellàtae. There are differences of opinion regarding the number of families recognized and in some cases the names used for them. A synopsis of North American spiders, as followed in this book, is given here, with other names and arrangements in parentheses. Families marked with an asterisk are relatively rare or are not likely to be encountered by the general collector.

Suborder Orthógnatha (Avicularìoidea)—mygalomorphs: tarantulas and their relatives
    Ctenìzidae—trap-door spiders
    Theraphòsidae (Avicularìidae)—tarantulas
    *Antrodiaètidae (Theraphòsidae in part: Brachybothriìnae)—folding-door tarantulas
    *Mecicobothrìidae (Theraphòsidae in part: Hexurìnae)—sheet-web tarantulas

    *Diplùridae (Theraphòsidae in part)—funnel-web tarantulas
    Atýpidae—purse-web spiders
Suborder Labidógnatha (Argiopòidea)—true spiders
  Section Cribellàtae—hackled-band spiders
    *Hypochìlidae—four-lunged spiders
    *Oecobìidae—oecobiid spiders
    *Filistátidae—filistatid spiders
    *Zorópsidae—zoropsid spiders
    Amaurobìidae (Dictỳnidae in part)—white-eyed spiders
    *Dinòpidae (Deinòpidae)—ogre-faced spiders
    Ulobòridae—uloborid spiders
    Dictỳnidae—hackled-band weavers
  Section Ecribellàtae—plain-thread weavers
    *Dysdéridae—dysderid six-eyed spiders
    *Caponìidae—caponiid spiders
    Segestrìidae (Dysdéridae in part)—segestriid six-eyed spiders
    *Oonópidae—minute jumping spiders
    Scytòdidae—spitting spiders
    Diguètidae (Scytòdidae in part)—diguetid six-eyed spiders
    *Plectreùridae (Scytòdidae in part—plectreurid spiders
    Loxoscélidae (Scytòdidae in part)—recluse spiders
    *Leptonètidae—cave spiders
    *Prodidómidae—prodidomid spiders
    Gnaphòsidae (Drassòdidae, Drássidae)—hunting spiders
    *Zodarìidae—zodariid spiders
    *Homalonýchidae (Zodarìidae in part)—homalonychid spiders
    *Hersilìidae (Zodarìidae in part)—hersiliid spiders
    Phólcidae—long-legged or cellar spiders
    Theridìidae—comb-footed spiders
    Linyphìidae—sheet-web spiders
    Erigónidae (Micryphántidae; Linyphìidae in part)—dwarf spiders
    Mimètidae—spider-hunting spiders
    Aranèidae (Argiópidae, Epeìridae)—orb weavers
    Theridiosomátidae (Aranèidae in part)—ray spiders
    Tetragnáthidae (Aranèidae in part)—long-jawed orb weavers
    Thomísidae—crab spiders
    *Selenópidae—selenopid crab spiders
    Heteropódidae (Sparássidae)—giant crab spiders
    Cténidae—wandering spiders
    Clubiónidae—two-clawed hunting spiders or sac spiders
    Anyphaènidae (Clubiónidae in part)—anyphaenid spiders

Agelènidae (Agalènidae)—grass or funnel-web
    spiders
Hahnìidae (Agelènidae in part)—hahniid sheet-
    web spiders
Pisáuridae—nursery-web and fishing spiders

Lycòsidae—wolf or ground spiders
Oxyòpidae—lynx spiders
*Lyssománidae—lyssomanid spiders
Saltícidae (Áttidae)—jumping spiders

Key to the Families of Spiders

Groups in this key marked with an asterisk are relatively rare, or are unlikely to be encountered by the general collector.

1.	Fangs of the chelicerae moving vertically or forward and backward, parallel to the median plane of the body; 2 pairs of book lungs; no cribellum; stout-bodied spiders, mostly western and tropical (suborder Orthógnatha) **2**	
1'.	Fangs of the chelicerae moving laterally or in and out; usually only 1 pair of book lungs (if 2, then a cribellum is present) (suborder Labidógnatha) **7**	
2(1).	Anal tubercle well separated from spinnerets; abdomen with 1–3 sclerotized terga **3**	
2'.	Anal tubercle immediately adjacent to spinnerets; abdomen without sclerotized terga **5**	
3(2).	Endites well developed; labium fused to sternum; carapace with a transverse pit; widely distributed ....**Atýpidae**	p. 118
3'.	Endites weakly developed; labium not fused to sternum; carapace with a longitudinal pit or groove; mostly western United States **4***	
4(3').	Chelicerae with a group of apical teeth on mesal margin; labium about as long as wide; 4 spinnerets, last segment of posterior pair a little longer than preceding segment ....**Antrodiaètidae***	p. 118
4'.	Chelicerae without such teeth on mesal margin; labium much wider than long; usually 6 spinnerets, last segment of posterior pair nearly twice as long as preceding segment ....**Mecicobothrìidae***	p. 118
5(2').	Tarsi with 2 claws and with claw tufts; large (40 mm or more in length), robust, hairy spiders, occurring in the South and West ....**Theraphòsidae**	p. 118
5'.	Tarsi with 3 claws and without claw tufts; length less than 30 mm **6**	
6(5').	Chelicerae with group of apical teeth on mesal margin; anterior portion of carapace higher than posterior portion; anterior spinnerets separated by less than their own length; basal segment of posterior spinnerets as long as or longer than remaining segments combined; length 15–28 mm ....**Ctenìzidae**	p. 117
6'.	Chelicerae without such teeth on mesal margin; carapace flattened, anterior portion no higher than posterior portion; anterior spinnerets separated by at least their own length; the 3 segments of posterior spinnerets of about equal length; length about 15 mm ....**Diplùridae***	p. 118
7(1').	With cribellum in front of spinnerets (Figure 6–8B, *crb*) and calamistrum on hind metatarsi (Figure 6–7B, *clm*); if cribellum and calamistrum are rudimentary (males of *Filistàta*), eyes are all on raised tubercle and pedipalps longer than body (section Cribellàtae) **8**	
7'.	With neither cribellum nor calamistrum; eyes and pedipalps not as above (section Ecribellàtae) **15**	

8(7). With 2 pairs of book lungs, posterior pair about halfway between epigastric furrow and spinnerets; length 5–14 mm; in southern mountains . . . .**Hypochìlidae*** p. 118

8'. With 1 pair of book lungs **9**

9(8'). Anal tubercle large, 2-segmented, fringed with long hairs; 8 eyes in compact group, posterior median eyes triangular or irregular in shape; length 2–4 mm . . . .**Oecobìidae** p. 118

9'. Anal tubercle small, unsegmented, without conspicuous fringe of hairs; arrangement of eyes variable, posterior median eyes round **10**

10(9'). Tarsi with 2 claws and with claw tufts; cribellum divided; eyes in 2 rows; rare southwestern spiders . . . .**Zorópsidae*** p. 118

10'. Tarsi with 3 claws and usually without claw tufts; cribellum and eyes variable **11**

11(10'). Chelicerae fused together at base, each with apical tooth which with the fang forms a sort of claw; tracheal spiracle considerably anterior to spinnerets; labium fused to sternum; the 8 eyes in a compact group; length 9–18 mm; southern United States . . . .**Filistátidae*** p. 118

11'. Chelicerae not fused together at base, and without apical tooth; tracheal spiracle close to spinnerets; labium not fused to sternum **12**

12(11'). Eight eyes, all light colored (Figure 6–6E); tarsi with trichobothria; cribellum divided; length 4.5–12.0 mm . . . .**Amauróbìidae** p. 118

12'. Six or 8 eyes; if 8, then some or all are dark colored; tarsi usually without trichobothria; cribellum divided or undivided; length 1.7–8.0 mm **13**

13(12'). Eight eyes, all dark colored **14**

13'. Either 8 eyes and only anterior median ones dark, or 6 eyes and all pearly white; cribellum undivided; length 1.7–6.0 mm . . . .**Dictỳnidae** p. 118

14(13). Femora with trichobothria; 8 eyes, in 2 recurved rows; cribellum divided; length 2.4–8.0 mm . . . .**Ulobòridae** p. 118

14'. Femora without trichobothria; eyes in 2 or 3 rows, first row of 4 eyes; posterior eyes often large . . . .**Dinòpidae*** p. 118

15(7'). One pair of book lungs and not more than 1 pair of tracheal spiracles; usually 6 or 8 eyes **16**

15'. Book lungs lacking, and with 2 pairs of tracheal spiracles; 2 eyes; rare southwestern spiders . . . .**Caponìidae*** p. 119

16(15). A pair of spiracles behind book lungs; 6 eyes or none **17**

16'. A single spiracle (or none) between epigastric furrow and spinnerets; 6 or 8 eyes **19**

17(16). Median eyes larger than lateral ones; pair of tracheal spiracles inconspicuous; minute spiders, about 1 mm in length . . . .**Oonópidae*** p. 119

17'. Median eyes not larger than lateral ones (Figure 6–6F); the pair of tracheal spiracles conspicuous; length 7–17 mm **18**

18(17'). Third pair of legs directed backward; sternum with lateral extensions between coxae; cephalothorax and legs reddish brown, abdomen dirty white; length 12–13 mm; eastern United States . . . .**Dysdéridae*** p. 119

18'. Third pair of legs directed forward; sternum without lateral extensions between coxae; color brownish; length 7–10 mm; widely distributed. . . . .**Segestrìidae** p. 119

19(16').	Tibiae and metatarsi of first and second legs with series of long spines and series of shorter spines between each 2 long ones; length 5–8 mm. ....**Mimètidae**

p. 120

19'.	Spines on first and second tibiae and metatarsi not as above **20**
20(19').	The 6 spinnerets about equal in size; widely distributed **21**
20'.	The 2 anterior spinnerets large, 2 posterior pairs small (*Lùtica*, recorded from Oregon, and *Zodàrion*, from Pennsylvania) ....**Zodariidae***

p. 119

21(20)	Chelicerae fused together at base, each with apical tooth which with the fang forms a sort of claw **22**
21'.	Chelicerae not fused together at base, and without apical tooth **26**
22(21).	Tarsi usually long, flexible, and with many pseudosegments; spiracles lacking; eyes in 2 groups of 3 each, with or without pair of smaller eyes between groups (Figure 6–6H); labium broader than long; length 2–6 mm ....**Phólcidae**

p. 120

22'.	Tarsi not greatly elongated, without pseudosegments; spiracle present, at least one-sixth the distance from the epigastric furrow to spinnerets; eyes not as above; labium longer than broad; length variable; mostly western species **23**
23(22').	Eight eyes, in 2 rows; labium not fused to sternum; 3 tarsal claws; about 12.5 mm in length; western and southwestern United States ......**Plectreùridae***

p. 119

23'.	Six eyes, in three groups of 2 each (Figure 6–6I); labium fused to sternum; 2 or 3 tarsal claws; length variable **24**
24(23').	Anterior row of eyes in nearly straight line; carapace only two-thirds as wide as long; 3 tarsal claws; length 5.6–9.5 mm; western United States. ....**Diguètidae***

p. 119

24'.	Median pair of eyes distinctly anterior to lateral eyes; carapace more than two-thirds as wide as long; 2 or 3 tarsal claws; length 3.5–15.0 mm; widely distributed **25**
25(24').	Carapace flat, with conspicuous median furrow in posterior portion; sternum pointed posteriorly; tarsi with 2 claws; length 6.0–8.0 mm; mostly southern and western United States. ....**Loxoscélidae**

p. 119

25'.	Carapace much arched posteriorly and without conspicuous median furrow; sternum rounded posteriorly; tarsi with 3 claws; length 3.5–15.0 mm; widely distributed ....**Scytòdidae**

p. 119

26(21').	Tarsi with 2 claws, with or without claw tufts **27**
26'.	Tarsi with 3 claws, without claw tufts (Figure 6–7C); spurious claws sometimes present **39**
27(26).	Tracheal spiracles well anterior to spinnerets, at least one-third the distance to epigastric furrow ....**Anyphaènidae**

p. 122

27'.	Tracheal spiracle immediately in front of spinnerets **28**
28(27').	Claw tufts present (Figure 6–7D) **29**
28'.	Claw tufts absent **38**
29(28).	Eight eyes in 2 rows, 6 in front row, the posterior pair far apart; body very flat, legs laterograde, i.e., turned so that morphological dorsal surface is posterior and anterior surface appears to be dorsal, fitted for running laterally ....**Selenópidae***

p. 122

29'.	Eyes in 2–4 rows, only 2 or 4 eyes in first row; legs variable **30**
30(29').	Anterior median eyes dark colored, others light colored **31**

30'.   All eyes dark colored **32**

31(30).   Eyes in 2 rows of 4 each; tarsi with dense row of short hairs beneath; anterior
                 spinnerets not long and brushlike; chelicerae of normal size; length 4–15
                 mm; widely distributed . . . .**Gnaphòsidae**   p. 119

31'.   Eyes in 3 rows (4–2–2); tarsi (except possibly front ones) without dense row of
                 short hairs beneath; anterior spinnerets long and brushlike; chelicerae very
                 large; southern United States . . . .**Prodidómidae***   p. 119

32(30').   Hind coxae widely separated by the rounded sternum; a pair of spurious claws
                 present; southwestern United States . . . .**Homalonýchidae***   p. 120

32'.   Hind coxae approximated, sternum oval or elongate; no spurious claws; widely
                 distributed **33**

33(32').   At least 2 anterior pairs of legs laterograde (see couplet 29) **34**

33'.   Legs normal, not laterograde **35**

34(33).   Length 20 mm or more; colulus absent; apex of metatarsi with soft trilobate
                 membrane; southern United States . . . .**Heteropódidae**   p. 122

34'.   Length 15 mm or less; colulus present but small; apex of metatarsi sclerotized,
                 without trilobate membrane; widely distributed . . . .**Thomísidae**   p. 121

35(33').   Eyes in 4 rows of 2 each, anterior eyes much larger than others, those of third
                 row minute; chelicerae elongate and divergent; southern and southwestern
                 United States . . . .**Lyssománidae***   p. 122

35'.   Eyes in 2 or 3 rows; chelicerae usually not as above; widely distributed **36**

36(35').   Eyes in 3 rows (4–2–2), anterior median eyes much larger than others (Figure
                 6–6B); stocky spiders with short legs, often with scales and hairs of bright
                 colors and often iridescent . . . .**Saltícidae**   p. 122

36'.   Eyes not as above **37**

37(36').   Eyes in 2 rows of 4 each; length 3–15 mm . . . .**Clubiónidae**   p. 122

37'.   Eyes in 3 rows (usually 2–4–2), eyes of first row smaller than those of second
                 row; length 3.5–8.0 mm . . . .**Ctènidae**   p. 122

38(28').   At least first 2 pairs of legs laterograde (see couplet 29) . . . .**Thomísidae**   p. 121

38'.   Legs not laterograde, but fitted for running forward . . . .**Zodariidae***   p. 119

39(26').   Spinnerets in more or less transverse row; tracheal spiracle well in front of
                 spinnerets, at least one-third distance to epigastric furrow; length 3.5 mm
                 or less . . . .**Hahniidae**   p. 122

39'.   Spinnerets not in single transverse row (Figure 6–8C–E); size and location of
                 tracheal spiracles variable **40**

40(39').   Hind tarsi with ventral row of curved serrated bristles forming comb (Figure
                 6–7A); spiders hanging upside down in irregular webs . . . .**Theridiidae**   p. 120

40'.   Hind tarsi without such a row of bristles **41**

41(40').   Eyes in hexagonal group (Figure 6–6A); abdomen pointed apically (Figure
                 6–12A); legs with prominent spines; length 4–20 mm . . . .**Oxyòpidae**   p. 122

41'.   Eyes not as above; abdomen shape and leg spines variable **42**

42(41').   Tarsi with at least 1 pair of spurious claws and usually without trichobothria;
                 labium usually rebordered (with a thickened anterior edge) **43**

42'.   Tarsi without spurious claws and usually with trichobothria; labium not
                 rebordered **48**

43(42).   Labium rebordered; 8 eyes (rarely 6 or none) **44**

43'. Labium not rebordered; 6 eyes in compact group ....**Leptonètidae*** p. 119

44(43). All eyes the same color; clypeus usually narrower than height of median ocular area (area with the 4 median eyes); mostly weavers of orb webs **45**

44'. All eyes not the same color; clypeus usually as wide as or wider than median ocular area; mostly not building orb webs **46**

45(44). Femora with trichobothria (at least 1 at base of first and second femora); boss on chelicera rudimentary or absent; chelicerae usually large and powerful; length 3.5–9.0 mm ....**Tetragnáthidae** p. 121

45'. Femora without trichobothria; boss on chelicerae usually well developed; length 1.5–30 mm ....**Aranèidae** p. 120

46(44'). Sternum broadly truncate posteriorly; front femora much thicker than hind femora; legs without spines; chelicerae without stridulating ridges on outer surface; length 1.6–2.7 mm ....**Theridiosomátidae** p. 121

46'. Without above combination of characters **47**

47(46'). Pedipalps of females usually with a claw, those of male without apophysis (a subapical clawlike process); hind tibiae usually with 2 dorsal spines or bristles; length 1.5–8.0 mm; living in sheet webs ....**Linyphìidae** p. 120

47'. Pedipalps of female without claw, those of male with at least 1 apophysis; hind tibiae with single dorsal spine or bristle, or none; length usually less than 2 mm; usually living in debris ....**Erigónidae** p. 120

48(42'). Chelicerae with distinct boss **49**

48'. Chelicerae without boss ....**Hersilìidae*** p. 120

49(48). Tarsi with single row of trichobothria that increase in length distally; trochanters not notched; hind spinnerets often very long (Figure 6–8C); spiders living in funnel webs. ....**Agelènidae** p. 122

49'. Tarsi with numerous trichobothria, irregularly distributed; trochanters with curved notch at distal end on ventral side; hind spinnerets not particularly lengthened (Figure 6–8D); spiders not generally building webs **50**

50(49'). Eyes in 3 rows (4–2–2), those in middle row larger than others (Figure 6–6C); median claw with 1 tooth or none; anterior part of lorum (plate on dorsal side of abdominal pedicel) rounded behind, fitted into notch of posterior piece; body hairs usually simple; length 2.5–35.0 mm; egg sac carried attached to spinnerets, young carried on abdomen of mother ......**Lycòsidae** p. 122

50'. Eyes in 2 rows, the posterior row slightly recurved, the median eyes in second row little if any larger than others; median claw with 2 or 3 teeth; anterior piece of lorum with posterior notch into which posterior piece fits or transverse suture between the 2 pieces; body with plumose hairs; length 2–26 mm; egg sac held under cephalothorax, young not carried by mother ....**Pisáuridae** p. 122

SUBORDER **Orthógnatha**—Mygalomorphs: These spiders have large and powerful chelicerae that move in a plane more or less parallel to the median sagittal plane of the body. Most species are heavy-bodied and stout-legged. This group is largely tropical, but about 80 species occur in North America. Most of them occur in the South and Southwest, but a few occur as far north as Massachusetts and southeastern Alaska.

Family **Ctenizidae**—Trap-Door Spiders: These spiders are so called because they construct tunnels in the ground that are closed by a door hinged with silk. The door fits snugly and is usually camouflaged on the outside. The tunnels may be simple or branched, or they may contain side chambers that are closed off from the main tunnel by hinged doors. These spiders spend most of their time in the tunnels. When they feel prey passing overhead, they rush out, capture the prey, and take it down into the tunnel. These spiders occur in the South and West.

Family **Theraphòsidae**—Tarantulas: This group includes our largest spiders, some of which have a body about the size of one's thumb. They feed chiefly on insects, but may occasionally take small vertebrates. These spiders are often feared, but the U.S. species are actually less venomous than the much smaller black widow and the brown recluse. Some species have a dense covering of special hairs on the opisthosoma that cause intense skin irritation in humans; the effect is apparently mechanical and not chemical. Tarantulas are largely nocturnal, hiding during the day in various protected places. They occur in the West and Southwest.

Family **Antrodiaètidae**—Folding-Door Tarantulas: This is a small but widely distributed group whose members live in burrows in the ground. The burrows are closed by doors that meet in the middle of the opening. These are small mygalomorphs, with a body length of about 15 mm.

Family **Mecicobothrìidae**—Sheet-Web Tarantulas: Members of this group and the next can usually be recognized by the long spinnerets, which may be more than half the length of the opisthosoma. Most of these spiders have six spinnerets, while the Diplùridae have only four. *Microhexùra*, which occurs in the Pacific Northwest and in the Carolinas, has only four spinnerets. The sheet-web tarantulas occur chiefly along the Pacific Coast and construct webs similar to those of the funnel-web tarantulas.

Family **Diplùridae**—Funnel-Web Tarantulas: The web of one of these spiders is a sheet of silk, usually in the roots at the base of a tree or in rocks, with a tubular retreat at one side where the spider hides. The prey is entangled in the sheet of silk. American species occur in the West.

Family **Atýpidae**—Purse-Web Spiders: These spiders construct tubes of silk at the base of a tree, the tubes extending from a little way into the ground to about 150 mm above ground, and camouflage them with debris. If an insect lands on this tube, the spider bites through the tube, grabs the insect, and pulls it into the tube. These spiders are 10–30 mm in length and occur in the eastern states, extending as far north as Wisconsin and New England.

SUBORDER **Labidógnatha:** This group includes the vast majority of North American spiders. They differ from the Orthógnatha in having chelicerae

that move laterally, or in and out, and they are generally smaller. The chelicerae usually extend downward from the front of the prosoma, but in a few groups are angled forward. This suborder is divided into two sections, the Cribellàtae and the Ecribellàtae, on the basis of the presence or absence of a cribellum.

SECTION **Cribellàtae**—Hackled-Band Spiders: These spiders have a cribellum in front of the spinnerets (Figure 6–8B, *crb*) and a calamistrum (Figure 6–7B, *clm*). Their webs contain ribbonlike bands of silk, but the ribbonlike nature of these bands is usually visible only with considerable magnification.

Family **Hypochìlidae**—Four-Lunged Spiders: These spiders are so called because they have two pairs of book lungs (the Orthógnatha also have two pairs of book lungs). They make irregular webs on the underside of overhanging ledges, usually along streams. Most of them are brownish in color, have very long legs, are 5–14 mm in length, and occur in the mountains in the southeastern states.

Family **Oecobìidae:** These are tiny spiders, 2–4 mm in length, that make small flat webs over cracks in walls and on leaves. They are widely distributed and sometimes get into houses.

Family **Filistátidae:** These spiders live in tubes in wall crevices and similar places and have strands of silk radiating from the mouth of the tube. They occur from the southeastern states west to California.

Family **Zorópsidae:** These are rare spiders occurring in the Southwest; little is known of their habits.

Family **Amaurobìidae**—White-Eyed Spiders: These spiders construct irregular webs under stones, in rock crevices, and in debris. Most spiders have all or most of the eyes dark colored, but the amaurobiids have all eight eyes light colored. These spiders are widely distributed.

Family **Dinòpidae**—Ogre-Faced Spiders: These spiders are so called because two of their eight eyes are very large. The body is elongate, and the legs are relatively long. The dinopids occur in the southwestern states, but are quite rare.

Family **Ulobòridae:** These spiders spin orb webs, or sections of orbs, similar to those of the Aranèidae and related families. The spiral thread of their webs is a hackled (flat) band of silk. The uloborids are the only North American group of spiders that lack venom glands. These spiders are widely distributed, but are not common.

Family **Dictỳnidae**—Hackled-Band Weavers: This is the largest family of the cribellates, and its members are small (mostly less than 5 mm in length). These spiders construct irregular webs, usually at the tips of plants, but sometimes in crevices or on the ground. They are widely distributed and fairly common.

SECTION **Ecribellàtae**—Plain-Thread Weavers: These spiders lack a cribellum and a calamistrum and do not spin bandlike strands of silk. This group includes the majority of North American spiders.

Family **Dysdéridae**—Dysderid Six-Eyed Spiders: These spiders have six eyes, which are nearly contiguous and form an incomplete oval (two on each side and two posteriorly). They have two pairs of spiracles at the base of the abdomen (Figure 6–8A). The coxae of the two anterior pairs of legs are longer and thinner than those of the two posterior pairs. These spiders live under bark or stones, where they construct a retreat of silk, and they hunt prey from this retreat. The dysderids occur in the East, from New England to Nebraska and south to Georgia.

Family **Caponiidae**: The caponiids are rare spiders occurring in the Southwest. They are unique in having only two eyes. They occur in litter and under stones.

Family **Segestriidae**: These spiders are similar to the dysderids, but have the three anterior pairs of legs directed forward and the hind pair directed backward (the third pair is directed backward in dysderids). Segestriids construct tubular retreats in crevices, under bark and stones, and in similar situations.

Family **Oonópidae**—Minute Jumping Spiders: These spiders are only about a millimeter in length and are commonly found in buildings. They can generally be recognized by their jumping habits (a few do not jump).

Family **Scytòdidae**—Spitting Spiders: These spiders do not construct snares, but capture their prey by spitting out a mucilaginous substance that engulfs the prey and fastens it to the substrate. They frequently occur in the dark corners of buildings. The prosoma is somewhat rounded (dorsal view), and the legs are slender.

Family **Diguètidae**—Diguetid Six-Eyed Spiders: These spiders resemble the scytodids but have the prosoma more elongate, and the anterior row of eyes is nearly a straight line. Diguetids live in silken tubes attached to a series of overlapping silken disks that are arranged like shingles on a roof and attached to vegetation. A few members of this group occur in the Southwest.

Family **Plectreùridae**: These spiders resemble the scytodids, but they have eight eyes, the prosoma is more elongate, and the legs are thicker. They occur in the West and Southwest and are usually found under stones.

Family **Loxoscélidae**—Recluse Spiders: These are small, light-colored spiders, 6–10 mm in length, which have only six eyes (arranged in three widely separated dyads, as in the Scytòtidae and Diguètidae; see Figure 6–6I) and have chelicerae fused together at the base. The group is widely distributed but is more common in the South. Some species are quite venomous. The brown recluse spider, *Loxósceles reclùsa* Gertsch and Mulaik, is a venomous species occurring only in the East. It varies in color from grayish brown to deep reddish brown and has a dark fiddle-shaped mark on the prosoma (Figure 6–9). It usually occurs out of doors in sheltered places, but may sometimes occur indoors in basements, attics, and barns. It frequently occurs in clothing left hanging in a barn or outbuilding.

Family **Leptonètidae**—Cave Spiders: The leptonetids are small (1–3 mm in length), six-eyed, long-legged spiders, most of which live in caves. A few live in debris or under rocks.

Family **Prodidómidae**: The prodidomids are small spiders (2–4 mm in length) with long spreading chelicerae, that live under stones in dry areas in the southern states. They are quite rare.

Family **Gnaphòsidae**—Hunting Spiders: This is a fairly large group of small, dark-colored spiders, 4–15 mm in length, that construct a tubular retreat under stones and in debris and hunt at night from this retreat. Most species are uniformly brown or black, but some have a pattern of light markings. About 250 species occur in North America, and they are widely distributed.

Family **Zodariidae**: This group includes four species in the genus *Lùtica*, which occur in restricted coastal and island habitats in southern California.

Figure 6–9. Brown recluse spider, *Loxósceles reclùsa* Gertsch and Mulaik. (Courtesy of U.S. Public Health Service.)

These large, whitish spiders have the small posterior and median spinnerets concealed beneath the large anterior pair. These spiders bury themselves in sand, coming to the surface at night to wait for prey. In addition, a species of *Zodàrion* has been found in Pennsylvania.

Family **Homalonýchidae:** This is a tropical group, one species of which is occasionally found in the Southwest. This spider is 16–18 mm in length and somewhat brownish in color, with a row of small dark spots along the sides of the body.

Family **Hersiliidae:** One species in this tropical group, *Tàma mexicàna* (Cambridge), has been reported from southern Texas. A feature of this group is the very long spinnerets.

Family **Phólcidae**—Long-Legged or Cellar Spiders: These are small spiders, 2–6 mm in length, with very long and slender legs. Except for the body shape (opisthosoma petiolate, and rounded or elongate), they might be mistaken for daddy-longlegs. Most species are light-colored, gray or brown. Their webs, which are built in cellars and other dark places, are sheetlike or irregular, and the spider usually hangs upside down under the web. The female carries the egg sac in her chelicerae.

Family **Theridíidae**—Comb-Footed Spiders: This is a large (more than 200 North American species) and widespread group whose webs are an irregular network in which the spider usually hangs upside down. The webs are built in various protected places, sometimes in buildings. The prosoma is small, the opisthosoma large and rounded (some have the opisthosoma oddly shaped), and the legs usually bent. The common name of this group is derived from the comb of serrated bristles on the hind tarsi (Figure 6–7A). These combs are used in wrapping the prey in silk.

This group includes the widow spiders (*Latrodéctus*), which are quite venomous. Three species of *Latrodéctus* occur in the United States: *L. máctans* (Fabricius), which occurs in the eastern states north to southern New England; *L. variòlus* Walckenaer, which occurs in the eastern states north into southeastern Canada; and *L. hésperus* (Chamberlin and Ivie), which is the only species occurring in the West and ranges north into southwestern Canada. The widows are probably the most venomous spiders in the United States; their bite is sometimes fatal. The females are about 12 mm in length and shining black with reddish orange markings on the ventral side of the opisthosoma. This marking is shaped like an hourglass in *máctans* and *hésperus* and consists of two transverse bars in *variòlus*. The male, which is seen less often than the female, is marked like the female in *máctans* and *variòlus* but also has four

reddish orange stripes on the sides of the opisthosoma. The male of *L. hésperus* has a color pattern quite different from that of the female: the dorsum of the opisthosoma has a base color of greenish gray, with light tan bands and an orange middorsal line. These spiders get the name "widow" from the fact that the male is often (but not always) killed by the female after mating. Widow spiders are found under stones, about stumps, in holes in the ground, about outbuildings, and in similar places. Though these spiders are quite venomous, they seldom bite people. When disturbed they are much more likely to attempt to escape than to attack the intruder. The widow spiders are widely distributed over the United States and Canada, but are probably more abundant in the southern states.

This family includes many other common spiders, most of which occur out of doors. A common species occurring indoors, in the corners of rooms and in the angles of windows, is the house spider, *Achaearànea tepidariòrum* (Koch).

Family **Linyphìidae**—Sheet-Web Spiders: This is a large group of small spiders, mostly less than 7 mm in length, that are generally fairly common but are seldom noticed because of their small size. The opisthosoma is more elongate than in the theridiids and is usually brightly patterned. The webs of many of these spiders are often conspicuous, particularly when covered with dew. They are flat and sheetlike, sometimes bowl-shaped or domelike, and usually have an irregular mesh around or above the sheetlike part. The webs are usually built in weeds and bushes, and the spider spends most of its time on the underside of the web. Many members of this group live in litter.

Family **Erigónidae**—Dwarf Spiders: This is one of the largest families of spiders (several hundred North American species), but its members are very small; most are less than 2 mm in length, and some are less than 1 mm. Dwarf spiders are sometimes abundant in leaf litter and debris, and some may be collected by sweeping vegetation. Most of these spiders make small sheet webs.

Family **Mimètidae**—Spider-Hunting Spiders: These spiders are similar to many of the orb weavers (Aranèidae) in general appearance, but can be recognized by the characteristic spination on the tibiae and metatarsi of the first two pairs of legs: the larger spines are separated by a row of smaller spines. These spiders do not construct webs, but appear to feed largely, if not entirely, on other spiders. They may attack a passing spider or attack one in its web.

Family **Aranèidae**—Orb Weavers: This is a large and widely distributed group, and nearly all its members construct an orb web. There is considerable

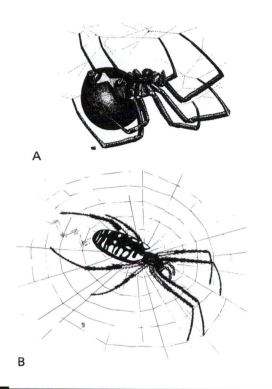

A

B

Figure 6–10. **A,** black widow spider, *Latrodéctus máctans* (Fabricus), female, hanging from its web; **B,** a garden spider, *Argiòpe aurántia* Lucas. (**A,** courtesy of Utah Agricultural Experiment Station.)

variation in size, color, and shape in this family, and the family is divided into five subfamilies.

Subfamily **Gasteracanthinae**—Spiny-Bellied Spiders: These small spiders are so called because of the spiny protuberances on the opisthosoma. They are usually found in woods, and their small orb webs are suspended between two trees a meter or two apart.

Subfamily **Nephilìnae**—Silk Spiders: These are so called because of the large amount and strength of their silk, which is sometimes used in the manufacture of fabrics. This group is largely tropical, but one species, *Néphila clávipes* (L.), is fairly common in the southern states. Females are about 22 mm in length, with the prosoma dark brown and the opisthosoma dark greenish with several pairs of small light spots, and there are conspicuous tufts of hairs on the femora and tibiae of the first, second, and fourth pairs of legs. Their webs are about a meter in diameter.

Subfamily **Metìnae:** This is a small group whose members live in caves, in wells, under ledges, and in similar places. Some species are brightly colored.

Subfamily **Argiopìnae**—Garden Spiders: Garden spiders are common in grassy or weedy areas. They

are often brightly colored, black and yellow, or black and red (Figure 6–10B). The web is constructed in grass or weeds and consists of a vertical orb with a dense net of silk extending through the middle. The spider rests head downward in the center of the web.

Subfamily **Araneìnae**—Typical Orb Weavers: This is the largest subfamily, and its members vary greatly in size and color.

Family **Theridiosomátidae**—Ray Spiders: These small spiders (less than 5 mm in length) are usually found near streams or other damp situations. The web is peculiar in that the radii unite in groups of three or four, and each group is connected to the center by a single thread. The web is drawn into a conical shape by a thread to a nearby twig, where it is held by the spider. When an insect gets into the web, the spider releases its line, allowing the web to spring back and entangle the insect. These spiders suspend their egg sacs on a stalk.

Family **Tetragnáthidae**—Long-Jawed Orb Weavers: These spiders have very long and protruding chelicerae, especially in the males. Most species are brownish in color and relatively long and slender, and the legs, especially the front pair, are very long. These spiders are usually found in marshy places.

Family **Thomísidae**—Crab Spiders: The crab spiders are somewhat crablike in shape and walk sideways or backward. The two anterior pairs of legs are usually stouter than the two posterior pairs (Figure 6–11). These spiders spin no webs, but forage for their prey or lie in ambush for it. Many species lie in wait for their prey on flowers and are able to capture flies or bees much larger than themselves. One of the most common species in this group is the goldenrod spider, *Misùmena vàtia* (Clerck), which is white or yellow with a red band on either side of the opistho-

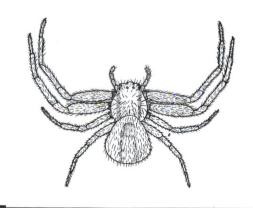

Figure 6–11. A crab spider, *Misùmenops* sp. (Thomísidae).

soma. This spider can change color (over a period of a few days), depending on the color of the flower.

Family **Selenópidae**—Selenopid Crab Spiders: These are tropical spiders of medium to large size that occur in the South and Southwest. They resemble thomisids, but are larger and flatter and have the six eyes in a single row. They occur under bark or rocks and sometimes enter houses.

Family **Heteropódidae**—Giant Crab Spiders: These spiders resemble the thomisids, but are larger (20–25 mm in length) and are largely confined to the southern states. In the South, they sometimes enter houses, where they feed on cockroaches. One species, *Heterópoda venatòria* (L.), is sometimes found in the North on shipments of bananas. A large spider found on bananas in the North is generally this species.

Family **Ctènidae**—Wandering Spiders: The wandering spiders are somewhat similar to the clubionids, but have the eyes in three rows instead of two. They do not construct webs, but wander over foliage or on the ground in search of prey. This group is chiefly tropical, and U.S. species occur principally in the southern states.

Family **Clubiónidae**—Two-Clawed Hunting Spiders: The clubionids are common spiders, 3–15 mm in length, which occur on foliage or on the ground. They do not spin webs for the capture of prey, but construct a tubular retreat under stones or in rolled-up leaves or folds of grasses. One species, *Chiracánthium inclùsum* (Hentz), can inflict an extremely painful bite. This spider is about 8 or 9 mm in length, is pale yellow or greenish with dark brown chelicerae, and occurs throughout the United States. Some members of this family are rather antlike in appearance.

Family **Anyphaènidae**: These are similar to the clubionids, but have the tracheal spiracle well anterior to the spinnerets, and the hairs of the claw tufts are somewhat flattened. They construct retreats of silken tubes in high weeds and shrubs and wander over foliage in search of prey.

Family **Agelènidae**—Grass and Funnel-Web Spiders: This is a large group (about 250 species in North America) of common spiders that build sheetlike webs in grass, under rocks or boards, and in debris. The webs of the larger species are somewhat funnel-shaped, with a tubular retreat leading down into the material in which the web is built. When an insect crosses the web, the spider dashes out, grabs the insect, and carries it back into the tubular retreat. Many of the smaller species construct a sheet web without a retreat. Agelenid sheet webs are most easily distinguished from those of linyphiids and erigonids by the fact that the agelenid spiders stand upright on the dorsal surface of the webs, while the

linyphiids and erigonids hang inverted under the sheet. The abundance of these spiders is most evident in early morning when the webs are covered with dew.

Family **Hahnìidae**—Hahniid Sheet-Web Spiders: The hahniids are small spiders, 1.5–3.2 mm in length, with the spinnerets in a single transverse row. They construct webs similar to those of the Agelènidae, without the funnellike retreat. The webs are very delicate and rarely seen unless covered with dew.

Family **Pisáuridae**—Nursery-Web and Fishing Spiders: These spiders resemble the wolf spiders (Lycòsidae), but have a different eye pattern (see key, couplet 50). The egg sac is carried by the female under her prosoma, held there by the chelicerae and pedipalps. Before the eggs hatch the female attaches the sac to a plant and builds a web around it—and stands guard nearby. The pisaurids forage for their prey and build webs only for their young. Some spiders in this group, particularly the fishing spiders in the genus *Dolómedes*, are quite large and may have a leg spread of 75 mm or more (Figure 6–12B). The *Dolómedes* spiders live near water; they may walk over the surface of the water or dive beneath it to feed on aquatic insects and sometimes small fishes.

Family **Lycòsidae**—Wolf or Ground Spiders: This is a large group of spiders that forage for their prey on the ground. Most of them are dark brown in color (Figure 6–13B) and can be recognized by the characteristic eye pattern (Figure 6–6C): four small eyes in the first row, two very large ones in the second row, and two small ones in the third row. The egg sac is carried about by the female, attached to her spinnerets. When the young hatch they are carried about for a time on the back of the female. The lycosids are widely distributed, and many are common spiders.

Family **Oxyòpidae**—Lynx Spiders: These spiders can generally be recognized by their eye pattern: eight eyes in an oval group (Figure 6–6A). The opisthosoma usually tapers to a point posteriorly (Figure 6–12A). These spiders chase their prey over foliage with great speed. Many can jump. They do not construct a web or retreat. They live in low vegetation and attach their egg sacs to foliage. These spiders are more common in the southern states.

Family **Lyssománidae**: The only member of this group occurring in our area is *Lyssómanes víridis* (Walckenaer), a pale green spider 6–8 mm in length, which occurs in the southern states. The chelicerae are of normal size and vertical in the female, but are very long and strongly diverging in the male. This species occurs in low bushes.

Family **Saltícidae**—Jumping Spiders: These spiders are small to medium in size, stout-bodied, and short-legged (Figure 6–13A), with a distinctive eye

Figure 6–12. **A,** a lynx spider, *Oxyòpes sálticus* Hentz (Oxyòpidae); **B,** a fishing spider, *Dolómedes* (Pisáuridae).

A

B

pattern (Figure 6–6B). The body is rather hairy and is often brightly colored or iridescent. Some species are antlike in appearance. The jumping spiders forage for their prey in the daytime. They approach a prey slowly and, when a short distance away, make a sudden leap onto it. They are good jumpers and can jump many times their own length. Before jumping they attach a silk thread—on which they can climb back if they miss their target. This is a large group, and its members are common spiders.

ORDER **Ricinùlei**[15]—Ricinuleids: This is a small group of rare tropical arachnids. They are somewhat

ticklike in appearance, and one of their distinctive features is a movable flap at the anterior end of the prosoma that extends over the chelicerae. The tarsi of the third pair of legs in the male are modified as copulatory organs. One species, *Cryptocéllus doròtheae* Gertsch and Mulaik, has been reported from the Rio Grande Valley of Texas. This arachnid is about 3 mm in length, is orange-red to brown in color, and occurs under objects on the ground. Some tropical species are larger (up to about 15 mm in length), and the majority have been taken in caves.

ORDER **Opiliònes**[16]—Harvestmen: These arachnids have the body rounded or oval, with the prosoma

[15]Ricinùlei: *Ricin*, a kind of mite or tick; *ulei*, small (a diminutive suffix).

[16]Opiliònes: from the Latin, meaning a shepherd.

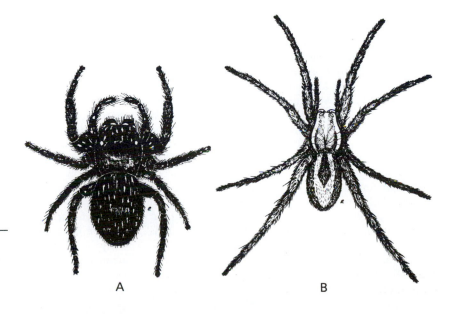

Figure 6–13. **A,** a jumping spider, *Phidíppus áudax* (Hentz) (Saltícidae); **B,** a wolf or ground spider, *Lycòsa* sp. (Lycòsidae).

A

B

and opisthosoma broadly joined. There are usually two eyes, generally located on each side of a median elevation. Scent glands are present, their ducts opening to the outside above the first or second coxae. These glands secrete a peculiar-smelling fluid when the animal is disturbed. Most species are predaceous or feed on dead animals or plant juices. The eggs are laid on the ground in the fall and hatch in the spring. Most species live a year or two. This order is divided into three suborders, the Cyphophthálmi, the Laniatòres, and the Palpatòres.

SUBORDER **Cyphophthálmi**—Mite Harvestmen: These are small, short-legged, mitelike forms, 3 mm in length or less, which differ from the other two suborders in having the scent glands opening on short conical processes. The eyes, if present, are far apart and indistinct. This group is represented in the United States by four species, which occur in the Southwest and the far West.

SUBORDER **Laniatòres**: This group is mainly tropical, but more than 60 species occur in the southern and western states, many of them in caves. These differ from the Palpatòres in having the tarsi on the third and fourth legs with two or three claws (or one claw with three teeth). The pedipalps are large and robust, and their tarsi are armed with a strong claw. The legs are not unusually long.

SUBORDER **Palpatòres**—Daddy-Longlegs: This group includes the harvestmen commonly called daddy-longlegs, which have very long and slender legs (Figure 6–14A). About 150 species occur in North America. These forms have the second pair of legs the longest, and the tarsi of all legs have just one claw. The pedipalps are smaller, their tarsi having a weak claw or none. Four families of this suborder occur in North America, but most of our species belong to the Phalángidae.

ORDER **Ácari**[17]—Mites and Ticks: The Ácari constitute a very large group of small to minute animals. More than 30,000 have been described, and it has been estimated that perhaps half a million more are still undescribed. The body is usually oval, with little (Figure 6–15, 6–16) or no (Figures 6–17 through 6–22) differentiation of the two body regions. Newly hatched young, called larvae, have only three pairs of legs (Figures 6–19B, 6–22A) and acquire the fourth pair after the first molt. A few mites have fewer than three pairs of legs (Figure 6–20). The instars between larva and adult are called nymphs.

The Ácari occur in practically all habitats in which any animal is found and rival the insects in their variations in habits and life histories. This

[17]Ácari: from the Greek, meaning a mite.

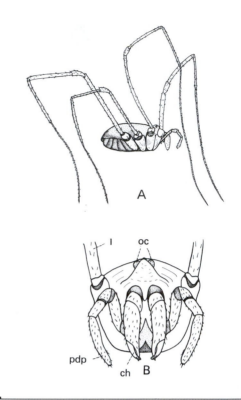

Figure 6–14. A harvestman or daddy-longlegs (Order Opiliònes). **A,** lateral view; **B,** anterior view. *ch,* chelicera; *l,* front leg; *oc,* eyes or ocelli; *pdp,* pedipalp. The harvestmen typically have two eyes located on a tubercle, and the chelicerae are clawlike, as shown in **B.**

group includes both aquatic and terrestrial forms, and the aquatic forms occur in both fresh and salt water. Ácari are abundant in soil and organic debris, where they usually outnumber other arthropods. Many are parasitic, at least during part of their life cycle, and both vertebrates and invertebrates (including insects) serve as hosts. Most of the parasitic forms are external parasites of their hosts. Many of the free-living forms are predaceous, and some of these prey on undesirable arthropods. Many are scavengers and aid in the breakdown of forest litter. Many are plant feeders, and some of these are injurious to crops. Some of the parasitic forms are pests of humans and animals, causing damage by their feeding and sometimes serving as vectors of disease. This group is of considerable biological and economic importance.

The groups of Ácari have been arranged differently by different authorities; we follow here the arrangement of Barnes (1987), but call the three major groups of Ácari "groups" rather than orders. This

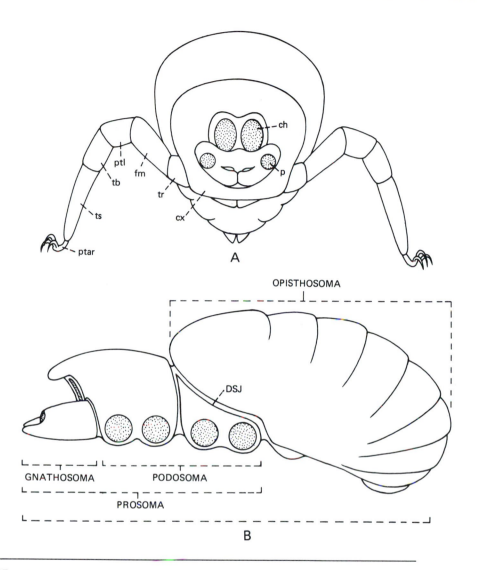

Figure 6–15.   A generalized acariform mite. **A,** anterior view; **B,** lateral view. *ch,* socket of chelicera; *cx,* coxa; *DSJ,* disjugal furrow; *fm,* femur; *p,* socket of palp; *ptar,* pretarsus; *ptl,* genu or patella; *tb,* tibia; *tr,* trochanter; *ts,* tarsus. (Courtesy of Johnston.)

arrangement (with other spellings, names, or arrangements in parentheses) is as follows:

Order Àcari—mites and ticks
    Group I. Opilioacarifórmes (Opilioacàrida, Notostigmàta; Parasitifórmes in part)
    Group II. Parasitifórmes
        Suborder Holothyrìna (Holothỳrida, Tetrastigmàta)
        Suborder Mesostigmàta (Gamàsida)
        Suborder Ixódida (Ixódides, Metastigmàta)—ticks

Group III. Acarifórmes
    Suborder Prostigmàta (Trombidifórmes, Actinèdida)
    Suborder Astigmàta (Sarcoptifórmes, Acarídida)
    Suborder Oribátida (Oribátei, Cryptostigmàta)

GROUP I. **Opilioacarifórmes:** The members of this group (Figure 6–16) are elongate and somewhat leathery, and have the abdomen segmented. They are brightly colored and are superficially similar to some of the harvestmen (Opiliònes). They are usually

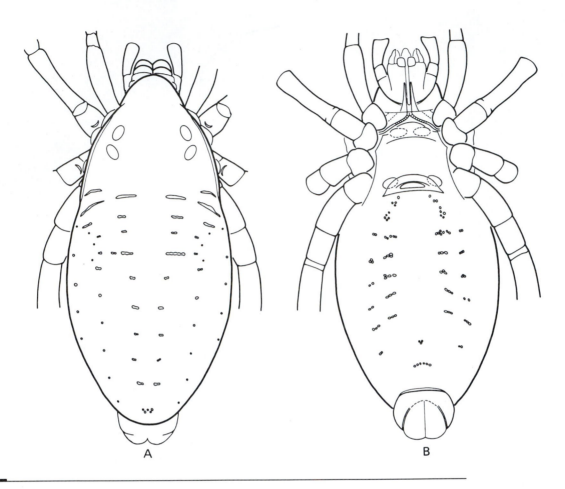

Figure 6–16.   A female opilioacariform mite. **A,** dorsal view; **B,** ventral view. (From Johnston, redrawn by van der Hammen.)

found under stones or in debris, and are omnivorous or predatory. Our species occur in the Southwest.

GROUP II. **Parasitifórmes:** These are medium-sized to large mites that have the abdomen unsegmented, and the tracheal system has ventrolateral spiracles.

SUBORDER **Holothyrìna:** The members of this group are fair-sized (2–7 mm in length), rounded or oval mites that occur in Australia, New Guinea, New Zealand, some islands in the Indian Ocean, and in the American tropics. They are found under stones or in decaying vegetation and are predaceous.

SUBORDER **Mesostigmàta:** This is the largest suborder of the Parasitifórmes and includes predaceous, scavenging, and parasitic forms. The majority are free-living and predaceous and are usually the dominant mites in leaf litter, humus, and soil. The parasitic mites in this group attack birds, bats, small mammals, snakes, insects, and rarely humans. One

parasitic species, the chicken mite, *Dermanýssus gállinae* (De Geer), is a serious pest of poultry. It hides during the day and attacks poultry and sucks their blood at night. This species also causes a dermatitis in man.

SUBORDER **Ixódida**—Ticks: Two families of ticks occur in North America, the Ixódidae or hard ticks and the Argásidae or soft ticks. Ticks are larger than most other Àcari and are parasitic, feeding on the blood of mammals, birds, and reptiles. Those attacking man are annoying pests, and some species serve as disease vectors. Ticks are the most important vectors of disease to domestic animals and second only to mosquitoes as vectors of disease to humankind. Certain ticks, especially engorging females feeding on the neck or near the base of the skull of their host, inject a venom that produces a paralysis; the paralysis may be fatal if the tick is not removed. The most important tick-borne diseases are Rocky

Mountain spotted fever, relapsing fever, Lyme disease, tularemia, Texas cattle fever, and Colorado tick fever.

Ticks lay their eggs in various places, but not on the host; the young seek out a host after hatching. Most species have a three-host life cycle: the larva feeds upon one host, drops off, and molts; the nymph feeds on a second; and the adult feeds on a third. The hard ticks take only one blood meal in each of their three instars. They remain on the host for several days while feeding, but usually drop off to molt. The soft ticks generally hide in crevices during the day and feed on their hosts at night; each instar may feed several times. The hard ticks ordinarily have two or three hosts during their development, while the soft ticks may have many hosts. The cattle tick that transmits Texas cattle fever feeds on the same host individual during all three instars, and the protist that causes the disease is transmitted transovarially, that is, through the eggs to the tick's offspring. The hard ticks (Figure 6–17) possess a hard dorsal plate called the scutum, and they have the mouthparts protruding anteriorly and visible from above. The soft ticks (Figure 6–18) lack a scutum and are soft-bodied, and the mouthparts are ventrally located and are not visible from above.

GROUP III. **Acarifórmes:** These are small mites that have the abdomen unsegmented, and the spiracles are near the mouthparts or absent.

SUBORDER **Prostigmàta:** This is a large group whose members vary considerably in habits. Some are free-living (occurring in litter, moss, or water) and vary in food habits; some are parasitic; and some are parasitic as larvae but predaceous as adults. This group includes the spider mites, gall mites, water mites, harvest mites, feather mites, and others.

The spider mites (Tetranýchidae) are plant feeders, and some species do serious damage to orchard trees, field crops, and greenhouse plants. They feed on the foliage or fruits and attack a variety of plants. They are widely distributed and sometimes occur in tremendous numbers. The eggs are laid on the plant and, during the summer, hatch in 4 or 5 days. There are four instars (Figure 6–19), and growth from egg to adult usually requires about 3 weeks. Most species overwinter in the egg stage. The immature instars are usually yellowish or pale in color, and the adults are yellowish or greenish. (These animals are sometimes called red mites, but they are seldom red.) Sex in these mites is determined by the fertilization of the egg. Males develop from unfertilized eggs, and females from fertilized eggs.

The gall mites (Eriophyòidea) are elongate and wormlike and have only two pairs of legs (Figure 6–20). A few species form small pouchlike galls on leaves, but the majority feed on leaves without forming galls and produces a rusting of the leaves. Some attack buds, and one forms the conspicuous witches'-broom twig gall on hackberry. Many gall mites are serious pests of orchard trees or other cultivated plants.

The water mites (Hydrachnídia, with 45 families in 9 superfamilies) include a number of common and widely distributed freshwater species and a few marine forms. A few species occur in hot springs. The larvae are parasitic on aquatic insects, and most nymphs and adults are predaceous. Water mites are small, round-bodied, usually brightly colored (red or

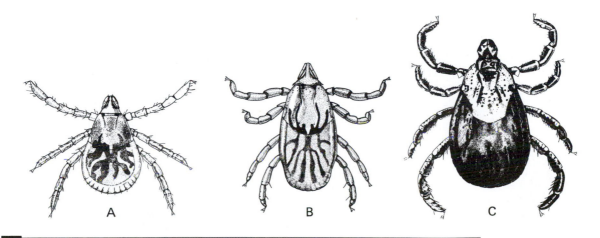

Figure 6–17. The American dog tick, *Dermacéntor variábilis* (Say) (Ixódidae). **A,** larva; **B,** nymph; **C,** adult (unengorged) female. (Courtesy of USDA.)

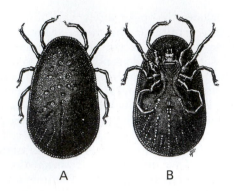

Figure 6–18. The fowl tick, *Árgas pérsicus* (Oken), adult female (Argásidae). **A,** dorsal view; **B,** ventral view. (Courtesy of USDA.)

green), and often quite common in ponds. They crawl on the bottom and on aquatic vegetation and lay their eggs on the undersides of leaves or on aquatic animals (mainly freshwater mussels). Water mite larvae (mostly in the genus *Arrenùrus*) are often abundant on the bodies of dragonflies and damselflies. They crawl from the nymph to the adult when the latter emerges and may remain there for a couple of weeks, feeding on the body fluids of the insect and eventually dropping off and developing into adults (if they happen to get into a suitable habitat).

The harvest mites (also called chiggers or redbugs) (Trombicùlidae) are ectoparasites of vertebrates in the larval stage, whereas the nymphs and adults are free-living and predaceous on small ar-

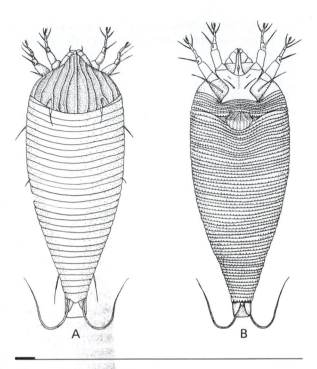

Figure 6–20. A gall mite, *Phyllocóptes variábilis* Hodgkiss, a species attacking sugar maple; 460×. **A,** dorsal view; **B,** ventral view. (Redrawn from Hodgkiss.)

thropods and arthropod eggs. Harvest mites lay their eggs among vegetation. On hatching, the larvae crawl over the vegetation and attach to a passing host. They insert their mouthparts into the outer layer of the skin, and their saliva partly digests the tissues beneath. The larvae remain on the host for a few days, feeding on tissue fluid and digested cellular material, and then drop off. These mites are small (Figure 6–22A) and are seldom noticed. Their bites, however, cause considerable irritation, and the itching persists for some time after the mites have left. On people, these mites seem to prefer areas where the clothing is tight. A person going into an area infested with chiggers can avoid being attacked by using a good repellent, such as dimethyl phthallate or diethyl toluamide. This material can be put on the clothing, or the clothing can be impregnated with it. A good material to reduce the itching caused by chiggers is tincture of benzyl benzoate. In the Orient, southern Asia, the Southwest Pacific, and Australia, certain harvest mites serve as vectors of scrub typhus, or tsutsugamushi disease. This disease caused more than 7,000 casualties in the U.S. armed forces during World War II.

The feather mites (19 families, in the superfamilies Analgòidea, Pterolichòidea, and Freyanòidea)

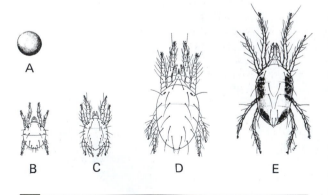

Figure 6–19. The fourspotted spider mite, *Tetránychus canadénsis* (McGregor). **A,** egg; **B,** first instar or larva; **C,** second instar, or protonymph; **D,** third instar, or deutonymph; **E,** fourth instar, adult female. (Courtesy of USDA, after McGregor and McDunough.)

constitute a large group whose members occur on the feathers or skin or (rarely) in the respiratory system of birds. Many are found on particular feathers or feather areas of their hosts. They are seldom of economic importance, though they often occur in considerable numbers on poultry or avian pets. They appear to be scavengers, feeding on feather fragments and oily secretions on the feathers. Some of those occurring on aquatic birds feed on diatoms.

The Tarsonèmidae is a large family of mites that includes species associated with insects or plants, and some cause human dermatitis. Some species live in the galleries of bark beetles, where they feed on the bark beetle eggs. They are carried from gallery to gallery on the bodies of the beetles. Species in the genus *Acaràpis* occur on the bodies of honey bees. *Acaràpis woodi* (Rennie) causes what is known as Isle of Wight disease in honey bees. A few species (*Tarsonèmus* and other genera) have been implicated in cases of human dermatitis.

SUBORDER **Astigmàta:** The mites in this group are mostly terrestrial and nonpredatory. Some are parasitic, and a few of the parasitic forms are important pests of people and animals. The most important mites in this group are probably those that infest stored foods and those that cause dermatitis in humans and animals.

The Acaròidea are principally scavengers, occurring in animal nests, stored foods, and plant tissues. Those occurring in stored foods (cereals, dried meats, cheese, and the like) not only damage or contaminate these materials, but they may get on people and cause a dermatitis called grocer's itch or miller's itch.

The most important mites in this suborder that cause dermatitis in humans are the families Psoróptidae and Sarcóptidae. The Psoróptidae include the mange mites, which attack various animals (Figure 6–21), and the Sarcóptidae include the itch or scab mites. These mites burrow into the skin and cause severe irritation, and the resulting scratching often causes additional injury or leads to secondary infection. One of the best treatments for scabies (infection by these mites) is the application of a solution of benzyl benzoate. Species of *Dermatophagòides* (Pyroglỳphidae) are common inhabitants of houses and have been implicated in house-dust allergies.

SUBORDER **Oribátida:** This is a large group of small mites (0.2–1.3 mm) that exhibit considerable variation in form. Some superficially resemble small beetles (Figure 6–22B) and are called beetle mites. Some species have winglike lateral extensions of the notum. In a few cases these extensions, called pteromorphs, are hinged, contain "veins," and are provided with muscles. Oribatid mites are found in leaf litter, under bark and stones, and in the soil. They are mainly scavengers. They make up a large percentage of the soil fauna and are important in breaking down organic matter and promoting soil fertility. Some species of Orbatulòidea have been found to serve as the intermediate hosts of certain tapeworms that infest sheep, cattle, and other ruminants.

ORDER **Pseudoscorpiònes**[18]—Pseudoscorpions: The pseudoscorpions are small arachnids, seldom more than 5 mm in length. They resemble true scorpions in having large chelate pedipalps, but the opisthosoma is short and oval, there is no sting (Figure 6–23), and the body is quite flat. The pseudoscorpions differ from most other arachnids in lacking a patellar segment in the legs. Eyes may be present or absent; if present, there are two or four, located at the anterior end of the prosoma.

This is a fair-sized group, with about 200 species in North America, and its members are common animals. They are found under bark and stones, in leaf litter and moss, between the boards of buildings, and in similar situations. They sometimes cling to and are carried about by large insects. They feed chiefly on small insects, which are caught with the pedipalps. Most species have venom glands that open on the pedipalps. These animals have silk glands, the ducts from which open on the chelicerae.[19] The silk is used in making a cocoon in which the animal overwinters.

[18]Pseudoscorpiònes: *pseudo*, false; *scorpiones*, scorpion.

[19]Another name given to this order, Chelonéthida, refers to this feature: *chelo*, claw; *neth*, spin.

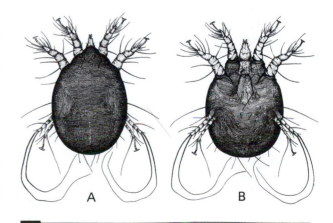

Figure 6–21.   The sheep scab mite, *Psoróptes òvis* (Hering), female. **A,** dorsal view; **B,** ventral view. (Courtesy of USDA.)

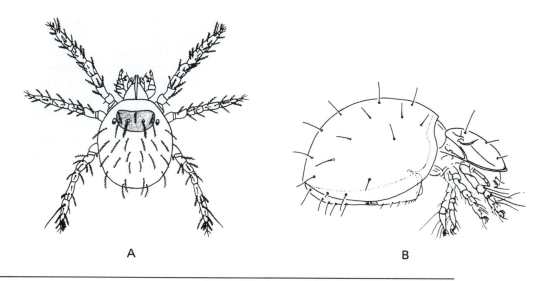

Figure 6–22.   **A,** a chigger, the larva of *Eutrombícula alfreddùgesi* (Oudemans), 215 ×; **B,** an oribatid mite (family Euphthiracàridae). (**A,** redrawn from a U.S. Public Health Service release; **B,** courtesy of the Institute of Acarology.)

ORDER **Solifùgae**[20]—Windscorpions: This is a fair-sized group of arachnids (about 120 species in North America) whose members occur chiefly in the arid or desert regions of the West (one species occurs in Florida). They are called by a variety of names: windscorpions (they run "like the wind"), sunscorpions, sunspiders, and camelspiders. They are 20–30 mm in length and are usually pale colored and somewhat hairy; the body is slightly constricted in the middle (Figure 6–4C). One of their most distinctive features is their very large chelicerae (often as long as the prosoma), giving them a very ferocious appearance.

[20]Solifùgae: *sol,* sun; *fugae,* flee (referring to the nocturnal habits of these animals).

They may bite, but do not have venom glands. The males have a flagellum on the chelicera. The fourth legs bear, on the ventral side of the coxae and trochanters, five short, broad, T-shaped structures (attached by the base of the T) called racket organs or malleoli, which are probably sensory in function.

Windscorpions are largely nocturnal, hiding during the day under objects or in burrows. They are fast-running and predaceous, sometimes even capturing small lizards. The pedipalps and first legs are used as feelers, and these animals run on the last three pairs of legs. Two families occur in the United States, the Ammotréchidae (first legs without claws, and anterior prosoma rounded or pointed) and the Eremobátidae (first legs with one or two claws, the anterior edge of prosoma straight).

Figure 6–23.   Pseudoscorpions. **A,** *Dactylochélifer copiòsus* Hoff; **B,** *Lárca granulàta* (Banks); **C,** *Pselaphochérnes párvus* Hoff. (Courtesy of Hoff and Illinois Natural History Survey.)

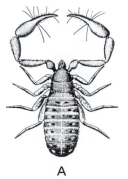

A   B   C

Class Pycnogónida[21]—Sea Spiders

The pycnogonids are marine, spiderlike forms with long legs. They are occasionally found under stones near the low-tide mark, but usually occur in deep water. They are predaceous and have a sucking proboscis. The body consists principally of prosoma; the opisthosoma is very small. The sea spiders vary in length from one to several centimeters. Little is known of their habits, for they are not common.

Collecting and Preserving Chelicerates

To obtain a large collection of chelicerates, one needs primarily to collect in as many different types of habitats as possible. Chelicerates are frequently very abundant, often as abundant as insects or more so. The general collector of insects is likely to encounter more spiders and mites than any other types of chelicerates; therefore, the following suggestions are concerned primarily with these groups.

Chelicerates occur in a great variety of situations and can often be collected with the same techniques and equipment used in collecting insects. Many may be taken by sweeping vegetation with an insect net. Many may be obtained with beating equipment, that is, using a sheet or beating umbrella beneath a tree or bush and beating the bush to knock off the specimens. The ground forms may be found running on the ground or under stones, boards, bark, or other objects. Many are to be found in the angles of buildings and similar protected places. Many of the smaller forms can be found in debris, soil litter, or moss and are best collected by means of sifting equipment such as a Berlese funnel (Figure 36–6) or a screen sieve or by means of pitfall traps. Many are aquatic or semiaquatic and may be collected in marshy areas with aerial collecting equipment or in water with aquatic equipment. The parasitic species (various mites and ticks) usually must be looked for on their hosts.

Many chelicerates are nocturnal, and collecting at night may prove more successful than collecting during the day. Very few are attracted to lights, but they may be spotted at night with a flashlight or a headlamp. The eyes of many spiders will reflect the light, and with a little experience one may locate many spiders at night by the use of a light. Scorpions are fluorescent and may be collected at night with a portable ultraviolet light to make them visible.

Chelicerates should be preserved in fluids rather than on pins or points. Many forms, such as the spiders, are very soft-bodied and shrivel when dry. They are usually preserved in 70–80% alcohol. There should be plenty of alcohol in the bottle in relation to the specimen, and it is often desirable to change the alcohol after the first few days. Many workers preserve mites in Oudeman's fluid, which consists of 87 parts of 70% alcohol, 5 parts of glycerine, and 8 parts of glacial acetic acid. The chief advantage of this fluid is that the mites die with their appendages extended so that subsequent examination is easier. Alcohol is not suitable for preserving gall mites. Such mites are best collected by wrapping infested plant parts in soft tissue paper and allowing them to dry. This dried material can be kept indefinitely, and the mites may be recovered for study by warming the dried material in Kiefer's solution (50 grams of resorcinal, 20 grams of diglycolic acid, 25 milliliters of glycerol, enough iodine to produce the desired color, and about 10 milliliters of water). Specialists on mites prefer specimens in fluid, rather than mounted on permanent microscopic slides, so that all aspects and structures can be studied.

Chelicerates may be collected by means of a net, forceps, vial, or small brush, or they may be collected by hand. In the case of biting or stinging forms, it is safer to use some method other than collecting them with the fingers. Specimens collected with a net can be transferred directly to a vial of alcohol, or they may be collected in an empty vial and later transferred to alcohol. Since some species are quite active, it is sometimes preferable to put them first into a cyanide bottle and transfer them to alcohol after they have been stunned and are quiet. Specimens collected from the ground or debris may be picked up with forceps or coaxed into a bottle, or the smaller specimens (found in any situation) may be picked up with a small brush moistened with alcohol.

Spider webs that are flat and not too large may be collected and preserved between two pieces of glass. One piece of glass is pressed against the web (which will usually stick to the glass because of the viscous material on some of the silk strands), and then the other piece of glass is applied to the first. It is often desirable to have the two pieces of glass separated by thin strips of paper around the edge of the glass. Once the web is between the two pieces of glass, the glass is bound together with lantern-slide binding tape. Spider webs are best photographed when they are covered with moisture (dew or fog) or dust. They may often be photographed dry, if illuminated from the side and photographed against a dark background.

---

[21]Pycnogónida: *pycno*, thick or dense; *gonida*, offspring (referring to the eggs).

Subphylum Crustàcea[22]—Crustaceans

The crustaceans comprise a large and varied group of arthropods, with more than 44,000 known species. Most of them are marine, but many occur in fresh water, and a few are terrestrial. In addition to the larger and more familiar types, such as lobsters, crayfish, crabs, and shrimp, there is a multitude of small to minute aquatic forms that are very important in aquatic food webs.

There is a great deal of variation in the appendages and body regions in this group, but typically there are two pairs of antennae, the functional jaws consist of endite lobes of the gnathal appendages, and many of the appendages are biramous. A biramous appendage bears a process at its base (arising from the second segment of the appendage) which is more or less leglike, giving the appendage a two-branched appearance (Figure 6–1C). There may be an exite lobe on the basal segment, as in trilobites, and in some cases this functions as a gill. There are differences in this group in the nature of the body regions. Sometimes there are two fairly distinct (and nearly equal-sized) body regions, the cephalothorax and the abdomen, with the cephalothorax bearing the antennae, gnathal appendages, and legs. Sometimes the abdominal appendages occupy only a small portion of the total body length. There is typically a terminal telson. The cephalothorax in many crustaceans is covered by a shieldlike portion of the body wall called the carapace. The abdomen lacks paired appendages except in the Malacóstraca.

The smaller crustaceans, particularly those in the Branchiópoda, Copépoda, and Ostrácoda, are abundant in both salt and fresh water. The chief importance of most species lies in the fact that they serve as food for larger animals and thus are an important part in the food webs leading to fish and other larger aquatic animals. A few species are parasitic on fish and other animals, and the barnacles are often a nuisance when they encrust pilings, boat bottoms, and other surfaces. Many of the small crustaceans can be easily maintained in indoor aquaria and are frequently reared as food for other aquatic animals.

Class Branchiópoda[23]

Most members of this group occur in fresh water. Males are uncommon in many species, and parthenogenesis is a common mode of reproduction. Both unisexual (parthenogenic) and bisexual reproduction occurs in many species, and the factors controlling the production of males are not well understood.

There are differences of opinion regarding the classification of these crustaceans, but four fairly distinct groups are usually recognized, the Anóstraca, Notóstraca, Conchóstraca, and Cladócera. The first two of these are sometimes placed in a group called the Phyllópoda, and the last two are sometimes called the Diplóstraca.

The Anóstraca,[24] or fairy shrimps (Figure 6–25A), have the body elongate and distinctly segmented, without a carapace and with 11 pairs of swimming legs, and the eyes are stalked. The fairy shrimps are often abundant in temporary pools. The Notóstraca,[25] or tadpole shrimps, have an oval convex carapace covering the anterior part of the body, 35–71 pairs of thoracic appendages, and two long filamentous caudal appendages. These animals range in size from about 10 to 50 mm and are restricted to

[22]Crustàcea: from the Latin, referring to the crustlike exoskeleton possessed by many of these animals.

[23]Branchiópoda: *branchio*, gill; *poda*, foot or appendage.

[24]Anóstraca: *an*, without; *ostraca*, shell.

[25]Notóstraca; *not*, back; *ostraca*, shell.

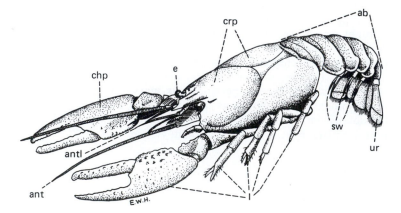

Figure 6–24. A crayfish (*Cámbarus* sp.), natural size. *ab*, abdomen; *ant*, antenna; *antl*, antennule; *chp*, cheliped; *crp*, carapace; *e*, eye; *l*, legs (including cheliped); *sw*, swimmerets; *ur*, uropod.

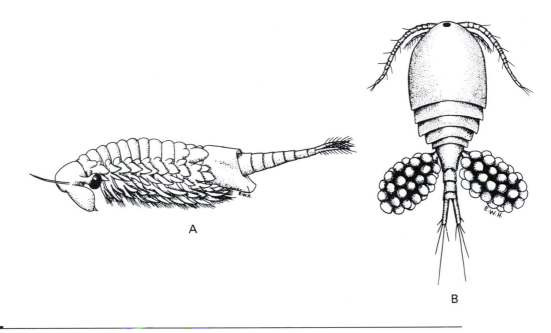

Figure 6–25.   Crustaceans. **A,** a fairy shrimp, *Eubránchipus* (subclass Branchiópoda, order Anóstraca), 6×; **B,** a female copepod, *Cỳclops* sp., 50×, with two egg sacs at posterior end of body.

the western states. The Conchóstraca,[26] or clam shrimps, have the body somewhat flattened laterally and entirely enclosed in a bivalved carapace, and they have 10–32 pairs of legs. Most species are 10 mm in length or less. The Cladócera,[27] or water fleas (Figure 6–26A), have a bivalved carapace, but the head is not enclosed in the carapace. There are 4–6 pairs of thoracic legs. The water fleas are 0.2–3.0 mm in length and are very common in freshwater pools.

There are three groups of small crustaceans occurring in fresh water that have a bivalved carapace, and these groups are likely to be confused. The Ostrácoda (Figure 6–26B,C) and Conchóstraca have the body completely enclosed in the carapace, whereas in the Cladócera (Figure 6–26A) the head is outside the carapace. The Ostrácoda have only three pairs of thoracic legs; the Conchóstraca have 10–32 pairs.

Class Copépoda[28]

Some of the copepods are free-swimming, and others are parasitic on fish. The parasitic forms are often peculiar in body form and quite unlike the free-swimming forms in general appearance. This group includes both marine and freshwater forms. The female of most copepods carries her eggs in two egg sacs located laterally near the end of the abdomen (Figure 6–25B). The parasitic copepods are often called fish lice, and they live on the gills or the skin or burrow into the flesh of their host. When numerous they may seriously injure the host. Some species serve as intermediate hosts of certain human parasites (for example, the fish tapeworm, *Diphyllobóthrium látum* L.).

Class Ostrácoda[29]

The ostracods have a bivalved carapace that can be closed by a muscle, and when the valves are closed the animal looks like a miniature clam (Figure 6–26B,C). When the valves of the carapace are open, the appendages are protruded and propel the animal through the water. Many species are parthenogenic. Most of the ostracods are marine, but there are also many common freshwater species.

[26]Conchóstraca: *conch,* shell or shellfish; *ostraca,* shell.

[27]Cladócera: *clado,* branch; *cera,* horn (referring to the antennae).

[28]Copépoda: *cope,* oar; *poda,* foot or appendage.

[29]Ostrácoda: from the Greek, meaning shell-like (referring to the clamlike character of the carapace).

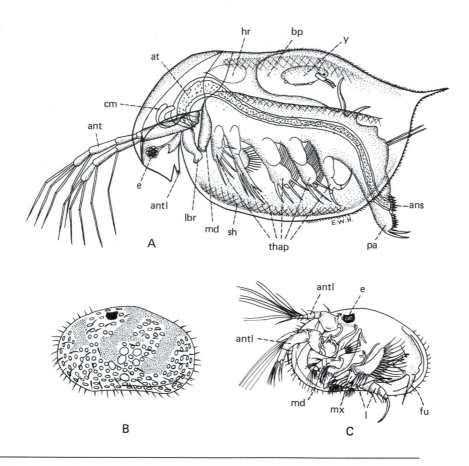

Figure 6–26.   Crustaceans. **A,** a water flea or cladoceran, *Dáphnia* sp., 25 × ; **B,** an ostracod, *Cypridópsis* sp., lateral view; **C,** same, but with left valve of carapace removed. *ans,* anus; *ant,* antenna; *antl,* antennule; *at,* alimentary tract; *bp,* brood pouch; *cm,* caecum; *e,* compound eye; *fu,* furca; *hr,* heart; *l,* first and second thoracic legs; *lbr,* labrum; *md,* mandible; *mx,* maxilla; *pa,* postabdomen; *sh,* bivalved shell; *thap,* thoracic appendages; *y,* developing young. (**C** modified from Kesling.)

Class Cirripèdia[30]

The best-known members of this group are the barnacles, the adults of which live attached to rocks, pilings, seaweeds, boats, or marine animals, and which are enclosed in a calcareous shell. A few species are parasitic, usually on crabs or mollusks. Most of the members living in this group are hermaphroditic; that is, each individual contains both male and female organs. Some barnacles, such as the goose barnacle (Figure 6–27A), have the shell attached to some object by means of a stalk. Others, such as the rock barnacle (Figure 6–27B), are sessile and do not have stalks.

The Smaller Crustacean Classes

Included here are the classes Cephalocàrida,[31] Mystacocàrida,[32] Branchiùra,[33] Tantulocàrida,[34] and Remipèdia.[35] The nine known species of Cephalocàrida are marine bottom-dwelling forms that often occur in very deep water. The Mystacocàrida are minute (mostly about 0.5 mm in length) marine forms living in the intertidal zone. Nine species of these have been described. The Branchiùra are ectoparasites on

---

[30]Cirripèdia: *cirri,* a curl of hair; *pedia,* foot or appendage.

[31]Cephalocàrida: *cephalo,* head; *carida,* a shrimp.

[32]Mystacocàrida: *mystaco,* mustache; *carida,* a shrimp.

[33]Branchiùra: *branchi,* gill; *ura,* tail.

[34]Tantulocàrida: *tantula,* little; *carida,* a shrimp.

[35]Remipèdia: *remi,* an oar; *pedia,* foot or appendage.

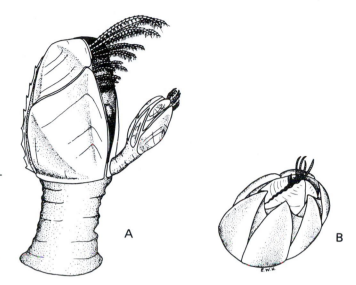

Figure 6–27.   Barnacles. **A,** a goose barnacle, *Lèpas* sp., 3×; **B,** a rock barnacle, *Balànus* sp., 2×. The basal stalk or peduncle of the goose barnacle is at the animal's posterior end; the biramous appendages protruding from the shell at the top of the figure are the posterior thoracic legs; a second small individual is shown attached to the first.

the skin or in the gill cavities of fish (both marine and freshwater). About 130 species are known. The Tantulocàrida (4 known species) are ectoparasites of deep-water crustaceans. The Remipèdia (8 known species) have the body long and wormlike, and occur in island caves connected to the sea.

Class Malacóstraca[36]

The Malacóstraca, the largest of the crustacean classes, include the larger and better known forms, such as the lobsters, crayfish, crabs, and shrimps. They differ from the preceding classes (sometimes referred to as the Entomóstraca) in having appendages (swimmerets or pleopods) on the abdomen. There are typically 19 pairs of appendages, the first 13 being cephalothoracic and the last 6 abdominal. The leglike appendages on the cephalothorax are often chelate. This class contains some 13 orders. Only the more common ones can be mentioned here.

ORDER **Amphípoda**[37]:   The body of an amphipod is elongate and more or less compressed; there is no carapace; and seven (rarely six) of the thoracic segments are distinct and bear leglike appendages. The abdominal segments are often more or less fused, and hence the six or seven thoracic segments make up most of the body length (Figure 6–28). This group contains both marine and freshwater forms. Many of them, such as the beach fleas (Figure 6–28B), live

on the beach, where they occur under stones or in decaying vegetation. Most of the amphipods are scavengers.

ORDER **Isópoda**[38]:   The isopods are similar to the amphipods in lacking a carapace, but are dorsoventrally flattened. The last seven thoracic segments are distinct and bear leglike appendages. The abdominal segments are more or less fused, and hence the thoracic segments (with their seven pairs of legs) make up most of the body length (Figure 6–29). The anterior abdominal appendages of the aquatic forms usually bear gills. The terminal abdominal appendages are often enlarged and feelerlike. The isopods are small (most are less than 20 mm in length), and most are marine, but some occur in fresh water and some are terrestrial. The marine forms generally live under stones or among seaweed, where they are scavengers or omnivores, but a few are wood-boring (apparently feeding chiefly on the fungi in the wood), and some are parasitic on fish or other crustaceans. The most common isopods away from the ocean are the sowbugs or woodlice—blackish, gray, or brownish animals usually found under stones, boards, or bark. Some sowbugs (often called pillbugs) are capable of rolling into a ball. In some areas sowbugs are important pests of cultivated plants.

ORDER **Stomatópoda**[39]—Mantis Shrimps: These are predaceous marine forms, mostly 5–36 cm in length, with the body dorsoventrally flattened. There are three pairs of legs, in front of which are five pairs of maxillipeds, the second of which is very

---

[36]Malacóstraca: *malac,* soft; *ostraca,* shell.

[37]Amphípoda: *amphi,* on both sides, double; *poda,* foot or appendage.

[38]Isópoda: *iso,* equal; *poda,* foot or appendage.

[39]Stomatópoda: *stomato,* mouth; *poda,* foot or appendage.

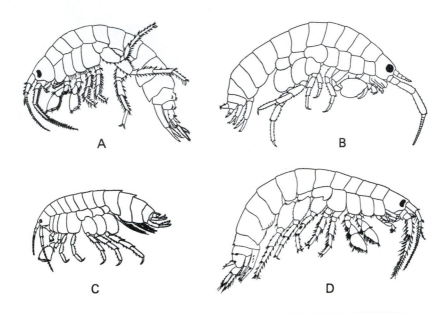

Figure 6–28. Amphipods. **A,** a common freshwater scud, *Dikerogámmarus fasciàtus* (Say), 10–15 mm in length; **B,** a sand flea or beach flea, *Orchéstia ágilis* Smith, abundant underneath seaweed along the coast near the high-tide mark; **C,** a common freshwater scud, *Hyalélla knickerbóckeri* (Bate), about 7 mm in length; **D,** a sea scud, *Gámmarus annulàtus* Smith, a common coastal form, about 15 mm in length. (Courtesy of Kunkle and the Connecticut State Geology and Natural History Survey; **C,** after Smith.)

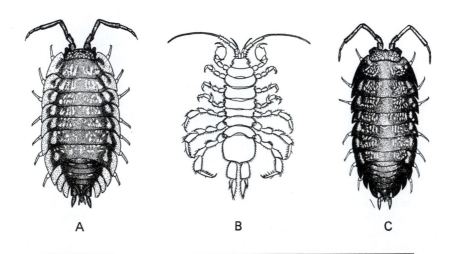

Figure 6–29. Isopods. **A,** *Oníscus aséllus* L., a common sowbug; **B,** *Aséllus commùnis* Say, a common freshwater isopod; **C,** *Cylísticus convéxus* (De Geer), a pillbug capable of rolling itself into a ball. (Courtesy of the Connecticut State Geology and Natural History Survey. **A** and **C,** courtesy of Kunkle, after Paulmier; **B,** courtesy of Kunkle, after Smith.)

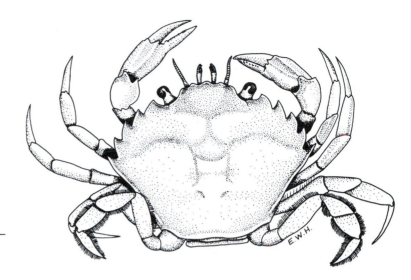

Figure 6–30. A green crab, *Carcínides* sp., 1½×.

large and chelate. A small carapace covers the body in front of the legs, and the abdomen is a little wider than the carapace. The mantis shrimps are often brightly colored: green, blue, red, or patterned. This group is principally tropical. U.S. species occur chiefly along the southern coasts.

ORDER **Decápoda**[40]: This order contains the largest and probably the best-known of the crustaceans, the lobsters, crayfish (Figure 6–24), crabs (Figure 6–30), and shrimps. The carapace of a decapod covers the entire thorax. Five pairs of the cephalothoracic appendages are leglike, and the first pair of these usually bears a large claw. The abdomen may be well developed (lobsters and crayfish), or it may be much reduced (crabs). This is a very important group, for many of its members are used as food, and their collection and distribution provide the basis of a large coastal industry.

Collecting and Preserving Crustàcea

The aquatic crustaceans must be collected by various types of aquatic collecting equipment. Most of them can be collected by a dip net. A white enamel dipper is the best means of collecting many of the smaller forms. The dipper is simply dipped into the water, and any small animals in the dipper can be easily seen. Forms so collected can be removed by means of an eye dropper or (if they are fairly large) by forceps. The smaller forms in ponds, lakes, and the ocean are often collected by means of a fine-mesh net called a plankton net, towed by a boat.

Many of the larger forms are collected by traps. Such traps (or "pots") are the standard means of collecting lobsters and crabs. The shore-dwelling and terrestrial forms can be collected by hand or forceps or possibly (for example, beach fleas) with an aerial insect net. The larger forms with well-developed claws should be handled with care, for the claw may inflict serious injury. The safest way to pick up a large crayfish or lobster is from above, grasping the animal at the back of the carapace.

One must collect in a variety of places to obtain a variety of Crustàcea. When collecting in water, one should investigate every possible aquatic niche. Some crustaceans are free-swimming; some burrow in the mud of the bottom; some occur under stones; and many are to be found on aquatic vegetation. The shore-dwelling forms are usually found under stones, debris, or decaying vegetation along the shore.

Crustaceans should be preserved in fluids (for example, 70–95% alcohol). Most of the smaller forms must be mounted on microscope slides for detailed study. Some of the smaller Malacóstraca can be preserved dry (for example, pinned) but specimens preserved in fluid are more satisfactory for study.

Subphylum Ateloceràta[41]

The members of this subphylum have a single pair of antennae and uniramous (unbranched) appendages. According to Manton (1977) the mandibles of these species differ from those of Crustacea in that

---

[40]Decápoda: *deca*, ten; *poda*, foot or appendage.

[41]Ateloceràta: *atelos*, defective; *keras*, horn; referring to the fact that the second antennae are present in these taxa only as embryonic rudiments.

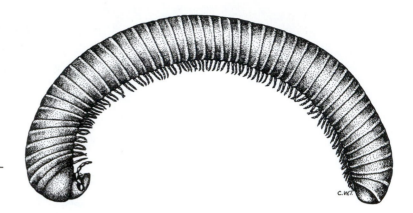

Figure 6–31. A common millipede, *Nárceus* sp. (order Spirobólida), 1½×.

the entire appendage makes up the functional portion of the mandible (and not only the basal portion). Manton placed the groups included below together with the Onychóphora as the phylum Uniràmia (concluding that the Arthrópoda is a polyphyletic taxon). We believe that this position has not been adequately supported. This conclusion requires that evidence be found indicating that one or more taxa now classified as arthropods are more closely related to a nonarthropod group. Until such evidence is available, we continue to treat the Arthrópoda as a monophyletic unit and do not consider the onychophorans to be arthropods.

Class Diplópoda[42]—Millipedes

The millipedes are elongate, wormlike animals with many legs (Figure 6–31). Most millipedes have 30 or more pairs of legs, and most body segments bear 2 pairs. The body is cylindrical or slightly flattened, and the antennae are short and usually seven-segmented. The external openings of the reproductive system are located at the anterior end of the body, between the second and third pairs of legs. One or both pairs of legs on the seventh segment of the male are usually modified into gonopods, which function in copulation. Compound eyes are usually present. The first tergum behind the head is usually large and is called the collum (Figure 6–32A).

The head in most millipedes is convex above, with a large epistomal area, and flat beneath. The bases of the mandibles form a part of the side of the head. Beneath the mandibles, and forming the flat ventral surface of the head, is a characteristic liplike structure called the gnathochilarium (Figure 6–32B, *gna*). The gnathochilarium is usually divided by su-

tures into several areas: a median more or less triangular plate, the mentum (*mn*); two lateral lobes, the stipites (*stp*); two median distal plates, the laminae linguales (*ll*); and usually a median transverse basal sclerite, the prebasilare (*pbs*), and two small laterobasal sclerites, the cardines (*cd*). The size and shape of areas differ among groups of millipedes, and the gnathochilarium often provides characters by which the groups are recognized.

Millipedes are usually found in damp places: under leaves, in moss, under stones or boards, in rotting wood, or in the soil. Many species are able to give off an ill-smelling fluid through openings along the sides of the body. This fluid is sometimes strong enough to kill insects that are placed in a jar with

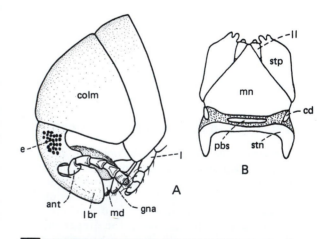

Figure 6–32. Head structure in a millipede (*Nárceus*, order Spirobólida). **A,** lateral view of head; **B,** gnathochilarium. *ant*, antenna; *cd*, cardo; *colm*, collum, tergite of the first body segment; *e*, eye; *gna*, gnathochilarium; *l*, first leg; *lbr*, labrum; *ll*, lamina lingualis; *md*, mandible, *mn*, mentum; *pbs*, prebasilare; *stn*, sternum of first body segment; *stp*, stipes.

---

[42]Diplópoda: *diplo*, two; *poda*, foot or appendage (referring to the fact that most body segments bear two pairs of legs).

the millipede, and it has been shown (in some cases at least) to contain hydrogen cyanide. Millipedes do not bite people. Most millipedes are scavengers and feed on decaying plant material, but some attack living plants and sometimes do serious damage in greenhouses and gardens, and a few are predaceous. These animals overwinter as adults in protected situations, and lay their eggs during the summer. Some construct nestlike cavities in the soil in which they deposit their eggs; others lay their eggs in damp places without constructing any sort of nest. The eggs are usually white and hatch within a few weeks. Newly hatched millipedes have only three pairs of legs. The remaining legs are added in subsequent molts.

There are a number of arrangements of orders and families in this group. We follow the arrangement of Chamberlin and Hoffman (1958), which is outlined here (with alternate names or arrangements in parentheses):

Subclass Pselaphógnatha (Pencillàta)
    Order Polyxénida
Subclass Chilógnatha
    Superorder Pentazònia (Opisthándria)
        Order Glomérida (Oniscomórpha)
    Superorder Helminthomórpha (Ológnatha, Eùgnatha)
        Order Polydésmida (Proterospermóphora)
        Order Chordeùmida (Chordeumátida, Nematóphora)
        Order Jùlida (Opisthospermóphora in part)
        Order Spirobólida (Opisthospermóphora in part)
        Order Spirostréptida (Opisthospermóphora in part)
        Order Cambálida (Opisthospermóphora in part)
    Superorder Colobógnatha
        Order Polyzonìida
        Order Platydésmida

Key to the Orders of Diplópoda

1. Adults with 13 pairs of legs; integument soft; body hairs forming long lateral tufts; 2–4 mm in length ....**Polyxénida**   p. 140

1'. Adults with 28 or more pairs of legs; integument strongly sclerotized; body hairs not forming long tufts; larger millipedes **2**

2(1'). Body with 14–16 segments and with 11–13 tergites; male gonopods at caudal end of body, modified from last 2 pairs of legs; southern and western United States ....**Glomérida**   p. 140

2'. Body with 18 or more segments; male gonopods modified from legs on seventh segment **3**

3(2'). Head small, often concealed, the mandibles much reduced; 8 pairs of legs anterior to the male gonopods..**4**

3'. Head and mandibles of normal size; 7 pairs of legs anterior to the male gonopods...**5**

4(3). Tergites with median groove; gnathochilarium with most of the typical parts; usually pink in color ....**Platydésmida**   p. 141

4'. Tergites without median groove; gnathochilarium consisting of a single plate or several indistinctly defined plates; usually cream colored .....**Polyzonìida**   p. 141

5(3'). Body with 18–22 segments; eyes absent; body more or less flattened, with lateral carinae ....**Polydésmida**   p. 141

5'. Body usually with 26 or more segments; eyes usually present; body usually cylindrical or nearly so, and only rarely (some Chordeùmida) with lateral carinae **6**

6(5'). Terminal segment of body with 1–3 pairs of setae-bearing papillae; lateral carinae sometimes present; collum not overlapping head; sternites not fused with pleurotergites; body with 26–30 segments ....**Chordeùmida**   p. 140

ORDER **Polyxénida**[43]: These millipedes are minute (2–4 mm in length) and soft-bodied, with the body very bristly. The group is a small one (five North American species), and its members are widely distributed but are not common. They are usually found under bark or in litter. The order contains a single genus, *Polýxenus*, in the family Polyxénidae.

ORDER **Glomérida**[44]—Pill Millipedes: These millipedes are so called because they can roll themselves into a ball. They are short and wide and resemble sowbugs, but have more than seven pairs of legs. Males have the gonopods at the posterior end of the body and clasperlike. The appendages of the seventh segment are not modified. These millipedes occur in the southeastern states and in California. U.S. species are small (8 mm or less in length), but some tropical species, when rolled, are nearly as big as golf balls.

ORDER **Polydésmida**[45]: The polydesmids are rather flattened millipedes, with the body keeled laterally and the eyes much reduced or absent. The tergites are divided by a transverse suture, a little anterior to the middle of the segment, into an anterior prozonite and a posterior metazonite. The metazonite is extended laterally as a broad lobe. The first and last two body segments are legless; segments 2–4

each have a single pair of legs; and the remaining segments each bear two pairs of legs. The anterior pair of legs on the seventh segment of the male is modified into gonopods. The diplosomites (those segments bearing two pairs of legs) are continuously sclerotized rings. There are no sutures between tergites, pleurites, and sternites.

This is a large group, with about 250 North American species. Many are brightly colored, and most of them have scent glands. *Óxidus grácilis* (Koch), a dark brown to black millipede, 19–22 mm in length and 2.0–2.5 mm wide, is a common pest in greenhouses. This order is divided into ten families, and its members occur throughout the United States.

ORDER **Chordeùmida**[46]: These millipedes have 26–30 segments, and the terminal tergite bears one to three pairs of hair-tipped papillae (spinnerets). The body is usually cylindrical. The head is broad and free and not overlapped by the collum. One or both pairs of legs on the seventh segment of the male may be modified into gonopods. This is a relatively large group, with about 170 species occurring in North America. A few are predaceous.

Three suborders of Chordeùmida occur in the United States. The suborder Chordeumídea, with nine families (in some classifications these millipedes are placed in a single family, the Craspedo-

[43]Polyxénida: *poly*, many; *xenida*, stranger or guest.

[44]Glomérida: from the Latin, meaning a ball of yarn (referring to the way these animals roll themselves into a ball).

[45]Polydésmida: *poly*, many; *desmida*, bands.

[46]Chordeùmida: from the Greek, meaning a sausage.

somátidae), are small (mostly 4–15 mm in length), soft-bodied millipedes with no keels on the metazonites and without scent glands. They are not very common. The suborder Lysiopetalídea, with one family, the Lysiopetálidae (= Callipódidae), contains larger millipedes that are usually keeled. These millipedes can coil the body into a spiral. The secretions of the scent glands are milky white and very odoriferous. The suborder Striariídea, with one family (the Striarìidae), have no scent glands, the anal segment three-lobed, and a high middorsal carina on the metazonite. These millipedes are mostly southern and western in distribution.

ORDER **Jùlida**[47]: This order and the next three are by some authorities combined into a single order, the Opisthospermóphora. These four groups have the body cylindrical, with 40 or more segments. The collum is large and hoodlike and overlaps the head. Either both pairs of legs on the seventh segment of the male are modified into gonopods or one pair is absent. Scent glands are present. The diplosomites are not differentiated into prozonite and metazonite. The millipedes in the order Jùlida have the stipites of the gnathochilarium broadly contiguous along the midline behind the laminae linguales. Segment 3 and the terminal segment are legless; segments 1, 2, and 4 have one pair of legs each; and the remaining segments have two pairs of legs each. More than a hundred species of julids occur in North America, and some of them reach a length of about 90 mm.

ORDER **Spirobólida**[48]: The millipedes in this order differ from the Jùlida in having the stipites of the gnathochilarium separated (Figure 6–32B) and from the following two orders in having one pair of legs each on segments 1–5. This group contains about 35 North American species, including some of the largest. *Nárceus americànus* (Beauvois), which is dark brown and narrowly ringed with red, may reach a length of 100 mm (Figure 6–31).

ORDER **Spirostréptida**[49]: The members of this order have one pair of legs each on segments 1–4, and the posterior pair of gonopods on the seventh segment of the male is rudimentary or absent. The stipites of the gnathochilarium are separated, but the laminae linguales are usually contiguous. This group is principally tropical, but three species occur in the Southwest.

ORDER **Cambálida**[50]: These millipedes are very similar to the Spirostréptida, but have the laminae linguales separated by the mentum and both pairs of legs on the seventh segment of the male modified into gonopods, and there are no legs on the fourth segment. The collum is quite large, and most species have prominent longitudinal ridges on the body. One species in this order, *Cámbala annulàta* (Say), is predaceous.

SUPERORDER **Colobógnatha**[51]: The members of this group have the head small and the mouthparts suctorial, and the body is somewhat flattened, with 30–60 segments. The first pair of legs on the seventh segment of the male is not modified into gonopods. This superorder contains two orders, the **Platydésmida**[52] and **Polyzonìida**,[53] which may be separated by the characters given in the key. These orders are represented in the United States by one and two families, respectively. *Polyzònium bivirgàtum* (Wood), which reaches a length of about 20 mm, occurs in rotten wood.

[51]Colobógnatha: *colobo*, shortened; *gnatha*, jaws.
[52]Platydésmida: *platy*, flat; *desmida*, bands.
[53]Polyzonìida: *poly*, many; *zoniida*, belt or girdle.

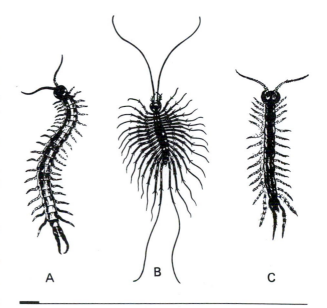

Figure 6–33. Centipedes. **A,** a large centipede, *Scolopéndra obscùra* Newport, about ¼ natural size; **B,** a house centipede, *Scutígera coleoptràta* (L.), about ½ natural size; **C,** a small centipede, *Lithòbius erythrocéphalus* Koch, about natural size. (Courtesy of USDA.)

[47]Jùlida: from the Greek, meaning a centipede.
[48]Spirobólida: *spiro*, spiral; *bolida*, throw.
[49]Spirostréptida: *spiro*, spiral; *streptida*, twisted.
[50]Cambálida: derivation unknown.

Class Chilópoda[54]—Centipedes

The centipedes are elongate, flattened animals with 15 or more pairs of legs (Figure 6–33). Each body segment bears a single pair of legs. The last two pairs are directed backward and are often different in form from the other pairs. The antennae consist of 14 or more segments. The genital openings are located at the posterior end of the body, usually on the next to last segment. Eyes may be present or absent; if present, they usually consist of numerous ommatidia. The head bears a pair of mandibles and two pairs of maxillae. The second pair of maxillae may be somewhat leglike in form or short with basal segments of the two maxillae fused together. The appendages of the first body segment behind the head are clawlike and function as poison jaws (Figure 6–34).

Centipedes are found in a variety of places, but usually occur in a protected situation such as in the soil, under bark, or in rotten logs. They are very active, fast-running animals and are predaceous. They feed on insects, spiders, and other small animals. All centipedes possess poison jaws with which they paralyze their prey. The smaller centipedes of the northern states are harmless to people, but the larger ones of the South and the tropics are able to inflict a painful bite. Centipedes overwinter as adults in protected situations and lay their eggs during the summer. The eggs are usually sticky and

become covered with soil, and they are deposited singly. In some species the male may eat the egg before the female can get it covered with soil.

Some centipedes produce silk, which is used in mating. The male makes a small web in which he deposits a package of sperm, and this package is then picked up by the female.

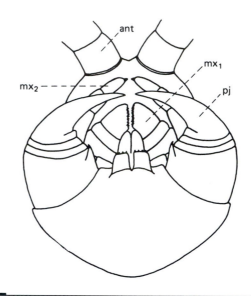

Figure 6–34. Head of centipede (*Scolopéndra*, order Scolopendromórpha), ventral view. *ant*, antenna; *mx₁*, first maxilla; *mx₂*, second maxilla; *pj*, poison jaw or toxicognath, a modified leg.

[54]Chilópoda: *chilo*, lip; *poda*, foot or appendage (referring to the fact that the poison jaws are modified legs)

Key to the Orders of Chilópoda

1.	Adults with 15 pairs of legs, newly hatched young with 7 pairs (subclass Anamórpha) **2**	
1'.	Adults and newly hatched young with 21 or more pairs of legs (subclass Epimórpha) **3**	
2(1).	Spiracles unpaired, 7 in number, located on middorsal line near posterior margin of tergites; antennae long and many-segmented; legs long (Figure 6–33B); eyes compound ....**Scutigeromórpha**	p. 143
2'.	Spiracles paired and located laterally; each leg-bearing segment with a separate tergite; antennae and legs relatively short (Figure 6–33C); eyes not compound, but consisting of single facets or groups of facets, or absent ....**Lithòbiomórpha**	p. 143
3(1').	Antennae with 17 or more segments; 21–23 pairs of legs; eyes usually 4 or more facets on each side.................................**Scolopéndromórpha**	p. 143
3'.	Antennae 14-segmented; 29 or more pairs of legs; eyes absent ....**Geophilomórpha**	p. 143

ORDER **Scutigeromórpha**[55]: This group includes the common house centipede, *Scutígera coleoptràta* (L.) (Figure 6–33B), which is found throughout the eastern United States and Canada. Its natural habitat is under logs and similar places, but it frequently enters houses where it feeds on flies, spiders, and the like. In houses it often frequents the vicinity of sinks and drains. It is harmless to people. This order contains the single family Scutigéridae.

ORDER **Lithòbiomórpha**[56]—Stone Centipedes: These are short-legged, usually brown centipedes with 15 pairs of legs in the adults (Figure 6–33C). They vary in length from about 4 to 45 mm. Some members of this order are quite common, usually occurring under stones or logs, under bark, and in similar situations. When disturbed, they sometimes use their posterior legs to throw droplets of a sticky material at their attacker. This order contains two families, the Henicópidae (4–11 mm in length, the legs without strong spines, and the eyes consisting of a single facet each or absent) and the Lithobìidae (10–45 mm in length, at least some legs with strong spines, and the eyes usually consisting of many facets).

ORDER **Scolopéndromórpha**[57]: This group is principally tropical and, in the United States, occurs mainly in the southern states. The scolopendrids include the largest North American centipedes, which reach a length of about 150 mm (Figure 6–33A). Some tropical species may be a half a meter or more in length. Many scolopendrids are greenish or yellowish in color. These are the most venomous centipedes in our area. The bite of the larger species is quite painful, and they can also pinch with their last pair of legs. Two families occur in this order in the United States, the Scolopéndridae (each eye with four facets) and the Cryptópidae (each eye with one facet).

ORDER **Geophilomórpha**[58]—Soil Centipedes: The members of this order are slender, with 29 or more pairs of short legs and large poisonous jaws, and are usually whitish or yellowish in color. Most species are small, but some may reach a length of 100 mm or more. They usually occur in the soil, in rotten logs, or in debris. When disturbed, they curl up and give off a secretion that seems to act as a repellent for potential predators. The five families in this order that occur in the United States are separated by characters of the mandibles.

Class Paurópoda[59]—Pauropods

Pauropods are minute, usually whitish myriapods, 1.0–1.5 mm in length. The antennae bear three apical branches. The nine pairs of legs are not grouped in double pairs as in the millipedes. The head is small and is sometimes covered by the tergal plate of the first body segment (Figure 6–35A). The genital ducts open near the anterior end of the body. Pauropods occur under stones, in leaf litter, and in similar places.

Class Sýmphyla[60]—Symphylans

The symphylans are slender, whitish myriapods, 1–8 mm in length, with 15–22 (usually 15) body segments and 10–12 pairs of legs (Figure 6–35B). The antennae are slender and many-segmented, and the head is well developed and distinct. The genital openings are located near the anterior end of the

[59]Paurópoda: *pauro*, small; *poda*, foot or appendage.

[60]Sýmphyla: from the Greek, meaning growing together.

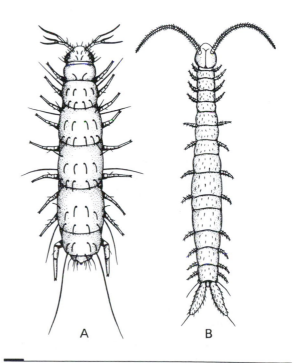

Figure 6–35. **A,** a pauropod, *Pauròpus* sp., 95×; **B,** a symphylan, *Scolopendrélla* sp., 16×. (**A** redrawn from Lubbock; **B,** redrawn from Comstock, after Latzel.)

[55]Scutigeromórpha: *scuti*, shield; *gero*, bear or carry; *morpha*, form.

[56]Lithòbiomórpha: *litho*, stone; *bio*, life; *morpha*, form.

[57]Scolopéndromórpha: *scolopendro*, centipede; *morpha*, form.

[58]Geophilomórpha: *geo*, earth; *philo*, loving; *morpha*, form.

body. Symphylans occur in humus soil, under stones, in decaying wood, and in other damp situations. The garden symphylan, *Scutigerélla immaculàta* (Newport), feeds on the roots of plants and is sometimes a pest of vegetable crops, of the seedlings of broadleaved trees, and in greenhouses.

Collecting and Preserving Myriapods

Myriapods may be killed in a cyanide bottle, but such specimens often become coiled or distorted. These animals are best killed and preserved in alcohol (about 75%) or in alcohol and glycerine (10 parts of alcohol to 1 part of glycerine). Millipedes may be picked up by hand or with forceps. Except in the case of the smaller specimens, it is well to handle centipedes with forceps, as the larger specimens can inflict a painful bite.

Class Hexápoda[61]

This class is included here to indicate its position in the phylum. Since the bulk of this book is concerned with this group, we need to say no more about them here.

[61]Hexápoda: *hexa*, six; *poda*, legs.

References

Anderson, D. T. 1979. Embryology and Phylogeny in Annelids and Arthropods. New York: Pergamon Press, 495 pp.

Barnes, R. D. 1987. (5th ed.). Invertebrate Zoology. Philadelphia: Saunders College Publishing, 893 pp.; illus.

Clarke, K. U. 1973. The Biology of Arthropods. New York: American Elsevier, 270 pp.; illus.

Cloudsley-Thompson, J. L. 1958. Spiders, Scorpions, Centipedes, and Mites. New York: Pergamon Press, 228 pp.; illus.

Eddy, S., and A. C. Hodson. 1950. Taxonomic Keys to the Common Animals of the North Central States Exclusive of the Parasitic Worms, Insects and Birds. Minneapolis: Burgess, 123 pp.; illus.

Gupta, A. P. 1979. Arthropod Phylogeny. New York: Van Nostrand–Reinhold, 762 pp.; illus.

Levi, H. V., L. R. Levi, and H. S. Zim. 1968. Spiders and Their Kin. New York: Golden Press, 160 pp.; illus. (most in color).

Manton, S. M. 1964. Mandibular mechanisms and the evolution of the arthropods. Phil. Trans. Roy. Soc. B 247:1–183; illus.

Manton, S. M. 1977. The Arthropoda. Habits, Functional Morphology, and Evolution. Oxford: Clarendon Press, 257 pp.; illus.

Pimentel, R. A. 1967. Invertebrate Identification Manual. New York: Reinhold, 150 pp.; illus.

Snodgrass, R. E. 1935. Principles of Insect Morphology. New York: McGraw-Hill, 677 pp.; illus.

Snodgrass, R. E. 1952. A Textbook of Arthropod Anatomy. Ithaca, N.Y.: Comstock, 363 pp.; illus.

Tiegs, O. W., and S. M. Manton. 1958. The evolution of the Arthropoda. Biol. Rev. 33:255–337; illus.

The Cheliceràta

Arthur, D. R. 1959. A Monograph of the Ixodoidea. Part V. The Genera *Dermacentor, Anocentor, Cosmiomma, Boophilus,* and *Margaropus.* Cambridge: Cambridge Univ. Press, 251 pp.; illus.

Atkins, J. A., C. W. Wingo, W. A. Soderman, and J. E. Flynn. 1958. Nectotic arachnidism. Amer. J. Trop. Med. Hyg. 7(2):165–184; illus.

Baker, E. W., T. M. Evans, D. J. Gould, W. B. Hull, and H. L. Keegan. 1956. A Manual of Parasitic Mites of Medical or Economic Importance. New York: National Pest Control Assoc., 170 pp.; illus.

Baker, E. W., and G. W. Wharton. 1952. An Introduction to Acarology. New York: Macmillan, 465 pp.; illus.

Beck, L., and H. Schubart. 1968. Revision der Gattung *Cryptocellus* Westwood 1874 (Arachnida: Ricinulei). Senckenberg Biol. 49:67–78.

Bishop, S. C. 1949. The Phalangida (Opiliones) of New York, with special reference to the species in the Edmund Niles Huyk Preserve. Proc. Rochester Acad. Sci. 9(3):159–235; illus.

Bristowe, W. S. 1939–1941. The Comity of Spiders. Vol. 1, Publ. 126, 228 pp., illus. (1939). Vol. 2, Publ. 128, 332 pp., illus. (1941). London: Ray Society. (These volumes are available in a 1-vol. reprint ed. by Johnson Reprints.)

Chamberlin, J. C. 1931. The arachnid order Chelonethida. Stanford Univ. Publ. Biol. Ser. 7(1):1–284; illus.

Chamberlin, R. V., and W. Ivie. 1944. Spiders of the Georgia region of North America. Bull. Univ. Utah 35(9):1–267; illus.

Comstock, J. H., and W. J. Gertsch. 1940. The Spider Book. New York: Doubleday, 729 pp.; illus.

Dondale, C. D., and J. H. Redner. 1978. The crab spiders of Canada and Alaska (Araneae: Philodromidae and Thomisidae). The Insects and Arachnids of Canada, Part 5. Ottawa: Can. Gov. Pub. Centre, 255 pp.; illus.

Dondale, C. D., and J. H. Redner. 1982. The sac spiders of Canada and Alaska (Araneae: Clubionidae and Anyphaenidae). The Insects and Arachnids of Canada, Part 9. Ottawa: Can. Gov. Pub. Centre, 194 pp.; illus.

Evans, G. O., J. H. Sheals, and D. Macfarlane. 1961. The Terrestrial Acari of the British Isles: An Introduction to Their Morphology, Biology, and Classification. London: British Museum, 219 pp.; illus.

Ewing, H. E. 1928. Scorpions of the western part of the United States, with notes on those occurring in northern Mexico. Proc. U.S. Natl. Mus. 73(9):1–24; illus.

Ewing, H. E. 1929. A synopsis of the order Ricinulei. Ann. Entomol. Soc. Amer. 22:583–600; illus.

Gertsch, W. J. 1979 (2nd ed.). American Spiders. New York: Van Nostrand, 274 pp.; illus.

Gertsch, W. J., and S. Mulaik. 1939. Report on a new ricinuleid from Texas. Amer. Mus. Novitat. No. 1037, 5 pp.; illus.

Gertsch, W. J., and S. Mulaik. 1940. The spiders of Texas. I. Bull. Amer. Mus. Nat. Hist. 77(6):307–340; illus.

Gorham, J. R., and T. B. Rheney. 1968. Envenomation by the spiders *Chiracanthium inclusum* and *Argiope aurantia*. Observations on arachnids in the United States. J. Amer. Med. Assoc. 206(9):1958–1962; illus.

Hoff, C. C. 1949. The pseudoscorpions of Illinois. Ill. Nat. Hist. Surv. Bull. 24(4):411–498; illus.

Hoff, C. C. 1959. List of the pseudoscorpions of North America north of Mexico. Amer. Mus. Novitat. No. 1875; 50 pp.

Johnson, J. D., and D. M. Allred. 1972. Scorpions of Utah. Gr. Basin Natur. 32(3):157–170; illus.

Johnston, D. E. 1968. An Atlas of the Acari. I. The Families of Parasitiformes and Opilioacariformes. Columbus: Acarology Laboratory, Ohio State Univ., 110 pp.; illus.

Kaston, B. J. 1948. Spiders of Connecticut. Conn. State Geol. Nat. Hist. Surv. Bull. 70:1–874; illus.

Kaston, B. J. 1970. Comparative biology of American black widow spiders. Trans. San Diego Soc. Nat. Hist. 16(3):33–82; illus.

Kaston, B. J. 1977. Supplement to the spiders of Connecticut. J. Arachn. 4(1):1–72.

Kaston, B. J. 1978 (3rd ed.). How to Know the Spiders. Dubuque, Iowa: Wm. C. Brown, 272 pp.; illus.

King, P. E. 1974. Pycnogonida. New York: St. Martin's, 144 pp.; illus.

Krantz, G. W. 1978 (2nd ed.). A Manual of Acarology. Corvallis: Oregon State Univ. Book Stores, 509 pp.; illus.

Martens, J. 1978. Spinnenriere, Arachnida: Weberknechte, Opiliones. Die Tierwelt Deutschlands 64:1–464; illus.

McCloskey, L. R. 1973. Marine flora and fauna of the northeastern United States: Pycnogonida. NOAA Tech. Rep. NMFS Circ. 386, 12 pp.; illus.

Muma, M. H. 1943. Common Spiders of Maryland. Baltimore: Natural History Society of Maryland, 173 pp.; illus.

Muma, M. H. 1951–1962. The arachnid order Solpugida in the United States. Bull. Amer. Mus. Nat. Hist. 97:31–141; illus. (1951). Amer. Mus. Novitat. No. 2902, Suppl. 1, 44 pp.; illus. (1962).

Muma, M. H. 1970. A synoptic review of North American, Central American, and West Indies Solpugida (Arthropoda: Arachnida). Arthropods of Florida and Neighboring Land Areas 5:1–62; illus.

Parrish, H. M. 1959. Deaths from bites and stings of venomous animals and insects. Amer. Med. Assoc. Arch. Intern. Med. 104:198–207.

Pritchard, A. E., and E. W. Baker. 1955. A revision of the spider mite family Tetranychidae. Mem. Pac. Coast Entomol. Soc. 2:1–472; illus.

Roe, R. M., and C. W. Clifford. 1976. Freeze-drying of spiders and immature insects using commercial equipment. Ann. Entomol. Soc. Amer. 69:497–499.

Roth, V. D. 1985. Spider genera of North America. Gainesville, Fla.: Amer. Arachnol. Soc., 176 pp.

Savory, T. 1977 (2nd ed.). Arachnida. New York: Academic Press, 350 pp.; illus.

Stahnke, H. L. 1974. Revision and keys to the higher categories of Vejovidae (Scorpionida). J. Arachn. 1(2):107–141.

Tuttle, D. M., and E. W. Baker. 1968. Spider Mites of Southwestern United States and Revisions of the Family Tetranychidae. Tucson: Univ. Arizona Press, 150 pp.; illus.

Vogel, B. R. 1968. A zodariid spider from Pennsylvania. J. N.Y. Entomol. Soc. 76:96–100.

Weygoldt, P. 1969. The Biology of Pseudoscorpions. Cambridge: Harvard Univ. Press, 145 pp.; illus.

Wingo, C. W. 1960. Poisonous spiders. Univ. Mo. Agr. Ext. Serv. Bull. No. 738, 11 pp.; illus.

The Crustàcea

Crowder, W. 1931. Between the Tides. New York: Dodd, Mead, 461 pp.; illus.

Edmondson, W. T. (Ed.). 1959. Fresh Water Biology. New York: Wiley, 1248 pp.; illus.

Green, J. 1961. A Biology of the Crustacea. Chicago: Quadrangle Books, 180 pp.; illus.

Klots, E. B. 1966. The New Book of Freshwater Life. New York: G. P. Putnam's, 398 pp.; illus.

Miner, R. W. 1950. Field Book of Seashore Life. New York: G. P. Putnam's, 888 pp.; illus.

Pennak, R. W. 1978 (2nd ed.). Fresh-Water Invertebrates of the United States. New York: Wiley Interscience, 803 pp.; illus.

Willoughby, L. G. 1976. Freshwater Biology. New York: Pica Press, 168 pp.; illus.

The Myriapods

Bailey, J. W. 1928. The Chilopoda of New York state, with Notes on the Diplopoda. N.Y. State Mus. Bull. 276:5–50; illus.

Chamberlin, R. V., and R. L. Hoffman. 1958. Checklist of the millipedes of North America. U.S. Natl. Mus. Bull. 212:1–236.

Eason, E. H. 1964. Centipedes of the British Isles. London: Frederick Wame, 294 pp.; illus.

Johnson, B. M. 1954. The millipedes of Michigan. Pap. Mich. Acad. Sci. 39(1953):241–252; illus.

Keeton, W. T. 1960. A taxonomic study of the millipede family Spirobolidae (Diplopoda, Spirobolida). Mem. Entomol. Soc. Amer. No. 17, 146 pp.; illus.

Shear, W. A. 1972. Studies in the millipede order Chordeumida (Diplopoda): A revision of the family Cleidogonidae and a reclassification of the order Chordeumida in the New World. Bull. Mus. Comp. Zool. Harvard 144(4):151–352; illus.

Chapter 7   Hexápoda[1]

Characters of the Hexápoda

The distinguishing characters of the Hexápoda may be listed briefly as follows:

Body

1. The body with three distinct regions: head, thorax, and abdomen

Head

2. One pair of antennae (rarely no antennae)
3. One pair of mandibles
4. One pair of maxillae
5. A hypopharynx
6. A labium

Thorax

7. Three pairs of legs, one on each thoracic segment (a few insects are legless, and some larvae possess additional leglike appendages—such as prolegs—on the abdominal segments)

Abdomen

8. The gonopore (rarely two gonopores) on the posterior portion of the abdomen
9. No locomotor appendages on the abdomen of the adult (except in some primitive hexapods); abdominal appendages, if present, located at the apex of the abdomen and consisting of a pair of cerci, an epiproct, and a pair of paraprocts
10. Flagellum of spermatozoa with 9 + 9 + 2 arrangement of microtubules

Classification of the Hexápoda

The class Hexápoda is divided into orders primarily on the basis of the structure of the wings and mouthparts, and the metamorphosis. There are differences of opinion among entomologists regarding the limits of some of the orders and the names that should be used for them. A few of the groups that we treat as a single order are divided into two or more orders by some authorities, and there are cases where two groups that we recognize as separate orders are combined into a single order by some authorities. A few of the groups that we treat as orders of hexapods (the entognathous orders) are considered by some to be separate classes of arthropods.

A synopsis of the orders of hexapods, as recognized in this book, is given in the following outline. Other names or arrangements are given in parentheses. Data on the sizes of the various orders are given in Table 7–1.

146   [1]Hexápoda: *hexa*, six; *poda*, foot.

Table 7–1
Relative Size of the Insect Orders, as Shown by the Number of Species and Families Occurring in Different Geographic Areas

| Order | Number of Species | | | | | Families in North America North of Mexico[e] |
	North Carolina[a]	Mt. Desert, Maine[b]	New York[c]	North America North of Mexico[d]	World[d]	
Protùra	0	0	1	19	200	3
Collémbola	169	1	200	677	6,000	7
Diplùra	1	1	2	64	659	4
Microcorýphia	1	0	2	20	250	2
Thysanùra	5	1	3	18	320	3
Ephemeróptera	121	44	61	611	2,000	17
Odonàta	148	81	159	407	4,870	11
Grylloblattària	0	0	0	10	20	1
Phásmida	4	0	2	29	2,000	4
Orthóptera	235	46	121	1,080	12,500	10
Mantòdea	2	0	2	20	1,500	1
Blattària	17	4	11	49	4,000	5
Isóptera	5	0	1	42	1,900	4
Dermáptera	7	0	4	20	1,100	6
Embiidìna	0	0	0	10	150	3
Plecóptera	94	31	59	537	1,500	9
Zoráptera	1	0	0	2	24	1
Psocóptera	37	25	36	340	2,400	26
Phthiráptera	175	186	64	1,000	5,500	16
Hemíptera	568	179	727	3,587	50,000	42
Homóptera	759	224	864	6,359	32,000	38
Thysanóptera	68	9	71	694	4,000	5
Neuróptera	68	35	61	350	4,670	15
Coleóptera	3,336	1,175	4,546	23,701	300,000	115
Strepsíptera	11	2	2	109	300	4
Mecóptera	27	5	20	68	480	5
Siphonáptera	14	10	26	320	2,300	8
Díptera	2,595	1,626	3,615	18,200	120,000	108
Trichóptera	161	96	174	1,261	7,000	23
Lepidóptera	1,428	1,479	2,439	11,286	112,000	75
Hymenóptera	2,463	1,107	2,300	17,200	108,000	78
Total	12,520	6,367	15,573	88,090	787,643	659

[a]From D. L. Wray, *Insects of North Carolina*, 3rd supplement (Raleigh: North Carolina Department of Agriculture, Division of Entomology, 1967), 181 pp.

[b]From W. Procter, *Biological Survey of the Mt. Desert Region*, Part VII: *The Insect Fauna* (Philadelphia: Wistar Institute Press, 1946), 566 pp.

[c]Mainly from M. D. Leonard, *A List of the Insects of New York*, Cornell University Agricultural Experiment Station Mem. 101 (1928), 1121 pp.

[d]From various sources, chiefly the USDA Yearbook for 1952, p. 6; the figures in most cases are approximate.

[e]The number recognized in this book.

Entógnatha
1. Protùra (Myrientómata)—proturans
2. Collémbola (Oligentómata)—springtails
3. Diplùra (Entógnatha, Entótrophi, Áptera)—diplurans

Insécta
4. Microcorýphia (Archaeógnatha; Thysanùra, Ectógnatha, and Ectótrophi in part)—bristletails

5. Thysanùra (Ectógnatha, Ectótrophi, Zygentòma)—silverfish, firebrats

Pterygòta—winged and secondarily wingless insects
6. Ephemeróptera (Ephemérida, Plectóptera)—mayflies
7. Odonàta—dragonflies and damselflies
8. Grylloblattària (Grylloblattòdea, Notóptera)—rock crawlers

9. Phásmida (Phasmátida, Phasmatóptera, Phasmatòdea, Cheleutóptera; Orthóptera in part)—walkingsticks and timemas
10. Orthóptera (Saltatòria, including Gryllóptera)—grasshoppers and crickets
11. Mantòdea (Orthóptera, Dictyóptera, Dictuóptera in part)—mantids
12. Blattària (Blattòdea; Orthóptera, Dictyóptera, Dictuóptera in part)—cockroaches
13. Isóptera (Dictyóptera, Dictuóptera in part)—termites
14. Dermáptera (Euplexóptera)—earwigs
15. Embiidìna (Embióptera)—webspinners
16. Plecóptera—stoneflies
17. Zoráptera—zorapterans
18. Psocóptera (Corrodéntia)—psocids
19. Phthiráptera (Mallóphaga, Anoplùra, Siphunculáta)—lice
20. Hemíptera (Heteróptera)—bugs
21. Homóptera (Hemíptera in part)—cicadas, hoppers, psyllids, whiteflies, aphids, and scale insects
22. Thysanóptera (Physápoda)—thrips
23. Neuróptera (including Megalóptera and Raphidiòdea)—alderflies, dobsonflies, fishflies, snakeflies, lacewings, antlions, and owlflies
24. Coleóptera—beetles
25. Strepsíptera (Coleóptera in part)—twisted-wing parasites
26. Mecóptera (including Neomecóptera)—scorpionflies
27. Siphonáptera—fleas
28. Díptera—flies
29. Trichóptera—caddisflies
30. Lepidóptera (including Zeuglóptera)—butterflies and moths
31. Hymenóptera—sawflies, ichneumonids, chalcids, ants, wasps, and bees

Phylogeny of the Hexápoda

Data on the phylogeny of hexapods are found chiefly in the fossil record and in comparative studies of present-day insects. Insect fossils are not abundant, but enough have been found to give us a general idea of insect history on the earth. A brief summary of the fossil record is given in Table 7–2. The data from comparative studies are interpreted differently by some people, who may attribute different degrees of importance to particular features, but certain general relationships are evident and can be outlined here.

Table 7–2
An Outline of the Fossil Record

Era	Millions of Years Ago[a]	Periods		Forms of Life
Cenozoic		Pleistocene		First man
	70	Tertiary	Pliocene Miocene Oligocene Eocene Paleocene	Age of mammals and flowering plants; rise of modern insect genera; insects in amber
Mesozoic	135 180 225	Cretaceous Jurassic Triassic	First birds First mammals	Age of reptiles; first flowering plants; most modern orders of insects; extinction of fossil insect orders
Paleozoic	270	Permian		Rise of most modern insect orders; extinction of many fossil orders
	350	Carboniferous		First winged insects (in several orders, most now extinct; some very large insects in this period); appearance of primitive reptiles
	400	Devonian		First hexapods (springtails); first land vertebrates (amphibians); age of fish

Table 7–2 (*Continued*)

Era	Millions of Years Ago[a]	Periods	Forms of Life
Paleozoic (*cont.*)	440	Silurian	First land animals (scorpions and millipedes); rise of fish
	500	Ordovician	First vertebrates (ostracoderms)
	600	Cambrian	First arthropods (trilobites, xiphosurans, and branchiopods)
Precambrian			Primitive invertebrates

[a]From the beginning of the period.

The fossil record for Precambrian time is quite scanty, but by the Cambrian period marine arthropods were present, consisting of trilobites, crustaceans, and xiphosurans. The first terrestrial arthropods—scorpions and millipedes—appeared later, in the Silurian period, and the first hexapods appeared in the Devonian. Relatively few fossils are known from the Devonian, but many are known from the Carboniferous and later periods.

The hexapods are believed to have arisen from a myriapod-like ancestor that had paired leglike appendages on each body segment. The change to the hexapod condition involved the development of a head, modification of the three segments behind the head as locomotory segments, and a loss or reduction of most of the appendages on the remaining body segments. The first insects were undoubtedly wingless (sometimes called apterygotes).

The Protùra, Diplùra, and Collémbola are very distinct groups. (Some authorities would put these in separate classes, concluding that the characteristics of "hexapods" evolved at least four times independently.) These animals are primitively wingless and have the lateral portions of the head prolonged and fused to the labium to form a pouch, thus enveloping the mandibles and maxillae. This latter characteristic gives rise to the name of the taxon containing these three orders, the Entógnatha. These orders represent early offshoots of the hexapod line. The oldest known hexapod fossils (from the Devonian) are clearly identifiable as Collémbola.

The other two primitively wingless orders are the Microcorýphia and Thysanùra. These creatures, as well as the winged insects, usually have the mouthparts exposed (hence the name Ectógnatha). Kristensen (1981) has suggested that the word *insects* be restricted to refer to these ectognathous species and that *hexapods* should include both the Entógnatha and Ectógnatha. Thus the two terms would not be synonymous, and the more general word *hex-apod* would refer to the fundamental characteristic of the species included, that is, the possession of six thoracic legs. We will use the terms in that sense in this book.

Two major lines developed within the winged insects, or Pterygòta: the Paleóptera and the Neóptera. These two groups differ (among other ways) in their ability to flex their wings: the Paleóptera cannot flex their wings over the abdomen,[2] while the Neóptera can. This wing flexion is effected by rotation of the third axillary sclerite about the posterior notal wing process (see Chapter 3). There were several orders of Paleóptera present in the late Paleozoic, but the only ones that have survived to the present are the Ephemeróptera and Odonàta.

The relationship among the orders of Neóptera are far from clear. There are several orders, generally referred to as the orthopteroid orders, that are characterized by simple metamorphosis, mandibulate mouthparts, a large anal lobe in the hind wing, cerci, and numerous Malpighian tubules. They include the present orders Orthóptera, Phásmida, Grylloblattària, Mantòdea, Blattària, Isóptera, Dermáptera, and Embiidìna. Some authorities classify these together as the taxon Polyneóptera. Among these, the Embiidìna do not have a large anal lobe in the hind wing, and it is uncertain whether this characteristic represents a secondary development. The position of the order Plecóptera is debated. They are sometimes placed within the Polyneóptera and sometimes separated by themselves in the group Paurometábola (or Pliconeóptera).

The hemipteroid groups (sometimes classified as the Paraneóptera) are characterized by simple metamorphosis, a trend toward haustellate mouthparts, no large anal lobe in the hind wing and the venation

[2]The only exception to this rule is the extinct order Diaphanapteròdea. These insects could flex the wings, but apparently by a still unknown mechanism different from that of the Neóptera.

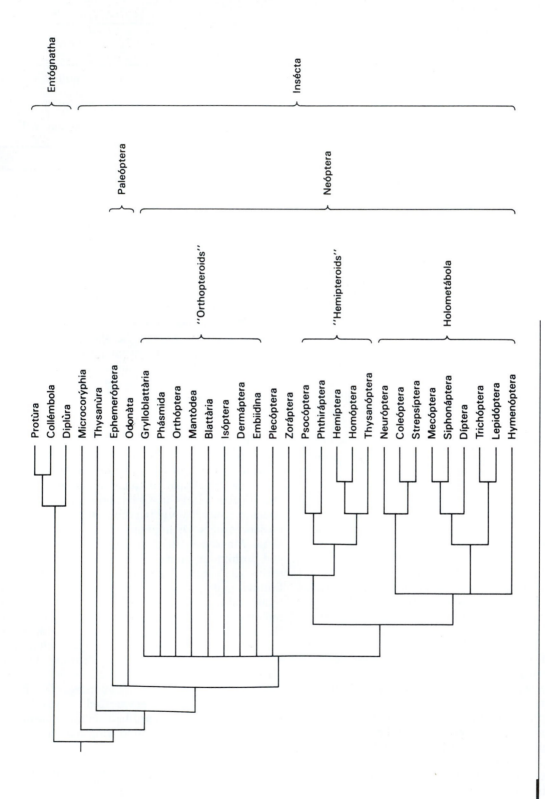

Figure 7–1. Phylogeny of the hexapod orders (after Kristensen 1981).

somewhat reduced, no cerci, and relatively few Malpighian tubules. This group certainly includes the Thysanóptera, Hemíptera, Homóptera, Psocóptera, and Phthiráptera. The Zoráptera may belong here or may have lost the structures just mentioned independently of the other hemipteroids.

Complete metamorphosis appeared with the common ancestor of the remaining nine orders, the Holometábola or Endopterygòta. The relationships among these orders are unclear, but there are at least three major lines: (1) the Hymenóptera; (2) the neuropteroids: the Neuróptera, Coleóptera, and Strepsíptera; and (3) the panorpoids: the Lepidóptera, Trichóptera, Mecóptera, Siphonáptera, and Díptera.

These concepts of the phylogeny of the insect orders are summarized in the diagram in Figure 7–1, which also shows the sequence in which the orders are treated in this book.

Key to the Orders of Hexapods

This key includes adults, nymphs, and larvae. The portion of the key covering nymphs and larvae should work for most specimens, but some very young or highly specialized forms may not key out correctly. The habitat is sometimes an important character in keying out larvae. Groups marked with an asterisk are unlikely to be encountered by the general collector.

1.	With well-developed wings (adults)	**2**
1′.	Wingless or with wings vestigial or rudimentary (nymphs, larvae, and some adults)	**30**
2(1).	Wings membranous, not hardened or leathery	**3**
2′.	Front wings hardened or leathery, at least at base (Figure 7–2); hind wings, if present, usually membranous	**24**
3(2).	With only one pair of wings	**4**

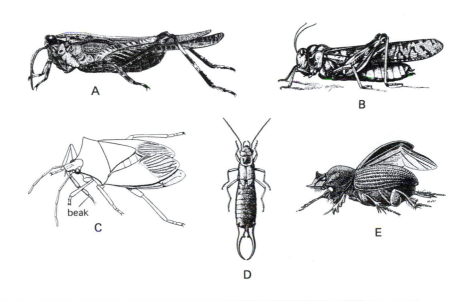

Figure 7–2.   Insects with front wings thickened and hind wings membranous. **A,** a pygmy grasshopper (Orthóptera); **B,** a band-winged grasshopper (Orthóptera); **C,** a stink bug (Hemíptera); **D,** an earwig (Dermáptera); **E,** a dung beetle (Coleóptera). (**A, C,** and **E** courtesy of Illinois Natural History Survey; **B,** courtesy of USDA; **D,** courtesy of Knowlton and the Utah Agricultural Experiment Station.)

3'.   With two pairs of wings **10**

4(3).   Body grasshopperlike; pronotum extending back over abdomen and pointed
           apically; hind legs enlarged (Figures 7–2A and 14–5) (pygmy grasshoppers,
           family Tetrígidae) ....**Orthóptera**   p. 208

4'.   Body not grasshopperlike; pronotum not as above; hind legs not so enlarged   **5**

5(4').   Antennae with at least 1 segment bearing a long lateral process; front wings
           minute, hind wings fanlike (Figure 29–1A–D); minute insects (male
           twisted-wing parasites) ....**Strepsíptera***   p. 479

5'.   Not exactly fitting the description above **6**

6(5').   Abdomen with 1–3 threadlike or stylelike caudal filaments; mouthparts
           vestigial **7**

6'.   Abdomen without threadlike or stylelike caudal filaments; mouthparts nearly
           always well developed, mandibulate or haustellate (Figure 7–3) **8**

7(6).   Antennae long and conspicuous; abdomen terminating in long style (rarely 2
           styles); wings with single forked vein (Figure 25–29A); halteres present,
           usually terminating in hooklike bristle; minute insects, usually less than 5
           mm in length (male scale insects) ....**Homóptera***   p. 312

7'.   Antennae short, bristlelike, inconspicuous; abdomen with two or three
           threadlike caudal filaments; wings with numerous veins and cells; halteres
           absent; usually over 5 mm in length (mayflies) ....**Ephemeróptera**   p. 175

8(6').   Tarsi nearly always 5-segmented; mouthparts haustellate; hind wings reduced
           to halteres (Figure 7–4A, *hal*) (flies) ....**Díptera**   p. 499

8'.   Tarsi 2- or 3-segmented; mouthparts variable; hind wings reduced or absent,
           not halterelike **9**

9(8').   Mouthparts mandibulate (some psocids) ....**Psocóptera***   p. 260

9'.   Mouthparts haustellate (some planthoppers and a few leafhoppers) **Homóptera**   p. 312

10(3').   Wings largely or entirely covered with scales; mouthparts usually in form of
           coiled proboscis; antennae many-segmented (Figure 7–4B) (butterflies and
           moths)..**Lepidóptera**   p. 588

10'.   Wings not covered with scales; mouthparts not in form of coiled proboscis;
           antennae variable **11**

11(10').   Wings long and narrow, veinless or with only 1 or 2 veins, fringed with long
           hairs (Figure 7–5A); tarsi 1- or 2-segmented, last segment swollen; minute
           insects, usually less than 5 mm in length (thrips) ....**Thysanóptera**   p. 350

11'.   Wings not as above, or if wings are somewhat linear, then tarsi have more than
           2 segments...**12**

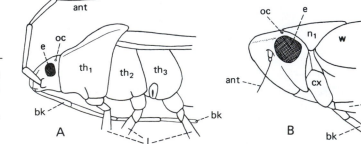

Figure 7–3. Lateral view of anterior part
of body of **A,** a lygaeid bug (Hemíptera), and
B, a froghopper (Homóptera). *ant,* antenna;
bk, beak; *cx,* front coxa; *e,* compound eye; *l,*
legs; *n₁,* pronotum; *oc,* ocellus; *th₁₋₃,*
thoracic segments; *w,* front wing.

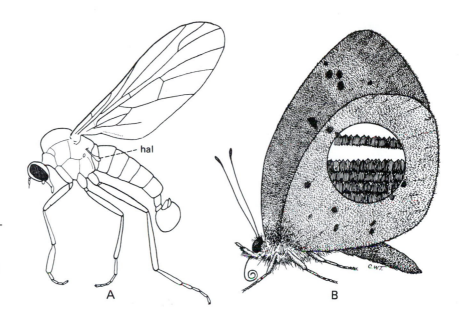

Figure 7–4. **A,** a dance fly (Díptera); **B,** a butterfly (Lepidóptera), with a section of the wing enlarged to show the scales. *hal,* haltere.

12(11′).	Front wings relatively large, usually triangular; hind wings small, usually rounded; wings at rest held together above body; wings usually with many veins and cells; antennae short, bristlelike, inconspicuous; abdomen with 2 or 3 threadlike caudal filaments (Figure 7–6); delicate, soft-bodied insects (mayflies) ....**Ephemeróptera** p. 175
12′.	Not exactly fitting the description above **13**
13(12′).	Tarsi 5-segmented **14**
13′.	Tarsi with 4 or fewer segments **17**
14(13).	Front wings noticeably hairy; mouthparts usually much reduced except for palps; antennae generally as long as body or longer; rather soft-bodied insects (caddisflies) ....**Trichóptera** p. 576
14′.	Front wings not hairy, at most with microscopic hairs; mandibles well developed; antennae shorter than body **15**
15(14′).	Rather hard-bodied, wasplike insects, abdomen often constricted at base; hind wings smaller than front wings, with fewer veins; front wings with 20 or fewer cells (sawflies, ichneumonids, chalcidoids, ants, wasps, and bees). ....**Hymenóptera** p. 605

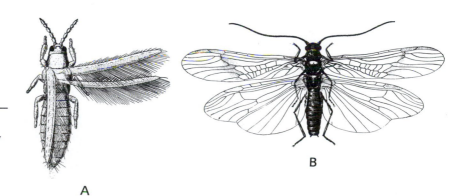

Figure 7–5. **A,** a thrips (Thysanóptera); **B,** a stonefly (Plecóptera). (**A,** courtesy of Illinois Natural History Survey; **B,** courtesy of USDA.)

Figure 7–6. A mayfly (Ephemeróptera). (Courtesy of Illinois Natural History Survey.)

15'.   Soft-bodied insects, not wasplike, abdomen not constricted at base; hind wings about same size as front wings and usually with about as many veins; front wings often with more than 20 cells **16**

16(15').   Costal area of front wing nearly always with numerous cross veins (Figure 7–7B), or if not (Coniopterýgidae, Figure 27–3A), then hind wings shorter than front wings; mouthparts not prolonged ventrally into beak (fishflies, dobsonflies, lacewings, and antlions) ....**Neuróptera**   p. 357

16'.   Costal area of front wings with not more than 2 or 3 cross veins (Figure 7–7A); mouthparts prolonged ventrally to form beaklike structure (Figures 30–1A and 30–2) (scorpionflies) ....**Mecóptera**   p. 482

17(13').   Hind wings as long as front wings and of same shape or wider at base; wings at rest held above the body or outstretched (never held flat over abdomen); wings with many veins and cells; antennae short, bristlelike, inconspicuous; abdomen long, slender (Figure 7–8); tarsi 3-segmented; length 20–85 mm (dragonflies and damselflies) ....**Odonàta**   p. 187

17'.   Not exactly fitting description above **18**

18(17').   Mouthparts haustellate **19**

18'.   Mouthparts mandibulate **20**

19(18).   Beak arising from front part of head (Figures 7–3A and 24–8) (gnat bugs) ....**Hemíptera***   p. 284

19'.   Beak arising from hind part of head (Figure 7–3B) (cicadas, some hoppers, aphids, some psyllids, and whiteflies) ....**Homóptera**   p. 312

20(18').   Tarsi 4-segmented; front and hind wings similar in size, shape, venation (Figure 17–1); cerci minute or absent (termites) ....**Isóptera**   p. 234

20'.   Tarsi with 3 or fewer segments; hind wings usually shorter than front wings; cerci present or absent **21**

21(20').   Hind wings with anal area nearly always enlarged and forming a lobe, which is folded fanwise at rest; venation varying from normal to very dense, the front wings usually with several cross veins between Cu_1 and M and between Cu_1 and Cu_2 (Figure 7–5B); cerci present, often fairly long; mostly 10 mm or more in length; nymphs aquatic, adults usually found near water (stoneflies) ....**Plecóptera**   p. 250

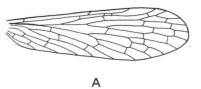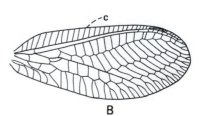

Figure 7–7. **A,** front wing of a scorpionfly (Mecóptera); **B,** front wing of a lacewing (Neuróptera).

A   B

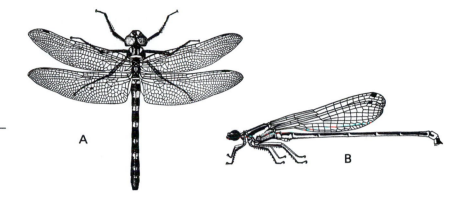

Figure 7–8. Odonàta. **A,** a dragonfly; **B,** a damselfly. (Courtesy of Kennedy and the U.S. National Museum.)

21'.	Hind wings without enlarged anal area and not folded at rest, with no extra cross veins; cerci present (but short) or absent; mostly 10 mm in length or less; nymphs not aquatic, adults not necessarily near water **22**	
22(21').	Tarsi 3-segmented, basal segment of front tarsi enlarged (Figure 19–1) (webspinners) ....**Embiidina***	p. 247
22'.	Tarsi 2- or 3-segmented, basal segment of front tarsi not enlarged **23**	
23(22').	Cerci present; tarsi 2-segmented; wing venation reduced (Figure 21–1A); antennae moniliform and 9-segmented (zorapterans) ....**Zoráptera***	p. 258
23'.	Cerci absent; tarsi 2- or 3-segmented; wing venation not particularly reduced (Figures 22–4 and 22–7); antennae not moniliform, usually long and hairlike, with 13 or more segments (Figure 22–8) (psocids) ....**Psocóptera**	p. 260
24(2').	Mouthparts haustellate, beak elongate and usually segmented (Figure 7–3) **25**	
24'.	Mouthparts mandibulate **26**	
25(24).	Beak arising from front of head (Figure 7–3A); front wings usually thickened at base, membranous at tip, the tips overlapping at rest (Figure 7–2C) (bugs) ....**Hemíptera**	p. 284
25'.	Beak arising from hind part of head, often appearing to arise at base of front legs (Figure 7–3B); front wings of uniform texture throughout, tips not, or but slightly, overlapping at rest (hoppers, some psyllids) ....**Homóptera**	p. 312
26(24').	Abdomen with forcepslike cerci (Figure 7–2D); front wings short, leaving most of abdomen exposed; tarsi 3-segmented (earwigs) ....**Dermáptera**	p. 242
26'.	Abdomen without forcepslike cerci, or if so, then front wings cover most of abdomen; tarsi variable **27**	
27(26').	Front wings without veins, usually meeting in straight line down middle of back; antennae generally with 11 or fewer segments; hind wings narrow, usually longer than front wings when unfolded, with few veins (Figure 7–2E) (beetles) ....**Coleóptera**	p. 370
27'.	Front wings with veins, either held rooflike over abdomen or overlapping over abdomen when at rest; antennae generally with more than 12 segments; hind wings broad, usually shorter than front wings, with many veins (Figure 14–9), usually folded fanwise at rest **28**	
28(27').	Tarsi with 4 or fewer segments; usually jumping insects, with hind femora more or less enlarged (Figures 14–1, 14–5, 14–7 through 14–9, and 14–13 through 14–17) (grasshoppers and crickets) ....**Orthóptera**	p. 208

28'.	Tarsi 5-segmented; running or walking insects, with hind femora not particularly enlarged (Figures 15–1 and 16-3) **29**	
29(28').	Prothorax much longer than mesothorax; front legs modified for grasping prey (Figure 15–1) (mantids) ....**Mantòdea**	p. 227
29'.	Prothorax not greatly lengthened; front legs not modified for grasping prey (Figure 16–3) (cockroaches) ....**Blattària**	p. 229
30(1').	Body usually insectlike, with segmented legs and usually also antennae (adults, nymphs, and some larvae) **31**	
30'.	Body more or less wormlike, body regions (except possibly head) not well differentiated, segmented thoracic legs absent; antennae present or absent (larvae and some adults) **77**	
31(30).	Front wings present but rudimentary; hind wings absent or represented by halteres; tarsi nearly always 5-segmented (some flies) ....**Díptera***	p. 499
31'.	Wings entirely absent, or with 4 rudimentary wings and no halteres; tarsi variable **32**	
32(31').	Antennae absent; length 1.5 mm or less (Figure 8–1); usually occurring in soil or leaf litter (proturans) ....**Protùra***	p. 165
32'.	Antennae usually present (sometimes small); size and habitat variable **33**	
33(32').	Ectoparasites of birds, mammals, or honey bees and usually found on host; body more or less leathery, usually flattened dorsoventrally or laterally **34**	
33'.	Free-living (not ectoparasitic), terrestrial or aquatic **37**	
34(33).	Tarsi 5-segmented; antennae short, usually concealed in grooves on head; mouthparts haustellate **35**	
34'.	Tarsi with fewer than 5 segments; antennae, mouthparts variable **36**	
35(34).	Body flattened laterally; usually jumping insects, with relatively long legs (Figure 7–9A) (fleas) ....**Siphonáptera**	p. 489
35'.	Body flattened dorsoventrally; not jumping insects, legs usually short (louse flies, bat flies, and bee lice) ....**Díptera***	p. 499
36(34').	Antennae distinctly longer than head; tarsi 3-segmented (bed bugs and bat bugs) ....**Hemíptera**	p. 284
36'.	Antennae not longer than head; tarsi 1-segmented (lice) ....**Phthiráptera**	p. 275
37(33').	Mouthparts haustellate, with conical or elongate beak enclosing stylets **38**	
37'.	Mouthparts mandibulate (sometimes concealed in head), not beaklike **42**	
38(37).	Tarsi 5-segmented; maxillary or labial palps present **39**	
38'.	Tarsi with 4 or fewer segments; palps small or absent **40**	
39(38).	Body covered with scales; beak usually in form of a coiled tube; antennae long and many-segmented (wingless moths) ....**Lepidóptera**	p. 588
39'.	Body not covered with scales; beak not coiled; antennae variable, but often short, with 3 or fewer segments (wingless flies) ....**Díptera***	p. 499
40(38').	Mouthparts in form of cone located basally on ventral side of head; palps present but short; body elongate, usually less than 5 mm in length; antennae about as long as head and prothorax combined, not bristlelike, 4- to 9-segmented; tarsi 1- or 2-segmented, often without claws (thrips) ....**Thysanóptera**	p. 350
40'.	Mouthparts in form of an elongate segmented beak; palps absent; other characters variable **41**	

41(40′).   Beak arising from front part of head; antennae 4- or 5-segmented, not bristlelike; tarsi usually 3-segmented; abdomen without cornicles (bugs) ....**Hemíptera**   p. 284

41′.   Beak arising from rear of head; antennae either with more than 5 segments (and tarsi 2-segmented) or bristlelike (and tarsi 3-segmented); abdomen often with pair of cornicles (Figure 25–6C) (aphids, hoppers, and others, adults and nymphs) ....**Homóptera**   p. 312

42(37′).   Abdomen distinctly constricted at base; antennae often elbowed; tarsi 5-segmented; hard-bodied, antlike insects (ants and wingless wasps) ....**Hymenóptera**   p. 665

42′.   Abdomen not particularly constricted at base; antennae not elbowed; tarsi variable **43**

43(42′).   Abdomen with 3 long threadlike caudal filaments and with stylelike appendages on some abdominal segments (Figure 7–9D); mouthparts mandibulate, but often more or less retracted into head; body nearly always covered with scales; terrestrial (silverfish, bristletails) **44**

43′.   Abdomen with only 2 threadlike caudal filaments or none; if with 3 (mayfly nymphs), then aquatic; other characters variable **45**

44(43).   Compound eyes large, usually contiguous; body somewhat cylindrical, with thorax arched; ocelli present; middle and hind coxae nearly always with styli; abdominal styli on segments 2–9 (Figure 9–1) ....**Microcoryphia**   p. 171

44′.   Compound eyes small and widely separated, or absent; body somewhat flattened dorsoventrally, thorax not arched; ocelli present or absent; middle and hind coxae without styli; abdominal segments 1–6 usually without styli ....**Thysanúra**   p. 172

45(43′).   Aquatic, often with tracheal gills **46**

45′.   Terrestrial, without tracheal gills **53**

46(45).   Nymphs; compound eyes and usually wing pads present **47**

46′.   Larvae; compound eyes and wing pads absent **49**

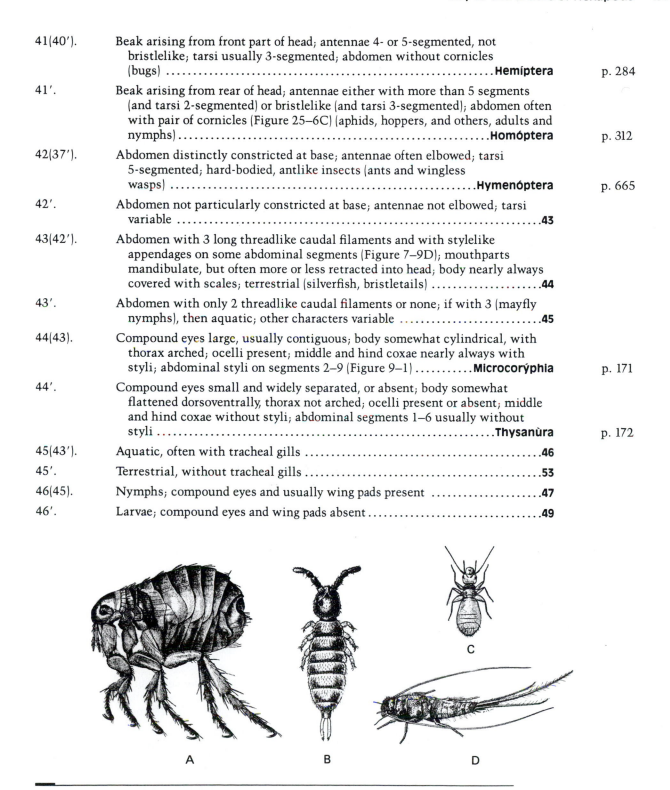

A   B   D   C

Figure 7–9.   Wingless hexapods. **A,** a human flea (Siphonáptera); **B,** springtail (Collémbola); **C,** psocid (Psocóptera); **D,** firebrat (Thysanúra). (**A** and **C,** courtesy of USDA; **B,** courtesy of Folsom and the U.S. National Museum; **D,** courtesy of Illinois Natural History Survey.)

57(56). Tarsi 5-segmented **58**

57'. Tarsi with 4 or fewer segments **62**

58(57). Mouthparts prolonged ventrally into snoutlike structure (Figure 30–6); body more or less cylindrical, usually less than 15 mm in length (wingless scorpionflies) ....**Mecóptera***   p. 482

58'. Mouthparts not as above; body shape and size variable **59**

59(58'). Antennae 5-segmented; Texas (some female twisted-wing parasites: Mengèidae) ....**Strepsíptera***   p. 479

59'. Antennae with more than 5 segments; widely distributed **60**

60(59'). Cerci 1-segmented; body and legs very slender (Figure 13–1) (walking-sticks) ....**Phásmida**   p. 205

60'. Cerci with 8 or more segments; body shape variable **61**

61(60'). Body flattened and oval, head more or less concealed from above by pronotum (Figure 16–3); ocelli usually present; widely distributed (cockroaches) ....**Blattària**   p. 229

61'. Body elongate and cylindrical, head not concealed from above by pronotum; ocelli absent; northwestern United States and western Canada (rock crawlers) ....**Grylloblattària***   p. 203

62(57'). Cerci forcepslike; tarsi 3-segmented **63**

62'. Cerci absent or, if present, not forcepslike; tarsi variable **64**

63(62). Antennae more than half as long as body; cerci short; western United States (timemas) ....**Phásmida***   p. 205

63'. Antennae usually less than half as long as body; cerci long (Figure 7–2D); widely distributed (earwigs) ....**Dermáptera**   p. 242

64(62'). Tarsi 3-segmented, basal segment of front tarsi enlarged (Figure 19–1) (webspinners) ....**Emblídìna***   p. 247

64'. Tarsi 2- to 4-segmented, basal segment of front tarsi not enlarged **65**

65(64'). Grasshopperlike insects, with hind legs enlarged and fitted for jumping; length usually over 15 mm (grasshoppers) ....**Orthóptera**   p. 208

65'. Not grasshopperlike, hind legs usually not as above; length less than 10 mm **66**

66(65'). Tarsi 4-segmented; pale, soft-bodied, wood- or ground-inhabiting insects (termites) ....**Isóptera**   p. 234

66'. Tarsi 2- or 3-segmented; color and habits variable **67**

67(66'). Cerci present, 1-segmented, terminating in long bristle; antennae 9-segmented, moniliform (Figure 21–1B–D); compound eyes and ocelli absent; tarsi 2-segmented (zorapterans) ....**Zoráptera***   p. 258

67'. Cerci absent; antennae with 13 or more segments, usually hairlike (Figure 7–9C); compound eyes and 3 ocelli usually present; tarsi 2- or 3-segmented (psocids) ....**Psocóptera**   p. 260

68(56'). Ventral prolegs present on 2 or more abdominal segments (Figures 30–1B and 34–3) **69**

68'. Abdominal prolegs absent or on terminal segment only **71**

69(68). With 5 pairs of prolegs (on abdominal segments 3–6 and 10) or fewer, prolegs with tiny hooks (crochets); several (usually 6) stemmata on each side of head (caterpillars, butterfly and moth larvae) ....**Lepidóptera**   p. 588

69'.   With 6 or more pairs of abdominal prolegs, prolegs without crochets; number of stemmata variable **70**

70(69').   Seven or more stemmata on each side of head; prolegs on segments 1–8 or 3–8, usually inconspicuous, pointed structures (Figure 30–1B) (scorpionfly larvae)..**Mecóptera***   p. 482

70'.   One stemma on each side of head; prolegs fleshy, not pointed, usually on abdominal segments 2–8 and 10, sometimes on 2–7 or 2–6 and 10 (Figure 35–37) (sawfly larvae) ....**Hymenóptera**   p. 665

71(68').   Mandible and maxilla on each side united to form sucking jaw that is often long (Figures 27–9B and 27–11); tarsi with 2 claws; labrum absent or fused with head capsule; maxillary palps absent (Planipénnia: larvae of lacewings and antlions). ....**Neuróptera**   p. 357

71'.   Mandibles and maxillae not as above; tarsi with 1 or 2 claws; labrum and maxillary palps usually present **72**

72(71').   Head and mouthparts directed forward (prognathous), head about as long along midventral line as along middorsal line, usually cylindrical or somewhat flattened **73**

72'.   Head and mouthparts directed ventrally (hypognathous), head much longer along middorsal line than along midventral line and usually rounded **75**

73(72').   Tarsi with 1 claw (some beetle larvae) ....**Coleóptera**   p. 370

73'.   Tarsi with 2 claws **74**

74(73').   Distinct labrum and clypeus present (Raphidiòdea: snakefly larvae) ....**Neuróptera**   p. 357

74'.   Labrum absent or fused with head capsule (most Adéphaga: beetle larvae) ....**Coleóptera**   p. 370

75(72').   Front legs distinctly smaller than other pairs; middle and hind legs projecting laterally much more than front legs; small group of stemmata (usually 3) on each side of head behind bases of antennae; tarsal claws absent; length less than 5 mm; usually found in moss (larvae of Borèidae) ....**Mecóptera***   p. 482

75'.   Legs not as above, front and middle legs about the same size and position; stemmata variable; tarsi with 1–3 claws; size and habitat variable **76**

76(75').   Tarsi with 1 or 2 claws; abdomen usually without caudal filaments; antennae variable (beetle larvae).......................................**Coleóptera**   p. 370

76'.   Tarsi usually with 3 claws; abdomen with 2 caudal filaments about one-third as long as body (Figure 29–1F); antennae usually short, 3-segmented (triungulin larvae of some beetles [Melòidae] and twisted-wing parasites) ....**Coleóptera* and Strepsíptera***   pp. 370, 479

77(30').   Aquatic (fly larvae) ....**Díptera**   p. 499

77'.   Not aquatic, but terrestrial or parasitic **78**

78(77').   Sessile, plant feeding; body covered by a scale or waxy material; mouthparts haustellate, long and threadlike (female scale insects) ....**Homóptera**   p. 312

78'.   Not exactly fitting description above **79**

79(78').   Head and thorax more or less fused, abdominal segmentation indistinct (Figure 29–1G); internal parasites of other insects (female twisted-wing parasites) ....**Strepsíptera***   p. 479

79'.   Head not fused with thorax, body segmentation distinct; habitat variable ...**80**

80(79').   Head distinct, sclerotized, usually pigmented and exserted **81**

80'.   Head indistinct, incompletely or not at all sclerotized, sometimes retracted into thorax **88**

81(80).   Head and mouthparts directed forward (prognathous), head about as long along midventral line as along middorsal line, usually cylindrical or somewhat flattened **82**

81'.   Head and mouthparts directed ventrally (hypognathous), head much longer along middorsal line than along midventral line and usually rounded **85**

82(81).   Terminal abdominal segment with a pair of short pointed processes; several long setae on each body segment (Figure 31–4) (flea larvae) ....**Siphonáptera***   p. 489

82'.   Not exactly fitting description above **83**

83(82').   Labium with protruding spinneret; antennae arising from membranous area at bases of mandibles; mandibles well developed, opposable; body usually more or less flattened; ventral prolegs usually with crochets; mostly leafminers in leaves, bark, or fruits (moth larvae) ....**Lepidóptera**   p. 588

83'.   Labium without spinneret; antennae, if present, arising from head capsule; prolegs without crochets **84**

84(83').   Mouthparts distinctly mandibulate, with opposable mandibles; spiracles usually present on thorax and 8 abdominal segments; body shape variable (beetle larvae) ....**Coleóptera**   p. 370

84'.   Mouthparts as above or with mouth hooks more or less parallel and moving vertically; spiracles variable, but usually not as above; body elongate (fly larvae) ....**Díptera**   p. 499

85(81').   Abdominal segments usually with 1 or more longitudinal folds laterally or lateroventrally; body C-shaped, scarabaeiform (Figure 28–37); 1 pair of spiracles on thorax, usually 8 pairs on abdomen (white grubs: beetle larvae) ....**Coleóptera**   p. 370

85'.   Abdominal segments without longitudinal folds, or if such folds present, then spiracles not as above **86**

86(85').   Head with adfrontal areas (Figure 34–3, *adf*); labium with projecting spinneret; antennae, if present, arising from membranous area at base of mandibles; often 1 or more (usually 6) stemmata on each side of head; ventral prolegs, if present, with crochets (moth larvae) ....**Lepidóptera**   p. 588

86'.   Head without adfrontal areas; labium without spinneret; antennae and stemmata not as above; prolegs, if present, without crochets **87**

87(86').   Mandibles not heavily sclerotized and not brushlike; spiracles usually present on thorax and most abdominal segments, posterior pair not enlarged; larvae occurring in plant tissues, as parasites, or in cells constructed by adults (Apócrita) ....**Hymenóptera**   p. 665

87'.   Mandibles usually brushlike; spiracles usually not as above—if present in several abdominal segments, posterior pair much larger than others; occurring in wet places, in plant tissues, or as internal parasites (fly larvae, mostly Nematócera) ....**Díptera**   p. 499

88(80').   Mouthparts of normal mandibulate type, with opposable mandibles and maxillae; antennae usually present (beetle larvae) ....**Coleóptera**   p. 370

88'.   Mouthparts reduced or modified, with only mandibles opposable, or with parallel mouth hooks present; antennae usually absent **89**

89(88').   Body behind "head" (first body segment) consisting of 13 segments, full-grown larvae usually with sclerotized ventral plate ("breast bone") located ventrally behind head (larvae of Cecidomyìidae) ....**Díptera**   p. 499

89'.   Body consisting of fewer segments; no "breast bone" **90**

90(89').   Mouthparts consisting of 1 or 2 (if 2, then parallel, not opposable) median, dark-colored, decurved mouth hooks (maggots; larvae of Muscomórpha) ....**Díptera**   p. 499

90'.   Mandibles opposable, but sometimes reduced, without mouth hooks as described above (larvae of Apócrita) ....**Hymenóptera**   p. 665

References

Arnett, R. H. 1985. American Insects: A Handbook of the Insects of America North of Mexico. New York: Van Nostrand Reinhold, 850 pp.; illus.

Borror, D. J., and R. E. White. 1970 (paperback ed., 1974). A Field Guide to the Insects of America North of Mexico. Boston: Houghton Mifflin, 404 pp.; illus.

Boudreaux, H. B. 1979. Arthropod Phylogeny with Special Reference to Insects. New York: Wiley, 320 pp.; illus.

Brues, C. T., A. L. Melander, and F. M. Carpenter. 1954. Classification of insects. Bull. Mus. Comp. Zool. Harvard No. 108, 917 pp.; illus.

Chinery, M. 1974. A Field Guide to the Insects of Britain and Northern Europe. Boston: Houghton Mifflin, 352 pp.; illus.

Chu, P. 1949. How to Know the Immature Insects. Dubuque, Iowa: Wm. C. Brown, 234 pp.; illus.

Commonwealth Scientific and Industrial Research Organization (CSIRO). 1970. The Insects of Australia. Carlton, Victoria: Melbourne Univ. Press, 1029 pp.; illus.

Comstock, J. H. 1949 (9th ed.). An Introduction to Entomology. Ithaca, N.Y.: Comstock, 1064 pp.; illus.

Daly, H. V., J. T. Doyen, and P. R. Ehrlich. 1978. An Introduction to Insect Biology and Diversity. New York: McGraw-Hill, 564 pp.; illus.

Elzinga, R. J. 1981 (2nd ed.). Fundamentals of Entomology. Englewood Cliffs, N.J.: Prentice-Hall, 432 pp.; illus.

Essig, E. O. 1958. Insects and Mites of Western North America. New York: Macmillan, 1050 pp.; illus.

Friedlander, C. P. 1977. The Biology of Insects. New York: Pica Press, 190 pp.; illus.

Grassé, P. P. (Ed.). 1949. Traité de Zoologie; Anatomie, Systématique, Biologie. Vol. 9. Insectes: Paleontologie, Géonémie, Aptérygotes, Ephéméroptères, Odonatoptères, Blattoptéroïdes, Orthoptéroïdes, Dermaptéroïdes, Coléoptères. Paris: Masson, 1117 pp.; illus.

Grassé, P. P. (Ed.). 1951. Traité de Zoologie; Anatomie, Systématique, Biologie, Vol. 10: Insectes Supérieurs et Hemiptéroïdes, Part I: Neuroptéroïdes, Mecoptéroïdes, Hemiptéroïdes, pp. 1–975. Part II, Hymenoptéroïdes, Psocoptéroïdes, Hemiptéroïdes, Thysanoptéroïdes, pp. 976–1948, illus. Paris: Masson.

Imms, A. D. 1947. Insect Natural History. New York: William Collins, 317 pp.; illus.

Jacques, H. E. 1947 (2nd ed.). How to Know the Insects. Dubuque, Iowa: Wm. C. Brown, 205 pp.; illus.

Kristensen, N. P. 1975. The phylogeny of hexapod "orders": A critical review of recent accounts. Z. Zool. Syst. Evolutions-Forsch. 13:1–44.

Kristensen, N. P. 1981. Phylogeny of insect orders. Annu. Rev. Entomol. 26:135–157.

Linsenmaier, W. 1972. Insects of the World (translated from German by L. E. Chadwick). New York: McGraw-Hill, 392 pp.; illus.

Lutz, F. E. 1935. Field Book of Insects. New York: Putnam, 510 pp.; illus.

Martynov, A. V. 1925. Über zwei Grundtypen der Flügel bei den Insekten und ihre Evolution. Z. Morphol. Okol. Tiere 4:465–501; illus.

Martynova, O. 1961. Paleoentomology. Annu. Rev. Entomol. 6:285–294.

Matheson, R. 1951 (2nd ed.). Entomology for Introductory Courses. Ithaca, N.Y.: Comstock, 629 pp.; illus.

Merritt, R. W., and K. W. Cummins. 1978. An Introduction to the Aquatic Insects of North America. Dubuque, Iowa: Kendall/Hunt, 512 pp.; illus.

Oldroyd, H. 1970. Elements of Entomology; An Introduction to the Study of Insects. London: Weidenfield & Nicolson, 312 pp.; illus.

Pennak, R. W. 1978 (2nd ed.). Fresh-Water Invertebrates of the United States. New York: Wiley Interscience, 803 pp.; illus.

Peterson, A. 1939. Keys to the orders of immature insects (exclusive of eggs and pronymphs) of North American insects. Ann. Entomol. Soc. Amer. 32:267–278.

Peterson, A. 1948. Larvae of Insects, Part I: Lepidoptera and Plant-Infesting Hymenoptera. Ann Arbor, Mich.: Edwards Bros., 315 pp.; illus.

Peterson, A. 1951. Larvae of Insects, Part II: Coleoptera, Diptera, Neuroptera, Siphonaptera, Mecoptera, Trichoptera. Ann Arbor, Mich.: Edwards Bros., 416 pp.; illus.

Richard, O. W., and R. G. Davies. 1977. Imm's General Textbook of Entomology, 2 vols. London: Chapman and Hall, vol. 1, pp. 1–418; vol. 2, pp. 419–1354; illus.

Romoser, W. S. 1973. The Science of Entomology. New York: Macmillan, 449 pp.; illus.

Ross, H. H. 1955. Evolution of the insect orders. Entomol. News 66:197–208.

Ross, H. H., C. A. Ross, and J. R. P. Ross. 1982 (4th ed.). A Textbook of Entomology. New York: Wiley, 666 pp.; illus.

Smart, J. 1963. Explosive evolution and the phylogeny of the insects. Proc. Linn. Soc. Lond. 174:125–126.

Stehr, F. (Ed.). 1987. Immature Insects. Dubuque, Iowa: Kendall/Hunt, 754 pp.; illus.

Swain, R. B. 1948. The Insect Guide. New York: Doubleday, 261 pp.; illus.

Swan, L. A., and C. S. Papp. 1972. The Common Insects of North America. New York: Harper & Row, 750 pp.; illus. (part color).

Usinger, R. L. (Ed.). 1956. Aquatic Insects of California, with Keys to North American Genera and California Species. Berkeley: Univ. California Press, 508 pp.; illus.

Chapter 8

The Entognathous Hexapods
Protùra, Collémbola, and Diplùra

These three orders and the two considered in Chapter 9 are all primitively wingless hexapods with simple metamorphosis. Some of the pterygotes also lack wings, but their wingless condition is a secondary one, since they are derived from winged ancestors.

The three orders treated in this chapter are grouped together as the Entógnatha because the mouthparts are more or less withdrawn into the head. The lateral portions of the head capsule are extended ventrally, fusing with the sides of the labium and labrum to form a pouch within which the mandibles and maxillae are concealed. In addition, in these orders the segments of the antennal flagellum (when present) are musculated; the tarsi are 1-segmented; compound eyes are either absent or the ommatidia reduced in number (8 or less); and the tentorium is rudimentary. Manton (1977) concluded that each of these three groups evolved the hexapodous condition independently and that each should be treated as a separate class. We follow here the conclusions of Boudreaux (1979) and the nomenclatural suggestions of Kristensen (1981) and group them as the Entógnatha. As such, they are the sister group of the insects (which includes the Microcorýphia, Thysanùra, and Pterygòta). Together the Entógnatha and Insécta make up the Hexápoda.

There are other differences of opinion regarding the taxonomic status of these groups and the names to be given them. Our arrangement is outlined as follows, with synonyms and other arrangements in parentheses:

Order Protùra (Myrientomàta)—proturans
    Eosentómidae
    Protentómidae (including Hesperentómidae)
    Acerentómidae
Order Collémbola—springtails
  Suborder Arthroplèona—elongate-bodied
    springtails
    Podùridae
    Hypogastrùridae (Podùridae in part)
    Onychiùridae (Podùridae in part)
    Isotómidae (Entomobrỳidae in part)
    Entomobrỳidae
  Suborder Symphyplèona—globular-bodied
    springtails
    Neélidae (Sminthùridae in part)
    Sminthùridae
Order Diplùra (Entótrophi)—diplurans
    Campodèidae
    Procampodèidae
    Anajapýgidae (Projapýgidae in part)
    Japỳgidae (Iapýgidae)

Order Protùra[1]—Proturans

The proturans are minute whitish hexapods, 0.6–1.5 mm in length. The head is somewhat conical, and there are no eyes or antennae (Figure 8–1). The mouthparts do not bite, but are apparently used to scrape off food particles which are then mixed with saliva and sucked into the mouth. The first pair of legs is principally sensory in function and is carried in an elevated position like antennae. Styli are present on the first three abdominal segments. Upon hatching from the egg, the proturan abdomen is composed of 9 segments. At each of the next three molts segments are added anterior to the apical portion (the telson), so that the adult abdomen appears to have 12 segments (11 metameric segments and the apical telson).

These hexapods live in moist soil or humus, in leaf mold, under bark, and in decomposing logs. They feed on decomposing organic matter and fungal spores. They are found worldwide, and approximately 200 species are known at present.

[1]Protùra: *prot*, first; *ura*, tail.

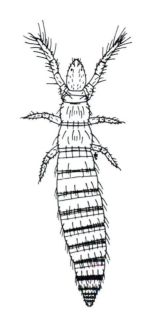

Figure 8–1. Dorsal view of a proturan, *Aceréntulus bárberi bárberi* Ewing. (Courtesy of Ewing and the Entomological Society of America.)

Key to the Families of Protùra

1. Tracheae present, thorax with 2 pairs of spiracles; abdominal appendages 2-segmented, with a terminal vesicle . . . . **Eosentómidae**   p. 165

1′. Tracheae and spiracles absent; abdominal appendages on segment 3 1-segmented, appendages with or without terminal vesicle **2**

2(1′). At least 2 pairs of abdominal appendages with terminal vesicle; most abdominal segments with single transverse row of dorsal setae . . . . **Protentómidae**   p. 165

2′. Only first pair of abdominal appendages with terminal vesicle; most abdominal segments with 2 transverse rows of dorsal setae   **Acerentómidae**   p. 165

The **Eosentómidae** contains eight North American species, all belonging to the genus *Eoséntomon*. The **Protentómidae** includes three rather rare North American species, one recorded from Maryland, one from Iowa, and a third from California. The **Acerentómidae** is a widely distributed group, with eight North American species.

Order Collémbola[2]—Springtails

The common name "springtail" is derived from the forked structure or furcula that propels these minute

[2]Collémbola: *coll*, glue; *embola*, a bolt or wedge (referring to the collophore).

hexapods through the air. The furcula arises on the ventral side of the fourth abdominal segment and, when at rest, is folded forward beneath the abdomen, where it is held in place by a clasplike appendage on the third abdominal segment called the retinaculum. Jumps are made when the animal is disturbed or during mating activities by extending the furcula downward and backward. A springtail 3 to 6 mm in length may be able to leap 75 to 100 mm. A large number of species, especially those dwelling in soil, have reduced or totally atrophied spring mechanisms.

Many collembolans have up to eight ommatidia on each side of the head, while others are reduced or totally blind. Mouthparts are somewhat elongate and concealed within the head. Some species are herbivorous or even carnivorous and have mandibles with well-developed molar plates. Others are fluid feeders and have styletlike mouthparts. These hexapods possess a tubelike appendage, the collophore, on the ventral side of the first abdominal segment; a bilobed eversible vesicle may be protruded at its apex. Originally it was believed that the collophore enabled the insect to cling to the surface on which it walked (hence the order name), but it is now known that this structure plays a role in water uptake.

Springtails, while very common and abundant, are seldom observed because of their small size (0.25–6 mm) and habit of living in concealed situations. Most species live in the soil or in such habitats as leaf litter, under bark, in decaying logs, and in fungi. Some species may be found on the surface of freshwater pools or along seashores; some occur on vegetation; and a few live in termite and ant nests, caves, or snow fields. Springtail populations are often very large; up to 100,000/m³ of surface soil, or literally millions per hectare.

Most soil-inhabiting springtails feed on decaying plant material, fungi, and bacteria. Others feed on arthropod feces, pollen, algae, and other materials. A few species may occasionally cause damage in gardens, greenhouses, or mushroom cellars.

Key to the Families of Collémbola

1.	Body elongate (Figure 8–2A–F), abdomen with 6 distinct segments (suborder Arthroplèona) **2**	
1′.	Body oval or globular (Figure 8–2G,H), abdomen with 4 basal segments fused, segments 5 and 6 forming small apical papilla (suborder Symphyplèona) **6**	
2(1).	Prothorax well developed, visible from above, with bristles or setae dorsally **3**	
2′.	Prothorax reduced, usually not visible from above, without bristles or setae dorsally **5**	
3(2).	Body dark-colored; eyes usually present; furcula present or absent **4**	
3′.	Body white; eyes absent; furcula usually absent ....**Onychiùridae**	p. 168
4(3).	Furcula long and flattened; found on surface of freshwater ponds ....**Podùridae**	p. 168
4′.	Furcula short or absent; habitats varied, but if found on the surface of water, then along the seashore, not on freshwater ponds ....**Hypogastrùridae**	p. 168
5(2′).	Fourth abdominal segment at least twice as long as third along middorsal line (Figure 8–2E,F); body scaly or with clavate setae; furcula always well developed ....**Entomobrỳidae**	p. 168
5′.	Third and fourth abdominal segments about same length along middorsal line (Figure 8–2D); body not scaly and with only simple setae; furcula often reduced ....**Isotómidae**	p. 168
6(1′).	Antennae as long as or longer than head; eyes present (Figure 8–2H) ....**Sminthùridae**	p. 168
6′.	Antennae much shorter than head; eyes absent (Figure 8–2G) ....**Neélidae**	p. 168

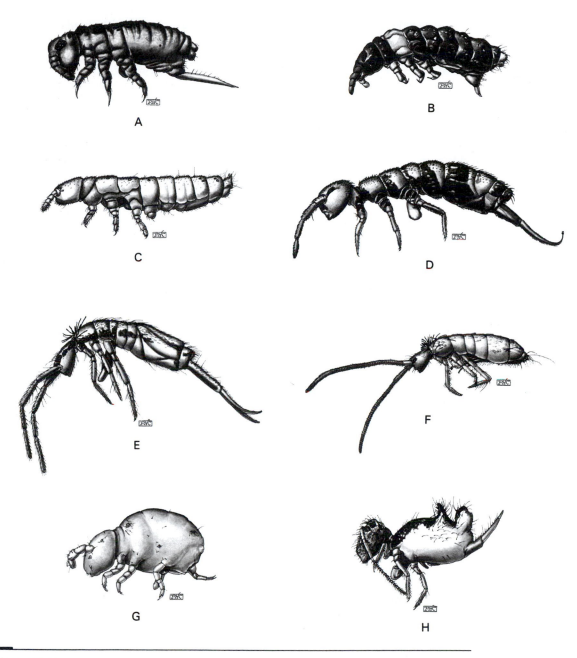

Figure 8–2.   Springtails. **A,** *Podùra aquática* (L.) (Podùridae); **B,** *Pseudachorùtes aureofasciàtus* (Harvey) (Hypogastrùridae); **C,** *Onychiùrus ramòsus* Folsom (Onychiùridae); **D,** *Isotomùrus trìcolor* (Packard) (Isotómidae); **E,** *Entomobrỳa sòcia* Denis (Entomobrỳidae); **F,** *Tomócerus elongàtus* Maynard (Entomobrỳidae); **G,** *Neélus minùtus* (Folsom) (Neélidae); **H,** *Sminthùrus floridànus* MacGillivray (Sminthùridae). (Courtesy of Peter H. Carrington and R. J. Snider.)

Family **Podùridae**: This family contains only one species, *Podùra aquática* L., a ubiquitous species that lives on the surface of freshwater ponds (Figure 8–2A). It is about 1.3 mm in length, and dark blue to reddish brown in color. This family is now considered to be more closely related to the Sminthùridae and Neélidae than the other Arthroplèona.

Family **Hypogastrùridae**: Members of this family are usually 1–2 mm in length, with short appendages (sometimes with the furcula reduced or lacking), ranging in color from cream, tan, purple, blue, and greenish, to black (Figure 8–2B). This is the largest family in the order, with 194 North American species. The snow flea, *Hypogastrùra nivícola* (Fitch), is a dark-colored species often found grazing on algae and fungal spores on snow during the winter. It is sometimes a pest in buckets of maple sap. *Neanùra muscòrum* (Templeton) is a flat species with lobed body segments armed with short, strong setae, lacking a furcula, and lives beneath loose bark or in leaf litter. Its mouthparts are formed into a cone. The seashore springtail, *Anùrida marítima* (Guérin), is a slate-blue species that is sometimes extremely abundant along seashores between tidemarks, where it is found on the surface of small pools, under stones and shells, and crawling over the shore. These springtails cluster in air pockets under submerged rocks at high tide.

Family **Onychiùridae**: The members of this family (66 North American species) are somewhat similar to the Hypogastrùridae. However, they differ markedly from that family by lacking pigment, eye patches, and a furcula (Figure 8–2C). They characteristically have pseudocelli (porelike structures) distributed on the antennal bases, head, and trunk segments. When disturbed, these insects are capable of exuding their noxious or toxic hemolymph through the pseudocelli. In culture, species of *Tullbérgia* and *Onychiùrus* have been shown to be parthenogenetic. It is probable that this form of reproduction is common among these soil-dwelling species. Members of the Onychiùridae are abundantly found in agricultural and forest soils.

Family **Isotómidae**: The 170 North American members of this family range in color from white, yellow, and green to blue, brown, and dark purple with longitudinal stripes or transverse bands. Often occurring in vast numbers, *Isotomùrus trìcolor* (Packard), is a common species found in marshes, as well as wet forest edges and sometimes freshwater pools (Figure 8–2D). *Metisótoma grándiceps* (Reuter) is carnivorous on other Collémbola. *Isótoma propín-*

qua Axelson is one of several collembolan species that exhibit ecomorphosis, a phenomenon that occurs when individuals developed at abnormally high temperatures differ morphologically from those developing at lower temperatures, resulting in individuals that are sometimes placed in different taxa.

Family **Entomobrÿidae**: This is a rather large group of species (138 North American species) of slender springtails that resemble the Isotómidae, but have a large fourth abdominal segment (Figure 8–2E,F). In addition, some species have robust setae, scales, very long antennae and legs, and striking color combinations. *Orchesélla hexfasciàta* Harvey is a common yellow species with purple markings, which is found in leaf litter and under bark. *Tomócerus flavéscens* (Tullberg) and *T. elongàtus* Maynard are commonly found in leaf litter and under bark. They are primarily nocturnal in their habits. The third antennal segment is much longer than segment 4, and the last two segments (3 and 4) are very flexible. *Lepidócyrtus paradóxus* Uzel is a dark blue species with a scaled body and enlarged mesothoracic segment, giving it the appearance of being "humpbacked." Another species, *Willòwsia búski* (Lubbock) is found in close association with man-made structures and very protected habitats. This is an extremely diverse family, which will probably be split into several families upon future revision.

Family **Neélidae**: This is a small group (7 North American species) of very small springtails (0.27–0.70 mm in length) that have been collected in wooded areas and in caves. Most species are found in organic soils or under bark. They lack eyes, and the antennae are reduced in length to less than the diameter of the head (Figure 8–2G). Several members of the family are pigmented, but most are colorless. The thorax is relatively large, giving the animal a seedlike shape. *Megalothòrax mínimus* (Willem) is one of our commonest species, reaching a length of 0.4 mm.

Family **Sminthùridae**: These springtails (99 North American species) range in size from 0.75 to 3 mm, and are oval-bodied active jumpers (Figure 8–2H). Many species are common on vegetation. Some, like *Bourletiélla horténsis* (Fitch), can be pests in gardens. Others, such as *Sminthùrus víridis* L., may be devastating on alfalfa in Europe and Australia. Still others may live under stones or bark or in leaf litter, while a few are found on freshwater pond surfaces. In woodland situations, *Pténothrix átra* (L.) and *P. marmoràta* (Packard) are commonly seen on mushrooms or living in old pine cones.

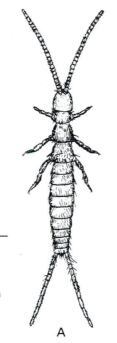
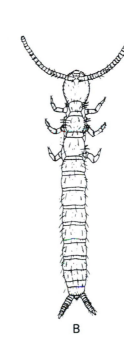
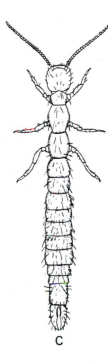

Figure 8–3. Diplurans. **A,** *Campòdea fòlsomi* Silvestri (Campodèidae); **B,** *Anajápyx vesiculòsus* Silvestri (Anajapýgidae); **C,** *Holojápyx diversiúngis* (Silvestri) (Japýgidae). (**A, C,** redrawn from Essig.)

A   B   C

Order Diplùra[3]—Diplurans

The diplurans appear somewhat similar to the silverfish and bristletails, but they lack a median caudal filament and thus have only two caudal filaments or appendages. The body is usually not covered with scales; compound eyes and ocelli are absent; the tarsi are 1-segmented; and the mouthparts are mandibulate and withdrawn into the head. Styli are present on abdominal segments 1–7 or 2–7. These hexapods are small (generally less than 7 mm in length) and usually pale in color. They are found in damp places in the soil, under bark, under stones or logs, in rotting wood, in caves, and in similar moist situations.

[3]Diplùra: *dipl*, two; *ura*, tail.

Key to the Families of Diplùra

1.	Cerci (of adults) 1-segmented and forcepslike (Figure 8–3C) ....**Japýgidae**	p. 170
1'.	Cerci many-segmented, not forcepslike (Figure 8–3A,B) **2**	
2(1').	Cerci long, about as long as antennae, and many-segmented (Figure 8–3A); widely distributed ....**Campodèidae**	p. 170
2'.	Cerci short, shorter than antennae, and 8-segmented (Figure 8–3B); California **3**	
3(2').	Styli on abdominal segments 2–7; antennal trichobothria beginning on third segment ....**Procampodèidae**	p. 170
3'.	Styli on abdominal segments 1–7; antennal trichobothria beginning on fifth segment ....**Anajapýgidae**	p. 170

Family **Campodèidae:** This is the largest family of diplurans (34 North American species), and contains those most often encountered. Most are about 6 mm in length. *Campòdea fòlsomi* Silvestri (Figure 8–3A) is a fairly common member of this family. It is found under stones in damp woods and in humus.

Family **Procampodèidae:** The only North American member of this family is *Procampòdea macswàini* Condé and Pagés, which occurs in California.

Family **Anajapýgidae:** This family is represented in the United States by a single rare species, *Anajápyx hermòsa* Smith, which has been taken in wet soil and humus in Placer County, California.

Family **Japýgidae:** This is a widely distributed group, but its members are not often encountered. They can be recognized by the 1-segmented forceps-like cerci (Figure 8–3C). Twenty-eight species occur in the United States, and all are small. Some tropical species are larger, and one Australian species of *Heterojápyx* reaches a length of 50 mm.

Collecting and Preserving Entógnatha

Most species can be collected by sifting debris or by looking under bark or stones or in fungi. Soil, leaf litter, or other material that may contain these species can be sprinkled onto a white surface and the insects found can be picked up with a moistened brush or aspirator. Many forms are most easily collected by means of a Berlese funnel (see page 751). The springtails that occur on vegetation with a white lected by sweeping the vegetation with a white enameled pan held at about a 30° angle to the ground. The hexapods falling or jumping into the pan can be easily seen and collected. The aquatic springtails can be collected with a dipper or tea strainer.

The best way to preserve these hexapods is in fluid—generally 80–85% alcohol. It is usually necessary to mount them on microscope slides for detailed study.

References

Bernard, E. C., and S. L. Tuxen. 1987. Class and order Protura, pp. 47–54 *in* F. W. Stehr (ed.), Immature Insects, vol. 1. Dubuque, Iowa: Kendall/Hunt, 754 pp.; illus.

Betsch, J.-M. 1980. Eléments pour une monographie des Collemboles Symphyplêones (Hexapodes, Aptérygotes). Mem. Mus. Nat. Hist. Natur., Serie A 116:1–227.

Boudreaux, H. B. 1979. Arthropod Phylogeny with Special Reference to Insects. New York: Wiley, 320 pp.; illus.

Christiansen, K. 1964. Bionomics of Collembola. Annu. Rev. Entomol. 9:147–178.

Christiansen, K. A., and P. F. Bellinger. 1980–1981. The Collembola of North America North of the Rio Grande. Grinnell, Iowa: Grinnell College, 1322 pp.

Christiansen, K. A., and R. J. Snider. 1984. Aquatic Collembola, pp. 82–93 *in* An Introduction to the Aquatic Insects, 2nd ed., ed. R. W. Merritt and K. W. Cummins. Dubuque, Iowa: Kendall/Hunt.

Ewing, H. E. 1940. The Protura of North America. Ann. Entomol. Soc. Amer. 33:495–551; illus.

Fjellberg, A. 1985. Arctic Collembola I—Alaskan Collembola of the families Poduridae, Hypogastruridae, Odontellidae, Brachystomellidae, and Neanuridae. Entomol. Scand. Suppl. No. 21, 126 pp.

Gisin, J. 1960. Collembolenfauna Europas. Geneva: Museum d'Histoire Naturelle, 312 pp.; illus.

Kristensen, N. P. 1981. Phylogeny of insect orders. Annu. Rev. Entomol. 26:135–157.

Lubbock, J. 1873. Monograph of the Collembola and Thysanura. London: Roy. Soc. Lond. 276 pp.; illus.

Manton, S. M. 1977. The Arthropoda, Habits, Functional Morphology, and Evolution. Oxford: Clarendon Press, 527 pp.; illus.

Paclt, J. 1956. Biologie der primär flügellosen insekten. Jena, Germany: Gustav Fischer Verlag, 258 pp.; illus.

Paclt, J. 1957. Diplura. Genera Insect. 212:1–122; illus.

Richards, W. R. 1968. Generic classification, evolution, and biogeography of the Sminthuridae of the world (Collembola). Mem. Entomol. Soc. Can. 53:1–54.

Salmon, J. T. 1964–1965. An index to the Collembola. Bull. Roy. Soc. New Zealand No. 7. Vol. 1, pp. 1–144 (1964). Vol. 2, pp. 145–644 (1964). Vol. 3, 645–651 (1965).

Smith, L. M. 1960. The families Projapygidae and Anajapygidae (Diplura) in North America. Ann. Entomol. Soc. Amer. 53:575–583; illus.

Snider, R. J. 1987. Class and order Collembola, pp. 55–64 *in* F. W. Stehr (ed.), Immature Insects, vol. 1. Dubuque, Iowa: Kendall/Hunt, 754 pp.; illus.

Szeptycki, A. 1979. Chaetotaxy of the Entomobryidae and its phylogenetical significance: Morpho-systematic studies on Collembola IV. Krakow: Pol. Akad. Nauk, 218 pp.

Tuxen, S. L. 1959. The phylogenetic significance of entognathy in entognathous apterygotes. Smithson. Misc. Coll. 137:379–416; illus.

Tuxen, S. L. 1964. The Protura: A Revision of the Species of the World with Keys for Determination. Paris: Hermann, 360 pp.; illus.

Wygodzinsky, P. 1987. Class and order Diplura, pp. 65–67 *in* F. W. Stehr (ed.), Immature Insects, vol. 1. Dubuque, Iowa: Kendall/Hunt, 754 pp.; illus.

Chapter 9

The Apterygote Insects
Microcorýphia and Thysanùra

The species in these two orders are small to medium-sized wingless creatures with simple metamorphosis. The Microcorýphia and Thysanùra are the closest living relatives of the winged insects (see Figure 7–1), but they differ in a number of respects. Some features of thoracic structure in the Pterygòta are correlated with the development of wings and are present even in the wingless members of that group. In the Pterygòta each thoracic pleuron (with rare exceptions) is divided by a pleural suture into an episternum and epimeron, and the thoracic wall is strengthened internally by furcae and phragmata. In the Microcorýphia and Thysanùra there are no pleural sutures, and furcae and phragmata are not developed. In addition, these orders usually have stylelike appendages on some of the pregenital abdominal segments. Such appendages are lacking in adult Pterygòta.

There are some differences between these orders and the other primitively wingless hexapods. The Microcorýphia and Thysanùra are ectognathous; that is, the mouthparts are more or less exposed and not covered by cranial folds. The segments of the antennal flagellum are without muscles; the tarsi are three- to five-segmented; compound eyes are usually present; and the tentorium is fairly well developed.

Microcorýphia[1]—Jumping Bristletails

The Microcorýphia are similar to the silverfish in the order Thysanùra. However, they are more cylindrical with the thorax somewhat arched; the compound eyes are large and contiguous; ocelli are always present; each mandible has a single point of articulation with the head capsule,[2] the tarsi are three-segmented; and the middle and hind coxae usually bear styli. (These styli are sometimes lacking on the middle coxae, or they may be completely absent.) The abdomen bears a pair of styli on segments 2–9, and segments 2–7 each bear three ventral sclerites (the coxopodites and a median sternum; the sternum is sometimes much reduced). Segments 1–7 usually bear 1 or 2 pairs of eversible vesicles.

These insects live in grassy or wooded areas under leaves, under bark, in dead wood, under stones, under rocks and cliffs, and in similar situations. Most are nocturnal, and their eyes glow at night when illuminated with a flashlight. The largest members of the order are about 15 mm in length.

[1]Microcorýphia: *micro*, small; *coryphia*, head.

[2]The retention of this primitive form of mandibular articulation is reflected in the other name commonly used for this order, Archaeógnatha: *archaeo*, old; *gnatha*, jaw.

The Microcorýphia are quite active and jump when disturbed, sometimes as far as 25–30 cm. The eversible vesicles on the abdomen function as water-absorbing organs. Before these insects molt they cement themselves to the substrate (the cement appears to be fecal material). If the cement fails, or if the substrate (such as sand) is not firm, they are unable to molt, and die. The bodies of these insects are covered with scales, which sometimes form distinctive patterns. The scales are often lost during the collecting process or when the insects are preserved in fluid. The jumping bristletails feed chiefly on algae, but feed also on lichens, mosses, decaying fruits, and similar materials.

Key to the Families of Microcorýphia

1.   The two basal antennal segments heavily scaled; sterna of abdominal segments 2–7 large and triangular, extending caudad at least half the length of coxopodite; abdominal segments 2–7 with at least 1 pair of eversible vesicles, some segments with 2 pairs ....**Machílidae**   p. 172

1'.   Antennae without scales; sterna of abdominal segments 2–7 very small, protruding only slightly or not at all between coxopodites, never extending as much as half the length of coxopodites (Figure 9–1B); abdominal segments 2–7 never with more than 1 pair of eversible vesicles, sometimes with none ....**Meinertéllidae**   p. 172

Family **Machílidae:**   These insects are brownish, elongate, and about 12 mm in length. There are 14 species in North America, and they are found in leaf litter, under bark, among rocks along the seashore, or in old stone walls. *Petròbius brevistỳlis* Carpenter is common in rocky cliffs along the New England seacoast, usually occurring 5 to 20 feet above the high tide mark.

Family **Meinertéllidae:**   These are similar in appearance to the machilids and are widely distributed. Six species occur in North America.

Order Thysanùra[3]—Silverfish

The silverfish are moderate-sized to small insects, usually elongate in form and somewhat flattened,

with three taillike appendages at the posterior end of the abdomen. The body is nearly always covered with scales. The mouthparts are mandibulate, and each mandible has two points of articulation with the head capsule. The compound eyes are small and widely separated (or absent), and ocelli may be present or absent. The tarsi are 3- to 5-segmented. The taillike appendages consist of the cerci and a median caudal filament. The abdomen is 11-segmented, but the last segment is often much reduced. Segments 2–7 each contain a single undivided ventral sclerite or a sternite and a pair of coxopodites, and there are styli on segments 2–9, 7–9, or 8–9.

[3]Thysanùra: *thysan*, bristle or fringe; *ura*, tail.

Key to the Families of Thysanùra

1.   Tarsi 5-segmented; ocelli present; body not covered with scales; northern California ....**Lepidotríchidae**   p. 173

1'.   Tarsi 3- or 4-segmented; ocelli absent; body usually covered with scales **2**

2(1').   Compound eyes present; body always covered with scales; widely distributed
....**Lepismátidae**   p. 174

2'.   Compound eyes absent; body with scales (Atelurìnae) or without scales
(Nicoletiìnae); Florida and Texas ....**Nicoletiìdae**   p. 173

Family **Lepidotríchidae**: This family is represented in the United States by a single species, *Tricholepídion gértschi* Wygodzinsky, which occurs under decaying bark of fallen Douglas fir in northern California. This insect is reddish, elongate, with a maximum body length of about 12 mm, with the antennae reaching a length of 9 mm and the caudal appendages 14 mm.

Family **Nicoletiídae**: This group contains two subfamilies, which differ in appearance and habits.

The Nicoletiìnae are slender and 7–19 mm in length; they lack scales; and the caudal filaments and antennae are relatively long (half as long as the body or longer). The Atelurìnae are oval (often with the body tapering posteriorly); the body is usually covered with scales; and the caudal filaments and antennae are shorter (usually less than half as long as the body). The Nicoletiìnae are subterranean or occur in caves and mammal burrows. The Atelurìnae are free-living or occur in ant or termite nests. Four species

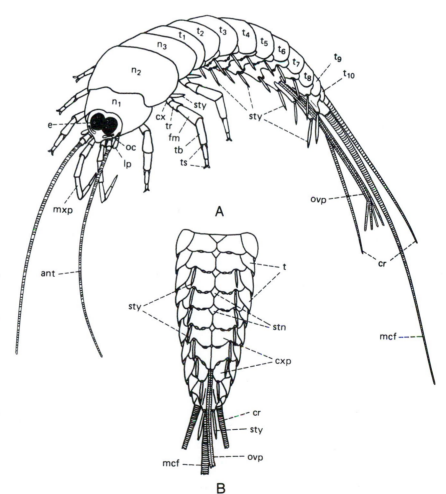

Figure 9–1. **A,** a jumping bristletail (Meinertéllidae), female; **B,** same, ventral view of abdomen. *ant*, antenna; *cr*, cerci; *cx*, coxa; *cxp*, coxopodite of abdominal appendages; *e*, compound eye; *fm*, femur; *lp*, labial palp; *mcf*, median caudal filament; *mxp*, maxillary palp; *n₁–n₃*, thoracic nota; *oc*, ocellus; *ovp*, ovipositor (in **A** the gonapophyses forming the ovipositor are shown separated at the apex); *stn*, abdominal sternites; *sty*, styli; *t*, terga; *tb*, tibia; *tr*, trochanter; *ts*, tarsus.

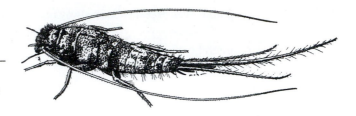

Figure 9–2.   The firebrat, *Thermòbia doméstica* (Packard). (Courtesy of the Illinois Natural History Survey.)

in this family have been reported from Florida and Texas.

Family **Lepismátidae:**   This group is represented in our area by 13 species, some of which are common and widely distributed. The best-known members of this family are the silverfish, *Lepísma saccharìna* L., and the firebrat, *Thermòbia doméstica* (Packard), which are domestic species inhabiting buildings. They feed on all sorts of starchy substances and frequently become pests. In libraries they feed on starch in books, bindings, and labels. In dwellings they feed on starched clothing, curtains, linens, silks, and the starch paste in wallpaper. In stores they feed on paper, vegetables, and foods that contain starch. The silverfish is gray in color, about 12 mm in length, and is found in cool, damp situations. The firebrat (Figure 9–2) is tan or brown in color, about the same size as the silverfish, and frequents the warm situations around furnaces, boilers, and steampipes. Both species are quite active and can run rapidly. The lepismatids that occur outside buildings are found in caves, in debris, under stones and leaves, and in ant nests.

Collecting and Preserving Apterygote Insects

Indoor species like the silverfish and firebrat can be trapped (see Chapter 36), or they can be collected with forceps or a moistened brush. Most outdoor species can be collected by sifting debris or by looking under bark or stones or in fungi. Soil, leaf litter, or other material that may contain these insects can be sprinkled onto a white surface, and the insects can be picked up with a moistened brush or aspirator. Many forms are most easily collected by means of a Berlese funnel (see page 751). The jumping bristletails can sometimes be most easily collected at night by shining a flashlight over the rocks or leaf litter where they occur. In some 15–20 minutes the insects will begin crawling toward the light.

The best way to preserve these insects is in fluid—generally 80–85% alcohol. The bristletails are perhaps better preserved in alcoholic Bouin's solution (see page 761).

References

Paclt, J. 1956. Biologie der primär flügellosen insekten. Jena, Germany: Gustav Fischer Verlag, 258 pp.; illus.

Paclt, J. 1963. Thysanura, family Nicoletiidae. Genera Insect., Fasc. 216e, 58 pp., illus.

Remington, C. L. 1954. The suprageneric classification of the order Thysanura (Insecta). Ann. Entomol. Soc. Amer. 47:277–286.

Slabaugh, R. E. 1940. A new thysanuran, and a key to the domestic species of Lepismatidae (Thysanura) found in the United States. Entomol. News 51:95–98; illus.

Smith, E. L. 1970. Biology and structure of some California bristletails and silverfish (Apterygota: Microcoryphia, Thysanura). Pan-Pac. Entomol. 46: 212–225; illus.

Wygodzinsky, P. 1961. On a surviving representative of the Lepidotrichidae (Thysanura). Ann. Entomol. Soc. Amer. 54:621–627; illus.

Wygodzinsky, P. 1972. A revision of the silverfish Lepismatidae, Thysanura) of the United States and the Caribbean area. Amer. Mus. Novitat. No. 2481, 26 pp.; illus.

Wygodzinsky, P. 1987. Order Microcoryphia, pp. 68–70 *in* F. W. Stehr (ed.), Immature Insects, vol. 1. Dubuque, Iowa: Kendall/Hunt, 754 pp.; illus.

Wygodzinsky, P. 1987. Order Thysanura, pp. 71–74 *in* F. W. Stehr (ed.), Immature Insects, vol. 1. Dubuque, Iowa: Kendall/Hunt, 754 pp.; illus.

Wygodzinsky, P., and K. Schmidt. 1980. Survey of the Microcoryphia (Insecta) of the northeastern United States and adjacent provinces of Canada. Amer. Mus. Novitat. No. 2071, 17 pp.

Chapter 10

Order Ephemeróptera[1]
Mayflies

Mayflies are small to medium-sized, elongate, very soft-bodied insects with two or three long threadlike tails. They are common near ponds and streams. The adults (Figure 10–1) have membranous wings with numerous veins. The front wings are usually large and triangular, and the hind wings are small and rounded. Some species have the front wings more elongate and the hind wings very small or absent. The wings at rest are held together above the body. The antennae are small, bristlelike, and inconspicuous. The immature stages are aquatic, and the metamorphosis is simple.

Mayfly nymphs are found in a variety of aquatic habitats. Some are streamlined in form and very active, while others are burrowing in habit. They can usually be recognized by the leaflike or plumose gills along the sides of the abdomen and the three (rarely two) long tails (Figure 10–2). Stonefly nymphs (Figures 20–2B and 20–3) are similar, but have only two tails (the cerci), and the gills are on the thorax (only rarely on the abdomen) and are not leaflike. Mayfly nymphs feed chiefly on algae and detritus. Many are most active at night.

When ready to transform to the winged stage, a mayfly nymph rises to the surface of the water and molts, and a winged form flies a short distance to the shore where it usually alights on vegetation. This stage is not the adult and is called a subimago. It molts once more, usually the next day, to become the adult. The subimago is dull in appearance and somewhat pubescent. There are hairs along the wing margin and on the caudal filaments (these areas are nearly always bare in the adults), and the genitalia are not fully developed. In a few genera there is no imago stage in the female; the subimago in these species mates and lays the eggs. The adult is usually smooth and shining; it has longer legs and tails than the subimago; and its genitalia are fully developed. The mayflies are the only insects that molt again after the wings become functional. The nymphs may require a year or two to develop, but the adults (which have vestigial mouthparts and do not feed) seldom live more than a day or two.

Adult mayflies often engage in rather spectacular swarming flights during which mating takes place. These swarms vary in size from small groups of individuals flying up and down in unison to large clouds of flying insects. The swarms of some species are 15 meters or more above the ground. The individuals in the swarm are usually all males. Sooner or later females enter the swarm, and a male will seize a female and fly away with her. Mating occurs in flight, and oviposition generally occurs very shortly thereafter (within minutes or, at most, a few hours).

[1]Ephemeróptera: *ephemera*, for a day, short-lived; *ptera*, wings (referring to the short life of the adults).

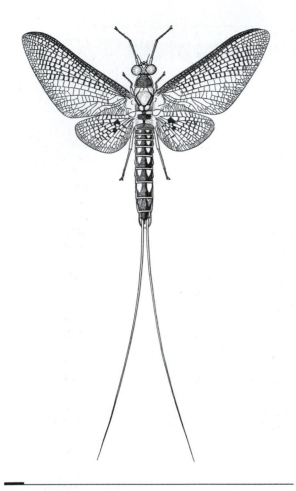

Figure 10–1.   A mayfly, *Hexagènia bilineàta* (Say) (Ephemeridae). (Courtesy of Needham and the U.S. Bureau of Fisheries.)

The eggs are laid on the surface of the water or are attached to objects in the water. In cases where the eggs are laid on the surface of the water, they may simply be washed off the end of the abdomen a few at a time, or they may all be laid in one clump. Each species has characteristic egg-laying habits.

Mayflies often emerge in enormous numbers from lakes and rivers and sometimes may pile up along the shore or on nearby roads and streets. Piles as deep as 1.2 meters have been observed in Illinois (Burks 1983), causing serious traffic problems. Such enormous emergences are often a considerable nuisance. Up until about the mid-1950s, mass emergences of this sort occurred along the shores of Lake Erie, but changes in the lake (increased pollution) have greatly reduced the number of these insects (and also the numbers of many fish), and their emergences now are not as striking as they used to be.

The chief importance of mayflies lies in their value as food for fish. Both adults and nymphs are an important food of many freshwater fish, and many artificial flies used by fishermen are modeled after these insects. Mayflies also serve as food for many other animals, including birds, amphibians, spiders, and many predaceous insects. Most species of mayflies in the nymphal stage are restricted to particular types of habitats. Hence, the mayfly fauna of an aquatic habitat may serve as an indicator of the ecological characteristics (including the degree of pollution) of that habitat.

Some Characters of the Ephemeróptera

The Head.   The compound eyes often differ in the two sexes, being generally larger and closer together in the male and smaller and farther apart in the female. In most of the smaller species, such as the Caènidae, the eyes are small and widely separated in both sexes. The eyes of the male are often larger or have upper facets that are a different color from the other facets. In the Baètidae and some Leptophlebìidae the upper facets are more or less stalked (such eyes are described as turbinate). The eyes of the female are usually uniform in color and facet size.

The Legs.   Most mayflies have the front legs of the male much longer than the other legs (the tibiae and tarsi being much elongated), sometimes as long as or longer than the body. The Polymitarcyidae have the middle and hind legs of the male and all the legs of the female vestigial.

The Wings.   Most mayflies have two pairs of wings, but in the Caènidae, Tricorýthidae, Baètidae, and some Leptophlebìidae the hind wings are greatly reduced or absent. The shape of the front wings is somewhat triangular in most mayflies, but the front wings are more elongate in those species having the hind wings reduced or absent. The wings are somewhat corrugated, with the veins lying either on a ridge or in a furrow. Some veins contain bullae, weakened areas that allow the wings to bend during flight.

There is considerable variation in the venational terminologies used in this group by different authorities. We use here the terminology of Edmunds and Traver (Figure 10–3), which is a little different from that used by many earlier workers. In addition, Kukalová-Peck (1985) has recently proposed a reinterpretation of mayfly venation, bringing it in line with her hypotheses on the fundamental structure of pterygote wings. Table 10–1 presents a comparison

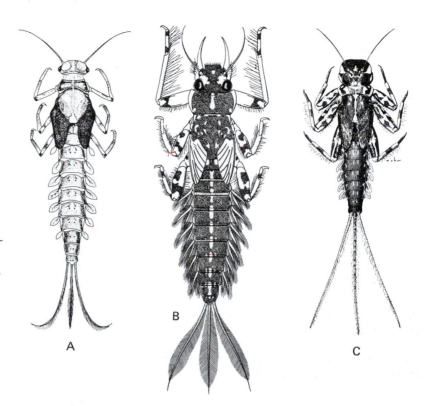

Figure 10–2.   Mayfly nymphs. **A,** *Baètis hiemàlis* Leonard (Baètidae); **B,** *Potamánthus* sp. (Potamánthidae); **C,** *Heptagènia diabàsia* Burks (Heptagenìidae). (**A,** courtesy of Leonard and the Entomological Society of America; **B,** courtesy of Needham and the U.S. Bureau of Fisheries; **C,** courtesy of Burks and the Entomological Society of America.)

of these three venational terminologies (veins labeled I are intercalaries).

The Abdomen. The abdomen of a mayfly is 10-segmented, with the caudal filaments arising on the tenth segment. Some mayflies have only two caudal filaments (the cerci), with the median filament vestigial or absent; others have all three filaments well developed. The sternum of segment 9 forms the subgenital plate. In the male there is a pair of clasperlike genital forceps on the distal margin of this plate and paired penes (rarely the penes are more or less fused) dorsal to this plate (Figure 10–5). The subgenital plate of the female, formed by the posterior part of the ninth sternum, varies in shape, and there are no claspers or penes. The character of the claspers is sometimes used in separating families, and both the claspers and the penes are usually very important in separating species.

Classification of the Ephemeróptera

We follow here the classification of McCafferty and Edmunds (1979), who divide the order Ephemeróptera into two suborders, which differ principally in characters of the nymphs, and divide each suborder into three superfamilies. Since the suborders and

Table 10–1
A Comparison of Venational Terminologies in the Ephemeróptera

Kukalová-Peck (1985)	Edmunds and Traver (1954b)[a]	Needham *et al.* (1935)[b]
C[c]	C	C
ScP	Sc	Sc
RA	R_1	R_1
RP1	R_2	R_2
RP2	IR_2	IR_2
—	R_3	IR_2
RP3–4	R_{4+5}	R_3
MA1–2	MA_1	R_4
—	IMA_1	IR_4
MA3–4	MA_2	R_5
MP1–2	MP_1	M_1
M supplements	IMP_1	IM_1
MP3–4	MP_2	M_2
CuA1–2	CuA	Cu_1
Cu supplements and CuA3–4	ICuA	ICu_1
CuP + AA1	CuP	Cu_2
AA2	1A	1A
IN	2A	2A

[a]Used in this book and by many present workers on the Ephemeróptera.

[b]Used by Burks (1953) and in previous editions of this book.

[c]The costal margin is formed by the fusion of PC, CA, CP, and ScA1–2; Sc3–4 forms the subcostal brace at the base of the wing (previously called the costal brace).

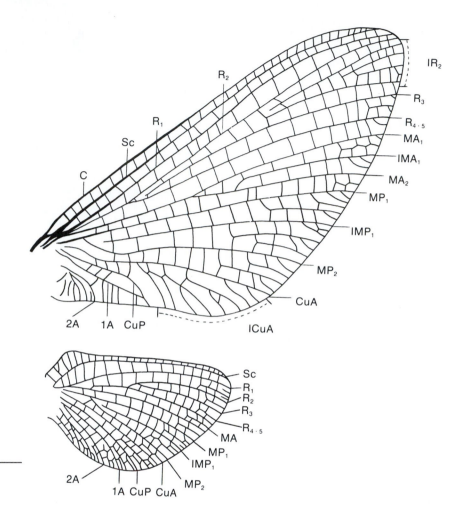

Figure 10–3.   Wings of
Pentagènia (Palingenìidae).

superfamilies are not very distinct (as far as adults
are concerned), we have omitted them from our discussion. This classification is outlined below, with
alternate names or arrangements in parentheses, and
with a list of the genera in each group. The numbers
in parentheses are the numbers of North American
species, and (with the genera) have been taken from
Edmunds (1984). The groups marked with an asterisk are relatively rare or are unlikely to be taken by
the general collector.

Suborder Schistonòta
  Superfamily Baetòidea
    Siphlonùridae (Siphlùridae; Baètidae in part)
      (56): *Acanthamétropus* (1), *Améletus* (31)
      Análetris (1), *Edmúndsius* (1), *Paraméletus*
      (4), *Siphlonísca* (1), *Siphlonùrus* (17)

Metretopódidae (Ametropódidae in part) (2):
  Metrétopus (1), *Siphloplécton* (1)
*Ametropódidae (3): *Amétropus* (3)
Baètidae (Baetìnae of Baètidae) (130): *Acerpénna*
  (2), *Apobaètis* (1), *Baètis* (35), *Baetòdes* (2),
  Callibaètis (23), *Centróptilum* (24), *Cloèon*
  (12), *Dactylobaètis* (2), *Diphètor* (2), *Fáll-
  ceon* (2), *Heterocloèon* (4), *Paracloeòdes* (2),
  Pseudocloèon (19)
Oligoneurìidae (32): *Lachlània* (3), *Homoeoneù-
  ria* (4), *Isonýchia* (25)
Heptagenìidae (Ecdùridae, Ecydonùridae; Ame-
  tropódidae in part) (127): *Anepèorus* (2),
  Arthroplèa (1), *Cinýgma* (3), *Cinýgmula*
  (11), *Epèorus* (19), *Heptagènia* (13), *Leuro-
  cùta* (10), *Macdúnnoa* (2), *Níxe* (12), *Iron-
  òdes* (6), *Pseudìron* (2), *Rhithrogèna* (21),
  Sténacron (7), *Stenonèma* (17), *Spínadis* (1)

Superfamily Leptophlebiòidea
Leptophlebìidae (Baètidae in part) (70): *Chorotérpes* (12), *Habrophlèbia* (1), *Habrophlebiòdes* (4), *Farròdes* (= *Homothràulus*) (1), *Leptophlèbia* (10), *Paraleptophlèbia* (33), *Thraulòdes* (5), *Traverélla* (4)
Superfamily Ephemeròidea
*Behningìidae (1): *Dolània* (1)
Potamánthidae (Epheméridae in part) (8): *Potamánthus* (8)
Epheméridae (13): *Ephémera* (7), *Hexagènia* (5), *Litobráncha* (1)
Palingenìidae (Epheméridae in part) (2): *Pentagènia* (2)
Polymitarcỳidae (Epheméridae in part) (6): *Éphoron* (2), *Campsùrus* (1), *Tórtopus* (3)

Suborder Pannòta
Superfamily Ephemerellòidea
Ephemeréllidae (Baètidae in part) (81): *Attenélla* (4), *Caudatélla* (5), *Dannélla* (2), *Drunélla* (15), *Ephemerélla* (28), *Eurylophélla* (12), *Serratélla* (14), *Timpanòga* (1)
Tricorýthidae (Caènidae in part, Ephemeréllidae in part) (14): *Leptohỳphes* (1), *Tricorythòdes* (13)
Superfamily Caenòidea
Neoepheméridae (Epheméridae in part) (4): *Neoephémera* (4)
Caènidae (Baètidae in part) (18): *Brachycércus* (5), *Caènis* (13)
Superfamily Prosopistomatòidea
Baetíscidae (Baètidae in part) (12): *Baetísca* (12)

Key to the Families of Ephemeróptera

The venational characters used are those of the front wing, unless otherwise indicated. Groups marked with an asterisk are relatively rare or are unlikely to be taken by the general collector. Keys to nymphs are given by Edmunds *et al.* (1963), Edmunds (1984), and Edmunds and Allen (1987).

1.   Wing venation greatly reduced, with only 3 or 4 longitudinal veins behind R_1 (Figure 10–4A); body black (*Homoeoneùria* and *Lachlània*) ...**Oligoneurìidae***   p. 183

1'.   Wing venation complete or only slightly reduced, with more than 4 longitudinal veins behind R_1; body color variable **2**

2(1'). Usually 4 or more long cubital intercalaries arising from CuP; male with penes longer than genital forceps; antennae of female arising from prominent anterolateral projections; southeastern United States ....**Behningìidae***   p. 184

2'.   With 3 or fewer long cubital intercalaries; male with penes shorter than genital forceps (Figure 10–5); antennae of female not as above; widely distributed **3**

3(2'). Bases of MP_2 and CuA bent sharply toward CuP (Figures 10–3, 10–4I, and 10–6A,B); MA in hind wing not forked, but hind wing with numerous veins and cross veins **4**

3'.   Bases of MP_2 and CuA not sharply bent toward CuP (rarely MP is unforked or is atrophied basally) (Figures 10–4D–H,J and 10–6C,D); hind wings variable (sometimes very small or absent); MA in hind wing forked or unforked **8**

4(3'). Hind wings with a prominent costal projection near base (Figure 10–4B) and 1A in front wing not forked; fork of MP in hind wing beyond middle of wing; basal costal cross veins weak or atrophied; both sexes with 3 well developed caudal filaments; eastern United States, mostly southeastern ....**Neoepheméridae***   p. 184

4'.   Hind wings without prominent costal projection near base, or 1A in front wing forked (Figure 10–3, 10–4I, and 10–6A,B); fork of MP in hind wings in basal half of wing (Figures 10–3, 10–6A,B); basal costal cross veins well developed; median caudal filament sometimes reduced or vestigial; widely distributed **5**

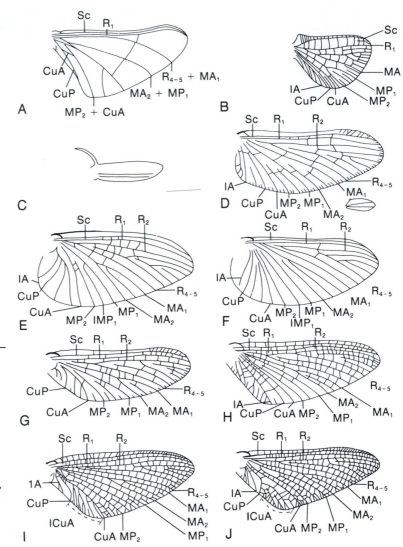

Figure 10–4. Wings of Ephemeróptera. **A,** *Lachlània,* Oligoneuriidae, front wing; **B,** *Neoephémera,* Neoepheméridae, hind wing; **C,** *Leptohýphes,* Tricorýthidae, hind wing of male; **D,** *Baètis,* Baètidae, front and hind wings; **E,** *Tricorythòdes,* Tricorýthidae, front wing; **F,** *Caènis,* Caènidae, front wing; **G,** *Ephemerélla,* Ephemeréllidae, front wing; **H,** *Baetísca,* Baetíscidae, front wing; **I,** *Potamánthus,* Potamánthidae, front wing; **J,** *Leptophlèbia,* Leptophlebìidae, front wing.

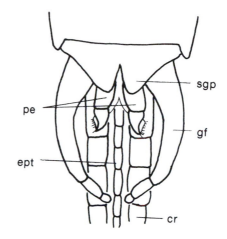

Figure 10–5. Apex of abdomen of male mayfly, *Leptophlèbia cùpida* (Say), ventral view. *cr*, lateral caudal filament (cercus); *ept*, median caudal filament (epiproct); *gf*, genital forceps; *pe*, penes; *sgp*, subgenital plate.

8(3').	Cubital intercalaries a series of veinlets, often forked or sinuate, extending from CuA to hind margin of wing; MA in hind wing usually forked (Figure 10–6D); hind tarsi 4-segmented **9**	
8'.	Cubital intercalaries not as above; MA in hind wing forked or unforked (hind wings sometimes reduced or absent); hind tarsi 4- or 5-segmented **10**	
9(8).	MP in hind wing forked near margin; front legs largely or entirely dark, middle and hind legs pale (*Isonýchia*) ....**Oligoneuriidae**	p. 183
9'.	MP in hind wing forked near base or middle of wing; leg color not as above ....**Siphlonùridae**	p. 183
10(8').	With 3 well-developed caudal filaments **11**	
10'.	With only 2 well-developed caudal filaments, median filament rudimentary or absent **14**	
11(10).	Hind wings present, usually relatively large with 1 or more veins forked; costal projection of hind wings, if present, shorter than wing width **12**	
11'.	Hind wings absent, or very small with only 2 or 3 simple veins and long costal projection that is as long as or longer than wing is wide (Figure 10–4C) **18**	
12(11).	Two more or less parallel cubital intercalaries present; 1A attached to hind margin of wing by series of veinlets; western United States ....**Ametropódidae***	p. 183
12'.	Cubital intercalaries not as above; 1A not attached to hind margin of wing as above; widely distributed **13**	
13(12').	Some short, basally detached marginal veinlets along outer margin of wing (Figure 10–4G); genital forceps of male with 1 short terminal segment ....**Ephemeréllidae**	p. 184
13'.	No basally detached marginal veinlets along outer margin of wing (Figure 10–4J); genital forceps of male with 2 or 3 short terminal segments (Figure 10–5) ....**Leptophlebiidae**	p. 183
14(10').	Cubital intercalaries absent and 1A extending to hind margin of wing (Figures 10–4D and 10–6C); hind wings without numerous long, free marginal veinlets **15**	
14'.	Cubital intercalaries present and 1A extending to outer margin of wing; hind wings with many long, free marginal veinlets ....**Baetíscidae**	p. 184

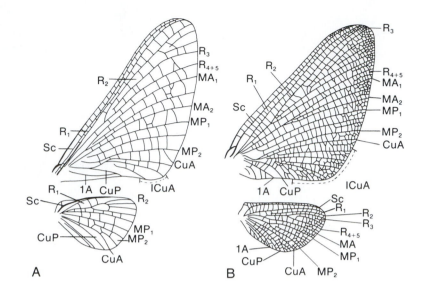

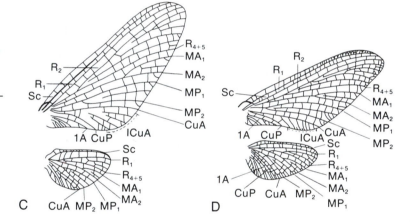

Figure 10–6. Wings of Ephemeróptera. **A,** *Campsùrus,* Campsurìnae, Polymitarcỳidae; **B,** *Éphoron,* Polymitarcỳinae, Polymitarcỳidae; **C,** *Stenonèma,* Heptageniìnae, Heptageniìdae; **D,** *Siphlonùrus,* Siphlonurìnae, Siphlonùridae.

and slender, apical segments elongate and more slender than basal segments, subgenital plate with a median notch (*Pseudìron*). . . . .**Heptageniidae***   p. 183

18(11′).   With 2 caudal filaments; bases of MA_2 and MP_2 atrophied; 1–2 short, basally detached marginal veinlets between main longitudinal veins (Figure 10–4D) . . . .**Baètidae**   p. 183

18′.   With 3 caudal filaments; bases of MA_2 and MP_2 usually well developed; no short, basally detached marginal veinlets between main longitudinal veins (Figure 10–4E,F) **19**

19(18′). MP_2 and IMP_2 extending less than three-fourths distance to wing base (Figure 10–4E); genital forceps of male 2- or 3-segmented; thorax usually black or gray . . . .**Tricorýthidae**   p. 184

19′. MP_2 and IMP_2 extending nearly to wing base (Figure 10–4F); genital forceps of male 1-segmented; thorax usually brown . . . .**Caènidae**   p. 184

Family **Siphlonùridae:**   The nymphs of these mayflies are streamlined in form and occur principally in rapidly flowing streams and rivers. At least some are predaceous on tube-dwelling midge larvae and other small aquatic insects. The adults resemble the Heptageniidae in having MA in the hind wing forked, but they do not have two parallel pairs of cubital intercalaries (compare Figure 10–6C,D), and the hind tarsi are four-segmented (five-segmented in Heptageniidae). This is a large and widely distributed group, and its members vary in size (measured by the length of the front wings) from 8 to 20 mm.

Family **Metretopódidae:**   The nymphs of this small group generally occur in large, slowly flowing streams, usually in shallow water near the shore. The adults have a wing venation similar to that of the Heptageniidae (Figure 10–6C), but the hind tarsi are four-segmented (five-segmented in the Heptageniidae). These mayflies are chiefly northern in distribution, occurring across Canada and south into the eastern United States.

Family **Ametropódidae:**   These mayflies have a wing venation similar to that of the Heptageniidae (Figure 10–6C), but they have three caudal filaments (two in the Heptageniidae), and the hind tarsi are four-segmented. The nymphs live buried in the silty sand in the bottoms of large rivers with a fairly strong current.

Family **Baètidae:**   This is the largest family of mayflies in North America, and its members are common and widely distributed. The nymphs occur in a variety of aquatic habitats. The adults are small (frong wings 2–12 mm), with the front wings elongate-oval and the hind wings very small or lacking.

Baetids (Figure 10–4D) differ from other mayflies that have the hind wings small or lacking (Caènidae, Figure 10–4F; Tricorýthidae, Figure 10–4E; and some Leptophlebìidae) in having only two caudal filaments, one or two short marginal veinlets between the main longitudinal veins, and the bases of MA_2 and MP_2 atrophied. The eyes of the male are divided, with the upper portion turbinate.

Family **Oligoneuriidae:**   The adults of two of the three genera in this family (*Homoeoneùria* and *Lachlània*) have the wing venation greatly reduced (Figure 10–4A). In the third genus (*Isonýchia*) the venation is fairly complete. It resembles that in Figure 10–6D, but MP in the hind wing is forked near the wing margin (see couplet 9 of key). The nymphs occur in fairly rapid streams with sandy bottoms.

Family **Heptageniidae:**   This is the second largest family of mayflies in North America, and its members are common and widely distributed. The nymphs are sprawling forms, usually dark-colored, with the head and body flattened (Figure 10–2C). Most species occur on the underside of stones in streams, but some occur in sandy rivers and boggy ponds. Adults have two caudal filaments and two pairs of cubital intercalaries that are more or less parallel (Figure 10–6C), and (except in *Arthroplèa*) MA in the hind wing is forked. The hind tarsi are five-segmented (appearing four-segmented in *Pseudìron*).

Family **Leptophlebìidae:**   This is a fairly large group, and its members are relatively common and widely distributed. The nymphs occur in a variety of aquatic habitats, usually in still water or in streams with a reduced current. Adults have three caudal filaments, and the venation (Figure 10–4J) is fairly complete. There are no detached veinlets, and CuP is rather strongly recurved. The eyes of the male are strongly divided, with the upper portion having larger facets. Adults range in size (measured by the length of the front wing) from 4 to 14 mm.

Family **Behningiidae:** This group is represented in the United States by a single rare species, *Dolània americàna* Edmunds and Traver, which has been found from South Carolina to Florida. The nymphs burrow in the sand at the bottom of large rivers.

Family **Potamánthidae:** The nymphs of this group live in the silt or sand at the bottom of swiftly flowing shallow water. The adults are pale in color, with the vertex and thoracic dorsum reddish brown, and the front wings are 7–13 mm in length. There are three caudal filaments, and the median filament is a little shorter than the lateral ones. The wing venation is similar to that of the Epheméridae, but 1A is forked near the wing margin (Figure 10–4I).

Family **Epheméridae:** These mayflies are medium-sized to large (front wings 10–25 mm), with two or three caudal filaments. The wings are hyaline or brownish and, in *Ephémera*, have dark spots. The nymphs are burrowing in habit and occur in the sand or silt at the bottoms of streams and lakes, sometimes in fairly deep water. Adults of *Hexagènia* (Figure 10–1) sometimes emerge from lakes in tremendous numbers.

Family **Palingeniidae:** This group is represented in the United States by two species of *Pentagènia*, which are not very common. They are very similar to the Epheméridae, but may be separated by the characters given in the key (couplet 7).

Family **Polymitarcỳidae:** These mayflies are similar to the Epheméridae, but have the middle and hind legs of the male, and all legs of the female, greatly reduced or vestigial. They are widely distributed, but are not very common. Some (Polymitarcyìnae) have a dense network of marginal veinlets (Figure 10–6B), and the genital forceps of the male are four-segmented. Others (Campsurìnae) have few marginal veinlets (Figure 10–6A), and the genital forceps of the male are two-segmented.

Family **Ephemeréllidae:** These mayflies are medium-sized (front wing 6–19 mm) and usually brownish, with three caudal filaments. They have short, basally detached marginal veinlets along the outer margin of the front wing, and the costal cross veins are reduced (Figure 10–4G). The ephemerellids are common and widely distributed mayflies. The The nymphs occur in a variety of aquatic habitats, usually under rocks or in debris in cool, clear, rapid streams or in small clear lakes.

Family **Tricorýthidae:** This group is largely trop-ical, but a few species range as far north as Utah and Maryland. The nymphs occur in rivers and streams. The adults are small (front wing 3–9 mm), with three caudal filaments. The front wings are elongate-oval (widened at the base in *Tricorythòdes*), without marginal veinlets, and with MP$_2$ atrophied at the base (Figure 10–4E). Hind wings are lacking except in males of *Leptohỳphes*, in which the hind wings are very small and have a long slender costal projection (Figure 10–4C).

Family **Neoepheméridae:** These mayflies are similar to the ephemerids, but they have the costal cross veins somewhat reduced and an acute costal projection near the base of the hind wing (10–4B). The nymphs occur in slow to moderately rapid streams, usually in debris. This is a small group whose members occur in the eastern United States. They are not very common.

Family **Caènidae:** These mayflies are quite small (front wing 2–6 mm), with three caudal filaments and with the hind wings lacking. They are similar to the Tricorýthidae, but have the fork of MA symmetrical and veins IMP$_1$ and MP$_2$ extending nearly to the wing base (Figure 10–4F). The nymphs occur in a variety of aquatic habitats, but usually in quiet water.

Family **Baetíscidae:** These mayflies are small to medium-sized (front wing 8–12 mm), with two caudal filaments (which are usually shorter than the body). The wings are often reddish or orange, at least basally. The front wing lacks cubital intercalaries and has 1A extending to the outer margin of the wing (Figure 10–4H). The nymphs occur principally in cool, fairly rapid streams.

Collecting and Preserving Ephemeróptera

Most adult mayflies are captured with a net, either from swarms or by sweeping vegetation. One sometimes needs a net with a very long handle for swarms high above the ground. Some mayflies may be taken at night at lights, especially when the nights are warm and the sky is overcast. Large numbers of adults can sometimes be obtained with a trap such as a Malaise trap (page 752 and Figure 36–7C). Curtains of netting placed over a stream will serve as a surface on which emerging mayflies alight and from which they can be collected.

If subimagoes are collected (usually recognizable by their dull appearance and pubescence), they should be allowed to molt to the adult stage. This is done by transferring them to small boxes (without actually handling them if possible, as they are very delicate). A cardboard box with a clear plastic window is good for this purpose.

Adults of many species are best obtained by rearing them from nymphs, in a container where the adults can be captured (see pages 772–774). Nymphs with black wing pads are nearly mature and are the best to select for rearing as they will usually transform to the winged stage in a day or two. When the subimago emerges, it is desirable to transfer it to a box where it can molt to the adult stage.

Mayfly nymphs can be collected in various types of aquatic habitats by the methods of collecting aquatic insects (page 754).

Adult mayflies are extremely fragile and must be handled with considerable care. They may be preserved dry, on pins or points or in paper envelopes,

or in alcohol. Specimens preserved dry retain their color better than those preserved in alcohol, but they sometimes become somewhat shriveled and are more subject to breakage. Adults preserved in alcohol should be preserved in 80% alcohol, preferably with 1% of ionol added.

Nymphs are best put directly into modified Carnoy fluid (glacial acetic acid, 10%; 95% ethanol, 60%; chloroform, 30%). After a day or so the Carnoy fluid is drained off and replaced with 80% alcohol. A good substitute for Carnoy fluid is Kahle's fluid (formalin, 11%; 95% ethanol, 28%; glacial acetic acid, 2%; water, 59%). This fluid should be drained off in about a week and replaced with 80% alcohol. If neither Carnoy nor Kahle's fluid is available, nymphs may be preserved in 95% alcohol.

References

Berner, L. 1950. The Mayflies of Florida. Gainesville: Univ. Florida Press, 287 pp.; illus.

Britt, N. W. 1962. Biology of two species of Lake Erie mayflies, *Ephoron album* (Say) and *Ephemera simulans* Walker. Bull. Ohio Biol. Surv. (New Ser.) 1(5):1–70; illus.

Burks, B. D. 1953 (reprinted 1975). The mayflies or Ephemeroptera of Illinois. Ill. Nat. Hist. Surv. Bull. 26(1): 1–216; illus.

Day, W. C. 1956. Ephemeroptera, *in* Aquatic Insects of California, ed. R. L. Usinger. Berkeley: Univ. California Press, pp. 79–105; illus.

Edmunds, G. F., Jr. 1959. Ephemeroptera, *in* Freshwater Biology, ed. W. F. Edmondson. New York: Wiley, pp. 908–916; illus.

Edmunds, G. F., Jr. 1962a. The principles applied in determining the hierarchic level of the higher categories of Ephemeroptera. Syst. Zool. 11:22–32; illus.

Edmunds, G. F., Jr. 1962b. The type localities of the Ephemeroptera of North America north of Mexico. Univ. Utah Biol. Ser. 12(5):1–39.

Edmunds, G. F., Jr. 1972. Biogeography and evolution of the Ephemeroptera. Annu. Rev. Entomol. 17:21–42; illus.

Edmunds, G. F., Jr. 1984. Ephemeroptera, *in* An Introduction to the Aquatic Insects of North America, 2nd ed., ed. R. W. Merritt and K. W. Cummins. Dubuque, Iowa: Kendall/Hunt, pp. 94–123; illus.

Edmunds, G. F., Jr., and R. K. Allen. 1957. A checklist of the Ephemeroptera of North America north of Mexico. Ann. Entomol. Soc. Amer. 50:317–324.

Edmunds, G. F., Jr., and R. K. Allen. 1987. Order Ephemeroptera, pp. 75–94 *in* F. W. Stehr (ed.), Immature Insects, vol. 1. Dubuque, Iowa: Kendall/Hunt, 754 pp.; illus.

Edmunds, G. F., Jr., R. K. Allen, and W. L. Peters. 1963. An annotated key to the nymphs of the families and subfamilies of mayflies (Ephemeroptera). Univ. Utah Biol. Ser. 13(1):1–49; illus.

Edmunds, G. F., Jr., L. Berner, and J. R. Traver. 1958. North American mayflies of the family Oligoneuriidae. Ann. Entomol. Soc. Amer. 51:375–382; illus.

Edmunds, G. F., Jr., S. L. Jensen, and L. Berner. 1976. The Mayflies of North and Central America. Minneapolis: Univ. Minnesota Press, 300 pp.; illus.

Edmunds, G. F., Jr., and J. R. Traver. 1954a. An outline of a reclassification of the Ephemeroptera. Proc. Entomol. Soc. Wash. 56:236–240.

Edmunds, G. F., Jr., and J. R. Traver. 1954b. The flight mechanics of the wings of Ephemeroptera with notes on the archetype wing. J. Wash. Acad. Sci. 44(12):390–400; illus.

Edmunds, G. F., Jr., and J. R. Traver. 1959. The classification of the Ephemeroptera. I. Ephemeroidea: Behningiidae. Ann. Entomol. Soc. Amer. 52:43–51; illus.

Hubbard, M. D., and W. L. Peters. 1976. The number of genera and species of mayflies (Ephemeroptera). Entomol. News 87:245.

Kukalová-Peck, J. 1985. Ephemeroid wing venation based upon new gigantic Carboniferous mayflies and basic morphology, phylogeny, and metamorphosis of pterygote insects. Can. J. Zool. 63:933–955; illus.

Leonard, J. W., and F. A. Leonard. 1962. Mayflies of Michigan Trout Streams. Bloomfield Hills, Mich.: Cranbrook Institute of Science, 137 pp.; illus.

McCafferty, W. P., and G. F. Edmunds, Jr. 1976. Redefinition of the family Palingeniidae and its implications for the higher classification of the Ephemeroptera. Ann. Entomol. Soc. Amer. 69:486–490; illus.

McCafferty, W. P., and G. F. Edmunds, Jr. 1979. The higher classification of the Ephemeroptera and its evolutionary basis. Ann. Entomol. Soc. Amer. 72:5–12; illus.

Needham, J. G. 1920. Burrowing mayflies of our larger lakes and streams. Bull. U.S. Bur. Fish. 36:269–292; illus.

Needham, J. G., J. R. Traver, and Y.-C. Hsu. 1935. The Biology of Mayflies, with a Systematic Account of North American Species. Ithaca, N.Y.: Comstock, 759 pp.; illus.

Pennak, R. W. 1978 (2nd ed.) Fresh-Water Invertebrates of the United States. New York: Wiley Interscience, 803 pp.; illus.

Peters, W. L., and G. F. Edmunds, Jr. 1970. Revision of the generic classification of the eastern hemisphere Leptophlebiidae (Ephemeroptera). Pac. Insects 12(1): 157–240; illus.

Thew, T. B. 1960. Revision of the genera of the family Caenidae (Ephemeroptera). Trans. Amer. Entomol. Soc. 86:187–205; illus.

Traver, J. R. 1932–1933. Mayflies of North Carolina. J. Elisha Mitchell Sci. Soc. 47(1):85–161, illus. (1932); 47(2):163–236 (1932); 49(2):141–206, illus. (1933).

Chapter 11

Order Odonàta[1]
Dragonflies and Damselflies

The Odonàta are relatively large and often beautifully colored insects that spend a large part of their time on the wing. The immature stages are aquatic, and the adults are usually found near water. All stages are predaceous and feed on various insects and other organisms and, from the human point of view, are generally very beneficial. The adults are harmless to people; that is, they do not bite or sting.

Adult dragonflies and damselflies are easily recognized (Figures 11–10 through 11–14). The four wings are elongate, many-veined, and membranous. The compound eyes are large and many-faceted and often occupy most of the head. The thorax is relatively small and compact (the prothorax is always small, and the other two thoracic segments make up most of the thorax), and the dorsal surface of the pterothorax, between the pronotum and the base of the wings, is formed by pleural sclerites. The antennae are very small and bristlelike. The abdomen is long and slender. The cerci are unsegmented and function as clasping organs in the male. The mouthparts are of the chewing type, and the metamorphosis is simple.

Present-day Odonàta vary in length from about 20 to more than 135 mm. The largest dragonfly known,[2] which lived about 250 million years ago and is known only from fossils, had a wingspread of about 71 cm (28 inches)! The largest dragonflies in the United States are about 85 mm in length, though they often look much larger when seen on the wing.

Odonàta nymphs are aquatic and breathe by means of gills. The gills of damselfly nymphs (Zygóptera) are in the form of three leaflike structures at the end of the abdomen (Figure 11–1). These nymphs swim by body undulations, the gills functioning like the tail of a fish. The gills of dragonfly nymphs (Anisóptera) (Figures 11–2 and 11–11A,B) are in the form of ridges in the rectum. When a dragonfly nymph breathes, it draws water into the rectum through the anus and then expels it. If the insect is in a hurry, this expulsion of water from the anus is the chief means of locomotion, and the insect moves by "jet propulsion."

The nymphs vary somewhat in habits, but all are aquatic and feed on various sorts of small aquatic organisms. They usually lie in wait for their prey, either on a plant or more or less buried in the mud. The prey is generally small, but some of the larger nymphs (particularly Aéshnidae) occasionally attack tadpoles and small fish. The nymphs have the labium

---

[1]Odonàta: from the Greek, meaning tooth (referring to the teeth on the mandibles).

[2]*Meganeurópsis permiàna* Carpenter, of the extinct order Meganisóptera.

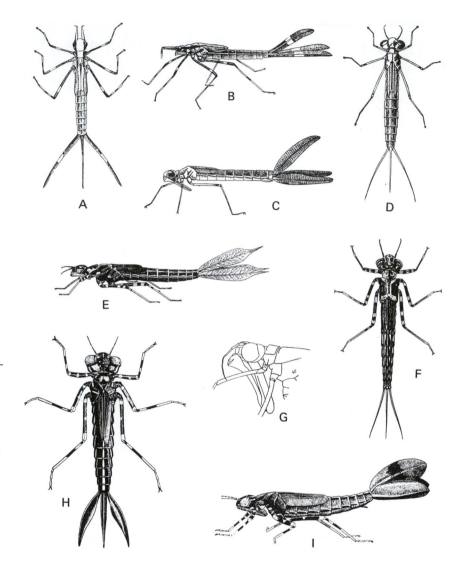

Figure 11–1. Nymphs of damselflies (Zygóptera), dorsal and lateral views. **A** and **B,** *Calópteryx aequábilis* (Say) (Calopterýgidae); **C** and **D,** *Léstes drỳas* Kirby (Léstidae); **E** and **F,** *Ischnùra cervùla* Selys (Coenagriónidae); **G,** head of *Léstes drỳas,* lateral view; **H** and **I,** *Árgia émma* Kennedy (Coenagriónidae). (Courtesy of Kennedy and the U.S. National Museum.)

modified into a peculiar segmented structure with which the prey is captured. The labium is folded under the head when not in use. When used, it is thrust forward, usually very quickly, and the prey is grabbed by two movable clawlike lobes (the lateral lobes or palps) at the tip of the labium (Figure 11–3). The labium, when extended, is usually at least a third as long as the body (Figure 11–11B).

When a nymph is fully grown, it crawls up out of the water, usually on a plant stem or rock (and usually early in the morning) and undergoes its final molt. The nymphs of some species wander many yards from the water before molting. Once out of the last nymphal skin, the adult expands to its full size in about half an hour. The flight of newly emerged adults is relatively feeble, and they are very easy to catch, but they make poor specimens. They are not

yet fully colored, and they are very soft-bodied. It is usually a few days before the insect's full powers of flight are developed, and it may be a week or two before the color pattern is fully developed. Many Odonàta have a color or color pattern in the first few days of their adult life that is quite different from what they will have after a week or two. Newly emerged, pale, soft-bodied adults are usually spoken of as *teneral* individuals.

The two sexes in the suborder Anisóptera are usually similarly colored, though the colors of the male are frequently brighter. In some of the Libellùlidae the two sexes differ in the color pattern of the wings. The two sexes are differently colored in most of the Zygóptera, and the male is usually the more brightly colored. In most of the Coenagriónidae the two sexes have a different color pattern. Some dam-

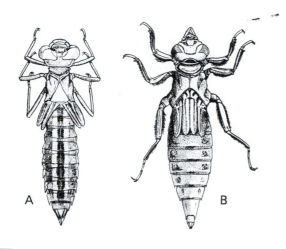

Figure 11–2. Nymphs of Aeshnòidea. **A,** *Aéshna verticàlis* Hagen (Aéshnidae); **B,** *Gómphus quádricolor* Walsh (Gómphidae). (Courtesy of Walker and the Canadian Entomologist.)

selflies have two or more different color phases in the female. For example, most females of *Ischnùra verticàlis* (Say) have a color pattern that is different from that of the male and are either orange and black (newly emerged) or rather uniformly bluish (older individuals), but a few females have a color pattern that is similar to that of the male.

Some species of Odonàta are on the wing for only a few weeks each year, whereas others may be seen throughout the summer or over a period of several months. Observations of marked individuals indicate that the average damselfly probably has a maximum adult life of 3 or 4 weeks, and some dragonflies may live 6 or 8 weeks. Most species have a single generation a year, with the egg or nymph (usually the nymph) overwintering. A few of the larger darners are known to spend 2 or 3 years in the nymphal stage.

Dragonflies and damselflies are peculiar among insects in having the copulatory organs of the male located at the anterior end of the abdomen, on the ventral side of the second abdominal segment. The male genitalia of other insects are located at the posterior end of the abdomen. Before mating, the male dragonfly must transfer sperm from the genital opening on the ninth segment to the structures on the second segment. This transfer is accomplished by bending the abdomen downward and forward.

The two sexes frequently spend considerable time "in tandem," with the male clasping the female by the back of the head or the prothorax with the appendages at the end of his abdomen. Copulation,

with the female bending her abdomen downward and forward and making contact with the second-segment genitalia of the male, usually occurs in flight.

Odonàta lay their eggs in or near water and may do so while in tandem or when alone. In some species where the female detaches from the male before beginning oviposition, the male will remain nearby "on guard" while the female is ovipositing and will chase off other males that come near. An unprotected female, after she begins ovipositing, may be interrupted by another male, who may grab her and fly off in tandem with her.

Females of the Gómphidae, Macromìidae, Corduliìidae, and Libellùlidae do not have an ovipositor, and the eggs are generally laid on the surface of the water by the female flying low and dipping her abdomen in the water and washing off the eggs. The females of most species in these groups are alone when ovipositing. A somewhat rudimentary ovipositor is developed in the Cordulegástridae, which oviposit by hovering above shallow water with the body in a more or less vertical position and repeatedly jabbing the abdomen into the water and laying the eggs in the bottom. The females of the other groups

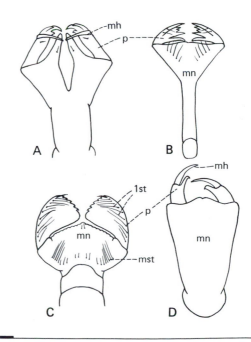

Figure 11–3. Labia of nymphal Odonàta. **A,** *Calópteryx* (Calopterýgidae); **B,** *Léstes* (Léstidae); **C,** *Plathèmis* (Libellùlidae); **D,** *Ànax* (Aéshnidae). *lst,* lateral setae; *mh,* movable hook or palp; *mn,* mentum; *mst,* mental setae; *p,* palp or lateral lobe. (Redrawn from Garman.)

(Aéshnidae, Petalùridae, and all Zygóptera) have a well-developed ovipositor (Figure 11–4E) and insert their eggs in plant tissues (in many species while still in tandem with the male). The eggs are usually inserted just below the surface of the water, no farther than the female can reach, but in a few cases (for example, some species of *Léstes*) the eggs are laid in plant stems above the water line, and in a few other cases (for example, some species of *Enallágma*) the female may climb down a plant stem and insert her eggs into the plant a foot or more below the surface of the water. The eggs usually hatch in 1 to 3 weeks. In some species (for example, *Léstes*), however, the eggs overwinter and hatch the following spring.

Most species of Odonàta have characteristic habits of flight. The flight of most common skimmers (Libellùlidae) is very erratic. They fly this way and that, often hovering in one spot for a few moments, and they seldom fly very far in a straight line. Many

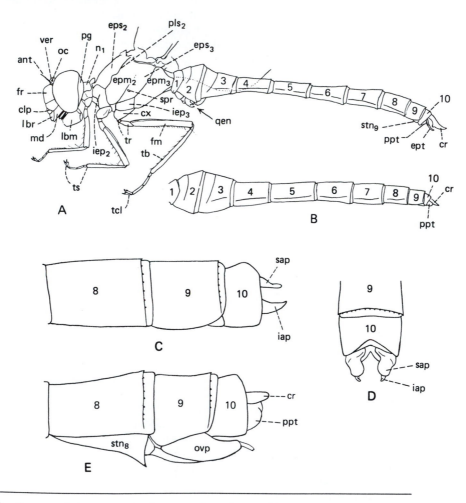

Figure 11–4.   Structural characters of Odonàta. **A,** lateral view of *Sympètrum intérnum* Montgomery, male; **B,** lateral view of abdomen of *S. intérnum*, female; **C,** terminal abdominal segments of *Enallágma hágeni* (Walsh), male lateral view; **D,** same, dorsal view; **E,** terminal abdominal segments of *E. hágeni*, female, lateral view. *ant*, antennae; *clp*, clypeus; *cr*, cerci or superior appendages; *cx*, coxa; *e*, compound eye; *epm₂*, mesepimeron; *epm₃*, metepimeron; *eps₂*, mesepisternum; *eps₃*, metepisternum; *ept*, epiproct or inferior appendage; *fm*, femur; *fr*, frons; *gen*, male copulatory apparatus; *iap*, interior appendage (paraproct); *iep₂*, mesinfraepisternum; *iep₃*, metinfraepisternum; *lbm*, labium; *lbr*, labrum; *md*, mandible; *n₁*, pronotum; *oc*, ocellus; *ovp*, ovipositor; *pg*, postgena; *pls₂*, mesopleural suture (or humeral suture); *ppt*, paraproct; *sap*, superior appendage (cercus); *spr*, spiracle; *stn*, sternum; *tb*, tibia; *tcl*, tarsal claws; *tr*, trochanter; *ts*, tarsus; *ver*, vertex; *1–10*, abdominal segments.

stream species fly relatively slowly up and down the stream, often patrolling a stretch of 90 meters or more. These dragonflies fly at a height and a speed that are characteristic for the species. Some of the gomphids, when flying over open land areas, fly with a very undulating flight, each undulation covering 1.2–1.8 meters vertically and 0.6–0.9 meters horizontally. Many of the corduliids and aeshnids fly from 1.8 to 6.1 meters or more above the ground, and their flight seems tireless. Many of the smaller damselflies fly only 25–50 mm above the surface of the water.

Most dragonflies feed on a variety of small insects that are caught on the wing in a basketlike arrangement of the legs. The dragonfly may alight and eat its prey or may eat it on the wing. The prey is chiefly small flying insects such as midges, mosquitoes, and small moths, but the larger dragonflies often capture bees, butterflies, or other dragonflies. Odonàta normally take only moving prey, but if captured they will eat or chew on almost anything that is put into their mouth—even their own abdomen!

Many pond species are frequently found with large numbers of small, rounded, usually reddish bodies attached to the under side of the thorax or abdomen; these bodies are larval water mites. The mite larvae attach to the dragonfly nymph and, when the nymph emerges, move onto the adult. The mites spend 2 or 3 weeks on the dragonfly, feeding on its blood and increasing in size, and eventually leave it. If they get back into water, they develop into adult mites, which are free-living and predaceous. The mite larvae do not appear to do a great deal of damage to the dragonflies. It is not unusual to find dragonflies with dozens of mite larvae on them.

Classification of the Odonàta

A synopsis of the Odonàta occurring in North America north of Mexico is given below, with synonyms and alternate spellings in parentheses. The numbers in parentheses following each family are the numbers of North American species, taken from Westfall (1984).

Suborder Anisóptera—dragonflies
   Superfamily Aeshnòidea
      Petalùridae (2)—graybacks
      Gómphidae (93)—clubtails
      Aéshnidae (Aéschnidae) (38)—darners
   Superfamily Cordulegastròidea (Aeshnòidea in part)
      Cordulegástridae (Cordulegastéridae) (8)—biddies
   Superfamily Libellulòidea
      Macromìidae (Epophthalmìidae) (10)—belted skimmers and river skimmers
      Cordulìidae (50)—green-eyed skimmers
      Libellùlidae (93)—common skimmers
Suborder Zygóptera—damselflies
      Calopterýgidae (Agriónidae, Agrìidae) (8)—broad-winged damselflies
      Léstidae (18)—spread-winged damselflies
      Protoneùridae (Coenagriónidae in part) (2)—protoneurid damselflies
      Coenagriónidae (Coenagrìidae, Agriónidae) (93)—narrow-winged damselflies

The separation of the families of Odonàta is based primarily on characters of the wings. There are three major interpretations of the wing venation in this order. We use the Comstock-Needham interpretation (which includes a number of special terms not used in other orders), illustrated in Figures 11–5 and 11–6. Riek and Kukalová-Peck (1984) have recently proposed a reinterpretation of dragonfly wing venation on the basis of fossil specimens; a comparison between their scheme and that used here is presented in Table 11–1. The separation of genera and species is based on wing venation, color pattern, structure of the genitalia, and other characters. Many species of Odonàta can be recognized in the field by their characteristic size, shape, color, or habits.

Key to the Families of Odonàta

This key deals only with adults. Westfall (1987) provides a key to the nymphs of Odonàta.

1.   Front and hind wings similar in shape and both narrowed at base (Figures 11–6 and 11–7D,F); wings at rest held either together above body or slightly divergent; head transversely elongate; males with 4 appendages at end of abdomen (figure 11–4C,D) (damselflies, suborder Zygóptera) **2**

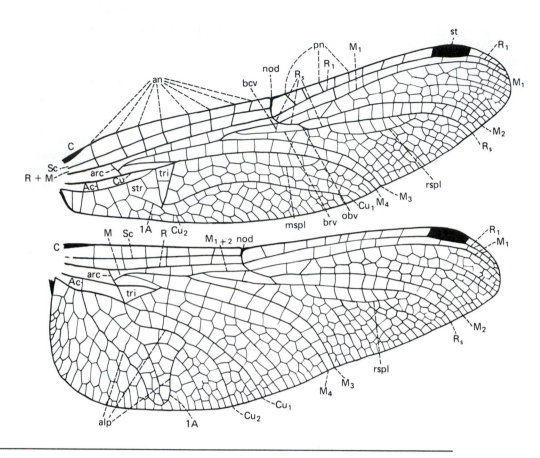

Figure 11–5. Wings of *Sympètrum rubicúndulum* (Say) (Libellùlidae), showing the Comstock-Needham system of terminology. *Ac*, anal crossing (A branching posteriorly from Cu; often called the cubitoanal cross vein); *alp*, anal loop (foot-shaped in this species); *an*, antenodal cross veins; *arc*, arculus (the upper part is M, and the lower part is a cross vein); *bcv*, bridge cross vein; *brv*, bridge vein; *mspl*, medial supplement; *nod*, nodus; *obv*, oblique vein; *pn*, postnodal cross veins; *rspl*, radial supplement; *st*, stigma; *str*, subtriangle (3-celled in this wing); *tri*, triangle (2-celled in front wing, 1-celled in hind wing). The usual symbols are used for the other venational characters.

1′.	Hind wings wider then front wings (Figures 11–5 and 11–7A–C); wings at rest held horizontally or nearly so; head not usually transversely elongate, but more rounded; males with 3 appendages at end of abdomen (Figure 11–4A) (dragonflies, suborder Anisóptera) **5**
2(1).	Ten or more antenodal cross veins (Figure 11–7D); wings not stalked, often with black or red markings ....**Calopterýgidae** p. 199
2′.	Two (rarely 3) antenodal cross veins (Figures 11–6 and 11–7F); wings stalked at base, either hyaline or lightly tinged with brownish (only rarely blackish) **3**
3(2′).	M₃ arising nearer arculus than nodus (Figure 11–6B); wings usually divergent above body at rest ....**Léstidae** p. 199
3′.	M₃ arising nearer nodus than arculus (Figure 11–6A), usually arising below nodus; wings usually held together above body at rest **4**

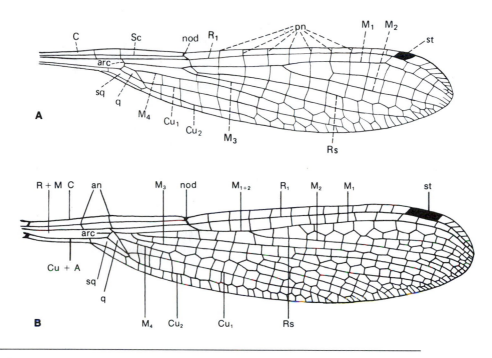

Figure 11–6. Hind wings of damselflies. **A,** *Enallágma* (Coenagriónidae); **B,** *Léstes* (Léstidae). *q*, quadrangle; *sq*, subquadrangle.

4(3′).	Cu₂ rudimentary or absent, Cu₁ short, forming, the anterior border of only 3 or 4 cells distal to arculus (Figure 11–7F); reddish or brownish damselflies; southern Texas ....**Protoneùridae**	p. 199
4′.	Cu₁ and Cu₂ well developed, both extending several cells distal to arculus (Figure 11–6A); color variable; widely distributed ....**Coenagriónidae**	p. 199
5(1′).	Triangles in front and hind wings similar in shape and about equidistant from arculus (Figure 11–7A); most of the costal and subcostal cross veins not in line; usually a brace vein (an oblique cross vein; Figure 11–7E, *bvn*) present behind proximal end of stigma **6**	
5′.	Triangles in front and hind wings usually not similar in shape, and triangle in front wing farther distad of arculus than triangle in hind wing (Figures 11–5 and 11–7B,C); most of costal and subcostal cross veins in line; no brace vein behind proximal end of stigma **9**	
6(5).	Brace vein present behind proximal end of stigma (Figure 11–7E, *bvn*) **7**	
6′.	No brace vein behind proximal end of stigma ....**Cordulegàstridae**	p. 196
7(6).	Compound eyes in contact for a considerable distance on dorsal side of head (Figure 11–8B) ....**Aéshnidae**	p. 194
7′.	Compound eyes separated on dorsal side of head (Figure 11–8A) or meeting at a single point only **8**	
8(7′).	Median lobe of labium notched (Figure 11–9A); stigma at least 8 mm in length ....**Petalùridae**	p. 194
8′.	Median lobe of labium not notched (Figure 11–9B); stigma less than 8 mm in length ....**Gómphidae**	p. 194

9(5').   Hind margin of compound eyes slightly lobed (Figure 11–8D); males with
           small lobe on each side of second abdominal segment (above genitalia), with
           inner margin of hind wing somewhat notched; anal loop rounded (Figure
           11–7B) or elongate, if foot-shaped with little development of "toe" (Figure
           11–7C) **10**

9'.   Hind margin of compound eyes straight or with very small lobe (Figure
           11–8C); males without small lobe on side of second abdominal segment,
           with inner margin of "toe" well developed (Figure 11–5) ....**Libellùlidae**   p. 197

10(9).   Anal loop rounded, without a bisector (Figure 11–7B); triangle in hind wing
           distad of arculus; 3 or more cu-a cross veins in hind wing ......**Macromìidae**   p. 196

10'.   Anal loop elongate, with a bisector (Figure 11–7C); triangle in hind wing
           opposite arculus or nearly so; 1 or 2 cu-a cross veins in hind
           wing ....**Corduliidae**   p. 197

SUBORDER **Anisóptera**—Dragonflies: Dragonflies have the hind wings wider at the base than the front wings, and the wings are held horizontal (or nearly so) at rest. The hind wings of the male in all but the Libellùlidae are somewhat notched at the anal angle (Figure 11–7A–C), while the hind wings of all Libellùlidae and the females of the other families have the anal angle rounded (Figure 11–5). The head is somewhat rounded and is seldom transversely elongate. The males have three appendages at the apex of the abdomen, two superior appendages (the cerci) and an inferior appendage (the epiproct). The females of some groups have a well-developed ovipositor, while those of other groups have the ovipositor either poorly developed or entirely absent (with the sternum of segment 8 more or less prolonged posteriorly to form an egg guide called the vulvar lamina). The nymphs have short appendages at the apex of the abdomen and have the gills in the rectum.

Family **Petalùridae**—Graybacks: Two species in this family occur in North America: *Tachópteryx thòreyi* (Hagen) in the eastern United States and *Tanýpteryx hágeni* (Selys) in the Northwest (California and Nevada to southern British Columbia). Adults of *T. thòreyi* are grayish brown and about 75 mm in length. They usually occur along small streams in wooded valleys, where they often alight on tree trunks. Adults of *T. hágeni* are a little smaller and blackish and are found at high elevations. The nymphs of this species occur in wet moss.

Family **Gómphidae**—Clubtails: This is a fairly large group, and most of its members occur along streams or lake shores. The clubtails are 50–75 mm in length and dark-colored, usually with yellowish or greenish markings (Figure 11–10D,E). They generally alight on a bare flat surface. Many species have the terminal abdominal segments swollen, hence the common name for the group. The largest genus in the family is *Gómphus*.

Family **Aéshnidae**—Darners: This group includes the largest and most powerful of the dragonflies; most of them are about 75 mm in length. The green darner, *Ànax jùnius* (Drury), a common and widely distributed species that occurs about ponds, has a greenish thorax, a bluish abdomen, and a targetlike mark on the upper part of the face (Figure 11–10A). The genus *Aéshna* contains a number of species, most of which are to be found near marshes in the latter part of the summer. They are dark-colored with blue or greenish markings on the thorax and

Table 11–1
Comparison of Interpretations of Dragonfly Venation

Comstock-Needham	Riek and Kukalová-Peck (1984)
C	Costal margin (PC + CA + CP + ScA)
Sc	ScP
R + M basally	Paired or fused stems of RA and RP
R_1	RA
Rs	Radial Supplement
M_{1+2}	RP1–2
M_1	RP1
M_2	RP2
M_3	RP3–4
M_4	MA
Cu basally	MP
Cu_1	MP
Cu_2	CuA
1A	CuP
Anal crossing	CuP crossing

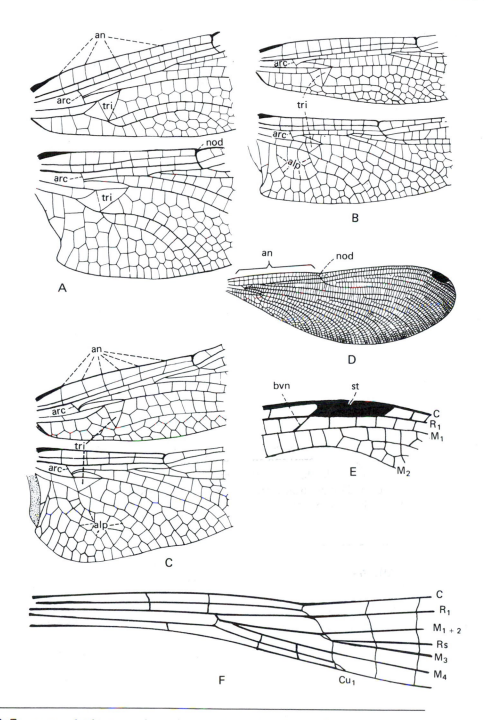

Figure 11–7.   Wings of Odonàta. **A,** base of wings of *Gómphus* (Gómphidae); **B,** base of wings of *Dídymops* (Macromìidae); **C,** base of wings of *Epithèca* (Cordulìidae); **D,** front wing of *Calópteryx* (Calopterýgidae); **E,** stigmal area of wing of *Aéshna* (Aéshnidae); **F,** base of front wing of *Protoneùra* (Protoneùridae). *alp,* anal loop; *an,* antenodal cross veins; *arc,* arculus; *bvn,* brace vein; *nod,* nodus; *st,* stigma; *tri,* triangle.

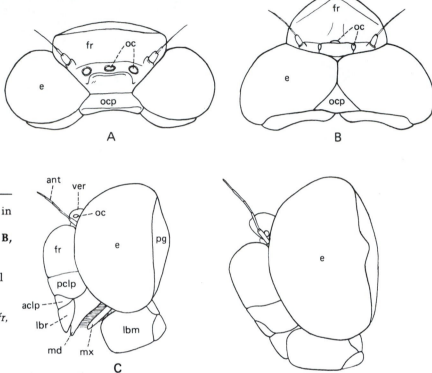

Figure 11–8.   Head structure in dragonflies. **A,** *Gómphus éxilis* Selys (Gómphidae), dorsal view; **B,** *Basiaèschna janàta* (Say) (Aéshnidae), dorsal view; **C,** *Sympètrum* (Libellùlidae), lateral view; **D,** *Epithèca* (Corduliìdae), lateral view. *aclp,* anteclypeus; *ant,* antenna; *e,* compound eye; *fr,* frons; *lbm,* labium; *lbr,* labrum; *md,* mandible; *mx,* maxilla; *oc,* ocellus; *ocp,* occiput; *pclp,* postclypeus; *pg,* postgena; *ver,* vertex.

abdomen (Figure 11–10B). One of the largest species in this family is *Epiaéschna hèros* (Fabricius), an early-summer species about 85 mm in length and dark brown with indistinct greenish markings on the thorax and abdomen.

Family **Cordulegástridae**—Biddies: The biddies are large brownish-black dragonflies with yellow markings (Figure 11–10C). They differ from the other Aeshnòidea in lacking a brace vein at the proximal end of the stigma. These dragonflies are usually found along small, clear, woodland streams. The adults fly slowly up and down the stream, 0.3 to 0.7 meter above the water, but if disturbed can fly very rapidly. The group is a small one, and all species in the United States belong to the genus *Cordulegáster.*

Family **Macromìidae**—Belted Skimmers and River Skimmers: The members of this group can be distinguished from the Corduliìdae, with which they were formerly classified, by the rounded anal loop that lacks a bisector (Figure 11–7B). Two genera occur in the United States, *Dídymops* and *Macròmia.* The belted skimmers (*Dídymops*) are light brown in color, with light markings on the thorax. They occur along boggy pond shores. The river skimmers (*Macròmia*) are large species that occur along lake shores and large streams. These dragonflies are dark brown with yellowish markings on the thorax and abdomen (Figure 11–11C,D), and they are extremely fast fliers. The eyes of the Macromìidae are greenish in life (in *Macròmia,* usually a brilliant green).

Figure 11–9.   Labia of adult dragonflies. **A,** *Tachópteryx* (Petalùridae); **B,** *Aéshna* (Aéshnidae). *lg,* ligula or median lobe; *mn,* mentum; *p,* palp or lateral lobe; *plg,* palpiger or squama.

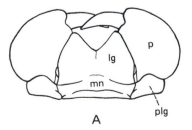

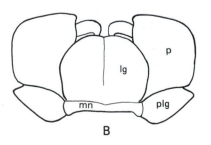

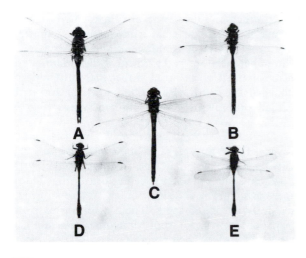

Figure 11–10. Aeshnòidea. **A,** *Ánax jùnius* (Drury), male (Aéshnidae); **B,** *Aéshna constrícta* Say, male (Aéshnidae); **C,** *Cordulegáster oblìquus* (Say), female (Cordulegástridae); **D,** *Dromogómphus spoliàtus* (Hagen), male (Gómphidae); **E,** *Gómphus extérnus* Hagen, male (Gómphidae). About one-third natural size.

Family **Corduliidae**—Green-Eyed Skimmers: These skimmers are mostly black or metallic in color and seldom have conspicuous light markings. The eyes of most species are brilliant green in life. The flight is usually direct, in many species interrupted by periods of hovering. Most members of this group are more common in the northern United States and Canada than in the South.

The genus *Epithèca* contains principally dark-colored dragonflies about 35 to 45 mm in length, often with brownish color at the base of the hind wing. They occur chiefly around ponds and swamps. The royal skimmer, *Epithèca prínceps* (Hagen), is the only corduliid in the Northeast with black spots beyond the base of the wing. It is about 75 mm in length, with three blackish spots in each wing: basal, nodal, and apical. It occurs about ponds. The largest genus in this group is *Somátochlora*, which includes the bog skimmers. Most of the bog skimmers are metallic in color and more than 50 mm in length, and they usually occur along small wooded streams or in bogs.

Family **Libellùlidae**—Common Skimmers: Most of the species in this group occur about ponds and

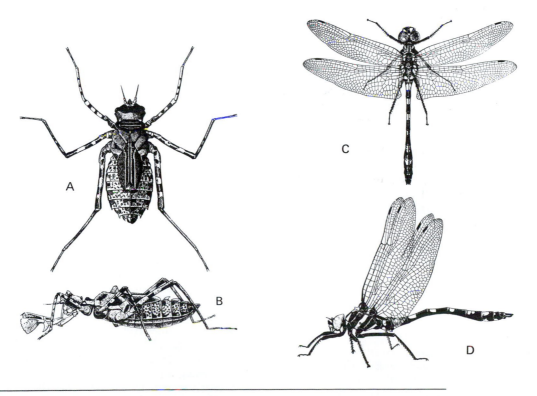

Figure 11–11. *Macròmia magnífica* MacLachlan (Macromìidae). **A,** nymph, dorsal view; **B,** nymph, lateral view, with labium extended; **C,** adult male, dorsal view; **D,** same, lateral view. (Courtesy of Kennedy and the U.S. National Museum.)

swamps, and many species are quite common. These dragonflies vary in length from about 20 to 75 mm, and many species have the wings marked with spots or bands. The flight is usually rather erratic. This is a large group, and only a few of the more common genera and species can be mentioned here.

The smallest libellulid in the United States is the dwarf skimmer, *Nannothèmis bélla* (Uhler), which is about 19 mm in length and occurs in bogs in the eastern states. The males are bluish with clear wings (Figure 11–12G), and the females are patterned with black and yellow and have the basal third or more of the wings yellowish brown. The large dragonflies that are common about ponds and have black or black and white spots on the wings are mostly species in the genus *Libéllula*. The tenspot skimmer, *L. pulchéla* Drury (Figure 11–12A), with a wingspread of about 90 mm, has three black spots (basal, nodal, and apical) on each wing, and the males have white spots between the black spots. The widow skimmer, *L. luctuòsa* Burmeister, which is slightly smaller, has the basal third or so of each wing blackish brown, and the males have a white band beyond the basal dark coloring of the wing (Figure 11–12B).

The white-tailed skimmer, *Plathèmis lýdia* (Drury), has a wingspread of about 65 mm. The male has a broad dark band across the middle of each wing and the dorsal side of the abdomen nearly white (Figure 11–12D). The females have the wings spotted as in the females of *L. pulchéla* and do not have a white abdomen. Spotted skimmers (*Celithèmis*) are medium-sized (wingspread of about 50 mm), mostly reddish or brownish with darker markings, and with reddish or brownish spots on the wings (Figure 11–12F).

The amber-winged skimmer, *Perithèmis ténera* (Say), with a wingspread of about 40 mm, has the wings amber-colored in the male and clear with brownish spots in the female. The dragonflies of the genus *Sympétrum* are medium-sized, late-summer, marsh-inhabiting insects. Their color varies from yellowish brown to a bright brownish red, and the wings are usually clear except for a small basal spot of yellowish brown. The white-faced skimmers (*Leucorrhínia*) have a wingspread of about 40 mm and are dark-colored, with a conspicuous white face. The most common species in the East is *L. intácta* Hagen, which has a yellow spot on the dorsal side of the seventh abdominal segment.

The blue pirate, *Pachydíplax longipénnis* (Burmeister), is a common pond species, particularly in the central and southern United States. It varies in color from a patterned brown and yellow to a uniform bluish, and the wings are often tinged with brownish (Figure 11–12C). It has a long cell just behind the stigma and has a wingspread of 50 to 65 mm. The green-jacket skimmer. *Erythèmis simplicicóllis* (Say), is a little larger than *P. longipénnis*. It has clear wings, and the body color varies from light green patterned with black to a uniform light blue (Figure 11–12H). The skimmers in the genera *Pantàla* and *Tràmea* are medium-sized to large (wingspread 75–100 mm), wide-ranging insects and have the base of the hind wings very broad. Those in *Pantàla* are yellowish brown with a light yellowish or brownish spot at the base of the hind wing. Those in *Tràmea* are largely black or dark reddish brown with a black or dark brown spot at the base of the hind wing (Figure 11–12E).

SUBORDER **Zygóptera**—Damselflies: Damselflies have the front and hind wings similar in shape, with both narrowed at the base, and the wings at rest are either held together above the body or slightly divergent. The wings of the two sexes are similar in shape. The head is transversely elongate. The males have four appendages at the apex of the abdomen: a pair of superior appendages (the cerci) and a pair of inferior appendages (the paraprocts). The females have an ovipositor, which usually gives the end of the abdomen a somewhat swollen appearance. The nymphs have three leaflike gills at the apex of the abdomen (Figure 11–1).

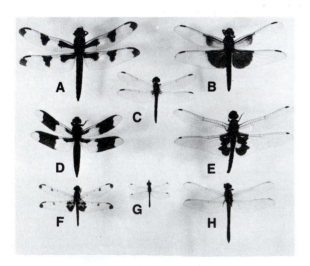

Figure 11–12.   Libellùlidae. **A,** *Libéllula pulchéla* Drury, male; **B,** *Libéllula luctuòsa* Burmeister, male; **C,** *Pachydíplax longipénnis* (Burmeister), male; **D,** *Plathèmis lýdia* (Drury), male; **E,** *Tràmea laceràta* Hagen, male; **F,** *Celithèmis elìsa* (Hagen), male; **G,** *Nannothèmis bélla* (Uhler), male; **H,** *Erythèmis simplicicóllis* (Say). About one-third natural size.

Family **Calopterýgidae**—Broad-Winged Damselflies: The members of this group are relatively large damselflies that have the base of the wings gradually narrowed, not stalked as in other families of Zygóptera. These insects occur along streams. Two genera occur in the United States, *Calópteryx* (= *Ágrion*) and *Hetaerìna*. The common eastern species of *Calópteryx* is the black-winged damselfly, *C. maculàta* (Beauvois). The wings of the male are black, and those of the female are dark gray with a white stigma. The body is metallic greenish black. The most common species of *Hetaerìna* is the American ruby-spot, *H. americàna* (Fabricius), which is reddish in color, with a red or reddish spot in the basal third or fourth of the wings.

The majority of the damselflies in the United States belong to the remaining families. Nearly all have clear wings that are stalked at the base and have only two antenodal cross veins. Most of them are between 25 and 50 mm in length.

Family **Léstidae**—Spread-Winged Damselflies: The members of this group occur chiefly in swamps, but the adults occasionally wander some distance from swamps. When alighting, these damselflies hold the body vertical, or nearly so, and the wings partly outspread. They usually alight on plant or grass stems. Most of the species in this group belong to the genus *Léstes*.

Family **Protoneùridae**: Two species in this tropical group, *Neoneùra àaroni* Calvert and *Protoneùra*

càra Calvert, occur in southern Texas. They are reddish or brownish in color, 32–37 mm in length, and occur along streams.

Family **Coenagriónidae**—Narrow-Winged Damselflies: This family is a large one, with many genera and species. These damselflies occur in a variety of habitats: some occur chiefly along streams, and others about ponds or swamps. Most of them are rather feeble fliers and, when alighting, usually hold the body horizontal and wings together over the body. The two sexes are differently colored in most species, with the males more brightly colored than the females. Many of these damselflies are beautifully colored, but the color usually fades after the insect dies.

The dancers (*Árgia*, Figure 11–13) are chiefly stream species and can be recognized by the long, close-set spines on the tibiae. The males of the violet dancer, *Árgia fumipénnis* (Burmeister), a common species occurring along streams and pond shores, are a beautiful violet color. The green damsels (*Nehalénnia*) are small, slender, bronzy-green insects usually found in bogs and swamps. The bicolored bog damsel, *Amphiágrion sàucium* (Burmeister), is a small, stout-bodied, red and black damselfly usually found in bogs. The largest genus in this family is *Enallágma*, which includes the bluets. Most species are light blue with black markings. Several species of *Enallágma* may be found about the same pond or lake. Among the forktails (Figure 11–4), the common forktail, *Ischnùra verticàlis* (Say), is a very com-

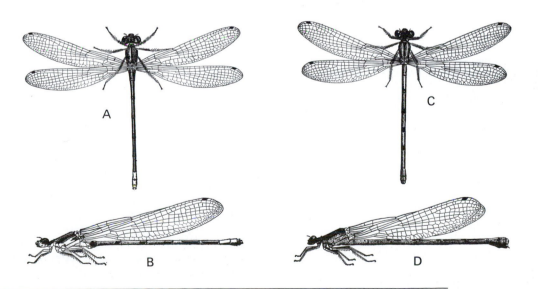

Figure 11–13. *Árgia émma* Kennedy (Coenagriónidae). **A** and **B**, male; **C** and **D**, female. (Courtesy of Kennedy and the U.S. National Museum.)

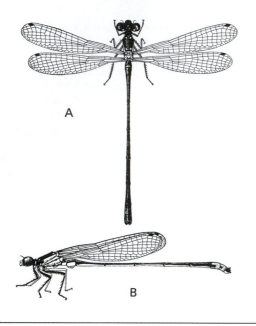

Figure 11–14. *Ischnùra cervùla* Selys, male (Coenagriónidae). **A,** dorsal view; **B,** lateral view. (Courtesy of Kennedy and the U.S. National Museum.)

mon species in the East and occurs nearly everywhere that any damselfly is to be found. The males are dark-colored, with green stripes on the thorax and blue on the tip of the abdomen. Most of the females are bluish green with faint dark markings (older individuals) or brownish orange with black markings (recently emerged individuals). A very few of the females are colored like the males.

Collecting and Preserving Odonàta

Many of the Odonàta are powerful fliers, and their capture often presents a challenge to the collector. Many are so adept on the wing that they can easily dodge a net, even when the net is swung as one would swing a baseball bat. The collector who wishes to catch these fast-flying insects must study their flight habits. Many species have particular beats along which they fly at rather regular intervals or have perches on which they frequently alight. One familiar with the insect's flight habits can often anticipate where it will fly and can be prepared for it. One should swing at a flying dragonfly from behind. If approached from the front, the insect can see the net coming and can usually dodge it. In stalking a specimen, one should use only the slowest motions until the final swing. Movements of the legs

and feet should be covered by vegetation as much as possible, for dragonflies often see motion below them better than that on a level with them.

The net used to capture Odonàta should be an open-mesh net with little air resistance so that it can be swung rapidly. The rim size and handle length may depend on the collector, but for many species it is desirable to have a relatively large rim (300–380 mm in diameter) and a net handle at least 1 meter long.

Dragonflies beyond the reach of a net (many specimens will fall in this category) may often be collected with a sling shot loaded with sand or with a gun loaded with dust shot. Many specimens so collected may be slightly damaged, but a slightly damaged specimen is usually better than none at all.

Odonàta occur in a great variety of habitats, and to obtain a large number of species, one should visit as many different habitats as possible. Two habitats that appear similar often contain different species, or the same habitat may harbor different species in different seasons. Many species have a short seasonal flight range, and one must be in the field at just the right season to collect them. Most species will be found near aquatic habitats—ponds, streams, marshes, and the like—but many are wide-ranging and may be found in meadows, woodlands, and the hillsides above aquatic habitats.

It is practically impossible to collect many Odonàta without wading, for they often fly at some distance (beyond net reach) out from the shores of a pond or stream. Many species, particularly damselflies, can be obtained by sweeping in the vegetation along and near the shores of ponds and marshes. Others patrol along the edge of the emergent vegetation, where the water is a few feet deep. Stream species, which are usually rare in collections and are often locally distributed, are best collected by wading streams (if the streams are small enough to wade in). It is often necessary to wade for considerable distances.

Killing jars for Odonàta should be relatively large and wide-mouthed and should contain several pieces of cleansing tissue. Specimens should be removed from the killing jars as soon as they are killed, since they may become discolored if left in too long. Mating pairs or pairs in tandem should be pinned together before they are put into the killing jar, so they can be associated later. Specimens collected in the field should be placed in envelopes, with the wings folded above the body. Ordinary letter envelopes will serve this purpose, and the collecting data can be written on the outside. After returning from the field, the collector can sort and mount the contents of the envelopes.

Most of the bright colors of the Odonàta fade after the insect dies. These colors are most likely to be retained if the specimens are dried rapidly in the sun, under a lamp, or in an oven. If one collects Odonàta in any numbers, they are best kept in triangular paper envelopes (Figure 36–8), one or two specimens to an envelope (never two species in the same envelope). If specimens are pinned, they may be pinned with the wings outspread, with the help of a spreading board, or they may be pinned sideways. It is usually preferable to pin the specimen sideways, with the pin passing through the thorax at the base of the wings and the left side of the insect uppermost. Some specimens, particularly dragonflies, will usually have to be placed in an envelope for a few days before they are pinned, so that the wings will stay together above the body. It is often necessary to support the abdomen of a pinned specimen with crossed insect pins under the abdomen, with a strip of narrow cardboard on the pin under the insect, or by bristling (a heavy bristle or a very slender insect pin shoved through the fresh specimen from frons to anus).

The nymphs of Odonàta may be collected by the various types of aquatic collecting equipment and methods described in Chapter 36. Nymphs should be preserved in 70–75% alcohol. Newly emerged adults and their exuviae should be preserved together in a pillbox, an envelope, or (preferably) alcohol. If full-grown nymphs are collected in the field, they may be brought back to the laboratory (preferably wrapped in a wet cloth or grass) and reared out in a fish-free balanced aquarium. A stick must be provided for the nymphs to crawl out of the water, and the aquarium should be covered with a screen or cloth.

References

Borror, D. J. 1945. A key to the New World genera of Libellulidae (Odonata). Ann. Entomol. Soc. Amer. 38:168–194; illus.

Byers, C. F. 1927. Key to the North American species of *Enallagma*, with a description of a new species (Odonata: Zygoptera). Trans. Amer. Entomol. Soc. 53:249–260; illus.

Byers, C. F. 1930. A contribution to the knowledge of Florida Odonata. Univ. Fla. Publ. Biol. Ser. No. 1; 327 pp.; illus.

Calvert, P. 1901–1909. Odonata, *in* Biologia Centrali Americana: Insecta Neuroptera. London: Dulau, pp. 17–342, Suppl. pp. 324–420; illus.

Corbet, P. S. 1963. A Biology of Dragonflies. Chicago: Quadrangle, 247 pp.; illus.

Fraser, F. C. 1957. A Reclassification of the Order Odonata. Sydney: Roy. Soc. Zool. New South Wales, 133 pp.; illus.

Garman, P. 1917. The Zygoptera, or damselflies, of Illinois. Ill. State Lab. Nat. Hist. Bull. 12(4):411–587; illus.

Garman, P. 1927. The Odonata or dragonflies of Connecticut. Conn. State Geol. Nat. Hist. Survey. Bull. 39, 331 pp.; illus.

Gloyd, L. K., and M. Wright. 1959. Odonata, *in* Freshwater Biology, ed. W. T. Edmondson. New York: Wiley, pp. 917–940; illus.

Howe, R. H. 1917–1923. Manual of the Odonata of New England. Mem. Thoreau Mus. Nat. Hist. 2:1–138; Suppl. pp. 1–14 (1921); illus.

Johnson, C. 1972. The damselflies (Zygoptera) of Texas. Bull. Fla. State Mus. Biol. Sci. 16(2):55–128; illus.

Johnson, C., and M. J. Westfall, Jr. 1970. Diagnostic keys and notes on the damselflies (Zygoptera) of Florida. Bull. Fla. State Mus. Biol. Sci. 15(2):45–89; illus.

Kennedy, C. H. 1915. Notes on the life history and ecology of the dragonflies of Washington and Oregon. Proc. U.S. Natl. Mus. 49:259–345; illus.

Kennedy, C. H. 1917a. Notes on the life history and ecology of the dragonflies of central California and Nevada. Proc. U.S. Natl. Mus. 52:483–635; illus.

Kennedy, C. H. 1917b. The dragonflies of Kansas. Bull. Kan. Univ. 18:127–145; illus.

Montgomery, B. E. 1962. The classification and nomenclature of calopterygine dragonflies (Odonata: Calopterygoidea). Verh. XI int. Kongr. Ent. Wien 1960, 3(1962):281–284.

Munz, P. A. 1919. A venational study of the suborder Zygoptera (Odonata), with keys for the identification of genera. Mem. Amer. Entomol. Soc. No. 3; 78 pp.; illus.

Musser, R. J. 1962. Dragonfly nymphs of Utah (Odonata: Anisoptera). Univ. Utah Biol. Ser. 12(6):1–66; illus.

Muttkowski, R. A. 1910. Catalogue of the Odonata of North America. Milwaukee Pub. Mus. Bull. 1(1):1–207.

Needham, J. G., and E. Broughton. 1927. The venation of the Libellulidae. Trans. Amer. Entomol. Soc. 53:157–190; illus.

Needham, J. G., and E. Fisher. 1936. The nymphs of North American libelluline dragonflies (Odonata). Trans. Amer. Entomol. Soc. 62:107–116; illus.

Needham, J. G., and H. B. Heywood. 1929. A Handbook of the Dragonflies of North America. Springfield, Ill.: C. C. Thomas, 378 pp.; illus.

Needham, J. G., and M. J. Westfall, Jr. 1955 (reprinted 1975). A Manual of the Dragonflies of North America (Anisoptera). Los Angeles: Univ. California Press, 615 pp.; illus.

Pennak, R. W. 1978 (2nd ed.). Fresh-water invertebrates of the United States. New York: Wiley Interscience, 803 pp.; illus.

Riek, E. F., and J. Kukalová-Peck. 1984. A new interpretation of dragonfly wing venation based upon early Upper Carboniferous fossils from Argentina (Insecta: Odonatoidea) and basic character states in pterygote wings. Can. J. Zool. 62:1150–1166; illus.

Ris, F. 1909–1919. Collections Zoologiques du Baron Edm. de Selys Longchamps. Bruxelles: Hayez, Impr. des Academies, Fasc. IX–XVI, Libellulinen 4–8, 1278 pp.; illus.

Robert, A. 1963. Libellules du Québec. Bull. 1, Serv. de la Faune, Ministère du Tourisme, de la Chasse et de la Pêche, Prov. Québec; 223 pp.; illus.

Smith, R. F., and A. E. Pritchard. 1956. Odonata, *in* Aquatic Insects of California, ed. R. L. Usinger. Berkeley: Univ. California Press, pp. 106–153; illus.

Tillyard, R. J. 1917. The Biology of Dragonflies. Cambridge: The University Press, 396 pp.; illus.

Walker, E. M. 1912. North American dragonflies of the genus *Aeshna*. Univ. Toronto Studies, Biol. Ser. No. 11, 214 pp.; illus.

Walker, E. M. 1925. The North American dragonflies of the genus *Somatochlora*. Univ. Toronto Studies, Biol. Ser. No. 26, 202 pp.; illus.

Walker, E. M. 1953. The Odonata of Canada and Alaska, vol. 1: General, the Zygoptera—Damselflies. Toronto: Univ. Toronto Press, 292 pp.; illus.

Walker, E. M. 1958. The Odonata of Canada and Alaska, vol. 2: The Anisoptera—Four Families. Toronto: Univ. Toronto Press, 318 pp.; illus. (Covers the Aeshnoidea and Cordulegastroidea.)

Walker, E. M., and P. S. Corbet. 1975. The Odonata of Canada and Alaska, vol. 3: The Anisoptera—Three Families. Toronto: Univ. Toronto Press, 307 pp.; illus. (Covers the Libelluloidea.)

Westfall, M. J., Jr. 1984. Odonata, *in* An Introduction to the Aquatic Insects of North America, 2nd ed., ed. R. W. Merritt and K. W. Cummins. Dubuque, Iowa: Kendall/Hunt, 126–176; illus.

Westfall, M. J., Jr. 1987. Order Odonata, pp. 95–177 *in* F. W. Stehr (ed.), Immature Insects, vol. 1. Dubuque, Iowa: Kendall/Hunt, 754 pp.; illus.

Wright, M., and A. Peterson. 1944. A key to the genera of anisopterous dragonfly nymphs of the United States and Canada (Odonata, suborder Anisoptera). Ohio J. Sci. 44(4):151–166; illus.

Chapter 12

Order Grylloblattària
Rock Crawlers

The first member of this group was not discovered until 1914 when Walker described *Grylloblátta campodeifórmis* from Banff, Alberta. Rock crawlers are slender, elongate, wingless insects, usually about 15–30 mm in length (Figure 12–1). The body is pale in color and finely pubescent. The eyes are small or absent and there are no ocelli. The antennae are long and filiform, consisting of 23–45 segments; the cerci are long, with either 5 or 8 segments; and the sword-shaped ovipositor of the female is nearly as long as the cerci.

There are only 20 species of rock crawlers in the world (Japan, Siberia, northwestern United States, and western Canada). Thirteen species, all belonging to the genus *Grylloblátta* in the family *Grylloblátti-dae*, have been described from North America.

Rock crawlers live in cold places such as the talus slopes at the edges of glaciers and in ice caves, often at high elevations. They are mainly nocturnal, and their principal food appears to be dead insects and other organic matter found on the snow and ice fields. They are soft-bodied, and probably best preserved in alcohol.

Some specialists consider grylloblattids to be living remnants of the extinct order Protorthóptera, and some still consider them merely a disjunctive, primitive subfamily of Orthóptera, a notion not too difficult to accept.

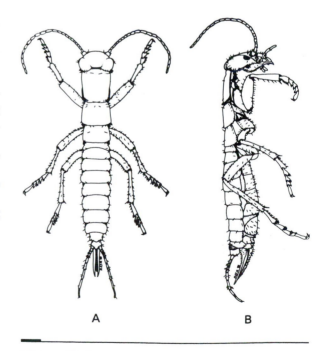

Figure 12–1. A rock crawler, *Grylloblatta* sp. **A,** dorsal view; **B,** lateral view.

References

Gurney, A. B. 1948. The taxonomy and distribution of the Grylloblattidae. Proc. Entomol. Soc. Wash. 50:86–102; illus.

Gurney, A. B. 1953. Recent advances in the taxonomy and distribution of *Grylloblatta* (Orthoptera: Grylloblattidae). J. Wash. Acad. Sci. 43:325–332.

Gurney, A. B. 1961. Further advances in the taxonomy and distribution of *Grylloblatta* (Orthoptera: Grylloblattidae). Proc. Biol. Soc. Wash. 74:67–76.

Helfer, J. R. 1972 (2nd ed.). How to Know the Grasshoppers, Cockroaches, and Their Allies. Dubuque, Iowa; William C. Brown, 359 pp.; illus.

Kamp, J. W. 1963. Descriptions of two new species of Grylloblattidae and the adult of *Grylloblatta barberi*, with an interpretation of their geographic distribution. Ann. Entomol. Soc. Amer. 56:53–68; illus.

Kamp. J. W. 1970. The cavernicolous Grylloblattoidea of the western United States. Ann. Speleology 25:223–230.

Kamp. J. W. 1973. Taxonomy, distribution and zoogeographic evolution of *Grylloblatta* in Canada (Insecta: Notoptera). Can. Entomol. 105:1235–1249.

Nickle, D. A. 1987. Order Grylloblattodea (Notoptera), pp. 143–144 *in* F. W. Stehr (ed.), Immature Insects, vol. 1. Dubuque, Iowa: Kendall/Hunt, 754 pp.; illus.

Rentz, D. C. F. 1982. A review of the systematics, distribution and bionomics of the North American Grylloblattidae, *in* Biology of the Notoptera, ed. H. Ando. Nagano, Japan: Kashiyo-Insatsu, 194 pp.; illus.

Vickery, V. R., and D. K. McE. Kevan. 1985. The grasshoppers, crickets, and related insects of Canada and adjacent regions: Ulonata: Dermaptera, Cheleutoptera, Notoptera, Dictuoptera, Grylloptera, and Orthoptera; The Insects and Arachnids of Canada, Part 14. Ottawa: Can. Govt. Publ. Centre, 918 pp.; illus.

Walker, E. M. 1914. A new species of Orthoptera, forming a new genus and family. Can Entomol. 46:93–99; illus.

Chapter 13   **Order Phásmida**
Walkingsticks and Leaf Insects

The members of this order do not have the hind femora enlarged (and they do not jump), and the tarsi are usually five-segmented (three-segmented in the Timèmidae). The species in our area have the body elongated and sticklike, and the wings are either much reduced or entirely absent. Some tropical forms (leaf insects) are flattened and expanded laterally (and have at least the hind wings well developed), and very greatly resemble leaves. These insects lack tympana and stridulatory organs; the cerci are short and one-segmented; and the ovipositor is short and concealed.

The walkingsticks are slow-moving herbivorous insects that are usually found on trees or shrubs. They are very similar to twigs in appearance, and this mimicry probably has protective value. Walkingsticks are able to emit a foul-smelling substance from glands in the thorax, a behavior that serves as a means of defense. Unlike most insects, the walkingsticks are able to regenerate lost legs, at least in part. These insects are usually not sufficiently numerous to do much damage to cultivated plants but, when numerous, may do serious damage to trees.

The eggs are not laid in any particular situation, but are simply scattered on the ground. There is a single generation a year, with the egg stage overwintering. The eggs often do not hatch the following spring, but hatch the second year after they are laid. For this reason walkingsticks are generally abundant only in alternate years. The young are usually greenish in color, and the adults are brownish.

The walkingsticks are widely distributed (more than 2000 species worldwide), but the group is most diverse in the tropics, especially in the Indo-Malayan region, and in the Nearctic is better represented in the southern states. All walkingsticks in the United States are wingless except *Áplopus màyeri* Caudell, which occurs in southern Florida. This species has short oval front wings, and the hind wings project 2 or 3 mm beyond the front wings. Some tropical walkingsticks are around a foot or so in length.

Classification of the Phásmida

Timèmidae—timema walkingsticks
Pseudophasmátidae (Bacuncùlidae)—striped walkingsticks
Heteronemìidae—common walkingsticks
Phasmátidae (Bacterìidae)—winged walkingsticks

Key to the Families of Phásmida

1.   Tarsi 3-segmented ....**Timèmidae**   p. 206

1'.   Tarsi 5-segmented **2**

2(1').   Mesothorax never more than 3 times as long as prothorax; middle and hind
                  tibiae deeply emarginate apically, receiving base of tarsi in
                  repose ....**Pseudophasmátidae**   p. 206

2'.   Mesothorax at least 4 times as long as prothorax; middle and hind tibiae not
                  deeply emarginate apically **3**

3(2').   Adults with short wings; first abdominal tergum as long as or longer than
                  metanotum (longer than wide); head with 2 stout spines on
                  vertex ....**Phasmátidae**   p. 206

3'.   Wings absent; first abdominal tergum much shorter than metanotum
                  (subquadrate); vertex without stout spines ....**Heteronemìidae**   p. 206

Family **Timèmidae**—Timema Walkingsticks: These insects are much stouter and shorter than most other walkingsticks and somewhat resemble earwigs. They are short-legged, apterous, 15–30 mm in length, and greenish to pink in color. The tarsi are all three-segmented and have unequal pretarsal claws. There are nine known species, all belonging to the genus *Tímema*, which occur in deciduous trees in California, Arizona, and Nevada. At least one species is parthenogenetic. Timemas are usually collected by beating foliage.

Family **Pseudophasmátidae**—Striped Walkingsticks: These insects have the tergum of the first abdominal segment at least as long as the thoracic metanotum, with which it is completely fused, and the middle and hind tibiae are broadly and deeply emarginate apically, receiving the base of the tarsus in repose. They are brownish yellow (male) or brown (female) with a dark median and two lateral dorsal stripes. They possess defensive glands from which they can squirt a thick milky fluid. Our fauna is restricted to two species of *Anisomórpha*, both of which occur in Florida. They are found in grass or on bushes all year long.

Family **Heteronemìidae**—Common Walkingsticks: These insects are more sticklike than the other three families of Phásmida. There are 20 species in 7 genera in our area; 10 of the species belong to the genus *Diápheromèra*. The common walkingstick in the northeastern states is *D. femoràta* (Say) (Figure 13–1), which sometimes becomes abundant enough to seriously defoliate forest trees. This family contains the longest insect in the United States, *Megaphásma dénticrus* (Stål), which reaches a length of 150–180 mm. It occurs in the South and Southwest.

Family **Phasmátidae**—Winged Walkingsticks: There are more than 100 Neotropical species in this family, but only one, *Áplopus màyeri* Caudell, occurs in our area (southern Florida), feeding on bay cedar and other shore vegetation. It is 80–130 mm in length and is our only walkingstick with wings. The head has two stout spines on the vertex.

Figure 13–1. A walkingstick, *Diápheromèra femoràta* (Say). (Courtesy of the Ohio Agricultural Research and Development Center.)

Collecting and Preserving Phásmida

Walkingsticks are relatively large and slow-moving and, once found, are fairly easy to collect. The best time for collecting the adults of most species is from midsummer to late fall. Adults should be pinned in

about the middle of the body (from front to rear). If the specimen is very soft-bodied, the body should be supported by a piece of cardboard or by pins; otherwise, it will sag at either end.

References

Bedford, G. O. 1978. Biology and ecology of the Phasmatodea. Annu. Rev. Entomol. 23:125–149.

Bradley, J. C., and B. S. Galil. 1977. The taxonomic arrangement of the Phasmatodea with keys to the subfamilies and tribes. Proc. Entomol. Soc. Wash. 79:176–208.

Helfer, J. R. 1963. How to Know the Grasshoppers, Cockroaches, and Their Allies. Dubuque, Iowa: Wm. C. Brown, 353 pp.

Henry, L. M. 1937. Biological notes on *Timema californica* Scudder. Pan-Pac. Entomol. 13:137–141.

Nickle, D. A. 1987. Order Phasmatodea, pp. 145–146 *in* F. W. Stehr (ed.), Immature Insects, vol. 1. Dubuque, Iowa: Kendall/Hunt, 754 pp.; illus.

Strohecker, H. F. 1966. New *Timema* from Nevada and Arizona (Phasmodea: Timemidae). Pan-Pac. Entomol. 42:25–26.

Vickery, V. R., and D. K. McE. Kevan. 1985. The grasshoppers, crickets, and related insects of Canada and adjacent regions: Ulonata: Dermaptera, Cheleutoptera, Notoptera, Dictuoptera, Grylloptera, and Orthoptera; The Insects and Arachnids of Canada, Part 14. Ottawa: Can. Govt. Publ. Centre, 918 pp.; illus.

Chapter 14

Order Orthóptera[1]
Grasshoppers, Crickets, and Katydids

The order Orthóptera contains a rather varied assemblage of insects, many of which are very common and well known. Most of them are plant feeders, and some of these are important pests of cultivated plants. A few are predaceous, a few are scavengers, and a few are more or less omnivorous.

The Orthóptera may be winged or wingless, and the winged forms usually have four wings. The front wings are usually elongate, many-veined, and somewhat thickened and are referred to as tegmina (singular, tegmen). The hind wings are membranous, broad, and many-veined, and at rest they are usually folded fanwise beneath the front wings. Some species have one or both pairs of wings greatly reduced or absent. The body is elongate; the cerci are well developed (containing from one to many segments); and the antennae are relatively long (sometimes longer than the body) and many-segmented. Many species have a long ovipositor, which is sometimes as long as the body. In others the ovipositor is short and more or less hidden. The tarsi are usually three- to four-segmented. The mouthparts are of the chewing type (mandibulate), and the metamorphosis is simple.

Sound Production in the Orthóptera

A great many types of insects "sing," but some of the best known insect songsters (grasshoppers and crickets) are in the order Orthóptera. The songs of these insects are produced chiefly by stridulation, that is, by the rubbing of one body part against another (Figure 14–1). The singing Orthóptera usually possess auditory organs—oval eardrums or tympana, located on the sides of the first abdominal segment (short-horned grasshoppers) or at the base of the front tibiae (long-horned grasshoppers and crickets; Figure 14–4B, tym). These tympana are relatively insensitive to changes in pitch, but are capable of responding to rapid and abrupt changes in intensity. The songs of grasshoppers and crickets play an important role in their behavior, and the songs of different species are usually different. The significant differences are in rhythm.

The crickets (Grýllidae) and long-horned grasshoppers (Tettigoniidae) produce their songs by rubbing a sharp edge (the scraper) at the base of the front wing along a filelike ridge (the file) on the ventral side of the other front wing (Figure 14–2B–D). The bases of the front wings at rest lie one above the other. The left one is usually uppermost in the long-horned grasshoppers, and the right is usually uppermost in the crickets. Both front wings possess a file and a scraper, but the file is usually longer in the

[1]Orthóptera: *Ortho*, straight; *ptera*, wings.

Figure 14–1. A field cricket singing (note elevated position of front wings). (Courtesy of R. D. Alexander.)

upper wing and the scraper is better developed in the lower wing. In the long-horned grasshoppers the lower (right) front wing usually contains more membranous area than the upper one. The file on the lower front wing and the scraper on the upper one are usually nonfunctional.

When the song is produced, the front wings are elevated (Figure 14–1) and moved back and forth; generally, only the closing stroke of the wings produces a sound. The sound produced by a single stroke of the front wings is called a pulse. Each pulse is composed of a number of individual tooth strikes of the scraper on the file. The pulse rate in a given insect varies with the temperature, being faster at higher temperatures. In different species it varies from 4 to 5 per second to more than 200 per second.

The songs of different species differ in the character of the pulses, in the pulse rate, and in the way the pulses are grouped. The pulses of crickets (Figure 14–3A,B,D–F) are relatively musical; that is, they can usually be assigned a definite pitch, which in different species may range from 1500 to 10,000 Hz (hertz, or cycles per second). The pulses of long-horned grasshoppers (Figure 14–12) are more noise-like; that is, they contain a wide band of frequencies and cannot be assigned a definite pitch. The principal frequencies in the songs of some Orthóptera are quite high, between 10,000 and 20,000 Hz, and may be nearly or quite inaudible to some people. The pulses may be delivered at a regular rate for a considerable period, producing a prolonged trill (Figure 14–3E,F) or buzz (Figure 14–12D). They may be delivered in short bursts, a second or less in length, separated by silent intervals of a second or more (some tree crickets). They may be delivered in short series of a few pulses each (Figure 14–3A,B,D), producing chirps. They may be delivered in regularly alternating series of fast and slow pulses (meadow grasshoppers; Figure 14–12B). Or the pulse rhythm may be more complex.

The band-winged grasshoppers (Oedipodìnae) usually make their noises by snapping their hind wings in flight. The noises so produced are crackling or buzzing. The slant-faced grasshoppers (Acridìnae) "sing" by rubbing the hind legs across the front wings, producing a soft rasping sound. The hind

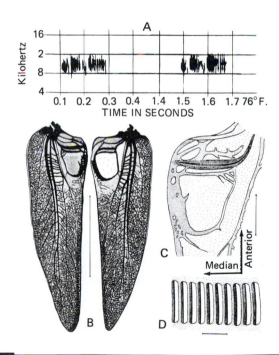

Figure 14–2. Song and sound-producing structures of the big green pine-tree katydid, *Hubbéllia marginífera* (Walker) (Tettigonìidae, Tettigonìinae). **A,** audiospectrograph of two pulses of the song (4 KHz is approximately the pitch of the top note of the piano); **B,** front wings, dorsal view (line = 10 mm); **C,** ventral surface of basal portion of left front wing showing the file (line = 1 mm); **D,** several teeth of the file (line = 0.1 mm). (Courtesy of R. D. Alexander.)

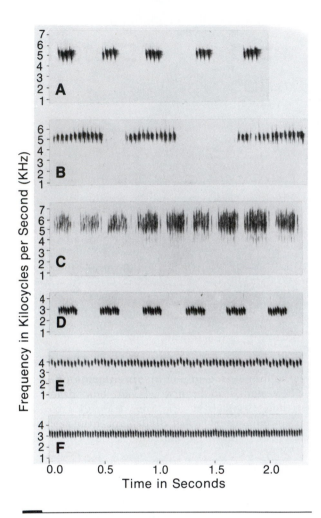

Figure 14–3. Audiospectrographs of cricket songs. **A,** calling song; **B,** aggressive song, and **C,** courtship song of a field cricket, *Grýllus pennsylvánicus* Burmeister; **D,** calling song of snowy tree cricket, *Oecánthus fúltoni* Walker; **E,** calling song of the tree cricket, *Oecánthus argentínus* Saussure; **F,** calling song of the tree cricket, *Oecánthus latipénnis* Riley. The pulse rate in **E** is 34 per second, and that in **F** is 44 per second.

Each type is produced in certain circumstances, and each produces a characteristic reaction by the other individuals. The loudest and most commonly heard sound is the "calling song" (Figures 14–3A,D–F), which serves primarily to attract the female. The female, if she is at the same temperature as the singing male, is able to recognize the song of her species and move toward the male. The males of some species produce an aggressive song in the presence of another male (Figure 14–3B); this type of song is generally produced when a male's territory is invaded by another male. The field and ground crickets (Gryllìnae and Nemobiìnae) produce a special courtship song in the presence of a female (Figure 14–3C), which usually leads to copulation. A few Orthóptera (for example, the northern true katydid) produce "alarm" or "disturbance" sounds when disturbed or threatened with injury.

The majority of the singing Orthóptera sing only at night (Tettigoniìdae and many Grýllidae); some sing only in the daytime (band-winged grasshoppers); and some sing both day and night (field, ground, and some tree crickets). Many species (for example, some of the cone-headed grasshoppers and tree crickets) "chorus"; that is, when one starts to sing, other nearby individuals begin to sing also. In a few cases (for example, the snowy tree cricket) the individual pulses of the chorusing individuals may be synchronized, making it seem to a listener that only one insect is singing; in other cases the synchronization is less evident. In the case of the northern true katydid, a group whose songs are synchronized will alternate their songs with those of another such group, producing the pulsating "katy did, katy didn't" sound commonly heard on summer evenings in the East.

Classification of the Orthóptera

Until rather recently, this order included not only the grasshoppers, crickets, and katydids, but also the mantids (order Mantòdea), walkingsticks (Phásmida), cockroaches (Blattària), and rock crawlers (Grylloblattària). Few will argue that these groups along with the earwigs (Dermáptera), webspinners (Embiidìna), and termites (Isóptera) are relatively primitive Neóptera, and they are generally referred to as the orthopteroid orders. Some current workers elevate several groups which we here call subfamilies to family status (e.g., Phaneroptéridae, Eneoptéridae, Stenopelmátidae, etc.). We have chosen to maintain a conservative approach to the classification of the orthopteroid orders while admitting that

femora of these insects are usually provided with a series of short peglike structures that function something like a file (Figure 14–4H, *strp*).

The females of a few Orthóptera may make a few soft noises, but most of the singing is done by the males. The short-horned grasshoppers usually move about while singing. The crickets and long-horned grasshoppers are usually stationary. Many Orthóptera, particularly some of the crickets and long-horned grasshoppers, are capable of producing two or more different types of sounds (Figure 14–3A–C).

many of the affinities pointed out by other authors (e.g., between termites, cockroaches, and mantids) certainly have merit and that many of the subfamilies we recognize may deserve family rank.

A synopsis of North American Orthóptera, as treated in this book, is given here. Other spellings, names, and arrangements are given in parentheses. The groups marked with an asterisk are relatively rare or are unlikely to be taken by a general collector.

Suborder Caelífera
  Superfamily Acridòidea
    Tetrígidae (Acrydìidae; Acrídidae in part)—pygmy grasshoppers and grouse locusts
    *Eumastácidae (Acrídidae in part)—monkey grasshoppers
    *Tanaocéridae (Eumastácidae in part)—desert long-horned grasshoppers
    Acrídidae (Locústidae)—short-horned grasshoppers
      Romaleìnae (Cyrtacanthacridìnae in part)—lubber grasshoppers
      Cyrtacanthacridìnae (including Catantopìnae and Melanoplìnae)—spur-throated grasshoppers
      Acridìnae (Truxalìnae; including Gomphocerìnae)—slant-faced grasshoppers
      Oedipodìnae—band-winged grasshoppers
  Superfamily Tridactylòidea
    Tridactýlidae (Grýllidae in part, Gryllotálpidae in part)—pygmy mole crickets
Suborder Ensífera
  Tettigonìidae—long-horned grasshoppers
    Copiphorìnae—cone-headed grasshoppers

Phaneropterìnae—katydids
Pseudophyllìnae—true katydids
*Listroscelìnae (Decticìnae in part)—listrosceline grasshoppers
Conocephalìnae—meadow grasshoppers
Decticìnae—shield-backed grasshoppers
*Tettigoniìnae—pine-tree katydids
*Sagìnae—matriarchal katydid
*Meconematìnae—drumming katydid
*Prophalangópsidae (Tettigonìidae in part)—hump-winged crickets
Gryllacrídidae (Gryllácridae, Stenopelmátidae; Tettigonìidae in part)—wingless long-horned grasshoppers
Gryllacridìnae (Gryllacrìnae)—leaf-rolling grasshoppers
Rhaphidophorìnae (Ceuthophilìnae)—cave or camel crickets
Stenopelmatìnae—Jerusalem, sand, or stone crickets
Grýllidae—crickets
Oecanthìnae—tree crickets
Eneopterìnae—bush crickets
Trigonidiìnae—bush, sword-bearing, or sword-tailed crickets
*Mogoplistìnae—scaly crickets
*Myrmecophilìnae—ant-loving crickets
Nemobiìnae (Gryllìnae in part)—ground crickets
Gryllìnae—house and field crickets
*Brachytrupìnae (Gryllìnae in part)—short-tailed crickets
Gryllotálpidae (Grýllidae in part)—mole crickets

Key to the Families of Orthóptera

Adults (and some nymphs) of North American Orthóptera may be identified to family by means of the following key. Families marked with an asterisk are relatively rare and are unlikely to be taken by a general collector.

1.   Front legs much dilated and modified for digging (Figure 14–18); tarsi 3-segmented; length 20–35 mm ....**Gryllotálpidae**   p. 224

1'.   Front legs not so enlarged, or if they are slightly enlarged (Tridactýlidae) the front and middle tarsi are 2-segmented and the insect is less than 10 mm in length **2**

2(1').   Front and middle tarsi 2-segmented, hind tarsi 1-segmented or absent; front legs somewhat dilated and fitted for digging; abdomen with apparently 2 pairs of stylelike cerci; 4–10 mm ....**Tridactýlidae**   p. 217

2'.   Tarsi 3- or 4-segmented, or if front and middle tarsi are 2-segmented (Tetrígidae), then hind tarsi are 3-segmented; front legs not dilated; abdomen with a single pair of cerci; length usually over 10 mm **3**

3(2'). Hind tarsi 3-segmented, front and middle tarsi 2- or 3-segmented; ovipositor short; antennae usually short, seldom more than half as long as the body (Figures 14–5, 14–7 through 14–9); auditory organs (tympana), if present, on sides of first abdominal segment **4**

3'. Tarsi 3- or 4-segmented; ovipositor usually elongate; antennae long, usually as long as body or longer (Figures 14–1, 14–11, 14–13 through 14–17); auditory organs, if present, at base of front tibiae (Figure 14–4B, *tym*) **7**

4(3). Pronotum prolonged backward over abdomen and tapering posteriorly (Figure 14–5); front wings vestigial; no arolia; front and middle tarsi 2-segmented, hind tarsi 3-segmented . . . .**Tetrígidae** p. 213

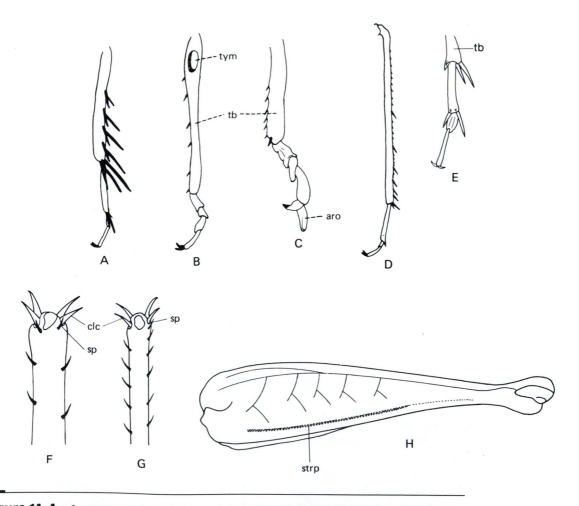

Figure 14–4. Leg structure in Orthóptera. **A–E,** tibiae and tarsi; **F–G,** apical portion of left hind femur; **H,** hind femur, mesal view. **A,** *Nemòbius* (Nemobiìnae, Grýllidae), hind leg; **B,** *Scuddèria* (Phaneropterìnae, Tettigonìidae), front leg; **C,** *Schistocérca* (Cyrtacanthacridìnae, Acrídidae); **D,** *Oecánthus* (Oecanthìnae, Grýllidae), hind leg; **E,** *Phyllopálpus* (Trigonidiìnae, Grýllidae), hind tarsus; **F,** *Romàlea* (Romaleìnae, Acrídidae); **G,** *Melánoplus* (Cyrtacanthacridìnae, Acrídidae); **H,** Acridìnae (Acrídidae). *aro,* arolium; *clc,* movable spines or calcaria; *sp,* immovable spines; *strp,* stridulatory pegs; *tb,* tibia; *tym,* tympanum.

4'.	Pronotum not prolonged backward over abdomen (Figures 14–7 through 14–9); front wings usually well developed if hind wings are present; arolia present (Figure 14–4C); all tarsi 3-segmented **5**	
5(4').	Antennae shorter than front femora; wings absent; 8–25 mm in length; occurring in the chaparral country of the southwestern United States ....**Eumastácidae***	p. 213
5'.	Antennae longer than front femora; wings nearly always present; size variable, but usually over 15 mm in length; widely distributed **6**	
6(5').	Wings and tympana nearly always present; antennae not unusually long; males without a file on third abdominal tergum; widely distributed ......**Acrídidae**	p. 214
6'.	Wings and tympana absent; antennae very long, in males longer than body; males with a file on third abdominal tergum; southwestern United States ....**Tanaocéridae***	p. 214
7(3').	At least middle tarsi, and usually all tarsi, 4-segmented (Figures 14–4B, 14–10E); ocelli usually present; ovipositor sword-shaped **8**	
7'.	All tarsi 3-segmented (Figure 14–4A,D,E); ocelli present or absent; ovipositor cylindrical or needle-shaped ....**Grýllidae**	p. 222
8(7).	Wings present (but sometimes very small) and with fewer than 8 principal longitudinal veins; males with stridulatory structures on front wings (Figure 14–2B–D); front tibiae with tympana; color variable, but often green **9**	
8'.	Wings usually absent, but if present, then with 8 or more principal longitudinal veins; males lacking stridulatory structures on front wings; front tibiae with or without tympana; color usually gray or brown ....**Gryllacrídidae**	p. 220
9(8).	Antennal sockets located about halfway between epistomal suture and top of head; wings reduced, broad in male, minute in female; ovipositor extremely short; hind femora extending to about tip of abdomen; northwestern United States and southwestern Canada ....**Prophalangópsidae***	p. 220
9'.	Antennal sockets located near top of head; wings and ovipositor variable; hind femora usually extending beyond tip of abdomen ....**Tettigoniidae**	p. 217

SUBORDER **Caelífera:** The Caelífera are jumping Orthóptera, with the hind femora more or less enlarged; they include the short-horned grasshoppers and the pygmy mole crickets. The antennae are nearly always relatively short, and the tarsi contain three or fewer segments. The tympana, if present, are located on the sides of the first abdominal segment. The species that stridulate usually do so by rubbing the hind femora over the tegmina or abdomen or snapping the wings in flight. All have the cerci and ovipositor short.

Family **Tetrígidae**—Pygmy Grasshoppers and Grouse Locusts: The pygmy grasshoppers may be recognized by the characteristic pronotum, which extends backward over the abdomen and is narrowed poste-riorly (Figure 14–5). Most species are between 13 and 19 mm in length, and the females are usually larger and heavier bodied than the males. These are among the few grasshoppers that winter as adults. The adults are most often encountered in the spring and early summer. The pygmy grasshoppers are not of very much economic importance.

Family **Eumastácidae**—Monkey Grasshoppers: The members of this group occur on bushes or trees in the chaparral country of the Southwest. They are wingless and remarkably agile. Their common name refers to their ability to progress through small trees and shrubs. Adults are slender, 8–25 mm in length, and usually brownish in color. The face is somewhat slanting; the vertex is pointed; and the antennae are

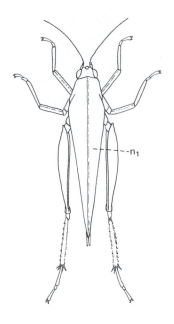

Figure 14–5.   A pygmy grasshopper, *Tettigídea lateràlis* (Say), $3\frac{1}{2}\times$. n_1, pronotum.

very short (not reaching the rear edge of the pronotum). Monkey grasshoppers do not have a stridulatory organ on the sides of the third abdominal segment, as do the Tanaocéridae. This group is principally tropical, with 12 species occurring in the United States. They occur from central California, southern Nevada, and southwestern Utah south to southern California and southeastern Arizona.

Family **Tanaocéridae**—Desert Long-Horned Grasshoppers: The members of this family resemble the monkey grasshoppers in being wingless and very

active, and they occur in the deserts of the Southwest. They are grayish to blackish in color, relatively robust, and 8–25 mm in length. The face is less slanting than in the monkey grasshoppers, and the vertex is rounded. The antennae are long and slender, longer than the body in the male and shorter than the body in the female. Males have a stridulatory organ on the sides of the third abdominal segment. These grasshoppers are very seldom encountered. They are nocturnal and are likely to be found early in the season. Three species occur in the United States (in the genera *Tanaócerus* and *Mohavácris*); they occur from southern Nevada to southern California.

Family **Acrídidae**—Short-Horned Grasshoppers: This family includes most of the grasshoppers that are so common in meadows and along roadsides from midsummer until fall. The antennae are usually much shorter than the body; the auditory organs (tympana) are located on the sides of the first abdominal segment; the tarsi are three-segmented; and the ovipositor is short. Most are gray or brownish in color, and some have brightly colored hind wings. These insects are plant feeders and are often very destructive to vegetation. Most species pass the winter in the egg stage, the eggs being laid in the ground. A few overwinter as nymphs, and a very few overwinter as adults.

Many males in this group sing (during the day), either by rubbing the inner surface of the hind femur against the lower edge of the front wing or by snapping the hind wings in flight. Males in the former group (most slant-faced grasshoppers) have a row of tiny stridulatory pegs on the inner surface of the hind femur (Figure 14–4H, *strp*), and the sound produced is usually a low buzzing sound. In the latter group (band-winged grasshoppers) the song is a sort of crackling sound.

Key to the Subfamilies of Acrídidae

There are differences of opinion regarding the number of subfamilies in this family. We follow Rehn and Grant (1961), who recognize four subfamilies in our fauna. Most genera of these subfamilies may be separated by the following key:

1.	Hind tibiae with both inner and outer immovable spines at tip (Figure 14–4F); prosternum usually with median spine or tubercle ....**Romaleinae**	p. 215
1'.	Hind tibiae with only the inner immovable spine at tip, outer one absent (Figure 14–4G); prosternum with or without median spine or tubercle **2**	
2(1').	Prosternum with median spine or tubercle (Figure 14–6A, *tub*); hind wings usually hyaline; hind femora of males without row of stridulatory pegs ....**Cyrtacanthacridinae**	p. 215

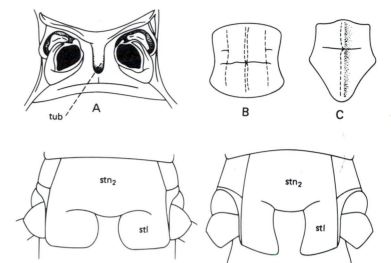

Figure 14–6. **A,** prothorax of *Melánoplus* (Cyrtacanthacridinae, Acrídidae), ventral view; **B,** pronotum of *Syrbùla* (Acridinae, Acrídidae), dorsal view; **C,** pronotum of *Chortóphaga* (Oedipodinae, Acrídidae), dorsal view; **D,** mesothorax of *Melánoplus* (Cyrtacanthacridinae, Acrídidae), ventral view; **E,** same, *Schistocérca* (Cyrtacanthacridinae, Acrídidae). *stl,* mesosternal lobe; *stn₂,* mesosternum; *tub,* prosternal tubercle.

2′.	Prosternum without median spine or tubercle; color of hind wings variable, but if hyaline, then hind femora of males usually with row of stridulatory pegs (Figure 14–4H, *strp*) **3**
3(2′).	Face vertical or nearly so; pronotum with strong median ridge, caudal margin produced backward and angulate mesally (Figure 14–6C); hind wings usually colored; antennae slender, cylindrical, not flattened; wings long, reaching or surpassing tip of abdomen; grasshoppers that often stridulate in flight; hind femora of males without row of stridulatory pegs ...**Oedipodinae** p. 216
3′.	Face usually slanting backward, sometimes very strongly so; pronotum flat, or with low median ridge; caudal margin of pronotum truncate or rounded, not angulate mesally (Figure 14–6B); hind wings usually hyaline; antennae usually slightly flattened, sometimes strongly so; wings variable in length, sometimes short and not reaching tip of abdomen; grasshoppers that do not stridulate in flight, but usually with row of stridulatory pegs on hind femora of male (Figure 14–4H, *strp*), which are rubbed against the tegmina when the insect is at rest ....**Acridinae** p. 216

Subfamily **Romaleinae**—Lubber Grasshoppers: These are robust, usually large grasshoppers (length mostly 25–75 mm) that are chiefly western in distribution. Some species have the wings short and do not fly, and some have the hind wings brightly colored. The only species in this group that normally occurs in the East is *Romàlea guttàta* (Houttuyn), which occurs from North Carolina and Tennessee to Florida and Louisiana. This insect is 40–75 mm in length, with short wings, and the hind wings are red with a black border. This species is often used for morphological studies in beginning biology and entomology classes.

Subfamily **Cyrtacanthacridinae**—Spur-Throated Grasshoppers: Most grasshoppers in this group can be recognized by the presence of a median spine or tubercle on the prosternum. Most of them have the face vertical or nearly so, but a few, such as the slender grasshopper, *Leptýsma marginicóllis* (Serville), have the face very slanting and may be confused with some Acridinae. The males lack a row of stridulatory pegs on the inner surface of the hind femora, while most Acridinae have such pegs.

Uvarov (1966) places the grasshoppers that we treat here as Cyrtacanthacridinae in two subfamilies, the Cyrtacanthacridinae and the Catantopìnae, which differ in the shape of the mesosternal lobes: rounded and about as long as wide in the Catantopìnae (Figure 14–6D); somewhat rectangular and longer than wide in the Crytacanthacridìnae (Figure 14–6E). Uvarov puts the genus *Schistocérca* in the Cyrtanthacridìnae and most other genera in our area in the Catantopìnae. The species in the genus *Schistocérca* are large and often brightly colored (Figure 14–7A).

The largest genus in this subfamily is *Melánoplus*, and here belong our most common grasshoppers—and the ones that are most destructive. Most of the damage done to crops in the United States by spur-throated grasshoppers is caused by four species of *Melánoplus*: the migratory grasshopper, *M. sanguínipes* (Fabricius) (Figure 14–7C); the differential grasshopper, *M. differentiàlis* (Thomas) (Figure 14–7B); the two-striped grasshopper, *M. bivittàtus* (Say); and the red-legged grasshopper, *M. femurrùbrum* (De Geer).

Some species of spur-throated grasshoppers occasionally increase to tremendous numbers and migrate considerable distances, causing damage of catastrophic proportions. The migrating hordes of these insects may contain millions upon millions of individuals and literally darken the sky. From 1874 to 1877 great swarms of migratory grasshoppers appeared in the plains east of the Rocky Mountains and migrated to the Mississippi valley and to Texas, destroying crops whenever they stopped in their flight. This migratory behavior follows a tremendous buildup in numbers, resulting from a combination of favorable environmental conditions. When the numbers decrease, the insects remain stationary.

Subfamily **Acridìnae**—Slant-Faced Grasshoppers: The slanting face of these grasshoppers (Figure 14–8) will distinguish them from most other Acrídidae, except the very slender grasshoppers in the Cyrtanthacridìnae. Males of most genera have a row of tiny stridulatory pegs on the inner surface of the hind femur (Figure 14–4H, *strp*). These pegs are lacking in the other subfamilies in our area. The Acridìnae usually lack a prosternal spine or tubercle, and the hind wings are usually hyaline.

Uvarov (1966) places the grasshoppers that we treat here as Acridìnae in two subfamilies, the Acridìnae and the Gomphocerìnae, which differ in the presence of stridulatory pegs on the hind femur of the males (present in the Gomphocerìnae and absent in the Acridìnae). Uvarov puts the genus *Radinonòtum* (very slender grasshoppers occurring in the southwestern states) in the Acridìnae and most other genera in our area in the Gomphocerìnae.

The Acridìnae are not as abundant as the Cyrtacanthacridìnae and Oedipodìnae and are most likely to be found along the borders of marshes, in wet meadows, and in similar places. They are rarely numerous enough to do much damage to vegetation.

Subfamily **Oedipodìnae**—Band-Winged Grasshoppers: These insects have the hind wings brightly

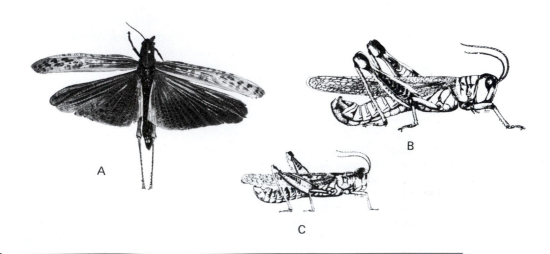

Figure 14–7. Spur-throated grasshoppers. **A**, *Schistocérca americàna* (Drury), with wings outspread; **B**, *Melánoplus differentiàlis* (Thomas); **C**, *Melánoplus sanguínipes* (Fabricius). (**A**, courtesy of the Ohio Agricultural Research and Development Center; **B–C**, courtesy of USDA.)

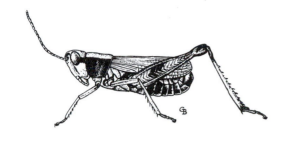

Figure 14–8. A slant-faced grasshopper, *Chloeáltis conspérsa* Harris. (Courtesy of Institut de Biologie Générale, Université de Montréal.)

Family **Tettigoniidae**—Long-horned Grasshoppers and Katydids: The members of this family can usually be recognized by the long hairlike antennae, the four-segmented tarsi, the auditory organs (when present) located at the base of the front tibiae, and the laterally flattened bladelike ovipositor. Most species have well-developed stridulating organs and are noted songsters. Each species has a characteristic song. The winter is usually passed in the egg stage, and in many species the eggs are inserted into plant tissues. Most species feed on plants, but a few prey on other insects.

colored, and they generally frequent areas of sparse vegetation. They often alight on bare ground, with the hind wings concealed and the front wings blending with the background. These insects are quite conspicuous in flight, owing to the bright colors of the hind wings and the crackling sound sometimes made by the wings. The Oedipodìnae are the only short-horned grasshoppers that stridulate while flying (the stridulation producing the crackling sound).

One of the more common species in this group is the Carolina grasshopper, *Dissosteìra carolìna* (L.), in which the hind wings are black with a pale border (Figure 14–9A). The clear-winged grasshopper, *Cámnula pellùcida* (Scudder), is an important pest species in this group. It has clear hind wings.

Family **Tridactýlidae**—Pygmy Mole Crickets: These tiny crickets (length 4–10 mm) are burrowing in habit and usually occur along the shores of streams and lakes. They are very active jumpers, and when one is approached, it may seem to disappear suddenly. The tridactylids are peculiar among the Orthóptera in having what appear to be two pairs of cerci: four slender, stylelike appendages at the apex of the abdomen. These insects have no tympanal organs, and the males do not sing. Only two species occur in North America, but they are widely distributed.

SUBORDER **Ensífera**: The Ensífera are jumping Orthóptera, with the hind femora more or less enlarged. They include the long-horned grasshoppers and crickets. The antennae are nearly always long and hairlike, and the tarsi are three- or four-segmented. The tympana, if present, are located on the upper ends of the front tibiae. The species that stridulate do so by rubbing the edge of one front wing over a filelike ridge on the ventral side of the other front wing. Nearly all have the ovipositor relatively long, either sword-shaped or cylindrical.

Figure 14–9. Band-winged grasshoppers. **A,** *Dissosteìra carolìna* (L.); **B,** *Spharágemon bólli* Scudder. (**B,** courtesy of Institut de Biologie Générale, Université de Montréal.)

Key to the Subfamilies of Tettigoniidae[2]

1.   Front wings oval and convex, costal field broad, with many parallel transverse veins; prosternal spine present; color green ....**Pseudophyllinae**   p. 219

1'.   Front wings variable in shape, but costal field without transverse veins as described above; other characters variable **2**

2(1').   Dorsal surface of first tarsal segment grooved laterally (Figure 14–10E); prosternal spine usually present (Figure 14–10D); front wings about as long as hind wings **3**

2'.   Dorsal surface of first tarsal segment smoothly rounded; prosternal spines absent; hind wings usually longer than front wings ....**Phaneropterinae**   p. 219

3(2).   Anterior portion of vertex conical, sometimes acuminate, extending well beyond basal antennal segment (Figure 14–10C, *ver*) ....**Copiphorinae**   p. 219

3'.   Anterior portion of vertex usually not conical or acuminate, not extending beyond basal antennal segment (Figure 14–10A,B, *ver*) **4**

4(3').   Anterior portion of vertex laterally compressed, much less than half as wide as basal antennal segment (Figure 14–10A, *ver*); southwestern United States ....**Listroscelinae**   p. 219

4'.   Anterior portion of vertex variable, but always more than half as wide as basal antennal segment; widely distributed **5**

[2]The subfamilies Saginae and Meconematinae, each containing one species that has been introduced and established in the United States, are not included in this key. These subfamilies are discussed in the text.

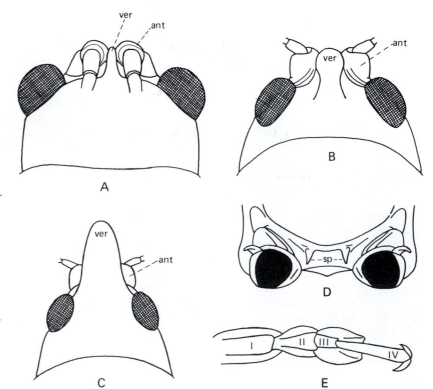

Figure 14–10. Characters of Tettigoniidae. **A,** head of *Réhnia* (Listroscelinae), dorsal view; **B,** head of *Orchélimum* (Conocephalinae), dorsal view; **C,** head of *Neoconocéphalus* (Copiphorinae), dorsal view; **D,** prothorax of *Orchélimum* (Conocephalinae), ventral view; **E,** hind tarsus of *Neoconocéphalus* (Copiphorinae), dorsal view. *ant,* base of antenna; *sp,* prosternal spine; *ver,* vertex; *I–IV,* tarsal segments.

5(4').	One or more spines on dorsal surface of front tibiae **6**	
5'.	No spines on dorsal surface of front tibiae ....**Conocephalinae**	p. 220
6(5).	Pronotum extending back to abdomen (except in a few long-winged forms); wings usually greatly reduced; front wings usually gray, brown, or spotted; prosternal spines present or absent; widely distributed ....**Decticinae**	p. 220
6'.	Pronotum never extending back to abdomen; wings always well developed; front wings green, rarely spotted with brown; prosternal spines present; southeastern United States ....**Tettigoniinae**	p. 220

Subfamily **Copiphorinae**—Cone-Headed Grasshoppers: The cone-heads are long-bodied grasshoppers that have the head conical (Figure 14–11) and the ovipositor long and swordlike. They occur in two color phases, green and brown. They are generally found in high grass or weeds and are rather sluggish. Their jaws are very strong, and person handling these insects carelessly may receive a healthy nip. This group is a small one, with only a few genera. The more common eastern species belong to the genus *Neoconocéphalus*. The songs of cone-heads vary. In most cases the song is a prolonged buzz (Figure 14–12D), but in *N. énsiger* (Harris), a common eastern species, it is a rapid series of lisping notes (Figure 14–12C). These insects generally sing only at night.

Subfamily **Phaneropterinae**—Katydids: The members of this and the next subfamily are commonly called katydids and are well known for their songs, which are usually heard in the evening and at night. The katydids in this family can be recognized by the absence of spines on the prosternum, and the hind wings are longer than the front wings. About 10 genera occur in the United States. The three most common genera in the East are *Scuddèria* (bush katydids), *Microcéntrum* (angular-winged katydids), and *Amblycórypha* (round-headed katy-dids). *Scuddèria* has the front wings nearly parallel-sided (Figure 14–13B,C); *Microcéntrum* has the front wings somewhat angled, with the hind femora not extending beyond the front wings (Figure 14–13A); *Amblycórypha* has the front wings elongate-oval, and the hind femora extend beyond the apex of the front wings. These katydids are normally green, but pink forms occasionally occur, especially in *Amblycórypha*. These color forms are not distinct species.

Subfamily **Pseudophyllinae**—True Katydids: These katydids are principally arboreal in habit, living in the foliage of trees and shrubs. The northern true katydid, *Pterophýlla camellifòlia* (Fabricius), is the insect whose "katy did, katy didn't" song is heard so commonly on summer evenings in the Northeast. Its song contains from two to five pulses (Figure 14–12A). The southern representatives of this katydid sing a somewhat longer and faster song, containing up to about a dozen pulses.

Subfamily **Listroscelinae**: These grasshoppers are very similar to the Decticinae, and the U.S. genera (*Neobarréttia* and *Réhnia*) were formerly placed in the Decticinae. This subfamily is principally tropical in distribution and is represented in the United States by a few species in the South Central States, from Texas north to Kansas.

Figure 14–11.   A cone-headed grasshopper, *Neoconocéphalus énsiger* (Harris). **A,** male; **B,** female. (Courtesy of the Institut de Biologie Générale, Université de Montréal.)

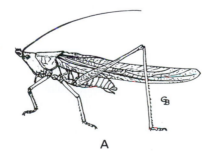
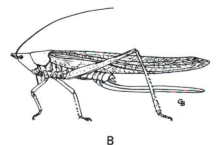

A   B

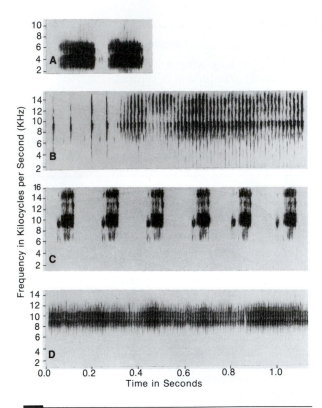

Figure 14–12. Audiospectrographs of the songs of long-horned grasshoppers (Tettigonìidae). **A,** northern true katydid, *Pterophýlla camellifòlia* (Fabricius), a 2-pulse song, the pulses uttered at the rate of about 5 per second; **B,** a meadow grasshopper, *Orchélimum nígripes* Scudder; **C,** a cone-headed grasshopper, *Neoconocéphalus énsiger* (Harris), the pulses produced at the rate of about 5 per second; **D,** another cone-headed grasshopper, *N. nebrascénsis* (Brunner), the pulses produced at the rate of about 146 per second. **B, C,** and **D** show only a part of the long-continued song of these insects.

Subfamily **Conocephalìnae**—Meadow Grasshoppers: These are small to medium-sized, slender bodied, usually greenish grasshoppers (Figure 14–14) that are found principally in wet grassy meadows and along the margins of ponds and streams. Two genera are common in the eastern United States, *Orchélimum* (usually over 18 mm in length) and *Conocéphalus* (usually less than 17 mm in length).

Subfamily **Decticìnae**—Shield-Backed Grasshoppers: These insects are brownish to black, short-winged, and usually 25 mm or more in length. The pronotum extends back to the abdomen. Most spe-

cies are cricketlike in appearance. The eastern species, most of which belong to the genus *Atlánticus*, occur in the dry upland woods. The majority of the Decticìnae occur in the West, where they may occur in fields or woods. Some of the western species often do serious damage to field crops. The Mormon cricket, *Ánabrus símplex* Haldeman, is a serious pest in the Great Plains states, and the coulee cricket, *Peránabrus scabricóllis* (Thomas), often does considerable damage in the arid regions of the Pacific Northwest. The work of gulls in checking an outbreak of the Mormon crickets in Utah is now commemorated by a monument to the gull in Salt Lake City.

Subfamily **Sagìnae**: *Sàga pèdo* (Pallas), the matriarchal katydid, has been introduced from Europe and is established in Michigan. This insect has raptorial front and middle legs and is predaceous on other insects.

Subfamily **Meconematìnae**: *Meconèma thalassìnum* (De Geer), the drumming katydid, has been introduced from Europe and is established in New York State. It is a small, delicate, greenish insect, with a rounded head, and the antennae are inserted between the eyes. This subfamily is well represented by some 200 species in the Palearctic region and Africa.

Subfamily **Tettigonìinae**: This group contains a single U.S. species, *Hubbéllia margìnifera* (Walker), the big green pine-tree katydid, which occurs in the southeastern United States. The song and song-producing structures of this katydid are illustrated in Figure 14–2.

Family **Prophalangópsidae**—Hump-Winged Crickets: This family is represented in North America by two species of *Cyphodérris*, which occur in the mountains of the northwestern United States and southwestern Canada. Adults are brownish with light markings, relatively robust, and about 25 mm in length. In the Tettigonìidae the left front wing is uppermost, and its file is the functional one. In this group either front wing may be uppermost, and the males may switch the position of the wings while singing. The song of *C. monstròsa* Uhler is a loud, very high-pitched (12–13 kHz) trill about 2 seconds in length or less, which has a slight pulsating quality that is apparently due to the switching of the front wings during the song.

Family **Gryllacrídidae**—Wingless Long-Horned Grasshoppers: The members of this family are brown or gray in color and lack auditory organs. The wings are vestigial or completely lacking. The three subfamilies occurring in the United States may be separated by the following key:

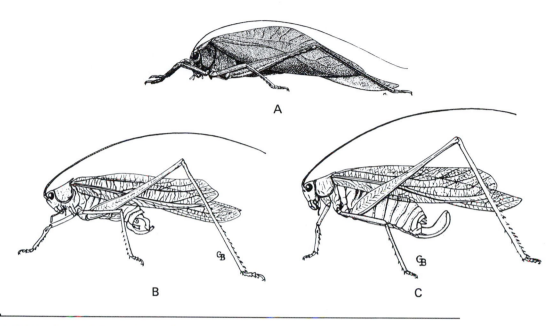

A

B   C

Figure 14–13.   Bush Katydids. **A,** *Microcéntrum rhombifòlium* (Saussure); **B,** *Scuddèria furcàta* Brunner, male; **C,** *S. furcàta* Brunner, female. (**A,** Hebard, 1934, courtesy of the author and the Illinois Natural History Survey; **B** and **C,** courtesy of Institut de Biologie Générale, Université de Montréal.)

Key to the Subfamilies of Gryllacrídidae

1.	Antennae at base contiguous or nearly so ....**Rhaphidophorìnae**	p. 222
1′.	Antennae at base separated by a distance equal to or greater than length of first antennal segment **2**	
2(1′).	Tarsi lobed, more or less flattened dorsoventrally; hind femora extending beyond apex of abdomen; eastern United States ....**Gryllacridìnae**	p. 222
2′.	Tarsi not lobed and more or less flattened laterally; hind femora not extending beyond apex of abdomen; western United States ....**Stenopelmatìnae**	p. 222

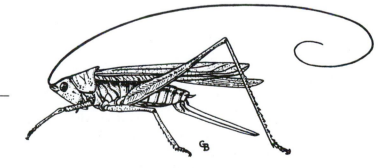

Figure 14–14.   A meadow grasshopper, *Conocéphalus fasciàtus* (De Geer), female. (Courtesy of Institut de Biologie Générale, Université de Montréal.)

Subfamily **Gryllacridinae**—Leaf-rolling Grasshoppers: This group is represented in the United States by one species: *Camptonòtus carolinènsis* (Gerstaecker), which occurs in the East from New Jersey to Indiana and south to Florida and Mississippi. This insect is nocturnal and feeds chiefly on aphids. During the day they spend their time in a shelter formed of a leaf rolled up and tied with silk that is spun from the insect's mouth.

Subfamily **Rhaphidophorinae**—Cave or Camel Crickets: These insects are brownish and rather humpbacked in appearance (Figure 14–15) and are found in caves, in hollow trees, under logs and stones, and in other dark moist places. The antennae are often very long. Most of the species in this group belong to the genus *Ceuthóphilus* with 114 species in the United States and Canada.

Subfamily **Stenopelmatinae**—Jerusalem, Sand, or Stone Crickets: These insects are 20–50 mm in length, and the head and abdomen are rather large and robust. They are usually brownish in color with black bands on the abdomen. They are generally found under stones or in loose soil. Four species of *Stenopelmàtus* and five species of *Cnemotéttix* represent this family in North America. They occur in the West and are common in the Pacific Coast states.

Figure 14–15.   A cave cricket, *Ceuthóphilus maculàtus* (Harris), female. (Courtesy of Hebard and the Illinois Natural History Survey.)

Family **Grýllidae**—Crickets: The crickets resemble the long-horned grasshoppers in having long tapering antennae, stridulating organs on the front wings of the male, and the auditory organs on the front tibiae, but differ from them in having not more than three tarsal segments, the ovipositor usually needlelike or cylindrical rather than flattened, and the front wings bent down rather sharply at the sides of the body. Many of these insects are well-known songsters, and each species has a characteristic song. Most species overwinter as eggs, laid generally in the ground or vegetation. This family is represented in the United States by eight subfamilies, which may be separated by the following key:

Key to the Subfamilies of Grýllidae

1.	Wingless, broadly oval; hind femora much enlarged; eyes small and ocelli lacking; length 2–4 mm; insects living in ant nests ....**Myrmecophilinae**	p. 224
1′.	Without the above combination of characters **2**	
2(1′).	Second tarsal segment somewhat expanded laterally, flattened dorsoventrally (Figure 14–4E) **3**	
2′.	Second tarsal segment small, flattened laterally (Figure 14–4A,D) **4**	
3(2).	Hind tibiae with small teeth between longer spines; ovipositor cylindrical, usually straight; length 11–23 mm ....**Eneopterinae**	p. 223
3′.	Hind tibiae without small teeth between longer spines; ovipositor compressed, upcurved; length 4.0–8.5 mm ....**Trigonidiinae**	p. 223
4(2′).	Wings very short or absent; hind tibiae without long spines (but with apical spurs); body covered with scales; hind femora stout; southern United States ....**Mogoplistinae**	p. 223
4′.	Wings usually well developed; hind tibiae nearly always with long spines (Figure 14–4A); body not covered with scales; hind femora only moderately enlarged; widely distributed **5**	
5(4′).	Ocelli present; head short, vertical (Figures 14–1, 14–17); hind tibiae without teeth between spines (Figure 14–4A); black or brown insects **6**	

5'.   Ocelli absent; head elongate, horizontal (Figure 14–16); hind tibiae usually with minute teeth between spines (Figure 14–4D); usually pale green insects . . . . **Oecanthinae**   p. 223

6(5).   Spines of hind tibiae long and movable (Figure 14–4A); last segment of maxillary palps at least twice as long as preceding segment; body usually less than 12 mm in length . . . . **Nemobiinae**   p. 224

6'.   Spines of hind tibiae stout and immovable; last segment of maxillary palps only slightly longer than preceding segment; body usually over 14 mm in length **7**

7(6').   Ocelli arranged in nearly a transverse row; ovipositor very short, often not visible; southeastern United States . . . . **Brachytrupinae**   p. 224

7'.   Ocelli arranged in an obtuse triangle; ovipositor at least half as long as hind femora; widely distributed . . . . **Gryllinae**   p. 224

Subfamily **Oecanthinae**—Tree Crickets: Most tree crickets are slender, whitish or pale green insects (Figure 14–16). All are excellent singers. Some species occur in trees and shrubs; others occur in weedy fields. The snowy tree cricket, *Oecánthus fúltoni* Walker, a shrub inhabitant, chirps at a very regular rate, which varies with the temperature (Figure 14–3D). Adding 40 to the number of its chirps in 15 seconds gives a good approximation of the temperature in degrees Fahrenheit. Most species of tree crickets deliver loud trills. Some of the tree-inhabiting species have songs consisting of short bursts of pulses. Most of our tree crickets belong to the genus *Oecánthus*. The two-spotted tree cricket, *Neoxàbea bipunctàta* (De Geer), differs from *Oecánthus* in lacking teeth on the hind tibiae, in having the hind wings much longer than the front wings, and in its buffy coloration. Tree crickets lay their eggs in bark or on stems (Figure 3–34E) and often seriously damage twigs by their egg laying.

Subfamilies **Eneopterìnae** and **Trigonidiìnae**—Bush Crickets: The bush crickets are principally bush- or tree-inhabiting and are rarely found on the ground (where one would find the somewhat similar ground crickets). They differ from other crickets in having the second tarsal segment distinct and somewhat flattened and expanded laterally (Figure 14–4E). This segment is quite small and somewhat compressed in other crickets (Figure 14–4D). The Eneopterìnae differ from the Trigonidiìnae in being much larger (length 11–23 mm in the Eneopterìnae and 4.0–8.5 mm in the Trigonidiìnae) and in the shape of the ovipositor and the character of the spines on the hind tibiae (see key to subfamilies, couplet 3). Both groups are small and occur only in the eastern states.

The most common species in the Eneopterìnae is the jumping bush cricket. *Orócharis saltàtor* Uhler, which is grayish brown in color and 14–16 mm in length. The two most common species in the Trigonidiìnae are Say's bush cricket, *Anáxipha exígua* (Say), which is brownish in color and 6–8 mm in length, and the handsome or red-headed bush cricket, *Phyllopálpus pulchéllus* Uhler, which is blackish, with the head and pronotum red, and 6–7 mm in length. The species of *Cyrtóxipha* (Trigonidiìnae), which occur in the Southwest, are pale green in color.

Subfamily **Mogoplistìnae**—Scaly Crickets: The members of this group are small, wingless or very

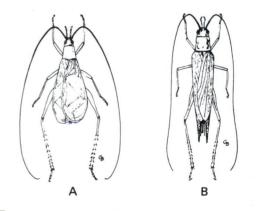

Figure 14–16.   A tree cricket, *Oecánthus quadrimaculàtus* Beutenmüller. **A,** male, **B,** female. (Courtesy of Institut de Biologie Générale, Université de Montréal.)

short-winged, slender-bodied, flattened insects that are chiefly tropical in distribution. They occur on bushes or beneath debris in sandy localities near water. The body is covered with translucent scales that are easily rubbed off. The members of this group occurring in the southern states are 5–13 mm in length.

Subfamily **Myrmecophilìnae**—Ant-Loving Crickets: These crickets are small (2–4 mm in length) and broadly oval, with greatly dilated hind femora. They live in ant nests and feed (at least in part) on secretions from the ants. Of the half dozen or so North American species, only one, *Myrmecóphila pergándei* Bruner, occurs in the East (from Maryland to Nebraska).

Subfamily **Nemobiìnae**—Ground Crickets: These crickets (Figure 14–17A) are common insects in pastures, in meadows, along roadsides, and in wooded areas. They are less than 13 mm in length and are usually brownish in color. The songs of most species are soft, high-pitched, and often pulsating trills or buzzes.

Subfamily **Gryllìnae**—House and Field Crickets: These crickets are very similar to the ground crick-

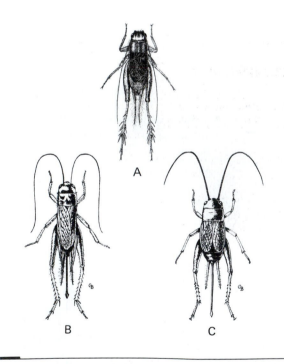

Figure 14–17. **A**, a ground cricket, *Allonemòbius fasciàtus* (De Geer), male; **B**, the house cricket, *Achèta domésticus* (L.); **C**, a field cricket, *Grýllus pennsylvánicus* Burmeister. (**A**, courtesy of Hebard and the Illinois Natural History Survey; **B** and **C**, courtesy of Institut de Biologie Générale, Université de Montréal.)

Figure 14–18. The northern mole cricket, *Neocurtílla hexadáctyla* (Perty). (Courtesy of Hebard and the Illinois Natural History Survey.)

ets, but are generally larger (more than 13 mm in length), and they vary in color from brownish to black. The field crickets (Figure 14–1) are very common insects in pastures, in meadows, along roadsides, and in yards, and some enter houses. The several species of *Grýllus* are very similar morphologically and were formerly considered to represent a single species. Now several species are recognized, which differ chiefly in habits, life history, and song. Most species of *Grýllus* chirp (Figure 14–3A), but one species occurring in the Southwest, *G. rùbens* Scudder, produces a more or less long trill. The most common species of *Grýllus* in the East is probably the northern field cricket, *G. pennsylvánicus* Burmeister (Figure 14–17C). The house cricket, *Achèta domésticus* (L.), a species introduced into the United States from Europe, which often enters houses, differs from the native species of *Grýllus* in having the head light-colored with dark cross bars (Figure 14–17B). The members of this group sing both day and night. Other genera in this subfamily (*Miogrýllus* and *Gryllòdes*) occur in the southern states.

Subfamily **Brachytrupìnae**—Short-Tailed Crickets: These crickets get their common name from the fact that their ovipositor is very short and often not visible, rather than long and slender as in most other crickets. The short-tailed crickets are burrowing in habit and usually occur in colonies, their burrows going 0.3 meter or more into the ground. They spend most of the time during the day in their burrows and generally come out only at night. A single species of short-tailed cricket occurs in the southeastern states, *Anurogrýllus mùticus* (De Geer). This insect is 12 to 17 mm in length and yellowish brown in color.

Family **Gryllotálpidae**—Mole Crickets: Mole crickets are brownish, very pubescent insects with short antennae, and the front legs are very broad and spade-like (Figure 14–18). These insects burrow in moist soil, usually near ponds and streams, often 150–200 mm below the surface. There is a tympanum on the front tibia, and the males sing. Only seven species of mole crickets occur in North America, six in the

East and one in the West. The most common eastern species is *Neocurtílla hexadáctyla* (Perty) (Figure 14–18). This insect is generally 25–30 mm in length, and its song is much like that of the snowy tree cricket (*Oecánthus fúltoni* Walker) but is lower pitched. Mole crickets sometimes damage crops such as peanuts, tobacco, strawberries, and garden vegetables in the South Atlantic and Gulf Coast states.

Collecting and Preserving Orthóptera

Many of the Orthóptera, because they are relatively large and numerous, are fairly easy to collect. The best time for collecting most species is from midsummer to late fall, though a few species should be looked for in early summer. The more conspicuous forms such as the grasshoppers and crickets, are most easily collected with a net, either by sweeping vegetation or by aiming for particular individuals. Some of the more secretive species may be collected at night by listening for their songs and then locating them with a flashlight, or by means of various sorts of baited traps. Some forms can be caught by putting molasses or a similar material in the bottom of a trap like that shown in Figure 36–7A. The insects so collected can simply be picked out of the trap.

Most nymphs and some soft-bodied adult specimens should be preserved in alcohol, but most adults can be pinned. Grasshoppers should be pinned through the right side of the rear part of the pronotum or through the right tegmen. Crickets should be pinned through the right tegmen, in about the middle (from front to rear) of the body. If the specimen is very soft-bodied, the body should be supported by a piece of cardboard or by pins; otherwise, it will sag at either end. In the case of grasshoppers, it is desirable to spread the wings, at least on one side (as in Figure 14–9A), in order that the color and venation of the hind wing can be seen. It is sometimes desirable to eviscerate some of the larger grasshoppers before they are pinned to facilitate drying and preservation. A short incision may be made on the right or left side of the body near the base of the abdomen and as much of the viscera removed as possible.

References

Alexander, R. D. 1957a. Sound production and associated behavior in insects. Ohio J. Sci. 57:101–113; illus.

Alexander, R. D. 1957b. The taxonomy of the field crickets of the eastern United States (Orthoptera, Gryllidae: *Acheta*). Ann. Entomol. Soc. Amer. 50:584–602; illus.

Alexander, R. D., and D. J. Borror. 1956. The songs of insects (a 12-inch long-play phonograph record). Ithaca, N.Y.; Cornell Univ. Press.

Alexander, R. D., and T. J. Walker. 1962. Two introduced field crickets new to eastern United States (Orthoptera: Gryllidae). Ann. Entomol. Soc. Amer. 55:90–94 (includes a discussion of the status of the names *Gryllus* and *Acheta*).

Ball, E. D., E. R. Tinkham, R. Flock, and C. T. Vorheis. 1942. The grasshoppers and other Orthoptera of Arizona. Ariz. Agr. Expt. Sta. Tech. Bull. No. 93:257–373; illus.

Blatchley, W. S. 1920. Orthoptera of Northeastern America. Indianapolis: Nature, 785 pp.; illus.

Brooks, A. R. 1958. Acridoidea of south Alberta, Saskatchewan, and Manitoba (Orthoptera). Can. Entomol. Suppl. 9:1–92; illus.

Brusven, M. A. 1967. Differentiation, ecology, and distribution of immature slant-faced grasshoppers (Acridinae) in Kansas. Kan. Agr. Expt. Sta. Tech. Bull. No. 149, 59 pp.; illus.

Cantrell, I. J. 1968. An annotated list of the Dermaptera, Dictyoptera, Phasmatoptera, and Orthoptera of Michigan. Mich. Entomol. 1:299–346; illus.

Chopard, L. 1938. La Biologie des Orthoptères. Paris, Lachevalier, 541 pp.; illus.

Dirsch, V. M. 1975. Classification of the Acridomorphoid Insects. Oxford, England: E. W. Classey, 178 pp.; illus.

Froeschner, R. C. 1954. The grasshoppers and other Orthoptera of Iowa. Iowa State Coll. J. Sci. 29:163–354; illus.

Grant, H. J., Jr., and D. Rentz. 1967. Biosystematic review of the family Tanaoceridae, including a comparative study of the proventriculus (Orthoptera: Tanaoceridae). Pan-Pac. Entomol. 43:65–74; illus.

Hebard, M. 1934. The Dermaptera and Orthoptera of Illinois. Ill. Nat. Hist. Surv. Bull. 20:125–179; illus.

Helfer, J. R. 1972 (2nd ed.). How to Know the Grasshoppers, Cockroaches, and Their Allies. Dubuque, Iowa; Wm. C. Brown, 359 pp.; illus.

Hubbell, T. H. 1936. A monographic revision of the genus *Ceuthophilus* (Orthoptera, Gryllacrididae, Rhaphidophorinae). Univ. Fla. Publ. Biol. Sci. Ser. 2(1):1–551; illus.

Jago, N. D. 1971. A revision of the Gomphocerinae of the world with a key to the genera (Orthoptera: Acrididae). Proc. Acad. Nat. Sci. Philadelphia 123(8):204–343; illus.

Love, R. E., and T. J. Walker. 1979. Systematics and acoustic behavior of the scaly crickets (Orthoptera: Gryllidae: Mogoplistinae) of eastern United States. Trans. Amer. Entomol. Soc. 105:1–66; illus.

Morse, A. P. 1920. Manual of the Orthoptera of New England. Proc. Boston Soc. Nat. Hist. 35(6):197–556; illus.

Nickle, D. A., T. J. Walker, and M. A. Brusven. 1987. Order Orthoptera, pp. 147–170 *in* F. W. Stehr (ed.), Immature Insects, vol. 1. Dubuque, Iowa: Kendall/Hunt, 754 pp.; illus.

Otte, D. 1981. The North American Grasshoppers, vol. 1: Acrididae, Gomphocerinae and Acridinae. Cambridge, Mass.: Harvard Univ. Press, 275 pp.; illus.

Otte, D. 1984. The North American Grasshoppers, vol. 2: Acrididae, Oedipodinae. Cambridge, Mass.: Harvard Univ. Press, 366 pp.; illus.

Rehn, J. A. G., and H. J. Grant, Jr. 1961. A monograph of the Orthoptera of North America (north of Mexico), vol. 1. Acad. Nat. Sci. Philadelphia Monogr. No. 12, 257 pp.; illus.

Rehn, J. A. G., and M. Hebard. 1918. A study of the North American Eumastacidae (Orthoptera: Acrididae). Trans. Amer. Entomol. Soc. 44:223–250; illus.

Rentz, D., and J. D. Burchim. 1968. Revisionary studies of nearctic Decticinae. Mem. Pac. Coast Entomol. Soc. 3:1–173; illus.

Rentz, D. C. F., and D. B. Weissman. 1981. Faunal affinities, systematics, and bionomics of the Orthoptera of the California Channel Islands. Univ. Calif. Publ. Entomol. 94:1–240; illus.

Strohecker, H. F., W. M. Middlekauff, and D. C. Rentz. 1968. The grasshoppers of California. Bull. Calif. Insect Surv. 10:1–177; illus.

Uvarov, B. P. 1928. Locusts and grasshoppers. London: Imperial Bureau of Entomology, 352 pp.; illus.

Uvarov, B. P. 1966. Grasshoppers and Locusts: A Handbook of General Acridology, vol. 1: Anatomy, Physiology, and Development, Phase Polymorphism, Introduction to Taxonomy. Cambridge: Cambridge Univ. Press, 481 pp.; illus.

Vickery, V. R., and D. K. McE. Kevan. 1985. The grasshoppers, crickets, and related insects of Canada and adjacent regions: Ulonata: Dermaptera, Cheleutoptera, Notoptera, Dictuoptera, Grylloptera, and Orthoptera. The Insects and Arachnids of Canada, Part 14. Ottawa: Can. Govt. Publ. Centre, 918 pp.; illus.

Vickerey, V. R., and D. E. Johnstone. 1970. Generic status of some Nemobiinae (Orthoptera: Gryllidae) in northern North America. Ann. Entomol. Soc. Amer. 63:1740–1749; illus.

Vickerey, V. R., and D. E. Johnstone. 1973. The Nemobiinae (Orthoptera: Gryllidae) of Canada. Can. Entomol. 105:623–645; illus.

Waldon, B. H. 1911. The Euplexoptera and Orthoptera of Connecticut. Conn. State Geol. Nat. Hist. Surv. Bull. 16:39–169; illus.

Walker, T. J. 1962. The taxonomy and calling songs of the United States tree crickets (Orthoptera: Gryllidae: Oecanthinae). I. The genus *Neoxabea* and the *niveus* and *varicornis* groups of the genus *Oecanthus*. Ann. Entomol. Soc. Amer. 55:303–322; illus.

Walker, T. J. 1963. The taxonomy and calling songs of the United States tree crickets (Orthoptera: Gryllidae: Oecanthinae). II. The *nigricornis* group of the genus *Oecanthus*. Ann. Entomol. Soc. Amer. 56:772–789; illus.

Walker, T. J. 1966. Annotated checklist of the Oecanthinae (Orthoptera: Gryllidae) of the world. Fla. Entomol. 49:265–277.

Chapter 15

Order Mantòdea[1]
Mantids

Mantids are large, elongate, rather slow-moving insects that are striking in appearance because of their peculiarly modified front legs (Figure 15–1). The prothorax is greatly lengthened and movably attached to the pterothorax; the front coxae are very long and mobile; and the front femora and tibiae are armed with strong spines and fitted for grasping prey. The head is freely movable. Mantids are the only insects that can ''look over their shoulder.'' These insects are highly predaceous and feed on a variety of insects (including other mantids). They usually lie in wait for their prey with the front legs in an upraised position. This position has given rise to the common names ''praying mantid'' and ''soothsayer'' that are often applied to these insects.

Mantids overwinter in the egg stage, and the eggs are deposited on twigs or grass stems in a styrofoam-like egg case or ootheca secreted by the female. Each egg case may contain 200 or more eggs. If brought into the house and kept warm, the eggs will hatch in late winter or early spring, and the nymphs, unless supplied with food, will eat each other until one large nymph remains.

There are more than 1500 species in eight families of mantids in the world, most of which are tropical. In the United States and Canada there are only 20 species, all belonging to the family **Mántidae.** The

[1]Mantòdea, from the Greek, meaning a soothsayer or a kind of grasshopper.

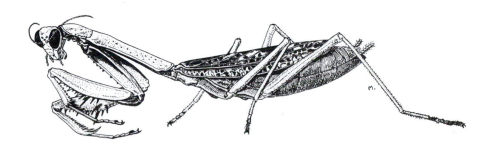

Figure 15–1. The Carolina mantid, *Stagmomántis carolìna* (Johannsen). (Courtesy of Hebard and the Illinois Natural History Survey.)

Carolina mantid, *Stagmomántis carolìna* (Johann-son), which is about 50 mm in length (Figure 15–1), is the most common of several species of mantids occurring in the southern states. The large mantid (75–100 mm in length) that is locally common in the northern states is an introduced species, the Chinese mantid, *Tenódera aridifòlia sinénsis* Saussure. This species was introduced in the vicinity of Philadelphia about 75 years ago and has since become rather widely distributed through the transportation of egg masses. The European mantid, *Mántis religiòsa* L., a pale-green insect about 50 mm in length, was introduced in the vicinity of Rochester, New York, about 75 years ago and now occurs throughout most of the eastern states.

The female mantid usually eats the male immediately after or actually during mating. No males are known for *Brunnéria boreàlis* Scudder, a fairly common species in the South and Southwest.

Mantids are highly touted as biological control agents, and one can buy them to place in gardens to help control pest insects. This practice is not rec-ommended because the mantids cannot possibly keep up with populations of damaging insects. In addition, mantids do not discriminate between destructive and useful insects and sometimes become a pest themselves, especially around beehives, where they may have a real feast of honey bees going to and from the hive.

Collecting and Preserving Mantòdea

Mantids are relatively large and slow-moving and, once found, are fairly easy to collect. The best time for collecting the adults of most species is from midsummer to late fall. The egg masses are large and fairly conspicuous, especially on the bare twigs of trees during the winter. Adults should be pinned through the right tegmen, in about the middle of the body (from front to rear). If the specimen is very soft-bodied, the body should be supported by a piece of cardboard or by pins; otherwise, it will sag at either end.

References

Blatchley, W. S. 1920. Orthoptera of Northeastern America. Indianapolis: Nature, 785 pp.; illus.

Gurney, A. B. 1951. Praying mantids of the United States. Smithson. Inst. Rep. 1950:339–362.

Hebard, M. 1934. The Dermaptera and Orthoptera of Illinois. Ill. Nat. Hist. Surv. Bull. 20:125–179; illus.

Helfer, J. R. 1972 (2nd ed.). How to Know the Grasshoppers, Cockroaches, and Their Allies. Dubuque, Iowa: Wm. C. Brown, 359 pp.; illus.

Nickle, D. A. 1987. Order Mantodea, pp. 140–142 *in* F. W. Stehr (ed.), Immature Insects, vol. 1. Dubuque, Iowa: Kendall/Hunt, 754 pp.; illus.

Vickery, V. R., and D. K. McE. Kevan. 1985. The grasshoppers, crickets, and related insects of Canada and adjacent regions: Ulonata: Dermaptera, Cheleutoptera, Notoptera, Dictuoptera, Grylloptera, and Orthoptera. The Insects and Arachnids of Canada, Part 14. Ottawa: Can. Govt. Publ. Centre, 918 pp.; illus.

Chapter 16

Order Blattària
Cockroaches

Cockroaches are cursorial insects with five-segmented tarsi and none of the legs modified for digging or grasping. They are very fast runners, as anyone who attempts to step on one soon discovers. The body is oval and flattened and the head is concealed from above by the pronotum. Tympana and stridulating organs (usually) are absent. Wings are generally present, though in some species they are much reduced. The females of many species have shorter wings than the males. The cerci are one- to many-segmented and usually fairly long; the antennae are long and filiform. These insects are rather general feeders. The eggs are enclosed in capsules or oothecae, which may be deposited immediately after they are formed, carried about on the abdomen of the female until they hatch, or carried internally in a uterus or brood pouch for the full gestation period.

Cockroaches are primarily tropical insects, and most of our species occur in the southern part of the United States. Some tropical species are occasionally brought into the North in shipments of bananas or other tropical fruits. The most commonly encountered cockroaches in the North are those that invade houses, where they are often serious pests. None is known to be a specific vector of disease, but they feed on all sorts of things in a house. They contaminate food, they have an unpleasant odor, and their presence is often very annoying.

Classification of the Blattària

There is much difference of opinion regarding the classification of cockroaches. The 40-odd major groups are variously treated as tribes, subfamilies, or families by different authorities. We follow here the classification of McKittrick (1964), who groups the 50 or so North American species into five families. A synopsis of the North American Blattària, as treated in this book, is given here. The groups marked with an asterisk are relatively rare or are unlikely to be taken by a general collector.

*Cryptocércidae—brown-hooded cockroach
Bláttidae—oriental, American, and other
   cockroaches
*Polyphágidae—sand cockroaches and others
Blattéllidae—German, wood, and other
   cockroaches
Blabéridae—giant cockroaches and others

229

Key to the Families of the Blattària

1.   Length 3 mm or less; found in ant nests (*Attáphila, Myrmecoblátta*) ....**Polyphágidae*** p. 232

1'.   Length over 3 mm; almost never found in ant nests **2**

2(1').   Middle and hind femora with numerous spines on ventroposterior margin **3**

2'.   Middle and hind femora without spines on ventroposterior margin, or with hairs and bristles only, or 1 or 2 apical spines **7**

3(2).   Pronotum and front wings densely covered with silky pubescence; length 27 mm or more (tropical species accidental in the United States) (*Nyctibòra*) ....**Blattéllidae*** p. 232

3'.   Pronotum and front wings glabrous or only very sparsely pubescent **4**

4(3').   Ventroposterior margin of front femora with row of spines that either decrease gradually in size and length distally or are nearly equal in length throughout (Figure 16–1A) **5**

4'.   Ventroposterior margin of front femora with row of heavy spines proximally and more slender and shorter spines distally (Figure 16–1B) **6**

5(4).   Female subgenital plate divided longitudinally (Figure 16–2C); male styli similar, slender, elongate, and straight (Figure 16–2D); length 18 mm or more (*Blátta, Periplanèta, Eurycòtis, Neostylopỳga*) ....**Bláttidae** p. 231

5'.   Female subgenital plate entire, not divided longitudinally (Figure 16–2B); male styli variable, often modified, asymmetrical, or unequal in size (Figure 16–2E); length variable, but usually less than 18 mm (*Supélla, Cariblátta, Symplòce, Pseùdomops, Blattélla*) ....**Blattéllidae** p. 232

6(4').   Front femora with only 1 apical spine; supra-anal plate weakly bilobed; color glossy light brown, with sides and front of pronotum and basal costal part of front wings yellowish; 15–20 mm in length; Florida Keys (*Phoetàlia, Epilámpra*) ....**Blabéridae*** p. 232

6'.   Front femora with 2 or 3 apical spines; supra-anal plate not bilobed; size and color variable; widely distributed (*Ectòbius, Latiblattélla, Ischnóptera, Parcoblátta, Euthlastoblátta, Aglaópteryx*)........................**Blattéllidae** p. 232

7(2').   Distal portion of abdomen (usually including cerci) covered by produced seventh dorsal and sixth ventral abdominal sclerites, subgenital plate absent; wingless, body almost parallel-sided, shining reddish brown, finely punctate, 23–29 mm in length; widely distributed, usually found in rotting logs ....**Cryptocércidae*** p. 231

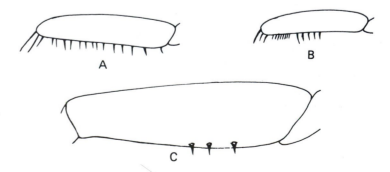

Figure 16–1. Front femora of Blattària. **A,** *Periplanèta* (Bláttidae); **B,** *Parcoblátta* (Blattéllidae); **C,** *Blàberus* (Blabéridae).

7'.   Distal portion of abdomen not so covered, subgenital plate present; wings usually well developed (absent in some females); usually oval in shape; size and color variable; mostly southern United States **8***

8(7').   Hind wings with an apical portion (intercalated triangle or appendicular area) that folds over when wings are in resting position (Figure 16–2A, *it*); 8.5 mm in length or less, and glossy yellowish in color, often beetlelike in appearance; southeastern United States (*Chorisoneùra, Plectóptera*) . . . .**Blattéllidae***   p. 232

8'.   Hind wings not as above **9***

9(8').   Front femora with 1 to 3 spines on ventroposterior margin and 1 at tip (Figure 16–1C); length over 40 mm; arolia present; southern Florida (*Bláberus, Hemiblábera*) . . . .**Blabéridae***   p. 232

9'.   Front femora without spines on ventroposterior margin and with 1 or a few at tip; size variable; arolia present or absent; eastern and southern United States **10***

10(9'). Wings well developed, the anal area of hind wings folded fanwise at rest; frons flat, not bulging; length over 16 mm, or pale green in color (*Panchlòra, Pycnoscèlus, Nauphoèta, Leucophaèa*) . . . .**Blabéridae***   p. 232

10'.   Anal area of hind wings flat, not folded fanwise at rest (some females are wingless); frons thickened and somewhat bulging; usually (except some *Arenivàga*) less than 16 mm in length and never green (*Holocómpsa, Eremoblátta, Compsòdes, Arenivàga*) . . . .**Polyphágidae***   p. 232

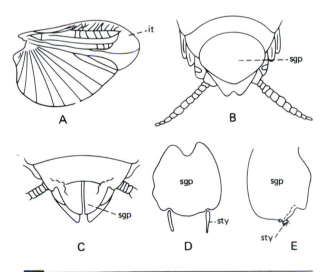

Figure 16–2. **A,** hind wing of *Chorisoneùra* (Blattéllidae); **B,** apex of abdomen of female cockroach (Blattéllidae), ventral view; **C,** apex of abdomen of female cockroach (Bláttidae), ventral view; **D,** subgenital plate of male cockroach (Bláttidae), ventral view; **E,** same (Blattéllidae). *it,* intercalated triangle; *sgp,* subgenital plate; *sty,* stylus.

Family **Cryptocércidae:**   The only cryptocercid in the United States is the brown-hooded cockroach, *Cryptocércus punctulàtus* Scudder, which occurs in hilly or mountainous areas from New York to Georgia in the East and from Washington to California in the West. This cockroach is wingless, 23–29 mm in length, and shining reddish brown with the dorsal surface finely punctured, and it is somewhat elongate and parallel-sided. It occurs in decaying logs, particularly oak logs. This cockroach has intestinal protists that break down the cellulose ingested (as in termites).

Family **Bláttidae:**   The cockroaches in this group are relatively large insects (most are 25 mm or more in length). Several species are important household pests. One of the most common pest species in this group is the oriental cockroach, *Blátta orientàlis* L., which is about 25 mm long, dark brown, and broadly oval with short wings (Figure 16–3D,E). Several species of *Periplanèta* also invade houses, one of the most common being the American cockroach, *P. americàna* (L.) (Figure 16–3B). This species is about 27–35 mm in length and reddish brown with well-developed wings. One blattid occurring in Florida, *Eurycòtis floridàna* (Walker) (brown to black with

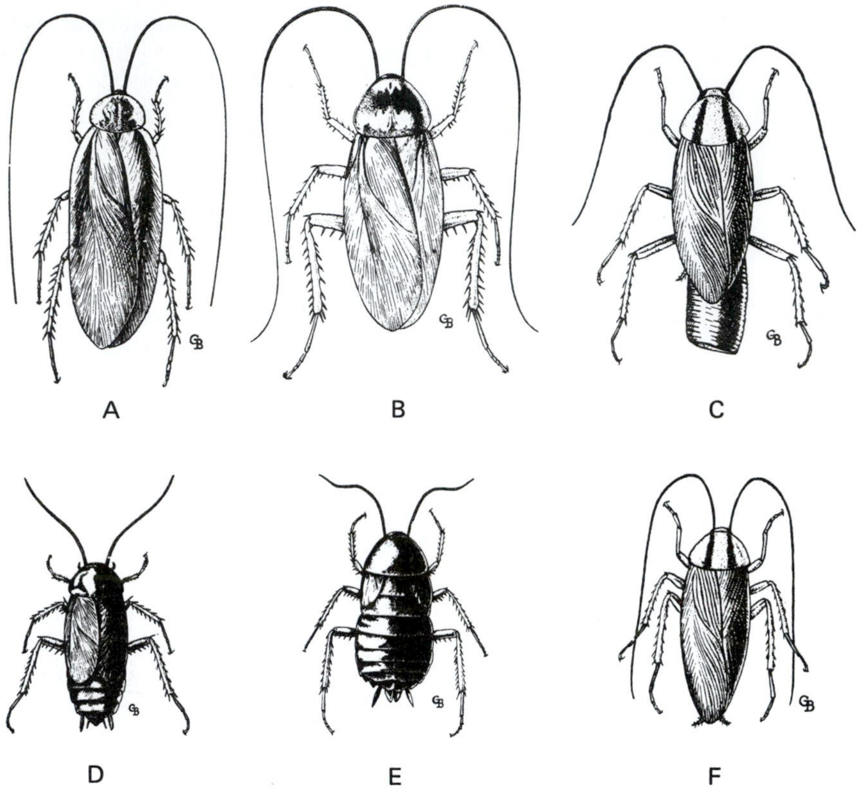

Figure 16–3. Some common cockroaches. **A,** a wood cockroach, *Parcoblátta pennsylvánica* (De Geer) (Blattéllidae); **B,** the American cockroach, *Periplanèta americàna* (L.) (Bláttidae); **C,** the German cockroach, *Blattélla germánica* (L.), female (Blattéllidae); **D,** the oriental cockroach, *Blátta orientàlis* (L.), male (Bláttidae); **E,** same, female; **F,** the German cockroach, male. **A,** slightly enlarged; **B, D,** and **E** about natural size; **C** and **F,** 2×. (Courtesy of Institut de Biologie Générale, Université de Montréal.)

very short wings, and 30–39 mm in length), which occurs under various sorts of cover outdoors, emits a very smelly liquid and is sometimes called the stinking cockroach.

Family **Polyphágidae:** These are mostly small cockroaches that have the pronotum rather hairy. The winged forms have the anal area of the hind wings flat at rest (not folded fanwise). They occur in the southern states, from Florida to California. Most species occurring in the Southwest (*Arenivàga* and *Eremoblátta*) are found in desert areas (some of these burrow in the sand like moles) and have the females wingless. Some *Arenivàga* are nearly 25 mm in length. Other species are 6.5 mm in length or less. *Attáphila fungícolla* (Wheeler) is 3 mm in length or less and occurs in southern Texas and Louisiana in the nests of leaf-cutting ants.

Family **Blattéllidae:** This is a large group of small cockroaches, most of them 12 mm in length or less. Several species invade houses. One of the most important of these is the German cockroach, *Blattélla germánica* (L.) (Figure 16–3C,F), which is light brown with two longitudinal stripes on the pronotum. An-

other is the brown-banded cockroach, *Supélla longipálpa* (Fabricius). A number of species in this group occur outdoors. The most common such species in the North are the wood cockroaches, *Parcoblátta* spp. (Figure 16–3A), which live in litter and debris in woods. Most of the species in this group occur in the South, where they may be found in litter and debris outdoors, under signs on trees, and in similar situations. The Asian cockroach, *Blattélla asahìnae* Mizukoba, morphologically very similar to *B. germánica*, is now established in Florida (first detected in 1986).

Family **Blabéridae:** This group is principally tropical, and our species are nearly all restricted to the southern states. The group includes the largest U.S. cockroaches (*Bláberus* and *Leucophaèa*), which may reach a length of 50 mm. Most species are brownish, but one occurring in southern Texas, *Panchlòra nívea* (L.), is pale green. Most members of this group are found outdoors in litter or debris. A few get into houses occasionally, for example, the Surinam cockroach, *Pycnoscèlus surinaménsis* (L.), and the Madeira cockroach, *Leucophaèa madèrae* (Fabricius). The Madeira cockroach (38–51 mm in length) is able to stridulate, and it gives off an offensive odor.

Collecting and Preserving Blattària

Cockroaches are mainly nocturnal creatures, and night is often the best time to collect them. They may be found by searching in leaf litter or under bark, or by overturning fallen logs. Many species, including the common household pests, can be caught by putting molasses or a similar bait in the bottom of a trap like that shown in Figure 36–7A. The insects so collected can simply be picked out of the trap.

Most nymphs and some soft-bodied adult specimens should be preserved in alcohol, but most adults can be pinned. The pin should be placed through the right tegmen, in about the middle (from front to rear) of the body. If the specimen is very soft-bodied, the body should be supported by a piece of cardboard or by pins; otherwise, it will sag at either end.

References

Deyrup, M., and F. W. Fisk. 1984. A myrmecophilous cockroach new to the United States (Blattaria: Polyphagidae). Entomol. News 95:183–185.

Fisk, F. W. 1987. Order Blattodea, pp. 120–131 *in* F. W. Stehr (ed.), Immature Insects, vol. 1. Dubuque, Iowa: Kendall/Hunt, 754 pp.; illus.

Hebard, M. 1917. The Blattidae of North America north of the Mexican boundary. Mem. Amer. Entomol. Soc. 2:1–284; illus.

Helfer, J. R. 1972 (2nd ed.). How to Know the Grasshoppers, Cockroaches, and Their Allies. Dubuque, Iowa: Wm. C. Brown, 359 pp.; illus.

McKittrick, F. A. 1964. Evolutionary studies of cockroaches. Cornell Univ. Agr. Exp. Sta. Mem. No. 189; 197 pp.; illus.

McKittrick, F. A. 1965. A contribution to the understanding of the cockroach-termite affinities. Ann. Entomol. Soc. Amer. 58:18–22.

Princis, K. 1960. Zur Systematik der Blattarien. Eos, Revista Española Entomol. 36(4):427–449; illus.

Princis, K. 1969. Fam. Blattellidae. Orthopterorum Catalogus 13:713–1038.

Rehn, J. W. H. 1950. A key to the genera of North American Blattaria, including established adventives. Entomol. News 61(3):64–67.

Rehn, J. W. H. 1951. Classification of the Blattaria as indicated by their wings (Orthoptera). Mem. Amer. Entomol. Soc. No. 14, 134 pp.; illus.

Roth, L. M. 1970. Evolution and taxonomic significance of reproduction in Blattaria. Annu. Rev. Entomol. 15:75–96.

Roth, L. M., and E. R. Willis. 1957. The medical and veterinary importance of cockroaches. Smithson. Misc. Coll. 134(10), 147 pp.; illus.

Vickery, V. R., and D. K. McE. Kevan. 1985. The grasshoppers, crickets, and related insects of Canada and adjacent regions: Ulonata: Dermaptera, Cheleutoptera, Notoptera, Dictuoptera, Grylloptera, and Orthoptera. The Insects and Arachnids of Canada, Part 14. Ottawa: Can. Govt. Publ. Centre, 918 pp.; illus.

Chapter 17

Order Isóptera[1]
Termites

Termites are medium-sized, cellulose-eating social insects comprising the order Isóptera, a relatively small group of insects, consisting of approximately 1900 species worldwide. They live in highly organized and integrated societies, or colonies, with the individuals differentiated morphologically into distinct forms or castes—reproductives, workers, and soldiers—which perform different biological functions. The wings (present only in the reproductive caste) are four in number and membranous. The front and hind wings are almost equal in size (Figure 17–1), hence the name Isóptera. The antennae are moniliform or filiform. The mouthparts of the workers and reproductives are of the chewing type. The metamorphosis is simple. The nymphs have the potential to develop into any one of the castes. Experiments have shown that hormones and inhibitory pheromones secreted by the reproductives and soldiers regulate caste differentiation.

Though termites are popularly referred to as "white ants," they are not ants, nor are they closely related to ants, which are grouped with bees and wasps in the Hymenóptera, whose social system has evolved independently of that in the Isóptera. Termites are most closely related to the cockroaches,

both having probably evolved from a primitive cockroachlike ancestor. The primitive living species *Mastotérmes darwiniénsis* Froggatt from Australia has affinities with some cockroaches, such as the folded anal lobe in the hind wing and an egg mass resembling the ootheca of cockroaches. This and other evidence of relationship to primitive Blattària suggest that termites evolved in the late Permian, approximately 200 million years ago (though the known fossil termites date only from the Cretaceous, about 120 million years ago). The termite society is therefore the oldest.

There are many important differences between termites and ants. Termites are soft-bodied and usually light-colored, while ants are hard-bodied and usually dark. The antennae in termites are not elbowed as in ants. The front and hind wings of termites are nearly equal in size and are held flat over the abdomen at rest, while in ants the hind wings are smaller than the fore wings and the wings at rest are usually held above the body. In termites, the wings, when shed, break along a suture, leaving only the wing base, or "scale," attached to the thorax. The abdomen in termites is broadly joined to the thorax, whereas in ants it is constricted at the base, forming the characteristic hymenopteran petiole, or "waist." The sterile castes (workers and soldiers) in termites are made up of both sexes, and reproductives and sterile castes develop from fertilized eggs.

---

[1]Isóptera: *iso*, equal; *ptera*, wings. This chapter was written, with minor editorial changes by the authors, by Kumar Krishna.

Figure 17–1. A winged termite. (Courtesy of USDA.)

In ants, the sterile castes are made up of females only, and all females, sterile and reproductive, develop from fertilized eggs, while the reproductive males develop from unfertilized eggs.

Termite Castes

The reproductive function in the termite society is carried out by the primary reproductives, the king and queen—most commonly one pair to a colony—which develop from fully winged (macropterous) adults (Figure 17–2A). They are heavily sclerotized and have compound eyes. The king is generally small, but in many species the queen develops an enlarged abdomen as a result of her increasing egg-laying capacity, and in some tropical species she can reach a size as great as 11 cm (compared with 1–2 cm for the king). The winged reproductives from which the king and queen develop are produced in large numbers seasonally. They leave the colony in a swarming or colonizing flight, shed their wings along a suture, and, as individual pairs, seek a nesting site, mate, and establish new colonies. In some species one emergence a year occurs; in others, many. In the most common eastern species, *Reticulitérmes flávipes*, it occurs in the spring; in many western species, it occurs in late summer.

In the initial stages of colony foundation, the reproductives feed the young and tend to the nest, but these household duties are soon taken over by young nymphs and workers.

If it happens that the king and queen die or part of the colony is separated from the parent colony, supplementary reproductives develop within the nest and take over the function of the king and queen. The supplementary reproductives are slightly sclerotized and pigmented, with short wing pads (brachypterous) or no wing pads (apterous) and reduced compound eyes. They develop from nymphs

and achieve sexual maturity without reaching the fully winged adult stages and without leaving the nest.

The worker and soldier castes, made up of both sexes, are sterile, wingless, in most species blind, and in some species polymorphic, that is, of two distinct sizes (Figure 17–2C,D).

The workers are usually the most numerous individuals in a colony. They are pale and soft-bodied, with mouthparts adapted for chewing. They perform most of the work of the colony: nest building and repair, foraging, and feeding and grooming the other members of the colony. Because of its feeding function, the worker caste causes the widespread destruction for which termites are notorious. In the primitive families a true worker caste is absent, and its functions are carried out by wingless nymphs called pseudergates, which may molt from time to time without change in size.

The soldier has a large, dark, elongated, highly sclerotized head, adapted in various ways for defense. In the soldiers of most species, the mandibles are long, powerful, hooked, and modified to operate with a scissorslike action to behead, dismember, or lacerate enemies or predators (usually ants). In the soldiers of some genera, such as *Cryptotérmes*, the head is short and truncated in front and is used in defense to plug entrance holes in the nest.

The mechanical means of defense are sometimes supplemented or displaced by chemical means, in which a sticky and toxic fluid is secreted by the frontal gland and ejected through an opening onto the enemy. In *Coptotérmes* and *Rhinotérmes*, the gland occupies a large portion of the head. In the subfamily Nasutitermitinae, the mechanism of defense is exclusively chemical: the mandibles are reduced, the frontal gland is greatly enlarged, and the head has developed a snout, or nasus (Figure 17–2B), through which a sticky, repellent secretion is squirted at the enemy.

In a few genera, such as *Anoplotérmes*, the soldier caste is absent, and the nymphs and workers defend the colony.

Habits of Termites

Termites frequently groom each other with their mouthparts, probably as a result of the attraction of secretions that are usually available on the body. The food of termites is composed of the cast skins and feces of other individuals, dead individuals, and plant materials such as wood and wood products.

Some termites live in moist subterranean habitats and others live in dry habitats aboveground. The

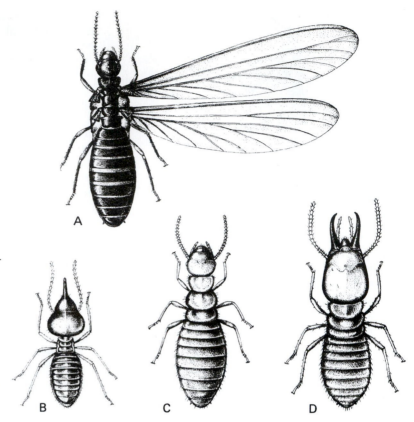

Figure 17–2. Castes of termites. **A,** sexual winged adult, *Amitérmes tubifórmans* (Buckley), 10 × (Termítidae); **B,** nasute soldier of *Tenuirostritérmes tenuiróstris* (Desneux), 15 × (Termítidae); **C,** worker, and **D,** soldier of *Prorhinotérmes símplex* (Hagen), 10 × (Rhinotermítidae). (Courtesy of Banks and Snyder and the U.S. National Museum.)

subterranean forms normally live in wood buried beneath or in contact with the soil. They may enter wood remote from the soil, but must maintain a passageway or connecting gallery to the soil, from which they obtain moisture. Some species construct earthen tubes between the soil and wood aboveground. These tubes are made of dirt mixed with a secretion from a pore on the front of the head (the fontanelle; Figure 17–3, *fon*). The nests may be entirely subterranean, or they may protrude above the surface: some tropical species have nests (termitaria) 9 meters high. The drywood termites, which live aboveground (without contact with the ground), live in posts, stumps, trees, and buildings constructed of wood. Their chief source of moisture is metabolic water (water resulting from the oxidation of food).

The cellulose in a termite's food is digested by myriads of flagellated protists living in the termite's digestive tract. A termite from which these flagellates have been removed will continue to feed, but it will eventually starve to death because its food is not digested. This association is an excellent example of symbiosis, or mutualism. Some termites har-

bor bacteria rather than flagellates. Termites engage in a unique form of anal liquid exchange (trophallaxis), and it is by this means that intestinal microorganisms are transmitted from one individual to another.

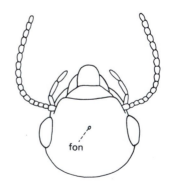

Figure 17–3. Head of *Prorhinotérmes*, dorsal view, showing fontanelle (*fon*). (Modified from Banks and Snyder.)

Key to the Families of Isóptera (Winged Adults)

1.   Fontanelle usually present (Figure 17–3, *fon*); wings with only 2 heavy veins in anterior part of wing beyond scale, R usually without anterior branches (Figure 17–4A) **2**

1′.   Fontanelle absent; wings with 3 or more heavy veins in anterior part of wing beyond scale, R with 1 or more anterior branches (Figure 17–4B) **3**

2(1).   Scale of front wing longer than pronotum; pronotum flat; cerci 2-segmented; widely distributed ....**Rhinotermítidae**   p. 238

2′.   Scale of front wing shorter than pronotum; pronotum saddle-shaped; cerci 1- or 2-segmented; southwestern United States ....**Termítidae**   p. 239

3(1′).   Ocelli present; shaft of tibiae without spines; antennae usually with fewer than 21 segments; cerci short, 2-segmented; Florida and western United States ....**Kalotermítidae**   p. 238

3′.   Ocelli absent; shaft of tibiae usually with spines; antennae usually with more than 21 segments; cerci long, 4-segmented; western United States and southern British Columbia ....**Hodotermítidae**   p. 238

Key to the Families of Isóptera (Soldiers)

1.   Mandibles vestigial, the head produced anteriorly into a long noselike projection (nasute soldiers; Figure 17–2B) ....**Termítidae**   p. 239

1′.   Mandibles normal, head not as above **2**

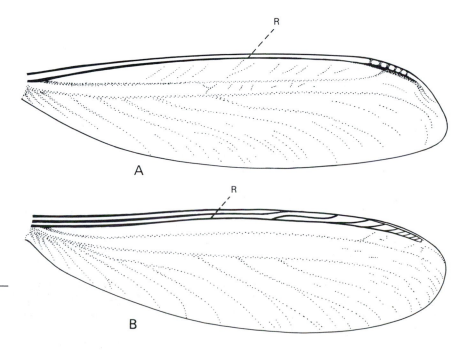

Figure 17–4. Wings of termites. **A**, Rhinotermítidae; **B**, Kalotermítidae.

2(1').	Head longer than broad (Figure 17–2D); mandibles with or without prominent marginal teeth **3**	
2'.	Head short, hollowed out; mandibles without marginal teeth; southern United States (powderpost termites) ....**Kalotermítidae**	p. 238
3(2).	Mandibles with one or more prominent marginal teeth; southern and western United States **4**	
3'.	Mandibles without marginal teeth (Figure 17–2D); widely distributed ....**Rhinotermítidae**	p. 238
4(3).	Mandibles with only 1 prominent marginal tooth; head narrowed anteriorly ....**Termítidae**	p. 239
4'.	Mandibles with more than 1 prominent marginal tooth; head not narrowed anteriorly **5**	
5(4').	Third antennal segment modified; hind femora swollen ....**Kalotermítidae**	p. 238
5'.	Third antennal segment not modified; hind femora variable **6**	
6(5').	Hind femora swollen; antennae with at least 23 segments; shaft of tibiae with spines ....**Hodotermítidae**	p. 238
6'.	Hind femora not, or only slightly, swollen; antennae with fewer than 23 segments; shaft of tibiae without spines ....**Kalotermítidae**	p. 238

Family **Kalotermítidae:** This family is represented in the United States by 16 species and includes drywood, dampwood, and powderpost termites. These termites have no worker caste, and the young of the other castes perform the work of the colony. The kalotermitids lack a fontanelle and do not construct earthen tubes.

The drywood termites (*Incisitérmes, Pterotérmes,* and *Marginitérmes*) attack dry sound wood and do not have a ground contact. Most infestations are in buildings, but furniture, utility poles, and piled lumber may also be attacked. Adults are cylindrical in shape and about 13 mm in length, and the reproductives are pale brown in color. *Incisitérmes mìnor* (Hagen) and *Marginitérmes húbbardi* (Banks) are important species in the southwestern states.

The dampwood termites in this family (*Neotérmes* and *Paraneotérmes*) attack moist dead wood, tree roots, and the like. They occur in Florida and the western United States.

The powderpost termites (*Cryptotérmes* and *Calcaritérmes*) usually attack dry wood (without a soil contact) and reduce it to powder. They occur in the southern United States. *Cryptotérmes brévis* (Walker) is an introduced species in the United States. It occurs along the Gulf Coast near Tampa and New Orleans and has been found as far north as Tennessee. It was probably introduced in furniture. It attacks furniture, books, stationery, dry goods, and building timbers and frequently does a great deal of damage. It is found in buildings, never outdoors. Where it is found, its colonies are numerous but small.

Family **Hodotermítidae**—Dampwood Termites: This group includes three species of *Zootermópsis,* which occur along the Pacific Coast north to southern British Columbia. The adults are 13 mm or more in length, are somewhat flattened, and lack a fontanelle. There is no worker caste. These termites attack dead wood, and although they do not require a ground contact, some moisture in the wood is required. They generally occur in dead, damp, rotting logs, but frequently damage buildings, utility poles, and lumber, particularly in coastal regions where there is considerable fog.

The most common species in this group are *Z. nevadénsis* Banks and *Z. angusticóllis* (Hagen). *Zootermópsis nevadénsis* is a little over 13 mm long and lives in relatively dry habitats (especially dead tree trunks). The wingless forms are pale with a darker head, and the winged forms are dark brown with the head chestnut or orange. *Zootermópsis angusticóllis* is larger (about 18 mm long) and generally occurs in damp dead logs. Adults are pale with a brown head.

Family **Rhinotermítidae:** This group is represented in the United States by nine species (with one species extending northward into Canada) and includes the subterranean termites (*Reticulitérmes* and *Heterotérmes*) and the dampwood termites in the genus *Prorhinotérmes* (Figure 17–2C,D). The subterranean termites are widely distributed, but the dampwood termites occur only in Florida. These termites are small (adults are about 6–8 mm long). Wingless forms are very pale (soldiers have a pale brown head), and winged forms are black. There is a fontanelle on the front of the head (Figure 17–3, *fon*). The members of this group always maintain contact with the soil. They often construct earthen tubes to wood not in contact with the soil. The eastern subterranean termite, *Reticulitérmes flávipes* (Kollar) (Figure 17–5), is probably the most destructive species in the order and is the only termite occurring in the Northeast.

Coptotérmes formosànus Shiraki, a native of mainland China and Taiwan and a serious pest, has been introduced into Louisiana, Florida, and Texas. The soldiers can be recognized by their oval heads and a large fontanelle opening in the front margin of the head. The nest is underground or in wood.

Family **Termítidae:** This group is represented in the United States by 14 species in the Southwest. It includes the soldierless termites (*Anoplotérmes*), the desert termites (*Amitérmes* and *Gnáthamitérmes*), and the nasutiform termites (*Nasutitérmes* and *Tenuiróstritérmes*). The soldierless termites burrow under logs or cow chips and are not of economic importance. The desert termites are subterranean and occasionally damage the wood of buildings, poles,

and fence posts. The nasutiform termites attack trees or other objects on the ground and maintain a ground contact.

Economic Importance of Termites

Termites hold two positions from the economic point of view. On the one hand, they may be very destructive, since they feed upon and often destroy various structures or materials that people use: wooden portions of buildings, furniture, books, utility poles, fence posts, many fabrics, and the like (Figure 17–6). On the other hand, they are beneficial in that they assist in the conversion of dead trees and other plant products to substances that can be used by plants.

Reticulitérmes flávipes is the common termite throughout the eastern United States. This species occurs in buried wood, fallen trees, and logs. It must maintain a ground connection to obtain moisture. It cannot initiate a new colony in the wood in a house; the nest in the soil must be established first. Once the soil nest is established, these termites may enter buildings from the soil in one of five ways: (1) through timbers that are in direct contact with the soil, (2) through openings in rough stone foundations, (3) through openings or cracks in concrete-block foundations, (4) through expansion joints or cracks in concrete floors, or (5) by means of earthen tubes constructed over foundations or in hidden cracks and crevices in masonry.

Infestations of the subterranean termite in a building may be recognized by the swarming of the reproductives in the spring in or about the building, by mud protruding from cracks between boards or beams or along basement joists, by the earthen tubes extending from the soil to the wood, or by the hollowness of the wood in which the insects have been tunneling. A knife blade can easily be pushed into a timber hollowed out by termites, and such wood readily breaks apart.

Subterranean termites in buildings are controlled by two general methods: by proper construction of the buildings to render them termite-proof, and by the use of chemicals. The former involves construction in which no wood is in contact with the ground and in which the termites cannot reach the wooden part of the building through outside steps, through sills, or through the foundation. Control by chemicals involves their application to the wood or to the soil. Utility poles and fence posts, which must be in contact with the ground, may be rendered termite-proof by chemical treatment.

Figure 17–5. A group of eastern subterranean termites, *Reticulitérmes flávipes* (Kollar); note the soldier in the right central position of the picture. (Courtesy of Davidson.)

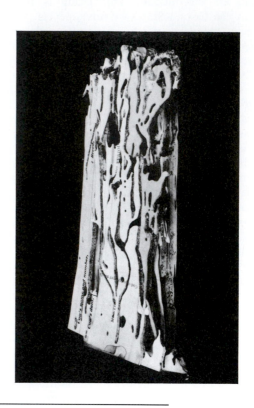

Figure 17–6. Termite damage. (Courtesy of Davidson.)

The best method of eliminating drywood termites is by fumigation. For such termites in buildings, a large tent of plastic or other impervious material is placed over the entire building. This is a rather expensive procedure. Drywood termites may also be eliminated by drilling holes in infested timbers, forcing a small amount of a poison dust into the holes, and then plugging up the holes. Termites constantly groom one another, and once a few individuals get this dust on themselves, the other individuals of the colony will eventually obtain it and be killed.

Collecting and Preserving Isóptera

Termites can be found by turning over dead logs or by digging into dead stumps. They may be collected with forceps or a moistened brush, or they may be shaken out of infested timbers onto a paper. Termites should be preserved in 70–80% alcohol. Most individuals are very soft-bodied and shrivel or become distorted if mounted on pins or points. It is often necessary to mount these insects on microscope slides for detailed study.

References

Araujo, R. L. 1977. Catálogo dos Isoptera do Novo Mondo. Rio de Janeiro: Academia Brasileira de Ciencias, 92 pp.

Banks, N., and T. E. Snyder. 1920. A revision of the Nearctic termites, with notes on their biology and distribution. Bull. U.S. Natl. Mus. No. 108, 228 pp.; illus.

Berger, B. G. 1947. How to recognize and control termites in Illinois. Ill. Nat. Hist. Surv. Circ. No. 41, 44 pp.; illus.

Ebeling, W. 1968. Termites: identification, biology, and control of termites attacking buildings. Calif. Agr. Expt. Sta. Extension Service Manual No. 38, 68 pp.

Ebeling, W. 1975. Isoptera: termites, pp. 118, 130–167, in Urban Entomology. Berkeley: Univ. California Press.

Ernst, E., and R. L. Araujo. 1986. A Bibliography of Termite Literature, 1966–1978. Chichester, England: Wiley, 903 pp.

Kofoid, C. A., S. F. Light, A. C. Horner, M. Randall, W. B. Herms, and E. E. Bowe, eds. 1934. Termites and Their Control. Berkeley: Univ. California Press, 734 pp.; illus.

Krishna, K. 1961. A generic revision and phylogenetic study of the family Kalotermitidae (Isoptera). Bull. Amer. Mus. Nat. Hist. 122(4):307–408; illus.

Krishna, K. 1966. A key to eight termite genera. Coop. Econ. Insect Rep. (USDA) 16(47):1091–1098.

Miller, E. M. 1949. A Handbook of Florida Termites. Coral Gables, Fla.: Univ. Miami Press, 30 pp.

Skaife, S. H. 1961. Dwellers in Darkness. New York: Doubleday, 180 pp.; illus.

Snyder, T. E. 1935. Our Enemy the Termite. Ithaca, N.Y.: Comstock, 196 pp.; illus.

Snyder, T. E. 1949. Catalogue of the termites (Isoptera) of the world. Smithson. Misc. Coll. 112(3953), 490 pp.

Snyder, T. E. 1954. Order Isoptera—The Termites of the United States and Canada. New York: Natl. Pest Control Assoc., 64 pp.; illus.

Snyder, T. E. 1956. Annotated subject-heading bibliography of termites, 1350 B.C. to A.D. 1954. Smithson. Misc. Coll. 130(4258), 305 pp.

Snyder, T. E. 1961. Supplement to the annotated subject-heading bibliography of termites, 1955 to 1960. Smithson. Misc. Coll. 143(3), 137 pp.

Snyder, T. E. 1968. Second supplement to the annotated subject-heading bibliography of termites, 1961–1965. Smithson. Misc. Coll. 152, 188 pp.

Vickery, V. R., and D. K. McE. Kevan. 1985. The grasshoppers, crickets, and related insects of Canada and adjacent regions: Ulonata: Dermaptera, Cheleutoptera, Notoptera, Dictuoptera, Grylloptera, and Orthoptera. The Insects and Arachnids of Canada, Part 14. Ottawa: Can. Govt. Publ. Centre, 918 pp.; illus.

Weesner, F. M. 1960. Evolution and biology of the termites. Annu. Rev. Entomol. 5:153–170.

Weesner, F. M. 1965. The Termites of the United States: A Handbook. Elizabeth, N. J.: Natl. Pest Control Assoc., 71 pp.

Weesner, F. M. 1987. Order Isoptera, pp. 132–139 in Immature Insects, ed. F. W. Stehr. Dubuque, Iowa: Kendall/Hunt.

Chapter 18

Order Dermáptera[1]
Earwigs

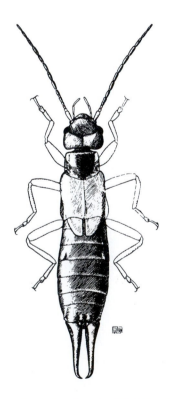

Earwigs are elongate, slender, somewhat flattened insects that resemble rove beetles but have forceps-like cerci (Figure 18–1). Adults may be winged or wingless, with one or two pairs of wings. If winged, the front wings are short, leathery, and veinless (and are usually called tegmina or elytra), and the hind wings (when present) are membranous and rounded, with radiating veins. At rest the hind wings are folded beneath the front wings with only the tips projecting. The tarsi are three-segmented; the mouthparts are of the chewing type; and the metamorphosis is simple.

Immature earwigs have fewer antennal segments than adults, with segments added at each molt. Immatures can be told from adults by the combination of a malelike ten-segmented abdomen (adult females have only eight apparent segments) with femalelike straight forceps (adult male forceps usually have the inner margin distinctly curved) (Figure 18–2).

Earwigs are largely nocturnal in habit and hide during the day in cracks, in crevices, under bark, and in debris. They feed mainly on dead and decaying vegetable matter, but some occasionally feed on living plants, and a few are predaceous. Some of the winged forms are good fliers, but others fly only rarely. The eggs are laid in burrows in the ground or

Figure 18–1. The European earwig, *Forfícula auriculària* L., female, about 4×. (Courtesy of Fulton and the Oregon Agricultural Experiment Station.)

[1]Dermáptera: *derma*, skin; *ptera*, wings (referring to the texture of the front wings).

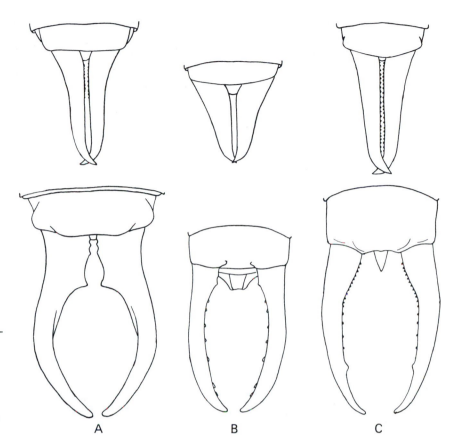

Figure 18–2. Anal forceps of Dermáptera. **A,** *Forfícula auriculària* L.; **B,** *Làbia mìnor* (L.); **C,** *Dòru lineàre* (Eschscholtz). Upper figures, forceps of female; lower figures, forceps of male.

A   B   C

in debris, generally in clusters, and are guarded by the female until they hatch. Earwigs overwinter in the adult stage.

Some species of earwigs have glands opening on the dorsal side of the third and fourth abdominal segments, from which they emit a foul-smelling fluid that serves as a means of protection. Some species can squirt this fluid 75–100 mm.

The name "earwig" is derived from an old superstition that these insects enter people's ears. This belief is entirely without foundation. Earwigs do not bite, but, if handled, will attempt to pinch with their cerci, and the abdomen is quite maneuverable. The larger earwigs, especially the males, can inflict a painful pinch.

Classification of the Dermáptera

The order Dermáptera is usually divided into three suborders, the Arixenìna, the Diploglossàta (Hemimerìna), and the Forficulìna. Some authorities consider the Arixenìna to be a family (Arixénidae) of the Forficulìna. The Arixenìna are Malayan ectoparasites of bats, and the Diploglossàta are South African parasites of rodents. The Forficulìna is the only suborder occurring in North America. Twelve of the 22 North American species of earwigs have been introduced from Europe or from the tropics. Our species represent six families, adults of which may be separated by the following key.

Key to the Families of Dermáptera

1.   Second tarsal segment extending distally beneath base of third (Figure
            18–3D); antennae with 12–16 segments **2**

1'.   Second tarsal segment not extending distally beneath base of third (Figure
            18–3C); antennae with 10–31 segments **3**

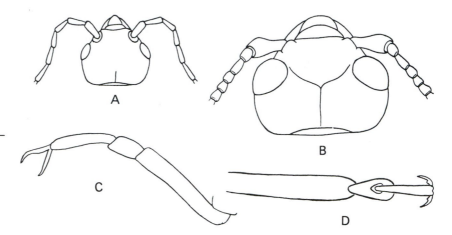

Figure 18–3. Characters of the Dermáptera. **A,** head of *Làbia mìnor* (L.), dorsal view; **B,** head of *Labidùra ripària* Pallas, dorsal view; **C,** tarsus of *Labidùra*; **D,** tarsus of *Forfícula*.

2(1).	Distal extension of second tarsal segment dilated, broader than third segment (Figure 18–3D), and without dense brush of hairs beneath; antennae with 12–16 segments; color usually yellowish or brownish; widely distributed ....**Forficùlidae** p. 245
2'.	Distal extension of second tarsal segment not dilated, no wider than third segment, and with dense brush of hairs beneath; antennae 12-segmented; color black; California ....**Chelisóchidae** p. 245
3(1').	A large padlike arolium between tarsal claws; male forceps curved strongly inward; recorded near Miami, Florida ....**Pygidicrànidae** p. 244
3'.	No arolium between tarsal claws; male forceps not strongly curved (Figure 18–2B,C); widely distributed **4**
4(3').	Antennae with 25–30 segments; pronotum light brown with 2 dark longitudinal stripes; length 20–30 mm; southern United States, from North Carolina to Florida and California ....**Labidùridae** p. 245
4'.	Antennae with 10–24 segments; pronotum uniformly colored; length 4–25 mm; widely distributed...**5**
5(4').	Antennae with 14–24 segments; tegmina present as rounded flaps not meeting at inner basal margins, or absent; right forceps of male more strongly curved than left; length 9–25 mm ....**Carcinophòridae** p. 244
5'.	Antennae with 10–16 segments; tegmina normally developed and meeting along entire midline; male forceps symmetrical; length less than 20 mm ....**Labìidae** p. 245

Family **Pygidicrànidae:** This family is represented in the United States by a single species, *Pyragrópsis búscki* (Caudell), which is fully winged and 12–14 mm in length. This insect has been collected in southern Florida and also occurs in Cuba, Jamaica, and Hispaniola.

Family **Carcinophòridae** (Psalídidae, Anisolàbidae; Labidùridae in part)—Seaside and Ring-Legged Earwigs: The seaside earwig, *Anisólabis maritìma* (Bo-nelli), is a wingless, blackish brown insect 20–25 mm in length with 20–24 antennal segments. It is an introduced species that is predaceous and usually found beneath debris along seashores. It now occurs locally along the Atlantic, Pacific, and Gulf coasts. The genus *Euboréllia* contains six North American species, which are 9–18 mm in length with 14–20 antennal segments. These earwigs are usually found in debris and occur mainly in the southern states.

The most common species is the ring-legged earwig, *E. annùlipes* (Lucas), a wingless species that is widely distributed and sometimes invades houses. *Euboréllia cincticóllis* (Gerstaecker) was introduced into California and Arizona. This species has three morphs, with individuals exhibiting well-developed wings, shortened front wings with the hind wings reduced or absent, or lacking both pairs of wings altogether.

Family **Labìidae**—Little Earwigs: This family contains eight North American species in three genera, with the most common species being *Làbia mìnor* (L.), an introduced species. This insect is 4–7 mm in length and covered with golden hair. It is a good flier and can be found flying during the early evening or attracted to lights at night. *Màrava pulchélla* (Audinet-Serville) is a larger (8–10 mm in length), shining reddish brown species in which individuals can possess either well-developed wings or short front wings with the hind wings reduced or absent. This insect is found in the southern states. The genus *Vóstox* contains three species, one of which, *V. apicedentàtus* (Caudell), is 9–12 mm in length and fairly common around dead leaves and cacti in the desert regions of the Southwest.

Family **Labidùridae**—Striped Earwigs: This group includes a single North American species, *Labidùra ripària* (Pallas), an introduced species that occurs in the southern part of the United States, from North Carolina south to Florida and west to California. This species is most readily recognized by its large size (length 20–30 mm) and the longitudinal dark stripes on the pronotum and tegmina. It is nocturnal and predaceous, hiding under debris during the day.

Family **Chelisóchidae**—Black Earwigs: This group includes a single North American species, *Chelísoches mòrio* (Fabricius), which is a native of the tropics (islands in the Pacific) but has become established in California. This insect is black and 16–20 mm in length.

Family **Forficùlidae**—European and Spine-Tailed Earwigs: The most common member of this family is the European earwig, *Forfícula auriculària* L., a brownish black insect 15–20 mm in length (Figure 18–1). It is widely distributed throughout southern Canada south to North Carolina, Arizona, and California. It occasionally causes substantial damage to vegetable crops, cereals, fruit trees, and ornamental plants. The spine-tailed earwigs (*Dòru*) are a little smaller (12–18 mm in length), and are so called because the male has a short median spine on the terminal abdominal segment (Figure 18–2C).

Collecting and Preserving Dermáptera

Earwigs generally must be looked for in various protected places: in debris, in cracks and crevices, under bark, and about the roots of grasses and sedges. They are not often collected with a net. Some will come to lights at night, and some may be taken in pitfall traps (Figure 36–7A). They are normally preserved dry, on either pins or points. If pinned, they are pinned through the right tegmen, as are beetles.

References

Blatchley, W. S. 1920. Orthoptera of Northeastern America. Indianapolis: Nature, 784 pp.; illus.

Brindle, A. 1966. A revision of the subfamily Labidurinae (Dermaptera: Labiduridae). Ann. Mag. Nat. Hist. (13)9:239–269; illus.

Brindle, A. 1971a. A revision of the Labiidae (Dermaptera) of the Neotropical and Nearctic regions. II. Geracinae and Labiinae. J. Nat. Hist. 5:155–182.

Brindle, A. 1971b. A revision of the Labiidae (Dermaptera) of the Neotropical and Nearctic regions. III. Spongiphorinae. J. Nat. Hist. 5:521–568.

Brindle, A. 1971c. The Dermaptera of the Caribbean. Stud. Fauna Curaçao and Other Caribbean Islands, 131, 38: 1–75.

Brindle, A. 1987. Order Dermaptera, pp. 171–178 *in* F. W. Stehr (ed.), Immature Insects, vol. 1. Dubuque, Iowa: Kendall/Hunt, 754 pp.; illus.

Cantrell, I. J. 1968. An annotated list of the Dermaptera, Dictyoptera, Phasmatoptera, and Orthoptera of Michigan. Mich. Entomol. 1:299–346; illus.

Eisner, T. 1960. Defense mechanisms of arthropods. II. The chemical and mechanical weapons of an earwig. Psyche, 67:62–70; illus.

Giles, E. T. 1963. The comparative external morphology and affinities of the Dermaptera. Trans. Roy. Entomol. Soc. Lond. 115:95–164; illus.

Gurney, A. B. 1972. Important recent name changes among earwigs of the genus Doru (Dermaptera, Forficulidae). Coop. Econ. Insect Rep. (USDA) 22(13):182–185.

Hebard, M. 1934. The Dermaptera and Orthoptera of Illinois. Ill. Nat. Hist. Surv. Bull. 20(3):125–279; illus.

Helfer, J. R. 1972 (2nd ed.). How to Know the Grasshoppers, Cockroaches, and Their Allies. Dubuque, Iowa: Wm. C. Brown, 359 pp.; illus.

Hinks, W. D. 1955–1959. A Systematic Monograph of the Dermaptera of the World Based on Material in the British Museum (Natural History). Part I, Pygidicranidae, Subfamily Diplatyinae, 132 pp.; illus. (1955). Part II, Pygidicranidae Excluding Diplatyinae, 218 pp.; illus. (1959). London: British Museum (Natural History).

Hoffman, K. M. 1987. Earwigs (Dermaptera) of South Carolina, with a key to the eastern North American species and a checklist of the North American fauna. Proc. Entomol. Soc. Wash. 89:1–14; illus.

Knabke, J. J., and A. A. Grigarick. 1971. Biology of the African earwig, *Euborellia cincticollis* (Gerstaecker) in California and comparative notes on *Euborellia annulipes* (Lucas). Hilgardia 41:157–194.

Langston, R. L., and J. A. Powell. 1975. The earwigs of California. Bull. Calif. Insect Surv. 20:1–25; illus.

Popham, E. J. 1965. A key to the Dermaptera subfamilies. Entomologist 98:126–136.

Popham, E. J. 1965. Towards a natural classification of the Dermaptera. Proc. 12th Int. Congr. Entomol. Lond. (1964): 114–115.

Steinmann, H. 1978. A systematic survey of the species belonging to the genus *Labidura* Leach, 1815 (Dermaptera). Acta Zool. Acad. Sci. Hung. 25:415–423.

Vickery, V. R., and D. K. McE. Kevan. 1985. The grasshoppers, crickets, and related insects of Canada and adjacent regions: Ulonata: Dermaptera, Cheleutoptera, Notoptera, Dictuoptera, Grylloptera, and Orthoptera. The Insects and Arachnids of Canada, Part 14. Ottawa: Can. Govt. Publ. Centre, 918 pp.; illus.

Chapter 19

Order Embiidìna[1]
Web-Spinners

The web-spinners are small, slender, chiefly tropical insects, represented by 11 species in the southern United States. The body of adult males is somewhat flattened, but that of females and young is cylindrical. Most species are about 10 mm in length. The antennae are filiform; ocelli are lacking; the mouthparts are of the chewing type; and the head is prognathous. The legs are short and stout; the tarsi are three-segmented; and the hind femora are greatly enlarged. The basal segment of the front tarsus is enlarged and contains silk glands. The silk is spun from a hollow hairlike structure on the ventral surface of the basal and second tarsal segments. The males of most species are winged, but some are wingless or have only vestigial wings. Both winged and wingless males may occur in the same species. The females are always wingless. The wings are similar in size, shape, and venation, and the venation is somewhat reduced (Figure 19–1A). The venation is characterized by certain blood-sinus veins (Sc, R_1, Cu, and 1A), which stiffen for flight by blood pressure. When not in use the wings are very flexible. The abdomen is ten-segmented with rudiments of the eleventh, and bears a pair of cerci. The cerci are generally two-segmented, but the adult males of some species have the left cercus 1-segmented. The terminal appendages of the female are always symmetrical, but they are asymmetrical in the male. The web-spinners undergo simple metamorphosis. Some species (only one in the United States) are parthenogenetic.

Web-spinners live in silken galleries spun in leaf litter, under stones, in soil cracks, in bark crevices, and in epiphytic plants. In most silk-producing insects the silk is spun by modified rectal glands or by salivary glands opening near the mouth, but in web-spinners the silk is produced by glands in the front tarsi. All instars, even the first, are able to spin silk. Most species live in colonies made up of a parent female and her brood. Web-spinners often feign death when disturbed, but on occasion can move very rapidly, usually running backward. The eggs are elongate-oval and are usually laid in a single-layered patch in the galleries. They are coated in most species with a paste of chewed habitat material or fecal pellets. Females guard their eggs and early-stage nymphs. Web-spinners feed mostly on dead plant materials, which also constitute the substrate of their galleries. These insects are easily cultured in tubes or jars, and this is the best method of securing adult males, which are usually required for identification to family.

[1]Embiidìna: from *embio*, lively. This chapter was written by Dr. Edward S. Ross, with minor editorial changes by the authors.

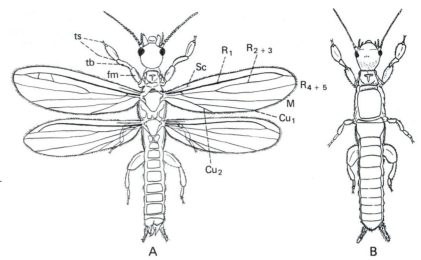

Figure 19–1. A web-spinner, *Oligótoma sáundersii* (Westwood). **A,** winged male; **B,** wingless female. *fm,* femur; *tb,* tibia; *ts,* tarsus. (Redrawn from Essig.)

Key to the Families of Embiidìna

1.	Adults and immatures with two bladderlike papillae on ventral surface of basal segment of hind tarsus (*Haploémbia*) ....**Oligotómidae** (in part)	p. 248
1′.	Adults and immatures with only one bladderlike papilla on ventral surface of hind tarsus **2**	
2(1′).	Mandibles of adult males dentate apically, left cercus 2-segmented, inner surface of basal segment lacking peglike setae **3**	
2′.	Mandibles of adult males not dentate apically, left cercus 1-segmented, inner surface of apex with a few peglike setae ....**Anisembìidae**	p. 248
3(2).	R_{4+5} forked ....**Teratembìidae**	p. 248
3′.	R_{4+5} not forked ....**Oligotómidae** (in part)	p. 248

Family **Anisembìidae:** Anisembìidae are represented in the United States by three species: *Anisémbia texàna* (Melander) of the South Central states, and *Dactylocérca rùbra* (Ross) and *D. áshworthi* Ross of the Southwest. In arid habitats both winged and wingless males occur in colonies of *A. texàna.* In marginal habitats the males are always wingless.

Family **Teratembìidae** (Oligembìidae): This family is represented in the United States by five species: *Oligémbia húbbardi* (Hagen) of Florida, *O. melanùra* Ross of Louisiana and Texas, *Diràdius lobàtus* (Ross) in the lower Rio Grande valley of Texas, *D. caribbeànus* (Ross), in the Florida Keys, and *D. vandỳkei* (Ross) of the Southwest.

Family **Oligotómidae:** The Oligotómidae are represented in the United States by three introduced Old World species: *Oligótoma saundérsii* (Westwood) of the southeastern states, *O. nìgra* Hagen, of the Southwest (extending as far east as San Antonio, Texas), and *Haploémbia soliéri* (Rambur) of the Southwest (extending as far north as southern Oregon). The last species is parthenogenetic, but a bisexual form has recently been introduced into central California.

Collecting and Preserving Embiidìna

The males, which are generally more easily identified than the females, are best collected at lights. In their normal habitat these insects are probably most readily collected during and following the rainy season, while the soil is damp. Many specimens collected at this time may be immatures, but they can be reared to maturity (males and females) in jars containing some dried grass and leaves that are kept somewhat moist.

Web-spinners should be preserved in 70% alcohol. For detailed study it may be desirable to clear the specimens in KOH and mount them on microscope slides (see Ross 1940, p. 634).

References

Ross, E. S. 1940. A revision of the Embioptera of North America. Ann. Entomol. Soc. Amer. 33:629–676; illus.

Ross, E. S. 1944. A revision of the Embioptera of the New World. Proc. U.S. Natl. Mus. 94(3175):401–504; illus.

Ross, E. S. 1970. Biosystematics of the Embioptera. Annu. Rev. Entomol. 15:157–171.

Ross, E. S. 1984. A synopsis of the Embiidina of the United States. Proc. Entomol. Soc. Wash. 86:82–93; illus.

Ross, E. S. 1987. Order Embiidina (Embioptera), pp. 179–183 in F. W. Stehr (ed.), Immature Insects, vol. 1, Dubuque, Iowa: Kendall/Hunt, 754 pp.; illus.

Chapter 20

Order Plecóptera[1]
Stoneflies

Stoneflies are mostly medium-sized or small, somewhat flattened, soft-bodied, rather drab-colored insects found near streams or rocky lake shores. They are poor fliers and are seldom found far from water. Most species have four membranous wings (Figure 20–1). The front wings are elongate and rather narrow and usually have a series of cross veins between M and Cu_1 and between Cu_1 and Cu_2. The hind wings are slightly shorter than the front wings and usually have a well-developed anal lobe that is folded fanwise when the wings are at rest. A few species of stoneflies have the wings reduced or absent, usually in the male. Stoneflies at rest hold the wings flat over the abdomen (Figure 20–2A). The antennae are long, slender, and many-segmented. The tarsi are three-segmented. Cerci are present and may be long or short. The mouthparts are of the chewing type, though in many adults (which do not feed) they are somewhat reduced. The stoneflies undergo simple metamorphosis, and the nymphal stages of development are aquatic.

Stonefly nymphs (Figures 20–2B and 20–3) are somewhat elongate, flattened insects with long antennae and long cerci, and often with branched gills on the thorax and about the bases of the legs. They are very similar to mayfly nymphs, but lack a median caudal filament; that is, they have only two tails, while mayfly nymphs nearly always have three. Stonefly nymphs have two tarsal claws and mayfly nymphs have only one, and the gills are different: mayfly nymphs have leaflike gills along the sides of the abdomen (Figure 10–2). Stonefly nymphs are often found under stones in streams or along lake shores (hence the common name of these insects), but may occasionally be found anywhere in a stream where food is available. A few species are known to live in underground water, and their nymphs sometimes appear in wells or other drinking water supplies. Some species are plant feeders in the nymphal stage, and others are predaceous or omnivorous. Some species of stoneflies emerge, feed, and mate during the fall and winter months. The nymphs of these species are generally plant feeders, and the adults feed chiefly on blue-green algae and are diurnal in feeding habits. The species that emerge during the summer vary in nymphal feeding habits. Many do not feed as adults.

In many species of stoneflies the sexes get together in response to acoustic signals. The males drum by tapping the tip of the abdomen on the substrate. Virgin females respond to this drumming, and answer with a drumming of their own either during or immediately after the male drumming.

[1]Plecóptera: *pleco*, folded or plaited; *ptera*, wings (referring to the fact that the anal region of the hind wings is folded when the wings are at rest).

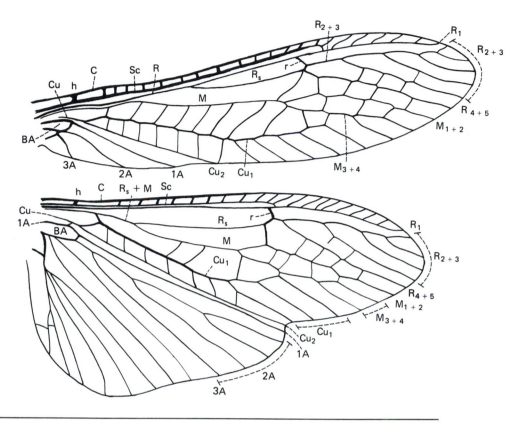

Figure 20–1.   Wings of a perlid stonefly. *BA,* basal anal cell.

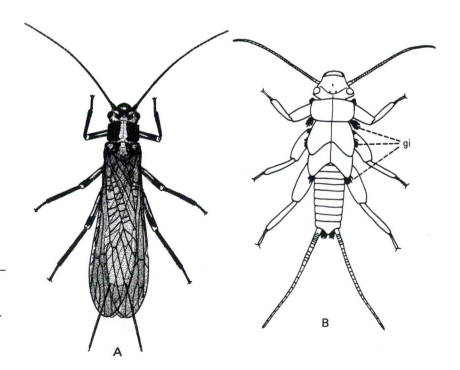

Figure 20–2.   **A,** an adult stonefly, *Cliopérla clio* Newman (Perlódidae); **B,** a stonefly nymph. **gi,** gills. (Courtesy of Frison and the Illinois Natural History Survey; **B,** redrawn from Frison.)

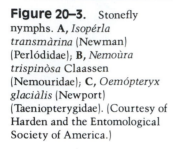

Figure 20–3. Stonefly nymphs. **A,** *Isopérla transmàrina* (Newman) (Perlódidae); **B,** *Nemoùra trispinòsa* Claassen (Nemouridae); **C,** *Oemópteryx glaciàlis* (Newport) (Taeniopterygidae). (Courtesy of Harden and the Entomological Society of America.)

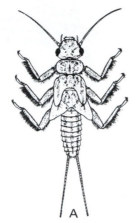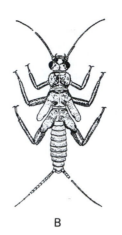

The males drum throughout their adult life, and the signals are species-specific.

Classification of the Plecóptera

This order in North America is divided into two groups of families on the basis of the structure of the labium (couplet 1 of key, and Figure 20–4). Different authorities recognize different numbers of families; we follow here the arrangement of Stark *et al.* (1986), who recognize nine families in North America. This arrangement is outlined below, with alternate names and arrangements in parentheses. The numbers in parentheses, representing the numbers of North American species, are from Stark *et al.* (1986).

Group Euhológnatha (Filipálpia, Hológnatha) (280)
    Taeniopterýgidae (Nemoùridae in part) (33)—winter stoneflies
    Nemoùridae(Nemourìnae of Nemoùridae) (64)—spring stoneflies
    Leùctridae (Nemoùridae in part) (52)—rolled-winged stoneflies
    Capnìidae (Nemoùridae in part) (131)—small winter stoneflies
Group Systellógnatha (Setipálpia, Subulipálpia) (257)
    Pteronarcỳidae (Pteronárcidae) (10)—giant stoneflies
    Peltopérlidae (17)—roachlike stoneflies
    Pérlidae (44)—common stoneflies

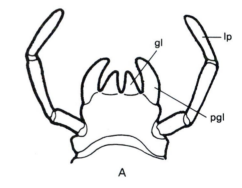

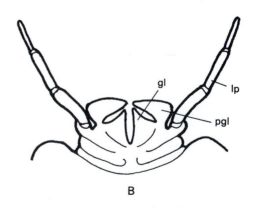

Figure 20–4. Labia of adult stoneflies, ventral views. **A,** *Pteronárcys* (Pteronarcỳidae); **B,** *Pérla* (Pérlidae). *gl,* glossa; *lp,* labial palp; *pgl,* paraglossa.

Perlódidae (including Isopérlidae) (114)—perlodid stoneflies

Chloropérlidae (72)—green stoneflies

The principal characters used to separate the families of stoneflies are wing venation, characters of the tarsi, and the gill remnants. The gill remnants are usually shriveled and difficult to see in pinned and dried specimens. Their location on the thorax is shown in Figure 20–5. The characters of the gill remnants are much easier to study in specimens that are preserved in alcohol.

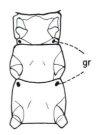

Figure 20–5. Thorax of *Acroneùria* (Pérlidae), ventral view. *gr*, gill remnants. (Redrawn from Frison, courtesy of the Illinois Natural History Survey.)

Key to the Families of Plecóptera

Keys to nymphs are given by Claassen (1931), Jewett (1956), Pennak (1978), Harper (1984), and Stewart and Stark (1984).

1.	Labium with glossae and paraglossae about the same size, labium thus appearing to have 4 similar terminal lobes (Figure 20–4A)	**2**
1'.	Labium with glossae very small, appearing to have 2 terminal lobes (the paraglossae), each with a small basomesal lobe (the glossae) (Figure 20–4B)	**7**
2(1).	Basal tarsal segment short, much shorter than third segment (Figure 20–6E)	**3**
2'.	Basal tarsal segment longer, nearly as long as or longer than third segment (Figure 20–6A–D)	**4**

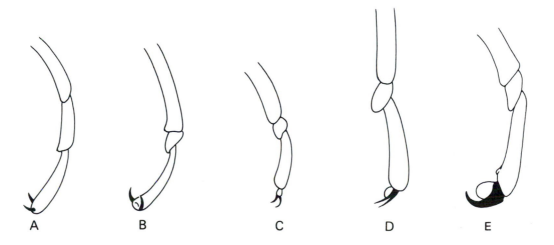

Figure 20–6. Hind tarsi of Plecóptera. **A,** *Taeniópteryx* (Taeniopterygidae); **B,** *Leùctra* (Leuctridae); **C,** *Nemoùra* (Nemouridae); **D,** *Allocápnia* (Capniidae); **E,** *Pteronárcys* (Pteronarcỳidae).

3(2).   Anal area of front wing with 2 series of cross veins (Figure 20–7A); 3 ocelli; gill remnants on sides of first 2 or 3 abdominal segments; large stoneflies, usually over 25 mm in length ....**Pteronarcýidae**   p. 256

3'.   Anal area of front wing with no rows of cross veins (Figure 20–7B–E); 2 ocelli; no gill remnants on abdominal segments; length less than 25 mm ....**Peltopérlidae**   p. 256

4(2').   Second segment of tarsi about as long as each of the other two segments (Figure 20–6A) ....**Taeniopterýgidae**   p. 254

4'.   Second segment of tarsi much shorter than each of the other two segments (Figure 20–6B–D) **5**

5(4').   Cerci short and 1-segmented; front wing with 4 or more cubital cross veins, 2A forked (Figure 20–7C) **6**

5'.   Cerci long and with 4 or more segments; front wing with only 1 or 2 cubital cross veins, 2A not forked (Figure 20–7E) ....**Capniidae**   p. 256

6(5).   Front wings flat at rest, with an apical cross vein (Figure 20–7D, *apc*) ....**Nemoùridae**   p. 254

6'.   Front wings at rest bent down around sides of abdomen, without an apical cross vein (Figure 20–7C) ....**Leùctridae**   p. 254

7(1').   Front wing with cu-a (if present) opposite basal anal cell, or distad of it by no more than its own length; remnants of branched gills on thorax (Figure 20–5) ....**Pérlidae**   p. 256

7'.   Front wing with cu-a (if present) usually distad of basal anal cell by more than its own length; no remnants of branched gills on thorax (some Perlódidae may have remnants of unbranched or fingerlike gills on thorax) **8**

8(7').   Hind wings with anal lobe well developed, with 5–10 anal veins; front wing with no forked vein arising from basal anal cell; pronotum rectangular, the corners acute or narrowly rounded (Figure 20–8B,D); length 6–25 mm ....**Perlódidae**   p. 256

8'.   Hind wings with anal lobe reduced (rarely absent), and usually with no more than 4 anal veins; front wing sometimes with forked vein arising from basal anal cell; pronotum with corners rounded (Figure 20–8C); length 15 mm or less ....**Chloropérlidae**   p. 256

GROUP **Euhológnatha:** These stoneflies have the glossae and paraglossae similar in size (Figure 20–4A). They are principally plant feeders, both as adults and nymphs. This is the larger of the two groups, and contains about three-fifths of the North American species.

Family **Taeniopterýgidae**—Winter Stoneflies: The members of this family are dark brown to black insects, generally 13 mm or less in length, which emerge from January to April. The nymphs (Figure 20–3C) are phytophagous and occur in large streams and rivers. Some adults are flower feeders. Two common eastern species in this group are *Taeniópteryx maùra* (Pictet), 8–12 mm in length, which emerges

from January to March, and *Strophópteryx fasciàta* (Burmeister), 10–15 mm in length, which emerges during March and April.

Family **Nemoùridae**—Spring Stoneflies: The adults of this family are brown or black in color, and appear from April to June. The nymphs (Figure 20–3B) are plant feeders, and usually occur in small streams with sandy bottoms.

Family **Leùctridae**—Rolled-Winged Stoneflies: These stoneflies are for the most part 10 mm or less in length and brown or black in color. The wings at rest are bent down over the sides of the abdomen. These insects are most common in hilly or mountainous regions, and the nymphs usually occur in small

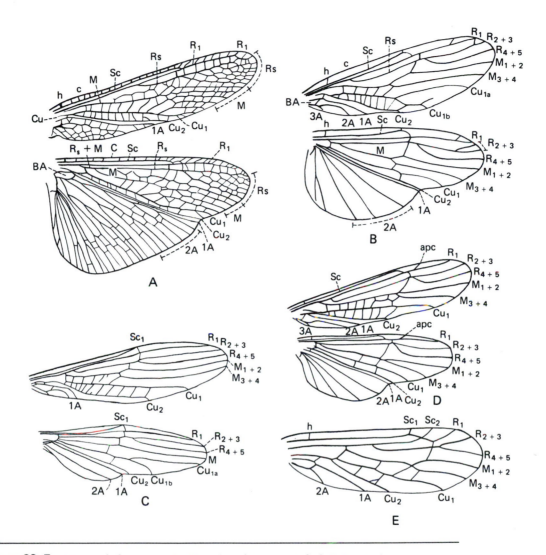

Figure 20–7. Wings of Plecóptera. **A,** *Pteronárcys* (Pteronarcýidae); **B,** *Taenionèma* (Taeniopterygidae); **C,** *Leùctra* (Leuctridae); **D,** *Nemoùra* (Nemouridae); **E,** front wing of a capniid, *apc,* apical cross vein. *BA,* basal anal cell.

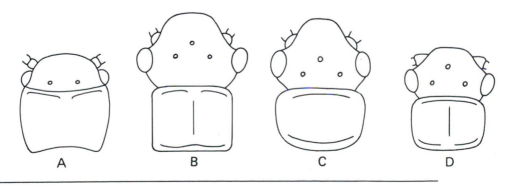

Figure 20–8. Head and pronotum of Plecóptera. **A,** *Peltopérla* (Peltopérlidae); **B,** *Isogenòides* (Perlódidae); **C,** *Chloropérla* (Chloropérlidae); **D,** *Isopérla* (Perlódidae). (Redrawn from Frison, courtesy of the Illinois Natural History Survey.)

streams. The adults appear from March to December.

Family **Capniidae**—Small Winter Stoneflies: This is the largest family in the order, and its members, which are blackish in color and mostly 10 mm in length or less, emerge during the winter months. The wings are short or rudimentary in some species. Most of the capniids occurring in the East belong to the genus *Allocápnia*.

GROUP **Systellógnatha**: These stoneflies have the glossae very small and appearing as a basomesal lobe of the paraglossae (Figure 20–4B). They are mostly predaceous as nymphs and nonfeeding as adults.

Family **Pteronarcyidae**—Giant Stoneflies: This family includes the largest insects in the order; females of a common eastern species, *Pteronárcys dorsàta* (Say), may sometimes reach a length (measured to the wing tips) of 65 mm. The nymphs are plant feeders and occur in medium-sized to large rivers. The adults are nocturnal in habit and often come to lights. They do not feed. They appear in late spring to early summer.

Family **Peltopérlidae**—Roachlike Stoneflies: This family is so called because the nymphs are somewhat cockroachlike in appearance. Most of these stoneflies are western or northern in distribution. The most common eastern species are brown and 12–18 mm in length.

Family **Pérlidae**—Common Stoneflies: This family contains the stoneflies most often collected. The adults are nonfeeding spring and summer forms, and most of them are 20–40 mm in length. The nymphs are mostly predaceous.

Two eastern species in this family have only two ocelli, *Perlinélla éphyre* (Newman) and *Neopérla clýmene* (Newman). Both are about 12 mm in length and brown, with somewhat grey wings. *Neopérla clýmene* has the ocelli close together, and *P. éphyre* has them far apart. *Perlinélla drỳmo* (Newman), 10–20 mm in length, is brown, with two black spots on the yellow head, and it has a row of cross veins in the anal area of the front wing. *Perlésta plácida* (Hagen), 9–14 mm in length and nocturnal in habit, and *Agnetìna capitàta* (Pictet), 20–24 mm in length and diurnal in habit, have the costal edge of the front wing yellow. One of the largest and most common genera is *Acroneùria*. The adults in this genus are relatively large (20–40 mm in length), and the males have a disklike structure in the middle of the posterior portion of the ninth abdominal sternum.

Family **Perlódidae**: The most common members of this family (Figure 20–2A) usually have green wings and the body yellow or green and are 6–15 mm

in length. The adults are chiefly pollen feeders and diurnal in habit. Other less common species are brown or black in color and 10–25 mm in length. The nymphs are omnivores or carnivores.

Family **Chloropérlidae**—Green Stoneflies: The adults of this family are 6–15 mm in length and yellow or green in color. They appear in the spring. *Haplopérla brévis* (Banks), a common eastern species, is 6–9 mm in length and bright green in color and has no anal lobe in the hind wing. The stoneflies belonging to the genus *Allopérla*, of which there are several eastern species, are 8–15 mm in length and have a small anal lobe in the hind wing.

Collecting and Preserving Plecóptera

During the warmer days in the fall, winter, and spring, adults of the winter species may be found resting on bridges, fence posts, and other objects near the streams in which the nymphs develop. Many species may be collected by sweeping the foliage along the banks of streams. Bridges are a favorite resting place for many species throughout the year. Many of the summer forms are attracted to lights. The nymphs are to be found in streams, usually under stones or in the bottom debris.

Both adult and nymphal stoneflies should be preserved in alcohol. Pinned adults often shrink, with the result that some characters, particularly those of the genitalia and the gill remnants, are difficult to make out.

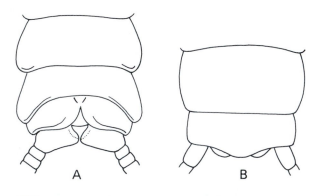

Figure 20–9. Terminal abdominal segments of male Plecóptera, dorsal view. **A,** *Isogenòides* (Perlódidae); **B,** *Isopérla* (Perlódidae). (Redrawn from Frison, courtesy of the Illinois Natural History Survey.)

References

Baumann, R. W. 1987. Order Plecoptera, pp. 186–195 *in* F. W. Stehr (ed.), Immature Insects, vol. 1. Dubuque, Iowa: Kendall/Hunt, 754 pp.; illus.

Baumann, R. W., A. R. Gaufin, and R. F. Surdick. 1977. The stoneflies (Plecoptera) of the Rocky Mountains. Mem. Amer. Entomol. Soc. 31, 208 pp.; illus.

Claassen, P. W. 1931. Plecoptera nymphs of America (north of Mexico). Thomas Say Foundation Publ. 3, 199 pp.; illus.

Frison, T. H. 1935. The stoneflies, or Plecoptera, of Illinois. Ill. Nat. Hist. Surv. Bull. 20(4):281–471; illus.

Frison, T. H. 1942. Studies of North American Plecoptera, with special reference to the fauna of Illinois. Ill. Nat. Hist. Surv. Bull. 22(2):231–355; illus.

Gaufin, A. R., A. V. Nebeker, and J. Sessions. 1966. The stoneflies (Plecoptera) of Utah. Univ. Utah Biol. Ser. 14:9–89; illus.

Harper, P. P. 1984. Plecoptera, pp. 182–230 *in* An Introduction to the Aquatic Insects of North America, 2nd ed., ed. R. W. Merritt and K. W. Cummins. Dubuque, Iowa: Kendall/Hunt.

Hitchcock, S. W. 1974. Guide to the insects of Connecticut. Part VII. The Plecoptera or stoneflies of Connecticut. Conn. State Geol. Nat. Hist. Surv. Bull. 107:1–262; illus.

Illies, J. 1965. Phylogeny and zoogeography of the Plecoptera. Annu. Rev. Entomol. 10:117–140; illus.

Jewett, S. G., Jr. 1956. Plecoptera, pp. 155–181 *in* Aquatic Insects of California, ed. R. L. Usinger. Berkeley: Univ. California Press; illus.

Jewett, S. G., Jr. 1959. The stoneflies (Plecoptera) of the Pacific Northwest. Ore. State Monogr. No. 3, 95 pp.; illus.

Kondratieff, B. C., and R. F Kirchner. 1987. Additions, taxonomic corrections, and faunal affinities of the stoneflies of Virginia, USA. Proc. Entomol. Soc. Wash. 89:24–30.

Needham, J. G., and P. W. Claassen. 1925. A monograph of the Plecoptera or stoneflies of America north of Mexico. Thomas Say Foundation Publ. 2, 397 pp.; illus.

Pennak, R. W. 1978 (2nd ed.). Fresh-Water Invertebrates of the United States. New York: Wiley Interscience, 803 pp.; illus.

Ricker, W. E. 1952. Systematic studies in Plecoptera. Ind. Univ. Stud. Sci. Ser. 18:1–200; illus.

Ricker, W. E. 1959. Plecoptera, pp. 941–957 *in* Fresh-Water Biology, ed. W. T. Edmondson. New York: Wiley; illus.

Ross, H. H., and W. E. Ricker. 1971. The classification, evolution, and dispersal of the winter stonefly genus *Allocapnia*. Ill. Biol. Monogr. No. 43, 240 pp.

Stark, B. P., S. W. Szczytko, and R. W. Baumann. 1986. North American Stoneflies (Plecoptera): Systematics, distribution, and taxonomic references. Gr. Basin Natur. 46:383–397.

Stewart, K. W., and B. P. Stark. 1984. Nymphs of North American Perlodinae genera (Plecoptera: Perlodidae). Gr. Basin Natur. 44:373–415; illus.

Surdick, R. F., and K. C. Kim. 1976. Stoneflies (Plecoptera) of Pennsylvania, a synopsis. Bull. Penn. State Univ. Coll. Agr. 808:1–73; illus.

Surdick, R. F. 1985. Nearctic genera of Chloroperlinae (Plecoptera: Chloroperlidae). Ill. Biol. Monogr. No. 54: 1–146; illus.

Szczytko, S. W., and K. W. Stewart. 1979. The genus *Isoperla* (Plecoptera) of western North America; holomorphology and systematics, and a new stonefly genus *Cascadoperla*. Mem. Amer. Entomol. Soc. 32, 120 pp.; illus.

Unzicker, J. D., and V. H. McCaskill. 1982. Plecoptera, *in* Aquatic Insects and Oligochaetes of North and South Carolina. Mahomet, Ill.: Midwest Aquatic Enterprises, 837 pp.; illus.

Chapter 21

Order Zoráptera[1]
Zorapterans

The zorapterans are minute insects, 3 mm or less in length, and may be winged or wingless. The winged forms are generally dark-colored, and the wingless forms are usually pale. The zorapterans are a little like termites in general appearance and are gregarious.

Both winged and wingless forms occur in both sexes. The wings are four in number and membranous, with a much reduced venation and with the hind wings smaller than the front wings (Figure 21–1A). The wings of the adult are eventually shed, as in ants and termites, leaving stubs attached to the thorax. The antennae are moniliform and nine-segmented as adults. The wingless forms (Figure 21–1D) lack both compound eyes and ocelli, but the winged forms have compound eyes and three ocelli. The tarsi are two-segmented, and each tarsus bears two claws. The cerci are short and unsegmented and terminate in a long bristle. The abdomen is short, oval, and ten-segmented. The mouthparts are of the chewing type, and the metamorphosis is simple. Apparently there are four juvenile instars in the common species in our area.

Some wingless males of certain species have a cephalic fontanelle. This is true of *Zorótypus húbbardi* Caudell. The gland may secrete a pheromone, which helps keep the largely blind gregarious assemblage together in their dark habitat. Delamare Deboutteville (1956) considered the zorapteran fontanelle as probably homologous with that of termites.

The order Zoráptera contains a single family, the **Zorotýpidae,** and a single genus, *Zorótypus.* In 1978, New listed 28 described species of zorapterans, and since then two more species have been found in southeast Tibet. Three species occur in the United States. *Zorótypus húbbardi* has been taken in a number of localities in the southeastern United States, from Maryland and southern Pennsylvania westward to southern Iowa and southward to Florida and Texas; *Z. snỳderi* Caudell occurs in Florida and Jamaica; and *Z. swèzeyi* Caudell is known from Hawaii. *Zorótypus húbbardi* is commonly found under slabs of wood buried in piles of old sawdust. Colonies are also found under bark and in rotting logs. The principal food of zorapterans appears to be fungus spores, but they are known to eat small dead arthropods.

Collecting and Preserving Zoráptera

Zorapterans are to be looked for in the habitats indicated previously and are generally collected by sifting debris or by means of a Berlese funnel (Figure 36–6). Where zorapterans are abundant, an aspirator is most useful. They should be preserved in 70% alcohol and may be mounted on microscope slides for detailed study.

---

[1]Zoráptera: *zor,* pure, *aptera,* wingless. Only wingless individuals were known when this order was described, and the wingless condition was thought to be a distinctive feature of the order.

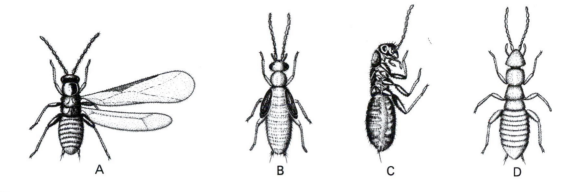

Figure 21–1. *Zorotýpus húbbardi* Caudell. **A,** winged adult; **B,** nymph of winged form; **C,** dealated winged adult, lateral view; **D,** wingless adult. (Courtesy of Caudell.)

References

Caudell, A. N. 1918. *Zorotypus hubbardi,* a new species of the order Zoraptera from the United States. Can. Entomol. 50:375–381.

Caudell, A. N. 1920. Zoraptera not an apterous order. Proc. Entomol. Soc. Wash. 22:84–97.

Caudell, A. N. 1927. *Zorotypus longiceratus,* a new species of Zoraptera from Jamaica. Proc. Entomol. Soc. Wash. 29:144–145.

Delamare Deboutteville, C. 1956. Zoraptera, *in* Taxonomist's Glossary of Genitalia in Insects, ed. S. L. Tuxen. Copenhagen: Munksgaard.

Gurney, A. B. 1938. A synopsis of the order Zoraptera, with notes on the biology of *Zorotypus hubbardi* Caudell. Proc. Entomol. Soc. Wash. 40:57–87.

Gurney, A. B. 1959. New distribution records for *Zorotypus hubbardi* Caudell (Zoraptera). Proc. Entomol. Soc. Wash. 61:183–184.

Gurney, A. B. 1974. Class Insecta, Order Zoraptera, *in* Status of the Taxonomy of the Hexapoda of Southern Africa, ed. W. G. H. Coaton. RSA Dept. Agr. Tech. Serv., Entomol. Mem. 38:32–34.

New, T. R. 1978. Notes on Neotropical Zoraptera, with descriptions of two new species. Syst. Entomol. 3:361–370.

Riegel, G. T. 1963. The distribution of *Zorotypus hubbardi* (Zoraptera). Ann. Entomol. Soc. Amer. 56:744–747.

Riegel, G. T. 1969. More Zoraptera records. Proc. North Central Branch, Entomol. Soc. Amer. 23(2):125–126.

Riegel, G. T. 1987. Order Zoraptera, pp. 184–185 *in* Immature Insects, ed. F. W. Stehr. Dubuque, Iowa: Kendall/Hunt.

Riegel, G. T., and S. J. Eytalis. 1974. Life history studies on Zoraptera. Proc. North Central Branch, Entomol. Soc. Amer. 29:106–107.

Riegel, G. T., and M. B. Ferguson. 1960. New state records of Zoraptera. Entomol. News 71(8):213–216.

St. Amand, W. 1954. Records of the order Zoraptera from South Carolina. Entomol. News 65(5):131.

Chapter 22

Order Psocóptera[1]
Psocids

The psocids are small, soft-bodied insects, most of which are less than 6 mm in length. Wings may be present or absent, and both long-winged and short-winged individuals occur in some species. The winged forms have four membranous wings (rarely two, with the hind wings vestigial). The front wings are a little larger than the hind wings, and the wings at rest are usually held rooflike over the abdomen. The antennae are generally fairly long; the tarsi are two- or three-segmented; and cerci are lacking. Psocids have mandibulate mouthparts, and the clypeus is large and somewhat swollen. The metamorphosis is simple (Figure 22–1).

Some 72 genera and about 340 species of psocids are known from the United States and Canada, but most people see only a few species that occur in houses or other buildings. Most of the species found in buildings are wingless and, because they often live among books or papers, are usually called booklice. The majority of the psocids are outdoor species with well-developed wings. They occur on the bark or foliage of trees and shrubs, under bark or stones, or in dead leaves. These psocids are sometimes called barklice.

Some psocids feed on algae and lichens. Others feed on molds, cereals, pollen, fragments of dead insects, and similar materials. The term "lice" in the names "booklice" and "barklice" is somewhat misleading, for none of these insects is parasitic, although a few are phoretic on birds and mammals. Relatively few are louselike in appearance. The species occurring in buildings rarely cause much damage, but are frequently a nuisance.

The eggs of psocids are laid singly or in clusters and are sometimes covered with silk or debris. Most species pass through six nymphal instars. Some species are gregarious, living under thin silken webs. One southern species, *Archipsòcus nòmas* Gurney, often makes rather conspicuous webs on tree trunks and branches.

Certain psocids (species of *Liposcèlis* and *Rhyopsòcus*) have been found capable of acting as intermediate hosts of the fringed tapeworm of sheep, *Thysanosòma ostiniòides* Diesing.

Classification of the Psocóptera

A number of different classifications have been used in this order, and they differ in the principal criteria used in dividing up the order, in the number of families recognized, and in the placement of some genera. The principal classifications are those of

---

[1]Psocóptera: *psoco*, rub small; *ptera*, wings (referring to the gnawing habits of these insects). This chapter was prepared by Edward L. Mockford.

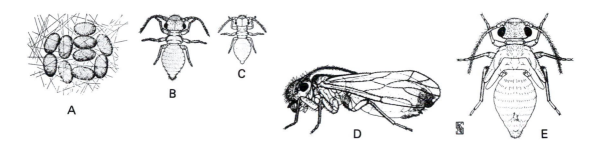

Figure 22–1.   Developmental stages of the psocid *Ectopsocópsis cryptomèriae* (Enderlein) (Ectopsòcidae). **A,** eggs; **B,** third instar; **C,** first instar; **D,** adult female; **E,** sixth instar. (Courtesy of Sommerman.)

Pearman (1936), Roesler (1944), Badonnel (1951), and Smithers (1972). We follow here the arrangement of Badonnel with minor revisions.

A synopsis of the Psocóptera occurring in the United States and Canada is given here, with alternate names and arrangements in parentheses. The groups marked with an asterisk are seldom encountered.

Suborder Trogiomórpha
  Lepidopsòcidae
  Trogìidae (Atrópidae)
  Psoquíllidae (Trogìidae in part)
  Psyllipsòcidae (Psocatrópidae)
  *Prionoglàridae (Psyllipsòcidae, in part)
Suborder Troctomórpha
  Liposcèlidae
  Pachytróctidae
  *Sphaeropsòcidae (Pachytróctidae in part)
  Amphientómidae

Suborder Psocomórpha (Eupsòcida)
  Epipsòcidae
  *Ptiloneùridae (Epipsòcidae in part)
  Caecilìidae (Polypsòcidae)
  Amphipsòcidae (Stenopsòcidae, Polypsòcidae)
  *Asiopsòcidae (Caecilìidae)
  Elipsòcidae (Pseudocaecilìidae in part)
  Philotársidae (Pseudocaecilìidae in part)
  Mesopsòcidae (Pseudocaecilìidae in part)
  Lachesíllidae (Pseudocaecilìidae in part)
  Peripsòcidae (Pseudocaecilìidae in part)
  Ectopsòcidae (Pseudocaecilìidae in part, Peripsòcidae in part)
  Pseudocaecilìidae
  Trichopsòcidae (Pseudocaecilìidae in part)
  Archipsòcidae (Pseudocaecilìidae in part)
  *Hemipsòcidae (Pseudocaecilìidae in part)
  Myopsòcidae
  Psòcidae

Key to the Families of Psocóptera

The families marked with an asterisk are small and are unlikely to be encountered by the general collector. This key is based on adults (for a key to nymphs see Mockford 1987). All psocid nymphs have two-segmented tarsi, either no wing pads or fleshy wing pads (Figure 22–1E), and no external genitalia (Figure 22–2F). It is necessary to make at least temporary slide preparations for some parts of this key; see the section "Collecting and Preserving Psocóptera."

1.   Antennae with more than 20 segments; segments never secondarily annulated; tarsi 3-segmented (suborder Trogiomórpha) **2**

1'.   Antennae with 17 or fewer segments; if more than 13 segments present, some or all flagellar segments secondarily annulated (Figure 22–3A); tarsi 2- or 3-segmented **6**

2(1).   Female with ovipositor valvulae of opposite sides separated by a space or touching only at or near their apices (Figure 22–2A); subgenital plate not

(*text continued on page 263*)

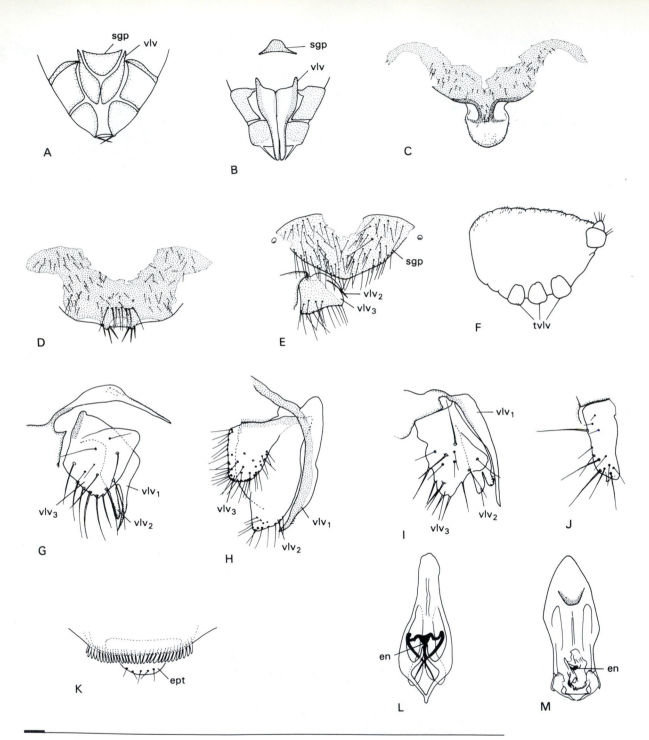

Figure 22–2. Abdominal structures of Psocóptera. **A,** *Psyllipsòcus*, female (Psyllipsòcidae), terminal abdominal segments, ventral view; **B,** *Echmépteryx*, female (Lepidopsòcidae), terminal abdominal segments, ventral view; **C,** subgenital plate of female *Mesopsòcus* (Mesopsòcidae); **D,** subgenital plate of female *Elipsòcus* (Elipsòcidae); **E,** subgenital plate and left ovipositor valvulae of *Archipsòcus* (Archipsòcidae); **F,** lateral view of abdomen of nymph of Amphipsòcidae; **G,** ovipositor valvulae of *Trichopsòcus* (Trichopsòcidae); **H,** ovipositor valvulae of *Peripsòcus* (Peripsòcidae); **I,** ovipositor valvulae of *Nepiomórpha* (Elipsòcidae); **J,** left ovipositor valvulae of *Lachesílla* (Lachesíllidae); **K,** comb of tenth abdominal tergum of *Ectopsòcus* male (Ectopsòcidae); **L,** phallosome of *Peripsòcus* male (Peripsòcidae); **M,** phallosome of *Ectopsòcus* male (Ectopsòcidae). *en,* endophallus; *ept,* epiproct; *sgp,* subgenital plate; *tv,* transverse vesicle; *vlv*$_{1-3}$, ovipositor valvulae 1–3.

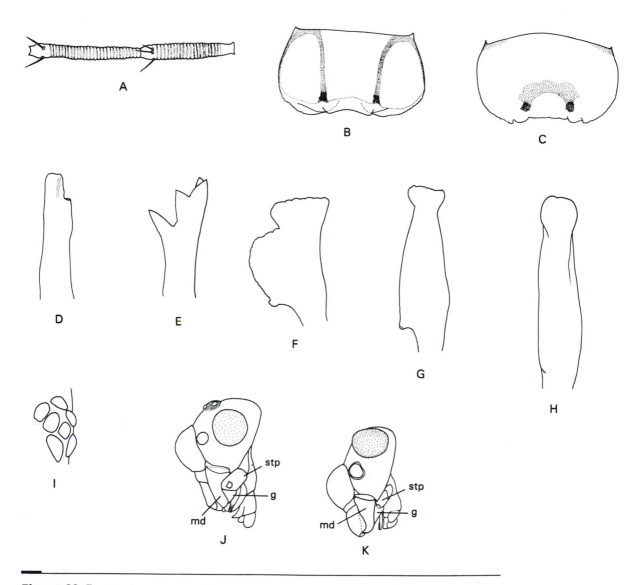

Figure 22–3.   Head structures of Psocóptera. **A,** flagellar segments 1 and 2 of *Liposcèlis* (Liposcèlidae); **B,** labrum of *Loneùra* (Ptiloneùridae); **C,** labrum of *Indiopsòcus* (Psòcidae); **D,** distal end of lacinia of *Speléketor* (Prionoglàridae); **E,** distal end of lacinia of *Psyllipsòcus* (Psyllipsòcidae); **F,** distal end of lacinia of *Asiopsòcus* (Asiopsòcidae); **G,** distal end of lacinia of *Teliapsòcus* (Amphipsòcidae); **H,** distal end of lacinia of *Caecílius* (Caecilìidae); **I,** ocular elements of *Liposcèlis* (Liposcèlidae); **J,** lateral view of head of *Teliapsòcus*; **K,** lateral view of head of *Mesopsòcus* (Mesopsòcidae). *g*, galea; *md*, mandible; *stp*, stipes.

much reduced (Figure 22–2A); in long-winged forms, veins Cu_2 and 1A of front wing ending together or very close on wing margin (Figure 22–4B); hind wings with one closed cell; wings never clothed in scales or dense hairs; venation persistent in short-winged forms **3**

2′.   Female with ovipositor valvulae of opposite sides touching along ventral midline (Figure 22–2B); subgenital plate much reduced; in long-winged forms, veins Cu_2 and 1A of front wing ending separately on wing margin (Figure 22–4C); hind wing with no closed cells, or if one present then at least front wing densely clothed with scales or hairs (Figure 22–4D); wings reduced in some forms (venation absent in some of these) **4**

3(2). Sc of front wing describing a curve and rejoining R_1 distally (Figure 22–4A); lacinia totally absent or at least lacking terminal tines (Figure 22–3D) ....**Prionoglàridae***   p. 270

3'. Segment of Sc in front wing absent from near wing base to base of pterostigma (Figure 22–4B); lacinia persistent in adult and with terminal tines (Figure 22–3E) ....**Psyllipsòcidae**   p. 270

4(2'). Body and front wings densely clothed in scales or long hairs or both (Figure 22–4D); front wings usually well developed, usually pointed apically (Figure 22–4C), never reduced to pads extending less than one-fourth length of abdomen ....**Lepidopsòcidae**   p. 270

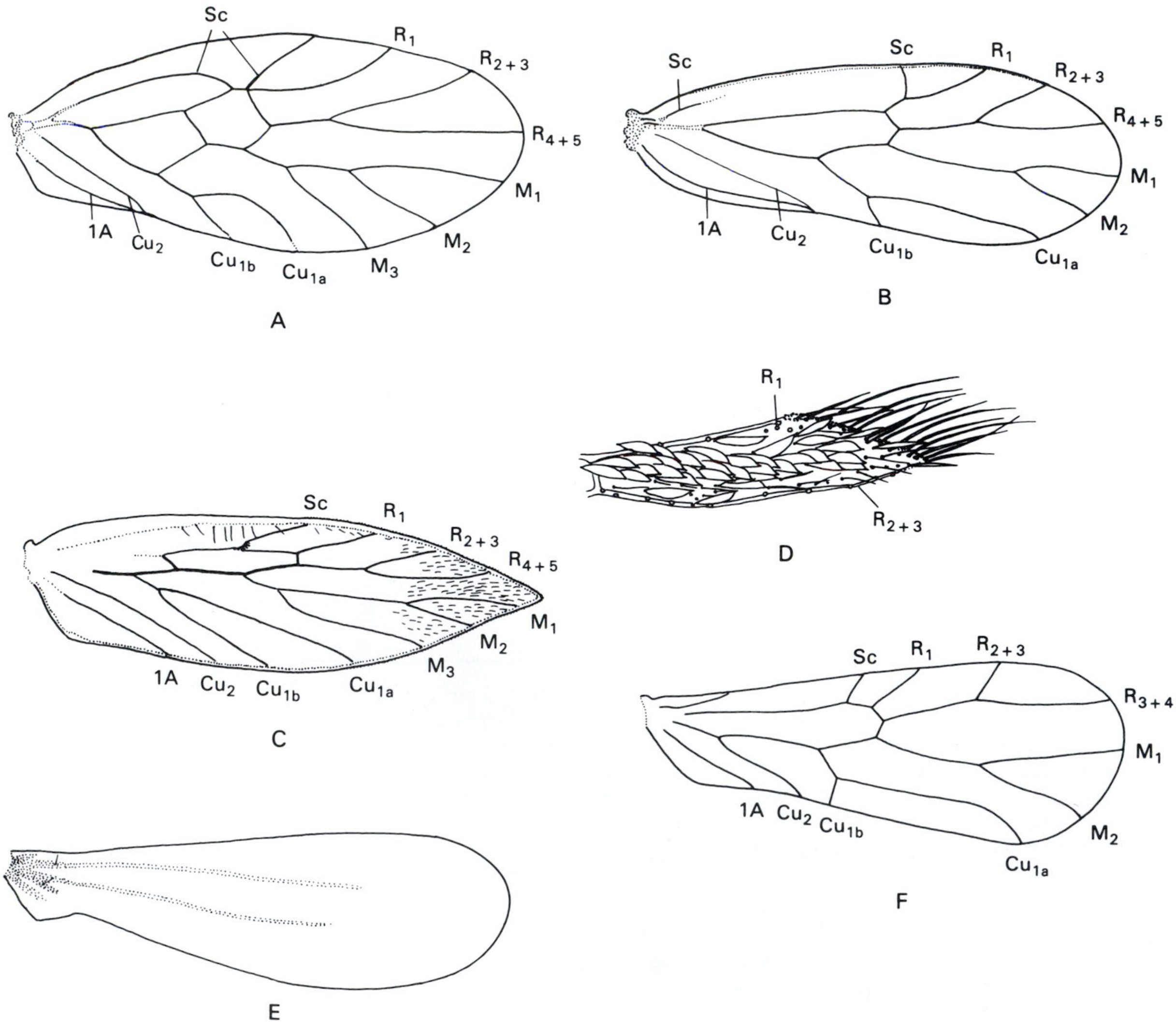

Figure 22–4. Front wings of Trogiomórpha and Troctomórpha. **A,** *Speléketor* (Prionoglàridae); **B,** *Psyllipsòcus* (Psyllipsòcidae); **C,** *Echmépteryx,* scales and marginal hairs removed (Lepidopsòcidae); **D,** *Echmépteryx,* cell R_1, enlarged, scales and marginal hairs intact; **E,** *Embidopsòcus* (Liposcèlidae); **F,** *Nanopsòcus* (Pachytróctidae).

4'.   Body and wings never scaled; front wings variably developed, from fully
           developed to nearly absent **5**

5(4').   Front wings well developed or reduced, but always with veins (Figure 22–5C);
           hind wings developed or absent ....**Psoquíllidae**   p. 270

5'.   Front wings reduced to tiny scales or buttons (Figure 22–5B), never with veins
           ....**Trogíidae**   p. 270

6(1').   Antennae 11- to 17-segmented, with secondary annulations (Figure 22–3A)
           (suborder Troctomórpha) **7**

6'.   Antennae 13-segmented, lacking secondary annulations (suborder
           Psocomórpha) **10**

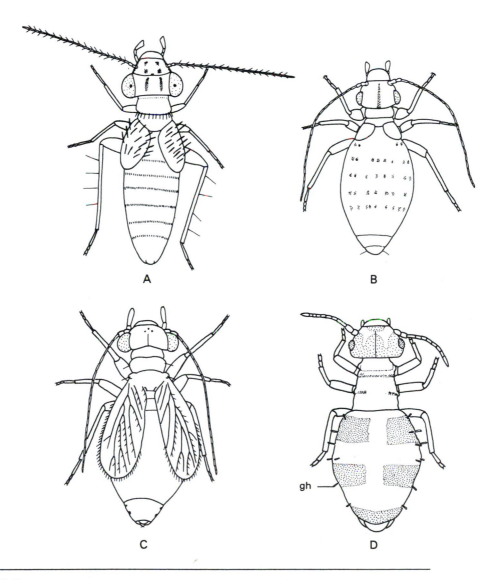

Figure 22–5.   Short-winged Psocóptera. **A,** *Lepólepis occidentàlis* Mockford
(Lepidopsòcidae); **B,** *Trògium pulsatòrium* (L.) (Trogìidae); **C,** *Rhyopsòcus béntonae*
Sommerman (Psoquíllidae); **D,** *Nepiomórpha perpsocòides* Mockford (Elipsòcidae). *gh,* gland
hair.

7(6).   Wings, when present, never scaled; either held flat over back when at rest with
             front wing of one side largely covering that of other side, or front wings
             elytriform; wings frequently reduced or absent **8**

7'.   Wings always present, not held flat over back in repose; front wings clothed
             with scales, never elytriform ....**Amphientómidae**   p. 272

8(7).   Front wings, when present, with complete venation (Figure 22–4F);
             mesothorax and metathorax distinctly separate in both winged and wingless
             forms ....**Pachytróctidae**   p. 272

8'.   Front wings, when present, with venation greatly reduced (Figure 22–4E); in
             all apterous forms mesothorax and metathorax indistinguishably fused **9**

9(8').   In alate forms both front and hind wings present, flat and delicate; eyes near
             vertex, hemispherical, compound; in apterous forms eyes removed from
             vertex, each consisting of six or fewer smaller ocelloids (Figure 22–3I);
             thoracic sterna broad and bearing setae (Figure 22–6A) ....**Liposcèlidae**   p. 271

9'.   In alate forms front wings convex, elytriform; in all forms eyes removed from
             vertex, composed of few ocelloids, none greatly enlarged; thoracic sterna
             narrow, without setae ....**Sphaeropsòcidae***   p. 272

10(6').   Head long dorsoventrally; labrum with two oblique, strongly sclerotized ridges
             internally that are clearly visible externally (Figure 22–3B); wings usually
             much reduced; long-winged forms with Rs and M of front wing not
             touching, connected by distinct cross vein (Figure 22–7A,B) **11**

10'.   Head short, wide; labrum internally on either side with only small sclerotized
             tubercle, the two sometimes connected by sclerotized arch; below arch, or
             between the pair of tubercles lies a clear semicircular area bordering anterior

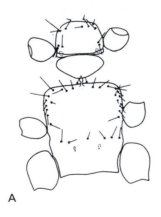

A

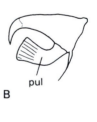

B

Figure 22–6.   Thoracic
structures of Psocóptera. **A,** thoracic
sterna and leg bases of *Embidopsòcus*
(Liposcèlidae); **B,** tarsal claw of
Teliapsòcus (Amphipsòcidae); **C,**
mesosternum of *Mesopsòcus*
(Mesopsòcidae); **D,** mesosternum of
Trichadenotécnum (Psòcidae). *pul,*
pulvillus; *pcb* precoxal bridge; *tn,*
trochantin.

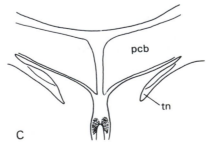

C

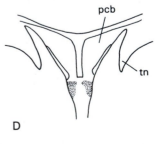

D

margin (Figure 22–3C); long-winged forms with Rs and M of front wing variable, joined together for short distance, or at a point, or by cross vein **12**

11(10).   Front wing with one anal vein (Figure 22–7A) or wings greatly reduced; tarsi 2-segmented . . . . **Epipsòcidae**   p. 272

11′.   Front wings never reduced, with 2 anal veins (Figure 22–7B); tarsi 3-segmented . . . . **Ptiloneùridae***   p. 272

12(10′).   Mandibles elongate, concave posteriorly (Figure 22–3J), the concavity filled by bulging stipes and galea; labrum broad; preapical denticle never present on tarsal claws (Figure 22–6B) **13**

12′.   Mandibles short, not decidedly concave posteriorly (Figure 22–3K), the stipes and galea relatively flat; labrum rounded, closely adhering to contour of mandibles; preapical denticle present or absent on tarsal claws **15**

13(12).   Abdomen ventrally with 2 or 3 transverse vesicles capable of being inflated (Figure 22–2F); lacinial tip variable but not extremely broad (Figure 22–3G,H) **14**

13′.   Abdomen ventrally lacking transverse vesicles, lacinial tip very broad (Figure 22–3F) . . . . **Asiopsòcidae***   p. 272

14(13).   Setae of front wing veins relatively short, slanting distally, mostly single-ranked (Figure 22–7C) . . . . **Caecilìidae**   p. 272

14′.   Setae of front wing veins relatively long, upright, mostly in more than one rank (Figure 22–7D), or if as above, then hind wing lacking marginal setae . . . . **Amphipsòcidae**   p. 272

15(12′).   Wings fully developed or only slightly reduced **16**

15′.   Wings greatly reduced; venational characters not usable **30**

16(15).   Mesothoracic precoxal bridges narrow at point of junction with trochantin (Figure 22–6D), trochantin broad basally, tapering distally **17**

16′.   Mesothoracic precoxal bridges wide at point of junction with trochantin (Figure 22–6C), trochantin narrow throughout **19**

17(16).   Tarsi 2-segmented **18**

17′.   Tarsi 3-segmented . . . . **Myopsòcidae**   p. 273

18(17).   Cu$_{1a}$ of front wing joined directly to M; M in front wing 3-branched (Figure 22–7K) . . . . **Psòcidae**   p. 273

18′.   Cu$_{1a}$ in front wing joined to M by a cross vein; M in front wing 2-branched (Figure 22–7L) . . . . **Hemipsòcidae***   p. 273

19(16′).   Margin of front wing with "crossing hairs" between veins R$_{4+5}$ and Cu$_{1a}$ (Figure 22–7J) **20**

19′.   Margin of front wing without "crossing hairs" **22**

20(19).   Tarsi 3-segmented . . . . **Philotársidae**   p. 272

20′.   Tarsi 2-segmented **21**

21(20′).   Surface of front wing densely hairy, venation of front wing obscure (Figure 22–7F); forms living in colonies under dense webs . . . . **Archipsòcidae**   p. 272

21′.   Surface of front wing with hairs largely confined to veins and margin; venation of both wings distinct; solitary forms living freely or under sparse webbing . . . . **Pseudocaecilìidae**   p. 272

22(19′).   Tarsi 3-segmented **23**

22′.   Tarsi 2-segmented **24**

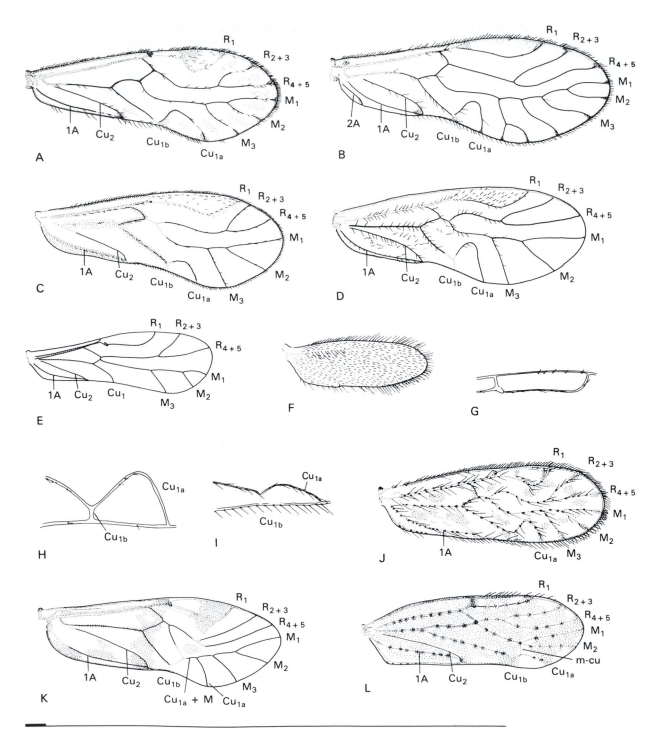

Figure 22–7. Front wings of Psocomórpha. **A,** *Epipsòcus* (Epipsòcidae); **B,** *Loneùra* (Ptiloneùridae); **C,** *Caecílius* (Caecilìidae); **D,** *Teliapsòcus* (Amphipsòcidae); **E,** *Palmícola,* male (Elipsòcidae); **F,** *Archipsòcus,* female (Archipsòcidae); **G,** pterostigma of *Ectopsòcus* (Ectopsòcidae); **H,** cell Cu$_{1a}$ of *Lachesílla* (Lachesíllidae); **I,** cell Cu$_{1a}$ of *Trichopsòcus* (Trichopsòcidae); **J,** *Aaroniélla* (Philotársidae); **K,** *Indiopsòcus* (Psòcidae); **L,** *Hemipsòcus* (Hemipsòcidae).

23(22). Wings bare; subgenital plate with single central posteriorly directed lobe (Figure 22–2C) ....**Mesopsòcidae**   p. 272

23'. Wings with obvious hairs on veins and margins; subgenital plate never with central posteriorly directed lobe, usually with two lobes (Figure 22–2D) ....**Elipsòcidae**   p. 272

24(22'). Vein Cu$_1$ in front wing branched (i.e., Cu$_{1a}$ present) **25**

24'. Vein Cu$_1$ in front wing simple (i.e., Cu$_{1a}$ absent) **27**

25(24). Cubital loop in front wing low (Figure 22–7I); numerous setae on veins and margins of wings; females with 3 complete pairs of ovipositor valvulae (Figure 22–2G) **26**

25'. Cubital loop in front wing higher (Figure 22–7H) or joined to M; setae sparse or absent on veins and margins of wings; ovipositor valvulae reduced to a single valvula on each side (Figure 22–2J) ....**Lachesíllidae**   p. 272

26(25). Pale delicate forms found on foliage ....**Trichopsòcidae**   p. 272

26'. Darker-bodied forms found on tree trunks and stone outcrops (males of *Reuterélla*) ....**Elipsòcidae**   p. 272

27(24'). Pterostigma constricted basally (as in Figure 22–7A–E,J,K); if M of fore wing 3-branched, setae sparse or absent on veins and margin of wing; if M of fore wing 2-branched, setae abundant on veins and wing margin **28**

27'. Pterostigma not constricted basally (Figure 22–7G); M of fore wing 3-branched ....**Ectopsòcidae**   p. 272

28(27). M in front wing 2-branched; setae abundant on veins and margin of front wing (*Notiopsòcus*) ....**Asiopsòcidae***   p. 272

28'. M in front wing 3-branched; setae sparse or absent on veins and margin of front wing **29**

29(28'). Free-living forms (females) with body beset with "gland hairs," i.e., hairs widest apically; solitary forms (males) living under dense webbing; third valvula of ovipositor large, covering most of second in normal position (Figure 22–2I) (*Nepiomórpha* and *Palmícola*) ....**Elipsòcidae**   p. 272

29'. Body without "gland hairs"; forms not living under webs; third valvula of ovipositor much smaller than second (Figure 22–2H) ....**Perípsòcidae**   p. 272

30(15'). Tarsi 3-segmented; only females, all with single central posterior projection on subgenital plate (Figure 22–2C); large, robust forms with wings reduced to tiny knobs, length 4–5 mm ....**Mesopsòcidae**   p. 272

30'. Tarsi 2-segmented; smaller forms, including males **31**

31(30'). Males and females both bearing a conspicuous white crosslike mark dorsally on abdomen (Figure 22–5D) and body beset with gland hairs (Figure 22–5D, see couplet 29) (*Nepiomórpha*) ....**Elipsòcidae**   p. 272

31'. Body not marked as above; gland hairs, if present, very restricted in distribution **32**

32(31'). Females with two pairs of ovipositor valvulae (Figure 22–2E) or none; subgenital plate evenly rounded on its posterior margin (Figure 22–2E); males never with transverse comb on posterior margin of tenth abdominal tergum; subtropical and tropical forms living under dense webs ....**Archipsòcidae**   p. 272

32'. Females with either one pair or three pairs of ovipositor valvulae; posterior margin of subgenital plate variously developed; males with transverse comb on posterior margin of tenth abdominal tergum; either free-living forms,

SUBORDER **Trogiomórpha:** The members of this suborder have more than 20 antennal segments, the labial palps are two-segmented, and the tarsi are three-segmented. Antennal flagellar segments are never secondarily annulated, although rings of microtrichia that resemble annulations are sometimes present.

Family **Lepidopsòcidae:** These psocids occur on trees, shrubs, and stone outcrops. The wings are slender, usually pointed apically, and wings and body are usually covered with scales. The group is primarily tropical, with 13 species in the United States. *Echmépteryx hàgeni* (Packard) is common on trees and stone outcrops throughout the eastern states.

Family **Trogìidae:** Most members of this family have the wings reduced but none are completely wingless. Species of *Cerobàsis* are common on shrubs and trees in the Southwest. A few species occur in buildings: *Lepinòtus inquilìnus* Heyden is often found in granaries, and *Trògium pulsatòrium* (L.) occurs in houses, barns, and granaries in the

Northeast. Females of some trogiids produce a sound by tapping the abdomen on the substrate.

Family **Psoquíllidae:** Members of this family may be fully winged or have the wings in various stages of reduction, but always with distinct venation. *Psoquílla marginepunctàta* Hagen occurs in houses in the Southeast. Species of *Rhyopsòcus* occur in dead leaves hanging on plants and in ground litter in the southern states.

Family **Psyllipsòcidae:** The psyllipsocids are pale-colored and occur in a variety of situations. *Psyllipsòcus rambùrii* Selys-Longchamps occurs in damp, dark places such as cellars and caves. It is common about the openings of wine and vinegar barrels. *Psyllipsòcus oculàtus* Gurney occurs on persistent dead leaves of yucca plants in arid areas of the Southwest. Both long- and short-winged individuals occur in most species.

Family **Prionoglàridae:** This family is represented in the United States by the genus *Speléketor,* medium-sized, rather pale forms with broad, unmarked wings. They occur in caves and on the skirts of the palm *Washingtònia filífera* in the Southwest.

SUBORDER **Troctomórpha:** The members of this suborder have more than 13 but fewer than 20 antennal segments with the flagellar segments secondarily annulated (Figure 22–3A). The labial palpi are two-segmented, and the tarsi are three-segmented.

Family **Liposcèlidae:** Most members of this group occur under bark, in dead leaves and dead grass, and in bird and mammal nests. They are either fully winged with wings held flat over the back at rest, or completely wingless. Several species of *Liposcèlis* occur commonly in buildings. They are found in dusty places where the temperature and humidity are high, on shelves, in cracks of windowsills, behind loose wallpaper, and in similar situations. They are wingless psocids about 1 mm in length with enlarged hind femora (Figure 22–8D).

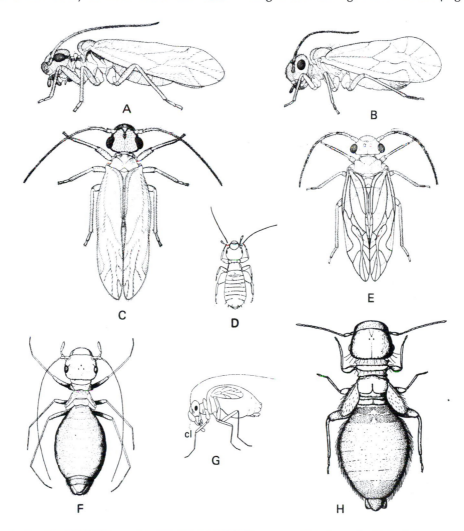

Figure 22–8.   Psocids. **A,** *Caecílius mánteri* Sommerman, female, lateral view (Caeciliidae); **B,** *Anomopsòcus amábilis* (Walsh), female, lateral view (Lachesíllidae); **C,** *Caecílius mánteri,* female, dorsal view; **D,** *Liposcèlis* sp., dorsal view (Liposcèlidae); **E,** *Anomopsòcus amábilis,* female, dorsal view; **F,** *Psyllipsòcus rambùrii* Selys, short-winged female, dorsal view (Psyllipsòcidae); **G,** *Psocathròpus* sp., lateral view (Psyllipsòcidae), *cl,* clypeus; **H,** *Archipsòcus nòmas* Gurney, short-winged female, dorsal view (Archipsòcidae). (**A–C, E,** courtesy of Sommerman; **F,** courtesy of Gurney; **D** and **G** reprinted by permission of Pest Control Technology, National Pest Control Association; **A, E,** courtesy of the Entomological Society of Washington; **B, E, F,** courtesy of the Entomological Society of America; **H,** courtesy of the Washington Academy of Science.)

Family **Pachytróctidae:** Only six species in this family occur in the United States. *Nanopsòcus oceánicus* Pearman occurs in houses in the Southeast. It and several species of *Tapinélla* occur on leaves of native palms in the Gulf states.

Family **Sphaeropsòcidae:** These are small psocids with elytriform front wings. Two species have been found in ground litter in California.

Family **Amphientómidae:** These psocids resemble the Lepidopsòcidae in having the wings and body covered with scales. They are mainly tropical, but one species of *Stimulopálpus* has been introduced from Asia and occurs commonly on cement structures and stone outcrops in forest areas from Virginia and North Carolina west to Illinois.

SUBORDER **Psocomórpha:** The antennae in these psocids usually have fewer than 13 segments, never more. The labial palps are one-segmented, and the tarsi are two- or three-segmented.

Family **Epipsòcidae:** This family is represented in the United States by three species. Two species of *Bertkàuia* are moderately common, one on shaded rock outcrops and adjacent tree trunks, the other in forest ground litter. A species of *Epipsòcus*, probably introduced from the American tropics, occurs in southern Florida.

Family **Ptiloneùridae:** This is a neotropical group closely related to the Epipsòcidae. It is represented in the United States by a single rare species occurring on stone outcrops in southern Arizona.

Family **Caeciliidae:** These are leaf-inhabiting psocids on both conifers and broad-leaf trees. Most are long-winged, but some ground-litter species have both long-winged and short-winged females. Twenty-eight species are known in the United States.

Family **Amphipsòcidae:** These psocids resemble the caeciliids but are larger with relatively longer hairs on wings and antennae. They are also leaf inhabitants. Three species are known in the United States.

Family **Asiopsòcidae:** These psocids appear to be inhabitants of twigs of small trees and shrubs. One species of *Asiopsòcus* occurs in southern Arizona. The tropical genera *Notiopsòcus* and *Pronotipsòcus* each have a representative in southern Florida.

Family **Elipsòcidae:** This family includes forms with 2- as well as 3-segmented tarsi. Several species of *Elipsòcus* occur on conifers and broad-leaf trees in the Pacific states, some of them introduced from Europe. *Reuterélla helvimácula* Enderlein, also known from Europe, occurs on stone outcrops and tree trunks in several northern states. Species of *Palmícola* occur on palms, oaks, and conifers in the southeastern states.

Family **Philotársidae:** This is one of several families in which setae of the posterodistal margin of the front wing form a series of crossing pairs (Figure 22–7J). North American species have three tarsal segments. Although only five species are known from the United States, these insects may become abundant locally in late summer. *Philotársus kwakiùtl* Mockford is common on conifers in the Pacific Northwest. *Aaroniélla eertmóedi* Mockford is often abundant on trunks and branches of trees and on stone outcrops in the southern part of the Midwest.

Family **Mesopsòcidae:** These are relatively large psocids found on branches of coniferous and broadleaf trees. Only three species of this primarily Old World family occur in the United States. *Mesopsòcus unipunctàtus* (Müller) occurs across the northern United States as well as northern Europe, and south in the Appalachians to North Carolina and on the Pacific coast to southern California. It is one of the first psocids to mature in the spring. The female is very short-winged and the male is long-winged.

Family **Lachesíllidae:** The members of this large family are inhabitants of persistent dead leaves of a great variety of plants. Some inhabit foliage of conifers. Although 54 species are now known in the United States, the number of species in Latin America is much larger.

Family **Peripsòcidae:** This is one of two families in which there is no cubital loop in the front wing; that is, vein Cu_1 is simple. The peripsocids are medium-sized inhabitants of twigs, branches, and trunks of conifers and broad-leaf trees. Some 14 species are now known in the United States.

Family **Ectopsòcidae:** This is another family in which the cubital loop is absent in the front wing. These are relatively small inhabitants of persistent dead leaves. *Ectopsocópsis cryptomèriae* (Enderlein) seems to thrive in agricultural situations where few other psocids exist. It occasionally invades food-storage warehouses. Ten species of ectopsocids occur in the United States.

Family **Pseudocaecíliidae:** This is another family which shows pairs of crossing hairs on the posterodistal margin of the front wing. North American species have two tarsal segments. Only three species occur in the United States, all of them probably introduced. *Pseudocaecílius citrícola* (Ashmead) is a common yellow species on citrus trees in Florida.

Family **Trichopsòcidae:** These are pale, delicate leaf-inhabiting forms superficially resembling caeciliids. Only two species occur in the United States. *Trichopsòcus clàrus* (Banks) is common in coastal California.

Family **Archipsòcidae:** This is a third family in which there are pairs of crossing hairs on the posterodistal margin of the fore wing. This tropical family is restricted in North America to Florida, the Gulf Coast, and the Atlantic Coast north to South Carolina. Archipsocids are communal web spinners. Males are short-winged, while females occur in short- and long-winged forms. About ten species occur in the United States.

Family **Hemipsòcidae:** This is primarily a tropical family, with only two species in the United States, both in the Southeast. *Hemipsòcus pretiòsus* Banks occurs on leaf litter and dead persistent leaves of small palms in southern Florida.

Family **Myopsòcidae:** Although this group is largely tropical, it is represented in the fauna of our area by ten species, all of which are 4–5 mm in length and have mottled front wings. They occur on shaded stone outcrops and shaded cement structures, such as bridges, as well as tree trunks and branches.

Family **Psòcidae:** This is the largest family in the United States, with some 75 species. Psòcidae are moderate-sized to large psocids with the cubital loop always joined to M for a distance in the front wing. Generally, they inhabit branches and trunks of various kinds of trees, foliage of conifers, and shaded rock outcrops. *Cerastipsòcus venòsus* Burmeister is a large, dark-colored species that forms herds of up to several hundred individuals on tree trunks and branches. It occurs throughout the eastern United States.

Collecting and Preserving Psocóptera

The psocids that live outdoors can often be collected by beating branches of trees and shrubs and sweeping grasses. Coniferous trees and fallen branches with persistent dead leaves often are sites where psocids are concentrated. Some species are found under loose bark, on stone outcrops, in ground litter, and in bird and mammal nests. Indoor species can be found in old papers and books, in stored grain and cereal products, and on wood surfaces in such sites as musty cellars. Individuals can be picked up with an aspirator or a small brush moistened with alcohol.

Psocids may be preserved in 70–80% alcohol, but some color fading occurs in these preservatives. Specimens mounted on pins or points keep their colors better, but they shrivel and must be restored in liquids for study.

It is often necessary to mount specimens or parts, such as legs, wings, mouthparts, and terminal abdominal segments, on microscope slides for study. For this, parts other than legs or wings should be partially cleared by soaking in a cold 10–15% aqueous solution of KOH for several minutes. They can then be washed in water and mounted in Hoyer's medium (see Chapter 36). Undigested material in the hindgut must be teased out with fine needles with the specimen under water.

References

Badonnel, A. 1951. Ordre des Psocoptères, *in* Traité de Zoologie, ed. P. P. Grassé, vol. 10, fasc. 2: 1301–1340. Paris: Masson; illus.

Chapman, P. J. 1930. Corrodentia of the United States of America. I. Suborder Isotecnomera. J. N.Y. Entomol. Soc. 39:54–65; illus.

Eertmoed, G. E. 1966. The life history of *Peripsocus quadrifasciatus* (Psocoptera: Peripsocidae). J. Kan. Entomol. Soc. 39:54–65; illus.

Eertmoed, G. E. 1973. The phenetic relationships of the Epipsocetae (Psocoptera): The higher taxa and the species of two new families. Trans. Amer. Entomol. Soc. 99:373–414; illus.

García Aldrete, A. N. 1974. A classification above species level of the genus *Lachesilla* Westwood (Psocoptera: Lachesillidae). Folia Entomol. Mex. 27:1–88.

Gurney, A. B. 1950. Corrodentia, pp. 129–163 *in* Pest Control Technology, Entomology Section. New York: Natl. Pest Control Assoc.; illus.

Lee, S. S., and I. W. B. Thornton. 1967. The family Pseudocaeciliidae (Psocoptera)—A reappraisal based on the discovery of new Oriental and Pacific species. Pac. Insects Monogr. No. 18, 114 pp.; illus.

Mockford, E. L. 1955a. Notes on some eastern North American psocids with descriptions of two new species. Amer. Midl. Nat. 53(2):436–441; illus.

Mockford, E. L. 1955b. Studies of the reuterelline psocids (Psocoptera). Proc. Entomol. Soc. Wash. 57:97–108; illus.

Mockford, E. L. 1957. Life history studies on some Florida insects of the genus *Archipsocus* (Psocoptera). Bull. Fla. State Mus. 1:253–274; illus.

Mockford, E. L. 1959. The *Ectopsocus briggsi* complex in the Americas (Psocoptera: Peripsocidae). Proc. Entomol. Soc. Wash. 61:260–266; illus.

Mockford, E. L. 1963. The species of Embidopsocinae of the United States (Psocoptera: Liposcelidae). Ann. Entomol. Soc. Amer. 56:25–37; illus.

Mockford, E. L. 1965. The genus *Caecilius* (Psocoptera: Caeciliidae). Part I. Species groups and the North American species of the *flavidus* group. Trans. Amer. Entomol. Soc. 91:121–166; illus.

Mockford, E. L. 1966. The genus *Caecilius* (Psocoptera: Caeciliidae). Part II. Revision of the species groups, and the North American species of the *fasciatus, confluens,* and *africanus* groups. Trans. Amer. Entomol. Soc. 92:133–172; illus.

Mockford, E. L. 1969. The genus *Caecilius* (Psocoptera: Caeciliidae). Part III. The North American species of the *alcinus, caligonus,* and *subflavus* groups. Trans. Amer. Entomol. Soc. 95:77–151; illus.

Mockford, E. L. 1971a. Parthenogenesis in psocids (Insecta: Psocoptera). Amer. Zool. 11:327–339; illus.

Mockford, E. L. 1971b. *Peripsocus* species of the *albogut-tatus* group (Psocoptera: Peripsocidae). J. N.Y. Entomol. Soc. 79:89–115; illus.

Mockford, E. L. 1978. A generic classification of family Amphipsocidae (Psocoptera: Caecilietae). Trans. Amer. Entomol. Soc. 104:139–190.

Mockford, E. L. 1987. Order Psocoptera, pp. 196–214 *in* F. W. Stehr (ed.), Immature Insects. Dubuque, Iowa: Kendall/Hunt, 754 pp.

Mockford, E. L., and A. B. Gurney. 1956. A review of the psocids, or book-lice and bark-lice, of Texas (Psocoptera). J. Wash. Acad. Sci. 46:353–368; illus.

Mockford, E. L., and D. M. Sullivan. 1986. Systematics of the graphocaeciliine psocids with a proposed higher classification of the family Lachesillidae (Psocoptera). Trans. Amer. Entomol. Soc. 112:1–80.

New, T. R. 1974. Psocoptera. Roy. Entomol. Soc. Lond. Handbooks Identif. Brit. Insects 1(7):1–102; illus.

New, T. R. 1987. Biology of the Psocoptera. Oriental Insects 21:1–109.

Pearman, J. V. 1928. On sound production in the Psocoptera and on a presumed stridulatory organ. Entomol. Mon. Mag. 64:179–186; illus.

Pearman, J.V. 1936. The taxonomy of the Psocoptera; preliminary sketch. Proc. Roy. Entomol. Soc. Lond. Ser. B, 5(3):58–62.

Roesler, R. 1944. Die Gattungen der Copeognathen. Stn. Entomol. Ztg. 105:117–166.

Smithers, C. N. 1965. A bibliography of the Psocoptera (Insecta). Austral. Zool. 13:137–209.

Smithers, C. N. 1967. A catalog of the Psocoptera of the world. Austral. Zool. 14:1–145.

Smithers, C. N. 1972. The classification and phylogeny of the Psocoptera. Austral. Mus. Mem. 14:1–349.

Sommerman, K. M. 1943. Bionomics of *Ectopsocus pumilis* (Banks) (Corrodentia: Caeciliidae). Psyche 50:55–63; illus.

Sommerman, K. M. 1944. Bionomics of *Amapsocus amabilis* (Walsh) (Corrodentia: Psocidae). Ann. Entomol. Soc. Amer. 37:359–364; illus.

Sommerman, K. M. 1946. A revision of the genus *Lachesilla* north of Mexico (Corrodentia; Caeciliidae). Ann. Entomol. Soc. Amer. 39:627–661.

Chapter 23

Order Phthiráptera[1]
Lice

The lice are small wingless ectoparasites of birds and mammals. These insects are often divided into two separate orders, the Mallóphaga (chewing lice) and Anoplùra (sucking lice). The suborder Anoplùra contains several species that are parasites of domestic animals and two species that attack humans. These insects are irritating pests, and some are important vectors of disease. Many chewing lice (suborders Amblýcera and Ischnócera) are pests of domestic animals, particularly poultry. These lice cause considerable irritation, and heavily infested animals appear run-down and emaciated. If they are not actually killed by the lice, they are rendered easy prey for various diseases. Different species of lice attack different types of poultry and domestic mammals, and each species usually infests a particular part of the host's body. None of the chewing lice is known to attack people. Those who handle birds or other infested animals may occasionally get the lice on themselves, but the lice do not stay long. The control of chewing lice usually involves treatment of the infested animal with a suitable dust or dip. A third suborder of chewing lice, the Rhynchophthirìna, contains only two species, parasites of the Indian elephant and the wart hog.

The Anoplùra feed on the blood of their host. The mouthparts of a sucking louse consist of three piercing stylets that are normally carried withdrawn into a stylet sac in the head (Figure 23–1). The mouthparts are highly specialized and difficult to homologize with those of other sucking insects. There is a short rostrum (probably the labrum) at the anterior end of the head, from which the three piercing stylets are protruded. The rostrum is eversible and is armed internally with small recurved teeth. The stylets are about as long as the head and, when not in use, are withdrawn into a long saclike structure lying below the alimentary canal. The dorsal stylet probably represents the fused maxillae. Its edges are curved upward and inward to form a tube that serves as a food channel. The intermediate stylet is very slender and contains the salivary channel; this stylet is probably the hypopharynx. The ventral stylet is the principal piercing organ; it is a trough-shaped structure and is probably the labium. There are no palps. When an anopluran feeds, the stylets are everted through a rostrum at the front of the head. The rostrum is provided with tiny hooks with which the louse attaches to its host while feeding. The chewing lice have mandibulate mouthparts and feed on bits of hair, feathers, or skin of the host. Ocelli are absent, and eyes are usually reduced or absent. The antennae are short and three- to five-segmented.

[1]Phthiráptera: *phthir*, lice; *a*, without; *ptera*, wings.

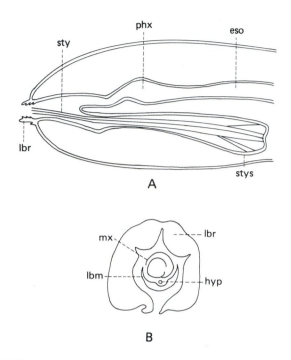

Figure 23–1.   Mouth parts of a sucking louse. **A**, sagittal section of head; **B**, cross section through rostrum. *eso*, esophagus; *hyp*, intermediate stylet (probably hypopharynx); *lbm*, ventral stylet (probably labium); *lbr*, rostrum (probably labrum); *mx*, dorsal stylet (probably the fused maxillae); *phx*, pharynx; *sty*, stylets; *stys*, stylet sac. (Redrawn from Snodgrass.)

The tarsi of sucking lice are one-segmented and are provided with a single large claw that usually fits against a thumblike process at the end of the tibia. This claw forms an efficient mechanism for hanging to the hairs of the host.

The Phthiráptera undergo simple metamorphosis. The females of most species lay from 50 to 150 eggs, nearly always attaching them to the hairs or feathers of the host. The eggs usually hatch in about a week, and the developing louse goes through three nymphal instars in most species.

Classification of the Phthiráptera

There is disagreement among entomologists on the higher classification of the lice. Many American workers place them in two orders, the Anoplùra and Mallóphaga. British, German, and Australian workers generally recognize a single order, the Phthiráptera, with four suborders (one of which is the Anoplùra). The sucking lice clearly form a distinct phylogenetic branch and deserve separate recognition at some level. It is the classification of the chewing lice that causes problems. Kim and Ludwig (1978b, 1982) have forcefully argued the hypothesis that the characteristics that distinguish lice from their closest relatives, the Psocóptera, have evolved numerous times in parallel as a result of the ectoparasitic niche they occupy. Therefore, they advocate that two orders, Mallóphaga and Anoplùra, be recognized. However, the relationships among the suborders of lice are poorly understood. Kim and Ludwig (1982) summarize the evidence for and against several alternative schemes. The only common component is that all lice together form a monophyletic unit whose sister-group is the Psocóptera. Until the phylogeny is better understood, we will recognize a single order of lice, the Phthiráptera. We follow here the familial classification of Kim *et al.* (1986) within the suborder Anoplùra. These groups, with synonyms and other arrangements in parentheses, are as follows:

Suborder Amblýcera (Mallóphaga in part)
    Gyrópidae—lice of guinea pigs
    Boopìidae (Boópidae)—lice of marsupials and
        dogs
    Menopónidae—lice of birds
    Laemobothrìidae—lice of birds
    Ricínidae—lice of birds
Suborder Ischnócera (Mallóphaga in part)
    Philoptéridae—lice of birds
    Trichodéctidae—lice of mammals
Suborder Anoplùra
    Echinophthirìidae—lice of seals, sea lions, walruses, and the river otter
    Enderleinéllidae (Hoplopleùridae in part)—lice of
        squirrels
    Haematopínidae—lice of ungulates (pigs, cattle,
        horses, deer)
    Hoplopleùridae—lice of rodents and insectivores
    Linognáthidae—lice of even-toed ungulates (cattle, sheep, goats, deer) and canids (dogs,
        foxes, coyotes)
    Pecaroècidae—lice of peccaries
    Pedicùlidae—the head and body lice of humans
    Polyplácidae (Hoplopleùridae in part)—lice of rodents and insectivores
    Pthíridae (Phthíridae, Phthirìidae)—the crab
        louse of humans

Key to the Families of Phthiráptera

1. Head as wide as or wider than prothorax (Figures 23–2 through 23–4); mouthparts mandibulate; parasites of birds (with 2 tarsal claws) and mammals (with 1 tarsal claw) **2**

1'. Head usually narrower than prothorax (Figures 23–5, 23–6); mouthparts haustellate; parasites of mammals, with 1 large tarsal claw (Suborder Anoplùra) **8**

2(1). Antennae more or less clubbed and usually concealed in grooves; maxillary palps present (Figure 23–2A and 23–3) (Suborder Amblýcera) **3**

2'. Antennae filiform and exposed; maxillary palps absent (Figures 23–2B and 23–4) (Suborder Ischnócera) **7**

3(2). With 1 tarsal claw or none; parasitic on guinea pigs ....**Gyrópidae**   p. 280

3'. With 2 tarsal claws; parasitic on birds, marsupials, and dogs **4**

4(3'). Antennae 5-segmented and strongly clubbed; legs long and slender; parasitic on marsupials and dogs ....**Boopiidae**   p. 280

4'. Antennae 4-segmented and less strongly clubbed; legs not particularly long and slender; parasitic on birds **5**

5(4'). Antennae in grooves on sides of head; head broadly triangular and expanded behind eyes (Figure 23–2A) ....**Menopónidae**   p. 280

5'. Antennae in cavities that open ventrally; head not broadly triangular and expanded behind eyes (Figure 23–3) **6**

6(5'). Sides of head with conspicuous swelling in front of eye at base of antenna (Figure 23–3A) ....**Laemobothriidae**   p. 280

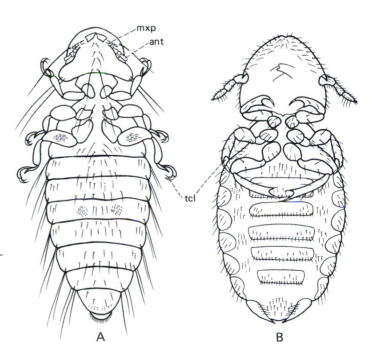

Figure 23–2. **A,** shaft louse of chickens, *Ménopon gállinae* (L.) (Menopónidae), ventral view of female; **B,** cattle-biting louse, *Bovícola bòvis* (L.) (Trichodéctidae), ventral view of female, *ant,* antenna; *mxp,* maxillary palp; *tcl,* tarsal claws.

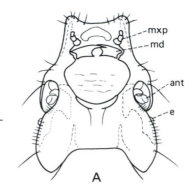
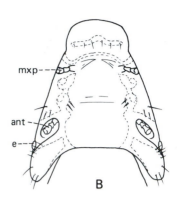

Figure 23–3.   **A,** head of *Laemobòthrion* (Laemobothrìidae), ventral view; **B,** head of a ricinid (Ricínidae), ventral view. *ant*, antenna; *e*, eye; *md*, mandible; *mxp*, maxillary palp.

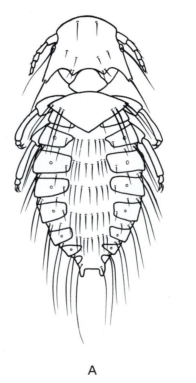
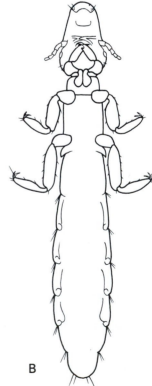

Figure 23–4.   Philoptéridae. **A,** the large turkey louse, *Chelopístes meleágridis* (L.), dorsal view; **B,** *Anatícola crassicòrnis* (Scopoli), a louse of the blue-winged teal, ventral view.

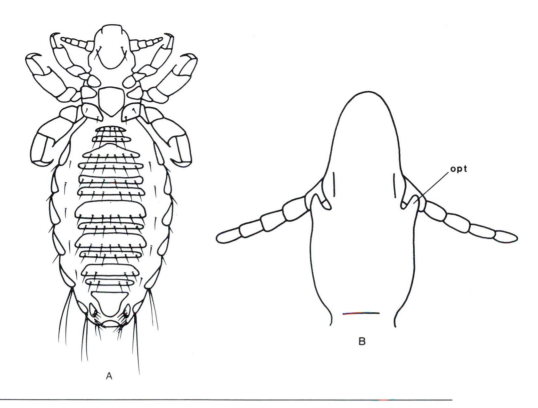

Figure 23–5. **A,** the spined rat louse, *Pólyplax spinulòsa* (Burmeister), female, ventral view (Polyplácidae); **B,** head of the hog louse, *Haematópinus sùis* (L.), dorsal view (Haematopínidae). *opt*, ocular point.

9'.	Head without eyes but with prominent ocular points (Figure 23–5B, *opt*); parasites of ungulates ....**Haematopínidae**	p. 281
10(9).	Head long and slender, much longer than thorax; southwestern United States, on peccaries ....**Pecaroècidae**	p. 281
10'.	Head about as long as thorax (Figure 23–6); parasites of humans **11**	
11(10').	Abdomen about as long as its basal width, and with prominent lateral lobes (Figure 23–6B); middle and hind legs stouter than front legs ....**Pthíridae**	p. 282
11'.	Abdomen much longer than its basal width, and without lateral lobes (Figure 23–6A); middle and hind legs not stouter than front legs ....**Pedicùlidae**	p. 281
12(8').	Body thickly covered with short stout spines, abdomen with scales; parasites of seals, walruses, and the river otter ....**Echinophthiríidae**	p. 281
12'.	Body with only a few setae, abdomen without scales; parasites of terrestrial mammals **13**	
13(12')	Front and middle legs similar in size and shape, both smaller, more slender than hind legs; parasites of squirrels ....**Enderleinéllidae**	p. 281
13'.	Front legs smallest of the three pairs, middle and hind legs similar in size and shape (Figure 23–5A), or hind legs larger; parasites of ungulates, canids, rodents, and insectivores **14**	
14(13').	Front coxae widely separated; parasites of even-toed ungulates and canids..**Linognáthidae**	p. 281

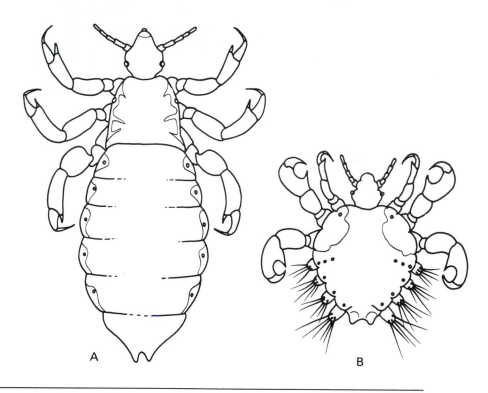

Figure 23–6. Human lice. **A,** the body louse, female; **B,** the crab louse, female. 20×.

14′.	Front coxae contiguous or nearly so; parasites of rodents and insectivores ...**15**
15(14′).	Hind legs largest of the three pairs; sternite of second abdominal segment extending laterally on each side to articulate with the tergite ....**Hoplopleúridae** p. 281
15′.	Middle and hind legs similar in size and shape (Figure 23–5A); sternite of second abdominal segment not extending laterally on each side and not articulating with tergite ....**Polyplácidae** p. 282

Family **Gyrópidae:** The members of this group are chiefly confined to Central and South America. Two species occur in the United States on guinea pigs.

Family **Boopíidae:** This group is represented in the United States by two species of *Heterodóxus*: *H. longitársus* (Piaget), a kangaroo louse that is sometimes a severe pest of dogs in the San Francisco Bay area of California, and *H. spíniger* (Enderlein), which occurs on dogs and coyotes in the southwestern

states. Most members of this family occur in Australia, where they are parasites of marsupials.

Family **Menopónidae:** This is a large group whose members attack birds. Two important pests of poultry in this group are the chicken body louse, *Menacánthus stramíneus* (Nitzsch), and the shaft louse, *Ménopon gállinae* (L.) (Figure 23–2A).

Family **Laemobothríidae:** This is a small group of very large lice whose members are parasites of water birds and birds of prey.

Family **Ricínidae:** This is a small group whose members are parasites of birds, chiefly sparrows, other passerine birds, and hummingbirds.

Family **Philoptéridae:** This is the largest family in the order and contains species parasitizing a wide variety of birds. Two important pests of poultry in this group are the chicken head louse, *Cuclotogáster heterógrapha* (Nitzsch), and the large turkey louse, *Chelopístes meleágridis* (L.) (Figure 23–4A).

Family **Trichodéctidae:** The trichodectids are parasites of mammals. Some important pest species in this group are the cattle-biting louse, *Bovícola bòvis* (L.) (Figure 23–2B); the horse-biting louse, *B. équi* (Denny); and the dog-biting louse, *Trichodéctes cànis* (De Geer).

Family **Echinophthiríidae:** The six North American species in this group attack aquatic mammals (seals, sea lions, walruses, and the river otter). At least some species burrow into the skin of their host.

Family **Enderleinéllidae:** This is a widely distributed group, with ten North American species, whose members are parasites of squirrels. They may be recognized by the fact that the front and middle legs are similar in size and more slender than the hind legs. Most of the North American species belong to the genus *Enderleinéllus. Micróphthirus uncinàtus* (Ferris), a parasite of flying squirrels, is less than 0.5 mm in length, and is the smallest louse in this order.

Family **Haematopínidae:** The lice in this group attack pigs, cattle, horses, and deer. They differ from other sucking lice in having ocular points on the sides of the head behind the eyes (Figure 23–5B, *opt*). This family contains four North American species, including the hog louse, *Haematópinus sùis* (L.); the horse sucking louse, *H. ásini* (L.); and two species of *Haematópinus* that attack cattle.

Family **Hoplopleùridae:** The members of this group (16 North American species) attack rodents, hares, moles, and shrews. These lice differ from other Anoplùra attacking these hosts (Polyplácidae) in the form of the sternite of the second abdominal segment and the relative size of the different legs (see key, couplet 15).

Family **Linognáthidae:** This group includes ten North American species that are parasites of cattle, sheep, goats, deer, reindeer, dogs, coyotes, and foxes. It includes the dog sucking louse, *Linógnathus setòsus* (Olfers); the goat sucking louse, *L. stenópsis* (Burmeister); and the long-nosed cattle louse, *L. vítuli* (L.). The last species differs from the haematopinids attacking cattle in lacking ocular points on the head.

Family **Pecaroècidae:** This group includes a single North American species, *Pecaroècus javáli* Babcock and Ewing, which occurs in the Southwest on peccaries. This species is the largest North American anopluran, and may reach a length of 8 mm.

Family **Pedicùlidae:** This group includes the head and body lice of humans, *Pedículus humànus cápitis* (De Geer) and *P. h. humànus* L., respectively, which are considered varieties of a single species (*P. humànus* L.). These lice (Figure 23–6A) are narrower and more elongate than crab lice. The head is only a little narrower than the thorax, and the abdomen lacks lateral lobes. Adults are 2.5–3.5 mm in length.

The head and body lice have a similar life history, but differ somewhat in habits. The head louse occurs chiefly on the head, and its eggs are attached to the hair. The body louse occurs chiefly on the body, and its eggs are laid on clothing, chiefly along the seams. The eggs hatch in about a week, and the entire life cycle from egg to adult requires about a month. Lice feed at frequent intervals, and individual feedings last a few minutes. Body lice usually hang onto clothing while feeding, and often remain on clothing when it is removed. The head louse is transmitted from person to person through the promiscuous use of combs, hair brushes, and caps. The body louse is transmitted by clothing and bedding, and at night may migrate from one pile of clothes to another.

The body louse (also called "cootie" or "seam squirrel") is an important vector of human disease. The most important disease it transmits is epidemic typhus, which frequently occurs in epidemic proportions and may have a high mortality rate. Body lice become infected by feeding on a typhus patient and are able to infect another person a week or so later. Infection results from scratching the feces of the louse, or the crushed louse itself, into the skin. This disease is not transmitted by the bite of the louse. Another important louse-borne disease is a type of relapsing fever that is transmitted by the infected louse being crushed and rubbed into the skin. Neither the feces nor the bite of the louse is infective. A third louse-borne disease is trench fever, which occurred in epidemic proportions during World War I, but since then has not been very important.

People who bathe and change clothes regularly seldom become infested with lice, but when they go for long periods without doing so and live in crowded conditions, lousiness is likely to be prevalent. The latter conditions are often common during wartime, when living quarters are crowded and people go for long periods without a change of clothes. If a louse-borne disease such as typhus gets started in a population that is heavily infested with body lice, it can spread quickly to epidemic proportions.

The control of body lice usually involves dusting

individuals with an insecticide. Clothing must also be treated, for the eggs are laid on it, and adult lice often cling to clothing when it is removed. The treatment of clothing usually involves fumigation or sterilization by heat.

Epidemics of typhus have occurred in many military campaigns and have often caused more casualties than actual combat. Up to the time of World War II, there were no simple and easily applied controls for body lice. DDT, which first came into use during this war, proved ideal for louse control. In the fall of 1943, when a typhus epidemic threatened Naples, Italy, the dusting of thousands of people in Naples with DDT brought the epidemic under complete control in only a few months. In the years since then, body lice have developed resistance to DDT, and this insecticide is no longer as effective in their control as it used to be.

Family **Polyplácidae:** This family is the largest family in the suborder, with 27 North American species. Its members attack rodents, hares, moles, and shrews. Some species in other parts of the world attack primates (monkeys and lemurs).

Family **Pthíridae:**   The only member of this family in our area is the crab louse of man, *Pthírus pùbis* (L.) (Figure 23–6B), but there is an African species (*P. goríllae* Ewing) that attacks gorillas. *Pthírus pùbis* is broadly oval and somewhat crab-shaped, with the claws of the middle and hind legs very large, the head much narrower than the thorax, and the abdominal segments with lateral lobes. Adults are 1.5–2.0 mm in length. This louse occurs chiefly in the pubic region, but in hairy individuals may occur almost anywhere on the body. The eggs (nits) are attached to body hairs. The crab louse is an irritating pest, but is not known to transmit any disease.

Collecting and Preserving Phthiráptera

The only effective way to find lice is to examine their hosts carefully. Hosts other than domestic animals usually must be shot or trapped. Lice may occasionally be found still attached to museum skins of birds or mammals. Small host animals collected in the field to be examined later should be placed in a tightly closed bag. Any lice that fall or crawl off the host can then be found in the bag. Different species or, preferably, different individuals should be placed in separate bags so as to be certain of the host relationship.

All parts of the host should be examined, since different species of lice often occur on different parts of the same host. The best way to locate lice is to go over the host carefully with forceps, or a comb can often be used to advantage. The lice will sometimes fall off if the host is shaken over a sheet of paper. Lice may be picked up with forceps or with a camel's-hair brush moistened with alcohol.

Lice should be preserved in 70–75% alcohol, along with collection and host data. A different vial should be used for the lice from each host, and the collection data (on a penciled label inside the vial) should include the host species, the date, the locality, and the name of the collector.

Lice must be mounted on microscope slides for detailed study; specimens preserved on pins or points are usually unsatisfactory. Specimens to be mounted are first cleared for a day or so in cold potassium hydroxide. It is sometimes desirable to stain the specimen before mounting it on a slide. Kim *et al.* (1986, pp. 3–5) give detailed directions for collecting and mounting Anoplùra.

References

Clay, T. 1970. The Amblycera (Phthiraptera: Insecta). Bull. Brit. Mus. (Nat. Hist.) Entomol. 25:73–98.

Emerson, K. C. 1972. Checklist of the Mallophaga of North America (north of Mexico). Part I: Suborder Ischnocera, 200 pp. Part II: Suborder Amblycera, 118 pp. Part III: Mammal host list, 28 pp. Part IV: Bird host list, 216 pp. Dugway, Utah: Desert Test Center.

Emerson, K. C., and R. D. Price. 1981. A host-parasite list of the Mallophaga on mammals. Misc. Publ. Entomol. Soc. Amer. 12(1):1–72.

Ewing, H. E. 1924. Taxonomy, biology, and distribution of the Gyropidae. Proc. U.S. Natl. Mus. 63(20):1–42.

Ewing, H. E. 1929. A manual of external parasites. Springfield, Ill.: Charles C. Thomas, 225 pp.; illus. (Especially Chap. 4, pp. 127–152).

Ferris, G. F. 1919–1933. Contributions toward a monograph of the sucking lice. Stanford Univ. Publ. Biol. Sci. 2:1–634; illus.

Ferris, G. F. 1951. The sucking lice. Mem. Pac. Coast Entomol. Soc. 1:1–321; illus.

Hopkins, G. H. E., and T. Clay. 1952. A Check List of the Genera and Species of Mallophaga. London: British Museum (Nat. Hist.), 362 pp.

Kim, K. C. (Ed.) 1985. Coevolution of parasitic arthropods and mammals. New York: Wiley, 800 pp.; illus.

Kim, K. C. 1987. Order Anoplura, pp. 224–245 *in* F. W. Stehr (ed.), Immature Insects. Dubuque, Iowa: Kendall/Hunt, 754 pp.; illus.

Kim, K. C., and H. W. Ludwig. 1978a. The family classification of the Anoplura. Syst. Entomol. 3:249–284; illus.

Kim, K. C., and H. W. Ludwig. 1978b. Phylogenetic relationships of parasitic Psocodea and taxonomic position of the Anoplura. Ann. Entomol. Soc. Amer. 71:910–922; illus.

Kim, K. C., and H. W. Ludwig. 1982. Parallel evolution, cladistics, and classification of parasitic Psocodea. Ann. Entomol. Soc. Amer. 75:537–548; illus.

Kim, K. C., H. D. Pratt, and C. J. Stojanovich. 1986. The sucking lice of North America. University Park: Pennsylvania State University. Press, 241 pp.; illus.

Price, R. D. 1987. Order Mallophaga, pp. 215–223 *in* F. W. Stehr (ed.), Immature Insects. Dubuque, Iowa: Kendall/Hunt, 754 pp.; illus.

Werneck, F. L. 1948–1950. Os Malófagos de Mamíferos. Parte I: Amblycera e Ischnocera (Philopteridae e parte de Trichodectidae), 243 pp. (1948). Parte II: Ischnocera (continuação de Trichodectidae) e Rhynchophthirina, 207 pp. (1950). Rio de Janeiro: Edição da Revista Brasileira de Biologia.

Chapter 24

Order Hemíptera[1]
Bugs

The term *bug* is used by the general public for a great many different animals and by entomologists for occasional insects in other orders (for example, mealybugs, lightningbugs). When used for an insect in the order Hemíptera, the *bug* of the name is written as a separate word. The Hemíptera are sometimes called the "true" bugs, to distinguish them from occasional insects in other orders to which the term *bug* is applied.

One of the most distinctive features of the Hemíptera, and one from which the order gets its name, is the structure of the front wings. In most Hemíptera the basal portion of the front wing is thickened and leathery, and the apical portion is membranous. This type of wing is called a hemelytron (plural, hemelytra). The hind wings are entirely membranous and are slightly shorter than the front wings. The wings at rest are held flat over the abdomen, with the membranous tips of the front wings overlapping.

The mouthparts of the Hemíptera are of the piercing-sucking type and are in the form of a slender, usually segmented beak that arises from the front part of the head and generally extends back along the ventral side of the body, sometimes well

beyond the bases of the hind legs (Figure 24–1B, *bk*). The segmented portion of the beak is the labium, which serves as a sheath for the four piercing stylets (two mandibles and two maxillae). The maxillae fit together in the beak to form two channels, a food channel and a salivary channel (Figure 3–17). There are no palps, though certain tiny lobelike structures on the beak of some aquatic bugs are thought by some authorities to represent palps.

The Hemíptera and the Homóptera are very similar in many respects and are grouped by some authorities in a single order, the Hemíptera, with the two groups as the suborders Homóptera and Heteróptera (the latter including the true bugs). The two groups differ principally in the structure of the wings and in the location of the beak. The front wings in the Homóptera have a uniform texture throughout, either leathery or membranous (hence the name *homo*, uniform; *ptera*, wings). In the Hemíptera the basal portion of the front wings is usually thickened. The beak in the Hemíptera arises from the front part of the head, whereas in the Homóptera it arises from the posterior part of the head (Figure 7–3).

The antennae are fairly long in most of the terrestrial Hemíptera and consist of four or five segments. The compound eyes are nearly always well developed, but the ocelli (two in number) may be present or absent (always absent in nymphs). Most

[1]Hemíptera: *hemi*, half; *ptera*, wings (referring to the fact that the front wings usually have the basal portion thickened and the distal portion membranous).

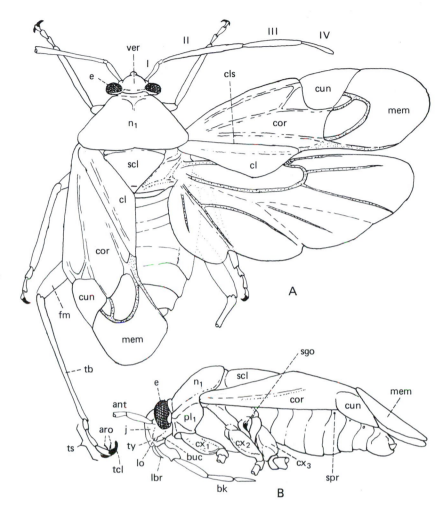

Figure 24–1.   Structure of a bug, *Lỳgus oblineàtus* (Say), family Míridae. **A,** dorsal view; **B,** lateral view. *ant*, antenna; *aro*, arolia; *bk*, beak; *buc*, buccula; *cl*, clavus; *cls*, claval suture; *cor*, corium; *cun*, cuneus; *cx*, coxa; *e*, compound eye; *fm*, femur; *j*, jugum; *lbr*, labrum; *lo*, lorum; *mem*, membrane; n_1, pronotum; pl_1, propleuron; *scl*, scutellum; *sgo*, scent gland opening; *spr*, spiracle; *tb*, tibia; *tcl*, tarsal claw; *ts*, tarsus; *ty*, tylús; *ver*, vertex; *I–IV*, antennal segments.

adult Hemíptera have scent glands that open on the sides of the thorax, whereas the scent glands of the nymphs are located on the dorsal surface of the abdomen. These glands (Figure 24–1B, *sgo*) give off a characteristic odor, particularly when the insect is disturbed. This odor is often unpleasant to people. Most of the Hemíptera have well-developed wings, but some species are wingless, some are brachypterous (wings short, the front wings usually lacking the membrane), and in some species both long-winged and brachypterous forms occur.

Hemíptera usually lay their eggs in or on plants or in crevices, or in some cases the eggs are simply dropped. Some eggs are relatively plain, but others are more elaborate (Figure 3–35). The members of this order undergo simple metamorphosis, and most of them have five nymphal instars.

The Hemíptera are a large and widely distributed group of insects. Most species are terrestrial, but many are aquatic. Many feed on plant juices, and some of these are serious pests of cultivated plants. Others are predaceous, and some of these are very beneficial to man. Still others attack humans and other animals and suck blood, and a few of these act as disease vectors.

Classification of the Hemíptera

We follow the classification of Štys and Kerzhner (1975) in dividing this order into seven suborders (indicated by the suffix -*morpha*). A synopsis of the Hemíptera occurring in North America is given below. Synonyms, alternate spellings, and other arrangements are given in parentheses. Groups marked with an asterisk are relatively rare or are unlikely to be taken by a general collector.

Suborder Enicocephalomórpha
 *Enicocephálidae—unique-headed bugs, gnat
   bugs
Suborder Dipsocoromórpha
 *Dipsocòridae (Cryptostemmátidae in part, Cer-
   atocómbidae)—jumping ground bugs
 *Schizoptéridae (Cryptostemmátidae in part)—
   jumping ground bugs
Suborder Nepomórpha—aquatic bugs
 Nèpidae—waterscorpions
 Belòstomátidae (Belòstomidae)—giant water bugs
 Coríxidae—water boatmen
 *Ochtéridae—velvety shore bugs
 Gelastocòridae (Galgùlidae)—toad bugs
 Naucòridae—creeping water bugs
 Notonéctidae—backswimmers
 Plèidae—pygmy backswimmers
Suborder Gerromórpha (Amphibicorìzae in part)—
   semiaquatic bugs
 Mesovelìidae—water treaders
 Hydrométridae—water measurers or marsh
   treaders
 Hèbridae—velvet water bugs
 *Macrovelìidae—macroveliid shore bugs
 Velìidae—broad-shouldered water striders, riffle
   bugs
 Gérridae—water striders
Suborder Leptopodomórpha
 Sáldidae—shore bugs
 *Leptopódidae—spiny shore bugs
Suborder Cimicomórpha
 *Thaumastocòridae—royal palm bugs
 Tíngidae—lace bugs
 *Microphỳsidae—microphysid bugs
 Míridae (including Isometópidae)—leaf bugs,
   plant bugs
 Nàbidae—damsel bugs
 Anthocòridae—minute pirate bugs
 Cimícidae—bed bugs
 *Polycténidae—bat bugs
 Reduvìidae (including Phymátidae and Ploiarì-
   idae)—assassin bugs, ambush bugs, thread-
   legged bugs
Suborder Pentatomomórpha
 Arádidae—flat bugs
 Piesmátidae—ash-gray leaf bugs
 Berýtidae (Neídidae)—stilt bugs
 Lygaèidae—seed bugs
 Lárgidae—largid bugs
 Pyrrhocòridae—red bugs, cotton stainers
 Corèidae—squash bugs, leaf-footed bugs
 Alỳdidae (Corìscidae)—broad-headed bugs
 Rhopálidae (Corìzidae)—scentless plant bugs
 Cýdnidae—burrower bugs
 Thyreocòridae (Corimelaènidae)—negro bugs

Scutelléridae—shield-backed bugs
Pentatómidae (including Podópidae)—stink bugs
Acanthosomátidae (Pentatómidae in part)—acan-
   thosomatid stink bugs

Characters Used in Identifying Hemíptera

The principal characters used in separating the families of the Hemíptera are those of the antennae,
beak, legs, and wings. Features of the thorax and
abdomen (particularly the symmetry or asymmetry
of the genitalia, the nature of the phallus and spermatheca, and the position of the spiracles and trichobothria), and such general characters as size,
shape, color, and habitat are sometimes used in separating families.

The antennae may be either four- or five-segmented.[2] In the Nepomórpha they are very short and
concealed in grooves on the underside of the head; in
the other suborders they are fairly long and conspicuous. The beak is usually three- or four-segmented
and in some groups fits into a groove on the prosternum when not in use. In the Pentatomòidea the five-
segmented antennae are often hidden beneath a ridge
on the side of the head.

The posterolateral angles of the pronotum are
sometimes referred to as the humeral angles, or the
humeri. The disk is the central dorsal portion of the
pronotum. It sometimes bears slightly raised areas
(the calli) anteriorly. In some cases the anterior border of the pronotum is more or less separated from
the rest of the pronotum by a groove or suture, thus
forming a collar. A few Hemíptera have the pronotum more or less two-parted, or divided into an anterior and a posterior lobe (for example, Figures
24–22C, 24–26B,F). Laterally the pronotum may be
sharp-edged (in which case it is described as "margined") or rounded.

The front legs in many of the predaceous Hemíptera are more or less modified into grasping structures and are spoken of as being raptorial. A raptorial
leg (Figure 24–2) usually has the femur enlarged and
armed with large spines on the ventroposterior margin. The tibia fits tightly against this armed surface,
and often it, too, bears conspicuous spines.

The Hemíptera generally have two or three tarsal
segments, the last of which bears a pair of claws.
The claws are apical in most of the Hemíptera, but

---

[2]In a few Hemíptera, some of the Reduvìidae, for example,
one of the antennal segments may be divided into several subsegments. In counting the antennal segments, the minute segments
between the larger segments are not counted.

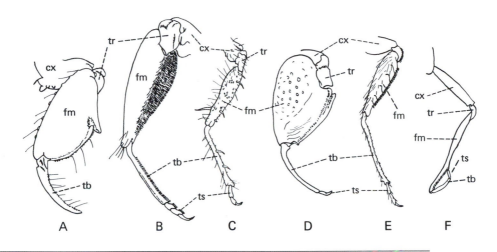

Figure 24–2.   Raptorial front legs of Hemíptera. **A,** *Phýmata* (Reduvìidae); **B,** *Lethócerus* (Belostomátidae); **C,** *Sìnea* (Reduvìidae); **D,** *Pelócoris* (Naucòridae); **E,** *Nàbis* (Nàbidae); **F,** *Ránatra* (Nèpidae). *cx,* coxa; *fm,* femur; *tb,* tibia; *tr,* trochanter; *ts,* tarsus.

in the water striders (Gérridae and Veliidae) they are anteapical; that is, they arise slightly proximad of the tip of the last tarsal segment (Figure 24–3C,D). Many Hemíptera have arolia, or lobelike pads, one at the base of each tarsal claw (Figure 24–3A, *aro*).

The hemelytra are subject to considerable modification in different groups of bugs, and special names are given to the different parts of the hemelytron (Figure 24–4). The thickened basal part of the hemelytron consists of two sections, the corium (*cor*) and the clavus (*cl*), which are separated by the claval suture (*cls*). The thin apical part of the hemelytron is the membrane (*mem*). In some Hemíptera a narrow strip of the corium along the costal margin is set off from the remainder of the corium by a suture; this is the embolium (Figure 24–4C, *emb*). In a few Hemíptera a cuneus (Figure 24–4A, *cun*) is set off by a suture in the apical part of the corium. The membrane usually contains veins, the number and arrangement of which often serve to separate different families.

The principal difficulties likely to be encountered in using the key are those involving the interpretation of certain characters and those resulting from the small size of some specimens. It is often necessary to use high magnification to determine the number of segments in the beak, particularly in small specimens.

Figure 24–3.   Tarsi of Hemíptera. **A,** hind tarsus of *Lygaèus* (Lygaèidae); **B,** middle tarsus of *Nàbis* (Nàbidae); **C,** front tarsus of *Gérris* (Gérridae); **D,** front tarsus and tibia of *Rhagovèlia* (Velìidae). *aro,* arolia; *tb,* tibia; *tcl,* tarsal claw.

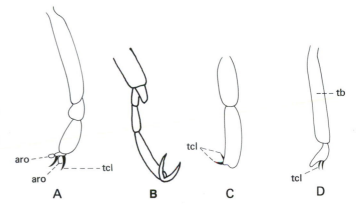

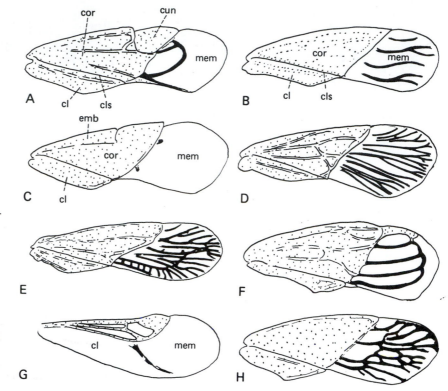

Figure 24–4.   Hemelytra of Hemíptera. **A,** *Lỳgus* (Míridae); **B,** *Ligyrócorus* (Lygaèidae); **C,** *Òrius* (Anthocòridae); **D,** *Bòisea* (Rhopálidae); **E,** *Nàbis* (Nàbidae); **F,** *Sáldula* (Sáldidae); **G,** *Mesovèlia* (Mesovelìidae); **H,** *Lárgus* (Lárgidae). *cl,* clavus; *cls,* claval suture; *cor,* corium; *cun,* cuneus; *emb,* embolium; *mem,* membrane.

Key to the Families of Hemíptera

This key is based on adults, but it will work for some nymphs. Families marked with an asterisk are relatively rare or are unlikely to be taken by a general collector. Some brachypterous forms may not key out correctly in this key, because they either lack ocelli or do not show the wing characteristics used in the key.

1.	Compound eyes present **2**	
1'.	Compound eyes absent; ectoparasites of bats, 3.5–4.5 mm in length; western United States . . . .**Polycténidae***	p. 301
2(1).	Antennae shorter than head, usually (except Ochtéridae*) hidden in cavities beneath eyes (Figure 24–5A); no arolia; aquatic or semiaquatic (suborder Nepomórpha) **3**	
2'.	Antennae as long as or longer than head, usually free and visible from above; arolia present or absent; habits variable **10**	
3(2).	Ocelli present (Figure 24–5B); length 10 mm or less; shore species **4**	
3'.	Ocelli absent; size variable; aquatic species **5**	
4(3).	Antennae hidden; front legs shorter than middle legs; eyes strongly protuberant (Figure 24–12); beak short, concealed by front femora . . . .**Gelastocòridae**	p. 295
4'.	Antennae exposed; front legs as long as middle legs; eyes not strongly protuberant; beak long, extending at least to hind coxae . . . .**Ochtéridae***	p. 295
5(3').	Front tarsi 1-segmented and modified into scoop-shaped structures (Figure 24–6); beak very short and hidden, appearing 1-segmented; dorsal surface of body usually with fine transverse lines . . . .**Coríxidae**	p. 295

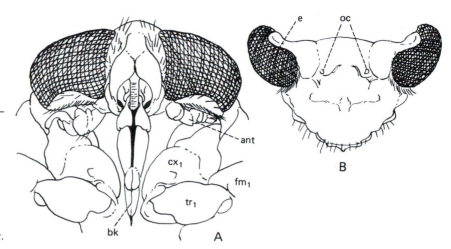

Figure 24–5. Head structure in Nepomórpha. **A,** *Lethócerus* (Belostomátidae), ventroanterior view; **B,** *Gelastócoris* (Gelastocòridae), dorsoanterior view. *ant* antenna; *bk*, beak; *cx₁*, front coxa; *e*, compound eye; *fm*, femur; *oc*, ocelli; *tr*, trochanter.

5′.	Front tarsi not as above; beak segmentation clearly evident; dorsal surface of body not as above **6**	
6(5′).	Body with 2 long terminal filaments (Figure 24–9); tarsi 1-segmented..**Nèpidae**	p. 294
6′.	Body without terminal filaments or, at most, with short ones (Figure 24–10); tarsi variable **7**	
7(6′).	Hind legs long and oarlike (Figure 24–14); hind tarsi without claws; length 5–16 mm ....**Notonéctidae**	p. 296
7′.	Hind legs not unusually lengthened; hind tarsi with claws; length variable ...**8**	
8(7′).	Oval, beetlelike, convex, 3 mm in length or less; front legs not raptorial ....**Plèidae***	p. 296
8′.	More than 3 mm in length, often more than 20 mm; not strongly convex; front legs raptorial with femora thickened **9**	
9(8′).	Membrane of hemelytra with veins; abdomen with short terminal filaments (Figure 24–10); length over 20 mm ....**Belostomátidae**	p. 294
9′.	Membrane of hemelytra without veins; abdomen without terminal filaments (Figure 24–13); length 5–16 mm ....**Naucòridae**	p. 296
10(2′).	Body linear, head as long as entire thorax, and legs very slender (Figure 24–16); aquatic or semiaquatic bugs ....**Hydrométridae**	p. 297
10′.	Body of various forms, but if linear, then head shorter than thorax and the insect terrestrial **11**	
11(10′).	Tarsal claws, especially on front legs, anteapical (Figure 24–3C,D); tip of last tarsal segment more or less cleft; aquatic, surface inhabiting **12**	
11′.	Tarsal claws apical; tip of last tarsal segment entire **13**	
12(11).	Middle legs arising closer to hind legs than to front legs; hind femora extending well beyond apex of abdomen (Figure 24–17A); all tarsi 2-segmented; ocelli present but small; usually over 5 mm in length ......**Gérridae**	p. 298
12′.	Middle legs usually arising about midway between front and hind legs; if middle legs arise closer to hind legs than front legs (*Rhagovèlia*), then front tarsi apparently 1-segmented (Figure 24–17B); hind femora extending little if any beyond apex of abdomen; tarsi 1-, 2-, or 3-segmented; ocelli absent, 1.6–5.5 mm in length ....**Velìidae**	p. 298

13(11′).	Antennae 4-segmented **14**	
13′.	Antennae 5–segmented **43**	
14(13).	Prosternum with a median, finely striated, longitudinal groove (Figure 24–7B, *stg*); beak short, 3-segmented, its tip fitting into prosternal groove; front legs usually raptorial ....**Reduviidae**	p. 301
14′.	Prosternum without such a groove; beak longer, its tip not fitting into prosternal groove, 3- or 4-segmented; front legs variable **15**	
15(14′).	Front wings with numerous closed cells (reticulately sculptured), without distinct division into corium, clavus, and membrane (Figure 24–18); pronotum with triangular process that extends back over scutellum; tarsi 1- or 2-segmented; ocelli absent; small somewhat flattened bugs, usually less than 5 mm in length ....**Tíngidae**	p. 299
15′.	Front wings with a variable arrangement of cells, but corium, membrane, and usually also clavus differentiated; pronotum usually without triangular process that extends back over scutellum; tarsi, ocelli, and size variable **16**	
16(15′).	Ocelli present **17**	
16′.	Ocelli absent **36**	
17(16).	Tarsi, at least on hind legs, 2-segmented **18**	
17′.	Tarsi, at least on hind legs, 3-segmented **23**	
18(17).	Antennae with 2 basal segments short and thick, third and fourth segments very slender (Figure 24–7A); 2 mm in length or less **24***	
18′.	Not exactly fitting the above description **19**	

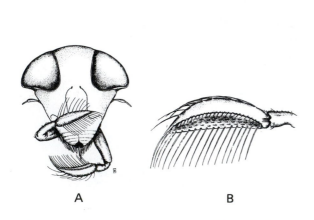

Figure 24–6. *Coríxa* (Coríxidae). **A,** head, anterior view; **B,** front leg. (Courtesy of Hungerford.)

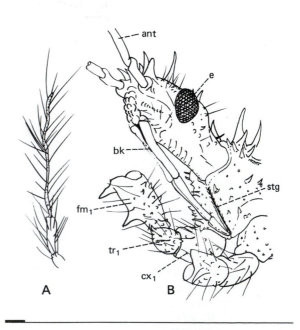

Figure 24–7. **A,** antenna of *Cryptostemátida* (Dipsocòridae); **B,** head of *Sìnea* (Reduvìidae). *ant*, antenna; *bk*, beak; *cx*, coxa; *e*, compound eye; *fm*, femur; *stg*, prosternal groove; *tr*, trochanter.

19(18').	Clavus and membrane of hemelytra similar in texture (as in Figure 24–4G) (some are brachypterous); body densely clothed with short velvety hairs; stout-bodied, semiaquatic bugs (*Merragàta*) ....**Hèbridae***	p. 297
19'.	Clavus and membrane of hemelytra different in texture; body not as above **20**	
20(19').	Hemelytra with a cuneus; shining black, 1.2 mm in length, recorded from Maryland and the District of Columbia ....**Microphỳsidae***	p. 299
20'.	Hemelytra without a cuneus **21**	
21(20').	Corium and clavus reticulated, with an irregular network of small cells; juga extending considerably beyond tylus; pronotum with longitudinal ridges (Figure 24–24) ....**Piesmátidae**	p. 303
21'.	Corium and clavus not as above; juga not extending considerably beyond tylus; pronotum without longitudinal ridges **22***	
22(21').	Elongate bugs 3–5 mm in length (Figure 24–8); front wings entirely membranous, corium and membrane not differentiated; front legs raptorial; beak 4-segmented; widely distributed, but rare ....**Enicocephálidae***	p. 294
22'.	Oblong-oval, somewhat flattened bugs, 2–3 mm in length; front wings with corium and membrane differentiated; front legs not raptorial; beak 3-segmented; occurring in Florida on royal palm ....**Thaumastocòridae***	p. 299
23(17').	Antennae with 2 basal segments short and thick, third and fourth very slender (Figure 24–7A); tarsi and beak 3-segmented; length 3.5 mm or less **24***	
23'.	Antennal segments similar, not as above; tarsi and size variable **26**	
24(18,23).	Head (including eyes), pronotum, front wings, front legs very spiny; third and fourth antennal segments not hairy; front femora thickened; 3.5 mm in length; California ....**Leptopódidae***	p. 299
24'.	Body not spiny; third and fourth antennal segments hairy (Figure 24–7A); 1–2 mm in length; widely distributed **25***	
25(24').	Eyes projecting outward, not overlapping front angles of pronotum; head and tibiae with strong bristles; second antennal segment about twice as long as first ....**Dipsocòridae***	p. 294
25'.	Eyes projecting outward and backward, overlapping front angles of pronotum; head and tibiae without strong bristles; first 2 antennal segments about equal in length ....**Schizoptéridae***	p. 294
26(23').	Hemelytra with a cuneus; small to minute bugs, 1.2–5.0 mm in length, usually 2–3 mm **27**	
26'.	Hemelytra without a cuneus; size variable **28**	
27(26).	Beak 3–segmented (Figure 24–21B) ....**Anthocòridae**	p. 301
27'.	Beak 4-segmented (Isometopìnae) ....**Míridae***	p. 299
28(26').	Beak 3-segmented **29**	
28'.	Beak 4-segmented **30**	
29(28).	Membrane of hemelytra with 4 or 5 long closed cells (Figure 24–4F) ...**Sáldidae**	p. 298
29'.	Membrane of hemelytra without veins, more or less confluent with the membranous clavus (Figures 24–4G, 24–15A) ....**Mesovelìidae***	p. 297
30(28').	Bugs resembling mesoveliids in general appearance (Figure 24–15A), but with closed cells in the front wings, pronotum with a median backward-projecting lobe that covers scutellum; western United States ....**Macrovelìidae***	p. 297
30'.	Without the above combination of characters **31**	

31(30′).   Tips of front and middle tibiae with broad flat apical process (Figure 24–3B); arolia absent; membrane of hemelytra (when developed) with numerous marginal cells (Figures 24–4E, 24–20A) (Nabìnae) ....**Nàbidae**   p. 300

31′.   Tips of front and middle tibiae without such a process; arolia present (Figure 24–3A); membrane of hemelytra variable **32**

32(31′).   Body and appendages long and slender; first segment of antennae long and enlarged apically, last segment spindle-shaped; femora clavate (Figure 24–25) ....**Berýtidae**   p. 303

32′.   Body shape variable; antennae and femora not as above **33**

33(32′).   Membrane of hemelytra with only 4 or 5 veins (Figure 24–4B) ....**Lygaèidae**   p. 304

33′.   Membrane of hemelytra with many veins (Figure 24–4D) **34**

34(33′).   Usually dark-colored, over 10 mm in length; scent glands present, opening between middle and hind coxae (Figure 24–1B, *sgo*) **35**

34′.   Usually pale-colored, less than 10 mm in length; scent glands absent ....**Rhopálidae**   p. 307

35(34).   Head narrower and shorter than pronotum (Figure 24–29A–C); bucculae (lateral view) extending backward beyond base of antennae; hind coxae more or less rounded or quadrate ....**Corèidae**   p. 306

35′.   Head nearly as wide and as long as pronotum (Figure 24–29D); bucculae (lateral view) shorter, not extending backward beyond base of antennae; hind coxae more or less transverse ....**Alýdidae**   p. 307

36(16′).   Tarsi 1-segmented; beak 3-segmented; front legs raptorial, the front femora slightly swollen; elongate, slender, 3.5–5.0 mm in length, with constriction near middle of body; yellowish or greenish yellow with reddish brown markings; eastern United States (Carthasìnae) ....**Nàbidae***   p. 300

36′.   Tarsi 2- or 3-segmented; beak 3- or 4-segmented; front legs usually not raptorial; size, shape, color variable **37**

37(36′).   Beak short, 3-segmented, fitting into groove in prosternum (Figure 24–7B); front femora more or less enlarged, raptorial; head more or less cylindrical, usually with transverse suture near eyes (Emesìnae and Saicìnae) ....**Reduvìidae**   p. 301

37′.   Beak longer, 3- or 4-segmented, not fitting into groove in prosternum; front femora and head variable **38**

38(37′).   Beak 3-segmented; wings vestigial (Figure 24–21A); ectoparasites of birds and mammals ....**Cimícidae**   p. 301

38′.   Beak 4-segmented (only 2–3 segments can be seen in some Arádidae); wings usually well developed **39**

39(38′).   Hemelytra with cuneus, the membrane with 1 or 2 closed cells, rarely with other veins (Figure 24–4A); rarely (for example, *Hálticus*; Figure 24–19A) membrane absent, in which case cuneus lacking, hind femora enlarged; mesosternum and metasternum formed of more than 1 sclerite ......**Míridae**   p. 299

39′.   Hemelytra without cuneus, membrane not as above; mesosternum and metasternum formed of a single sclerite **40**

40(39′).   Tarsi 2-segmented, without arolia; body very flat; usually dull-colored, gray, brown, or black (Figure 24–23) ....**Arádidae**   p. 303

40′.   Tarsi 3-segmented, with arolia; body not particularly flattened; often brightly colored **41**

41(40′).   Elongate, shining black bugs, 7–9 mm in length; front femora moderately swollen and armed beneath with 2 rows of teeth (*Cnemòdus*) .....**Lygaèidae**   p. 304

41′.   Color variable, but usually not shining black; 8–18 mm in length; front femora not swollen and usually not armed with teeth **42**

42(41′).   Pronotum margined laterally; sixth visible abdominal sternum entire in both sexes ....**Pyrrhocòridae**   p. 306

42′.   Pronotum rounded laterally; sixth visible abdominal sternum of female cleft to base ....**Lárgidae**   p. 305

43(13′).   Tarsi 2-segmented; body densely clothed with velvety pubescence; hemelytra with clavus and membrane similar in texture and without veins; the two basal antennal segments thicker than others; semiaquatic bugs, 3 mm in length or less (*Hèbrus*; Figure 24–15B) ....**Hèbridae***   p. 297

43′.   Tarsi usually 3-segmented (2-segmented in Acanthosomátidae); body not covered with velvety pubescence; hemelytra with clavus and membrane differentiated, membrane usually with veins; the 2 basal antennal segments similar to others; terrestrial; usually over 3 mm in length **44**

44(43′).   Tips of front and middle femora with broad flat apical process (Figure 24–3B); scutellum only about one-fifth as long as abdomen; shining black bugs 5–7 mm in length; body elongate and narrowed anteriorly, the pronotum distinctly narrower than the widest part of the abdomen (Prostemmìnae: *Pàgasa*) ....**Nàbidae***   p. 300

44′.   Tips of front and middle tibiae without such a process; size variable; color variable, but if shining black then body is oval or shield-shaped **45**

45(44′).   Tibiae armed with strong spines (Figure 24–30A); color usually shining black; length 8 mm or less **46**

45′.   Tibiae not armed with strong spines (Figure 24–30B); color rarely shining black; usually over 8 mm in length **47**

46(45).   Scutellum very large, broadly rounded posteriorly, covering most of abdomen (Figure 24–31A); length usually 3–4 mm ....**Thyreocòridae**   p. 307

46′.   Scutellum more or less triangular, not extending to apex of abdomen (Figure 24–31B); length up to about 8 mm ....**Cÿdnidae**   p. 307

47(45′).   Scutellum very large, broadly rounded posteriorly, covering most of the abdomen (Figure 24–32); corium of hemelytra narrow, not extending to anal margin of wing **48**

47′.   Scutellum shorter, usually narrower posteriorly and more or less triangular (Figures 24–33, 24–34), if large and broadly rounded posteriorly (*Stíretrus*, family Pentatómidae, subfamily Asopìnae), colors are bright and contrasting; corium of hemelytra broad, extending to anal margin of wing **49**

48(47).   Sides of pronotum with a prominent tooth or lobe in front of humeral angle (Figure 24–32B); length 3.5–6.5 mm (*Amauróchrous*) ....**Pentatómidae***   p. 307

48′.   Sides of pronotum without such a tooth or lobe (Figure 24–32A); length 8–10 mm ....**Scutelléridae**   p. 307

49(47′).   Tarsi 2-segmented; sternum of thorax with median longitudinal ridge or keel ....**Acanthosomátidae**   p. 308

49′.   Tarsi 3-segmented; sternum of thorax usually without median longitudinal keel ....**Pentatómidae**   p. 307

SUBORDER **Enicocephalomórpha:** This suborder includes a single North American family, the Enicocephálidae, which was formerly thought to be related to the Reduvìidae because of similarities in head structure. It is now believed to be sufficiently different from other Hemíptera to constitute a separate suborder and probably represents the sister group of the rest of the order.

Family **Enicocephálidae**—Unique-Headed Bugs or Gnat Bugs: These are small (2–5 mm in length), slender, predaceous bugs that have a peculiarly shaped head and the front wings entirely membranous (Figure 24–8). They usually occur under stones or bark or in debris, where they feed on various small insects. Some species form large swarms and fly about like gnats or midges. This is a small group (four North American species), and its members are rather rare.

SUBORDER **Dipsocoromórpha:** This group contains a few small and seldom-encountered bugs whose position in the order is not well understood.

Families **Dipsocòridae and Schizoptéridae**—Jumping Ground Bugs: These are minute oval bugs, 1.0–1.5 mm in length, which live in moist places on the ground, beneath dead leaves, or in moist soil. The Schizoptéridae jump actively when disturbed. Only seven species in these two families occur in the United States. They are principally southern in distribution and uncommon.

SUBORDER **Nepomórpha:** The Nepomórpha are aquatic (rarely shore-inhabiting). The antennae are shorter than the head and usually concealed in grooves on the underside of the head. Trichobothria are absent.

Family **Nèpidae**—Waterscorpions: The waterscorpions are predaceous aquatic bugs with raptorial front legs and with a long caudal breathing tube formed by the cerci. The breathing tube is often almost as long as the body and is thrust up to the surface as the insect crawls about on aquatic vegetation. These insects move slowly and prey on various types of small aquatic animals, which they capture with their front legs. Waterscorpions can inflict a painful bite when handled. They have well-developed wings, but seldom fly. The eggs are inserted into the tissues of aquatic plants.

Three genera and 12 species of waterscorpions occur in the United States and Canada. The nine species of *Ránatra* are slender and elongate with very long legs and are somewhat similar to walkingsticks in appearance (Figure 24–9B). Our only species of *Nèpa, N. apiculàta* Uhler, has the body oval and somewhat flattened (Figure 24–9A). The body shape in *Curícta* is somewhat intermediate between those of *Ránatra* and *Nèpa*. Our most common waterscorpions belong to the genus *Ránatra; N. apiculàta* is less common and occurs in the eastern states; the two species of *Curícta* are relatively rare and occur in the Southwest.

Family **Belostomátidae**—Giant Water Bugs: This family contains the largest bugs in the order, some of which (in the United States) may reach a length of 65 mm. One species in South America is more than 100 mm long. These bugs are elongate-oval and somewhat flattened, with the front legs raptorial (Figure 24–10). They are fairly common in ponds and lakes, where they feed on other insects, snails, tadpoles, and even small fish. They frequently leave the water and fly about, and because they are often attracted to lights, they are sometimes called electric light bugs. Giant water bugs can inflict a painful bite if handled carelessly. In some species (*Belostòma* and *Ábedus*), the eggs are laid on the back of the male, which carries them about until they hatch. The eggs of other species (*Lethócerus*) are attached to aquatic vegetation.

The 19 species of giant water bugs in North America are classified in three genera: *Lethócerus, Belostòma*, and *Ábedus*. The first two are widely distributed, while *Ábedus* occurs only in the South and West. The species of *Lethócerus* are our largest belostomatids (45–65 mm in length) (Figure 24–10) and have the basal segment of the beak very short. Most species of *Belostòma* are about 25 mm in length, and they have the membrane of the hemelytra well developed. *Ábedus* has the membrane of the hemelytra much reduced. One species occurring in

Figure 24–8. A gnat bug, *Systellóderes bìceps* (Say), 15×. (Courtesy of Froeschner and the American Midland Naturalist.)

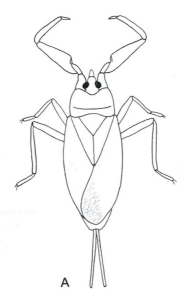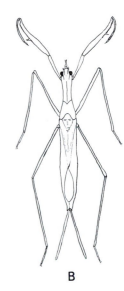

Figure 24–9. Waterscorpions. **A,** *Nèpa apiculàta* Uhler, 2×; **B,** *Ránatra fúsca* Palisot de Beauvois, about natural size.

the Southwest (usually in streams) is 27–37 mm in length, but a relatively rare species occurring in the southeastern states is only 12–15 mm in length.

Family **Coríxidae**—Water Boatmen: This is the largest family in the suborder, with about 120 North American species, and its members are common insects in freshwater ponds and lakes. They occasionally occur in streams, and a few species occur in the brackish pools just above the high-tide mark along the seashore. The body is elongate-oval (Figure 24–11), somewhat flattened, and usually dark gray in color. The dorsal surface of the body is often cross-lined. The middle and hind legs are elongate, and the hind legs are oarlike. The beak is broad, conical, and unsegmented; the front wings are uniform in texture throughout and the front tarsi are scoop-shaped (Figure 24–6B). Like all other aquatic bugs, they lack gills and obtain air at the surface of the water. They frequently carry a bubble of air under water, either on the surface of the body or under the wings. They swim rapidly, usually in a somewhat erratic fashion, but often cling to vegetation for long periods.

Most water boatmen feed on algae and other minute aquatic organisms. A few are predaceous, feeding on midge larvae and other small aquatic animals. They are apparently able to take in solid particles of food, not just liquids. Unlike most other aquatic bugs, water boatmen will not bite people.

The eggs of water boatmen are usually attached to aquatic plants. In some parts of the world (for example, certain parts of Mexico) water boatmen eggs are used as food. They are collected from aquatic plants, dried, and later ground into flour. Water boatmen are an important item of food for many aquatic animals.

Family **Ochtéridae**—Velvety Shore Bugs: These are oval-bodied insects 4–5 mm in length that occur along the shores of quiet streams and ponds, but they are uncommon. They are velvety bluish or black in color and are predaceous. Seven species occur in the United States.

Family **Gelastocòridae**—Toad Bugs: These bugs superficially resemble small toads, in both appearance and hopping habits. They are short and broad,

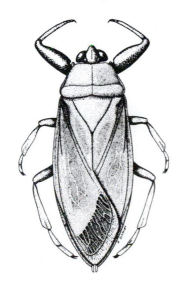

Figure 24–10. A giant water bug, *Lethócerus gríseus* (Say), about natural size.

have large projecting eyes (Figure 24–12), and are usually found along the moist margins of ponds and streams. One has to examine them closely to be certain they are not toads. Toad bugs feed on other insects. They capture their prey by leaping on it and grasping it in their front legs. The eggs are laid in the sand. This family is a small one, with only seven species occurring in North America.

Family **Naucòridae**—Creeping Water Bugs: These bugs are brownish in color, broadly oval and somewhat flattened, and 9–13 mm in length. The front femora are greatly thickened (Figure 24–13). They are most common in quiet water, where they may be found in submerged vegetation or in debris. Some occur in streams. They feed on various small aquatic animals. They bite quite readily—and painfully—when handled. There are about 20 North American species, only two of which (in the genus *Pelócoris*) occur in the East.

Family **Notonéctidae**—Backswimmers: The backswimmers are so named because they swim upside down. They are very similar to the water boatmen in shape (Figure 24–14), but have the dorsal side of the body more convex and usually light-colored. They frequently rest at the surface of the water, with the body at an angle and the head down, and with the long hind legs extended. They can swim rapidly, using the hind legs like oars.

Backswimmers are predaceous, feeding on other insects and occasionally on tadpoles and small fish. They frequently attack animals larger than themselves and feed by sucking the body juices from their prey. A common method of capturing prey is to drift up under it after releasing hold of a submerged plant to which the attacker has been clinging. These in-

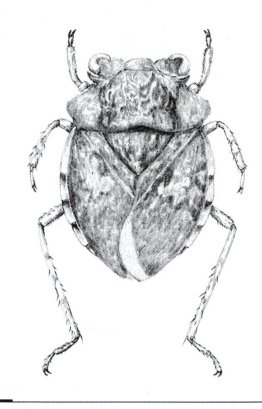

Figure 24–12.   A toad bug, *Gelastócoris oculàtus* (Fabricius), $7\frac{1}{2} \times$.

sects will bite people when handled, and the effect is much like a bee sting. Backswimmer eggs are deposited in the tissues of aquatic plants or glued to the surface of a plant.

Males of many species of backswimmers stridulate during courtship, by rubbing the front legs against the beak. The structure of the stridulatory areas often provides characters of value in separating species.

There are 34 species of backswimmers in North America, in three genera: *Buénoa*, *Notonécta*, and *Martárega*. The species of *Buénoa* are small (5–9 mm in length) and slender, with the antennae three-segmented, the hemelytra glabrous, and the scutellum distinctly shorter than the claval commissure. The other two genera are usually larger (8–17 mm in length) and a little stouter. The antennae are four-segmented, and the hemelytra are usually longer than the claval commissure. Most of the species, and most specimens collected, belong to the genus *Notonécta*.

Family **Plèidae**—Pygmy Backswimmers: These bugs are similar to the Notonéctidae, but are very small (1.6–2.3 mm in length) and have the dorsal

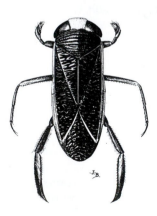

Figure 24–11.   A water boatman, *Hesperocoríxa atopodónta* (Hungerford), 7 ×. (Courtesy of Slater and Baranowski and the Wm. C. Brown Company.)

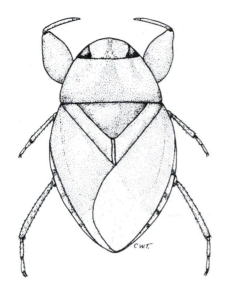

Figure 24–13. A creeping water bug, *Pelócoris femoràtus* (Palisot de Beauvois), 5×.

surface of the body very convex, with the wings forming a hard shell. Seven species occur in our area.

SUBORDERS **Gerromórpha and Leptopodomórpha:** The members of these suborders are semiaquatic or shore-inhabiting; they have conspicuous antennae; and they have three pairs of trichobothria on the head.

Family **Mesoveliidae**—Water Treaders: These bugs are usually found crawling over floating vegetation at the margins of ponds or pools or on logs projecting from the water. When disturbed they run rapidly over

the surface of the water. They are small (5 mm in length or less), slender, and usually greenish or yellowish green in color (Figure 24–15A). Within a species, some adults are winged and some are wingless. These insects feed on small aquatic organisms on and just beneath the surface of the water.

Family **Hydrométridae**—Water Measurers or Marsh Treaders: These bugs are small (about 8 mm in length), usually grayish in color, and very slender. They resemble tiny walking-sticks (Figure 24–16). The head is very long and slender, with the eyes conspicuously bulging laterally. These insects are usually wingless. They occur in shallow water among vegetation and feed on minute organisms. They frequently walk very slowly over surface vegetation or over the surface of the water. The eggs, which are elongate and about one-fourth as long as the adult, are laid singly and glued to objects near the water. Only seven species, all belonging to the genus *Hydrómetra*, occur in North America.

Family **Hèbridae**—Velvet Water Bugs: The hebrids are small (less than 3 mm in length) oblong bugs with a broad-shouldered appearance (Figure 24–15B), and the entire body is covered with velvety hairs. They occur on the surface of shallow pools where there is an abundance of aquatic vegetation and in damp soil near the water's edge. They are believed to be predaceous. This group contains 15 North American species, in two genera: *Merragàta* (antennae four-segmented) and *Hèbrus* (antennae five-segmented).

Family **Macroveliidae:** This group is represented in North America by a single species, *Macrovèlia*

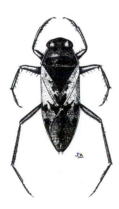

Figure 24–14. A backswimmer, *Notonécta insulàta* Kirby, 4×. (Courtesy of Slater and Baranowski and the Wm. C. Brown Company.)

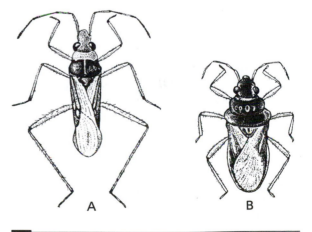

Figure 24–15. **A,** a water treader, *Mesovèlia mulsánti* White, 9×; **B,** a velvet water bug, *Hèbrus sobrìnus* Uhler, 16×. (Courtesy of Froeschner and the American Midland Naturalist.)

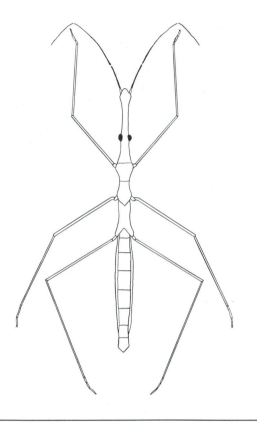

Figure 24–16. A water measurer, *Hydrómetra mártini* Kirkaldy, 7½×.

hórnii Uhler, which occurs in the West. This species resembles a mesoveliid in appearance (see Figure 24–15A), but differs in having six closed cells in the hemelytra, and the pronotum has a backward projecting lobe that covers the scutellum. It occurs along the shores of springs and streams, usually in moss or other protected places. It does not run about on the water surface, but it has never been taken more than a few feet from the water's edge.

Family **Veliidae**—Broad-Shouldered Water Striders, Riffle Bugs: These water striders are small (1.6–5.5 mm in length) and brown or black in color, often with silvery markings. They are usually wingless. They live on the surface of the water or on the adjacent shore and feed on various small insects. Members of the genus *Rhagovèlia* (Figure 24–17B) are gregarious, and a single sweep of a dip net may sometimes yield up to 50 or more specimens. These veliids occur on or near the riffles of small streams, but members of other genera are usually found in quieter parts of streams or on ponds. Three widely distributed genera, with more than 30 species, occur

in the United States: *Rhagovèlia*, *Microvèlia*, and *Paravèlia*.

Family **Gérridae**—Water Striders: The water striders are long-legged insects (Figure 24–17A) that live on the surface of the water, running or skating over the surface and feeding on insects that fall onto the water. The front legs are short and are used in capturing food; the middle and hind legs are long and are used in locomotion. Most species are black or dark-colored, and the body is long and narrow.

The tarsi of water striders are clothed with fine hairs and are difficult to wet. This tarsal structure enables a water strider to skate around on the surface of the water. If the tarsi become wet, the insect can no longer stay on the surface film, and it will drown unless it can crawl up on some dry surface. When the tarsi dry again, they function normally.

These insects are common on quiet water in small coves or protected places. They often occur in large numbers. Species inhabiting small intermittent streams burrow down in the mud or under stones when the stream dries up and remain dormant until the stream fills with water again. The adults hibernate in such situations. Except for one genus, the water striders are restricted to fresh water. The species in the genus *Halóbates* live on the surface of the ocean, often many miles from land. Winged and wingless adults occur in many species, and the insect moves from one aquatic situation to another when in the winged stage. The eggs are laid at the surface of the water on floating objects.

Family **Sáldidae**—Shore Bugs: The shore bugs are small, oval, flattened, usually brown or black and white bugs that are often common along shores of

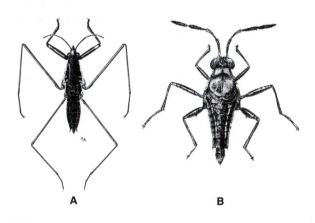

A   B

Figure 24–17. Water striders. **A,** *Gérris* sp. (Gérridae), 5×; **B,** *Rhagovèlia obèsa* Uhler (Velìidae), 10×. (Courtesy of Slater and Baranowski and the Wm. C. Brown Company.)

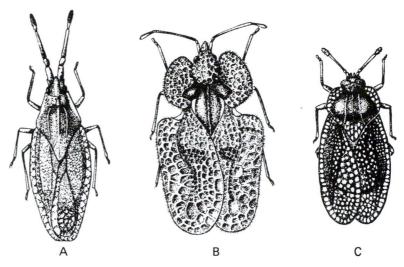

Figure 24–18.   Lace bugs. **A,** *Àtheas miméticus* Heidemann, 18×; **B,** the sycamore lace bug, *Corythùca ciliàta* (Say), 13×; **C,** *Acalýpta lilliànis* Bueno, 14×. (**A** and **B** redrawn from Froeschner and the American Midland Naturalist; **C,** redrawn from Osborn and Drake and the Ohio Biological Survey.)

A   B   C

streams, ponds, or the ocean. Some are burrowing in habit. When disturbed, they fly quickly for a short distance and then scurry under vegetation or into a crevice. They are predaceous on other insects. The shore bugs can usually be recognized by the four or five long closed cells in the membrane of the hemelytra (Figure 24–4F). There are about 70 North American species of shore bugs.

Family **Leptopódidae**—Spiny Shore Bugs: This is an Old World group, one species of which, *Patàpius spinòsus* (Rossi), has been introduced into California. It may be found from Butte County south to Los Angeles County. This bug is 3.3 mm in length and is yellowish brown with two dark brown transverse bands on the hemelytra.

SUBORDERS **Cimicomórpha and Pentatomomórpha:** These bugs are all terrestrial; they almost always have conspicuous antennae; and they usually have trichobothria. The majority are plant feeders, feeding on sap, flowers, fruits, or even mature seeds. A few are predaceous.

Family **Thaumastocòridae**—Royal Palm Bugs: This group is represented in the United States by a single species, *Xylastódoris lutèolus* Barber, which occurs in Florida. This insect is 2.0–2.5 mm in length, flattened, oblong-oval, and pale yellowish with reddish eyes. It feeds on the royal palm.

Family **Tíngidae**—Lace Bugs: This is a fairly large group (about 140 North American species) of small (less than 5 mm in length) bugs that have the dorsal surface of the body rather elaborately sculptured (Figure 24–18). This lacelike appearance is found only in the adults; the nymphs are usually spiny. These bugs are plant feeders, and while most species feed on herbaceous plants, some of our most common species feed on trees. Their feeding causes a

yellow spotting of the leaf, but with continued feeding the leaf becomes entirely brown and falls off. Some species do considerable damage to trees. The eggs are usually laid on the underside of the leaves. *Corythùca ciliàta* (Say) (Figure 24–18B), a common species that is somewhat milky in color, feeds chiefly on sycamore.

Family **Microphỳsidae:** This family is represented in the United States by a single species, *Mallochìola gagàtes* (McAtee and Malloch). This bug resembles a mirid in having a cuneus, but it has ocelli, symmetrical male genitalia, and tarsi that are two-segmented. It is broadly oval and somewhat flattened, shining black, and 1.2 mm in length. It is known only from Maryland and the District of Columbia.

Family **Míridae**—Plant Bugs or Leaf Bugs: This is the largest family in the order (about 1750 North American species), and its members are to be found on vegetation almost everywhere. Some are very abundant. Most species are plant feeders, but a few are predaceous on other insects. Some of the plant-feeding species are pests of cultivated plants.

The mirids are soft-bodied bugs, mostly 4–10 mm in length, that may be variously colored. Some species are brightly marked with red, orange, green, or white. Members of this group can be recognized by the presence of a cuneus and only one or two closed cells at the base of the membrane (Figure 24–1 and 24–4A). The antennae and beak are four-segmented, and ocelli are lacking (present in the Isometopìnae).

Figure 24–19 illustrates some of the more important mirids that attack cultivated plants. The meadow plant bug, *Leptoptérna dolobràta* (L.) (Figure 24–19D), is abundant in meadows and pastures in

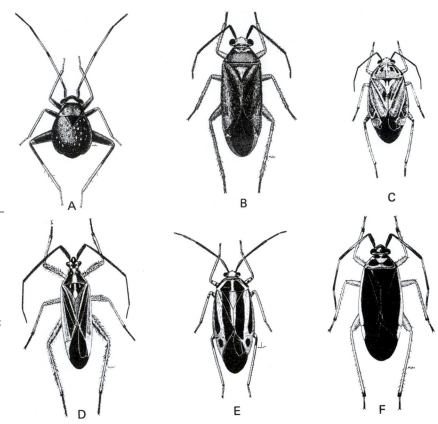

Figure 24–19. Plant or leaf bugs (Míridae). **A,** garden fleahopper, *Hálticus bractàtus* (Say), female, 10×; **B,** apple red bug, *Lygídea méndax* Reuter, female, 5×; **C,** tarnished plant bug, *Lỳgus lineolàris* (Palisot de Beauvois), 4×; **D,** meadow plant bug, *Leptoptérna dolobràta* (L.), male 4×; **E,** four-lined plant bug, *Poecilocápsus lineàtus* (Fabricius), 4×; **F,** rapid plant bug, *Adelphócoris rápidus* (Say), 4×. (Redrawn from the Illinois Natural History Survey.)

early summer and does considerable damage to grass. It is 7–9 mm in length. The tarnished plant bug, *Lỳgus lineolàris* (Palisot de Beauvois) (Figure 24–19C), is brown in color with a Y-shaped mark on the scutellum. It is a very common bug and often causes serious damage to legumes, vegetables, and flowers. This species occurs throughout the eastern and central states. Other species of *Lỳgus* are serious crop pests in the West. The four-lined plant bug *Poecilocápsus lineàtus* (Fabricius) (Figure 24–19E), is yellowish or greenish with four longitudinal black stripes on the body. It feeds on a large number of plants and sometimes causes serious damage to currants, gooseberries, and some ornamental flowers. The apple red bug, *Lygídea méndax* Reuter (Figure 24–19B), a red and black bug about 6 mm in length, was at one time a serious pest of apples in the Northeast, but has become less important in recent years. The rapid plant bug, *Adelphócoris rápidus* (Say) (Figure 24–19F), is 7–8 mm in length and dark brown with yellowish margins on the front wings. It feeds chiefly on dock, but sometimes injures cotton and legumes. The garden fleahopper, *Hálticus bractàtus*

(Say) (Figure 24–19A), is a common leaf bug that is often brachypterous. It is a shining black, jumping bug, 1.5–2.0 mm in length, that feeds on many cultivated plants but is often a pest of legumes. The front wings of the female (the sex illustrated) lack a membrane and resemble the elytra of a beetle. The males have normal wings, but the membrane is short.

This family is divided into a number of subfamilies, one of which, the Isometopìnae, is sometimes given family rank. These mirids, commonly called jumping ground bugs, differ from other mirids in having ocelli. They are found on bark and dead twigs, and they jump quickly when disturbed. The group is a small one, with less than a dozen North American species, all relatively rare.

Family **Nàbidae**—Damsel Bugs: The nabids are small bugs (3.5–11.0 mm in length) that are relatively slender with the front femora slightly enlarged (Figure 24–20), and the membrane of the hemelytra (when developed) has a number of small cells around the margin (Figures 24–4E and 24–20A). These bugs are predaceous on many different types of insects,

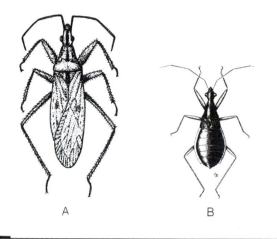

Figure 24–20.   Damsel bugs. **A,** *Nàbis americóferus* Carayon, 5×; **B,** *Nabícula subcoleoptràta* (Kirby), 4×. (**A,** redrawn from Froeschner and the American Midland Naturalist; **B,** courtesy of Slater and Baranowski and the Wm. C. Brown Company.)

including aphids and caterpillars. Whether the name "damsel" bug is appropriate for such predaceous insects perhaps depends on one's point of view.

The most commonly encountered damsel bugs are pale yellowish to brownish with well-developed wings. *Nàbis americóferus* Carayon (Figure 24–20A) is common throughout the United States. Some of the nabids occur in both long-winged and short-winged forms, but the long-winged forms are in many cases quite rare and it is the short-winged forms that are usually encountered. A fairly common nabid of this sort is *Nabícula subcoleoptràta* (Kirby), a shining black insect (Figure 24–20B) usually found in meadows, where it feeds chiefly on the meadow plant bug, *Leptoptérna dolobràta*.

Family **Anthocòridae**—Minute Pirate Bugs: These bugs are small (2–5 mm in length), elongate-oval, and somewhat flattened, and many species are black with whitish markings (Figure 24–21B). Most species are predaceous, feeding on various small insects and insect eggs. The insidious flower bug, *Òrius insidiòsus* (Say) (Figure 24–21B), is an important predator on the eggs and larvae of the corn earworm and many other pests. The bite of this bug is surprisingly painful for such a tiny insect. The common species of anthocorids are usually found on flowers, but some species occur under loose bark, in leaf litter, and in decaying fungi. About 70 species occur in North America.

Family **Cimícidae**—Bed Bugs: The bed bugs are flat, broadly oval, wingless bugs about 6 mm in length (Figure 24–21A) that feed by sucking blood from birds and mammals. The group is a small one, but some of the species are widely distributed and well known. The common beg bug that attacks people is *Cìmex lretulàrius* L. This species is sometimes a pest in houses, hotels, barracks, and other living quarters. It also attacks animals other than humans. A tropical species, *Cìmex hemípterus* (Fabricius) also bites people. Other species in this family attack bats and various birds.

The common bed bug is largely nocturnal and, during the day, hides in cracks in a wall, under the baseboard, in the springs of a bed, under the edge of a mattress, under wallpaper, and in similar places. Its flatness makes it possible for it to hide in very small crevices. Bed bugs may be transported from place to place on clothing or in luggage or furniture, or they may migrate from house to house. They lay their eggs, 100–250 per female, in cracks. Development to the adult stage requires about two months in warm weather. The adults may live for several months and can survive long periods without food. Bed bugs are important primarily because of their irritating bites; they are apparently unimportant as disease vectors.

Family **Polycténidae**—Bat Bugs: Only two rare species of bat bugs occur in the United States, one in Texas and the other in California. They are ectoparasites of bats. These bugs are wingless and lack compound eyes and ocelli. The front legs are short and flattened, and the middle and hind legs are long and slender. The body is generally covered with bristles. These bugs are 3.5–4.5 mm in length.

Family **Reduviidae**—Assassin Bugs, Ambush Bugs, and Thread-Legged Bugs: This is a large group (more

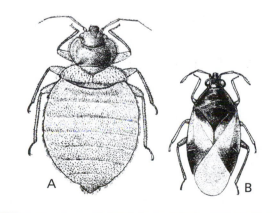

Figure 24–21.   **A,** the common bed bug, *Cìmex lectulàrius* (L.), 7×; **B,** insidious flower bug, *Òrius insidiòsus* (Say), 16×. (Courtesy of Froeschner and the American Midland Naturalist.)

than 160 North American species) of predaceous bugs, and many species are fairly common. They are often blackish or brownish in color, but many are brightly colored. The head is usually elongate with the part behind the eyes necklike. The beak is short and three-segmented, and its tip fits into a stridulatory groove in the prosternum (Figure 24–7B). The abdomen in many species is widened in the middle, exposing the lateral margins of the segments beyond the wings. Most species are predaceous on other insects, but a few are bloodsucking and frequently

bite people. Many species will inflict a painful bite if carelessly handled.

One of the largest and most easily recognized assassin bugs is the wheel bug, *Àrilus cristàtus* (L.), a grayish bug 28–36 mm in length, with a semicircular crest on the pronotum that terminates in teeth and resembles a cogwheel (Figure 24–22B). This species is fairly common in the East. The masked hunter, *Redùvius personàtus* (L.), is a brownish black bug (it resembles the reduviid shown in Figure 24–22C) 17–22 mm in length that is often found in

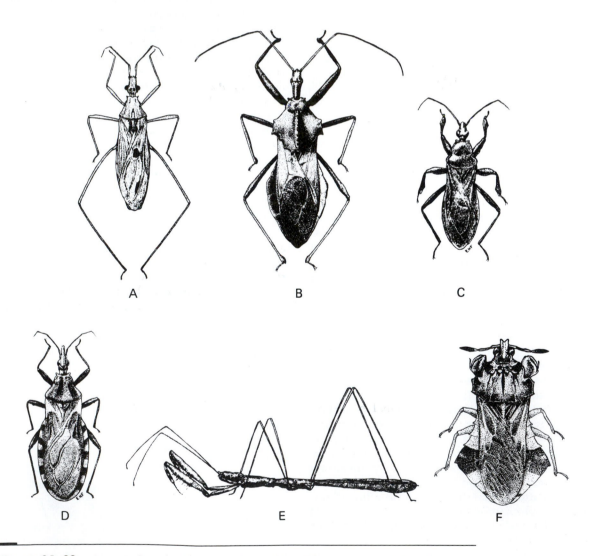

Figure 24–22. Assassin bugs (**A–D**), a thread-legged bug (**E**), and an ambush bug (**F**). **A,** *Narvèsus carolinénsis* Stål, 2½×; **B,** the wheel bug, *Àrilus cristàtus* (L.) 1½×; **C,** *Melanoléstes pìcipes* (Herrich-Schäffer), 2×; **D,** a bloodsucking conenose, *Triátoma sanguisùga* (LeConte), 2×; **E,** *Bárce ùhleri* (Banks), 5½×; **F,** *Phýmata fasciàta georgiénsis* Melin, 4½×. (Courtesy of Froeschner and the American Midland Naturalist.)

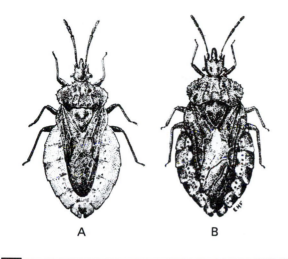

Figure 24–23. Flat bugs (Arádidae). **A,** *Áradus inornàtus* Uhler, 4½×; **B,** *Áradus acùtus* (Say), 5½×. (Redrawn from Froeschner and the American Midland Naturalist.)

houses. It feeds on bed bugs, but it will also bite people. The nymphs are soft-bodied and cover themselves with dust particles. They are often called "dust bugs" or "masked bedbug hunters."

The assassin bugs in the genus *Triátoma* also invade houses and bite people. They feed at night, biting any exposed parts (such as the face) of people sleeping. These bugs are sometimes called kissing bugs (because of their tendency to bite people about the mouth) or Mexican bed bugs. In South America species of this genus serve as vectors of a trypanosome disease of man known as Chagas' disease (several cases of this disease have recently been found in the United States). Armadillos, opossums, and certain rats also serve as a host for the trypanosome causing this disease.

Ambush bugs (Phymatìnae) are small stout-bodied bugs with the front femora much thickened and the terminal antennal segment swollen (Figure 24–22F). Most of the ambush bugs are about 13 mm in length or less, yet they are able to capture insects as large as fair-sized bumble bees. They lie in wait for their prey on flowers, particularly goldenrod, where they are excellently concealed by their greenish yellow color. They feed principally on large bees, wasps, and flies.

The thread-legged bugs (Emesìnae) are very slender and long-legged and resemble walkingsticks (Figure 24–22E). They occur in old barns, cellars, and dwellings, and outdoors beneath loose bark and in grass tufts, where they catch and feed on other in-sects. One of the largest and most common of the thread-legged bugs is *Emesàya brevipénnis* (Say), a widely distributed species that is 33–37 mm in length. Most of the thread-legged bugs are smaller (down to 4.5 mm in length). *Bárce ùhleri* (Banks) (Figure 24–22E) is 7–10 mm in length.

Family **Arádidae**—Flat Bugs: Nearly a hundred species in this group occur in North America. They are 3–11 mm in length, usually dark brownish, very flat bugs (Figure 24–23), with the body surface somewhat granular. The wings are well developed but small and do not cover the entire abdomen. The antennae and beak are four-segmented (sometimes only 2–3 segments of the beak visible); the tarsi are two-segmented; and there are no ocelli. These insects are usually found under loose bark or in crevices of dead or decaying trees. They feed on the sap of fungi.

Family **Piesmátidae**—Ash-Gray Leaf Bugs: These small bugs (2.5–3.5 mm in length) can usually be recognized by their reticulately sculptured corium and clavus, the two-segmented tarsi, the ridges of the pronotum, and the juga extending well beyond the tylus (Figure 24–24). They are plant feeders and are probably found most often on pigweed (*Amaránthus*), but feed also on other plants. The ten North American species in this group belong to the genus *Piésma.*

Family **Berýtidae**—Stilt Bugs: The stilt bugs are slender and elongate and have the legs and antennae very long and slender (Figure 24–25). They resemble the water measurers (Figure 24–16) and thread-legged bugs (Figure 24–22E), but the head is not greatly elongate and they never occur on the surface of the

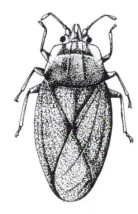

Figure 24–24. An ash-gray leaf bug, *Piésma cinèrea* (Say), 15×. (Redrawn from Froeschner and the American Midland Naturalist.)

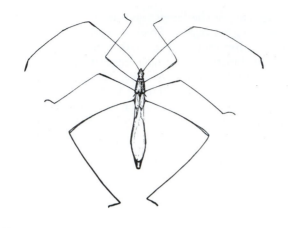

Figure 24–25. A stilt bug, *Jálysus wickhami* Van Duzee, 3½×. (Courtesy of Froeschner and the American Midland Naturalist.)

water (as do water measurers). In addition, they do not have the front legs raptorial (as do the thread-legged bugs). They occur in vegetation and feed chiefly on plants, though some species may be partly predaceous. They are 5–9 mm in length and usually brownish in color. They are rather sluggish insects.

Family **Lygaèidae**—Seed Bugs: This is the second-largest family in the order in North America, with more than 250 species, and many of its members are common bugs. Most of them, including the species having the front femora enlarged and appearing rap-torial, feed on seeds. The Blissìnae (which includes the chinch bug) feed on the sap of the host plant, and the big-eyed bugs (Geocorìnae; Figure 24–26C) usu-ally feed on other insects.

There is a great deal of variation in size, shape, and color in this family (Figure 24–26), but its mem-bers can usually be recognized by the four-seg-mented antennae, four-segmented beak, ocelli, and four or five simple veins in the membrane of the hemelytra (Figure 24–4B). They differ from the leaf bugs (Míridae) in lacking a cuneus and in possessing ocelli, and they are harder-bodied. They differ from the Corèidae, Alỳdidae, and Rhopálidae in having only a few veins in the membrane of the hemelytra. The lygaeids vary in length from about 2 to 18 mm, and many species are conspicuously marked with spots or bands of red, white, or black.

The chinch bug (Figure 24–27) is probably the most injurious bug in this family, attacking wheat, corn, and other cereals. Sometimes it becomes a serious pest of turf grasses. It is about 3.5 mm in length and is black with white front wings. Each front wing has a black spot near the middle of the costal margin. Both long-winged and short-winged forms occur in this species (Figure 24–27C,D).

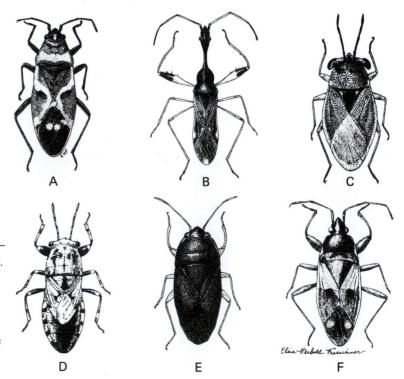

Figure 24–26. Seed bugs (Lygaèidae). **A,** the small milkweed bug, *Lygaèus kálmii* Stål, 3×; **B,** *Myódocha sérripes* Olivier, 4×; **C,** a big-eyed bug, *Geócoris púnctipes* (Say), 8×; **D,** *Phlégyas abbreviàtus* (Uhler), 8×; **E,** *Aphànus illuminàtus* (Distant), 6×; **F,** *Eremócoris fèrus* (Say). (Courtesy of Froeschner and the American Midland Naturalist.)

Figure 24–27. The chinch bug, *Blíssus leucópterus* (Say). **A,** fourth instar nymph; **B,** fifth instar nymph; **C,** adult; **D,** short-winged adult. (Courtesy of USDA.)

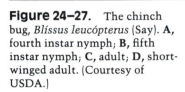

A   B   C   D

Chinch bugs overwinter as adults in grass clumps, fallen leaves, fence rows, and other protected places. They emerge about the middle of April and begin feeding on small grains. The eggs are laid during May, either in the ground or in grass stems near the ground, and hatch about a week or ten days later. Each female may lay several hundred eggs. The nymphs feed on the juices of grasses and grains and reach maturity in four to six weeks. By the time these nymphs become adult, the small grains (wheat, rye, oats, and barley) are nearly mature and no longer succulent, and the adults (along with nymphs nearly adult) migrate to other fields of more succulent grain, usually corn. They migrate on foot, often in great numbers. The females lay eggs for a second generation on the corn, and this generation reaches maturity in late fall and then seeks out places of hiberna-tion. When chinch bugs are abundant, whole fields of grain may be destroyed.

Several species in this group are brightly marked with red and black. The small milkweed bug, *Lygaèus kálmii* Stål (Figure 24–26A), has a red X-shaped area on the hemelytra and a broad red band across the base of the pronotum. The large milkweed bug, *Oncopéltus fasciàtus* (Dallas), is broadly banded with red and black.

The big-eyed bugs (subfamily Geocorìnae; Figure 24–26C) are unusual among the lygaeids in being at least partly predaceous. They are oval, somewhat flattened, usually yellowish or brownish in color, and generally seen running about on the ground or on foliage.

Family **Lárgidae:** These bugs are similar to the pyrrhocorids in appearance and habits (Figure

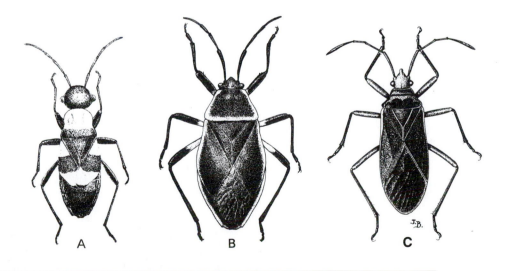

A   B   C

Figure 24–28. **A,** *Árhaphe carolìna* (Herrich-Schäffer) (Lárgidae), 4×; **B,** *Lárgus succínctus* (L.) (Lárgidae), 3×; **C,** the cotton stainer, *Dysdércus suturéllus* (Herrich-Schäffer) (Pyrrhocòridae), 4×. (**A** and **B,** courtesy of Froeschner and the American Midland Naturalist; **C,** courtesy of Slater and Baranowski and the Wm. C. Brown Company.)

24–28A,B). Some of them, such as *Árhaphe carolìna* (Herrich-Schäffer), are very antlike in appearance and have short hemelytra (Figure 24–28A). These bugs occur principally in the southern states.

Family **Pyrrhocòridae**—Red Bugs and Cotton Stainers: These are medium-sized (11–17 mm in length), elongate-oval bugs that are usually brightly marked with red or brown and black. They resemble large lygaeids, but lack ocelli and have many branched veins and cells in the membrane of the hemelytra (as in Figure 24–4H). An important pest species in this family is the cotton stainer, *Dysdércus suturéllus* (Herrich-Schäffer) (Figure 24–28C), which is a serious pest of cotton in some parts of the South. It stains the cotton fibers by its feeding and greatly reduces their value. This family is a small one (seven North American species), and its members are limited to the southern states.

Family **Corèidae**—Leaf-Footed Bugs: This is a moderate-sized group (about 80 North American species) whose members have well-developed scent glands. These glands open on the sides of the thorax between the middle and hind coxae (Figure 24–1B,

sgo). Most species give off a distinct odor (sometimes pleasant, sometimes not) when handled. The coreids are mostly medium-sized to large, somewhat elongate, and dark-colored, with the head narrower and shorter than the pronotum (Figure 24–29A–C). Some species have the hind tibiae expanded and leaflike (Figure 24–29A), hence the name "leaf-footed bugs" for this group.

The majority of the Corèidae are plant feeders, but a few are predaceous. The squash bug, *Ánasa trístis* (DeGeer) (Figure 24–29C), a serious pest of cucurbits, is dark brown in color and about 13 mm in length. It has one generation a year and passes the winter in the adult stage in debris and other sheltered places. The males of many species of coreids have the hind femora enlarged and armed with a series of sharp spines. These males establish territories and defend them vigorously from other males. The mesquite bug, *Thàsus acutángulus* Stål, is one of the largest coreids (35–40 mm in length). It is common on mesquite in Arizona and New Mexico. The nymphs form aggregations which, when disturbed, simultaneously produce a noxious vapor. If a tree

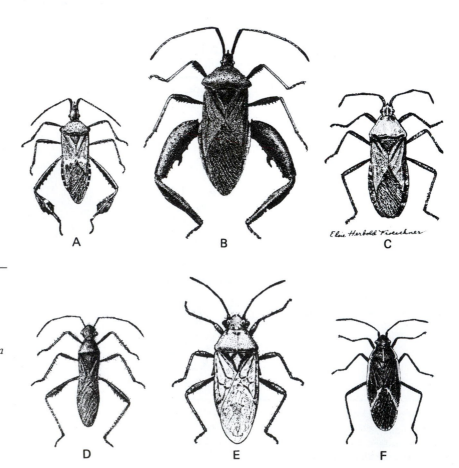

Figure 24–29. **A,** a leaf-footed bug, *Leptoglóssus clypeàlis* (Heidemann), 1½×; **B,** *Acanthocéphala femoràta* (Fabricius), male (Corèidae), 1½×; **C,** the squash bug, *Ánasa trístis* (DeGeer), 2×; **D,** a broad-headed bug, *Alỳdus eurínus* (Say), 2×; **E,** a scentless plant bug, *Arhýssus lateràlis* (Say), 5×; **F,** the box elder bug, *Bòisea trivittàtus* (Say), 2×. (Redrawn from Froeschner.)

with mesquite bugs on it is located in a suburban yard, the homeowner may be considerably upset by the presence of so many big bugs.

Family **Alÿdidae**—Broad-Headed Bugs: These bugs are similar to the Corèidae, but the head is broad and nearly as long as the pronotum, and the body is usually long and narrow (Figure 24–29D). They might well be called stink bugs, as they often "stink" much worse than the members of the Pentatómidae (to which the name "stink bug" is usually applied). They give off an odor reminiscent of someone with a bad case of halitosis. The openings of the scent glands are conspicuous oval openings between the middle and hind coxae. These bugs are fairly common on the foliage of weeds and shrubs along roadsides and in woodland areas. Most broad-headed bugs are either yellowish brown or black. Some of the black species have a red band across the middle of the dorsal side of the abdomen. A common brown species in the Northeast is *Pròtenor belfrágei* Haglund; it is 12–15 mm in length. Some of the black species (for example, *Alÿdus*; Figure 24–29D) look very much like ants in their nymphal stage, and the adults in the field look much like some of the spider wasps.

Family **Rhopálidae**—Scentless Plant Bugs: These bugs differ from the coreids in lacking well-developed scent glands. They are usually light-colored and smaller than the coreids (Figure 24–29E,F). Some are very similar to the orsilline lygaeids, but can be distinguished by the numerous veins in the membrane of the hemelytra (Figure 24–4D). They occur principally on weeds, but a few (including the box elder bug) are arboreal. All are plant feeders.

The box elder bug, *Bòisea trivittàtus* (Say), is a common and widely distributed species in this group. It is blackish with red markings and 11–14 mm in length (Figure 24–29F). It often enters houses and other sheltered places in the fall, sometimes in considerable numbers. It feeds on box elder and occasionally other trees.

Family **Cÿdnidae**—Burrower Bugs: These bugs are a little like stink bugs in general appearance and antennal structure, but they are a little more oval and have the tibiae spiny (Figure 24–30A). They are black or reddish brown in color and less than 8 mm in length (Figure 24–31B). They are usually found beneath stones or boards, in sand, or about the roots of grass tufts. They apparently feed on the roots of plants. They are most likely to be seen by the general collector when they come to lights at night.

Family **Thyreocòridae**—Negro Bugs: These bugs are small (mostly 3–6 mm in length), broadly oval, strongly convex, shining black bugs that are somewhat beetlelike in appearance (Figure 24–31A). The

scutellum is very large and covers most of the abdomen and wings. These insects are common on grasses, weeds, berries, and flowers.

Family **Scutellèridae**—Shield-Backed Bugs: These look much like stink bugs (Pentatómidae), but the scutellum is very large and extends to the apex of the abdomen. The wings are visible only at the edge of the scutellum (Figure 24–32A). Most species in the northern part of the United States and Canada are brown or yellow, but many tropical species are brightly colored, even iridescent. The scutellerids are 8–10 mm in length, and are plant feeders.

Family **Pentatòmidae**—Stink Bugs: This is a large and well-known group (more than 200 North American species), and its members are easily recognized by their round or ovoid shape and five-segmented antennae. They can be separated from other bugs having five-segmented antennae by the characters given in the key. Stink bugs are the most common and abundant of the bugs that produce a disagreeable odor, but some other bugs (particularly the broad-headed bugs) produce an odor that is stronger and more disagreeable than that produced by stink bugs. Many stink bugs are brightly colored or conspicuously marked.

The family Pentatómidae is divided into five subfamilies, the Asopìnae, Discocephalìnae, Edessìnae, Podopìnae, and Pentatomìnae. The Pentatomìnae, which contains most of the species in the family, are plant feeders, and have the basal segment of the beak slender and at rest lying between the bucculae, which are parallel. The Asopìnae, which are predaceous, have the basal segment of the beak short and thick, with only the base lying between the bucculae, which converge behind the beak.

Figure 24–30.   **A,** a tibia of *Pangaèus* (Cýdnidae); **B,** tibia of *Murgántia* (Pentatómidae).

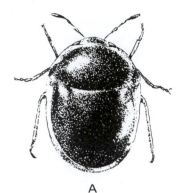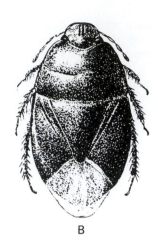

Figure 24–31. **A,** a negro bug, *Allócoris pulicària* (Germar), 6½×; **B,** a burrower bug, *Pangaèus bilineàtus* (Say), 7½×. (Courtesy of Froeschner and the American Midland Naturalist.)

A   B

The eggs of stink bugs, which are usually barrel-shaped and have the upper end ornamented with spines, are usually laid in groups, like so many little brightly colored barrels lined up side by side (Figure 3–35).

One rather important pest species in this group is the harlequin bug, *Murgántia histriónica* (Hahn) (Figure 24–33B). This brightly colored insect is often very destructive to cabbage and other cruciferous plants, particularly in the southern part of the United States. The other stink bugs that are plant feeders (Figures 24–33A,C, 24–34) usually attack grasses or other plants and usually are not of very great economic importance. The spined soldier bug, *Pódisus maculivéntris* (Say) (Figure 24–33D), is predaceous on lepidopterous larvae. The terrestrial turtle bugs, *Amauróchrous* spp., 3.5–6.5 mm in length, are similar to the shield-backed bugs, but may be separated by the characters given in the key

(couplet 48). These were formerly placed in a family by themselves, the Podópidae, which has been reduced to the subfamily Podopinae.

Family **Acanthosomátidae:** This is a small group closely related to the Pentatómidae, but readily separated from them by having only two instead of three tarsal segments. The females of several of the species in our area guard the eggs and young nymphs. *Elasmùcha lateràlis* (Say) is fairly common on birch trees in the northern states and southern Canada.

Collecting and Preserving Hemíptera

The aquatic bugs can be collected by means of the aquatic collecting equipment and methods described in Chapter 36. A few aquatic species, particularly water boatmen and giant water bugs, may often be collected at lights. One should examine a

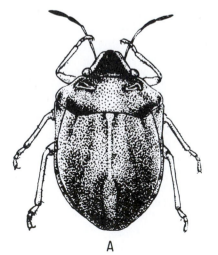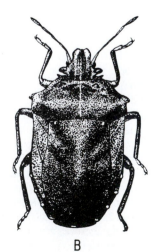

Figure 24–32. **A,** a shield-backed bug, *Homaèmus párvulus* (Germar); **B,** a terrestrial turtle bug, *Pòdops cínctipes* (Say), 8×. (Courtesy of Froeschner and the American Midland Naturalist.)

A   B

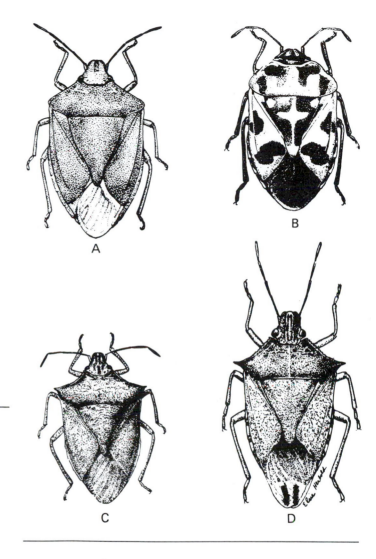

Figure 24–33. Stink bugs. **A,** *Thyánta custàtor* (Fabricius), 4½×; **B,** harlequin bug, *Murgántia histriónica* (Hahn), 4×; **C,** one-spot stink bug, *Euschístus variolàrius* (Palisot de Beauvois), 3×; **D,** spined soldier bug, *Pódisus maculivéntris* (Say), 4½×. **A–C,** Pentatomìnae; **D,** Asopìnae. (Courtesy of Froeschner and the American Midland Naturalist.)

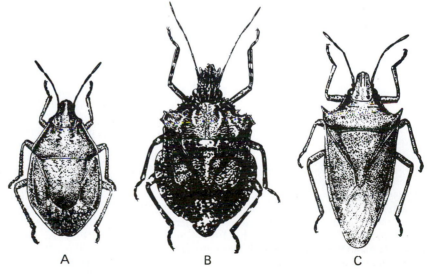

Figure 24–34. Stink bugs (subfamily Pentatomìnae). **A,** *Coènus dèlius* (Say), 3½×; **B,** *Brochýmena arbòrea* (Say), 3×; **C,** *Oebálus púgnax* (Fabricius), 4½×. (Courtesy of Froeschner and the American Midland Naturalist.)

variety of aquatic habitats, since different species occur in different types of situations. Terrestrial forms may be collected with a net (particularly by sweeping vegetation), at lights, or by examining such specialized habitats as in leaf litter, under bark, and in fungi.

A laboratory squeeze bottle of 70% alcohol with a long exit tube is sometimes useful in capturing active ground-dwelling bugs such as shore bugs. A hit with a squirt of alcohol will slow down the insect so that it can be picked up with forceps.

The best type of killing bottle for most Hemíptera is a small vial such as that shown in Figure 36–4A, which should be partly filled with small pieces of cleansing tissue or lens paper. One should have several such vials, since large and heavy-bodied specimens should not be put into the same vial with small and delicate specimens. After specimens have been killed, they should be taken from the vial and placed in pillboxes that are partly filled with cleansing tissue or Cellucotton.

Most Hemíptera are preserved dry on pins or points. The larger specimens should be pinned through the scutellum, and the smaller specimens through the right hemelytron. Care must be taken in pinning a bug not to destroy structures on the ventral side of the thorax that will be used in identification. Most Hemíptera less than 10 mm in length should be mounted on points. Specimens mounted on points should be mounted so that the beak, legs, and ventral side of the body are not embedded in glue. The best way to mount a small bug on a point is to bend the tip of the point down and glue the bug to the point by the right side of the thorax. If a specimen is mounted dorsal side up on the tip of a point (Figure 36–14A), the point should not extend beyond the middle of the ventral side of the insect.

It is desirable to mount these insects, particularly the soft-bodied ones, as soon as possible after they are captured. A field catch can be stored in 70 or 75% alcohol until the specimens can be mounted, but alcohol will cause some colors to fade. All nymphs should be preserved in alcohol.

References

Blatchley, W. S. 1926. Heteroptera or True Bugs of Eastern North America, with Special Reference to the Faunas of Indiana and Florida. Indianapolis: Nature, 1116 pp.; illus.

Bobb, M. L. 1974. The insects of Virginia. No. 7. The aquatic and semi-aquatic Hemiptera of Virginia. Va. Polytech. Inst. State Univ. Res. Div. Bull. 67, 196 pp.; illus.

Britton, W. E., ed. 1923. The Hemiptera or sucking insects of Connecticut. Part 4. Bull. Conn. Geol. Nat. Hist. Surv., No. 34, 807 pp.; illus.

Brooks, A. R. and L. A. Kelton. 1967. Aquatic and semi-aquatic Heteroptera of Alberta, Saskatchewan, and Manitoba (Hemiptera). Mem. Entomol. Soc. Can. 51: 1–92; illus.

Carvalho, J. C. de Melo. 1957–1960. A catalogue of the Miridae of the World (1758–1956), Parts 1–4. Bibliography and general index, Part 5. General Catalogue of the Hemiptera, Fasc. 7. Arch. Mus. Rio de Janeiro, 44: 1–158 (1957); 45:1–216 (1958); 47:1–161 (1958); 48: 1–384 (1959); 51:1–194 (1960).

China, W. E., and N. C. E. Miller. 1959. Check-list and keys to the families and subfamilies of the Hemiptera-Heteroptera. Bull. Brit. Mus. (Nat. Hist.) Entomol. 8(1): 1–45; illus.

Decoursey, R. M. 1971. Keys to the families and subfamilies of the nymphs of North American Hemiptera-Heteroptera. Proc. Entomol. Soc. Wash. 73:413–429; illus.

Drake, C. J., and N. T. Davis. 1960. The morphology, phylogeny, and higher classification of the family Tingidae, including the descriptions of a new genus and species of the subfamily Vianaidinae (Hemiptera-Heteroptera). Entomol. Amer. 39:1–100; illus.

Drake, C. J., and F. A. Ruhoff. 1960. Lace-bug genera of the world (Hemiptera: Tingidae). Proc. U.S. Natl. Mus. 122: 1–105; illus.

Drake, C. J., and F. A. Ruhoff. 1965. Lacebugs of the world: A catalogue (Hemiptera: Tingidae). Bull. U.S. Natl. Mus. 243, 634 pp.; illus.

Fracker, S. B. 1913. A systematic outline of the Reduviidae of North America. Proc. Iowa Acad. Sci. 19:217–247.

Froeschner, R. C. 1941–1961. Contributions to a synopsis of the Hemiptera of Missouri. Part 1: Scutelleridae, Podopidae, Pentatomidae, Cydnidae, Thyreocoridae. Amer. Midl. Nat. 26(1):122–146; illus. (1941). Part 2: Coreidae, Aradidae, Neididae. Amer. Midl. Nat. 27(3):591–609; illus. (1942). Part 3: Lygaeidae, Pyrrhocoridae, Piesmidae, Tingidae, Enicocephalidae, Phymatidae, Ploiariidae, Reduviidae, Nabidae. Amer. Midl. Nat. 31(3):638–683; illus. (1944). Part 4: Hebridae, Mesoveliidae, Cimicidae, Anthocoridae, Cryptostemmatidae, Isometopidae, Miridae. Amer. Midl. Nat. 42(1):123–188; illus. (1949). Part 5: Hydrometridae, Gerridae, Veliidae, Saldidae, Ochteridae, Gelastocoridae, Naucoridae, Belostomatidae, Nepidae, Notonectidae, Pleidae, Corixidae. Amer. Midl. Nat. 67(1):208–240; illus. (1961).

Froeschner, R. C. 1960. Cydnidae of the Western Hemisphere. Proc. U.S. Natl. Mus. 111:337–680; illus.

Herring, J. L., and P. D. Ashlock. 1971. A key to the nymphs of the families of Hemiptera (Heteroptera) of America north of Mexico. Fla. Entomol. 54:207–213; illus.

Hoffman, R. L. 1971. The insects of Virginia, No. 4: Shield bugs (Hemiptera; Scutelleroidea; Scutelleridae, Corimelaenidae, Cydnidae, Pentatomidae). Va. Polytech. Inst. State Univ. Res. Div. Bull. 67, 61 pp.; illus.

Hungerford, H. B. 1948. The Corixidae of the Western Hemisphere. Univ. Kan. Sci. Bull. 32:1–827; illus.

Hungerford, H. B. 1959. Hemiptera, pp. 958–972 *in* Fresh-Water Biology, ed. W. T. Edmundson. New York: Wiley; illus.

Kelton, L. A. 1978. The Anthocoridae of Canada and Alaska (Heteroptera: Anthocoridae). The Insects and Arachnids of Canada, Part 4. Ottawa: Can. Govt. Publ. Centre, 101 pp.; illus.

Kelton, L. A. 1980. The plant bugs of the prairie provinces of Canada (Heteroptera: Miridae). The Insects and Arachnids of Canada, Part 8. Ottawa: Can. Govt. Publ. Centre, 408 pp.; illus.

Knight, H. H. 1941. The plant bugs or Miridae of Illinois. Ill. Nat. Hist. Surv. Bull. 22(1):1–234; illus.

Knight, H. H. 1968. Taxonomic review; Miridae of the Nevada test site and the western United States. Brigham Young Univ. Sci. Bull. Ser. 9(3):1–282; illus.

Lawson, F. A. 1959. Identification of the nymphs of the common families of Hemiptera. J. Kan. Entomol. Soc. 32:88–92; illus.

Lent, H., and P. Wygodzinsky. 1979. Revision of the Triatominae (Hemiptera, Reduviidae), and their significance as vectors of Chagas' disease. Bull. Amer. Mus. Nat. Hist. 163(3):125–520; illus.

Matsuda, R. 1977. The Aradidae of Canada (Hemiptera: Aradidae). The Insects and Arachnids of Canada, Part 3. Ottawa: Can. Govt. Publ. Centre, 116 pp.; illus.

McPherson, J. E. 1982. The Pentatomoidea (Hemiptera) of northeastern North America. Carbondale: Southern Illinois Univ. Press; 241 pp.

Miller, N. C. E. 1956. Biology of the Heteroptera. London: Methuen, 1972 pp. (Reprinted 1971 by Entomological Reprint Specialists, Los Angeles.)

Parshley, H. M. 1925. A bibliography of the North American Hemiptera-Heteroptera. Northampton, Mass.: Smith College, 252 pp.

Pennak, R. W. 1978 (2nd ed.). Fresh-Water Invertebrates of the United States. New York: Wiley Interscience, 803 pp.; illus.

Readio, P. A. 1927. Studies on the biology of the Reduviidae of America north of Mexico. Univ. Kan. Sci. Bull. 17: 1–128; illus.

Schaefer, C. W. 1964. The morphology and higher classification of the Coreoidea (Hemiptera-Heteroptera), Parts 1 and 2. Ann. Entomol. Soc. Amer. 57:670–684; illus.

Schaefer, C. W. 1965. The morphology and higher classification of the Coreoidea (Hemiptera-Heteroptera), Part 3: The families Rhopalidae, Alydidae, and Coreidae. Misc. Publ. Entomol. Soc. Amer. 5(1):1–76; illus.

Schuh, R. T. 1986. The influence of cladistics on heteropteran classification. Ann. Rev. Entomol. 31:67–93.

Scudder, G. G. E. 1963. Adult abdominal characters of the Lygaeoid-Coreoid complex of the Heteroptera, and a classification of the group. Can. J. Zool. 41:1–14; illus.

Slater, J. A. 1964. A Catalogue of the Lygaeidae of the World, vols. 1 and 2. Storrs: Univ. Connecticut. 1688 pp.

Slater, J. A. 1982. Hemiptera, pp. 417–447 *in* Synopsis and Classification of Living Organisms, ed. S. Parker. New York: McGraw-Hill.

Slater, J. A., and R. M. Baranowski. 1978. How to Know the True Bugs. Dubuque, Iowa: Wm. C. Brown, 256 pp.; illus.

Štys, P., and I. Kerzhner. 1975. The rank and nomenclature of higher taxa in recent Heteroptera. Acta Entomol. Bohemoslovaca 72:65–79.

Sweet, M. H. 1960. The seed bugs: A contribution to the feeding habits of the Lygaeidae (Hemiptera-Heteroptera). Ann. Entomol. Soc. Amer. 53:317–321.

Torre-Bueno, J. R. de la. 1939–1941. A synopsis of the Hemiptera-Heteroptera of America north of Mexico. Entomol. Amer. 19:141–304; illus. (1939); 21:41–122 (1941).

Usinger, R. L. 1943. A revised classification of the Reduvoidea with a new subfamily from South America (Hemiptera). Ann. Entomol. Soc. Amer. 36:602–618; illus.

Usinger, R. L. 1956. Aquatic Hemiptera, pp. 182–228 *in* Aquatic Insects of California, ed. R. L. Usinger. Berkeley: Univ. California Press; illus.

Usinger, R. L. 1966. Monograph of the Cimicidae (Hemiptera-Heteroptera). Thomas Say Found. Publ. 7:1–585; illus.

Van Duzee, E. P. 1917. Catalogue of the Hemiptera of America north of Mexico, excepting the Aphididae, Coccidae, and Aleyrodidae. Calif. Univ. Publ. Tech. Bull. 2, 902 pp.

Chapter 25

Order Homóptera[1]
Cicadas, Hoppers, Psyllids, Whiteflies, Aphids, and Scale Insects

This order contains a large and diverse group of insects closely related to the Hemíptera. They exhibit considerable variation in body form, and many species are rather degenerate in structure. The life history of some Homóptera is very complex, involving bisexual and parthenogenetic generations, winged and wingless individuals and generations, and sometimes regular alternations of food plants. All the Homóptera are plant feeders, and many species are serious pests of cultivated plants. Some species transmit plant diseases. A few Homóptera are beneficial and serve as a source of shellac, dyes, or other materials.

The mouthparts are similar to those of the Hemíptera. They are sucking, with four piercing stylets (the mandibles and maxillae). The beak arises from the back of the head, in some cases appearing to arise between the front coxae. In the Hemíptera, however, the beak arises from the front of the head. In some adults the mouthparts are vestigial or lacking.

Winged Homóptera usually have four wings. The front wings have a uniform texture throughout, either membranous or slightly thickened, and the hind wings are membranous. The wings at rest are usually held rooflike over the body, with the inner mar-

gins overlapping slightly at the apex. In some groups one or both sexes may be wingless, or both winged and wingless individuals may occur in the same sex. Male scale insects have only one pair of wings, on the mesothorax.

The members of this group usually undergo simple metamorphosis. The development in whiteflies and male scale insects resembles complete metamorphosis in that the last nymphal instar is quiescent and pupalike.

The antennae are very short and bristlelike in some Homóptera and longer and usually filiform in others. Ocelli may be present or absent. If present, there are either two or three. The compound eyes are usually well developed.

Classification of the Homóptera

Some authorities consider the insects here treated as Homóptera to represent a suborder of the Hemíptera, with the insects we treat as Hemíptera representing the second suborder (the Heteróptera). We believe there are enough differences between the Homóptera and the Hemíptera (Heteróptera) to warrant their recognition as separate orders.

The order Homóptera is divided into two suborders, the Auchenorrhýncha and the Sternorrhýncha, each of which is further divided into superfamilies

[1]Homóptera: *homo*, alike, uniform; *ptera*, wings (referring to the fact that the front wings are uniform in texture throughout).

312

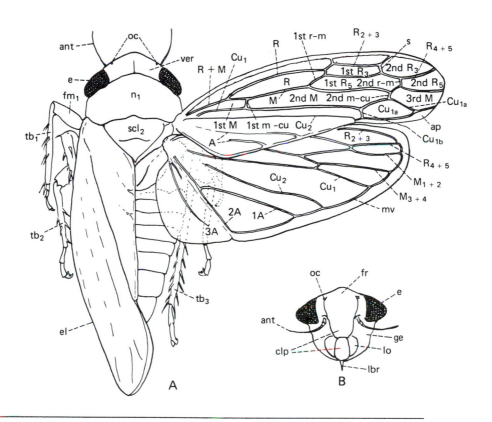

Figure 25–1. Structure of a leafhopper, *Paraphlépsius irroràtus* (Say). **A,** dorsal view; **B,** anterior view of head. *ant*, antenna; *ap*, appendix; *clp*, clypeus; *e*, compound eye; *el*, elytron or front wing; *fm*, femur; *fr*, frons; *ge*, gena; *lbr*, labrum; *lo*, lorum; *mv*, marginal vein; n_1 pronotum; *oc*, ocelli; scl_2, mesoscutellum; *tb*, tibia; *ver*, vertex. The venational terminology follows the Comstock-Needham system, except for the veins posterior to the media. Students of the leafhoppers usually use a different terminology for the venational characters of the front wing; a comparison of their terminology with that used here is given in the following table:

Veins		Cells	
Terms in This Figure	Other Terms	Terms in This Figure	Other Terms
R + M	first sector	R	discal cell
R	outer branch of first sector	1st R_3	outer anteapical cell
M	inner branch of first sector	2nd R_3	first apical cell
Cu_1	second sector	1st R_5	anteapical cell
Cu_2	claval suture	2nd R_5	second apical cell
A	claval veins	2nd M	inner anteapical cell
1st m-cu	first cross vein	3rd M	third apical cell
2nd m-cu	apical cross vein	Cu_{1a}	fourth apical cell
s	apical cross vein		
1st r-m	cross vein between sectors		
2nd r-m	apical cross vein		

and families. There are differences of opinion regarding the taxonomic status that should be given the various groups in this order. Some of the groups that we treat as superfamilies (especially the Fulgoròidea, Aphidòidea, and Coccòidea) are regarded as families by some entomologists. Other entomologists regard as superfamilies some of the groups that we treat as families (especially the families of Cicadòidea). The arrangement followed in this book is as follows:

Suborder Auchenorrhýncha—cicadas and hoppers
    Superfamily Cicadòidea
        Cicàdidae—cicadas
        Membràcidae—treehoppers
        Aetaliónidae (Aethaliónidae; Membràcidae in part)—aetalionid treehoppers
        Cercópidae—froghoppers, spittlebugs
        Cicadéllidae (Jássidae)—leafhoppers
    Superfamily Fulgoròidea—planthoppers
        Delphácidae (Areopódidae)—delphacid planthoppers
        Dérbidae—derbid planthoppers
        Cixìidae—cixiid planthoppers
        Kinnàridae—kinnarid planthoppers
        Dictyophàridae—dictyopharid planthoppers
        Fulgòridae—fulgorid planthoppers
        Achìlidae—achilid planthoppers
        Tropidùchidae—tropiduchid planthoppers
        Flàtidae—flatid planthoppers
        Acanalonìidae (Amphiscépidae; Íssidae in part)—acanaloniid planthoppers
        Íssidae (including Nogodínidae)—issid planthoppers
Suborder Sternorrhýncha (Gularóstria)
    Superfamily Psyllòidea
        Psýllidae (Psyllìidae, Chérmidae)—psyllids or jumping plantlice
    Superfamily Aleyrodòidea
        Aleyròdidae (Aleuròdidae)—whiteflies

Superfamily Aphidòidea
    Aphídidae (Àphidae)—aphids or plantlice
    Eriosomátidae (Aphídidae in part)—woolly and gall-making aphids
    Adélgidae (Chérmidae; Phylloxèridae in part)—pine and spruce aphids
    Phylloxèridae (Adélgidae in part)—phylloxerans
Superfamily Coccòidea—scale insects
    Margaròdidae (Monophlèbidae)—giant coccids and ground pearls
    Orthezìidae—ensign coccids
    Kérridae (Laccifèridae, Tachardìidae)—lac scales
    Cóccidae (Lecanìidae)—soft scales, wax scales, tortoise scales
    Aclérdidae—aclerdid scales
    Cryptocóccidae—cryptococcid scales
    Kermèsidae (Kérmidae, Hemicóccidae)—gall-like coccids
    Asterolecanìidae—pit scales
    Lecanodiaspídidae—lecanodiaspidid scales
    Cerocóccidae (Asterolecanìidae in part)—cerococcid scales
    Dactylopìidae (Cóccidae)—cochineal insects
    Diaspídidae—armored scales
    Conchaspídidae (Eriocóccidae in part)—conchaspidid scales
    Phoenicocóccidae—the red date scale
    Pseudocóccidae—mealybugs
    Eriocóccidae (Pseudocóccidae in part)—eriococcid scales

The superfamilies and families of the Auchenorrhýncha are separated principally on the basis of the ocelli, the position of the antennae, the form of the pronotum, and the spination of the legs. The superfamilies of the Sternorrhýncha are separated on the basis of the number of antennal and tarsal segments, the structure and venation of the wings, and other characters. The families of scale insects are separated on the basis of characters of the female.

Key to the Families of Homóptera

The student should have no particular difficulty in running winged specimens through this key, but may have trouble with some of the wingless forms. The separation of the families of scale insects is based on females (unless otherwise indicated), which generally must be mounted on microscope slides in order to run them through the key. Some wingless Aphidòidea can be separated only if one is familiar with their life history.

1.   Tarsi 3-segmented; antennae very short and bristlelike; beak arising from back of head; active insects (suborder Auchenorrhýncha) **2**

1'. Tarsi 1- or 2-segmented (when legs are present); antennae usually long and filiform; beak, when present, arising between front coxae; often not active insects (suborder Sternorrhýncha) **18**

2(1). Antennae separated from front of head by a vertical carina, thus arising on sides of head beneath eyes (Figure 25–2C); tegulae usually present; 2 anal veins in front wing usually meeting apically to form a Y-vein (Figure 25–3A,B, *clv*) (Superfamily Fulgoròidea) **3**

2'. Antennae not separated from front of head by a vertical carina, thus arising on front of head between eyes (Figures 25–2A, 25–15); tegulae usually absent, no Y-vein in anal area of front wing (Figures 25–1A, 25–4A) (superfamily Cicadòidea) **13**

3(2). Hind tibiae with broad movable apical spur (Figure 25–3C, *sp*); a large group of small to minute forms, many dimorphic (with wings well developed or short), the sexes often very different ....**Delphácidae**   p. 333

3'. Hind tibiae without broad movable apical spur **4**

4(3'). Anal area of hind wings reticulate, with many cross veins ....**Fulgòridae**   p. 334

4'. Anal area of hind wings not reticulate, without cross veins **5**

5(4'). Second segment of hind tarsi with 2 apical spines (1 on each side) and with apex usually rounded or conical (Figure 25–3D) **6**

5'. Second segment of hind tarsi with a row of apical spines and with apex truncate or emarginate **9**

6(5). Front wings with numerous costal cross veins, longer than body, at rest held almost vertically at sides of body (Figure 25–17F); clavus with numerous small pustulelike tubercles ....**Flàtidae**   p. 335

6'. Front wings without numerous costal cross veins (except sometimes apically), variable in size and position at rest; clavus without numerous small pustulelike tubercles **7**

7(6'). Front wings longer than abdomen, with a series of cross veins between costal margin and apex of clavus separating off apical, more densely veined portion of the wing; slender, greenish or yellowish to brownish, 7–9 mm in length; southeastern United States, Florida to Louisiana ....**Tropidùchidae**   p. 334

7'. Front wings without differentiated apical portion as described above; variable in length **8**

8(7'). Front wings very broad, venation reticulate, longer than body, at rest held almost vertically at sides of body (Figure 25–17E); hind tibiae without spines except at apex ....**Acanaloniidae**   p. 335

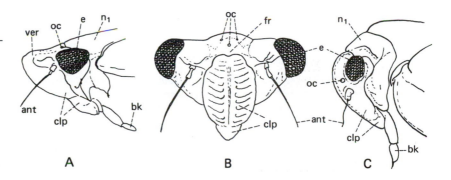

Figure 25–2. Head structure in Homóptera. **A,** froghopper (*Philaènus*), lateral view; **B,** cicada (*Magicicàda*), anterior view; **C,** planthopper (*Anórmenis*), lateral view. *ant,* antenna; *bk,* beak; *clp,* clypeus; *e,* compound eye; *fr,* frons; *n₁,* pronotum; *oc,* ocelli; *ver,* vertex.

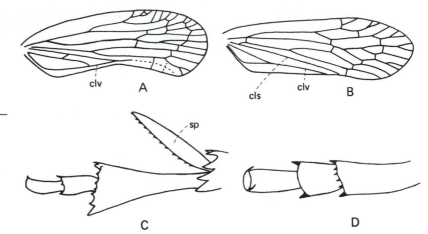

Figure 25–3. Characters of Fulgoròidea. **A,** front wing of *Epíptera* (Achìlidae); **B,** front wing of *Cíxius* (Cixìidae); **C,** hind tarsus of a delphacid; **D,** hind tarsus of *Anórmenis* (Flàtidae). *cls,* claval suture; *clv,* claval vein; *sp,* apical spur of tibia.

8′.	Front wings variable in size and shape, often shorter than abdomen, but if longer than abdomen, then usually oval; hind tibiae usually with spines on sides, in addition to apical ones ....**Íssidae**	p. 335
9(5′).	Terminal segment of beak short, not more than 1½ times as long as wide ....**Dérbidae**	p. 333
9′.	Terminal segment of beak longer, at least twice as long as wide **10**	
10(9′).	Front wings overlapping at apex (Figure 25–17C); claval vein (a Y vein) extending to apex of clavus (Figure 25–3A, *clv*); body somewhat flattened ....**Achìlidae**	p. 334
10′.	Front wings usually not overlapping at apex; claval vein not reaching apex of clavus (Figure 25–3B, *clv*); body not particularly flattened **11**	
11(10′).	Head prolonged in front (Figure 25–17G–I), or if not, then frons bears 2 or 3 carinae, or the tegulae are absent and the claval suture is obscure; no median ocellus ....**Dictyophàridae**	p. 334
11′.	Head not prolonged in front (Figure 25–17A,D) or only moderately so; frons either without carinae or with median carina only; tegulae present; claval suture distinct; median ocellus usually present **12**	
12(11′).	Abdominal terga 6–8 chevron-shaped, sometimes sunk below rest of terga; 3–4 mm in length; western United States ....**Kinnàridae**	p. 334
12′.	Abdominal terga 6–8 rectangular; size variable; widely distributed ....**Cixìidae**	p. 333
13(2′).	Three ocelli (Figure 25–2B); large insects with front wings membranous (Figure 25–9); males usually with sound-producing organs ventrally at base of abdomen (Figure 25–11); not jumping insects ....**Cicàdidae**	p. 322
13′.	Two (rarely 3) ocelli (Figure 25–1B) or none; smaller insects, sometimes with front wings thickened; sound-producing organs generally absent; usually jumping insects **14**	
14(13′).	Pronotum extending back over abdomen and concealing the scutellum (Figure 25–12) or at least with a median backward-projecting process that partly conceals the scutellum (Figure 25–5A); hind tibiae usually without distinct spurs or long spines **15**	
14′.	Pronotum not extending back over abdomen, the scutellum nearly always well exposed (Figures 25–5B, 25–13, 25–15); hind tibiae with or without distinct spurs or spines **16**	

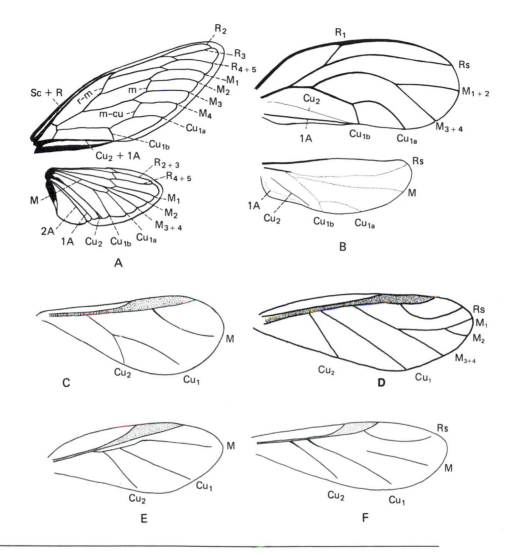

Figure 25–4. Wings of Homóptera. **A,** Cicàdidae (*Magicicàda*); **B,** Psýllidae (*Psýlla*); **C,** Phylloxèridae (*Phyllóxèra*); **D,** Aphídidae (*Longistígma*); **E,** Adélgidae (*Adélges*); **F,** Eriosomátidae (*Cólopha*). **C–F,** front wings.

15(14).	Pronotum with a narrow, median, backward-projecting process that only partly conceals scutellum and extends between wings for one-fourth their length or less (Figure 25–5A), often with a pair of ridges or leaflike processes dorsally; beak extending to hind coxae (*Microcéntrus*) ....**Aetaliónidae** p. 325
15′.	Pronotum broadly extended backward over wings and abdomen, completely covering scutellum and extending to middle of wings or farther, often with spines or other processes or appearing arched (Figure 25–12); beak not extending to hind coxae. ....**Membràcidae** p. 325
16(14′).	Hind tibiae with 1 or more rows of small spines (Figure 25–6A); hind coxae transverse ....**Cicadéllidae** p. 325
16′.	Hind tibiae without spines or with 1 or 2 stout ones laterally and a crown of short spines at tip (Figure 25–6B); hind coxae short and conical **17**

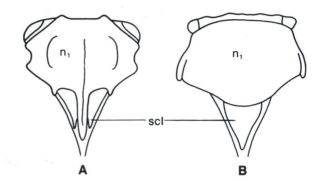

Figure 25–5. Pronotum and associated structures in Aetaliónidae, dorsal view. **A,** *Microcéntrus;* **B,** *Aetálion.* n_1, pronotum; *scl,* scutellum.

17(16′).	Hind tibiae without spines, but hairy; beak extending to hind coxae; head largely covered dorsally by pronotum (Figure 25–5B), the face vertical or nearly so; Florida, southern Arizona, and California (*Aetálion*) . . **Aetaliónidae**	p. 325
17′.	Hind tibiae with 1 or 2 stout spines laterally and a crown of short spines at tip (Figure 25–6B); head usually not largely covered by pronotum (Figure 25–13), the face slanting backward; beak length variable; widely distributed . . . . **Cercópidae**	p. 325
18(1′).	Tarsi 2-segmented, with 2 claws; winged forms with 4 wings; mouthparts usually well developed in both sexes, with beak long **19**	
18′.	Tarsi 1-segmented, with a single claw (when legs are present); female wingless and often legless, scalelike, or grublike and wax-covered; male with only 1 pair of wings and without beak (superfamily Coccòidea) **24**	
19(18).	Antennae with 5–10 (usually 10) segments; front wings often thicker than hind wings; jumping insects . . . . **Psýllidae**	p. 335
19′.	Antennae with 3–7 segments; wings membranous or opaque whitish; not jumping insects **20**	
20(19′).	Wings usually opaque, whitish, and covered with whitish powder; hind wings nearly as large as front wings; no cornicles . . . . **Aleyròdidae**	p. 335
20′.	Wings membranous and not covered with whitish powder; hind wings much smaller than front wings (Figure 25–6C); cornicles often present (superfamily Aphidòidea) **21**	
21(20′).	Front wings with 4 or 5 (rarely 6) veins behind stigma extending to wing margin (Rs present) (Figure 25–4D,F); cornicles usually present (Figure	

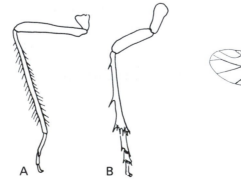

Figure 25–6. **A,** hind leg of a leafhopper (Cicadéllidae); **B,** hind leg of a froghopper (Cercópidae); **C,** a winged aphid (Aphídidae). *crn,* cornicle. (**C,** courtesy of USDA.)

	25–6C); antennae generally 6-segmented; sexual females oviparous, parthenogenetic females viviparous **22**	
21'.	Front wings with only 3 veins behind stigma extending to wing margin (Rs absent) (Figure 25–4C,E); cornicles absent; antennae 3- to 5-segmented; all females oviparous..**23**	
22(21).	Cornicles nearly always present and conspicuous; M in front wing branched (Figure 25–4D); females, and usually also males, with functional mouthparts; without abundant wax glands ....**Aphídidae**	p. 336
22'.	Cornicles indistinct or lacking; M in front wing not branched (Figure 25–4F); sexual forms with mouthparts atrophied and not functional; wax glands usually abundant ....**Eriosomátidae**	p. 338
23(21').	Wings at rest held rooflike over body; Cu₁ and Cu₂ in front wing separated at base (Figure 25–4E); apterous parthenogenetic females covered with waxy flocculence; on conifers ....**Adélgidae**	p. 339
23'.	Wings at rest held horizontal; Cu₁ and Cu₂ in front wing stalked at base (Figure 25–4C); apterous parthenogenetic females not covered with waxy flocculence (at most, covered with a powdery material) ....**Phylloxèridae**	p. 340
24(18').	Abdominal spiracles present (Figure 25–7A, *spr*); male usually with compound eyes and ocelli **25**	
24'.	Abdominal spiracles absent (Figure 25–8B); male with ocelli only **26**	
25(24).	Anal ring distinct, with numerous pores and 6 long setae; antennae 3- to 8-segmented (Figure 25–7A) ....**Ortheziidae**	p. 342
25'.	Anal ring reduced, without pores or setae; antennae 1- to 13-segmented ....**Margaròdidae**	p. 341
26(24').	A large dorsal spine present near center of abdomen, anterior spiracles much larger than posterior ones; southwestern United States ....**Kérridae**	p. 342
26'.	No large dorsal spine in center of abdomen; all spiracles about equal in size; widely distributed **27**	
27(26').	Anal opening covered by 2 triangular plates (Figure 25–7D, *anp*) (except *Physokérmes*); abdomen with well-developed anal cleft (Figure 25–7D, *anc*) ....**Cóccidae**	p. 342
27'.	Anal opening covered by single plate or none; anal cleft, if present, not well developed **28**	
28(27').	Anus covered by single oval or triangular plate; caudal margin of body with furrows or ridges ....**Aclérdidae**	p. 342
28'.	No plate covering anal opening; caudal margin of body without furrows or ridges **29**	
29(28').	Anal ring surrounded by short stout setae; cluster pore plate present, just below each posterior thoracic spiracle; northeastern United States, on sugar maple ....**Cryptocóccidae**	p. 343
29'.	Anal ring not surrounded by short stout setae; no cluster pore plates; widely distributed, on various host plants **30**	
30(29').	Dorsum with 8-shaped pores (shaped like the figure 8) (Figure 25–7C, *mpo*)..**31**	
30'.	Dorsum without 8-shaped pores **34**	
31(30).	8-shaped pores on dorsum and in submarginal band on venter; antennae 1- to 9-segmented; on various host plants **32**	
31'.	8-shaped pores restricted to dorsum; antennae 5-segmented; on oaks ....**Kermèsidae**	p. 343

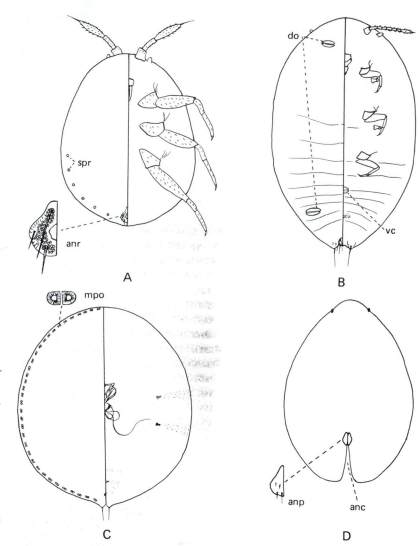

Figure 25–7. Characters of female scale insects (diagrammatic). **A,** Orthezìidae; **B,** Pseudocóccidae; **C,** Asterolecanìidae; **D,** Cóccidae. In **A–C** the left side represents a dorsal view, and the right side a ventral view. *anc,* anal cleft; *anp,* anal plate; *anr,* anal ring; *do,* dorsal ostioles; *mpo,* marginal 8-shaped pores; *spr,* abdominal spiracles; *vc,* ventral circulus. (Figure prepared by Dr. Michael Kosztarab.)

32(31).	A sclerotized anal plate present; antennae 1- to 9-segmented **33**	
32'.	No sclerotized anal plate present; antennae 1-segmented .....**Asterolecanìidae**	p. 343
33(32).	Antennae 1-segmented, with associated cluster of 5–7 locular pores; anal plate triangular ....**Cerocóccidae**	p. 343
33'.	Antennae 7- to 9-segmented, without associated cluster of 5–7 locular pores; anal plate triangular, much wider than long ....**Lecanodiaspídidae**	p. 343
34(30').	Locular pores usually in clusters, with common duct, scattered over dorsum; body with numerous, thick, truncate setae; on cacti ....**Dactylopìidae**	p. 344
34'.	Pores not arranged as above, setae usually not truncate; on various host plants **35**	
35(34').	Terminal abdominal segments fused to form pygidium (Figure 25–8, *py*); anal opening simple; body covered by thin shieldlike scale **36**	
35'.	Terminal abdominal segments not fused to form pygidium; anal opening often with setae; body not covered by thin shieldlike scale **37**	

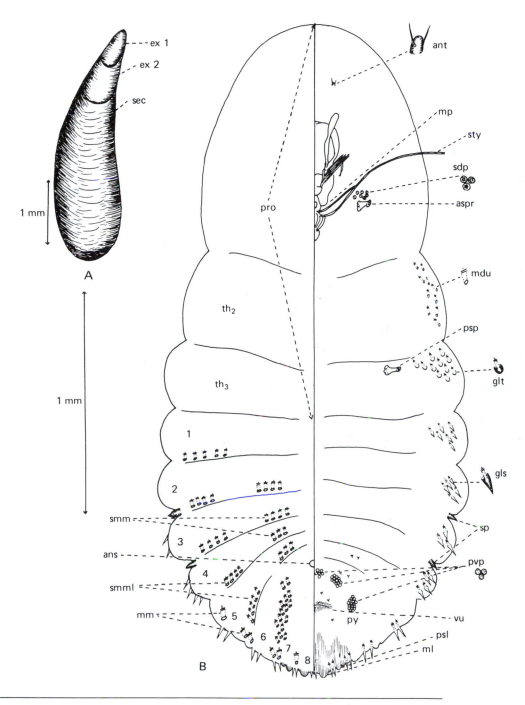

Figure 25–8.   Characters of scale insects. **A,** scale of female; **B,** diagrammatic drawing of a female armored scale. The left side of **B** represents a dorsal view, and the right side a ventral view. *ans,* anus; *ant,* antenna; *aspr,* anterior spiracle; *ex 1,* first exuvium; *ex 2,* second exuvium; *gls,* gland spines; *glt,* gland tubercle; *mdu,* microduct; *ml,* median lobe; *mm,* marginal macroduct; *mp,* mouthparts; *pro,* prosoma; *psl,* paired second lobe; *psp,* posterior spiracle; *pvp,* perivulvar pores; *py,* pygidium; *sdp,* spiracular disc pore; *sec,* secretion of adult; *smm,* submedian macroduct; *smml,* submarginal macroducts; *sp,* spur; *sty,* stylets; *th₂,* mesothorax; *th₃,* metathorax; *vu,* vulva. (Figure prepared by Dr. Michael Kosztarab.)

SUBORDER **Auchenorrhýncha:** The members of this suborder (cicadas and hoppers) are active insects, being good fliers or jumpers. Their tarsi are three-segmented, and their antennae are very short and bristlelike. The cicadas are relatively large insects, with membranous wings and three ocelli. The hoppers are small to minute insects, with the front wings usually more or less thickened, and they usually have two ocelli (or none). The males of many Auchenorrhýncha are able to produce sound, but except for the cicadas these sounds are nearly inaudible to humans.

Family **Cicàdidae**—Cicadas: The members of this family can usually be recognized by their characteristic shape and their large size (Figure 25–9). This group contains the largest Homóptera in the United States, some of which reach a length of about 50 mm. The smallest cicadas are a little less than 25 mm in length.

Figure 25–9. A dog-day cicada, *Tibìcen pruinòsa* (Say), about natural size. (Courtesy of Carl Mohr and the Illinois Natural History Survey.)

A conspicuous characteristic of cicadas is their ability to produce sound. Other Homóptera (for example, leafhoppers) can produce sounds, but their sounds are very weak. The sounds produced by cicadas are generally quite loud. The sounds are produced by the males, and each species has a characteristic song. One who is familiar with these songs can identify the species by song alone (Figure 25–10). Each species also produces a somewhat different sound (a disturbance squawk or "protest" sound) when handled or disturbed, and some species have a special song (termed a courtship song) that is produced by a male approaching a female.

Cicada sounds are produced by a pair of tymbals located dorsally at the sides of the basal abdominal segment (Figure 25–11, *tmb*). The tymbals consist of a posterior plate and several riblike bands lying in a membrane and are sometimes completely exposed above. In the dog-day cicadas (*Tibìcen* spp.) they are covered above by an abdominal flap. The hearing organs, or tympana (*tym*), lie posteriorly in a ventral cavity through which the tymbals or tymbal spaces are exposed below. This space often has a yellowish membrane (*mem*) connecting anteriorly to the thorax and is covered over ventrally by a pair of thoracic flaps called opercula (*op*). Internally, the last thoracic segment and up to five abdominal segments are nearly entirely filled by a large tracheal air sac that functions as a resonance chamber. A pair of large muscles runs through this air sac from above the tympana to the large plate of the tymbals, and their contractions cause the ribs to bend suddenly and

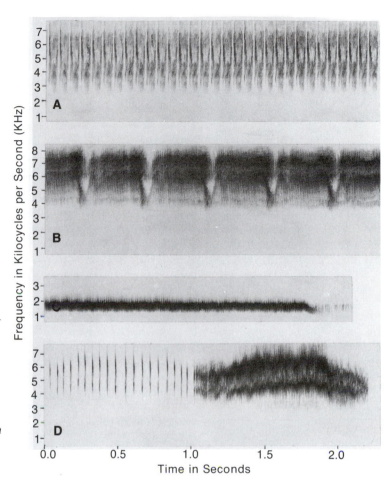

Figure 25–10. Audiospectrographs of cicada calling songs. **A,** a dog-day cicada, *Tibìcen chloromèra* (Walker), about two seconds from near the middle of the song; **B,** another dog-day cicada, sometimes called the scissors-grinder cicada, *T. pruinòsa* (Say), a portion of the song; **C,** a periodical cicada, *Magicicàda septéndecim* (L.), the end of the song; **D,** a part of the song of another periodical cicada, *M. cássini* (Fisher).

produce the sounds. The air sacs and general body tension, plus other structures, control the volume and quality of the sounds. There are also stridulating and wing-banging groups of cicadas, which produce their characteristic sounds by these other means.

Two common types in this family are the dog-day cicadas (various species) (Figure 25–9) and the periodical cicadas (*Magicicàda*). The dog-day cicadas are mostly large blackish insects, usually with greenish markings, that appear each year in July and August. The periodical cicadas, which occur in the eastern United States, differ from other eastern species in that they have the eyes and wing veins reddish, they are smaller than most other eastern species, and the adults appear in late May and early June. The life cycle of dog-day cicadas is unknown, but two Japanese woodland species are known to require seven years to mature. The shortest known cicada life cycle is four years, for a grassland species. In dog-day cicadas, even with long life cycles, the broods overlap so that some adults appear each year.

The life cycle of the periodical cicadas lasts 13 to 17 years, and in any given area adults are not present each year.

There are at least 13 broods of 17-year cicadas and 5 of 13-year cicadas. These broods emerge in different years and have different geographic ranges. The 17-year cicadas are generally northern and the 13-year cicadas southern, but there is considerable overlap, and both life-cycle types may occur in the same woods (but would emerge together only once every 221 years). The emergence of some of the larger broods is a very striking event, as the insects in these broods may be extremely numerous. The large broods of 17-year cicadas that have occurred in central and southern Ohio in recent years appeared in 1973 (Brood XIII), 1974 (Brood XIV), and 1987 (Brood X).

There are six species of periodical cicadas, three with a 17-year cycle and three with a 13-year cycle. The three species in each life-cycle group differ in size, color, and song (see Table 25–1). Each 17-year

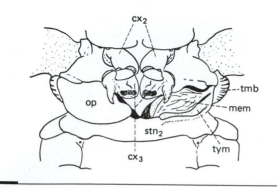

Figure 25–11. Thorax of a cicada (*Magicicàda*), ventral view, showing the sound-producing organs; the operculum at the right has been removed. *cx*, coxa; *mem*, membrane; *op*, operculum; *stn*, abdominal sternum; *tmb*, tymbal; *tym*, tympanum.

species has a similar or sibling species with a 13-year cycle, from which it can be separated only by differences in life cycle and distribution. Most broods of each life-cycle type contain more than one species, and many contain all three.

Cicadas deposit their eggs in the twigs of trees and shrubs. The twigs are usually so severely injured by this egg laying that the terminal part of the twig dies. The eggs generally hatch in a month or so (some species overwinter as eggs) and the nymphs drop to the ground, enter the soil, and feed on roots, particularly of perennial plants. The nymphs remain in the ground until they are ready to molt the last time. In the case of the periodical cicadas, this period is 13–17 years. When the last nymphal instar digs its way out of the ground, it climbs up on some object, usually a tree, and fastens its claws in the bark, and

Table 25–1
Summary of the Periodical Cicadas (*Magicicàda*)[a]

Characteristics	17-Year Cycle	13-Year Cycle
Body length 27–33 mm Propleura and lateral extensions of pronotum between eyes and wing bases reddish Abdominal sterna primarily reddish brown or yellow Song: "phaaaaaroah," a low buzz, 1–3 seconds in length, with a drop in pitch at the end (Figure 25–10C)	Linnaeus' 17-year cicada, *M. septéndecim* (L.)	Riley's 13-year cicada, *M. trédecim* Walsh and Riley
Body length 20–28 mm Propleura and lateral extensions of pronotum between eyes and wing bases black Abdominal sterna all black, or a few with a narrow band of reddish brown or yellow on apical third; this band often constricted or interrupted medially Last tarsal segment with apical half or more black Song: 2–3 seconds of ticks alternating with 1- to 3-second buzzes that rise and then fall in pitch and intensity (Figure 25–10D)	Cassin's 17-year cicada, *M. cássini* (Fisher)	Cassin's 13-year cicada, *M. tredecássini* Alexander and Moore
Body length 19–27 mm Propleura and lateral extensions of pronotum between eyes and wing bases black Abdominal sterna black basally, with a broad apical band of reddish yellow or brown on posterior half of each sternum; this band not interrupted medially Last tarsal segment entirely brownish or yellowish or, at most, the apical third black Song: 20–40 short high-pitched phrases, each like a short buzz and tick delivered together, at the rate of 3–5 per second, the final phrases shorter and lacking the short buzz	The little 17-year cicada, *M. septendécula* Alexander and Moore	The little 13-year cicada, *M. tredécula* Alexander and Moore

[a]Data from Alexander and Moore (1962).

the final molt then takes place. The adult stage lasts a month or more.

The principal damage done by cicadas is caused by the egg laying of the adults. When the adults are numerous, as in years when the periodical cicadas emerge, they may do considerable damage to young trees and nursery stock.

Family **Membràcidae**—Treehoppers: The members of this group can be recognized by the large pronotum that covers the head, extends back over the abdomen, and often assumes peculiar shapes (Figure 25–12). Many species appear more or less humpbacked. Others have spines, horns, or keels on the pronotum, and some species are shaped like thorns. The wings are largely concealed by the pronotum. These insects are rarely more than 10 or 12 mm long.

Treehoppers feed chiefly on trees and shrubs, and most species feed only on specific types of host plants. Some species feed on grass and herbaceous plants in the nymphal stage. The treehoppers have one or two generations a year and usually pass the winter in the egg stage.

Only a few species in this group are considered of economic importance, and most of their damage is caused by egg laying. The buffalo treehopper, *Stictocéphala bizonia* Kopp and Yonke (Figure 25–12C), is a common pest species that lays its eggs in the twigs of apple and several other trees. The eggs are placed in slits cut in the bark, and the terminal portion of the twig beyond the eggs often dies. The eggs overwinter and hatch in the spring, and the nymphs drop to herbaceous vegetation where they complete their development, returning to the trees to lay their eggs.

Family **Aetaliónidae**—Aetalionid Treehoppers: Two genera in this family occur in our area, *Microcéntrus* which is widely distributed, and *Aetálion*, which occurs in Florida, southern Arizona, and California. *Microcéntrus* resembles a membracid, but the pronotum has only a narrow median backward-projecting process that extends a short distance between the wings and only partly covers the scutellum (Figure 25–5A). It was formerly placed in the subfamily Centrotìnae of the Membràcidae, but has been transferred to the family Aetaliónidae by Hamilton (1971). *Aetálion* resembles a large cercopid, but lacks spines on the hind tibiae characteristic of that group. The pronotum extends farther forward over the head (Figure 25–5B), and the face is vertical. The beak in the aetalionids extends to the hind coxae. It is shorter in most other hoppers, but is even longer in some cercopids (extending beyond the hind coxae in *Aphróphora* of the Cercópidae). *Microcéntrus càryae* (Fitch),

a widely distributed species, occurs on hickory, oak, and other trees. *Aetálion* also occurs on trees and is sometimes tended by ants or (in the tropics) meliponine bees (Àpidae).

Family **Cercópidae**—Froghoppers or Spittlebugs: Froghoppers are small hopping insects, rarely over 13 mm in length, some species of which vaguely resemble tiny frogs in shape (Figure 25–13). They are very similar to the leafhoppers, but can be distinguished by the spination of the hind tibiae (Figure 25–6A,B). They are usually brown or gray in color. Some species have a characteristic color pattern.

These insects feed on shrubs, trees, and herbaceous plants, the different species feeding on different host plants. The nymphs surround themselves with a frothy spittlelike mass (Figure 25–14) and are usually called spittlebugs. These masses of spittle are sometimes quite abundant in meadows. Each mass contains one or more greenish or brownish spittlebugs. After the last molt the insect leaves the spittle and moves about actively.

The spittle is derived from fluid voided from the anus and from a mucilaginous substance secreted by the epidermal glands on the seventh and eighth abdominal segments. Air bubbles are introduced into the spittle by means of the caudal appendages of the insect. A spittlebug usually rests head downward on the plant, and as the spittle forms, it flows down over and covers the insect. It lasts some time, even when exposed to heavy rains, and provides the nymph with a moist habitat. The adults do not produce spittle.

The most important economic species of spittlebug in the eastern states is *Philaènus spumàrius* (L.) (Figure 25–13), a meadow species that causes serious stunting, particularly to clovers. This insect lays its eggs in late summer in the stems or sheaths of grasses and other plants, and the eggs hatch the following spring. There is one generation a year. There are several color forms of this species. Most of the spittlebugs attack grasses and herbaceous plants, but a few attack trees. *Aphróphora permutàta* Uhler and *A. saratogénsis* (Fitch) are important pests of pine.

Family **Cicadéllidae**—Leafhoppers: The leafhoppers constitute a very large group (about 2500 North American species), and they are of various forms, colors, and sizes (Figure 25–15). They are similar to froghoppers and aetalionids in the genus *Aetálion*, but they have one or more rows of small spines extending the length of the hind tibiae. They rarely exceed 13 mm in length, and many are only a few millimeters in length. Many are marked with a beautiful color pattern.

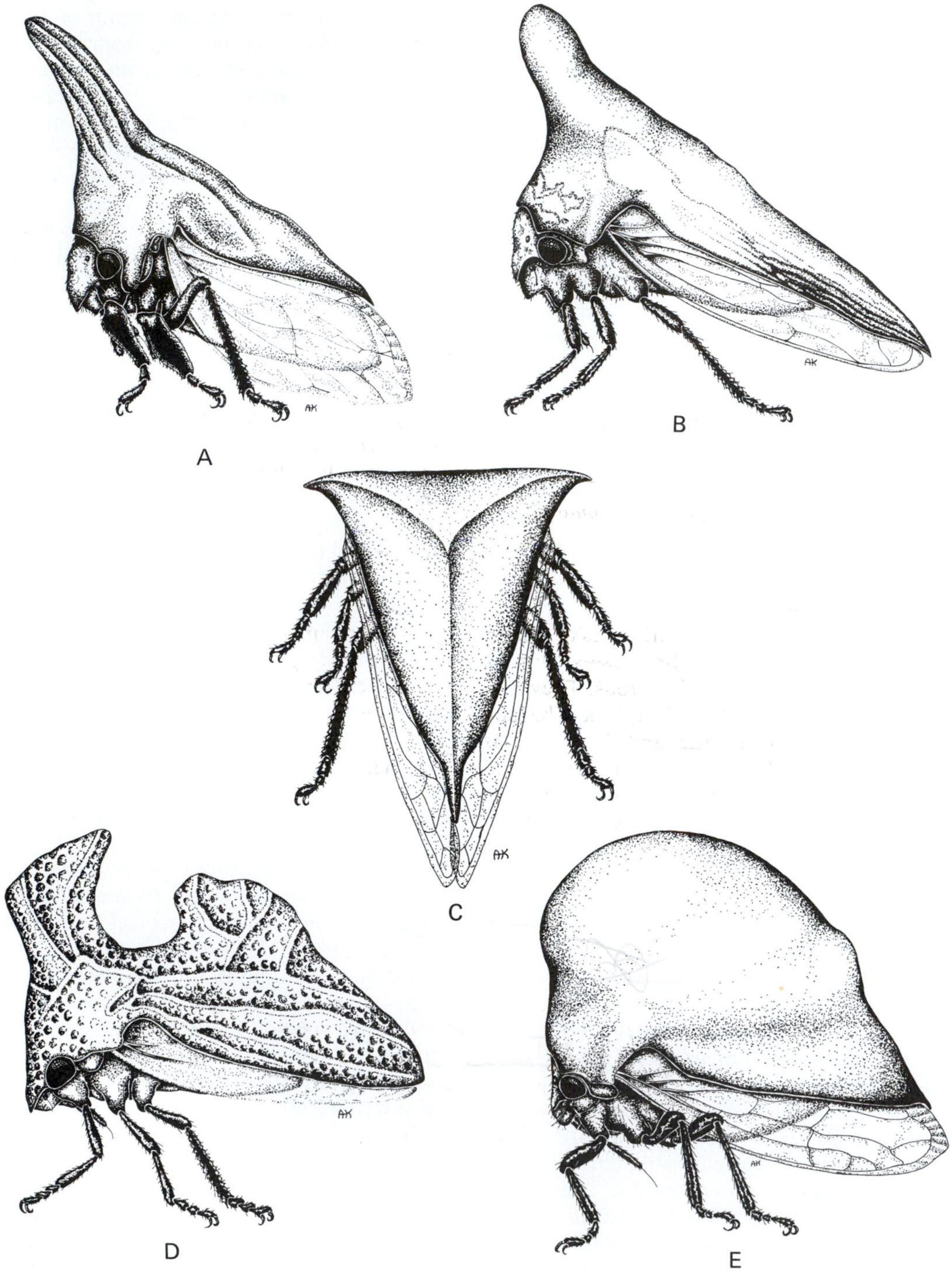

Figure 25–12. Treehoppers. **A**, *Campylénchia látipes* (Say); **B**, *Thèlia bimaculàta* (Fabricius); **C**, *Stictocéphala bizonia* Kopp and Yonke; **D**, *Ent̀ylia concìsa* Walker, **E**, *Archàsia galeàta* (Fabricius). **A, B, D,** and **E,** lateral views; **C,** dorsal view.

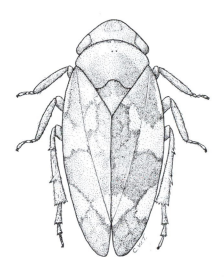

Figure 25–13. A froghopper, *Philaènus spumàrius* (L.).

Leafhoppers occur on almost all types of plants, including forest, shade, and orchard trees, shrubs, grasses, and many field and garden crops. They feed principally on the leaves of their food plant. The food of most species is quite specific, and the habitat is therefore well defined. In many cases a specialist in this group can examine a series of specimens taken in a given habitat and can describe that habitat and often determine the general region of the country from which the specimens came.

Most leafhoppers have a single generation a year, but a few have two or three. The winter is usually passed in either the adult or the egg stage, depending on the species.

There are many economically important pest species in this group, and they cause five major types of injury to plants. (1) Some species remove excessive amounts of sap and reduce or destroy the chlorophyll in the leaves, causing the leaves to become covered with minute white or yellow spots. With continued feeding the leaves turn yellowish or brownish. This type of injury is produced on apple leaves by various species of *Erythroneùra*, *Typhlocỳba*, and *Empoásca*. (2) Some species interfere with the normal physiology of the plant, for example, by mechanically plugging the phloem and xylem vessels in the leaves so that transport of food materials is impaired. A browning of the outer portion of the leaf, and eventually of the entire leaf, results. The potato leafhopper, *Empoásca fàbae* (Harris) (Figure 25–15A), causes this type of injury. (3) A few species injure plants by ovipositing in green twigs, often causing the terminal portion of the twigs to die. Various species of *Gyponàna* cause damage of this sort. Their egg punctures are similar to those of the buffalo treehopper but smaller. (4) Many species of leafhoppers act as vectors of the organisms that cause plant diseases. Aster yellows, corn stunt, phloem necrosis of elm, Pierce's disease of grape, phony peach, potato

Figure 25–14. Spittle mass of the spittlebug *Philaènus spumàrius* (L.). (Courtesy of the Illinois Natural History Survey.)

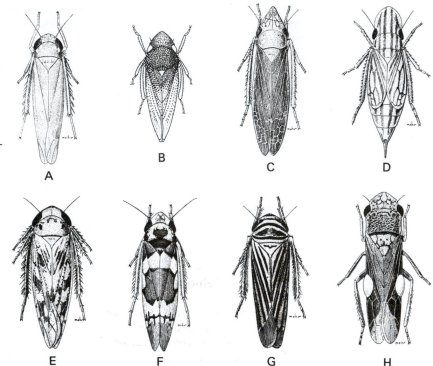

Figure 25–15. Leafhoppers. **A,** the potato leafhopper, *Empoásca fàbae* (Harris) (Typhlocybìnae); **B,** *Xerophloèa màjor* Baker (Ledrìnae); **C,** *Draeculacéphala móllipes* (Say) (Cicadellìnae); **D,** *Hécalus lineàtus* (Uhler) (Hecalìnae); **E,** the beet leafhopper, *Circùlifer tenéllus* (Baker) (Deltocephalìnae); **F,** *Erythroneùra vìtis* (Harris) (Typhlocybìnae); **G,** *Tylozỳgus bifidus* (Say) (Cicadellìnae); **H,** *Oncometòpia undàta* (Fabricius) (Cicadellìnae). (Courtesy of the Illinois Natural History Survey.)

yellow dwarf, curly top in sugar beets, and other plant diseases (see Table 2–1, Chapter 2) are transmitted by leafhoppers, chiefly species in the subfamilies Agalliìnae, Cicadellìnae, and Deltocephalìnae. (5) Some species cause stunting and leaf curling that results from the inhibition of growth on the undersurface of the leaves where the leafhoppers feed. The potato leafhopper, *Empoásca fàbae* (Harris), produces injury of this type.

Many species of leafhoppers emit from the anus a liquid called honeydew. It is composed of unused portions of plant sap to which are added certain waste products of the insect.

Many of the leafhoppers (as well as some of the other hoppers) are known to produce sound (Ossiannilsson 1949). These sounds are all quite weak; some can be heard if the insect is held close to one's ear, while others can only be heard when amplified. These sounds are produced by the vibration of tymbals located dorsolaterally at the base of the abdomen (on the first or second segment). The tymbals are thin-walled areas of the body wall, and are not very conspicuous from an external view. The sounds produced by leafhoppers of the genus *Empoásca* (Shaw et al. 1974) are of up to five types (depending on the species): one or two types of "common" sounds, disturbance sounds, courtship sounds, and sounds by the female. Most of these sounds are different in different species and are believed to play a role in species recognition by the insects.

Metcalf (1962–1968) considers the leafhoppers to represent a superfamily (the Cicadellòidea) and divides them into a number of families. The differences between these families are not as great as those between the families of Fulgoròidea, and most leafhopper specialists prefer to treat the leafhoppers as a single family divided into subfamilies. There are differences of opinion as to the leafhopper subfamilies to be recognized and the names to be given them. The arrangement followed in this book is outlined here, with other names and arrangements in parentheses. Following each subfamily is a list of the genera in that group mentioned in this book.

Family Cicadéllidae
    Ledrìnae (Xerophloeìnae)—*Xerophloèa*
    Dorycephalìnae (Dorydiìnae in part)—
        Dorycéphalus
    Hecalìnae (Dorydiìnae in part)—*Hécalus,*
        Parábolocràtus
    Megophthalmìnae (Ulopìnae; Agalliìnae in part)
    Agalliìnae—*Aceratagállia, Agállia, Agalliàna,*
        Agalliópsis
    Macropsìnae—*Macrópsis*

Idiocerìnae (Eurymelìnae)—*Idiócerus*
Gyponìnae—*Gyponàna*
Iassìnae (including Bythoscopìnae)
Penthimiìnae—*Penthímia*
Koebeliìnae—*Koebèlia*
Coelidiìnae (Jassìnae)—*Tinobrégmus*
Nioniìnae—*Niònia*
Aphrodìnae—*Aphròdes*
Xestocephalìnae—*Xestocèphalus*
Neocoelidiìnae—*Paracoelídia*
Cicadellìnae (Tettigellìnae, Tettigoniellìnae; including Evacanthìnae)—*Agrosòma, Carneocéphala, Cuérna, Draeculacéphala, Friscànus,*

Graphocéphala, Helochàra, Homalodísca, Hórdnia, Keonólla, Neokólla, Oncometòpia, Pagarònia, Sibòvia, Tylozỳgus
Typhlocybìnae (Cicadellìnae)—*Empoásca, Erythroneùra, Kunzeàna, Typhlocỳba*
Deltocephalìnae (Athysanìnae, Euscelìnae; including Balcluthìnae)—*Acinópterus, Chlorotéttix, Circùlifer, Colladònus, Dálbulus, Éndria, Euscelídius, Eùscelis, Excultànus, Fieberiélla, Graminélla, Macrósteles, Norvellìna, Paraphlépsius, Paratànus, Pseudotéttix, Scaphòideus, Scaphytòpius, Scleroràcus, Texanànus*

Key to the Subfamilies of Cicadéllidae

1.   Front wings without cross veins basad of apical cross veins (Figure 25–16F); longitudinal veins indistinct basally; ocelli often absent; apex of first segment of hind tarsus sharp-tipped; slender, fragile leafhoppers . . . . **Typhlocybìnae**   p. 333

1′.   Front wings with cross veins basad of apical cross veins (Figure 25–16H); longitudinal veins distinct basally; ocelli present; apex of first segment of hind tarsus truncate; usually relatively robust leafhoppers **2**

2(1′).   Episterna of prothorax easily visible in anterior view, not largely concealed by genae (Figure 25–16A, *eps*₁) **3**

2′.   Episterna of prothorax largely or entirely concealed by genae in anterior view (Figure 25–16B–E,G) **4**

3(2).   Ocelli on crown, remote from eyes and from anterior margin of crown (Figure 25–16L); dorsum covered with rounded pits (Figure 25–15B) . . . . **Ledrìnae**   p. 332

3′.   Ocelli on lateral margins of head, just in front of eyes (Figure 25–16J,K); dorsum not covered with rounded pits . . . . **Dorycephalìnae**   p. 332

4(2′).   Ocelli on crown (usually disk of crown), frontal sutures extending over margin of crown nearly to ocelli; clypellus broad above and narrowed below; clypeus usually swollen (Figure 25–16E) . . . . **Cicadellìnae**   p. 333

4′.   Without combination of characters above **5**

5(4′).   Frontal sutures terminating at or slightly above antennal pits, or ocelli near disk of crown and remote from eyes, or both **6**

5′.   Frontal sutures extending beyond antennal pits to or near ocelli, ocelli never on disk of crown **11**

6(5).   Lateral margins of pronotum carinate, moderately long; ledge or carina above antennal pits transverse or nearly so **7**

6′.   Lateral margins of pronotum short and not carinate, or only feebly so; ledge above antennal pits, if present, oblique **9**

7(6).   Face in profile concave; front wings with appendix very large, first (inner) apical cell large (equal in area to second and third apical cells combined) . . . . **Penthimiìnae**   p. 332

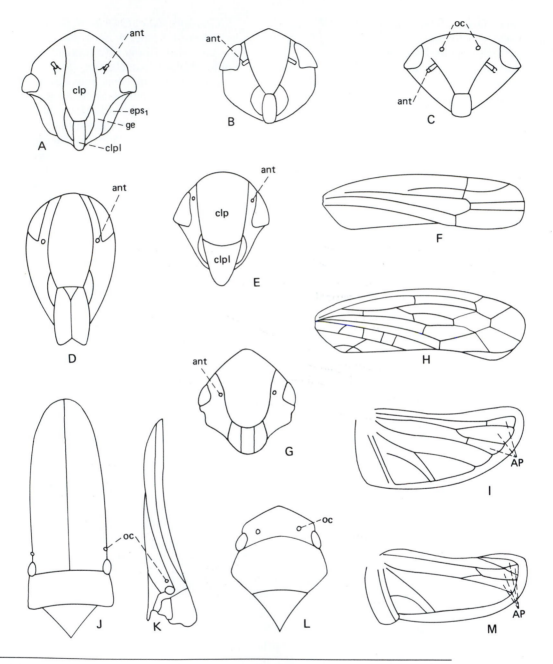

Figure 25–16. Characters of leafhoppers. **A,** face of *Xerophloèa víridis* (Fabricius) (Ledrìnae); **B,** face of *Paraphlépsius irroràtus* (Say) (Deltocephalìnae); **C,** face of *Idiócerus alternàtus* (Fitch) (Idiocerìnae); **D,** face of *Tinobrégmus vittàtus* Van Duzee (Coelidiìnae); **E,** face of *Sibòvia occatòria* (Say) (Cicadellìnae); **F,** front wing of *Kunzeàna marginélla* (Baker) (Typhlocybìnae); **G,** face of *Parabolocràtus víridis* (Uhler) (Hecalìnae); **H,** front wing of *Éndria inímica* (Say) (Deltocephalìnae); **I,** hind wing of *Macrópsis víridis* (Fitch) (Macropsìnae); **J,** head, pronotum, and scutellum of *Dorycéphalus platyrhýnchus* (Osborn), dorsal view (Dorycephalìnae); **K,** same, lateral view; **L,** head, pronotum, and scutellum of *Xerophloèa víridis* (Fabricius), dorsal view (Ledrìnae); **M,** hind wing of *Aceratagállia sanguinolénta* (Provancher) (Agalliìnae). *ant,* antenna; *AP,* apical cells; *clp,* clypeus; *clpl,* clypellus; *eps_1,* episternum of prothorax; *ge,* gena; *oc,* ocellus.

7'.   Face in profile not concave, usually distinctly convex; front wings with
           appendix normal or small, first apical cell not enlarged **8**

8(7').   Ocelli on crown, usually remote from anterior margin of head ......**Gyponìnae**   p. 332

8'.   Ocelli on anterior margin of crown ....**Iassìnae**   p. 332

9(6').   Hind wings always present, with 3 apical cells (Figure 25–16I, *AP*); pronotum
           extending forward beyond anterior margins of eyes; distance between ocelli
           usually greater than twice distance from ocellus to eye ....**Macropsìnae**   p. 332

9'.   Hind wings present or absent, if present with 4 apical cells (Figure 25–16M,
           AP); pronotum not extending forward beyond anterior margins of eyes;
           distance between ocelli not more than twice distance from ocellus to eye..**10**

10(9').   Face with carinae replacing frontal sutures above antennal pits; western
           United States ....**Megophthalmìnae**   p. 332

10'.   Face without such carinae; widely distributed ....**Agalliìnae**   p. 332

11(5').   Dorsum with circular pits; pronotum extending forward beyond anterior
           margins of eyes; shining black leafhoppers ....**Nioniìnae**   p. 332

11'.   Dorsum without such pits; pronotum not extending forward beyond anterior
           margins of eyes; color variable **12**

12(11').   Distance between ocelli less than distance between antennal pits, or clypellus
           much wider distally than basally and extending to or beyond apex of genae
           ....**13**

12'.   Distance between ocelli equal to or greater than distance between antennal
           pits, or clypellus parallel-sided and usually not extending to apex of genae..**14**

13(12).   Clypeus long and narrow, of nearly uniform width (Figure 25–16D); crown not
           wider than eye; costal margin of hind wings of macropterous forms
           expanded for short distance near base; head narrower than pronotum
           ....**Coelidiìnae**   p. 332

13'.   Clypeus short, broad, wider above (Figure 25–16C); crown wider than eye;
           costal margin of hind wings not expanded basally; head usually wider than
           pronotum ....**Idiocerìnae**   p. 332

14(12').   Ocelli on face ....**Koebeliìnae**   p. 332

14'.   Ocelli on or near margin of head **15**

15(14').   Clypeus extended laterally over bases of antennae, thus forming relatively deep
           antennal pits; small leafhoppers with head rounded, eyes small, clypeus
           ovate, antennae near margin of eyes, and ocelli distant from
           eyes ....**Xestocephalìnae**   p. 333

15'.   Clypeus not extended laterally over bases of antennae to form antennal pits;
           variable leafhoppers, but not having combination of characters above **16**

16(15').   Distinct ledge or carina above each antennal pit **17**

16'.   Without ledge or carina above each antennal pit **18**

17(16).   Ledge above each antennal pit oblique; face strongly convex (viewed from
           above) ....**Neocoelidiìnae**   p. 333

17'.   Ledge above each antennal pit transverse; face broad and relatively
           flat ....**Aphrodìnae**   p. 333

18(16').   Lower margins of genae sinuate (Figure 25–16G); body usually elongate,
           somewhat flattened; crown flat or nearly so, strongly produced, with
           anterior margin acute or foliaceous; lateral margins of pronotum carinate, as
           long as or longer than width of eye in dorsal view ....**Hecalìnae**   p. 332

18'.   Lower margins of genae not sinuate, or if so, then head not produced and body
            not flattened; lateral margins of pronotum short and, if carinate, usually
            only feebly so ....**Deltocephalìnae**   p. 333

Subfamily **Ledrìnae:**   This group is represented in our area by about eight species of *Xerophloèa*. They are grass feeders and sometimes become pests of forage crops. They have the dorsum covered with numerous pits, and the ocelli are on the disk of the crown (Figure 25–15B).

Subfamily **Dorycephalìnae:**   This is another small group (about nine North American species) of grass feeders, and they are chiefly southern in distribution. They are elongate and somewhat flattened. The head is long, with the margin thin and foliaceous (Figure 25–16J,K).

Subfamily **Hecalìnae:**   These leafhoppers (Figure 25–15D) are similar to the Dorycephalìnae, but have the episterna of the prothorax largely or entirely concealed in anterior view. They feed chiefly on grasses.

Subfamily **Megophthalmìnae:**   The members of this small group (seven North American species) are known only from California. Their food plants are unknown.

Subfamily **Agalliìnae:**   This is a fairly large group (about 70 North American species) in which the head is short, the ocelli are on the face, and the frontal sutures terminate at the antennal pits. The food habits of these leafhoppers are rather varied. A few species in this group act as vectors of plant diseases. For example, species of *Aceratagállia*, *Agállia*, and *Agalliópsis* serve as vectors of potato yellow dwarf.

Subfamily **Macropsìnae:**   In this group (more than 50 North American species) the head is short and broad, and the ocelli are on the face. The anterior margin of the pronotum extends forward beyond the anterior margins of the eyes. The dorsal surface, from the crown to the scutellum, is somewhat roughened—rugulose, punctate, or striate. These leafhoppers feed on trees and shrubs.

Subfamily **Idiocerìnae:**   This group (about 75 North American species) is similar to the Macropsìnae, but the pronotum does not extend forward beyond the anterior margins of the eyes. These leafhoppers feed on trees and shrubs.

Subfamily **Gyponìnae:**   This is a large group (more than 140 North American species) of relatively robust and somewhat flattened leafhoppers, which have the ocelli on the crown remote from the eyes and back from the anterior margin of the head. The crown is variable in shape and may be produced and foliaceous or short and broadly rounded in front. Some species feed on herbaceous plants, and others feed on trees and shrubs. One species, *Gyponàna angulàta* (Spangberg), acts as a vector of aster yellows, and another, *G. lámina* DeLong, acts as a vector of peach X-disease.

Subfamily **Iassìnae:**   These leafhoppers are relatively robust and somewhat flattened, with the head short and the ocelli on the anterior margin of the crown, about midway between the eyes and the apex of the head. The group is a small one (23 North American species), and its members occur chiefly in the West. Little is known about their food plants, but some species are known to feed on shrubs.

Subfamily **Penthimiìnae:**   This group is represented in our area by only two species of *Penthímia*, which occur in the East. They are short, oval, and somewhat flattened. The ocelli are located on the crown about halfway between the eyes and the midline, and the front wings are broad with a large appendix. Their food plants are not known.

Subfamily **Koebeliìnae:**   This group is represented in the United States by four species of *Koebèlia*, which occur in the West and feed on pine. The head is wider than the pronotum, and the crown is flat with a foliaceous margin and a broad shallow furrow in the midline. The ocelli are on the face.

Subfamily **Coelidiìnae:**   This is a small group (ten North American species) of relatively large and robust leafhoppers. The clypeus is long and narrow and of nearly uniform width (Figure 25–16D; in most other leafhoppers the clypeus is wider dorsally). The head is narrower than the pronotum, with the eyes large and the crown small, and the ocelli are on the anterior margin of the crown. This group is mainly Neotropical, and its known food plants are shrubs and herbaceous plants.

Subfamily **Nioniìnae:**   This group is represented in our area by a single species, *Niònia pálmeri* (Van Duzee), which occurs in the southern states. Its food plants are not known. This leafhopper is shining black, with the crown short and broad, and with the ocelli on the anterior margin and distant from the eyes. The anterior margin of the pronotum extends forward beyond the anterior margins of the eyes, and the anterior part of the dorsum bears numerous circular pits.

Subfamily **Aphrodínae:** This is a small group (six North American species), but its members are common and widely distributed. They are short, broad, and somewhat flattened, with the ocelli on the anterior margin of the crown. The head and pronotum are rugulose or coarsely granulate. Species of *Aphródes* are known to act as vectors of aster yellows, clover stunt, and clover phyllody.

Subfamily **Xestocephalínae:** This is a small group (3 species of *Xestocéphalus*) but a widely distributed one, whose members are small and robust, with the head and eyes small. The crown is rounded anteriorly, with the ocelli on the anterior margin.

Subfamily **Neocoelidiínae:** This is a small group (26 North American species), and many of its members are rather elongate in form. The face is strongly convex, and the ocelli are on the crown near the anterior margin and the eyes. Some species (*Paracoelídia*) occur on pine.

Subfamily **Cicadellínae:** This is a fairly large group (nearly a hundred North American species), with many common species. Most are relatively large, and some are rather robust. The ocelli are on the crown, and the frontal sutures extend over the margin of the head nearly to the ocelli. Some members of this group are very strikingly colored. One of our largest and most common species is *Graphocéphala coccínea* (Foerster), which is similar in size and shape to *Draeculacéphala móllipes* (Say) (Figure 25–15C), but has the wings reddish striped with bright green. The nymphs of this species are bright yellow. This species is often found on forsythia and other ornamental shrubs. Many species in this group serve as vectors of plant disease: species of *Carneocéphala*, *Cuérna*, *Draeculacéphala*, *Friscànus*, *Graphocéphala*, *Helochàra*, *Homalodísca*, *Neokólla*, *Oncometòpia*, and *Pagarònia* serve as vectors of Pierce's disease of grape. Species of *Draeculacéphala*, *Graphocéphala*, *Homalodísca*, and *Oncometòpia* serve as vectors of phony peach.

Subfamily **Typhlocybínae:** This is a large group (more than 700 North American species, more than half of which are in the genus *Erythroneùra*) of small, fragile, and often brightly colored leafhoppers (Figure 25–15A,F). The ocelli may be present or absent, and the venation of the front wings is somewhat reduced, with no cross veins except in the apical portion. The food plants are varied. This group includes a number of pest species in the genera *Empoásca*, *Erythroneùra*, and *Typhlocýba*.

Subfamily **Deltocephalínae:** This is the largest subfamily of leafhoppers (more than 1150 North American species), and its members are variable in form and food plants. The ocelli are always on the anterior margin of the crown, and there is no ledge above the antennal pits. Many members of this group are important vectors of plant diseases. Aster yellows is transmitted by species of *Scaphytòpius*, *Macrósteles*, *Paraphlépsius*, and *Texanànus*. Curly top of sugar beets is transmitted by *Circùlifer tenéllus* (Baker). Phloem necrosis of elm is transmitted by *Scaphòideus luteòlus* Van Duzee. Clover phyllody is transmitted by species of *Macrósteles*, *Chlorotéttix*, *Colladònus*, and *Eùscelis*. And corn stunt is transmitted by species of *Dálbulus* and *Graminélla*.

SUPERFAMILY **Fulgoròidea**—Planthoppers: This is a large group, but its members are seldom as abundant as the leafhoppers or froghoppers. The species in the United States are seldom more than 10 or 12 mm long, but some tropical species reach a length of 50 mm or more. Many of the planthoppers have the head peculiarly modified, with that part in front of the eyes greatly enlarged and more or less snout-like (Figure 25–17, especially G–I).

The planthoppers differ from the leafhoppers in having only a few large spines on the hind tibiae and from both the leafhoppers and the froghoppers in having the antennae arising below the compound eyes. The ocelli are usually located immediately in front of the eyes, on the side (rather than the front or dorsal surface) of the head (Figure 25–2C). There is often a sharp angle separating the side of the head (where the compound eyes, antennae, and ocelli are located) and the front.

The food plants of these insects range from trees and shrubs to herbaceous plants and grasses. The planthoppers feed on the plant juices and, like many other Homóptera, produce honeydew. Many of the nymphal forms are ornamented with wax filaments. Very few planthoppers cause economic damage to cultivated plants.

Family **Delphácidae:** This is the largest family of planthoppers, and its members can be recognized by the large flattened spur at the apex of the hind tibiae (Figure 25–3C, *sp*). Most species are small, and many have reduced wings. The sugarcane leafhopper, *Perkinsiélla saccharícida* Kirkaldy, which at one time was a very destructive pest in Hawaii, is a member of this family.

Family **Dérbidae:** These planthoppers are principally tropical and feed on woody fungi. Most species are elongate with long wings and are rather delicate in build (Figure 25–17K).

Family **Cixíidae:** This is one of the larger families of planthoppers. Its members are widely distributed, but most species are tropical. Some species are subterranean feeders on the roots of grasses during their nymphal stage. The wings are hyaline and frequently ornamented with spots along the veins (Figure 25–17A,D).

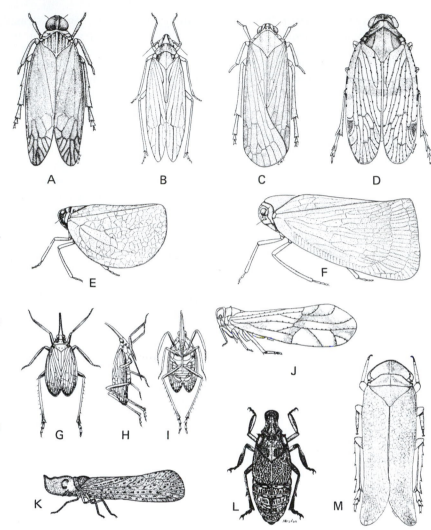

Figure 25–17. Planthoppers. **A,** *Oècleus boreàlis* Van Duzee (Cixìidae); **B,** *Sternocrànus dorsàlis* Fitch (Delphácidae); **C,** *Catònia impunctàta* (Fitch) (Achìlidae); **D,** *Cíxius angustàtus* Caldwell (Cixìidae); **E,** *Acanalònia bivittàta* (Say) (Acanalonìidae); **F,** *Anórmenis septentrionàlis* (Spinola) (Flàtidae); **G,H,** and **I,** *Scòlops pérdix* Uhler (Dictyophàridae), dorsal, lateral, and ventral views; **J,** *Liburniélla ornàta* (Stål) (Delphácidae); **K,** *Apáche degeèrii* (Kirby) (Dérbidae); **L,** *Fitchiélla róbertsoni* (Fitch) (Íssidae); **M,** *Cyrpóptus belfrágei* Stål (Fulgòridae). (Courtesy of Osborn and the Ohio Biological Survey.)

Family **Kinnàridae:** These planthoppers resemble the Cixìidae, but are quite small and have no dark spots on the wings. Our six species (*Oeclídius*) occur in the Southwest, but some West Indies species might occur in southern Florida.

Family **Dictyophàridae:** The members of this group are chiefly grass feeders and are generally found in meadows. The most common eastern members of this group (*Scòlops*; Figure 25–17G–I) have the head prolonged anteriorly into a long slender process. Other dictyopharids have the head somewhat triangularly produced anteriorly or not at all produced.

Family **Fulgòridae:** This group contains some of the largest planthoppers, some tropical species having a wingspread of about 150 mm. Our largest fulgorids have a wingspread of a little more than 25 mm and a body length of about 13 mm. Some tropical

species have the head greatly inflated anteriorly, producing a peanutlike process. This was believed to be luminous, thereby giving rise to the name "lanternflies" for these insects. Most of our species (for example, Figure 25–17M) have the head short. The members of this family can generally be recognized by the reticulated anal area of the hind wings.

Family **Achìlidae:** These planthoppers can usually be recognized by their overlapping front wings (Figure 25–17C). Most species are brownish, and vary in length from about 4 to 10 mm. The nymphs usually live under loose bark or in a depression in dead wood.

Family **Tropidùchidae:** This is a tropical group, but three species have been found in Florida. The most common is probably *Pelitròpis rotulàta* Van Duzee, which has three longitudinal keels on the vertex, pronotum, and scutellum, those on the scutellum meeting anteriorly. This species also occurs in Louisiana.

Family **Flàtidae:** These planthoppers have a wedge-shaped appearance when at rest (Figure 25–17F), and there are usually numerous cross veins in the costal area of the front wings. Most species are either pale green or dark brown in color. They appear to feed chiefly on vines, shrubs, and trees and are usually found in wooded areas.

Family **Acanaloniidae:** These planthoppers are somewhat similar to the Flàtidae, but have a slightly different shape (Figure 25–17E), and they do not have many cross veins in the costal area of the front wings. These planthoppers are usually greenish, with brown markings dorsally.

Family **Íssidae:** This is a large and widely distributed group. Most of them are dark-colored and rather stocky in build, and some have short wings and a weevillike snout (Figure 25–17L).

SUBORDER **Sternorrhýncha:** The members of this suborder are for the most part relatively inactive insects, and some (for example, most scale insects) are quite sedentary. The tarsi are one- or two-segmented, and the antennae (when present) are usually long and filiform. Many members of this suborder are wingless, and some scale insects lack legs and antennae and are not very insectlike in appearance.

Family **Psýllidae**—Jumping Plantlice or Psyllids: These insects are small, 2–5 mm in length, and usually resemble miniature cicadas in form (Figures 25–18B, 25–19, 25–20B). They are somewhat

Figure 25–19. The potato psyllid, *Paratriòza cockerélli* (Sulc). (Courtesy of Knowlton and Janes and the Entomological Society of America.)

similar to the aphids, but have strong jumping legs and relatively long antennae. The adults of both sexes are winged, and the beak is short and three-segmented. The nymphs of many species produce large amounts of a white waxy secretion, causing them to superficially resemble the woolly aphids. The jumping plantlice feed on plant juices, and as in the case of most of the Homóptera, the food-plant relationships are quite specific.

Two important pest species in this group, the pear psylla, *Psýlla pyrícola* Foerster, and the apple sucker, *Psýlla máli* (Schmidberger), have been imported from Europe. A western species, the potato or tomato psyllid, *Paratriòza cockerélli* (Sulc) (Figure 25–19), transmits a virus that causes psyllid yellows in potatoes, tomatoes, peppers, and eggplants. This disease causes a reduction in yield resulting from the dwarfing and discoloration of the plant.

The cottony alder psyllid, *Psýlla floccòsa* (Patch), is a common member of this group occurring in the Northeast. The nymphs feed on alder and produce large amounts of wax, and groups of the nymphs on alder twigs resemble masses of cotton (Figure 25–18A). These insects may sometimes be confused with the woolly alder aphid, *Procíphilus tessellàtus* (Fitch). The psyllid is to be found on the alder only during the early part of the summer, but the aphid occurs up until fall. The adults of the cottony alder psyllid (Figure 25–18B) are pale green in color.

A few of the psyllids are gall-making forms. Species of *Pachypsýlla* produce small galls on the leaves of hackberry (Figure 25–20).

Family **Aleyròdidae**—Whiteflies: The whiteflies are minute insects, rarely more than 2 or 3 mm in length, that resemble tiny moths. The adults of both sexes are winged, and the wings are covered with a white dust or waxy powder. The adults are usually active whitish insects that feed on leaves.

The metamorphosis of whiteflies is somewhat different from that of most other Homóptera. The first-instar young are active, but subsequent immature instars are sessile and look like scales. The

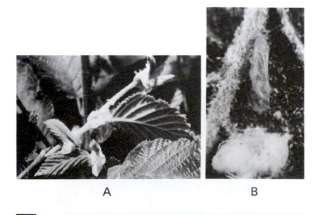

A   B

Figure 25–18. The alder psyllid, *Psýlla floccòsa* (Patch). **A,** groups of nymphs on alder (these groups form white cottony masses on the twigs, particularly at the base of leaf petioles); **B,** a newly emerged adult; below the adult is the cast skin of the nymph, still covered with the cottony secretions characteristic of the nymphs of this species.

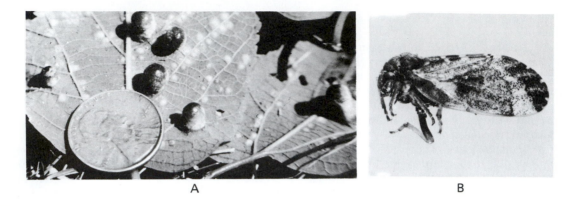

A   B

Figure 25–20. **A,** galls of *Pachypsýlla celtidismámma* (Riley) on hackberry; **B,** adult of *Pachypsýlla* sp., 20×. (**A,** courtesy of Moser; **B,** courtesy of the Ohio Agricultural Research and Development Center.)

scalelike covering is a waxy secretion of the insect and has a rather characteristic appearance (Figure 25–21). The wings develop internally during metamorphosis, and the early instars are usually called larvae. The next to the last instar is quiescent and is usually called a pupa. The wings are everted at the molt of the last larval instar.

The whiteflies are most abundant in the tropics and subtropics, and the most important pest species in the United States are those that attack citrus trees and greenhouse plants. The damage is done by sucking sap from the leaves. One of the most serious pests in this group is *Aleurocánthus wóglumi* Ashby, which attacks citrus trees and is well established in the West Indies and Mexico. An objectionable sooty fungus often grows on the honeydew excreted by whiteflies and interferes with photosynthesis. This fungus is more prevalent in the South and in the tropics than in the North.

Family **Aphídidae**—Aphids or Plantlice: The aphids constitute a large group of small, soft-bodied insects that are frequently found in large numbers sucking the sap from the stems or leaves of plants. Such aphid groups often include individuals in all stages of development. The members of this family can usually be recognized by their characteristic pearlike shape, a pair of cornicles at the posterior end of the abdomen, and the fairly long antennae. Winged forms can usually be recognized by the venation and the relative size of the front and hind wings (Figure 25–6C). The wings at rest are generally held vertically above the body.

The members of this family are very similar to the Eriosomátidae, but differ in having the cornicles nearly always developed, the wax glands much less

abundant, the sexual female (and usually also the male) with functional mouthparts, and the ovipositing female producing more than one egg.

The cornicles of aphids are tubelike structures arising from the dorsal side of the fifth or sixth abdominal segment. These cornicles secrete a defensive fluid. In some species the body is more or less covered with white waxy fibers, secreted by dermal

Figure 25–21. "Pupae" of mulberry whiteflies, *Tetraleuròdes mòri* (Quaintance). (Courtesy of the Ohio Agricultural Research and Development Center.)

glands. Aphids also excrete honeydew, which is emitted from the anus. The honeydew consists mainly of excess sap ingested by the insect, to which are added excess sugars and waste material. This honeydew may be produced in sufficient quantities to cause the surface of objects beneath to become sticky. Honeydew is a favorite food of many ants, and some species, for example, the corn root aphid, *Anuràphis maidirádicis* (Forbes), are tended like cows by certain species of ants.

The life cycle of many aphids is rather unusual and complex (Figure 25–22). Most species overwinter in the egg stage, and these eggs hatch in the spring into females that reproduce parthenogenetically and give birth to living young. Several generations may be produced during the season in this way, with only females being produced and the young being born alive. The first generation or two usually consists of wingless individuals, but eventually winged individuals appear. In many species these winged forms migrate to a different host plant, and the reproductive process continues. In the latter part of the season the aphids migrate back to the original host plant species, and a generation consisting of both males and females appears. The individuals of this bisexual generation mate, and the females lay the eggs, which overwinter.

Enormous populations of aphids can be built up in a relatively short time by this method of repro-

duction. The aphids would be a great deal more destructive to vegetation were it not for their numerous parasites and predators. The principal parasites of aphids are braconids and chalcidoids, and the most important predators are ladybird beetles, lacewings, and the larvae of some syrphid flies.

This family contains a number of serious pests of cultivated plants. Aphids cause a curling or wilting of the food plant by their feeding (Figure 2–5B), and they serve as vectors of a number of important plant diseases. Several diseases are transmitted by aphids, including the mosaics of beans, sugarcane, and cucumbers, by species of *Àphis*, *Macrosìphum*, and *Mỳzus;* beet mosaic by *Àphis rùmicis* L.; and cabbage ring spot, crucifer mosaic, and potato yellow dwarf by *Mỳzus pérsicae* (Sulzer) (see Table 2–1, Chapter 2).

The rosy apple aphid, *Dysàphis plantagínea* (Passerini), overwinters on apple and related trees and passes the early summer generations there, then migrates to the narrow-leaved plantain as the secondary host. Later in the season migration back to apple takes place (Figure 25–22). The apple grain aphid, *Rhopalosìphum fítchii* (Sanderson), has apple as its primary host plant and migrates in early summer to grasses, including wheat and oats. Other species of importance are the apple aphid, *Àphis pòmi* De Geer; the cotton aphid, *A. gossýpii* Glover; the potato aphid, *Macrosìphum euphòrbiae* (Thomas); the rose

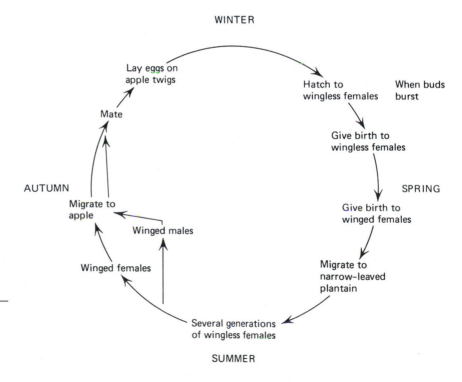

Figure 25–22. Diagram of the life history of the rosy apple aphid, *Dysàphis plantagínea* (Passerini).

WINTER

Lay eggs on apple twigs

Hatch to wingless females   When buds burst

Mate

Give birth to wingless females

AUTUMN   SPRING

Give birth to winged females

Migrate to apple   Winged males

Winged females

Migrate to narrow-leaved plantain

Several generations of wingless females

SUMMER

aphid, *M. ròsae* (L.); the pea aphid, *Acyrthosìphon pìsum* (Harris); and the cabbage aphid, *Brevicòryne brássicae* (L.). The largest aphid in the East is the giant bark aphid, *Longistígma càryae* (Harris), 6 mm in length, which feeds on hickory, sycamore, and other trees (Figure 25–23).

The corn root aphid, *Anuràphis maidirádicis* (Forbes), is sometimes a serious pest of corn, and it has an interesting relationship with ants. The eggs of this aphid pass the winter in the nests of field ants, chiefly those in the genus *Làsius.* In the spring, the ants carry the young aphids to the roots of smart-weed and other weeds, where the aphids feed. Later in the season, the ants transfer the aphids to the roots of corn. When the aphid eggs are laid in the fall, they are gathered by the ants and stored in their nest for the winter. All during the season the aphids are tended by the ants, which transfer them from one food plant to another. The ants feed on the honeydew produced by the aphids.

Family **Eriosomátidae**—Woolly and Gall-Making Aphids: The cornicles are reduced or absent in this group, and wax glands are abundant. The sexual forms lack mouthparts, and the ovipositing female produces only one egg. Nearly all members of this family alternate between host plants. The primary host (on which the overwintering eggs are laid) is usually a tree or shrub, and the secondary host is a herbaceous plant. These aphids may feed either on the roots of the host plant or on the part of the plant above the ground. Many species produce galls or malformations of the tissues of the primary host, but usually do not produce galls on the secondary host.

The woolly apple aphid, *Eriosòma lanígerum* (Hausmann) (Figure 25–24), is a common and important example of this group. This species feeds principally on the roots and bark and can be recognized by the characteristic woolly masses of wax on its body. These aphids usually overwinter on elm, and the first generations of the season are spent on that host. In early summer, winged forms appear and migrate to apple, hawthorn, and related trees. Later in the season some of these migrate back to elm, where the bisexual generation is produced and the overwintering eggs are laid. Other individuals migrate from the branches of the apple tree to the roots, where they produce gall-like growths. The root-inhabiting forms may remain there a year or more, passing through several generations. This aphid transmits perennial canker.

The woolly alder aphid, *Procíphilus tessellàtus* (Fitch), is often found in dense masses on the branches of alder and maple. All the generations may be passed on alder, or the species may overwinter on maple and migrate to alder in the summer and then back to maple in the fall, where the sexual forms are produced. The species may overwinter in either the egg or the nymphal stage.

Some of the more common gall-making species in this group are *Cólopha ulmícola* (Fitch), which causes the cockscomb gall on elm leaves (Figure 25–25A; *Hormàphis hamamélidis* (Fitch), which

Figure 25–23.   **A,** a colony of apterous females and nymphs of the giant bark aphid, *Longistígma càryae* (Harris); **B,** a winged female of the giant willow aphid, *Làchnus salígnus* (Gmelin). (**A,** courtesy of the Illinois Natural History Survey; **B,** courtesy of the Ohio Agricultural Research and Development Center.)

A   **B**

Figure 25–24.   A colony of woolly apple aphids, *Eriosòma lanígerum* (Hausman). (Courtesy of the Ohio Agricultural Research and Development Center.)

causes the cone gall on the leaves of witch hazel; *Hamamelístes spinòsus* Shimer, which forms a spiny gall on the flower buds of witch hazel (Figure 25–25B); and *Pémphigus pópulitransvérsus* Riley, which forms a marble-shaped gall on the petioles of poplar leaves (Figure 25–25C).

Family **Adélgidae**—Pine and Spruce Aphids: The members of this group feed only on conifers. They form cone-shaped galls on spruce and, on other hosts, occur as white cottony tufts on the bark, branches, twigs, needles, or cones, depending on the species. Most species alternate between two different conifers in their life history, forming galls only on the primary host tree (spruce). All the females are oviparous. The antennae are five-segmented in the winged forms, four-segmented in the sexual forms, and three-segmented in the wingless parthenogenetically reproducing females. The body is often covered with waxy threads, and the wings at rest are held rooflike over the body. Cu_1 and Cu_2 in the front wing are separated at the base (Figure 25–4E).

The eastern spruce gall aphid, *Adélges abiètis* (L.), is a fairly common species attacking spruce in southeastern Canada and the northeastern part of the United States and forming pineapple-shaped galls on the twigs (Figure 25–26). It has two generations a year, and both generations consist entirely of females. There is no bisexual generation. Both generations occur on spruce. Partly grown nymphs pass the winter attached to the base of spruce buds. The nymphs mature into females the following April or May and lay their eggs at the base of the buds. The feeding of these females on the needles of the new shoots causes the needles to swell. The eggs hatch in about a week, and the nymphs settle on the needles that have become swollen by the feeding of the mother. The twig swelling continues and a gall is formed, and the nymphs complete their development in cavities in the gall. Later in the summer, winged females emerge from the galls and lay their eggs on the needles of nearby branches. These eggs hatch, and the nymphs overwinter.

This group contains two genera, *Adélges* and *Píneus*, whose members attack spruce and various other conifers. Perhaps the most important species in the West is Cooley's spruce gall aphid, *Adélges*

Figure 25–25. Aphid galls. **A**, elm cockscomb gall, caused by *Cólopha ulmícola* (Fitch); **B**, spiny bud gall of witch hazel, caused by *Hamamelístes spinòsus* Shimer; **C**, leaf petiole gall of poplar, caused by *Pémphigus pópulitransvérsus* Riley; **D**, vagabond gall of poplar, caused by *Pémphigus vagabúndus* Walsh. (**A–C**, courtesy of the Illinois Natural History Survey; **D**, courtesy of the Ohio Agricultural Research and Development Center.)

cooleyi (Gillette), which is also widely distributed in eastern North America and in Europe. The galls of this species on spruce are 12–75 mm long and light green to dark purple in color, and each chamber in the gall contains from 3 to 30 wingless aphids. The alternate host of this species in the West is Douglas fir, where the insects form white cottony tufts on new needles, shoots, and developing cones. A severe infestation may cause a heavy shedding of foliage, and the damage, particularly in Christmas tree areas, may be considerable.

Family **Phylloxèridae**—Phylloxerans: The antennae in this group are three-segmented in all forms, and the wings at rest are held flat over the body. Cu_1 and Cu_2 in the front wing are stalked at the base

(Figure 25–4C). These insects do not produce waxy threads, but some species are covered with a waxy powder. The phylloxerans feed on plants other than conifers, and the life history is often very complex.

The grape phylloxera, *Daktulosphaìra vitifòliae* (Fitch), is a common and economically important species in this group. This minute form attacks both the leaves and the roots of grape, forming small galls on the leaves (Figure 25–27) and gall-like swellings on the roots. The European grapes are much more susceptible to the attacks of this insect than are the native American grapes.

Some of the phylloxerans produce galls on trees. One such species occurring in the East is the hickory gall aphid, *Phylloxèra caryaecáulis* (Fitch) (Figure

Figure 25–26. Eastern spruce gall, caused by *Adélges abiètis* (L.). (Courtesy of the Ohio Agricultural Research and Development Center.)

25–28). These galls reach a diameter of 16–18 mm, and each contains a large number of aphids.

SUPERFAMILY **Coccòidea**—Scale Insects: This group is a large one and contains forms that are minute and highly specialized. Many are so modified that they look very little like other Homóptera. The females are wingless and usually legless and sessile, and the males have only a single pair of wings (rarely, the males, too, are wingless). The males lack mouthparts and do not feed; the abdomen terminates in one (rarely two) long stylelike process (Figure 25–29A); and the hind wings are reduced to small halterelike processes that usually terminate in a hooked bristle. The antennae of the female may be lacking or may have up to 11 segments; the antennae of the male have 10–25 segments. Male scale insects look very much like small gnats, but they can usually be recognized by the absence of mouthparts and the presence of a stylelike process at the end of the abdomen.

The development of scale insects varies somewhat in different species, but in most cases it is rather complex. The first-instar nymphs have legs and antennae and are fairly active insects; they are often called crawlers. After the first molt, the legs and antennae are often lost and the insect becomes sessile, and a waxy or scalelike covering is secreted and covers the body. In the armored scales (Diaspídidae), this covering is often separate from the body of the insect. The females remain under the scale covering when they become adult and produce their eggs or give birth to their young there. The males develop much like the females, except that the last instar preceding the adult is quiescent and is often called a pupa. The wings develop externally in the pupa.

Family **Margaròdidae**—Giant Coccids and Ground Pearls: This family contains about 41 North American species and includes some of the largest species in the superfamily. Some species of *Llavèia* and *Cal-*

Figure 25–27. Galls on grape leaves caused by the grape phylloxera, *Daktulosphaìra vitifòliae* (Fitch). (Courtesy of the Ohio Agricultural Research and Development Center.)

Figure 25–28. Galls of the hickory gall aphid, *Phylloxèra caryaecáulis* (Fitch). **A,** gall on a hickory leaf; **B,** two galls cut open to show the insects inside. (Courtesy of the Ohio Agricultural Research and Development Center.)

lipáppus may reach a length of about 25 mm. The name "ground pearls" comes from the pearllike appearance of the wax cysts of females in the genus *Margaròdes,* which live on the roots of plants. The cysts of some tropical species are used in making varnish. The cottony cushion scale, *Icérya púrchasi* Maskell, is an important pest of citrus in the West. Several species in the genus *Matsucóccus* are pests of pines.

Family **Ortheziidae**—Ensign Coccids: The females in this group are distinctly segmented, elongate-oval, and covered with hard, white, waxy plates (Figure 25–30A). Some have a white egg sac at the posterior end of the body. These insects may occur on almost any part of the host plant, but are perhaps most often found on the roots. There are 27 species of ensign coccids in the United States, 21 of which are in the genus *Orthèzia.* One of these, *O. insígnis* Browne, is a common and important greenhouse pest.

Family **Kérridae**—Lac Scales: The females in this group are globular in form and legless and live in cells of resin. Six species of *Tachardiélla* occur in the Southwest, where they feed on cactus and other desert plants. They all produce lac, some of which is highly pigmented.

Most members of this family are tropical or subtropical in distribution, and one, the Indian lac insect, *Láccifer lácca* (Kerr), is of considerable commercial value. It occurs on fig, banyan, and other plants in Sri Lanka, Taiwan, India, Indochina, and the Philippine Islands. The bodies of the females become covered with heavy exudations of wax or lac and are sometimes so numerous that the twigs are coated with lac to a thickness of 5–15 mm. The twigs are cut and the lac is melted off, refined, and used in the production of shellac and varnishes. About 4 million pounds of this material is harvested annually.

Family **Cóccidae**—Soft Scales, Wax Scales, and Tortoise Scales: The females of this group are elongate-oval, usually convex but sometimes flattened, with a hard smooth exoskeleton or a covering of wax. Legs are usually present, and the antennae are either absent or much reduced. The males may be winged or wingless.

This is a fair-sized group, with about 85 North American species, a number of which are important pests. The brown soft scale, *Cóccus hesperídium* L., and the black scale, *Saissètia òleae* (Bernard), are important pests of citrus in the South. The hemispherical scale, *Saissètia cóffeae* (Walker), is a common pest of ferns and other plants in homes and greenhouses. Several species in this group attack shade and fruit trees. The tulip-tree scale, *Toumeyélla liriodéndri* (Gmelin), is one of the largest scale insects in the United States, the adult female being about 8 mm in length. The cottony maple scale, *Pulvinària innumerábilis* (Rathvon), is a relatively large species (about 6 mm in length) whose eggs are laid in a large cottony mass that protrudes from the end of the scale (Figure 25–31). Soft scales belonging to the genus *Lecànium* (Figure 25–32) attack a variety of plants and are often pests in greenhouses.

The Chinese wax scale, *Erícerus pèla* Chavannes, is an interesting and important oriental species. The males secrete large amounts of a pure white wax, which is used in making candles. Wax is also produced by the wax scales of the genus *Ceroplástes.* The Indian wax scale, *C. ceríferus* Anderson, produces a wax that is used for medicinal purposes.

Family **Aclérdidae:** This is a small family (15 North American species), most of whose members feed on grasses. These scales usually occur beneath the leaf sheaths or at the base of the plant, sometimes among the roots. One of our species feeds on Spanish moss, and some tropical species attack orchids.

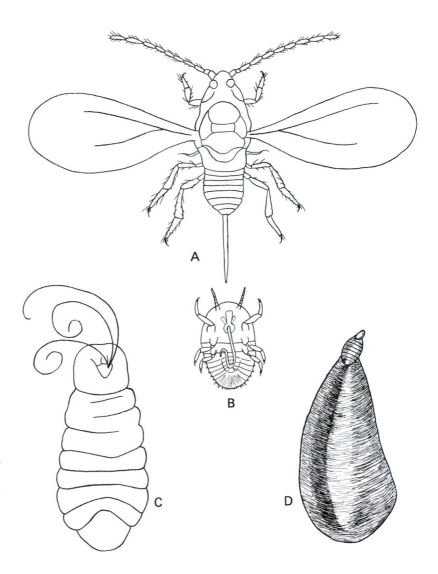

Figure 25–29. Stages of the oystershell scale, *Lepidósaphes úlmi* (L.). **A,** adult male; **B,** newly hatched young, or crawler; **C,** adult female; **D,** scale of female. (Redrawn from various sources.)

Family **Cryptocóccidae**: This family is represented in the United States by two species of *Cryptocóccus*, which occur in the northeastern states. They are found in bark crevices of sugar maple.

Family **Kermèsidae**—Gall-like Coccids: The females in this group are rounded and resemble small galls (Figure 25–30B). About 30 species occur in the United States, and they are found on the twigs or leaves of oak.

This family includes the tamarisk manna scale, *Trabutìna mannípara* (Ehrenberg), which is believed to have produced the manna mentioned in the Bible. This species feeds on plants in the genus *Támarix*, and the females excrete large amounts of honeydew. In arid regions the honeydew solidifies on the leaves and accumulates in thick layers to form a sweet sugarlike material called manna.

Family **Asterolecaniidae**—Pit Scales: These insects are called pit scales because many of them produce gall-like pits in the bark of their hosts. This group is a small one, with 15 species in the United States, and they attack a variety of hosts. Some occur on the bark, and others occur on the leaves of the host.

Family **Lecanodiaspídidae**: This group is represented in the United States by about five species of *Lecanodiáspis*. Some of these are fairly common and are occasionally pests of azalea, holly, and other ornamentals.

Family **Cerocóccidae**: This group is represented in our area by seven species of *Cerocóccus*, which occur on a variety of host plants. *Cerocóccus kálmiae* Ferris is occasionally a pest of azalea. The oak wax scale, *C. quércus* Comstock, occurs on oak in Cali-

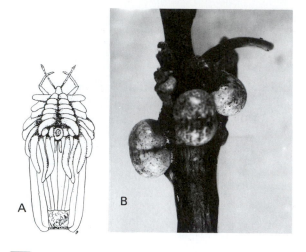

Figure 25–30.   **A,** an ensign coccid, *Orthèzia solidáginis* (Sanders), female; **B,** bur oak gall-like coccid, *Kérmes pubéscens* (Bogue). (**A,** redrawn from Sanders; **B,** courtesy of the Ohio Agricultural Research and Development Center.)

fornia and Arizona, and the wax in which it is encased was once used as chewing gum by the Indians.

Family **Dactylopiidae**—Cochineal Insects: These insects resemble the mealybugs in appearance and habits. The females are red in color, elongate-oval in shape, and distinctly segmented, and the body is covered with white waxy plates. The group is represented in the United States by five species of *Dactylòpius*, which occur on cactus (*Opúntia* and *Nopàlea*). A Mexican species, *D. cóccus* Costa, is an important source of a crimson dye for natives of Mexico. Mature females are brushed from the cacti and dried, and the pigments are extracted from their dried bodies. These insects were commercially important until about 1875, when aniline dyes were introduced.

Family **Diaspídidae**—Armored Scales: This is the largest family of scale insects (more than 300 North American species), and it contains a number of very important pest species. The females are very small and soft-bodied and are concealed under a scale covering that is usually free from the body of the insect underneath. The scale covering is formed of wax secreted by the insect, together with the cast skins of the early instars. The scales vary in different species. They may be circular or elongate, smooth or rough, and variously colored. The scales of the male are usually smaller and more elongate than those of the female. The adult females have the body small, flattened, and disklike, and the segmentation is fre-

quently obscure. They have neither eyes nor legs, and the antennae are absent or vestigial. The males are winged and have well-developed legs and antennae.

Reproduction may be bisexual or parthenogenetic. Some species are oviparous, and others give birth to living young. The eggs are laid under the scale. The first-instar young, or crawlers, are active insects and may travel some distance. They are able to live several days without food. A species is spread in this crawler stage, either by the locomotion of the crawler itself or by the crawlers' being transported on the feet of birds or by other means. Eventually the crawlers settle down and insert their mouthparts into the host plant. The females remain sessile the remainder of their lives.

These insects injure plants by sucking sap and, when numerous, may kill the plant. The armored scales feed principally on trees and shrubs and may sometimes heavily encrust the twigs or branches. Several species are important pests of orchard and shade trees.

The San Jose scale, *Quadraspidiòtus perniciòsus* (Comstock) (Figure 25–33), is a very serious pest. It first appeared in California about 1880, probably from the Orient, and has since spread throughout the United States. It attacks a number of different trees and shrubs, including orchard trees, shade trees, and ornamental shrubs, and when numerous it may kill the host plant. The scale is somewhat circular in shape. This species gives birth to living young.

The oystershell scale, *Lepidósaphes úlmi* (L.), is another important species. It is so named because of

Figure 25–31.   The cottony maple scale, *Pulvinària innumerábilis* (Rathvon). (Courtesy of the Ohio Agricultural Research and Development Center.)

Figure 25–32. The terrapin scale, *Lecànium nigrofasciàtum* Pergande (Cóccidae).

the shape of its scale (Figure 25–34). This widely distributed species attacks a number of plants, including most fruit trees and many ornamental trees and shrubs. Plants heavily infested are often killed. The oystershell scale lays eggs which overwinter under the scale of the female.

A number of other armored scales are somewhat less important than the two just mentioned. The scurfy scale, *Chionáspis fúrfura* (Fitch), is a common whitish scale that attacks a number of trees and shrubs. The rose scale, *Aulacáspis ròsae* (Bouché), is a reddish insect with a white scale and attacks various types of berries and roses. Heavily infested plants look as though they have been whitewashed. The pine needle scale, *Phenacáspis pinifòliae* (Fitch), is common throughout the United States on pine, and sometimes attacks other evergreens.

Several tropical or subtropical species in this group attack citrus or greenhouse plants. The California red scale, *Aonidiélla auràntii* (Maskell), is an important pest of citrus in California. The female has a circular scale slightly larger than that of the San Jose scale.

Family **Conchaspídidae:** Only one species in this group occurs in the United States: *Conchàspis angraèci* Cockerell occurs in California and Florida, where it is found on orchids. The females are similar to those of the Diaspídidae, but they have well-developed legs, and the antennae are four-segmented.

Family **Phoenicocóccidae:** This group is represented in the United States by a single species, the red date scale, *Phoenicocóccus márlatti* (Cockerell), which occurs on the date palm in the southwestern states. It is usually found at the bases of the leaf petioles or under the fibrous covering of the trunk.

Family **Pseudocóccidae**—Mealybugs: The name "mealybug" is derived from the mealy or waxy secretions that cover the bodies of these insects. The body of the female is elongate-oval and segmented and has well-developed legs (Figure 25–35). Some species lay eggs, and others give birth to living young. When eggs are laid, they are placed in loose cottony wax. Mealybugs may be found on almost any part of the host plant.

Figure 25–33. The San Jose scale, *Quadraspidiòtus perniciòsus* (Comstock). (Courtesy of the Ohio Agricultural Research and Development Center.)

This is a large group, with more than 300 species in our area. There are three important pest species in this group. The citrus mealybug, *Planocóccus cítri* (Risso) and the citrophilus mealybug, *Pseudocóccus frágilis* Brain, are serious pests of citrus and also attack greenhouse plants. The longtailed mealybug, *Pseudocóccus longispìnus* (Targioni-Tozzetti), is often found in greenhouses, where it attacks a variety of plants.

Family **Eriocóccidae:** These insects are similar to the pseudococcids, but the body is bare or only lightly covered with wax. This is a widely distributed group, with about 55 species in the United States. The European elm scale, *Eriocóccus spùrius* (Modeer), is a common pest of elms in North America and Europe. A sooty mold develops on the honeydew secreted by this insect. The azalea bark scale, *Eriocóccus azàleae* Comstock, is an important pest of azaleas.

Figure 25–34. The oystershell scale, *Lepidósaphes úlmi* (L.). (Courtesy of the Ohio Agricultural Research and Development Center.)

Collecting and Preserving Homóptera

The methods of collecting and preserving Homóptera vary with the group concerned. The active species are collected and preserved much like other insects, but special techniques are used for such forms as the aphids and scale insects.

Most of the active species of Homóptera are best collected by sweeping. Different species occur on

Figure 25–35. The citrus mealybug, *Planocóccus cítri* (Risso). (Courtesy of the Ohio Agricultural Research and Development Center.)

different types of plants, and one should collect from as many different types of plants as possible to secure a large number of species. The smaller hopping species may be removed from the net with an aspirator, or the entire net contents can be stunned and sorted later. Forms that are not too active can be collected from foliage or twigs directly into a killing jar, without using a net. Some of the cicadas, which spend most of their time high in trees, may be collected with a long-handled net. They may be dislodged with a long stick in the hope that they will land within net range, or they may be shot. A slingshot loaded with sand or fine shot, or a rifle or shotgun loaded with dust shot, may be used to collect cicadas that are out of reach of a net.

Cicadas, the various hoppers, whiteflies, and psyllids are usually mounted dry, on either pins or points. If a larger hopper is pinned, it should be pinned through the right wing. Whiteflies and psyllids are sometimes preserved in fluids and mounted on microscope slides for study. Aphids that are pinned or mounted on points usually shrivel. These insects should be preserved in fluids and mounted on microscope slides for detailed study.

Scale insects may be preserved in two general ways: the part of the plant containing the scales may be collected, dried, and mounted (pinned or in a Riker mount), or the insect may be specially treated and mounted on a microscope slide. No special techniques are involved in the first method, which is satisfactory if one is interested only in the form of the scale. The insects themselves must be mounted on microscope slides for detailed study. The best way to secure male scale insects is to rear them. Very few are ever collected with a net.

In mounting a scale insect on a microscope slide, the scale is removed and the insect is cleaned, stained, and mounted. Some general suggestions for mounting insects on microscope slides are given on pages 761–763. The following procedures are specifically recommended for mounting scale insects:

1. Place the dry scale insect, or fresh specimens that have been in 70% alcohol for at least 2 hours, in 10% potassium hydroxide until the body contents are soft.
2. While the specimen is still in the potassium hydroxide, remove the body contents by making a small hole in the body (at the anterior end or at the side where no taxonomically important characters will be damaged) and pressing the insect.
3. Transfer the specimen to acetic acid alcohol for 20 minutes or more. Acetic acid alcohol is made by mixing 1 part of acetic acid, 1 part of distilled water, and 4 parts of 95% alcohol.
4. Stain in acid fuchsin for 10 minutes or more. Then transfer to 70 percent alcohol for 5 to 15 minutes, to wash out excess stain.
5. Transfer the specimen to 95% alcohol for 5 to 10 minutes.
6. Transfer the specimen to 100% alcohol for 5 to 10 minutes.
7. Transfer the specimen to clove oil for 10 minutes or more.
8. Mount in balsam.

Aphids should be preserved in 80 or 85% alcohol and can often be collected from the plant directly into a vial of alcohol. Winged forms are usually necessary for specific identification and should be mounted on microscope slides.

References

Alexander, R. D., and T. E. Moore. 1962. The evolutionary relationships of 17-year and 13-year cicadas, and three new species (Homoptera, Cicadidae, *Magicicada*). Misc. Publ. Mus. Zool. Univ. Mich. No. 121; 59 pp.; illus.

Annand, P. N. 1928. A contribution toward a monograph of the Adelginae (Phylloxeridae) of North America. Stanford Univ. Publ. Biol. Sci. 6(1):1–146; illus.

Beirne, B. P. 1956. Leafhoppers (Homoptera: Cicadellidae) of Canada and Alaska. Can. Entomol. Suppl. 2:1–180; illus.

Britton, W. E. (ed.). 1923. The Hemiptera or sucking insects of Connecticut. Conn. State Geol. Nat. Hist. Surv. Bull. 34, 807 pp.; illus.

Caldwell, J. S. 1938. The jumping plant lice of Ohio (Homoptera, Chermidae). Ohio Biol. Surv. Bull. 6(5):229–281; illus.

Crawford, D. L. 1914. Monograph of the jumping plant lice or Psyllidae of the New World. U.S. Natl. Mus. Bull. 85, 186 pp.; illus.

DeLong, D. M. 1948. The leafhoppers, or Cicadellidae, of Illinois (Eurymelinae-Balcluthinae). Ill. Nat. Hist. Surv. Bull. 24(2):91–376; illus.

DeLong, D. M. 1971. The bionomics of leafhoppers. Annu. Rev. Entomol. 16:179–210.

Delong, D. M., and P. H. Freytag. 1967. Studies of the world Gyponinae (Homoptera, Cicadellidae): A synopsis of the genus *Ponana*. Contrib. Amer. Entomol. Inst. 1(7):1–86; illus.

Deitz, L. L. 1975. Classification of the higher categories of the New World treehoppers (Homoptera: Membracidae). N.C. Agr. Expt. Sta. Bull. 225, 177 pp.; illus.

Doering, K. 1930. Synopsis of North American Cercopidae. J. Kan. Entomol. Soc. 3:53–64, 81–108; illus.

Dozier, H. L. 1926. The Fulgoridae or planthoppers of Mississippi, including those of possible occurrence. Miss. Agr. Expt. Sta. Bull. 14; 151 pp.; illus.

Duffels, J. P., and P. A. van der Laan. 1985. Catalogue of the Cicadoidea (Homoptera, Auchenorrhyncha), 1956–1980. The Hague: Junk, 414 pp.

Dybas, H. S., and M. Lloyd. 1974. The habitats of 17-year periodical cicadas (Homoptera: Cicadidae: *Magicicada* spp.). Ecol. Monogr. 44(3):279–324; illus.

Eastop, V. F., and D. H. R. Lambers. 1976. Survey of the World's Aphids. The Hague: Junk, 574 pp.; illus.

Evans, J. W. 1946–1947. A natural classification of the leafhoppers (Jassoidea, Homoptera). Part 1: External morphology and systematic position. Trans. Roy. Entomol. Soc. Lond. 96(3):47–60; illus. (1946). Part 2: Aetalionidae, Hyticidae, Eurymelidae. Trans. Roy. Entomol. Soc. Lond. 97(2):39–54; illus. (1946). Part 3: Jassidae. Trans. Roy. Entomol. Soc. Lond. 98(6):105–271; illus. (1947).

Evans, J. W. 1963. The phylogeny of the Homoptera. Annu. Rev. Entomol. 8:77–94; illus.

Fennah, R. G. 1956. Homoptera: Fulgoroidea. Insects of Micronesia 6(3),72 pp.; illus.

Ferris, G. F. 1937–1955. Atlas of the Scale Insects of North America. Stanford, Calif.: Stanford Univ. Press. 7 vol.; illus.

Forsythe, H. Y., Jr. 1976. Distribution and species of 17-year cicadas in broods V and VIII in Ohio. Ohio J. Sci. 76(6):254–258; illus.

Funkhouser, W. D. 1937. Biology of the Membracidae of the Cayuga Lake Basin. Cornell Univ. Agr. Expt. Sta. Mem. No. 11:177–445; illus.

Hamilton, K. G. A. 1971. Placement of the genus *Microcentrus* in the Aetalionidae (Homoptera: Cicadelloidea), with a redefinition of the family. J. Georgia Entomol. Soc. 6(4):229–236; illus.

Hamilton, K. G. A. 1982. The spittlebugs of Canada (Homoptera: Cercopidae). The Insects and Arachnids of Canada, Part 10. Ottawa: Can. Gov. Pub. Centre, 102 pp.; illus.

Hanna, M., and T. E. Moore. 1966. The spittlebugs of Michigan. Pap. Mich. Acad. Sci. 51:39–73; illus.

Harris, K. F., and K. Maramorosch. 1977. Aphids as Virus Vectors. New York: Academic Press, 570 pp.

Hottes, F. C., and T. H. Frison. 1931. The plant lice, or Aphididae, of Illinois. Ill. Nat. Hist. Surv. Bull. 19(3): 121–447; illus.

Howell, J. O., and M. L. Williams. 1976. An annotated key to the families of scale insects (Homoptera: Coccoidea) of America, north of Mexico, based on characteristics of the adult female. Ann. Entomol. Soc. Amer. 69: 181–189; illus.

Kennedy, J. S., and H. L. G. Stroyan. 1959. Biology of aphids. Annu. Rev. Entomol. 4:139–160.

Kopp, D. D., and T. R. Yonke. 1973–1974. The treehoppers of Missouri. J. Kan. Entomol. Soc.; Part 1, 46:42–64 (1973); Part 2, 46:233–276 (1973); Part 3, 46:375–421 (1973); Part 4, 46:80–130 (1974); illus.

Kramer, J. P. 1966. A revision of the New World leafhoppers of the subfamily Ledrinae (Homoptera: Cicadellidae). Trans. Amer. Entomol. Soc. 92:469–502; illus.

Kramer, J. P. 1971. A taxonomic study of the North American leafhoppers of the genus *Deltocephalus* (Homoptera: Cicadellidae: Deltocephalinae). Trans. Amer. Entomol. Soc. 97:413–439; illus.

Kramer, J. P. 1983. Taxonomic study of the planthopper family Cixiidae in the United States (Homoptera: Fulgoroidea). Trans. Amer. Entomol. Soc. 109:1–58.

Lambers, D. H. R. 1966. Polymorphism in Aphididae. Annu. Rev. Entomol. 11:47–78; illus.

Linnavuori, R. 1959. Revision of the neotropical Deltocephalinae and some related subfamilies (Homoptera). Ann. Zool. Soc. Vanamo 20:1–370; illus.

MacGillivray, A. D. 1921. The Coccidae. Urbana, Ill.: Scarab, 502 pp.

McKenzie, H. L. 1967. The Mealybugs of California. Berkeley: Univ. California Press, 525 pp.; illus.

Metcalf, Z. P. 1923. Fulgoridae of eastern North America. J. Elisha Mitchell Sci. Soc. 38:139–230; illus.

Metcalf, Z. P. 1954–1958. General Catalogue of the Homoptera. Raleigh: North Carolina State College. Fasc. 4, Fulgoroidea. Part 11: Tropiduchidae, 176 pp. (1954). Part 12: Nogodinidae, 84 pp. (1954). Part 15: Issidae, 570 pp. (1958). Part 16: Ricaniidae, 208 pp. (1955). Part 17: Lophopidae, 84 pp. (1955). Part 18: Eurybrachidae and Gengidae, 90 pp. (1956).

Metcalf, Z. P. 1960–1962. General Catalogue of the Homoptera. Raleigh: North Carolina State College. Fasc. 7, Cercopoidea: A bibliography of the Cercopoidea, 266 pp. (1960). Part 1: Macherotidae, 56 pp. (1960). Part 2: Cercopidae, 616 pp. (1961). Part 3: Aphrophoridae, 608 pp. (1962). Part 4: Clastopteridae, 66 pp. (1962).

Metcalf, Z. P. 1962–1963. General Catalogue of the Homoptera. Raleigh: North Carolina State College. Fasc. 8, Cicadoidea: A bibliography of the Cicadoidea, 234 pp. (1962). Part 1: Cicadidae, 492 pp. (1963). Part 2: Tibicinidae, 919 pp. (1963).

Metcalf, Z. P. 1962–1968. General Catalog of the Homoptera. USDA, Agric. Res. Serv. Fasc., 6, Cicadelloidea. Part 1: Tettigellidae, 730 pp. (1965). Part 2: Hylicidae, 18 pp. (1962). Part 3: Gyponidae, 299 pp. (1962). Part 4: Ledridae, 147 pp. (1962). Part 5: Ulopidae, 101 pp. (1962). Part 6: Evancanthidae, 63 pp. (1963). Part 7: Nirvanidae, 35 pp. (1963). Part 8: Aphrodidae, 268 pp. (1963). Part 9: Hecalidae, 123 pp. (1963). Part 10: Euscelidae, Section 1, pp. 1–1077; Section 2, pp. 1078–2074; Section 3, pp. 2075–2695 (1967). Part 11: Coelidiidae, 182 pp. (1964). Part 12: Eurymelidae, 43 pp. (1965). Part 13: Macropsidae, 261 pp. (1966). Part 14: Agallidae, 173 pp. (1966). Part 15: Iassidae, 229 pp. (1966). Part 16: Idioceridae, 237 pp. (1966). Part 17: Cicadellidae, 1513 pp. (1968).

Metcalf, Z. P., and V. Wade. General catalogue of the Homoptera. A supplement to fascicle 1—Membracidae of the general catalogue of the Homoptera. A catalogue of fossil Homoptera (Homoptera: Auchenorrhyncha). N.C. Agr. Expt. Sta. Pap. No. 2049; 245 pp.

Moore, T. E. 1966. The cicadas of Michigan (Homoptera: Cicadidae). Pap. Mich. Acad. Sci. 51:75–96; illus.

Morrison, H., and A. V. Renk. 1957. A selected bibliography of the Coccoidea. USDA Agr. Res. Serv. Misc. Publ. 734, 222 pp.

Oman, P. W. 1949. The Nearctic leafhoppers (Homoptera: Cicadellidae), a generic classification and check list. Entomol. Soc. Wash. Mem. No. 3, 253 pp.; illus.

Osborn, H. 1938. The Fulgoridae of Ohio. Ohio Biol. Surv. Bull. 6(6):283–349; illus.

Osborn, H. 1940. The Membracidae of Ohio. Ohio Biol. Surv. Bull. 7(2):51–101; illus.

Ossiannilsson, F. 1949. Insect drummers: A study of the morphology and function of the sound-producing organs of Swedish Homoptera Auchenorrhyncha. Opusc. Entomol. Suppl. 10:1–146; illus.

Shaw, K. C., A. Vargo, and O. V. Carlson. 1974. Sounds and associated behavior of *Empoasca* (Homoptera: Cicadellidae). J. Kan. Entomol. Soc. 47:284–307; illus.

Smith, C. F. 1972. Bibliography of the Aphididae of the world. N.C. Agr. Expt. Sta. Tech. Bull. 216, 717 pp.

Wade, V. 1966. General catalogue of the Homoptera: Species index of the Membracoidea and fossil Homoptera (Homoptera: Auchenorrhyncha). A supplement to fascicle 1, Membracidae of the general catalogue of the Homoptera. N.C. Agr. Expt. Sta. Pap. No. 2160(2), 40 pp.

Way, M. J. 1963. Mutualism between ants and honeydew-producing Homoptera. Annu. Rev. Entomol. 8:307–344.

Williams, M. L., and M. Kosztarab. 1972. Morphology and systematics of the Coccidae of Virginia, with notes on their biology (Homoptera: Coccoidea). Va. Polytech. Inst. State Univ. Res. Div. Bull. 74, 215 pp.; illus.

Young, D. A. 1952. A reclassification of western hemisphere Typhlocybinae (Homoptera, Cicadellidae). Univ. Kan. Sci. Bull. 35:3–217.

Young, D. A. 1968. Taxonomic study of the Cicadellinae (Homoptera: Cicadellidae), Part 1: Proconiini. Smithson. Inst. Bull. 261, 287 pp.; illus.

Young, D. A. 1977. Taxonomic study of the Cicadellinae (Homoptera: Cicadellidae), Part 2: New World Cicadellini and the genus *Cicadella*. N.C. Agr. Expt. Sta. Bull. 235, 1135 pp.; illus.

Chapter 26

Order Thysanóptera[1]
Thrips

The thrips are minute, slender-bodied insects 0.5–5.0 mm in length (some tropical species are nearly 14 mm in length). Wings may be present or absent. The wings when fully developed are four in number, very long and narrow with few or no veins, and fringed with long hairs. The fringe of hairs on the wings gives the order its name.

The mouthparts (Figure 26–1) are of the sucking type, and the proboscis is a stout, conical, asymmetrical structure located posteriorly on the ventral surface of the head. The labrum forms the front of the proboscis; the basal portions of the maxillae form the sides; and the labium forms the rear. There are three stylets: one mandible (the left one; the right mandible is vestigial) and the laciniae of the two maxillae. Both maxillary and labial palps are present, but short. The hypopharynx is a small median lobe in the proboscis. The mouthparts of thrips have been termed "rasping-sucking," but it is probable that the stylets pierce rather than rasp the tissues fed upon. The food ingested is generally in liquid form, but minute spores are sometimes ingested.

The antennae are short and four- to nine-segmented. The tarsi are one- or two-segmented, with one or two claws, and are bladderlike at the tip. An ovipositor is present in some thrips. In others, the tip of the abdomen is tubular and an ovipositor is lacking.

The metamorphosis of thrips is somewhat intermediate between simple and complete (Figure 26–2). The first two instars have no wings externally and are usually called larvae. In at least some cases, the wings are developing internally during these two instars. In the suborder Terebrántia, the third and fourth instars (only the third instar in *Franklíno-thrips*) are inactive, do not feed, and have external wings; the third instar is called the prepupa, and the fourth the pupa. The pupa is sometimes enclosed in a cocoon. In the suborder Tubulífera, the third and fourth instars are prepupae (the third does not have external wings), and the fifth instar is the pupa. The stage following the pupa is the adult. This type of metamorphosis resembles simple metamorphosis in that more than one preadult instar (except in *Franklínothrips*) has external wings. It resembles complete metamorphosis in that at least some of the wing development is internal, and there is a quiescent (pupal) instar preceding the adult.

The two sexes of thrips are similar in appearance, but the males are usually smaller. Parthenogenesis occurs in many species. Those thrips that have an ovipositor usually insert their eggs in plant tissues. The thrips that lack an ovipositor usually lay their eggs in crevices or under bark. Young thrips

[1]Thysanóptera: *thysano*, fringe; *ptera*, wings.

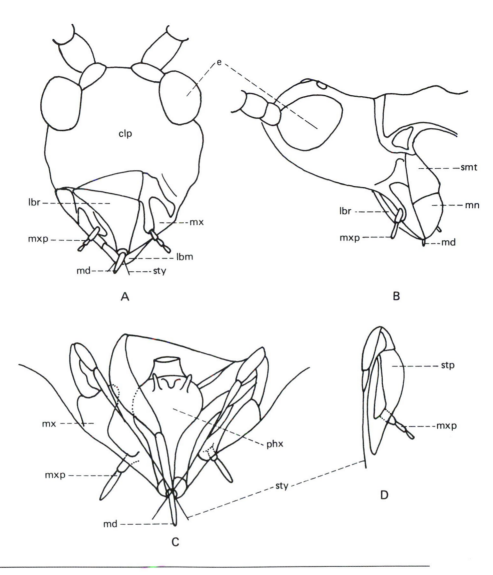

Figure 26–1.   Mouthparts of a thrips. **A,** head, ventro-anterior view; **B,** head, lateral view; **C,** mouth parts, posterior view; **D,** a maxilla. *clp,* clypeus; *e,* compound eye; *lbm,* labium; *lbr,* labrum; *md,* left mandible; *mn,* mentum; *mx,* maxilla; *mxp,* maxillary palp; *phx,* pharynx; *smt,* submentum; *stp,* stipes; *sty,* maxillary stylet. (Redrawn from Peterson 1915.)

are relatively inactive. Generally there are several generations a year.

A great many of the thrips are plant feeders, attacking flowers, leaves, fruits, twigs, or buds. They feed on a great many types of plants. They are particularly abundant in the flower heads of daisies and dandelions. They destroy plant cells by their feeding, and some species act as vectors of plant disease. Many species are serious pests of cultivated plants. A few thrips feed on fungus spores, and a few are predaceous on other small arthropods. These insects sometimes occur in enormous numbers, and a few species may bite people.

Classification of the Thysanóptera

This order is divided into two suborders, the Terebrántia and the Tubulífera, which differ in the shape of the last abdominal segment and the development of the ovipositor. The Terebrántia have the last abdominal segment more or less conical or rounded,

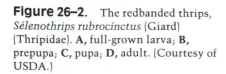

Figure 26–2.   The redbanded thrips, *Sélenothrips rubrocínctus* (Giard) (Thrípidae). **A,** full-grown larva; **B,** prepupa; **C,** pupa; **D,** adult. (Courtesy of USDA.)

and the females usually have a well-developed ovipositor. The Tubulífera have the last abdominal segment tubular, and the females lack an ovipositor. Five families of thrips occur in North America, four of them in the suborder Terebrántia. These families may be separated by the following key. The families of Terebrántia are separated largely by characters of the antennae, particularly the number of antennal segments and the nature of the sensoria on the third and fourth segments. These sensoria are circular or oval areas near the apex of the segments or are in the form of simple or forked sense cones.

Key to the Families of Thysanóptera

1.   Last abdominal segment tubular (Figures 26–3C, 26–4C), females without an ovipositor; front wings, if present, either veinless or with short median vein that does not extend to wing tip, membrane without microscopic hairs; antennae 4- to 8-segmented (suborder Tubulífera) . . . .**Phlaeothrípidae**   p. 355

1'.   Last abdominal segment broadly rounded or conical (Figures 26–3A,B, 26–4A,B,D–G), females usually with sawlike ovipositor (Figure 26–3A,B); front wings, if present, with 1 or 2 longitudinal veins, membrane with microscopic hairs; antennae 4- to 9-segmented (suborder Terebrántia) **2**

2(1').   Antennae 9-segmented, sensoria on third and fourth segments in form of longitudinal flat areas (Figure 26–5A, *sa*); ovipositor curved upward (Figure 26–3B); front wings relatively broad, with tips rounded . . . . . .**Aeolothrípidae**   p. 354

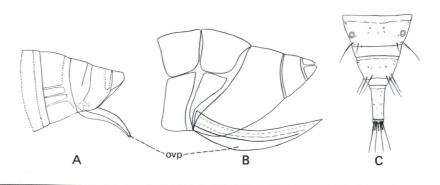

Figure 26–3.   Abdominal structures of Thysanóptera. **A,** apex of abdomen of the pear thrips, *Taèniothrips incónsequens* (Uzel) (Thrípidae), lateral view, showing the decurved ovipositor; **B,** apex of abdomen of *Mélanothrips* (Aeolothrípidae), lateral view, showing the upcurved ovipositor; **C,** apex of abdomen of *Háplothrips hispánicus* Priesner (Phlaeothrípidae), dorsal view. *ovp,* ovipositor. (Modified from Pesson.)

2'.   Antennae 6- to 9-segmented, sensoria on third and fourth segments in form of flat areas that are not longitudinal (Figure 26–5B,C, *sa*), or protrude as simple or forked sense cones (Figure 26–5D,E, *scn*); ovipositor, when developed, curved downward (Figure 26–3A); front wings narrower, usually pointed at tip **3**

3(2').   Sensoria of third and fourth antennal segments in form of slender, simple, or forked sense cones located preapically (Figure 26–5D,E, *scn*) ....**Thrípidae**   p. 354

3'.   Sensoria of third and fourth antennal segments in form of flat areas encircling apex of segment (Figure 26–5B,C, *sa*), or short blunt sense cone at outer tip of segment **4**

4(3').   Antennae 8-segmented, sensoria of third and fourth segments in form of flat apical area (Figure 26–5B, *sa*); color light yellowish brown; ovipositor weakly developed; pronotum with longitudinal suture on each side; front and hind femora thickened (Figure 26–4G) ....**Merothrípidae**   p. 354

4'.   Antennae 9-segmented, sensoria of third and fourth segments forming a band of small, flat, circular areas around apex of segment (Figure 26–5C, *sa*; *Héterothrips*, widely distributed), or in the form of a short, blunt sense cone at outer tip of segment (*Òligothrips*, California and Oregon) ..**Heterothrípidae**   p. 354

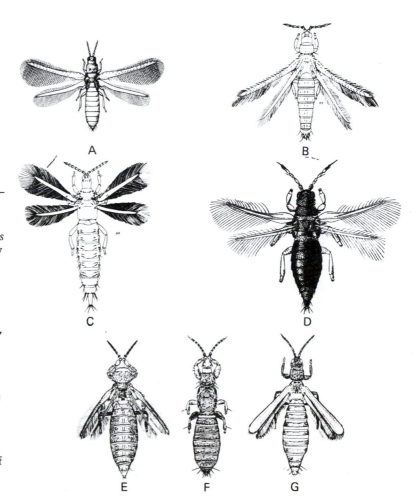

Figure 26–4. Thrips. **A,** gladiolus thrips, *Taèniothrips símplex* (Morison) (Thrípidae); **B,** pear thrips, *Taèniothrips incónsequens* (Uzel) (Thrípidae); **C,** lily bulb thrips, *Lìothrips vanèeckei* Priesner (Phlaeothrípidae); **D,** greenhouse thrips, *Hèliothrips haèmorrhoidàlis* (Bouché) (Thrípidae); **E,** a banded thrips, *Stòmatothrips crawfordi* Stannard (Aeolothrípidae); **F,** *Héterothrips sálicis* (Shull) (Heterothrípidae); **G,** a large-legged thrips, *Mérothrips mòrgani* Hood (Merothrípidae). (**A,** courtesy of the Utah Agricultural Experiment Station; **B,** courtesy of Bailey and the University of California Experiment Station; **C,** courtesy of Bailey and the California Department of Agriculture; **D,** courtesy of USDA; **E–G,** courtesy of Stannard and the Illinois Natural History Survey.)

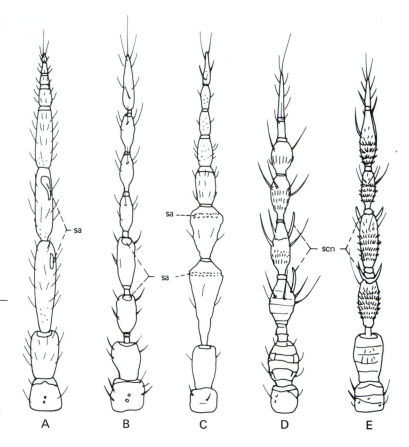

Figure 26–5. Antennae of Thysanóptera. **A,** *Aeòlothrips* (Aeolothrípidae); **B,** *Mérothrips* (Merothrípidae); **C,** *Héterothrips* (Heterothrípidae); **D,** *Cáliothrips* (Thrípidae); **E,** *Thríps* (Thrípidae). *sa,* sensoria; *scn,* sense cone. (Redrawn from Stannard, courtesy of the Illinois Natural History Survey.)

Family **Aeolothrípidae**—Broad-Winged or Banded Thrips: The front wings in this group are relatively broad, with two longitudinal veins extending from the base of the wing nearly to the tip, and usually with several cross veins. The adults are dark in color and often have the wings banded or mottled (Figure 26–4E). The most common species in this group is the banded thrips, *Aeólothrips fasciàtus* (L.). The adult is yellowish to dark brown, with three white bands on the wings. The larvae are yellowish, shading into orange posteriorly. The adults are about 1.6 mm in length. This species occurs on various plants and is often common in the flower heads of clover. It feeds on other thrips, aphids, mites, and other small insects. It is widely distributed and occurs in Europe, Asia, Africa, and Hawaii as well as in North America.

Family **Merothrípidae**—Large-Legged Thrips: The members of this group may be recognized by the enlarged front and hind femora and by the two longitudinal sutures on the pronotum. The only common species in this family is *Mérothrips mòrgani* Hood (Figure 26–4G), which occurs in the eastern United States under bark, in debris, and in fungi.

Family **Heterothrípidae:** Two genera in this small family occur in North America, *Héterothrips* (widely distributed; Figure 26–4F) and *Òligothrips* (California and Oregon). The several species of *Héterothrips* occur on trees (buckeye, oak, and willow) and flowers (azalea, wild rose, and jack-in-the-pulpit) and in the buds of wild grape. Our only species of *Òligothrips*, *O. oreìos* Moulton, occurs in the blossoms of madrone and manzanita.

Family **Thrípidae**—Common Thrips: This family is the largest in the order and contains most of the species that are of economic importance. The wings are narrower than in the Aeolothrípidae and are more pointed at the tip. The antennae are six- to nine-segmented. These thrips are mostly plant feeders, and a number of species are serious pests of cultivated plants.

The pear thrips, *Taèniothrips incónsequens* (Uzel) (Figure 26–4B) attacks the buds, blossoms, young leaves, and fruits of pears, plums, cherries, and other plants. The adults are brown with pale wings and 1.2–1.3 mm in length. This species has a single generation a year and overwinters as a pupa in the soil. The adults emerge in early spring, attack the fruit trees, and oviposit on the petioles of the leaves and fruits. The young feed until about June, when they drop to the ground and remain dormant until about October, at which time they pupate and go into hibernation. This species occurs on the east and west coasts of the United States.

The gladiolus thrips, *Taèniothrips símplex* (Morison), is a serious pest of gladiolus, injuring the leaves and greatly reducing the size, development, and color of the flowers. It is very similar to the pear thrips in appearance (Figure 26–4A). The onion thrips, *Thríps tabàci* Lindeman, is a widely distributed species that attacks onions, tobacco, beans, and many other plants. It is a pale yellowish or brownish insect 1.0–1.2 mm in length. It transmits the virus that causes spotted wilt disease in tomatoes and other plants. The greenhouse thrips, *Hèliothrips haèmorrhoidàlis* (Bouché) (Figure 26–4D), is a tropical species that occurs outdoors in the warmer parts of the world and is a serious pest in greenhouses in the North. The male of this species is very rare. The flower thrips, *Frankliniélla trítici* (Fitch), is a common and widely distributed pest of grasses, grains, truck crops, weeds, trees, and shrubs. It is a slender yellow and orange insect 1.2–1.3 mm in length. The six-spotted thrips, *Scòlothrips sexmaculàtus* (Pergande), is a little less than a millimeter in length and is yellow with three black spots on each front wing. It is predaceous on plant-feeding mites. The grain thrips, *Lìmothrips cereàlum* (Haliday), is a dark brown to black thrips, 1.2–1.4 mm in length, that feeds on cereals and grasses. It is sometimes quite abundant, and it may bite people.

Family **Phlaeothrípidae:** The family Phlaeothrípidae is a rather large group, most species of which are larger and stouter-bodied than the thrips in the suborder Terebrántia. One Australian species, *Idólothrips marginàtus* Haliday, is 10–14 mm in length. These thrips are mostly dark brown or black, often with light-colored or mottled wings. Most of them are spore feeders. Some are predaceous, feeding on small insects and mites. A few are plant feeders, and some of these may be of economic importance. The lily bulb thrips, *Lìothrips vanèeckei* Priesner, is a dark-colored species about 2 mm in length (Figure 26–4C) that feeds on lilies and injures the bulbs. The black hunter, *Léptothrips máli* (Fitch), is a fairly common predaceous species. *Aleuródothrips fasciapénnis* Franklin, which is common in Florida, is predaceous on whiteflies. *Háplothrips leucánthemi* (Schrank) is a black thrips that is common in daisy flowers.

Collecting and Preserving Thysanóptera

Thrips may be found on flowers, foliage, fruits, bark, and fungi and in debris. The species occurring on vegetation are most easily collected by sweeping. They may be removed from the net by stunning the entire net contents and sorting out the thrips later, or the net contents may be shaken out onto a paper and the thrips picked up with an aspirator or with a moistened camel's-hair brush. Dark species are best seen on a light paper, and light species on a dark paper. If host data are desired, the specimens should be collected directly from the host plant. The best way to collect flower-frequenting species is to collect the flowers in a paper bag and examine them later in the laboratory. The species that occur in debris and in similar situations are usually collected by means of a Berlese funnel (Figure 36–6) or by sifting the material in which they occur. Bark- and branch-inhabiting species can be collected with a beating umbrella.

Thrips should be preserved in liquid and mounted on microscope slides for detailed study. They may be mounted on points, but specimens so mounted are usually not very satisfactory. The best killing solution is AGA, which contains 8 parts of 95% alcohol, 5 parts of distilled water, 1 part of glycerine, and 1 part of glacial acetic acid. After a few weeks, specimens should be transferred from this solution to alcohol (about 80%) for permanent preservation.

References

Bailey, S. F. 1940. The distribution of injurious thrips in the United States. J. Econ. Entomol. 33(1):133–136.

Bailey, S. F. 1951. The genus *Aeolothrips* Haliday in North America. Hilgardia 21(2):43–80; illus.

Bailey, S. F. 1957. The thrips of California, Part 1: Suborder Terebrantia. Bull. Calif. Insect Surv. 4(5):143–220; illus.

Cott, H. E. 1956. Systematics of the Suborder Tubulifera (Thysanoptera) in California. Berkeley: Univ. California Press, 216 pp.; illus.

Hinds, W. E. 1902. Contribution to a monograph of the insects in the order Thysanoptera inhabiting North America. Proc. U.S. Natl. Mus. 26(1310):79–242; illus.

Lewis, T. 1973. Thrips, Their Biology, Ecology and Economic Importance. New York: Academic Press, 350 pp.

Moulton, D. 1911. Synopsis, catalogue, and bibliography of North American Thysanoptera. USDA Bur. Entomol. Plant Quarantine Tech. Ser. No. 21, 56 pp.; illus.

O'Neill, K., and R. S. Bigelow. 1964. The *Taeniothrips* of Canada. Can. Entomol. 96:1219–1239; illus.

Peterson, A. 1915. Morphological studies on the head and mouthparts of the Thysanoptera. Ann. Entomol. Soc. Amer. 8:20–67; illus.

Priesner, H. 1926–1928. Die Thysanopteren Europas. Vienna: Verlag Fritz Wagner, Abh. 1–2: 342 pp., illus.

(1926). Abh. 3: pp. 343–570 (1927). Abh. 4: pp. 571–755 (1928).

Priesner, H. 1949. Genera Thysanopterorum: Keys for the identification of the order Thysanoptera. Bull. Soc. Fouad 1er Entomol. 33:31–157.

Stannard, L. J. 1957. The phylogeny and classification of the North American genera of the suborder Tubulifera (Thysanoptera). Ill. Biol. Monogr. No. 25, 200 pp.; illus.

Stannard, L. J. 1968. The thrips, or Thysanoptera, of Illinois. Ill. Nat. Hist. Surv. Bull. 29(4):215–552; illus.

Watson, J. R. 1923. Synopsis and catalogue of the Thysanoptera of North America. Univ. Fla. Agr. Expt. Sta. Bull. No. 168, 100 pp.

Chapter 27

Order Neuróptera[1]
Alderflies, Dobsonflies, Fishflies, Snakeflies, Lacewings, Antlions, and Owlflies

The Neuróptera are soft-bodied insects with four membranous wings that usually have a great many cross veins and extra branches of the longitudinal veins (hence the order name). There are generally a number of cross veins along the costal border of the wing, between the C and Sc. The radial sector often bears a number of parallel branches. The front and hind wings in our species are similar in shape and venation and are usually held rooflike over the body at rest. The mouthparts are mandibulate; the antennae are generally long and many-segmented; the tarsi are five-segmented; and cerci are absent.

These insects undergo complete metamorphosis. The larvae are generally campodeiform, with mandibulate mouthparts. Most larvae are predaceous, but those of the Sisýridae feed on freshwater sponges, and those of the Mantíspidae are parasitic in the egg sacs of spiders. The mandibles of Megalóptera and Raphidiòdea larvae are relatively short, while those of Planipénnia larvae are long and sicklelike. In the Planipénnia the feeding is done by sucking the body fluids of the victim through a narrow channel formed between the mandible and maxilla. The pupae are naked in the Megalóptera and Raphidiòdea, but in the Planipénnia pupation occurs in a silken cocoon.

The silk is produced by the Malpighian tubules and is spun from the anus.

Adult Neuróptera are found in a variety of situations, but those whose larvae are aquatic (Siálidae, Corydálidae, and Sisýridae) generally occur near water. The adults are rather weak fliers. Most adults are predaceous. Some take only relatively weak prey, and adults of the Megalóptera probably feed little or not at all.

Classification of the Neuróptera

The insects here included in the order Neuróptera are by some authorities divided into three orders, Megalóptera, Raphidiòdea, and Neuróptera. Some authorities would include the Raphidiòdea in the Megalóptera. We are treating these three groups as suborders.

An outline of the groups in the order is given here. Alternative names or spellings are given in parentheses, and groups that are rare or unlikely to be taken by the general collector are marked with an asterisk.

Suborder Megalóptera (Sialòdea)
    Siálidae—alderflies
    Corydálidae—dobsonflies and fishflies

---

[1]Neuróptera: *neuro*, nerve (referring to the wing veins); *ptera*, wings.

357

Suborder Raphidiòdea (Raphidiòidea)—snakeflies
    Raphidìidae—raphidiid snakeflies
    Inocellìidae—inocelliid snakeflies
Suborder Planipénnia (Neuróptera in the narrow sense)
    Superfamily Coniopterygòidea
      *Coniopterỳgidae—dusty-wings
    Superfamily Ithonòidea
      *Ithònidae—ithonid lacewings
    Superfamily Hemerobiòidea
      Mantíspidae—mantidflies
      Hemerobìidae (including Sympherobìidae)—brown lacewings
      Chrysòpidae—common lacewings, green lacewings
      *Dilàridae—pleasing lacewings
      *Beròthidae—beaded lacewings
      *Polystoechòtidae—giant lacewings
      Sisýridae—spongillaflies
    Superfamily Myrmeleontòidea
      Myrmeleóntidae—antlions
      Ascaláphidae—owlflies

Two slightly different interpretations of wing venation are encountered in this order, that of Comstock and that of Carpenter and others. Most present workers, particularly those studying the Raphidiòdea and Planipénnia—following Martynov (1928), Carpenter (1936, 1940), and others—believe that an anterior branch of the media (labeled MA in our figures) persists in this order, branching from M near the base of the wing and usually fusing with Rs for a short distance. The differences in these two interpretations may be summarized as follows:

Comstock	Carpenter
R_4	R_{4+5}
R_5	MA
Basal r-m	Base of MA
M	MP
M_{1+2}	MP_{1+2}
M_{3+4}	MP_{3+4}
Cu_1	CuA
Cu_2	CuP

We have followed Comstock's interpretation in labeling our figures of the Megalóptera and Coniopterýgidae and the interpretation of Carpenter and others in labeling our figures of other wings in this order.

Key to the Families of Neuróptera

The families marked with an asterisk in this key are relatively rare or are unlikely to be encountered by the general collector. Keys to larvae are given by Peterson (1951).

1.   Hind wings broader at base than front wings, with enlarged anal area that is folded fanwise at rest (Figure 27–1A,B); longitudinal veins usually not forking near wing margin; larvae aquatic (suborder Megalóptera) **2**

1'.   Front and hind wings similar in size and shape, hind wings without enlarged anal area that is folded fanwise at rest (Figures 27–1C,D, 27–2, 27–3, 27–4) **3**

2(1).   Ocelli present; fourth tarsal segment cylindrical; body usually 25 mm or more in length; wings hyaline or with smoky areas ....**Corydálidae**   p. 363

2'.   Ocelli absent; fourth tarsal segment dilated and deeply bilobed; body usually less than 25 mm in length; wings usually smoky (Figure 27–5) ......**Siálidae**   p. 363

3(1'). Wings with relatively few veins, Rs usually with only 2 branches (Figure 27–3A); wings covered with whitish powder; minute insects ....**Coniopterýgidae***   p. 363

3'.   Wings with many veins, Rs usually with more than 2 branches (Figures 27–1C,D, 27–2, 27–3B,C, 27–4); wings not covered with whitish powder; size variable, but usually not minute **4**

4(3'). Prothorax elongate (Figure 27–8)..**5**

4'.   Prothorax of normal size, not elongate **7**

5(4).   Front legs raptorial, arising from anterior end of prothorax (Figure 27–8B); mantid-like insects, widely distributed ....**Mantíspidae**   p. 365

5'.   Front legs not raptorial, arising from posterior end of prothorax (Figure 27–8A); western United States (suborder Raphidiòdea) **6**

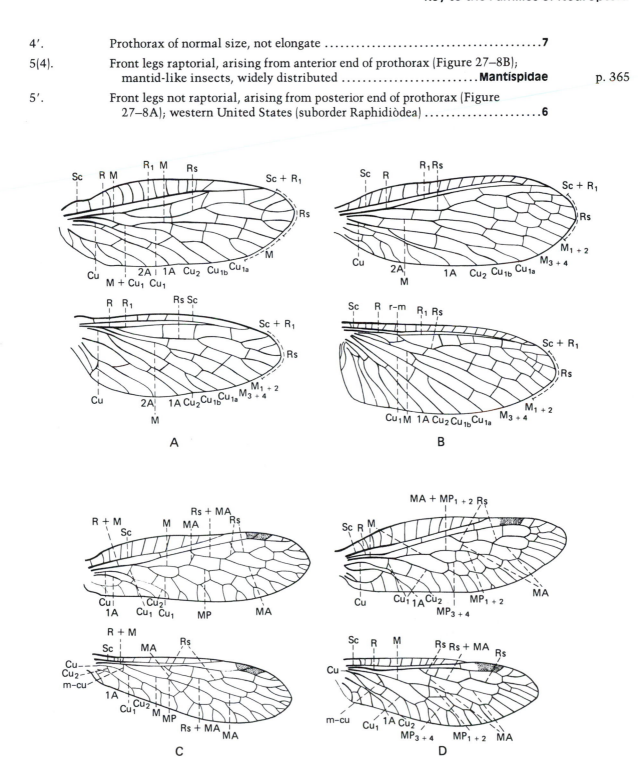

Figure 27–1.   Wings of Neuróptera. **A,** *Sìalis* (Siálidae); **B,** *Nigrònia* (Corydálidae); **C,** *Agúlla* (Raphidìidae); **D,** *Inocéllia* (Inocéllìidae). The venation in **A** and **B** is labeled with the interpretation of Comstock, and in **C** and **D** with the interpretation of Carpenter (1936) and others. MA, anterior media; MP, posterior media.

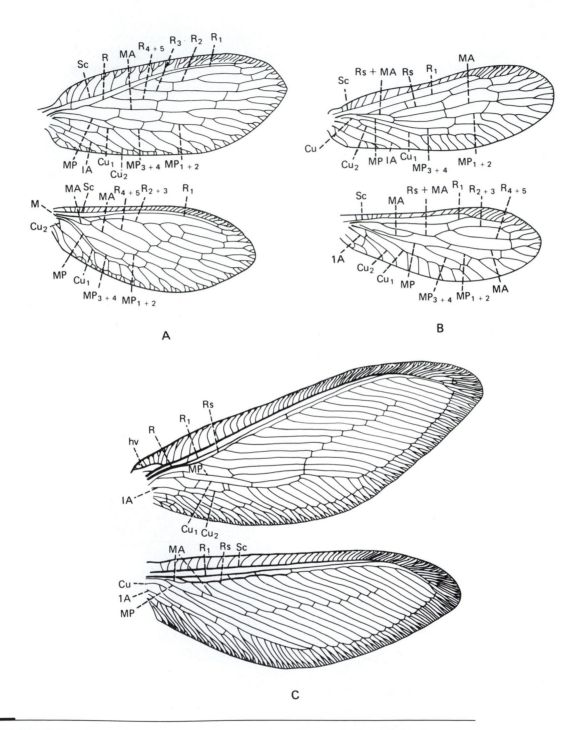

Figure 27–2.   Wings of Neuróptera. **A,** *Ameromicròmus* (Hemerobìidae); **B,** *Climàcia* (Sisýridae); **C,** *Polystoechòtes* (Polystoechòtidae). The venation is labeled with the interpretation of Carpenter (1940) and others. *hv,* humeral or recurrent vein; MA, anterior media; MP, posterior media.

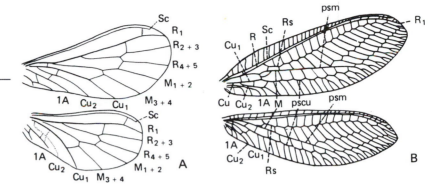

Figure 27–3. Wings of Neuróptera. **A,** *Coniópteryx* (Coniopterýgidae); **B,** *Chrysòpa* (Chrysòpidae). The venation is labeled with the interpretation of Comstock. *pscu,* pseudocubitus; *psm,* pseudomedia.

6(5').   Ocelli present; stigma in front wing with a cross vein; hind wings with Cu$_2$ and 1A fused for short distance, basal m-cu transverse (Figure 27–1C) ....**Raphidìidae**   p. 363

6'.   Ocelli absent; stigma in front wing without cross vein; hind wings with Cu$_2$ and 1A separate, basal m-cu oblique (Figure 27–1D) ....**Inocellìidae**   p. 363

7(4').   Antennae clubbed or knobbed; insects with abdomen long and slender, resembling dragonflies or damselflies in general appearance (Figure 27–10) (superfamily Myrmeleontòidea) **8**

7'.   Antennae filiform, moniliform, or pectinate, not clubbed or knobbed; usually not particularly resembling dragonflies or damselflies in appearance **9**

8(7).   Antennae about as long as head and thorax together (Figure 27–10); hypostigmatic cell (cell behind the point of fusion of Sc and R$_1$; Figure 27–4A, *hcl*) very long, several times as long as wide; eyes entire ....**Myrmeleóntidae**   p. 366

8'.   Antennae nearly or quite as long as body; hypostigmatic cell short, not more than 2 or 3 times as long as wide (Figure 27–4D, *hcl*); eyes entire (Neuroptyngìnae) or divided horizontally (Ascalaphìnae) ....**Ascaláphidae**   p. 367

9(7').   At least some, usually many, of costal cross veins forked (Figure 27–2A,C) **10**

9'.   All (or nearly all) of the costal cross veins simple (Figures 27–2B and 27–3B) **13**

10(9).   Front wings apparently with 2 or more radial sectors (Figure 27–2A: R$_2$, R$_3$, R$_{4+5}$) ....**Hemerobìidae**   p. 365

10'.   Front wings with only 1 radial sector, which has 2 or more branches (Figure 27–2C, Rs) **11***

11(10').   Front wings with a recurrent humeral vein (Figure 27–2C, *hv*), 16–34 mm in length **12***

11'.   Front wings without a recurrent humeral vein, 9–13 mm in length ....**Beróthidae***   p. 366

12(11).   Sc and R$_1$ in front wing fused distally; Rs in front wing with many branches, cross veins between them forming a fairly distinct gradate vein; free basal portion of MA in hind wing longitudinal (Figure 27–2C); widely distributed ....**Polystoechòtidae***   p. 366

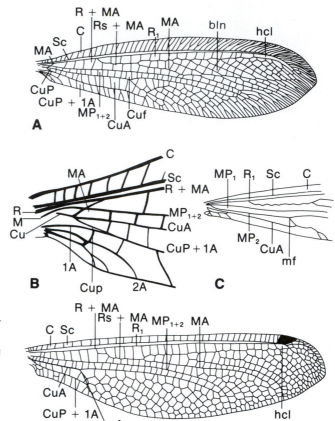

Figure 27–4.   Wings of Myrmeleontòidea. **A,** front wing of *Dendròleon* (Myrmeleóntidae); **B,** base of the same wing as **A,** enlarged to show detail; **C,** base of hind wing of *Dendròleon,* with most cross veins not shown; **D,** front wing of an ascalaphid. *bln,* banksian line; *cuf,* cubital fork (fork of CuA); *hcl,* hypostigmatic or truss cell; *mf,* medial fork (fork of MP₂).

12′.	Sc and R_1 in front wing not fused distally; Rs in front wing with only a few branches, cross veins between them scattered and not forming a distinct gradate vein; free basal part of MA in hind wing short and oblique; southern California . . . .**Ithònidae***	p. 365
13(9′).	Sc and R_1 in front wing not fused near wing tip, Rs appearing unbranched (Figure 27–3B); wings, at least in life, often greenish; very common insects . . . .**Chrysòpidae**	p. 365
13′.	Sc and R_1 in front wing fused or separate apically, Rs appearing branched (Figure 27–2B); wings not greenish; uncommon insects **14**	
14(13′).	Antennae pectinate in male, filiform in female; female with exserted ovipositor about as long as body; hind wing about as long as front wing in male, about two-thirds as long as front wing in female; front wing 3.0–5.5 mm in length . . . .**Dilàridae***	p. 366
14′.	Antennae filiform in both sexes; female without exserted ovipositor; hind wing with free basal part of MA present, longitudinal (Figure 27–2B); wings elongate-oval, hind wing nearly as long as front wing 3.4–7.0 mm in length . . . .**Sisýridae**	p. 366

SUBORDER **Megalóptera:** The members of this suborder have the hind wings broader at the base than the front wings, and this enlarged anal area is folded fanwise at rest. The longitudinal veins do not have branches near the wing margin, as do those of many of the other insects in this order. Ocelli may be present or absent. The larvae are aquatic, with lateral abdominal gills, and with normal jaws (not elongate and sicklelike, as in the Planipénnia). The pupae are not in cocoons.

Family **Siálidae**—Alderflies: The alderflies (Figure 27–5) are dark-colored insects, about 25 mm in length or less, and are usually found near water. The larvae are aquatic and are usually found under stones in streams. They are predaceous on small aquatic insects. The larvae of alderflies (Figure 27–6C) differ from those of the Corydálidae in that they have a terminal filament, seven pairs of lateral filaments, and no hooked anal prolegs. *Sìalis infumàta* Newman is a common eastern species that is about 19 mm in length and has smoky wings.

Family **Corydálidae**—Dobsonflies and Fishflies: These insects are similar to the alderflies, but are in general larger (usually over 25 mm in length) and have ocelli. They are soft-bodied, have a rather fluttery flight, and are usually found near water. Some species are attracted to lights and may be found some distance from water. The larvae (Figure 27–6A,B) are aquatic and usually occur under stones in streams. They differ from alderfly larvae in that they have a pair of hooked anal prolegs, no terminal filament, and eight pairs of lateral filaments. These larvae are sometimes called hellgrammites and are frequently used as bait by fishermen. The jaws can inflict a painful nip.

The largest insects in this group are the dobsonflies (*Corýdalus* and *Dysmicohérmes*), which have front wings 50 mm or more in length. A common eastern species (Figure 27–7) has a wingspread of about 130 mm, and the males have extremely long mandibles. The smaller species in this group (front wings less than 50 mm in length) are called fishflies. Most of them belong to the genera *Chauliòdes*, *Neohérmes*, and *Nigrònia*. Dobsonflies and some of the fishflies have clear wings, but other fishflies (species of *Nigrònia*) have the wings black or smoky with a few small clear areas. Fishflies in the genera *Chauliòdes* and *Nigrònia* have the antennae serrate or pectinate.

SUBORDER **Raphidiòdea:** These insects are peculiar in having the prothorax elongate, somewhat as in the Mantíspidae, but the front legs are similar to the other legs and are borne at the posterior end of the prothorax (Figure 27–8A). These insects can

Figure 27–5. An alderfly, *Sìalis mòhri* Ross. (Courtesy of the Illinois Natural History Survey.)

raise the head above the rest of the body, much like a snake preparing to strike. The adults are predaceous, but are capable of catching only small and weak prey. The female (which has a long ovipositor) lays her eggs in clusters in crevices in bark, and the larvae are usually found under bark. The larvae feed principally on small insects such as aphids and caterpillars. The snakeflies are restricted to the western states.

Family **Raphidiìdae:** This family is represented in North America by 17 species of *Raphídia*, which are widely distributed through the West, occurring from central Texas and California north to British Columbia and Alberta. They vary in size, with the front wings ranging from 6 to 17 mm in length. Females are usually a little larger than males.

Family **Inocelliidae:** This group is represented in our area by one species of *Inocéllia*, which occurs from California and Nevada north to British Columbia. Inocelliids are larger than most raphidiids, with the front wing varying in length from 11 to 17 mm. They also have longer and thicker antennae and a larger, darker pterostigma than rhaphidiids.

SUBORDER **Planipénnia:** This suborder includes the dusty-wings, lacewings, antlions, and owlflies. Some authorities include only these insects in the order Neuróptera. The adults lack ocelli; the front and hind wings (in our species) are similar in size and shape; and the longitudinal veins in the wings often have branches near the wing margin. The larvae have long sicklelike mandibles, and the food is sucked up through a channel formed between the mandible and maxilla. Pupation occurs in a silken cocoon.

Family **Coniopterýgidae**—Dusty-Wings: These are minute insects, 3 mm in length or less, and are

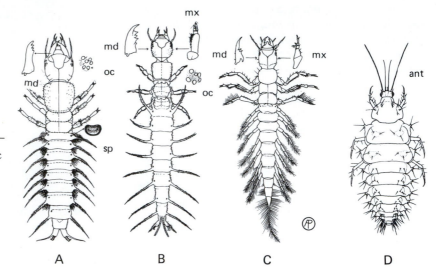

Figure 27–6. Larvae of aquatic Neuróptera; **A,** *Corýdalus* (Corydálidae); **B,** *Chauliòdes* (Corydálidae); **C,** *Sìalis* (Siálidae); **D,** *Climàcia* (Sisýridae). *ant,* antenna; *md,* mandible; *mx,* maxilla; *oc,* ocelli; *sp,* spiracle. (Courtesy of Peterson; reprinted by permission.)

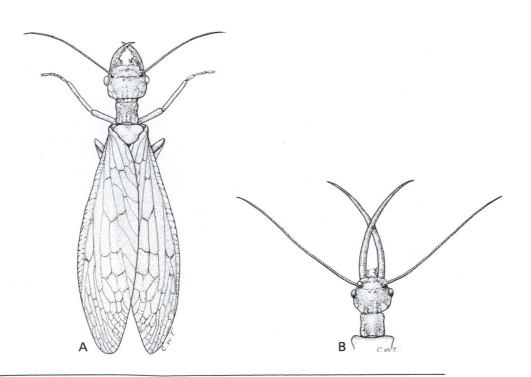

Figure 27–7. A dobsonfly, *Corýdalus cornùtus* (L.). **A,** female; **B,** head of male showing the greatly enlarged mandibles; about natural size.

covered with a whitish powder. The group is a small one, and its members are relatively rare. The larvae feed on small insects and insect eggs.

Family **Ithònidae:** This family is represented in the United States by a single very rare species, *Oliárces clàra* Banks, which has been taken in southern California. This insect has a wingspread of 35–40 mm and resembles a *Sìalis* with bleached wings. The larvae are scarabaeiform and plant-feeding.

Family **Mantíspidae**—Mantidflies: These insects resemble mantids in having the prothorax lengthened and the front legs enlarged and fitted for grasping prey (Figure 27–8B). They have a wingspread of 25 mm or so. The larvae of some species (e.g., *Plèga*) feed primarily on the larvae of wasps and bees, while those of other species (e.g., *Mantíspa* and *Climaciélla*) feed on spider eggs. Mantidflies undergo hypermetamorphosis: the first-instar larvae are active and campodeiform, and the subsequent larval insects are scarabaeiform. These insects are more common in the South.

Family **Hemerobìidae**—Brown Lacewings: These insects resemble common lacewings (Chrysòpidae), but are brownish instead of green and generally smaller, and they have a different wing venation. The chrysopids have a single distinct radial sector, while the hemerobiids appear to have from two to four (that is, two to four veins branch off R_1). Most hemerobiids appear to have three or four radial sectors. Two genera that appear to have only two (*Pséctra* and *Sympheròbius*) are placed by some authorities in a separate family, the Sympherobìidae. Some species have a recurved and branched humeral vein in the front wing. Brown lacewings are generally found in wooded areas, and are much less common than the Chrysòpidae. The eggs are laid on plants, but are not stalked. The larvae are predaceous. This is the third largest family in the order, with 58 North American species.

Family **Chrysòpidae**—Common Lacewings: This is the second largest family in the order (87 North American species), and its members are common insects—usually occurring in grass and weeds and on the foliage of trees and shrubs. Most of them are greenish in color with copper-colored eyes (Figure 27–9A). The species of *Eremóchrysa* (western) are often tan and resemble hemerobiids. Some chrysopids give off a rather disagreeable odor when handled. The larvae of most species are predaceous, chiefly on aphids, and are sometimes called aphidlions (Figure 27–9B). Some larvae pile debris on their backs and carry it around. The adults may be predaceous (e.g., *Chrysòpa*), feed on pollen (e.g., *Meleòma*), or feed on honeydew (e.g., *Eremóchrysa*). The eggs are usually laid on foliage, and each egg is laid at the end of a tiny stalk (Figure 27–9C). The larvae pupate in silken cocoons that are generally attached to the underside of leaves. The largest and most commonly

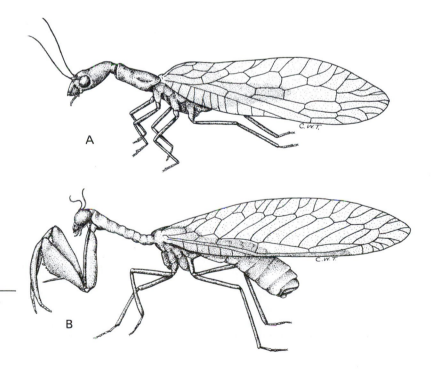

Figure 27–8. **A,** a snakefly, *Raphídia adníxa* (Hagen); **B,** a mantispid, *Mantíspa cincticòrnis* Banks.

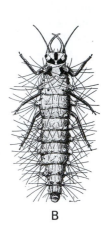

Figure 27–9.   Adult (**A**), larva (**B**), and eggs (**C**) of a common lacewing, *Chrysòpa* sp. (**A** and **B,** courtesy of the Illinois Natural History Survey.)

encountered genus in this family is *Chrysòpa* (Figures 27–3B, 27–9).

Family **Dilàridae**—Pleasing Lacewings: This group contains two very rare North American species. *Nallàchius americànus* (MacLachlan), which has MP in the front wing forked near the wing margin, has been recorded from several eastern states, from Michigan to Georgia; *N. pulchéllus*, which has MP in the front wing forked near its base, has been recorded from Cuba and Arizona. Unlike most Neuróptera, these insects commonly rest with the wings outspread and resemble small moths. The female has an ovipositor that is a little longer than the body. Males have plumose antennae. The eggs are laid in crevices or under bark, and the larvae are predaceous.

Family **Beròthidae**—Beaded Lacewings: This family is represented in North America by ten rather rare species in the genus *Lomamỳia*. Adults are frequently attracted to lights at night and resemble slender caddisflies. In some species the outer margin of the front wing is somewhat indented just behind the apex, and the females of some species have scales on the wings and thorax. The eggs are stalked. The larvae are predaceous on termites. The prey is first immobilized by a gas discharged from the anus (an example of an allomone), and its use by berothids in predation is unique among insects.

Family **Polystoechòtidae**—Giant Lacewings: These lacewings have a wingspread of 40–75 mm. They are quite rare, and only two species are known in North America. The larvae are terrestrial and predaceous.

Family **Sisÿridae**—Spongillaflies: The spongillaflies look very much like tiny brownish lacewings. They are usually found near ponds or streams, for the larvae (Figure 27–6D) are aquatic and feed on freshwater sponges. When full grown, the larvae emerge from the water and pupate in silken cocoons attached to objects near the water. These cocoons are constructed inside hemispherical cocoon covers.

There are six species of spongillaflies in North America, three in each of the genera *Climàcia* and *Sísyra*. These genera differ in the forking of Rs. *Climàcia* has a single fork in Rs, located below the pterostigma (Figure 27–2B), while *Sísyra* has two forks in this vein, located well proximad of the pterostigma.

Family **Myrmeleóntidae**—Antlions: This is the largest family in the order (89 North American species). Its members are widely distributed, but are most abundant in the South and West and a little less common in the northern part of the United States. The adults of this group resemble damselflies, with a long slender abdomen (Figure 27–10). They differ from damselflies in being softer-bodied, in having relatively long clubbed antennae, and in having quite different wing venation (compare Figures 27–4A and 11–6). They are rather feeble fliers and are often attracted to lights. The wings are clear in some species and irregularly spotted in others (Figure 27–10).

Antlion larvae, or doodlebugs, are queer-looking creatures with long sicklelike jaws (Figure 27–11A). Most of them (Acanthoclisìnae and Dendroleontìnae) either lie in wait for their prey on the surface of the ground (generally in sandy areas) or buried just beneath the surface, or they give chase on the surface. Most larvae move both forward and backward equally well. Some species in this family (the Myr-

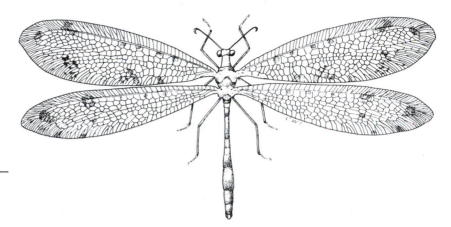

Figure 27–10. An adult antlion, *Dendróleon obsolétum* (Say).

meleontìnae) capture their prey by means of pitfalls. They conceal themselves in the bottom of a small conical pit, made in sand or dust, and feed on ants and other insects that fall into this pit. The pits are generally 35–50 mm across and are usually found in dry situations such as under overhanging cliffs or under buildings. It is not always easy to dig one of these larvae from its pit, because the larvae remain motionless when disturbed and, when dug up, are covered with a layer of sand or dust and are easily overlooked. Antlion larvae pupate in the soil, in a cocoon made of sand and silk.

This group contains several distinctive venational features, some of which are of taxonomic value: (1) a characteristic fork in the basal third of the wing (the trigonal fork of Comstock), formed by the forking of the CuA in the front wing and of MP_2 in the hind wing; (2) the prefork area (trigonal loop of Comstock), the area between MP_2 and CuA + 1A in the front wing; (3) the hypostigmatic cell (the truss cell of Comstock), a long cell behind the point of fusion of Sc and R_1 in the distal part of the wing

(Figure 27–4, *hcl*); and (4) the presectoral cross veins, those basad of the separation of Rs + MA from R_1, extending between Rs + MA and MP in the front wing and between Rs + MA and MP_1 in the hind wing. Some species have a fairly distinct gradate vein called the banksian line, extending lengthwise in the distal half or third of the wing (Figure 27–4A, *bln*).

Our species of antlions are arranged in three subfamilies, the Acanthoclisìnae, Myrmeleontìnae, and Dendroleontìnae. Some authorities consider the Dendroleontìnae a tribe (the Dendroleontìni) of the subfamily Myrmeleontìnae. The Acanthoclisìnae occur only in the West, but the other two subfamilies are widely distributed. More than half of our species belong to the Dendroleontìnae. It is only the larvae of the Myrmeleontìnae that construct pitfalls.

Family **Ascaláphidae**—Owlflies: These are large dragonflylike insects with long clubbed antennae. They are fairly common in the South and Southwest, but are quite rare in the northern states. Most species lay their eggs on twigs, and a week or so after

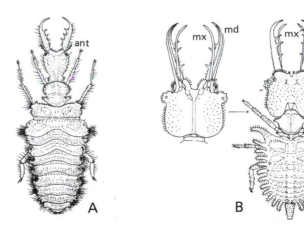

Figure 27–11. Larvae of Myrmeleontòidea. **A,** *Myrméleon immaculàtus* De Geer (Myrmeleóntidae); **B,** *Ascalóptynx appendiculàtus* (Fabricius) (Ascaláphidae). *ant*, antennae; *md*, mandible; *mx*, maxilla; *oc*, ocelli. (Courtesy of Peterson; reprinted by permission.)

hatching the larvae climb down to the ground, where they live in litter. The larvae of a few species may be arboreal. Some larvae cover themselves with debris; others have a coloration that renders them inconspicuous. The larvae are predaceous. They lie in wait for their prey with their large jaws wide open. The closing of the jaws on a prey is apparently triggered by contact, and the prey is usually paralyzed within seconds by the bite of the ascalaphid larva. Pupation occurs in litter, in a silken cocoon, and lasts from a few weeks to a few months. Some adults are diurnal, and some are nocturnal. Most of our species fly at dusk, flying up to 10 m above the ground by the time of complete darkness. The flight of the adults is strong and dragonfly-like, with periods of hovering and rapid flight, the adults feeding on small insects. Adults spend much of their time resting—usually head down on a vertical twig, with the body projecting from the twig at about a right angle—thus resembling a small twig. They are apparently unable to fly off directly from a resting position, but must go through a warm-up of several minutes, vibrating their wings. The adults of some species have some

color in the wings, the color developing a few days after the adults emerge.

Collecting and Preserving Neuróptera

Most Neuróptera can be collected with an insect net by sweeping vegetation. Adults of the Siálidae, Corydálidae, and Sisýridae are generally to be found near the aquatic habitats (ponds and streams) in which the larvae live. The best way to collect many Neuróptera, particularly representatives of the less common groups, is at lights.

Adult Neuróptera are preserved in alcohol, or on pins or points, or in envelopes. All are relatively soft-bodied, and pinned specimens often sag or shrivel and become distorted. Many pinned specimens need some support for the abdomen, at least until the insect has dried. Very small forms can be mounted on points, but preservation in alcohol is better. Large elongate forms, such as dobsonflies and antlions, can be preserved in envelopes.

References

Adams, P. A. 1956. New antlions from the southwestern United States (Neuroptera: Myrmeleontidae). Psyche 63:82–108; illus.

Banks, N. 1906. A revision of the Nearctic Coniopterygidae. Proc. Entomol. Soc. Wash. 8:77–86; illus.

Banks, N. 1927. Revision of Nearctic Myrmeleontidae. Bull. Mus. Comp. Zool. Harvard 68:1–84; illus.

Bickley, W. E., and E. G. MacLeod. 1956. A synopsis of the Nearctic Chrysopidae with a key to the genera (Neuroptera). Proc. Entomol. Soc. Wash. 58:177–202; illus.

Carpenter, F. M. 1936. Revision of the Nearctic Raphidiodea (recent and fossil). Proc. Amer. Acad. Arts Sci. 71(2):89–157; illus.

Carpenter, F. M. 1940. A revision of the Nearctic Hemerobiidae, Berothidae, Sisyridae, Polystoechotidae, and Dilaridae (Neuroptera). Proc. Amer. Acad. Arts Sci. 74(7):193–280; illus.

Carpenter, F. M. 1951. The structure and relationships of *Oliarces* (Neuroptera). Psyche 58:32–41; illus.

Chandler, H. P. 1956. Megaloptera, pp. 229–233 *in* Aquatic Insects of California, ed. R. L. Usinger. Berkeley: Univ. California Press; illus.

Davis, K. C. 1903. Sialididae of North and South America. N.Y. State Mus. Bull. 68:442–486; illus.

Froeschner, R. C. 1947. Notes and keys to the Neuroptera of Missouri. Ann. Entomol. Soc. Amer. 40:123–136; illus.

Glorioso, M. J. 1981. Systematics of the dobsonfly subfamily Corydalinae (Megaloptera: Corydalidae). Syst. Entomol. 6:253–290; illus.

Gurney, A. B. 1947. Notes on Dilaridae and Berothidae, with special reference to the immature stages of the Nearctic genera (Neuroptera). Psyche 54:145–169; illus.

Gurney, A. B., and S. Parfin. 1959. Neuroptera, pp. 973–980 *in* Freshwater Biology, ed. W. T. Edmondson. New York: Wiley; illus.

Henry, C. S. 1977. The behavior and life histories of two North American ascalaphids. Ann. Entomol. Soc. Amer. 70:176–195; illus.

Johnson, J. B., and K. S. Hagen. 1981. A neuropterous larva uses an allomone to attack termites. Nature 289:506–507.

Johnson, V. 1976. A new genus and species of Coniopterygidae (Neuroptera) from New Mexico. Psyche 83:192–195; illus.

Lambkin, K. J. 1986a. A revision of the Australian Mantispidae (Insecta: Neuroptera) with a contribution to the classification of the family. I. General and Drepanicinae. Austral. J. Zool., Suppl. Ser. 116:1–142.

Lambkin, K. J. 1986b. A revision of the Australian Mantispidae (Insecta: Neuroptera) with a contribution to the classification of the family. II. Calomantispinae and Mantispinae. Austral. J. Zool., Suppl. Ser. 117:1–113.

MacLeod, E. G., and K. E. Redborg. 1982. Larval platymantispine mantispids (Neuroptera: Planipennia): Possibly a subfamily of general predators. Neuroptera Int. 2:37–41.

Martynov, A. 1928. Permian fossil insects of northeast Europe. Trav. Mus. Geol. Acad. Sci. USSR 4:1–117.

Meinander, M. 1972. A revision of the family Coniopterygidae. Acta Zool. Fenn. 136:1–357; illus.

Parfin, S. 1952. The Megaloptera and Neuroptera of Minnesota. Amer. Midl. Nat. 47(2):421–434.

Parfin, S., and A. B. Gurney. 1956. The spongillaflies with special reference to those of the western hemisphere (Sisyridae, Neuroptera). Proc. U.S. Natl. Mus. 105(3360): 421–529; illus.

Peterson, A. 1951. Larvae of Insects, Part 2: Coleoptera, Diptera, Neuroptera, Siphonaptera, Mecoptera, Trichoptera. Ann Arbor, Mich.: Edwards Bros., 416 pp.; illus.

Redborg, K. E., and E. G. MacLeod. 1985. The developmental ecology of *Mantispa uhleri* Banks (Neuroptera: Mantispidae). Ill. Biol. Monogr. No. 53, 130 pp.

Rehn, J. W. H. 1939. Studies in North American Mantispidae (Neuroptera). Trans. Amer. Entomol. Soc. 65:237–263; illus.

Ross, H. H. 1937. Nearctic alderflies of the genus *Sialis*. Ill. Nat. Hist. Surv. Bull. 21(3):57–78; illus.

Smith, R. C. 1922. The biology of the Chrysopidae. N.Y. (Cornell) Agr. Expt. Sta. Mem. 58:1285–1377; illus.

Stange, L. A. 1970. Revision of the antlion tribe Brachyneurini of North America (Neuroptera: Myrmeleontidae). Univ. Calif. Publ. Entomol. 55:1–192; illus.

Tauber, C. A. 1969. Taxonomy and biology of the lacewing genus *Meleoma* (Neuroptera: Chrysopidae). Univ. Calif. Publ. Entomol. 58:1–94; illus.

Throne, A. L. 1971a. The Neuroptera—suborder Planipennia of Wisconsin, Part 1: Introduction and Chrysopidae. Mich. Entomol. 4(3):65–78; illus.

Throne, A. L. 1971b. The Neuroptera—suborder Planipennia of Wisconsin, Part 2: Hemerobiidae, Polystoechotidae, and Sisyridae. Mich. Entomol. 4(3):79–87; illus.

Withycombe, C. L. 1925. Some aspects of the biology and morphology of the Neuroptera, with special reference to the immature stages and their phylogenetic significance. Trans. Entomol. Soc. Lond. 1924: 303–411; illus.

Chapter 28

Order Coleóptera[1]
Beetles

The order Coleóptera is the largest order of insects and contains about 40% of the known species in the Hexápoda. More than a quarter of a million species of beetles have been described, and about 30,000 of these occur in the United States and Canada. These vary in length (in the United States) from less than a millimeter up to about 75 mm. Some tropical species reach a length of about 125 mm. The beetles vary considerably in habits and are to be found almost everywhere. Many species are of great economic importance.

One of the most distinctive features of the Coleóptera is the structure of the wings. Most beetles have four wings, with the front pair thickened, leathery, or hard and brittle, and usually meeting in a straight line down the middle of the back and covering the hind wings (hence the order name). The hind wings are membranous, are usually longer than the front wings, and when at rest, are usually folded up under the front wings (Figure 28–1). The front wings of a beetle are called elytra (singular, *elytron*). The elytra normally serve only as protective sheaths. The hind wings are the only ones ordinarily used for flight. The front or hind wings are greatly reduced in a few beetles.

The mouthparts in this order are of the chewing type, and the mandibles are well developed. The mandibles of many beetles are stout and are used in crushing seeds or gnawing wood. In others they are slender and sharp. In the snout beetles the front of the head is drawn out into a more or less elongated snout with the mouthparts at the end.

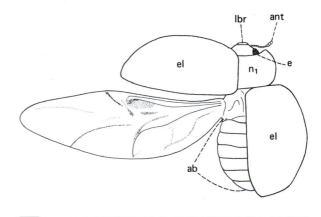

Figure 28–1. Dorsal view of a ladybird beetle (*Adàlia* sp.), with the left wings extended. *ab*, abdomen, *ant*, antenna; *e*, compound eye; *el*, elytron; *lbr*, labrum; *n*, pronotum.

[1]Coleóptera: *coleo*, sheath; *ptera*, wings (referring to the elytra).

The beetles undergo complete metamorphosis. The larvae vary considerably in form in different families. Most beetle larvae are campodeiform or scarabaeiform, but some are platyform, some are elateriform, and a few are vermiform.

Beetles may be found in almost every type of habitat in which any insect is found, and they feed on all sorts of plant and animal materials. Many are phytophagous; many are predaceous; some are scavengers; others feed on mold or fungi; and a very few are parasitic. Some are subterranean in habit; many are aquatic or semiaquatic; and a few live as commensals in the nests of social insects. Some of the phytophagous species are free feeders on foliage; some bore into the wood or fruits; some are leaf miners; some attack the roots; and some feed on parts of the blossoms. Any part of a plant may be fed upon by some type of beetle. Many beetles feed on stored plant or animal products, including many types of foods, clothing, and other organic materials. One Californian species is remarkable for its ability to bore through the lead sheathing of telephone cables. Many beetles are of value to humans because they destroy injurious insects or act as scavengers.

The life cycle in this order varies in length from four generations a year to one generation in several years. Most species have one generation a year. The winter may be passed in any of the life stages, depending on the species. Many overwinter as partly grown larvae; many overwinter as pupae in chambers in the soil or in wood or in other protected situations; and many overwinter as adults. Relatively few species overwinter as eggs.

Sound Production in the Coleóptera

Sound production has been reported in about 50 families of Coleóptera, but the sounds produced are generally rather weak, and they have been less studied than the sounds of Orthóptera and cicadas. Relatively little is known of the role these sounds play in behavior.

Beetles produce sounds in three principal ways: (1) in the course of normal activities such as flying and feeding, (2) by striking some part of the body against the substrate, and (3) by stridulation.

Flight sounds, produced by the movements of the wings, are similar to those produced by other flying insects. Feeding sounds are dependent upon the size of the beetles and the material fed upon, but in some cases these sounds may be fairly loud. A large wood-boring beetle larva feeding in a log can sometimes be heard from several feet away. Feeding sounds, such as those of wood-boring larvae or grain-feeding bee-

tles, probably play no role in communication from one beetle to another but are communicative from the human point of view—in indicating the presence (and feeding) of the insects in the material concerned.

Adult deathwatch beetles (*Anòbium* and *Xestòbium* spp., family Anobìidae) produce sounds by striking the lower parts of their heads against the walls of their galleries (in wood). In quiet surroundings these sounds are quite apparent. In Arizona and California, adults of *Eupsóphulus castàneus* Horn (Tenebriónidae) cause some annoyance by tapping their abdomens against screen doors and windows, producing a surprisingly loud noise. Another tenebrionid, *Eusáttus reticulàtus* (Say), produces a sound by rapidly tapping the apex of the abdomen against the ground.

When a click beetle on its back "jumps" (see page 430), there is a distinct clicking sound. It is not clear whether the click is caused by the body striking the substrate or the prosternal peg stopping abruptly in the mesosternal notch.

Most sounds in the Coleóptera, including the sounds that may be involved in communication, are produced by stridulation. The stridulatory structures may be located on almost any part of the body and involve an area bearing a series of ridges (the "file") and a "scraper," usually a hard ridge, knob, or spine, which is rubbed against the file. Most stridulatory structures are on adults, but there are a few cases in the beetles where the larvae, or even the pupae, stridulate.

The stridulatory structures in beetles may involve the head and pronotum (Nitidùlidae, Tenebriónidae, Endomýchidae, Curculiónidae), head appendages (usually mouthparts; certain Scarabaeìdae), pronotum and mesonotum (common in the Cerambýcidae), leg and thorax (Anobìidae, Bostríchidae), leg and abdomen (some Scarabaeìdae), leg and leg (adult and larval Passálidae, Lucànidae, and some Scarabaeìdae), abdomen and hind wings (Passálidae), and elytra and abdomen (Hydrophílidae, Curculiónidae, Scolýtidae).

Little is known about auditory mechanisms in the beetles. They do not possess tympana, but certain chordotonal organs and sensillae have been found to be sensitive to vibration. These organs are usually located on either the legs or the antennae.

Beetle stridulations are produced in four general sorts of situations: (1) when the insect is handled or attacked ("stress" sounds); (2) in aggressive situations, such as fighting; (3) in calling (attracting the opposite sex); and (4) prior to mating (a "courtship" sound). It is probable that most beetles that stridulate produce stress sounds, and such sounds may be of value to the beetle in deterring potential predators. Stress sounds may be the only ones some beetles produce, while in other beetles (for example, the hydrophilid genus *Beròsus* and scolytids), other types of sounds besides stress sounds may be produced.

Beetle sounds vary in their character, depending on the species and how the sounds are produced, but most are of a quality that might be described as a chirp, a squeak, or a rasping sound. Most contain a broad band of frequencies (Figures 4–3D, 28–2). Stress sounds and some aggressive sounds are generally produced at an irregular rate of, at most, only a few per second. In calling and courtship sounds the chirps are produced at a faster, regular rate, which differs in different species (Figure 28–2).

The sounds produced by beetles in the genus *Beròsus* (Hydrophílidae) are of two sorts, an alarm sound and a premating sound. The alarm sound, produced when the beetle is handled (and sometimes spontaneously), consists of irregularly spaced chirps, 1–3 or so per second. The premating sound is a rapid series of short chirps lasting 0.3–3.6 seconds, with the chirps uttered rapidly at a regular rate. The premating sounds of different sympatric species are different and are believed to act as a species-isolating mechanism.

In *Dendróctonus* (Scolýtidae), both sexes stridulate, and the sounds produced are of three general types: (1) simple chirps (each produced by a single movement of the stridulatory apparatus); (2) interrupted chirps (each produced by a single movement of the stridulatory apparatus, but interrupted by one or more brief moments of silence); and (3) clicks (each a single spike of sound, produced by females when alone in the bark). Stridulation occurs during stress situations (for example, when a beetle is handled), during aggression, and during courtship. The sounds made by females in the bark may have a territorial function; that is, they may limit the density of the burrows. Males emit interrupted chirps both while fighting a rival male and when attracted to the gallery of a virgin female. A female responds to male stridulation at the gallery entrance by simple chirps. The courting behavior in the gallery involves the male emitting simple chirps while the female is silent.

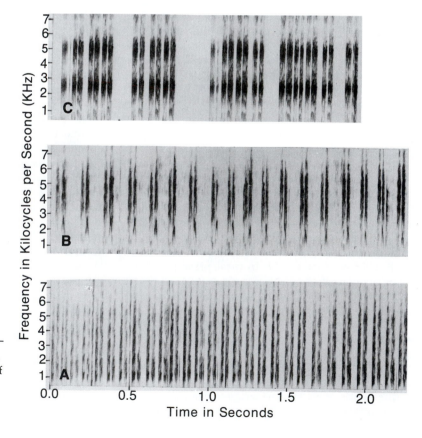

Figure 28–2. Audiospectrographs of the stridulations of three species of snout beetles: **A**, *Conotràchelus carínifer* Casey; **B**, *C. nàso* LeConte; **C**, *C. posticàtus* Casey.

Classification of the Coleóptera

There are differences of opinion among coleopterists with regard to the relationships of the various groups of beetles, the groups that should be given family status, and their arrangement into superfamilies. The arrangement of suborders, superfamilies, and families followed in this book is taken from various sources, principally Crowson (1968), Arnett (1968), and Lawrence (1982). Many authorities give family status to more groups than we do in this book.

An outline of the groups in the order Coleóptera, as they are treated in this book, is given here. Names in parentheses represent different spellings, synonyms, or other treatments of the group. Families marked with an asterisk are relatively rare or are not very likely to be taken by the general collector. Most of the common names of families are those given by Arnett (1968).

Suborder Archostémata
  *Cupédidae (Cupésidae, Cùpidae)—reticulated beetles
  *Micromálthidae—micromalthid beetles
Suborder Myxóphaga
  *Sphaerìidae (Sphaèridae)—minute bog beetles
  *Hydroscáphidae (Hydrophílidae in part)—skiff beetles
Suborder Adéphaga
  Rhysòdidae (Rhyssòdidae)—wrinkled bark beetles
  Cicindèlidae—tiger beetles
  Carábidae (including Pàussidae and Omophrónidae)—ground beetles
  Halíplidae—crawling water beetles
  *Amphizòidae—trout-stream beetles
  *Notéridae (Dytíscidae in part)—burrowing water beetles
  Dytíscidae—predaceous diving beetles
  Gyrìnidae—whirligig beetles
Suborder Polýphaga
  Superfamily Staphylinòidea
    *Hydraènidae (Limnebìidae; Hydrophílidae in part)—minute moss beetles
    Ptilìidae (Ptílidae, Trichopterýgidae; including Limulòdidae)—feather-winged beetles and horseshoe crab beetles
    Agýrtidae (Sílphidae in part)—agyrtid beetles
    *Leiòdidae (Lìodidae, Anisotómidae, Leptodíridae, Catópidae; Sílphidae in part)—round fungus beetles
    *Leptìnidae (including Platypsýllidae)—mammal-nest beetles and beaver parasites
    *Scydmaènidae—antlike stone beetles

    *Dasycéridae (Lathridìidae in part)—dasycerid beetles
    Sílphidae—carrion beetles
    Staphylìnidae (including Micropéplidae, Scaphidìidae, and Brathínidae)—rove beetles
    Pseláphidae (including Clavigéridae)—short-winged mold beetles
  Superfamily Hydrophilòidea
    Hydrophílidae (including Hydróchidae and Sperchèidae)—water scavenger beetles
    *Georýssidae—minute mud-loving beetles
    *Sphaerítidae—false clown beetles
    Histéridae—hister beetles
  Superfamily Eucinetòidea
    *Eucinètidae (Dascíllidae in part)—plate-thigh beetles
    Clámbidae—fringe-winged beetles
    Scírtidae (Helòdidae, Cyphónidae; Dascíllidae in part)—marsh beetles
  Superfamily Dascillòidea
    Dascíllidae (Dascýllidae; including Karumìidae)—soft-bodied plant beetles
    Rhipicéridae (Sandálidae in part)—cedar beetles
  Superfamily Scarabaeòidea
    Lucànidae—stag beetles
    Passálidae—bess beetles
    Scarabaèidae (including Acanthocéridae, Geotrùpidae, Ochodaèidae, Hybosòridae, Glaphýridae, Trógidae, Ceratocánthidae, Pleocómidae, and Diphyllostómidae)—scarab beetles
  Superfamily Byrrhòidea
    Býrrhidae—pill beetles
  Superfamily Buprestòidea
    Bupréstidae (including Schizópidae)—metallic wood-boring beetles
  Superfamily Dryopòidea
    *Eulichádidae (Dascíllidae in part)—eulichadid beetles
    *Callirhípidae (Rhipicéridae in part, Sandálidae in part)—callirhipid beetles
    Ptilodactýlidae (Dascíllidae in part)—ptilodactylid beetles
    *Chelonarìidae—chelonariid beetles
    Heterocéridae—variegated mud-loving beetles
    *Limníchidae (including Lutróchidae; Dascíllidae in part)—minute marsh-loving beetles
    Dryópidae (Párnidae)—long-toed water beetles
    Elmidae (Elmínthidae, Helmínthidae, Hélmidae)—riffle beetles
    Psephènidae (including Eubrìidae)—water-penny beetles

Superfamily Elateròidea
  *Artematópidae (Eurypogónidae; Dascíllidae in part: Macropogonìni)—artematopid beetles
  *Cerophýtidae—cerophytid beetles
  Elatéridae (including Plastocéridae)—click beetles
  *Cebriónidae—cebrionid beetles
  Thróscidae (Trixágidae)—throscid beetles
  *Perothópidae (Eucnèmidae in part)—perothopid beetles
  Eucnèmidae (Melásidae)—false click beetles
Superfamily Cantharòidea
  Brachypséctridae (Dascíllidae in part)—the Texas beetle
  Lýcidae—net-winged beetles
  *Phengòdidae—glowworms
  *Telegeùsidae—telegeusid beetles
  Lampýridae—lightningbugs, fireflies
  Canthàridae (including Ométhidae and Chauliognáthidae)—soldier beetles
Superfamily Dermestòidea
  *Derodóntidae—tooth-necked fungus beetles
  *Nosodéndridae—wounded-tree beetles
  Derméstidae (including Thoríctidae and Thylodrìidae)—dermestid or skin beetles
Superfamily Bostrichòidea
  Bostríchidae (Bostrýchidae, Apátidae; including Psòidae)—branch and twig borers
  Lýctidae (Bostríchidae in part)—powderpost beetles
  Anobìidae—anobiid beetles
  Ptìnidae (including Gnóstidae)—spider beetles
Superfamily Lymexylòidea
  Lymexýlidae (Lymexylónidae)—ship-timber beetles
Superfamily Cleròidea
  Trogossítidae (Ostómidae, Ostomátidae, Trogosítidae, Temnochìlidae)—bark-gnawing beetles
  Cléridae (including Corynètidae = Korynètidae)—checkered beetles
  Melýridae (Malachìidae plus Dasýtidae)—soft-winged flower beetles
Superfamily Cucujòidea
  *Sphíndidae—dry-fungus beetles
  Nitidùlidae (including Smicrípidae and Cybocephálidae)—sap beetles
  Rhizophágidae (Nitidùlidae in part; including Monotómidae)—root-eating beetles
  Cucùjidae (including Laemophloèidae, Passándridae, Silvànidae, and Prostómidae)—flat bark beetles
  Cryptophágidae (including Biphýllidae = Diphýllidae)—silken fungus beetles

Langurìidae—lizard beetles
Erotýlidae (including Dácnidae)—pleasing fungus beetles
Phalácridae—shining flower beetles
Cerylónidae (Murmidìidae; Colydìidae in part)—cerylonid beetles
Corylóphidae (Orthopéridae)—minute fungus beetles
Coccinéllidae (including Epiláchnidae)—ladybird beetles
Endomýchidae (including Mycetaèidae and Merophysìidae)—handsome fungus beetles
Lathridìidae—minute brown scavenger beetles
Bytùridae (Derméstidae in part)—fruitworm beetles
Superfamily Tenebrionòidea
  Mycetophágidae—hairy fungus beetles
  Cìidae (Císidae, Cìòidae)—minute tree-fungus beetles
  Melandrỳidae (including Synchròidae, Tetratómidae, Scraptìidae, Anaspídidae, and Serropálpidae)—false darkling beetles
  Mordéllidae—tumbling flower beetles
  Rhipiphòridae—wedge-shaped beetles
  Colydìidae (including Adiméridae, Bothridéridae, Merýcidae, and Monoèdidae)—cylindrical bark beetles
  Monómmidae (Monommátidae)—monommid beetles
  Tenebriónidae (including Zophéridae and Archeocrýpticidae)—darkling beetles
  Allecùlidae (Cistèlidae)—comb-clawed beetles
  Lagrìidae—long-jointed beetles
  *Cephalòidae—false longhorn beetles
  Melòidae (Lýttidae; including Tetraonýchidae)—blister beetles
  Oedeméridae—false blister beetles
  Myctéridae (including Hemipéplidae)—mycterid beetles
  Pyrochròidae—fire-colored beetles
  Salpíngidae (including Aegialítidae = Eurystèthidae, Inopéplidae, Othnìidae, Pỳthidae, Dacodéridae, Elacátidae, and Bòridae)—narrow-waisted bark beetles
  Anthícidae (including Cononòtidae and Pedílidae)—antlike flower beetles
  *Euglénidae (Adéridae, Hylophílidae, Xylophílidae; Anthícidae in part)—antlike leaf beetles
Superfamily Chrysomelòidea
  Cerambýcidae (including Distenìidae, Parándridae, and Spondýlidae)—long-horned beetles
  Brùchidae (Larìidae, Mylábridae; including Acanthoscélidae)—seed beetles

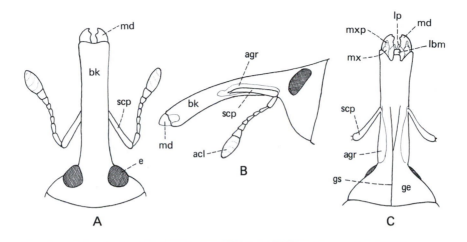

Figure 28–3. Head of a snout beetle (*Pissòdes*, Curculiónidae). **A,** dorsal view; **B,** lateral view; **C,** ventral view. *acl,* antennal club; *agr,* scrobe, groove in beak for reception of antenna; *bk,* beak or snout; *e,* compound eye; *ge,* gena; *gs,* gular suture; *lbm,* labium; *lp,* labial palp; *md,* mandible; *mx,* maxilla; *mxp,* maxillary palp; *scp,* scape of antenna.

Chrysomélidae (including Cassídidae, Crypto-cephálidae, Híspidae, and Ságridae)—leaf beetles
Superfamily Curculionòidea (Rhynchóphora)
Anthríbidae (Platystómidae, Bruchélidae, Chorágidae, Platyrrhìnidae)—fungus weevils
Bréntidae (Brénthidae)—straight-snouted weevils
Attelábidae (Curculiónidae in part)—leaf-rolling weevils
Rhynchítidae (Curculiónidae in part)—tooth-nosed weevils
Nemonýchidae (Rhinomacéridae, Cimbéridae; Curculiónidae in part)—pine-flower snout beetles
*Oxycorýnidae (including Allocorýnidae; Curculiónidae in part)—oxycorynid weevils
Apiónidae (including Cyládidae; Curculiónidae in part)—apionid weevils
Ithycéridae (Curculiónidae in part)—the New York weevil
Curculiónidae (including Cossónidae, Rhyn-chophòridae)—snout beetles or weevils
Platypódidae—pin-hole borers
Scolýtidae (including Ípidae)—bark beetles or engraver beetles, and ambrosia beetles

Characters Used in the Identification of Beetles

The principal characters of beetles used in identification are those of the head, antennae, thoracic sclerites, legs, elytra, and abdomen. Occasionally, characters such as size, shape, and color are used. In most cases the ease of recognizing these characters depends on the size of the beetle. Some characters require careful observation, often at high magnification, for accurate interpretation.

Head Characters

The principal head character used involves the development of a snout. In the Curculionòidea the head is more or less prolonged forward into a snout; the mouthparts are reduced in size and are located at the tip of the snout; and the antennae usually arise on the sides of it. The basal antennal segment often fits into a groove (the *scrobe;* Figure 28–3, *agr*) on the snout. In many cases (Figure 28–3) the snout is quite distinct, and occasionally it may be as long as the body or longer. In other cases (for example, the Scolýtidae and Platypódidae) the snout is poorly developed and not very evident as such. The families in the Curculionòidea are sometimes placed in a separate group, the Rhynchóphora. These beetles differ from most of the other members of the order in having gular sutures fused (Figure 28–3C). There is some development of a snout in a few beetles outside this superfamily, but such beetles have the gular sutures separated (Figure 28–4, *gs*).

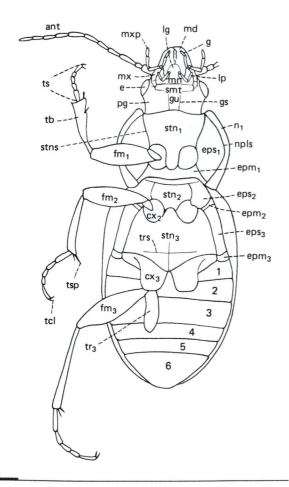

Figure 28–4. Ventral view of a ground beetle (*Omàseus* sp.). *ant,* antenna; *cx,* coxa; *e,* compound eye; *epm₁,* proepimeron; *epm₂,* mesepimeron; *epm₃,* metepimeron; *eps₁,* proepisternum; *eps₂,* mesepisternum; *eps₃,* metepisternum; *fm,* femur; *g,* galea; *gs,* gular suture; *gu,* gula; *lg,* ligula; *lp,* labial palp; *md,* mandible; *mn,* mentum; *mx,* maxilla; *mxp,* maxillary palp; *n₁,* pronotum; *npls,* notopleural suture; *pg,* postgena; *smt,* submentum; *stn₁,* prosternum; *stn₂,* mesosternum; *stn₃,* metasternum; *stns,* prosternal suture; *tb,* tibia; *tcl,* tarsal claws; *tr,* trochanter; *trs,* transverse suture on metasternum; *ts,* tarsus; *tsp,* tibial spurs; *1–6,* abdominal sterna.

Antennae

The antennae of beetles are subject to considerable variation in different groups, and these differences are used in identification. The term *clubbed,* as used in the key, refers to any condition in which the terminal segments are larger than the segments preceding them, including *clavate* (the terminal segments enlarging gradually and only slightly, as in Figure 3–15D,E); *capitate* (the terminal segments abruptly enlarged, as in Figure 28–5F–I); *lamellate* (the terminal segments expanded on one side into rounded or oval plates, as in Figure 28–6A,C–G); and *flabellate* (the terminal segments expanded on one side into long, thin, parallel-sided, tonguelike processes, as in Figure 28–6B). The distinction between some of these antennal variations (for example, between filiform and slightly clubbed or between filiform and serrate) is not very sharp, and some conditions might be interpreted in different ways. This fact is taken into account in the key, as specimens will key out correctly from either alternative at many places in the key.

The number of terminal antennal segments that form the club (in clubbed antennae) often serves as a key character. The antennal segments between the scape (the basal segment) and the club are often referred to as the funiculus (or funicle).

Thoracic Characters

The pronotum and scutellum are normally the only thoracic areas visible from above. The other thoracic areas are usually visible only in a ventral view. The pronotum, when viewed from above, may vary greatly in shape, and its posterior margin may be convex, straight, or sinuate (Figure 28–7E–G). Laterally, the pronotum may be margined (with a sharp keellike lateral edge) or rounded. The surface of the pronotum may be bare or pubescent, and it may be smooth or with various punctures or dents, ridges, grooves, tubercles, or other features. The scutellum (the mesoscutellum) is usually visible as a small triangular sclerite immediately behind the pronotum, between the bases of the elytra. Only occasionally is it rounded or heart-shaped, and sometimes it is concealed.

The chief thoracic characters apparent in a ventral view that are of importance in identification are the various sutures, the shape of certain sclerites, and the particular sclerites that are adjacent to the front and middle coxae. A few beetles (the Adéphaga, Myxóphaga, and Cupédidae) have notopleural sutures (Figure 28–4, *npls*), which separate the pronotum from the propleura. Most beetles have proster-

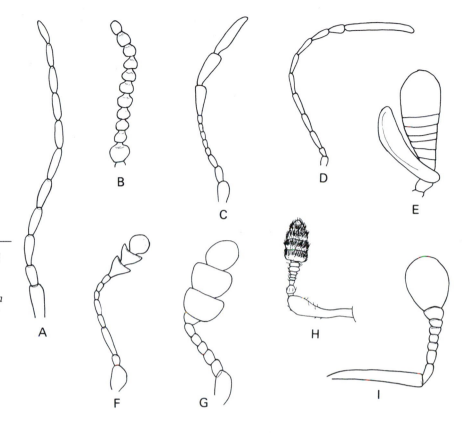

Figure 28–5.   Antennae of Coleóptera. **A,** *Hárpalus* (Carábidae); **B,** *Rhysòdes* (Rhysòdidae); **C,** *Trichodésma* (Anobìidae); **D,** *Arthrómacra* (Lagrìidae); **E,** *Dineùtus* (Gyrìnidae); **F,** *Lobìopa* (Nitidùlidae); **G,** *Derméstes* (Derméstidae); **H,** *Hylurgópinus* (Scolýtidae); **I,** *Hololépta* (Histéridae). (**H,** redrawn from Kaston.)

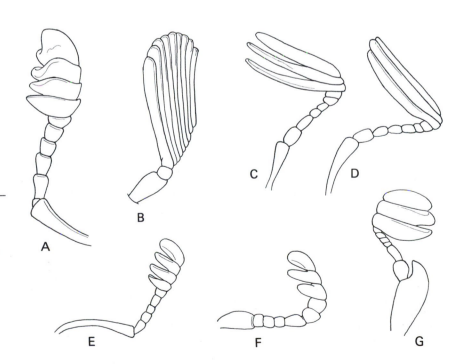

Figure 28–6.   Antennae of Coleóptera. **A,** *Nicróphorus* (Sílphidae); **B,** *Sándalus,* male (Rhipicéridae); **C,** *Phyllóphaga* (Scarabaèidae), the terminal segments expanded; **D,** same, terminal segments together forming a club; **E,** *Lucànus* (Lucànidae); **F,** *Odontotaènius* (Passálidae); **G,** *Tróx* (Scarabaèidae).

nal sutures (Figure 28–4, *stns*), which separate the prosternum from the rest of the prothorax. The anterior margin of the prosternum is usually straight. When it is somewhat convex (as in Figure 28–8A), it is said to be lobed. The prosternum often has a process or lobe extending backward between the front coxae, and sometimes (for example, in click beetles; Figure 28–8A) this process is spinelike.

When the sclerites of the prothorax extend posteriorly around the front coxae, these coxal cavities are said to be closed (Figure 28–7B). When the sclerite immediately behind the front coxae is a sclerite of the mesothorax, these cavities are said to be open

(Figure 28–7A). When the middle coxae are surrounded by sterna and are not touched by any pleural sclerite, these coxal cavities are said to be closed (Figure 28–7D). When at least some of the pleural sclerites reach the middle coxae, these coxal cavities are said to be open (Figure 28–7C).

Leg Characters

The coxae of beetles vary greatly in size and shape. In some cases they are globose or rounded and project only slightly. When they are more or less elongate

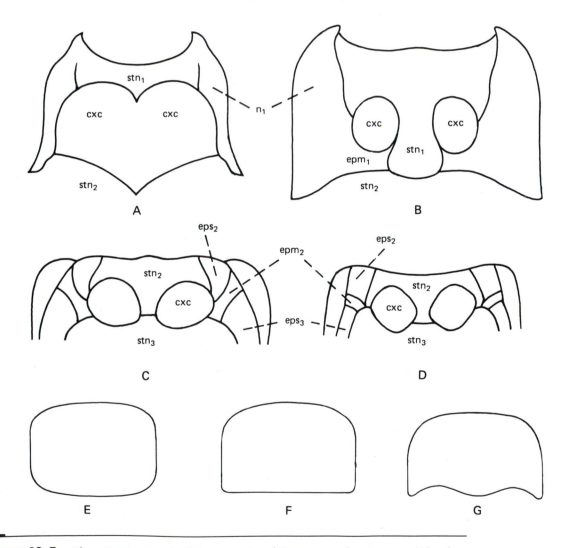

Figure 28–7.   Thoracic structure in Coleóptera. **A** and **B,** prosterna showing open (**A**) and closed (**B**) coxal cavities; **C** and **D,** mesosterna showing open (**C**) and closed (**D**) coxal cavities; **E–G,** pronota with posterior margin convex (**E**), straight (**F**), or sinuate (**G**), *cxc,* coxal cavity; *epm_1,* proepimeron; *epm_2,* mesepimeron; *eps_2,* mesepisternum; *eps_3,* metepisternum; *stn_1,* prosternum; *stn_2,* mesosternum; *stn_3,* metasternum.

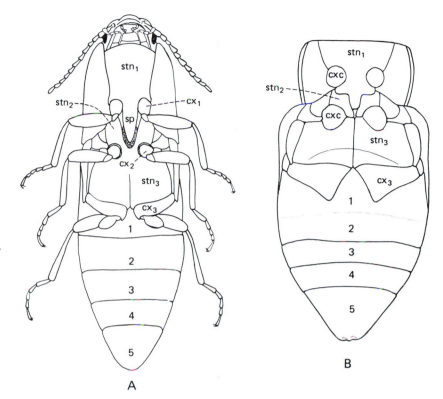

Figure 28–8. **A,** ventral view of a click beetle (*Agriòtes*); **B,** ventral view of the thorax and abdomen of a metallic wood-boring beetle (*Chrysóbothris*). *cx,* coxa; *cxc,* coxal cavity; *sp,* prosternal spine; *stn₁,* prosternum; *stn₂,* mesosternum; *stn₃,* metasternum; *1–5,* abdominal sterna.

laterally without projecting very much, they are said to be *transverse*. Sometimes they are more or less conical and project ventrad noticeably. A few beetles have a small sclerite, the trochantin, located in the anterolateral portion of the coxal cavity (Figure 28–9B, *tn*).

Many beetles when disturbed draw their appendages in close to the body and "play dead." Such beetles often have grooves in the body or in certain leg segments into which the appendages fit when so retracted. Beetles with retractile legs usually have grooves in the coxae (particularly the middle or hind coxae) into which the femora fit when the legs are retracted, and they may have grooves in other leg segments.

The number and relative size and shape of the tarsal segments are very important characters for the identification of beetles. It is necessary to examine the tarsi of almost any beetle one wishes to run through the key. The number of tarsal segments in most beetles varies from three to five. It is usually the same on all tarsi, but some groups have one less segment in the hind tarsi than in the middle and front tarsi, and others have fewer segments in the front tarsi. The tarsal formula is an important part of any group description and is given as 5–5–5, 5–5–4, 4–4–4, 3–3–3, and so on, indicating the num-

ber of tarsal segments on the front, middle, and hind tarsi, respectively. Most Coleóptera have a 5–5–5 tarsal formula.

In a few groups, including some very common beetles, the next to the last tarsal segment is very small and inconspicuous. In such cases this segment may be very difficult to see unless very carefully examined under high magnification. These tarsi thus appear to have one segment less than they actually have and are so described in the key. For example, a five-segmented tarsus like the one shown in Figure 28–10A is described in the key as "apparently 4-segmented."

A few groups have the basal tarsal segment very small (Figure 28–10D) and visible only if the tarsus is properly oriented.

If the tarsi of a beetle appear to be four-segmented and the third segment is relatively large and more or less U-shaped (Figure 28–10A), they are generally five-segmented, with the fourth segment very small. If the tarsi appear to be four-segmented and the third segment is slender and not greatly different from the terminal segment, then they either are actually four-segmented or are five-segmented with the basal segment very small.

The tarsal claws of beetles are subject to some variation. In most cases they are simple, that is,

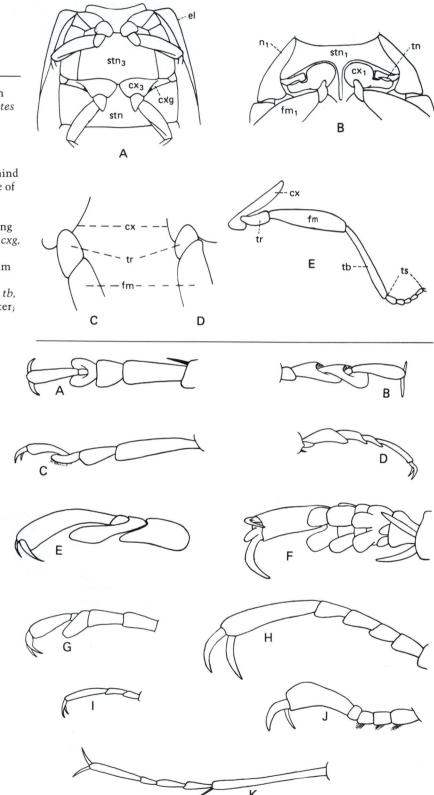

Figure 28–9. Leg structure in Coleóptera. **A,** thorax of *Derméstes* (Derméstidae), ventral view, showing grooved hind coxae; **B,** prothorax of *Psephènus* (Psephènidae), ventral view, showing trochantin; **C,** base of hind leg of *Àpion* (Apiónidae); **D,** base of hind leg of *Conotràchelus* (Curculiónidae); **E,** hind leg of *Trichodésma* (Anobìidae), showing interstitial trochanter. *cx,* coxa; *cxg,* groove in coxa; *el,* elytron; *fm,* femur; *n₁,* pronotum; *stn,* sternum of first abdominal segment; *stn₁,* prosternum; *stn₃,* metasternum; *tb,* tibia; *tn,* trochantin; *tr,* trochanter; *ts,* tarsus.

Figure 28–10. Tarsi of Coleóptera. **A,** *Megacyllène,* (Cerambýcidae); **B,** *Necròbia* (Cléridae); **C,** *Nacérda* (Oedeméridae), hind leg; **D,** *Trichòdes* (Cléridae); **E,** *Chilócorus* (Coccinéllidae); **F,** *Sándalus* (Rhipicéridae); **G,** *Scólytus* (Scolýtidae); **H,** *Psephènus* (Psephènidae); **I,** a lathridiid, **J,** *Párandra* (Cerambýcidae); **K,** *Plátypus* (Platypódidae).

without branches or teeth, but in some cases they are toothed, pectinate, or cleft (Figure 28–11).

The Elytra

The elytra normally meet in a straight line down the middle of the body. This line of union of the elytra is called the suture. The suture may extend to the tips of the elytra, or the tips may be slightly separated. The anterolateral angles of the elytra are called the humeri. The elytra usually slope gradually from the suture to the outer edge. When they are abruptly bent down laterally, the bent-down portion is called the epipleura (plural, *epipleurae*).

The elytra vary principally in shape, length, and texture. They are usually parallel-sided anteriorly and tapering posteriorly. Sometimes they are more or less oval or hemispherical. The elytra of some beetles are truncate at the apex. The elytra in some groups are variously sculptured, with ridges, grooves or striae, punctures, tubercles, and the like. In other cases they are quite smooth. If the elytra appear hairy under low or medium magnification, they are said to be pubescent. The elytra of some beetles are quite hard and stiff and curve around the sides of the abdomen to some extent. In others they are soft and pliable and lie loosely on top of the abdomen without firmly embracing it.

The Abdomen

The structure of the first abdominal segment serves to separate the two principal suborders of the Coleóptera. In the Adéphaga the hind coxae extend backward and bisect the first abdominal sternum so that, instead of extending completely across the body, this sternum is divided and consists of two lateral pieces separated by the hind coxae (Figures 28–4 and 28–12A). In the Polýphaga the hind coxae extend backward a different distance in different groups, but the first abdominal sternum is never completely divided, and its posterior edge extends completely across the body.

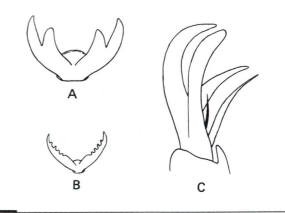

Figure 28–11. Tarsal claws of Coleóptera. **A,** toothed (coccinellid); **B,** pectinate (alleculid); **C,** cleft (meloid).

The number of visible abdominal sterna varies in different groups and is repeatedly used in the key. In a few cases (for example, the Bupréstidae) the first two visible sterna are more or less fused together, and the suture between them is much less distinct than the other abdominal sutures (Figure 28–8B). If the sutures between the abdominal sterna are all equally distinct, then no segments are said to be fused.

The last abdominal tergum is often called the pygidium and is sometimes exposed beyond the tips of the elytra.

Other Characters

Characters such as size, shape, or color should not prove particularly difficult. The term *base* is used to distinguish the two ends of body parts. When speaking of an appendage, the base is the end nearest the body. The base of the head or pronotum is the posterior end, and the base of the elytra or abdomen is the anterior end. The segments of the tarsi or antennae are numbered from the base distad.

Key to the Families of Coleóptera

The following key is rather long, not only because this is the largest order of insects, but also because there is quite a bit of variation in many families. The key is constructed to take this variation into account and also to provide for specimens whose characters are somewhat borderline. Many specimens will key out correctly from either alternative at certain points in the key. Groups marked with an asterisk are relatively rare or are not very likely to be taken by the general collector. This key is to adults. Keys to larvae are given by Peterson (1951) and Brues *et al.* (1954).

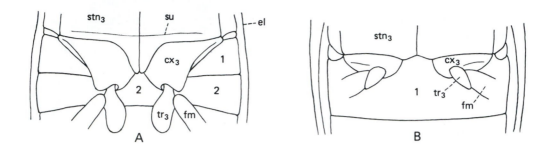

Figure 28–12. Base of abdomen, ventral view, showing difference between Adéphaga and Polýphaga. **A,** tiger beetle (Adéphaga); **B,** pleasing fungus beetle (Polýphaga). cx_3, hind coxa; el, elytron; fm, hind femur; stn_3, metasternum; su, transverse metasternal suture; tr_3, hind trochanter; *1, 2,* abdominal sterna.

1.	Form beetlelike, elytra present **2**	
1′.	Larviform, elytra and hind wings absent (females) **244***	
2(1).	Hind coxae expanded into large plates that conceal most of the abdomen (Figure 28–19B); antennae 11-segmented and filiform; small aquatic beetles, 5 mm in length or less ....**Halíplidae**	p. 410
2′.	Hind coxae not so expanded; other characters variable **3**	
3(2′).	First visible abdominal sternum divided by hind coxae, posterior margin of sternum not extending completely across abdomen; hind trochanters large and offset toward midline, femora almost touching coxae (Figure 28–12A); prothorax usually with notopleural sutures (Figure 28–4, *npls*); tarsi nearly always 5–5–5; antennae usually filiform (suborder Adéphaga) **4**	
3′.	First visible abdominal sternum not divided by hind coxae, posterior margin of sternum extending completely across abdomen, hind trochanters small (Figure 28–12B); prothorax usually without notopleural sutures; tarsi and antennae variable **11**	
4(3).	Aquatic beetles, hind legs fringed with hairs and more or less flattened, fitted for swimming; metasternum without transverse suture in front of hind coxae **5**	
4′.	Usually terrestrial beetles, hind legs not fringed or modified for swimming; metasternum usually with transverse suture just in front of hind coxae (Figure 28–4, *trs*) **8**	
5(4).	Two pairs of compound eyes, one dorsal and one ventral (Figure 28–13C); antennae very short, stout (Figure 28–5E); oval, blackish beetles (Figure 28–23), 3–15 mm in length ....**Gyrínidae**	p. 412
5′.	One pair of compound eyes; antennae long and slender **6**	
6(5′).	Scutellum exposed; length 1–40 mm ....**Dytíscidae**	p. 410
6′.	Scutellum not visible; size variable **7**	
7(6′).	Hind tarsi with 2 curved claws of equal length; abdomen with 5 visible sterna; front coxal cavities closed behind; length 1.2–5.5 mm ....**Notéridae***	p. 410
7′.	Hind tarsi with single straight claw; abdomen with 6 visible sterna; front coxal cavities open behind; length usually over 5 mm ....**Dytíscidae**	p. 410
8(4′).	Metasternum with transverse suture just in front of hind coxae (Figure 28–4, *trs*); antennae usually slender, most segments much longer than broad **9**	

8'.   Metasternum without transverse suture in front of hind coxae; antennae short
           and thick or moniliform **10**

9(8).   Antennae arising from front of head, above mandibles; clypeus produced
           laterally beyond bases of antennae; mandibles long, sickle-shaped, toothed;
           elytra usually without grooves or rows of punctures; head, including eyes,
           usually as wide as or wider than pronotum (Figure 28–17); mostly 10–24 mm
           in length ....**Cicindèlidae**   p. 408

9'.   Antennae arising more laterally, on sides of head between eye and base of
           mandible; clypeus not produced laterally beyond bases of antennae;
           mandibles usually not as above; elytra often with longitudinal grooves or
           rows of punctures; head, including eyes, usually narrower than pronotum
           (Figure 28–18); length 4–35 mm ....**Carábidae**   p. 409

10(8').   Body slender and elongate, 5.5–7.5 mm in length (Figure 28–16); pronotum
           with at least 3 longitudinal grooves; terrestrial beetles, widely distributed
           ....**Rhysòdidae**   p. 408

10'.   Body oval and blackish, 11–16 mm in length; pronotum not as above; occurring
           in mountain streams in western United States ....**Amphizòidae***   p. 410

11(3').   Prothorax with notopleural sutures (as in Figure 28–4) **12***

11'.   Prothorax without notopleural sutures **14**

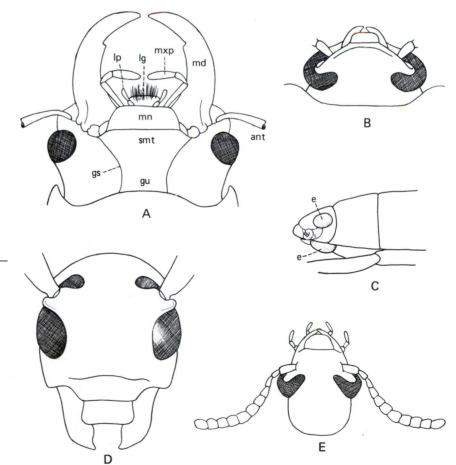

Figure 28–13.   Heads of
Coleóptera. **A,** *Pseudolucànus*
(Lucànidae), ventral view; **B,**
Diapèris (Tenebriónidae),
dorsal view; **C,** *Dineùtus*
(Gyrìnidae), lateral view; **D,**
Sapérda (Cerambýcidae),
anterior view; **E,** *Brùchus*
(Brùchidae), dorsal view. *ant,*
base of antenna; *e,* compound
eye; *gs,* gular suture; *gu,* gula;
lg, ligula; *lp,* labial palp; *md,*
mandible; *mn,* mentum; *mxp,*
maxillary palp; *smt,*
submentum.

12(11).   Tarsi 5–5–5; elongate, parallel-sided, covered with scales, 7–11 mm in length; elytra covering entire abdomen, with several longitudinal ridges between which are rows of large square punctures; antennae filiform; widely distributed ....**Cupédidae***   p. 407

12'.   Tarsi 3–3–3; oval in shape, 1.5 mm in length or less; elytra not as above, sometimes short; antennae usually clubbed; western United States **13***

13(12').   Abdomen with 3 visible sterna, the second short; antennae 11-segmented, with 3-segmented club; hind coxae large, contiguous; elytra completely covering abdomen; length 0.5–0.75 mm (see also 45) ....**Sphaeriidae***   p. 408

13'.   Abdomen with 6 or 7 visible sterna; antennae 9-segmented, with a 1-segmented club; hind coxae small, separated; elytra short, exposing about 3 abdominal segments; length about 1.5 mm ....**Hydroscáphidae***   p. 408

14(11').   Palps very short, generally rigid and not visible; prosternal sutures usually lacking; labrum nearly always lacking; head often prolonged into a beak or snout, with antennae arising far in front of eyes on snout (Figures 28–3, 28–89A, 28–91 through 28–97); tarsi 5–5–5, often appearing 4–4–4; antennae filiform or clubbed, often elbowed and clubbed **15**

14'.   Palps longer, flexible, and usually evident; prosternal sutures nearly always present (Figure 28–4, *stns*); head rarely prolonged into a beak (if it is, antennae arise near eyes and are not elbowed); labrum usually present; tarsi variable **17**

15(14).   Antennae filiform or moniliform; head prolonged into a beak extending straight forward (Figure 28–90G,H); body parallel-sided or nearly so (Figure 28–89A) ....**Bréntidae**   p. 461

15'.   Antennae clubbed, sometimes also elbowed; beak, if developed, usually more or less decurved; shape variable **16**

16(15').   Head prolonged into a distinct beak or snout (Figure 28–3); basal segment of antennae often received in grooves on snout; antennae often reaching base of pronotum or beyond; tarsi apparently 4–4–4; front tibiae usually without a series of teeth externally or prolonged distally into a stout spur; size and shape variable **235**

16'.   Head broad and short beyond eyes, not prolonged into a distinct snout; basal segment of antennae not received in grooves; antennae short, scarcely extending beyond anterior edge of pronotum; tarsi 5–5–5, sometimes appearing 4–4–4; front tibiae with a series of teeth externally or prolonged distally into a stout spur, antennae with a large compact club; length 9 mm or less **116**

17(14').   Elytra short, leaving one or more complete abdominal segments exposed **18**

17'.   Elytra covering tip of abdomen or leaving only a part of last abdominal segment exposed...**40**

18(17).   Tarsi with apparently 3 or fewer segments **19**

18'.   Tarsi with more than 3 segments **23**

19(18).   Elytra very short, leaving 3 or more abdominal segments exposed **20**

19'.   Elytra longer, leaving only 1 or 2 abdominal segments exposed **22**

20(19).   Antennae 2-segmented; tarsi 3–3–3, basal 2 segments very small; tarsi with 1 claw; head and pronotum much narrower than elytra; brownish yellow beetles, 2.5 mm in length or less, living in ant nests (Clavigerinae) ....**Pseláphidae***   p. 416

20′.	Not exactly fitting the above description **21**	
21(20′).	Abdomen with 5 or 6 visible sterna, usually more or less oval; antennae abruptly clubbed; length less than 6 mm ....**Peseláphidae**	p. 416
21′.	Abdomen with 6 or 7 visible sterna, usually parallel-sided; antennae moniliform or slightly clavate; size variable ....**Staphylìnidae***	p. 414
22(19′).	Last visible abdominal sternum very long; hind wings without fringe of hairs; body elongate, parallel-sided; antennae 10-segmented, with 2-segmented club; southern United States (*Smícrips*) ....**Nitidùlidae***	p. 438
22′.	Last visible abdominal sternum not unusually long; hind wings with fringe of hairs or absent; body more or less oval; antennae 9- to 11-segmented, with a 2- to 3-segmented club **47**	
23(18′).	Antennae elbowed and clubbed (Figure 28–5I); tarsi 5–5–5 (rarely 5–5–4); shiny, hard-bodied, usually black beetles, 0.5–10.0 mm in length (Figure 28–24A) ....**Histéridae**	p. 417
23′.	Antennae not elbowed **24**	
24(23′).	Tarsi 5–5–5, 5–4–4, or 4–4–4 ....**25**	
24′.	Tarsi 5–5–4 ....**152**	
25(24).	Tarsi apparently 4–4–4 ....**26**	
25′.	Tarsi 5–5–5 or 5–4–4 ....**29**	
26(25).	Third tarsal segment very small, concealed in notch of second; hind wings with fringe of hairs; abdomen with 6 visible sterna, first very long; oval convex beetles, 5 mm in length or less ....**Corylóphidae**	p. 441
26′.	Third tarsal segment not as above; hind wings without fringe of hairs **27**	
27(26′).	Antennae filiform, moniliform, serrate, or slightly clavate **28**	
27′.	Antennae with abrupt club **35**	
28(27).	Head somewhat prolonged into broad quadrate muzzle; antennae usually filiform or serrate; elytra pubescent; brownish or yellowish, more or less oval beetles, with only tip of abdomen exposed (Figure 28–80), generally less than 5 mm in length ....**Brùchidae**	p. 454
28′.	Head not as above; antennae filiform to slightly clavate; elytra pubescent or bare; size, shape, color, and length of elytra variable **184**	
29(25′).	Maxillary palps very long, nearly as long as antennae, last segment very long and straplike; antennae filiform; elytra short, exposing more than half of abdomen; hind wings not folded, extending beyond elytra; slender brownish beetles, 4–6 mm in length; Arizona and California ....**Telegeùsidae***	p. 432
29′.	Not exactly fitting the above description **30**	
30(29′).	Small, oval, somewhat flattened, louselike insects, 2–4 mm in length; found in nests of small mammals or ground-nesting bees, or on beavers; abdomen with 6 visible sterna; eyes reduced or lacking ....**Leptìnidae***	p. 414
30′.	Not exactly fitting the above description **31**	
31(30′).	Body very flat, dorsal and ventral surfaces flat and parallel; pronotum somewhat triangular, much narrowed basally; front coxae rounded; generally less than 6 mm in length (*Inopéplus*) ....**Salpíngidae***	p. 449
31′.	Body not unusually flattened, or pronotum not as above **32**	
32(31′).	Antennae lamellate (Figure 28–6,A,C,D) or with abrupt club **33**	
32′.	Antennae filiform, moniliform, serrate, pectinate, or slightly clavate **36**	

33(32). Antennae lamellate, terminal segments expanded on one side to form lopsided club; usually over 10 mm in length **34**

33'. Antennae not lamellate, club symmetrical **35**

34(33). The terminal antennal segments expanded laterally into rounded lobes not capable of being united to form a compact club (Figure 28–6A); elytra usually black or orange and black; length 15–35 mm (*Nicróphorus*; Figure 28–26B)..**Sílphidae** p. 414

34'. The 3 or 4 terminal antennal segments expanded laterally into oval or elongate lobes capable of being united into a compact club (Figure 28–6C,D); color and size variable ....**Scarabaèidae** p. 419

35(27',33'). Antennae 10-segmented with 1- or 2-segmented club; first and fifth visible abdominal sterna longer than others; third tarsal segment short, fourth as long as or longer than first three combined; length 3 mm or less **80**

35'. Antennae 11-segmented, with 3-segmented club; abdominal sterna not as above; length variable, but usually over 3 mm ....**Nitidùlidae** p. 438

36(32'). Small, elongate, dark-colored beetles, 1.7–2.2 mm in length, with yellow legs and antennae; first 2 antennal segments large, antennae filiform or moniliform, scarcely extending beyond head; head wider than pronotum; pronotum narrowed posteriorly; 3 or 4 abdominal segments exposed beyond elytra ....**Micromálthidae*** p. 407

36'. Not exactly fitting the above description **37**

37(36'). Abdomen with 7 or 8 visible sterna **38**

37'. Abdomen with 5 or 6 visible sterna **39**

38(37). Antennae moniliform or clavate, rarely filiform; at least 4 abdominal segments exposed beyond elytra; pronotum usually margined laterally; length 1–20 mm ....**Staphylìnidae** p. 414

38'. Antennae filiform, serrate, or pectinate; other characters variable **193**

39(37'). Elytra bare, shining, truncate, exposing 1 or 2 abdominal segments; antennae clavate; last abdominal segment sharply pointed (Figure 28–28); length 2–7 mm (Scaphidiìnae) ....**Staphylìnidae** p. 414

39'. Elytra pubescent, their length variable; antennae clavate or filiform; last abdominal segment not sharply pointed; length 5–20 mm **232**

40(17'). Terminal segments of antennae enlarged, forming club of various sorts (Figures 28–5C,F–I, 28–6) **41**

40'. Antennae not clubbed, but filiform, moniliform, serrate, pectinate, or gradually and only very slightly enlarged distally **151**

41(40). Maxillary palps long, slender, usually as long as antennae or longer (Figure 28–29) **42**

41'. Maxillary palps much shorter than antennae **43**

42(41). Abdomen with 5 visible sterna; antennae with last 3 segments pubescent; length 1–40 mm ....**Hydrophílidae** p. 417

42'. Abdomen with 6 or 7 visible sterna; antennae with last 5 segments pubescent; length 2 mm or less ....**Hydraènidae*** p. 412

43(41'). All tarsi with apparently 4 or fewer segments **44**

43'. Tarsi 5–5–5, 5–5–4, or 5–4–4 ....**104**

44(43). Tarsi apparently 3–3–3, 2–3–3, or 2–2–3 ....**45**

44'.   Some or all tarsi apparently 4-segmented; second tarsal segment dilated and spongy pubescent beneath, third slender and much shorter than fourth (see also 44") **51**

44".   Some or all tarsi apparently 4-segmented, but second and third segments not as in 44'. **55**

45(44). Body oval, convex, shining, blackish, 0.5–0.75 mm in length; abdomen short, appearing 3-segmented; first segment a triangular piece between hind coxae, second a narrow transverse band, third occupying most of abdomen; antennae short, not extending beyond middle of pronotum, 11-segmented; western United States ....**Sphaeriidae***   p. 408

45'.   Not exactly fitting the above description **46**

46(45'). Hind wings fringed with hairs that often project beyond elytra; length usually less than 2 mm **47**

46'.   Hind wings not fringed with hairs; length usually over 2 mm **49**

47(22',46). Minute (mostly less than 1 mm in length) convex beetles, shaped a little like a horseshoe crab, with abdomen tapering posteriorly; compound eyes, hind wings absent; tarsi 2-segmented, or 3-segmented with first segment minute and concealed in apex of tibia; antennae short, retractile into grooves on underside of head, with 2-segmented club; prosternal process broad and long, extending backward under mesosternum; abdomen with 5–7 visible sterna; living in ant nests (Limulodinae) ....**Ptiliidae***   p. 412

47'.   Not exactly fitting the above description **48**

48(47'). Antennae 11-segmented, with whorls of long hairs, 2 basal segments not enlarged; first visible abdominal sternum not unusually long; fringe on hind wings long; length 1 mm or less ....**Ptiliidae**   p. 412

48'.   Antennae 9- to 11-segmented, without whorls of long hairs, 2 basal segments enlarged; first abdominal segment very long; fringe on hind wings short; length usually over 1 mm ....**Corylóphidae**   p. 441

49(46'). Pronotum margined laterally, its base as wide as base of elytra; head much narrower than pronotum, usually not visible from above; antennal club 3- to 5-segmented; oval, convex, shiny beetles, usually capable of tucking head and prothorax under body and rolling into a ball (Figure 28–24B) ....**Leiódidae***   p. 413

49'.   Not exactly fitting the above description **50**

50(49'). Second tarsal segment dilated; tarsi actually 4-segmented, but third segment minute, fused to base of fourth, and difficult to see (Figure 28–10E); oval, convex beetles, often brightly colored.....................................**51**

50'.   Second tarsal segment not dilated; color and shape variable **52**

51(44',50). Tarsal claws toothed at base (Figure 28–11A); antennae short, antennae and head often hidden from above; anterior margin of pronotum straight or nearly so, not extended forward at sides; first visible abdominal sternum with curved coxal lines ....**Coccinéllidae**   p. 441

51'.   Tarsal claws simple; head and antennae easily visible from above; anterior margin of pronotum broadly excavated, produced forward at sides; first visible abdominal sternum without curved coxal lines ....**Endomýchidae**   p. 442

52(50'). Elytra covering entire abdomen **53**

52'.   Elytra truncate, exposing last abdominal segment **80**

53(52). First visible abdominal sternum long, often as long as next 3 sterna combined; first 3 abdominal sterna more or less fused together, front coxae globular, widely separated; elytra shiny, with sparse pubescence; length usually more than 3 mm ....**Colydiidae**   p. 444

53'. First visible abdominal sternum not unusually long, all sterna freely movable; front coxae somewhat conical, contiguous or separated; elytra usually pubescent; length 3 mm or less (see also 53") **54**

53". First visible abdominal sternum not unusually long, all the sterna more or less fused and immovable; front coxae globular, usually slightly separated; elytra shiny or pubescent; length 0.5–11.0 mm ....**Anthríbidae**   p. 461

54(53'). Front coxal cavities open; front coxae contiguous ....**Dasycéridae***   p. 414

54'. Front coxal cavities closed, or if open, then front coxae are separated ....**Lathridiidae**   p. 443

55(44"). First tarsal segment broad, flat, oval, with dense pad of short hairs beneath, second and third segments minute, second arising from upper surface of first near its base, fourth large, long; head and pronotum of about equal width, parallel-sided; elytra parallel-sided, about one-third wider than pronotum; reddish yellow or tawny, with black antennae and scutellum, and with 5 elongate black marks on each elytron; 2 mm in length; Florida (*Monoèdus*) ....**Colydiidae***   p. 444

55'. Not exactly fitting the above description **56**

56(55'). Tibiae dilated, very spiny; body broad and flat, mandibles and labrum projecting forward prominently; first and fourth tarsal segments much longer than second and third; last 7 antennal segments forming short serrate club; semiaquatic, mud-inhabiting beetles; 4.0–6.5 mm in length (Figure 28–47A) ....**Heterocéridae**   p. 428

56'. Not exactly fitting the above description **57**

57(56'). Stout, cylindrical or slightly oval beetles, 1–9 (usually 5 or less) mm in length (Figure 28–99); antennae short, elbowed, scarcely reaching beyond front of pronotum, with large solid club (Figure 28–5H); front tibiae with series of teeth externally, or produced distally into stout spur; eyes oval, emarginate, or divided ....**Scolýtidae**   p. 474

57'. Not exactly fitting the above description **58**

58(57'). Front tarsi with a different number of segments from middle and hind tarsi   **59**

58'. All tarsi apparently 4–4–4 ....**60**

59(58). Tarsi 3–4–4; elytra pubescent; elongate-oval, somewhat flattened beetles, 1.5–6.0 mm in length, often brightly patterned (males) (Figure 28–65A) ....**Mycetophágidae**   p. 443

59'. Tarsi 4–3–3; elytra bare; oval, convex, brownish or black beetles (see also couplet 49) (males of *Aglyptìnus*) ....**Leiòdidae***   p. 413

60(58'). Elytra bare or with a few scattered hairs **61**

60'. Elytra pubescent **85**

61(60). Third tarsal segment more or less lobed beneath **62**

61'. Third tarsal segment slender or small, not lobed beneath **66**

62(61). Body elongate and usually very flat, length 4 mm or less (Silvanìnae) ....**Cucùjidae**   p. 439

62'. Body not unusually flattened; size and shape variable **63**

63(62').	Elongate, somewhat cylindrical beetles, 5.5–12.0 mm in length, usually with pronotum yellow or red and elytra black (Figure 28–62D) ....**Languriidae**	p. 440
63'.	Body shape and color variable, usually not as above **64**	
64(63').	Antennal club usually not very abrupt, segments gradually enlarging distally, club usually consisting of more than 3 segments **65**	
64'.	Antennal club abrupt, 3-segmented (Figure 28–5F); oval, convex beetles, less than 5 mm in length **74**	
65(64).	Oval, convex, dark-colored beetles, 5–10 mm in length with head deflexed and not visible from above (Figure 28–41); front coxae transverse ......**Býrrhidae**	p. 426
65'.	Size, shape, and color variable, but if oval and convex, then front coxae not transverse ....**Chrysomélidae**	p. 455
66(61').	Body extremely flattened, elongate, more or less parallel-sided; front coxae rounded; length 2–12 mm ....**Cucùjidae**	p. 439
66'.	Body not unusually flattened; front coxae transverse; size variable **67**	
67(66').	A pair of ocelli present near compound eyes (Figure 28–14C); elytra with rows of large square punctures; brownish beetles, 3–6 mm in length (*Laricòbius*) ....**Derodóntidae***	p. 433
67'.	Ocelli absent; elytra, color, size variable **68**	
68(67').	Head scarcely or not at all visible from above; body shape variable **69**	
68'.	Head easily visible from above; body usually elongate **77**	

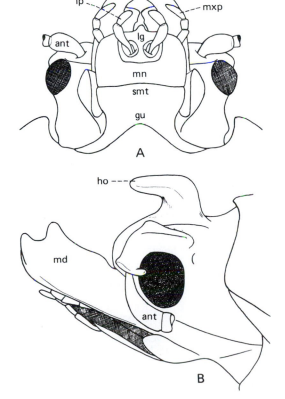

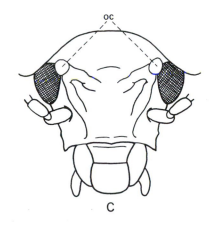

Figure 28–14. Heads of Coleóptera. **A,** ventral view, and **B,** lateral view, of *Odontotaènius disjúnctus* (Illiger) (Passálidae); **C,** *Derodóntus* (Derodóntidae). *ant,* base of antenna; *gu,* gula; *ho,* horn; *lg,* ligula; *lp,* labial palp; *md,* mandible; *mn,* mentum; *mxp,* maxillary palp; *oc,* ocelli, *smt,* submentum.

69(68).   Elongate, cylindrical, dark-colored beetles, usually less than 12 mm in length (one western species is about 50 mm in length); pronotum tuberculate, sometimes with blunt hornlike processes; elytra usually with ridges or punctures (Figure 28–54); tarsi actually 5–5–5, but fourth segment very small and difficult to see ....**Bostríchidae**   p. 435

69'.   Oval, convex beetles, not as above; usually less than 3 mm in length **70**

70(69').   Antennal club relatively abrupt, 3-segmented **71**

70'.   Antennae more gradually enlarged distally, club with more than 3 segments **76**

71(70).   Abdomen with 6 visible sterna, first very long; basal 2 antennal segments enlarged ....**Corylóphidae**   p. 441

71'.   Abdomen with 5 (rarely 6) visible sterna, first not unusually long **72**

72(71').   Front coxae flattened, nearly contiguous; length 3 mm or less ....**Georýssidae***   p. 417

72'.   Front coxae conical, or if small and flat, then separated **73**

73(72').   Front coxae conical, prominent; beetles often capable of tucking the head and prothorax under body and rolling into a ball ....**Leiòdidae***   p. 413

73'.   Front coxae round, flat, or transverse; beetles not capable of rolling into a ball **74**

74(64',73'). Front coxae transverse; hind coxae separated; oval convex beetles less than 2 mm in length (*Cybocéphalus*) ....**Nitidùlidae***   p. 438

74'.   Front coxae oval or rounded; hind coxae usually contiguous or nearly so; length 5 mm or less **75**

75(74').   Abdomen with 5 visible sterna; head visible from above; pygidium exposed ....**Anthríbidae**   p. 461

75'.   Abdomen with 5 visible sterna; head visible from above; pygidium concealed (see also 75") ....**Phalácridae**   p. 441

75".   Abdomen with 6 visible sterna; head usually not visible from above; pygidium variable ....**Corylóphidae**   p. 441

76(70').   Front coxae conical and prominent; beetles often capable of tucking head and prothorax under the body and rolling into a ball ....**Leiòdidae***   p. 413

76'.   Front coxae transverse and separated ....**Býrrhidae**   p. 426

77(68').   Abdomen with 6 visible sterna, first very long; basal 2 antennal segments enlarged ....**Corylóphidae**   p. 441

77'.   Abdomen with 5 visible sterna **78**

78(77').   Antennae 10-segmented with 1- or 2-segmented club; slender beetles **79**

78'.   Antennae 8- to 11-segmented, club at least 3-segmented **81**

79(78).   Head and eyes prominent; length 6 mm or less **80**

79'.   Head small, partly retracted into prothorax, eyes usually more or less concealed; length 1–18 mm ....**Colydìidae**   p. 444

80(35, 52',79). Front coxae rounded or transverse ....**Rhizophágidae**   p. 439

80'.   Front coxae conical, prominent (*Phyllobaènus, Isohydnócera*) ....**Cléridae**   p. 437

81(78').   Pronotum with distinct lateral margins; eyes oval, not abruptly convex from sides of head; size variable; widely distributed............................**82**

81'.   Pronotum without distinct lateral margins; eyes round, abruptly convex from sides of head; length 7–28 mm; mostly western United States (Psoìnae) (see also 129) ....**Bostríchidae**   p. 435

82(81).	Front coxae transverse **83**	
82'.	Front coxae rounded **84**	
83(82).	Pronotum rather widely separated from elytra except at attachment point in center (Figure 28–58); tarsi actually 5-segmented, but first segment very short and difficult to see ....**Trogossítidae**	p. 437
83'.	Pronotum contiguous with base of elytra completely across body; tarsi actually 4-segmented; oval, convex beetles; less than 2 mm in length (*Cybocéphalus*) ....**Nitidùlidae***	p. 438
84(82').	Tarsi actually 5-segmented, but fourth segment small and difficult to see; anterior margin of pronotum not produced forward at sides ....**Erotýlidae**	p. 440
84'.	Tarsi actually 4-segmented; anterior margin of pronotum produced forward at sides (Mycetaeìnae) (see also 84")..............................**Endomýchidae**	p. 442
84".	Tarsi actually 4-segmented; anterior margin of pronotum only slightly concave (see also 53 and 79') ....**Colydìidae**	p. 444
85(60').	Third tarsal segment more or less lobed beneath **86**	
85'.	Third tarsal segment slender or small, not lobed beneath **94**	
86(85).	Antennal club distinct, of 3 or fewer segments **87**	
86'.	Antennal club less distinct, composed of more than 3 segments **91**	
87(86).	Head produced anteriorly into broad muzzle; base of pronotum as wide as base of elytra; gular sutures present or absent **88**	
87'.	Head not produced anteriorly into broad muzzle; width of pronotum variable; gular sutures present **89**	
88(87).	Pronotum posteriorly with keellike lateral margins and usually a transverse ridge; gular sutures absent; labrum separated from face by suture; tibiae without apical spurs; length 0.5–11.0 mm ....**Anthríbidae**	p. 461
88'.	Pronotum rounded laterally; gular sutures present; labrum not separated from face by suture; tibia with 2 small movable apical spurs; length 3–5 mm (Cimberìnae) ....**Nemonýchidae**	p. 462
89(87').	Lateral margins of pronotum toothed (Figure 28–62B); length less than 3 mm (*Oryzaéphilus*) ....**Cucùjidae**	p. 439
89'.	Lateral margins of pronotum not toothed; length usually over 3 mm **90**	
90(89').	Base of pronotum as wide as and contiguous with base of elytra; front coxae more or less transverse; tarsi 5–5–5, fourth segment small, second and third lobed beneath; usually uniformly colored beetles, generally less than 5 mm in length (Figure 28–65B) ....**Bytùridae**	p. 443
90'.	Base of pronotum usually narrower than, and slightly separated from, base of elytra; front coxae somewhat conical, rarely transverse; tarsi 5–5–5, first or fourth segment small, segments 1–3 or 1–4 lobed beneath; often brightly patterned; 3–24 mm in length (Figure 28–59) ....**Cléridae**	p. 437
91(86').	Head produced anteriorly into a rather broad muzzle; pygidium exposed; first tarsal segment very long; usually grayish or brownish oval beetles **Brùchidae**	p. 454
91'.	Head not as above; pygidium covered or exposed, but if exposed, then body elongate, nearly parallel-sided **92**	
92(91').	Oval, convex, usually dark-colored beetles, with head deflexed and scarcely or not at all visible from above (Figure 28–41); front coxae transverse **Býrrhidae**	p. 426
92'.	Body elongate, nearly parallel-sided; head not deflexed, usually conspicuous from above; front coxae usually conical, rarely transverse.................**93**	

93(92'). Sides of pronotum serrate (Figure 28–62B); length less than 3 mm
(*Oryzaéphilus*) ....**Cucùjidae**   p. 439

93'.   Sides of pronotum not serrate (Figure 28–59); length 5 mm or more ...**Cléridae**   p. 437

94(85'). Oval, convex beetles, 2 mm in length or less, often capable of deflecting the
head and prothorax and rolling into a ball; hind coxae dilated into broad
plates that conceal hind legs in repose; antennae with 10 or fewer segments,
club 2-segmented; hind wings fringed with long hairs ....**Clámbidae***   p. 417

94'.   Not exactly fitting the above description **95**

95(94'). First 3 or 4 visible abdominal sterna more or less fused together **96**

95'.   All abdominal sterna freely movable **98**

96(95).   Apical segment of maxillary palps needlelike, much more slender than preceding segments (*Cérylon, Philothérmus*) ....**Cerylónidae**   p. 441

96'.   Apical segment of maxillary palps not needlelike, its diameter as great as or
greater than that of preceding segments **97**

97(96'). Antennae 10-segmented, with solid 2-segmented club, usually received in cavities beneath front corners of thorax; front coxae enclosed behind by mesosternum; oval beetles; 1.5 mm in length or less ....**Cerylónidae**   p. 441

97'.   Antennae usually 11-segmented, club 2- or 3-segmented; front coxae usually
distant from mesosternum; body generally elongate and cylindrical, but if
oval, then usually over 1.5 mm in length and with front corners of pronotum
produced forward (see also 53) ....**Colydìidae**   p. 444

98(95'). Head scarcely or not at all visible from above **99**

98'.   Head easily visible from above **102**

99(98).   Antennal club compact, 3- or 4-segmented; elongate-cylindrical beetles **100**

99'.   Antennal club not very compact, usually of 5 or more segments; oval, convex
beetles **101**

100(99). Length 3 mm or less; tarsi actually 4–4–4, with basal 3 tarsal segments short,
fourth long; front coxae separated ....**Cìidae**   p. 443

100'.   Length usually over 3 mm; tarsi actually 5–5–5, basal tarsal segment longer
than others; front coxae contiguous ....**Bostríchidae**   p. 435

101(99'). Length 5–10 mm; eighth antennal segment about same size as seventh or
ninth; front coxae transverse ....**Býrrhidae**   p. 426

101'.   Length 2–5 mm; eighth antennal segment smaller than seventh or ninth; front
coxae large, prominent, conical or quadrate ....**Leiòdidae***   p. 413

102(98'). Elongate, cylindrical, uniformly colored beetles (Figure 28–56B); antennae
with an abrupt 2-segmented (rarely 3-segmented) club; head slightly constricted behind eyes, about as wide as pronotum ....**Lýctidae**   p. 435

102'.   Elongate-oval, often patterned beetles; antennal club less abrupt, composed
of 3–5 segments; head not constricted behind eyes, narrower than
pronotum **103**

103(102'). Pronotum truncate anteriorly (Figure 28–65A); tibiae with apical
spurs ....**Mycetophágidae**   p. 443

103'.   Pronotum excavated anteriorly, sides produced forward (Figure 28–63C); tibiae
without apical spurs (Mycetaeìnae) ....**Endomýchidae**   p. 442

104(43'). Hind tarsi 3- or 4-segmented **105**

104'.   All tarsi 5-segmented **106**

105(104). Oval, convex, shiny beetles, 1–6 mm in length; antennae with 3- to 5-segmented club; 6 (rarely 5) visible abdominal sterna; pronotum margined laterally, as broad at base as base of elytra; tarsi 5–5–4; beetles often capable of tucking head and prothorax under body and rolling into a ball .....**Leiòdidae*** — p. 413

105'. Not exactly fitting the above description **152**

106(104'). Antennae distinctly lamellate (Figure 28–6C–G) or flabellate (Figure 28–6B), terminal segments expanded on one side to form a lopsided club (slightly asymmetrical in some Trogossítidae) **107**

106'. Antennae not lamellate or flabellate, club usually symmetrical **113**

107(106). First tarsal segment very small and difficult to see; pronotum rather widely separated from base of elytra except at attachment point in center (Figure 28–58); length 5–20 mm ....**Trogossítidae** — p. 437

107'. First tarsal segment of normal size **108**

108(107'). Antennae flabellate, terminal 5 or more segments expanded laterally into long, thin, parallel-sided tonguelike lobes (as in Figure 28–6B) **109**

108'. Antennae lamellate, terminal 3 or 4 segments expanded laterally into oval or elongate lobes capable of being united into compact ball (Figure 28–6C,D,G) (see also 108") ....**Scarabaèidae** — p. 419

108". Antennae with terminal (or intermediate) segments expanded laterally into rounded or flattened lobes that are not capable of being united into compact ball (Figure 28–6E,F) **111**

109(108). Front tibiae dilated, flattened, coarsely scalloped or toothed along outer edge; ventral surface of body clothed with long hair; stout-bodied, striped (*Polyphýlla*) or unicolorous (*Pleócoma*) beetles, 17–43 mm in length; western United States ....**Scarabaèidae** — p. 419

109'. Not exactly fitting the above description **110**

110(109'). Tarsi with hairy projection between claws, basal 4 segments with lobes beneath (Figure 28–10F); mandibles large and projecting forward; antennae not received in grooves on front; 16–24 mm in length (Figure 28–31) ....**Rhipicéridae** — p. 418

110'. Tarsi not as above; mandibles small and inconspicuous; antennae often received in transverse grooves on front; usually less than 16 mm in length ....**Eucnèmidae** — p. 431

111(108"). Last tarsal segment long, nearly as long as preceding segments combined, with long claws (as in Figure 28–10H); most antennal segments broader than long; length 6 mm or less; generally aquatic beetles ....**Dryópidae** — p. 429

111'. Last tarsal segment and claws not so lengthened; antennae lamellate; length over 7 mm **112**

112(111'). Mentum deeply emarginate (Figure 28–14A); head with short, dorsal, anteriorly directed horn (Figure 28–14B); first antennal segment not greatly lengthened (Figure 28–6F); pronotum with deep median groove and elytra with longitudinal grooves; shining black beetles; 30–40 mm in length (Figure 28–32C) ....**Passálidae** — p. 418

112'. Mentum entire (Figure 28–13A); head without such a horn (except in *Sinodéndron*); first antennal segment greatly lengthened (Figure 28–6E); pronotum without median groove; elytra often smooth; brown or black beetles; 8–40 mm in length ....**Lucànidae** — p. 418

113(106'). A pair of ocelli present near compound eyes (Figure 28–14C); elytra with rows of punctures (*Derodóntus*) or polished dark spots (*Peltástica*); lateral margins of pronotum toothed (*Derodóntus*; Figure 28–52) or thin and entire (*Peltástica*); brownish beetles, 3–6 mm in length ....**Derodóntidae*** p. 433

113'. Ocelli absent; other characters variable **114**

114(113'). Dorsum with rows of short hair tufts (easily abraded), not particularly shiny; tibiae dilated, flat; basal 4 tarsal segments short, fifth about as long as others combined; black, oval, convex beetles; 4–6 mm in length; usually found in tree wounds ....**Nosodéndridae*** p. 433

114'. Not exactly fitting the above description **115**

115(114'). Antennae short, elbowed, scarcely reaching beyond anterior edge of pronotum, with large compact club; front tibiae with series of teeth externally, or prolonged distally into stout spur; more or less cylindrical beetles, 9 mm in length or less **116**

115'. Not exactly fitting the above description **117**

116(16', 115). Tarsi very slender, basal segment as long as next 3 combined (Figure 28–10K); head as broad as or broader than pronotum; eyes round, prominent; body slender and cylindrical; antennal club unsegmented (Figure 28–98) ....**Platypódidae** p. 474

116'. Basal tarsal segment not as long as next 3 combined (Figure 28–10G); head not broader than pronotum; eyes oval, emarginate, or divided, not prominent; body stouter, cylindrical to slightly oval; antennal club usually segmented or annulated (Figure 28–99) ....**Scolýtidae** p. 474

117(115'). Last tarsal segment very long, with long claws (as in Figure 28–10H); first 3 visible abdominal sterna usually more or less fused together; elongate or oval beetles, 1–8 mm in length, usually aquatic or shore-inhabiting **187**

117'. Tarsi and abdominal sterna not as above; mostly terrestrial beetles **118**

118(117'). Elytra distinctly pubescent **119**

118'. Elytra bare or with only a few scattered hairs **133**

119(118). Hind corners of pronotum prolonged backward into points that tightly embrace base of elytra; front coxae rounded or oval, separated; prosternum prolonged backward into median process that is received by mesosternum; oblong-oval; slightly flattened, black or brownish beetles, mostly 2–5 mm in length ....**Thróscidae** p. 431

119'. Not exactly fitting the above description **120**

120(119'). Head narrowed behind eyes into narrow neck; femora usually clavate; body antlike, brown or black, 1–5 (usually less than 3) mm in length (Figure 28–25B) ....**Scydmaénidae*** p. 414

120'. Head and body not as above; femora usually not clavate; size variable **121**

121(120'). Head scarcely or not at all visible from above **122**

121'. Head prominent, easily visible from above..................................**126**

122(121). Antennae clavate, club not abrupt; front coxae transverse, separated; hind coxae large, extending to lower edge of elytra; oval, convex, usually dark-colored beetles, 5–10 mm in length (Figure 28–41) ....**Býrrhidae** p. 426

122'. Antennae usually with distinct club of 3–5 segments; coxae variable **123**

123(122'). Front coxae conical and prominent **124**

123'. Front coxae small, usually rounded, not prominent **125**

124(123). Antennal club of about 5 segments, club not abrupt; tarsal segments subequal in length; oval, uniformly colored beetles, 3–5 mm in length .....**Leiódidae*** p. 413

124′.   Antennal club abrupt, 3-segmented; last tarsal segment longer than others; oval or elongate beetles, uniformly colored or patterned, 1–12 mm in length (Figure 28–53) ....**Derméstidae**   p. 433

125(123′).   Tibiae with apical spines or spurs; hind coxae not grooved for reception of femora; elytra often with apical spines or teeth; pronotum often tuberculate; length usually 3–10 mm (one western species reaches a length of about 50 mm) ....**Bostríchidae**   p. 435

125′.   Tibial spurs very small or lacking; hind coxae grooved for reception of femora; elytra without apical spines or teeth; pronotum not tuberculate; length 1–9 mm ....**Anobiidae**   p. 436

126(121′).   Front coxae conical, prominent **127**

126′.   Front coxae rounded, oval, or transverse, not prominent **128**

127(126).   Brownish, oval, uniformly colored beetles, 2–5 mm in length; base of pronotum as wide as base of elytra; found in nests of small mammals or ground-nesting bees or on mountain beavers ....**Leptinidae***   p. 414

127′.   Elongate or elongate-oval beetles, not particularly flattened, usually brightly colored, 3–24 mm in length (Figure 28–59); base of pronotum usually narrower than base of elytra; not found in situations listed above ....**Cléridae**   p. 437

128(126′).   Front coxae oval or globose; first visible abdominal segment longer than any other; elongate-oval, usually yellowish brown beetles, 1–5 mm in length, with silky pubescence ....**Cryptophágidae**   p. 440

128′.   Front coxae and size variable; first visible abdominal segment variable in length, but if somewhat lengthened, then not agreeing with the above description **129**

129(128′).   Antennae with 10 or fewer segments; first tarsal segment shorter than second; front coxae small, about as long as wide, front coxal cavities open behind; head including eyes wider than pronotum; length 7–28 mm; mostly western United States (Psoìnae) (see also 81′) ....**Bostríchidae**   p. 435

129′.   Antennae nearly always 11-segmented; other characters variable **130**

130(129′).   Front coxae nearly always transverse **131**

130′.   Front coxae globose or oval **132**

131(130).   Tarsi slender, segments not lobed, basal segment very short; body pubescence sparse; pronotum often separated from base of elytra except at attachment point in center (Figure 28–58) length 5–20 mm ....**Trogossítidae**   p. 437

131′.   Some tarsal segments dilated or lobed beneath, first segment not unusually short; body densely pubescent; pronotum contiguous with base of elytra; length less than 5 mm (Figure 28–65B) (see also 131″) ....**Bytùridae**   p. 443

131″.   The 3 basal tarsal segments dilated or lobed beneath, fourth smaller and without brush of hairs; body pubescence sparse; oval, somewhat flattened beetles (Figure 28–61C) ....**Nitidùlidae**   p. 438

132(130′).   Elongate-oval, somewhat flattened beetles; head narrower than pronotum; first visible abdominal sternum short, visible only in angle between hind coxae; Quebec (*Lendòmus*)..**Mycetophágidae***   p. 443

132′.   Elongate, parallel-sided, more or less cylindrical beetles; head nearly as wide as pronotum (Figure 28–56B); first visible abdominal sternum longer; widely distributed (see also 132″) ....**Lýctidae**   p. 435

132″.   Elongate, parallel-sided, flattened beetles, head nearly as wide as pronotum (Figure 28–62A,B); first visible abdominal sternum longer; widely distributed (Silvanìnae) ....**Cucùjidae**   p. 439

133(118').   Body oval, convex; head much narrower than pronotum **134**

133'.   Body elongate, or if oval, then more or less flattened; head width variable   **138**

134(133).   Front coxae conical, prominent; pronotum margined laterally; length 1–5 mm; usually capable of tucking head and prothorax under body and rolling into a ball ....**Leiòdidae***   p. 413

134'.   Front coxae globose or transverse, usually not prominent; pronotum and size variable **135**

135(134').   Maxillary palps long, nearly as long as antennae; antennae 8- or 9-segmented, with pubescent club; head visible from above; dung-inhabiting beetles, 1–7 mm in length (Sphaeridìnae) ....**Hydrophílidae**   p. 417

135'.   Maxillary palps much shorter than antennae; antennae 11–segmented **136**

136(135').   Length 5–10 mm; antennae clavate, club not abrupt; hind coxae large, extending to lower edge of elytra ....**Býrrhidae**   p. 426

136'.   Length 1–6 mm; antennal club abrupt, 3-segmented **137**

137(136').   Length 1–3 mm; basal 3 tarsal segments broad, fourth small; pygidium covered by elytra ....**Phalácridae**   p. 441

137'.   Length about 6 mm; tarsi slender; pygidium exposed ....**Sphaerítidae***   p. 417

138(133').   Head not visible from above; elongate, cylindrical, dark-colored beetles, usually less than 12 mm in length (one western species reaches a length of about 50 mm); pronotum tuberculate, sometimes with blunt hornlike processes ....**Bostríchidae**   p. 435

138'.   Head prominent, easily visible from above; size, shape, pronotum variable..**139**

139(138').   Body very flat, dorsal and ventral surfaces parallel; fourth tarsal segment usually small; elongate, generally parallel-sided, usually reddish or brownish beetles, 2–12 mm in length (Figure 28–62A) ....**Cucùjidae**   p. 439

139'.   Body not so flat, dorsal surface slightly convex; fourth tarsal segment generally not unusually small **140**

140(139').   Front coxae conical or quadrate, prominently projecting; 5–6 visible abdominal sternites; flattened, oval, usually blackish beetles (Figure 28–26), 3.0–16.0 mm in length **141**

140'.   Front coxae usually globose or transverse, not prominently projecting; 5 visible abdominal sternites; other characters variable **142**

141(140).   Antennae clavate, seventh segment nearly as wide as long; elytra usually with 9 striae each; abdomen with 6 visible sternites in male, 5 in female ....**Agýrtidae***   p. 413

141'.   Antennae only slightly clavate, seventh segment twice as long as wide or nearly so, *or* elytra with 3 or fewer striae each and antennae distinctly clavate or capitate; abdomen with 6 visible sternites in both sexes ....**Sílphidae**   p. 414

142(140').   Antennae with 10 or fewer segments and 3-segmented club; first tarsal segment much shorter than second; front coxal cavities open behind; length 7–28 mm; western United States (*Psòa*) ....**Bostríchidae**   p. 435

142'.   Antennae 11-segmented (if 10-segmented, then body length is less than 4 mm) **143**

143(142').   Front coxae transverse **144**

143'.   Front coxae globose **147**

144(143).   Antennae 10-segmented, with 2-segmented club; length 3 mm or less; southern United States (*Smícrips*) ....**Nitidùlidae***   p. 438

144'.   Antennae nearly always 11-segmented, club with at least 3 segments; usually over 3 mm in length **145**

145(144').   The 3 basal tarsal segments about same size and with a dense brush of hairs beneath, fourth segment smaller and without brush of hairs **146**

145'.   The 4 basal tarsal segments with long hairs below, the fourth segment as large as the third, and the first segment short (Trogossitinae) ....**Trogossítidae**   p. 437

146(145).   Oval or elongate, 1.5–12.0 mm in length; pronotum more or less quadrate, at most only slightly wider than head; elytra sometimes short and exposing tip of abdomen ....**Nitidúlidae**   p. 438

146'.   Oval or elongate-oval, 3–20 mm in length; pronotum more or less trapezoidal, narrower anteriorly, at base distinctly wider than head; elytra covering entire abdomen ....**Erotýlidae**   p. 440

147(143').   Body oval to elongate-oval; head distinctly narrower than pronotum; pronotum margined laterally; often marked with red, yellow, or orange; length 3–20 mm ....**Erotýlidae**   p. 440

147'.   Body elongate, parallel-sided; head about as wide as pronotum **148**

148(147').   Pygidium exposed; first visible abdominal sternum about as long as sterna 2–4 combined; length 4 mm or less (Figure 28–60B) ....**Rhizophágidae**   p. 439

148'.   Pygidium concealed; first visible abdominal sternum not as long as sterna 2–4 combined; length usually over 5 mm **149**

149(148').   Fourth tarsal segment very small, first of normal size; antennae with 4-segmented club; usually black beetles, with pronotum yellowish or reddish (Figure 28–62D), 5.5–12.0 mm in length ....**Langúriidae**   p. 440

149'.   First tarsal segment very small, fourth of normal size; antennae with 2-segmented (rarely 3-segmented) club; uniformly colored, black or brownish beetles, 2–20 mm in length **150**

150(149').   Blackish beetles, 10–20 mm in length; western United States (*Polýcaon*) ....**Bostríchidae**   p. 435

150'.   Usually brownish beetles, 2–7 mm in length; widely distributed ......**Lýctidae**   p. 435

151(40').   Tarsi 5–5–4 (rarely appearing 4–4–3) **152**

151'.   Tarsi apparently 3–3–3, 4–4–4, or 5–5–5 (4–5–5 in male *Cóllops*, family Melýridae) **177**

152(24', 105', 151.)   Front coxal cavities closed behind **153**

152'.   Front coxal cavities open behind **160**

153(152).   Tarsal claws pectinate (Figure 28–11B); elongate-oval, pubescent, usually black or brown beetles, 4–12 mm in length (Figure 28–68B) ....**Allecúlidae**   p. 446

153'.   Tarsal claws not pectinate; size and color variable **154**

154(153').   Last antennal segment lengthened, as long as preceding 3 or 4 segments combined, antennae filiform (Figure 28–66B); head and pronotum narrower than elytra; elongate, dark-colored, shiny beetles, 6–15 mm in length ...**Lagríidae**   p. 446

154'.   Last antennal segment not so lengthened, or antennae clubbed; size, shape and color variable **155**

155(154').   Five visible abdominal sterna, with suture separating the 2 basal segments poorly defined, so that these segments appear as one large segment; coxae widely separated; apical tarsal segment longer than the others combined;

eyes small, round, and protruding; blackish, shiny beetles, 2–4 mm in length; living in rock cracks below the high tidemark along the Pacific Coast (Aegialitinae) ....**Salpíngidae*** p. 449

155′. Not exactly fitting the above description **156**

156(155′). Antennae 11-segmented (rarely 10-segmented), arising beneath frontal ridge; antennae filiform, moniliform, or slightly clubbed, only rarely capitate or flabellate; eyes often emarginate; shape and color variable (Figure 28–69); length 2–35 mm; a large and widely distributed group ....**Tenebriónidae** p. 445

156′. Antennae 10- or 11-segmented, with distinct club, not arising beneath frontal ridge; eyes round **157***

157(156′). Antennae 11-segmented, moniliform or with 3-segmented club **158***

157′. Antennae 10-segmented, club of 1 or 2 segments; length less than 5 mm **159***

158(157). Antennae with 3-segmented club; often with mottled coloration; eyes large, prominent; body not particularly flattened; resembling tiger beetles (Othniinae) ....**Salpíngidae*** p. 449

158′. Antennae moniliform; straw-colored; eyes not particularly prominent; body very flat; resembling a cucujid (*Hemipéplus*) ....**Myctéridae*** p. 448

159(157′). Elongate slender beetles; elytra bare or nearly so; pygidium exposed (some males) ....**Rhizophágidae*** p. 439

159′. Oblong convex beetles; elytra pubescent, covering pygidium ....**Sphíndidae*** p. 438

160(152′). Oval, black, somewhat flattened beetles, 5–12 mm in length (Figure 28–68A); antennae with abrupt club of 2 or 3 segments, received in grooves on underside of prothorax; legs retractile ....**Monómmidae** p. 444

160′. Not exactly fitting the above description **161**

161(160′). Pronotum with sharp lateral margins **162**

161′. Pronotum with rounded lateral margins **165**

162(161). Body elongate, very flat, dorsal and ventral surfaces parallel ....**Cucùjidae** p. 439

162′. Body not so flattened **163**

163(162′). Body somewhat wedge-shaped, as high as or higher than wide, humpbacked, head bent down, abdomen pointed apically (Figure 28–67); length 14 mm or less, usually less than 8 mm ....**Mordéllidae** p. 443

163′. Not exactly fitting the above description **164**

164(163′). Antennae with distinct 3-segmented club; pronotum without depressions near posterior margin; first segment of hind tarsi not greatly lengthened; length 1–5 mm ....**Cryptophágidae** p. 440

164′. Antennae filiform or nearly so; pronotum with 2 depressions near posterior margin (Figure 28–66A); first segment of hind tarsi elongate, much longer than any other segment; length 3–20 mm ....**Melandrỳidae** p. 443

165(161′). Tarsal claws pectinate, with large pad beneath each claw; head elongate, somewhat diamond-shaped, gradually narrowing behind eyes to narrow neck; pronotum narrow anteriorly, about as wide as base of elytra posteriorly, somewhat bell-shaped, yellowish to brownish beetles, 3–20 mm in length ....**Cephalòidae*** p. 446

165′. Not exactly fitting the above description **166**

166(165′). Pronotum with 2 dents or depressions near posterior margin (Figure 28–66A), at base about as wide as base of elytra; first segment of hind tarsi much longer than any other segment **167**

166'.   Pronotum without such dents or depressions; other characters variable **168**

167(166). Front of head distinctly prolonged anterior to eyes (somewhat as in Figure 28–90G); bases of antennae distant from eyes; eyes round (Mycterìnae) ....**Myctéridae**   p. 448

167'.   Front of head only slightly projecting anterior to eyes; bases of antennae very close to eyes; eyes elongate-oval ....**Melandrỳidae**   p. 443

168(166'). Penultimate segment of all tarsi dilated, densely hairy beneath; middle coxae conical, prominent, contiguous; pronotum widest in anterior half, at base narrower than elytra; tarsal claws usually simple, rarely with basal tooth; abdomen with 5 visible sterna; elongate, soft-bodied beetles, 3.5–20.0 mm in length (Figure 28–72A). ....**Oedeméridae**   p. 448

168'.   Not exactly fitting the above description **169**

169(168'). Antennae usually pectinate, flabellate, or plumose, rarely serrate **170**

169'.   Antennae (at least terminal segments) filiform **172**

170(169). Length 3 mm or less; eyes emarginate; penultimate tarsal segment very small, tarsi sometimes appearing 4–4–3 (*Emelìnus*) ....**Euglénidae***   p. 449

170'.   Length 4 mm or more; eyes usually not emarginate; penultimate tarsal segment not unusually small, tarsi distinctly 5–5–4 ....**171**

171(170'). Pronotum as wide at base as base of elytra, dark-colored; body somewhat wedge-shaped, higher than wide; elytra often tapering to a point posteriorly; length 4–15 mm ....**Rhipiphòridae**   p. 444

171'.   Pronotum distinctly narrower than base of elytra, often reddish or yellowish, body dorsoventrally flattened; elytra rounded apically, usually widest behind middle; length 6–20 mm (Figure 28–72B) ....**Pyrochròidae**   p. 448

172(169'). Tarsal claws cleft to base (Figure 28–11C), or toothed; abdomen with 6 visible sterna; length 3–30 mm ....**Melòidae**   p. 446

172'.   Tarsal claws simple; abdomen usually with 5 visible sterna; length 12 mm or less **173**

173(172'). Head abruptly narrowed posteriorly to form a slender neck **174**

173'.   Head not abruptly narrowed posteriorly **176**

174(173). Length more than 6 mm; hind coxae contiguous; head constricted well behind eyes; body elongate (Figure 28–73B) ....**Anthícidae**   p. 449

174'.   Length less than 6 mm; hind coxae contiguous or separated; head constricted just behind eyes. **175**

175(174'). Eyes oval; pronotum sometimes with anterior hornlike process extending forward over head (Figure 28–73A); penultimate tarsal segment easily visible, tarsi distinctly 5–5–4; first 2 visible abdominal sterna not fused; length 2–4 mm ....**Anthícidae**   p. 449

175'.   Eyes emarginate; pronotum without anterior hornlike process; penultimate tarsal segment very small, tarsi sometimes appearing 4–4–3; first 2 visible abdominal sterna more or less fused together; length 1.5–3.0 mm
    ....**Euglénidae***   p. 449

176(173'). Elytra long, covering entire abdomen; body not particularly flattened; pronotum widest in middle, narrower at base and apex (Figure 28–68C); length 2–15 mm (Salpingìnae) ....**Salpíngidae**   p. 449

176'.   Elytra short, exposing 2 or more abdominal segments; body strongly flattened; pronotum triangular, very narrow at base, widest anteriorly; length 6 mm or less (Inopeplìnae) ....**Salpíngidae***   p. 449

187(117, 186'). Antennae 10- or 11-segmented, basal 2 segments relatively long, remaining segments short and broad; elytra distinctly pubescent; front coxae transverse; oval, convex beetles, 1–4 mm in length ....**Limníchidae*** p. 428

187'. Antennae 7- to 11-segmented, segments generally not as above; elytra pubescent or bare; front coxae variable; elongate-oval beetles, 1–8 mm in length **188**

188(187'). Front coxae transverse, trochantin exposed; elytra bare or pubescent; antennae short, with most segments broader than long ....**Dryópidae** p. 429

188'. Front coxae globose or oval, trochantin concealed; elytra bare; antennae longer and more slender ....**Élmidae** p. 429

189(185'). Abdomen with 7 or 8 visible sterna; elytra usually soft **190**

189'. Abdomen with 5 or 6 visible sterna; elytra variable **195**

190(189). Ocelli present on front or vertex **191***

190'. Ocelli absent **192**

191(190). Two ocelli on vertex between eyes; second visible abdominal sternum with transverse ridge along front edge; length 2.5–7.5 mm (Omaliìni) ....**Staphylìnidae*** p. 414

191'. Only 1 ocellus present, on front of head between eyes; large, hairy, median swelling on first visible abdominal sternum; pale, straw-colored beetles, about 2.5 mm in length, with long slender antennae (males of *Thylódrias*) ....**Derméstidae*** p. 433

192(190'). Middle coxae separated; elytra usually with reticulate sculpturing; flattened beetles, usually widest in posterior half, often brightly colored, 5–18 mm in length (Figure 28–50A) (some species, chiefly western, have the head prolonged into a prominent snout) ....**Lýcidae** p. 431

192'. Middle coxae contiguous or nearly so; elytra not reticulate; elongate, usually parallel-sided beetles **193**

193(38', 192'). Head more or less concealed by pronotum, usually not visible from above (Figure 28–51A); mesal margins of metepisterna straight or nearly so (Figure 28–15A); abdomen often with luminescent organs (yellowish areas on underside); length, 5–20 mm ....**Lampýridae** p. 432

193'. Head not concealed by pronotum, easily visible from above (Figure 28–51B); mesal margins of metepisterna variable; abdomen without luminescent organs; size variable **194**

194(193'). Mesal margins of metepisterna more or less curved (Figure 28–15B); antennae 11-segmented, filiform or serrate (rarely pectinate); elytra usually broadly rounded apically; length 18 mm or less ....**Canthàridae** p. 432

194'. Mesal margins of metepisterna straight; antennae 12-segmented, pectinate or plumose; elytra narrowed, more or less pointed apically (Figure 28–50B); length 10–30 mm ....**Phengòdidae*** p. 432

195(189'). The first 2 visible abdominal sterna partly fused together, suture between them very weak (Figure 28–8B); metasternum usually with transverse suture (Figure 28–8B); hard-bodied, usually metallic (especially ventrally) ....**Bupréstidae** p. 426

195'. All visible abdominal sterna separated by equally distinct sutures; metasternum usually without transverse suture (Figure 28–8A); soft- or hard-bodied, seldom metallic **196**

196(195'). Head scarcely or not at all visible from above; oval or elongate-oval, usually convex beetles, generally 10 mm in length or less **197**

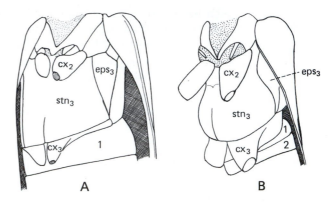

Figure 28–15.   Lateroventral views of thorax and base of abdomen. **A**, *Photùris* (Lampýridae); **B**, *Chauliógnathus* (Canthàridae). *cx*, coxa; *eps₃*, metepisternum; *stn₃*, metasternum; *1–2*, abdominal sterna.

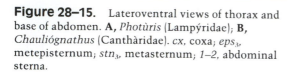

196′.	Head prominent from above; size and shape variable **208**	
197(196).	Hind corners of pronotum prolonged backward into points that tightly embrace base of elytra; front coxae small, rounded; prosternum prolonged backward as a process that fits into mesosternum **198**	
197′.	Hind corners of pronotum not prolonged backward as points; other characters variable **199**	
198(197).	Oblong-oval beetles, widest in middle of body; usually brownish or blackish in color, mostly 2–5 mm in length...................................**Thróscidae**	p. 431
198′.	Elongate, more or less cylindrical beetles, parallel-sided; brownish to black; generally more than 5 mm in length (Figure 28–49D) ....**Eucnèmidae**	p. 431
199 (197′).	Oval, convex beetles, 4–5 mm in length, with head completely ventral and retracted into prothorax, partly concealing eyes; basal antennal segment small, completely concealed, second and third segments much larger, flattened, situated tightly in groove in prosternum, remaining segments flattened, serrate, exposed (extending along mesosternum); middle coxae widely separated; hind coxae grooved for reception of femora; legs strongly retractile; posterior margin of pronotum sinuate, with row of large punctures; southeastern United States ....**Chelonariidae***	p. 428
199′.	Not exactly fitting the above description **200**	
200(199′).	Third tarsal segment conspicuously lobed beneath, fourth very small and difficult to see; scutellum heart-shaped, notched anteriorly; antennae serrate (females) or pectinate (some males); pale brown or tan, more or less elongate beetles, 4–6 mm in length ....**Ptilodactýlidae**	p. 427
200′.	Not exactly fitting the above description **201**	
201(200′).	At least one tarsal segment with prominent lobes beneath **202**	
201′.	Tarsal segments slender, usually without lobes beneath (small lobes are present in some Anobìidae) **204**	
202(201).	Hind coxae grooved for reception of femora; length 4–10 mm **203**	
202′.	Hind coxae not grooved for reception of femora; length 2–4 mm (see also couplet 230) ....**Scírtidae**	p. 417
203(202).	Antennae long, slender, moniliform, extending posteriorly to middle of elytra or beyond; tarsi with segments 2–4 lobed beneath, with fourth segment very short; elongate pubescent beetles; 4.0–7.5 mm in length .....**Artematópidae**	p. 430

203'. Antennae stout, clavate, short, seldom extending much beyond base of pronotum; tarsi variable; oval, convex beetles; 5–10 mm in length (Figure 28–41)
....**Býrrhidae**   p. 426

204(201'). Hind trochanters quadrate; front coxae contiguous **205**

204'. Hind trochanters triangular; front coxae variable **206***

205(204). Hind coxae grooved for reception of femora; antennae usually with last 3
segments elongate (Figure 28–5C), rarely pectinate, flabellate, filiform or
serrate; short-legged, not spiderlike; 1.1–9.0 mm in length (Figure 28–57)
....**Anobiidae**   p. 436

205'. Hind coxae not grooved; antennae filiform, last 3 segments not elongated
(*Gnóstus*, occurring in ant nests in Florida, has antennae 3-segmented); long-
legged, brownish, spiderlike beetles; 2–4 mm in length (Figure 28–56A)
....**Ptìnidae**   p. 437

206(204'). Hind coxae dilated into broad oblique plates that extend to elytra and cover
most of first visible abdominal sternum; tarsal segments decreasing in
length distally; oval convex beetles; 3 mm in length or less (Figure 28–30A)
....**Eucinètidae***   p. 417

206'. Hind coxae not dilated into broad oblique plates; size and shape variable
....**207***

207(206'). Oval, convex beetles; 2–5 mm in length ....**Leiòdidae***   p. 413

207'. Elongate beetles; 3–14 mm in length ....**Dascíllidae***   p. 418

208(196'). Middle and hind trochanters very long, hind trochanters nearly as long as
femora; pronotum wider than long, but a little narrower at base than base of
elytra, hind angles pointed but not projecting backward beyond level of middle of rear edge of pronotum; elongate, slightly flattened, black beetles;
6.0–8.5 mm in length; Pennsylvania and California ....**Cerophýtidae***   p. 430

208'. Middle and hind trochanters of normal size; other characters usually not as
above **209**

209(208'). Antennae serrate, pectinate, or flabellate **210**

209'. Antennae filiform or moniliform **219**

210(209). Posterior corners of pronotum prolonged backward as sharp points **211**

210'. Posterior corners of pronotum not prolonged backward, base of pronotum
straight, sinuate, or somewhat convex **215**

211(210). Front coxae conical, prominent; prosternum not prolonged backward as spinelike process **212**

211'. Front coxae small, rounded; prosternum prolonged backward as spinelike
process **213**

212(211). Mandibles large, prominent, apical half sharply bent, apices acute; length over
10 mm; southeastern United States ....**Callirhípidae**   p. 427

212'. Mandibles short, not prominent, with blunt apices; length 5–6 mm; Texas,
Utah, and California ....**Brachypséctridae***   p. 431

213(211'). Prothorax appearing firmly attached to mesothorax and not very movable;
front coxae partly covered by prosternal spine; oblong-oval beetles, usually
brownish or blackish, 2–5 mm in length, sometimes capable of clicking and
jumping ....**Thróscidae**   p. 431

213'. Prothorax loosely attached to mesothorax and freely movable; front coxae laterad of prosternal spine; elongate beetles, usually over 5 mm in length,
generally able to click and jump **214**

214(213').   Labrum fused to front; antennae arising well in front of eyes, often received in grooves on front and prosternum; prosternum not lobed in front, anterior margin straight or nearly so; more or less cylindrical beetles; usually 15 mm in length or less (*Palaeóxenus dòhrni* Horn, from southern California, brilliant orange and black, 15–20 mm in length) (Figure 28–49D) . . .**Eucnèmidae**   p. 431

214'.   Labrum distinct; antennae usually arising near eyes, above base of mandibles, usually not received in grooves on front (but sometimes received in grooves on prosternum); prosternum usually lobed in front (anterior margin usually arcuate); somewhat flattened beetles; size variable, up to about 35 mm in length (Figure 28–49A,C) . . . .**Elatéridae**   p. 430

215(210').   Elongate, slender, cylindrical beetles, 9.0–13.5 mm in length, brown or black with yellow appendages; antennae short, not extending beyond middle of prothorax, filiform or serrate; head about as wide as pronotum, somewhat narrowed behind eyes; tarsal segments slender, without lobes beneath, as long as or longer than tibiae; elytra with short pubescence; maxillary palps of male flabellate; eastern United States . . . .**Lymexýlidae**   p. 437

215'.   Not exactly fitting the above description **216**

216(215').   Pronotum more or less trapezoidal in shape, posterior corners angulate, posterior margin sinuate; body pubescence when present usually short **217**

216'.   Pronotum quadrate or somewhat oval, posterior corners rounded, posterior margin straight or convex; body pubescence long; often brightly colored beetles **232**

217(216).   Length usually less than 10 mm; front coxae transverse; elytral pubescence moderate to dense; usually brownish; antennae 11-segmented . . . .**Dascíllidae**   p. 418

217'.   Length more than 10 mm; front coxae conical, prominent; elytral pubescence when present fine, short; brown to black beetles; antennae 11- or 12-segmented **218**

218(217').   Tarsi lobed beneath (Figure 28–10F); widely distributed . . . .**Rhipicéridae**   p. 418

218'.   Tarsi not lobed beneath; northern California (see also 218") . . . .**Eulichádidae**   p. 427

218".   Tarsi not lobed beneath; southeastern United States . . . .**Callirhípidae**   p. 427

219(209').   Body antlike; head narrowed behind eyes to a narrow neck; pronotum and elytra oval in dorsal view; length 6 mm or less **220***

219'.   Body not antlike; size variable **221**

220(219).   Abdomen with 6 visible sterna; pronotum long-pubescent; femora clavate (Figure 28–25B); widely distributed . . . .**Scydmaènidae***   p. 414

220'.   Abdomen with 5 visible sterna; pronotum bare; femora slender; northeastern United States and California (Brathinìnae) . . . .**Staphylìnidae***   p. 414

221(219').   Body very flat, dorsal and ventral surfaces parallel . . . .**Cucùjidae**   p. 439

221'.   Body not so flat, dorsal surface more or less convex **222**

222(221').   Posterior corners of pronotum prolonged backward as sharp points; prosternum prolonged backward as spinelike process that fits into cavity in mesosternum (Figure 28–8A) **223**

222'.   Posterior corners of pronotum not prolonged backward as sharp points, or prosternum not as above **225**

223(222).   Labrum distinct, separated from front of head by suture; prosternum usually lobed in front (anterior margin usually arcuate), extending forward under mouthparts (Figure 28–8A); antennae arising near eyes, above base of mandibles; body somewhat flattened; union of prothorax and mesothorax loose, beetles able to click and jump; length 3–35 mm ....**Elatéridae**   p. 430

223′.   Labrum usually not distinct, suture separating it from front of head indistinct or absent; prosternum not, or but slightly, lobed in front, anterior margin straight or nearly so; antennae arising well in front of eyes; body more or less cylindrical; union of prothorax and mesothorax not very loose, beetles sometimes able to click and jump; length 3–20 mm **224**

224(223′).   Tarsal claws pectinate; mandibles large, usually prominent .....**Perothópidae***   p. 431

224′.   Tarsal claws simple; mandibles small, inconspicuous ....**Eucnèmidae**   p. 431

225(222′).   Body very pubescent, hairs long; mandibles long, bent, hooklike, extending forward from head; eyes round, bulging; pronotum trapezoidal, about as wide as head anteriorly, narrower than base of elytra posteriorly; tibiae dilated apically, with 2 long apical spurs; tarsi long, slender, longer than tibiae; abdomen with 6 visible sterna; light brown beetles, 20–25 mm in length; southern United States ....**Cebriónidae***   p. 431

225′.   Not exactly fitting the above description **226**

226(225′).   Length nearly always more than 10 mm; elytra bare, brown, shining (*Párandra*) or black and punctate (*Spóndylis* and *Scaphinus*) ....**Cerambýcidae**   p. 449

226′.   Length variable, but if more than 10 mm, then elytra are pubescent **227**

227(226′).   Elongate, slender, cylindrical beetles, 9.0–13.5 mm in length, brown or black with yellow appendages; antennae short, not extending beyond middle of prothorax; head about as wide as pronotum, somewhat narrowed behind eyes; pronotum margined laterally; tarsal segments slender, without lobes beneath, tarsi as long as or longer than tibiae; maxillary palps of male flabellate; eastern United States. ....**Lymexýlidae**   p. 437

227′.   Not exactly fitting the above description **228**

228(227′).   Brownish oval beetles, usually less than 3 mm in length, found in nests of small mammals or ground-nesting bees or on mountain beavers; abdomen with 6 visible sterna; front coxae globular; eyes usually reduced; tip of abdomen exposed beyond elytra ....**Leptìnidae***   p. 414

228′.   Size and color variable; not found in situations listed above, or there are only 5 visible abdominal sterna and elytra cover entire abdomen; eyes well developed; front coxae variable, but usually not globular **229**

229(228′).   Hind trochanters quadrate, as long as or longer than wide; pronotum distinctly narrower than elytra at their widest point; elytra oval and convex, bare or pubescent; legs long, femora sometimes swollen or clavate; small, brownish, spiderlike beetles, 2–4 mm in length (*Gnóstus*, occurring in ant nests in Florida, has the antennae 3-segmented) ....**Ptìnidae**   p. 437

229′.   Hind trochanters small, triangular; elytra pubescent; shape usually not as above **230**

230(229′).   Oval or elongate-oval, convex beetles, 2–4 mm in length; hind femora often swollen; pronotum more or less quadrate, about twice as wide as long, posterior margin sinuate; 5 visible abdominal sterna; front coxae conical; usually found near water, larvae aquatic ....**Scírtidae**   p. 417

230′.   Elongate or elongate-oval, convex or flattened beetles, usually more than 4 mm in length; pronotum trapezoidal, quadrate, or oval, usually as long as or longer than wide, posterior margin sinuate, straight, or convex; 5 or 6 visible abdominal sterna; front coxae variable; habitats variable **231**

231(230').   Pronotum quadrate or trapezoidal, posterior margin sinuate; body usually con-
               vex, more or less cylindrical; usually brownish beetles, 3–14 mm in length
               ....**Dascíllidae**   p. 418

231'.   Pronotum quadrate or oval, posterior margin straight or convex; body some-
               what flattened; often brightly colored beetles, 3–24 mm in length **232**

232 (39',   Middle coxae rounded, not prominent; hind coxae flat or oval, projecting but
216', 231').   slightly below ventral surface of abdomen; pronotum usually rounded later-
               ally; eyes often emarginate ....**Cléridae**   p. 437

232'.   Middle coxae conical, prominent; hind coxae prominent, extending ventrally
               below ventral surface of abdomen; pronotum margined laterally; eyes
               round **233**

233(232').   Elytra short, exposing at least 3 abdominal segments; antennae usually
               slightly clavate ....**Staphylínidae**   p. 414

233'.   Elytra longer, not more than 2 abdominal segments exposed; antennae filiform
               or slightly serrate **234**

234(233').   Antennae 10- or 11-segmented, inserted on front above base of mandibles, sock-
               ets facing anteriorly; hind coxae transverse; body pubescence usually long
               and erect; length 5–10 mm. ....**Melýridae**   p. 438

234'.   Antennae 11-segmented, inserted between eyes and distant from base of man-
               dibles, sockets facing dorsally; hind coxae triangular, prominent; body pu-
               bescence usually short and recumbent; length 1–15 mm ....**Cantháridae**   p. 432

235(16).   Maxillary palps normal, segmented, flexible; labrum present; gular sutures
               distinct, separate; 3.0–4.5 mm in length ....**Nemonýchidae**   p. 462

235'.   Maxillary palps rigid, segments usually invisible, palps often concealed; gular
               sutures usually fused; size variable **236**

236(235').   Trochanters elongate, femora attached at their apices, thus distant from coxae
               (Figure 28–9C); small, pear-shaped beetles, usually black, 4.5 mm in length
               or less ....**Apiónidae**   p. 462

236'.   Trochanters short, triangular, femora attached at their sides, contiguous with
               or closely adjacent to coxae (Figure 28–9D); size, shape, and color
               variable **237**

237(236').   Antennae elbowed; beak usually with antennal scrobes ....**Curculiónidae**   p. 464

237'.   Antennae not elbowed; beak usually lacking antennal scrobes **238**

238(237').   Pronotum margined laterally; elytra short, rounded apically, exposing parts of
               about 3 abdominal segments; oval, slightly flattened, metallic indigo blue
               beetles, 2.8–3.2 mm in length; eastern North America (Pterocolinae)
               ....**Rhynchítidae**   p. 462

238'.   Pronotum rounded laterally; elytra longer; other characters variable, but color
               usually not as above **239**

239(238').   Antennae 10-segmented, last segment elongate, swollen (Figure 28–90A,B);
               pronotum narrowed posteriorly; body antlike, 5–6 mm in length, with pro-
               notum reddish, elytra blue-black (Figure 28–91); southern United States
               (Cyladìnae) ....**Apiónidae**   p. 462

239'.   Antennae 11-segmented, club usually 3-segmented; pronotum not narrowed
               posteriorly **240**

240(239').   Hind femora short, very broad, upper margins slightly crenulate; antennae not
               arising on beak, but about halfway between base of beak and eye; beak long,

	slender, decurved; hind coxae separated; length 3.5–4.2 mm; southern Florida. . . . .**Oxycorýnidae**	p. 462
240'.	Hind femora slender or somewhat clavate, upper margins not crenulate; antennae arising on beak; beak and size variable **241**	
241(240').	Segments of antennal club usually separate and forming a loose club (Figure 28–90C); length usually less than 7 mm **242**	
241'.	Segments of antennal club firmly united, forming a compact club (Figure 28–90D); size variable **243**	
242(241).	Mandibles flat and toothed on inner and outer edges (Figure 28–90I); beak long, nearly parallel sided; tibiae with short, straight terminal spur (Figure 28–90F) . . . .**Rhynchítidae**	p. 462
242'.	Mandibles stout, pincers-shaped, not toothed on outer edge (Figure 28–90J); beak short, widened distally; tibiae with 2 large, curved terminal spurs (Figure 28–90E) . . . .**Attelábidae**	p. 462
243(241').	Hind femora long, spiny; body broadly oval, 3 mm in length or less (Tachygonìnae) . . . .**Curculiónidae**	p. 464
243'.	Hind femora clavate, not spiny; body elongate, 12–18 mm in length . . . .**Ithycéridae**	p. 463
244(1').	Tarsi with 1 claw; head almost completely retracted into prothorax; body elongate, cylindrical, more than 10 mm in length, often over 20 mm in length; often with luminous area on each side of most segments . . . . . .**Phengòdidae***	p. 432
244'.	Tarsi with 2 claws; head prominent, not retracted into thorax **245***	
245(244').	Body oval, dorsoventrally flattened, straw-colored; 3 mm in length or less (Thylódrias) . . . .**Derméstidae***	p. 433
245'.	Body narrow, somewhat laterally flattened; usually over 3 mm in length . . . .**Rhipiphòridae***	p. 444

SUBORDER **Archostémata:** Coleopterists do not agree on the relationships of the two families here considered as representing the suborder Archostémata. The Cupédidae are considered by most authorities to be a very primitive group meriting subordinal rank, but some (for example, Arnett 1968) would place the Micromálthidae in the suborder Polýphaga because they lack notopleural sutures. The two families in this suborder are small (only five North American species) and seldom encountered.

Family **Cupédidae**—Reticulated Beetles: This is a small and little known group, with only four species occurring in the United States. All are densely scaly, with the elytra reticulate and the tarsi distinctly five-segmented. The prosternum extends backward as a narrow process that fits into a groove in the mesosternum, much as in click beetles. The common species in the eastern United States, *Cùpes cóncolor* Westwood, is 7–10 mm in length and brownish gray in color. In the Rocky Mountains and the Sierra Nevada the most common species is *Priácma serràta* (LeConte), which is gray with faint black bands across the elytra. These beetles are usually found under bark.

Family **Micromálthidae:** This family includes a single rare species, *Micromálthus débilis* LeConte, which has been taken in several localities in the eastern United States and in British Columbia and New Mexico. The adults are 1.8–2.5 mm in length, elongate and parallel-sided, dark, and shiny, with yellowish legs and antennae. The tarsi are five-segmented. This insect has a remarkable life cycle, with paedogenetic larvae. The larvae are able to reproduce (both oviparously and viviparously) parthenogenetically. These beetles have been found in decaying logs, principally oak and chestnut logs.

SUBORDER **Myxóphaga:** The suborder contains two small families of tiny beetles that occur in water or wet places and apparently feed on filamentous algae (to which the suborder name refers). The Myxóphaga are distinguished by the character of the wings and mouth parts and by the presence of notopleural sutures. All have three-segmented tarsi and clubbed antennae. The two families of Myxóphaga are usually keyed out on the basis of their having notopleural sutures (from couplet 11 in the key). The Sphaerìidae are very tiny, and the notopleural sutures may be very difficult to see, so we have also keyed out this family from couplet 11′ (notopleural sutures lacking).

Family **Sphaerìidae**—Minute Bog Beetles: The sphaeriids are tiny (0.5–0.75 mm in length), oval, convex, shining, blackish beetles with a large, prominent head and capitate antennae that are found in mud and under stones near water, among roots of plants, and in moss in boggy places. They differ from other similarly shaped beetles found in these situations in having three-segmented tarsi and in the character of the abdomen (see key, couplet 45). The group is represented in the United States by two or three species that occur in the eastern states, Texas, southern California, and Washington.

Family **Hydroscáphidae**—Skiff Beetles: The skiff beetles are about 1.5 mm in length, with three-segmented tarsi and short elytra, and are similar in general appearance to rove beetles. The antennae are eight-segmented, with a one-segmented club. They occur in the filamentous algae growing on rocks in streams. The group is represented in the United States by a single species, *Hydróscapha nàtans* LeConte, which occurs in southern California, southern Nevada, and Arizona.

SUBORDER **Adéphaga:** The members of this suborder have the hind coxae dividing the first visible abdominal sternum (Figure 28–12A). The posterior margin of this sternum does not extend completely across the abdomen, but is interrupted by the hind coxae. Nearly all the Adéphaga have filiform antennae and 5–5–5 tarsi; they have notopleural sutures; and most of them are predaceous.

Family **Rhysòdidae**—Wrinkled Bark Beetles: The members of this group are slender, brownish beetles 5.5–7.5 mm in length with three fairly deep longitudinal grooves on the pronotum and with the antennae moniliform (Figure 28–16). The pronotal grooves are complete in *Omoglýmmius*, but are present on only about the posterior third of the pronotum in *Clinídium*. These beetles are usually found under the bark of decaying beech, ash, elm, or pine. Eight species occur in the United States, one of each genus in the West, and the others in the East.

Family **Cicindèlidae**—Tiger Beetles: Adult tiger beetles are usually metallic or iridescent in color

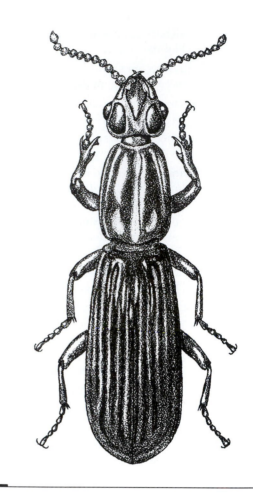

Figure 28–16. A wrinkled bark beetle, *Clinídium scúlptilis* Newman, 14×. (Courtesy of Arnett.)

and often have a definite color pattern. They can usually be recognized by their characteristic shape (Figure 28–17), and most of them are 10–20 mm in length. Most of our tiger beetles belong to the genus *Cicindèla*. Some authorities consider tiger beetles to be a subfamily of Carabidae.

Most tiger beetles are active, usually brightly colored insects found in open sunny situations. They are often common on sandy beaches. They can run or fly rapidly and are very wary and difficult to approach. They take flight quickly, sometimes after running a few feet, and usually alight some distance away facing the pursuer. They are predaceous and feed on a variety of small insects, which they capture with their long sicklelike mandibles. When handled, they can sometimes administer a painful bite.

The larvae are predaceous and live in vertical burrows in the soil in dry paths or fields or in sandy

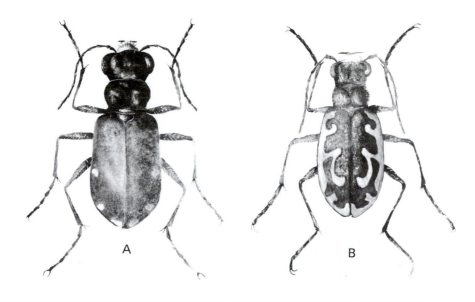

Figure 28–17.   Tiger beetles. **A,** *Cicindèla sexguttàta* (Fabricius); **B,** *C. hirticóllis* Say, 3½ × .

beaches. They prop themselves at the entrance of their burrow, with the traplike jaws wide apart, waiting to capture some passing insect. The larva has hooks on the fifth abdominal tergum with which it can anchor itself in its burrow and thus avoid being pulled out when it captures a large prey. After the prey is subdued, it is dragged to the bottom of the burrow, often 0.3 meter underground, and eaten.

Family **Carábidae**—Ground Beetles: This is the third largest family of beetles in North America (the Staphylìnidae and Curculiónidae are larger), with more than 2200 species in our area. Its members exhibit considerable variation in size, shape, and color. Most species are dark, shiny, and somewhat flattened, with striate elytra (Figure 28–18).

Ground beetles are commonly found under stones, logs, leaves, bark, or debris or running about on the ground. When disturbed, they run rapidly, but seldom fly. Most species hide during the day and feed at night. Many are attracted to lights. Nearly all are predaceous on other insects, and many are very beneficial. The members of a few genera (for example, *Scaphinòtus*; Figure 28–18B) feed on snails. The larvae are also predaceous and occur in burrows in the soil, under bark, or in debris.

The largest and most brilliantly colored ground beetles belong to the genus *Calosòma*. These are often called caterpillar hunters, since they feed chiefly on caterpillars, particularly those that attack trees and shrubs. Most of these beetles are 25 mm or more in length. When handled, they give off a very disagreeable odor. *Calosòma sycophánta* L., a bril-

liant greenish beetle with a dark-blue pronotum, was introduced from Europe to aid in the control of the gypsy moth. These beetles are attracted to lights.

The species in the genus *Bráchinus* are called bombardier beetles because they eject from the anus what looks like a puff of smoke. This is a glandular fluid that is ejected with a popping sound and that vaporizes into a cloud when it comes in contact with the air. The discharge of some species may irritate tender skin. This apparently serves as a means both of protection and of offense.

A few of the carabids are plant feeders. Adults of *Stenolòphus lecóntei* (Chaudoir), the seed-corn beetle, and *Clivìna impréssifrons* LeConte, the slender seed-corn beetle, sometimes attack corn seeds in the soil and prevent them from sprouting. This behavior occasionally causes considerable damage, especially during cold springs when germination is delayed.

The members of the genus *Ómophron*, called round sand beetles (and formerly placed in a separate family, the Omophrónidae), differ from other carabids in having the scutellum concealed. They are small (5–8 mm in length), oval convex beetles that occur in wet sand along the shores of lakes and streams. They may be found running over the sand or burrowing in it (particularly under stones) and may occasionally be found running over the surface of the water. They run when disturbed and seldom fly. Adults and larvae are predaceous, but the larvae occasionally feed on seedlings of crops planted in moist soil.

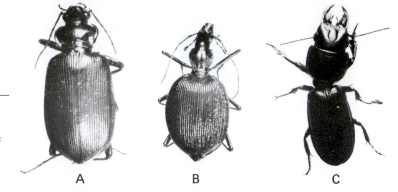

Figure 28–18. Ground beetles. **A,** *Calosòma scrutàtor* (Fabricius); **B,** *Scaphinòtus guyòti* (LeConte); **C,** *Scarites subterràneus* (Fabricius). All figures slightly enlarged. (**C,** courtesy of the Illinois Natural History Survey.)

Family **Halíplidae**—Crawling Water Beetles: The haliplids are small, oval, convex beetles 2.5–4.5 mm in length, that live in or near water. They are usually yellowish or brownish with black spots (Figure 28–19A) and may be distinguished from similar aquatic beetles by their very large and platelike hind coxae (Figure 28–19B). They are fairly common in and about ponds, swimming or moving about rather slowly. They frequently occur in masses of vegetation on or near the surface of the water. The adults feed chiefly on algae and other plant materials. The larvae (Figure 28–20B) are predaceous. There are 70 species of Halíplidae in North America. The two common eastern genera in this group can be separated by the presence or absence of two black spots at the base of the pronotum. These spots are present in *Peltódytes* (Figure 28–19A) and absent in *Háliplus*.

Family **Amphizòidae**—Trout-Stream Beetles: This family contains five species in the genus *Amphizòa*, four occurring in western North America and one in eastern Tibet. These beetles are oval, dark-colored, and 11.0–15.5 mm in length. Adults and larvae of most species occur in the cold water of mountain streams, where they crawl about on submerged objects or on driftwood. One species occurring near Seattle lives in relatively warm quiet water. The larvae do not have gills and must obtain oxygen at the water surface. They frequently crawl out of the water onto twigs or floating objects. When dislodged, they float until they can grasp another object, as they apparently do not swim. The adults swim very little and often run about on stream shores at night. Both adults and larvae are predaceous, feeding largely (if not entirely), on stonefly nymphs.

Family **Notéridae**—Burrowing Water Beetles: These beetles are very similar to the dytiscids, but have the scutellum hidden and have two equal claws on the hind tarsus. They are broadly oval, smooth, brownish to black beetles, 1.2–5.5 mm in length, and are similar to the dytiscids in habits. The com-

mon name of this group refers to the larvae, which burrow into the mud around the roots of aquatic plants and apparently feed on algae. There are 17 species in North America.

Family **Dytíscidae**—Predaceous Diving Beetles: This is a large group of aquatic beetles (475 species in North America) that are usually very common in ponds and quiet streams. The body is smooth, oval, and very hard, and the hind legs are flattened and fringed with long hairs to form excellent paddles. These beetles obtain air at the surface of the water, but can remain submerged for long periods because they carry air in a chamber under the elytra. They often hang head downward from the surface of the water. These insects may leave the water at night and fly to lights.

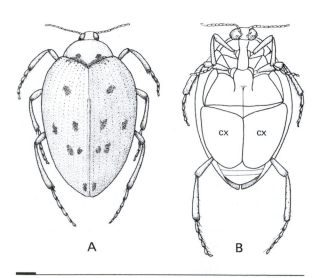

Figure 28–19. A crawling water beetle, *Peltódytes edéntulus* (LeConte), 11 ×. **A,** dorsal view; **B,** ventral view. *cx*, hind coxa.

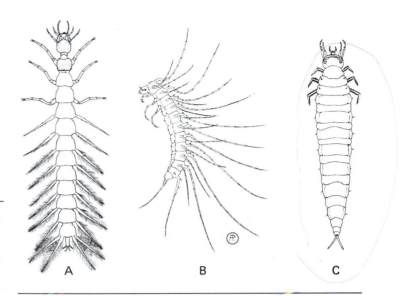

Figure 28–20.   Larvae of aquatic beetles. **A,** *Dineùtus* (Gyrìnidae); **B,** *Peltódytes* (Halíplidae), lateral view; *C, Hydróphilus triangulàris* (Say) (Hydrophílidae). (Courtesy of Peterson; reprinted by permission.)

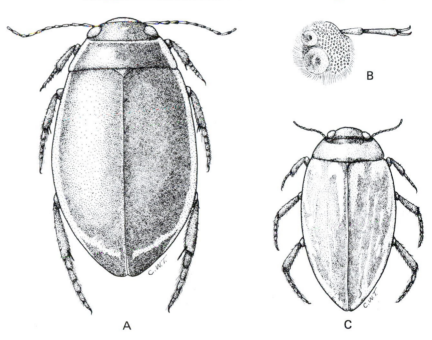

Figure 28–21.   Predaceous diving beetles. **A,** *Dytíscus verticàlis* (Say), female, 2×; **B,** same, front tarsus of male; **C,** *Coptótomus interrogàtus* (Fabricius), 7×.

The dytiscids are very similar to another group of beetles common in fresh water, the Hydrophílidae. The adults of these two groups may be distinguished by the structure of the antennae and the maxillary palps and sometimes by the structure of the metasternum. The dytiscids have long filiform antennae and very short maxillary palps (Figure 28–21), whereas the antennae of the hydrophilids are short and clubbed, and the maxillary palps are nearly always as long as or longer than the antennae (Figure 28–29). The metasternum in many hydrophilids is prolonged posteriorly into a long spine (Figure 28–29B). An excellent field character for separating these two groups is their method of swimming. The dytiscids move the hind legs simultaneously, like oars, whereas the hydrophilids move the hind legs alternately, as though they were running through the water.

Both adults and larvae of the dytiscids are highly predaceous and feed on a variety of small aquatic animals, including small fish. The larvae (Figure 28–22) are often called water tigers. They have long

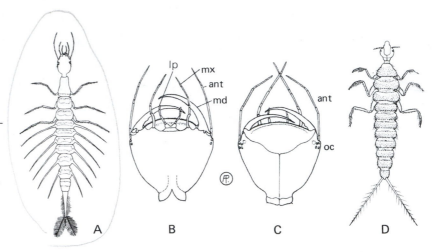

Figure 28–22. Larvae of Dytíscidae. **A,** *Coptótomus*; **B,** head of *Dytíscus*, ventral view; **C,** same, dorsal view; **D,** *Hydróporus*. *ant,* antenna; *lp,* labial palp; *md,* mandible; *mx,* maxilla; *oc,* ocelli. (Courtesy of Peterson; reprinted by permission.)

sicklelike jaws, which are hollow, and when they attack a prey they suck out its body fluids through the channels in the jaws. These larvae are very active and will not hesitate to attack an animal much larger than themselves.

Adult dytiscids vary in length from 1.2 to 40 mm. Most of them are brownish, blackish, or greenish. The males of some species (Figure 28–21B) have peculiar front tarsi bearing large suction disks that are used in holding the smooth slick elytra of the female at the time of mating. Some of the larger species have a pale yellow band along the lateral margins of the pronotum and elytra (Figure 28–21A). A few members of this group have the tarsi appearing 4–4–5.

Family **Gyrínidae**—Whirligig Beetles: The gyrinids are oval black beetles that are commonly seen swimming in endless gyrations on the surface of ponds and quiet streams. They are equally at home on the surface of the water or beneath it. They are extremely rapid swimmers, swimming principally by means of the strongly flattened middle and hind legs, which move simultaneously (as in Dytíscidae). The front legs are elongate and slender (Figure 28–23). These insects are peculiar in having each compound eye divided. They have a pair of compound eyes on the upper surface of the head and another pair on the ventral surface (Figure 28–13C). The antennae are very short and somewhat clubbed and have the third segment greatly expanded and somewhat earlike (Figure 28–5E). The two basal abdominal sterna are fused, and the suture separating them is indistinct.

Adult whirligig beetles are principally scavengers, feeding chiefly on insects that fall onto the surface of the water. The larvae (Figure 28–20A) are predaceous, feeding on a variety of small aquatic animals, and are often cannibalistic. Many of the adults give off a characteristic fruity odor when han-

dled. The adults are often gregarious, forming large swarms on the surface of the water.

The eggs of whirligig beetles are laid in clusters or rows on the undersides of the leaves of aquatic plants, particularly water lilies and pondweed. Pupation occurs in mud cells on the shore or on aquatic plants.

Most of our 58 species of whirligig beetles belong to the genera *Gyrínus* and *Dineùtus*. The species of *Dineùtus* are 8.5–15.5 mm in length and the scutellus is hidden (Figure 28–23A).

SUBORDER **Polýphaga:**   The members of this suborder differ from most other beetles in that the first visible abdominal sternum is not divided by the hind coxae, and its posterior margin extends completely across the abdomen. The hind trochanters are usually small, not large, and offset toward the midline as in the Adéphaga (Figure 28–12B), and notopleural sutures are lacking. This suborder includes the remaining families of beetles, which vary greatly in the form of the antennae, the tarsal formula, and other characters.

Family **Hydraènidae**—Minute Moss Beetles: These beetles are similar to the hydrophilids, but differ in having six or seven abdominal sterna (only five in the Hydrophílidae). They are elongate or oval, dark-colored beetles, 1.2–1.7 mm in length, and occur in matted vegetation along stream margins, in wet moss, and along the seashore. Both larvae and adults feed on algae. There are 36 species in North America.

Family **Ptilíidae**—Feather-Winged Beetles: This family includes some of the smallest beetles known. Few exceed 1 mm, and many are less than 0.5 mm in length. The body is oval, the hind wings bear a long fringe of hairs that often extends out from beneath the elytra, and the antennae bear whorls of long hairs. These beetles occur in rotting wood, dung, and leaf litter and feed chiefly on fungus

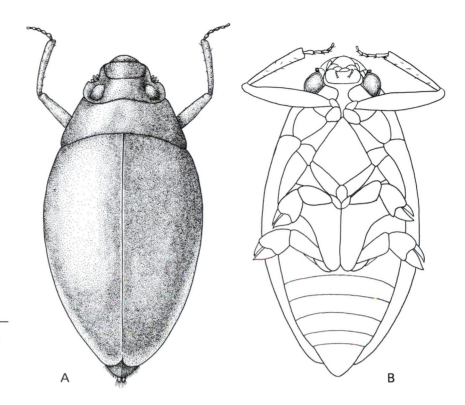

Figure 28–23. A whirligig beetle, *Dineùtus americànus* (Say), 7×. **A,** dorsal view, **B,** ventral view.

spores. More than 100 species occur in North America.

This family includes the horseshoe crab beetles, formerly placed in Limulòdidae, which are usually a millimeter or less in length and are somewhat similar to horseshoe crabs in general appearance. They are oval in shape, with the elytra short and the abdomen somewhat tapering, and yellowish to brownish in color. Hind wings and compound eyes are absent. These beetles are found in ant nests, where they usually ride on the ants, feeding on exudations from their bodies. The group is a small one (four species in the United States), but is widely distributed.

Family **Agýrtidae:** This is a small group (six North American species) formerly included in the Sílphidae. These beetles are 4–14 mm in length, oblong to elongate in shape, slightly flattened, and glabrous. They are found in decaying animal or vegetable matter. One species has been reported in Indiana and Kentucky. The other species occur in the Pacific Coast states.

Family **Leiòdidae**—Round Fungus Beetles: The leiodids, with about 135 species in our area, are a variable group that was formerly divided into at least two families. The Leiodìnae are convex, shiny, oval beetles, 1.5–6.5 mm in length, and brown to black in color (Figure 28–24B). Many species when dis-

turbed tuck the head and prothorax under the body and roll into a ball, thus concealing all the appendages. These beetles occur in fungi, under bark, in decaying wood, and in similar places. The Catopìnae (formerly placed in the family Leptodíridae) are elongate-oval, somewhat flattened, brownish to black, pubescent, and 2–5 mm in length. They often have faint cross striations on the elytra and pronotum,

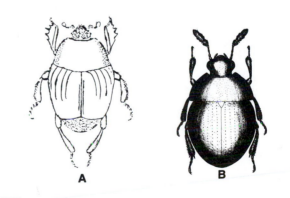

Figure 28–24. **A,** a hister beetle, *Geomyzáprinus góffi* (Ross), 6×; **B,** a round fungus beetle, *Anisótoma globòsa* Hatch, 15×. (**A,** courtesy of Ross and the Entomological Society of America; **B,** courtesy of Wheeler and Blackwell Scientific Publications.)

and most of them have the eighth antennal segment shorter and smaller in diameter than the seventh and ninth segments. Most of these beetles occur in carrion, but some are found in fungi, some feed on slime molds, and others occur in ant nets. The highly modified *Glaciacavícola bathyscòides* Westcott is known only from Idaho ice caves.

Family **Leptinidae**—Mammal-Nest Beetles and Beaver Parasites: The leptinids are brownish, oblong-oval, louselike beetles, 2–5 mm in length, with the eyes reduced or absent. The species of *Leptinus* (two in North America) occur in the nests and fur of mice, shrews, and moles and occasionally in the nests of ground-nesting Hymenóptera. The species of *Leptinúllus* (two in North America) occur in the nests and fur of beavers, one species on the common beaver (*Cástor*) and the other on the mountain beaver (*Aplodóntia*). The single species of *Platypsýlla*, *P. castòris* Ritsema, is an ectoparasite of the common beaver.

Family **Scydmaènidae**—Antlike Stone Beetles: The members of this group are antlike in shape (Figure 28–25B), long-legged, brownish, somewhat hairy beetles, 1–5 mm in length. The antennae are slightly clavate, and the femora are often clavate (Figure 28–25B). They occur under stones, in moss and leaf litter, and in ant nests. These beetles are secretive in habit, but sometimes fly about in numbers at twilight.

Family **Dasycéridae:** This family includes the genus *Dasýcerus*, which was formerly placed in the family Lathridìidae. It includes only two species in our area, one in North Carolina and Georgia and the other in California. These beetles differ from the Lathridìidae in having the front coxal cavities open behind and the front coxae contiguous. Their habits are similar to those of the Lathridìidae.

Family **Sílphidae**—Carrion Beetles: The common species in this group are relatively large and often brightly colored insects that occur about the bodies of dead animals. The body is soft and somewhat flattened, the antennae are clubbed (clavate or capitate), and the tarsi are five-segmented. Silphids range in length from 3 to 35 mm, but most species are over 10 mm.

Two common genera in this group are *Sílpha* and *Nicróphorous* (= *Necrophórus*). In *Sílpha* (Figure 28–26A) the body is broadly oval and flattened, 10–24 mm in length, and the elytra are rounded or acute at the apex and almost cover the abdomen. In some species (for example, *S. americàna* L.) the pronotum is yellowish with a black spot in the center. In *Nicróphorus* (Figure 28–26B) the body is more elongate, the elytra are short and truncate apically, and most species are red and black in color. The beetles of the genus *Nicróphorus* are often known as burying beetles. They excavate beneath the dead body of a mouse or other small animal, and the body sinks into the ground. These beetles are remarkably strong. A pair may move an animal as large as a rat several feet to get it to a suitable spot for burying. After the body is buried, the eggs are laid on it. Both adults and larvae feed on carrion and are usually found beneath the bodies of dead animals.

Other species of silphids occur in various types of decaying animal matter. Some occur in fungi, a few occur in ant nests, and at least one species, *Sílpha bituberòsa* LeConte, feeds on plant materials. A few are predaceous on maggots and other animals that occur in decaying organic matter. In some species (for example, *Nicróphorus*) the newly hatched larvae are fed carrion regurgitated by the parent beetles.

Family **Staphylìnidae**—Rove Beetles: The rove beetles (Figures 28–27 and 28–28) are slender and elongate and can usually be recognized by the very short elytra. The elytra are usually not much longer than their combined width, and a considerable portion of the abdomen is exposed beyond their apices (Figure 28–27). There are six or seven visible abdominal sterna, which will separate them from short-winged Nitidùlidae (such as *Conótelus*). The hind wings are well developed and, when at rest, are folded under the short elytra. Rove beetles are active insects

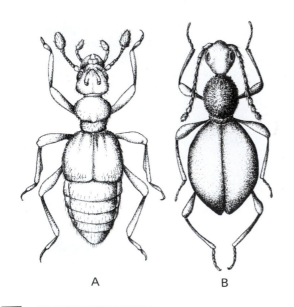

Figure 28–25. **A,** short-winged mold beetle, *Trimiomélba dùbia* (LeConte) (Pseláphidae), 30×; **B,** an antlike stone beetle, *Eucónnus clàvipes* (Say) (Scydmaènidae), 18×. (Redrawn from Arnett.)

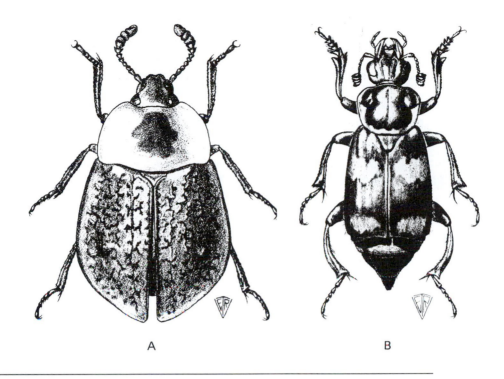

Figure 28–26. Carrion beetles. **A,** *Sílpha americàna* L.; **B,** *Nicróphorus sàyi* Laporte; 3×. (Courtesy of Arnett.)

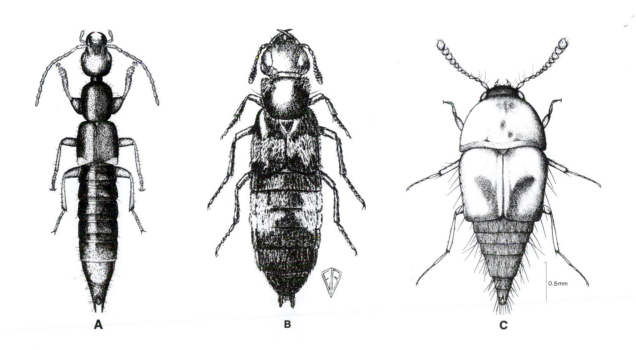

Figure 28–27. Rove beetles. **A,** *Lathròbium angulàre* LeConte, 8×; **B,** *Creóphilus maxillòsus* (L.), 4×; **C,** *Sepedóphilus scríptus* (Horn), 7½×. (**A,** courtesy of Watrous; **B,** courtesy of Arnett; **C,** courtesy of Campbell.)

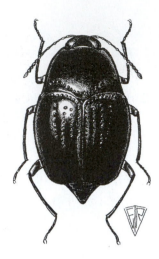

Figure 28–28.   A rove beetle, *Scaphídium quadriguttàtum pìceum* Melsheimer, 7×. (Courtesy of Arnett.)

and run or fly rapidly. When running, they frequently raise the tip of the abdomen, much as scorpions do. The mandibles are very long, slender, and sharp and usually cross in front of the head. Some of the larger rove beetles can inflict a painful bite when handled. Most of these beetles are black or brown in color. They vary considerably in size, but the largest are about 25 mm in length.

This is one of the two largest families of beetles, with nearly 3200 North American species. These beetles occur in a variety of habitats, but are probably most often seen about decaying materials, particularly dung or carrion. They also occur under stones and other objects on the ground, along the shores of streams and the seashore, in fungi and leaf litter, and in the nests of birds, mammals, ants, and termites. Most species appear to be predaceous. The larvae usually occur in the same places and feed on the same things as the adults. A few are parasites of other insects.

Family **Pseláphidae**—Short-Winged Mold Beetles: The pselaphids are small yellowish or brownish beetles, 0.5–5.5 (mostly about 1.5) mm in length, and most of them are found under stones and logs, in rotting wood, and in moss. A few occur in ant, termite, and mammal nests. These beetles have short truncate elytra and resemble rove beetles, but have only three tarsal segments (most rove beetles have more), the pronotum is narrower than the elytra, and the antennae are usually abruptly clubbed (Figure 28–25A). This group is a large one, with about 650 species occurring in North America.

The members of one subfamily of pselaphids, the Clavigerìnae, are peculiar in having the antennae two-segmented and the tarsi with only one claw. These beetles occur in ant nests, where they are "milked" by the ants for a secretion on which the ants feed. Most pselaphids are thought to be predators.

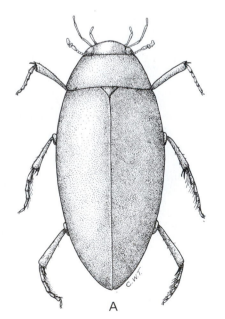
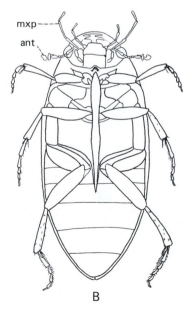

Figure 28–29.   A water scavenger beetle, *Hydróphilus triangulàris* Say. **A,** dorsal view; **B,** ventral view. *ant,* antenna; *mxp,* maxillary palp.

A

B

Family **Hydrophílidae**—Water Scavenger Beetles: The hydrophilids are oval, somewhat convex beetles that can be recognized by the short clubbed antennae and the long maxillary palps (Figure 28–29). Most species are aquatic and are very similar in general appearance to the Dytíscidae. The aquatic species are generally black in color, and they vary in length from a few millimeters up to about 40 mm. The metasternum in some species is prolonged posteriorly as a sharp spine (Figure 28–29B). This spine may be jabbed into the fingers of a person who is careless in handling one of these insects.

The water scavenger beetles differ somewhat from the dytiscids in habits. They rarely hang head downward from the surface of the water, as the dytiscids frequently do, and they carry air with them below the water in a silvery film over the ventral side of the body. In swimming, the hydrophilids move opposite legs alternately, whereas the dytiscids move opposite legs simultaneously, like a frog. The adults are principally scavengers, as the common name implies, but the larvae are usually predaceous. The larvae of the water scavenger beetles (Figure 28–20C) differ from those of the predaceous diving beetles in that they have only a single tarsal claw (dytiscid larvae have two), and the mandibles are usually toothed. The larvae are voracious and feed on all sorts of aquatic animals.

The hydrophilids (284 North American species) are common insects in ponds and quiet streams. A large and common species, *Hydróphilus triangulàris* Say, is shining black and about 40 mm in length (Figure 28–29). Most hydrophilids are aquatic, but a few (subfamily Sphaeridiìnae) are terrestrial and occur in dung. These differ from the aquatic hydrophilids in having the first segment of the hind tarsi rather long, and the maxillary palps are usually shorter than the antennae. The most common dung-inhabiting species is *Sphaerídium scarabaeòides* (L.), which has a faint red spot and a fainter yellow spot on each elytron. Some of the aquatic species are attracted to lights at night. The aquatic species lay their eggs in silken cases, which are usually attached to aquatic plants. The full-grown larvae leave the water to pupate in earthen cells underground.

Family **Georýssidae**—Minute Mud-Loving Beetles: This group includes two small and rare North American species, one widely distributed (Maine to Washington) and the other in Idaho and California. *Georýssus pusíllus* LeConte is about 1.7 mm in length, black, and broadly oval in shape. These beetles occur in the mud along the banks of lakes and streams and apparently feed on algae.

Family **Sphaerítidae**—False Clown Beetles: This group is represented in North America by a single species that occurs in carrion, manure, and decaying fungi from Alaska to northern Idaho and California. This species, *Sphaerìtes polìtus* Mannerheim, is 3.5–5.5 mm in length and black with a metallic bluish luster. It is very similar to some of the hister beetles, but the antennae are not elbowed, the tibiae are less expanded and lack teeth externally, and only the last abdominal segment is exposed beyond the elytra.

Family **Histéridae**—Hister Beetles: Hister beetles are small (0.5–10.0 mm in length), broadly oval beetles that are usually shining black in color. The elytra are cut off square at the apex, exposing one or two apical abdominal segments (Figure 28–24A). The antennae (Figure 28–5I) are elbowed and clubbed. The tibiae are dilated, and the anterior ones are usually toothed or spined. Hister beetles are generally found in or near decaying organic matter such as dung, fungi, and carrion, but are apparently predaceous on other small insects living in these materials. Some species, which are very flat, occur under the loose bark of stumps or logs. A few live in the nests of ants or termites. A few species are elongate and cylindrical; these live in the galleries of wood-boring insects. When disturbed, the hister beetles usually draw in their legs and antennae and become motionless. The appendages fit so snugly into shallow grooves on the ventral side of the body that it is often difficult to see them, even with considerable magnification. Around 500 species occur in the United States and Canada.

Family **Eucinètidae**—Plate-Thigh Beetles: The eucinetids are small (2.5–3.0 mm in length), oval, convex beetles that have the head deflexed and not visible from above (Figure 28–30A). There are six visible abdominal sterna, and the hind coxae are dilated into broad plates that extend to the elytra and cover most of the first visible abdominal sternum (hence the common name). Eight species occur in our area (in the East and in California), and they are generally found under bark or in fungi.

Family **Clámbidae**—Fringe-Winged Beetles: The clambids are minute (about 1 mm in length), oval, convex, brownish to black beetles that are capable of tucking the head and prothorax under the body and rolling into a ball. They resemble the leiodids in this respect, but differ from leiodids in being pubescent, in having the hind coxae dilated into broad plates, and in having a fringe of long hairs on the hind wings. These beetles occur in decaying plant material. The group is small (12 North American species), and its members are not often encountered.

Family **Scírtidae**—Marsh Beetles: The scirtids are oval beetles, 2–4 mm in length (Figure 28–30B), and occur on vegetation in swampy places and in damp

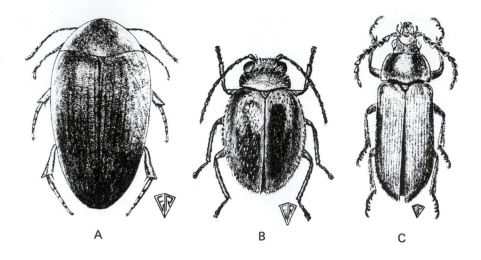

Figure 28–30.   **A,** a plate-thigh beetle, *Eucinètus terminàlis* LeConte (Eucinètidae), 16×; **B,** a marsh beetle, *Prionocỳphon limbàtus* LeConte (Scírtidae), 6×; **C,** a soft-bodied plant beetle, *Dascíllus dàvidsoni* LeConte (Dascíllidae), 3×. (Courtesy of Arnett.)

rotting debris. There are 37 species in North America. Some have enlarged hind femora and are active jumpers. The larvae, which have long slender antennae, are aquatic.

Family **Dascíllidae**—Soft-Bodied Plant Beetles: The dascillids are oval to elongate, soft-bodied, pubescent beetles, mostly 3–14 mm in length. The head is usually visible from above, and some species have relatively large and conspicuous mandibles (Figure 28–30C). They are most likely to be found on vegetation near water, but are not very common. This group contains 25 North American species.

Family **Rhipicéridae**—Cedar Beetles: The cedar beetles are elongate-oval, brownish beetles, 12–24 mm in length, with orange antennae and prominent mandibles (Figure 28–31). The antennae are flabellate in the male and serrate to pectinate in the female. These beetles superficially resemble june beetles and are good fliers. The larvae are parasites of cicada nymphs. This group is small (six North American species of *Sándalus*) but is widely distributed.

Family **Lucànidae**—Stag Beetles: The lucanids are sometimes called pinchingbugs because of the large mandibles of the males (Figure 28–32A). In some males the mandibles are half as long as the body or longer and are branched like the antlers of a stag (hence the name "stag beetles"). Stag beetles are closely related to the Scarabaèidae, but the terminal segments of the antennae cannot be held tightly together as in the scarabs (Figure 28–6C,D,G). Our stag beetles vary in length from about 10 to 60 mm. Most

of the larger ones are 25–40 mm in length. There are 31 species in the United States and Canada.

These insects are usually found in woods, but some species occur on sandy beaches. The adults are often attracted to lights at night. The larvae are found in decaying wood and are similar to the white grubs that are found in grassy soil. They feed on the juices of the decaying wood.

Family **Passálidae**—Bess Beetles: These beetles are called by a variety of names: bessbugs, bessiebugs, betsy beetles, patent-leather beetles, and horned passalus beetles. Three species occur in the

Figure 28–31.   A cedar beetle, *Sándalus petrophỳa* Knoch, female (Rhipicéridae), 3×. (Courtesy of Arnett.)

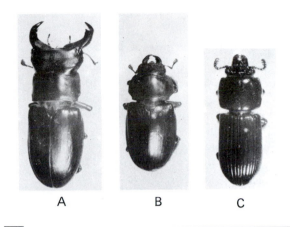

Figure 28–32. **A,** male, and **B,** female, of a stag beetle, *Pseudolucànus caprèolus* (L.); **C,** a bessbug, *Odontotaènius disjúnctus* (Illiger). About natural size.

United States, only one of which occurs in the East. The eastern species, *Odontotaènius disjúnctus* (Illiger) (Figure 28–32C), is a shining black beetle, 32–36 mm in length, with longitudinal grooves in the elytra and a characteristic horn on the head. (Figure 28–14B). This family is closely related to the Lucànidae, but differs in that the mentum of the labium is deeply notched. The two western species of the family occur in southern Texas.

The passalids are somewhat social, and their colonies occur in galleries in decaying logs. The adults are able to produce a squeaking sound by rubbing roughened areas on the underside of the wings across similar areas on the dorsal side of the abdomen. The larvae also stridulate. This sound is produced when the insect is disturbed. Normally, however, it probably serves as a means of communication. The adults prepare food (decaying wood) with their salivary secretions and feed it to the young. The passalids are fairly common insects.

Family **Scarabaèidae**—Scarab Beetles: This group contains about 1400 North American species, and its members vary greatly in size, color, and habits. The scarabs are heavy-bodied, oval or elongate, usually convex beetles, with the tarsi 5-segmented (rarely, the front tarsi are absent) and the antennae 8- to 11-segmented and lamellate. The last three (rarely more) of the antennal segments are expanded into platelike structures that may be spread apart (Figure 28–6C) or united to form a compact terminal club (Figure 28–6D). The front tibiae are more or less dilated, with the outer edge toothed or scalloped.

The scarabs vary considerably in habits. Many are dung feeders or feed on decomposing plant materials, carrion, and the like. Some live in the nests or burrows of vertebrates or in the nests of ants or termites. A few feed on fungi. Many feed on plant materials such as grasses, foliage, fruits, and flowers, and some of these are serious pests of lawns, golf greens, or various agricultural crops. The larvae are strongly curved and C-shaped and in many species are the damaging ("white grub") stage.

Key to the Subfamilies of the Scarabaèidae

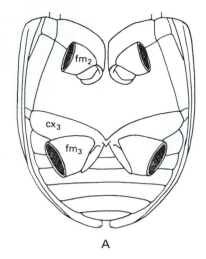
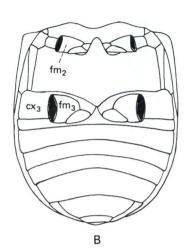

A   B

Figure 28–33. Ventral views of thorax and abdomen of Scarabaèidae. **A,** a dung-feeding scarab (*Aphòdius*, Aphodiìnae); **B,** a plant-feeding scarab (*Pelidnòta*, Rutelìnae). *cx₃*, hind coxa; *fm₂*, middle femur; *fm₃*, hind femur.

4(3).   Antennal club 3-segmented, with at least some club segments pubescent; elytra striate; widely distributed ....**Geotrupìnae**   p. 422

4′.   Antennal club 5- to 7-segmented, club segments bare or only sparsely hairy; elytra not striate; rare western beetles (*Pleócoma, Benedíctia*) ....**Pleocomìnae**   p. 423

5(3′).   Elytra tapering posteriorly, tips distinctly separated and short, exposing 2 or 3 abdominal terga; body very hairy; brownish in color and 13–18 mm in length; rare beetles ....**Glaphyrìnae**   p. 423

5′.   Not exactly fitting the above description **6**

6(5′).   Antennae 10-segmented with 3-segmented club, basal segment of club hollowed out and receiving next segment (which is largely concealed in repose); blackish beetles, glabrous and shining, about 7 mm in length; hind legs arising about middle of body (as in Figure 28–33B); southern and western United States ....**Hybosorìnae**   p. 422

6′.   Not exactly fitting the above description **7**

7(6′).   Hind legs situated far back on body, usually closer to tip of abdomen than to middle legs (Figure 28–33A); abdominal spiracles covered by elytra; segments of antennal club usually hairy; dung feeders **8**

7′.   Hind legs usually situated at about middle of body, closer to middle legs than to tip of abdomen (Figure 28–33B); at least 1 (often more) of the abdominal spiracles not covered by elytra; segments of antennal club smooth or only sparsely hairy; plant feeders **11**

8(7).   Hind tibiae with 1 apical spur (Figure 28–34C); pygidium partly exposed; middle coxae widely separated; scutellum small, usually not visible ....**Scarabaeìnae**   p. 421

8′.   Hind tibiae usually with 2 apical spurs (Figure 28–34A); pygidium usually covered by elytra; middle coxae approximated (Figure 28–33A); scutellum well developed and visible **9**

9(8′).   Antennae 9-segmented; size and color variable **10**

9′.   Antennae 10-segmented; reddish brown beetles, 5–6 mm in length ....**Ochodaeìnae**   p. 422

10(9). Clypeus expanded, mandibles not visible from above, clypeus usually notched at apex ....**Aphodiinae**   p. 422

10'. Mandibles not concealed by clypeus and visible from above; clypeus not notched at apex ....**Aegialiinae**   p. 422

11(7'). Tarsal claws (at least on hind legs) of unequal size, outer claw larger (Figure 28–34B); hind tibiae with 2 apical spurs; pygidium exposed; often brightly colored beetles ....**Rutelinae**   p. 424

11'. Tarsal claws, at least on hind legs, of equal size (except in some males of Dynastìnae, which have horns on the head or pronotum, and in *Hóplia*, subfamily Melolonthìnae, 6–9 mm in length, which has only 1 simple claw on the hind legs), or hind tibiae without apical spurs **12**

12(11'). Tarsal claws usually toothed or bifid; clypeus not emarginate laterally, bases of antennae usually not visible from above; generally only 1 pair of abdominal spiracles exposed below edges of elytra ....**Melolonthìnae**   p. 423

12'. Tarsal claws simple; clypeus variable, generally emarginate laterally, so that bases of antennae are visible from above; usually at least 2 pairs of abdominal spiracles exposed below edges of elytra **13**

13(12'). Front coxae transverse; body usually convex above; mandibles bent, expanded and leaflike, and generally visible from above; males often with large horns on head or pronotum (Figure 28–39); lateral margins of elytra without shallow emargination behind humeri; length 20–60 mm ....**Dynastìnae**   p. 424

13'. Front coxae conical and more or less prominent; body convex or flattened above; mandibles not bent and leaflike, usually not visible from above; no horns on head or pronotum; lateral margins of elytra often with shallow emargination behind humeri (Figure 28–40); size variable **14**

14(13'). Body flattened above; lateral margins of elytra usually with shallow emargination behind humeri (Figure 28–40); size and color variable, but if 7 mm in length or less (*Válgus*), then elytra truncate apically and do not cover entire abdomen, hind coxae are widely separated, and color usually dark; widely distributed ....**Cetoniinae**   p. 425

14'. Body convex above; lateral margins of elytra without shallow emargination behind humeri; 4–7 mm in length, light brown in color; elytra not truncate at apex, covering entire abdomen; hind coxae approximated; rare western beetles (*Ácoma*) ....**Pleocomìnae**   p. 423

Subfamily **Scarabaeìnae** (= **Coprìnae**)—Dung Beetles and Tumblebugs: These beetles are robust, 5–30 mm in length, and feed chiefly on dung. Most of them are dull black, but some are metallic green in color. The tumblebugs (principally *Cánthon* and *Deltochìlum*) are black and about 25 mm in length or less, with the middle and hind tibiae rather slender, and there are no horns on the head or pronotum. Other genera in this subfamily have the middle and hind tibiae swollen at the tip and often have a horn on the head. In *Phanaèus* (Figure 28–35C,D), which is usually a little less than 25 mm in length, the body is a brilliant green with the pronotum golden, and the males have a long horn on the top of the head.

The dung beetles in the genera *Còpris* and *Dichotòmius* (= *Pinòtus*) are black, with conspicuous striae on the elytra. *Còpris*, about 18 mm in length or less, has eight striae on each elytron, and *Dichotòmius* (about 25 mm long and very robust) has seven. Other genera in this subfamily are generally less than 10 mm in length.

The tumblebugs are usually common in pastures and are interesting insects to watch. They chew off a piece of dung, work it into a ball, and roll this ball a considerable distance. They usually work in pairs, one pushing and the other pulling, rolling the ball with their hind legs. The ball is then buried in the soil, and the eggs are laid in the ball. The larvae are

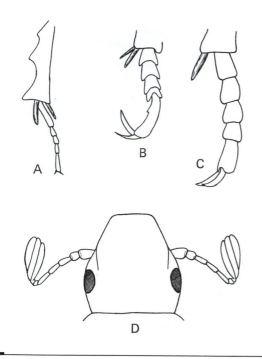

Figure 28–34.   Characters of Scarabaèidae. **A,** hind tibia and tarsus of *Aphòdius* (Aphodiìnae); **B,** hind tarsus of *Popíllia* (Rutelìnae); **C,** hind tarsus of *Cánthon* (Scarabaèinae); **D,** head of *Macrodáctylus* (Melolonthìnae), dorsal view.

thus assured a food supply, and the location of the ball provides protection.

The sacred scarab of ancient Egypt, *Scarabaèus sàcer* L., is a member of this group and has habits similar to those of the tumblebugs. In Egyptian mythology the ball of dung represented the earth and its rotation.

Subfamily **Aphodiìnae**—Aphodian Dung Beetles: This is a fairly large group (more than 200 North American species) of small dung beetles, and some are quite common, particularly in cow dung. They are usually black, or red and black. One species, *Ataènius sprétulus* (Haldeman), has recently become an important pest of turf grasses, especially on golf courses.

Subfamily **Aegialiìnae**: The members of this group are similar to the Aphodiìnae, but have the mandibles visible from above. The group is a small one (about 20 species in North America), and most of its members (including all the eastern species) belong to the genus *Aegiàlia*.

Subfamily **Ochodaeìnae**: This is a small group (19 species in our area), and most of its members occur in the western states. One species, *Ochodaèus músculus* (Say), a reddish-brown oval beetle, 5–6 mm in length, with striate elytra, occurs in the northern states.

Subfamily **Hybosorìnae**: These beetles are about 7 mm in length, brownish black to black in color, and shaped a little like a miniature june beetle. Three rare species occur in the United States, one in the southeastern states and the other two in Arizona and California.

Subfamily **Geotrupìnae**—Earth-Boring Dung Beetles: These beetles are very similar to some of the other dung-feeding scarabs, but have the antennae 11-segmented. They are stout-bodied, convex, oval beetles that are black or dark brown in color (Figure 28–35A). The elytra are usually grooved or striate, the tarsi are long and slender, and the front tibiae are broadened and toothed or scalloped on the outer edges. The elytra completely cover the abdomen. These beetles vary in length from 5 to 25 mm and

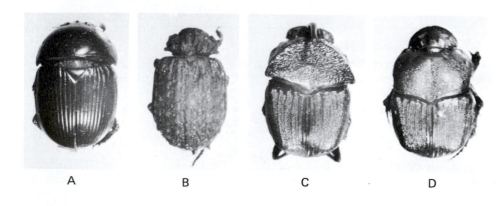

Figure 28–35.   Scarab beetles. **A,** an earth-boring dung beetle, *Geotrùpes spléndidus* (Fabricius); **B,** a skin beetle, *Tróx scabròsus* Beauvois; **C,** male, and **D,** female, of a dung beetle, *Phanaèus víndex* MacLachlan; 1½×.

are found beneath cow dung, horse manure, or carrion. Some occur in logs or decaying fungi. The larvae occur in or beneath dung or carrion. They feed on this material and hence are of value to humankind as scavengers.

Subfamily **Pleocominae**—Rain Beetles: These beetles are so called because the males fly and seek mates during the fall rains. The females are wingless. The 37 species are western in distribution and relatively rare. The larvae live in the soil and feed on the roots of trees and grasses. The adults live in burrows in the ground, usually coming out only at dusk or after a rain. The members of the genus *Pleócoma* are stout-bodied, relatively large (about 25 mm in length), and rather pubescent. The burrows of *P. fimbriàta* LeConte are about 25 mm in diameter and up to 0.6 meter in depth. The members of the genus *Ácoma* are much smaller, 4–7 mm in length, and light brown in color.

Subfamily **Glaphyrinae**: The members of this group are elongate and brownish and have the body very hairy. The elytra are short, exposing two or three abdominal terga. They taper posteriorly and are separated at the apex. These beetles are 13–18 mm in length. Our species belong to the genus *Lichnánthe*. Some occur in the Northeast and some in the West. All are quite rare.

Subfamily **Ceratocanthinae**: These beetles are round, blackish, and 5–6 mm in length, with the middle and hind tibiae greatly dilated and bearing rows of spines along their entire length. When disturbed, these beetles draw in their legs and antennae and form a hemispherical mass, and in this position they remain motionless. They occur under bark, in rotten logs and stumps, and occasionally on flowers. Three species occur in the United States: two species of *Cloeòtus*, which are widely distributed throughout the East, and *Acanthócerus aèneus* MacLeay, which occurs in the Southeast.

Subfamily **Troginae**—Skin Beetles: The members of this group have the dorsal surface of the body very rough. The second antennal segment arises before the tip of the first instead of from its apex (Figure 28–6G). These beetles are oblong, convex, dark brown in color (and often covered with dirt), and shaped much like june beetles (Figure 28–35B). They are usually found on old, dry animal carcasses, where they feed on the hide, feathers, hair, or dried tissues on the bones. They represent one of the last stages in the succession of insects living in animal carcasses. Some species occur in owl pellets, beneath bark, or on roots. When disturbed, these beetles draw in their legs and lie motionless, resembling dirt or rubbish, and are often overlooked. They overwinter as adults beneath leaves and in debris. Two

genera occur in the United States: *Tróx* (widely distributed) and *Glarèsis* (western United States).

Subfamily **Melolonthinae**—June Beetles, Chafers, and Others: This is a large and widely distributed group, and all its members are plant feeders. Many species are of considerable economic importance. The best-known beetles in this group are the june beetles or may beetles, sometimes called junebugs, which are usually brown in color and are common around lights in the spring and early summer (Figure 28–36A). Most of them belong to the genus *Phyllóphaga* (= *Lachnostérna*), which contains more than

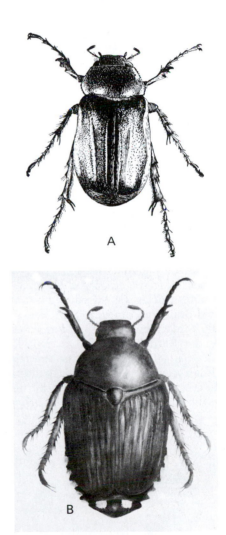

Figure 28–36. Plant-feeding scarabs. **A**, a june beetle, *Phyllóphaga portoricénsis* Smythe, 1½×; **B**, Japanese beetle, *Popíllia japónica* Newman, 4½×. (**A**, courtesy of Wolcott and the Journal of Agriculture of the University of Puerto Rico.)

200 eastern species. The adults feed at night on foliage and flowers. The larvae (Figure 28–37) are the well-known white grubs that feed in the soil on the roots of grasses and other plants. White grubs are very destructive insects and do a great deal of damage to pastures, lawns, and such crops as corn, small grains, potatoes, and strawberries. The life cycle usually requires two or three years to complete. The greatest damage to field crops occurs when fields are rotated from grass or meadow to corn.

This subfamily also contains the chafers (*Macrodáctylus*). The rose chafer, *M. subspinòsus* (Fabricius), is a slender, tan, long-legged beetle that feeds on the flowers and foliage of roses, grapes, and various other plants. It often feeds on peaches and other fruits. The larvae are small white grubs that occur in light soil and often do serious damage to roots. Poultry that eat these beetles become extremely ill and quite often are killed.

Most of the other beetles in this subfamily are robust, oval, and brownish and resemble june beetles (though most are smaller). The beetles in the genus *Dichelónyx* are elongate and slender, with the elytra greenish or bronze in color, and the tarsal claws are simple.

Subfamily **Rutelìnae**—Shining Leaf Chafers: The larvae of these beetles feed on plant roots, and the adults feed on foliage and fruits. Many of the adults are very brightly colored. A number of important pest species are included in this subfamily.

One of the most serious pests in this group is the Japanese beetle, *Popíllia japónica* Newman (Figure 28–36B). This species was introduced into the eastern United States on nursery stock from Japan in about 1916. Since then, it has spread over a large part of the eastern United States, where it is a serious pest on lawns, golf courses, fruits, and shrubbery. The adult is a very pretty insect. The head and thorax are bright green, the elytra are brownish tinged with green on the edges, and there are white spots along

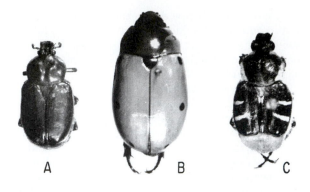

Figure 28–38. Plant-feeding scarabs. **A,** the hermit flower beetle, *Osmodérma eremícola* Knoch (Cetoniìnae), slightly enlarged; **B,** the grape pelidnota, *Pelidnòta punctàta* (L.) (Rutelìnae), 1½×; **C,** a flower beetle, *Trichiotìnus texànus* (Horn) (Cetoniìnae), 4×.

the sides of the abdomen. This species has one generation a year and overwinters in the larval stage in the soil.

Another rather common and destructive species is the grape pelidnota, *Pelidnòta punctàta* (L.). The adult is 25 mm or more in length and looks a little like a large june beetle, but is yellowish with three black spots on each elytron (Figure 28–38B). Most of the damage done by this species is done by the adult. The larvae feed chiefly in rotting wood.

The members of the genus *Cotálpa* are usually large beetles, uniform green or yellowish above and dark beneath. The larvae do considerable damage to the roots of berries, corn, and grass. One distinctive species in this genus is *C. lanígera* (L.), 20–26 mm in length and entirely yellow with a metallic luster. It occurs on or near catalpa trees.

From Baja California to Utah the common members of the Rutelìnae are the black and reddish brown members of the genus *Paracotálpa* (= *Pocálta*). In Texas and Arizona are found the real jewels of this subfamily, species belonging to the genus *Plusiòtis*. These large scarabs are a brilliant green, sometimes with added longitudinal lines of metallic golden color. They are favored items among collectors.

Subfamily **Dynastìnae**—Rhinoceros Beetles, Hercules Beetles, and Elephant Beetles: This group contains some of the largest North American beetles, a few of which may reach a length of 65 mm. The dorsal surface of the body is rounded and convex, and the males usually have horns on the head or pronotum (Figure 28–39). The females lack these horns.

The largest Dynastìnae are the Hercules beetles (*Dynástes*), which occur principally in the southern states. *Dynástes títyus* (L.), the eastern species, is

Figure 28–37. White grubs (*Phyllóphaga* sp.). (Courtesy of the Ohio Agricultural Research and Development Center.)

Figure 28–39.   The eastern Hercules beetle, *Dynástes títyus* (L.); male at left, female at right. About natural size.

50–65 mm in length and greenish gray mottled with large black areas. The pronotal horn of the male extends forward over the head (Figure 28–39). The western species, *D. gránti* Horn, is similar, but is slightly larger and has a longer pronotal horn. The elephant beetles (*Stratègus*) are big brown scarabs, 35–50 mm in length, that occur from Rhode Island to Kansas and Texas. They have three horns on the pronotum in the male (one in the female), but none on the head. In the rhinoceros beetle, *Xyloríctes jamaicénsis* (Drury), a dark brown scarab a little over 25 mm in length, the males have a single large upright horn on the head. (The females have a small tubercle instead of a horn.) The larva of this species feeds on the roots of ash trees. The rhinoceros beetle occurs from Connecticut to Arizona. The members of the genus *Phileùrus*, which are about 25 mm long and have two horns on the head, occur in the southern and southwestern states.

The smaller members of this subfamily, particularly the species in the genera *Lígyrus* and *Euetheòla*, are often serious pests of corn, sugarcane, and cereal crops. Both adult and larval stages cause damage.

Subfamily **Cetoniìnae**—Flower Beetles and Others: The members of this group are principally pollen feeders and are common on flowers. Many occur under loose bark or in debris, and a few occur in ant nests. The larvae feed on organic matter in the soil, and some species damage the roots of plants. This subfamily includes the goliath beetles of Africa, which are among the largest insects known. Some species reach a length of 100 mm or more.

Several genera in this subfamily (including *Cótinis*, *Euphòria*, and *Cremastocheìlus*) have the mes-

epimera visible from above, between the hind angles of the pronotum and the humeri of the elytra (Figure 28–40). The members of the genus *Cótinis* are more than 18 mm long and have the scutellum small and covered by a median backward-projecting lobe of the pronotum. Those of *Euphòria* and *Cremastocheìlus* are smaller and have the scutellum large and exposed (Figure 28–40). The green june beetle, *Cótinis nítida* (L.), is a common dark-green beetle nearly 25 mm long. The adults feed on grapes, ripening fruits, and young corn, and the larvae often seriously damage lawns, golf courses, and various crops. The beetles in the genus *Euphòria* are somewhat bumblebee-like and are often called bumble flower beetles. They are brownish yellow and black, are very pubescent, and act much like bumblebees. These beetles do not extend their elytra in flight. Instead, the hind wings are extended through shallow emarginations at the sides of the elytra (Figure 28–40).

Perhaps the least-known and most interesting members of this subfamily are those in the genus *Cremastocheìlus*. These beetles, which are 9–15 mm in length, are kept captive in ant nests to provide the ants with a nutritive fluid. The ants cling to the beetle's thorax and gnaw at pubescent glandular areas on the exposed mesepimera. More than 30 species belonging to this genus are known in the United States.

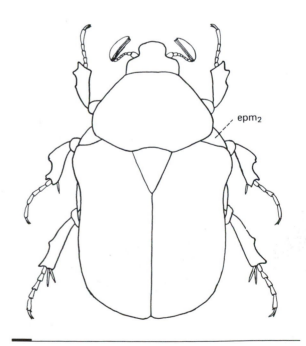

Figure 28–40.   A bumble flower beetle, *Euphòria índa* (L.) (Cetoniìnae), 5×. *epm₂*, mesepimeron.

In the other common genera of Cetoniìnae the mesepimera are not visible from above. The hermit flower beetle, *Osmodérma eremícola* Knoch, is a brownish black insect about 25 mm in length, with the elytra longer than wide (Figure 28–38A). The larvae feed in decaying wood, and the adults are frequently found under dead bark or in tree cavities. The adults emit a very disagreeable odor when disturbed. In *Válgus* and *Trichiotìnus* the elytra are about as long as wide. The members of *Válgus* are small, less than 7.5 mm in length, and are brown in color and covered with scales. *Trichiotìnus* beetles are brightly colored and pubescent (Figure 28–38C). The adults of these two genera occur on various types of flowers, and the larvae live in decaying wood.

Family **Býrrhidae**—Pill Beetles: The pill beetles (Figure 28–41) are oval, convex, and 1.5–10.0 mm in length. The head is bent downward and concealed from above, and the wide hind coxae extend to the elytra. These insects usually occur in sandy situations, such as lake shores, where they may be found under debris. Species of *Býrrhus* and *Cỳtilus* occasionally damage forest tree seedlings. When disturbed, they draw in their legs, with the femora fitting into coxal grooves, and remain motionless. There are 72 species recorded for the United States and Canada.

Family **Bupréstidae**—Metallic Wood-Boring Beetles: The adults of this group are 3–100 mm (usually less than 20 mm) in length and are often rather metallic—coppery, green, blue, or black—especially on the ventral side of the body and on the dorsal surface of the abdomen. They are hard-bodied and compactly built and usually have a characteristic shape (Figures 28–42 and 28–43). Many adult buprestids are attracted to dead or dying trees and logs and to slash. Others occur on the foliage of trees and shrubs. These beetles run or fly rapidly and are often difficult to catch. Some are colored like the bark and are very inconspicuous when they remain motionless. Many of the larger beetles in this group are common in sunny situations. There are about 675 North American species of Bupréstidae.

Most buprestid larvae bore under bark or in wood, attacking either living trees or newly cut or dying logs and branches. Many do serious damage to trees and shrubs. The eggs are usually laid in crevices in the bark. The larvae, on hatching, tunnel under the bark, and some species eventually bore into the wood. The galleries under the bark are often winding and filled with frass. The galleries in the wood are oval in cross section and usually enter the wood at an angle (Figure 28–44). Pupation occurs in the galleries. Because buprestid larvae usually have the anterior end expanded and flattened (Figure 28–45), they are often known as flat-headed borers. The larvae of some species make winding galleries under the bark of twigs (Figure 28–46B); others make galls (Figure 28–46A); and one species girdles twigs.

The larvae of *Chrysóbothris femoràta* (Olivier) attack a number of trees and shrubs and frequently do serious damage to fruit trees. The larvae of different species of *Ágrilus* attack raspberries, blackberries, and other shrubs. *Ágrilus champlàini* Frost makes galls in ironwood (Figure 28–46A), and *A. ruficóllis* (Fabricius) makes galls in raspberry and blackberry. *Ágrilus arcuàtus* (Say) is a twig girdler. The adults of the genus *Ágrilus* are rather long and narrow (Figure 28–43C); most are dark-colored with metallic shades, and some have light markings. The larvae of the species of *Bráchys* (Figure 28–42D) are leaf miners. Most buprestids fly when disturbed, but the beetles in the genus *Bráchys* draw up their legs, "play dead," and fall off the foliage onto the ground. These smaller buprestids are usually found on foliage.

Family **Eulichádidae**: This group includes a single North American species, *Stenócolus scutellàris* LeConte, which has previously been included in the family Dascíllidae. This species, which occurs in the mountains of northern California, is 15–25 mm in length and shaped like a click beetle, with a vestiture of fine hairs. The mandibles are prominent and strongly bent apically, with the apex scooplike. The larvae occur in streams and probably feed on decaying vegetation.

Family **Callirhípidae**: The only North American species in this family is *Zénoa pìcea* (Beauvois), an

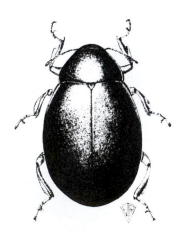

Figure 28–41. A pill beetle, *Amphicýrta déntipes* Erichson, 5×. (Courtesy of Arnett.)

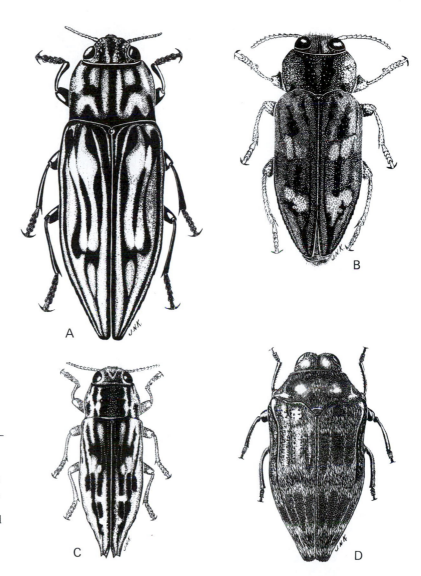

Figure 28–42. Metallic wood-boring beetles. **A,** *Chalcóphora fórtis* LeConte, which breeds in dead white pine; **B,** *Chrysóbothris florícola* Gory, which breeds in pine; **C,** *Dicérca lépida* LeConte, which breeds in dead ironwood and hawthorn; **D,** *Bráchys ovátus* Weber, which mines in oak leaves. (Courtesy of Knull.)

elongate, dark-brown, shiny beetle, 11–15 mm in length. Its antennae are short flabellate in both sexes. This is a rare beetle found under logs and bark and is known from Ohio, Indiana, Pennsylvania, Kansas, Louisiana, and Florida.

Family **Ptilodactýlidae:** The members of this group are elongate-oval in shape, brownish in color, and 4–6 mm in length, and the head is generally not visible from above. The antennae are serrate in the female and pectinate in the male (segments 4–10 each bear a slender basal process about as long as the segment). The tarsi are 5–5–5, with the third segment lobed beneath and the fourth often minute. The ptilodactylids occur on vegetation chiefly in swampy places. Some larvae are aquatic and others occur in moist dead logs.

Family **Chelonariidae:** Only one rare species of chelonariid occurs in the United States, *Chelonàrium lecóntei* Thomson, which occurs in the Southeast, from North Carolina to eastern Texas and south to Florida and Louisiana. This insect is oval, convex, 4–5 mm in length, and black with patches of white pubescence on the elytra. The legs are retractile. The basal antennal segments are situated in a prosternal groove, and the remaining segments extend back along the mesosternum. The larvae of these beetles are aquatic, and the adults are found on vegetation.

Family **Heterocéridae**—Variegated Mud-Loving Beetles: The heterocerids are a group of flattened, oblong, pubescent beetles (Figure 28–47A) that live in mud or sand along the banks of streams or lakes. Superficially they resemble small scarabs. Most of

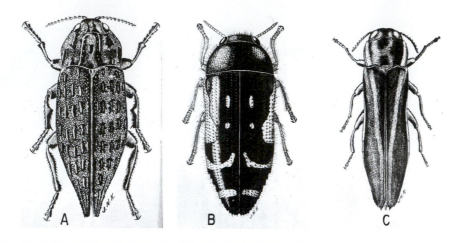

Figure 28–43.   Metallic wood-boring beetles. **A,** *Dicérca tenebròsa* (Kirby), 3½× ; **B,** *Ácmaeodèra pulchélla* (Herbst), 6× ; **C,** *Ágrilus bilineàtus* (Weber), 6×. (Courtesy of Knull.)

them are blackish or brownish with bands or spots of dull yellow and are 4–6 mm in length. The tibiae are armed with rows of heavy flattened spines. The tarsi are 4–4–4, with segments 1 and 4 much longer than 2 and 3. The antennae are short, with the last seven segments forming an oblong serrate club. The front and middle tibiae are greatly dilated and spiny and are used in burrowing. These beetles may often be forced to leave their burrows in the stream bank when the shore is flooded with water splashed up from the stream. There are 31 species in the United States and Canada.

Family **Limníchidae**—Minute Marsh-Loving Beetles: The members of this and the two following families have the tarsal claws quite long (as in Figure 28–10H), and the first three visible abdominal sterna are more or less fused together. The larvae of most species (and usually also the adults) are aquatic. The limnichids are small (1–4 mm in length), oval, convex beetles that have the body clothed with fine pubescence. The most common limnichids (*Lutròchus*) have 11 antennal segments. These beetles are usually found in the wet sand or soil along the margins of streams.

Family **Dryópidae**—Long-Toed Water Beetles: The dryopids are elongate-oval, 1–8 mm in length, and dull gray or brown, with the head more or less withdrawn into the prothorax (Figure 28–47B). Some species have the body covered with a fine pubescence. The antennae are very short, with most segments broader than long, and are concealed beneath the prosternal lobe. These beetles usually cling to objects in a stream. Sometimes they are found crawling

about on the bottoms of streams or along the shores. The adults may leave the stream and fly about, especially at night. Most known larvae are vermiform and live in soil or decaying wood (rather than in water). Thirteen species occur in our area.

Family **Élmidae**—Riffle Beetles: These beetles generally occur on the stones or debris in the riffles of streams. A few species occur in ponds or swamps, and a few are terrestrial. Riffle beetles are somewhat cylindrical in shape, with the elytra very smooth or somewhat ridged (Figure 28–47C), and most of them

Figure 28–44.   Galleries of buprestid larvae. (Courtesy of Davidson.)

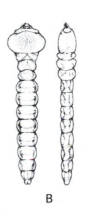
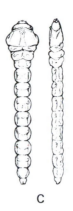
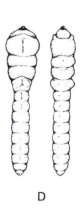

Figure 28–45. Larvae of Buprestidae. **A,** *Chrysóbothris trinérva* (Kirby); **B,** *Melanóphila drúmmondi* (Kirby); **C,** *Dicérca tenebròsa* (Kirby); **D,** *Acmaeodèra prórsa* Fall. Dorsal view at left in each figure, lateral view at right. (Courtesy of USDA.)

A   B   C   D

are 3.5 mm in length or less. The larvae of most species, which occur in the same situations as the adults, are long and slender. Those of *Phanócerus* are somewhat flattened and elliptical. There are 85 species in the United States and Canada.

Family **Psephènidae**—Water-Penny Beetles: These beetles derive their common name from the peculiar shape of the larvae (Figure 28–48A,B). The larvae (called water pennies) are very flat and almost cir-

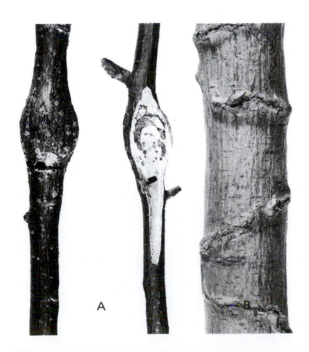

Figure 28–46. **A,** galls of *Ágrilus champlàini* Frost, in ironwood (*Ostrỳa*); **B,** the work of *Ágrilus bilineàtus carpìni* Knull on blue beech (*Carpìnus*). (Courtesy of Knull.)

cular and occur on the undersides of stones or other objects in streams and wave-swept shores. *Psephènus hérricki* (DeKay) is a common eastern species. The adult is a somewhat flattened blackish beetle, 4–6 mm in length (Figure 28–48C), which is usually found on stones in the water or along the shore of the streams where the larvae occur. Thirteen other species, mostly western, occur in the United States.

Family **Artematópidae:** This is a small family (eight North American species) formerly placed in the Dascíllidae (subfamily Dascíllinae), which they strongly resemble. They are elongate pubescent beetles, 4.0–7.5 mm in length, with the head deflexed and with long filiform antennae. The tarsi usually have the fourth segment small and segments 2–4 lobed. Species of *Eurypògon* are frequently taken by sweeping vegetation.

Family **Cerophýtidae:** This group includes two very rare species of *Ceróphytum*, one occurring in the East and the other in California. These beetles are elongate-oblong in shape, somewhat flattened, 7.5–8.5 mm in length, and brownish to black in color. The hind trochanters are very long, nearly as long as the femora. These beetles occur in rotten wood and under dead bark.

Family **Elatéridae**—Click Beetles: The click beetles constitute a large group (about 885 North American species), and many species are quite common. These beetles are peculiar in being able to "click" and jump. In most of the related groups, the union of the prothorax and mesothorax is such that little or no movement at this point is possible. The clicking is made possible by the flexible union of the prothorax and mesothorax, and by a prosternal spine that fits into a groove on the mesosternum (Figure 28–8A).

If one of these beetles is placed on its back on a smooth surface, it is usually unable to right itself by means of its legs. It bends its head and prothorax

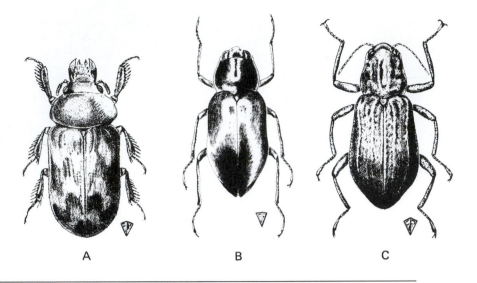

Figure 28–47.   **A,** a variegated mud-loving beetle, *Neoheterócerus pállidus* (Say) (Heterocéridae), 9×; **B,** a long-toed water beetle, *Hélichus lithóphilus* (Germar) (Dryópidae), 8×; **C,** a riffle beetle, *Stenélmis crenàta* (Say) (Élmídae), 8×. (Courtesy of Arnett.)

backward, so that only the extremities of the body are touching the surface on which it rests. Then, with a sudden jerk and clicking sound, the body is straightened out. This movement snaps the prosternal spine into the mesosternal groove and throws the insect into the air, spinning end over end. If the insect does not land right side up, it continues snapping until it does.

The click beetles can usually be recognized by their characteristic shape (Figure 28–49A,C). The body is elongate, usually parallel-sided, and rounded at each end. The posterior corners of the pronotum are prolonged backward into sharp points or spines. The antennae are usually serrate (occasionally filiform or pectinate). Most of these beetles are between 12 and 30 mm in length, but a few exceed these limits. The largest and most easily recognized species is the eyed click beetle, *Álaus oculàtus* (L.), a

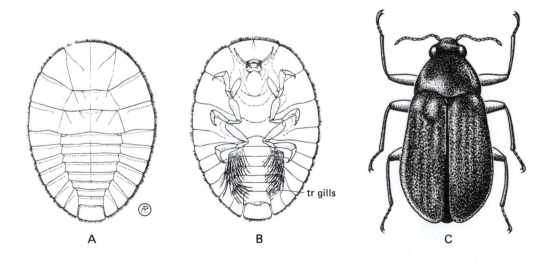

Figure 28–48.   Psephènidae. **A,** dorsal view, and **B,** ventral view, of a water penny, the larva of *Psephènus hérricki* (DeKay); **C,** adult water penny beetle, *Psephènus hérricki* (DeKay), 8×. *tr gills,* tracheal gills. (**A** and **B,** courtesy of Peterson; **C,** courtesy of Arnett.)

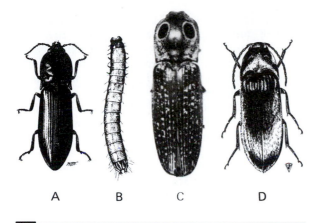

Figure 28–49. **A,** adult, and **B,** larva, of a click beetle, *Ctenícera nóxia* (Hyslop) (slightly enlarged); **C,** the eyed click beetle, *Álaus oculàtus* (L.) (about natural size); **D,** a false click beetle, *Aneláes drùryi* (Kirby), 3×. (**A** and **B,** courtesy of USDA; **D,** courtesy of Arnett.)

mottled-gray beetle with the pronotum bearing two large black eyelike spots (Figure 28–49C). This species may reach about 40 mm or more in length. Most elaterids are inconspicuously colored with black or brown.

Adult click beetles are phytophagous and occur on flowers, under bark, or on vegetation. Most larvae are slender, hard-bodied, and shiny and are commonly called wireworms (Figure 28–49B). The larvae of many species are very destructive, feeding on newly planted seeds and the roots of beans, cotton, potatoes, corn, and cereals. Many elaterid larvae occur in rotting logs, and some of these feed on other insects. Pupation occurs in the ground, under bark, or in dead wood.

Species of *Pyróphorus* in the southern states and in the tropics have two light-producing spots on the posterior edge of the prothorax and one on the abdomen. The light is much stronger than that of the lampyrids, and a large number flying about at night is a striking sight.

Family **Cebriónidae**: The cebrionids are elongate brownish beetles, 15–25 mm in length, with the mandibles hooklike and extending forward in front of the head. Some have the body quite hairy. The larvae and females (which are wingless) live in the ground. The males are excellent fliers and are largely nocturnal. All of the 18 North American species are southern in distribution.

Family **Thróscidae**: This is a small group (27 North American species) of oblong-oval brownish to black beetles that are mostly 5 mm in length or less.

They are similar to the elaterids, but are more oval in shape. Some (*Aulonothróscus* and *Tríxagus*) have the antennae clubbed. The prosternum is lobed anteriorly and almost conceals the mouthparts. The prothorax appears rather solidly fused to the mesothorax, but at least some of these beetles can click and jump like an elaterid. The adults are found chiefly on vegetation and in leaf litter. They are primarily in litter in cool weather, but fly or climb onto nearby vegetation in warm weather. They do not seem to have any preferences for particular species of plants.

Family **Perothópidae**: These beetles are similar to the Eucnèmidae, but have the prothorax free and the tarsal claws pectinate. They are 10–18 mm in length, brownish in color, and found on the trunks and branches of old beech trees. Three species of *Pérothops* occur in the United States from Pennsylvania to Florida and in California. The larvae are unknown.

Family **Eucnèmidae**—False Click Beetles: This family (71 species in our area) is very closely related to the Elatéridae. Its members are relatively rare beetles usually found in wood that has just begun to decay, chiefly in beech and maple. Most of them are brownish in color and about 10 mm in length or less (Figure 28–49D). The pronotum is quite convex above; the antennae are inserted rather close together on the front of the head; and there is no distinct labrum. These beetles quiver their antennae almost constantly, a habit not occurring in the Elatéridae. Some, like the click beetles, can click and jump.

Family **Brachypséctridae**: This family is represented in the United States by a single very rare species, *Brachypséctra fúlva* LeConte, a yellowish brown beetle 5–6 mm in length, which is sometimes referred to as the Texas beetle. It resembles a click beetle in general appearance, but does not have the prosternal spine and mesosternal fossa characteristic of the Elatéridae. This insect is known from Texas, Utah, and California.

Family **Lýcidae**—Net-Winged Beetles: The lycids (83 North American species) are elongate softwinged beetles, 5–18 mm in length. They are somewhat similar to the soldier beetles, but may be readily recognized by the peculiar network of raised lines on the elytra, with the longitudinal ridges more distinct than the transverse ridges (Figure 28–50A). Some western species (*Lýcus*) have a distinct snout. The elytra in some species are slightly widened posteriorly. The adults occur on foliage and tree trunks, usually in wooded areas. They feed on the juices of decaying plant materials and occasionally on other insects. The larvae are predaceous.

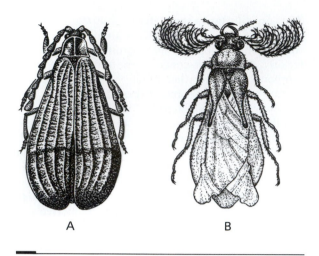

Figure 28–50.   **A,** a net-winged beetle, *Calópteron terminàle* (Say); **B,** adult male of a glowworm, *Phengòdes plumòsa* Olivier; 4×. (Courtesy of Arnett.)

One of the more common members of this group is *Calópteron reticulàtum* (Fabricius), 11–19 mm in length. The elytra are yellow, with the posterior half and a narrow cross band in the anterior part black. This insect's pronotum is black, margined with yellow. Most lycids are blackish, but many are brightly colored with red, black, or yellow. They are apparently distasteful to predators, and their coloration is mimicked by other beetles (certain Cerambýcidae) and some moths (for example, certain Arctìidae; Figure 34–82C).

Family **Phengòdidae**—Glowworms: This is a small group (25 species in North America) of relatively uncommon beetles closely related to the Lampýridae. Most of them are broad and flat, with the elytra short and pointed and the posterior part of the abdomen covered only by the membranous, fan-shaped, nonfolding hind wings (Figure 28–50B). The antennae are usually serrate, but in some males they may be pectinate or plumose. These insects vary in length from 10 to 30 mm and are found on foliage or on the ground. The adult females of all known species are wingless and luminescent, as in the Lampýridae, and look much like larvae. The larvae are predaceous.

Family **Telegeùsidae:** The Telegeùsidae are represented in North America by two species of small, rare beetles that occur in Arizona and California. Their most distinctive character is the form of the maxillary and labial palps, which have the terminal segment tremendously enlarged. The tarsi are five-segmented; the antennae are serrate; and the seven or eight abdominal segments are less than half cov-

ered by the short elytra. The telegeusids are slender and 5–8 mm in length, resembling small rove beetles. The hind wings do not fold, but extend back over the abdomen beyond the tips of the elytra. Females, which are probably larviform, and larvae of telegeusids are unknown.

Family **Lampýridae**—Lightningbugs or Fireflies: Many members of this common and well-known group possess a "taillight"—segments near the end of the abdomen with which the insects are able to produce light. These luminous segments can be recognized, even when they are not glowing, by their yellowish green color. During certain seasons, usually early summer, these insects fly about in the evenings and are conspicuous by their blinking yellow lights.

The lampyrids are elongate and very soft-bodied beetles, 5–20 mm in length, in which the pronotum extends forward over the head so that the head is largely or entirely concealed from above (Figure 28–51A). The elytra are soft, flexible, and rather flat except for the epipleurae. Most of the larger members of this group have luminescent organs, but many of the smaller ones do not.

The light emitted by these insects is unique in being cold. Nearly 100% of the energy given off appears as light. In the electric arc light, only 10% of the energy is light, and the other 90% is given off as heat. The light given off by a firefly is produced by the oxidation of a substance called luciferin, which is produced in the cells of the light-producing organs. These organs have a rich tracheal supply, and the insect controls the emission of light by controlling the air supply to the organs. When air is admitted, the luciferin (in the presence of an enzyme called luciferinase) is almost instantly oxidized, releasing the energy as light. The flashing of fireflies serves primarily as a means of getting the sexes together, and each species has a characteristic flash rhythm (see also page 85). Females of some predatory species imitate the flashes of other species and thus lure amorous but hapless males of those species to their doom.

During the day the lampyrids are usually found on vegetation. The larvae are predaceous and feed on various smaller insects and on snails. The females of many species are wingless and look very much like larvae. These wingless females and most lampyrid larvae are luminescent and are often called "glowworms." There are about 125 species of fireflies in the United States and Canada, mostly in the East and the South.

Family **Canthàridae**—Soldier Beetles: The cantharids are elongate, soft-bodied beetles, 1–15 mm in length, that are very similar to the lightningbugs

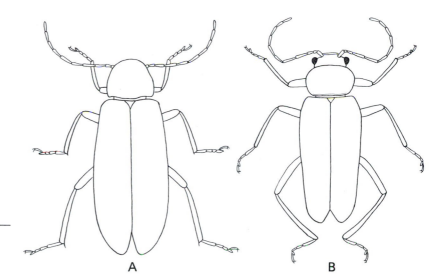

Figure 28–51. **A,** a lightning-bug (*Photùris*); **B,** a soldier beetle (*Chauliógnathus*); 3¾×.

(Lampýridae), but the head protrudes forward beyond the pronotum and is visible from above (not concealed by the pronotum as in the Lampýridae). These beetles do not have light-producing organs.

Adult soldier beetles are usually found on flowers. The larvae are predaceous on other insects. One common species, *Chauliógnathus pennsylvánicus* (DeGeer) (Figure 28–51B), about 13 mm in length, has each elytron yellowish with a black spot or stripe. Members of other genera are yellowish, black, or brown in color. There are 468 species of soldier beetles in North America.

Family **Derodóntidae**—Tooth-Necked Fungus Beetles: The derodontids (9 North American species) are small, usually brownish beetles, 3–6 mm in length (Figure 28–52), and have a pair of ocelli on the head near the inner margins of the compound eyes (Figure 28–14C). The members of the genus *Derodóntus* have three or four strong teeth or notches along the lateral margins of the pronotum. Other genera lack these teeth. The elytra completely cover the abdomen, and each bears many rows of large square punctures or polished dark spots. These beetles occur in woody fungi and under the bark of rotting logs. *Laricòbius erichsònii* Rosenhauer has been introduced from Europe into Oregon, where it is established as an important predator of the balsam woolly aphid.

Family **Nosodéndridae:** This family includes two species of *Nosodéndron*, one occurring in the East and the other in the West. The eastern species, *N. unicólor* Say, is an oval, convex, black beetle 5–6 mm in length. It occurs in oozing tree wounds (sometimes in good numbers), under the bark of dead logs, and in debris. The nosodendrids are similar to

the Býrrhidae, but they have the head visible from above, and the elytra bear rows of short yellow hair tufts.

Family **Derméstidae**—Dermestid or Skin Beetles: This group (129 North American species) contains a number of very destructive and economically important species. The dermestids are mostly scavengers and feed on a great variety of plant and animal products, including leather, furs, skins, museum specimens, woolen or silk materials, rugs, stored food materials, and carrion. Most of the damage is done by the larvae.

Adult dermestids are small, oval or elongate-oval, convex beetles with short clubbed antennae, and

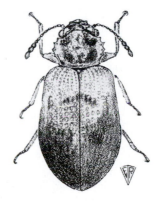

Figure 28–52. A tooth-necked fungus beetle, *Derodóntus maculàtus* Melsheimer, 15×. (Courtesy of Arnett.)

they vary in length from 2 to 12 mm. They are usually hairy or covered with scales (Figure 28–53A–C). All adults except members of the genus *Derméstes* have a median ocellus (which is sometimes very small). They may be found in the materials mentioned previously, and many feed on flowers. Some are black or dull-colored, but many have a characteristic color pattern. The larvae are usually brownish and are covered wtih long hairs (Figure 28–53D–F).

The larger dermestids belong to the genus *Derméstes*. The larder beetle, *D. lardàrius* L., is a common species in this genus. It is a little more than 6 mm long and is black with a light brown band across the base of the elytra. It feeds on a variety of stored foods, including meats and cheese, and occasionally damages the specimens in insect collections.

Some of the smaller dermestids are often common in houses and may do serious damage to carpets, upholstery, and clothing. Two common species of this type are the black carpet beetle, *Attagènus megátoma* (Fabricius), and the carpet beetle, *Anthrènus scrophulàriae* (L.). The former is a grayish black beetle, 3.5–5.0 mm in length (Figure 28–53B), and the latter is a pretty little black-and-white patterned species, 3–5 mm in length (Figure 28–53A). Most of

the damage done by these species is done by the larvae. The adults are often found on flowers.

This is one group of insects that every entomology student will encounter sooner or later. All the student has to do to get some dermestids is to make an insect collection and not protect it against these pests. The dermestids will eventually find the collection and ruin it. Many species in this group are serious pests in homes, markets, and food-storage places.

This group contains one of the worst stored-products pests in the world, the khapra beetle, *Trogodérma granàrium* Everts. A native of India, this beetle is frequently intercepted at ports of entry into this country, and in 1953 it became established in California, Arizona, and New Mexico. It is now apparently eradicated in the United States.

While many of the dermestids are serious pests, they are nevertheless of value as scavengers, aiding in the removal of dead organic matter. Some of the species that feed on carrion, notably species of *Derméstes*, have been used by vertebrate zoologists to clean skeletons for study.

One species in this family, *Thylódrias contráctus* Motschulsky, is unusual in having the antennae filiform and the female wingless and larviform.

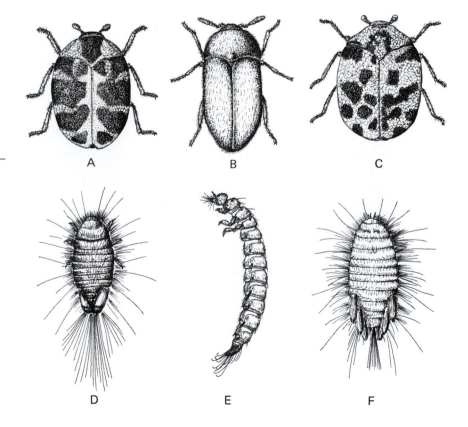

A   B   C

D   E   F

Figure 28–53. Dermestid beetles. **A,** the carpet beetle, *Anthrènus scrophulàriae* (L.), adult; **B,** the black carpet beetle, *Attagènus megátoma* (Fabricius), adult; **C,** the furniture carpet beetle, *Anthrènus flávipes* LeConte, adult; **D,** larva of *A. scrophulàriae* (L.), dorsal view; **E,** larva of *A. megátoma* (Fabricius), lateral view; **F,** larva of *A. flávipes* LeConte, dorsal view. (**E,** courtesy of Peterson; other figures, courtesy of the Cornell University Agricultural Experiment Station.)

Family **Bostríchidae**—Branch and Twig Borers: Most of the beetles in this group (more than 60 North American species) are elongate and somewhat cylindrical, and the head is bent down and scarcely visible from above (Figure 28–54). The antennae are straight, with a loose three- or four-segmented club. Most species vary in length from 3.5 to 12.0 mm, but one western species, *Dinápate wrìghti* Horn, which breeds in palms, reaches a length of 52 mm. Most species in this group are wood-boring and attack living trees, dead twigs and branches, or seasoned lumber. The apple twig borer, *Amphícerus bicaudàtus* (Say), attacks the twigs of apple, pear, cherry, and other trees. *Rhizopértha domínica* (Fabricius), the lesser grain borer, is a major cosmopolitan pest of stored grain.

One species in this family that occurs in the West, *Scobícia déclivis* (LeConte), is rather unusual in that the adults often bore into the lead sheathing of telephone cables. This insect normally bores in the wood of oak, maple, and other trees. It apparently does not feed as it bores into the cables. The beetles make holes in the sheathing about 2.5 mm in diameter that allow moisture to enter the cable, causing a short-circuiting of the wires and a consequent interruption of service. This insect is commonly known as the lead-cable borer or short-circuit beetle.

The bostrichids in the subfamily Psoìnae, which occur principally in the West, differ from other bostrichids in that the head is large and easily visible from above, and the mandibles are large and strong. The members of the genus *Polýcaon* are 14–28 mm long, are brown or black in color, and often cause great damage to orchards in California and Oregon by severely pruning the trees. The larvae tunnel through the heartwood of these trees, but the adults seldom enter the wood. *Psòa maculàta* (LeConte), 6 mm long, is the ''spotted limb borer'' of California. It breeds only in dead twigs of trees or shrubs and is usually bluish black or greenish with dense gray hair and with a few large lighter spots on the elytra.

Family **Lýctidae**—Powderpost Beetles: These beetles derive their name from the fact that they bore

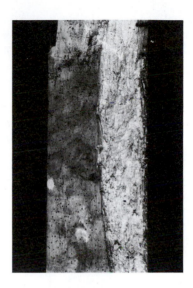

Figure 28–55. A board damaged by powderpost beetles, showing exit holes of the beetles.

into dry and seasoned wood and reduce it to a powder. Species of *Lýctus* may completely destroy furniture, wooden beams (particularly in barns and cabins), tool handles, and hardwood floors. They live beneath the surface for months, and timbers from which the adults have emerged may be peppered with tiny holes, as though fine shot had been fired into them (Figure 28–55). These beetles do not enter wood that is painted or varnished. The powerpost beetles are slender and elongate (Figure 28–56B),

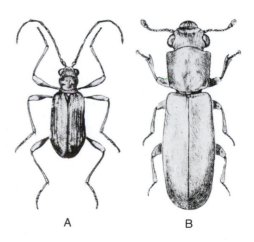

A   B

Figure 28–56. **A,** a spider beetle, *Ptìnus fúr* (L.), 5×; **B,** a powderpost beetle, *Trogoxỳlon parallelopípedum* (Melsheimer), 10×. (Courtesy of Arnett.)

Figure 28–54. A bostrichid beetle, *Ápate mónacha* Fabricius. (Courtesy of Wolcott and the Journal of Agriculture of the University of Puerto Rico.)

uniformly colored brown to black, and 2–7 mm in length. The head is prominent from above, and the antennae have a two-segmented club. There are 11 species in our area.

Family **Anobiidae:**   The anobiids are cylindrical to oval, pubescent beetles, 1–9 mm in length. The head is deflexed and is usually concealed from above by the hoodlike pronotum. Most of them have the last three antennal segments enlarged and lengthened (Figures 28–5C, 28–57B,D–F). A few have these segments lengthened but not enlarged, and a few have the antennae serrate or pectinate. More than 300 species occur in North America.

Most anobiids live in dry vegetable materials such as logs and twigs or under the bark of dead trees. Others pass the larval stage in fungi or in the seeds and stems of various plants. Some species, such as *Xestòbium rufovillòsum* (De Geer) (Figure 28–57F), are called deathwatch beetles because as they bore through wood they make a ticking sound that is audible to the human ear when conditions are quiet (as at a wake).

Some of the anobiids are common and destructive pests. The drugstore beetle, *Stegòbium paníceum* (L.) (Figure 28–57E), infests various drugs and cereals. The cigarette beetle, *Lasiodérma serricòrne* (Fabricius) (Figure 28–57C), is common in dried tobacco, museum specimens, insect collections, and various household products. In some parts of the United States it is a common household pest, infest-

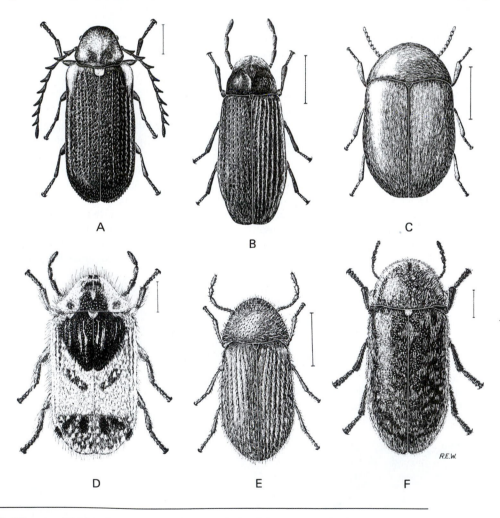

Figure 28–57.   Anobiid beetles. **A,** *Eucràda humeràlis* (Melsheimer); **B,** the furniture beetle, *Anòbium punctàtum* (De Geer); **C,** the cigarette beetle, *Lasiodérma serricòrne* (Fabricius); **D,** *Trichodésma gibbòsa* (Say); **E,** the drugstore beetle, *Stegòbium paníceum* (L.); **F,** a deathwatch beetle, *Xestòbium rufovillòsum* (De Geer). The lines represent 1 mm. (Courtesy of White and the Ohio Biological Survey.)

ing paprika, pepper, chili powder, pet foods, cereals, and other materials. Some wood-boring species, such as the furniture beetle, *Anòbium punctàtum* (De Geer) (Figure 28–57B), bore in timbers, woodwork, and furniture. *Hemicoèlus gibbicóllis* (LeConte), the Pacific powderpost beetle, damages buildings along the Pacific Coast from California to Alaska, feeding chiefly in well-seasoned wood.

Family **Ptìnidae**—Spider Beetles: The ptinids are long-legged beetles, 1–5mm in length, that have the head and pronotum much narrower than the elytra and are somewhat spiderlike in appearance (Figure 28–56A). The head is nearly or completely concealed from above. Many species are minor pests of stored grain products. Some feed on both plant and animal products and are known to attack museum specimens. One species is known to pass its larval stages in rat droppings, and another (*Ptìnus califòrnicus* Pic) feeds on the pollen provisions in nests of solitary bees. There are around 50 species in North America.

Family **Lymexýlidae**—Ship-Timber Beetles: This group is represented in the United States by three rare species that occur under bark and in dead logs and stumps. They cause much of the pin-hole damage in chestnut. These beetles are long and narrow and 9.0–13.5 mm in length; the head is bent down and narrowed behind the eyes to form a short neck; the antennae are filiform to serrate; the tarsi are five-segmented; and the maxillary palps in the males are long and flabellate. These beetles are called ship-timber beetles because one European species has been very destructive to ship timbers. One of our two species, *Hylecoètus lùgubris* Say, is commonly called the sapwood timberworm.

Family **Trogossítidae**—Bark-Gnawing Beetles: This group (64 species in the United States and Canada) contains two subfamilies that differ rather markedly in shape. The Trogossitìnae are elongate, with the head about as wide as the pronotum and with the pronotum rather widely separated from the base of the elytra (Figure 28–58), and the Peltìnae are oval or elliptical, with the head only about half as wide as the pronotum, and the pronotum rather closely joined to the base of the elytra. The Peltìnae are very similar to some nitidulids (for example, Figure 28–61C), but may be separated by the characters given in the key (couplet 144). Most Peltìnae have long erect hairs on the elytra, while the similarly shaped nitidulids have the elytra bare or short-pubescent. The Trogossitìnae are chiefly predaceous on insects under bark, but the Peltìnae feed chiefly on fungi.

Trogossitids are 2.6–20.0 mm in length, and most are brownish or blackish. A few are bluish or greenish. The cadelle, *Tenebròides mauritánicus* (L.) (cf. Figure 28–58), occurs commonly in granaries. It

is believed to feed both on other insects in the grain and on the grain itself. *Temnochìla viréscens* (Fabricius), a rather common and widely distributed species, is a bright blue-green beetle about 20 mm in length. It can administer a vicious bite from its powerful mandibles. Adults and larvae of trogossitids are generally found under bark, in woody fungi, and in dry vegetable matter.

Family **Cléridae**—Checkered Beetles: The clerids are elongate, very pubescent beetles 3–24 (mostly 5–12) mm in length, and many are brightly colored. The pronotum is usually narrower than the base of the elytra and sometimes narrower than the head (Figure 28–59). The tarsi are 5-segmented, but in many species the first or the fourth segment is very small and difficult to see. The antennae are usually clubbed, but are sometimes serrate, pectinate, or (rarely) filiform. There are 266 species of Cléridae in our area.

Most of the checkered beetles are predaceous as both adults and larvae. Many are common on or within tree trunks and logs, where they prey on the larvae of various wood-boring insects (chiefly bark beetles). Others occur on flowers and foliage. A few (for example, *Trichòdes*; Figure 28–59E) are pollen feeders in the adult stage and sometimes also in the larval stage. *Trichòdes* larvae sometimes develop in the egg pods of grasshoppers or in the nests of bees and wasps.

Some of the clerids, which have the fourth tarsal segment very small and difficult to see, have been placed by some authorities in a separate family, the

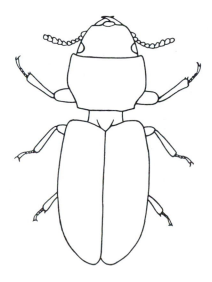

Figure 28–58. A trogossitid beetle, *Tenebròides* sp., $7\frac{1}{2}\times$.

Corynètidae. These beetles are similar in general appearance and habits to the other clerids. One species in this group, *Necròbia rùfipes* De Geer (Figure 28–59D), the red-legged ham beetle, is occasionally destructive to stored meats.

Family **Melýridae**—Soft-Winged Flower Beetles: The members of this family (520 species in North America) are elongate-oval, soft-bodied beetles 10 mm in length or less. Many are brightly colored with brown or red and black (Figure 28–60A). Some melyrids (Malachiìnae) have peculiar orange-colored structures along the sides of the abdomen, which may be everted and saclike or withdrawn into the body and inconspicuous. Some melyrids have the two basal antennal segments greatly enlarged. Most adults and larvae are predaceous, but many are common on flowers. Our most common species belong

to the genus *Cóllops* (Malachiìnae); *C. quadrimaculàtus* (Fabricius) is reddish, with two bluish black spots on each elytron.

Family **Sphíndidae**—Dry-Fungus Beetles: The sphindids are broadly oval to oblong, convex, dark brown to black beetles, 1.5–3.0 mm in length. They have a 5–5–4 tarsal formula, and the 10–segmented antennae terminate in a 2- or 3-segmented club. The sphindids occur in slime molds on dead trees, logs, and stumps and on dry fungi, such as the shelf fungi on tree trunks. Six relatively rare species occur in the United States.

Family **Nitidùlidae**—Sap Beetles: The members of this family (183 North American species) vary considerably in size, shape, and habits. Most of them are small, 12 mm in length or less, and elongate or oval, and in many the elytra are short and expose the

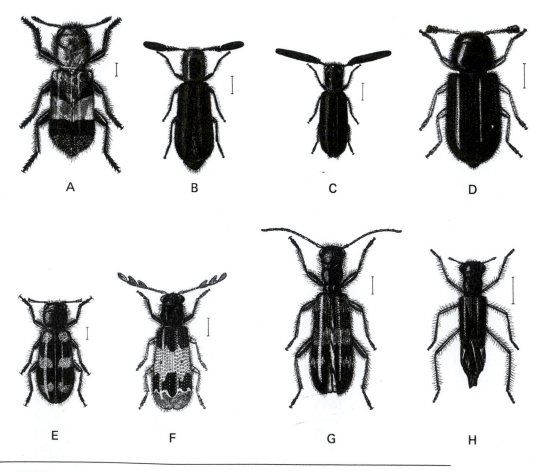

Figure 28–59.   Checkered beetles. **A,** *Enóclerus ichneumòneus* (Fabricius); **B,** *Monophýlla terminàta* (Say), female, **C,** same, male; **D,** the red-legged ham beetle, *Necròbia rùfipes* (De Geer); **E,** *Trichòdes núttalli* (Kirby); **F,** *Corinthíscus leucophaéus* (Klug); **G,** *Cymatodèra undulàta* (Say); **H,** *Isohydnócera curtipénnis* (Newman). The lines represent 1 mm. (Courtesy of Knull and the Ohio Biological Survey.)

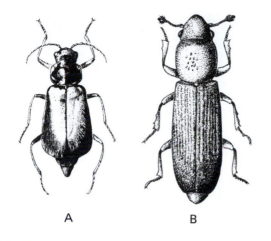

A   B

Figure 28–60. **A,** a soft-winged flower beetle, *Maláchius aèneus* (L.) (Melýridae), 5×; **B,** a root-eating beetle, *Rhizóphagus bipunctàtus* (Say) (Rhizophágidae), 18×. (Redrawn from Arnett.)

terminal abdominal segment (Figure 28–61). The antennae usually have a three-segmented club, but some have the terminal segment annulated, causing the club to appear four-segmented (Figure 28–61 B,C). Most nitidulids are found where plant fluids are fermenting or souring—for example, around decaying fruits or melons, flowing sap, and some types of fungi. A few occur on or near the dried carcasses or dead animals, and several occur in flowers. Others are very common beneath the loose bark of dead stumps and logs, especially if these are damp enough to be moldy.

Two members of the genus *Glischróchilus*, *G. quadrisignàtus* (Say) and *G. fasciàtus* (Oliver), both shiny black with two yellowish spots on each elytron, are called picnic beetles. They frequently become so abundant at such affairs that, although they cause no damage, people are driven indoors. *Carpóphilus lùgubris* Murray (Figure 28–61B), the dusky sap beetle, is a serious pest of sweet corn, especially corn grown for canning. The larvae feed inside the kernels at the tip of the ear and are frequently missed during the canning operation.

Family **Rhizophágidae**—Root-Eating Beetles: These beetles are small, slender, dark-colored, and 1.5–3.0 mm in length (Figure 28–60B). They usually occur under bark or in rotten wood. A few species live in ant nests, and some occur in bark beetle galleries, where they feed on the eggs and young of bark beetles. The antennae are ten-segmented with a one- or two-segmented club; the last tarsal segment is elongate and the other segments are short; the tip of the abdomen is exposed beyond the elytra; and the first and fifth abdominal sterna are longer than the others. One subfamily, the Monotomìnae (sometimes given family rank), has the head abruptly constricted into a narrow neck a little way behind the eyes, and the body is covered with short dense pubescence (to which dirt often adheres). Fifty-four species occur in North America.

Family **Cucùjidae**—Flat Bark Beetles: Most of the beetles in this group (about 80 North American species) are extremely flat and are either reddish, brownish, or yellowish in color. Most cucujids are found under the bark of freshly cut logs, chiefly maple, beech, elm, ash, and poplar. The largest cucujids, which belong to the genera *Cucùjus* and *Catogènus*, reach a length of about 13 mm. Our only species of *Cucùjus*, *C. clávipes* Fabricius, is uniform red in color (Figure 28–62A). A common species of

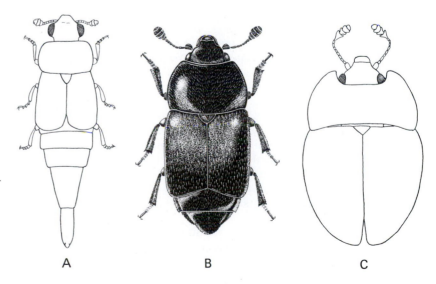

Figure 28–61. Representative Nitidùlidae. **A,** *Conótelus obscùrus* Erichson, 15×; **B,** *Carpóphilus lùgubris* Murray, the dusky sap beetle, 15×; **C,** *Lobìopa* sp., 7½×.

A   B   C

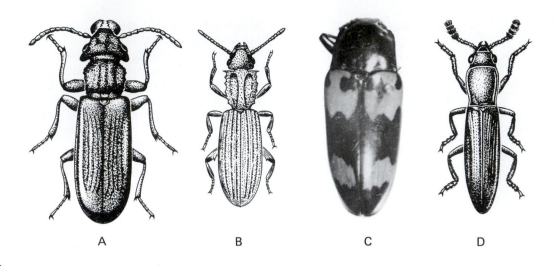

Figure 28–62.   **A,** a flat bark beetle, *Cucùjus clávipes* Fabricius (Cucùjidae), 4×; **B,** the saw-toothed grain beetle, *Oryzaéphilus surinaménsis* (L.) (Cucùjidae), 17×; **C,** a pleasing fungus beetle, *Megalodácne hèros* (Say) (Erotýlidae), 2½×; **D,** adult of the clover stem borer, *Langùria mozárdi* Latreille (Langurìidae), 6×. (**A,** courtesy of Arnett; **B** and **D,** courtesy of USDA.)

Catogènus, C. rùfus (Fabricius), is brown and has the elytra grooved.

Most of the cucujids are predaceous on mites and small insects, which they find under bark. Some species, including those of *Catogènus*, are parasitic in the larval stage on species of Cerambýcidae and Bracónidae and undergo hypermetamorphosis. A few species feed on stored grain or meal. One of the most important of these is the saw-toothed grain beetle, *Oryzaéphilus surinaménsis* (L.), so called because of the toothed lateral margins of the pronotum (Figure 28–62B).

Three of our cucujid genera (*Catogènus, Scalídia,* and *Prostòmis*) are sometimes assigned to a separate family, the Prostòmidae (= Passándridae). The members of these genera have the maxillae concealed by large, corneous, porrect plates formed by the genae, on the ventral side of the head.

Family **Cryptophágidae**—Silken Fungus Beetles: These beetles (about 150 species in our area) are 1–5 mm in length, elongate-oval in shape, yellowish brown, and covered with a silky pubescence. They feed on fungi, decaying vegetation, and similar materials and usually occur in decaying vegetable matter. Some species occur in nests of wasps or bumble bees.

Most cryptophagids have the prosternum extending back to the mesosternum. Two genera in which the prosternum is short and does not reach the me-

sosternum (*Anchòrius* and *Diplocoèlus*) are sometimes placed in a separate family, the Biphýllidae.

Family **Langurìidae**—Lizard Beetles: The lizard beetles are narrow and elongate, 2–10 mm in length, and usually have the pronotum reddish and the elytra black (Figure 28–62D). The tarsi are 5–5–5, with the fourth segment very small and segments 1–3 densely pubescent beneath. The antennae are 11-segmented with a 3- to 6-segmented club. The adults feed on the leaves and pollen of many common plants, including goldenrod, ragweed, fleabane, and clover. The larvae are stem borers. The larvae of the clover stem borer (*Langùria mozárdi* Latreille) attack clover and sometimes cause considerable damage. There are 38 species in our area.

Family **Erotýlidae**—Pleasing Fungus Beetles: The erotylids are small to medium-sized, oval, and usually shiny beetles that are found on fungi or may be attracted to sap. They often occur beneath the bark of dead stumps, especially where rotting fungus abounds. Some of the erotylids are brightly patterned with orange or red and black. The species in this group that have the tarsi distinctly five-segmented are by some authorities placed in a separate family, the Dácnidae. The largest species of dacnids (*Megalodácne*) are about 20 mm in length and are black with two orange-red bands across the elytra (Figure 28–62C). In other erotylids the fourth tarsal segment is very small, so that the tarsi appear four-segmented. These beetles are smaller, 8 mm in length or less. There are about 50 North American species and some are fairly common insects.

Family **Phalácridae**—Shining Flower Beetles: The phalacrids are oval, shining, convex beetles, 1–3 mm in length (Figure 28–63A) and usually brownish in color. Adults are sometimes quite common on the flowers of goldenrod and other composites. The larvae feed on fungus spores. About 125 species occur in our area.

Family **Cerylónidae**: This family includes a group of genera formerly placed in the Colydìidae (*Cérylon*, *Philothérmus*, *Euxéstus*, and five genera in the subfamily Murmidiìnae). They are somewhat more oval and flattened than most colydiids and 2–3 mm in length. The antennae are ten-segmented with an abrupt 1- or 2-segmented club and are received in a cavity of the prothorax, and the coxae are widely separated. The 18 North American species in this group are widely distributed. *Cérylon castàneum* Say is fairly common under dead bark, but the other species are relatively rare.

Family **Corylóphidae**—Minute Fungus Beetles: These beetles are rounded or oval and generally less than 1 mm in length. The tarsi are four-segmented, but the third segment is small and concealed in a notch of the bilobed third segment, and the tarsi appear three-segmented. The antennae are clubbed, and the club is usually three-segmented. The hind wings are fringed with hairs. These beetles occur in decaying vegetable matter and in debris, where they apparently feed on fungus spores. Sixty species occur in our area.

Family **Coccinéllidae**—Ladybird Beetles: The ladybird beetles are a well-known group of small (0.8–10 mm in length), oval, convex, and often brightly colored insects containing about 475 North American species. The head is concealed from above by the expanded pronotum. They may be distinguished from the chrysomelids, many of which have a similar shape, by the three distinct tarsal segments (chrysomelids appear to have four tarsal segments). Most of the ladybird beetles are predaceous, as both larvae and adults, and feed chiefly on aphids. They are frequently quite common, particularly on vegetation where aphids are numerous. Ladybirds hibernate as adults, frequently in large aggregations, under leaves or in debris.

The larvae of ladybird beetles (Figure 28–64C) are elongate, somewhat flattened, and covered with minute tubercles or spines. They are usually spotted or banded with bright colors. These larvae are usually found in aphid colonies.

Two fairly common phytophagous species in this group are serious garden pests; the Mexican bean beetle, *Epilàchna varivéstis* Mulsant, and the squash beetle, *E. boreàlis* (Fabricius). The Mexican bean beetle is yellowish, with eight spots on each elytron.

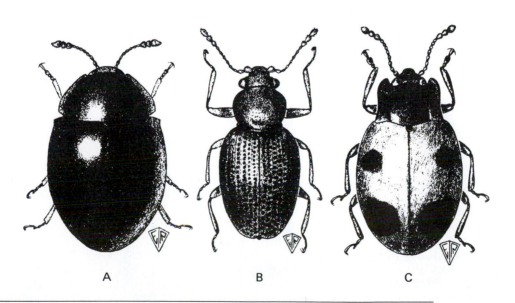

Figure 28–63.   **A,** a shining flower beetle, *Phálacrus polìtus* Melsheimer (Phalácridae), 25×; **B,** a minute brown scavenger beetle, *Melanophthálma americàna* Mannerheim (Lathridìidae), 26×; **C,** a handsome fungus beetle, *Endómychus biguttàtus* Say (Endomýchidae), 12½×. (Courtesy of Arnett.)

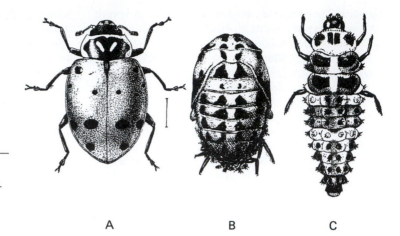

Figure 28–64. A ladybird beetle, *Hippodàmia convérgens* Guérin-Méneville. **A,** adult; **B,** pupa; **C,** larva. The line at the right of the adult indicates the actual size. (Courtesy of USDA.)

A   B   C

The squash beetle is pale orange-yellow, with three spots on the pronotum and a dozen or so large spots arranged in two rows on the elytra, plus a large black dot near the tip of the elytra. These two species are the only large ladybird beetles in the United States that are pubescent. The larvae of these species are yellow and oval in shape, with forked spines on the body. Both larvae and adults are phytophagous, and they are often very destructive.

Except for the two species of *Epiláchna*, the ladybird beetles are a very beneficial group of insects. They feed on aphids, scale insects, and other injurious insects and mites. During serious outbreaks of aphids or scale insects, large numbers of ladybird beetles are sometimes imported into the infested areas to serve as a means of control. The cottony cushion scale, *Icérya púrchasi* Maskell, a pest of citrus in California, has been kept under control for a number of years by means of a ladybird beetle, *Rodòlia cardinàlis* (Mulsant), imported from Australia.

Family **Endomýchidae**—Handsome Fungus Beetles: These are small oval beetles, mostly 3–8 mm in length. They are smooth and shiny and usually brightly colored. They are somewhat similar to the Coccinéllidae, but the head is easily visible from above. The pronotum is broadly excavated or grooved laterally, with the sides produced forward (Figure 28–63C), and the tarsal claws are simple. Some members of this group (the Mycetaeìnae, with 17 North American species) have the tarsi appearing four-segmented, with the third segment easily visible. The others (15 North American species, in four subfamilies) have the third tarsal segment very small, and the tarsi appear three-segmented. Most of the endomychids occur under bark, in rotting wood, in fungi, or in decaying fruits and feed on fungus and mold. A few of the Mycetaeìnae are found on flowers. One species, *Mycetaèa subterrànea* (Fabricius), is occasionally a pest in granaries and warehouses because it spreads mold infection.

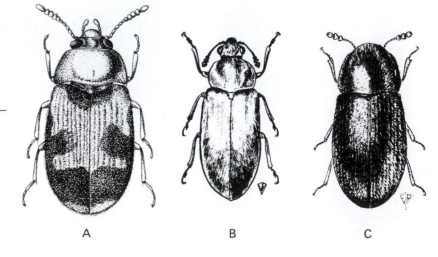

Figure 28–65. **A,** a hairy fungus beetle, *Mycetóphagus punctàtus* Say (Mycetophágidae), 8×; **B,** a fruitworm beetle, *Bytùrus unicólor* Say (Bytùridae), 8×; **C,** a minute tree-fungus beetle, *Cís fùscipes* Mellie (Cìidae), 14×. (Courtesy of Arnett.)

A   B   C

Family **Lathridìidae**—Minute Brown Scavenger Beetles: The lathridiids (128 North American species) are elongate-oval, reddish brown beetles, 1–3 mm in length (Figure 28–63B). The pronotum is narrower than the elytra, and each elytron bears six or eight rows of punctures. The tarsi are three-segmented (Figure 28–10I) or (males) 2–3–3 or 2–2–3. These beetles are found in moldy material (including stored food products) and debris and sometimes on flowers.

Family **Bytùridae**—Fruitworm Beetles: The byturids are small, oval, hairy beetles, pale brown to orange in color and mostly 3.5–4.5 mm in length, with clubbed antennae (Figure 28–65B). The second and third tarsal segments are lobed beneath. The group is a small one, with only two species in the United States. The only common eastern species is *Bytùrus unícolor* Say, a reddish yellow to blackish beetle 3.5–4.5 mm in length that feeds on the flowers of raspberry and blackberry. The larva, which is called the raspberry fruitworm, sometimes does serious damage to berries.

Family **Mycetophágidae**—Hairy Fungus Beetles: The mycetophagids are broadly oval, flattened, rather hairy beetles, 1.5–5.5 mm in length (Figure 28–65A). They are brown to black in color and often brightly marked with reddish or orange. These beetles occur under bark, in shelf fungi, and in moldy vegetable material. There are 26 species of mycetophagids in our area. *Typhaèa stercòrea* (L.), the hairy fungus beetle, is a fairly common pest in stored products.

Family **Cìidae**—Minute Tree-Fungus Beetles: The ciids are brownish to black beetles, 0.5–6.0 mm in length, and similar in appearance to the Scolýtidae and Bostríchidae (Figure 28–65C). The body is cylindrical; the head is deflexed and not visible from above; the tarsi are four-segmented (with the first three segments short and the fourth long); the antennae terminate in a three-segmented club, and sexual dimorphism is usually evident. These beetles (85 species in North America) occur under bark, in rotting wood, or in dry woody fungi, often in considerable numbers. They feed on fungi.

Family **Melandrỳidae**—False Darkling Beetles: The members of this group (142 North American species) are elongate-oval, somewhat flattened beetles usually found under bark or logs. Some species occur on flowers and foliage, others in fungi. They are mostly dark-colored and 3–20 mm in length. They can usually be recognized by the 5–5–4 tarsal formula, the open front coxal cavities, and the two impressions near the posterior border of the pronotum (Figure 28–66A). The most common melandryids are the oval, black, eastern members of *Pénthe*, which are 5–15 mm long and are common under old dead bark; *P. pimèlia* (Fabricius) is entirely black, and *P. obliquàta* (Fabricius) has a bright orange scutellum. Some members of this family, which have the head strongly and abruptly constricted just behind the eyes, have been placed in a separate family, the Scraptìidae, by some authorities.

Family **Mordéllidae**—Tumbling Flower Beetles: These beetles have a rather characteristic body shape (Figure 28–67): the body is somewhat wedge-shaped and humpbacked, the head is bent down, and the abdomen is pointed apically and extends beyond the tips of the elytra. Most mordellids (more than 200 North American species) are black or mottled gray in color, and the body is covered with a dense pubescence. Most of them are 3–7 mm in length, but some reach a length of 14 mm. These beetles are common on flowers, especially the composites. They are quite active and run or fly quickly when disturbed. Their

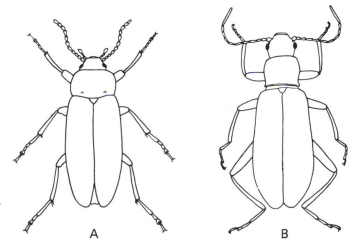

Figure 28–66. **A,** a melandryid, *Émmesa labiàta* (Say); **B,** a lagriid, *Arthrómacra* sp.; 4 ×.

A

B

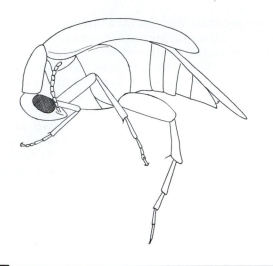

Figure 28–67. A tumbling flower beetle, *Mordélla marginàta* Melsheimer, 15×.

common name is derived from the tumbling movements they make in attempting to escape capture. The larvae live in decaying wood and in plant pith. Some are predaceous.

Family **Rhipiphòridae**—Wedge-Shaped Beetles: These beetles, 4–15 mm in length, are similar to the Mordéllidae, but have the abdomen blunt instead of pointed at the apex. The elytra are more or less pointed apically and usually do not cover the tip of the abdomen. In some species the elytra are quite

short. The antennae are pectinate in the males and serrate in the females. These beetles occur on flowers, particularly goldenrod, but they are not very common. They are sometimes found in the burrows of halictid bees. The larval stages are parasitic on various wasps (Véspidae, Scolìidae, and Tiphìidae) and bees (Halíctidae and Anthophorìnae). They undergo hypermetamorphosis similar to that in the Melòidae. Some females in this family are wingless and larviform. There are 44 North American species.

Family **Colydiidae**—Cylindrical Bark Beetles: The colydiids are hard-bodied, shiny beetles, 1–8 mm in length. Some species are oval or oblong and slightly flattened, and some are elongate and cylindrical. The antennae are 10- or 11-segmented and terminate in a 2- or 3-segmented club, and the tarsi are 4-segmented. These beetles occur under dead bark, in shelf fungi, or in ant nests. Many species are predaceous, others are plant feeders, and a few species (in the larval stage) are ectoparasites of the larvae and pupae of various woodboring beetles. There are 87 species in North America.

Family **Monómmidae**: The monommids (Figure 28–68A) are black oval beetles, 5–12 mm in length, and are flattened ventrally and convex dorsally. They have a 5–5–4 tarsal formula with the first segment relatively long. The anterior coxal cavities are open behind, the legs are strongly retractile, and the antennae terminate in a 2- or 3-segmented club and are received in grooves on the underside of the prothorax. The adults are found in leaf litter, and the larvae

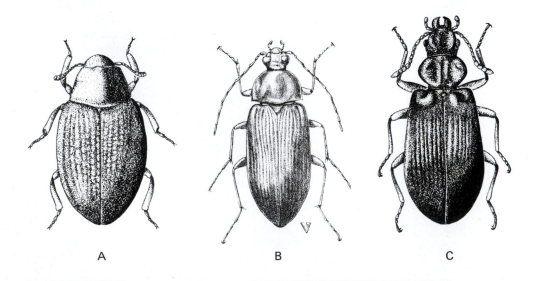

A   B   C

Figure 28–68. **A,** a monommid beetle, *Hypóphagus opúntiae* Horn, 3½×; **B,** a comb-clawed beetle, *Capnóchroa fuliginòsa* (Melsheimer) (Allecùlidae), 4½×; **C,** a narrow-waisted bark beetle, *Pỳtho nìger* Kirby (Salpíngidae), 4×. (Courtesy of Arnett.)

live in rotten wood. The group is a small one, with the eight species occurring in the southern states, from Florida to southern California.

Family **Tenebriónidae**—Darkling Beetles: The tenebrionids are a large and varied group, but can be distinguished by the 5–5–4 tarsal formula, the front coxal cavities closed behind (Figure 28-7B), the eyes usually notched (Figure 28-13B), the antennae nearly always 11-segmented and either filiform or moniliform, and five visible abdominal sterna. Most tenebrionids are black or brownish (Figure 28–69), but a few, for example, *Diapèris*, (Figure 28–69B), have red markings on the elytra. Many are black and smooth and resemble ground beetles. Some of the species that feed on the bracket fungi are brownish and rough-bodied and resemble bits of bark. One such species, *Bolitothèrus cornùtus* (Panzer), has two hornlike protuberances extending forward from the pronotum (Figure 28–69I). The fungus-inhabiting members of the genus *Diapèris* are somewhat similar in general appearance to the ladybird beetles (Figure 28–69B). Some of the tenebrionids are very hard-bodied.

Throughout the arid regions of the United States these beetles take over the ecological niche that is occupied by the Carábidae in the more verdant areas,

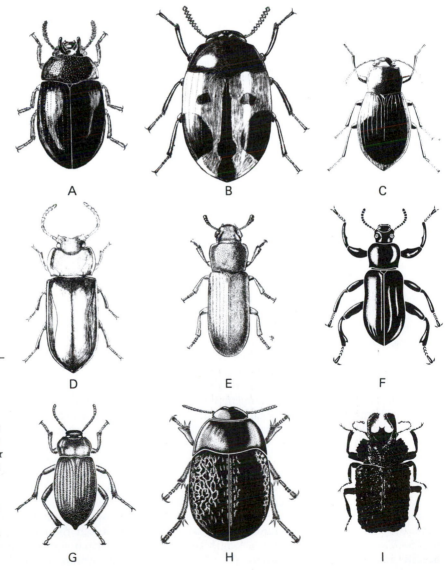

Figure 28–69. Darkling beetles (Tenebriónidae). **A,** *Neomìda bicòrnis* (Fabricius), 8×; **B,** *Diapèris maculàta* (Olivier), 6×; **C,** *Hèlops aèreus* Germar, 4×; **D,** *Adelìna plàna* (Say), 7×; **E,** the confused flour beetle, *Tribòlium confùsum* du Val, 10×; **F,** *Merìnus laèvis* (Olivier), 1¼×; **G,** *Eleòdes suturàlis* (Say) ¾×; **H,** *Eusáttus póns* Triplehorn, 3×; **I,** *Bolitothèrus cornùtus* (Panzer), male, 3×. (**E,** courtesy of USDA; **I,** courtesy of Liles.)

A   B   C

D   E   F

G   H   I

being very common under stones and rubbish and beneath loose bark, and even being attracted to lights at night.

The most distinctive habit of the members of the extremely large genus *Eleòdes* (Figure 28–69G) is the ridiculous position they assume when running from possible danger: the tip of the abdomen is elevated to an angle of about 45 degrees from the ground, and the beetles almost seem to be standing on their head as they run. When disturbed or picked up, they emit a reddish black fluid with a very disagreeable odor.

Most tenebrionids feed on plant materials of some sort. A few are common pests of stored grain and flour and are often very destructive. The beetles in the genus *Tenèbrio* are black or dark brown and 13–17 mm in length, and they feed on grain products in both larval and adult stages. The larvae are commonly called mealworms and are quite similar to wireworms. The members of the genus *Tribòlium* are oblong brown beetles, 5 mm or less in length (Figure 28–69E). Both adults and larvae commonly occur in flour, cornmeal, dog food, cereals, dried fruits, and similar materials.

The genera *Zòpherus*, *Phloeòdes*, *Nòserus*, and *Phellópsis* are sometimes placed in a separate family, the Zophéridae, and are commonly called "ironclads." All lack hind wings and have the elytra fused together. They are very hard-bodied (and difficult to pin). All are western except *Phellópsis obcordàta* (Kirby), which occurs in New England on shelf fungi.

This is the fifth largest family of beetles, with upward of 1000 North American species, and many of its members are common insects. Most of our species are western; only about 140 species occur in the East.

Family **Allecùlidae**—Comb-Clawed Beetles: The members of this family are small beetles, 5–15 mm in length, elongate-oval, and usually brownish or black with a somewhat glossy or shiny appearance resulting from the pubescence on the body (Figure 28–68B). They can be distinguished from related groups (those with 5–5–4 tarsal formula and closed front coxal cavities) by the pectinate tarsal claws (Figure 28–11B). The adults are found on flowers and foliage, on fungi, and under dead bark. The larvae resemble wireworms and live in rotting wood, plant debris, or fungi. There are 185 species in North America.

Family **Lagrìidae**—Long-Jointed Beetles: The lagriids are slender beetles, similar to darkling beetles, that can usually be recognized by their characteristic shape (Figure 28–66B), their 5–5–4 tarsal formula, and the elongate apical antennal segment (Figure 25–5D). They are 10–15 mm in length and dark metallic in color. The adults are found on foliage or

occasionally under bark. The larvae breed in plant debris and under the bark of fallen trees. Thirty-three species are recorded for North America.

Family **Cephalòidae**—False Longhorn Beetles: These beetles are elongate, convex, and somewhat similar to a cerambycid in shape (hence the common name). They are brownish to dark in color and 8–20 mm in length, and the head is somewhat diamond-shaped, narrowed behind the eyes to form a slender neck. They have a 5–5–4 tarsal formula, the tarsal claws (of six of our ten species) are pectinate, and there is a long (broad to narrow) pad under each claw. Little is known of the habits of these beetles, except that the adults are sometimes found on flowers and the larvae have been found in very old rotten logs.

Family **Melòidae**—Blister Beetles: The blister beetles (more than 300 North American species) are usually narrow and elongate; the elytra are soft and flexible; and the pronotum is narrower than either the head or the elytra (Figure 28–70). These beetles are called blister beetles because the body fluids of the commoner species contain cantharadin, a substance that often causes blisters when applied to the skin.

Several species of blister beetles are important pests, feeding on potatoes, tomatoes, and other plants. Two of these are often called the "old-fashioned potato beetles": *Epicáuta vittàta* (Fabricius) (with orange and black longitudinal stripes) and *Epicáuta pestífera* Werner (black, with the margins of the elytra and the sutural stripe gray; Figure 28–70C). These beetles are 12–20 mm in length. The black blister beetle, *E. pennsylvánica* (De Geer), is a common black meloid, 7–13 mm in length, that is usually found on the flowers of goldenrod.

The larvae of many blister beetles are considered beneficial, for they feed on grasshopper eggs. A few live in bee nests in the larval stage, where they feed on bee eggs and on the food stored in the cells with the eggs.

The life history of the blister beetles in the genus *Epicáuta* is rather complex. These insects undergo hypermetamorphosis, with the different larval instars being quite different in form (Figure 28–71). The first larval instar, an active, long-legged form called a triungulin, seeks out a grasshopper egg or a bee nest and then molts. In the species that develop in bee nests, the triungulin usually climbs on a flower and attaches itself to a bee that visits the flower. The bee carries the triungulin to the nest, whereupon the triungulin attacks the bee's eggs. The second instar is somewhat similar to the triungulin, but the legs are shorter. In the third, fourth, and fifth instars the larva becomes thicker and somewhat scarabaeiform. The sixth instar has a darker

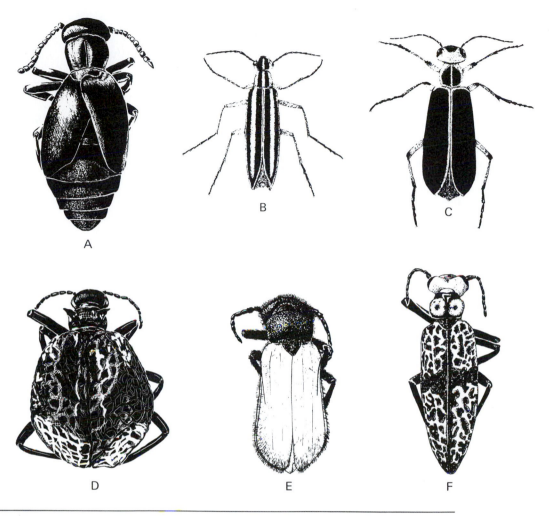

Figure 28–70.   Blister beetles. **A,** *Melòe laèvis* Leach, 2 × ; **B,** the three-striped blister beetle, *Epicàuta lemniscàta* (Fabricius), 2 × ; **C,** *Epicàuta pestífera* Werner, 2 × ; **D,** *Cysteodèmus armàtus* LeConte, 2½ × ; **E,** *Tricrània stánsburyi* (Haldeman), 4 × ; **F,** *Tegrodèra eròsa alòga* (Skinner), 2 × . (**B** and **C,** courtesy of Baerg and the Arkansas Agricultural Experiment Station; others, courtesy of Noller and the Arizona Agricultural Experiment Station.)

and thicker exoskeleton and lacks functional appendages. This instar is usually known as the coarctate larva or pseudopupa, and it is the instar that hibernates. The seventh instar is small, white, and active (though legless) but apparently does not feed and soon transforms to the true pupa.

The members of the genus *Melòe*, some of which are about 25 mm in length, have very short elytra that overlap just behind the scutellum, and the hind wings are lacking. These insects are dark blue or black in color (Figure 28–70A). They are sometimes called oil beetles, for they often exude an oily substance from the joints of the legs when disturbed.

The blister beetles in the genus *Nemógnatha* are unique in having the galeae prolonged into a sucking tube as long as or longer than the body. These beetles are usually brownish in color (sometimes blackish, or brown and black) and 8–15 mm in length. They are widely distributed.

Most of the blister beetles are elongate and somewhat cylindrical, but the species of *Cysteodèmus*, which occur in the Southwest from Texas to southern California, have the elytra broadly oval and very convex, superficially resembling spiders (Figure 28–70D). These beetles are black, often with bluish or purplish highlights, and about 15 mm in length.

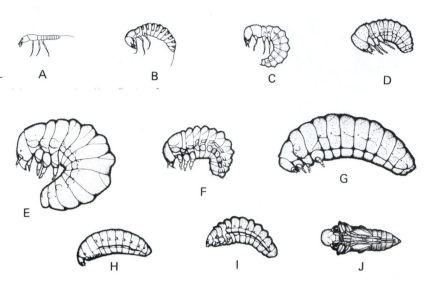

Figure 28–71. Larval and pupal instars of the black blister beetle, *Epicàuta pennsylvánica* (De Geer), showing hypermetamorphosis. **A,** newly hatched first instar, or triungulin; **B,** fully fed first instar; **C,** second instar; **D,** third instar; **E,** fourth instar; **F,** newly molted fifth instar; **G,** gorged fifth instar; **H,** sixth instar (coarctate larva or pseudopupa); **I,** seventh instar; **J,** pupa. (Courtesy of Horsfall and the Arkansas Agricultural Experiment Station.)

Family **Oedeméridae**—False Blister Beetles: The oedemerids are slender, soft-bodied beetles, 5–20 mm in length (Figure 28–72A). Many are black with an orange pronotum, while others are pale with blue, yellow, red, or orange markings. These beetles have a 5–5–4 tarsal formula, and the penultimate tarsal segment is dilated and densely hairy beneath (Figure 28–10C). The pronotum is anteriorly broadened and posteriorly narrower than the base of the elytra, and the eyes are often emarginate. The adults are usually found on flowers or foliage and are attracted to lights at night. The larvae live in moist decaying wood, especially driftwood. The larvae of the wharf borer, *Nacérdes melanùra* (L.), feed in very moist wood such as pilings under wharves, under buildings near water, and in greenhouses. The adult is 7–15 mm in length and reddish yellow with the tips of the elytra black. There are 86 species in the United States and Canada.

Family **Myctéridae**: Some members of this family (*Hemipéplus*, two species, found in Florida and Georgia) strongly resemble cucujiids. They are elongate, slender, very flat, yellowish beetles, 8–12 mm in length, with the front coxal cavities closed. These beetles are found under bark. Other mycterids (Mycterìnae) have the front coxal cavities open, and some of them (for example, *Mýcterus*, about 10 mm in length) have the head extended anteriorly, much like the broad-nosed weevils. The body is more robust and not at all flattened. These beetles are generally found under rocks, in debris, or in vegetation. Both adults and larvae are said to be predaceous. The Mycterìnae have been placed in the Salpíngidae, but differ from them in having the penultimate tarsal segment lobed. (In the Salpíngidae this segment is slender and similar to the other segments.)

Family **Pyrochròidae**—Fire-Colored Beetles: The pyrochroids (15 species in our area) are 6–20 mm in length and are usually black, with the pronotum reddish or yellowish. The head and pronotum are narrower than the elytra, and the elytra are somewhat broader posteriorly. The antennae are serrate to pectinate (rarely filiform), and in the males almost

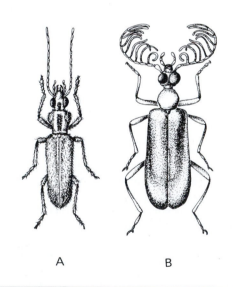

Figure 28–72. **A,** a false blister beetle, *Óxacis trimaculàta* Champion (Oedeméridae), 3×; **B,** a fire-colored beetle, *Dendròides canadénsis* LeConte (Pyrochròidae), 3×. (Courtesy of Arnett.)

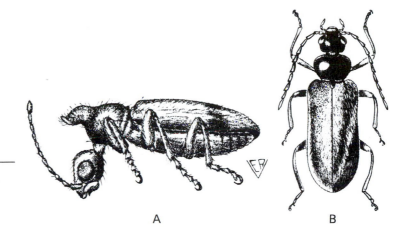

Figure 28–73.   Antlike flower beetles.
A, *Notóxus mónodon* Fabricius, 12×; **B,**
Pedìlus lùgubris Say, 5×. (Courtesy of
Arnett.)

A   B

plumose (Figure 28–72B), with long slender processes on segments 3–10. The eyes are often quite
large. The short-lived adults are found on foliage and
flowers and sometimes under bark. The larvae occur
under the bark of dead trees.

Family **Salpíngidae**—Narrow-Waisted Bark Beetles: The common name of this group refers to the
fact that some of the larger species (for example,
Pỳtho and *Lecóntia*, 10–30 mm in length) have the
pronotum narrowed basally, causing them to resemble ground beetles superficially (Figures 28–68C).
Most of our 40 species of salpingids are black, elongate, and somewhat flattened. The adults and larvae
are predaceous. The adults occur under rocks and
bark, in leaf litter, and on vegetation. The species of
Aegialìtes, which occur along the Pacific Coast from
California to Alaska, live in rock cracks below the
high tidemark along the seacoast. These beetles are
elongate-oval, 3–4 mm in length, and black with a
metallic luster. Five species of *Elacàtis* (false tiger
beetles) occur in the United States. They were formerly placed in a separate family, Othnìidae, now
considered a part of Salpíngidae.

Family **Anthícidae**—Antlike Flower Beetles: These
beetles are 2–12 mm in length and somewhat antlike
in appearance, with the head deflexed and strongly
constricted behind the eyes, and with the pronotum
oval. The pronotum in many species (*Notóxus*, Figure 28–73A and *Mycinotársus*) has an anterior hornlike process extending forward over the head. Anthicids generally occur on flowers and foliage; some
occur under stones and logs and in debris; and a few
occur on sand dunes. There are nearly 160 species in
our area.

Family **Euglénidae**—Antlike Leaf Beetles: The eu-
glenids (44 North American species) are reddish yellow to dark in color and 1.5–3.0 mm in length. They
are very similar to the anthicids, but may be sepa-

rated by the characters given in the key (couplet 175).
They are found on foliage and flowers.

Family **Cerambýcidae**—Long-Horned Beetles: This
family is a large one, with about 1000 species occurring in the United States and Canada, and its
members are all phytophagous. Most of the long-
horns are elongate and cylindrical with long antennae; the eyes are usually strongly notched or even
completely divided; and many of these beetles are
brightly colored. They vary from 3 to 60 mm in
length. The tarsi appear four-segmented with the
third segment bilobed, but are actually five-segmented. The fourth segment is small and concealed

Figure 28–74.   Galleries of the poplar borer, *Sapérda
calcaràta* Say. (Courtesy of the Ohio Agricultural
Research and Development Center.)

in the notch of the third and is often very difficult to see (Figure 28–10A). Both the Cerambýcidae and Chrysomélidae have this type of tarsal structure, and these groups are sometimes difficult to separate. They can usually be separated by the characters given in the key (couplet 184).

Most adult cerambycids, particularly the brightly colored ones, feed on flowers. Many, usually not brightly colored, are nocturnal in habit and during the day may be found under bark or resting on trees or logs. Some of these make a squeaking sound when picked up.

Most of the Cerambýcidae are wood-boring in the larval stage, and many species are very destructive to shade, forest, and fruit trees and to freshly cut logs. The adults lay their eggs in crevices in the bark, and the larvae bore into the wood. The larval tunnels in the wood (Figure 28–74) are circular in cross section (thereby differing from most buprestid tunnels, which are oval in cross section) and usually go straight in a short distance before turning. Different species attack different types of trees and shrubs. A few will attack living trees, but most species appear to prefer freshly cut logs or weakened and dying trees or branches. A few girdle twigs and lay their eggs just above the girdled band. Some bore into the stems of herbaceous plants. The larvae (Figure 28–75) are elongate, cylindrical, whitish, and almost legless and differ from the larvae of the Buprestidae in that the anterior end of the body is not

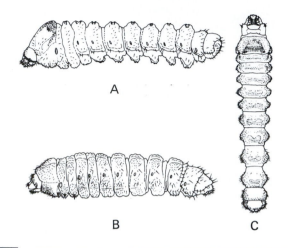

Figure 28–75. Cerambycid larvae. **A,** dogwood twig borer, *Obèrea tripunctàta* (Swederus), lateral view; **B,** twig pruner, *Elaphidionòides villòsus* (Fabricius), lateral view; **C,** linden borer, *Sapérda véstita* Say, dorsal view. (Courtesy of Peterson.)

broadened and flattened. They are often called round-headed borers, to distingush them from the flat-headed borers (larvae of Bupréstidae).

This family is divided into several subfamilies, which can generally be separated by the following key.

Key to the Subfamilies of Cerambýcidae

1.	Tarsi distinctly 5-segmented, fourth segment plainly visible (Figure 28–76E); antennae short, rarely surpassing base of pronotum, second segment more than half as long as third **2**	
1′.	Tarsi appearing 4-segmented, fourth segment very small and concealed in notch of dilated third segment, which has pubescent pads beneath (Figure 28–10A); antennae variable in length, but usually surpassing base of pronotum, second segment rarely half as long as the third **3**	
2(1).	Pronotum margined laterally; third tarsal segment entire or feebly emarginate; shining brown (Figure 28–77F); widely distributed. ....**Parandrìnae**	p. 451
2′.	Pronotum rounded laterally; third tarsal segment deeply bilobed; blackish; mostly southeastern and western United States ....**Spondylìnae**	p. 451
3(1′).	Pronotum margined laterally; front coxae transverse ....**Prionìnae**	p. 452
3′.	Pronotum rounded laterally (sometimes with lateral spine or tubercle); front coxae usually globular or conical, rarely transverse **4**	
4(3′).	Last segment of maxillary palps pointed apically (Figure 28–76C); face vertical or slanting backward ....**Lamiìnae**	p. 452

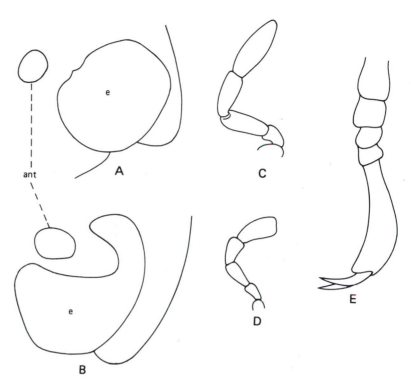

Figure 28–76.   Characters of Cerambýcidae. **A** and **B,** dorsolateral views of the left compound eye and the base of the antenna. **A,** base of antenna not surrounded by eye (*Toxòtus,* Lepturìnae); **B,** base of antenna partly surrounded by eye (*Elaphídion,* Cerambycìnae); **C** and **D,** maxillary palps; **C,** *Monochàmus* (Lamiìnae); **D,** *Anoplodèra* (Lepturìnae); **E,** hind tarsus of *Párandra* (Parandrìnae). *ant,* base of antenna; *e,* compound eye.

4′.	Last segment of maxillary palps blunt or truncate apically (Figure 28–76D); face slanting forward or subvertical **5**
5(4′).	Second antennal segment longer than broad, nearly half as long as third segment; head short, not narrowed behind eyes; front coxae somewhat globular; rather flattened, usually brownish beetles, with relatively short antennae . . . . **Asemìnae** p. 452
5′.	Second antennal segment usually very short, not much longer than broad, much less than half as long as third; other characters variable **6**
6(5′).	Front coxae conical; head somewhat elongate, narrowed behind eyes; base of antennae usually not surrounded by eyes (Figure 28–76A); often with a broad-shouldered appearance, the elytra narrowing posteriorly (Figures 28–77A–D,H, 28–78D) . . . . **Lepturìnae** p. 454
6′.	Front coxae variable, but usually not conical; head generally short and not narrowed behind eyes; base of antenna usually partly surrounded by eye (Figure 28–76B) (if not, then front coxae are globose or transverse); elytra generally parallel-sided in anterior two-thirds of their length (Figures 28–77E, 28–78B,C,F) . . . . **Cerambycìnae** p. 454

Subfamilies **Parandrìnae** and **Spondylìnae:**   These beetles differ from other cerambycids in having the fourth tarsal segment plainly visible and the tarsi obviously five-segmented (Figure 28–76E). The subfamily Parandrìnae contains two species in the genus *Párandra.* These beetles are elongate-oval, somewhat flattened, bright reddish brown, and 9–18 mm in length (Figure 28–77F). They look a little like small lucanids. They live under the bark of dead pine trees. The larvae burrow in dry dead wood of logs and stumps. The subfamily Spondylìnae contains two species: *Spóndylis upifórmis* Mannerheim, which oc-

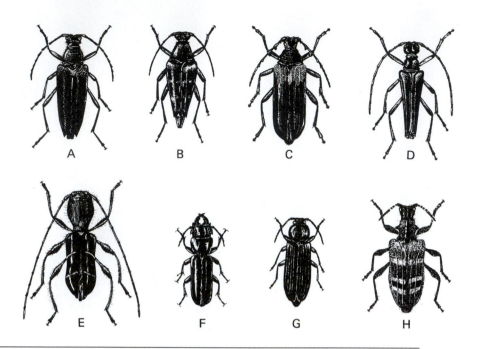

Figure 28–77. Long-horned beetles. **A,** *Anoplodèra canadénsis* (Olivier) (Lepturìnae); **B,** *Typócerus decéptus* Knull (Lepturìnae); **C,** *Desmócerus palliàtus* (Forster) (Lepturìnae); **D,** *Toxòtus cylindricóllis* (Say) (Lepturìnae); **E,** *Eudérces pìni* (Olivier) (Cerambycìnae); **F,** *Párandra polìta* Say (Parandrìnae); **G,** *Ásemum striàtum* (L.) (Asemìnae); **H,** *Rhàgium inquísitor* (L.) (Lepturìnae). (Courtesy of Knull and the Ohio Biological Survey.)

curs from the Great Lakes westward, and *Scaphìnus mùticus* (Fabricius), which occurs in the Southeast. These beetles are black, not particularly shiny, and 8–20 mm in length. Their habits are similar to those of *Párandra.*

Subfamily **Prionìnae:** This group contains our largest cerambycids, some of which may reach a length of about 75 mm. The Prionìnae differ from the two preceding subfamilies in having the tarsi appearing four-segmented and from the following subfamilies in having the pronotum margined laterally. Most of them have spines or teeth along the margins of the pronotum, and some have the antennae serrate and containing 12 or more segments. The most common species in this group belong to the genus *Priònus.* These beetles (Figure 28–78E) are broad and somewhat flattened, blackish brown in color, with three broad teeth on the lateral margins of the pronotum, and 17–60 mm in length (some western members of this genus are even larger). The antennae contain 12 or more segments, and are serrate in the female. The members of the genus *Ergàtes,* which occur in the West, are also dark brown but

have eight or ten small spines on each side of the pronotum, and the eyes are deeply emarginate. They are 35–65 mm in length. *Orthosòma brùnneum* (Forster), a fairly common eastern species, is long and narrow, light reddish brown, and 24–48 mm in length. It has two or three teeth on the lateral margins of the pronotum.

Subfamily **Asemìnae:** The members of this group are elongate, parallel-sided, somewhat flattened beetles, usually black (sometimes with the elytra brownish), and mostly 10–20 mm in length, with relatively short antennae (Figure 28–77G). Most of them have the eyes deeply emarginate (the eyes are completely divided in *Tetròpium*) and partly surrounding the bases of the antennae. The larvae of these beetles attack principally dead pine trees and pine stumps.

Subfamily **Lamiìnae:** The members of this subfamily can be recognized by the pointed terminal segment of the maxillary palps (Figure 28–76C) and the rather vertical face. They are elongated, parallel-sided, and usually somewhat cylindrical, with the pronotum often a little narrower than the base of the

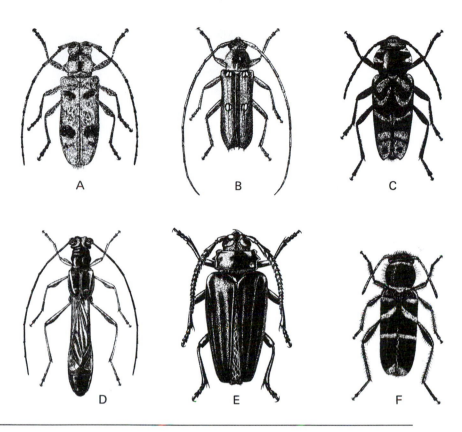

Figure 28–78.   Long-horned beetles. **A,** *Gòes tigrìnus* (De Geer) (Lamiìnae), 1¼×; **B,** *Ebùria quadrigemìnàta* (Say) (Cerambycìnae), 1¼×; **C,** the sugar maple borer, *Glycòbius speciòsus* (Say) (Cerambycìnae) (natural size); **D,** *Necýdalis méllita* (Say) (Lepturìnae); 2×; **E,** *Priònus imbricòrnis* (L.) (Prionìnae) (natural size); **F,** *Clýtus marginicóllis* Castelnau (Cerambycìnae), 3×. (Courtesy of Knull and the Ohio Biological Survey.)

elytra (Figures 28–78A, 28–79). This group is a large one, and many species are of considerable economic importance.

The beetles in the genus *Monochàmus* (Figure 28–79) are often called sawyer beetles. They are usually over 25 mm in length and are either black or a mottled gray in color. The first antennal segment has a scarlike area near the tip. The antennae of the males are sometimes twice as long as the body. In the females the antennae are about as long as the body. The larvae feed on evergreens, usually on freshly cut logs, but they may sometimes attack living trees. The holes made by the larvae are at least as large in diameter as a lead pencil, and those of some species are nearly 13 mm in diameter.

The genus *Sapérda* contains a number of important pest species. These beetles are about 25 mm in length and are sometimes strikingly colored. *Sapérda cándida* Fabricius is white, with three broad, brown longitudinal stripes on the back. The larva

bores in apple and other trees and is commonly called the round-headed apple tree borer. Other important species in this genus are the poplar borer, *S. calcaràta* Say, and the elm borer, *S. tridentàta* Olivier.

The species in the genus *Obèrea* are very slender and elongate. The raspberry cane borer, *O. bimaculàta* (Olivier), is black, with the pronotum yellow and bearing two or three black spots. The larvae are often serious pests in canes of raspberries and blackberries.

The species of *Tetraòpes* are about 13 mm in length and are red with black spots. The compound eyes are divided so that there are apparently two compound eyes on each side of the head. The red milkweed beetle, *T. tetraophthálmus* (Forster), is a common species feeding on milkweed.

The twig girdler, *Oncíderes cingulàta* (Say), lays its eggs under the bark near the tips of living branches of hickory, elm, apple, and other deciduous trees. Before the egg is deposited, the beetle gnaws

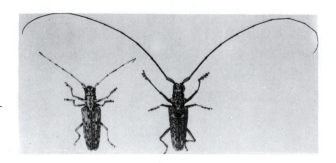

Figure 28–79. The northeastern sawyer beetle, *Monochàmus notàtus* (Drury), female at left, male at right. About $\frac{1}{2}\times$. (Courtesy of Knull.)

a deep groove around the twig, girdling it. The twig eventually dies and drops to the ground, and the larva completes its development in the twig.

Subfamily **Lepturìnae**: The long-horns in this group resemble those in the Cerambycìnae in having the terminal segment of the maxillary palps blunt or truncate at the apex (Figure 28–76D). They differ from the Cerambycìnae in having the front coxae conical, and the bases of the antennae are usually not surrounded by the eyes (Figure 28–76A). Many Lepturìnae have the elytra tapering posteriorly or the pronotum narrower than the base of the elytra, giving them a rather broad-shouldered appearance.

A striking eastern species in this group is the elderberry long-horn, *Desmócerus palliàtus* (Forster) (Figure 28–77C). This is a dark blue beetle about 25 mm long, with the basal third of the elytra orange-yellow, and with segments 3–5 of the antennae thickened at the tips. The adult occurs on the flowers and foliage of elderberry, and the larva bores in the pith of this plant. Several other species of *Desmócerus* occur on elderberry in the western states. They are similar in general coloration, with the males having brilliant scarlet elytra and a black pronotum. The females have very dark green elytra bordered narrowly with red along the outer margin.

This subfamily contains many species found on flowers. In most of them the elytra are broadest at the base and narrowed toward the apex (Figure 28–77A,B,D,H). Some common genera are *Sticto-pleptùra*, *Typócerus*, *Toxòtus*, and *Stenócorus*. Most of these beetles are brightly colored, often with yellow and black bands or stripes. In many cases the elytra do not cover the tip of the abdomen. All are excellent fliers.

Subfamily **Cerambycìnae**: This group is a large one, and its members vary considerably in size and general appearance. One of the most strikingly marked species in this subfamily is the locust borer, *Megacyllène robíniae* (Forster), the larva of which bores into the trunks of black locust. The adult is black with bright yellow markings and is relatively common on goldenrod in late summer. Another eas-

ily recognized species in this group is *Ebùria quad-rigeminàta* (Say), a brownish species 14–24 mm in length, which has two pairs of elevated ivory-colored swellings on each elytron (Figure 28–78B). The members of some genera in this group (*Smòdicum* and others) are somewhat flattened and have relatively short antennae. Others (for example, *Eudérces*; Figure 28–77E) are small, less than 9 mm in length, and somewhat antlike in appearance.

Family **Brùchidae**—Seed Beetles: The members of this family (134 species in our area) are short, stout-bodied beetles, mostly less than 5 mm in length, with the elytra shortened and not covering the tip of the abdomen. The body is often somewhat narrowed anteriorly (Figure 28–80) and is usually dull grayish or brownish in color. The head is produced anteriorly into a short broad snout.

The larvae of most bruchids feed inside seeds and pupate in the seeds. The adults generally oviposit on seeds that are fully developed or nearly so, but some oviposit on the flowers or young fruits. Some species develop in stored dry seeds. Some of the seed beetles, particularly those attacking leguminous plants, are serious pests.

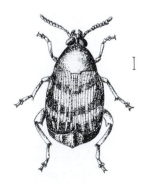

Figure 28–80. The bean weevil, *Acanthoscélides obtéctus* (Say). The line at the right represents the actual length. (Courtesy of USDA.)

Two common species in this family are the bean weevil, *Acanthoscélides obtéctus* (Say) (Figure 28–80), and the pea weevil, *Brùchus pisòrum* (L.). These beetles lay their eggs on the pods of beans or peas, and the larvae bore into the seeds. The adults emerge through little round holes cut in the seed. The bean weevil may breed indoors throughout the year in stored dried beans, but the pea weevil attacks the peas only in the field and does not oviposit on dried peas. These insects cause serious damage in stored seeds that are not protected. The homemaker frequently sees bean weevils for the first time when the beetles try to escape through the windows, and she does not account for their appearance until she later empties a sack of dried beans and finds them full of holes.

Family **Chrysomélidae**—Leaf Beetles: The leaf beetles are closely related to the Cerambýcidae, both groups having a similar tarsal structure (Figure 28–10A) and both being phytophagous. The leaf bee-tles usually have much shorter antennae and are smaller and more oval in shape than the cerambycids. The chrysomelids in the United States are almost all less than 12 mm in length; most of the cerambycids are larger. Many chrysomelids are brightly colored.

Adult leaf beetles feed principally on flowers and foliage. The larvae are phytophagous, but vary quite a bit in appearance and habits. Some larvae are free feeders on foliage; some are leaf miners; some feed on roots; and some bore in stems. Many members of this family are serious pests of cultivated plants. Most species overwinter as adults.

The family Chrysomélidae is a large one with about 1500 North American species assigned to 188 genera. It is divided into a number of subfamilies, and those occurring in North America may be separated by the key below. Groups in this key marked with an asterisk are relatively rare or unlikely to be taken by the general collector.

Key to the Subfamilies of Chrysomélidae

1.	Head largely or entirely concealed under prothorax; prothorax and elytra widened; body oval or circular and convex (Figure 28–88B,E); mouth located posteriorly on ventral side of head, the mouthparts directed caudad (Figure 28–81A) ....**Cassidìnae**	p. 460
1'.	Body not as above, or if oval and convex then the mouthparts are located anteriorly and are directed ventrad or forward **2**	
2(1').	Mouthparts located ventrally on head and directed ventrally or caudad (as in Figure 28–81A); body usually narrower anteriorly and widest posteriorly; elytra usually roughened by ridges or rows of punctures (Figure 28–87) ....**Hispìnae**	p. 460
2'.	Mouthparts located anteriorly on head and directed ventrad or forward; elytra usually not as above **3**	
3(2').	Abdominal sternites 2–4 narrowed medially; pygidium usually exposed; robust, subcylindrical beetles, mostly less than 6 mm in length, with head usually retracted into prothorax to eyes (Figure 28–81C); elytra sometimes tuberculate **4**	
3'.	Abdominal sternites 2–4 not narrowed medially; pygidium usually covered by elytra; size and shape variable; elytra not tuberculate **8**	
4(3).	Prosternum with lateral antennal grooves; legs retractile; elytra tuberculate ....**Chlamisìnae**	p. 458
4'.	Prosternum without lateral antennal grooves; legs not retractile; elytra not tuberculate **5**	
5(4').	Antennae filiform or slightly clavate **6**	
5'.	Antennae serrate or pectinate **7**	
6(5).	Base of pronotum narrower than base of elytra; southern Texas ....**Megascelìnae***	p. 458

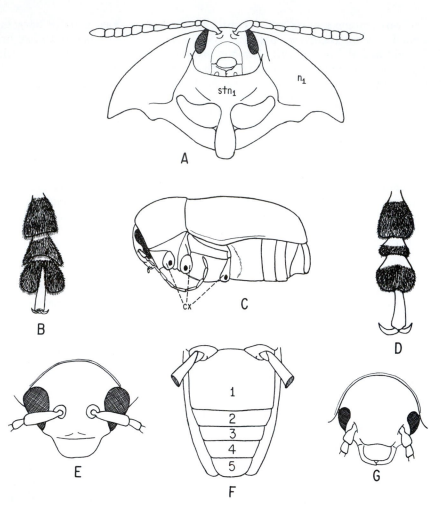

Figure 28–81. Characters of Chrysomélidae. **A,** head and prothorax of *Chelymórpha* (Cassidìnae), ventral view; **B,** tarsus of *Diabrótica* (Galerucìnae), ventral view; **C,** body of *Cryptocéphalus* (Cryptocephalìnae), lateral view; **D,** tarsus of *Leptinotársa* (Chrysomelìnae), ventral view; **E,** head of *Diabrótica* (Galerucìnae), anterior view; **F,** abdomen of *Donàcia* (Donaciìnae), ventral view; **G,** head of *Chrýsochus* (Eumolpìnae), anterior view. *cx,* coxa; n_1, pronotum; stn_1, prosternum; 1–5, abdominal sterna.

6'.	Base of pronotum as wide as base of elytra, or nearly so; widely distributed ....**Cryptocephalìnae**	p. 458
7(5').	Head more or less constricted behind eyes; eyes usually large and deeply emarginate ....**Zeugophorìnae**	p. 458
7'.	Head usually not constricted behind eyes; eyes usually not large or deeply emarginate...**Clytrìnae**	p. 458
8(3').	Pronotum margined laterally **9**	
8'.	Pronotum rounded laterally (may be denticulate or with flattened, sharp lobes medially) **14**	
9(8).	Antennae widely separated at base, farther apart than length of first antennal segment (Figure 28–81 G) **10**	
9'.	Antennae close together at base, closer than length of first antennal segment (Figure 28–81 E) **13**	
10(9).	Prosternum with lateral antennal grooves; small, round or oval, convex beetles, shining blue, green, or bronze; Florida and California ....**Lamprosomatìnae***	p. 458
10'.	Prosternum without lateral antennal grooves; color variable **11**	

11(10').   Tibiae each with two tibial spurs; pronotum narrower at base than base of elytra; elongate, flattened, cucujid-like beetles; southwestern United States ....**Aulacoscelinae***   p. 457

11'.   Tibiae each with one tibial spur or none; pronotum variable but often with base as wide as base of elytra; body usually convex; widely distributed **12**

12(11').   Front coxae oval or transverse; third tarsal segment, seen from beneath, entire apically or with a slight median notch (Figure 28–81 D) ....**Chrysomelinae**   p. 459

12'.   Front coxae rounded; third tarsal segment, seen from beneath, distinctly bilobed (Figure 28–81 B) ....**Eumolpinae**   p. 459

13(9').   Hind femora slender; elytra soft ....**Galerucinae**   p. 459

13'.   Hind femora swollen; elytra usually firm ....**Alticinae**   p. 460

14(8').   First abdominal sternum very long (Figure 28–81 F); antennae long, usually about half as long as body (Figure 28–82), close together at base; elongate, metallic, semiaquatic beetles ....**Donaciinae**   p. 457

14'.   First abdominal sternum not unusually long; antennae shorter, usually less than half as long as body, widely separated at base (Figure 28–81 G); color variable **15**

15(14').   Front coxae contiguous or nearly so; base of pronotum much narrower than base of elytra; body elongate and more or less parallel-sided. **16**

15'.   Front coxae broadly separated by prosternum; base of pronotum almost as wide as base of elytra; body round or oval, convex and usually shining ....**Eumolpinae**   p. 459

16(15).   Punctures of elytra in rows; elytra not pubescent; pronotum without lateral teeth ....**Criocerinae**   p. 458

16'.   Punctures of elytra not in rows, or if in rows, then pronotum has small lateral teeth and elytra have scattered pubescence **17**

17(16').   Procoxal cavities open behind; elytra pubescent or at least with a few conspicuous setae; pronotum with lateral margins denticulate or with flattened, sharp lobes medially ....**Synetinae**   p. 457

17'.   Procoxal cavities closed behind; elytra glabrous; pronotum with lateral margins not interrupted by teeth or lobes ....**Orsodacninae**   p. 457

Subfamily **Aulacoscelinae** (**Sagrinae** in part):   This group is represented by three rare species, which occur in New Mexico, Arizona, and California. The adults are leaf feeders, and the larvae are unknown.

Subfamily **Donaciinae**—Long-Horned Leaf Beetles: These beetles are elongate and slender and have long antennae (Figure 28–82). They are dark-colored and metallic, 5.5–12.0 mm in length, usually black, greenish, or coppery. They are active, fast-flying beetles and, in this respect, resemble the tiger beetles. The long-horned leaf beetles are seldom seen far from water. The adults are generally found on the flowers or foliage of water lilies, pondweed, and other aquatic plants. The eggs are usually laid on the undersides of the leaves of water lily, in a whitish cresent-shaped mass near a small circular hole cut in the leaf by the adult. The larvae feed on the submerged parts of aquatic plants and obtain air through the plant stems. They pupate in cocoons that are fastened to vegetation below the water surface.

Subfamily **Orsodacninae**:   This subfamily contains only one species, *Orsodácne átra* (Ahrens), a widely distributed beetle that is extremely variable in coloration, 7–8 mm in length, and found chiefly on willow and dogwood flowers.

Subfamily **Synetinae**:   This subfamily consists of only two genera, *Tricholèma* (one species, *T. anómala* Crotch, in California and Oregon) and *Synèta* (eight species, generally distributed in the northern United States as far south as North Carolina and Utah).

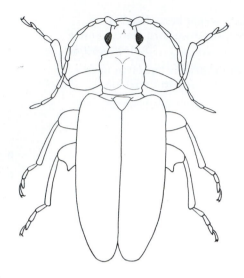

Figure 28–82. A long-horned leaf beetle, *Donàcia* sp., 7½×.

Synèta álbida LeConte, which damages the buds of many kinds of fruit trees along the North Pacific Coast, is the only member of this group that has much economic importance.

Subfamily **Criocerinae:** The members of this subfamily have the head narrowed behind the eyes to form a slender neck, and the punctures of the elytra are arranged in rows. Three genera occur in the United States, *Crióceris, Oulèma,* and *Lèma.* Some of these beetles are important pests.

The genus *Crióceris* includes two species, both imported from Europe, which attack asparagus and often cause serious damage. Both species are about 7 mm in length. The striped asparagus beetle, *C. aspáragi* (L.) has a red prothorax and light yellow markings on the bluish green elytra (Figure 28–83A). The spotted asparagus beetle, *C. duodecimpunctàta* (L.), is brownish, with six large black spots on each elytron. Adults and larvae of *C. aspáragi* feed on the new shoots and cause damage to the growing plants. The larvae of *C. duodecimpunctàta* feed inside the berries and do not injure the shoots.

The cereal leaf beetle, *Oulèma melánopus* (L.) is blue-black with a red pronotum and about 6 mm in length (Figures 28–83B, 28–84A). This is a serious introduced pest of grains in some sections of the Midwest (chiefly Michigan, Ohio, and Indiana). Both adults and larvae feed on the leaves of grain (and on various grasses).

About a dozen species of *Lèma* occur in the eastern and southern United States. The most important

species is probably the three-lined potato beetle, *L. trilínea* White, which feeds on potato and related plants. This beetle is 6–7 mm in length and reddish yellow with three broad black stripes on the elytra.

Subfamily **Megascelinae:** This is a tropical group that is represented in the United States by a single species, *Megascèlis texàna* Linell, which has been recorded from the Brownsville area of Texas.

Subfamily **Zeugophorinae:** This is a small group, represented in the United States by nine species of *Zeugóphora.* The adults are 3–4 mm in length and occur chiefly on poplar, hickory, and oak.

Subfamilies **Clytrìnae, Cryptocephalìnae, Chlami-sinae (= Chlamysìnae or Chlamydìnae), and Lampro-somatinae**—Case-Bearing Leaf Beetles: The members of these groups are small, robust, somewhat cylindrical beetles that have the head buried in the prothorax almost to the eyes (Figure 28–81C). When disturbed, they draw in their legs, fall to the ground, and remain motionless. Most of these beetles are dark-colored, often with reddish or yellowish markings. The larvae are small fleshy grubs that crawl about dragging a small protective case, usually made of their own excrement. These cases are shorter than the body, and the posterior portion of the larva is bent downward and forward in the case. The larvae of most case-bearing leaf beetles feed on leaves. The larvae of some Chlamisìnae live in ant nests, where they feed on vegetable debris. Pupation of these beetles occurs within the case.

The members of these four subfamilies can be separated by the characters given in the key. The first three of these subfamilies are large and widely dis-

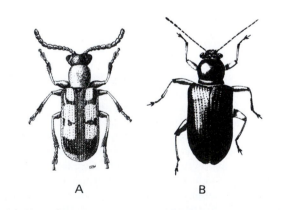

A   B

Figure 28–83. Criocerine leaf beetles. **A,** the striped asparagus beetle, *Crióceris aspáragi* (L.); **B,** the cereal leaf beetle, *Oulèma melánopus* (L.). (**A,** courtesy of the Utah State Agricultural College; **B,** courtesy of the Ohio Agricultural Research and Development Center.)

Figure 28–84. Leaf beetles. **A,** the cereal leaf beetle, *Oulèma melánopus* (L.); **B,** the striped cucumber beetle, *Acalýmma vittàtum* (Fabricius); **C,** the spotted cucumber beetle, *Diabrótica undecimpunctàta hówardi* Barber; **D,** a flea beetle (Alticinae). (Courtesy of the Ohio Agricultural Research and Development Center.)

tributed groups. The Lamprosomatìnae are represented in the United States by only two species, one occurring in Florida and the other in California.

Subfamily **Eumolpìnae:** These are oblong convex beetles that are usually brown to black. Some are metallic in color or are yellowish and spotted. The dogbane beetle, *Chrýsochus auràtus* (Fabricius), which occurs on dogbane and milkweed, is one of the most brilliantly colored of the leaf beetles. It has an iridescent blue-green color with a coppery tinge and is 8–11 mm in length. A closely related species, *C. cobaltìnus* LeConte, occurs in the Far West. It is darker and bluer than *C. auràtus* and is 9–10 mm in length.

The western grape rootworm, *Bròmius obscùrus* (L.), causes serious damage to grape crops from Alaska to New Mexico and also occurs in Europe and Siberia. Similar species found on grapes in the East belong to the genus *Fídia* and are small, oval, hairy, and dark brown to black in color.

Subfamily **Chrysomelìnae:** Most of the members of this large subfamily are oval, convex, brightly colored, and 3.5–12.0 mm in length, and they have the head sunk into the prothorax almost to the eyes. The Colorado potato beetle, *Leptinotársa decemlineàta* (Say), is the best-known and most important species in this group. This is a large, yellow beetle striped with black (Figure 28–85) and is a very serious pest of potato plants over most of the United States. Apparently the common name of this insect is inappropriate because both the beetle and its native host plants, several species of nightshade (*Solànum*), originated in Mexico. The beetle did adapt to the cultivated potato and rapidly spread eastward, but from Nebraska, not Colorado. Since the introduction of the potato, this beetle has spread throughout the United States (except California and Nevada) and has been transported to Europe, where it is also a serious pest. This group includes the genus *Chrysolìna*, species of which were introduced into California from Europe to control Klamath weed (see page 9).

Most of the other species in this subfamily feed on various wild plants and are of little economic importance. Species of *Labidómera* (relatively large red and black beetles) feed on milkweed; *Phratòra* (metallic blue or purple) feed on willow and poplar; and *Callìgrapha* (whitish, with dark streaks and spots) feed on willow, alder, and other plants.

Subfamily **Galerucìnae:** The members of this group are small soft-bodied beetles, mostly 2.5–11.0 mm in length, and most of them are yellowish with dark spots or stripes. The spotted cucumber beetle, *Diabrótica undecimpunctàta hówardi* Barber (Figure 28–84C), and the striped cucumber beetle, *Acalýmma vittàtum* (Fabricius) (Figure 28–84B), feed on cucumbers and related plants. These beetles do serious damage to cucurbits by their feeding, and they act as vectors of cucurbit wilt. The wilt bacilli pass the winter in the alimentary tract of the beetles, and new plants are inoculated when the beetles begin to

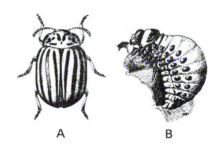

Figure 28–85. The Colorado potato beetle, *Leptinotársa decemlineàta* (Say). **A,** adult; **B,** larva. (Courtesy of the Utah Agricultural Experiment Station.)

feed on them in the spring. The larvae of these two species are small, white, and soft-bodied and feed on the roots and underground stems of cucurbits. The larva of the spotted cucumber beetle also feeds on the roots of corn and other plants and is sometimes called the southern corn rootworm.

Two other corn rootworms—the northern corn rootworm, *Diabrótica bárberi* Smith and Lawrence, and the western corn rootworm, *D. virgífera* LeConte—are serious pests of corn in the Midwest. Both adults and larvae cause damage, the larvae by feeding on the roots and the adults by feeding in the silk. The latter activity prevents pollination and consequent kernel development.

The elm leaf beetle, *Xanthogalerùca lutèola* (Müller), is another important pest species in this group. It is a greenish yellow beetle with a few black spots on the head and pronotum and a black stripe down the outer margin of each elytron.

Subfamily **Alticìnae (Halticìnae)**—Flea Beetles: The flea beetles are small jumping leaf beetles that have the hind femora greatly enlarged. Most of them are blue or greenish, but many are black or black with light markings (Figure 28–86). A number of the flea beetles are very important pests of garden and field crops. *Épitrix hirtipénnis* (Melsheimer) attacks tobacco; *E. cucùmeris* (Harris) feeds on potatoes and cucumbers; and *E. fúscula* Crotch feeds on eggplant and tomatoes. These are small blackish beetles about 2 mm in length. *Áltica chalýbea* Illiger, a blue-black beetle 4–5 mm in length, feeds on the buds and leaves of grape. Adult flea beetles feed on the leaves of the food plant and eat tiny holes in them. The leaves of a heavily infested plant look as if small shots had been fired into them. The larvae usually feed on the roots of the same plant.

The corn flea beetle, *Chaetocnèma pulicària* Melsheimer, is a vector of Stewart's disease of corn. The causative organism, a bacterium, overwinters in the alimentary tract of the adult beetle and is transmitted to seedling corn when the beetle feeds. This disease is especially important in early planted sweet corn. In some instances entire fields have been destroyed by the disease.

Subfamily **Hispìnae**—Leaf-Mining Leaf Beetles: These beetles are 4–7 mm in length, elongate, and peculiarly ridged (Figure 28–87). Most of them are leaf-mining in the larval stage, and some are rather serious pests. The locust leaf miner, *Odontòta dorsàlis* (Thunberg), an orange-yellow beetle with a broad black stripe down the middle of the back (Figure 28–87), is a serious pest of black locust. Its mines are irregular blotches in the terminal half of the leaflet and, when numerous may cause considerable defoliation.

Subfamily **Cassidìnae**—Tortoise Beetles: The tortoise beetles are broadly oval or circular, with the elytra wide and the head largely or entirely covered by the pronotum. Some of them are shaped very much like ladybird beetles. Many of the smaller tortoise beetles (5–6 mm in length) are very brilliantly colored, often with golden color or markings. The mottled tortoise beetle, *Deloyála guttàta* (Olivier), has black markings on a reddish gold background, and the golden tortoise beetle, *Charidotélla bìcolor* (Fabricius), is brilliant gold or bronzy without the black markings. One of the largest members of this subfamily is the argus tortoise beetle, *Chelymórpha cassídea* (Fabricius), which is 9.5–11.5 mm in length and shaped very much like a box turtle. It is red with six black spots on each elytron and one black spot along the suture overlapping both elytra (Figure 28–88B).

The larvae of tortoise beetles are elongate-oval and somewhat flattened. At the posterior end of the body is a forked process that is usually bent upward and forward over the body. Cast skins and excrement are attached to this process, forming a parasol-like

Figure 28–86. Flea beetles (Alticìnae). **A,** the potato flea beetle, *Épitrix cucùmeris* (Harris); **B,** the spinach flea beetle, *Disonýchia xanthómelas* (Dalman); **C,** the eggplant flea beetle, *Épitrix fùscula* Crotch. (Courtesy of USDA.)

A

B

C

Figure 28–87.   Adult of the locust leaf miner, *Odontòta dorsàlis* (Thunberg), 7× (Hispìnae). (Courtesy of the Ohio Agricultural Research and Development Center.)

shield over the body (Figure 28–88A). The larvae and adults of tortoise beetles feed principally on morning glories and related plants.

SUPERFAMILY **Curculionòidea:** The members of this group are sometimes called snout beetles, as most of them have the head more or less prolonged anteriorly into a beak or snout. This term is less appropriate (and is seldom used) for the Platypódidae and Scolýtidae, as the snout is scarcely developed in these two families. The Curculionòidea were formerly placed in a subdivision of the order called the Rhynchóphora.

Certain other characters besides the development of a snout distinguish the Curculionòidea from the beetles already described. The gular sutures are nearly always confluent, or lacking, with no gula developed (Figure 28–3C) (they are short but widely separated in the Nemonýchidae). Prosternal sutures are lacking (except in the Anthríbidae), and in most of them the palps are rigid or invisible and the labrum is absent (Figure 28–3A,B). The mouthparts are small and more or less hidden in most of these beetles. The mandibles, located at the tip of the snout, are usually the only mouthpart structures easily visible without dissection. The tarsi are five-segmented, but usually appear four-segmented (the fourth segment is generally very small).

This is a large and important group of beetles, with more than 3100 species occurring in North America. Practically all feed on plant materials, and most of the larvae are burrowing in habit, infesting nuts, twigs, and the like. The larvae are whitish, usually C-shaped, more or less cylindrical, and usu-

ally legless. A great many are of considerable economic importance as pests of field or garden crops, of forest, shade, and fruit trees, or of stored products.

There are differences of opinion regarding the classification of the beetles in this superfamily. The Bréntidae, Anthríbidae, Scolýtidae, and Platypódidae are almost universally recognized as distinct families by different authorities. We follow here, with slight modification, the arrangement of O'Brien and Wibmer (1982), who divide the remaining snout beetles into seven families.

Family **Anthríbidae**—Fungus Weevils: The anthribids are elongate-oval, 0.5–30.0 (usually less than 10.0) mm in length, with the beak short and broad and the antennae not elbowed (Figure 28–89B). Some species have slender antennae that may be longer than the body (hence they look a little like some Cerambýcidae), and others have short antennae with a three-segmented club. The elytra always cover the base of the pygidium, which is always partly exposed in lateral view but is usually not visible from above. The adults of this group are usually found on dead twigs or beneath loose bark. The larvae vary in habits. Some breed in woody fungi; some breed in the fungi of certain crops (for example, corn smut); some feed in seeds; and a few bore in dead wood. The introduced coffee bean weevil, *Araècerus fasciculàtus* (De Geer), is an important pest of seeds, berries, and dried fruits. There are 79 species of Anthríbidae in the United States and Canada.

Family **Bréntidae**—Straight-Snouted Weevils: The brentids are narrow, elongate, cylindrical beetles, 5.2–42.0 mm in length, usually reddish or brownish

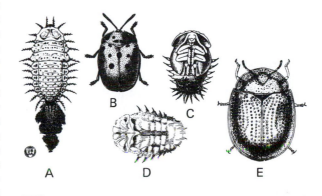

Figure 28–88.   Tortoise beetles (Cassidìnae). **A–D,** the argus tortoise beetle, *Chelymórpha cassídea* (Fabricius), 1½×; **E,** the eggplant tortoise beetle, *Cássida pallídula* Boheman, 5×. **A,** larva, with the anal fork extended and covered with fecal material; **B,** adult; **C,** pupa, ventral view; **D,** pupa, dorsal view. (Courtesy of USDA.)

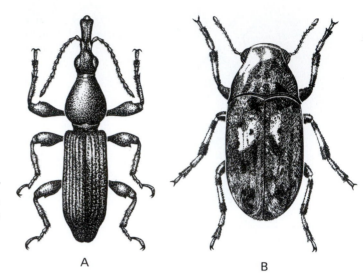

Figure 28–89.   A, a straight-snouted weevil, *Arrhenòdes minùtus* (Drury) (Bréntidae), 4×; **B,** a fungus weevil, *Eupàrius marmòreus* (Olivier) (Anthríbidae), 6½×; (**A,** courtesy of Arnett; **B,** courtesy of Pierce and the U.S. National Museum.)

A   B

and shining, with the snout projecting forward (Figure 28–89A). The snout is generally longer and more slender in the female than in the male (Figure 28–90G,H). This group is principally tropical, and only six species occur in North America. The only common eastern species is *Arrhenòdes minùtus* (Drury), which usually occurs under the loose bark of dead oak, poplar, and beech trees. The larvae are wood-boring and sometimes attack living trees.

Family **Attelábidae**—Leaf-Rolling Weevils: These beetles are short and robust, 3–6 mm in length, and are somewhat similar to the Rhynchítidae. Most of them are black, reddish, or black with red markings. The most interesting characteristic of this group is their method of laying eggs, from which their common name is derived. When a female is ready to oviposit, she cuts two slits near the base of the leaf, from each edge to the midrib, and rolls the part of the leaf beyond these cuts into a neat and solid ball. A single egg is laid near the tip of the leaf, usually on the underside, before the leaf is rolled up. She then gnaws the midrib of the leaf (at the end of the basal cuts) partly in two, and the leaf roll eventually drops to the ground. The larva feeds on the inner portion of this leaf roll and pupates either in the roll or in the ground.

Most of the ten species of leaf-rolling weevils in the United States belong to the genus *Attélabus*. Most species occur on oak, hickory, or walnut, but one species (*A. nígripes* LeConte, red and 3.5–4.5 mm in length) feeds on sumac, and another (*A. rhóis* Boheman, 4.5–5.5 mm in length and dark reddish to black) feeds on alder and hazelnut.

Family **Rhynchítidae**—Tooth-Nosed Weevils: These beetles are so named because of the teeth on the edges of the mandibles (Figure 28–90I). They are 1.5–6.5 mm in length and usually occur on low vegetation. There are about 50 North American species of these weevils. A common species in this group is the rose curculio, *Merhynchìtes bìcolor* (Fabricius), which occurs on roses. The adult is about 6 mm in length and is red, with the snout and the ventral side of the body black, and it has a broad-shouldered appearance. The larvae feed in rose fruits. Other species in this group breed in buds, fruits, and nuts.

Family **Nemonýchidae**—Pine-Flower Snout Beetles: This is a small group, with only ten species occurring in North America. These beetles are 3.0–4.5 mm in length, with the snout about as long as the prothorax and somewhat flattened and narrowed at the base. They differ from other families of Curculionòidea in having the labrum distinct and the palps flexible. The larvae of these beetles develop in the staminate flowers of various conifers. Adults are usually found on conifers, but may occasionally be found on plum or peach trees.

Family **Oxycorýnidae:**   Only one species in this family occurs in the United States, *Rhopalótria slóssoni* (Schaeffer), which occurs in southern Florida. The adults and larvae feed on the male cones of arrowroot (*Zàmia*). The adults have the elytra black, with an elongate reddish yellow mark near each humerus.

Family **Apiónidae:**   The members of this group are small (4.5 mm in length or less), somewhat pear-shaped, and usually blackish in color, and the antennae are usually not elbowed. Most of our 150 species

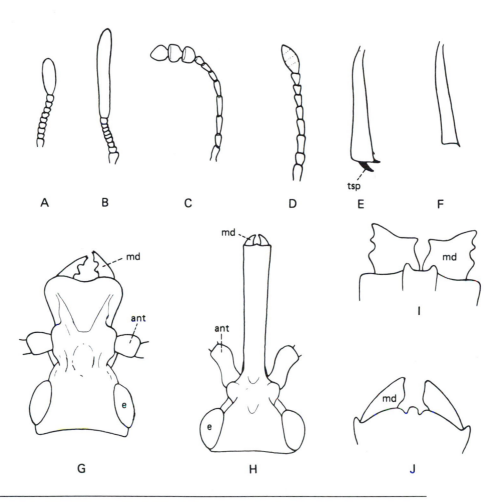

Figure 28–90.   Characters of snout beetles. **A–D,** antennae; **E–F,** tibiae; **G–H,** heads; **I–J,** tip of snout. **A,** *Cỳlas,* female (Apiónidae); **B,** same, male; **C,** *Rhynchìtes* (Rhynchítidae); **D,** *Ithýcerus* (Ithycéridae); **E,** *Attélabus* (Attelábidae); **F,** *Rhynchìtes* (Rhynchítidae); **G,** *Arrhenòdes,* male (Bréntidae); **H,** same, female; **I,** *Rhynchìtes* (Rhynchítidae); **J,** *Attélabus* (Attelábidae). *ant,* antenna; *e,* compound eye; *md,* mandible; *tsp,* tibial spur.

belong to the genus *Àpion,* most of which occur on legumes. The larvae bore into the seeds, stems, and other parts of the plant. Adults of the introduced hollyhock weevil, *A. longiróstre* Olivier, feed on the leaves and buds of the hollyhock, and the larvae feed on the seeds of this plant. The pine gall weevil, *Podàpion gallícola* Riley, forms galls on the twigs of pine trees. The sweet potato weevil, *Cỳlas formicàrius elegántulus* (Summers), is an introduced species that occurs principally in the southern states. This beetle is slender, elongate, antlike, and 5–6 mm in length. The pronotum is reddish brown and the elytra are blue-black (Figure 28–91). The larvae are often called sweet potato root borers. This insect is a serious pest of sweet potatoes because the larvae

bore in the vines and roots, and the plants are often killed. The larvae may continue to burrow through the tubers after they are harvested, and adults may emerge after the sweet potatoes are in storage or on the market.

Family **Ithycéridae:** This family includes a single species, the New York weevil, *Ithýcerus noveboracénsis* (Forster), which occurs in eastern North America west to Nebraska and Texas. This beetle is shiny black, clothed with patches of gray and brown pubescence, and has the scutellum yellowish. It is 12–18 mm in length. The adults of this beetle occur principally on the limbs and foliage of hickory, oak, and beech trees. The larvae develop on the roots of these same trees.

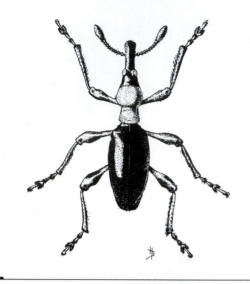

Figure 28–91. The sweet potato weevil, *Cỳlas formicàrius elegántulus* (Summers), female. (Courtesy of USDA.)

Family **Curculiónidae**—Snout Beetles: The members of this family are by far the most commonly encountered Curculionòidea. They may be found almost everywhere, and more than 2600 species occur in North America. They show considerable variation in size, shape, and the form of the snout. The snout is fairly well developed in most species, with the antennae arising about the middle of the snout. (Figure 28–3B). In some of the nut weevils (Figure 28–93C) the snout is long and slender, as long as the body or longer.

All snout beetles (except a few occurring in ant nests) are plant feeders, and many are serious pests. Almost every part of a plant may be attacked, from the roots upward. The larvae usually feed inside the tissues of the plant, and the adults drill holes in fruits, nuts, and other plant parts.

Most snout beetles, when disturbed, will draw in their legs and antennae, fall to the ground, and remain motionless. Many are colored like bits of bark or dirt, and when they remain motionless they are very dfficult to see. Some snout beetles (for example, *Conotràchelus*, subfamily Cryptorhynchìnae) are able to stridulate by rubbing hardened tubercles on the dorsum of the abdomen against filelike ridges on the underside of the elytra. These sounds in *Conotràchelus* (Figure 28–2) are extremely weak and usually can be heard only by holding the insect to one's ear.

There are differences of opinion among coleopterists regarding the limits of the family Curculiónidae. We follow here the arrangement of O'Brien and Wibmer (1982), who divide the Curculiónidae into 33 subfamilies.

Key to the Subfamilies of Curculiónidae

This key should serve to identify the vast majority of the specimens the general collector is likely to encounter. It does not include Acicnemidìnae (one introduced species), Amalactìnae (one introduced species), Raymondionymìnae (three species, California), Cholìnae (three species, one in Arizona and two introduced into orchid houses), Petalochilìnae (three species, southeastern United States), and Cionìnae (one species introduced from Europe into Louisiana and Canada).

1.	Antennae elbowed; beak usually with antennal scrobes **2**		
1'.	Antennae not elbowed; beak usually lacking antennal scrobes **Tachygonìnae**	p. 473
2(1).	Tarsi slender, third segment not bilobed; tarsal claws simple; beak short and broad, at rest fitting into cavity in front of front coxae; prosternum a triangular plate in front of front coxae ....**Thecesternìnae**	p. 470
2'.	Third tarsal segment usually strongly bilobed; tarsal claws variable; beak variable in size and shape, either beak not fitting into cavity in front of front coxae, prosternum not a triangular plate in front of front coxae, or beak extending beyond front coxae **3**		
3(2').	Beak stout, quadrate, usually shorter than prothorax, often expanded laterally toward apex, and with 1 or more longitudinal grooves; mandibles relatively large, with apical projection or cusp that is deciduous and leaves a round or		

oval scar when it falls off (Figure 28–92H, *scr*) or with many fine scales or setae laterally (the broad-nosed weevils) **4**

3′.   Beak usually slender and longer than prothorax, if shorter then lacking a median longitudinal groove; mandibles usually small, lacking a deciduous cusp or scar, and glabrous or with a few minute setae laterally **8**

4(3).   Anterior margin of prothorax with postocular lobes (Figure 28–92F, *pol*) that sometimes partly cover the eyes; eyes more or less transverse **5**

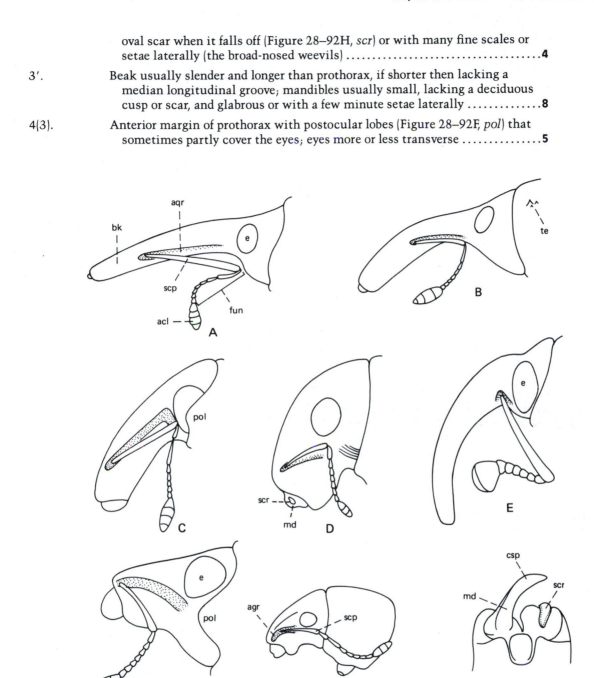

Figure 28–92.   Characters of snout beetles. **A–G,** heads, lateral view; **H,** tip of snout, ventral view. **A,** *Anthónomus* (Anthonomìnae); **B,** *Mágdalis* (Magdalìnae); **C,** *Listronòtus* (Cylindrorhinìnae); **D,** *Pandeletèlius* (Tanymecìnae); **E,** *Rhodobaènus* (Rhynchophorìnae); **F,** *Eudiagògus* (Leptopiìnae); **G** and **H,** *Pantómorus* (Brachyderìnae). *acl,* antennal club; *agr,* scrobe; *bk,* beak of snout; *csp,* cusp of mandible; *e,* compound eye; *fun,* funiculus (antennal segments between scape and club); *md,* mandible; *pol,* postocular lobe of prothorax; *scp,* scape, the basal antennal segment; *scr,* scar left on mandible where cusp has broken off; *te,* teeth on prothorax.

4'.	Anterior margin of prothorax without postocular lobes; eyes more or less rounded and usually well in front of prothorax **6**	
5(4).	Mandibles with 3 large setae ....**Eremninae**	p. 470
5'.	Mandibles with 4 or more large setae ....**Leptopiinae**	p. 470
6(4').	Prothorax with a group of long fine hairs extending anteriorly from anterior margin behind eyes (Figure 28–92D) ....**Tanymecinae**	p. 470
6'.	Prothorax without such hairs **7**	
7(6').	Antennal scrobe vaguely defined posteriorly; scape usually passing above middle of eye when retracted next to head ....**Otiorhynchinae**	p. 470
7'.	Antennal scrobe fairly well defined posteriorly, bent ventrally, scape passing below eye when retracted next to head (Figure 28–92G) ....**Brachyderinae**	p. 470
8(3').	Scape of antenna arising near eye, usually extending past posterior margin of eye, and not fitting into the short scrobe (Figure 28–92E); funiculus 6-segmented; basal two-thirds or more of antennal club dark, shining, and not annulated, the rest pale and not shining (Figure 28–92E); third tarsal segment usually not bilobed; pygidium generally exposed ....**Rhynchophorinae**	p. 473
8'	Scape of antenna usually arising more apically, fitting into scrobe, and not extending beyond posterior margin of eye; antennal club either not as above, or if first segment of club is glabrous, then funiculus is 7-segmented or the prosternum has an apical channel; third tarsal segment usually bilobed; pygidium generally covered **9**	
9(8').	Beak at rest fitting into median channel in prosternum **10**	
9'.	Beak at rest not fitting into median channel in prosternum **14**	
10(9).	Eyes partly covered by postocular lobes of prothorax when beak is in repose **11**	
10'.	Eyes not covered when beak is in repose; eyes elongate-oval, pointed ventrally ....**Zygopinae**	p. 473
11(10).	Pygidium covered by elytra; tibiae with an uncus (as in Figure 28–93G,I) ...**12**	
11'.	Pygidium exposed, tibiae without an uncus, but often mucronate (as in Figure 28–93H,I) ....**Ceutorhynchinae**	p. 473
12(11).	Antennal club nearly evenly pubescent; hind tibiae with apical comb of setae **13**	
12'.	First segment of antennal club nearly glabrous; hind tibiae without apical comb of setae; tarsi narrow, third segment not bilobed ....**Cryptorhynchinae**	p. 472
13(12).	Body with dense varnishlike coating; third tarsal segment often no wider than first two segments; front coxae contiguous; tarsal claws simple and free (as in Figure 28–93D) (Bagoini) ....**Erirrhininae**	p. 472
13'.	Body without dense varnishlike coating; third tarsal segment bilobed, usually wider than first two segments; front coxae separated, or tarsal claws toothed or connate...**Cryptorhynchinae**	p. 472
14(9').	Mesepimera extending upward, sometimes visible in dorsal view between prothorax and elytra (Figure 28–93A); elytra not produced anteriorly over base of prothorax **15**	
14'.	Mesepimera not as above, not visible in dorsal view **16**	
15(14).	Funiculus 6-segmented; tarsal claws simple or toothed ....**Ceutorhynchinae**	p. 473
15'.	Funiculus 7-segmented; tarsal claws simple, free, or connate, or with a single claw ....**Baridinae**	p. 473

16(14′).   Front coxae separated by piece of prosternum; second abdominal sternum about as long as or longer than third and fourth together; tarsal claws usually simple **17**

16′.   Front coxae contiguous **21**

17(16).   Eyes separated by distance not greater than maximum diameter of antennal club; front femora toothed, sometimes strongly so; pygidium concealed or exposed **18**

17′.   Eyes separated by distance greater than maximum diameter of antennal club, or lacking; front femora not toothed; pygidium concealed **19**

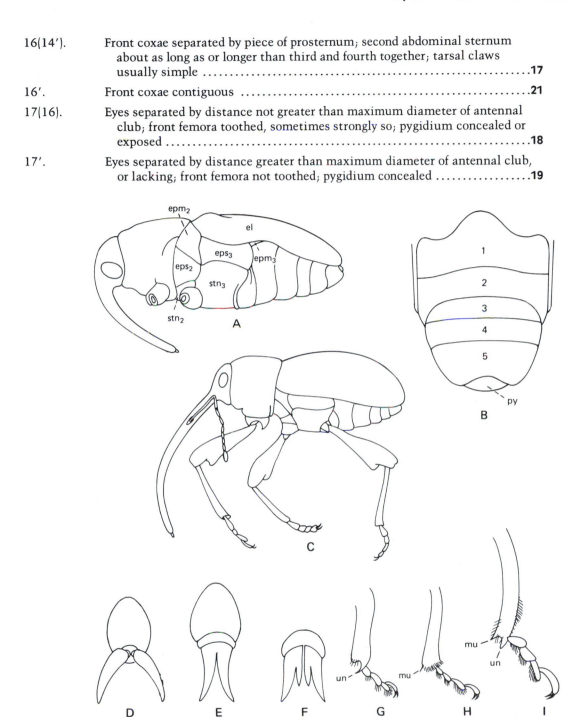

Figure 28–93.   Characters of snout beetles. **A,** lateral view of body of *Odontocorỳnus* (Baridìnae); **B,** ventral view of abdomen of *Miccotrògus* (Tychiìnae); **C,** a nut weevil, *Curcùlio* sp., lateral view (Curculionìnae); **D–F,** tarsal claws; **D,** claws free and simple (*Ophriástes,* Leptopiìnae). **E,** claws connate (*Clèonus,* Cleonìnae), **F,** claws toothed (*Rhyssemàtus,* Cryptorhynchìnae); **G–I,** tibia and tarsus; **G,** tibia uncinate (*Laemosáccus,* Magdalìnae), **H,** tibia mucronate (*Tỳchius,* Tychiìnae), **I,** tibia mucronate and uncinate (*Erethístes,* Cholìnae). *el,* elytron; *epm₂,* mesepimeron; *eps₂,* mesepisternum; *eps₃,* metepisternum; *mu,* mucro; *py,* pygidium; *stn₂,* mesosternum; *stn₃,* metasternum; *un,* uncus; 1–5, abdominal sterna.

18(17).   Base of elytra produced over base of prothorax; elytra black, usually with a reddish area; pygidium exposed; beak more or less cylindrical (*Laemosáccus*) ....**Magdalinae**   p. 472

18′.   Base of elytra not produced over base of prothorax; elytra unicolorous; pygidium exposed (*Piazorhìnus*) or more or less concealed (*Odóntopus*); beak slightly flattened apically ....**Prionomerìnae**   p. 472

19(17′).   Outer surface of apex of hind tibiae with apical comb of setae laterad of base of uncus; scutellum minute or not visible; dorsal margin of scrobe directed toward lower half of eye ....**Hylobìinae**   p. 471

19′.   Outer surface of apex of hind tibiae without apical comb of setae laterad of base of uncus **20**

20(19′).   Hind tibiae with apical dorsal comb of setae, the comb about as long as width of tibia at apex; beak usually about as long as prothorax ....**Pissodìnae**   p. 471

20′.   Hind tibiae without apical comb of setae; beak usually shorter than prothorax ....**Cossonìnae**   p. 474

21(16′).   Suture between second and third abdominal sterna strongly produced backward laterally, reaching or surpassing suture between third and fourth sterna (Figure 28–93B); hind coxae distant from margin of elytra; beak tapered apically ....**Tychìinae**   p. 472

21′.   Suture between second and third abdominal sterna straight or, at most, only slightly produced backward laterally, not reaching suture between third and fourth sterna **22**

22(21′).   Tarsal claws connate at base (Figure 28–93E) **23**

22′.   Tarsal claws free at base (as in Figure 28–93D) (*Brachybàmus*, Erirrhinìnae, has only 1 tarsal claw) **26**

23(22).   Funiculus 5-segmented; pygidium exposed ....**Gymnetrìnae**   p. 472

23′.   Funiculus 7-segmented **24**

24(23′).   Elytra with acute lateral tubercle behind humeri; tibiae angulate on inner surface near middle (*Stérnechus*) ....**Hylobìinae**   p. 471

24′.   Elytra without such lateral tubercles; tibiae not angulate on inner surface near middle **25**

25(24′).   Eyes distant from anterior margin of prothorax; anterior margin of prothorax with long postocular hairs and not produced into postocular lobes ....**Cleonìnae**   p. 471

25′.   Eyes concealed by postocular lobes on anterior margin of prothorax; prothorax without long postocular hairs (Smicronychìni, western United States) ....**Erirrhinìnae**   p. 472

26(22′).   Tarsal claws simple (*Brachybàmus*, Erirrhinìnae, has only 1 tarsal claw); second abdominal sternum longer than third, usually as long as third and fourth together **27**

26′.   Tarsal claws with a basal tooth or process (as in Figure 28–93F); abdominal sterna 2–4 usually about equal in length **34**

27(26).   Hind tibiae uncinate, uncus more than half as long as tarsal claws (Figure 28–93G,I) **28**

27′.   Hind tibiae unarmed apically, or mucronate with mucro not more than half as long as tarsal claws (as in Figure 28–93H) **31**

28(27).   Metepimera visible, their vestiture and sculpturing similar to those of metepisterna **29**

28'. Metepimera normally covered by elytra, their vestiture and sculpturing finer than those on metepisterna **30**

29(28). Uncus on hind tibiae projecting from slightly behind anterior margin of tibia; body usually without scales dorsally but with stellate scales ventrally . . . .**Magdalinae**   p. 472

29'. Uncus on hind tibiae projecting from anterior margin of tibia; body clothed dorsally and ventrally with narrow elongate scales (*Lépyrus*) . . . .**Cleoninae**   p. 471

30(28'). Dorsal surface of body covered with round scales and usually with varnishlike coating on top of scales; frons usually at least as wide as base of beak in dorsal view; hind coxae separated by distance equal to or greater than greatest diameter of the coxae . . . .**Erirrhininae**   p. 472

30'. Dorsal surface of body with narrow scales, or elongate and fairly broad scales, without varnishlike coating; frons much narrower than base of beak in dorsal view; hind coxae separated by distance distinctly less than greatest diameter of the coxae . . . .**Hylobiinae**   p. 471

31(27'). Dorsal margin of scrobe directed toward dorsal margin of eye and bent abruptly downward in front of eye (Figure 28–92C); prothorax with postocular lobes . . . .**Cylindrorhininae**   p. 470

31'. Dorsal margin of scrobe not reaching dorsal margin of eye and not bent downward in front of eye; prothorax lacking postocular lobes, or if such lobes are present, then beak is more slender than greatest width of middle femora **32**

32(31'). Front coxae much closer to hind margin of prosternum than to front margin . . . .**Erirrhininae**   p. 472

32'. Front coxae about equidistant from anterior and posterior margins of prosternum **33**

33(32'). Eyes nearly round; beak slender, longer than prothorax, rather glabrous, width in profile at base of antennae much less than width of eye . . . .**Anthonominae**   p. 472

33'. Eyes transversely oval; beak stout, densely and rather uniformly setose . . . .**Hyperinae**   p. 471

34(26'). Front coxae about equidistant from anterior and posterior margins of prosternum **35**

34'. Front coxae much closer to hind margin of prosternum than to front margin **38**

35(34). Prothorax longer than wide, wider in middle than at base; hind tibiae with small uncus. . . . .**Otidocephalinae**   p. 472

35'. Prothorax wider than long **36**

36(35'). Hind tibiae uncinate, uncus longer than tarsal claws (Figure 28–93G); basal tarsal segment longer than fourth; eyes transversely oval . . . .**Magdalinae**   p. 472

36'. Hind tibiae unarmed or mucronate, or if apparently uncinate, uncus is distinctly shorter than tarsal claws; basal tarsal segment shorter than fourth **37**

37(36'). Hind tibiae with apical comb of setae perpendicular to long axis of tibia; hind tibiae not narrowed apically; hind femora not much stouter than middle femora . . . .**Anthonominae**   p. 472

37'. Apical comb of setae on hind tibiae oblique, ascending for distance greater than width of tibiae at apex; hind tibiae narrowed apically; hind femora stouter than middle femora . . . .**Rhynchaeninae**   p. 472

38(34′).	Pronotum with anterolateral toothlike projections (Figure 28–92B) ....**Magdalinae**	p. 472
38′.	Pronotum without such projections **39**	
39(38′).	Prothorax oval, longer than wide, narrowed at base; hind tibiae uncinate; antennal scrobes located more ventrally; body nearly glabrous ....**Otidocephalinae**	p. 472
39′.	Prothorax wider than long, not wider in middle than at base; hind tibiae unarmed or mucronate; antennal scrobes located laterally **40**	
40(39′)	Femora with stout triangular tooth; elytra with slender elongate scales; beak slender, often as long as body or longer (Figure 28–93C) ....**Curculioninae**	p. 472
40′.	Femora without such a tooth; elytra with inconspicuous, short fine setae ....**Erirrhininae**	p. 472

Subfamily **Brachyderinae (Thylacitinae):** The members of this and the four following subfamilies are commonly called the broad-nosed weevils, because of the character of the beak (see key to subfamilies, couplet 3). Most of them are flightless because the elytra are grown together along the suture and the hind wings are vestigial. This is a large and widely distributed group (nearly 100 North American species) containing some important pests. The most important species in this group are the white-fringed beetles (four species of *Graphógnathus*), which are serious agricultural pests in the southern states. These beetles are about 12 mm long, with the edges of the elytra whitish and with two longitudinal white stripes on the head and pronotum (Figure 28–94A). The white-fringed beetles are parthenogenetic; no males are known. Another injurious species in this group is the Fuller rose weevil, *Pantómorus cervìnus* (Boheman), 7–9 mm in length, which is especially common in the Far West. It attacks roses and many greenhouse plants, as well as citrus and other fruit trees. The larvae live in the soil and feed on the roots of the host plant, and the adults feed on the leaves. Members of the genus *Sitòna* (mostly pale in color and 4–5 mm in length) attack and seriously damage clovers.

Subfamily **Tanymecinae:** This is a smaller group (41 North American species), mostly western. The larvae feed on a variety of herbaceous plants, shrubs, and trees. One species of importance in the Southeast is the citrus root weevil, *Pachnaèus lìtus* (Germar).

Subfamily **Otiorhynchinae (Brachyrhininae):** This is a large and widely distributed group of broad-nosed weevils, with about 100 North American species. Most of them are small (generally 6 mm in length or less). Members of the genus *Otiorhýnchus* are very common and feed on a variety of plants. The strawberry root weevil, *O. ovàtus* (L.), often causes serious injury to strawberries, and the black vine weevil, *O. sulcàtus* (Fabricius), is an important pest of yew (*Táxus*). The larvae of these species feed on the roots of the host plants.

Subfamily **Leptopiinae:** This is a large group, with 153 North American species. Most species are western, and some are brightly colored. The larvae feed chiefly on various herbaceous plants and shrubs.

Subfamily **Eremninae:** Only three species of Eremninae occur in North America. The most common species in the East is the Asiatic oak weevil, *Cyrtepístomus castàneus* (Roelofs), a species introduced from Japan and found on the foliage of oaks and other trees. This weevil is about 6 mm in length, dark brown, and covered with light green scales (especially laterally).

Subfamily **Cylindrorhininae:** Most members of this group breed in aquatic or subaquatic plants, and the adults are found near water. A few are pests of vegetables. The vegetable weevil, *Listróderes costiróstris obliquus* (Klug), attacks many different vegetables and is an important pest in the Gulf States and in California. The carrot weevil, *Listronòtus oregonénsis* (LeConte), is a pest of carrots and other vegetables in the East.

Subfamily **Thecesterninae**—Bison Snout Beetles: This group includes seven U.S. species, one of which occurs in the East. The eastern species, *Thecestérnus áffinis* LeConte, is a dull black beetle covered with brownish yellow scales and 6.5–9.0 mm in length. When at rest the head and beak are completely with-

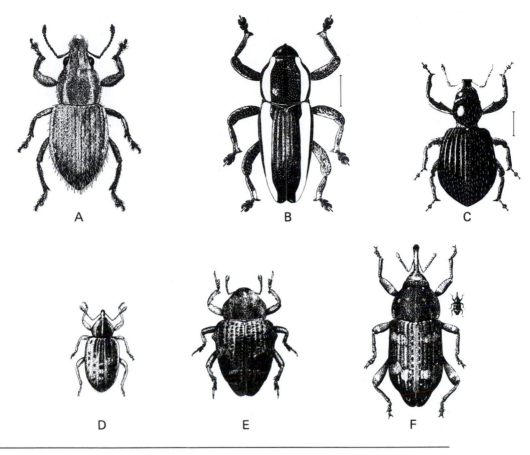

Figure 28–94.   Snout beetles. **A,** a white-fringed beetle, *Graphógnathus leucolòma* (Boheman), 3½× (Brachyderìnae); **B,** *Barìnus bivittàtus* (LeConte) (line = 1 mm) (Baridìnae); **C,** an antlike weevil, *Mýrmex subglàber* (Schaeffer) (line = 1 mm) (Otidocephalìnae); **D,** the alfalfa weevil, *Hỳpera pòstica* (Gyllenhal) (Hyperìnae), 5×; **E,** the bean stalk weevil, *Stérnechus paludàtus* (Casey) (Hylobiìnae); **F,** the white pine weevil, *Pissòdes stròbi* (Peck) (insert is about one-half natural size) (Pissodìnae). (**A, D, E,** and **F,** courtesy of USDA; **B** and **C,** courtesy oˊ Sleeper.)

drawn into a large cavity in the front of the prothorax. The Thecesternìnae occur under stones or dried cow dung. They are not common.

Subfamily **Hyperìnae**—Clover Weevils: Most members of this small group (seven North American species, in the genus *Hỳpera*) feed on various clovers and are important clover pests. The alfalfa weevil, *H. pòstica* (Gyllenhal) (Figure 28–94D), and the clover leaf weevil, *H. punctàta* (Fabricius), feed on the growing tips of the plant and skeletonize the leaves; *H. mèles* (Fabricius) feeds in the clover heads. These beetles are dark-colored and 3–8 mm in length.

Subfamily **Cleonìnae:**   The most common beetles in this group are those in the genus *Líxus*, which are elongate and cylindrical, 10–15 mm in length, with the curved beak nearly as long as the prothorax. They usually occur on weeds near water. *Líxus concàvus*

Say, which breeds in the stems of dock, sunflower, and occasionally rhubarb, is commonly called the rhubarb curculio. The adult is blackish, covered with gray pubescence. More than 100 species of Cleonìnae occur in North America, 69 of them in the genus *Líxus*.

Subfamily **Hylobiìnae** (including **Ithaurìnae**):   Most members of this group are dark-colored and of moderate size (Figure 28–95). Several species (especially species of *Hylòbius*) are important pests of pine and other conifers. The bean stalk weevil, *Stérnechus paludàtus* (Casey) (Figure 28–94E) is a member of this subfamily.

Subfamily **Pissodìnae**—Pine Weevils: The members of this group are usually brownish and cylindrical, and most are 8–10 mm in length (Figure 28–94F). Many species are important pests of coni-

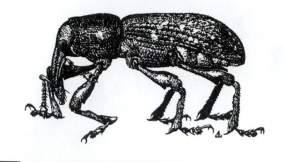

Figure 28–95.   The pales weevil, *Hylòbius pàles* (Herbst) (Hylobiìnae), 5× (Courtesy of USDA.)

fers. The larvae tunnel in the terminal leader of a young tree and kill it, and one of the lateral branches becomes the terminal leader, giving rise to a tree with a bend partway up the trunk. Such a tree is of little value for lumber. The white pine weevil, *Pissòdes stròbi* (Peck), is a common species attacking white pine. Other species of *Pissòdes* attack other conifers.

Subfamily **Erirrhinìnae:**   This is a large and widely distributed group, with 179 species reported from North America. The adults are usually found near water, as the larvae of many species develop in various aquatic plants.

Subfamily   **Otidocephalìnae**—Antlike   Weevils: These small shiny weevils have the prothorax oval and narrowed at the base and are somewhat antlike in appearance (Figure 28–94C). Some species develop in cynipid galls on oak, and some develop in twigs and stems. This group is a small one (in North America), and its members, most of which are in the genus *Mýrmex*, are not very common.

Subfamily **Magdalìnae:**   These small cylindrical weevils can usually be recognized by the toothlike processes on the anterior corners of the pronotum (Figure 28–92B, *te*). The larvae attack trees, usually tunneling in the twigs or under the bark. A few are pests of orchard or shade trees.

Subfamily **Curculioniìnae**—Acorn and Nut Weevils: These weevils are usually light brown in color and have a very long and slender snout that may be as long as the body or longer (Figure 28–93C). The adults bore into acorns and other nuts with their long snouts and lay their eggs in some of these feeding holes. The larvae develop inside the nut. Our species (27 in North America) belong to the genus *Curcùlio*; *C. nàsicus* Say and *C. occidéntis* (Casey) attack hazelnuts and *C. cáryae* (Horn), the pecan weevil, is a major pest of pecan.

Subfamily **Anthonomìnae:**   Nearly 200 species of Anthonomìnae occur in North America (more than

100 in the genus *Anthónomus*), and several are important pests of cultivated plants. The adults usually feed on fruits and lay their eggs in some of the feeding pits, and the larvae develop inside the fruits. The boll weevil, *A. gràndis* Boheman, is a well-known and serious pest of cotton in the southern states. It entered the United States from Mexico in the late 1800s and has since spread over most of the cotton-growing sections of the country. The adults are about 6 mm in length, reddish to brown in color, with a slender snout about half as long as the body. They feed on the fruit or bolls and flower buds and lay their eggs in the holes made in feeding. The larvae feed inside the buds and bolls and eventually destroy them. Other species of economic importance in this group are the strawberry weevil, *A. signàtus* Say; the cranberry weevil, *A. músculus* Say; and the apple curculio, *Tachypteréllus quadrigíbbus* (Say).

Subfamily   **Rhynchaenìnae**—Flea Weevils: These weevils are so called because of their jumping habits. The hind femora are relatively stout. The larvae are leaf miners and mine in the leaves of willow, elm, alder, cherry, and apple. The group is widely distributed and is represented in our area by 16 species of *Rhynchaènus*.

Subfamily **Prionomerìnae:**   The five North American species in this group occur in the East. The larvae are leaf miners in sassafras, tulip tree, and oak.

Subfamily **Tychiìnae:**   The larvae of most Tychiìnae feed on the seeds of various legumes, and the adults occur on the flowers. The clover seed weevil, *Tỳchius piciróstris* (Fabricius), is an important pest of clover in the Northwest.

Subfamily **Gymnetrìnae:**   Only seven species in this subfamily occur in North America, but some of these are fairly common insects. Some species develop in the seed pods of mullein (*Verbáscum*), some develop in the seed pods of *Lobèlia*, and another develops in galls at the base of plantain (*Plantágo*).

Subfamily **Cryptorhynchìnae:**   Many members of this large group (187 North American species) have the elytra rough and tuberculate. When at rest the beak is usually drawn back into a groove in the prosternum. The most important pest species in this group is the plum curculio, *Conotràchelus nénuphar* (Herbst) (Figure 28–96), which attacks plum, cherry, peach, apple, and other fruits. The females lay their eggs in little pits they eat in the fruits and then cut a crescent-shaped incision beside the pit containing the egg. The larvae develop in the fruits and pupate in the soil. The adult is about 6 mm in length, dark-colored, and has two prominent tubercles on each elytron. The genus *Conotràchelus* is a large one (62 North American species), and its members are

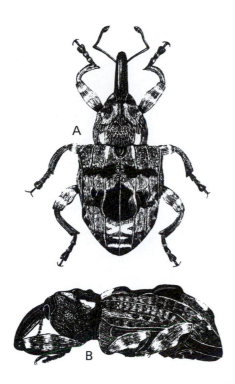

Figure 28–96.   The plum curculio, *Conotràchelus nénuphar* (Herbst). **A,** dorsal view; **B,** lateral view of an individual feigning death. (Courtesy of Rings and the Ohio Agricultural Research and Development Center.)

widely distributed. The larvae develop in various fruits and twigs.

Subfamily **Zygopìnae:**   This is a widely distributed group that is represented in North America by 40 species, which feed on various herbaceous plants and trees (including conifers).

Subfamily **Tachygonìnae**—Toad Weevils: These weevils are usually found on the foliage of oak, elm, or locust. The larvae are leaf miners in these trees. Adults at rest usually hang downward from the leaves, hanging by means of their spiny hind femora. They frequently walk about on the underside of the leaves. This group is represented in the United States by nine species of *Tachygònus*, which occur from the East to Arizona. They are not common.

Subfamily **Ceutorhynchìnae:**   This is a large and widely distributed group (145 North American species) and includes some important pests. The grape curculio, *Crapònius inaequàlis* (Say), a blackish, very broadly oval beetle about 3 mm in length, feeds on the foliage of grape. The larvae develop in the grape berries. The iris weevil, *Monónychus vulpéculus* (Fabricius), attacks iris. The larvae develop in the seed

pods, and the adults feed in the flowers. The cabbage curculio, *Ceutorhýnchus ràpae* Gyllenhal, is a pest of cabbage.

Subfamily **Baridìnae:**   This is the largest subfamily of the Curculiónidae, with about 500 North American species. These beetles are small and stout-bodied (Figure 28–94B) and can generally be recognized by the upward-extending mesepimera, which are sometimes visible from above (Figure 28–93A). Most species feed on various herbaceous plants; a few attack cultivated plants. The potato stalk borer, *Trichobàris trinotàta* (Say), attacks potato, eggplant, and related plants. The larvae bore in the stems, and the adults feed on the leaves. *Trichobàris mucòrea* (LeConte) damages tobacco in the same way. The grape cane gallmaker, *Ampeloglýpter sesóstris* (LeConte), a stout-bodied reddish brown beetle, 3–4 mm in length, makes galls on the shoots of grape.

Subfamily **Rhynchophorìnae**—Billbugs and Grain Weevils: These beetles are stout-bodied and cylindrical and are of varying size. Some of our largest snout beetles belong to this group. The antennae arise close to the eyes, and the scape extends posterior to the eye (Figure 28–92E). The basal two-thirds or more of the antennal club is smooth and shining. One of the largest of the billbugs is *Rhynchóphorus cruentàtus* (Fabricius), which is 20–30 mm in length and occurs on palms. The cocklebur weevil, *Rhodobaènus tredecimpunctàtus* (Illiger), a common eastern billbug, is 7–11 mm in length. It is reddish with small black spots on the elytra. The genus *Sphenóphorus* (Figure 28–97) includes the corn billbugs, which occur on various grasses including timothy and corn. The adults feed on the foliage, and the larvae bore into the stalks. Among the most important pests in this group are the granary weevil, *Sitóphilus granàrius* (L.), and the rice weevil, *S. orỳzae* (L.). These are small brownish insects, 3–4 mm in

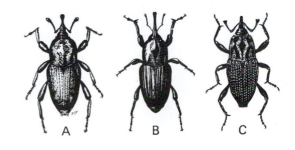

Figure 28–97.   Billbugs (Rhynchophorìnae), 2×. **A,** the curlewbug, *Sphenóphorus callòsus* (Olivier); **B,** the maize billbug, *S. màidis* Chittenden; **C,** the timothy billbug, *S. zèae* (Walsh). (Courtesy of USDA.)

length, that attack stored grain (wheat, corn, rice, and so forth). Both adults and larvae feed on the grain, and the larvae develop inside the grains.

Subfamily **Cossonìnae**—Broad-Nosed Bark Beetles: The Cossonìnae can usually be recognized by the broad short beak and the long curved spine at the apex of each front tibia. These beetles are 1.5–6.5 mm in length, and most of them occur under the loose dead bark of trees and under logs and stones. A few occur under driftwood and along the seacoast.

Family **Platypódidae**—Pin-Hole Borers: The beetles in this group are elongate, slender, and cylindrical with the head slightly wider than the pronotum (Figure 28–98). They are brownish in color and 2–8 mm in length. The tarsi (which are 5–5–5) are very slender, with the first segment longer than the remaining segments combined (Figure 28–10K). The antennae are short and geniculate and have a large unsegmented club. Our only genus is *Plátypus*, with seven species in the United States.

These beetles are wood-boring and bore in living trees, but seldom attack a healthy tree. They attack both deciduous trees and conifers. The larvae feed on fungi that are cultivated in their galleries.

Family **Scolýtidae**—Bark Beetles or Engravers, and Ambrosia Beetles: The scolytids are small cylindrical beetles, rarely more than 6 or 8 mm in length, and usually brownish or black in color (Figure 28–99). The antennae are short and geniculate and have a large, usually annulated club. The family contains

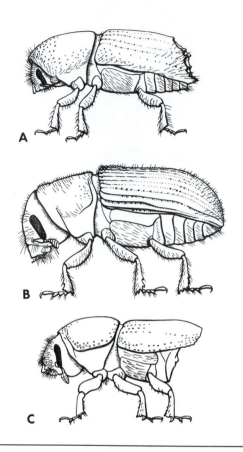

Figure 28–99.   Bark beetles. **A,** the pine engraver, *Íps pìni* (Say); **B,** the Douglas fir beetle, *Dendróctonus pseudotsùgae* Hopkins; **C,** the fir engraver, *Scólytus ventràlis* (LeConte). (Courtesy of Rudinsky and Ryker, Oregon State Agricultural Experiment Station.)

two groups: the bark beetles, which feed on the inner bark of trees, and the ambrosia beetles, which bore into the wood of trees and feed on an "ambrosial" form of a fungus, which they cultivate. Bark beetles differ from ambrosia beetles in having a large spine or projection at the apex of the front tibiae.

The bark beetles live within the bark of trees, usually right at the surface of the wood, and feed on the succulent phloem tissue. Some species, especially in *Íps,* and *Scólytus,* deeply score the sapwood and are often called engravers. Although all bark beetles feed in dying trees, some species may infest living trees, especially conifers, and kill them. Most of the economically important scolytids are in three genera: *Dendróctonus, Íps,* and *Scólytus.* The death of an infested tree is brought about by the fungi (called blue-stain or brown-stain) introduced by the adult beetles and spread by the larvae. As adults and larvae interrupt the flow of nutrients by feeding in

Figure 28–98.   A pinhole borer, *Plátypus wílsoni* Swaine, 12×. (Courtesy of Arnett.)

the phloem, the fungus spreads inward and clogs the water transport vessels in the sapwood, suppressing the flow of lethal pitch into the beetle galleries. The destructive bark beetles exhibit a remarkable coordination of their flying population in a tightly synchronized mass attack, overwhelming the tree's defenses by sheer numbers. Both males and females respond to a combination of odors from the resin of the host tree and chemical signals (aggregation pheromones) from the first colonists. As a result, thousands of beetles may infest the same tree simultaneously.

In monogamous species such as *Dendróctonus pseudotsùgae* Hopkins, the Douglas fir beetle, the female bores the gallery, releases pheromone, and accepts one male as her mate. In polygamous species such as *Íps pìni* (Say), the pine engraver (Figure 28–99A), the male does the initial boring but constructs only a nuptial chamber in which to mate with the several females he accepts into his harem. Each female bores her own egg gallery out from the nuptial chamber.

As a female bark beetle constructs her egg gallery, the male cooperates with her by following along behind her, removing boring dust and shoving it out the entry hole. The female lays her eggs in little notches at intervals along the sides of the gallery. When the eggs hatch, the tiny, C-shaped, legless larvae begin eating their way through the phloem at right angles to the egg gallery. As the larvae grow and molt, moving farther away from the adult gallery, the frass-filled larval mines become larger, forming characteristic patterns (Figure 28–100). When the larvae complete their growth, they pupate at the ends of their mines. The adults emerge through round holes they bore through the bark. After a brood emerges, the surface of an infested tree appears peppered with shot holes.

Bark beetles have a greater impact economically on the timber-producing forests of North America than any other group of insects, being credited with the death of more than 4 billion board feet of sawtimber annually—over 90% of the total insect-caused mortality. Most of the tree mortality caused by bark beetles is caused by five species of *Dendróctonus*: the southern pine beetle, *D. frontàlis* Zimmerman, in the South; and the Douglas fir beetle, *D. pseudotsùgae* (Figure 28–99B); western pine beetle, *D. brevicòmis* LeConte; mountain pine beetle, *D. ponderòsae* Hopkins; and spruce beetle, *D. obèsus* (Mannerheim), in the West. Trees infested by bark beetles are recognized by fading foliage on groups of trees, by reddish brown frass or hardened pitch tubes on the trunk, or by evidence of large-scale woodpecker work on the bark. Patch killing of trees results from an aggregation of beetles flying to a source of attractant pheromone initially in one of the trees.

Each species of bark beetle has a characteristic pattern of adult and larval galleries and a rigid preference for a particular tree species. Many, if not all, scolytids transport tree fungi. Destructive species inoculate trees with blue- or brown-stain fungi, and ambrosia beetles depend on their fungi for food. The Dutch elm disease, transmitted by elm bark beetles, is caused by a fungus introduced from Europe with the smaller European elm bark beetle, *Scólytus multistriàtus* (Marsham). These beetles have spread the disease clear across the United States, from Boston to Portland, Oregon, in 75 years, completely eliminating American elms in many urban areas.

One agriculturally important species of bark beetle is the clover root borer, *Hylastinus obscùrus* (Marsham), which often causes serious damage to clover. The larvae tunnel in the roots of clover and kill them.

Figure 28–100.   Semidiagrammatic drawing of a portion of a log containing galleries of bark beetles (Scolýtidae). The bark is cut through two entrance galleries, each with its accumulation of fine frass near the outside opening of the gallery. Three sets of galleries of different age are shown. In the one at the left the larvae are full grown, and some have already pupated. There is one empty pupal cell with its exit hole at the lower left corner of the cutaway section. Another entrance hole is evidenced by the frass accumulation on the bark at the left. (Courtesy of Kaston and the Connecticut Agricultural Experiment Station.)

Ambrosia beetles bore into the wood of trees, forming galleries in which both adults and larvae live. Only living or freshly killed trees, with a high moisture content, are infested. Although these beetles do not eat wood, the fungi that they cultivate stain the wood, reducing its value. The presence of these beetles can cause entire shiploads of timber or lumber to be refused at a foreign port. The larvae of ambrosia beetles develop in small cells adjoining the main galleries, and in most species the larvae are fed by the adults. Each species usually feeds on one particular type of fungus. When the females emerge and fly to another tree, they carry conidia of the fungus from the natal tree to the new host and introduce the fungus into the gallery they excavate. After the eggs hatch, the females care for the larvae until they are full grown and pupate, keeping the larval niches supplied with fresh fungus, or "ambrosia," and preventing the niche from being choked with frass or excess growth of fungus.

Collecting and Preserving Coleóptera

Since this is such a large and varied group, most of the methods discussed in Chapter 36 for collecting and preserving insects are applicable here. Several general collecting procedures, however, may be noted: (1) many species may be taken by sweeping in a variety of situations; (2) many species, often strikingly colored, may be taken on flowers; (3) a number of species, such as the carrion beetles and others, may be obtained by means of suitably baited traps; (4) a number of species are attracted to lights at night and may be collected at lights or in a light trap; (5) beetles of many groups are to be found under bark, in rotting wood, under stones, and in similar situations; (6) many species may be obtained by sifting debris or leaf litter; and (7) many beetles are aquatic and may be collected by the various aquatic equipment and methods described in Chapter 36.

Most beetles are preserved pinned (through the right elytron) or on points. When a beetle is mounted on a point, it is important that it be mounted so that the ventral side of the body and the legs are visible. The tip of the point may be bent down and the specimen attached to this bent-down tip by the right side of the thorax. It may sometimes be desirable to mount two specimens on the same point (when one is sure they are the same species), one dorsal side up and the other ventral side up. Many of the more minute beetles must be preserved in alcohol (70–80%) and mounted on a microscope slide for detailed study.

References

Arnett, R. H., Jr. 1967. Recent and future systematics of the Coleoptera in North America. Ann. Entomol. Soc. Amer. 60:162–170; illus.

Arnett, R. H., Jr. 1968. The Beetles of the United States (a Manual for Identification). Ann Arbor, Mich.: American Entomological Institute, 1112 pp.; illus. This work originally appeared in 1960–1962, published in looseleaf sections (fascicles) by the Catholic University of America Press, Washington, D.C. The 1968 edition is essentially a reprinting of the original work bound in a single volume, with the same pagination (the indexes to individual fascicles are omitted, but their page numbers are retained) but with some changes in the introductory sections and some errors in the original work corrected.

Arnett, R. H., Jr. (Ed.). 1978. Bibliography of Coleoptera of North America North of Mexico, 1758–1948. Gainesville, Fla.: Flora and Fauna Publications, 180 pp.

Blatchley, W. S. 1910. An Illustrated and Descriptive Catalogue of the Coleoptera or Beetles (Exclusive of the Rhynchophora) Known to Occur in Indiana. Indianapolis: Nature, 1385 pp.; illus.

Blatchley, W. S., and C. W. Leng. 1916. Rhynchophora or Weevils of Northeastern North America. Indianapolis: Nature, 682 pp.; illus.

Böving, A. G., and F. C. Craighead. 1931. An Illustrated Synopsis of the Principal Larval Forms of the Order Coleoptera. Entomol. Amer. (n.s.) 11(1–4):1–351; illus.

Bradley, J. C. 1930. A Manual of the Genera of Beetles of America North of Mexico. Ithaca, N.Y.: Daw, Illiston, 360 pp.

Bright, D. E., Jr. 1976. The bark beetles of Canada and Alaska. The Insects and Arachnids of Canada, Part 2. Ottawa: Can. Govt. Publ. Centre, 241 pp.; illus.

Brues, C. T., A. L. Melander, and F. M. Carpenter. 1954. Classification of insects. Bull. Mus. Comp. Zool. Harvard, 73, 917 pp.; illus.

The Coleopterists Bulletin. A quarterly journal containing papers on the Coleoptera, published by the Coleopterists Society, Field Museum of Natural History, Chicago, Illinois.

Cornell, J. F. 1972. Larvae of the families of Coleoptera: A bibliographic survey of recent papers and tabular summary of seven selected English language contributions. Coleop. Bull. 26:81–96.

Crowson, R. A. 1960. The phylogeny of the Coleoptera. Annu. Rev. Entomol. 5:111–134.

Crowson, R. A. 1968 (2nd ed.). The Natural Classification of the Families of Coleoptera. Oxford, England: E. W. Classey, 195 pp.; illus.

Dillon, E. S., and L. S. Dillon. 1961. A Manual of the Common Beetles of Eastern North America. Evanston, Ill.: Row, Peterson, 884 pp.; illus.

Edwards, J. G. 1949. Coleoptera or Beetles East of the Great Plains. Ann Arbor, Mich.: J. W. Edwards, 181 pp.; illus.

Edwards, J. G. 1950. A Bibliographic Supplement to Coleoptera or Beetles East of the Great Plains, Applying Particularly to Western United States. Published by the author, San Jose State College, San Jose, Calif., pp. 182–212.

Gordon, R. D. 1985. The Coccinellidae (Coleoptera) of America north of Mexico. J. N.Y. Entomol. Soc. 93:1–912; illus.

Hatch, M. H. 1927. A systematic index to the keys for the determination of Nearctic Coleoptera. J. N.Y. Entomol. Soc. 35:279–306.

Hatch, M. H. 1953. The Beetles of the Pacific Northwest, Part 1: Introduction and Adephaga. Seattle: Univ. Washington Press, 340 pp.; illus.

Hatch, M. H. 1957. The Beetles of the Pacific Northwest, Part 2: Staphyliniformia. Univ. Wash. Publ. Biol. 16:1–384; illus.

Hatch, M. H. 1961. The beetles of the Pacific Northwest, Part 3: Pselaphidae and Diversicornia I. Univ. Wash. Publ. Biol. 16:1–503; illus.

Hatch, M. H. 1965. The beetles of the Pacific Northwest, Part 4: Macrodactyles, Palpicornes, and Heteromera. Univ. Wash. Publ. Biol. 16:1–268; illus.

Hatch, M. H. 1973. The Beetles of the Pacific Northwest, Part 5: Rhipiceroidea, Sternoxi, Phytophaga, Rhynchophora, and Lamellicornia. Seattle: Univ. Washington Press, 650 pp.; illus.

Headstrom, R. 1977. The Beetles of America. Cranbury, N.J.: A. S. Barnes, 488 pp.; illus.

Jacques, H. E. 1953. How to Know the Beetles. Dubuque, Iowa: William C. Brown, 372 pp.; illus.

Kingsolver, J. M. (Ed.). 1978– . A Catalogue of the Coleoptera of America North of Mexico. This series is being published by the USDA in the Agriculture Handbook series, each family in a different release and usually by a different author. The first family to be covered in this series was the Heteroceridae, published in 1978. It is likely to be a number of years before this series is completed.

Kissinger, D. G. 1964. Curculionidae of America North of Mexico: A Key to the Genera. South Lancaster, Mass.: Taxonomic, 143 pp.; illus.

Lawrence, J. F. 1982. Coleoptera, pp. 482–553 in S. Parker (Ed.), Synopsis and Classification of Living Organisms. New York: McGraw-Hill; illus.

Leech, H. B., and H. P. Chandler. 1956. Aquatic Coleoptera, pp. 293–371 in Aquatic Insects of California, ed. R. L. Usinger. Berkeley: Univ. California Press; illus.

Leech, H. B., and M. W. Sanderson. 1959. Coleoptera, pp. 981–1023 in Freshwater Biology, ed. W. T. Edmondson. New York: Wiley; illus.

Leng, C. W., A. J. Mutchler, R. E. Blackwelder, and R. M. Blackwelder. 1920–1948. Catalogue of the Coleoptera of America North of Mexico. Mt. Vernon, N.Y.: John D. Sherman. Original catalogue, 470 pp. (1920). First Supplement, by C. W. Leng and A. J. Mutchler, 78 pp. (1927). Second and Third Supplements, by C. W. Leng and A. J. Mutchler, 112 pp. (1933). Fourth Supplement, by R. E. Blackwelder, 146 pp. (1939). Fifth Supplement, by R. E. Blackwelder and R. M. Blackwelder, 87 pp. (1948).

Linsley, E. G. 1961–1964. The Cerambycidae of North America, Part 1: Introduction; Univ. Calif. Publ. Entomol. 18: 1–135, illus. (1961). Part 2: Taxonomy and Classification of the Parandrinae, Prioninae, Spondylinae, and Aseminae; Univ. Calif. Publ. Entomol. 19:1–103, illus. (1962). Part 3: Taxonomy and classification of the subfamily Cerambycinae, tribes Opsimini through Megaderini; Univ. Calif. Publ. Entomol. 20:1–188 (1962). Part 4: Taxonomy and classification of the subfamily Cerambycinae, tribes Elaphidionini through Rhinotragini; Univ. Calif. Publ. Entomol. 21:1–165, illus. (1963). Part 5: Taxonomy and classification of the subfamily Cerambycinae, tribes Callichromini through Ancylocerini; Univ. Calif. Publ. Entomol. 22:1–197, illus. (1964).

Linsley, E. G., and J. A. Chemsak. 1972–1976. Cerambycidae of North America, Part 6: Taxonomy and classification of the subfamily Lepturinae. Univ. Calif. Publ. Entomol. 69:1–138, illus. (1972); 80:1–186; illus. (1976).

Moore, I., and E. F. Legner. 1979. An illustrated guide to the genera of Staphylinidae of America north of Mexico, exclusive of the Aleocharinae (Coleoptera). Berkeley: Univ. of California, Div. of Agric. Sci., 332 pp. illus.

O'Brien, C. W., and G. J. Wibmer. 1982. Annotated checklist of the weevils (Curculionidae sensu lato) of North America, Central America, and the West Indies (Coleoptera: Curculionoidea). Mem. Amer. Entomol. Inst. 34, 382 pp.

Papp, C. S. 1983. Introduction to North American beetles. Sacramento, Calif.: Entomography Publications, 335 pp.; illus.

Pennak, R. W. 1978 (2nd ed.). Fresh-Water Invertebrates of the United States. New York: Wiley Interscience, 803 pp.; illus.

Peterson, A. 1951. Larvae of Insects, Part 2: Coleoptera, Diptera, Neuroptera, Siphonaptera, Mecoptera, Trichoptera. Ann Arbor, Mich.: Edwards Bros., 416 pp.; illus.

Reichert, H. 1973. A critical study of the suborder Myxophaga, with a taxonomic revision of the Brazilian Torridincolidae and Hydroscaphidae (Coleoptera). Arq. Zool. (São Paulo), 24(2):73–162; illus.

Rudinsky, J. A., P. T. Oester, and L. C. Ryker. 1978. Gallery initiation and male stridulation of the polygamous bark beetle Polygraphus rufipennis. Ann. Entomol. Soc. Amer. 71:317–321; illus.

Rudinsky, J. A., and L. C. Ryker. 1976. Sound production in Scolytidae: Rivalry and premating stridulation of male Douglas fir beetle. J. Insect Physiol. 22:997–1003.

Ryker, L. C., and J. A. Rudinsky. 1976a. Sound production in Scolytidae: Aggressive and mating behavior in the mountain pine beetle. Ann. Entomol. Soc. Amer. 69:677–680; illus.

Ryker, L. C., and J. A. Rudinsky. 1976b. Sound production in Scolytidae: Acoustic signals of male and female *Dendroctonus valens* LeConte. Z. Ang. Entomol. 80:113–118.

Van Tassell, E. R. 1965. An audiospectrographic study of stridulation as an isolating mechanism in the genus *Berosus* (Coleoptera: Hydrophilidae). Ann. Entomol. Soc. Amer. 58:407–413; illus.

White, R. E. 1983. A field guide to the beetles of North America. Boston: Houghton Mifflin, 368 pp.; illus.

Wood, S. L. 1978. A reclassification of the subfamilies of Scolytidae (Coleoptera). Ann. Entomol. Soc. France 14(1):95–122.

Wood, S. L. 1979. Family Platypodidae. Catalogue of the Coleoptera of America North of Mexico, Fasc. 141, 4 pp.

Wood, S. L. 1982. The bark and ambrosia beetles of North and Central America (Coleoptera Scolytidae), a taxonomic monograph. Gr. Basin Natur. Mem. 6, 1359 pp.; illus.

Wood, S. L. 1986. A reclassification of the genera of Scolytidae (Coleoptera). Gr. Basin Natur. Mem. 10, 126 pp.; illus.

Chapter 29

Order Strepsíptera[1]
Twisted-Wing Parasites

The Strepsíptera are minute insects, most of which are parasitic on other insects. The two sexes are quite different. The males are free-living and winged, whereas the females are wingless and often legless, and in the parasitic species they do not leave the host.

Male Strepsíptera (Figure 29–1A–D) are somewhat beetlelike in appearance, with protruding, raspberry-like eyes, and the antennae often have elongate processes on some segments. The front wings are reduced to clublike structures that resemble the halteres of the Díptera. The hind wings are large and membranous, fanlike, and have a reduced venation (only longitudinal veins). The adult females of the free-living species (Figure 29–1E) have a distinct head, with simple four- or five-segmented antennae, chewing mouthparts, and compound eyes. The females of the parasitic species usually lack eyes, antennae, and legs; the body segmentation is very indistinct; and the head and thorax are fused (Figure 29–1G). The metamorphosis is complete.

The life history of the parasitic forms in this order is rather complex and involves hypermetamorphosis. A male, upon emerging, seeks out and mates with a female, which never leaves its host. The female produces large numbers—up to several thousand—of tiny larvae, which escape from its body and the body of the host to the soil or to vegetation. These larvae, which are called triungulins, have well-developed eyes and legs (Figure 29–1F) and are fairly active insects. They locate and enter the body of the host. Once there, the larva molts into a legless wormlike stage that feeds in the host's body cavity. After several molts, it pupates inside the last larval skin. The male, on emerging, leaves its host and flies about. The female remains in the host, with the anterior part of its body protruding between the abdominal segments of the host. After the young are produced, it dies.

Species of Orthóptera, Hemíptera, Homóptera, Hymenóptera, and Thysanúra serve as the hosts of Strepsíptera. The host is not always killed, but it may be injured. The shape or color of the abdomen may be changed, or the sex organs may be damaged. The developing male strepsipteran usually causes more damage to its host than the female.

Many entomologists (for example, Abdullah 1974) place the Strepsíptera in the order Coleóptera (usually as a single family, the Stylópidae), largely because of the similarity in life history (hypermetamorphosis) between these insects and Melòidae and Rhipiphòridae. The status of the Strepsíptera is controversial, but we follow Pierce (1964), who presented convincing evidence that they should be treated as a separate order.

[1]Strepsíptera: *strepsi*, twisted; *ptera*, wings.

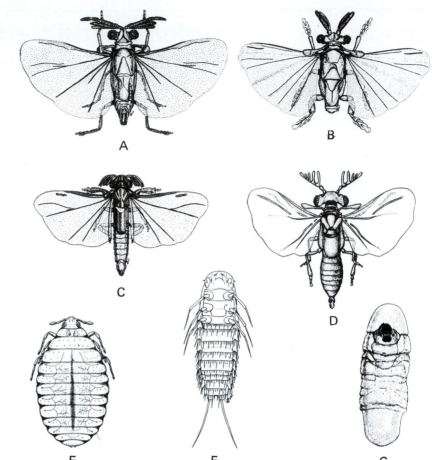

Figure 29–1. Strepsíptera. **A,** *Triozócera texàna* Pierce (Mengèidae), male; **B,** *Neostÿlops shánnoni* Pierce (Stylópidae), male; **C,** *Halcitóphagus oncometòpiae* (Pierce) (Halictophágidae), male; **D,** *Halictóphagus serràtus* Bohart (Halictophágidae), male; **E,** *Eoxènos laboulbénei* Peyerimhoff (Mengèidae), female; **F,** *Stylops califòrnica* Pierce (Stylópidae), triungulin, ventral view; **G,** *Halictóphagus oncometòpiae*, female, ventral view. (**A–C, F,** and **G,** courtesy of Pierce; **D,** courtesy of Bohart; **E,** courtesy of Parker and Smith; **A–C** and **F–G,** courtesy of the U.S. National Museum; **D–E,** courtesy of the Entomological Society of America.)

Key to the Families of Strepsíptera (Males)

1.	Tarsi 5-segmented, with claws; antennae 6- or 7-segmented, the third and fourth segments each with a long lateral process (Figure 29–1A) ....**Mengèidae**	p. 481
1'.	Tarsi with 4 or fewer segments and without claws; antennae with 4–7 segments, the lateral processes variable **2**	
2(1').	Tarsi 4-segmented; antennae 4- to 6-segmented, the third segment with a long lateral process (Figure 29–1B) ....**Stylópidae**	p. 481
2'.	Tarsi 2- or 3-segmented; antennae 4- to 7-segmented, the lateral processes variable **3**	
3(2').	Tarsi 2-segmented; antennae 4-segmented, the third segment with a long lateral process ....**Elénchidae**	p. 481
3'.	Tarsi 3-segmented; antennae 7-segmented, the third and fourth segments each with a long lateral process (Figure 29–1C,D) ....**Halictophágidae**	p. 481

Family **Mengèidae:** This family is represented in the United States by two species. *Triozócera texàna* Pierce occurs in the southeastern states, from Georgia to Texas. It is a parasite of the cydnid *Pangaèus bilineàtus* (Say). *Perissozócera cryóphila* Johnson has been reported from Kentucky and Georgia. The host and females of this species are unknown.

Family **Stylópidae:** This is the largest family in the order, with 70 species in the United States and Canada. Most of its members are parasitic on bees (Andrènidae, Halíctidae, and Hylaeìnae), but some are parasitic on wasps (Polistìnae, Eumenìnae, and Sphecìnae).

Family **Elénchidae:** This group is small (two North American species in the genus *Elénchus*), but its members are widely distributed. They are parasites of planthoppers (Fulgoròidea).

Family **Halictophágidae:** This is the second-largest family in the order, with about 14 North American species. Its members are parasites of leafhoppers, planthoppers, treehoppers, and pygmy mole crickets.

Collecting and Preserving Strepsíptera

The most satisfactory way to collect Strepsíptera is to collect parasitized hosts and rear out the parasites. Bees, wasps, leafhoppers, planthoppers, and other insects may harbor Strepsíptera. The parasitized hosts can often be recognized by the distorted abdomen, and one end of the parasite sometimes protrudes from between two of the abdominal segments. Some Strepsíptera occur under stones, and a few (males) may be attracted to lights. Males of *Stỳlops* are attracted to virgin females in hosts (bees) that are placed in screen cages and may be collected on or flying about the cages (MacSwain 1949).

Strepsíptera should be preserved in alcohol and, for detailed study, mounted on microscope slides.

References

Abdullah, M. 1974. World Entomophaga Abdullah, a new suborder of Coleoptera including Strepsiptera (Insecta). Zool. Beit. 20(2):177–211; illus.

Bohart, R. M. 1936–1937. A preliminary study of the genus *Stylops* in California. Pan-Pac. Entomol. 12:9–18, illus. (1936); 13:49–57, illus. (1937).

Bohart, R. M. 1941. A revision of the Strepsiptera with special reference to the species of North America. Univ. Calif. Publ. Entomol. 7(6):91–160; illus.

Bohart, R. M. 1943. New species of *Halictophagus* with a key to the genus in North America (Strepsiptera, Halictophagidae). Ann. Entomol. Soc. Amer. 36:341–359; illus.

Johnson, V. 1972. The female and host of *Triozocera mexicana* (Strepsiptera: Mengeidae). Ann. Entomol. Soc. Amer. 66:671–672; illus.

Johnson, V. 1976. A new genus and species of Strepsiptera from southeastern United States. J. Kan. Entomol. Soc. 49:580–582; illus.

Kinzelbach, R. K. 1971. Morphologische Befunde an Fächerfluglern und ihre phylogenetische Bedeutung (Insecta: Strepsiptera). Zoologica 119(1,2):1–256.

MacSwain, J. W. 1949. A method for collecting male *Stylops*. Pan-Pac. Entomol. 25:89–90.

Pierce, W. D. 1909. A monographic revision of the twisted-winged insects comprising the order Strepsiptera. Bull. U.S. Natl. Mus. No. 66, 232 pp.; illus.

Pierce, W. D. 1918. The comparative morphology of the order Strepsiptera together with records and descriptions of insects. Proc. U.S. Natl. Mus. 54(2242):391–501; illus.

Pierce, W. D. 1964. The Strepsiptera are a true order, unrelated to the Coleoptera. Ann. Entomol. Soc. Amer. 57:603–605.

Silvestri, F. 1942. Nuove osservazione sulla *Mengenilla parvula* Silvestri (Insecta Strepsiptera). Pontif. Acad. Sci. Acta Rome 6:95–96.

Ulrich, W. 1966. Evolution and classification of the Strepsiptera. Proc. 1st Int. Congr. Parasitol. 1:609–611.

Chapter 30

Order Mecóptera[1]
Scorpionflies and Hangingflies

The scorpionflies and hangingflies are medium-sized (about 9–22 mm long), slender-bodied insects with the head prolonged below the eyes as a beak, or rostrum (Figure 30–1A, 30–2). The rostrum is formed primarily by elongation of the clypeus. Its posterior surface consists partly of the lengthened maxillae and labium, but the mandibles are not unusually elongate and are at the lower end of the rostrum. In the (relatively uncommon) Panorpódidae, the rostrum is short (Figure 30–5A). Most Mecóptera have four long, narrow membranous wings. The front and hind wings are similar in size and shape and have a similar venation.

The wing venation of Mecóptera is very near the generalized pattern hypothesized by Comstock (cf. Figure 3–10), with most of the longitudinal veins and their branches present and with numerous cross veins. A distinctive venational feature of this order is the fusion in the hind wing of Cu_1 with M for a short distance near the wing base, and a similar fusion of Cu_2 with 1A (Figures 30–3, 30–5B). In the front wing of the Bittácidae, likewise, Cu_1 fuses with M for a short distance.

The common name scorpionflies is derived from the genital segment of males of the family Panórpidae, which is bulbous and often curved forward above the back, like a scorpion's sting. These insects cannot sting, however, and are quite harmless.

Scorpionflies undergo complete metamorphosis, with fairly rapid development of the larva followed by a prolonged prepupal stage. Pupation occurs in an oblong cell excavated by the larva in the soil. Larvae of Panórpidae and Bittácidae are eruciform, with short, pointed prolegs on abdominal segments 1–8 (Figure 30–1B). Those of Panorpódidae and Boréidae are somewhat scarabaeiform, without prolegs, but they lack tarsal claws and have the middle and hind legs projecting laterally more than the front legs. Larval Panórpidae are unusual among holometabolous larvae in having compound eyes of approximately 30 ommatidia each. Eyes of bittacid larvae have only seven ommatidia in a circular cluster, boreids have only three, and panorpodids are eyeless. The larvae of Meropèidae remain unknown.

Mecóptera are judged to be one of the most primitive of generalized orders of Holometábola. Fossil Mecóptera appear first in strata of lower Permian age, and at that time Mecóptera were apparently one of the major orders. Many more families and genera are known as fossils than are extant today.

[1]Mecóptera: *meco*, long; *ptera*, wings. This chapter was written by George W. Byers.

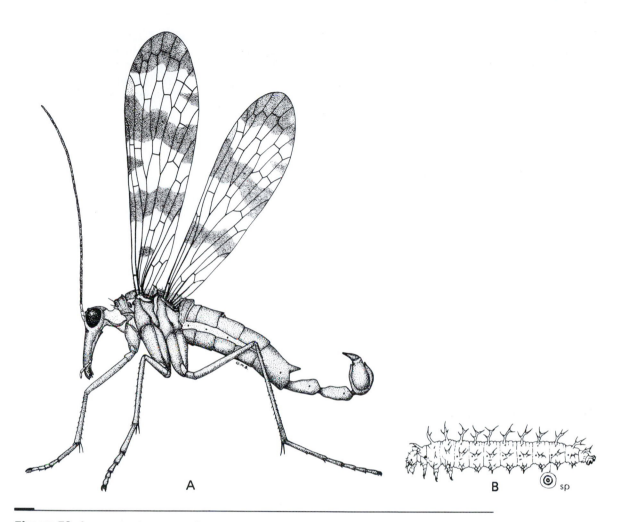

Figure 30–1. **A,** a male scorpionfly, *Panórpa hélena* Byers; **B,** larva of a hangingfly (*Bíttacus*); *sp,* spiracle. (**B,** courtesy of Peterson; reprinted by permission.)

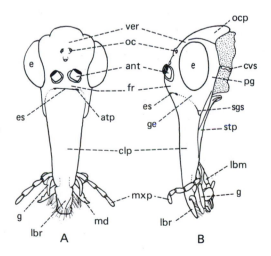

Figure 30–2. Head of *Panórpa.* **A,** anterior view; **B,** lateral view. *ant,* antenna; *atp,* anterior tentorial pit; *clp,* clypeus; *cvs,* cervical sclerite; *e,* compound eye; *es,* epistomal sulcus; *fr,* frons; *g,* galea; *ge,* gena; *lbm,* labium; *lbr,* labrum; *md,* mandible; *mxp,* maxillary palp; *oc,* ocelli; *ocp,* occiput; *pg,* postgena; *sgs,* subgenal sulcus; *stp,* stipes; *ver,* vertex. (Redrawn from Ferris and Rees.)

Classification of the Mecóptera

Five families of Mecóptera are represented in North America (there are four other families, restricted to southern South America and the Australian region). The majority of specimens encountered by general collectors belong to just two families, the Panórpidae and the Bittácidae. Families of Mecóptera are defined largely on the basis of wing venation and tarsal structure, but the classification is supported by details of adult and larval morphology, feeding habits, and other aspects of the biology of the insects.

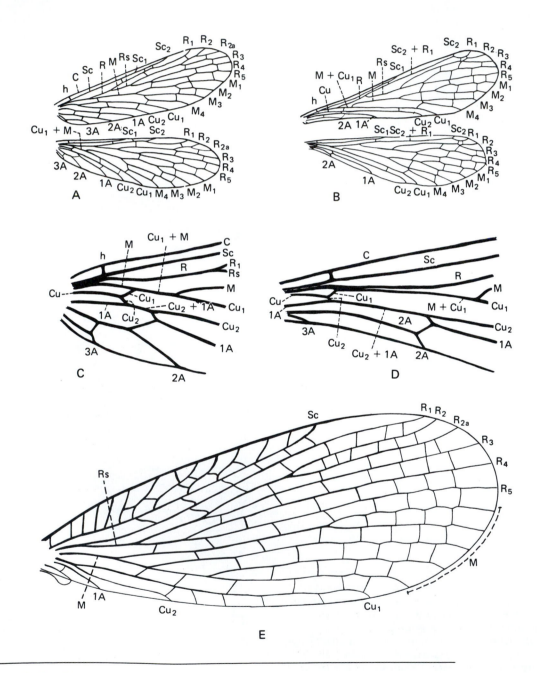

Figure 30–3. Wings of Mecóptera. **A,** *Panórpa* (Panórpidae); **B,** *Bíttacus* (Bittácidae); **C,** base of hind wing of *Panórpa*; *D,* base of hind wing of *Bíttacus*; **E,** front wing of *Mérope* (Meropèidae).

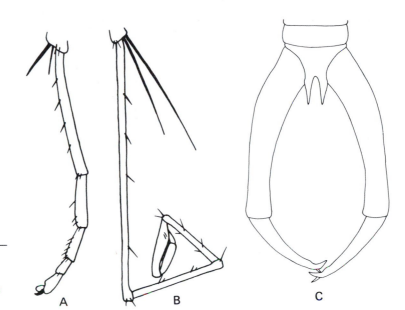

Figure 30–4. **A,** tarsus of *Panórpa* (Panórpidae); **B,** tarsus of *Bíttacus* (Bittácidae); **C,** anal appendages of a male *Mérope* (Meropèidae).

Key to the Families of Mecóptera

1.	Tarsi each with one large claw (Figure 30–4B); tarsi raptorial, fifth tarsal segment folding back against fourth ....**Bittácidae** p. 486
1′.	Tarsi each with two small claws (Figure 30–4A); fifth tarsal segment not folding back against fourth..**2**
2(1′).	Wings reduced to hardened, slender hooks in male and to short, roughly oval, sclerotized pads in female (Figure 30–6); small (2–7.4 mm), dark brown to black insects ....**Borèidae** p. 487
2′.	Wings nearly always well developed and membranous, never sclerotized; body yellowish brown to brown, rarely blackish, 9–25 mm long **3**
3(2′).	Wings narrow, 3.5 or more times as long as their greatest width (if wings reduced, rostrum very short); M with 4 branches (Figures 30–1A, 30–3A, 30–5B); genital claspers of male with bulbous basal segment, cheliform apical segment; ocelli conspicuous, on raised tubercle **4**
3′.	Wings broad, about 2.4 times as long as their greatest width; M with 5 or more branches, venation reticulate (Figure 30–3E); genital claspers of male with long, slender basal and apical segments (Figure 30–4C); ocelli absent ....**Meropèidae** p. 487
4(3).	Rostrum elongate, more than twice as long as width at base (Figure 30–2); wings well developed in both sexes, usually patterned with transverse bands or spots; R_2 branched ....**Panórpidae** p. 486
4′.	Rostrum short, only slightly longer than width at base (Figure 30–5A); wings well developed in males, slightly to greatly reduced in females, uniformly yellowish brown or paler along cross veins; R_2 not branched **Panorpódidae** p. 486

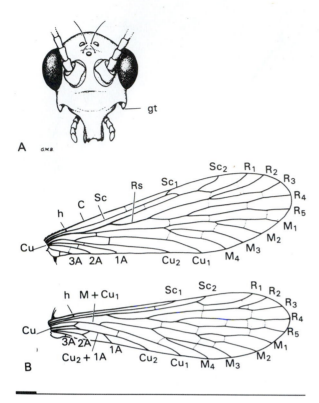

Figure 30–5. Characters of *Brachypanórpa oregonénsis* McLachlan (Panorpódidae). **A**, face of female, anterior view; **B**, wings of male. *gt*, genal tooth.

Family **Panórpidae**—Common Scorpionflies: In this family the genital appendages of males are enlarged, forming a bulblike structure that is carried above the back, resembling the sting of a scorpion (Figure 30–1A). The abdomen of the female tapers posteriorly and bears two short, fingerlike apical cerci. Most of these scorpionflies are sordid yellowish brown, but some are darker brown to nearly black. Their wings are usually transversely banded with interspersed spots, or they may be only spotted. One southeastern species, *Panórpa lùgubris* Swederus, is dark reddish brown with almost totally black wings. While most scorpionflies are 10 to 15 mm in length, males of *Panórpa nuptiàlis* Gerstaecker, of the south-central United States, may attain a length of 25 mm. Scorpionflies are most commonly found on low, broad-leaved plants at edges of woods or in open shade beneath deciduous trees. Both adults and larvae feed primarily on dead insects, less often on other dead animal matter. Adults occasionally feed on insects trapped in spiders' webs. Pupation occurs in an oblong cell prepared by the fourth-instar larva just beneath the soil surface. There are about 40 species known from eastern North America (south-eastern Canada to northern Florida and westward to southern Manitoba and eastern Texas), all of which belong to the Holarctic genus *Panórpa*. Several species are widespread, such as *P. hélena* Byers (Figure 30–1A), but most have ecologically and geographically restricted ranges.

Family **Bittácidae**—Hangingflies: Bittacids are slender-bodied, about 12–22 mm long, light yellowish brown to reddish brown, with long, slender legs and narrow wings. They resemble large crane flies, particularly in flight. Their wings are narrower near the base than are those of Panórpidae (Figure 30–A,B). One species in central California, *Apterobíttacus ápterus* (MacLachlan), is wingless. Unable to stand on surfaces, adult bittacids spend most of their time hanging by their front legs or front and middle legs from stems or edges of leaves. They are predaceous, capturing their prey by means of their raptorial hind tarsi, either while hanging or by flying up plant stems while making sweeping movements of the hind legs. Prey, grasped by the hind tarsi, is then held up to the mouthparts, pierced, and the hemolymph and soft parts sucked out. Their prey includes small, soft-bodied insects such as flies, moths, caterpillars, and aphids, and occasionally spiders. Male hangingflies lure females for mating by emitting a sex attractant pheromone from everted vesicles on the dorsum of the abdomen and subsequently offering the female a captured prey insect as a nuptial meal (Thornhill 1978).

Seven species of *Bíttacus* occur in eastern North America and California. A single species of *Orobíttacus* is known from central California. All these bittacids hold the wings alongside the abdomen when suspended. *Hylobíttacus apicàlis* (Hagen) of the eastern United States hangs with its wings outspread and, unlike the other species, has conspicuously darkened wing tips.

Family **Panorpódidae**—Short-Faced Scorpionflies: Two species of *Brachypanórpa* occur in the southern Appalachian Mountains and two in montane regions of the northwestern United States. These dull yellowish to yellowish brown scorpionflies have a short rostrum (Figure 30–5A). The genital appendages of males are enlarged, as in Panórpidae, but are not carried forward above the back. In one eastern species and one western species, females have rudimentary wings extending only to the base of the abdomen, while in the other species in each region the females have wings reaching the tip of the abdomen or slightly beyond. The eyeless, somewhat scarabaeiform larvae have been found in soil beneath grassy areas in woods and are presumed to feed on plant matter. Adults scrape surfaces of herbaceous vegetation for nourishment.

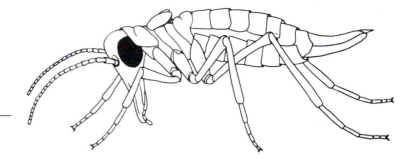

Figure 30–6. A snow scorpionfly, *Bòreus brumàlis* (Fitch), female.

Family **Meropèidae**—Earwigflies: A single species, *Mérope tùber* Newman, occurs in the eastern United States and adjacent Canada. It is a dull brownish insect, 10–12 mm long, somewhat flattened, with relatively broad wings having numerous cross veins (Figure 30–3E). The male has greatly elongated, forcepslike claspers at the apex of the abdomen (Figure 30–4C). This species ranges from southeastern Ontario to Georgia and westward to Minnesota and Kansas. It is secretive in habits and is sometimes found beneath logs and rocks. Once regarded as rare, it is fairly frequently taken at lights or in various kinds of traps (Byers 1973). Its only known near relative is a species in southwestern Australia.

Family **Borèidae**—Snow Scorpionflies: These small (2–7.4 mm) insects reach the adult form in winter. They are most often seen on the surface of snow because of their movement and dark, contrasting color. However, they may also be found in mosses on which their larvae feed. The slender, hardened, hooklike wings of the male are used to grasp the female, which is carried on his back, in mating. The family is represented in eastern North America by two species, *Bòreus brumàlis* Fitch (Figure 30–6), a shiny

black species, and *B. nivoriùndus* Fitch, which is brown. In the West, there are seven additional species of *Bòreus*, the most widespread and common being *B. califòrnicus* Packard, two species of *Hesperobòreus* and one of the aberrant *Caurìnus*.

Collecting and Preserving Mecóptera

Panórpidae and Bittácidae can be readily collected individually with a net. They are rather weak fliers and when alarmed ordinarily fly only a few meters. Sweeping may be effective when the vegetation is not dense, and is almost necessary to obtain the flightless females of *Brachypanórpa*. Boreids may be handpicked from snow surface or extracted from mosses. Malaise traps and chemical traps have proved most useful for catching *Mérope*, and may also trap *Panórpa*. Bittácidae often are attracted to lights. Panorpids are usually pinned. Drying bittacids in paper envelopes or folded paper triangles, then gluing them on points, will avoid much breakage of legs and wings. Boreids should be preserved in 75% ethanol or glued onto points.

References

Byers, G. W. 1954. Notes on North American Mecoptera. Ann. Entomol. Soc. Amer. 47:484–510; illus.

Byers, G. W. 1963. The life history of *Panorpa nuptialis* (Mecoptera: Panorpidae). Ann. Entomol. Soc. Amer. 56:142–149; illus.

Byers, G. W. 1965. Families and genera of Mecoptera. Proc. 12th Int. Congr. Entomol. London (1964); 123.

Byers, G. W. 1973. Zoogeography of the Meropeidae (Mecoptera). J. Kan. Entomol. Soc. 46:511–516; illus.

Byers, G. W. 1987. Order Mecoptera, pp. 246–252 *in* F. W. Stehr (ed.), Immature Insects. Dubuque, Iowa: Kendall/Hunt, 754 pp.; illus.

Byers, G. W., and R. Thornhill. 1983. Biology of the Mecoptera. Annu. Rev. Entomol. 28:203–228.

Carpenter, F. M. 1931a. Revision of Nearctic Mecoptera. Bull. Mus. Comp. Zool. Harvard 72:205–277; illus.

Carpenter, F. M. 1931b. The biology of the Mecoptera. Psyche 38:41–55.

Cooper, K. W. 1972. A southern California *Boreus*, *B. notoperates*, n. sp. 1: Comparative morphology and systematics (Mecoptera: Boreidae). Psyche 79:269–283; illus.

Cooper, K. W. 1974. Sexual biology, chromosomes, development, life histories and parasites of *Boreus*, especially of *B. notoperates*, a southern California *Boreus* (Mecoptera: Boreidae), II. Psyche 81:84–120; illus.

Hinton, H. E. 1958. The phylogeny of the panorpoid orders. Annu. Rev. Entomol. 3:181–206.

Kaltenbach, A. 1978. Mecoptera (Schnabelhafte, Schnabelfliegen). Handbuch der Zoologie 4(2) 2/28:1–111. Berlin: de Gruyter.

Penny, N. D. 1977. A systematic study of the family Boreidae (Mecoptera). Univ. Kan. Sci. Bull. 51:141–217.

Setty, L. R. 1940. Biology and morphology of some North American Bittacidae. Amer. Midl. Nat. 23(2):257–353; illus.

Thornhill, R. 1978. Sexually selected predatory and mating behavior of the hangingfly *Bittacus stigmatus* (Mecoptera: Bittacidae). Ann. Entomol. Soc. Amer. 71:597–601; illus.

Tillyard, R. J. 1935. The evolution of the scorpion-flies and their derivatives (Order Mecoptera). Ann. Entomol. Soc. Amer. 28:1–45; illus.

Webb, D. W., N. D. Penny, and J. C. Martin. 1975. The Mecoptera, or scorpionflies, of Illinois. Ill. Nat. Hist. Surv. Bull. 31(7):250–316; illus.

Willmann, R. 1987. The phylogenetic system of the Mecoptera. Syst. Entomol. 12:519–524; illus.

Chapter 31

Order Siphonáptera[1]
Fleas

Fleas are small wingless insects that feed as adults on the blood of birds and mammals. Many species are very annoying because of their bites; a few act as disease vectors; a few serve as the intermediate host of certain tapeworms; and a few burrow into the skin of their host.

The body of an adult flea (Figures 31–1, 31–2) is strongly flattened laterally and is provided with numerous backward-projecting spines and bristles. Most fleas are jumping insects and have long legs with the coxae greatly enlarged. The antennae are short and lie in grooves in the head. The mouthparts (Figure 31–3) are of the sucking type, with three piercing stylets (the epipharynx and two maxillary stylets), and both maxillary and labial palps are well developed. Both sexes are bloodsucking. Eyes may be present or absent. The metamorphosis is complete.

A few species of fleas (including some that attack humans) are worldwide in distribution and attack a wide range of hosts, but most species are more or less restricted both as to their hosts and geographic distribution. Most species of fleas are limited to hosts in a particular order or family, and a few are limited to a single species of host. About three-fourths of all the species of fleas are parasites of rodents, and about 5% are parasites of birds. The rest attack various mammals, including people.

Fleas differ in their relationship to their host, ranging from those that are on the host only when feeding and spend most of their time in the nest or den of the host to species that spend all or most of their time on the body of the host. The extreme of the latter end of this range is seen in fleas of the genus *Túnga*, females of which spend their lives imprisoned in the tissues of their host. It is probable that most fleas fall somewhere between these two extremes, but information on this point is not available for many genera.

The eggs of fleas vary in size, shape, and color, but in most species where they are known they are white, ovoid, and nonadhesive. They are frequently deposited while the adult female is feeding, and soon fall off into the nest or den of the host. Some species lay their eggs off the host, usually in or near its nest or den. The incubation period is dependent on temperature, and may vary from a few days to a few months. The eggs hatch into tiny, whitish, legless larvae, which are sparsely covered with bristly hairs and have a pair of blunt terminal appendages (Figure 31–4). Eyes are lacking. There are three larval instars, which differ little except in size. Only the head and mouthparts are sclerotized.

[1]Siphonaptera: *siphon*, a tube; *aptera*, wingless. We are indebted to Dr. Robert E. Lewis for most of the material in this chapter.

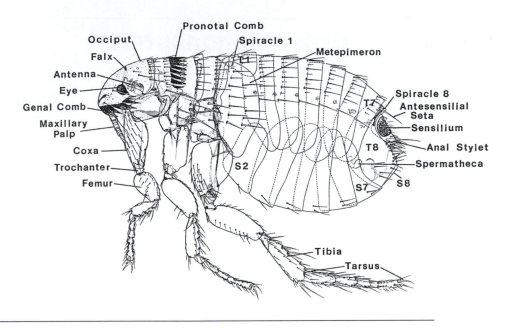

Figure 31–1.   An adult cat flea, *Ctenocephálides fèlis* (Bouché). (Figure prepared by Robert E. Lewis.)

Flea larvae are quite active, but they are seldom seen because they hide in the nesting material of their host. They feed on organic material, including droplets of dried blood that have been passed by the adults during feeding, fecal material, and other productions of their host, and probably some plant material. When fully developed the larva spins a silken cocoon into which grains of sand and other debris are incorporated.

The most important disease transmitted by fleas is plague, or black death, an acute infectious disease caused by the bacillus *Pasteurélla péstis* (Lehmann and Neumann). Three forms of plague occur in human beings: bubonic, pneumonic, and septocemic. The bubonic type is transmitted by fleas. Bubonic plague is a very serious disease because it often occurs in epidemic form and has a high mortality rate. Plague is primarily a disease of rodents and is spread from one rodent to another by fleas. Rodents thus serve as a reservoir for the disease. The disease in wild rodents is often called sylvatic plague. Fleas may transmit plague in three ways: (1) by regurgitation of the plague bacilli at the time of biting, a result of the blocking of the digestive tract by clumps of bacilli; (2) by infected feces of fleas being scratched into the skin; and (3) by the host ingesting an infected flea. Most plague transmission is by the first method.

Endemic typhus is a mild form of typhus caused by a *Rickéttsia*. It is primarily a disease of rodents (chiefly rats), but may be transmitted to people by fleas and to some extent by body lice.

Fleas serve as the intermediate host of two species of tapeworms that occasionally infest humans, *Dipylídium canìnum* (L.), usually a parasite of dogs, and *Hymenólepis diminùta* (Rudolphi), usually a parasite of rats. Larval fleas become infested with the tapeworm by ingesting the tapeworm eggs (which are passed in the feces of an infected host). Infection of the primary host (human, dog, or rat) follows the ingestion of a flea harboring the intermediate stage of the tapeworm.

Classification of the Siphonáptera

Several classifications of this order have been proposed in the past, but we follow here the classification of Smit (1982). This arrangement puts the North American fleas in eight families, and is outlined as follows (with a list of the North American genera):

Superfamily Hystrichopsyllòidea
  Hystrichopsýllidae
    Hystrichopsyllìnae—fleas of small rodents and
      insectivores: *Hystrichopsýlla, Atyphlóceras*

Ctenophthálmidae[2]
  Ctenophthalmìnae—fleas of small rodents and
      insectivores: *Carterétta, Ctenophthálmus*
  Doratopsyllìnae—fleas of shrews: *Corrodop-
      sýlla, Doratopsýlla*
  Rhadinopsyllìnae—fleas of small mammals,
      mostly rodents: *Corypsýlla, Nearctopsýlla,*

*Paratyphlóceras, Rhadinopsýlla,
  Trichopsyllòides*
Neopsyllìnae—fleas of small rodents: *Neop-
  sýlla, Tamióphila, Catallàgia, Delotèlis,
  Epitédia, Maríngis, Phalacropsýlla*
Anomiopsyllìnae—fleas of small rodents: *An-
  omiopsýllus, Callistopsýllus, Conorhinop-
  sýlla, Megarthroglóssus, Stenistómera*
Stenoponiìnae—fleas of small rodents:
  Stenopònia

[2]Lewis and Lewis (1985) include the six subfamilies of this family in the Hystrichopsýllidae.

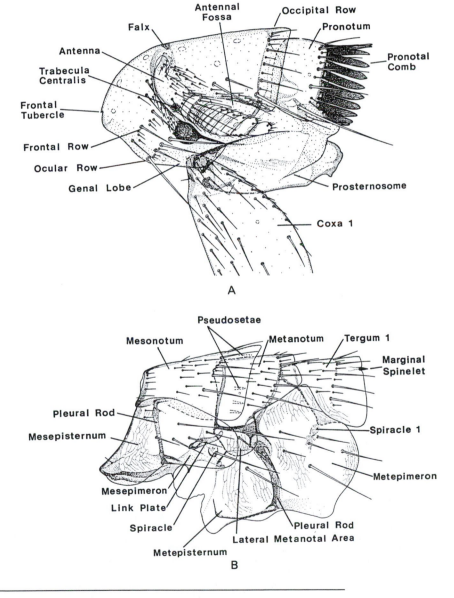

Figure 31–2. A ceratophyllid flea, showing structures of taxonomic importance. **A,** head and prothorax; **B,** mesothorax and metathorax. (Figure prepared by Robert E. Lewis.)

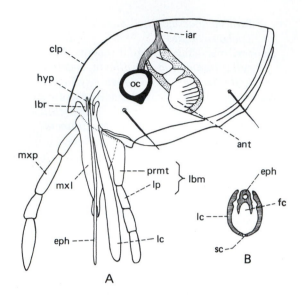

Figure 31–3.   Mouthparts of a flea. **A,** lateral view of head, somewhat diagrammatic, with stylets separated and left maxilla not shown; **B,** cross section through stylets. *ant,* antenna; *clp,* clypeus; *eph,* epipharynx; *fc,* food channel; *hyp,* hypopharynx; *iar,* interantennal ridge; *lbm,* labium; *lbr,* labrum; *lc,* lacinia; *lp,* labial palp; *mxl,* maxillary lobe; *mxp,* maxillary palp; *oc,* ocellus; *prmt,* prementum; *sc,* salivary channel. (**A,** modified from Snodgrass; **B,** redrawn from Matheson, by permission of Comstock Publishing Company.)

Superfamily Ceratophyllòidea
  Ceratophýllidae
    Ceratophyllìnae[3]—mostly fleas of rodents: *Aethèca, Amalàreus, Amàradix, Amphálius, Ceratophýllus, Dactylopsýlla, Dasypsýllus, Eumolpiànus, Foxélla, Jellisònia, Kòhlsia, Maláraeus, Margopsýlla, Megábothris, Mioctenopsýlla, Nosopsýllus, Opisodàsys, Orchopèas, Oropsýlla, Pleochaètis, Plusaètis, Spicàta, Tarsopsýlla*
    Leptopsyllìnae—mouse fleas: *Leptopsýlla, Peromyscopsýlla*
    Amphipsyllìnae—fleas of various rodents: *Amphipsýlla, Ctenophýllus, Dolichopsýllus, Geusíbia, Odontopsýllus, Ornithóphaga*
  Ischnopsýllidae
    Ischnopsyllìnae—bat fleas: *Myodopsýlla, Nycteridopsýlla, Sternopsýlla*
Superfamily Malacopsyllòidea
  Rhopalopsýllidae
    Rhopalopsyllìnae—fleas of rodents: *Polygènis, Rhopalopsýllus*

Superfamily Vermipsyllòidea
  Vermipsýllidae
    Vermipsyllìnae—fleas of carnivores: *Chaetopsýlla*
Superfamily Pulicòidea
  Pulícidae
    Xenopsyllìnae—oriental rat flea: *Xenopsýlla*
    Archaeopsyllìnae—cat and dog fleas: *Ctenocephálides*
    Hectopsyllìnae—fleas of birds: *Hectopsýlla*
    Pulicìnae—sticktight and human fleas: *Echidnóphaga, Pùlex*
    Spilopsyllìnae—mostly fleas of rabbits: *Actenopsýlla, Cediopsýlla, Euhoplopsýllus, Hoplopsýllus*
  Túngidae[4]—chigoe fleas: *Túnga*

Characters Used in the Identification of Siphonáptera

The characters used in the identification of fleas are best seen in specimens that are cleared and mounted on microscope slides. Identification at the species level in this order depends heavily on characters of the male genitalia, but identification at higher levels depends on a variety of characters.

Head (Figures 31–1, 31–2A).   The head consists of an anterior and posterior portion, separated by an oblique groove on each side, the antennal fossa. The preantennal part of the head bears the mouthparts, as well as the eyes and genal comb when these are present. The eyes vary from well developed to totally absent, and resemble ocelli in structure. A genal comb may be present or absent. When present, it may be composed of from 2 to 15 or more spines on each side. In some fleas a linear tentorium may be seen projecting anteriorly in front of the eye. The frontal area of the head usually bears a frontal tubercle. The upper ends of the antennal fossae are sometimes connected by an interantennal suture with internal sclerotized margins. Collectively these structures form the falx.

Thorax (Figures 31–1, 31–2).   The prothorax is somewhat L-shaped, consisting of an arched dorsal pronotum and a ventral, gutter-shaped prosternosome. The caudal margin of the pronotum frequently

[3]Lewis and Lewis (1985) give this group family rank.

[4]Lewis and Lewis (1985) consider the Tungìnae a subfamily of Pulícidae, including in it two tribes: Tungìni and Hectopsyllìni.

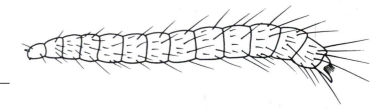

Figure 31–4.   Larva of a flea.

bears a comb of pigmented spines. The pleurosternal sclerite of the mesothorax is usually divided into an anterior mesepisternum and a posterior mesepimeron by a vertical pleural rod. The metathorax also has a pleural rod, but this may be reduced or lost in those fleas that have lost their ability to jump.

Legs.   Spiniform bristles on the coxae are short stout bristles, usually located near the apex of the coxa. Internal ridges on the coxae are thickenings, usually apparent in a cleared specimen as a dark line extending the length of the coxa.

Abdomen (Figure 31–1).   The abdomen is ten-segmented, but the first segment is reduced (it lacks a sternum), and segments 8–10 are modified into paragenital structures, which are used extensively in species identification. Some species have a striarium—that is, an area of close-set and parallel striae—on the metepimeron or basal abdominal segment. The sensilium (Figure 31–1) is a plate (or pair of plates) located at the apex of the abdomen on the dorsal side of the body, just behind the last unmodified abdominal tergum. Antepygidial bristles are large bristles located just in front of the sensilium.

Key to the Families and Subfamilies of Siphonáptera

1.	Middle coxae with an internal ridge; hind tibiae usually with an apical tooth; sensilium usually with 16 or more pits on each side **2**	
1′.	Middle coxae without an internal ridge; hind tibiae without an apical tooth; sensilium with 8–14 pits on each side (family Pulícidae) **14**	
2(1).	Anterior tentorial arm present; genal and pronotal combs absent; mesopleural rod not forked; ventral margin of pronotum not bilobed; fifth tarsal segment with 4 pairs of plantar bristles; frontal tubercle sunk in a groove and directed forward and upward (Figure 31–5C) ....**family Rhopalopsýllidae**	p. 496
2′.	Without the above combination of characters **3**	
3(2′).	Combs, marginal spinelets, antepygideal bristles, spiniform bristles on inner side of hind coxae, and anal stylet of female, all absent; parasites of carnivores ....**family Vermipsýllidae**	p. 496
3′.	Some or all of the above structures present **4**	
4(3′).	Mesonotum with marginal spinelets; dorsal surface of sensilium flat; female with 1 spermatheca **5**	
4′.	Mesonotum without marginal spinelets; dorsal surface of sensilium more or less convex; female with 1 or 2 spermathecae **8**	
5(4).	Interantennal suture well developed; genal comb consisting of two broad spines (Figure 31–5A); eyes absent or vestigial; parasites of bats ....**family Ischnopsýllidae**	p. 496
5′.	Interantennal suture usually weakly or not at all developed; genal comb, if present, not as above; eyes present or absent; parasites of animals other than bats (family Ceratophýllidae) **6**	

6(5′). Interantennal suture and genal comb present (Figure 31–5B)
....**subfamily Leptopsyllinae** p. 496

6′. Interantennal suture usually absent; genal comb present or absent **7**

7(6′). Genal comb present or absent; an arch of the tentorium usually visible in front
of eye...**subfamily Amphipsyllinae** p. 496

7′. Genal comb absent; no arch of the tentorium in front of eye
....**subfamily Ceratophyllinae** p. 496

8(4′). Club of male antennae extending onto prosternosome; female with 2
spermathecae ....**family Hystrichopsýllidae** p. 495

8′. Club of male antenna not extending onto prosternosome; female with 1
spermatheca (family Ctenophthálmidae) **9**

9(8′). Labial palps with at most 2 segments; genal comb well developed and with at
least 9 spines; first abdominal tergum with a well-developed comb
....**subfamily Stenoponiinae** p. 496

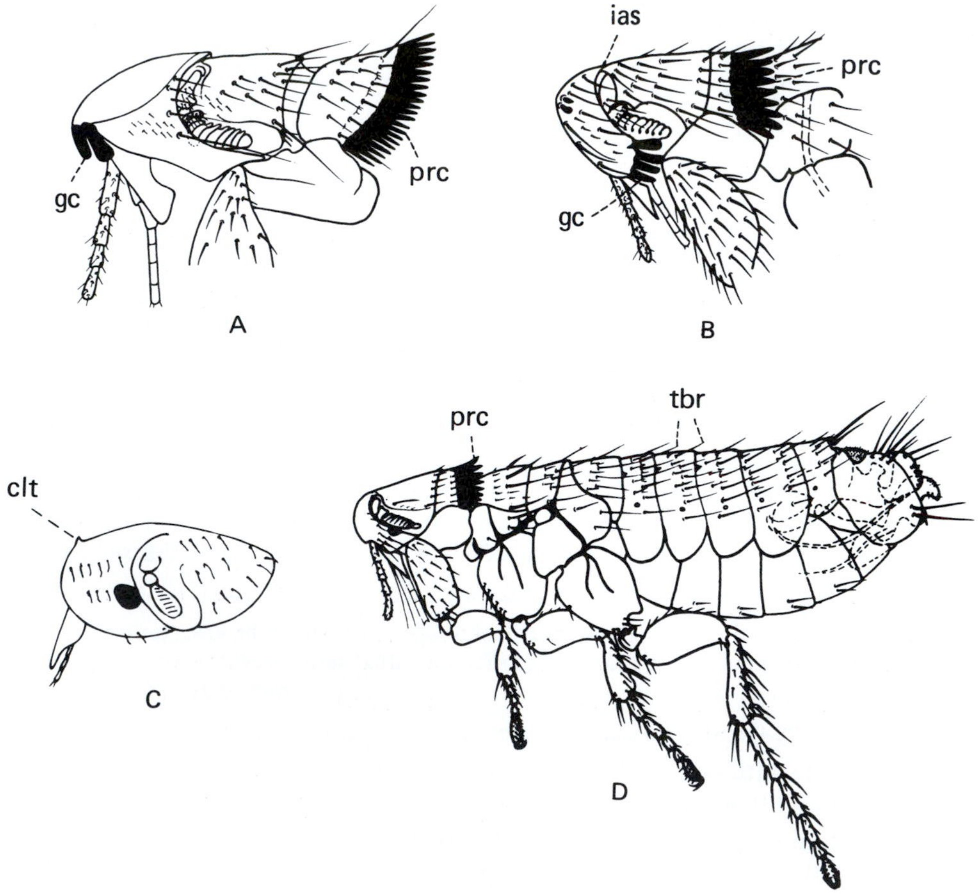

Figure 31–5. **A,** head and prothorax of a bat flea, *Myodopsýlla insígnis* (Rothschild)
(Ischnopsýllidae); **B,** head and prothorax of a mouse flea, *Leptopsýlla ségnis* (Schönherr)
(Ceratophýllidae); **C,** head of *Rhopalopsýllus* (Rhopalopsýllidae); **D,** a rodent flea, *Orchopèas
leucòpus* (Baker) (Ceratophýllidae). *clt,* clypeal tubercle; *gc,* genal comb; *ias,* interantennal
suture; *prc,* pronotal comb; *tbr,* tergal bristles (2 rows on most terga).

9'. Labial palps with at least 4 segments; genal comb present or absent, if present rarely with as many as 9 spines; first abdominal tergum without well-developed comb **10**

10(9'). Antennal club 7- or 8-segmented; pleural ridge of metathorax incomplete or absent ....**subfamily Rhadinopsyllinae**   p. 496

10'. Antennal club 9-segmented; pleural ridge of metathorax present and complete **11**

11(10'). Genal comb, if present, consisting of 2 overlapping spines, or if absent then striarium present on basal abdominal segment ......**subfamily Neopsyllinae**   p. 496

11'. Genal comb not as above, or if absent then striarium also absent **12**

12(11'). Genal comb usually present; abdominal tergites 2–7 with at least 2 rows of bristles **13**

12'. Genal comb absent; abdominal tergites 2–7 with only 1 distinct row of bristles, anterior row vestigial ....**subfamily Anomiopsyllinae**   p. 496

13(12). Genal comb of 4 well-developed, uniformly spaced spines, none of which is behind the eye; sensilium with 13 pits on each side......................... ....**subfamily Doratopsyllinae**   p. 496

13'. Genal comb of 3 or 5 spines, with 1 spine concealed behind another in lateral view, or 1 spine behind eye; sensilium with more than 13 pits on each side ....**subfamily Ctenophthalminae**   p. 496

14(1'). Inner side of hind coxae with spiniform bristles; sensilium with 14 pits on each side **15**

14'. Inner side of hind coxae without spiniform bristles; sensilium with 8 pits on each side **18**

15(14). Club of antennae symmetrical, elliptical in outline ...**subfamily Spilopsyllinae**   p. 496

15'. Club of antennae asymmetrical, its anterior segments foliaceous and extending backward, club more or less spherical in outline **16**

16(15'). Pleural rod of mesothorax present **17**

16'. Pleural rod of mesothorax absent ....**subfamily Pulicinae**   p. 496

17(16). Falx strongly sclerotized; genal and pronotal combs present, at least as a vestige ....**subfamily Archaeopsyllinae**   p. 496

17'. Falx absent or weakly sclerotized; genal and pronotal combs absent ....**subfamily Xenopsyllinae**   p. 496

18(14'). Anterior apical corner of hind coxae projecting ventrad as a broad tooth; no tooth at base of hind femora ....**family Túngidae**   p. 497

18'. Hind coxae without an apical tooth; hind femora with a large basal tooth ....**subfamily Hectopsyllinae**   p. 496

Family **Hystrichopsýllidae:** In another classification (Lewis and Lewis 1985) this family is one of the largest in the order, including in addition to the Hystrichopsyllìnae the groups now placed in the family Ctenophthálmidae. As defined here, this family includes only 17 Nearctic species, most of which attack small rodents and insectivores. One species, *Hystrichopsýlla schéfferi* Chapin, is a parasite of the mountain beaver from northern California to British Columbia.

Family **Ctenophthálmidae:** This is the second-largest family in the order, with 125 North American species. Most of these fleas are western in distribution, and most are parasites of small rodents.

Subfamily **Ctenophthalmìnae:** This is a small group, containing two species of *Carterétta* that occur in the Southwest on small rodents and two species of *Ctenophthálmus*, which are widely distributed and parasitize principally moles and shrews.

Subfamily **Doratopsyllìnae:** This group includes six species, most of which are widely distributed, that occur on shrews.

Subfamily **Rhadinopsyllìnae:** Most of the 29 North American species in this group occur in the West. Two species, *Paratyphlóceras oregonénsis* Ewing and *Trichopsyllòides oregonénsis* Ewing, occur on the mountain beaver in the Pacific Northwest. The remaining species are mostly parasites of moles, shrews, and small rodents.

Subfamily **Neopsyllìnae:** Six of the 50 North American species in this group occur in the East, and the rest occur in the West. These fleas are chiefly parasites of small rodents: chipmunks, ground squirrels, rats, and mice.

Subfamily **Anomiopsyllìnae:** One of our 34 species in this group, *Conorhinopsýlla stánfordi* Stewart, a parasite of flying squirrels, occurs in the East. The remaining species occur in the West, where they parasitize various small rodents.

Subfamily **Stenoponìinae:** Two species of *Stenopònia* occur in our area, one in the East and the other in the Southwest. They are parasites of small rodents.

Family **Ceratophýllidae:** This is the largest family of fleas, with 143 North American species. Most species are parasites of rodents, but about 12% are parasites of birds.

Subfamily **Ceratophyllìnae:** This is the largest of the North American subfamilies, with 118 species. Most of these are parasites of various rodents, and most are western in distribution. The species of *Dasypsýllus, Mioctenopsýlla,* and a few species of *Ceratophýllus* are parasites of birds; *C. gállinae* (Shrank) is a pest of poultry in both the United States and Europe. The rat flea, *Nosopsýllus fasciàtus* (Bosc), may transmit endemic typhus and serve as the intermediate host of the tapeworm *Hymenólepis diminùta.*

Subfamily **Leptopsyllìnae:** This small group (13 North American species) parasitizes small rodents. Most species are western, but the European mouse flea, *Leptopsýlla ségnis* (Schönherr), is worldwide in distribution.

Subfamily **Amphipsyllìnae:** Eleven of the 12 North American species in this group are western in distribution, and most are parasites of small rodents. One species, *Dolichopsýllus stylòsus* (Baker), is a parasite of the mountain beaver from British Columbia to northern California. The eastern species, *Odontopsýllus multispinòsus* (Baker), is a parasite of rabbits.

Family **Ischnopsýllidae:** The members of this family are parasites of bats. They can usually be recognized by the characteristic genal comb (Figure 31–5A). They have a rather distinct interantennal suture on the dorsal surface of the head, and the eyes are vestigial. Eleven species occur in the United States, two in the East and the rest in the West.

Family **Rhopalopsýllidae:** This group is principally Neotropical, but three species occur in the southwestern states from Florida to Texas. They are parasites of various small rodents and opossums.

Family **Vermipsýllidae:** This is a small group, with only six North American species, all in the genus *Chaetopsýlla.* These fleas are parasites of various carnivores, such as bears, foxes, wolves, and raccoons.

Family **Pulícidae:** This is a large family, of worldwide distribution, but only 14 species occur in our area, grouped in five subfamilies.

Subfamily **Xenopsyllìnae:** This group contains a single species that has been introduced: the oriental rat flea, *Xenopsýlla cheòpis* (Rothschild). This flea is the principal vector of bubonic plague (from rat to rat and rat to human); it serves as a vector of endemic typhus; and it may serve as the intermediate host of the tapeworm *Hymenólepis diminùta.*

Subfamily **Archaeopsyllìnae:** This group includes two North American species, the cat and dog fleas, *Ctenocephálides fèlis* (Bouché) and *C. cànis* (Curtis), which attack domestic pets, sometimes livestock, and sometimes people. The dog flea serves as the intermediate host of the dog tapeworm, *Dipylídium canìnum.*

Subfamily **Hectopsyllìnae:** This group includes a single North American species, *Hectopsýlla psittàcii* Frauenfeld, a parasite of cliff swallows in California.

Subfamily **Pulicìnae:** This group includes the sticktight flea, *Echidnóphaga gallinàcea* (Westwood), and three species of *Pùlex.* The sticktight flea attacks poultry, and occasionally other birds and mammals. The adults tend to congregate in masses on the host, usually on the head, and often remain attached for several days or even weeks. The best known species of *Pùlex* is the so-called human flea, *P. írritans* L., a cosmopolitan species that attacks people and other animals. The other two North American species of

Pùlex attack peccaries, ground squirrels, and other animals.

Subfamily **Spilopsyllinae:** This group includes six North American species, most of which are western. The one species of *Actenopsýlla* is a parasite of sea birds on the west coast; the three species of *Cediopsýlla* and the one species of *Euhoplopsýllus* are parasites of rabbits; and the one species of *Hoplopsýllus* is a parasite of rabbits and ground squirrels.

Family **Túngidae:** The members of this group are more or less permanent parasites in the adult stage. They have a small thorax and short legs, and the abdomen of the female, when full of eggs, is greatly enlarged. The group is mainly tropical, but one species, the chigoe flea, *Túnga pénetrans* (L.), may occur in the southern states.

Males and virgin females of the chigoe flea live like other fleas, feeding on a variety of mammalian hosts, but after mating the female burrows into the skin of humans or other animals, usually on the feet. Where the female burrows into the skin a painful ulcerlike sore develops. In this location, nourished by the surrounding tissues of the host, the abdomen of the female swells (with the development of the eggs) and may get as large as a pea. The eggs are discharged to the outside, and fall to the ground and develop. After all the eggs are discharged, the body of the female is usually expelled by the pressure of the surrounding tissues. These fleas usually burrow between the toes or under the toenails, and the sores if untreated may become gangrenous.

Collecting and Preserving Siphonáptera

Fleas may be collected from host animals or from their nests. The methods suggested for collecting Phthiráptera (Chapter 23) will also apply to Siphonáptera. Fleas should be preserved in 75% ethyl alcohol; formaldehyde-based preservatives should not be used, as they fix the tissues in a way that makes it impossible to properly clear the fleas for examination under the microscope.

Mammal nests are usually difficult to locate, but once found they may continue to yield adult fleas for an extended period if not permitted to dry out. Bird nests are usually easy to locate, but most nests in open areas will not contain fleas. The bird nests most likely to contain fleas are those on the ground, in natural cavities, and in holes in trees, or mud nests on buildings or cliff faces. Nest material should be examined by placing it on a white background and thoroughly picking it apart. Live fleas and other insects can be picked up with an aspirator or with a camel's-hair brush moistened with alcohol. Nesting material should be kept for a few weeks, moistened periodically, and examined every few days for newly emerged adults.

In areas such as yards or buildings where fleas are particularly abundant, they may be collected by sweeping, or one may simply walk about in such an area and collect the fleas as they jump on one's clothing. In the latter case the fleas are most easily seen if one wears white clothing.

References

Ewing, H. E., and I. Fox. 1943. The fleas of North America. USDA Misc. Publ. 500, 128 pp.; illus.

Fox, I. 1940. Fleas of Eastern United States. Ames: Iowa State College Press, 191 pp.; illus.

Holland, G. P. 1985. The fleas of Canada, Alaska and Greenland (Siphonaptera). Mem. Entomol. Soc. Can. No. 130; illus.

Hopkins, G. H. E., and M. Rothschild. 1953–1971. An illustrated catalogue of the Rothschild Collection of fleas (Siphonaptera) in the British Museum. London: British Museum (Nat. Hist.). Vol. 1: Tungidae and Pulicidae, 361 pp.; illus. (1953). Vol. 2: Coptopsyllidae, Vermipsyllidae, Stephanocircidae, Ischnopsyllidae, Hypsophthalmidae, and Xiphiopsyllidae, 445 pp.; illus. (1956). Vol. 3: Hystrichopsyllidae (Acedestiinae, Anomiopsyllinae, Hystrichopsyllinae, Neopsyllinae, Rhadinopsyllinae, and Stenoponiinae), 559 pp.; illus. (1962). Vol. 4: Hystrichopsyllidae (Ctenophthalminae, Dinopsyllinae, Doratopsyllinae, and Listropsyllinae), 549 pp.; illus. (1966). Vol. 5: Leptopsyllidae and Ancistropsyllidae, 530 pp.; illus. (1971).

Hubbard, C. A. 1947. Fleas of western North America. Ames: Iowa State College Press, 533 pp.; illus.

Jellison, W. L., and N. E. Good. 1942. Index to the literature of Siphonaptera of North America. U.S. Public Health Service, Nat. Inst. Health Bull. 178, 193 pp.

Layne, J. N. 1971. Fleas (Siphonaptera) of Florida. Fla. Entomol. 54:35–51.

Lewis, R. E. 1972–1975. Notes on the geographic distribution and host preferences in the order Siphonaptera. Part 1: Pulicidae; J. Med. Entomol. 9:511–520 (1972). Part 2: Rhopalopsyllidae, Malacopsyllidae and Vermipsyllidae; J. Med. Entomol. 10:255–260 (1973). Part 3: Hystrichopsyllidae; J. Med. Entomol. 11:147–167 (1974). Part 4: Coptopsyllidae, Pygiopsyllidae, Stephanocircidae and Xiphiopsyllidae; J. Med. Entomol. 11:403–413 (1974). Part 5: Ancistropsyllidae, Chimaeropsyllidae, Ischnopsyllidae, Leptopsyllidae, and Macropsyllidae; J. Med. Entomol. 11:525–540 (1974). Part 6: Ceratophyllidae; J. Med. Entomol. 11:658–676 (1975).

Lewis, R. E., and J. H. Lewis. 1985. Notes on the geographical distribution and host preferences in the order Siphonaptera, Part 7: New taxa described between 1972 and 1983 with a supraspecific classification of the order. J. Med. Entomol. 22:134–152.

Mardon, D. K. 1981. An illustrated catalogue of the Rothschild Collection of fleas in the British Museum. London: British Museum (Nat. Hist.). Vol. 6: Pygiopsyllidae, 298 pp.; illus.

Rothschild, M. 1975. Recent advances in our knowledge of the order Siphonaptera. Annu. Rev. Entomol. 20:241–259.

Smit, F. G. A. M. 1982. Siphonaptera, pp. 557–563 *in* S. P. Parker (Ed.), Synopsis and Classification of Living Organisms, vol. 2. New York: McGraw-Hill.

Smit, F. G. A. M. 1983. Key to genera and subgenera of Ceratophyllidae, pp. 1–36 *in* Traub *et al.*, 1983.

Traub, R., M. Rothschild, and J. F. Haddow. 1983. The Rothschild Collection of Fleas: The Ceratophyllidae: Key to the genera and host relationships, with notes on their evolution, zoogeography and medical importance. London: Academic Press, 288 pp.; illus.

Chapter 32

Order Díptera[1]
Flies

The Díptera constitute one of the largest orders of insects, and its members are abundant in individuals and species almost everywhere. Most of the Díptera can be readily distinguished from other insects to which the term *fly* is applied (sawflies, stoneflies, caddisflies, dragonflies, and others) by the fact that they possess one pair of wings. These are the front wings, and the hind wings are reduced to small knobbed structures called halteres, which function as organs of equilibrium. There are occasional insects in a few other orders that have only one pair of wings (some mayflies, some beetles, male scale insects, and others), but none of these, except male scale insects, has the hind wings reduced to halteres. The Díptera are sometimes spoken of as the two-winged flies, to distinguish them from the "flies" in other orders. In the common names of Díptera, the *fly* of the name is written as a separate word, whereas in the common names of flies in other orders, the *fly* of the name is written together with the descriptive word.

The majority of the Díptera are relatively small and soft-bodied insects, and some are quite minute, but many are of great economic importance. The mosquitoes, black flies, punkies, horse flies, stable flies, and others are bloodsucking and are serious

pests of humans and animals. Many of the bloodsucking flies, and some of the scavenging flies such as the house flies and blow flies, are important vectors of disease. The causative organisms of malaria, yellow fever, filarasis, dengue, sleeping sickness, typhoid fever, dysentery, and other diseases are carried and distributed by Díptera. Some flies, such as the Hessian fly and the apple maggot, are important pests of cultivated plants. On the other hand, many flies are useful as scavengers; others are important predators or parasites of various insect pests; others aid in the pollination of useful plants; and some are enemies of noxious weeds.

The mouthparts of the Díptera are of the sucking type, but there is considerable variation in mouthpart structure within the order. In many flies the mouthparts are piercing; in others they are sponging or lapping (pages 40–42); and in a few flies the mouthparts are so poorly developed as to be nonfunctional.

The Díptera undergo complete metamorphosis, and the larvae of many are called maggots. The larvae are generally legless and wormlike. In the primitive families (Nematócera) the head is usually well developed and the mandibles move laterally. In the higher families (Brachýcera) the head is reduced and the mouth hooks move in a vertical plane. In some families of Brachýcera (infraorders Tabanomórpha and Asilomórpha) the head of the larva is sclerotized

---

[1]Díptera: *di*, two; *ptera*, wings.

and more or less retractile, while in others (infraorder Muscomórpha) there is no sclerotization of the head at all except for the mouthparts. The pupae of the Nematócera are of the obtect type, while those of other Díptera are coarctate; that is, the pupal stage is passed inside the last larval cuticle, which is called a puparium.

Dipterous larvae occur in many kinds of habitats, but a large proportion of them live in water—in all sorts of aquatic habitats including streams, ponds, lakes, temporary puddles, and brackish and alkaline water. The larvae that feed on plants generally live within some tissue of the plant, as leaf miners, gall insects, stem borers, or root borers. The predaceous larvae live in many different habitats: in water, in the soil, under bark or stones, or on vegetation. Many species feed during the larval stage in decaying plant or animal matter. Some fly larvae live in some rather unusual habitats: one species (*Helaeomÿia petròlei* (Coquillett), family Ephÿdridae) lives in pools of crude petroleum. Other ephydrids breed in the Great Salt Lake.

Adult Díptera feed on various plant or animal juices, such as nectar, sap, or blood. Most species feed on nectar, but many are bloodsucking, and many are predaceous on other insects.

Classification of the Díptera

The classification of the Díptera followed in this book is that used in volumes 1 and 2 of the *Manual of Nearctic Diptera* (McAlpine *et al.* 1981–1987). This arrangement is outlined below, with alternate names, spellings, and arrangements in parentheses. The groups marked with an asterisk are relatively rare or are unlikely to be taken by a general collector.

Suborder Nematócera (Nemócera; Orthórrhapha in part)—long-horned flies
  Infraorder Tipulomórpha
    Superfamily Tanyderòidea
      *Tanydéridae—primitive crane flies
    Superfamily Tipulòidea
      Tipùlidae—crane flies
  Infraorder Blephariceromórpha
    Superfamily Blephariceròidea
      *Blepharicéridae (Blepharocéridae, Blepharocerátidae)—net-winged midges
    Superfamily Deuterophlebiòidea
      *Deuterophlebìidae—mountain midges
    Superfamily Nymphomyiòidea
      *Nymphomyìidae—nymphomyiid flies
  Infraorder Axymyiomórpha
    Superfamily Axymyiòidea

      Axymyìidae (Pachyneùridae in part)—axymyiid gnats
  Infraorder Bibionomórpha
    Superfamily Pachyneuròidea
      *Pachyneùridae (Cramptonomyìidae)—pachyneurid gnats
    Superfamily Bibionòidea
      Bibiónidae—march flies
    Superfamily Sciaròidea
      Mycetophílidae (Fungivòridae in part)—fungus gnats
      Sciáridae (Fungivòridae in part)—dark-winged fungus gnats, root gnats
      Cecidomyìidae (Cecidomÿidae, Itonídidae)—gall midges or gall gnats
  Infraorder Psychodomórpha
    Superfamily Psychodòidea
      Psychòdidae—moth flies and sand flies
    Superfamily Trichoceròidea
      *Trichocéridae (Trichocerátidae, Petaurístidae)—winter crane flies
    Superfamily Anisopodòidea
      Anisopódidae (Rhÿphidae, Silvicólidae, Phrynèidae; including Mycetobìidae)—wood gnats
    Superfamily Scatopsòidea
      Scatópsidae—minute black scavenger flies
      *Synneùridae (Hyperoscelídidae)—synneurid gnats
  Infraorder Ptychopteromórpha
    Superfamily Ptychopteròidea
      Ptychoptéridae (Liriopèidae)—phantom crane flies
  Infraorder Culicomórpha
    Superfamily Culicòidea
      Díxidae (Culícidae in part)—dixid midges
      Chaobòridae (Corèthridae; Culícidae in part)—phantom midges
      Culícidae—mosquitoes
    Superfamily Chironomòidea
      *Thaumalèidae (Orphnephílidae)—solitary midges
      Simulìidae (Melusínidae)—black flies or buffalo gnats
      Ceratopogónidae (Helèidae)—biting midges, punkies, no-see-ums
      Chironómidae (Tendipédidae)—midges
Suborder Brachýcera (including Cyclórrhapha and Orthórrhapha in part)—short-horned flies
  Infraorder Tabanomórpha (Orthórrhapha in part)
    Superfamily Tabanòidea
      *Pelecorhýnchidae (Tabánidae in part,

Xylophágidae in part)—pelecorhyn-
chid flies

Tabánidae—horse flies and deer flies

Atherícidae (Rhagiónidae in part)—ath-
ericid flies

Rhagiónidae (Léptidae)—snipe flies

Superfamily Stratiomyòidea

Xylophágidae (Erínnidae; Rhagiónidae in
part)—xylophagid flies

Xylomỳidae (Xylomỳiidae; Xylophágidae
in part)—xylomyid flies

Stratiomỳidae (Stratiomỳiidae; including
Chiromỳzidae)—soldier flies

Infraorder Asilomórpha (Orthórrhapha in part)

Superfamily Asilòidea

Therévidae—stiletto flies

*Scenopínidae (Omphrálidae)—window
flies

*Vermileónidae (Rhagiónidae in part)—
worm lions

Mỳdidae (Mydàidae, Mydásidae)—mydas
flies

*Apiocéridae (Apiocerátidae)—flower-
loving flies

Asílidae (including Leptogástridae—robber flies and grass flies

Superfamily Bombyliòidea

*Acrocéridae (Acrocerátidae, Cýrtidae,
Henópidae, Oncòdidae)—small-
headed flies

*Nemestrínidae—tangle-veined flies

Bombylìidae—bee flies

*Hilarimórphidae (Rhagiónidae in
part)—hilarimorphid flies

Superfamily Empidòidea

Empídidae (Émpidae)—dance flies

Dolichopódidae (Dolichópidae)—long-
legged flies

Infraorder Muscomórpha (Cyclórrhapha)—circular-seamed flies

Division Aschìza

Superfamily Lonchopteròidea

Lonchoptéridae (Musidóridae)—spear-
winged flies

Superfamily Platypezòidea

*Platypèzidae (Clythìidae)—flat-footed
flies

Phòridae—humpbacked flies

Superfamily Syrphòidea

Sýrphidae—syrphid flies or flower flies

Pipuncùlidae (Dorilàidae, Dorylàidae)—
big-headed flies

Division Schizóphora (including Pupípara)—
muscoid flies

Section Acalyptràtae—acalyptrate muscoid
flies

Superfamily Conopòidea

Conópidae—thick-headed flies

Superfamily Neriòidea

*Cypselosomátidae—cypselosomatid
flies

Micropèzidae (including Tỳlidae and Ca-
lobátidae = Trepidarìidae)—stilt-
legged flies

*Nerìidae—cactus flies

Superfamily Diopsòidea

*Tanypèzidae (Micropèzidae in part)—
tanypezid flies

*Stróngylophthalmyìidae (Psìlidae in
part)—strongylophthalmyiid flies

Psìlidae—rust flies

*Diópsidae—stalk-eyed flies

Superfamily Tephritòidea

Lonchaèidae (Sapromỳzidae in part)—
lonchaeid flies

Otítidae (Ortálidae, Ortalídidae)—picture-winged flies

Platystomátidae (Otítidae in part)—picture-winged flies

*Pyrgòtidae—pyrgotid flies

Tephrítidae (Trypétidae, Trupanèidae,
Trypanèidae, Euribìidae)—fruit flies

*Richardìidae (Otítidae in part, includ-
ing Thyreophòridae)—richardiid
flies

*Palloptéridae (Sapromỳzidae in part)—
flutter flies

Piophílidae (including Neottiophílidae)—
skipper flies

Superfamily Opomyzòidea

Clusìidae (Clusiòdidae, Heteroneùri-
dae)—clusiid flies

Acartophthálmidae (Clusìidae in part)—
acartophthalmid flies

Odinìidae (Odínidae, Agromỳzidae in
part)—odiniid flies

Agromỳzidae (Phytomỳzidae)—leaf
miner flies

*Opomỳzidae (Geomỳzidae)—opomyzid
flies

Anthomỳzidae (Opomỳzidae in part)—
anthomyzid flies

*Aulacigástridae (Aulacigastéridae; An-
thomỳzidae in part; Drosophílidae
in part)—aulacigastrid flies

*Periscelídidae (Periscélidae)—perisceli-
did flies

Asteìidae (Astíidae)—asteiid flies

Milichìidae (Phyllomỳzidae)—milichiid
flies
*Carnidae (Milichìidae in part)—carnid
flies
Braùlidae (Pupípara in part)—bee lice
Superfamily Sciomyzòidea
Coelópidae (Phycodròmidae)—seaweed
flies
*Dryomỳzidae (including Helcomỳzi-
dae)—dryomyzid flies
Sciomỳzidae (Tetanocéridae, Tetanocerá-
tidae)—marsh flies
*Ropaloméridae (Rhopaloméridae)—ro-
palomerid flies
Sépsidae—black scavenger flies
Superfamily Lauxaniòidea
Lauxanìidae (Sapromỳzidae)—lauxaniid
flies
Chamaemyìidae (Chamaemỳidae, Och-
thiphílidae)—aphid flies
Superfamily Sphaeroceròidea
Heleomỳzidae (Helomỳzidae)—heleomy-
zid flies
*Trixoscelídidae (Trixoscélidae, Trichos-
célidae; Chyromỳidae in part)—trix-
oscelidid flies
Chyromỳidae (Chyromyìidae)—chyro-
myid flies
*Rhinotòridae—rhinotorid flies
Sphaerocèridae (Sphaerocerátidae, Bor-
bòridae, Cypsélidae)—small dung
flies
Superfamily Ephydròidea
Curtonòtidae (Cyrtonòtidae; Drosophíli-
dae in part)—curtonotid flies
Drosophílidae—pomace flies, vinegar
flies, small fruit flies
*Diastátidae (Drosophílidae in part)—
diastatid flies
*Camíllidae (Drosophílidae in part)—
camillid flies
Ephýdridae (Hydréllidae, Notiophíli-
dae)—shore flies
Chlorópidae (Oscínidae, Titanìidae)—
grass flies
*Cryptochètidae (Chamaemyìidae in
part, Agromỳzidae in part)—crypto-
chetid flies
*Tethínidae (Opomỳzidae in part)—teth-
inid flies
*Canácidae (Canacèidae)—beach flies
Section Calyptràtae—calyptrate muscoid
flies
Superfamily Muscòidea
Scathophágidae (Scatophágidae, Scato-

mỳzidae, Scopeumátidae, Cordylùri-
dae, Anthomyìidae in part)—dung
flies
Anthomyìidae (Anthomỳidae; Múscidae
in part)—anthomyiid flies
Múscidae (including Glossínidae and
Fannìidae)—muscid flies: house fly,
face fly, horn fly, stable fly, tsetse
flies, and others
Superfamily Oestròidea
Calliphòridae (Metopìidae in part)—blow
flies
Sarcophágidae (Stephanosomátidae; Me-
topìidae in part)—flesh flies
*Oéstridae (including Cuterébridae,
Gasterophílidae, and Hypodermáti-
dae)—warble flies and bot flies
Rhinophòridae (Tachínidae in part)—
rhinophorid flies
Tachínidae (Larvaevòridae; including
Phasìidae = Gymnosomátidae, and
Dexìidae)—tachinid flies
Superfamily Hippoboscòidea
*Hippobóscidae (Pupípara in part)—
louse flies
*Nycteribìidae (Pupípara in part)—bat
flies
*Stréblidae (Pupípara in part)—bat flies

Characters Used in the Identification of Díptera

The principal characters used in the identification of
Díptera are those of the antennae, legs, wings, and
chaetotaxy (the arrangement of the bristles, chiefly
of the head and thorax). Occasionally various other
characters are used, such as those of the head, and
the size, shape, and color of the insect.

Antennae

The antennae vary quite a bit from family to family,
and to some extent within a single family. Occasionally they may differ in the two sexes of the same
species (e.g., mosquitoes; see Figure 32–37). Basically, the antennae of a fly consist of three segments:
the scape (the basal segment), pedicel, and flagellum.
In the Nematócera the flagellum is divided into four
or more distinct and movable subdivisions (which
we call segments, but which are sometimes called
flagellomeres). In some of the Brachýcera the third
antennal segment is subdivided, but the divisions
are not as distinct as those between the three basic
segments, and such a segment is said to be annulated

(Figure 32–1C,D,F). This annulation is sometimes difficult to see unless the antenna is properly illuminated. In a few cases it may be difficult to decide whether such an antenna is three-segmented or many-segmented. The third antennal segment in many Brachýcera bears an elongate process, a style or an arista. A style is usually terminal and fairly rigid, while an arista is usually dorsal and is bristlelike. Both styles and aristae may appear segmented, though the segments (particularly in an arista) are often difficult to see. An arista may be bare, pubescent, or plumose. In some of the Muscomórpha the form of the second antennal segment may serve to separate different groups: for example, the calyptrate and acalyptrate groups of muscoid flies differ in the form of the second antennal segment (Figure 32–14A,B).

Legs

The principal leg characters used in separating groups of flies are the structure of the empodium, the presence or absence of tibial spurs, and the presence of certain tibial bristles. The empodium (Figure 32–2, *emp*) is a structure arising from between the claws on the last tarsal segment. It is bristlelike or absent in most flies, but in a few families (Figure 32–2B) it is large and membranous and resembles the pulvilli in appearance. The pulvilli are pads at the apex of the last tarsal segment, one at the base of each claw (Figure 32–2, *pul*). A fly may thus have two pads (the pulvilli), three pads (the pulvilli and a pulvilliform empodium), or no pads (pulvilli absent) on the last tarsal segment. Tibial spurs are spinelike structures, usually located at the distal end of the tibia. Preapical tibial bristles are bristles on the outer or dorsal surface of the tibia just proximad of the apex (Figure 32–23B, *ptbr*).

Wings

Considerable use is made of wing characters, especially the venation, in the identification of flies, and it is often possible to identify a fly to family or beyond by the wings alone. The venation in this order is relatively simple, and the tendency in many families is toward reduction in the number of veins. Sometimes the wing's color, its shape, or the character of the lobes at the base of the wing is useful in identification.

In most fly wings there is an incision on the posterior side of the wing near the base that separates off a small basal lobe, called the alula. Distal to the alula is the anal angle of the wing, and the lobe there is called the anal lobe (Figure 32–4B, *C, al*). At the extreme base of the wing, basad of the alula, there are often two lobes called the calypteres (singular, *calypter*). The one next to the alula is the upper

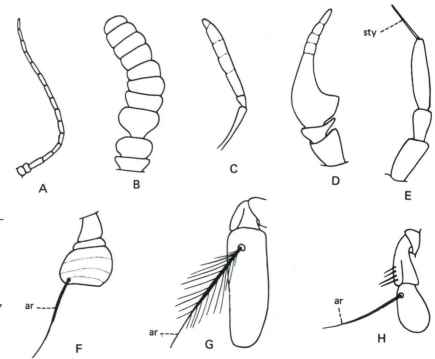

Figure 32–1. Antennae of Díptera. **A,** Mycetophílidae (*Mycomỳia*); **B,** Bibiónidae (*Bíbio*); **C,** Stratiomỳidae (*Stratiomys*); **D,** Tabánidae (*Tabánus*); **E,** Asìlidae (*Asìlus*); **F,** Stratiomỳidae (*Ptécticus*); **G,** Calliphòridae (*Callíphora*); **H,** Tachínidae (*Epálpus*). *ar*, arista; *sty*, style.

calypter, and the other one the lower calypter. The calypteres may vary in size and shape in different groups.

There are two different venational terminologies commonly used in this order, that of Comstock-Needham and an older system in which the principal longitudinal veins are numbered. Most authorities use the Comstock-Needham terminology, but not all agree with the Comstock-Needham interpretation, particularly regarding the veins posterior to M_2. Figure 32–3 shows a generalized dipteran wing, labeled with the Comstock-Needham terminology through M_2 and comparing three major interpretations of the veins posterior to M_2. We follow the Comstock-Needham interpretation in this book, but occasionally use terms of the older system, especially for certain wing cells. Table 32–1 compares the different venational terminologies used for dipteran wing venation, and Figure 32–4 shows some dipteran wings labeled with these terminologies.

A closed cell is one that does not reach the wing margin (for example, the anal or 1A cell in Figure 32–4). When the thickening of the anterior edge of the wing (the costa) ends near the wing tip (as in Figure 32–7B–F,J), the costa is said to extend only to the wing tip. Where there is no abrupt thinning of the anterior margin of the wing near the wing tip (as in Figure 32–7G–I), the costa is said to continue around the wing.

Many of the muscoid flies have one or two points in the costa where the sclerotization is weak or lacking, or where the vein appears to be broken. Such

(text continued on page 506)

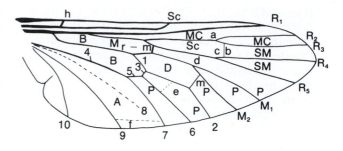

Figure 32–3.   Generalized dipteran venation (Comstock-Needham terminology for the veins), with a comparison of the major interpretations of the veins behind M_2, and notes on the occurrence of some venational characters through the order. *A,* anal cell; *B,* basal cells; *D,* discal cell; *MC,* marginal cells; *P,* posterior cells; *SM,* submarginal cells.

Interpretations of the Veins behind M_2

Vein Number	Comstock[a]	Tillyard[b]	McAlpine[c]
1	M_3	M_{3+4}	M_3
2	M_3	M_3	M_3
3	$m-cu$	M_4	$m-cu$
4	Cu	Cu_1	CuA
5	Cu_1	M_4	CuA_1
6	Cu_1	M_4	CuA_1
7	Cu_2	Cu_1	CuA_2
8[d]	1A	Cu_2	CuP
9	2A	1A	A_1
10	3A	2A	A_2

[a]The terminology used in this book.

[b]Tillyard 1926.

[c]McAlpine *et al.* 1981. In wings where the M_3 of Comstock fuses with the Cu_1 of Comstock, these authors do not recognize an M_3. If M_{1+2} is forked they call its branches M_1 and M_2, but if it is not forked they call it M (see Figure 32–4).

[d]Nearly always weak, often completely absent.

Occurrence of Some Venational Characters:

a   (forking of R_{2+3}): In some Nematócera only.

b   (r cross vein): In some Brachýcera only.

c   (forking of R_{4+5}): In Tanydéridae and some Psychòdidae of the Nematócera, and in most of the infraorders Tabanomórpha and Asilomórpha of the Brachýcera (no Muscomórpha).

d   (forking of M_{1+2}): In a few Nematócera, most Tabanomórpha and Asilomórpha, and only in the Lonchoptéridae of the Muscomórpha.

e   (fusion of veins 2 and 6): In some Nematócera, some Tabanomórpha and Asilomórpha, and all Muscomórpha.

f   (distal fusion of veins 7 and 9): In the Brachýcera only (many Tabanomórpha and Asilomórpha, and most Muscomórpha).

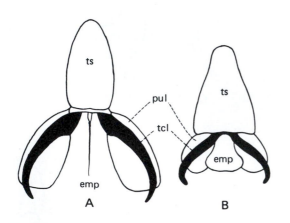

Figure 32–2.   Tip of tarsus, dorsal view. **A,** robber fly, with the empodium bristlelike; **B,** horse fly, with the empodium pulvilliform. *emp,* empodium; *pul,* pulvilli; *tcl,* tarsal claw; *ts,* last tarsal segment.

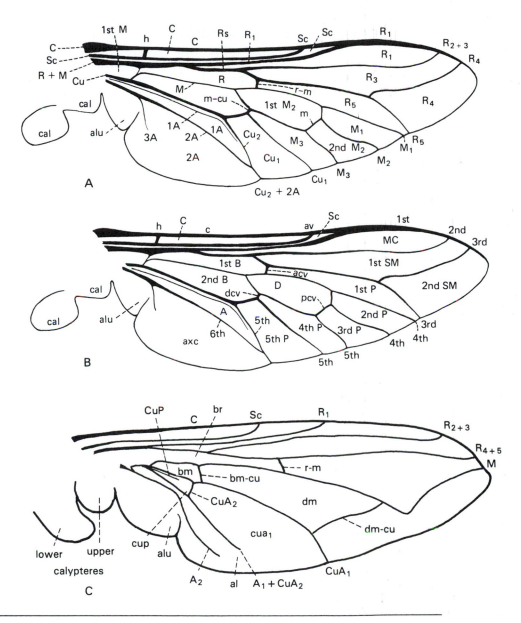

Figure 32–4. Wings of a horse fly (**A** and **B**) and a calyptrate muscoid fly (**C**), showing venational terminologies. **A,** Comstock-Needham system; **B,** an older system, in which the longitudinal veins are numbered; **C,** wing of a calyptrate muscoid showing the terminology used by McAlpine *et al.* (1981). For a key to the lettering in **A** and the longitudinal veins in **C,** see page 32. Labeling in **B:** *A,* anal cell; *acv,* anterior cross vein; *alu,* alula; *av,* auxiliary vein; *axc,* axillary cell; *B,* basal cells (first and second); *C,* costal cell; *c,* costal vein; *cal,* calypteres or squamae; *D,* discal cell; *dcv,* discal cross vein; *h,* humeral cross vein; *MC,* marginal cell; *P,* posterior cells; *pcv,* posterior cross vein; *Sc,* subcostal cell; *SM,* submarginal or apical cells (first and second). Labeling in **C:** *al,* anal lobe; *alu,* alula; *bm,* basal medial cell; *bm-cu,* basal medio-cubital cross vein; *br,* basal radial cell; *cua₁,* anterior cubital cell; *cup,* posterior cubital cell; *dm,* discal medial cell, *dm-cu,* discal medio-cubital cross vein.

points are termed costal breaks and may occur near the end of R_1 or the humeral cross vein (Figures 32–19B, 32–20C–E, *cbr*). Costal breaks are best seen with transmitted light. A few muscoids have a series of long hairs or bristles along the costa beyond the end of R_1 (Figure 32–19A,H). The costa in such cases is said to be spinose.

Chaetotaxy

In the identification of certain flies, particularly the muscoid groups, much use is made of the number, size, position and arrangement of the larger bristles on the head and thorax. The terminology used in the chaetotaxy of flies is illustrated in Figures 32–5 and

Table 32–1
A Comparison of Díptera Venational Terminologies

Veins

Comstock	Tillyard (1926)	McAlpine *et al.* (1981)	Old System
C	C	C	Costal
Sc	Sc	Sc	Auxiliary
R_1	R_1	R_1	First longitudinal
R_{2+3}	R_{2+3}	R_{2+3}	Second longitudinal
R_{4+5}	R_{4+5}	R_{4+5}	Third longitudinal
M_{1+2}	M_{1+2}	M_{1+2} or M^a	Fourth longitudinal
m–cu	base of M_4	m–cu	Discal cross vein
Cu	Cu	CuA	Fifth longitudinal
base of Cu_1	m–cu	base of CuA_1	Fifth longitudinal
Cu_1	M_4	CuA_1	Fifth longitudinal
Cu_2	Cu_1	CuA_2	Fifth longitudinal
$1A^b$	Cu_2	CuP	—
2A	1A	A_1	Sixth longitudinal
h	h	h	Humeral cross vein
r–m	r–m	r–m	Anterior cross vein
m	m	m–m	Posterior cross vein
M_3	M_{3+4} and M_3	M_3	Fifth longitudinal

Cells

Comstock	Tillyard (1926)	McAlpine *et al.* (1981)	Old System
C	C	c	Costal
Sc	Sc	sc	Subcostal
R	R	br^c	First basal
M	M	bm^d	Second basal
R_1, R_2	R_1, R_2	r_1, r_2	Marginal
R_3	R_3	r_3, r_{2+3}^e	First submarginal
R_4	R_4	r_4	Second submarginal
R_5	R_5	r_5, r_{4+5}^f	First posterior
M_1	M_1	m_1	Second posterior
1st M_2	1st M_2	d (discal)	Discal
2nd M_2	2nd M_2	m_2	Third posterior
M_3	M_3	m_3	Fourth posterior
Cu_1	M_4	cua_1	Fifth posterior
1A	Cu_2	cup	Anal
2A	1A	a_1	Axillary

[a]When no M_3 is recognized and this vein is not forked.

[b]Usually weak, often lacking.

[c]Basal radial cell.

[d]Basal medial cell.

[e]When R_{2+3} is not forked.

[f]When R_{4+5} is not forked.

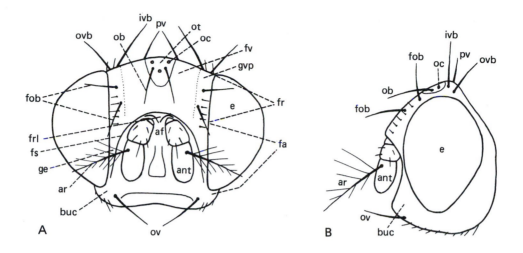

Figure 32–5.   Areas and chaetotaxy of the head of a drosophilid fly. **A,** anterior view; **B,** lateral view. *af,* antennal fossa; *ant,* antenna; *ar,* arista; *buc,* bucca; *e,* compound eye; *fa,* face; *fob,* fronto-orbital bristles; *fr,* frons; *frl,* frontal lunule; *fs,* frontal suture; *fv,* frontal vitta; *ge,* gena; *gvp,* genovertical or orbital plate; *ivb,* inner vertical bristle; *ob,* ocellar bristle; *oc,* ocellus; *ot,* ocellar triangle; *ov,* oral vibrissae; *ovb,* outer vertical bristle; *pv,* postvertical bristles.

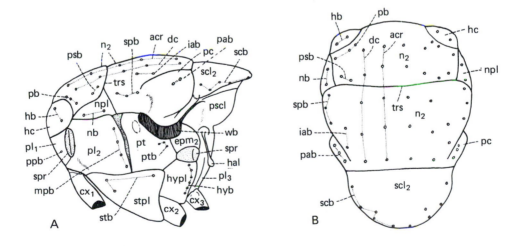

Figure 32–6.   Areas and chaetotaxy of the thorax of a blow fly. **A,** lateral view; **B,** dorsal view. *acr,* acrostichal bristles; *cx,* coxa; *dc,* dorsocentral bristles; *epm₂,* mesepimeron; *hal,* haltere; *hb,* humeral bristles; *hc,* humeral callus; *hyb,* hypopleural bristles; *hypl,* hypopleuron; *iab,* intra-alar bristles; *mpb,* mesopleural bristles; *n₂,* mesonotum; *nb,* notopleural bristles; *npl,* notopleuron; *pab,* postalar bristles; *pb,* posthumeral bristles; *pc,* postalar callus; *pl₁,* propleuron; *pl₂,* mesopleuron; *pl₃,* metapleuron; *ppb,* propleural bristle; *psb,* presutural bristles; *pscl,* postscutellum; *pt,* pteropleuron; *ptb,* pteropleural bristles; *scb,* scutellar bristles; *scl₂,* mesoscutellum; *spb,* supra-alar bristles; *spr,* spiracle; *stb,* sternopleural bristles; *stpl,* sternopleuron; *trs,* transverse suture; *wb,* base of wing.

32–6. The frontal bristles (not shown in Figure 32–5) are located in the middle of the front, between the ocellar triangle and the frontal suture.

Head and Thoracic Sutures

The principal head suture used in the identification of flies is the frontal suture (Figure 32–5, *fs*). This suture is usually in the shape of an inverted ∪, extending from above the bases of the antennae lateroventrad toward the lower margins of the compound eyes. This suture is commonly called the frontal suture by dipterists, but it is not the same as the frontal sutures in Figure 3–13. It is actually a ptilinal suture and marks the break in the head wall through which the ptilinum was everted at the time of the fly's emergence from the puparium (see page 548).

Between the apex of the ∪ and the bases of the antennae is a small crescent-shaped sclerite called the frontal lunule (*frl*). The presence of a frontal suture distinguishes the muscoid flies (division Schizóphora of the suborder Brachýcera) from other flies. In cases where the complete suture is difficult to see, the flies possessing it can be recognized by the presence of a frontal lunule above the bases of the antennae.

A transverse suture across the anterior part of the mesonotum (Figure 32–6, *trs*) separates most of the calyptrate from the acalyptrate muscoids. The calyptrate muscoids usually have sutures in the lateroposterior portions of the mesonotum, which separate the postalar calli (Figure 32–6, *pc*). These sutures are lacking in the acalyptrate muscoids.

The terms used by McAlpine *et al.* (1981) for the various thoracic areas are for the most part different from the terms we use. Hence their terms for most of the thoracic bristles are a little different from ours. A comparison of these two terminologies is given in Table 32–2.

Size

In the keys and descriptions in this chapter, "medium-sized" means about the size of a house fly or a blue-bottle fly. "Small" means smaller, and "large" means larger than this size. "Very small" or "minute" means less than 3 mm in length, and "very large" means 25 mm or more.

Identification of Díptera

The identification of Díptera is based on a number of characters, but the nature of the wing venation and antennae will generally enable one to determine approximately where in the order a specimen belongs. Table 32–3 summarizes the principal characters of the venation and antennae in four groups in the order.

Some difficulty may be encountered with small or minute specimens, and a microscope with considerable magnification (90–120×) may be necessary for examining such specimens. Acalyptrate muscoids (which key out from couplet 74) in which the head or the thoracic bristles are broken off or embedded in glue (specimens on a point) may be difficult or impossible to run through the key.

Table 32–2
Comparison of Terminologies of Thoracic Areas

This Book		McAlpine *et al.* (1981)	
Symbol	Name of Area	Symbol	Name of Area
hc	humeral callus	pprn	postpronotum
npl	notopleuron	npl	notopleuron
pscl	postscutellum	sbsctl	subscutellum
pl_1	propleuron	prepm	proepimeron
pl_2	mesopleuron	anepst	anepisternum
pt	pteropleuron	anepm	anepimeron
stpl	sternopleuron	kepst	katepisternum
hypl	hypopleuron	mr	meron
epm_2	mesepimeron	ktg	katatergite

Table 32–3
Characters of the Suborders of Díptera[a]

Character	Nematócera	Tabanomórpha and Asilomórpha	Muscomórpha
Branches of Rs	1–4	Usually 3	2
Fork of R_{2+3}	Sometimes present	Absent	Absent
Fork of R_{4+5}	Usually absent	Usually present	Absent
Discal cell	Usually open	Usually closed	Usually closed
Number of posterior cells	2–5	3–5	3
Anal cell	Open	Usually long and closed near wing margin	Usually short and closed far from wing margin
Antennae	With 6 or more segments	3- or 4-segmented, usually stylate	3-segmented, aristate
Key couplet with which to start	3	30	45[b]

[a]Applies to most members of each of the four groups; exceptions may occur.

[b]For most families in this group; a few families will key out earlier in the key.

Key to the Families of Díptera

Families in the following key marked with an asterisk are relatively rare or are unlikely to be taken by a general collector. Keys to larvae are given by Hennig (1948–1952), Peterson (1951), and McAlpine *et al.* (1981).

1.	Wings present and well developed, longer than thorax **2**	
1'.	Wings greatly reduced, usually shorter than thorax, or absent **140***	
2(1).	Wings extremely narrow, pointed apically, with greatly reduced venation and no closed cells, with a very long fringe; antennal flagellum elongate, annulated basally, clubbed; eyes separated dorsally but contiguous ventrally; small aquatic flies, less than 2 mm in length, slender, pale, weakly sclerotized; found in rapid streams in Quebec, New Brunswick, Maine ....**Nymphomyíidae***	p. 536
2'.	Without the above combination of characters **3**	
3(2').	Antennae composed of 6 or more freely articulated segments (Figure 32–1A,B), in some males very long plumose (Figure 32–37B,D); Rs 1–4 branched, if 3-branched, it is nearly always R_{2+3} that is forked; palps usually with 3–5 segments (suborder Nematócera) **4**	
3'.	Antennae composed of 5 or fewer (usually 3) segments, third segment sometimes annulated (appearing divided into subsegments, but these are not as distinct as the three main antennal segments), often bearing a terminal or dorsal style or arista (Figure 32–1C–H), never long plumose; Rs 2- or 3-branched (rarely unbranched), if 3-branched it is nearly always R_{4+5} that is forked; palps with not more than 2 segments (suborder Brachýcera) **30**	
4(3).	Mesonotum with V-shaped suture; legs long and slender (Figure 32–25A) **5**	
4'.	Mesonotum without V-shaped suture; legs variable **8**	
5(4).	Ocelli present; V-shaped suture on mesonotum incompletely developed in middle; 3A short, half as long as 2A or shorter, and curved ....**Trichocéridae***	p. 540

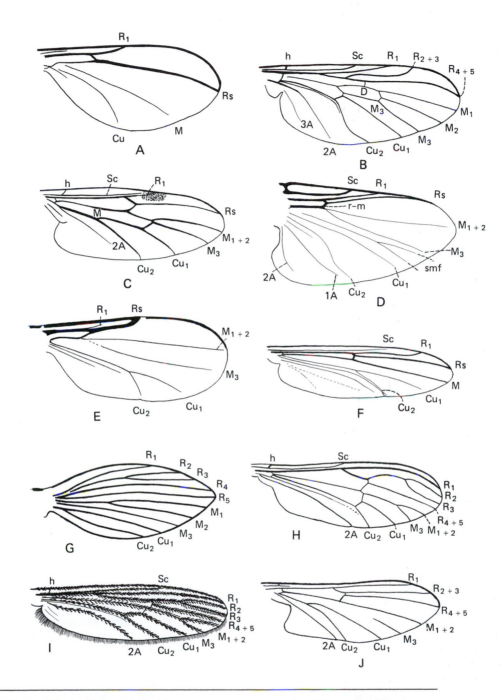

Figure 32–7. Wings of Nematócera. **A,** Cecidomyìidae; **B,** Anisopódidae (*Silvícola*); **C,** Bibiónidae (*Bíbio*); **D,** Simulìidae (*Simùlium*); **E,** Ceratopogónidae; **F,** Chironómidae; **G,** Psychòdidae (*Psychòda*); **H,** Díxidae (*Díxa*); **I,**Culícidae (*Psoróphora*); **J,** Blepharicéridae (*Blepharícera*). *D,* discal cell; *smf,* submedian fold.

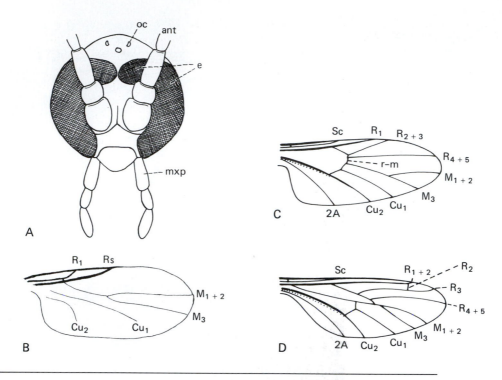

Figure 32–8.   **A,** head of *Scìara* (Sciáridae), anterodorsal view; **B,** wing of a scatopsid; **C,** wing of *Mycetòbia* (Anisopódidae); **D,** wing of *Axymỳia* (Axymyìidae). *ant,* antenna; *e,* compound eye; *mxp,* maxillary palp; *oc,* ocellus.

21′.	Basal cells variable; Rs simple or forked, if forked the fork is distad of r-m, or r-m is obliterated by the fusion of Rs and M; Sc and 2A variable; a large and widespread group ....**Mycetophilidae**[2]	p. 537
22(9′).	C ending at or near wing tip (Figure 32–7A–F) **23**	
22′.	C continuing around wing tip, though often weaker behind (Figure 32–7G–I) **25**	
23(22).	Wings broad, posterior veins weak (Figure 32–7D); antennae about as long as head; dark-colored flies, rarely over 3 mm in length, with a somewhat humpbacked appearance ....**Simuliidae**	p. 545
23′.	Wings narrower and posterior veins stronger (Figure 32–7E,F); antennae much longer than head; habitus usually not as above **24**	
24(23′).	M usually 2-branched (Figure 32–7E), M_3 rarely weak or absent; head rounded behind; metanotum rounded, without median furrow or keel; legs of moderate length, hind pair the longest; pulvilli absent; anterior thoracic spiracle nearly round; female mouthparts usually with mandibles and fitted for piercing ....**Ceratopogonidae**	p. 546
24′.	M unbranched (Figure 32–7F); head flattened behind; metanotum generally with median furrow or keel; legs long, front legs usually the longest; pulvilli present or absent; anterior thoracic spiracle distinctly oval; mouthparts without mandibles, not fitted for piercing ....**Chironomidae**	p. 546
25(22′).	First tarsal segment much shorter than second, tarsi sometimes appearing 4-segmented; small fragile midges with weakly veined wings, the wings usually with fewer than 7 longitudinal veins (Figure 32–7A) ....**Cecidomyiidae**	p. 538
25′.	First tarsal segment longer than second, tarsi clearly 5-segmented; other characters variable **26**	
26(25′).	Antennae short, about as long as head, two basal segments thick, globose; wings with 6–7 veins reaching wing margin ....**Thaumaleidae***	p. 545
26′.	Antennae at least twice as long as head, 2 basal segments not as above; wings with 9–11 veins reaching wing margin **27**	
27(26′).	Wings broad, pointed apically, usually densely hairy, and often held rooflike over body at rest; Rs usually 4-branched, M 3-branched (Figure 32–7G) ....**Psychodidae**	p. 540
27′.	Wings usually long and narrow, or if broad not pointed apically, and not densely hairy though there may be scales along the wing veins or wing margin; Rs with 3 or fewer branches, M 2-branched (Figure 32–7H,I) **28**	
28(27′).	Proboscis long, extending far beyond clypeus (Figure 32–37); scales present on wing veins and wing margin, usually also on body ....**Culicidae**	p. 541
28′.	Proboscis short, barely extending beyond clypeus; no scales on wing veins or body **29**	
29(28′).	R_{2+3} somewhat arched at base (Figure 32–7H); wing veins with short inconspicuous hairs; antennae with short sparse hairs ....**Dixidae**	p. 541
29′.	R_{2+3} nearly straight at base; wing veins with long, dense, conspicuous hairs; antennae with abundant long hairs in distinct whorls ....**Chaoboridae**	p. 541

---

[2]*Hesperodes johnsoni* Coquillett, reported from Massachusetts and New Jersey, lacks ocelli. It is 12 mm in length, is a member of the subfamily Keroplatinae, and has a wing venation similar to that shown in Figure 32–30B).

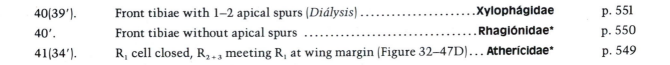

40(39′).   Front tibiae with 1–2 apical spurs (*Diálysis*) ....**Xylophágidae**   p. 551

40′.   Front tibiae without apical spurs ....**Rhagiónidae***   p. 550

41(34′). R_1 cell closed, R_{2+3} meeting R_1 at wing margin (Figure 32–47D)... **Atherícidae***   p. 549

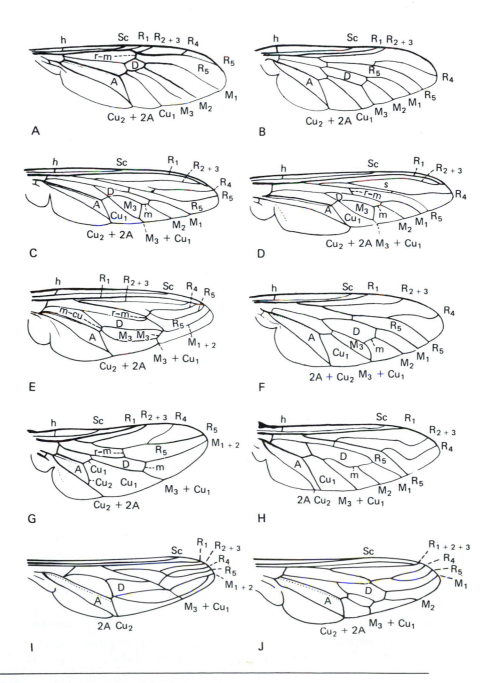

Figure 32–9.   Wings of Brachýcera. **A**, Stratiomỳidae; **B**, Rhagiónidae; **C**, Asìlidae (*Effèria*); **D**, Asìlidae (*Prómachus*); **E**, Mỳdidae (*Mỳdas*); **F**, Therévidae; **G**, Scenopínidae; **H**, Bombylìidae; **I**, Nemestrínidae (*Neorhynchocéphalus*); **J**, Apiocéridae (*Apiócera*). *A*, anal cell; *D*, discal (first M_2) cell.

41'. R_1 cell open, R_{2+3} meeting C well beyond end of R_1 ....**42**

42(41').   Wings narrowed basally, without an alula; scutellum bare; slender flies, about 5 mm in length; western United States ....**Vermileónidae***   p. 552

42'.   Wings not so narrow basally, alula nearly always present; scutellum hairy; size variable, but mostly over 5 mm in length; widely distributed ...**Rhagiónidae**   p. 550

43(30').   Coxae widely separated (Figure 32–15A); body somewhat flattened; ectoparasites of birds or mammals **44***

43'.   Coxae close together (ventral view); body usually not particularly flattened; not ectoparasitic **45**

44(43).   Compound eyes large, horizontally oval, at least three-fourths as high as head; palps slender and elongate, forming a sheath for proboscis; anterior veins strong and crowded forward, posterior veins weak (Figure 32–20G) or absent; ectoparasites of birds and mammals other than bats ....**Hippobóscidae***   p. 573

44'.   Compound eyes small or absent, if present rounded and not more than half as high as head; palps broader than long, projecting leaflike in front of head; wings uniformly veined; ectoparasites of bats ....**Stréblidae***   p. 573

45(43').   Wings with branches of R strongly thickened and crowded into anterior base of wing, 3–4 weak veins behind R, with no cross veins beyond base of wing (Figure 32–10G); hind legs long, femora flattened laterally; small, humpbacked flies, 1–4 mm in length (Figure 32–59) ....**Phòridae**   p. 557

45'.   Without the above combination of characters **46**

46(45').   Wings pointed at apex, with no cross veins except at base (Figure 32–10H); third antennal segment rounded, with terminal arista; small, slender, brownish or yellow flies, 2–5 mm in length ....**Lonchoptéridae**   p. 556

46'.   Wings rounded at apex, almost always with cross veins beyond base of wing; antennae, size, shape, and color variable **47**

47(46').   Rs 3-branched **48**

47'.   Rs 2-branched or unbranched **55**

48(47).   The branches of Rs and M_1 (or M_{1+2}) ending before wing tip (Figure 32–9E); large asilidlike flies **49**

48'. M_1 (or M_{1+2}) ending behind wing tip; size and form variable **50**

49(48).   With 1 ocellus or none; antennae long, appearing 4-segmented, clubbed (Figures 32–52); widely distributed ....**Mỳdidae**   p. 552

49'.   With 3 ocelli; antennae shorter, about as long as head, appearing 3-segmented, third segment tapering, not clubbed; occuring in arid regions of the West ....**Apiocéridae***   p. 553

50(48').   Vertex sunken, top of head concave between compound eyes (Figure 32–53D), eyes never holoptic ....**Asìlidae**   p. 553

50'.   Vertex not sunken, the eyes often holoptic in males **51**

51(50').   With 5 posterior cells, m-cu present, M_3 and Cu_1 separate or fused at base only (Figure 32–9F) ....**Therévidae**   p. 551

51'.   With 4 or fewer posterior cells, if with 5 (some *Caenòtus*, family Bombylìidae, Figure 32–50C) then bases of M_3 and Cu_1 fused and m-cu absent **52**

52(51'). M_{1+2} ending at or in front of wing tip (Figure 32–9G) or fused distally with R_{4+5}; 3 posterior cells ....**Scenopínidae**   p. 552

52'. M_1 (or M_{1+2}) ending behind wing tip; 3 or 4 posterior cells (Figure 32–9H, 32–10A) **53**

53(52').   Anal cell open (Figure 32–9H), or closed near wing margin and apex acute; body often hairy and robust **54**

53'.   Anal cell closed far from wing margin (Figure 32–10A) or absent, or if closed near wing margin apex is not acute; body rarely hairy, usually not robust ....**Empídidae**   p. 555

54(53).   Discal cell present, or if absent then R_{4+5} and M_{1+2} are similarly forked; wings hyaline or patterned; usually over 5 mm in length ....**Bombyliidae**   p. 555

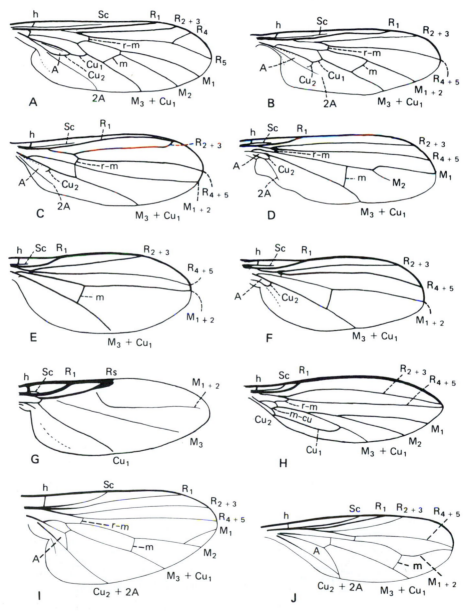

Figure 32–10.   Wings of Brachýcera. **A–C,** Empídidae; **D–F,** Dolichopódidae; **G,** Phòridae; **H,** Lonchoptéridae, female; **I,** Platypèzidae; **J,** Pipuncùlidae. *A,* anal (1A) cell.

54′.   Discal cell absent; R_{4+5} and M_{1+2} similarly forked, each fork shorter than its stem; wings hyaline to pale brown; small flies, usually less than 5 mm in length ....**Hilarimórphidae***   p. 555

55(47′).   Second antennal segment longer than third, third segment with a dorsal arista (*Sépedon*) ....**Sciomỳzidae**   p. 564

55′.   Second antennal segment not or scarcely longer than third, arista variable ...**56**

56(55′).   Hind tarsi, at least in male, nearly always with 1 or more segments expanded or flattened; wings relatively broad basally, anal angle well developed; anal cell closed some distance from wing margin, pointed apically (Figure 32–10I); M_{1+2} often forked apically; no frontal suture; arista terminal; small, usually black flies, less than 10 mm in length ....**Platypèzidae***   p. 556

56′.   Without the above combination of characters **57**

57(56′).   Anal cell elongate, longer than second basal cell, usually pointed apically, and narrowed or closed near wing margin (Figures 32–10J, 32–11); no frontal suture; head bristles usually lacking **58**

57′.   Anal cell usually shorter, closed some distance from wing margin or lacking; if anal cell is elongate and pointed apically (Figure 32–19C), then a frontal suture is present and head bristles are usually present **62**

58(57).   Proboscis usually very long and slender, often twice as long as head or longer, often folding; face broad, with grooves below antennae; abdomen clavate, bent downward at apex (Figure 32–63); R_5 cell closed, pointed apically (Figure 32–11D) ....**Conópidae**   p. 559

58′.   Proboscis short; face narrow, without grooves below antennae; abdomen and R_5 cell variable **59**

59(58′). R_5 cell closed; usually a spurious vein crossing r-m between R_{4+5} and M_{1+2} (Figure 32–11A–C) ....**Sýrphidae**   p. 557

59′. R_5 cell open, though sometimes narrowed apically; no spurious vein **60**

60(59′).   Head very large, hemispherical, face very narrow (Figures 32–12B, 32–62); proboscis small and soft...**Pipuncùlidae**   p. 557

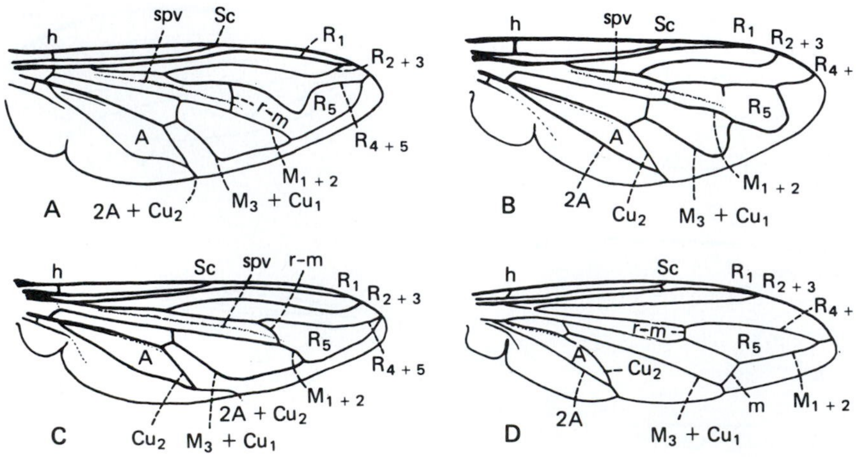

Figure 32–11.   Wings of Sýrphidae (**A–C**) and Conópidae (**D**). **A**, *Erístalis*; **B**, *Mìcrodon*; **C**, *Spilomỳia*; **D**, *Physocéphala*. *A*, anal (1A) cell; *spv*, spurious vein.

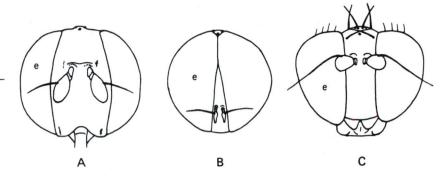

Figure 32–12. Heads of Díptera, anterior view. **A,** Sýrphidae (*Metasýrphus*); **B,** Pipunculidae (*Pipúnculus*); **C,** Dolichopódidae (*Dolíchopus*). *e,* compound eye.

60'.	Head not unusually large, face normal; proboscis slender and rigid **61**	
61(60').	R_{2+3} usually very short and ending in R_1, rarely lacking or ending in C beyond end of R_1; minute flies, 1.2–4.0 mm in length, rather stocky in build, with a humpbacked appearance, usually brownish or grayish in color; mostly western United States (Cyrtosiinae and Mythicomyiinae) ....**Bombyliidae**	p. 555
61'.	R_{2+3} ending in C well beyond end of R_1; relatively slender flies, usually black in color, size variable (Hybotìnae) ....**Empididae**	p. 555
62(57').	Frontal suture absent (Figure 32–12) **63**	
62'.	Frontal suture present (Figures 32–5A, 32–21, 32–24) (Schizóphora: muscoid flies) **65**	
63(62).	Head very large, hemispherical, face very narrow (Figures 32–12B, 32–62) (*Chálarus*) ....**Pipunculidae**	p. 557
63'.	Head not unusually large; face variable **64**	
64(63').	The r-m cross vein located in basal fourth of wing, or absent; fork of Rs usually swollen (Figure 32–10D–F); male genitalia often folded forward under abdomen (Figure 32–58); body usually metallic ....**Dolichopódidae**	p. 556
64'.	The r-m cross vein located beyond basal fourth of wing, fork of Rs usually not swollen (Figure 32–10B,C); male genitalia terminal, not folded forward under abdomen (Figure 32–57); body not metallic ....**Empididae**	p. 555
65(62').	Mouth opening small, mouthparts vestigial (Figure 32–13A); body hairy but not bristly, insect beelike in appearance, 9–25 mm in length; R_5, sometimes also M_{1+2}, ending before wing tip (Figure 32–16E,F); bot and warble flies ....**Oéstridae***	p. 570
65'.	Mouth opening normal, mouthparts present, functional; body usually with bristles; size, R_5, M_{1+2} variable **66**	
66(65').	Second antennal segment with a longitudinal suture on outer side (Figure 32–14A); thorax usually with a complete transverse suture (Figure 32–14C); lower (innermost) calypter usually large (calyptrate muscoid flies, except *Loxócera*, family Psìlidae). **67**	
66'.	Second antennal segment without such a suture (Figure 32–14B); thorax usually without complete transverse suture (Figure 32–14D); lower calypter usually small or rudimentary (acalyptrate muscoid flies) **74**	
67(66).	Hypopleura and pteropleura with row of bristles (Figure 32–15B); R_5 cell narrowed or closed distally **68**	
67'.	Hypopleura usually without bristles; if hypopleural bristles are present then there are no pteropleural bristles, or proboscis is rigid and fitted for piercing, or R_5 cell is not narrowed distally **71**	

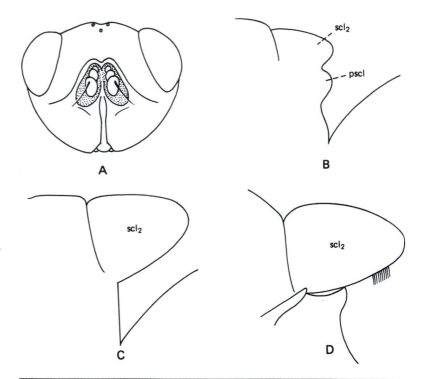

Figure 32–13. Characters of muscoid flies. **A,** head of a horse bot fly (*Gasteróphilus*), anterior view; **B–D,** posterior part of the thorax, lateral view: **B,** *Hypodérma* (Oestrìnae); **C,** a robust bot fly (Cuterebrìnae); **D,** an anthomyiid. *pscl,* postscutellum; *scl₂,* mesoscutellum.

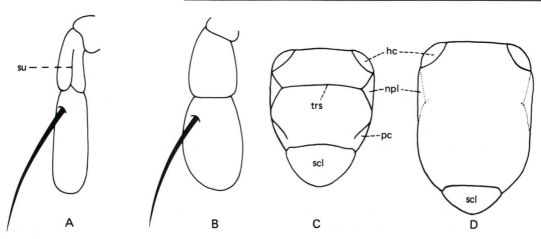

Figure 32–14. Antennae (**A, B**) and mesonota (**C, D**) of muscoid flies. **A,** calyptrate, showing suture (*su*) on second segment; **B,** acalyptrate, which lacks a suture on the second segment; **C,** calyptrate; **D,** acalyptrate. *hc,* humeral callus; *npl,* notopleuron; *pc,* postalar callus; *scl,* scutellum; *su,* suture; *trs,* transverse suture.

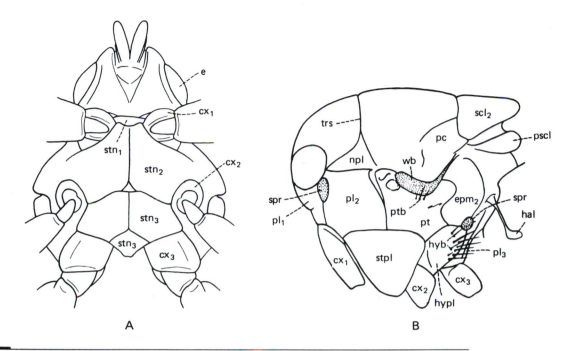

Figure 32–15. Thorax structure in muscoids. **A,** thorax of a hippoboscid (*Lýnchia*), ventral view; **B,** thorax of a tachinid (*Ptilodéxia*), lateral view. *cx,* coxa; *e,* compound eye; *epm₂,* mesepimeron; *hal,* haltere; *hc,* humeral callus; *hyb,* hypopleural bristles; *hypl,* hypopleuron; *npl,* notopleuron; *pc,* postalar callus; *pl₁,* propleuron; *pl₂,* mesopleuron; *pl₃,* metapleuron; *pscl,* postscutellum; *pt,* pteropleuron; *ptb,* pteropleural bristles; *scl₂,* mesoscutellum; *spr,* spiracle; *stn₁,* prosternum; *stn₂,* mesosternum; *stn₃,* metasternum; *stpl,* sternopleuron; *trs,* transverse suture; *wb,* base of wing. Only the hypopleural and pteropleural bristles are shown in **B.**

69(68′).	Postscutellum weakly developed; calypters narrow, their inner margins bending away from scutellum; M_{1+2} bending forward apically and meeting R_{4+5}, R_5 cell closed ....**Rhinophòridae**	p. 571
69′.	Postscutellum not at all developed; calypters not as above; M_{1+2} bending forward distally, but R_5 cell narrowly open at wing margin (as in Figure 32–16A) **70**	
70(69′).	Usually 2 (rarely 3) notopleural bristles, hindmost posthumeral bristle located laterad of presutural bristle (Figure 32–17A); arista usually plumose beyond basal half; body often metallic, the thorax rarely or never with black stripes on a gray background ....**Calliphòridae**	p. 569
70′.	Usually 4 notopleural bristles, and hindmost posthumeral bristle located even with or mesad of presutural bristle (Figure 32–17B); arista generally plumose only in basal half; body not metallic, the thorax often with black stripes on a gray background ....**Sarcophágidae**	p. 569
71(67′).	Third antennal segment longer than arista (Figure 32–18); oral vibrissae absent; mesonotum without bristles except above wings (*Loxócera*)..**Psílidae**	p. 560
71′.	Third antennal segment not so lengthened; oral vibrissae present; mesonotum with bristles **72**	
72(71′).	Sixth vein ($Cu_2 + 2A$) usually reaching wing margin, at least as a fold (Figure 32–16C), or if not (some Scathophágidae) then lower calypter linear and R_5 cell not narrowed apically **73**	

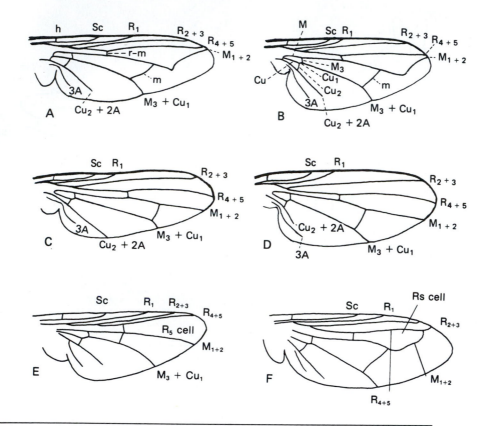

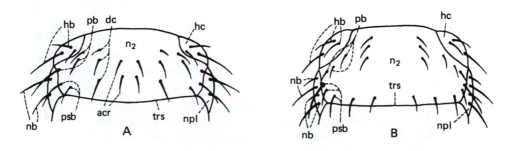

Figure 32–16. Wings of calyptrate muscoid flies. **A,** Tachínidae; **B,** Múscidae (*Músca*); **C,** Scathophágidae; **D,** Múscidae (*Fánnia*); **E,** *Gasteróphilus* (Oèstridae, Gasterophilìnae); **F,** *Oèstrus* (Oèstridae, Oestrìnae).

Figure 32–17. Anterior part of mesonotum of **A,** a blow fly (*Callíphora*), and **B,** a flesh fly (*Sarcóphaga*). *acr,* acrostichal bristles; *dc,* dorsocentral bristles; *hb,* humeral bristles; *hc,* humeral callus; *n₂,* mesonotum; *nb,* notopleural bristles; *npl,* notopleuron; *pb,* posthumeral bristles; *psb,* presutural bristles; *trs,* transverse suture.

Figure 32–18. Head of *Loxócera* (Psìlidae), lateral view.

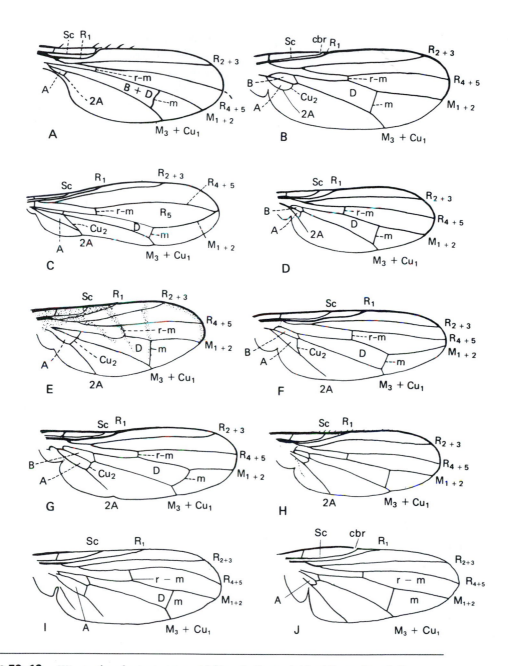

Figure 32–19.   Wings of acalyptrate muscoid flies. **A,** Curtonòtidae (*Curtonòtum*); **B,** Piophílidae (*Pióphila*); **C,** Micropèzidae (*Taeniáptera*); **D,** Lauxanìidae (*Physegénua*); **E,** Platystomátidae (*Rivéllia*); **F,** Otítidae (*Acrostícta*); **G,** Sciomỳzidae (*Sépedon*); **H,** Heleomỳzidae (*Amoebalèria*); **I,** Dryomỳzidae (*Neurostèna*); **J,** Lonchaèidae (*Lonchaèa*). *A,* anal cell; *B,* second basal cell; *cbr,* costal break; *D,* discal (first M₂) cell.

72′. Sixth vein never reaching wing margin, even as a fold (Figure 32–16B,D); R_5 cell variable, but often narrowed apically (Figure 32–16B) ....**Múscidae** p. 568

73(72). Scutellum with fine erect hairs on ventral surface (Figure 32–13D), or if such hairs absent (Fucelliìnae) then cruciate frontal bristles present; usually 2–4 sternopleural bristles ....**Anthomyìidae** p. 567

73′. Scutellum without fine hairs on ventral surface; cruciate frontal bristles absent; usually only 1 sternopleural bristle ....**Scathophágidae** p. 567

74(66′). Proboscis very long and slender, often two or more times as long as head, elbowed; second antennal segment longer than first; abdomen often clavate (Figure 32–63); anal cell usually long and pointed, longer than second basal cell (except in *Dalmánnia* and *Stylogáster*; in *Stylogáster* the ovipositor is slender and as long as rest of body) ....**Conópidae** p. 559

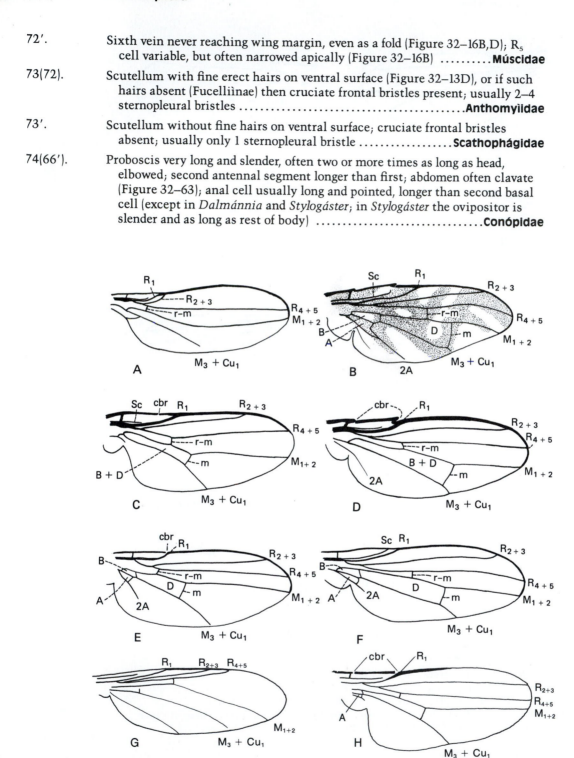

Figure 32–20. Wings of acalyptrate muscoid flies. **A,** Asteìidae (*Astèia*) (redrawn from Curran); **B,** Tephrítidae; **C,** Chlorópidae (*Epichlòrops*); **D,** Ephýdridae (*Éphydra*); **E,** Agromỳzidae (*Agromỳza*); **F,** Chamaemyìidae (*Chamaemyìa*); **G,** Hippobóscidae (*Lýnchia*); **H,** Milichìidae. *A,* anal cell; *B,* second basal cell; *cbr,* costal break; *D,* discal (first M_2) cell.

74'. Proboscis usually short and stout, rarely longer than head; second antennal segment usually shorter than first (if longer, then anal cell is shorter than second basal cell); anal cell usually very short, or absent **75**

75(74'). Sc complete or nearly so, ending in C or just short of it, and free from R_1 distally (Figures 32–19, 32–20F); anal cell present **76**

75'. Sc incomplete, not reaching C, often fusing with R_1 distally (Figure 32–20A,B); anal cell present or absent **108**

76(75). Ocelli present; size variable; wings with or without coloring **77**

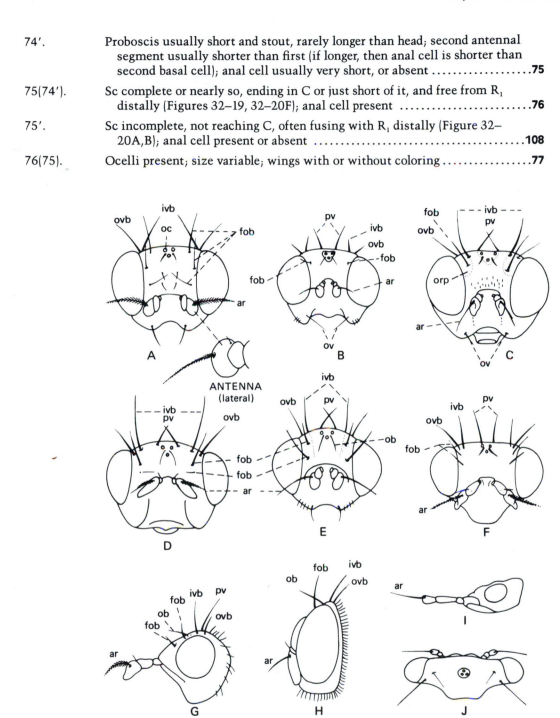

Figure 32–21. Heads of acalyptrate muscoid flies. **A–F,** anterior view; **G–I,** lateral view; **J,** dorsal view. **A,** Clusìidae (*Clùsia*); **B,** Piophílidae (*Pióphila*); **C,** Heleomỳzidae (*Heleomỳza*); **D,** Lauxaniidae (*Camptoprosopélla*); **E,** Chamaemyìidae (*Chamaemỳia*); **F, G,** Sciomỳzidae (*Tetanócera*); **H,** Lonchaèidae (*Lonchaèa*); **I,** Nerìidae (*Odontoloxòzus*); **J,** Diópsidae (*Sphyracéphala*). *ar,* arista; *fob,* fronto-orbital bristles; *ivb,* inner vertical bristles; *ob,* ocellar bristles; *oc,* ocellus; *orp,* orbital plate; *ov,* oral vibrissae; *ovb,* outer vertical bristles; *pv,* postvertical bristles.

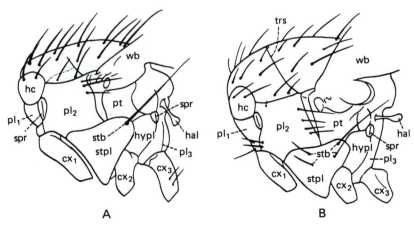

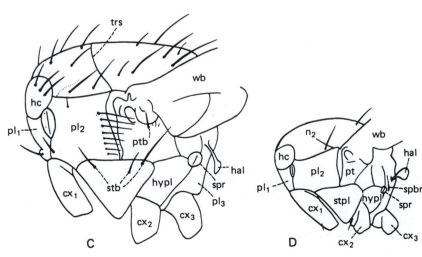

Figure 32–22. Thorax of muscoid flies, lateral view. **A,** Scathophágidae (*Scathóphaga*); **B,** Anthomyìidae (*Anthomỳia*); **C,** Múscidae (*Músca*); **D,** Sépsidae (*Themìra*). *cx*, coxa; *hal*, haltere; *hc*, humeral callus; *hypl*, hypopleuron; *n₂*, mesonotum; *pl₁*, propleuron; *pl₂*, mesopleuron; *pl₃*, metapleuron; *pt*, pteropleuron; *ptb*, pteropleural bristles; *spbr*, spiracular bristle; *spr*, spiracle; *stb*, sternopleural bristles; *stpl*, sternopleuron; *trs*, transverse suture; *wb*, base of wing.

80'.   Eyes not prominently bulging and vertex not sunken; femora, size, color variable, but usually not as above; widely distributed **82**

81(80). A series of cross veins between C and R_{2+3}; R_1 ending close to Sc; R_5 cell not narrowed distally; Arizona and New Mexico ....**Rhinotóridae***   p. 565

81'.   No cross veins between C and R_{2+3}; R_1 ending far beyond Sc; R_5 cell not narrowed distally; Florida ....**Ropaloméridae***   p. 564

82(80'). Oral vibrissae present (Figure 32–21A,C, *ov*) **83**

82'.   Oral vibrissae absent (Figure 32–21F–I) **91**

83(82). Costa spinose (Figure 32–19A,H) **84**

83'.   Costa not spinose **87**

84(83). Second basal and discal cells confluent (Figure 32–19A, *B + D*); arista plumose ....**Curtonòtidae***   p. 566

84'.   Second basal and discal cells separated (Figure 32–19B, *B* and *D*); arista usually not plumose **85**

85(84'). Postverticals diverging; anal vein (2A) reaching wing margin; 4 or 5 sterno-pleurals; 2 pairs of fronto-orbitals; ocellar triangle large (*Actenóptera*) ....**Piophílidae***   p. 561

85'.   Postverticals converging; other characters usually not as above **86**

86(85'). Orbital plates long, reaching nearly to level of antennae; ocellar bristles laterad of median ocellus; 2 or 3 pairs of fronto-orbitals; 2A never reaching wing margin ....**Trixoscelídidae***   p. 565

86'.   Orbital plates short, not reaching level of antennae (Figure 32–21C); ocellar bristles between median and lateral ocelli (Figure 32–21C); 1–2 pairs of fronto-orbitals; 2A variable, sometimes (Figure 32–19H) reaching wing margin ....**Heleomỳzidae**   p. 565

87(83'). Second basal and discal cells confluent (as in Figure 32–19A, *B + D*); postverticals lacking ....**Aulacigástridae***   p. 563

87'.   Second basal and discal cells separated (Figure 32–19B, *B* and *D*); postverticals present **88**

88(87'). Two to 4 pairs of fronto-orbitals (Figure 32–21A); second antennal segment usually with angular projection on outer side (Figure 32–21A); arista subapical; color variable ....**Clusiidae**   p. 561

88'.   At most 2 pairs of fronto-orbitals (Figure 32–21B); second antennal segment without angular projection on outer side; arista subbasal (Figure 32–21B); usually shining black or metallic bluish **89**

89(88'). Postverticals diverging (Figure 32–21B); 2A not reaching wing margin (Figure 32–19B) ....**Piophílidae**   p. 561

89'.   Postverticals converging; 2A variable **90***

90(89'). 2A reaching wing margin; 1 pair of fronto-orbitals (*Borborópsis* and *Oldenber-giélla*, western Canada and Alaska) ....**Heleomỳzidae***   p. 565

90'.   2A not reaching wing margin; 2 pairs of fronto-orbitals; widely distributed ....**Chyromỳidae***   p. 565

91(82'). Sc apically bent forward at almost a 90° angle and usually ending before reaching C (Figure 32–20B); C broken near end of Sc; wings usually patterned (Figures 32–66A, 32–67) ....**Tephrítidae**   p. 560

91'.   Sc apically bent toward C at a less abrupt angle and usually reaching C (Figure 32–19F); C not broken near end of Sc; wings variable **92**

92(91′).   C broken only near humeral cross vein; postverticals widely separated and diverging ....**Acartophthálmidae***   p. 562

92′.   C entire, broken only near end of Sc, or broken both near humeral cross vein and end of Sc; postverticals variable **93**

93(92′).   R₅ cell closed or much narrowed apically (Figure 32–19C); slender flies, the legs usually long and slender...**94**

93′.   R₅ cell open, usually not narrowed apically; body shape and legs variable, but usually not as above **96**

94(93,115).   Arista apical (Figure 32–21I), southwestern United States ....**Nerïidae***   p. 560

94′.   Arista dorsal; widely distributed...**95**

95(94′).   Head in profile higher than long, eyes large, distinctly higher than long; anal cell rounded apically; no sternopleural bristles ....**Tanypèzidae***   p. 560

95′.   Head in profile as long as or longer than high, eyes smaller, not much higher than long; anal cell square or pointed apically; 1 sternopleural bristle or none ....**Micropèzidae**   p. 560

96(93′).   Some or all tibiae with 1 or more preapical dorsal bristles (Figure 32–23B); C entire (Figure 32–19D,G,I); body usually light-colored, at least in part **97**

96′.   Tibiae usually without preapical dorsal bristles; if such bristles are present then either ovipositor is long and sclerotized, or R₁ is setulose above, or the vein forming end of the anal cell is bent (Figure 32–19F); C entire or broken near end of Sc; color variable...**99**

97(96).   Postverticals converging (Figure 32–21D); 2A short, not reaching wing margin (Figure 32–19D); small flies, rarely over 6 mm in length ....**Lauxanïidae**   p. 565

97′.   Postverticals parallel, diverging, or absent; 2A reaching wing margin, at least as a fold; size variable **98**

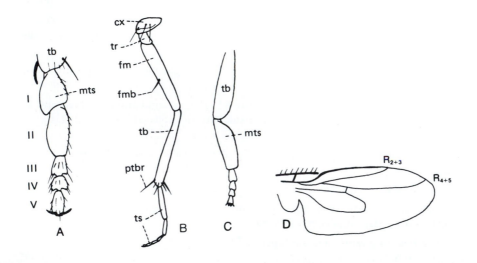

Figure 32–23.   **A,** hind tarsus of *Copromỳza* (Sphaerocéridae); **B,** middle leg of *Tetanócera* (Sciomỳzidae); **C,** hind leg of *Agathomỳia* (Platypèzidae); **D,** wing of *Leptócera* (Sphaerocéridae). *cx,* coxa; *fm,* femur; *fmb,* femoral bristle; *mts,* first tarsal segment; *ptbr,* preapical tibial bristles; *tb,* tibia; *tr,* trochanter; *ts,* tarsus; *I–V,* tarsal segments.

98(97′).   Femora with bristles, and a characteristic bristle usually present near middle
           of anterior face of middle femur (Figure 32–23B); R₁ ending at middle of wing
           (Figure 32–19G); antennae usually projecting forward and face generally
           produced (Figure 32–21G) . . . .**Sciomyzidae***   p. 564

98′.   Femoral bristles not developed; R₁ ending beyond middle of wing (Figure
           32–19I); antennae usually not projecting forward . . . .**Dryomyzidae***   p. 564

99(96′).   Cu₂ bent distad in middle, anal cell with acute distal projection posteriorly
           (Figures 32–19F, 32–20B); wings usually patterned . . . .**Otitidae**   p. 560

99′.   Cu₂ straight or curved basad, anal cell without acute distal projection posteri-
           orly (Figure 32–19E); wing color variable **100**

100(99′). Costa broken near end of Sc **101**

100′.   Costa not broken near end of Sc (Figures 32–19E,F, 32–20F) **105**

101(100). Second abdominal segment usually with lateral bristles; femora often
           thickened and spinose; wings usually patterned . . . .**Richardiidae***   p. 561

101′.   Second abdominal segment without lateral bristles; femora not thickened. .**102**

102(101′). With 1 to several upcurved bristles below compound eye; 3–5 pairs of
           lateroclinate fronto-orbitals; postverticals diverging; seashore species
           . . . .**Canácidae***   p. 567

102′.   Without upcurved bristles below compound eye; fewer than 3 (usually 1) pair
           of lateroclinate fronto-orbitals; postverticals parallel or diverging; widely
           distributed **103**

103(102′). Head hemispherical in profile, eyes large, oval or semicircular (Figure 32–21H);
           third antennal segment elongate (Figure 32–21H); postverticals diverging;
           2A usually sinuate; small, shining blackish flies with broad flat abdomen;
           female with lancelike ovipositor . . . .**Lonchaeidae**   p. 560

103′.   Head more or less rounded in profile, eyes smaller, rounded or slightly oval;
           postverticals parallel or slightly divergent; 2A not sinuate; pale-colored flies,
           or with yellow or reddish markings **104***

104(103′). Costa spinose (as in Figure 32–19A); eyes oval; Arizona and California
           (*Omomyia*) . . . .**Richardiidae***   p. 561

104′.   Costa not spinose; eyes round; northern United States and
           Canada . . . .**Pallopteridae***   p. 561

105(100′). Postverticals converging (Figure 32–21E) or absent; R₁ bare above; small flies,
           usually gray in color . . . .**Chamaemyiidae**   p. 565

105′.   Postverticals diverging or absent; R₁ bare or setulose above; small to medium-
           sized flies, usually dark and shining **106**

106(105′). Eyes horizontally oval, about twice as long as high; length 1.5–2.5 mm; grayish
           flies with yellowish markings on sides of thorax and abdomen, and on front;
           recorded from New Mexico, Oregon, New Brunswick, and Newfoundland
           (*Cremifània*) . . . .**Chamaemyiidae***   p. 565

106′.   Without the above combination of characters **107**

107(106′). Anal cell relatively long, its anterior side more than one-fourth as long as
           posterior side of discal cell (Figure 32–19E); sternopleural bristles lacking;
           R₁ setulose above . . . .**Platystomátidae**   p. 560

107′.   Anterior side of anal cell less than one-fourth as long as posterior side of discal
           cell; sternopleural bristles usually present; R₁ bare or setulose above
           . . . .**Otitidae**   p. 560

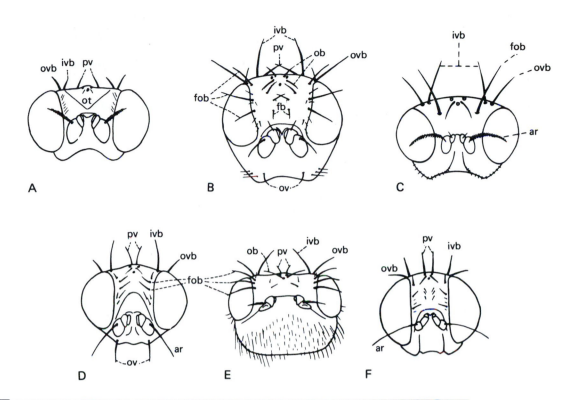

Figure 32–24.   Heads of acalyptrate muscoid flies, anterior view. **A,** Chlorópidae (*Diplotòxa*); **B,** Tethínidae (*Tethìna*); **C,** Opomỳzidae (*Opomỳza*); **D,** Agromỳzidae (*Agromỳza*); **E,** Ephýdridae (*Éphydra*); **F,** Milichìidae (*Milíchia*). *ar*, arista; *fb*, frontal bristles; *fob*, fronto-orbital bristles; *ivb*, inner vertical bristles; *ob*, ocellar bristles; *ot*, ocellar triangle; *ov*, oral vibrissae; *ovb*, outer vertical bristles; *pv*, postvertical bristles.

121(120).	Ocellar triangle large (as in Figure 32–24A); 3–5 pairs of lateroclinate fronto-orbitals; postverticals diverging; flies occurring along the seashore ....**Canácidae***	p. 567
121'.	Ocellar triangle small; other characters variable **122**	
122(121').	Wings strongly narrowed at base, anal angle not distinct (*Geomỳza*) ....**Opomỳzidae***	p. 563
122'.	Wings not so narrow at base, and with distinct anal angle **123**	
123(122').	Postverticals diverging...**124**	
123'.	Postverticals converging or absent **125**	
124(123).	Wings patterned; preapical tibial bristles usually present; 2 reclinate and 1 inclinate pairs of fronto-orbitals ....**Odiníidae***	p. 562
124'.	Wings hyaline, not patterned; preapical tibial bristles absent; fronto-orbitals usually not as above ....**Agromỳzidae**	p. 562
125(123').	All fronto-orbitals directed outward (Figure 32–24B) ....**Tethínidae***	p. 567
125'.	Some or all fronto-orbitals reclinate, none directed outward **126**	
126(125').	Mesopleura bare ....**Anthomỳzidae³**	p. 563

³The Cypselosomátidae will key out here if one cannot see the costal break near the humeral cross vein; see the account of the Cypselosomátidae, p. 559.

126'.   Mesopleura setulose . . . .**Chyromyidae***   p. 565

127(120').   Sternopleural bristles present; sometimes with spur in apical section of M$_{1+2}$ extending into second posterior cell . . . .**Opomyzidae***   p. 563

127'.   Sternopleural bristle absent; M$_{1+2}$ without spur in apical section **128**

128(127').   Mesopleura with large bristle in addition to fine hairs; usually 2 notopleural bristles . . . .**Strongylophthalmyiidae***   p. 560

128'   Mesopleura without large bristle, with fine hairs only; 1 notopleural bristle . . . .**Psilidae**   p. 560

129(117').   Anal cell present; postverticals usually well developed and converging; oral vibrissae usually present **130**

129'.   Anal cell absent; postverticals and oral vibrissae variable **138**

130(129).   Ocellar bristles present, well developed; frons never with bright orange band; arista variable **131**

130'.   Ocellar bristles absent or very weak; frons with bright orange band near anterior margin; arista plumose (*Aulacigáster*) . . . .**Aulacigástridae***   p. 563

131(130).   Middle tibiae with preapical dorsal bristle; face tuberculate; arista bare or pubescent, not plumose (*Cinderélla*) . . . .**Heleomyzidae***   p. 565

131'.   Middle tibiae usually without preapical dorsal bristle; face not tuberculate; arista variable, but often plumose **132**

132(131').   All fronto-orbitals similarly oriented; arista short-pubescent; postverticals slightly converging; Arizona and Utah . . . .**Cypselosomátidae***   p. 559

132'.   Fronto-orbitals not similarly directed; arista variable, but often plumose; postverticals variable; widely distributed **133**

133(132').   At least 1 pair of fronto-orbitals bent inward (Figure 32–24F); oral vibrissae sometimes weak **134**

133'.   No fronto-orbitals bent inward; oral vibrissae well developed **135**

134(133).   Genae broad, with a row of bristles in middle; proboscis short and stout . . . .**Cárnidae***   p. 564

134'.   Genae usually narrow, if broad then bristles confined to lower margin; proboscis variable, but often slender . . . .**Milichiidae**   p. 564

135(133').   Costa spinose (Figure 32–19A); arista long-plumose; proclinate fronto-orbital arising below reclinate one . . . .**Curtonòtidae***   p. 566

135'.   Costa usually not spinose, or if spinose (Diastátidae) bristles short, extending beyond middle of wing; fronto-orbitals variable. **136**

136(135').   Costa spinose, bristles short, extending nearly to wing tip; proclinate fronto-orbital arising above reclinate one; arista short-plumose . . . .**Diastátidae***   p. 566

136'.   Costa not spinose; proclinate fronto-orbital usually arising below reclinate one; arista long-plumose. **137**

137(136').   Sternopleural bristle present; body not metallic; anal cell well developed, closed apically; widely distributed, common flies . . . .**Drosophílidae**   p. 566

137'.   Sternopleural bristle absent; body metallic; anal cell poorly developed, open apically; Ontario . . . .**Camíllidae***   p. 566

138(129').   Face strongly convex, usually without oral vibrissae (Figure 32–24E); postverticals, if present, diverging . . . .**Ephýdridae**   p. 566

138'.   Face somewhat concave; oral vibrissae and postverticals variable **139***

139(138'). Arista plumose; tibiae with preapical dorsal bristle; body metallic; Ontario . . . .**Camíllidae***   p. 566

139'. Arista slightly pubescent, not plumose; middle tibiae without preapical dorsal bristle; widely distributed . . . .**Cárnidae***   p. 564

140(1'). Antennal flagellum elongate, annulated basally, and clubbed; eyes separated dorsally but contiguous ventrally; small aquatic flies, less than 2 mm in length, slender, pale, weakly sclerotized; found in rapid streams in Quebec, New Brunswick, and Maine . . . .**Nymphomyíidae***   p. 536

140'. Without the above combination of characters **141***

141(140'). Antennae with 6 or more freely articulated segments; palps usually with 3–5 segments (Nematócera) **142***

141'. Antennae consisting of 3 or fewer segments; palps not segmented (Brachýcera) **149***

142(141). Mesonotum with a V-shaped suture (as in Figure 32–25) . . . .**Tipùlidae***   p. 535

142'. Mesonotum without a V-shaped suture **143***

143(142'). Compound eye consisting of a single facet; ocelli absent; head and thorax small, well sclerotized, abdomen thick, weakly sclerotized, and indistinctly segmented; antennae thick, 8-segmented; length 3.4 mm; found in leaf litter in Virginia (*Baeonòtus*) . . . .**Cecidomyíidae***   p. 538

143'. Without the above combination of characters **144***

144(143'). At least 1 ocellus present **145***

144'. Ocelli absent (*Clùnio*, Florida; *Eretmóptera*, California) . . . .**Chironómidae***   p. 546

145(144). Tibiae with apical spurs **146***

145'. Tibiae without apical spurs **147***

146(145). Scutellum and halteres present; tarsal claws simple; wings present but only about half normal size; abdomen normal-sized (*Cobóldia*) . . . . . .**Scatópsidae***   p. 541

146'. Scutellum, halteres, and wings absent; tarsal claws variable; abdomen some-times greatly swollen . . . .**Cecidomyíidae***   p. 538

147(145'). Eyes meeting above bases of antennae (some females of *Bradỳsia* and *Epítapus*) . . . .**Sciáridae***   p. 538

147'. Eyes not meeting above bases of antennae **148***

148(147'). Palps 1-segmented; length about 2 mm (females of *Pnýxia*) . . . .**Sciáridae***   p. 538

148'. Palps with 3 or more segments; length at least 4 mm (females of *Baeoptero-gỳna*, Yukon Territory and Alaska; and some *Boletìna*, widely distributed) . . . .**Mycetophílidae***   p. 537

149(141'). Thorax very short, in dorsal view less than half as long as head, resembling abdominal segments; scutellum absent; parasitic on honey bee . . .**Braùlidae***   p. 564

149'. Thorax at least as long as head, differing from abdominal segments; scutellum present; habits variable, but not parasitic on honey bees **150***

150(149'). Coxae widely separated (Figure 32–15A); abdominal segmentation sometimes obscure; tarsal claws toothed; ectoparasites of bats, birds, or mammals **151***

150'. Coxae usually contiguous; abdominal segmentation distinct; tarsal claws sim-ple; usually not ectoparasitic, but sometimes (Cárnidae) associated with nestling birds **153***

151(150).   Head narrow and folding back into a groove on mesonotum; first tarsal segment very long, as long as rest of tarsus; spiderlike insects parasitic on bats ....**Nycteribíidae***   p. 573

151′.   Head broader and not folding back onto mesonotum; first tarsal segment short, about as long as second; ectoparasites of birds and mammals **152***

152(151′).   Compound eyes present, large, usually vertically oval, at least three-fourths as high as head; palps elongate, forming a sheath for proboscis; parasites of mammals other than bats, and birds ....**Hippobóscidae***   p. 573

152′.   Compound eyes present or absent, if present small and round, never more than half as high as head; palps broad and projecting leaflike on front of head; parasites of bats ....**Stréblidae***   p. 573

153(150′).   Frontal suture and frontal lunule present **154***

153′.   Frontal suture and frontal lunule absent **161***

154(153).   First segment of hind tarsi short and swollen, shorter than second segment (Figure 32–23A) ....**Sphaerocéridae***   p. 565

154′.   First segment of hind tarsi not swollen, longer than second segment **155***

155(154′).   Propleuron with a vertical ridge (some *Conioscinélla*) ....**Chlorópidae***   p. 566

155′.   Propleuron without a vertical ridge **156***

156(155′).   Face strongly convex (some females of *Hyadìna* and *Nastíma*) ......**Ephýdridae***   p. 566

156′.   Face concave **157***

157(156′).   Postverticals present; at least 2 pairs of fronto-orbitals **158***

157′.   Postverticals absent; only 1 pair of fronto-orbitals (some *Geomỳza*) ....**Opomỳzidae***   p. 563

158(157).   Postverticals parallel or nearly so; gena with a pair of strong bristles in middle; associated with birds (*Cárnus*) ....**Cárnidae***   p. 564

158′.   Postverticals converging; gena without a row of strong bristles in middle; not associated with birds **159***

159(158′).   Some or all tibiae with a preapical dorsal bristle; frons without strong fronto-orbitals on lower half **160***

159′.   Tibiae without preapical dorsal bristles; frons with 2 pairs of strong fronto-orbitals on lower half (some *Anthomỳza*) ....**Anthomỳzidae***   p. 563

160(159).   Arista plumose; frons with a pair of proclinate fronto-orbitals (mutant *Drosóphila*) ....**Drosophílidae***   p. 566

160′.   Arista bare or short-pubescent; no proclinate fronto-orbitals (some *Lutomỳia*) ....**Heleomỳzidae***   p. 565

161(153′).   Antennae apparently consisting of a single globular segment with a 3-segmented arista; hind femora laterally flattened (some females) ......**Phòridae***   p. 557

161′.   Antennae with obviously 2 or 3 segments; arista, if present, 2-segmented; hind femora not flattened **162***

162(161′).   Vertex convex; compound eyes bare; proboscis elongate and projecting (*Chersodròmia*) ....**Empídidae***   p. 555

162′.   Vertex excavated; compound eyes pubescent; proboscis short and retracted (females of some *Campsicnèmus*) ....**Dolichopódidae***   p. 556

SUBORDER **Nematócera**—Long-Horned Flies: This suborder contains a little less than one-third of the North American species of flies (nearly 5300), in 24 of the 108 families. Its members can be recognized by their many-segmented antennae, which are usually long. Most nematocerans are small, slender, and long-legged and are mosquito-like or midgelike in appearance. The wing venation varies from very complete (Tanydéridae) to greatly reduced (e.g., the Cecidomyìidae). This suborder contains the only Díptera that have the radius 5-branched. The larvae, except in the Cecidomyìidae, have a well-developed head, with the mandibles toothed or brushlike and moving laterally. Most of them live in water or in moist habitats. The pupae are obtect.

The group contains many flies of considerable economic importance. Many are bloodsucking and serious pests of man and animals (mosquitoes, punkies, black flies, and sand flies), and some of these serve as disease vectors. A few flies in this suborder (some Cecidomyìidae) are important pests of cultivated plants. The aquatic larvae of the Nematócera are an important item in the food of many freshwater fishes.

Family **Tanydéridae**—Primitive Crane Flies: This group is represented in North America by four species, of which one, *Protoplàsa fítchii* Osten Sacken, occurs in the East. The tanyderids are medium-sized insects with banded wings, and their larval stages

occur in wet sandy soil at the margins of large streams.

Family **Tipùlidae**—Crane Flies: This family is the largest in the order, with more than 1600 species occurring in North America. Many crane flies are common and locally abundant insects. They may be mistaken for large mosquitoes, but even those with elongate mouthparts are not able to bite. A few are smaller than the smallest mosquitoes. The legs are usually long and slender (Figure 32–25) and are easily broken off. The body is usually elongate and slender, and the wings are long and narrow. Some crane flies are quite large. *Holorùsia grándis* (Bergroth) of the western states, has a body length sometimes exceeding 35 mm and a wingspan of nearly 70 mm. Many species have clouded or patterned wings. Tipulids differ from Trichocéridae in lacking ocelli, from Tanydéridae in having four or fewer branches of the radius, and from Ptychoptéridae in having two anal veins (Figure 32–26).

Crane flies are found chiefly in damp habitats with abundant vegetation. There are, however, grassland species and even a few in deserts. Small, wingless, spiderlike species of *Chiònea* may be found on snow in winter. Larvae of many species are aquatic or semiaquatic. Others occur in the soil or in fungi, mosses, and decaying wood. Most eat decomposing plant matter, but certain aquatic groups are predaceous. Larvae of a few species feed on roots of young plants and if abundant may damage rangelands and seedling crops. Adult crane flies usually live only a few days, and probably most do not feed. However, some with long, slender mouthparts (e.g., subgenus *Geranomỳia* of the large genus *Limònia*) are known to take nectar from various flowers.

There are three subfamilies of Tipùlidae: the Tipulìnae, Cylindrotomìnae, and Limoniìnae. Most large crane flies belong to the Tipulìnae. These are characterized by having the terminal segment of the maxillary palps slender and longer than the penultimate segment, and the antennae are normally 13-segmented. In the Limoniìnae and Cylindrotomìnae the terminal segment of the maxillary palps is short, about like the others, and the antennae usually have 14 to 16 segments. The nine North American species of Cylindrotomìnae are not commonly collected. They may be recognized by the fusion of veins R_1 and R_{2+3} well before the wing tip (Figure 32–26C). Nearly all small crane flies (but a few large ones and many of medium size) belong to the Limoniìnae, in which veins R_1 and R_{2+3} are not fused (Figure 32–26D) and R_2 often has the form of a short cross vein between R_1 and R_3, or is absent.

Family **Blepharicéridae**—Net-Winged Midges: These insects are long-legged, mosquito-like or tipulid-like

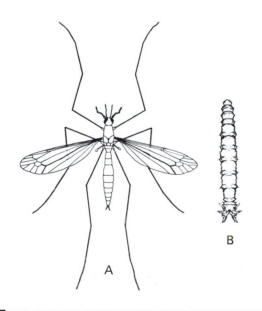

Figure 32–25. A crane fly (*Típula* sp., family Tipùlidae). **A,** adult; **B,** larva. (**B,** courtesy of Johannsen and the Cornell University Agricultural Experiment Station.)

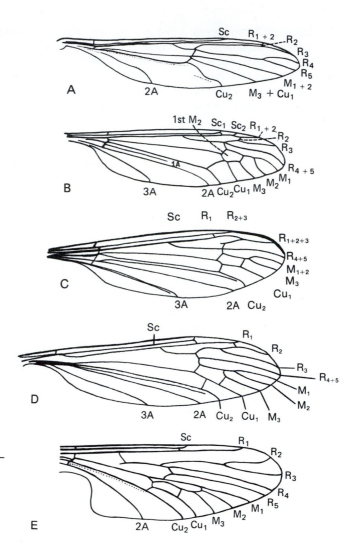

Figure 32–26.   Wings of crane flies. **A,** *Bittacomórpha* (Ptychoptéridae); **B,** *Típula* (Tipùlidae, Tipulìnae); **C,** Cylindrotomìnae (Tipùlidae); **D,** Limoniìnae (Tipùlidae); **E,** *Protoplàsa* (Tanydéridae).

insects, 3–13 mm in length. They differ from the Tipùlidae in lacking the V-shaped suture on the mesonotum. They sometimes have a network of fine lines between the wing veins; the anal angle of the wing is well developed; and the base of M_3 is lacking (Figure 32–7J). The adults are found near fast-flowing streams but are not common. The larvae live in swift water, clinging to rocks by means of a series of ventral suckers.

Family **Deuterophlebìidae**—Mountain Midges: These midges are peculiar in having broad fanlike wings, and the males have extremely long antennae (about four times as long as the body). Four species of *Deuterophlèbia* are known from the West (Colorado to California, north to Alberta), where the larvae occur in swift-flowing streams.

Family **Nymphomyìidae:**   Our only representative of this family is *Palaeodípteron wálkeri* Ide, which

has been collected in streams in Quebec, New Brunswick, and Maine. It is a pale, delicate insect, 1.5–2.5 mm in length. The wings are very narrow and pointed apically, with a much reduced venation and a very long fringe. Most of the specimens of this species that have been collected may have had the wings broken off, with only stubs left. The halteres are well developed, and the legs are long and slender. The compound eyes are separated dorsally and contiguous ventrally, and there is a single ocellus on each side of the head beneath the compound eye. The larvae occur among aquatic mosses on stones in small, rapidly flowing streams.

Family **Axymyìidae:**   This family includes two North American species, *Axymyìa furcàta* McAtee, which occurs in the East, and another species of *Axymyìa* that has been found in Oregon. These are medium-sized, stout-bodied flies, resembling some of the march flies (*Bíbio*) in appearance, with short antennae and a characteristic wing venation (Figure 32–8D). The larvae occur in cavities in moist rotting wood. These insects are relatively rare, and little is known of the habits of the adults.

Family **Pachyneúridae:** This group includes a single North American species, *Cramptonomỳia spénceri* Alexander, which occurs in the Northwest (Oregon, Washington, and British Columbia). This is a medium-sized, long-legged, slender, tipulid-like fly. The wings have a cross vein between the branches of Rs, a closed discal cell, and a dark spot near the end of R_1, and the antennae are slender and about as long as the head and thorax combined. This is a rare fly, and its immature stages are unknown. The larvae of other genera in the family occur in rotten wood.

Family **Bibiónidae**—March Flies: The march flies are small to medium-sized, usually dark-colored, hairy or bristly flies, with short antennae that arise low on the face (Figure 32–27). Many have a red or yellow thorax. The wings often have a dark spot near the end of R_1 (Figure 32–7C). The adults are most common in spring and early summer, and are sometimes abundant. The larvae live in decaying organic matter and among plant roots.

One member of this family, *Plècia neárctica* Hardy (Figure 32–27), which occurs in the Gulf States, sometimes (usually in May and September) occurs in enormous swarms. Cars driving through such swarms become spattered with these flies, which may clog radiator fans and cause the car to overheat, or spatter the windshield and obscure the driver's vision. If they are not soon cleaned off, they may damage the car's finish. Because pairs are often seen in copulo, these insects are commonly called "lovebugs." They are a particular problem in the northern part of penisular Florida and in other Gulf States.

Family **Mycetophílidae**—Fungus Gnats: The fungus gnats are slender, mosquito-like insects with elongated coxae and long legs (Figure 32–28). They are usually found in damp places where there is an abundance of decaying vegetation or fungi. The group is a large one, with more than 600 North American species, and many of its members are common insects. Most fungus gnats are about the size of mosquitoes, but a few are 13 mm or more in length. The larvae of most species live in fungi, moist soil, or decaying vegetation. Some species are pests in mushroom cellars. The larvae of the Keroplatìnae spin mucous webs. Some of these are fungus

Figure 32–27. A mating pair of "lovebugs," *Plècia neárctica* Hardy, a species of march fly. (Courtesy of Dwight Bennett.)

feeders, and others are predaceous. Some of the predaceous larvae, such as *Orfèlia fúltoni* (Fisher) (Figure 32–28), are luminescent (see page 84). Some adults of the Keroplatìnae, including some of our largest fungus gnats, feed on flowers.

Family **Sciáridae**—Dark-Winged Fungus Gnats, Root Gnats: These gnats are similar to the Mycetophílidae (Figure 32–29A), but have the eyes meeting above the bases of the antennae (Figure 32–8A) (except in *Pnýxia*), and the r-m cross vein is in line with and appears as a basal extension of Rs (Figure 32–30C,D). The sciarids are usually blackish insects and generally occur in moist shady places. The larvae of most species live in fungi, and some occasionally become pests in mushroom cellars. The larvae of a few species attack the roots of plants. One species, the potato scab gnat, *Pnýxia scàbiei* (Hopkins), attacks potatoes and serves as the vector of potato scab. The females of *P. scàbiei* have extremely short wings and no halteres. Sciarids are fairly common insects.

Family **Cecidomyiidae**—Gall Midges or Gall Gnats: The gall midges are small (mostly 1–5 mm in length), delicate flies with long legs and usually long antennae and with a reduced wing venation (Figures

Figure 32–28. A fungus gnat, *Orfèlia fúltoni* (Fisher), 8×. (Courtesy of Fulton and the Entomological Society of America.)

32–7A, 32–29B, 32–31). The group is a large one, with some 1200 North American species, about two-thirds of which are gall makers. Larvae of the others feed on plants (without producing galls) or live in decaying vegetation or wood, or in fungi. A few are predaceous on other small insects.

The larvae of gall midges are tiny maggots, with the head small and poorly developed and the mouth-

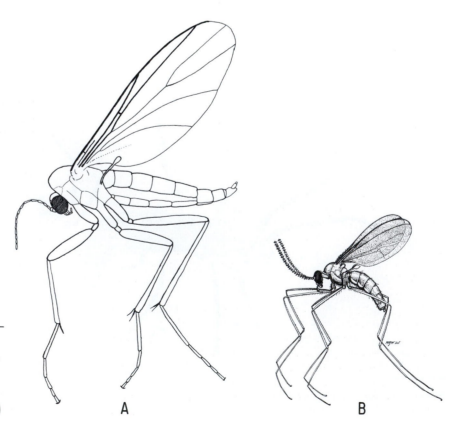

Figure 32–29. **A,** a dark-winged fungus gnat, *Scìara* sp., 15×, **B,** a cecidomyiid, *Aphidoléstes meridionàlis* Felt (which is predaceous on aphids). (**B,** courtesy of USDA.)

A   B

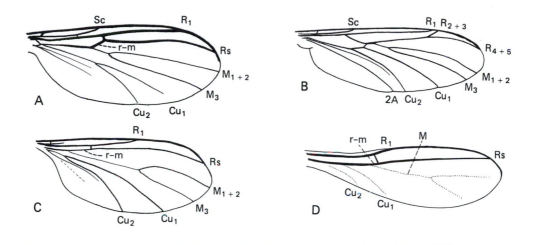

Figure 32–30.   Wings of Mycetophílidae (**A,B**) and Sciáridae (**C,D**). **A**, Sciophilìnae; **B**, Keroplatìnae; **C**, *Scìara*; **D**, *Pnýxia*, male.

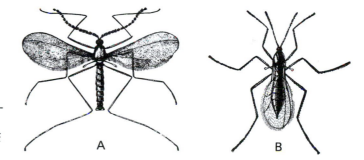

Figure 32–31.   The Hessian fly, *Mayetìola destrúctor* (Say). **A**, male; **B**, female. (Courtesy of USDA.)

parts minute. In the last larval instar of most species there is a characteristic T-shaped or clove-shaped sclerite on the ventral side of the prothorax called the "breastbone" or sternal spatula. Many of the larvae are brightly colored—red, orange, pink, or yellow.

The galls formed by gall midges occur on all parts of plants and are usually very distinctive. Many species of gall midges form a characteristic gall on a particular part of a particular species of plant. In some galls, such as the pine-cone willow gall and the maple leaf spot (Figure 32–32), only one larva develops. In others, such as the stem gall of willow, many larvae develop.

Paedogenesis (reproduction by larvae) occurs in several genera of gall midges. In *Miástor metralòas* Meinert, the larvae of which occur under bark, daughter larvae are produced inside a mother larva, and they eventually consume it and escape. These larvae may produce more larvae in a similar manner, through several generations, and the last larvae pupate.

One of the most important pest species in this group is the Hessian fly, *Mayetìola destrúctor* (Say), which is a serious pest of wheat (Figure 32–31). This insect overwinters as a full-grown larva in a puparium, under the leaf sheaths of winter wheat. The larvae pupate and the adults emerge in the spring. These adults oviposit on wheat, and the larvae feed between the leaf sheath and the stem, weakening the shoot or even killing it. The larvae pass the summer in a puparium, and the adults emerge in the fall and lay their eggs on the leaves of winter wheat. The damage to winter wheat can often be avoided by delaying the planting of wheat so that by the time the wheat has sprouted, the adult Hessian flies will have emerged and died.

Other species of economic importance in this family are the clover flower midge, *Dasineùra leguminícola* (Lintner), which is a serious pest of red clover throughout the United States; the chrysanthemum gall midge, *Rhopalomỳia chrysánthemi* (Ahlberg), a pest of chrysanthemums grown in greenhouses in various parts of the country; and the alfalfa

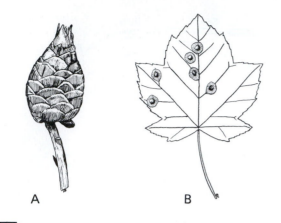

Figure 32–32.   Galls of cecidomyiids. **A**, the pine-cone willow gall, caused by *Rhabdóphaga strobilòides* (Osten Sacken); **B**, the maple leaf spot, caused by *Cecidomỳia ocellàris* Osten Sacken. (Redrawn from Felt.)

gall midge, *Asphondýlia wébsteri* Felt, which is sometimes a serious pest of alfalfa in the Southwest.

North American gall midges are grouped in three subfamilies, the Lestremiìnae, Porricondylìnae, and Cecidomyiìnae. The Lestremiìnae usually have ocelli; the basal tarsal segment is longer than the second; and M_{1+2} is present. The other two subfamilies lack ocelli and usually also M_{1+2}, and the first tarsal segment is much shorter than the second or the tarsi have fewer than five segments. The Cecidomyiìnae have the basal section of Rs very weak or lacking, while in the Porricondylìnae the basal section of Rs is present and as strong as the other veins. The gall-making cecidomyiids are in the subfamily Cecidomyiìnae. The larvae of the other two subfamilies live in decaying vegetation or wood, in fungi, or in plant tissues without producing galls. The larvae of some of the Cecidomyiìnae also live in fungi or in plant tissues without producing galls, and a few are predaceous.

The subfamily Lestremiìnae includes *Baeonòtus mìcrops* Byers, which was originally placed in a family by itself, the Baeonòtidae. *Baeonòtus mìcrops* lacks wings, halteres, and ocelli; the compound eyes are single-faceted; and the abdomen is large and indistinctly segmented. This insect was collected in forest soil, beneath oak-leaf litter, in Virginia.

Family **Psychòdidae**—Moth Flies and Sand Flies: The psychodids are small to minute, usually very hairy, mothlike flies. The most common species (Psychodìnae) hold the wings rooflike over the body. The adults occur in moist shady places, and they are sometimes abundant in drains or sewers. The larvae

occur in decaying vegetable matter, mud, moss, or water. The larvae of *Maruìna* (Psychodìnae), which occur in the West, live in fast-flowing streams.

This family is represented in the United States by 90 species, arranged in four subfamilies; Psychodìnae, Trichomyiìnae, Phlebotomìnae, and Bruchomyiìnae. In the Psychodìnae the eyes have a median extension extending above the base of the antennae. The other three subfamilies have the eyes oval, without a median extension. The Trichomyiìnae differ from the Phlebotomìnae and Bruchomyiìnae in having Rs three-branched, with only one longitudinal vein between the two forked veins in the wing. In the Phlebotomìnae and Bruchomyiìnae Rs is four-branched, with two veins between the two forked veins in the wing (as in Figure 32–7G). The Phlebotomìnae differ from the Bruchomyiìnae in having a long proboscis. Most of our psychodids (77 species) are in the subfamily Psychodìnae. The Trichomyiìnae contains only three species, the Phlebotomìnae nine, and the Bruchomyiìnae only one (which occurs in Florida).

Most psychodids are harmless to humans, but those in the subfamily Phlebotomìnae, often called sand flies, are bloodsucking. These occur in the southern states and in the tropics. Sand flies are known to act as vectors of several diseases in various parts of the world: pappataci fever (caused by a virus) in the Mediterranean region and in southern Asia; kala-azar and oriental sore (caused by leishmania organisms), which occur in South America, northern Africa, and southern Asia; espundia (caused by a leishmania), which occurs in South America; and Oroya fever or verruga peruana (caused by a bartonella organism), which occurs in South America.

Family **Trichocéridae**—Winter Crane Flies: The trichocerids are medium-sized flies that resemble the crane flies in the family Tipùlidae. They differ from the tipulids in having ocelli. They are usually seen in the fall or early spring, and some may be seen on mild days in winter. Adults may be found outdoors, sometimes in large swarms, or in caves, cellars, and similar dark places. The larvae occur in decaying vegetable matter.

Family **Anisopódidae**—Wood Gnats: This is a small group of gnats (nine North American species) that are usually found in moist places on foliage. Some species occasionally occur in large swarms consisting entirely of males. The larvae live in or near decaying organic matter, fermenting sap, and similar materials, and the adults are often attracted to flowing sap. Two subfamilies occur in our area, the Mycetobiìnae and Anisopodìnae. The Mycetobiìnae lack a discal cell, and the two basal cells are confluent because of the absence of the base of M

(Figure 32–8C). The Anisopodìnae have a discal cell, and the two basal cells are separated by the base of M (Figure 32–7B). The Mycetobiìnae contains a single rare but widely distributed species, *Mycetòbia divérgens* Walker. The most commonly encountered wood gnats are members of the Anisopodìnae, which often have faint spots on the wings.

Family **Scatópsidae**—Minute Black Scavenger Flies: These flies are black or brownish in color, usually 3 mm in length or less, and have short antennae. The veins near the costal margin of the wing (C, R_1, and Rs) are heavy, while the remaining veins are quite weak, and Rs ends at about one-half to three-fourths the wing length (Figure 32–8B). The larvae breed in decaying material and excrement. The group is a small one (74 North American species), but its members are sometimes fairly abundant.

Family **Synneùridae:**   These are rare flies similar to the Scatópsidae. They differ in having the palps four-segmented (one-segmented in the Scatópsidae). The larvae occur in decaying wood. Two species occur in North America. They have been taken from Quebec to California and north to Alaska.

Family   **Ptychoptéridae**—Phantom Crane Flies: These crane flies are similar to the tipulids, but they have only one anal vein reaching the wing margin and lack a closed discal cell. A fairly common species in this family, *Bittacomórpha clávipes* (Fabricius), has the long legs banded with black and white, and the basal segment of the tarsi is conspicuously swollen. These flies often drift with the wind, with their long legs extended. *Bittacomórpha* and *Bittacomorphélla* have the wings clear, and M_{1+2} is not forked (Figure 32–26A). In *Ptychóptera*, which resemble large fungus gnats, the wings are usually patterned, and M_{1+2} is forked. This is a small group, with only 16 North American species. The larvae live in decaying vegetable matter in marshes and swampy ponds.

Family **Díxidae**—Dixid Midges: The dixids are small, slender, mosquito-like flies with long legs and antennae. The wings lack scales, and the base of R_{2+3} is somewhat arched (Figure 32–7H). The adults do not bite. The larvae (Figure 32–33C) are aquatic and somewhat similar to the larvae of *Anópheles* mosquitoes, but do not have the thorax enlarged (cf. Figure 32–34C). They feed at the surface of the water like anopheline larvae, but the usual position is with the body bent into a U, and they move by alternately straightening and bending the body. The larvae feed on microorganisms and decayed organic matter. The group is a small one (42 North American species), but its members are fairly common.

Family **Chaobòridae**—Phantom Midges: These insects are very similar to mosquitoes, but differ in having a short proboscis and fewer scales on the wings. They do not bite. The larvae (Figure 32–33A,B) are aquatic and predaceous, and their antennae are modified into prehensile organs. The larvae of *Chaóborus* (Figure 32–33A) are almost transparent, giving rise to the name "phantom midges" for this group. The larvae of some species (e.g., *Mochlónyx*, Figure 32–33B) have a breathing tube and are very similar to mosquito larvae in appearance. Others (e.g., *Chaóborus*) do not have a breathing tube. The larvae occur in various sorts of pools and are sometimes very abundant. They frequently destroy large numbers of mosquito larvae. The group is a small one (19 North American species), but its members are fairly common insects.

Family **Culícidae**—Mosquitoes: This family is a large, abundant, well-known, and important group of flies. The larval stages are aquatic, and the adults can be recognized by the characteristic wing venation (Figure 32–7I), the scales along the wing veins, and the long proboscis. Mosquitoes are very important from the standpoint of human welfare because the females are bloodsucking, many species bite peo-

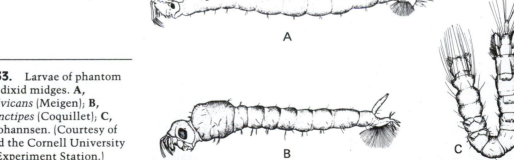

Figure 32–33.   Larvae of phantom (**A–B**) and (**C**) dixid midges. **A,** *Chaóborus flávicans* (Meigen); **B,** *Mochlónyx cínctipes* (Coquillet); **C,** *Díxa alíciae* Johannsen. (Courtesy of Johannsen and the Cornell University Agricultural Experiment Station.)

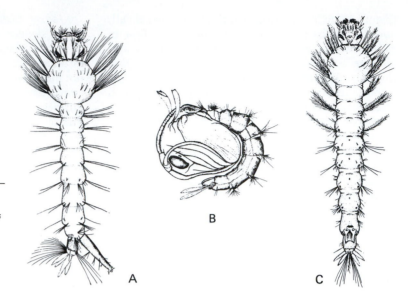

Figure 32–34. Larvae and pupa of mosquitoes. **A,** larva of *Cùlex pípiens* L.; **B,** pupa of *C. pípiens*; **C,** larva of *Anópheles punctipénnis* (Say). (After Johannsen, courtesy of the Cornell University Agricultural Experiment Station.)

ple, and they serve as vectors in the transmission of several important human diseases.

Mosquito larvae (Figure 32–34A,C), or wrigglers, occur in a variety of aquatic situations—in ponds and pools of various sorts, in the water in artificial containers, in tree holes, and in other situations—but each species usually occurs only in a particular type of aquatic habitat. The eggs (Figure 32–35) are laid on the surface of the water, either in "rafts" (*Cùlex*) or singly (*Anópheles*), or near water (*Aèdes*). In the latter case the eggs usually hatch when flooded. The larvae of most species feed on algae and organic debris, but a few are predaceous and feed on other mosquito larvae. Mosquito larvae breathe prin-

cipally at the surface, usually through a breathing tube at the posterior end of the body. The larvae of *Anópheles* lack a breathing tube and breathe through a pair of spiracular plates at the posterior end of the body.

Mosquito pupae (Figure 32–34B) are also aquatic and, unlike most insect pupae, are quite active and are often called tumblers. They breathe at the surface of the water through a pair of small trumpetlike structures on the thorax.

Most adult mosquitoes do not travel far from the water in which they spent their larval stage. *Aèdes aegýpti* (L.), the vector of yellow fever and dengue, seldom travels more than a few hundred yards from where it emerges. Some species of *Anópheles* may range as far as a mile from where they emerge. On the other hand, some of the salt-marsh mosquitoes—for example, *Aèdes sollícitans* (Walker) (Figure 32–36A)—may be found many miles from the larval habitat. Adult mosquitoes usually are active during the twilight hours or at night, or in dense shade. Many spend the day in hollow trees, under culverts, or in similar resting places. Some adults overwinter in such places. Only the female mosquitoes are bloodsucking. The males (and occasionally also the females) feed on nectar and other plant juices.

The sexes of most mosquitoes can be easily determined by the form of the antennae (Figure 32–37). The antennae of the males are very plumose, while those of the females have only a few short hairs. In most mosquitoes other than *Anópheles* (see below), the maxillary palps are very short in the female (Figure 32–37A) but are longer than the proboscis in the male (Figure 32–37B).

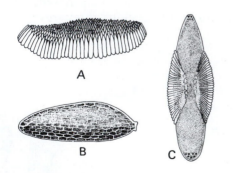

Figure 32–35. Eggs of mosquitoes. **A,** egg raft of *Cùlex réstuans* Theobald; **B,** egg of *Aèdes taeniorhýnchus* (Wiedemann); **C,** egg of *Anópheles quadrimaculàtus* Say, showing floats. (Courtesy of USDA, after Howard, Dyar, and Knab.)

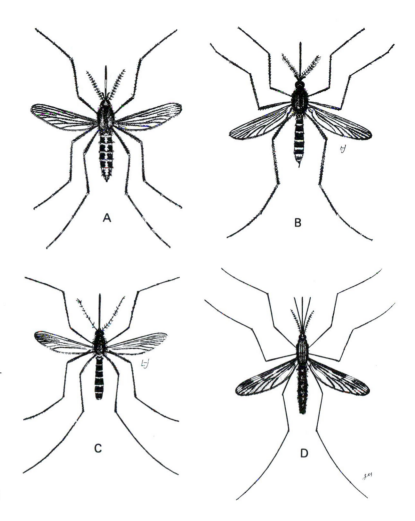

Figure 32–36. Common mosquitoes. **A,** the salt-marsh mosquito, *Aèdes sollícitans* (Walker); **B,** a woodland mosquito, *Aèdes stímulans* (Walker); **C,** the house mosquito, *Cùlex pípiens* L.; **D,** *Anópheles punctipénnis* (Say). *(Courtesy of Headlee and the New Jersey Agricultural Experiment Station.)*

Most of our mosquitoes (131 of the 150 species recorded from North America) belong to four genera: *Anópheles, Aèdes, Psoróphora,* and *Cùlex*. These genera contain the species that are most important from the human point of view. Adults of *Anópheles* are rather easily distinguished: the maxillary palps are long in both sexes (Figure 32–37C,D) and clubbed in the male (usually short in females of the other genera); the scutellum is evenly rounded (trilobed in the other genera); and the wings are usually spotted (not so in the other genera). The wing spotting in *Anópheles* is due to groups of differently colored scales on the wings. An *Anópheles* mosquito in a resting position has the body and proboscis in a straight line and at an angle to the surface on which the insect is resting (Figure 32–38A,B). Some species seem almost to "stand on their head" in a resting position. Adults of the other genera have the body in a resting position more or less parallel to the surface, with the proboscis bent down (Figure 32–38C). Adults of *Pso-*

róphora have a group of bristles (the spiracular bristles) immediately in front of the mesothoracic spiracle, while those of *Aèdes* and *Cùlex* lack spiracular bristles. *Psoróphora* mosquitoes are relatively large and have long erect scales on the hind tibiae. The best character to separate adults of *Aèdes* and *Cùlex* is the presence (*Aèdes*) or absence (*Cùlex*) of postspiracular bristles (a group of bristles immediately behind the mesothoracic spiracle). The tip of the abdomen of a female *Aèdes* is usually pointed, with the cerci protruding, and the thorax often has white or silvery markings. In *Cùlex* the tip of the female abdomen is generally blunt, with the cerci retracted, and the thorax is usually dull-colored.

The larvae of *Anópheles* differ from those of other mosquitoes in lacking a breathing tube (Figure 32–34C), and when at rest, they lie parallel to the surface of the water (Figure 32–39A). The larvae of the other three genera have a breathing tube (Figure 32–34A), and when at rest, they have the body at an angle to the surface of the water (Figure 32–39B). *Cùlex* larvae have several pairs of hair tufts on the breathing tube, and the tube is relatively long and slender. Larvae of *Aèdes* and *Psoróphora* have only a single pair of hair tufts on the breathing tube. The larvae of *Aèdes* and *Psoróphora* usually differ in the sclerotization of the anal segment (the sclerotization being completely around the segment in *Psoróphora* but usually not complete in *Aèdes*). The breathing tube in *Aèdes* larvae is relatively short and stout.

Anópheles larvae occur chiefly in ground pools, marshes, and places where there is considerable vegetation. The other mosquitoes breed in many places, but the most abundant *Aèdes* and *Psoróphora* mosquitoes breed in woodland pools and salt marshes,

and *Cùlex* in artificial containers. The woodland species that are so troublesome early in the season are largely species of *Aèdes* and have a single brood a year. Many species that breed in large bodies of water, borrow pits, or artificial containers may continue breeding through the season as long as weather conditions are favorable.

Mosquitoes act as vectors of several very important human diseases: malaria, caused by protists of the genus *Plasmòdium* and transmitted by certain species of *Anópheles*; yellow fever, caused by a virus and transmitted by *Aèdes aegýpti* (L.); dengue, caused by a virus and transmitted by *Aèdes aegýpti* (L.) and other species of *Aèdes*; filariasis, caused by a filarial worm and transmitted chiefly by species of

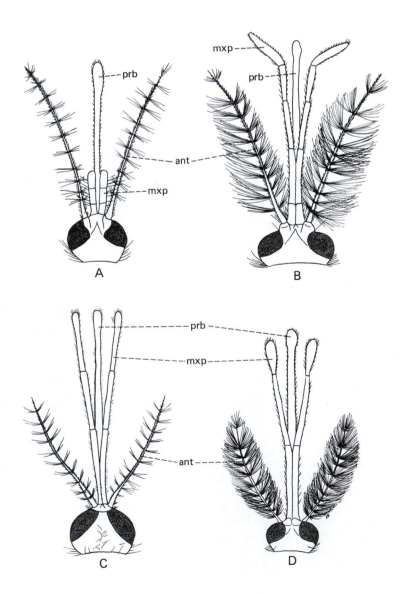

Figure 32–37.   Head structure in mosquitoes, showing sex characters. **A,** *Aèdes*, female; **B,** same, male; **C,** *Anópheles*, female; **D,** same, male. *ant*, antenna; *mxp*, maxillary palp; *prb*, proboscis.

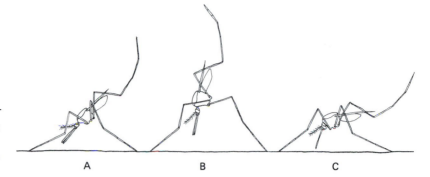

Figure 32–38.   Resting positions of mosquitoes. **A, B,** *Anópheles;* **C,** *Cùlex* (Redrawn from King, Bradley, and McNeel.)

A   B   C

Cùlex; and certain types of encephalitis, caused by a virus and transmitted by various species of mosquitoes (chiefly species of *Cùlex* and *Aèdes*).

Control measures against mosquitoes may be aimed at the larvae or at the adults. Measures aimed at the larvae may involve the elimination or modification of the larval habitats (for example, drainage) or may involve the treatment of the larval habitat with insecticides. Measures aimed at the adults may be in the nature of preventives (the use of protective clothing, screening, and the use of repellents) or insecticides (sprays or aerosols).

Family **Thaumalèidae**—Solitary Midges: The members of this family are small (3–4 mm in length), rather stocky flies with the head situated low on the thorax, and reddish yellow or brownish in color. Only seven species occur in the United States, two in the East and the other five in the West. They are quite rare. The adults are usually found along streams in which the larvae occur.

Family **Simuliidae**—Black Flies or Buffalo Gnats: The black flies are small, usually dark-colored insects with short legs, broad wings, and a humpbacked appearance (Figure 32–40). The females are bloodsucking. These insects are vicious biters and are serious pests in some sections of the country. The bites often cause considerable swelling and sometimes bleeding. Black flies sometimes attack livestock in such numbers and with such ferocity as to cause the death of the livestock, and there are

records of human deaths caused by these insects. Black flies have a wide distribution, but are most numerous in the north temperate and subarctic regions. The adults usually appear in late spring and early summer.

Black fly larvae occur in streams, where they attach to stones and other objects by means of a disklike sucker at the posterior end of the body. The larvae (Figure 32–41 C, G) are somewhat club-shaped, are swollen posteriorly, and move about like a measuringworm. Their locomotion is aided by silk spun from the mouth. They pupate in cone-shaped cases (Figure 32–41 B, E) attached to objects in the water. These larvae are sometimes extremely abundant. The adults are most frequently encountered near the streams where the larvae occur, but may occur at considerable distances from streams.

The black flies in the United States are not known to be vectors of any disease of man, but in Africa, Mexico, and Central America certain species in this group act as vectors of onchocerciasis, a disease caused by a filarial worm and characterized by large subcutaneous swellings. In some cases the worms may get into the eyes and cause partial or complete blindness.

Family **Ceratopogónidae**—Biting Midges, Punkies, or No-see-ums: These flies are very small but are often serious pests because of their bloodsucking habits, particularly along the seashore or along the shores of rivers and lakes. Their small size is responsible for

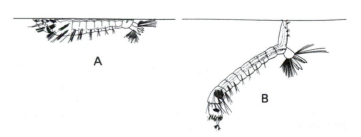

A

B

Figure 32–39.   Feeding positions of mosquito larvae. **A,** *Anópheles;* **B,** *Cùlex.* (Courtesy of USDA.)

the name "no-see-ums," and their bite is all out of proportion to their size. Many species in this group attack other insects and suck blood from the insect host as an ectoparasite. Punkies have been reported

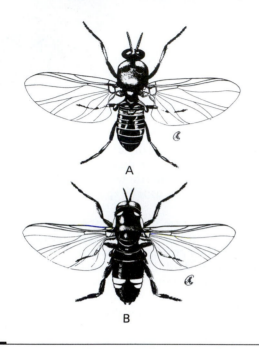

Figure 32–40. A black fly, *Simùlium nigricóxum* Stone. **A,** female; **B,** male. (Courtesy of Cameron and the Canadian Department of Agriculture.)

from mantids, walkingsticks, dragonflies, alderflies, lacewings, certain beetles, certain moths, crane flies, and mosquitoes. Some of the larger species prey on smaller insects. Some species (Figure 32–42B) have spotted wings. Most of the punkies that attack people belong to the genera *Culicòides* and *Leptocónops*. These insects apparently do not travel far from the place where the larvae occur, and one may often avoid punkie attacks by simply moving a few yards away.

Punkies are very similar to the midges (Chironómidae), but are generally stouter in build, with the wings broader and held flat over the abdomen (usually held more or less rooflike in the Chironómidae), and the wings are often strongly patterned (usually clear in Chironómidae). This is a large group, with about 500 North American species.

The larvae of punkies are aquatic or semiaquatic, occuring in sand, mud, decaying vegetation, and the water in tree holes. Those occurring along the seashore apparently breed in the intertidal zone. The feeding habits of the larvae are not well known, but they are probably scavengers.

Family **Chironómidae**—Midges: These insects are to be found almost everywhere. They are small (1–10 mm in length), delicate, and somewhat mosquitolike in appearance (Figure 32–43C), but they lack scales on the wings, and do not have a long proboscis (they do not bite). Their front legs are usually the longest, and the metanotum has a keel or furrow. The males usually have plumose antennae. Midges

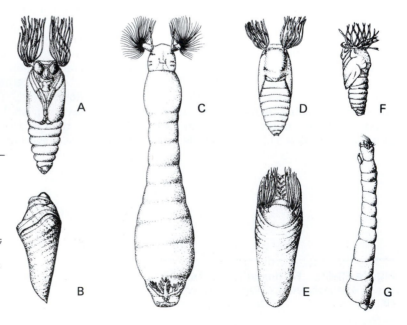

Figure 32–41. Immature stages of a black fly. **A–E,** *Simùlium nigricóxum* Stone; **F–G,** *S. píctipes* Hagen. **A,** pupa, ventral view; **B,** pupal case; **C,** larva, dorsal view; **D,** pupa, dorsal view; **E,** pupa in pupal case; **F,** pupa, lateral view; **G,** larva, lateral view. (**A–E,** courtesy of Cameron and the Canadian Department of Agriculture; **F–G,** courtesy of Johannsen and the Cornell University Agricultural Experiment Station.)

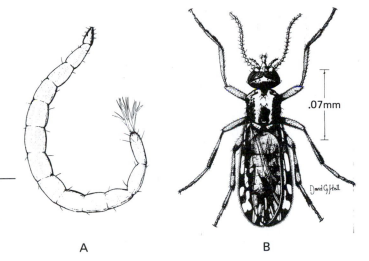

Figure 32–42. The little gray punkie, *Culicòides fùrens* (Poey) (Ceratopogónidae). **A,** larva; **B,** adult female; about 25 ×. (Courtesy of Dove, Hall, and Hull, and the Entomological Society of America.)

often occur in huge swarms, usually in the evening, and the humming of such a swarm can often be heard from a considerable distance.

This group is a large one, with about 760 North American species. The larvae of most midges (Figure 32–44B) are aquatic, and occur in all sorts of aquatic habitats. Some occur in decaying matter, soil, under bark, and similar habitats that are wet and rich in organic matter. Many of the aquatic forms live in tubes or cases composed of fine particles of the substrate cemented together with salivary secretion. The larvae of many species are red, because hemoglobin is present in the blood, and are known as bloodworms. Midge larvae swim by means of characteristic whipping movements of the body, something like the movements of mosquito larvae. Midge larvae are often very abundant, and are an important item of food for many freshwater fish and other aquatic animals.

SUBORDER **Brachýcera:** This suborder includes 84 of the 108 families and nearly 13,000 of the approximately 18,200 species of North American Díptera. Most of its members are relatively stout-bodied, and they vary greatly in size. The antennae are usually three-segmented, but the third segment is sometimes divided into subsegments, and it often bears a style or an arista.

The suborder Brachýcera is divided into three infraorders, the Tabanomórpha, Asilomórpha, and Muscomórpha. Some classifications of the Díptera limit the suborder Brachýcera to the 19 families in the Tabanomórpha and Asilomórpha, and put the 60 families of Muscomórpha in a third suborder, the Cyclórrhapha. Most of the Tabanomórpha and Asilomórpha (all except the Dolichopódidae, many Empídidae, and some Stratiomyìdae, Bombylìidae, and Acrocéridae) have Rs three-branched, with R_{4+5} forked (in few Asìlidae it may appear that it is R_{2+3}

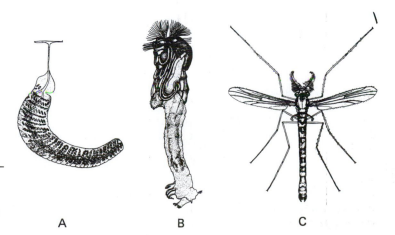

Figure 32–43. A midge, *Chirónomus plumòsus* (L.). **A,** egg mass; **B,** pupa, lateral view, with larval skin not completely shed; **C,** adult male. (Courtesy of Branch.)

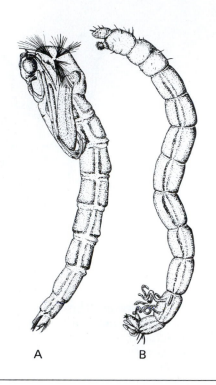

Figure 32–44.   Pupa (**A**) and larva (**B**) of *Chirónomus téntans* (Fabricius). (Courtesy of Johannsen and the Cornell University Agricultural Experiment Station.)

that is forked; see Figure 32–9D). All of the Muscomórpha have Rs two-branched, none has the third antennal segment annulated, and nearly all have an arista on the third antennal segment.

The pupae of Brachýcera are coarctate. In the Tabanomórpha and Asilomórpha the adult emerges from a T-shaped opening at one end. In the Muscomórpha the adult emerges from a circular opening at one end (hence the name Cyclórrhapha, sometimes used for these flies), and the members of this group are often called circular-seamed flies. Muscomórpha adults push out the end of the puparium with a structure called the ptilinum, which is everted from the front of the head, above the bases of the antennae. After emergence, the ptilinum is withdrawn into the head. In the Schizóphora the break in the head wall through which the ptilinum was everted is marked by the frontal suture (also called the ptilinal suture). This suture is lacking in the Aschìza.

Family **Pelecorhýnchidae**: This group includes eight rare North American species: seven species of *Glùtops* and one species of *Bequaertomỳia*. The species of *Glùtops* are less than 10 mm in length, and have R₄ and 2A relatively straight; *B. jònesi* (Cres-

son) is 13–15 mm in length, and has R_4 and 2A somewhat sinuate. A few species of *Glùtops* occur in the east, but the other species in the family are western. The larvae occur in the wet soil of swamps and stream banks, and are predaceous. The adults of a few species are known to feed on flowers.

Family **Tabánidae**—Horse Flies and Deer Flies: About 350 species of tabanids occur in North America, and many are quite common. They are medium-sized to large, rather stout-bodied flies. The females are bloodsucking and are often serious pests of livestock and people. The males feed chiefly on pollen and nectar and are often found on flowers. The two sexes are very easily separated by the eyes, which are contiguous in the males and separated in the females. The eyes are often brightly colored or iridescent. The larvae of most species are aquatic and predaceous, and the adults are generally encountered near swamps, marshes, ponds, and other situations where the larvae occur. Most horse flies are powerful fliers, and some species apparently have a flight range of several kilometers.

The two most common genera of tabanids, which include some 200 of the 350 North American species, are *Tabánus* and *Chrỳsops*. In *Tabánus* the hind tibiae lack apical spurs; the head is somewhat hemispherical in shape (slightly concave posteriorly in the female); and the third antennal segment (Figure 32–45A) has a toothlike process near the base. *Tabánus* is a large genus, with about a hundred North American species, and it includes some important pests. One of the largest flies in the genus is *T. atràtus* Fabricius, a black insect 25 mm or more in length (Figure 32–46E). The so-called greenheads, flies about 13 mm in length with green eyes and a yellowish brown body, are often serious pests on bathing beaches. In *Chrỳsops* the hind tibiae have apical spurs; the head is more rounded; the calypteres are smaller; and the third antennal segment

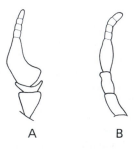

Figure 32–45.   Antennae of tabanids. **A,** *Tabánus atràtus* Fabricius; **B,** *Chrỳsops fuliginòsus* Wiedemann.

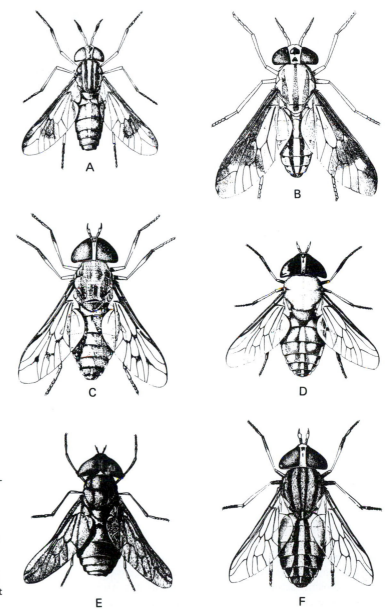

Figure 32–46. Horse and deer flies (Tabánidae). **A,** *Chrỳsops univittàtus* Macquart; **B,** *Chrỳsops pìkei* Whitney; **C,** *Tabánus súlcifrons* Macquart; **D,** *Tabánus quinquevittàtus* Wiedemann; **E,** *Tabánus atràtus* Fabricius; **F,** *Tabánus linèola* Fabricius. (Courtesy of Schwardt and Hall and the Arkansas Agricultural Experiment Station.)

(Figure 32–45B) is elongate and lacks a basal tooth-like process. Most members of this genus are about the size of a house fly or a little larger, brown or black in color, with dark markings on the wings (Figure 32–46A,B). These tabanids, called deer flies, are usually encountered near marshes or streams, and they frequently buzz around one's head or get in one's hair.

The eggs of tabanids are usually laid in masses on leaves or other objects near or over water. Most species overwinter in the larval stage and pupate during the summer.

Some of the tabanids, particularly certain species of *Chrỳsops,* are known to serve as vectors of disease. Tularemia and anthrax (and possibly other diseases) may be transmitted by tabanids in the United States, and in Africa a disease caused by the filarial worm *Lòa lòa* (Cobbold) is transmitted by deer flies.

Family **Atherícidae:** These flies were formerly placed in the Rhagiónidae, but differ from those now in the Rhagiónidae in lacking spurs on the front tibiae and in having the R_1 cell closed at the wing margin (Figure 32–47D). This group is a small one,

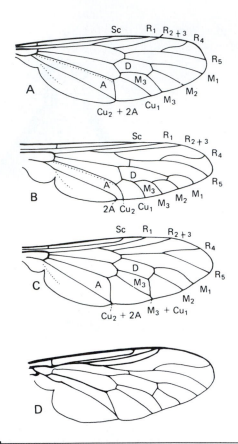

Figure 32–47.   Wings of Brachýcera. **A,** *Xylóphagus*, (Xylophágidae); **B,** *Coenomỳia* (Xylophágidae); **C,** *Xylomỳia* (Xylomỳidae); **D,** *Àtherix* (Atherícidae).

with only four North American species, and its members are not common. They are usually found in the vegetation bordering streams. The eggs are usually laid on the underside of bridges or on vegetation above a stream, and the larvae on hatching fall into the stream, where they live in the riffles and feed on midge larvae and other aquatic insects. In the case of *Àtherix* (widely distributed) the female remains on her egg mass and eventually dies there, and other females may lay eggs on this same mass until a ball of considerable size is formed—consisting of eggs and dead females. Females of *Suragìna concínna* (Williston), which occurs in southwest Texas and Mexico, are bloodsucking, feeding on people and cattle.

Family **Rhagiónidae**—Snipe Flies: Snipe flies are medium-sized to large, with the head somewhat rounded, the abdomen relatively long and tapering, and the legs rather long (Figure 32–48). Many species have spotted wings. The body may be bare or covered

with short hair. Most snipe flies are brownish or gray, but some are black with spots of white, yellow, or green. They are common in woods, especially near moist places, and are usually found on foliage. Both adults and larvae are predaceous on a variety of small insects. Most snipe flies do not bite but several species of *Symphoromỳia* are common biting pests in the western mountains and coastal areas.

This group includes the genus *Bolbomỳia*, which is sometimes placed in the Xylophágidae. It is a minute fly, 2–3 mm in length, dull black with smoky wings, and with characteristic antennae (see couplet 39 of key). Some other genera, formerly included in the Rhagiónidae, are in this book placed in other

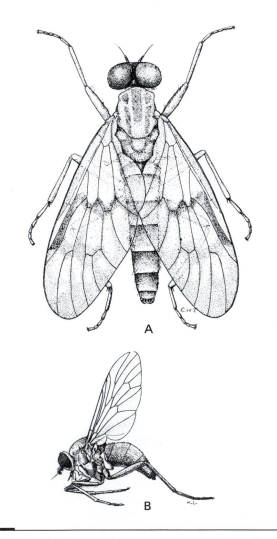

Figure 32–48.   Snipe flies. **A,** a common snipe fly, *Rhàgio mystàceus* (Macquart); **B,** a bloodsucking snipe fly, *Symphoromỳia átripes* Bigot. (**B,** courtesy of Ross and the Entomological Society of America.)

families: *Atherix* in the family Athericidae, *Vermileo* in the family Vermileónidae, and *Diálysis* in the family Xylophágidae.

Family **Xylophágidae:** Xylophagids are relatively uncommon flies of medium to large size. They are black in color, sometimes marked with yellow, or all reddish yellow. They usually occur in wooded areas, and feed on sap or nectar. The larvae occur in the soil (*Coenomỳia*), under bark (*Xylóphagus*), or in decaying logs (*Rachícerus*). The flies in the genus *Xylóphagus* are slender and ichneumonid-like, but other xylophagids are more robust. *Coenomỳia ferrugínea* Scopoli is large (14–25 mm in length) and usually reddish or brownish in color, with the eyes pubescent and the second to fifth posterior cells about as wide as long (Figure 32–47B). The flies in the genus *Rachícerus* are peculiar in having the antennae many-segmented and serrate or somewhat pectinate. They have the fourth posterior (M$_3$) cell closed; their eyes are emarginate just above the antennae; and they are 5–8 mm in length. Other xylophagids are 10 mm in length or less, and are quite rare.

Family **Xylomỳidae:** These are rather slender wasplike flies, 5–15 mm in length, rather brightly colored with pale markings on blackish background. The most common flies in this small group (ten North American species) are the species of *Xylomỳia*, which are slender and ichneumonid-like. They differ from xylophagids in the genus *Xylóphagus* (which are very similar in appearance) in having the M$_3$ cell closed (Figure 32–47C). The xylomyids are usually found in wooded areas. The larvae occur under bark, and are predaceous or scavengers.

Family **Stratiomyidae**—Soldier Flies: This is a fairly large group (more than 250 North American species), most of which are medium-sized or larger (to about 18 mm in length) and usually found on flowers. Many species are brightly colored and wasplike in appearance. The larvae occur in a variety of situations: some are aquatic and feed on algae, decaying materials, or small aquatic animals; some live in dung or other decaying materials; some occur under bark; and others are found in other situations.

In some species of soldier flies (e.g., *Stratìomys*, Figure 32–49A), the abdomen is broad and flat; the wings at rest are folded back together over the abdomen; and the antennae (Figure 32–1C) are long, with the third segment distinctly annulated. In other species (e.g., *Ptécticus*), the abdomen is elongate, usually narrowed at the base, and the third antennal segment (Figure 32–1F) appears globular, with an arista, and the annulations are very indistinct. Most soldier flies are dark-colored, with or without light markings, but some species are yellowish or light brown. The members of this family are most easily recognized by their wing venation: the branches of R are rather heavy and are crowded together in the anterior part of the wing, the wing membrane beyond the closed cells has fine longitudinal wrinkles, and the discal cell is small (Figure 32–9A).

Family **Therévidae**—Stiletto Flies: These flies are of medium size, are usually somewhat hairy or bristly, and often have the abdomen pointed (Figure 32–50A,B). They are superficially similar to some robber flies, but do not have the top of the head hollowed out between the eyes. This is a fair-sized group (about 130 North American species), but the adults are not common. They are most likely to be found in dry open areas such as meadows and beaches. Little is known of the feeding habits of the adults, but they are probably plant feeders. The larvae are

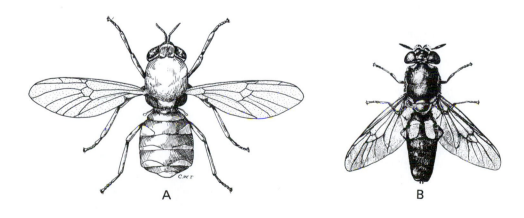

Figure 32–49. Soldier flies. **A,** *Stratìomys láticeps* Loew; **B,** *Hermàtia illùcens* (L.). (**B,** courtesy of USDA.)

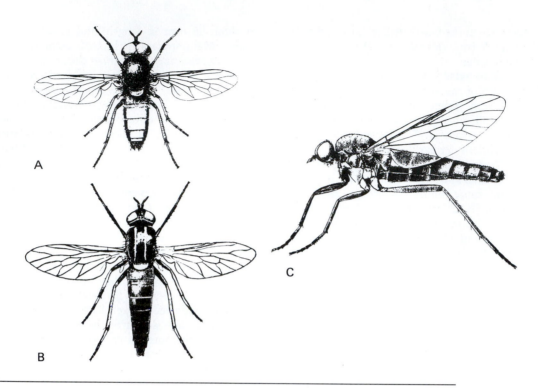

Figure 32–50. **A,** *Psilocéphala áldrichi* Coquillet, female (Therévidae); **B,** same, male; **C,** *Caenòtus inornátus* Cole, female (Bombylìidae). (Courtesy of Cole and the U.S. National Museum.)

predaceous and usually occur in sand or decaying wood.

Family **Scenopínidae**—Window Flies: The window flies are rather uncommon flies of medium or small size and are usually blackish in color. The common name is derived from the fact that one species, *Scenópinus fenestràlis* (L.) (Figure 32–51), is sometimes common on windows. The larva of this species is said to feed on the larvae of carpet beetles. The larvae of other species feed on decaying wood and fungi. This is a fair-sized group, with 136 North American species, most of which occur in the West.

Family **Vermileónidae**—Worm Lions: This group includes small (about 5 mm in length), slender, nearly bare flies with stylate antennae, a long slender abdomen, and slender legs. The wings are narrowed at the base, without an alula or a developed anal angle. The larvae of these flies construct pitfall traps in the sand, and they use these in capturing prey very much as antlions do (see Chapter 27). The adults feed on nectar. Only two species, in the genus *Vermíleo*, occur in the United States, from Colorado to New Mexico to California. The vermileonids are similar to the Rhagiónidae, with which they were once classified, but differ in having the wings more

narrowed at the base and in having apical spurs on the front tibiae.

Family **Mỳdidae**—Mydas Flies: The mydas flies are very large, elongate flies, with long four-segmented antennae. A Brazilian species, *Mỳdas hèros* Perty, which is 54 mm in length, is one of the largest dipterans known. There are 45 North American species in this family, and most of them are western. The species most likely to be encountered in the

Figure 32–51. A window fly, *Scenópinus fenestràlis* (L.). (Redrawn from USDA.)

East is *Mỳdas clavàtus* (Drury), which is black with the second abdominal segment yellow or orange (Figure 32–52). Little is known of the habits of the mydas flies, but the larvae occur in decaying wood and are predaceous. The adults are probably also predaceous.

Family **Apiocéridae**—Flower-Loving Flies: These are relatively large, elongate flies that resemble some of the robber flies (for example, Figure 32–53B,C), but they do not have the top of the head hollowed out between the eyes, and they have a different wing venation (M_1 and the veins anterior to it ending in front of the wing tip; see Figure 32–9J). This group is a small one (29 North American species), and its members are rather rare. They occur in the arid regions of the West, where they are often found on flowers.

Family **Asìlidae**—Robber Flies and Grass Flies: This is a large group, with nearly a thousand North American species, and many species are quite common. The adults are found in a variety of habitats, but each species usually occurs in a characteristic type of habitat. The adults are predaceous and attack a variety of insects, including wasps, bees, dragonflies, grasshoppers, and other flies. They often attack an insect as large as or larger than themselves. Most asilids capture their prey on the wing, but the grass flies (Leptogastrìnae) usually attack resting insects.

Some of the larger robber flies can inflict a painful bite if carelessly handled.

Robber flies have the top of the head hollowed out between the eyes (Figure 32–53D) and the face more or less bearded, and they have a stout thorax with long, strong legs. Most of them are elongate, with the abdomen tapering (Figure 32–53B,C), but some are stout-bodied, very hairy, and resemble bumble bees or other Hymenóptera (Figure 32–53A). Still others are very slender, almost damselfly-like (Figure 32–54). The larvae live in soil, decaying wood, and similar places and feed chiefly on the larvae of other insects.

The family Asìlidae is divided into four subfamilies, the Leptogastrìnae, Laphrìinae, Dasypogonìnae, and Asilìnae. The Leptogastrìnae have been placed in a separate family by some authorities. They are very slender and elongate (Figure 32–54), and they generally occur in grassy areas where they feed on small, soft-bodied, usually resting prey.

Family **Acrocéridae**—Small-Headed Flies: These are rather rare flies of small to medium size with a somewhat humpbacked appearance and with a very small head (Figure 32–55). Some have a long, slender proboscis and feed on flowers. Others have no proboscis and apparently do not feed in the adult stage. The larvae are internal parasites of spiders. The eggs

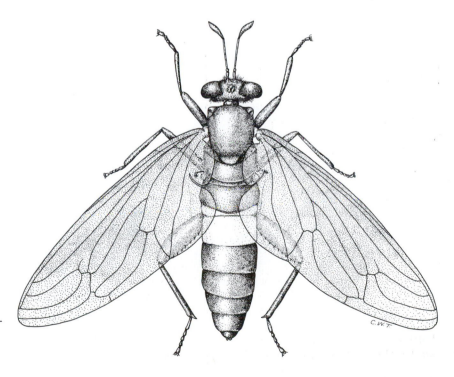

Figure 32–52. A mydas fly, *Mỳdas clavàtus* (Drury).

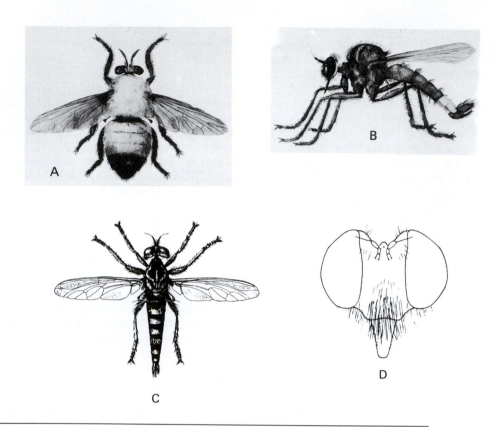

Figure 32–53.   Robber flies. **A,** *Láphria làta* Macquart; **B,** *Effèria* sp.; **C,** *Prómachus vertebràtus* (Say); **D,** head of *Effèria,* anterior view. (**C,** courtesy of USDA.)

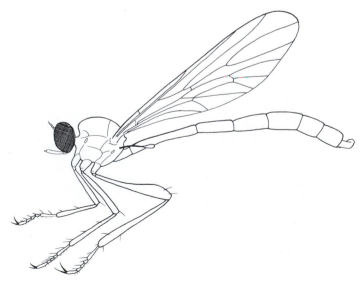

Figure 32–54.   A grass fly, *Psilónyx annulàtus* (Say). $7\frac{1}{2}\times$ (Leptogastrìnae, Asìlidae).

are laid in large numbers on vegetation and hatch into tiny flattened larvae called planidia. The planidia eventually attach to and enter the body of a passing spider. Pupation occurs outside the host, often in the host's web.

Family **Nemestrínidae**—Tangle-Veined Flies: These are medium-sized, rather stout-bodied flies, with a somewhat aberrant wing venation (Figure 32–9I). Some are hairy and beelike in appearance. They occur in open fields of fairly high vegetation. They hover persistently, and are very fast fliers. Some species occur on flowers. The group is a small one (six North American species), and its members are relatively rare. Most species are western. The species whose larvae are known are parasites of other insects: species of *Trichopsídea* parasitize grasshoppers, and species of *Hirmoneùra* attack scarabaeid beetle larvae. Nemestrinids are often important in controlling grasshopper populations.

Family **Bombyliidae**—Bee Flies: This is a large group (about 800 North American species), and its members are widely distributed. Bee flies are fairly common insects, probably more common in the arid areas of the Southwest than elsewhere. Most of them are stout-bodied, densely hairy flies of medium to large size. A few are slender and not very hairy, and a few are very small (some Mythicomyìinae are only 1.2 mm in length). Many have the proboscis long and slender.

Bee flies are found on flowers or hovering over or resting on the ground or grass in open sunny places.

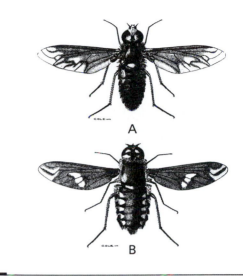

Figure 32–56.   Bee flies. **A,** *Poecilánthrax álpha* (Osten Sacken); **B,** *P. signatipénnis* (Cole). (Courtesy of Cole and the New York Entomological Society.)

They often visit water holes in arid regions. The wings at rest are usually held outstretched. Most species are very fast fliers, and when caught in an insect net, they buzz much like bees. Many have banded or spotted wings (Figure 32–56).

Bee fly larvae, as far as known, are either parasitic on the immature stages of other insects (Lepidóptera, Hymenóptera, Coleóptera, Díptera, and Neuróptera) or predaceous on grasshopper eggs.

Family **Hilarimórphidae**: The hilarimorphids are small (1.8–7.2 mm in length), robust, dark-colored flies, with the wings hyaline to pale brown. There are 30 species, all in the genus *Hilarimórpha*, in North America. They are widely distributed, but rare. Adults have been collected on willows along narrow gravel-bottomed streams. The immature stages are unknown.

Family **Empídidae**—Dance Flies: The dance flies are so named because the adults sometimes occur in swarms, flying with an up-and-down movement. This group is a large one (more than 725 North American species), and many species are fairly common. All are small, and some are minute (length, 1.5–12.0 mm). Most are dark-colored, but none are metallic. Most have a large thorax and a long tapering abdomen. The male genitalia are terminal and often are rather conspicuous (Figure 32–57).

Dance flies are found in a variety of situations, usually in moist places where there is an abundance of vegetation. They are predaceous on smaller insects (some are important predators of mosquitoes), but they often frequent flowers and feed on nectar.

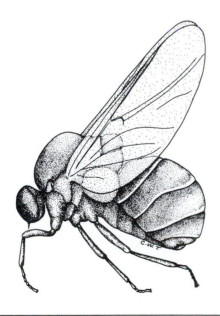

Figure 32–55.   A small-headed fly, *Ogcòdes* sp.

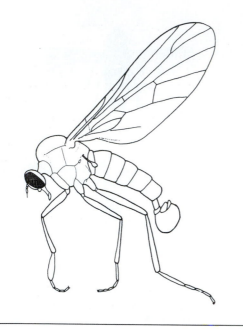

Figure 32–57.   A dance fly (Empídidae), 10×.

Many species of dance flies have rather interesting mating habits. The males sometimes capture prey and use it to attract females. Some species of *Hílara* and *Émpis* that occur in the Northwest construct balloons which they carry about as a means of attracting females. These balloons may be made of silk (spun from the basal segment of the front tarsi) or of a frothy material from the anus, and they usually contain prey.

Dance fly larvae occur in a great variety of situations: in the soil, decaying vegetation, or dung, under bark, or in water. All are probably predaceous.

Family **Dolichopódidae**—Long-Legged Flies: The dolichopodids are small to minute flies that are usually metallic in color: greenish, bluish, or coppery. They are superficially similar to many of the muscoid flies (Schizóphora) but lack a frontal suture and have a rather characteristic wing venation (Figure 32–10D–F): the r-m cross vein is very short or absent and is located in the basal fourth of the wing, and there is often a swelling of Rs where it forks. The male genitalia are usually large and conspicuous and folded forward under the abdomen (Figure 32–58). In the female the apex of the abdomen is pointed. The legs of the males are often peculiarly ornamented. Members of the genus *Melandèria*, which occur along the Pacific Coast, have the labellar lobes of the labium modified into mandible-like structures.

This group is a large one (more than 1230 North American species), and its members are abundant in many places, particularly near swamps and streams, in woodlands, and in meadows. Many species occur only in a particular type of habitat. The adults are predaceous on smaller insects. The adults of many species engage in rather unusual mating dances. The larvae occur in water or mud, in decaying wood, in grass stems, and under bark. Not much is known of their feeding habits, but at least some are predaceous. The larvae of the genus *Medètera* live under bark and are predaceous on bark beetles.

Family **Lonchoptéridae**—Spear-Winged Flies: The members of this group are slender, yellowish or brownish flies less than 5 mm in length, with the wings somewhat pointed at the apex and with a characteristic venation (Figure 32–10H). They are usually fairly common in moist, shady, or grassy places. The larvae occur in decaying vegetation. Males differ from females in venation: the M_3 cell is closed in the female (Figure 32–10H) and open in the male. Males are extremely rare, and these flies are probably parthenogenetic. This family contains only four North American species, in the genus *Lonchóptera*.

Family **Platypèzidae**—Flat-Footed Flies: These flies are so named because of the peculiarly shaped hind tarsi, which are usually flattened or otherwise modified (Figure 32–23C). The tarsi are generally more flattened in females than in males. The flat-footed flies are small, usually black or brown in color, and occur on low vegetation in damp woods. They often run about on leaves in an erratic, zigzag fashion. The males sometimes swarm in groups of up to

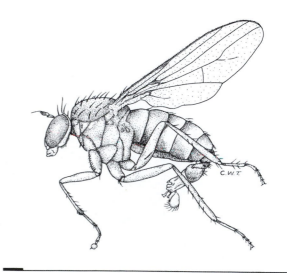

Figure 32–58.   A long-legged fly, *Dolíchopus pùgil* Loew, male.

50 or more, the swarms dancing in the air a meter or so above the ground, with the hind legs hanging down. Females enter these swarms to select mates. If the swarm is disturbed, as by a swinging net, the flies scatter and reform the swarm again a little higher up (out of net reach). Adults of the genus *Macrosània* are attracted to smoke, and are often called smoke flies. The larvae of flat-footed flies live in fungi.

Family **Phòridae**—Humpbacked Flies: The phorids are small or minute flies that are easily recognized by the humpbacked appearance (Figure 32–59), the characteristic venation (Figure 32–10G), and the laterally flattened hind femora. The adults are fairly common in many habitats but most abundant about decaying vegetation. The habits of the larvae are rather varied: some occur in decaying animal or vegetable matter; some occur in fungi; some are internal parasites of various other insects; and some occur as parasites or commensals in the nests of ants or termites. A few of the species that occur in ant or termite nests (and some others as well) have the wings reduced or lacking. More than 350 species occur in our area.

Family **Sýrphidae**—Syrphid Flies or Flower Flies: This is a large group (about 870 North American species), and many species are very abundant. Syrphids may be found almost everywhere, but different species occur in different types of habitats. The adults are often common about flowers and frequently do a great deal of hovering. Different species vary quite a bit in appearance (Figure 32–60), but (with a few exceptions) they can be recognized by the spurious vein in the wing between the radius and the media (Figure 32–11A–C, *spv*). Many are brightly colored and resemble various bees or wasps. Some look much like honey bees, others like bumble bees, and others like wasps, and the resemblance is often very striking. None of the syrphids will bite people.

Syrphid larvae vary considerably in habits and appearance (Figure 32–61). Many are predaceous on aphids; others live in the nests of social insects (ants, termites, or bees); others live in decaying vegetation or rotting wood; others live in highly polluted aquatic habitats; and a few feed on growing plants. The larvae of *Erístalis* (Figure 32–61D,E), which live in highly polluted water, have a very long breathing tube and are commonly called rattailed maggots. The adults of this genus (Figure 32–60D) resemble bees. Rattailed maggots are sometimes responsible for intestinal myiasis in humans.

Family **Pipuncùlidae**—Big-Headed Flies: The members of this group are small flies with the head very large and composed mostly of eyes (Figure 32–62). The wings are somewhat narrowed basally,

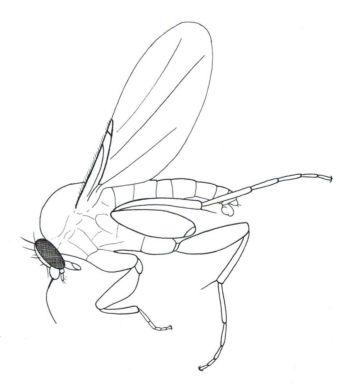

Figure 32–59. A humpbacked fly (Phòridae), 50×.

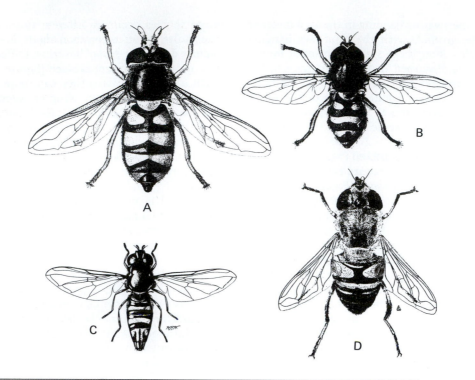

Figure 32–60.   Syrphid flies. **A**, *Dídea fasciàta* Macquart; **B**, *Sýrphus tòrvus* Osten Sacken; **C**, *Allográpta oblìqua* (Say); **D**, *Erístalis ténax* (L.). (**A** and **B**, courtesy of Metcalf and the Maine Agricultural Experiment Station; **C** and **D**, courtesy of USDA.)

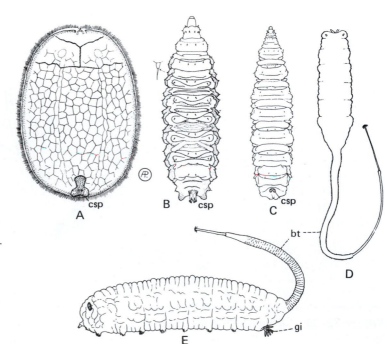

Figure 32–61.   Larvae of syrphid flies. **A**, *Mícrodon* sp., 50×; **B**, *Pipìza femoràlis* Loew, 50×; **C**, *Sýrphus víttafrons* Shannon, 3½×; **D, E**, *Erístalis* spp. (**D**, 2×; **E**, 3½×). *bt*, breathing tube; *csp*, caudal spiracle; *gi*, gills (Courtesy of Peterson; reprinted by permission.)

Figure 32–62. A big-headed fly, *Tomosvaryélla subviréscens* (Loew), female. (Courtesy of Knowlton and the Utah Agricultural Experiment Station.)

and the anal cell is usually long and closed near the wing margin (Figure 32–10J). The group is of moderate size (105 North American species), but its members are seldom common. The larvae are parasites of various hoppers, chiefly leafhoppers and planthoppers.

DIVISION **Schizóphora**—Muscoid Flies: The muscoid flies, with 60 families and more than 6000 North American species, make up about one-third of the order, and are to be found almost everywhere. They may be recognized by the presence of a frontal suture (Figure 32–5A, *fs*) on the lower part of the front of the head, arching up over the base of the antennae. Most are relatively stout-bodied, with a somewhat reduced wing venation (Figures 32–19, 32–20) and characteristic bristles on the head and thorax (which provide taxonomic characters).

Many of the muscoid flies are small, and their identification is often difficult. Identification is complicated by the fact that the distinction between families is often not very clear-cut, and many genera have been placed in different families by different authorities. Some species (e.g., the two species of *Latheticomỳia*, here placed in the family Cypselosomátidae) were originally described as being of uncertain family position.

The muscoids fall into two main groups, the Acalyptràtae (49 families, Conópidae through Canácidae) and the Calyptràtae (11 families, Scathophágidae though Stréblidae). These names refer to the development of the calypteres, which are large and well developed in most calyptrates and very small in the acalyptrates. These two groups also differ (with a few exceptions) in the structure of the second antennal segment (Figure 32–14A,B) and the sutures on the dorsal side of the thorax (Figure 32–14C,D) (see key, couplet 66). Each of these groups contains more than 3100 North American species.

Family **Conópidae**—Thick-Headed Flies: The conopids are medium-sized, brownish flies, many of

which superficially resemble small thread-waisted wasps (Figure 32–63). The abdomen is usually elongate and slender basally; the head is slightly broader than the thorax; and the antennae are long. All species have a very long and slender proboscis. In some species the proboscis is elbowed. The wing venation is similar to that in the Sýrphidae (Figure 32–11), but there is no spurious vein. Conopids may be distinguished from syrphids lacking a spurious vein by their long slender proboscis. In one genus (*Stylogáster*) the abdomen is slender and, in the female, terminates in a very long ovipositor that is as long as the rest of the body. The adults are usually found on flowers. The larvae are endoparasites, chiefly of adult bumble bees and wasps, and the flies usually oviposit on their hosts during flight.

Family **Cypselosomátidae:** This group contains two North American species of *Latheticomỳia*. This genus, along with the three new species in it (one occurring in Nicaragua), was described in 1956, and at the time of their description the author was uncertain of the family to which they belonged. In the USDA Catalog of Díptera (Stone *et al.* 1965) these species were not assigned to any family. McAlpine *et al.* (1981) placed them in the family Cypselosomátidae, which hitherto had been known only from the Old World. Only 14 specimens of the two United States species of *Latheticomỳia* are known. They were taken during late twilight at banana-baited traps, in Arizona and Utah.

The flies in this group that occur in the United States, *L. trìcolor* Wheeler and *L. lineàta* Wheeler, are 2.5–3.5 mm in length and black with yellow areas on the head, thorax, and legs. The front coxae are long and slender, nearly as long as the tibiae. The

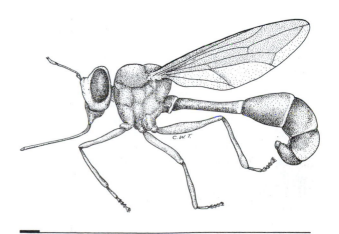

Figure 32–63. A thick-headed fly, *Physocéphala furcillàta* (Williston).

front femora have a few strong bristles ventrally in the distal half, and the hind femora have a single bristle at about three-fourths their length. The wings are hyaline; the anal cell is well developed; 2A does not reach the wing margin; and the second basal and discal cells are confluent.

Family **Micropèzidae**—Stilt-Legged Flies: The members of this group are small to medium-sized elongate flies with very long legs. The first posterior (R₅) cell is narrowed apically, and the anal cell is often long and pointed (Figure 32–19C). The adults are found near moist places. Only 27 species occur in North America, but the group is abundant in the tropics, where the larvae live in excrement.

Family **Nerìidae**—Cactus Flies: This group is represented in the United States by two species occurring in the Southwest. The most common species, *Odontoloxòzus longicòrnis* (Coquillett), ranges from southern Texas to southern California. It is slender, medium-sized, and grayish with brown markings, and it has long slender legs and long porrect antennae (Figure 32–21I). The larvae breed in decaying cacti, and the adults are usually found only on such cacti.

Family **Tanypèzidae**: The Tanypèzidae are medium-sized flies with rather long and slender legs. They occur in moist woods and are quite rare. Only two species occur in the United States (in the Northeast), and nothing is known of their immature stages.

Family **Strongylophthalmyìidae**: This group is very similar to the Psìlidae, with which it was formerly classified. The differences between this family and the Psìlidae are given in the key (couplet 128). This group contains a single widely distributed species, *Strongylophthalmỳia angustipénnis* Melander.

Family **Psìlidae**—Rust Flies: The psilids are small to medium-sized flies, usually rather slender, with long antennae. They have a peculiar ridge or weakening across the basal third of the wing. In the genus *Loxócera* the third antennal segment is very long and slender (Figure 32–18). The larvae live in the roots or galls of plants, and one species, *Psìla ròsae* Fabricius, the carrot rust fly, often does considerable damage to carrots, celery, and related plants.

Family **Diópsidae**—Stalk-Eyed Flies: This group is largely tropical, and only a single species, *Sphyracéphala brevicòrnis* (Say), occurs in North America. Most of the tropical species have the eyes situated at the ends of long stalks, but our species has relatively short eyestalks (Figure 32–21J). Adults of our species are blackish and about 4.5 mm in length, with the front femora distinctly swollen. This species has been reared in the laboratory (from eggs laid by overwintered adults), but little is known of its life history in the field. The larvae feed on wet or-

ganic matter and probably live in sphagnum bogs. Adults are usually found in or near such habitats, often on skunk cabbage.

Family **Lonchaèidae**: The lonchaeids are small, shining, blackish flies, with the abdomen in dorsal view oval and somewhat pointed apically. They occur chiefly in moist or shady places. The larvae are mostly secondary invaders of diseased or injured plant tissues. A few feed on pine cones, fruits, or vegetables. The group contains about 130 North American species, and adults are not very common.

Families **Otítidae** and **Platystomátidae**—Picture-Winged Flies: The picture-winged flies are a large group of small to medium-sized flies that usually have the wings marked with black, brown, or yellowish, and the body is often shining and metallic (Figure 32–64). They are usually found in moist places and are often very abundant. Little is known of their larval stages, but some feed on plants and occasionally damage cultivated plants, and some occur in decaying materials. These groups are most abundant in the tropics, but there are 96 species of Otítidae and 41 species of Platystomátidae in North America.

Family **Pyrgòtidae**: The pyrgotids are rather elongate flies of medium to large size, and they often have considerable coloring in the wings. The head is prominent and rounded, and there are no ocelli (Figure 32–65). This is a small group (eight North American species), and its members are not very common. The adults are mostly nocturnal and are often attracted to lights, and the larvae are parasites of adult june beetles.

Family **Tephrítidae**—Fruit Flies: The members of this group are small to medium-sized flies that usually have spotted or banded wings, the spotting often forming complicated and attractive patterns (Figures

Figure 32–64.   A picture-winged fly, *Euxésta stigmàtis* Loew, 6×. (Otítidae). (Courtesy of Wolcott and the Journal of Agriculture of the University of Puerto Rico.)

Figure 32–65.   *Pyrgòta undàta* Wiedemann
(Pyrgòtidae). (Courtesy of USDA.)

32–66, 32–67). They can be recognized by the structure of the subcosta, which apically bends forward at almost a right angle and then fades out. In most species the anal cell has an acute distal projection posteriorly (Figure 32–20B). The adults are found on flowers or vegetation. Some species have the habit of slowly moving their wings up and down while resting on vegetation and are often called peacock flies. This group is a large one (290 North American species), and many species are quite common.

The larvae of most tephritids feed on plants, and some are rather serious pests. The larva of *Rhagóletis pomonélla* (Walsh), usually called the apple maggot, tunnels in the fruits of apple and other orchard trees (Figure 32–66). Other species in this genus attack cherries. The Mediterranean fruit fly, *Cerátitis capitàta* (Wiedemann), attacks citrus and other fruits, and some years ago threatened to become a serious pest in the South. This species is now eradicated from the South. Species of the genus *Euròsta* form stem galls on goldenrod (Figure 32–68). The galls are rounded and thick-walled, with a single larva in the center. In the fall, the larva cuts a tunnel to the surface, overwinters as a larva in the gall, and pupates in the spring. A few of the tephritids are leaf miners in the larval stage.

Family **Richardìidae:** This is a small group (ten North American species) of uncommon to rare flies about which little is known. Most species have been taken at fruit-baited traps, and one species of *Omomỳia* has been taken on yucca. In *Omomỳia* (formerly classified in the family Thyreophòridae) the costa is spinose and the males are very hairy. These flies are known from Arizona and New Mexico. Most species in this family have patterned wings.

Family **Palloptéridae**—Flutter Flies: Our nine species in this group are rare and poorly known. They are medium-sized flies that usually have pictured wings and are found in moist shady places. The larvae of our species are unknown, but the larvae of European species are plant feeders in flower buds and stems or occur under the bark of fallen trees, where they prey on wood-boring beetle larvae.

Family **Piophílidae**—Skipper Flies: The skipper flies are usually less than 5 mm in length and are rather metallic black or bluish (Figure 32–69A). The larvae are mostly scavengers, and some live in cheese and preserved meats. The larvae of the cheese skipper, *Pióphila càsei* (L.), are often serious pests in cheese and meats. The name "skipper" refers to the fact that the larvae can jump. This family includes *Actenóptera hilarélla* (Zetterstedt), formerly placed in the family Neottiophílidae. This is a European species that has been reported from Quebec.

Family **Clusíidae:** The clusiids are small (mostly 3–4 mm in length) and relatively uncommon flies in which the wings are often smoky or marked with brown, especially apically. The body color varies from pale yellow to black. Some species have the thorax black dorsally and yellowish laterally. The larvae, which occur in decaying wood and under

Figure 32–66.   The apple maggot, *Rhagóletis pomonélla* (Walsh) (Tephrítidae). **A,** adult female, 7×; **B,** female puncturing skin of apple preparatory to depositing an egg; **C,** section of an apple showing an egg inserted at *a*, and a maggot tunneling into the pulp at *b*; **D,** an egg (greatly enlarged). (Courtesy of USDA.)

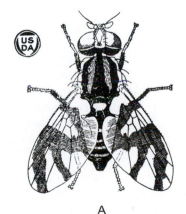

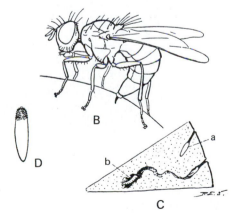

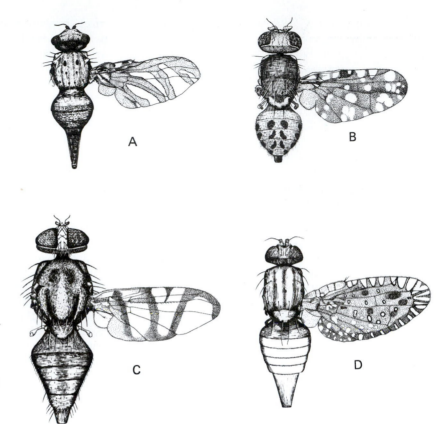

Figure 32–67. Fruit flies (Tephrítidae). **A,** *Peronỳma sarcinàta* (Loew); **B,** *Acidogòna melanùra* (Loew); **C,** *Zonosémata elécta* (Say); **D,** *Paracántha cúlta* (Wiedemann). (Courtesy of USDA.)

bark, are able to jump, much like the larvae of skipper flies.

Family **Acartophthálmidae:** This family is represented in North America by two rare species that

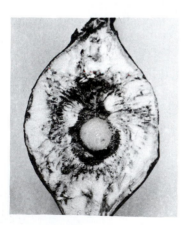

Figure 32–68. Gall of goldenrod gall fly, *Eurósta* sp. (Tephrítidae) cut open to show the larva. (Courtesy of the Illinois Natural History Survey.)

have been taken on rotten fungi and carrion from Massachusetts to Oregon and Alaska. One of these, *Acartophthálmus nigrìnus* (Zetterstedt), is about 2 mm long and is black with the front coxae and halteres yellow.

Family **Odiniídae:** This is a small group of uncommon flies, formerly placed in the family Agromýzidae. They differ from the Agromýzidae in having preapical tibial bristles and in having the wings patterned. The adults occur at fresh sap flows on trees, about woody fungi, on rotting tree trunks and stumps, and in similar places. Eleven species occur in the United States, most of them in the East.

Family **Agromýzidae**—Leaf-Miner Flies: These flies are small and usually blackish or yellowish in color (Figure 32–69B). The larvae are leaf miners, and the adults occur almost everywhere. Most species are more easily recognized by their mines than by the insects themselves. *Phytomỳza aquilegívora* Spencer is a fairly common species that makes a serpentine mine in the leaves of wild columbine (Figure 32–70B). *Agromỳza parvicòrnis* Loew makes a blotch mine in corn and several species of grasses. *Phytòbia clàra* (Melander) mines in the leaves of catalpa (Figure 32–70A). Most agromyzids make serpentine mines, that is, narrow winding mines that increase in width as the larva grows. This is the largest family of acalyptrate muscoids, with nearly 500 North American species.

Family **Opomýzidae:** The opomyzids are small to minute flies that are usually found in grassy areas. The known larvae feed in the stems of various grasses. Only 13 species occur in North America, and most of these occur in the West or in Canada; none is common. Ten of the species of opomyzids are in the genus *Geomýza*, which has the wings much narrowed at the base, without an alula and with no development of an anal lobe.

Family **Anthomýzidae:** These flies are small and somewhat elongate, and some species have pictured wings. This is a fairly small group (10 North American species), but its members are sometimes fairly common in grass and low vegetation, especially in marshy areas. The larvae live in marsh grasses and sedges.

Family **Aulacigástridae:** This group includes five relatively rare species that occur in the East, *Aulacigáster leucopèza* (Meigen), *Stenomìcra angustàta* Coquillett, and three species of *Cyamóps*. *Aulacigáster leucopèza* is a small blackish fly, about 2.5 mm in length, with the face banded with white, brown, and orange. Adults occur on (and larvae breed in) sap flows from tree wounds. The other four species are yellowish to brownish and are generally found in grasses.

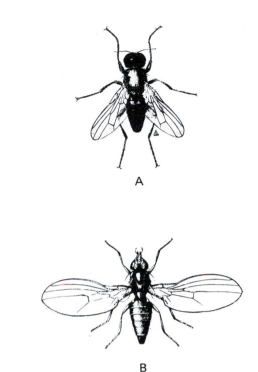

A

B

Figure 32–69.   **A,** adult of the cheese skipper, *Pióphila càsei* (L.) (Piophílidae); **B,** a leaf-miner fly, *Cerodóntha dorsàlis* (Loew) (Agromýzidae). (Courtesy of USDA.)

A

B

Figure 32–70.   Leaf mines of agromyzid flies. **A,** the catalpa leaf miner, *Phytòbia clàra* (Melander); **B,** the columbine leaf miner, *Phytomỳza aquilegívora* Spencer. (Courtesy of the Ohio Agricultural Research and Development Center.)

Family **Perisceliídidae:**   The three North American species in this family are widely distributed but rare. They are usually found around the sap flowing from tree wounds. One species has been reared from fermenting oak sap.

Family **Asteiidae:**   This family contains small to minute flies (usually 2 mm in length or less), most of which can be recognized by the distinctive venation (Figure 32–20A): R_{2+3} ending in the costa close to R_1. In *Leiomy̆za*, R_{2+3} ends well beyond R_1, at about three-fourths the wing length. Only 19 species occur in North America, and little is known of their habits.

Family **Milichiidae:**   The milichiids are small flies, usually black or silvery in color, and are sometimes fairly common in open areas. The larvae generally live in decaying plant or animal materials. Many of them have a slender proboscis. This group is a small one, with about three dozen North American species.

Family **Cárnidae:**   This small group (16 North American species) was formerly considered a subfamily of the Milichiidae. These flies may be separated from the Milichiidae by the characters given in the key (couplet 134). One species, *Cárnus hemápterus* Nitzsch, is a bloodsucking ectoparasite of birds.

Family **Braùlidae**—Bee Lice: This family contains a single species, *Braùla caèca* Nitzsch, which occurs in various parts of the world but is quite rare in North America. It is wingless and 1.2–1.5 mm in length and is found in bee hives, usually attached to the bees. The adults apparently feed on nectar and pollen at the bee's mouth.

Family **Coelòpidae**—Seaweed Flies: The members of this family are medium-sized to small flies, usually dark brown or black in color, and have the dorsum of the thorax conspicuously flattened and the body and legs very bristly (Figure 32–71). These flies occur along the seashore and are particularly abundant where various seaweeds have washed up. The larvae breed in the seaweed (chiefly kelp) in tremendous numbers, mainly just above the high tidemark in seaweed that has begun to rot. The adults swarming over the seaweed often attract large numbers of shore birds, which feed on them. Seaweed flies feed on flowers and sometimes cluster so thickly on the flowers near the shore that a single sweep of a net may yield a hundred or more individuals. Four of the five North American species occur along the Pacific Coast. The other, *Coelòpa frígida* (Fabricius), occurs along the Atlantic Coast from Rhode Island north.

Family **Dryomy̆zidae:**   This is a small group (11 North American species) of relatively rare flies that are similar to the Sciomy̆zidae. Three species in two

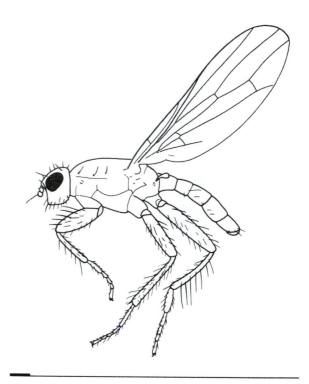

Figure 32–71.   A seaweed fly, *Coelòpa* sp. (Coelòpidae).

genera (*Helcomy̆za* and *Heterocheìla*, formerly placed in the family Helcomy̆zidae) occur along the Pacific coast from Oregon to Alaska. Their larvae live in rotting seaweed. The remaining species in the family are widely distributed and are usually found in moist woods. Their larvae occur in decaying organic matter.

Family **Sciomy̆zidae**—Marsh Flies: The marsh flies are small to medium-sized flies that are usually yellowish or brownish and have the antennae extending forward (Figure 32–72). Many species have spotted or patterned wings, and a characteristic bristle near the middle of the anterior face of the middle tibia. This is a fair-sized group (nearly 177 North American species), and many species are common insects. They usually occur along the banks of ponds and streams and in marshes, swamps, and woods. The larvae feed on snails, snail eggs, and slugs, generally as predators.

Family **Ropaloméridae:**   This is a small group of about 30 species, most of them occurring in Central and South America. They are of medium size and usually brownish or grayish in color, with the first posterior (R_5) cell narrowed apically, the femora thickened, and the hind tibiae often dilated. Our only species, *Rhy̆tidops floridénsis* (Aldrich), occurs

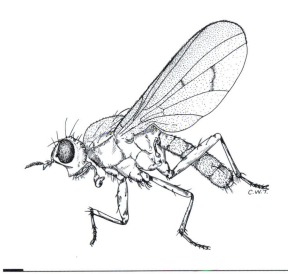

Figure 32–72.   A marsh fly, *Tetanócera vícina* Macquart (Sciomýzidae), 7½×.

in Florida, where adults are usually found around fresh palm exudates.

Family **Sépsidae**—Black Scavenger Flies: The sepsids are small, shining blackish flies (sometimes with a reddish tinge) that have the head spherical and the abdomen narrowed at the base (Figure 32–73). Many species have a dark spot along the costal margin of the wing near the tip. The larvae live in excrement and various types of decaying materials. The adults are common flies and are often found in considerable numbers near materials in which the larvae breed.

Family **Lauxaniidae:** Lauxaniids are small, relatively robust flies, rarely over 6 mm in length. Some have patterned wings, and they vary considerably in color. They can usually be distinguished from other acalyptrate muscoids by the complete subcosta, the lack of oral vibrissae, the postverticals converging, and the preapical tibial bristles. The group is a fairly large one (156 North American species), and its members are common in moist shady places. The larvae occur in decaying vegetation.

Family **Chamaemyìidae**—Aphid Flies: The chamaemyiids are small flies that are usually grayish in color with black spots on the abdomen. The larvae of most species are predaceous on aphids, scale insects, and mealybugs. One species has been reared from birds' nests.

Family **Heleomyzidae:** The heleomyzids are a fairly large group (113 North American species) of small to medium-sized flies, most of which are brownish in color. Many superficially resemble marsh flies (Sciomyzidae), but they have well-developed oral vibrissae, converging postvertical bristles (Figure 32–21 C), spinose costa (Figure 32–19 H), and smaller and less prominent antennae. The adults are usually found in moist shady places. The larvae of most species live in decaying plant or animal matter or in fungi.

Family **Trixoscelídidae:** The members of this family are small flies, mostly 2–3 mm in length, with the body yellow or dark and the wings hyaline, spotted, or clouded. Twenty-seven species are known in the United States, all but two occurring in the western states. *Spilochròa ornàta* (Johnson) (wings dark, with hyaline spots) occurs in Florida, and *Neóssos marylándica* Malloch (wings hyaline) has been reported from Maryland. These flies occur in grassy areas, woodlands, and deserts. *Neóssos marylándica* has been reared from puparia found in the nests of various song birds.

Family **Chyromỳidae:** This is a small (nine North American species) but widely distributed group of usually uncommon flies. Adults are usually taken on windows or on vegetation, and some have been reared from birds' nests and rotting wood.

Family **Rhinotòridae:** This is a small group of tropical flies, similar in general appearance and habits to the Ropaloméridae (page 564). Our only species, *Neorhinotòra divérsa* (Giglio-Tos), has been recorded in Arizona and New Mexico, where it was taken in banana-baited traps.

Family **Sphaerocéridae**—Small Dung Flies: The sphaerocerids are very small, black or brown flies that can usually be recognized by the character of

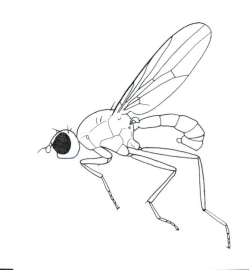

Figure 32–73.   A black scavenger fly (Sépsidae), 15×.

the hind tarsi (Figure 32–23A). Many have the longitudinal veins somewhat shortened and not reaching the wing margin (Figure 32–23D). This is a fair-sized group (241 North American species) whose members are common in swampy places near excrement. They often occur in large numbers about manure piles. The larvae live in excrement and refuse.

Family **Curtonòtidae:** This group is represented in North America by a single species, *Curtonòtum hélvum* (Loew), which occurs in the East. This species is about 6 mm in length, *Drosóphila*-like in appearance, and light yellowish brown with dark brown markings. It occurs in high grass in moist places. The larva is unknown.

Family **Drosophílidae**—Pomace Flies or Small Fruit Flies: These flies are 3–4 mm in length and usually yellowish in color (Figure 32–74), and they are generally found around decaying vegetation and fruits. This group is a large one (190 North American species), and many species are very common. The pomace flies are often pests in the household when fruits are present. The larvae of most species occur in decaying fruits and fungi. In the case of the larvae living in fruits, it has been shown that the larvae actually feed on the yeasts growing in the fruits. A few species are ectoparasitic (on caterpillars) or predaceous (on mealybug and other small Homóptera) in the larval stage. Several species in this group, because of their short life span, giant salivary gland chromosomes, and ease of culturing, have been used extensively in studies of heredity.

Family **Diastátidae:** This is a small (seven North American species) but widely distributed group whose members resemble the Drosophílidae but are usually dark-colored. They are relatively rare, and little is known of their habits.

Family **Camíllidae:** These flies resemble the Drosophílidae, but they are metallic, they lack sternopleural bristles, and they have the anal cell open apically. One species, *Camílla glàbra* (Fallén), has been reported from Ontario. Nothing is known of its biology.

Family **Ephýdridae**—Shore Flies: This is a large group (426 North American species), and some species are quite common. Shore flies are small to very small. Most of them are dark-colored, and a few have pictured wings. The adults are found in moist places: marshes, the shores of ponds and streams, and the seashore. The larvae are aquatic, and many species occur in brackish or even strongly saline or alkaline water. One western species, *Helaeomỳia petròlei* (Coquillett), breeds in pools of crude petroleum. These flies often occur in enormous numbers. Pools along the seashore may sometimes be alive with the adults, which walk or cluster on the surface of the water (for example, *Éphydra ripària* Fallén; Figure 32–75). Along the shore of Great Salt Lake, ephydrids may arise from the ground in clouds, and a few sweeps of a net may yield a cupful. At one time the Indians gathered the puparia from the lake and ate them.

Family **Chlorópidae**—Grass Flies: The chloropids are small and rather bare flies, and some species are brightly colored with yellow and black. They are very common in meadows and other places where there is considerable grass, though they may be found in a variety of habitats. The larvae of most species feed in grass stems, and some are serious pests of cereals. A few are scavengers, and a few are parasitic or predaceous. Some of the chloropids (for example, *Hippélates*), which breed in decaying vegetation and excrement, are attracted to animal secretions and feed on pus, blood, and similar materials. They are particularly attracted to the eyes and are sometimes called eye gnats. These flies may act as vectors of yaws and pinkeye. This is a fairly large group, with 290 North American species.

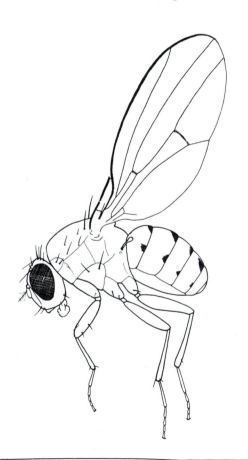

Figure 32–74. A pomace fly, *Drosóphila* sp., 20×.

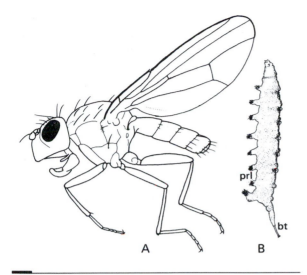

Figure 32–75.   A shore fly, *Éphydra ripària* Fallén. **A,** adult, 10×; **B,** larva, 4×. *bt,* breathing tube; *prl,* prolegs. (**B,** courtesy of Peterson; reprinted by permission.)

Family **Cryptochètidae:**   The flies in this group are somewhat similar to black flies (Simulìidae) and have habits similar to those of eye gnats (*Hippélates,* family Chlorópidae; see above). They can usually be recognized by the enlarged third antennal segment, which reaches nearly to the lower edge of the head and which lacks an arista but bears at its apex a short spine or tubercle. As far as known, the larvae are parasites of scale insects in the family Margaròdidae. This is principally an Old World group of flies, and only one species, *Cryptochèta icéryae* (Williston), occurs in the United States. It was introduced into California from Australia in the 1880s to control the cottony cushion scale, *Icérya púrchasi.* This fly is about 1.5 mm in length and stout-bodied, with the head and thorax dark metallic blue and the abdomen shiny green. The introduction was a successful one. This fly is probably a more important natural enemy of the cottony cushion scale than the ladybird beetle *Rodólia cardinális,* which was also introduced from Australia to control this scale insect.

Family **Tethínidae:**   Most tethinids are seashore species, occurring in beach grass, in salt marshes, and around seaweed washed up on the shore. The majority are found along the Pacific Coast. The inland species occur mainly in alkaline areas. This is a small group (24 North American species), and its members are uncommon flies.

Family **Canácidae**—Beach Flies: The canacids are small flies that resemble the ephydrids in appearance and habits, but they have only a single break in the costa, they have an anal cell, and the ocellar triangle is quite large (as in Figure 32–24A). Adults of the five rare North American species occur along the seashore in the southeastern states and in California. The larvae live in the algae washed up on the shore.

Section   **Calyptràtae**—Calyptrate Muscoid Flies: These flies occur nearly everywhere, often in large numbers. Some of the calyptrate groups are fairly distinct and easily recognized, but others are not, and there are differences of opinion about the taxonomic placement of some.

For purposes of identification, the families in this section may be divided into four groups:

1. Flat and leathery, with the coxae separated, and winged or wingless; ectoparasites of birds and mammals: Hippobóscidae, Stréblidae, and Nycteribìidae.
2. Robust, hairy, beelike, with the mouthparts reduced (bot and warble flies): Oéstridae.
3. Somewhat similar to a house fly in general appearance, usually with no hypopleural or pteropleural bristles, and the R_5 cell usually parallel-sided: Scathophágidae, Anthomyìidae, and Múscidae.
4. Similar to group 3, but with hypopleural and pteropleural bristles, and the R_5 cell narrowed or closed distally: Calliphòridae, Sarcophágidae, Rhinophòridae, and Tachínidae.

Family **Scathophágidae**—Dung Flies: The members of this group are very similar to the Anthomyìidae (the family in which they are sometimes placed), but differ in having no fine hairs on the underside of the scutellum, usually just one sternopleural bristle, and no cruciate frontal bristles.

Probably the most common members of the Scathophágidae are yellowish and quite hairy, and their larvae live in dung. Other species are dark-colored, and the larvae live in a variety of situations: some are plant feeders (a few of these are leaf miners); some feed in rotting seaweeds; and some are aquatic. The Scathophágidae are a large group (148 North American species) and contain many common species.

Family **Anthomyìidae:**   This is a large group (more than 500 North American species), and most are blackish and about the size of a house fly or smaller. They differ from the Múscidae in having the anal vein ($Cu_2 + 2A$) reaching the wing margin, at least as a fold. Most Anthomyìidae have fine hairs on the underside of the scutellum (Figure 32–13D). Those Anthomyìidae that lack these hairs (Fucellìinae) have cruciate frontal bristles and usually four sternopleural bristles, and they have the costa spinose.

Most of the Anthomyíidae are plant feeders in the larval stage, and many of these feed on the roots of the host plant. Some of these (Figure 32–76) are serious pests of garden or field crops. The larvae of the Fucelliìnae, a small group occurring chiefly in the West and in Canada, are aquatic and predaceous.

Family **Múscidae:** This is a large group (more than 700 North American species), and its members are to be found almost everywhere. Many are important pests. The house fly, *Músca doméstica* L., breeds in filth of all kinds and is often very abundant. It is known to be a vector of typhoid fever, dysentery, yaws, anthrax, and some forms of conjunctivitis. It

does not bite. The face fly, *Músca autumnàlis* De Geer, is an important pest of cattle. It gets its name from its habit of clustering on the face of cattle (Figure 2–6). The stable fly, horn fly, and tsetse flies are biting flies; but unlike mosquitoes, horse flies, and others, both sexes bite. The stable fly, *Stomóxys cálcitrans* (L.) (Figure 32–77), is very similar to the house fly in appearance (Figure 32–78). It breeds chiefly in piles of decaying straw. The horn fly, *Haematòbia írritans* (L.), which is similar to the house fly in appearance but smaller, is a serious pest of cattle that breeds in fresh cow dung. The tsetse flies, *Glossìna* spp., do not occur in the United States, but

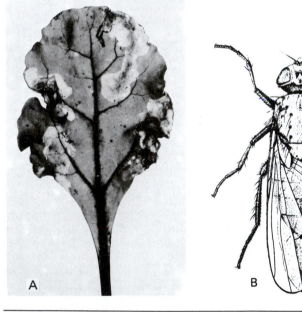

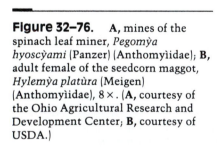

Figure 32–76. **A,** mines of the spinach leaf miner, *Pegomỳa hyoscỳami* (Panzer) (Anthomyìidae); **B,** adult female of the seedcorn maggot, *Hylemỳa platùra* (Meigen) (Anthomyìidae), 8×. (**A,** courtesy of the Ohio Agricultural Research and Development Center; **B,** courtesy of USDA.)

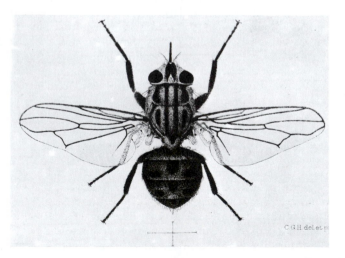

Figure 32–77. The stable fly, *Stomóxys cálcitrans* (L.). (Courtesy of the Illinois Natural History Survey.)

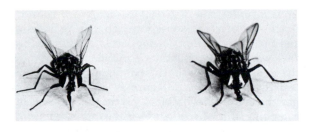

Figure 32–78.   Two common muscids, showing the difference in the shape of the proboscis. Left, stable fly; right, house fly. (Courtesy of the Illinois Natural History Survey.)

in Africa they are vectors of the trypanosomes that cause sleeping sickness and similar diseases of man and various animals.

Fánnia and its relatives (subfamily Fanniìnae) differ from other muscids in having 3A curved outward distally, so that Cu_2 + 2A if extended would meet it (Figure 32–16D). This group is sometimes given family rank. These flies look very much like small house flies and, in some areas, are a more important household pest than *M. doméstica*. The larvae breed in excrement and various types of decaying materials.

Family **Calliphòridae**—Blow Flies: Blow flies are to be found practically everywhere, and many species are of considerable economic importance. Most blow flies are about the size of a house fly or a little larger, and many are metallic blue or green (Figure 32–79). Blow flies are very similar to flesh flies (Sarcophágidae), and some authorities put the two groups in a single family, the Metopìidae. Blow flies are often metallic in color and have the arista of the antennae plumose at the tip, whereas flesh flies are blackish with gray thoracic stripes (Figure 32–80A) and have the arista bare or only the basal half plumose. Blow flies usually have two notopleural (rarely three) bristles, and flesh flies usually have four (Figure 32–17).

Most blow flies are scavengers, the larvae living in carrion, excrement, and similar materials. The most common species are those that breed in carrion. These species lay their eggs on bodies of dead animals, and the larvae feed on the decaying tissues of the animal. To most people a dead animal teeming with maggots (mostly the larvae of blow flies) is a nauseating thing, but it should be remembered that these insects are performing a valuable service in helping to remove dead animals from the landscape. The larvae of some of the species that breed in carrion, particularly *Phaenícia sericàta* (Meigen) and *Phórmia regína* (Meigen), when reared under aseptic

conditions, have been used in the treatment of such diseases as osteomyelitis in man. On the other hand, many of these flies may act as mechanical vectors of various diseases. Dysentery frequently accompanies high blow fly populations.

Some blow flies lay their eggs in open sores of animals or people. In some cases the larvae feed only on decaying or suppurating tissue, but in other cases they may attack living tissue. The screwworm fly, *Cochliomỳia hominivòrax* (Coquerel) (Figure 32–80B), is a species in the latter category. It lays its eggs in wounds or in the nostrils of its host, and its larvae may cause considerable damage. In recent years the number of screwworm flies in the South and Southwest has been greatly reduced by releasing large numbers of sterile male flies. The females mate only once, and if a female mates with a sterile male, its eggs fail to hatch.

Flies in this family are the "house flies" of the western United States, especially in the Southwest. They are far more common than *Músca* in houses in that part of the country.

When fly larvae become parasitic on humans or animals, the condition is spoken of as myiasis. Flies such as the screwworm may develop in surface wounds and cause cutaneous myiasis or in the nasal cavities and cause nasal myiasis. A few other flies in this group have been known to develop in the human intestine and cause intestinal myiasis. Myiasis in humans is relatively rare in the United States and Canada, and it is probably a more or less accidental occurrence. In the South and Southwest it has been very important in domestic animals.

Family **Sarcophágidae**—Flesh Flies: Flesh flies are very similar to some blow flies, but are generally blackish with gray thoracic stripes (never metallic)

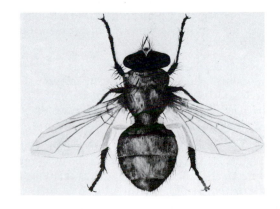

Figure 32–79.   A blow fly, *Lucília illústris* (Meigen).

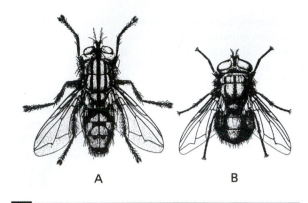

Figure 32–80. **A,** a flesh fly, *Sarcóphaga haemorrhoidàlis* (Fallén); **B,** the screwworm fly, *Cochliomỳia hominivòrax* (Coquerel) (Calliphòridae). (Courtesy of USDA.)

(Figure 32–80A). The adults are common insects and feed on various sugar-containing materials such as nectar, sap, fruit juices, and honeydew. The larvae vary considerably in habits, but nearly all feed on some sort of animal material. Many are scavengers, feeding on dead animals. Some are parasites of other insects (especially various beetles and grasshoppers). A few are parasites of vertebrates, usually developing in skin pustules, and some of these occasionally infest humans. Many species (most of the Miltogrammìnae) lay their eggs in the nests of various bees and wasps, where their larvae feed on the materials with which these nests are provisioned.

Family **Oéstridae**—Bot Flies and Warble Flies: The members of this group are robust, hairy, and somewhat beelike. The mouth opening is small, and the mouthparts are vestigial or lacking (Figure 32–13A). The larvae are endoparasites of mammals, and some are important pests of livestock.

The 47 North American species in this family are arranged in five genera and four subfamilies, as follows:

Cuterebrìnae: 34 species of *Cutérebra*
Gasterophilìnae: 4 species of *Gasteróphilus*
Hypodermatìnae: 3 species of *Hypodérma*
Oestrìnae: 1 species of *Oéstrus* and 5 species of *Cephenemỳia*

Gasteróphilus differs from the other oestrids in having M_{1+2} straight and reaching the wing margin behind the apex of the wing, and m is about opposite r-m (Figure 32–16E). The other oestrids have M_{1+2} bending forward apically and ending either in R_{4+5} (*Oéstrus,* Figure 32–16F) or in the wing margin in front of the wing tip (*Cutérebra, Hypodérma,* and

Cephenemỳia), and m is well distad of r-m. The Cuterebrìnae have the scutellum strongly projecting, and the postscutellum is not developed (Figure 32–13C), while the Hypodermatìnae and Oestrìnae have the scutellum quite short, and the postscutellum is usually well developed (Figure 32–13B). *Hypodérma* has the apical portion of M_{1+2} (the part beyond m) extending almost straight to the wing margin (Figure 32–81B), while in *Cephenemỳia* the apical portion of M_{1+2} continues in the same direction a short distance beyond m, then bends forward at a right angle and extends to the wing margin (much as in Figure 32–16A).

The Gasterophilìnae, or horse bot flies, are very similar to honey bees in appearance (Figure 32–81A). The larvae infest the alimentary tract of horses and are often serious pests. Three species occur commonly in the United States, *Gasteróphilus intestinàlis* (De Geer), *G. nasàlis* (L.), and *G. haemorrhoidàlis* (L.). A fourth species, G. *inérmis* Brauer, is very rare. In *G. intestinàlis* the eggs are laid on the legs or shoulders of the horse and are taken into the mouth when the animal licks these parts. In *G. nasàlis* the eggs are usually laid on the underside of the jaw, and the larvae are believed to make their way through the skin into the mouth. In *G. haemorrhoidàlis* the eggs are laid on the lips of the horse. The larvae develop in the stomach (*intestinàlis*), duodenum (*nasàlis*), or rectum (*haemorrhoidàlis*). When ready to pupate they pass out of the alimentary tract in the feces and pupate in the ground.

The Cuterebrìnae, or robust bot flies, are large, stout-bodied, rather hairy flies that resemble bees. Our species belong to the genus *Cutérebra,* the larvae of which are parasites of rabbits and rodents. One tropical species in this subfamily, *Dermatòbia hóminis* (L., Jr.) (Figure 32–81D), attacks livestock and occasionally people. This species lays its eggs on mosquitoes (principally mosquitoes in the genus *Psoróphora*). The eggs hatch and the larvae penetrate the skin when the mosquito feeds on livestock or humans. Stable flies and other muscids may also serve as carriers of *D. hóminis* eggs to humans.

The Hypodermatìnae include the ox warble flies, *Hypodérma bòvis* (L.) and *H. lineàtum* (de Villers). A third species of *Hypodérma* is a parasite of caribou. Ox warble flies are serious pests of cattle. The eggs of these flies are usually laid on the legs of cattle, and the larvae penetrate the skin and migrate, often by way of the esophagus, to the back, where they develop in swellings or "warbles" just under the skin. When full grown they escape through the skin and pupate in the ground. Adult ox warble flies are very fast fliers, and although they do not bite or injure the cattle when they oviposit, they are very

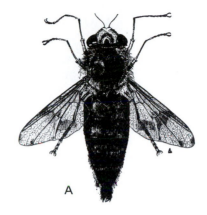

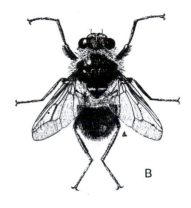

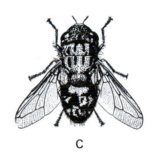

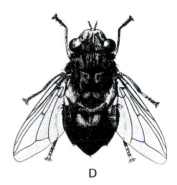

Figure 32–81.   Bot and warble flies (Oèstridae). **A,** a horse bot fly, *Gasteróphilus intestinàlis* (De Geer), female; **B,** ox warble fly, *Hypodérma lineàtum* (de Villers), female; **C,** sheep bot fly, *Oéstrus òvis* L., female; **D,** human bot fly or torsalo, *Dermatòbia hóminis* (L., Jr.), female. (Courtesy of USDA.)

annoying to cattle. Ox warble may seriously affect the health of cattle, and the holes made in the skin by the escaping larvae reduce the value of the hide when it is made into leather.

The subfamily Oestrínae includes the sheep bot fly, *Oéstrus òvis* L. (Figure 32–81 C), and five species of *Cephenemỳia*, which are parasites of cervids (deer, moose, elk, etc.). The sheep bot fly is viviparous and deposits its larvae in the nostrils of sheep (rarely, also in humans). The larvae feed in the frontal sinuses of the sheep.

Family **Rhinophòridae:**   These flies are similar to the tachinids (with which they were formerly classified) but differ in having the postscutellum weakly developed and the calypteres narrow. The eyes are sometimes hairy. The group is a small one, with only two North American species. *Melanóphora roràlis* (L.), which occurs in the East, is probably the most common species. It is a parasite of sowbugs.

Family **Tachínidae:**   This family is the second largest in the order (at least in North America), with about 1300 North American species, and its mem-

bers are to be found almost everywhere. It is a very valuable group, as the larval stages are parasites of other insects, and many species aid in keeping pest species in check.

Tachinids are usually relatively easy to recognize. Both the hypopleural and the pteropleural bristles are developed, and the postscutellum is prominent (Figure 32–15B). The ventral sclerites of the abdomen are usually overlapped by the terga, and the abdomen generally has a number of very large bristles in addition to the smaller ones. The first posterior (R_5) cell is narrowed or closed distally, and most species have the arista bare. Many tachinids are very similar in general appearance to muscids and flesh flies (Figure 32–82, 32–83A). Many are large, bristly, and beelike or wasplike in appearance.

Many different groups of insects are attacked by tachinids, and while most tachinids are more or less restricted to particular hosts, there are a few that may develop in a wide variety of hosts. Most tachinids attack the larvae of Lepidóptera, sawflies, and beetles, but some are known to attack Hemíptera,

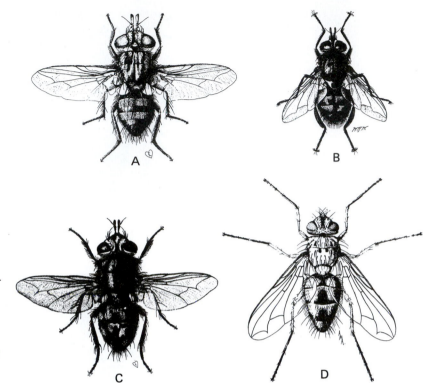

Figure 32–82.   Tachinid flies.
A, *Euphorócera claripénnis*
(Macquart); **B,** *Winthèmia
quadripustulàta* (Fabricius); **C,**
Árchytas marmoràtus (Townsend);
D, *Dexílla ventràlis* (Aldrich).
(Courtesy of USDA.)

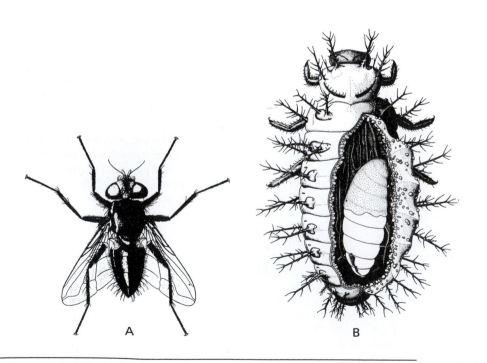

Figure 32–83.   The bean beetle tachinid, *Aplomyiópsis epiláchnae* (Aldrich). **A,** adult; **B,** a
bean beetle larva dissected to show a larva of this tachinid inside it. (Courtesy of USDA.)

Orthóptera, and some other orders, and a few attack other arthropods. A number of tachinids have been imported into the United States to aid in the control of introduced pests.

Most tachinids deposit their eggs directly on the body of their host, and it is not at all uncommon to find caterpillars with several tachinid eggs on them. Upon hatching, the tachinid larva usually burrows into its host and feeds internally (Figure 32–83B). When fully developed, it leaves the host and pupates nearby. Some tachinids lay their eggs on foliage. These eggs usually hatch into peculiar flattened larvae called planidia, which remain on the foliage until they can attach to a suitable host when it passes by. In other species that lay their eggs on foliage, the eggs hatch when they are ingested (along with the foliage) by a caterpillar. The tachinid larvae then proceed to feed on the internal organs of the caterpillar. An insect attacked by tachinids is practically always killed eventually.

Family **Hippobóscidae**—Louse Flies: This group includes both winged and wingless forms. Most of the winged forms are dark brownish in color and somewhat smaller than house flies. They are most likely to be found on birds. These flies are easily recognized by their flat shape and leathery appearance. They are the only flies likely to be found on living birds. The sheep ked, *Melóphagus ovìnus* (L.) (Figure 32–84), is a fairly common wingless louse fly. It is about 6 mm in length and reddish brown in color, and the adult is a parasite of sheep.

Families **Stréblidae** and **Nycteribìidae**—Bat Flies: These flies are ectoparasites of bats. Those in the family Stréblidae may be winged or wingless or may have the wings reduced. There are no ocelli, and the compound eyes are small or absent. The bat flies in the family Nycteribìidae are small, wingless, and spiderlike, with the head folded back into a groove on the dorsum of the thorax. The compound eyes are small and two-faceted. Only 15 species of bat flies occur in North America (8 in the Stréblidae, 7 in the Nycteribìidae), and they are very seldom encountered. They occur in the South and West.

Collecting and Preserving Díptera

The general methods of collecting Díptera are similar to those of collecting other insects. To obtain a large variety, one must collect in a variety of habitats. Many of the smaller species can be best collected by sweeping, putting the entire catch into the killing bottle, and examining it carefully later. Traps such as that shown in Figure 36–7B, using various types of baits, are useful collecting devices.

Most Díptera, particularly the smaller specimens, should be mounted as soon as possible after they are captured because they dry quickly and are likely to be damaged in mounting if they have dried out very much. Many of the smaller and more delicate specimens, such as midges, mosquitoes, and similar forms, should be handled very carefully in order to avoid rubbing off the minute hairs and scales, which are often important in identification, particularly if the specimen is ever identified to species. The only way to get good specimens of many of these delicate forms is to rear them and to get them into a killing jar without using a net.

The larger Díptera are preserved on pins, and the smaller specimens are mounted on points, minuten pins, or microscope slides. In pinning a fly, particularly the muscoids, it is important that the bristles on the dorsum of the thorax be kept intact; the pin should be inserted to one side of the midline. If the specimen is too small to pin this way, it should be mounted on a point. Specimens mounted on a point should be on their right side, with the wings together above the body and lying along the point, and the body at right angles to the point (Figure 36–14B). If a specimen to be mounted on a point dies with its wings bent down, the wings can often be snapped into the vertical position by gently squeezing the thorax with forceps. This procedure should be carried out as soon as possible after the insect dies. Some of the more minute specimens (especially Nematócera) should be preserved in fluids and must be mounted on microscope slides for detailed study.

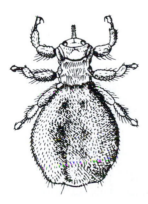

Figure 32–84.   The sheep ked, or sheep-tick, *Melóphagus ovìnus* (L.). (Courtesy of Knowlton, Madsen, and the Utah Agricultural Experiment Station.)

References

Alexander, C. P. 1967. The crane flies of California. Bull. Calif. Insect Surv. 8:1–269; illus.

Arnaud, P. H., Jr. 1978. A host-parasite catalog of North American Tachinidae (Diptera). USDA Misc. Publ. 1319; 860 pp.

Blanton, F. S., and W. W. Wirth. 1979. The sand flies (*Culicoides*) of Florida (Diptera: Ceratopogonidae). Arthropods of Florida and Neighboring Land Areas 10:1–204; illus.

Byers, G. W. 1969. A new family of nematocerous Diptera. J. Kan. Entomol. Soc. 42:366–371; illus. (Baeonotidae.)

Carpenter, S. J., and W. J. La Casse. 1955. Mosquitoes of North America (North of Mexico). Berkeley: Univ. California Press, 360 pp.; illus.

Cole, F. R. 1969. The flies of Western North America. Berkeley: Univ. California Press, 693 pp.; illus.

Curran, C. H. 1934. The Families and Genera of North American Diptera. New York: published by the author, 512 pp.; illus. (A reprint of this book has been published by Henry Tripp, Mount Vernon, N.Y., 1965.)

Diptera of Connecticut. 1942–1964. Guide to the insects of Connecticut, Part 6: The Diptera, or true flies of Connecticut. Bulletins of the Connecticut State Geological and Natural History Survey. First Fascicle, Bull. 64: External morphology, key to families: Tanyderidae, Ptychopteridae, Trichoceridae, Anisopodidae, and Tipulidae; by G. C. Crampton, C. H. Curran, C. P. Alexander, and R. B. Friend, 509 pp., illus. (1942). Second Fascicle, Bull. 68: Family Culicidae, the mosquitoes, by R. Matheson, 48 pp., illus. (1945). Third Fascicle, Bull. 69: Asilidae, by S. W. Bromley, 48 pp., illus. (1946). Fourth Fascicle, Bull. 75: Family Tabanidae, by G. B. Fairchild, and Family Phoridae, by C. T. Brues, 85 pp., illus. (1950). Fifth Fascicle, Bull. 80: Tendipedidae (Chironomidae), by O. A. Johannsen and H. K. Townes, Heleidae (Ceratopogonidae), by O. A. Johannsen and Fungivoridae (Mycetophilidae) by F. R. Shaw and E. G. Fisher, 250 pp., illus. (1952). Sixth Fascicle, Bull. 87: March flies and gall midges, Bibionidae, by D. E. Hardy, and Itonididae (Cecidomyiidae), by A. E. Pritchard and E. P. Felt, 218 pp., illus. (1958). Seventh Fascicle, Bull. 92: Psychodidae, by L. W. Quate, 54 pp., illus. (1960). Eighth Fascicle, Bull. 93: Scatopsidae and Hyperoscelidae, by E. F. Cook, Blepharoceridae and Deuterophlebiidae, by C. P. Alexander, and Dixidae, by W. R. Nowell, 115 pp., illus. (1963). Ninth Fascicle, Bull. 97: Simuliidae and Thaumaleidae, by A. Stone, 126 pp., illus. (1964).

Felt, E. P. 1940. Plant Galls and Gall Makers. Ithaca, N.Y.: Comstock, 364 pp.; illus.

Gillette, J. D. 1971. Mosquitoes. London: Weidenfeld and Nicolson, 274 pp.; illus.

Hall, D. G. 1948. The blow flies of North America. Thomas Say Foundation Publ. 4, 477 pp., illus.

Hennig, W. 1948–1952. Die Larvenformen der Dipteren. Berlin: Akademie-Verlag. Part 1: 185 pp., illus. (1948). Part 2: 458 pp., illus. (1950). Part 3: 628 pp., illus. (1952).

Huckett, H. C. 1965. The Muscidae of northern Canada, Alaska, and Greenland (Diptera). Mem. Entomol. Soc. Can. 42: 1–369; illus.

Hull, F. M. 1962. Robberflies of the World: The genera of the family Asilidae. U.S. Natl. Mus. Bull. 224 (2 vol.); 907 pp.; illus.

Ide, F. P. 1965. A fly of the archaic family Nymphomyiidae (Diptera) from North America. Can. Entomol. 97:496–507; illus.

James, M. T. 1960. The soldier flies or Stratiomyidae of California. Bull. Calif. Insect Surv. 6(5):79–122.

Johannsen, O. A. 1910–1912. The fungus gnats of North America. Maine Agr. Expt. Sta. Bull. 172:209–279; 180:125–192; 196:249–327; 200:57–146; illus.

Kessel, E. L., and E. A. Maggioncalda. 1968. A revision of the genera of Platypezidae, with descriptions of five new genera, and considerations of the phylogeny, circumversion, and hypopygia (Diptera). Weismann J. Biol. 26 (1):33–106; illus.

Knight, K. L., and A. Stone. 1973 (2nd ed.). A Catalog of the Mosquitoes of the World (Diptera: Culicidae). College Park, Md.; Thomas Say Foundation. Vol. 6, 611 pp. Supplement to Vol. 6 (1978, by K. L. Knight), 70 pp.

Maa, T. C. 1971. An annotated bibliography of batflies (Diptera: Streblidae, Nycteribiidae). Pac. Insects Monogr. 28:119–211.

Martin, C. H. 1968. The new family Leptogastridae (the grass flies) compared with the Asilidae (robber flies) (Diptera). J. Kan. Entomol. Soc. 41(1):70–100; illus.

Matheson, R. 1944. Handbook of the Mosquitoes of North America. Ithaca, N.Y.: Comstock, 314 pp.; illus.

McAlpine, J. F. 1963. Relationships of *Cremifania* Czerny (Diptera: Chamaemyiidae) and description of a new species. Can. Entomol. 95(3):239–253; illus.

McAlpine, J. F., B. V. Peterson, G. E. Shewell, H. J. Teskey, J. R. Vockeroth, and D. M. Wood. 1981–1987. Manual of Nearctic Diptera. Vol. 1, Monogr. No. 27, Research Branch, Agriculture Canada, 674 pp., illus. (1981). Vol. 2, Monogr. No. 28, Research Branch, Agriculture Canada, pp. 675–1332, illus. (1987).

McFadden, M. W. 1972. The soldier flies of Canada and Alaska (Diptera: Stratiomyidae). I. Beridinae, Sarginae, and Clitellariinae. Can. Entomol. 104:531–561.

Oldroyd, H. 1964. The Natural History of Flies. London: Weidenfeld and Nicolson, 324 pp.; illus.

Pechuman, L. L. 1973. Horse flies and deer flies of Virginia (Diptera: Tabanidae). Va. Polytech. Inst. State Univ. Res. Div. Bull. 81, 92 pp.; illus.

Pennak, R. W. 1978 (2nd ed.). Fresh-Water Invertebrates of the United States. New York: Wiley Interscience, 803 pp.; illus.

Peters, T. M., and E. F. Cook. 1966. The Nearctic Dixidae (Diptera). Misc. Publ. Entomol. Soc. Amer. 5(5):231–278; illus.

Peterson, A. 1951. Larvae of Insects, Part 2: Coleoptera, Diptera, Neuroptera, Siphonaptera, Mecoptera, Trichoptera. Ann Arbor, Mich.: Edwards Bros., 519 pp., illus.

Roback, S. D. 1951. A classification of the muscoid Calyptrate Diptera. Ann. Entomol. Soc. Amer. 44:327–361; illus.

Sabrosky, C. W. 1937. On mounting micro-Diptera. Entomol. News 48:102–107.

Spencer, K. A. 1969. The Agromyzidae of Canada and Alaska. Mem. Entomol. Soc. Can. 64:1–311; illus.

Steffan, W. A. 1966. A generic revision of the family Sciaridae (Diptera) of America north of Mexico. Univ. Calif. Publ. Entomol. 44:1–77; illus.

Steyskal, G. C. 1967. A key to the genera of Anthomyiinae known to occur in America north of Mexico, with notes on the genus *Ganperda* (Diptera: Anthomyiidae). Proc. Biol. Soc. Wash. 80:1–7; illus.

Stone, A. 1970. A synoptic catalog of the mosquitoes of the world, Supplement 4 (Diptera: Culicidae). Proc. Entomol. Soc. Wash. 72:137–171.

Stone, A., C. W. Sabrosky, W. W. Wirth, R. H. Foote, and J. R. Coulson. 1965. A catalog of the Diptera of America north of Mexico. USDA Agr. Handbook 276, 1969 pp.

Sublette, J. E. 1964. Chironomid midges of California. II. Tanypodinae, Podonominae, and Diamesinae. Proc. U.S. Natl. Mus. 115: 85–136; illus.

Thompson, P. H. 1967. Tabanidae of Maryland. Trans. Amer. Entomol. Soc. 93: 463–519; illus.

Tillyard, R. J. 1926. The Insects of Australia and New Zealand. Sydney: Angus and Robertson.

Vockeroth, J. R. 1969. A revision of the genera of the Syrphini (Diptera: Syrphidae). Mem. Entomol. Soc. Can. 62:1–176; illus.

Wirth, W. W., and A. Stone. 1956. Aquatic Diptera, pp. 372–482 *in* Aquatic Insects of California, ed. R. L. Usinger. Berkeley: Univ. California Press; illus.

Chapter 33

Order Trichóptera[1]
Caddisflies

The caddisflies are small to medium-sized insects, somewhat similar to moths in general appearance. The four membranous wings are rather hairy (and occasionally bear scales also), and they are usually held rooflike over the abdomen at rest. The antennae are long and slender. Most caddisflies are rather dull-colored insects, but a few are conspicuously patterned. The mouthparts are of the chewing type, with the palps well developed but with the mandibles much reduced. The adults feed principally on liquid foods. Caddisflies undergo complete metamorphosis, and the larvae are aquatic.

Caddisfly larvae are caterpillar-like, with a well-developed head and thoracic legs and a pair of hook-like appendages at the end of the abdomen. The abdominal segments bear filamentous gills (Figure 33–1). Caddisfly larvae occur in various types of aquatic habitats. Some occur in ponds or lakes, and others occur in streams. Some larvae are case makers, others construct nets under water, and a few are free-living.

The cases of the case-making larvae are made of bits of leaves, twigs, sand grains, pebbles, or other materials and are of various shapes (Figure 33–7). Each species builds a very characteristic type of case, and in some species the young larvae build a case different from that made by older larvae. The materials used in making the case are fastened together with silk, or they may be cemented together. Case-making larvae are plant feeders. The nets of the net-making species (found in streams) are made of silk spun from modified salivary glands and may be trumpet-shaped, finger-shaped, or cup-shaped, with the open end facing upstream. They are often attached to the downstream side of a rock or other object over which the water flows. The larvae spend their time near these nets (often in a crevice or retreat of some sort) and feed on the materials caught in the nets. The free-living caddisfly larvae, which construct neither cases nor nets, are generally predaceous.

The larvae fasten their cases to some object in the water when they have completed their growth, seal the opening (or openings) in the case, and pupate in the case. When the pupa is fully developed, it cuts its way out of the case with its mandibles (which are well developed in this stage), swims to the surface, then crawls out of the water onto a stone, stick, or similar object, and the adult emerges.

The wing venation of caddisflies (Figures 33–2A, 33–3) is rather generalized, and there are few cross veins. The subcosta is usually two-branched, the radius five-branched, the media four-branched in the front wing and three-branched in the hind wing, and the cubitus three-branched. The anal veins in the

[1]Trichóptera: *tricho*, hair; *ptera*, wings

Figure 33–1. Caddisfly larvae. **A,** *Hydróptila waubesiàna* Betten (Hydroptílidae), dorsal view at left, lateral view at right; **B,** *Rhyacóphila fenéstra* Ross (Rhyacophílidae); **C,** *Polycéntropus interrúptus* (Banks) (Psychomyíidae); **D,** *Hydropsỳche símulans* Ross (Hydropsỳchidae). (Courtesy of Ross and the Illinois Natural History Survey.)

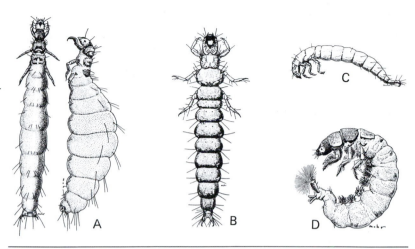

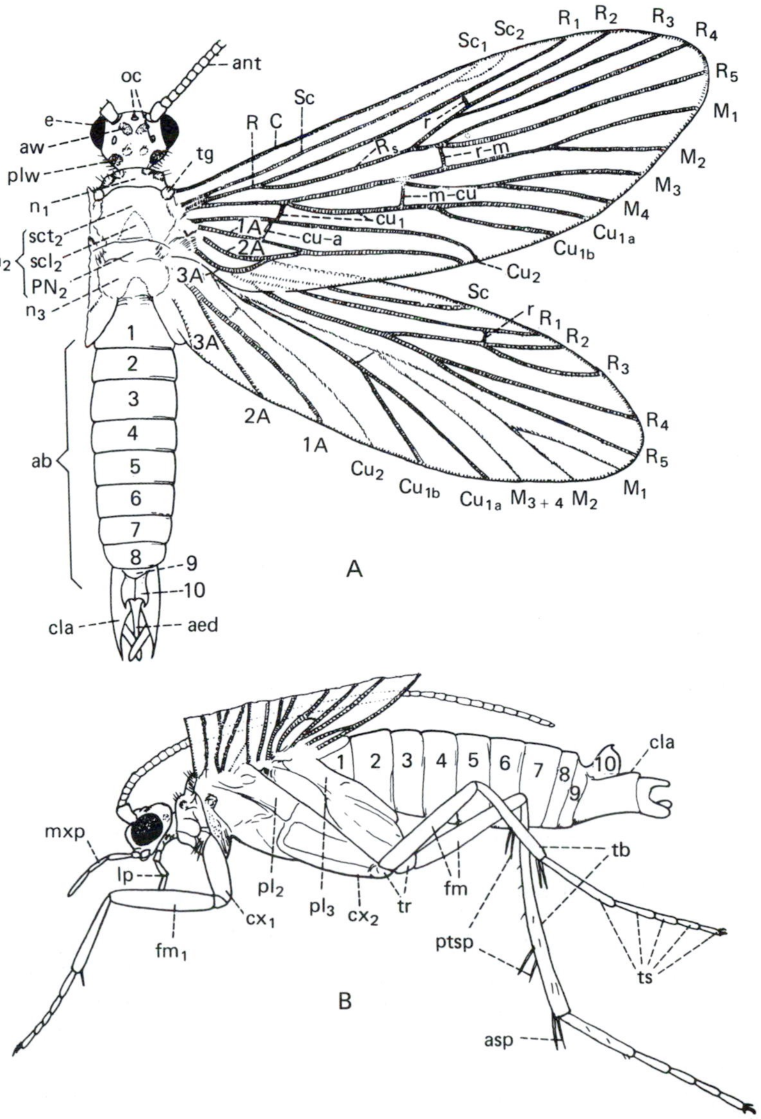

Figure 33–2. Structure of a caddisfly. **A,** dorsal view; **B,** lateral view. *ab,* abdomen; *aed,* aedeagus; *ant,* antenna; *asp,* apical spur; *aw,* anterior wart; *cla,* clasper; *cx,* coxa; *e,* compound eye; *fm,* femur; *lp,* labial palp; *mxp,* maxillary palp; *n₁,* pronotum; *n₂,* mesonotum; *n₃,* metanotum; *oc,* ocelli; *pl₂,* mesopleuron; *pl₃,* metapleuron; *plw,* posterolateral wart; *PN₂,* postnotum of mesothorax; *ptsp,* preapical tibial spur; *scl₂,* mesoscutellum; *sct₂,* mesoscutum; *tb,* tibia; *tg,* tegula; *tr,* trochanter; *ts,* tarsus; *1–10,* abdominal segments. (Redrawn from Ross.)

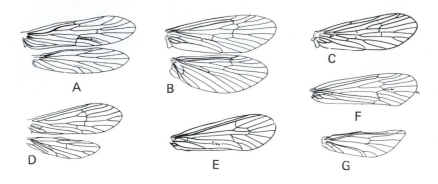

Figure 33–3. Wings of Trichóptera. **A,** *Dibùsa angàta* (Ross) (Hydroptílidae); **B,** *Aphropsỳche àprilis* Ross (Hydropsỳchidae); **C,** front wing of *Dolophilòdes distínctus* (Walker) (Philopotámidae); **D,** *Psychomỳia nómada* (Ross) (Psychomyìidae); **E,** front wing of *Sericóstoma crassicòrnis* (Walker) (Sericostomátidae); **F,** front wing of *Phanocèlia canadénsis* (Banks) (Limnephílidae); **G,** hind wing of *Helicopsỳche boreàlis* (Hagen) (Helicopsỳchidae). (Courtesy of Ross and the Illinois Natural History Survey.)

front wing usually form two Y veins near the base of the wing. Most species have a characteristic wing spot in the fork of R_{4+5}. Cu_2 in the hind wing usually fuses basally with 1A for a short distance. In naming the cubital and anal veins in this order, we follow the interpretation of Ross and others rather than that of Comstock. The veins we call Cu_{1a} and Cu_{1b} are called Cu_1 and Cu_2, respectively, by Comstock, who considers the remaining veins to be anal veins. In

some groups (for example, Figure 33–2A), the basal part of Cu_1 in the front wing appears like a cross vein, and what looks like the basal part of Cu_1 is really a mediocubital cross vein. (This cross vein is termed M_5 by Tillyard and others.)

The majority of the caddisflies are rather weak fliers. The wings are vestigial in the females of a few species. The eggs are laid in masses or strings of several hundred, either in the water or on objects

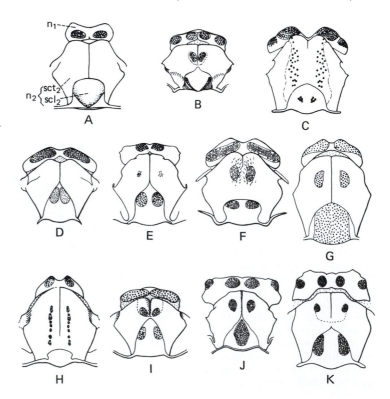

Figure 33–4. Pro- and mesonota of Trichóptera. **A,** *Hydropsỳche símulans* Ross (Hydropsỳchidae); **B,** *Psychomỳia flávida* Hagen (Psychomyìidae); **C,** *Anthripsòdes tàrsipunctàtus* (Vorheis) (Leptocéridae); **D,** *Beraèa górteba* Ross (Beraèidae); **E,** *Brachycéntrus numeròsus* (Say) (Brachycéntridae); **F,** *Helicopsỳche boreàlis* (Hagen) (Helicopsỳchidae); **G,** *Psilotrèta frontàlis* Banks (Odontocéridae); **H,** *Ganonèma americànum* (Walker) (Calamocerátidae); **I,** *Sericóstoma crassicòrnis* (Walker) (Sericostomátidae); **J,** *Goèra calcaràta* Banks (Goèridae); **K,** *Theliopsỳche* sp. (Lepidostomátidae). n_1, pronotum; n_2, mesonotum; scl_2, mesoscutellum; sct_2, mesoscutum. (Courtesy of Ross and the Illinois Natural History Survey.)

near the water. The adult in many species enters the water and attaches its eggs to stones or other objects. The eggs usually hatch in a few days, and in most species the larva requires nearly a year to develop. The adults usually live about a month. Adult caddisflies are frequently attracted to lights.

The chief biological importance of this group lies in the fact that the larvae are an important part of the food of many fish and other aquatic animals.

Classification of the Trichóptera

The arrangement of families followed here is that of Weaver and Morse (1986), who recognize 23 families in our area. This arrangement, with other arrangements or spellings in parentheses, is outlined below. Families that are rare or unlikely to be encountered by the general collector are indicated by an asterisk.

Suborder Annulipálpia
  Infraorder Curvipálpia
    Superfamily Hydropsychòidea
      *Ecnómidae
      Hydropsýchidae—net-spinning caddisflies
      Polycentropódidae (Polycentrópidae; Psychomyìidae in part)—trumpet-net and tube-making caddisflies
      Psychomyìidae—tube-making and trumpet-net caddisflies
      *Xiphocentrónidae
    Superfamily Philopotamòidea
      Philopotámidae—finger-net caddisflies or silken-tube spinners
  Infraorder Spicipálpia
    Superfamily Hydroptilòidea

Glossosomátidae (Rhyacophílidae in part)—saddle-case makers
      Hydroptílidae—microcaddisflies
    Superfamily Rhyacophilòidea
      *Hydrobiòsidae (Rhyacophílidae in part)
      Rhyacophílidae—primitive caddisflies
Suborder Integrepálpia
  Infraorder Planitentòria
    Superfamily Limnephilòidea
      *Goèridae (Limnephílidae in part)
      Limnephílidae—northern caddisflies
      *Uenòidae (Limnephílidae in part)
      Brachycéntridae
      *Lepidostomátidae
    Superfamily Phryganeòidea
      Phryganèidae—large caddisflies
  Infraorder Brevitentòria
    Superfamily Leptoceròidea
      Odontocéridae
      Calamocerátidae
      Leptocéridae—long-horned caddisflies
      Molánnidae
    Superfamily Sericostomatòidea
      *Beraèidae
      Helicopsýchidae—snail-case caddisflies
      *Sericostomátidae

Characters Used in Identifying Trichóptera

The characters used in separating families of adult caddisflies are principally those of the thoracic warts, the ocelli, the maxillary palps, the spurs and spines on the legs, and the wing venation.

The thoracic warts, which are of considerable

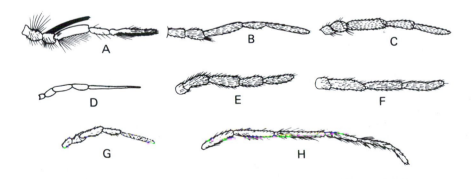

Figure 33–5. Maxillary palps of Trichóptera. **A,** *Psilotrèta* sp., male (Odontocéridae); **B,** *Dolóphilus shawnèe* Ross, male (Philopotámidae); **C,** *Rhyacóphila lobífera* Betten, male (Rhyacophílidae); **D,** *Macronèmum zebràtum* (Hagen) (Hydropsýchidae); **E,** *Banksìola selìna* Betten, female (Phryganèidae); **F,** *B. selìna*, male; **G,** *Cyrnéllus marginàlis* (Banks) (Psychomyìidae); **H,** *Triaenòdes tárda* Milne, male (Leptocéridae). (Courtesy of Ross and the Illinois Natural History Survey.)

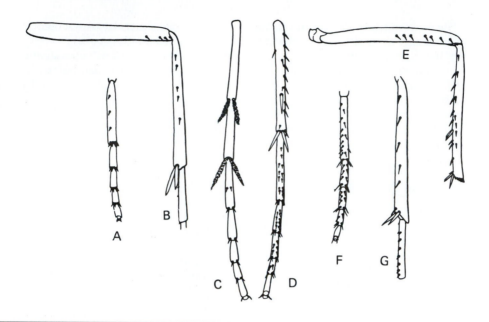

Figure 33–6.   Legs of Trichóptera. **A,** middle tarsus of *Beraèa górteba* Ross (Beraèidae); **B,** middle leg of *B. górteba;* **C,** middle tibia and tarsus of *Theliopsỳche coròna* Ross (Lepidostomátidae); **D,** middle tibia and tarsus of *Brachycéntrus numeròsus* (Say) (Brachycéntridae); **E,** middle leg of *Molánna unióphila* Vorheis (Molánnidae); **F,** middle tarsus of *Sericóstoma crassicòrnis* (Walker) (Sericostomátidae); **G,** middle tibia of *Sericóstoma crassicòrnis.* (Courtesy of Ross and the Illinois Natural History Survey.)

value in separating families, are wartlike or tubercle-like structures on the dorsum of the thorax and are often more hairy than the surrounding areas. They vary in size, number, and arrangement, and some of these variations are shown in Figure 33–4. These warts are very difficult to interpret in pinned specimens, since they are often destroyed or distorted by the pin. For this and other reasons, caddisflies should be preserved in alcohol rather than on pins.

The maxillary palps are nearly always five-seg-mented in females, but they may contain fewer segments in the males of some groups. The size and form of particular segments may differ in different families (Figure 33–5). Some variation in the spina-tion of the legs is shown in Figure 33–6. The most important variations are in the number of tibial spurs, which may vary up to a maximum of four—two apical and two near the middle of the tibia. Wing venation is not a very important character in sepa-rating the families of caddisflies.

Key to the Families of Trichóptera

Families marked with an asterisk in the key are small or unlikely to be encountered by the general collector. Keys to larvae are given by Denning (1956), Krafka (1915), Pennak (1978), Ross (1944, 1959), and Wiggins (1984).

1.   Mesoscutellum with posterior portion forming a flat triangular area with
         steep sides, and mesoscutum without warts; some wing hairs clubbed; hind
         wings narrow and pointed apically, often with a posterior fringe of hairs as
         long as wing is wide; antennae short (Figure 33–8F); small insects, usually
         less than 6 mm in length ....**Hydroptílidae**   p. 583

1'.   Mesoscutellum evenly convex, without a triangular portion set off by steep sides, or mesoscutum with warts; no wing hairs clubbed; hind wings usually broader and rounded apically, posterior fringe if present of shorter hairs; antennae usually as long as or longer than wings; length 5–40 mm .. **2**

2(1').   Ocelli present **3**

2'.   Ocelli absent **10**

3(2).   Maxillary palps 5-segmented, fifth segment 2 or 3 times as long as fourth (Figure 33–5B) ....**Philopotámidae**   p. 583

3'.   Maxillary palps with 3–5 segments, if 5-segmented then fifth segment about the same length as the fourth **4**

4(3').   Maxillary palps 5-segmented, second segment short, often more or less rounded, about same length as first segment (Figure 33–5C) **5**

4'.   Maxillary palps with 3–5 segments, if 5-segmented then second segment slender, longer than first **8**

5(4).   Second segment of maxillary palps rounded or globose (Figure 33–5C); widely distributed **6**

5'.   Second segment of maxillary palps cylindrical, not globose; southwestern United States ....**Hydrobiósidae***   p. 583

6(5).   Front tibiae with a preapical spur ....**Rhyacophílidae**   p. 583

6'.   Front tibiae without a preapical spur **7**

7(6').   Pronotal warts widely separated ....**Glossosomátidae**   p. 583

7'.   Pronotal warts close together but not actually in contact (*Palaeagápetus*)...**Hydroptílidae***   p. 583

8(4').   Middle tibiae with 2 preapical spurs ....**Phryganèidae**   p. 585

8'.   Middle tibiae with 1 preapical spur **9**

9(8').   Basal segment of antennae longer than head; mesoscutum with a pair of warts; mesoscutellum long, anterior apex acute, reaching middle of mesoscutum, with an elongate wart 3–4 times as long as wide; hind wings with anal area reduced, hind wings little wider than front wings; length 7 mm or less; western United States ....**Uenòidae***   p. 584

9'.   Basal segment of antennae shorter than head; mesoscutum variable; mesoscutellum shorter, anterior apex not acute and not reaching middle of mesoscutum, and with a broad wart less than 3 times as long as wide; anal area of hind wing broad, hind wings usually much wider than front wings; length 5–30 mm; widely distributed ....**Limnephílidae**   p. 584

10(2').   Maxillary palps with 5 or more segments **11**

10'.   Maxillary palps with fewer than 5 segments **16**

11(10).   Terminal segment of maxillary palps much longer than preceding segment, with numerous cross striae that are not possessed by the other segments (Figure 33–5G)...**12**

11'.   Terminal segment of maxillary palps without such cross striae, similar in structure and length to preceding segment, or some segments with long hair brushes (Figure 33–5A) **16**

12(11).   Mesoscutum with a pair of warts **13**

12'.   Mesoscutum without warts (Figure 33–4A) ....**Hydropsýchidae**   p. 583

13(12).   Mesoscutum with a pair of small rounded warts that are sometimes touching at midline (Figure 33–4B); widely distributed **14**

13′.   Mesoscutal warts large, somewhat quadrate, continuous along entire midline of mesoscutum; southern Texas ....**Xiphocentrónidae*** p. 583

14(13).   Front tibiae with a preapical spur, or if this spur absent (*Cernotina*, Polycentropódidae) then basal tarsal segment less than twice as long as longer apical spur **15**

14′.   Front tibiae without a preapical spur and basal tarsal segment at least twice as long as the longer apical spur ....**Psychomyiidae** p. 583

15(14).   R₁ in front wing branched; Texas ....**Ecnómidae*** p. 583

15′.   R₁ in front wing not branched; widely distributed ....**Polycentropódidae** p. 583

16(10′, 11′).   Tarsal segments, except basal one, with spines only around apex (Figure 33–6A); mesoscutum lacking warts and setae ....**Beraèidae*** p. 586

16′.   Tarsal segments with spines arranged irregularly (Figure 33–6F); mesoscutum with warts or setal areas **17**

17(16′).   Mesoscutal setae arising in area extending over almost entire length of mesoscutum (Figure 33–4C,H) **18**

17′.   Mesoscutal setae usually confined to a pair of warts (Figure 33–4F,G,I–K) ...**20**

18(17).   Basal segment of antennae at most twice as long as second; dorsum of head usually with posteromesal ridge ....**Calamocerátidae** p. 586

18′.   Basal segment of antennae at least 3 times as long as second; dorsum of head without posteromesal ridge **19**

19(18′).   Antennae much longer than body; middle tibiae without preapical spurs ....**Leptocéridae** p. 586

19′.   Antennae little if any longer than body; middle tibiae with 2 preapical spurs ....**Molánnidae** p. 586

20(17′).   Warts on dorsum of head very large, extending from eye to midline and anteriorly to middle of head; antennae never longer than front wing ....**Helicopsýchidae** p. 586

20′.   Warts on dorsum of head smaller, not as above, or antennae 1½ times as long as front wings **21**

21(20′).   Mesoscutellum with single large wart occupying most of sclerite (Figure 33–4G,J) **22**

21′.   Mesoscutellum with a pair of warts, or if appearing to have only 1 (Lepidostomátidae) then wart occupies only about anterior half of the sclerite **23**

22(21).   Mesoscutellar wart occupying most of sclerite (Figure 33–4G); maxillary palps always 5-segmented ....**Odontocéridae** p. 586

22′.   Mesoscutellar wart elongate and occupying only mesal portion of sclerite (Figure 33–4J); maxillary palps 5-segmented in female, 3-segmented in male ....**Goèridae*** p. 584

23(21′).   Pronotum with 1 pair of warts; mesoscutum with deep median fissure (Figure 33–4I) ....**Sericostomátidae** p. 586

23′.   Pronotum with 2 pairs of warts; median fissure of mesoscutum not as deep as above **24**

24(23').   Middle tibiae with an irregular row, middle tarsi with a double row of spines;
                middle tibiae with 1–2 preapical spurs situated at about two-thirds tibial
                length (Figure 33–6D), or preapical spurs lacking ....**Brachycéntridae**   p. 584

24'.   Middle tibiae without spines, and middle tarsi with only a scattered few in
                addition to apical ones (Figure 33–6C); middle tibiae with 2 preapical spurs
                arising from about midlength of the tibia ....**Lepidostomátidae**   p. 584

Family **Ecnómidae**:   This is a neotropical group, one species of which has recently been reported in Texas.

Family **Polycentropódidae**—Trumpet-Net and Tube-Making Caddisflies: These caddisflies vary in length from 4 to 11 mm. Most of them are brownish with mottled wings. The larvae occur in a variety of aquatic situations: some in rapid streams, some in rivers, and others in lakes. Some (e.g., *Polycéntropus*) construct trumpet-shaped nets that collapse rather rapidly when removed from the water. Others (e.g., *Phylocéntropus*) construct tubes in the sand at the bottoms of streams and cement the walls of these tubes to make a fairly rigid structure.

Family **Psychomyíidae**—Tube-Making and Trumpet-Net Caddisflies: The members of this group are very similar to the Polycentropódidae. They differ in leg characters, as indicated in the key (couplet 14). The larvae of these caddisflies construct silken tubes and spend their time in a retreat near the tube.

Family **Xiphocentrónidae**:   This group is represented in our area by a single species of *Xiphocéntron*, which occurs in southern Texas.

Family **Hydropsýchidae**—Net-Spinning Caddisflies: This is a large group (142 North American species), and many species are fairly common in small streams. The adults of both sexes have the maxillary palps five-segmented with the last segment elongate (Figure 33–5D). Ocelli are absent, and the mesoscutum lacks warts (Figure 33–4A). Most species are brownish, with the wings more or less mottled. The larvae occur in the parts of streams where the current is strongest. They construct a caselike retreat of sand, pebbles, or debris and, near this retreat, construct a cup-shaped net with the concave side of the net facing upstream. The larva feeds on materials caught in the net, and pupation occurs in the caselike retreat. These larvae are quite active, and if they are disturbed while feeding in the net, they back into their retreat very rapidly.

Family **Philopotámidae**—Finger-Net Caddisflies or Silken-Tube Spinners: These caddisflies vary in length from 6 to 9 mm and have the last segment of the maxillary palps elongate (Figure 33–5B). They are usually brownish with gray wings. Most females of *Dolophilòdes distínctus* (Walker) have the wings vestigial. The larvae live in rapid streams and construct finger-shaped or tubular nets that are attached to stones. These tubes have a large opening at the upstream end and a smaller one at the other end. Many such nets are frequently attached close together. The larva stays in the net and feeds on the food caught there. Pupation occurs in cases made of pebbles and lined with silk.

Family **Glossosomátidae**—Saddle-Case Makers: The adults in this group are usually brownish with the wings more or less mottled, and they vary in length from 3 to 13 mm. The antennae are short and the maxillary palps are five-segmented in both sexes. The larvae occur in rapid streams. The larvae make saddlelike or turtle-shaped cases (Figure 33–7A). These cases are oval, with the dorsal side convex and composed of relatively large pebbles, and the ventral side is flat and composed of smaller pebbles and sand grains. When these larvae pupate, the ventral side of the case is cut away and the upper part is fastened to a stone.

Family **Hydroptílidae**—Microcaddisflies: This is a large group (170 North American species) of small caddisflies that are 1.5 to 6 mm in length. They are quite hairy (Figure 33–8F), and most of them have a salt-and-pepper mottling. The larvae of most species occur in small lakes. These insects undergo a sort of hypermetamorphosis: the early instars are active and do not construct cases, but the later instars do make cases. The anal hooks are much larger in the active instars than in the later instars. The case is usually somewhat purse-shaped, with each end open (Figure 33–7B).

Family **Hydrobiósidae**:   The only members of this group in our area are three species of *Aropsỳche*, which occur in the Southwest. The larvae do not make cases, and are predaceous.

Family **Rhyacophílidae**—Primitive Caddisflies: These

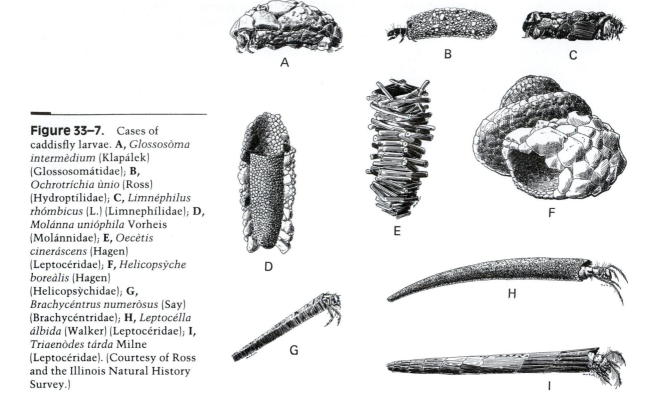

Figure 33–7. Cases of caddisfly larvae. **A,** *Glossosòma intermèdium* (Klapálek) (Glossosomátidae); **B,** *Ochrotríchia ùnio* (Ross) (Hydroptílidae); **C,** *Limnéphilus rhómbicus* (L.) (Limnephílidae); **D,** *Molánna unióphila* Vorheis (Molánnidae); **E,** *Oecètis cineráscens* (Hagen) (Leptocéridae); **F,** *Helicopsỳche boreàlis* (Hagen) (Helicopsỳchidae); **G,** *Brachycéntrus numeròsus* (Say) (Brachycéntridae); **H,** *Leptocélla álbida* (Walker) (Leptocéridae); **I,** *Triaenòdes tárda* Milne (Leptocéridae). (Courtesy of Ross and the Illinois Natural History Survey.)

insects are very similar to the Glossosomátidae (which were formerly considered a subfamily of the Rhyacophílidae), but they differ in habits. These caddisflies do not make cases and are predaceous. This is a fairly large group, and all but one of its approximately 100 North American species belong to the genus *Rhyacóphila*.

Family **Goèridae:** This is a small group that is represented in North America by 12 species. These caddisflies have the maxillary palps five-segmented in the females and three-segmented in the males. The larvae occur in streams and construct cases of small pebbles, with a large pebble glued to each side acting as ballast.

Family **Limnephílidae**—Northern Caddisflies: This family is the largest in the order, with nearly 300 species occurring in North America. Most species are northern in distribution. The adults vary in length from 7 to 23 mm, and most species are brownish with the wings mottled or patterned (Figure 33–8A). The maxillary palps are three-segmented in the males and five-segmented in the females. The larvae occur principally in ponds and slow-moving streams. The cases are made of a variety of materials,

and in some species the cases made by the young larvae are quite different from those made by older larvae. The larval stages of one species in this family, *Philocàsea démita* Ross, which occur in Oregon, live in moist leaf litter.

Family **Uenòidae:** This is a small group (13 North American species) whose members occur in the West. The larval cases are made of sand grains or small pebbles and are long, slender, tapered, and curved.

Family **Brachycéntridae:** Twenty-seven of the 31 North American species in this family belong to two genera, *Brachycéntrus* and *Micrasèma*. The young larvae of *Brachycéntrus* occur near the shores of small streams, where they feed principally on algae. Older larvae move to midstream and attach their cases (Figure 33–7G) to stones, facing upstream, and feed on both algae and small aquatic insects. The adults are 6–11 mm in length and dark brown to black, with the wings often tawny and checkered. The maxillary palps are three-segmented in the males and five-segmented in the females.

Family **Lepidostomátidae:** This group contains two American genera, *Lepidóstoma* and *Theliop-*

sỳche, with 70 species (65 of them in *Lepidòstoma*). The females have five-segmented maxillary palps, and the maxillary palps of the males are three-segmented or have a curiously modified one-segmented structure. The larvae occur principally in streams or springs. Their cases are mostly square in cross section and composed of leaf and bark fragments.

The cases of some species are cylindrical and composed of sand grains.

Family **Phryganèidae**—Large Caddisflies: The adults of this group are fairly large caddisflies (14–25 mm in length), and the wings are usually mottled with gray and brown (Figure 33–8B,E). The maxillary palps are four-segmented in the males (Figure

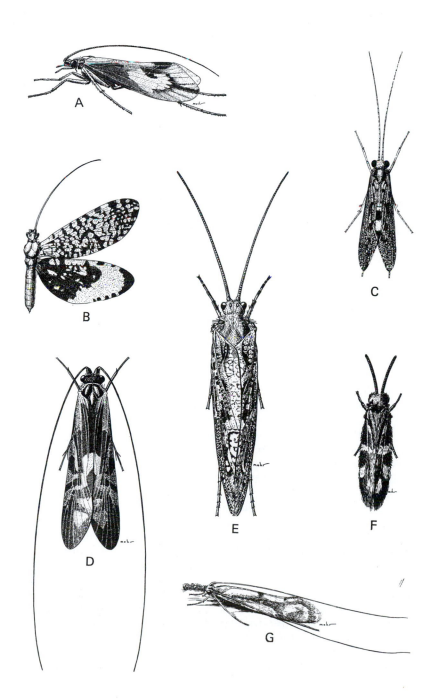

Figure 33–8. Adult caddisflies. **A,** *Platycéntropus radiàtus* (Say), male (Limnephílidae); **B,** *Eubasilíssa pardàlis* (Walker), female (Phryganèidae); **C,** *Hydropsỳche símulans* Ross, male (Hydropsỳchidae); **D,** *Macronèmum zebràtum* (Hagen), male (Hydropsỳchidae); **E,** *Phrygànea cinèrea* Walker, male (Phryganèidae); **F,** *Hydróptila hamàta* Morton, male (Hydroptílidae); **G,** *Triaenòdes tárda* Milne, male (Leptocéridae). (Courtesy of Ross and the Illinois Natural History Survey.)

33–5F) and five-segmented in the females (Figure 33–5E). The larvae occur principally in marshes and lakes; only a few are found in streams. The larval cases are slender, cylindrical, open at both ends, and usually made of narrow strips of plant materials glued together, often in a spiral.

Family **Odontocéridae:** The adults in this group are about 13 mm in length, the body is blackish, and the wings are grayish brown with light dots. The larvae live in the riffles of swift streams, where they construct cylindrical, often curved, cases of sand. When ready to pupate, large numbers attach their cases to stones, with the cases glued together and parallel.

Family **Calamocerátidae:** The adults of this group are orange-brown or brownish black, with the maxillary palps five- or 6-segmented. The larvae occur in both still and rapidly flowing water. The cases of most species are flat and composed of large pieces of leaves or bark. This group is a small one (five North American species), and most species occur in the West.

Family **Leptocéridae**—Long-Horned Caddisflies: These caddisflies are slender, often pale-colored, and 5–17 mm in length, and they have long slender antennae that are often nearly twice as long as the body (Figure 33–8G). The larvae occur in a variety of habitats, and there is considerable variation in the types of cases they make. Some species make long, slender, tapering cases (Figure 33–7H,I); some construct cases of twigs (Figure 33–7E); and some construct cornucopia-shaped cases of sand grains.

Family **Molánnidae:** This group is small (six North American species), and the known larvae live on the sandy bottoms of streams and lakes. The larval cases are shield-shaped and consist of a central cylindrical tube with lateral expansions (Figure 33–7D). The adults, which are 10–16 mm in length, are usually brownish gray with the wings somewhat mottled, and the maxillary palps are five-segmented in both sexes. The adults at rest sit with the wings curled about the body, which is held at an angle to the surface on which the insect rests.

Family **Beraèidae:** This family contains only three North American species, in the genus *Beraèa*, which occur in the Northeast and in Georgia. The adults are brownish in color and about 5 mm in length. The larval cases are curved, smooth, and made of sand grains.

Family **Helicopsỳchidae**—Snail-Case Caddisflies: This family contains the single genus *Helicopsỳche*, with five North American species. Adults can usu-

ally be recognized by the short mesoscutellum with its narrow transverse warts (Figure 33–4F) and the hamuli on the hind wings (Figure 33–3G). The adults are 5–7 mm in length and somewhat straw-colored, with the wings mottled with brown. The larvae construct cases of sand that are shaped like a snail shell (Figure 33–7F). During development the larvae occur on sandy bottoms, and when ready to pupate they attach their cases in clusters on stones. The cases are about 6 mm wide.

Family **Sericostomátidae:** This is a small group (12 North American species), the larvae of which occur in both lakes and streams. The larval cases are usually tapered, curved, short, smooth, and composed of sand grains, sometimes also with wood fragments.

Collecting and Preserving Trichóptera

Caddisfly adults are usually found near water. The habitat preferences of different species differ; hence, one should visit a variety of habitats to get a large number of species. The adults can be collected by sweeping in the vegetation along the margins of and near ponds and streams, by checking the underside of bridges, and by collecting at lights. The best way of collecting the adults is at lights. Blue lights seem more attractive than other colors.

Caddisfly larvae can be collected by the various methods of aquatic collecting discussed in Chapter 36. Many can be found attached to stones in the water; others will be found among aquatic vegetation; and still others can be collected with a dip net used to scoop up bottom debris or aquatic vegetation.

Both adult and larval caddisflies should be preserved in 80% alcohol. Adults may be pinned, but pinning frequently damages the thoracic warts that are used in separating families, and most dried specimens are more difficult to identify as to species than specimens preserved in alcohol. When using lights (for example, automobile headlights), one can easily collect large numbers by placing a pan containing about 6 mm of alcohol (or water containing a detergent) directly below the light. The insects will eventually fly into the alcohol and be caught. Specimens attracted to light may also be taken directly into a cyanide jar and then transferred to alcohol, or they may be picked off the light by dipping the index finger in alcohol and scooping up the insect rapidly but gently on the wet finger. An aspirator is a useful collecting device for the smaller species.

References

Betten, C. 1934. The caddis flies or Trichoptera of New York state. N.Y. State Mus. Bull. 292, 570 pp.; illus.

Denning, D. G. 1956. Trichoptera, pp. 237–270 *in* Aquatic Insects of California, ed. R. L. Usinger. Berkeley: Univ. California Press; illus.

Krafka, J., Jr. 1915. A key to the families of trichopterous larvae. Can. Entomol. 47:217–225; illus.

Lloyd, J. T. 1921. The biology of North American caddis fly larvae. Lloyd Libr. Bot. Pharm. Materia Med. Bull. 21 (Entomol. Ser. No. 1), 124 pp.; illus.

Merritt, R. W., and K. W. Cummins (Eds.). 1984 (2nd ed.). An Introduction to the Aquatic Insects of North America. Dubuque, Iowa: Kendall/Hunt, 722 pp.; illus.

Nimmo, A. P. 1971. The adult Rhyacophilidae and Limnephilidae (Trichoptera) of Alberta and eastern British Columbia and their post-glacial origins. Quaest. Entomol. 7(1):3–234; illus.

Pennak, R. W. 1978. (2nd ed.). Fresh-Water Invertebrates of the United States. New York: Wiley Interscience, 803 pp.; illus.

Ross, H. H. 1944. The caddis flies or Trichoptera of Illinois. Ill. Nat. Hist. Surv. Bull. 23(1):1–236; illus.

Ross, H. H. 1956. Evolution and Classification of the Mountain Caddisflies. Urbana: Univ. Illinois Press, 213 pp.; illus.

Ross, H. H. 1959. Trichoptera, pp. 1024–1049 *in* Fresh-Water Biology, ed. W. T. Edmondson. New York: Wiley; illus.

Ross, H. H. 1967. The evolution and past dispersal of the Trichoptera. Annu. Rev. Entomol. 12:169–206; illus.

Schmid, F. 1970. Le genre *Rhyacophila* et la famille des Rhyacophilidae (Trichoptera). Mem. Soc. Entomol. Can. No. 66, 230 pp.; illus.

Schmid, F. 1980. Genera des Trichoptères du Canada et des États adjacents. Les Insectes et Arachnides du Canada, Part 7. Agric. Can. Publ. 1692, 296 pp.

Smith, S. D. 1968. The Arctopsychinae of Idaho (Trichoptera: Hydropsychidae). Pan-Pac. Entomol. 44:102–112; illus.

Weaver, J. S., and J. C. Morse. 1986. Evolution of feeding and case-making behavior in Trichoptera. J. N. Amer. Benthol. Soc. 5(2):150–158; illus.

Wiggins, G. B. 1977. Larvae of North American Caddisfly Genera (Trichoptera). Toronto: Toronto Univ. Press, 401 pp.; illus.

Wiggins, G. B. 1984 (2nd ed). Trichoptera, pp. 271–311 *in* An Introduction to the Aquatic Insects of North America, ed. R. W. Merritt and K. W. Cummins. Dubuque, Iowa: Kendall/Hunt; illus.

Wiggins, G. B. 1987. Order Trichoptera, pp. 253–287 *in* F. W. Stehr (Ed.), Immature Insects. Dubuque, Iowa: Kendall/Hunt, 754 pp.; illus.

Chapter 34

Order Lepidóptera[1]
Butterflies and Moths

The butterflies and moths are common insects and well known to everyone. They are most readily recognized by the scales on the wings (Figure 34–1), which come off like dust on one's fingers when the insects are handled. Most of the body and legs are also covered with scales. This order is a large one, with more than 11,000 species occurring in the United States and Canada. Its members are to be found almost everywhere, often in considerable numbers.

The Lepidóptera have considerable economic importance. The larvae of most species are phytophagous, and many are serious pests of cultivated plants. A few feed on fabrics, and a few feed on stored grain or meal. On the other hand, the adults of many species are beautiful and much sought after by collectors, and many serve as the basis of art and design. Natural silk is the product of a member of this order.

The mouthparts of a butterfly or moth are usually fitted for sucking. A few species have vestigial mouthparts and do not feed in the adult stage, and the mouthparts in one family (the Micropterígidae) are of the chewing type. The labrum is small and is usually in the form of a transverse band across the lower part of the face, at the base of the proboscis. The mandibles are nearly always lacking. The pro-

boscis, when present, is formed by the appressed, longitudinally grooved galeae of the maxillae and is usually long and coiled. The maxillary palps are generally small or lacking, but the labial palps are

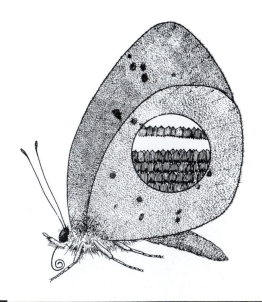

Figure 34–1. A butterfly with a section of the wing enlarged to show the scales.

[1]Lepidóptera: *lepido,* scale; *ptera,* wings.

nearly always well developed and usually extend forward in front of the face (Figure 34–2B).

The compound eyes of a butterfly or moth are relatively large and composed of a large number of facets. Most moths have two ocelli, one on each side close to the margin of the compound eye. Some species have sensory organs called chaetosemata near the ocelli.

Several families have auditory organs called tympana, which are believed to function in the detection of the high-frequency echolocating sounds of bats. The Pyrálidae and all of the Geometróidea except the Sematùridae have these organs on the anterior sternite of the abdomen, while in the Noctuòidea these organs are located ventrolaterally on the metathorax.

The members of this order undergo complete metamorphosis, and their larvae, usually called caterpillars, are a familiar sight. Many lepidopteran larvae have a grotesque or ferocious appearance that makes people afraid of them, but the vast majority are quite harmless when handled. Only a few give off an offensive odor, and only a very few temperate species have stinging body hairs. The ferocious appearance probably plays a role in defense by deterring potential predators.

The larvae of Lepidóptera are usually eruciform (Figure 34–3), with a well-developed head and a cylindrical body of 13 segments (3 thoracic and 10 abdominal). The head usually bears six stemmata on each side, just above the mandibles, and a pair of very short antennae. Each of the thoracic segments bears a pair of legs, and abdominal segments 3–6 and 10 usually bear a pair of prolegs. The prolegs are somewhat different from the thoracic legs. They are more fleshy and have a different segmentation, and they

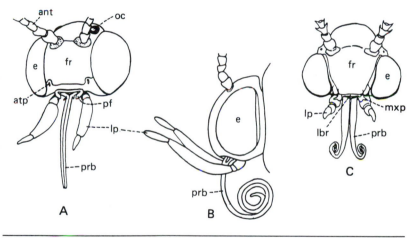

Figure 34–2. Head structure in Lepidóptera. **A,** *Synánthedon* (Sesìidae), anterior view; **B,** same, lateral view; **C,** *Hyphántria* (Arctìidae). *ant*, antenna; *atp*, anterior tentorial pit; *e*, compound eye; *fr*, frons; *lbr*, labrum; *lp*, labial palp; *mxp*, maxillary palp; *oc*, ocellus; *pf*, pilifer; *prb*, proboscis. (Redrawn from Snodgrass.)

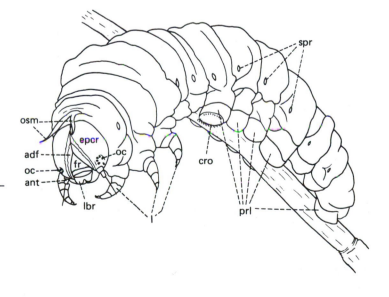

Figure 34–3. Larva of *Papílio* (Papiliónidae). *adf*, adfrontal area; *ant*, antenna; *cro*, crochets; *epcr*, epicranium; *fr*, frons; *l*, thoracic legs; *lbr*, labrum; *oc*, ocelli; *osm*, osmeterium (scent gland); *prl*, prolegs; *spr*, spiracles.

usually bear at their apex a number of tiny hooks called crochets. Some larvae, such as the measuring-worms and loopers, have fewer than five pairs of prolegs, and some lycaenids and leaf-mining Micro-lepidóptera have neither legs nor prolegs. The only other eruciform larvae likely to be confused with those of the Lepidóptera are the larvae of sawflies. Sawfly larvae (Figure 35–37) have only one stemma on each side, the prolegs do not bear crochets, and there are generally more than five pairs of prolegs. Most sawfly larvae are 25 mm or less in length, whereas many lepidopteran larvae are considerably larger.

Most butterfly and moth larvae feed on plants, but different species feed in different ways. The larger larvae generally feed at the edge of the leaf and consume all but the larger veins; the smaller larvae skeletonize the leaf or eat small holes in it. Many larvae are leaf miners, feeding inside the leaf, and their mines may be linear, trumpet-shaped, or blotchlike. A few are gall makers, and a few bore in the fruits, stems, wood, or other parts of the plant. A very few are predaceous on other insects.

The larvae of Lepidóptera have well-developed silk glands, which are modified salivary glands that open on the labium. Many larvae use this silk in making a cocoon, and some use it in making shelters. Leaf rollers and leaf folders roll or fold up a leaf, tie it in place with silk, and feed inside the shelter so formed. Other larvae tie a few leaves together and feed inside this shelter. Some of the gregarious species, such as the tent caterpillars and webworms, make a large shelter involving many leaves and even entire branches.

Pupation occurs in various situations. Many larvae form an elaborate cocoon and transform to the pupa inside it. Others make a very simple cocoon,

and still others make no cocoon at all. Many larvae pupate in some sort of protected situation. The pupae (Figure 34–4) are usually obtect, with the appendages firmly attached to the body. Moth pupae are usually brownish and relatively smooth, while butterfly pupae are variously colored and are often tuberculate or sculptured. Most butterflies do not make a cocoon, and their pupae are often called chrysalids (singular, *chrysalis*). The chrysalids of some butterflies (Danàidae, Nymphálidae, Satýridae, and Libythèidae) are attached to a leaf or twig by the cremaster, a spiny process at the posterior end of the body, and hang head downward (Figure 34–4B). In other cases (Lycaènidae, Piéridae, and Papiliónidae) the chrysalis is attached by the cremaster, but it is held in a more or less upright position by a silken girdle about the middle of the body (Figure 34–4A). Some moth larvae (certain Sphíngidae and Pyrálidae) pupate underground. A few moth larvae construct elaborate cocoons, for example, the network cocoon of *Uròdus* (Yponomeùtidae), which is attached to a branch by a long silken stalk.

Most of the Lepidóptera have one generation a year, usually overwintering as a larva or pupa. A few have two or more generations a year, and a few require two or three years to complete a generation. Many species overwinter in the egg stage, but relatively few overwinter as adults.

Classification of the Lepidóptera

There have been several arrangements of the major groups of Lepidóptera. One of the first was the division of the order into two suborders, Rhopalócera (butterflies) and Heterócera (moths), based principally on antennal characters. Later the order came

Figure 34–4. Pupae of Lepidóptera. **A,** *Papílio* (Papiliónidae); **B,** *Nýmphalis* (Nymphálidae); **C,** *Helìòthis* (Noctùidae), dorsal view; **D,** same, lateral view. *cre,* cremaster; *sp,* spiracle. (Courtesy of Peterson; reprinted by permission.)

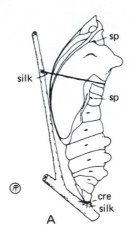
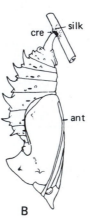

to be divided into two suborders on the basis of the wing venation and the nature of the wing coupling: the Jugàtae or Homoneùra and the Frenàtae or Heteroneùra. The Jugàtae usually had a jugum (and lacked a frenulum) and a similar venation in the front and hind wings, while the Frenàtae usually had a frenulum (but no jugum) and a reduced venation in the hind wings.

Past authorities have recognized two major divisions within the order, the Microlepidóptera and the Macrolepidóptera (the names referring to the insects' average size). As used in this book (and by most authorities using the terms), the Microlepidóptera includes the Monotrỳsia and the Ditrỳsia superfamilies Tineòidea through Pyralòidea (see the list below), and the Macrolepidóptera includes the remaining families of the Ditrỳsia.

Most recent arrangements have separated the Micropterígidae into a suborder by itself, the Zeuglóptera (some authorities would consider this an order, related to the Lepidóptera and Trichóptera), with the remaining Lepidóptera divided into two suborders, the Monotrỳsia and the Ditrỳsia, based principally on the number of genital openings in the female. This arrangement would place the Eriocranìidae, Acanthopteroctètidae, Hepiálidae, Nepticulòidea, and Incurvariòidea in the Monotrỳsia and the rest in the Ditrỳsia.

Some authorities (for example, Common 1975) believe the Eriocranìidae, Acanthopteroctètidae, and Hepiálidae are sufficiently different from the other groups originally included in the Monotrỳsia to remove them from that suborder and place them in two separate suborders, the Dacnonỳpha (for the Eriocranìidae and Acanthopteroctètidae) and the Exopòria (for the Hepiálidae and some related exotic families). We follow the latter arrangement in this book, dividing the Lepidóptera into five suborders: Zeuglóptera, Dacnonỳpha, Exopòria, Monotrỳsia, and Ditrỳsia.

Most lepidopterists have recognized a series of superfamilies in this order, but there is no final agreement about the number and family content of many of these groups. The classification of the Lepidóptera used in this book follows Hodges *et al.* (1983) and is outlined below (with alternate spellings, names, or arrangements in parentheses). The families marked with an asterisk either are relatively rare or are unlikely to be taken by a general collector.

Suborder Zeuglóptera (Jugàtae or Homoneùra, in part)
   Superfamily Micropterigòidea (Micropterygòidea)

*Micropterígidae (Micropterýgidae, Eriocephálidae)—mandibulate moths
Suborder Dacnonỳpha (Dachnonỳpha; Jugàtae or Homoneùra, in part)
   Superfamily Eriocraniòidea
      *Eriocranìidae—eriocraniid moths
      *Acanthopteroctètidae—acanthopteroctetid moths
Suborder Exopòria (Jugàtae or Homoneùra, in part)
   Superfamily Hepialòidea
      *Hepiálidae—ghost moths or swifts
Suborder Monotrỳsia (Frenàtae or Heteroneùra, in part)
   Superfamily Nepticulòidea (Stigmellòidea)
      *Nepticùlidae (Stigméllidae)—leaf miners
      *Opostégidae—opostegid moths
      *Tischerìidae—the apple-leaf trumpet miner and others
   Superfamily Incurvariòidea
      Incurvarìidae—incurvariid moths
      Prodóxidae (Incurvarìidae in part)—yucca moths
      Adèlidae (Incurvarìidae in part)—fairy moths
      *Heliozèlidae—shield bearers, leaf miners
Suborder Ditrỳsia (Frenàtae or Heteroneùra, in part)
   Superfamily Tineòidea (Tìnaeòidea)
      Tinèidae (Tinaèidae; including Acrolóphidae, Amydrìidae, Hieroxéstidae = Oinophílidae, and Setomórphidae)—clothes moths and others
      Psỳchidae (including Talaeporìidae)—bagworms
      *Lyonetìidae (including Bucculatrígidae)—lyonetiid moths
      Gracillarìidae (Gracilarìidae, Lithocollètidae; including Phyllocnístidae)—leaf blotch miners
   Superfamily Gelechiòidea
      Oecophòridae (Depressarìidae; including Stenómidae = Stenomátidae, Ethmìidae, Xyloríctidae, and Stathmopódidae = Tìnaegerìidae)—oecophorid moths
      *Lecithocéridae (Gelechìidae in part)—lecithocerid moths
      *Elachístidae (Cycnodìidae)—grass miners
      Coleophòridae (Mómphidae in part; Batrachedrìnae)—casebearers
      *Agonoxénidae (including Blastodácnidae)—agonoxenid moths
      *Blastobásidae (including Symmócidae and Holcopogónidae)—blastobasid moths
      *Mómphidae (Lavérnidae, Cosmopterígidae in part)—momphid moths
      *Scythrídidae (Scýthridae)—scythrid moths

*Cosmopterígidae (Cosmopterýgidae; including Walshìidae)—cosmopterigid moths

Gelechìidae—gelechiid moths

Superfamily Copromorphòidea (Alucitòidea)

*Copromórphidae—copromorphid moths

*Alucítidae (Orneòdidae)—many-plume moths

*Carposìnidae—carposinid moths

*Epermenìidae (Chaulìòdidae, Scythrídidae in part, Yponomeùtidae in part)—epermeniid moths

*Glyphipterígidae (Glyphipterýgidae)—glyphipterigid moths

Superfamily Yponomeutòidea

*Plutéllidae (Yponomeùtidae in part)—diamondback moths

Yponomeùtidae—ermine moths

*Ochsenheimerìidae—the cereal stem moth

*Argyresthìidae (Yponomeùtidae in part)—argyresthiid moths

*Douglasìidae (Glyphipterígidae in part)—leaf miners

*Acrolepìidae (Yponomeùtidae in part)—acrolepiid moths

*Heliodínidae (Schreckensteinìidae)—heliodinid moths

Superfamily Sesiòidea (Aegeriòidea)

Sesìidae (Aegerìidae)—clearwing moths

*Choreùtidae (Hemerophílidae; Glyphipterígidae in part)—choreutid moths

Superfamily Cossòidea

Cóssidae (including Hypóptidae and Zeuzéridae)—carpenter moths and leopard moths

Superfamily Tortricòidea

Tortrícidae (including Oleuthreùtidae, Chlidanòtidae, Cochýlidae, and Phalonìidae)—tortricid moths

Superfamily Zygaenòidea

*Zygaènidae (Pyromórphidae)—smoky moths and burnets

*Megalopỳgidae (Lagòidae)—flannel moths

*Epipyrópidae—planthopper parasites

*Dalcéridae (Acrágidae)—dalcerid moths

Limacòdidae (Cochlidìidae, Euclèidae)—slug caterpillars and saddleback caterpillars

Superfamily Pterophoròidea

Pterophòridae (including Agdístidae)—plume moths

Superfamily Pyralòidea

Pyrálidae (Pyralídidae; including Pyráustidae, Crámbidae, Gallerìidae, and Phycítidae)—snout moths, grass moths, and others

*Thyrídidae (Thỳridae)—window-winged moths

*Hyblaèidae (Noctùidae in part)—hyblaeid moths

Superfamily Hesperiòidea

Hesperìidae (including Megathỳmidae)—skippers

Superfamily Papilionòidea

Papiliónidae (including Parnassìidae)—swallowtails and parnassians

Piéridae (Ascìidae)—whites, sulphurs, and orange-tips

Lycaènidae (Cupidínidae, Rurálidae; including Riodínidae = Nemeobìidae = Erycínidae)—coppers, hairstreaks, blues, harvesters, and metalmarks

Libythèidae (Nymphálidae in part)—snout butterflies

Nymphálidae (Argyrèidae; including Heliconìidae, Ithomìidae, and Apatùridae)—brushfooted butterflies: fritillaries, checkerspots, crescentspots, anglewings, mourning cloaks, admirals, purples, heliconians, and others

Satýridae (Agapétidae; Nymphálidae in part)—satyrs, wood nymphs, and arctics

Danàidae (Lymnádidae; Nymphálidae in part)—milkweed butterflies

Superfamily Geometròidea

*Thyatíridae (Cymatophòridae)—thyatirid moths

Drepánidae—hook-tip moths

Geométridae—measuringworms, geometers, cankerworms, and others

*Epiplèmidae—epiplemid moths

*Sematùridae (Manidìidae)—sematurid moths

*Uranìidae—uraniid moths

Superfamily Mimallonòidea

Mimallónidae (Lacosòmidae, Perophòridae)—sack-bearers

Superfamily Bombycòidea

Lasiocámpidae—tent caterpillars, lappet moths, and others

*Apatelòdidae (Zanólidae)—apatelodid moths

*Bombýcidae—silkworm moths (introduced from Asia)

Saturnìidae (Attácidae; including Citheronìidae)—royal moths and giant silkworm moths

Superfamily Sphingòidea

Sphíngidae (Smerínthidae)—sphinx or hawk moths, hornworms

Superfamily Noctuòidea

Notodóntidae (Cerùridae)—prominents

*Dióptidae (Notodóntidae in part)—oakworms

Lymantrìidae (Lipáridae, Orgỳidae)—tussock moths, gypsy moths, and others

Arctìidae (including Lithosìidae, Ctenùchidae = Amátidae = Syntómidae = Euchromì-

idae = Nycteméridae)—tiger moths, footman moths, wasp moths, and others
Noctùidae (Phalaènidae; including Plusìidae, Nòlidae, and Agarístidae)—noctuid moths: underwings, cutworms, dagger moths, owlet moths, forester moths, and others

Characters Used in Identifying Lepidóptera

The principal characters used in identifying adult Lepidóptera are those of the wings (venation, method of wing union, wing shape, and scaling). Other characters used include the character of the antennae, mouthparts (principally the palps and proboscis), ocelli (whether present or absent), and legs, and frequently such general features as size and color.

Wing Venation

The wing venation in this order is relatively simple because there are few cross veins and rarely extra branches of the longitudinal veins, and the venation is reduced in some groups. There are differences of opinion regarding the interpretation of certain veins in the lepidopteran wing. We follow here the interpretation of Comstock.[2]

Two general types of wing venation occur in this order, homoneurous and heteroneurous. In homoneurous venation, the venation of the front and hind wings is similar; there are as many branches of R in the hind wing as in the front wing. In heteroneurous

[2]The mediocubital cross vein of the Comstock terminology is called M_4 by some authorities. The three branches of the media according to Comstock are M_1, M_2, and M_3. According to these other authorities, Comstock's Cu_1 and Cu_2 are Cu_{1a} and Cu_{1b}, his 1A is Cu_2, his 2A is 1A, and his 3A is 2A.

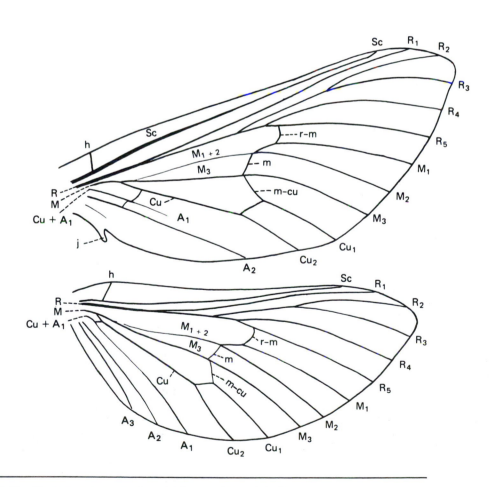

Figure 34–5. Homoneurous venation of *Sthenòpis* (Hepiálidae). *j*, jugum.

venation, the venation in the hind wing is reduced; Rs is always unbranched.

Homoneurous venation occurs in the suborders Zeuglóptera, Dacnonỳpha, and Exopòria. These groups have the subcosta simple or two-branched; the radius is five-branched (occasionally six-branched); the media is three-branched; and there are usually three anal veins (Figure 34–5).

The remaining suborders (Monotrỳsia and Ditrỳsia) have a heteroneurous venation. The radius in the front wing usually has five branches (occasionally fewer), but in the hind wing the radial sector is unbranched and R_1 usually fuses with the subcosta. The basal portion of the media is atrophied in many cases, with the result that a large cell, commonly called the discal cell, is formed in the central part of the wing. The first anal vein is often atrophied or fused with A_2. A somewhat generalized heteroneurous venation is shown in Figure 34–6.

The veins may fuse in various ways in the heteroneurous groups, and this fusing or stalking is used in the key. The subcosta in the front wing is nearly always free of the discal cell and lies between it and the costa. The branches of the radius arise from the anterior side of the discal cell or from its outer anterior corner. Two or more branches of the radius are frequently stalked, that is, fused for a distance beyond the discal cell. Certain radial branches occasionally fuse again beyond their point of separation, thus forming accessory cells (for example, Figure 34–17A, *acc*). The three branches of the media usually arise from the apex of the discal cell in both wings, though M_1 may be stalked with a branch of the radius for a distance beyond the apex of the discal cell (Figure 34–13). The point of origin of M_2 from the apex of the discal cell is an important character used in separating different groups: when it arises from the middle of the apex of the discal cell, as in Figure 34–20, or anterior to the middle, the vein (Cu) forming the posterior side of this cell appears three-branched; when M_2 arises nearer to M_3 than to M_1 (Figures 34–23 through 34–28), then the cubitus appears four-branched.

Variations in the venation of the hind wing of the heteroneurous groups involve principally the nature of the fusion of Sc + R_1 and the number of anal

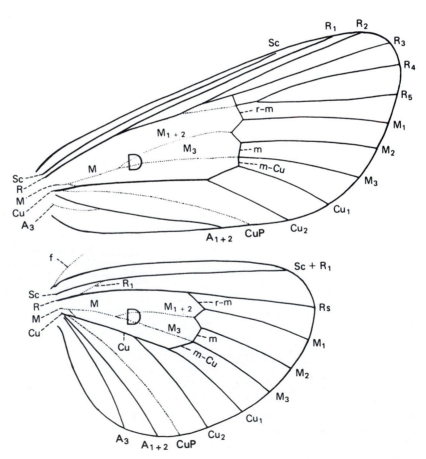

Figure 34–6. Generalized heteroneurous venation. The veins shown by dotted lines are atrophied or lost in some groups. *D*, discal cell; *f*, frenulum.

veins. In some cases R is separate from Sc at the base of the wing, and R_1 appears as a cross vein between Rs and Sc somewhere along the anterior side of the distal cell (Figure 34–17B). R_1 also fuses with Sc eventually, and judging from the pupal tracheation, the vein reaching the wing margin is Sc (the R_1 trachea is always small); however, this vein at the margin is usually called Sc $+$ R_1. In many cases Sc and R are fused basally, or they may be separate at the base and fuse for a short distance along the anterior side of the discal cell (Figures 34–26, 34–27). In the heteroneurous families most authorities call the 1A of Comstock CuP; his 2A, A_{1+2}; and his 3A, A_3.

Other Wing Characters

There are four general mechanisms whereby the wings on each side are caused to operate together: a fibula, a jugum, a frenulum, and an expanded humeral angle of the hind wing. A fibula is a small, more or less triangular lobe at the base of the front wing on the posterior side (Figure 34–34B, *fib*), which overlaps the base of the hind wing. This mechanism occurs in the Zeuglóptera and Dacnonỳpha. A jugum is a small fingerlike lobe at the base of the front wing (Figure 34–5, *j*), which overlaps the base of the anterior edge of the hind wing. This structure occurs in the Exopòria. A frenulum is a large bristle (males) or a group of bristles (most females) arising from the humeral angle of the hind wing and fitting under a group of scales near the costal margin (on the lower surface) of the front wing (Figure 34–6, *f*). A frenulum occurs in most Monotrỳsia and Ditrỳsia (except the butterflies and some moths). Those Monotrỳsia and Ditrỳsia that lack a frenulum usually have the humeral angle of the hind wing more or less expanded and fitting under the posterior margin of the front wing. A specialized wing coupling of interlocking spines and wing folding occurs in the Sesìidae.

Most of the Monotrỳsia (all but the Heliozèlidae) have minute hairlike spines on the wings (under the scales). These are termed aculeae, and such wings may be described as aculeate. The aculeae can be seen when the scales are bleached or removed. They are not movable at the base.

Most Lepidóptera have the front wings more or less triangular and the hind wings somewhat rounded, but many have the wings more elongate. Many of the smaller Microlepidóptera have the wings lanceolate; that is, both front and hind wings are elongate and pointed apically, and the hind wings are usually narrower than the front wings (as in

Figure 34–33), often with a broad fringe of hairlike scales.

Head Characters

The antennae of butterflies (Figure 34–7A,B) are slender and knobbed at the tip; those of moths (Figure 34–7C–E) usually filiform, setaceous, or plumose. The basal segment of the antennae in some of the Microlepidóptera is enlarged, and when the antenna is bent down and back this segment fits over the eye. Such an enlarged basal antennal segment is called an eye cap (Figure 34–29B). Most of the moths have a pair of ocelli located on the upper surface of the head close to the compound eyes (Figure 34–2A, *oc*). These ocelli often can be seen only by separating the hairs and scales. The mouthpart characters most often used in keys are the nature of the labial and maxillary palps and the proboscis. Certain exotic families do not conform to these distinctions between moths and butterflies.

Leg Characters

The leg characters of value in identification include the form of the tibial spurs and the tarsal claws, the presence or absence of spines on the legs, and occasionally the structure of the epiphysis. The epiphysis is a movable pad or spurlike structure on the inner surface of the front tibia that is probably used in cleaning the antennae. The front legs are very much reduced in some of the butterflies, particularly the Nymphálidae, Danàidae, Satýridae, and Libythèidae.

Studying Wing Venation in the Lepidóptera

It is often possible to make out venational details in a butterfly or moth without any special treatment of the wings, or in some cases venational details may be seen by putting a few drops of alcohol, ether, or xylene on the wings or by carefully scraping off a few of the wing scales. In many cases, however, it is necessary to bleach the wings in order to study all details of wing venation. A method of bleaching and mounting the wings of Lepidóptera is described here.

The materials needed for clearing and mounting lepidopteran wings are as follows:

1. Three watch glasses, one containing 95% alcohol, one containing 10% hydrochloric acid, and one containing equal proportions of aqueous solutions of sodium chloride and sodium hypochlorite. (Clorox serves fairly well in place of this mixture.)

2. A preparation dish of water, preferably distilled water.
3. Slides (preferably 50 by 50 mm), masks, and binding tape (or cover slips, and gummed labels with holes cut in the center).
4. Forceps and dissecting needle.

The procedure in clearing and mounting the wings is as follows:

1. Remove the wings from one side of the specimen, being careful not to tear them or to break any connections such as the frenulum between the front and hind wings. The frenulum is less likely to be broken if the front and hind wings are removed together.
2. Dip the wings in 95% alcohol for a few seconds to wet them.
3. Dip the wings in 10% hydrochloric acid for a few seconds.
4. Place the wings in the mixture of sodium chloride and sodium hypochlorite (or Clorox bleach) and leave them there until the color is removed. This process usually requires only a few minutes. If the wings are slow in clearing, dip them in the acid again and then return them to the bleaching solution.

5. Rinse the wings in water to remove the excess bleach.
6. Place the wings on the slide, centered and properly oriented (preferably with the base of the wings to the left). This procedure is most easily accomplished by floating the wings in water (for example, in a preparation dish) and bringing the slide up from underneath. The wings should be oriented on the slide while they are wet.
7. Allow the slide and wings to dry. If all the bleach has not been removed and some is deposited on the slide, place the slide again in water, carefully remove the wings, clean the slide, and remount the wings.
8. Place the mask on the slide around the wings (data, labeling, and the like should be put on the mask), put on the cover slide, and bind. Care should be taken before the slide is bound to make sure the wings are dry and both slides are perfectly clean.

Such a slide and the specimen from which the wings have been removed should always be labeled so that they can be associated. A wing slide of this sort will keep indefinitely and can be studied under the microscope or projected on a screen for demonstration. In the case of wings 13 mm or less in length, it is

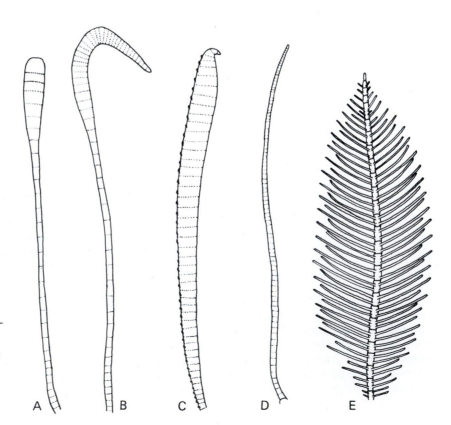

Figure 34–7.   Antennae of Lepidóptera. **A,** *Còlias* (Piéridae); **B,** *Epargỳreus* (Hesperìidae); **C,** *Hémaris* (Sphíngidae); **D,** *Drastèria* (Noctùidae); **E,** *Callosàmia* (Saturnìidae).

better not to use a mask. The mask may be thicker than the wings, and the wings may slip or curl after the slide is bound. The labeling can be put on a small strip of paper that is attached to the outside of the

slide with cellophane tape. Small wings can also be mounted under a cover slip, and the cover slip held down with a gummed slide label with a large hole cut from its center.

Key to the Families of Lepidóptera

This key is based to a considerable extent on wing venation, and it may sometimes be necessary to wet or mount the wings of a specimen in order to run it through the key. For the sake of brevity, the two anterior veins in the hind wing are referred to as Sc and Rs, though most of the first vein is usually Sc + R_1, and the base of the second vein may be R. Keys to the larvae are given by Forbes (1923–1960), Peterson (1948), and Stehr (1987). The groups marked with an asterisk are relatively rare or are unlikely to be taken by a general collector.

1.	Wings present and well developed **2**	
1'.	Wings absent or vestigial (females only) **116**	
2(1).	Front and hind wings similar in venation and usually also in shape; Rs in hind wing 3- or 4-branched (Figures 34–5, 34–34B); front and hind wings usually united by jugum or fibula; no coiled proboscis **3***	
2'.	Front and hind wings dissimilar in venation and usually also in shape; Rs in hind wing unbranched; no jugum or fibula, front and hind wings united by frenulum or by expanded humeral angle of hind wing; mouthparts usually in form of a coiled proboscis **6**	
3(2).	Wingspread 25 mm or more ....**Hepiálidae***	p. 622
3'.	Wingspread 12 mm or less **4***	
4(3').	Functional mandibles present; middle tibiae without spurs; Sc in front wing forked near its middle (Figure 34–34B) ....**Micropterígidae***	p. 621
4'.	Mandibles vestigial or absent; middle tibiae with 1 spur; Sc in front wing forked near its tip **5***	
5(4').	Ocelli present; M_1 in both wings not stalked with R_{4+5}; anal veins in front wing fused distally; widely distributed ....**Eriocraniidae***	p. 621
5'.	Ocelli absent; M_1 in both wings stalked with R_{4+5}; anal veins in front wing separate; western United States ....**Acanthopteroctètidae***	p. 622
6(2').	Antennae threadlike, swollen or knobbed at tip (Figure 34–7A,B); no frenulum; ocelli absent (butterflies and skippers) **7**	
6'.	Antennae of various forms, but usually not knobbed at tip (Figure 34–7C–E); if antennae are somewhat clubbed, then frenulum is present; ocelli present or absent (moths) **15**	
7(6).	Radius in front wing 5-branched, with all branches simple and arising from discal cell (Figure 34–8); antennae widely separated at base and usually hooked at tip (Figure 34–7B); hind tibiae usually with a middle spur; stout-bodied insects (skippers) ....**Hesperìidae**	p. 636
7'.	Radius in front wing 3- to 5-branched, and if 5-branched, then with some branches stalked beyond discal cell (Figures 34–9 through 34–14); antennae close together at base, never hooked at tip (Figure 34–7A); hind tibiae never with middle spur (butterflies) **8**	

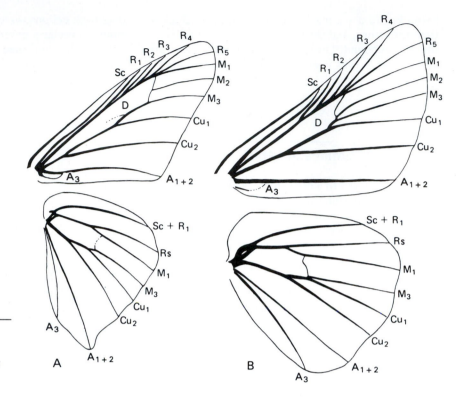

Figure 34–8. Wings of Hesperìidae. **A,** *Epargỳreus* (Pyrgìnae); **B,** *Pseudocopaeòdes* (Hesperìinae). *D,* discal cell.

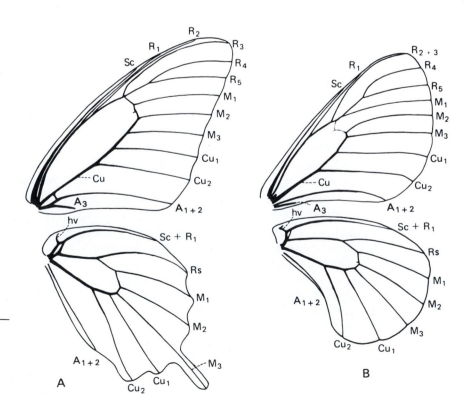

Figure 34–9. Wings of Papiliónidae. **A,** *Papílio* (Papilionìnae); **B,** *Parnássius* (Parnassìinae). *hv,* humeral vein.

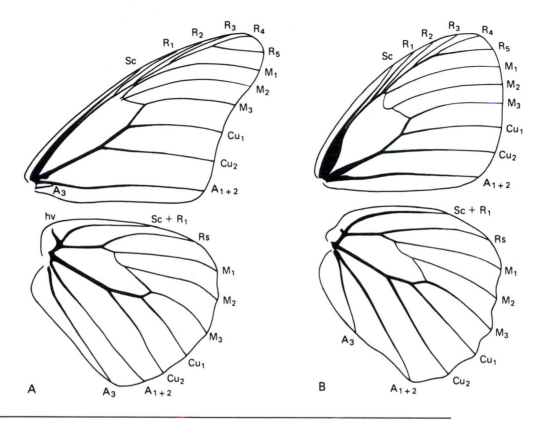

Figure 34–10. Wings of butterflies. **A,** *Danàus* (Danàidae); **B,** *Cercỳonis* (Satýridae). *hv,* humeral vein.

8(7′).   Cubitus in front wing apparently 4-branched, hind wing with single anal vein (Figure 34–9); hind wing often with 1 or more taillike prolongations on posterior margin ....**Papiliónidae**   p. 638

8′.   Cubitus in front wing apparently 3-branched, hind wing with 2 anal veins (Figures 34–10 through 34–14); hind wing usually without taillike prolongations on posterior margin **9**

9(8′).   Labial palps very long, longer than thorax, and thickly hairy (Figure 34–61 C) ....**Libythèidae***   p. 642

9′.   Labial palps of normal size, shorter than thorax **10**

10(9′).   Radius in front wing 5-branched (Figures 34–10 through 34–12, 34–13A); front legs usually reduced in size **11**

10′.   Radius in front wing 3- or 4-branched (Figures 34–13B, 34–14, 34–60); front legs usually of normal size **14**

11(10).   A$_3$ in front wing present but short, A$_{1+2}$ appearing to have a basal fork (Figure 34–10A); antennae not scaled above; relatively large, brownish butterflies (Figure 34–65A) ....**Danàidae**   p. 645

11′.   A$_3$ in front wing lacking, A$_{1+2}$ not appearing forked at base (Figures 34–10B, 34–11, 34–12A, 34–13A); antennae usually scaled above **12**

12(11′).   Some veins in front wing (especially Sc) greatly swollen at base (Figure 34–10B); front wings more or less triangular; antennae swollen apically but not

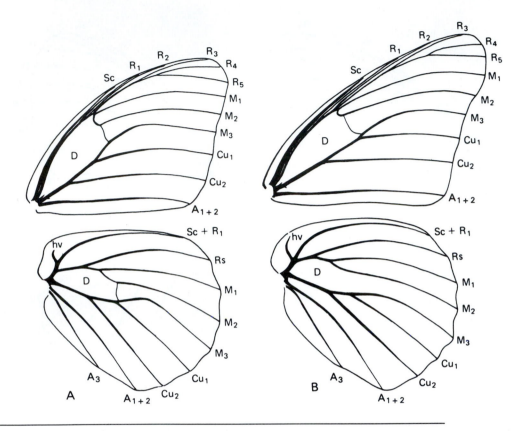

Figure 34–11. Wings of Nymphálidae. **A**, *Speyéria* (Argynnìnae) (discal cell in hind wing closed by a vestigial vein); **B**, *Limenìtis* (Limenitidìnae) (discal cell in hind wing open). *D*, discal cell; *hv*, humeral vein.

distinctly knobbed; small butterflies; usually brownish or grayish with eyespots in the wings (Figure 34–64) ....**Satýridae**   p. 644

12′.   Generally with no veins in front wing greatly swollen at base (Sc in front wing slightly swollen in some Nymphálidae); wing color and shape, and antennae, usually not as above **13**

13(12′).   M₁ in front wing stalked with R beyond discal cell (Figure 34–13A); front legs normal, or only slightly reduced, their claws bifid; small butterflies, usually white with black or orange markings (orange-tips) ....**Piéridae**   p. 639

13′.   M₁ in front wing not stalked with R beyond discal cell; front legs much reduced, without tarsal claws, not used in walking; usually medium-sized to large butterflies, and not colored as above ....**Nymphálidae**   p. 642

14(10′).   M₁ in front wing stalked with R beyond discal cell (Figure 34–13B); small to medium-sized butterflies, with white, yellow, or orange coloration, usually marked with black (Figure 34–59) ....**Piéridae**   p. 639

14′.   M₁ in front wing usually not stalked with R beyond discal cell (Figure 34–14); usually not colored as above ....**Lycaènidae**   p. 640

15(6′).   Wings, especially hind wings, deeply cleft or divided into plumelike lobes (Figure 34–52); legs long and slender, with long tibial spurs **16**

15′.   Wings entire, or front wings only slightly cleft **17**

16(15).   Each wing divided into 6 plumelike lobes ....**Alucítidae***   p. 628

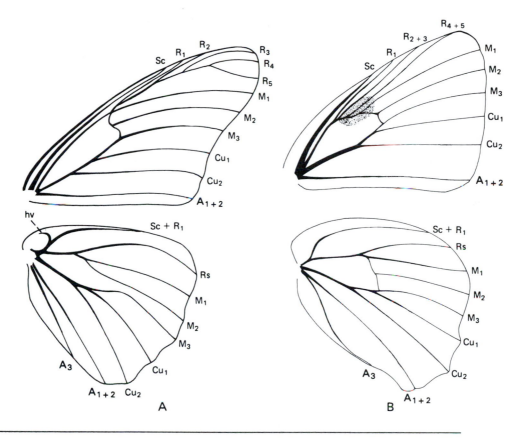

Figure 34–12.   Wings of butterflies. **A,** *Agráulis* (Heliconiìnae); **B,** *Thécla* (Theclìnae), male. *hv,* humeral vein. The dark spot in the wing of **B,** near the end of the discal cell, is a scent gland.

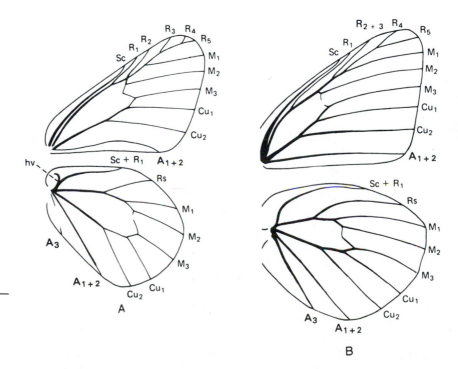

Figure 34–13.   Wings of Piéridae. **A,** an orange-tip (*Eùchloe*); **B,** a sulphur (*Còlias*). *hv,* humeral vein.

16'.   Front wings divided into 2–4 lobes, hind wings divided into 3 lobes (except
        (*Agdístis*) (Figure 34–52) . . . .**Pterophòridae**   p. 634

17(15'). A part of the wings, especially hind wings, devoid of scales (Figure 34–45);
        front wings long and narrow, at least 4 times as long as wide (Figure 34–46);
        hind margin of front wings and costal margin of hind wings with a series of
        recurved and interlocking spines and wing folds; wasplike day-flying
        moths . . . .**Sesìidae**   p. 630

17'.   Wings scaled throughout, or if with clear areas, then front wings are more
        triangular; wings without such interlocking spines **18**

18(17'). Hind wings much broader than their fringe, usually wider than front wings,
        never lanceolate; tibial spurs variable, often short or absent **19**

18'.   Hind wings with fringe as wide as wings or wider, hind wings usually no wider
        than front wings, often lanceolate (Figure 34–41); tibial spurs long, more
        than twice as long as width of tibia **63**

19(18). Hind wing with 3 anal veins behind discal cell **20**

19'.   Hind wing with 1–2 anal veins behind discal cell **31**

20(19). Hind wing with Sc and Rs fused for a varying distance beyond discal cell or
        separate but very closely parallel (Figure 34–15); Sc and R in hind wing
        separate along front of discal cell, or base of R atrophied . . . .**Pyrálidae**   p. 634

20'.   Hind wing with Sc and Rs widely separate beyond discal cell, base of R usually
        well developed **21**

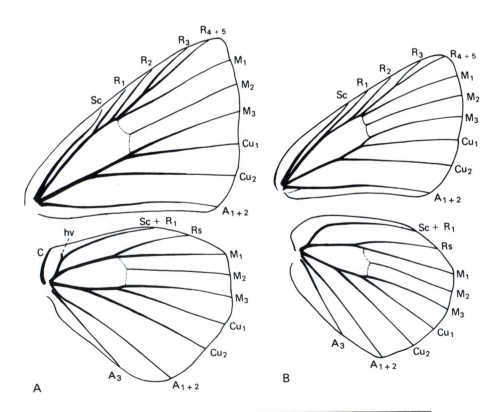

Figure 34–14.   Wings of Lycaènidae. **A,** *Lephelísca* (Riodinìnae); **B,** *Lycaèna* (Lycaenìnae).
hv, humeral vein.

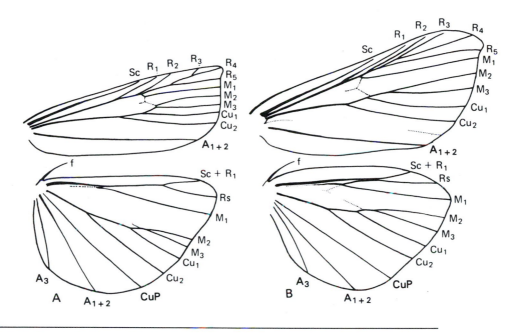

Figure 34–15.   Wings of Pyrálidae. **A,** *Crámbus* (Crambìnae); **B,** *Pýralis* (Pyralìnae). *f,* frenulum.

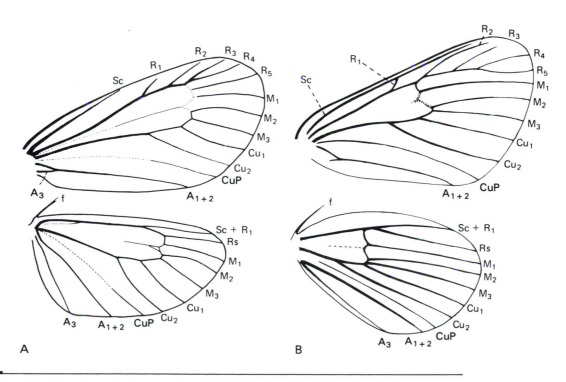

Figure 34–16.   **A,** wings of *Málthaca* (Zygaènidae); **B,** wings of *Megalopỳge* (Megalopỳgidae). *f,* frenulum.

21(20').   Sc and Rs in hind wing fused to near end of discal cell or at least fused beyond middle of cell (Figure 34–16) **22***

21'.   Sc and Rs in hind wing separate from base or fused for a short distance along basal half of cell (Figures 34–17, 34–18) **23**

22(21).   Wings largely or wholly blackish, thinly scaled; R₅ in front wing arising from discal cell (Figure 34–16A) ....**Zygaènidae***   p. 633

22'.   Wings largely yellowish or white, densely clothed with soft scales and hair; R₅ in front wing stalked beyond discal cell (Figure 34–16B) ....**Megalopỳgidae***   p. 633

23(21').   Front wing with an accessory cell (Figure 34–17A, *acc*) **24**

23'.   Front wing without an accessory cell (Figure 34–18) **27**

24(23).   Tibial spurs short, no longer than width of tibia; mouthparts often vestigial. **25**

24'.   Tibial spurs long, more than twice as long as width of tibia; mouthparts usually well developed **63**

25(24).   Front wing with some branches of R stalked, accessory cell extending beyond discal cell (Figure 34–17A) **26**

25'.   Front wing with no branches of R stalked, accessory cell not extending beyond discal cell; antennae bipectinate; small moths ....**Epipyrópidae***   p. 633

26(25).   Front wings subtriangular, about one-half longer than wide; wings densely clothed with soft scales and hair; Arizona ....**Dalcéridae***   p. 633

26'.   Front wings more elongate, at least twice as long as wide; wings more thinly scaled; widely distributed ....**Cóssidae**   p. 631

27(23').   M₂ in front wing arising about midway between M₁ and M₃, or closer to M₁, cubitus appearing 3-branched (Figures 34–17B, 34–18B); frenulum present or absent **28***

27'.   M₂ in front wing arising closer to M₃ than to M₁, cubitus appearing 4-branched; frenulum well developed (Figure 34–18A) **30**

28(27).   M₃ and Cu₁ in front wing stalked for a short distance beyond discal cell; frenulum well developed; California and Texas ....**Dióptidae***   p. 654

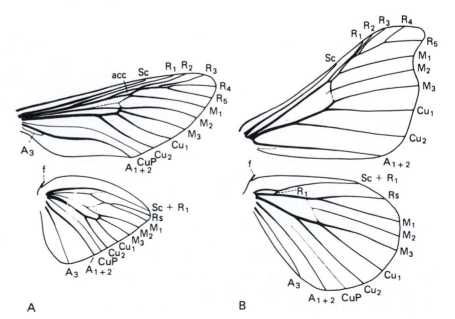

Figure 34–17. **A,** wings of *Prionoxýstus* (Cóssidae); **B,** wings of *Bómbyx* (Bombýcidae). *acc*, accessory cell; *f*, frenulum.

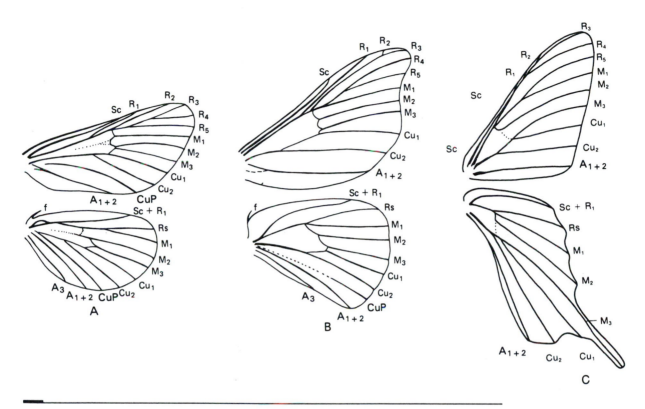

Figure 34–18. **A,** wings of *Euclèa* (Limacódidae); **B,** wings of *Cicínnus* (Mimallónidae); **C,** wings of *Urània* (Uranìidae). *f,* frenulum.

28'.   M₃ and Cu₁ in front wing not stalked beyond discal cell; frenulum small or absent; widely distributed **29***

29(28').   Front wing with R₂₊₃ and R₄₊₅ stalked independently of R₁; Sc and Rs in hind wing not connected by a cross vein (Figure 34–18B) ....**Mimallónidae***   p. 648

29'.   Front wing with R₂, R₃, R₄, and R₅ united on a common stalk; and Sc and Rs in hind wing connected basally by a cross vein (R₁) (Figure 34–17B) ....**Bombýcidae***   p. 649

30(27').   CuP absent in front wing, well developed in hind wing ......**Copromórphidae***   p. 628

30'.   CuP weak in both front and hind wings, often developed only near wing margin (Figure 34–31A,B) (see also 30") ....**Tortrícidae**   p. 632

30".   CuP complete in both front and hind wings (Figure 34–18A) ......**Limacòdidae**   p. 633

31(19').   Front wing with 2 distinct anal veins **32***

31'.   Front wing with single complete anal vein (Figures 34–19B, 34–20 through 34–28) or with A₁ and A₂ fusing near tip or connected by a cross vein (Figure 34–19A) **33**

32(31).   Ocelli present; front wing 3 or more times as long as wide (*Harrisìna*) ....**Zygaènidae***   p. 633

32'.   Ocelli absent; front wing not more than twice as long as wide .....**Hyblaèidae***   p. 636

33(31'.)   Front wing with a single complete vein behind discal cell (A₁₊₂), CuP at most represented by a fold, A₃ absent or meeting A₁₊₂ basally so that A₁₊₂ appears forked at base (Figures 34–19B, 34–20 through 34–28) **34**

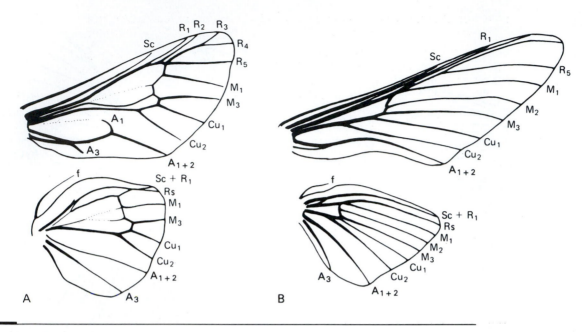

Figure 34–19. **A,** wings of *Thyridópteryx* (Psỳchidae); **B,** wings of *Hémaris* (Sphíngidae). *f,* frenulum.

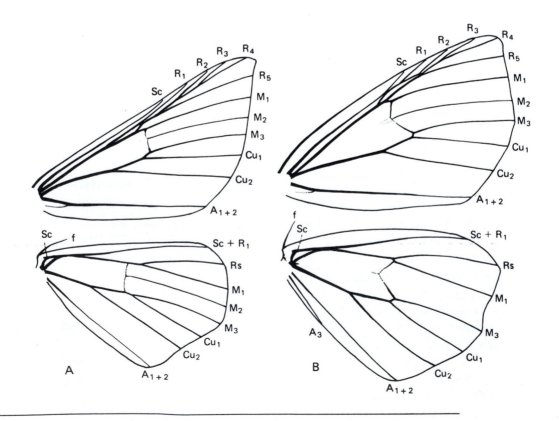

Figure 34–20. Wings of Geométridae. **A,** *Haemátopsis;* **B,** *Xanthótype. f,* frenulum.

33'.   Front wing with A$_1$ and A$_2$ fusing near tip (Figure 34–19A) or connected by a
         cross vein ....**Psýchidae**   p. 624

34(33). Antennae thickened, spindle-shaped (Figure 34–7C); Sc and Rs in hind wing
         connected by a cross vein near middle of discal cell, the two veins closely
         parallel to end of discal cell or beyond (Figure 34–19B); stout-bodied, often
         large moths (wingspread 50 mm or more) with narrow wings (Figure 34–77)
         ....**Sphíngidae**   p. 652

34'.   Antennae variable, rarely spindle-shaped; Sc and Rs in hind wing usually not
         connected by cross vein, or if such a cross vein is present, then the two veins
         strongly divergent beyond cross vein **35**

35(34'). M$_2$ in front wing arising about midway between M$_1$ and M$_3$, cubitus appearing
         3-branched (Figures 34–18B,C, 34–20 through 34–22), or (rarely) with M$_2$
         and M$_3$ absent, cubitus appearing to have fewer than 3 branches **36**

35'.   M$_2$ in front wing arising closer to M$_3$ than to M$_1$, cubitus appearing
         4-branched (Figures 34–23 through 34–28) **49**

36(35). Sc and Rs in hind wing swollen at base, fused to middle of discal cell, then
         diverging; M$_2$ and M$_3$ in front wing sometimes absent; small slender moths
         (Lithosiïnae) ....**Arctiidae**   p. 655

36'.   Sc and Rs in hind wing not fused at base, though they may be fused farther
         distad or connected by a cross vein **37**

37(36'). Antennae dilated apically; eyes hairy; Arizona ....**Sematuridae***   p. 647

37'.   Antennae not dilated apically, or if so, then eyes bare; widely distributed **38**

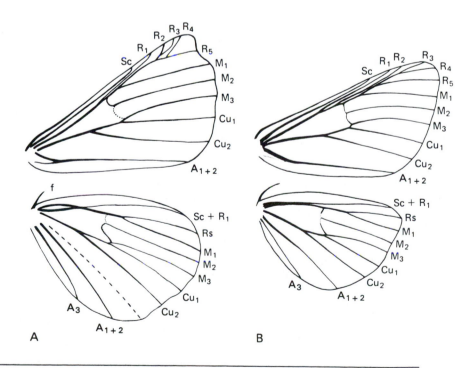

Figure 34–21.   **A,** wings of *Apatelòdes* (Apatelòdidae); **B,** wings of *Datàna* (Notodóntidae). *f,*
frenulum.

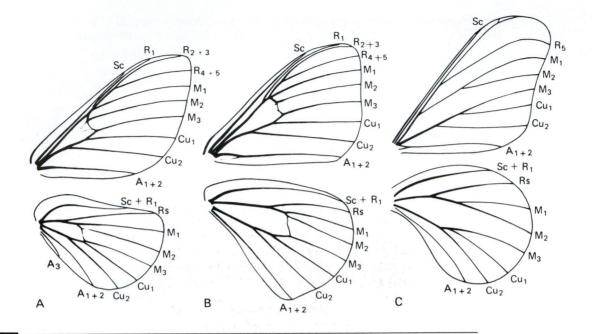

Figure 34–22. Wings of Saturnìidae. **A,** *Anisòta* (Citheroniìnae); **B,** *Autómeris* (Hemileucìnae); **C,** *Callosàmia* (Saturniìnae).

38(37').	Sc in hind wing strongly angled at base, usually connected to humeral angle of wing by strong brace vein; beyond the bend Sc fuses with or comes close to Rs for a short distance along discal cell (Figure 34–20) ....**Geométridae**	p. 645
38'.	Sc in hind wing straight or slightly curving at base, not of the above configuration **39**	
39(38').	Frenulum well developed; Sc and Rs in hind wing variable **40**	
39'.	Frenulum vestigial or absent; Sc and Rs in hind wing never fused but sometimes touching at a point beyond base or connected by a cross vein **45**	
40(39).	Sc in hind wing widely separated from Rs from near base of wing; M_1 in front wing stalked with R_5, which is well separated from R_4 ....**Epiplèmidae***	p. 647
40'.	Sc in hind wing close to Rs at least to middle of discal cell, often farther **41**	
41(40').	M_2 in hind wing arising nearer to M_3 than to M_1, cubitus appearing 4-branched; M_1 in hind wing arising from discal cell, not stalked with Rs beyond cell ....**Thyatíridae***	p. 645
41'.	M_2 in hind wing absent or arising midway between M_1 and M_3, or nearer to M_1, cubitus appearing 3-branched; M_1 in hind wing stalked with Rs for a short distance beyond discal cell (Figure 34–21) **42**	
42(41').	M_3 and Cu_1 in both front and hind wings stalked for a short distance beyond discal cell; slender, butterfly-like moths; California and Texas ....**Dióptidae***	p. 654
42'.	Not exactly fitting the above description **43**	
43(42').	Slender-bodied moths; tympanal hood at base of abdomen; Sc sinuous or swollen at base ....**Geométridae***	p. 645
43'.	Stout-bodied moths; no tympanal hood at base of abdomen **44**	

44(43').   Sc and Rs in hind wing close together and parallel along almost entire length of discal cell (Figure 34–21B); proboscis usually present; front wings fully scaled; tarsal claws with blunt tooth at base ....**Notodóntidae**   p. 654

44'.   Sc and Rs in hind wing separating near middle of discal cell (Figure 34–21A); proboscis lacking; front wings with 1 or 2 small clear spots near tip; tarsal claws simple ....**Apatelòdidae***   p. 649

45(39').   Sc and Rs in hind wing connected by a cross vein (Figure 34–17B); white moths of medium size ....**Bombýcidae***   p. 649

45'.   Sc and Rs in hind wing not connected by a cross vein (Figures 34–18B,C, 34–21A); color variable, but not white; size medium to large **46**

46(45').   Sc and Rs in hind wing separating near middle of discal cell, at the end of a long narrow basal areole; Rs and M_1 in hind wing stalked beyond discal cell (Figure 34–21A) ....**Apatelòdidae***   p. 649

46'.   Sc and Rs in hind wing separating at base of wing; Rs and M_1 in hind wing not stalked beyond discal cell (Figures 34–18B,C, 34–22) **47**

47(46'). M_2 in hind wing arising closer to M_1 than to M_3 (Figure 34–22); wingspread 25–150 mm ....**Saturniidae**   p. 649

47'. M_2 in hind wing arising about midway between M_1 and M_3 (Figure 34–18B,C); size variable **48***

48(47').   Hind wing with 1 anal vein (Figure 34–18C); large moths resembling a swallowtail butterfly; Texas ....**Uraniidae***   p. 647

48'.   Hind wing with 2 anal veins (Figure 34–18B); not swallowtail-like (Figure 34–70); widely distributed ....**Mimallónidae***   p. 648

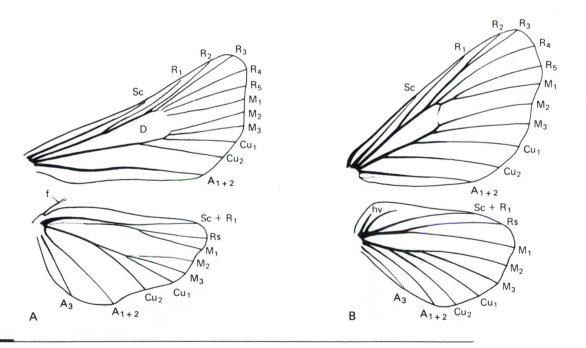

Figure 34–23.   **A,** wings of *Thỳris* (Thyrídidae); **B,** wings of *Malacosòma* (Lasiocámpidae). *f*, frenulum; *hv*, humeral veins.

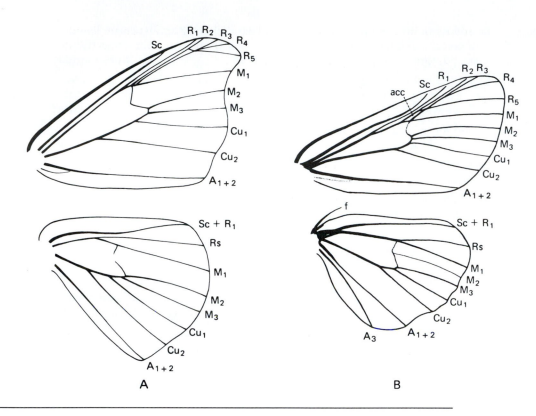

Figure 34–24.   **A,** wings of *Orèta* (Drepánidae); **B,** wings of *Alýpia* (Agaristìnae). *acc,* accessory cell; *f,* frenulum.

49(35').	All branches of R and M in front wing arising separately from the usually open discal cell (Figure 34–23A); wings generally with clear spots ....**Thyrídidae***	p. 636
49'.	Front wing with some branches of R or M fused beyond discal cell (Figures 34–23B, 34–24 through 34–28) **50**	
50(49').	Hind wing with humeral veins, without frenulum; Cu_2 in front wing arising in basal half or third of discal cell (Figure 34–23B) ....**Lasiocámpidae**	p. 648
50'.	Hind wing without humeral veins, usually with frenulum; Cu_2 in front wing arising in distal half of discal cell **51**	
51(50').	Frenulum absent or vestigial; Sc and Rs in hind wing approximated, usually parallel along discal cell or fusing beyond middle of cell (Figure 34–24A); apex of front wings usually sickle-shaped ....**Drepánidae**	p. 645
51'.	Frenulum well developed; Sc and Rs in hind wing not as above; apex of front wings usually not sickle-shaped **52**	
52(51').	Antennae swollen apically; Sc in hind wing fused with Rs for only a short distance at base of discal cell (Figure 34–24B); ocelli present; moths with a wingspread of about 25 mm, usually black with white or yellow spots in wings (Figure 34–86) (Agaristìnae) ....**Noctùidae**	p. 657
52'.	Antennae usually not swollen apically; Sc in hind wing variable; ocelli present or absent **53**	

53(52'). Sc in hind wing apparently absent (Figure 34–25A); day-flying moths (Figure 34–82) (Ctenuchìnae) . . . .**Arctìidae**   p. 655

53'. Sc in hind wing present and well developed **54**

54(53'). Sc and Rs in hind wing fused for a varying distance beyond discal cell or separate but very closely parallel (Figure 34–15); Sc and Rs in hind wing separate along front of discal cell, or base of Rs atrophied **55***

54'. Hind wing with Sc and Rs widely separate beyond discal cell, base of Rs usually well developed **56**

55(54). Front wings at least twice as long as wide, costal margin often irregular or lobed (if straight, M₂ and M₃ usually stalked); separation of Sc and Rs in hind wing generally well beyond discal cell; proboscis scaled; color variable, rarely white (Chrysaugìnae) . . . .**Pyrálidae***   p. 634

55'. Front wings less than twice as long as wide, costal margin straight; M₂ and M₃ not stalked; separation of Sc and Rs in hind wing about opposite end of discal cell; proboscis naked; white moths (*Eudeilínea*) . . . .**Drepánidae***   p. 645

56(54'). Apex of front wings sickle-shaped (Figure 34–24A); Sc and Rs in hind wing separate, more or less parallel along anterior side of discal cell (as in Figure 34–24A) (*Drépana*) . . . .**Drepánidae**   p. 645

56'. Apex of front wings not sickle-shaped; Sc and Rs in hind wing not as above (Figures 34–25B, 34–26 through 34–28) **57**

57(56'). Ocelli present **58**

57'. Ocelli absent **60**

58(57). Basal abdominal segment with 2 rounded domelike elevations (tympanal hoods) dorsolaterally, occupying the length of the segment, separated by a distance equal to their width; M₃ and Cu₁ in hind wing usually stalked (Figure 34–25B); black or brownish moths with white or yellow spots or bands in wings, sometimes with metallic tints; Gulf states and western United States (Pericopìnae). . . . . **Arctìidae***   p. 655

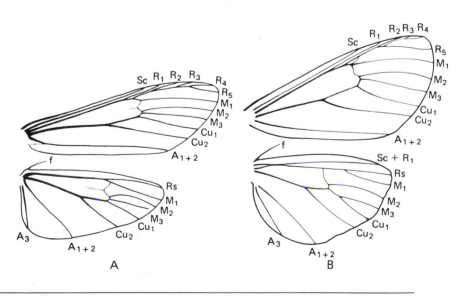

Figure 34–25. Wings of Arctìidae. **A,** *Císseps* (Ctenuchìnae); **B,** *Gnophaèla* (Pericopìinae). *f,* frenulum.

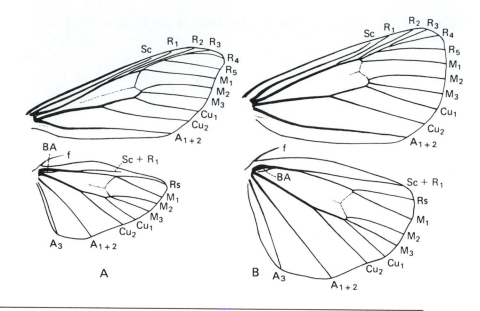

Figure 34–26.   Wings of Arctìidae. **A,** *Halisidòta;* **B,** *Apántesis. BA,* basal areole; *f,* frenulum.

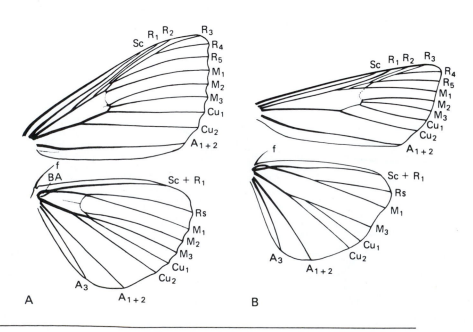

Figure 34–27.   Wings of Noctùidae, with M_2 in hind wing present and Cu appearing 4-branched (**A**), and M_2 in hind wing absent and Cu appearing 3-branched (**B**). *BA,* basal areole.

58'.   Tympanal hoods much smaller than above or not apparent; M_3 and Cu_1 in hind wing not stalked; color variable; widely distributed **59**

59(58').   Hind wing with Sc and Rs separating well before middle of discal cell, Sc not noticeably swollen at base; cubitus in hind wing appearing 3- or 4-branched (Figure 34–27); labial palps extending to middle of front or beyond; usually dark-colored moths ....**Noctùidae**   p. 657

59'.   Hind wing with Sc and Rs usually fused (beyond a small basal areole) to middle of discal cell, or if not, then Sc swollen at base; cubitus in hind wing appearing 4-branched (Figure 34–26); labial palps not exceeding middle of front; usually light-colored moths ....**Arctìidae**   p. 655

60(57').   Front wings with tufts of raised scales; Sc and Rs in hind wing fused (beyond a small basal areole) to near middle of discal cell; small moths (Nolìnae) ....**Noctùidae**   p. 657

60'.   Front wings smoothly scaled; Sc and Rs in hind wing not as above **61**

61(60').   Hind wing with a relatively large basal areole, Sc and Rs fused for only a short distance at end of areole (Figure 34–28) ....**Lymantrìidae**   p. 654

61'.   Hind wing with very small basal areole or none, Sc and Rs fused for varying distance along discal cell, at most to middle of cell **62**

62(61')   Labial palps short, usually not exceeding middle of face; size variable, wingspread up to about 40 mm; often brightly colored, reddish, yellowish, or white (Lithosiìnae) ....**Arctìidae**   p. 655

62'.   Labial palps longer, extending to middle of face or beyond; wingspread 20 mm or less; dull-colored moths (Hypenodìnae) ....**Noctùidae***   p. 657

63(18',24').   Basal segment of antennae enlarged, concave beneath, forming an eye cap (Figure 34–29B) **64**

63'.   Basal segment of antennae not forming an eye cap (Figure 34–29A) **68**

64(63).   Maxillary palps well developed, conspicuous; wing membrane aculeate (with minute spines under scales); proboscis scaled **65***

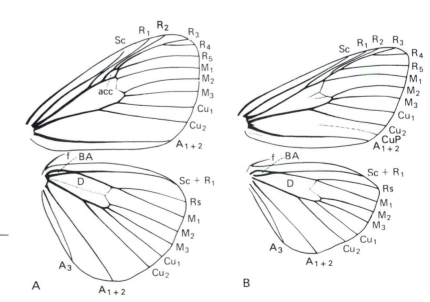

Figure 34–28. Wings of Lymantrìidae. **A,** Òrgyia; **B,** Lymántria. BA, basal areole; D, discal cell; f, frenulum.

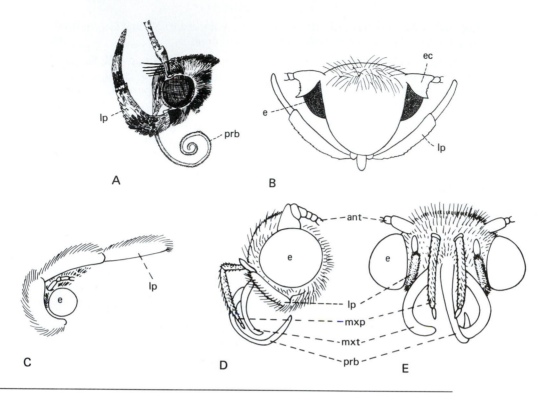

Figure 34–29.   Head structure in Microlepidóptera. **A,** *Pectinóphora* (Gelechìidae), lateral view; **B,** *Zenodòchium* (Blastobàsidae), anterior view; **C,** *Acrólophus* (Tinèidae), lateral view; **D,** lateral, and **E,** anterior views of *Tegetícula* (Prodóxidae). *ant,* antenna; *e,* compound eye; *ec,* eye cap; *lp,* labial palp; *mxp,* maxillary palp; *mxt,* maxillary tentacle; *prb,* proboscis. (**A,** redrawn from Busck; **B,** redrawn from Dietz.)

64′.   Maxillary palps vestigial; wing membrane not aculeate; proboscis naked
           (except Blastobàsidae). **66**

65(64).   Front wing with only 3 or 4 unbranched veins; wingspread usually over 3 mm;
           often white . . . .**Opostégidae***   p. 622

65′.   Front wing with branched veins (Figure 34–30A); wingspread 3 mm or less;
           often with metallic bands . . . .**Nepticùlidae***   p. 622

66(64′).   Labial palps minute and drooping, or absent; ocelli absent . . . .**Lyonetìidae***   p. 624

66′.   Labial palps of at least moderate size, upcurved or projecting forward; ocelli
           present or absent **67**

67(66′).   Wings pointed at apex; hind wing without discal cell; veins beyond discal cell
           in front wing diverging; no stigmalike thickening in front wing between C
           and R₁; proboscis naked (*Phyllocnístis*, etc.) . . . .**Gracillarìidae**   p. 625

67′.   Wings more or less rounded at apex; hind wing usually with a closed cell;
           veins beyond discal cell in front wing nearly parallel; front wing with
           stigmalike thickening between C and R₁ (as in Figure 34–30B); proboscis
           scaled (*Calosìma*) . . . .**Blastobàsidae***   p. 626

68(63′).   Maxillary palps well developed, folded in a resting position (Figure 34–29D,E)
           . . . .**69**

68'. Maxillary palps vestigial or, if present, projecting forward in a resting position
....**73**

69(68). Head smooth-scaled; R₅, when present, extending to costal margin of wing; strongly flattened moths; southern United States, Florida to California (Hieroxestìnae) ....**Tinèidae***   p. 623

69'. Head tufted, at least on vertex, or R₅ extending to outer margin of wing; widely distributed **70**

70(69'). R₅ in front wing extending to costal margin of wing or absent **71**

70'. R₅ in front wing extending to outer margin of wing ....**Acrolepìidae***   p. 630

71(70). Wing membrane aculeate (see couplet 64); antennae smooth, often very long; female with piercing ovipositor..**72**

71'. Wing membrane not aculeate; antennae usually rough, with a whorl of erect scales on each segment; ovipositor membranous, retractile ....**Tinèidae**   p. 623

72(71). Folded part of maxillary palps about half as long as width of head; dark-colored moths ....**Incurvarìidae**   p. 623

72'. Folded part of maxillary palps about two-thirds as long as width of head; mostly whitish moths ....**Prodóxidae**   p. 623

73(68'). First segment of labial palps as large as second or larger, palps recurved back over head and thorax (Figure 34–29C); ocelli absent; proboscis vestigial or absent; moderate-sized, stout, noctuid-like moths with eyes hairy (Acrolophiìnae) ....**Tinèidae***   p. 623

73'. Without the above combination of characters **74**

74(73'). Distal margin of hind wings concave, apex produced (Figure 34–31C); proboscis scaled ....**Gelechìidae**   p. 627

74'. Hind wings with distal margin rounded or trapezoidal, anal region well developed, venation complete or nearly so (Figures 34–31 A,B,D, 34–32); proboscis scaled or naked (see also 74") **75**

74". Wings lanceolate or linear, pointed or narrowly rounded at apex, anal region and venation often reduced (Figures 34–33, 34–34A) **90**

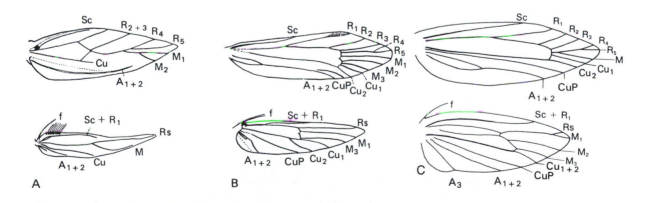

Figure 34–30. Wings of Microlepidóptera. **A,** *Obrússa* (Nepticùlidae); **B,** *Holcócera* (Blastobàsidae); **C,** *Ochsenheimèria* (Ochsenheimerìidae). *f,* frenulum. (**A,** redrawn from Braun; **B,** redrawn from Forbes; **C,** redrawn from Davis.)

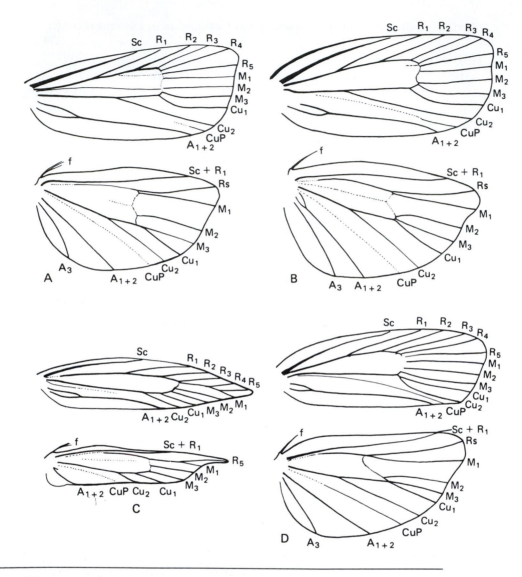

Figure 34–31. Wings of Microlepidóptera. **A** and **B**, Tortrícidae; **C**, Gelechìidae; **D**, Oecophòridae (*Stenòma*). *f*, frenulum.

75(74′).   CuP in front wing lacking **76***

75′.   CuP present in front wing, at least apically **78**

76(75).   Third segment of labial palps short and blunt, palps beaklike; R_5 rarely stalked with R_4, usually extending to outer margin of wing (Cochylìnae)
      ....**Tortrícidae***   p. 632

76′.   Third segment of labial palps long and slender, usually tapering, palps generally upturned to middle of front or beyond; R_5 in front wing usually stalked with R_4, extending to costal margin of wing **77***

77(76′).   Hind wing with all three branches of M present ....**Copromórphidae***   p. 628

77′.   Hind wing with M only 1- or 2-branched ....**Carposìnidae***   p. 628

78(75′).   Front wing with A_3 meeting A_{1+2} near its middle; Cu_2 arising at apex of discal cell, appearing as a continuation of the Cu stem, M unbranched, R_{4+5} stalked (Figure 34–30C); northeastern United States ....**Ochsenheimeriidae***   p. 629

78′.   Front wing with A_3 meeting A_{1+2} near its base, Cu_2 not as above, M usually 2- or 3-branched, R_{4+5} variable; widely distributed **79**

79(78′). Cu_2 in front wing arising in basal three-fourths of discal cell (Figure 34–31A,B); third segment of labial palps short and blunt, little if any longer than wide ....**Tortrícidae**   p. 632

79′. Cu_2 in front wing usually arising in distal fourth of discal cell (Figure 34–31D); labial palps variable, but third segment usually long and slender **80**

80(79′).   Labial palps and proboscis well developed **81**

80′.   Labial palps and proboscis vestigial (*Solenòbia*) ....**Psýchidae***   p. 624

81(80).   Vertex and upper part of face tufted with dense bristly hairs **82**

81′.   Upper face (and usually also vertex) smooth, with short scales **83**

82(81).   Wing membrane aculeate (see couple 64); antennae longer than wings in male; female with piercing ovipositor; day-flying ....**Adèlidae***   p. 623

82′.   Wing membrane usually not aculeate; antennae generally short; female with ovipositor membranous and retractile; generally nocturnal ....**Tinèidae**   p. 623

83(81′).   Rs and M_1 in hind wing arising close together, stalked or fused (Figure 34–31D) **84***

83′.   Rs and M_1 in hind wing well separated at their origin, at least half as far apart as at wing margin (Figure 34–32) **85**

84(83).   Front wings narrowly rounded or pointed apically (*Ceróstoma*) .....**Plutéllidae***   p. 629

84′.   Front wings broadly rounded or blunt apically (Figure 34–31D) (Stenomatìnae) ....**Oecophòridae***   p. 625

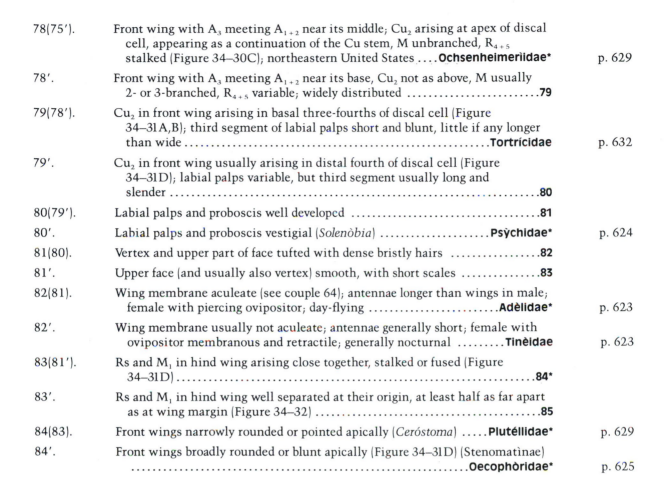

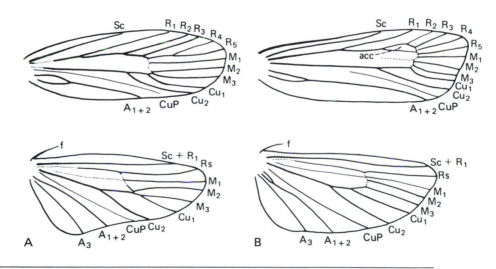

Figure 34–32.   Wings of Microlepidóptera. **A,** *Depressària* (Oecophòridae); **B,** *Átteva* (Yponomeùtidae). *acc,* accessory cell; *f,* frenulum.

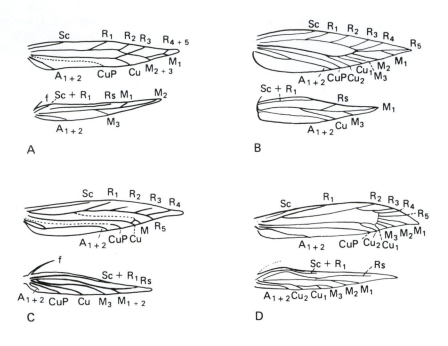

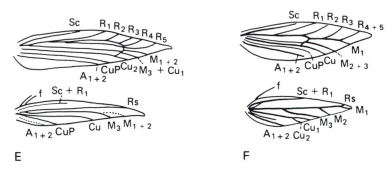

Figure 34–33. Wings of Microlepidóptera. **A,** *Bedéllia* (Lyonetìidae); **B,** *Tinágma* (Douglasìidae); **C,** *Coleóphora* (Coleophòridae); **D,** *Gracillària* (Gracillarìidae); **E,** *Tischèria* (Tischerìidae); **F,** *Antispìla* (Heliozèlidae). *f,* frenulum. (Redrawn from Comstock, by permission of the Comstock Publishing Company; **A,** after Clemens; **E** and **F,** after Spuler.)

89′. M_1 and M_2 in hind wing not stalked ....**Yponomeùtidae**   p. 629

90(74″).   Face and vertex with long bristly hairs; antennae usually rough, with 1 or 2
            whorls of erect scales on each segment; ocelli absent ....**Tinèidae**   p. 623

90′.   Face smooth-scaled; antennae variable; ocelli present or absent **91**

91(90′).   Front wing with closed discal cell **92**

91′.   Front wing without closed discal cell **115***

92(91).   Hind wing without discal cell, with R stem near middle of wing (well
            separated from Sc) and with a branch extending to C at about three-fifths
            the wing length (Figure 34–33B); R_5 in front wing free from R_4 but stalked
            with M_1; labial palps stout and drooping ....**Douglasiidae***   p. 629

92′.   Not exactly fitting the above description **93**

93(92′).   Discal cell in front wing somewhat oblique, its apex closer to hind margin of
            wing than to front margin, branches of Cu very short (Figure
            34–33C) **94**

93′.   Discal cell in front wing not oblique, its apex not much closer to hind margin
            of wing than to front margin, branches of Cu longer (Figures 34–30B,
            34–33D, F, 34–34A)...**96***

94(93).   Front wing with stigmalike thickening between C and R_1 (Figure 34–30B);
            scape of antenna with a row of long hairs ....**Blastobàsidae***   p. 626

94′.   Front wing without such a stigmalike thickening; scape of antenna
            variable **95**

95(94′).   Front tibiae slender, epiphysis apical or absent; antennae turned forward at rest
            ....**Coleophòridae**   p. 626

95′.   Front tibiae stout, epiphysis well developed, at middle of tibia; antennae
            turned backward at rest ....**Mómphidae*** and **Cosmopterígidae***   pp. 627, 627

96(93′).   Front wing with 5 veins reaching costal margin beyond Sc **97***

96′.   Front wing with 4 or fewer veins reaching costal margin beyond Sc **107***

97(96).   Accessory cell in front wing large, at least half as long as discal cell (Figure
            34–33E); vertex with a flat tuft covering base of antennae ......**Tischeriidae***   p. 622

97′.   Accessory cell in front wing smaller, less than half as long as discal cell, or
            absent; vertex usually not as above **98***

98(97′).   Vertex more or less tufted, or with rough bristly hair (*Parórnix*)
            ....**Gracillariidae***   p. 625

98′.   Vertex smooth-scaled **99***

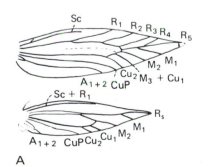

Figure 34–34. Wings of Lepidóptera. **A**, *Elachísta* (Elachístidae); **B**, *Micrópteryx* (Micropterígidae). *fib*, fibula. (Redrawn from Comstock by permission of the Comstock Publishing Company.)

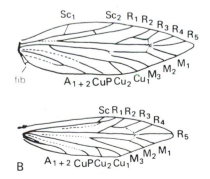

99(98′). R_1 in front wing arising basad of middle of discal cell, usually at about basal
               third (Figure 34–33D,E) **100***

99′. R_1 in front wing arising at or beyond middle of discal cell (Figures 34–30B,
               34–33F, 34–34A) **102***

100(99).   Front wing with stigmalike thickening between C and R_1 (Figure 34–30B); R_4
               and R_5 stalked ....**Blastobàsidae***   p. 626

100′.   Front wing without such a stigmalike thickening, R_4 and R_5 usually not
               stalked (Figure 34–33D) **101***

101(100′).   Third segment of labial palps pointed; maxillary palps folded over base of
               proboscis (*Limnacèia, Eteobàlea, Anóncia*) ....**Cosmopterígidae***   p. 627

101′.   Third segment of labial palps usually blunt; maxillary palps projecting
               forward, rudimentary, or absent ....**Gracillariìdae***   p. 625

102(99′).   Front wing with R_1 arising distinctly beyond middle of discal cell, M
               unbranched; venation of hind wing much reduced; tip of front wing drawn
               out to a narrow point ....**Gracillariìdae***   p. 625

102′.   Front wing with R_1 arising at about middle of discal cell, M usually 2- or
               3-branched; venation of hind wing usually complete; tip of front wing
               not as above **103***

103(102′).   Hind tarsi with more or less distinct groups of bristles near ends of segments;
               labial palps usually short, sometimes drooping; proboscis naked
               ....**Heliodínidae***   p. 630

103′.   Hind tarsi without such bristles; labial palps long, upcurved, third segment
               long and tapering; proboscis scaled **104***

104(103′). R_4 and R_5 in front wing stalked **105***

104′. R_4 and R_5 in front wing not stalked **106***

105(104).   Hind wings lanceolate, with complete venation (*Borkhausénia*)
               ....**Oecophòridae***   p. 625

105′.   Hind wings usually linear, with venation reduced ....**Cosmopterígidae***   p. 627

106(104′).   Several veins arising from end of discal cell between continuation of R and Cu
               stems ....**Agonoxénidae***   p. 626

106′.   No veins emerging from end of discal cell between continuation of R and Cu
               stems (*Hélice, Theísoa*, etc.).......................................**Gelechiìdae***   p. 627

107(96′).   Venation of front wing reduced, with 7 or fewer veins reaching wing margin
               from discal cell (Figure 34–33F) **108***

107′.   Venation of front wing complete or nearly so, with 8–10 veins reaching wing
               margin from discal cell **109***

108(107).   Vertex rough-scaled (*Cremastobombýcia, Phyllonorýcter = Lithocollètis*)
               ....**Gracillariìdae***   p. 625

108′.   Head entirely smooth-scaled ....**Heliozèlidae***   p. 623

109(107′).   Vertex more or less tufted; M_1 and M_2 in hind wing stalked **110***

109′.   Vertex smooth; usually no branches of M in hind wing stalked **111***

110(89,
   109).   Ocelli present ....**Plutéllidae***   p. 629

110′.   Ocelli absent ....**Argyresthiìdae***   p. 629

111(109′). R_1 in front wing arising at about two-thirds the length of discal cell; 9 veins in
               front wing reaching margin from discal cell ....**Scythrídidae***   p. 627

111'. R_1 in front wing usually arising near middle of discal cell or more basad; 8–10 veins in front wing reaching margin from discal cell **112***

112(111').   Labial palps long, upturned (as in Figure 34–29A); venation of front wing usually complete, with 10 veins reaching margin from discal cell **113***

112'.   Labial palps shorter, of moderate size or small, slightly upturned; venation of front wing somewhat reduced, with only 8 or 9 veins reaching margin from discal cell **114***

113(112).   Hind tibiae stiffly bristled, usually in tufts at the spurs; ocelli absent; proboscis naked ....**Epermeniidae***   p. 628

113'.   Hind tibiae without such bristles; ocelli present or absent; proboscis scaled ....**Agonoxénidae***, **Mómphidae***, and **Cosmopterígidae***   pp. 626, 627, 627

114(112').   Front wing with only 1 or 2 veins arising from apex of discal cell; hind wing with forked vein at apex (Figure 34–34A); proboscis scaled .....**Elachístidae***   p. 626

114'.   Front wing with at least 3 veins arising from apex of discal cell; hind wing without forked vein at apex; proboscis naked ....**Heliodínidae***   p. 630

115(91').   Front wings linear, with only 3 or 4 veins (*Cycloplàsis*) ....**Heliodínidae***   p. 630

115'.   Front wings lanceolate, with 7 veins reaching margin (*Coptodísca*) ....**Heliozèlidae***   p. 623

116(1').   Moth developing in, and usually never leaving, a sac or case constructed and carried about by the larva ....**Psýchidae**   p. 624

116'.   Moth not developing in a sac or case constructed by the larva **117**

117(116').   Ocelli present **118***

117'.   Ocelli absent **119**

118(117).   Proboscis present and naked; maxillary palps short, almost concealed; not aquatic ....**Tortrícidae***   p. 632

118'.   Proboscis small and scaled or vestigial; maxillary palps large; wings very small; aquatic moths (*Acéntropus*) ....**Pyrálidae***   p. 634

119(117').   Stout-bodied, short-legged, usually densely woolly; proboscis absent or vestigial ....**Lymantriidae**   p. 654

119'.   Slender-bodied, long-legged, hairy or scaly; proboscis present .....**Geométridae**   p. 645

SUBORDER **Zeuglóptera**: These moths differ from other Lepidóptera in having mandibulate mouthparts, with the mandibles well developed and the galeae short and not forming a proboscis. The venation of the front and hind wings is similar, and a fibula is present (Figure 34–34B). The larvae have eight pairs of short conical prolegs, each bearing a single claw.

Family **Micropterígidae**—Mandibulate Moths: This is a small group, with only two North American species, and its members are seldom encountered. One species *Epimartýria auricrenélla* (Walsingham), which has a wingspread of about 8 mm, occurs in the East, The larvae feed on mosses and liverworts, and the adults feed on pollen.

SUBORDER **Dacnonÿpha**: These moths resemble the Micropterígidae in having the venation of the front and hind wings similar. The middle tibiae bear a single spur (none in Micropterígidae). The females have a horny piercing ovipositor. There is a single genital opening in the female, behind the ninth sternum. Pupation occurs in the ground, and the pupae (which are exarate) have well-developed mandibles with which they chew their way out of the cocoon. The larvae are leaf miners. The adults have vestigial mandibles.

Family **Eriocraniidae**: These are small moths (wingspread 6.0–13.5 mm) that are similar to clothes moths in general appearance, but they have metallic markings in the wings. One of the best-known eastern species in this family is *Dyseriocrània auricyánea* (Walsingham). Its larvae make blotch mines in oak and chestnut and overwinter as pupae in the soil. The moths in this family typically fly very early in the year—February in north Florida and late March in Virginia.

Family **Acanthopteroctètidae:**   These moths resemble the Eriocranìidae, but may be separated by the characters given in the key (couplet 5). This family was established by Davis (1978a) with three known species occurring in the western states from northwestern Montana to southern California. The immature stages are unknown, but the larvae are presumed to be leaf miners. A fourth species has recently been found.

SUBORDER **Exopòria:**   These moths have the venation of the front and hind wings similar, and there is a well-developed jugum (Figure 34–5). The female has two genital openings, but that of the corpus bursae is very close to the egg pore on segment 9. The larvae are root borers.

Family **Hepiálidae**—Ghost Moths and Swifts: These are medium-sized to large moths, with wingspreads of 25–75 mm. Most of them are brown or gray with silvery spots in the wings (Figure 34–35). The name "swift" refers to the fact that some of these moths have an extremely rapid flight. They superficially resemble some of the Sphíngidae. The smaller moths in this family, with wingspreads of 25–50 mm, belong to the genus *Hepìalus*. Most of their larvae bore in the roots of herbaceous plants. The larger hepialids belong to the genus *Sthenòpis*. The larva of *S. argenteomaculàtus* (Harris) (Figure 34–35) bores in the roots of alder, and that of *S. thùle* Strecker bores in the roots of willows.

SUBORDER **Monotrỳsia:**   Females of this suborder have a single genital opening, located on segment 9. The venation of the front and hind wings is different (Rs is branched in the front wing but not in the hind wing); a frenulum is present; and the wings are aculeate (except in the Heliozèlidae).

Family **Nepticùlidae:**   The Nepticùlidae are minute moths, some species of which have a wingspread of only 3 mm. More than 80 species are known for North America. The wing venation is somewhat reduced, and the surface of the wings bears spinelike hairs or aculeae. The basal segment of the antenna is enlarged to form an eye cap; the maxillary palps are long; and the labial palps are short. The male has a well-developed frenulum, but the frenulum of the female consists of only a few small bristles. Most species in this group are leaf miners in trees or shrubs. The mines are linear when the larvae are young and are often broadened when the larvae become fully developed. The larvae usually leave the mines to pupate, spinning cocoons in debris on the surface of the soil. A few species in the genus *Ectoedèmia* are gall makers. Most of our species are in the genus *Stigmélla* (= *Nepticula*).

Family **Opostégidae:**   The Opostégidae are small moths with linear hind wings and with the radius, media, and cubitus of the front wings unbranched. The first segment of the antenna forms a large eye cap. The larvae are miners. This is a small group and contains the single genus *Opóstega*, with seven species in North America.

Family **Tischerìidae:**   The Tischerìidae are small moths in which the costal margin of the front wing is strongly arched and the apex is prolonged into a sharp point. The hind wings are long and narrow with a reduced venation (Figure 34–33E). The maxillary palps are small or absent. The larvae of most species make blotch mines in the leaves of oak or apple trees and blackberry or raspberry bushes. The apple-leaf trumpet miner, *Tischèria malifolièlla* Clemens, is a common species in the East and often

Figure 34–35.   A hepialid moth, *Sthenòpis argenteomaculàtus* Harris, 1.3×.

does considerable damage. The larva makes a trumpet-shaped mine in the upper surface of the leaf, overwinters in the mine, and pupates in the spring. There are two or more generations a year. About 50 species of Tischeriìdae occur in North America.

Family **Incurvariìdae:** These are small dark-colored moths with the wing venation very little reduced and the wing surface aculeate. The females have a piercing ovipositor. The larvae of the maple leaf cutter, *Paracleménsia acerifoliélla* (Fitch), are leaf mining when young and become casebearers when older. The older larvae cut out two circular pieces of the leaf and put them together to form a case. When the larva moves about, it carries this case with it and appears somewhat turtlelike. The winter is passed as a pupa inside the case. The adult moth is a brilliant steel blue or bluish green with an orange-colored head.

Family **Prodóxidae:** The moths in this group are often white, and the folded part of the maxillary palps is about two-thirds as long as the width of the head (Figure 34–29E, *mxp*). The best-known moths in this group are the yucca moths (*Tegetícula*), of which four species are known. The yucca is pollinated solely by these insects. The female moth collects pollen from the yucca flowers by means of long, curled, spinelike maxillary tentacles (palps) and then inserts her eggs into the ovary of another flower. After ovipositing, she thrusts the pollen she has collected onto the stigma of the flower in which the eggs have been laid. This action ensures fertilization and the development of the yucca seeds on which the larvae feed. The perpetuation of the yucca is assured, as more seeds are developed than are needed for the larvae. The bogus yucca moths of the genus *Prodóxus* lack the maxillary tentacles and cannot pollinate yuccas. Their larvae feed in the stems or fruits of these plants.

Family **Adèlidae**—Fairy Moths: These are small day-flying moths in which the antennae of the males are very long, usually more than twice as long as the wings. The larvae are leaf miners when young and case makers when older. They feed on the foliage of trees and shrubs. There are 18 North American species. The eastern species usually encountered is *Adèla caeruleélla* Walker.

Family **Heliozèlidae**—Shield Bearers: The heliozelids are small moths with lanceolate wings. The hind wings have no discal cell (Figure 34–33F). The larvae of the resplendent shield bearer, *Coptodísca splendoriferélla* (Clemens), are both leaf miners and casebearers. The larvae make a linear mine in apple, wild cherry, and related trees, and this mine is later widened. When full grown, the larva makes a case from the walls of its mine, lines it with silk, and

attaches it to a limb or to the trunk of the tree. There are two generations a year, with the larvae of the second generation overwintering in the cases. The front wings of the adult are dark gray at the base, with the outer portion bright yellow with brown and silver markings. Thirty-one species of heliozelids occur in North America.

SUBORDER **Ditrÿsia:** The females in this suborder have two genital openings, that of the corpus bursae on the sternum of segment 8 and the egg pore on the sternum of segment 9. The venation in the front and hind wings is different (Rs is branched in the front wing but not in the hind wing), and there is either a frenulum in the hind wing or the hind wing has the humeral angle somewhat expanded. This suborder includes the vast majority of the Lepidóptera and is divided into a number of superfamilies.

Family **Tinèidae:** Most of the tineids (about 135 North American species) are small moths, in which the venation is rather generalized (or somewhat reduced), the maxillary palps are usually large and folded, and the labial palps are short. The larvae of many species are casebearers. Some are scavengers or feed on fungi, and some feed on woolen fabrics. The species in this group that attack clothes and woolens (the clothes moths) are of considerable economic importance.

The most common clothes moth is the webbing clothes moth, *Tinèola bisselliélla* (Hummel). The adult is straw-colored, without dark spots on the wings, and has a wingspread of 12–26 mm. The larvae feed on hair fiber, woolens, silks, felt, and similar materials. They do not form cases. When full-grown the larva forms a cocoon of fragments of its food material fastened together with silk.

Second in importance among the clothes moths is the case-making clothes moth, *Tínea pellionélla* L. (Figure 34–36), which forms a case from silk and fragments of its food material. This case is tubular and open at each end. The larva feeds from within the case and pupates in it. The adult is brownish, with three dark spots on each front wing.

The clothes moth of the least importance in the United States is the carpet moth, *Trichóphaga tapetzélla* (L.), which builds rather long silken tubes or galleries to go through certain fabrics on which it may not feed. These tubes often have fragments of cloth woven in the silk. Where this species is found, it is quite destructive. The adult has a wingspread of 12–24 mm, and the front wings are black at the base and white in the apical portion.

One group of tineids, the burrowing webworms (formerly placed in a separate family, the Acrolóphidae) consists of small to medium-sized moths that resemble noctuids. The first segment of the labial

Figure 34–36. The case-making clothes moth, *Tínea pellionélla* (L.). **A,** larvae and cases; **B,** adult, 2½×. (Courtesy of the Ohio Agricultural Research and Development Center.)

palps is as large as the second or larger (Figure 34–29D); the eyes are usually hairy; and the venation is complete, with three anal veins in both front and hind wings. The 48 North American species in this group are placed in the genus *Acrólophus*. The larvae make a tubular web in the ground, sometimes extending as deep as 0.6 meter, into which they retreat when disturbed. They feed on the roots of grasses and also web in the blades at the surface. These insects often destroy entire young corn plants.

The genera *Phaeòses*, *Opogòna*, and *Oinóphila* have been placed in the Hieroxéstidae (= Oinophílidae), but are placed in the Tinèidae by Davis (1978b). They are small (wingspread 7.5–22.0 mm, mostly 15 mm or less) and usually rather plain-colored. They differ from most Tinèidae in having the head smooth-scaled and from many other Microlepidóptera in having the maxillary palps well developed (two-segmented and relatively short in *Phaeòses*, five-segmented and as long as the labial palps or longer in the other two genera). The moths occur in the southern states, from Florida to California. *Opogòna sácchari* (Bojer), the banana moth, has recently become established in southern Florida. It is destructive to ornamental nursery plants such as cane (*Dracaèna* spp.) and bamboo.

Family **Psýchidae**—Bagworms: These moths are so named because of the characteristic bags or cases that are made and carried about by the larvae. These bags are easily seen on trees during the winter after the leaves have fallen (Figure 34–37). The bags are composed of silk and portions of leaves and twigs. The larvae pupate in the bags, and most species overwinter as eggs in the bags. When the larvae hatch in the spring, they construct their cases and carry them about as they feed. When full-grown, they attach the case to a twig, close it, and pupate inside it.

The adult males of this group are generally small, with well-developed wings, but the females are wingless, legless, and wormlike and normally do not leave the bag in which they pupated. On emerging the males fly about and locate a bag containing a female. Mating takes place without the female's leaving the bag, and the eggs are later laid in the bag.

Thyridópteryx ephemeraefòrmis (Haworth) is a common species of bagworm, the larvae of which attack chiefly red cedar and arborvitae. The adult males are small, dark-colored, heavy-bodied moths with large clear areas in the wings.

Family **Lyonetìidae:** The Lyonetìidae are small moths with very narrow wings. The hind wings are often linear, with Rs extending through the center of the wing (Figure 34–33A). Ocelli and maxillary palps are usually lacking. The larvae are leaf miners or live in webs between the leaves. The apple bucculatrix, *Bucculàtrix pomifoliélla* Clemens, overwinters in rows of white, longitudinally ribbed cocoons on the twigs of apple. The adults emerge in the spring and oviposit on the lower surface of the leaves. The larvae enter the leaf and make a serpentine mine on the upper surface. Silken molting cocoons are made on the surface of the leaf before the pupal cocoons are formed. More than 120 species of lyonetiids occur in North America.

Figure 34–37. Bags of the bagworm, *Thyridópteryx ephemeraefòrmis* (Haworth). (Courtesy of the Ohio Agricultural Research and Development Center.)

Family **Gracillariidae**—Leaf Blotch Miners: This is a large group (275 North American species) of small to minute moths with lanceolate wings. The front wing usually lacks an accessory cell, and the hind wing in some species has a hump along the costal margin near the base (Figure 34–33D). The adult moths at rest have the anterior part of the body elevated, with the wing tips touching the surface on which the moth rests. The larvae usually make blotch mines, and the leaf is often folded.

The white-oak leaf miner, *Cameraria hamadry- adélla* (Clemens), is a common eastern species that feeds on various types of oak. The mines are on the upper surface of the leaves, and each mine contains a single larva. Many mines may occur on a single leaf (Figure 34–38A). The larvae are flattened, with only rudiments of legs and with the prothoracic segment enlarged. The larva pupates in a delicate cocoon inside the mine. It overwinters as a larva in dry leaves. The adult moth is white with broad irregular bronze bands on the front wings.

Some species of *Phyllocnístis* make winding serpentine mines in aspen leaves (Figure 34–38B). The larva usually starts near the tip of the leaf and mines toward the base, and it often has to go out toward the edge of the leaf to get across a large vein. It pupates in a silken cocoon at the end of the mine, usually at the basal edge of the leaf.

Family **Oecophoridae:** The 225 North American members of this family are arranged in six subfamilies, which have been considered families by some authorities.

Figure 34–39. Miscellaneous Microlepidóptera. **A,** *Diaphània hyalinàta* L. (Pyrálidae; adult of the melonworm); **B,** *Depressària pastinacélla* (Duponchel) (Oecophòridae, Depressariìnae; adult of the parsnip webworm); **C,** *Gnorimoschèma gallaesolidáginis* (Riley) (Gelechìidae; a goldenrod gall moth); **D,** *Stenòma algidélla* Walker (Oecophòridae, Stenomatìnae); **E,** *Harrisìna americàna* (Guérin) (Zygaènidae; adult of the grape leaf skeletonizer); **F,** *Thỳris lùgubris* Boisduval (Thyrídidae); **G,** *Valentínia glandulélla* (Riley) (Blastobàsidae; the acorn moth); **H,** *Geléchia cercerísélla* (Chambers) (Gelechìidae); **I,** *Stagmatóphora sexnotélla* Chambers (Cosmopterígidae). 1½ ×.

Subfamily **Depressariìnae:** These are small and somewhat flattened moths, with the wings relatively broad and rounded apically (Figure 34–39B). The venation (Figure 34–32A) is complete, with CuP preserved in the front wing, R_4 and R_5 in the front wing stalked or coalesced throughout their entire length, and Rs and M_1 in the hind wing separate and parallel. The parsnip webworm, *Depressària pastinacélla* (Duponchel), attacks parsnip, celery, and related plants. The larvae web together and feed on the unfolding blossom heads, and then burrow into the stems to pupate. The adults appear in late summer and hibernate in protected situations.

Subfamily **Oecophorìnae:** These moths are among the more colorful of the oecophorids. *Hofmannóphila pseudospretélla* (Stainton), is a minor household pest, originally from Europe. This group includes the Stathmopódidae, which was formerly placed in the Heliodínidae.

Subfamily **Ethmiìnae:** These differ from most other oecophorids in having M_2 in the hind wing arising closer to M_1 than to M_3. A few are plain-colored, but most are rather brightly patterned, often black and white. The larvae feed principally on the leaves and flowers of plants in the borage and water-leaf families (Boraginàceae and Hydrophyllàceae). *Éthmia discostrigélla* (Chambers) is a defoliator of

 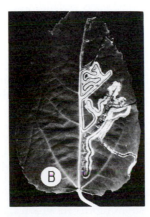

Figure 34–38. Leaf mines of Gracillaríidae. **A,** the white-oak leaf miner, *Cameraria hamadryadélla* Clemens; **B,** an aspen leaf miner, *Phyllocnístis* sp. (**A,** courtesy of the Ohio Agricultural Research and Development Center.)

mountain mahogany (*Cercocárpus*). Outbreaks of this insect deplete the winter ranges of big game in Oregon and other western areas. Most of our 50 species of Ethmiìnae occur in the West.

Subfamily **Peleopodìnae:** This is a tropical group, occurring in the United States only in the extreme South. Two species occur in our area.

Subfamily **Stenomatìnae:** These moths are larger than most Microlepidóptera, and the wings (Figure 34–31D) are relatively broad (Figure 34–39D). The larvae live in webs on the leaves of oaks and other trees. *Antaeótricha schlaègeri* (Zeller) is a fairly common eastern species. The adult has a wingspread of about 30 mm, and the wings are grayish white with dark markings. When at rest, this moth resembles bird excrement.

Subfamily **Chimabachìnae:** This is primarily a European group, and only one species, *Cheimóphila salicélla* (Hübner), occurs in our area.

Family **Lecithocéridae:** This is primarily a tropical group formerly considered a subfamily of the Gelechìidae. Only one species, *Deoclòna yuccasélla* Busck, occurs in our area. Most lecithocerids are day-flying, and are most numerous in the south Pacific and in tropical Asia.

Family **Elachístidae**—Grass Miners: The adults of this group have lanceolate hind wings that have a well-formed discal cell. The venation is only slightly reduced (Figure 34–34A). The larvae make blotch mines in grasses. The larvae of some species leave the mines and pupate in suspended webs. Most of the species in this small family (57 North American species) belong to the genus *Elachísta*.

Family **Coleophòridae**—Casebearers: The moths in this family are small, with very narrow, sharply pointed wings. The discal cell in the front wing is oblique, and veins Cu_1 and Cu_2 (when present) are very short. There are no ocelli or maxillary palps. About a hundred species, most of them in the genus *Coleóphora*, occur in the United States. The larvae are usually leaf miners when young and casebearers when they become larger. There are about 170 North American species of coleophorids.

The pistol casebearer, *Coleóphora malivorélla* Riley, is a common pest of apple and other fruit trees. The larvae construct pistol-shaped cases composed of silk, bits of leaves, and excrement, which they carry about. By protruding their heads from these cases, they eat holes in the leaves. They overwinter as larvae in the cases, and the moths appear in midsummer.

The cigar casebearer, *Coleóphora serratélla* (L.), also attacks apple and other fruit trees (Figure 34–40). This species is similar to the preceding casebearer except that the young larvae are miners

Figure 34–40.   Larvae (in their cases) of the cigar casebearer, *Coleóphora serratélla* (L.), on an apple leaf. (Courtesy of the Ohio Agricultural Research and Development Center.)

in the leaves for two or three weeks before making their cases.

This family includes the palm leaf skeletonizer, *Homáledra sabalélla* (Chambers), which occurs in the southern states, where its larvae feed on the upper surface of the leaves of the saw palmetto. A group of larvae make a delicate silken cover over the injured portion of the leaf and cover it with their droppings. *Homáledra* is in the subfamily Batrachedrìnae, a group previously included in the family Mómphidae.

Family **Agonoxénidae:** This is a small but widely distributed group, many of whose members have previously been placed in other families. Little is known of their larval habits, but at least some (for example, *Blastodácna*) are nut and fruit borers.

Family **Blastobàsidae:** The Blastobàsidae are small moths in which the hind wings are somewhat lanceolate and narrower than the front wings (Figure 34–30B). The membrane of the front wing is slightly thickened along the costa. The larva of the acorn moth, *Valentínia glandulélla* (Riley) (Figure 34–39G), feeds inside acorns that have been hollowed out by the larvae of acorn weevils. The larvae overwinter in the acorns, and the adults appear the following summer. Species of *Holcócera* attack conifers in the West. The larvae of *Zenodòchium coccivorèlla* (Chambers) are internal parasites of female gall-like coccids of the genus *Kérmes*. This species has been found in Florida. The subfamily Symmocìnae, which is mainly European but includes one North American species, is now included in the Blastobàsidae. There are 121 North American species of blastobasids.

Family **Mómphidae:** These moths are small, with the wings long and narrow and usually sharply pointed at the apex. They are very similar to the Cosmopterígidae, and since these families are separated principally by the structure of the male genitalia, some genera in these families cannot be separated by our key (which is based principally on wing venation). Many momphids are white, with the apex of the front wing patterned. Most of our 37 species are in the genus *Mómpha*.

Family **Scythrídidae:** This family is closely related to the Cosmopterígidae, and most species are day-fliers. Most of the 35 species in the family belong to the genus *Scýthris*. The larvae of *S. magnatélla* Busck feed on willow herbs (*Epilòbium*), folding over a portion of the leaf for an individual cell. Species in the genus *Areniscýthris* have very short wings, and their larvae build sand tubes at the base of their sand dune host shrub. This genus is largely western with one undescribed species in Florida.

Family **Cosmopterígidae:** This is a fair-sized group (180 North American species) of small moths that have the wings long and narrow and usually sharply pointed at the apex (Figure 34–41B). Some species are rather brightly colored. Most of these moths are leaf miners in the larval stage. The larvae of the cattail moth, *Lymnaècia phragmitélla* Stainton, feed in the heads of cattails. The pink scavenger caterpillar *Pyrodérces rìleyi* (Walsingham) (Figure 34–41B), feeds in cotton bolls. A somewhat aberrant member of this group, *Eucleménsia bassettélla* Clemens (placed in the subfamily Antequerìnae), is an internal parasite of female gall-like coccids of the genus *Kérmes*. Most species of the genus *Cosmópterix*, which look similar the world over, are dark-colored with a golden band near the apex of each front wing.

Family **Gelechìidae:** This family is one of the largest of the Microlepidóptera (about 650 North American species), and many species are fairly common. The moths are all rather small (Figure 34–39C,H). Veins R_4 and R_5 in the front wing are stalked at the base (rarely, they are fused for their entire length), and A_{1+2} is forked at the base. The hind wing usually has the outer margin somewhat pointed and recurved (Figure 34–31C). Gelechiid larvae vary in habits. Some are leaf miners; a few form galls; many are leaf rollers or leaf tiers; and one species is a serious pest of stored grain.

The Angoumois grain moth, *Sitotròga cerealélla* (Olivier), is an important pest of stored grain. The larva feeds in the kernels of corn, wheat, and other grains, and the emerging adult leaves a conspicuous emergence hole at one end of the kernel (Figure 34–42). The grain may become infested with this insect either in the milk stage of the growing grain

Figure 34–41. **A,** the pink bollworm, *Pectinóphora gossypiélla* (Saunders) (Gelechìidae); **B,** adult of the pink scavenger caterpillar, *Pyrodérces rìleyi* (Walsingham) (Cosmopterígidae); 4×. Inserts, lateral views of heads. (Courtesy of Busck and the USDA Journal of Agricultural Research.)

Figure 34–42. Injury to corn by the Angoumois grain moth. (Courtesy of Davidson.)

or in storage. Stored grain may be completely destroyed by it. The adult moth is light grayish brown with a wingspread of about 13 mm.

The pink bollworm, *Pectinóphora gossypiélla* (Saunders) (Figure 34–41A), is a serious pest of cotton in the South and Southwest. The larvae attack the bolls, and losses of up to 50% of the crop are not uncommon in fields that are infested with this insect.

Many species in the genus *Gnorimoschèma* form galls in the stems of goldenrod, different species attacking different species of goldenrod. The galls are elongate, spindle-shaped, and rather thin-walled (Figure 34–43). The larva pupates in the gall, but before pupating it cuts an opening (not quite completely through the wall) at the upper end of the gall. When the adult emerges it can easily push out through this opening. Pupation occurs in middle or late summer, and the adults (Figure 34–39C) emerge and lay their eggs on old goldenrod plants in the fall. The eggs hatch the following spring.

Phthorimaèa operculélla (Zeller), the potato tuberworm, is a pest of potatoes and related plants. The larvae mine in the leaves and bore into the tubers. *Aròga wébsteri* Clarke periodically defoliates and kills sagebrush over large areas of western range land. Species in the genus *Coleotechnìtes* are leaf miners in conifers. A few are sometimes serious pests.

Family **Copromórphidae:** This is a predominantly tropical group, with only five species occurring in the United States and Canada. They occur along the Pacific Coast from British Columbia to Mexico and east to Colorado. They are similar to the Carposìnidae but differ in having all three branches of M present in the hind wing. The larva of *Lotísma trigonàna* Walsingham is a fruit borer in *Arbùtus* and *Gaulthèria* (Ericàceae). The other species in the family are in the genus *Ellabélla*.

Family **Alucítidae**—Many-Plume Moths: The alucitids resemble the pterophorids, but have the wings split into six plumelike divisions. Only one named species in this family, *Alùcita hexadáctyla* L., occurs in the United States. The adults have a wingspread of about 13 mm. This insect, which was introduced, occurs in the northeastern states. Several undescribed species of Alucítidae are present in North America.

Family **Carposinidae:** The moths in this group have relatively broad wings with raised scale tufts on the front wings, and M_2 (and usually also M_1) in the hind wings is lacking. This group is a small one, with only 11 species in our area. The larvae whose habits are known bore into fruits, plant shoots, and the gummy enlargements of fruit trees. The larvae of the currant fruitworm, *Carposìna fernaldàna* Busck, feed on the fruits of the currant. The infested fruit eventually drops, and the larvae pupate in the soil.

Family **Epermeniidae:** This is a small group (11 North American species) of moths formerly placed in the Scythrídidae. The larvae of *Epermènia pimpinélla* Murtfeldt form puffy mines in parsley. The pupa is enclosed in a rather frail cocoon on the underside of a leaf or in an angle of a leaf stalk.

Family **Glyphipterígidae:** The members of this group are small diurnal moths, 7–15 mm in length, with relatively large ocelli and with the wings shaped much like those in Figure 34–30B. The larvae feed mostly as seed borers in sedges and rushes. Our most common species, *Diploschízia impigritélla* (Clemens), is found in the East, and also in the West from British Columbia to California and Nevada. Its

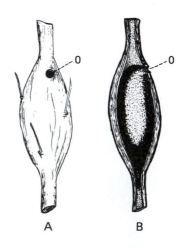

Figure 34–43. Gall of the goldenrod gall moth, *Gnorimoschèma* sp. (Gelechìidae). **A,** exterior view; **B,** a gall cut open. *o,* opening cut by the larva before pupating, through which the emerging adult escapes.

larva is a stem and leaf axil borer of *Cýperus*. Thirty-six species of glyphipterigids occur in our area.

Family **Plutéllidae**—Diamondback Moths: The Plutéllidae are similar to the Yponomeùtidae, but they hold their antennae forward when at rest, and M₁ and M₂ in the hind wings are stalked. The name "diamondback" refers to the fact that in the males of *Plutélla xylastélla* (L.) the wings, when folded, show a series of three yellow diamond-shaped marks along the line where the wings meet. This species is a pest of cabbage and other cruciferous plants. The larvae eat holes in the leaves and pupate in silken cocoons attached to the leaves. This group also includes the introduced mimosa webworm, *Homadáula anisocéntra* Meyrick, which is a serious defoliator of mimosa and honey locust. This insect was first recorded in the United States in 1942, in Washington, D.C. Since then it has spread southward to Florida and westward to Kansas and Nebraska, and there is a small colony in the vicinity of Sacramento, California. There are 52 species of plutellids in North America.

Family **Yponomeùtidae**—Ermine Moths: The Yponomeùtidae are small and usually brightly patterned moths with rather narrow wings (Figure 34–44). The branches of the main veins in the front wing are generally separate, and R₅ extends to the outer margin of the wing. Rs and M₁ in the hind wing are separate (Figure 34–32). The moths in the genus *Yponomeùta* have front wings that are white dotted with black. The larvae of *Y. padélla* (L.) feed in a common web on apple and cherry. The larvae of the ailanthus webworm, *Átteva punctélla* (Cramer), live in a frail silken web on the leaves of ailanthus and feed on the leaves. The pupae are suspended in loose webs. The front wings of the adult are bright yellow, marked with four transverse bands of lead blue, each enclosing a row of yellow spots (Figure 34–44). There are several forms of this species, with varying amounts of yellow spotting. The pine needle sheath miner, *Zelléria haimbáchi* Busck, is widely distributed and attacks various pines, sometimes doing quite a bit of damage. The first-instar larvae mine in needles, and later instars feed in the sheath at the base of the needle cluster, severing the needles and causing them to be shed. Each larva kills 6 to 10 needle clusters.

Family **Ochsenheimeriidae**: This is an Old World group, one species of which has apparently become established in the Northeast. This species is the cereal stem moth, *Ochsenheimèria vacculélla* F. von Roeslerstamm, which is a pest of winter wheat and rye in Europe and may become a similar pest in the United States. These are small (wingspread 11–14 mm), slender-bodied moths, with the front wings a mottled brownish and the hind wings pale. They may be recognized by the characters given in the key (couplet 78).

These moths oviposit in late summer on straw piles in the fields, and the eggs hatch in the spring. The young larvae mine in the leaf blades, and older larvae burrow into the stems. Pupation occurs between the leaves of the host plant, and the moths emerge in early June.

Family **Argyresthiidae**: These moths are closely related to the Yponomeùtidae, but the wings are narrower (hind wings lanceolate, with a reduced venation), and M₁ and M₂ in the hind wing are long-stalked. The Plutéllidae have a similar venation, but have ocelli (which are lacking in the Argyresthìidae). The larvae of these moths bore in twigs, buds, and fruits or are leaf miners, generally attacking various trees.

The genus *Argyrésthia* contains about 50 species whose members attack the leaves, buds, and twigs of various trees. The arborvitae leaf miner, *A. thuiélla* (Packard), attacks the leaves of cedar. The adults are white moths with the front wings spotted with brown and have a wingspread of about 8 mm. Many members of this group have metallic markings in the front wings. The adults often rest with the head against the substrate and the body held up on an angle.

Family **Douglasìidae**: The Douglasìidae are leaf miners in the larval stage, and the adults are small moths with lanceolate hind wings that lack a discal cell (Figure 34–33B). Rs in the hind wing separates from the media near the middle of the wing. The ocelli are large. Only five species of douglasiids occur in North America. The larvae of *Tinágma obscu-*

Figure 34–44.   An ermine moth, *Átteva* sp. (Yponomeùtidae), 2½×. (Courtesy of the Ohio Agricultural Research and Development Center.)

rofasciélla (Chambers) mine in the leaves of plants in the family Rosaceae.

Family **Acrolepiidae:** These small moths are similar to the Plutéllidae but have maxillary palps of the folded type (porrect in the Plutéllidae) and smooth labial palps (with a tuft in the Plutéllidae). This group is a small one, with only three North American species. One of these, *Acrolepiópsis incertéllus* (Chambers), occurs in the northern part of the United States, from New England to California. Its larva skeletonizes the leaves of *Smìlax* or bores in the stems of lilies. The adult's wings are gray-brown, with reddish iridescence and an oblique white stripe extending from the inner margin near the base to about the middle of the wing.

Family **Heliodínidae:** The heliodinids are small diurnal moths with hind wings that are very narrow and lanceolate and have a broad fringe. The adult at rest usually holds the hind legs elevated above the wings. The family is a small one (20 North American species), and the known larvae vary in habits. The larvae of *Cycloplàsis panicifoliélla* Clemens mine in the leaves of panic grass, forming at first a linear mine that is later enlarged to a blotch. When full grown, the larva cuts a circular piece from the leaf, folds it over to make a case, then drops to the ground and pupates in the case. The larvae of *Schreckensteìnia* feed on sumac and species of *Rùbus*. Heliodinids have a naked proboscis. Species with a scaled proboscis formerly included in this family (for example, the stathmopodines and *Eucleménsia*) have now been found to belong to gelechioid families.

Family **Sesiidae**—Clearwing Moths: The greater part of one or both pairs of wings in this family is devoid of scales, and many species bear a very striking resemblance to wasps (Figure 34–45). The front wings are long and narrow with the anal veins reduced, and the hind wings are broad with the anal area well developed (Figure 34–46). The sesiids have a wing-coupling mechanism somewhat similar to that in the Hymenóptera. Many species are brightly colored, and virtually all are active during the day. The two sexes are often differently colored, and in some cases they differ in the amount of clear area in the wings. The larvae bore in the roots, stems, canes, or trunks of plants or trees and often cause considerable damage. There are 115 species of sesiids in North America.

The peach tree borer, *Synánthedon exitiòsa* (Say), is one of the most important species in this family. The females lay their eggs on the trunks of peach trees near the ground, and the larvae bore into the tree just below the surface of the ground, often girdling the tree. There is one generation a year, and the larvae overwinter in their burrows in the tree.

The female has the front wings fully scaled, and the abdomen is marked with a broad orange band. The male has both the front and the hind wings largely clear, and the abdomen is ringed with several narrow yellow bands (Figure 34–45). The adults are active throughout the summer. The lesser peach tree borer, *S. píctipes* (Grote and Robinson), has similar habits, but the larvae generally bore into the trunk and larger branches. Both sexes resemble the male of *S. exitiòsa*.

The squash vine borer, *Melíttia cucúrbitae* (Harris), is a serious pest of squash and related plants. The larvae bore into the stems and often destroy the plant. The species overwinters as a pupa in the soil. The adults are a little larger than those of the peach tree borer and have the front wings olive green and the hind wings clear. The hind legs are heavily clubbed with a long fringe of orange-colored scales.

The currant borer, *Synánthedon tipulifórmis* (Clerck), is a small moth with a wingspread of about 18 mm. The larva bores in the stems of currants, and pupation occurs in the stems. The adults appear in early summer.

Sesiid sex pheromones have been synthesized for the capture of the males of such pest species as the peach tree borer, and these pheromones attract almost all male sesiids.

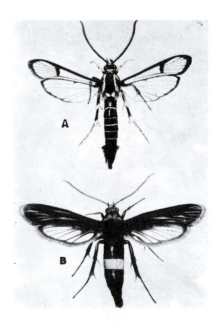

Figure 34–45. The peach tree borer, *Synánthedon exitiòsa* (Say) (Sesìidae), 1½×. **A,** male; **B,** female. (Courtesy of the Ohio Agricultural Research and Development Center.)

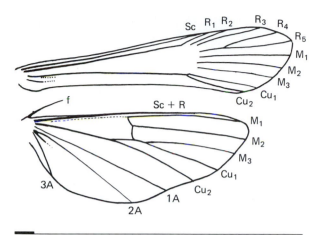

Figure 34–46.   Wings of *Synánthedon* (Sesiidae). *f,* frenulum.

Family **Choreùtidae:** These are small diurnal moths, somewhat similar to the Tortrícidae in general appearance but usually more colorful, with relatively broad wings, a scaled proboscis, and large ocelli. The larvae are mostly leaf tiers. The apple and thorn skeletonizer, *Choreùtes pariàna* (Clerck), is a pest of apple trees, especially in British Columbia. It ranges across southern Canada, going south into New England, Colorado, and Oregon. This species also occurs in Europe, from where it was introduced into North America. Tropical species sometimes come into Florida, and the total North American fauna of choreutids is about 40 species.

Family **Cóssidae**—Carpenter Moths and Leopard Moths: The cossids are wood-boring in the larval stage. The adults are medium-sized and heavy-bodied, and the wings are usually spotted or mottled. The carpenterworm, *Prionoxýstus robíniae* (Peck), is a common species that attacks various trees. The adult (Figure 34–47A) is a mottled gray and has a wingspread of about 50 mm. These insects may sometimes seriously damage trees. The leopard moth, *Zeùzera pyrìna* (L.), a slightly smaller moth with the wings pale and marked with large black dots (Figure 34–47B), has similar habits. These moths require two or three years to complete their life cycle. About 45 species occur in our area.

A

B

Figure 34–47.   Cossid moths. **A,** the carpenter moth, *Prionoxýstus robíniae* (Peck), $1\frac{1}{2}\times$; **B,** the leopard moth, *Zeùzera pyrìna* (L.), $1\frac{1}{2}\times$.

Family **Tortrícidae:**   This is one of the largest families of the Microlepidóptera, with about 1200 North American species, and many of its members are common moths. This group contains a number of important pest species. These moths are small, usually gray, tan, or brown; their wings have dark bands or mottled areas, or are occasionally colorful with metallic spots. The front wings are usually rather square-tipped. The wings at rest are held rooflike over the body. The larvae vary in habits, but many species are leaf rollers or leaf tiers, usually feeding on perennial plants. Many bore into various parts of the plant.

A tortricid that is an important pest of apples and other fruits is the codling moth, *Cydia pomonélla* (L.) (Figure 34–48). The adults appear in late spring and lay their eggs, which are flattened and transparent, on the surface of leaves. The young larvae crawl to young apples and chew their way into the fruits, usually entering by the blossom end. They are light-colored with a dark head. They complete their development in the fruits and pupate in the ground, under bark, or in similar situations. In the eastern United States there is a second generation in late summer, with the full-grown larvae overwintering in cocoons under the bark of apple trees and in other protected places.

The oriental fruit moth, *Graphólitha molésta* (Busck), is an oriental species that is widely distributed in the United States. It is a serious pest of peaches and other fruits. It has several generations a year. The larvae of the first generation bore into the young green twigs, and the later-generation larvae bore into the fruits much as the codling moth does. The winter is passed as a full-grown larva in a cocoon.

This group includes a number of important forest pests. Perhaps the most serious are the spruce budworms—*Choristoneùra,* particularly *C. fumiferàna*

Figure 34–49.   Larva (**A**) and adult (**B**) of the spruce budworm, *Choristoneùra fumiferàna* (Clemens). (Courtesy of the Ohio Agricultural Research and Development Center.)

(Clemens) in the East and *C. occidentàlis* Freeman in the West (Figure 34–49). These insects are very serious defoliators, feeding on the buds of new foliage, and they sometimes occur in outbreak numbers. Sustained attacks will kill a tree. The western black-headed budworm, *Ácleris gloveràna* (Walsingham), often causes extensive damage to various conifers in the West Coast states and in western Canada. It also sometimes occurs in outbreak numbers. The genus *Rhyaciònia* contains the pine tip moths—several species whose larvae mine in the buds and shoots of young pines. The attacked trees are seldom killed, but they are deformed, and their growth is retarded. The fruit tree leaf roller, *Árchips argyrospìlus* (Walker) (Figure 34–50A), is a rather common tortricid that makes an unsightly leaf nest in fruit and forest trees and often causes serious defoliation.

A number of other species in this family are occasionally destructive to various crops. The grape berry moth, *Endopìza viteàna* Clemens (Figure 34–50B), feeds in the larval stage in the berries of grape. It has two generations a year. The strawberry leaf roller, *Áncylis comptàna* (Frölich), attacks the foliage of strawberries and often does severe damage. The black-headed fireworm, *Rhopóbota naevàna* (Hübner), is a common pest that feeds on the heads

Figure 34–48.   The codling moth, *Cydia pomonélla* (L.), 3 ×. (Courtesy of the Ohio Agricultural Research and Development Center.)

Figure 34–50. **A**, adult of the fruit tree leaf roller, *Árchips argyrospìlus* (Walker), 2× (Tortrícidae); **B**, adult of the grape berry moth, *Endopìza viteàna* Clemens, 4× (Tortrícidae).

of clover, destroying unopened buds and decidedly reducing the crop of seed. This insect has three generations a year and passes the winter as a pupa.

A species in this family that is something of a curiosity is the Mexican jumping-bean moth, *Cỳdia deshaisiàna* (Lucas). The larva lives in the thin-walled seeds of *Sebastiàna* and, after consuming the inside of the seed, throws itself forcibly against the thin wall when disturbed, causing the jumping movements of the seed.

This family is divided into four subfamilies, the Clidanotìnae, Tortricìnae, Cochylìnae, and Olethreutìnae. Some authorities consider the Cochylìnae a tribe of the Tortricìnae.

The subfamily Cochylìnae includes a number of species whose larvae are web-spinners and borers. Most of them attack herbaceous plants. The adults are similar to other Tortrícidae, but vein CuP is completely lacking in the front wing, and Cu_2 in the front wing arises in the apical fourth of the discal cell; M_1 in the hind wing is usually stalked with Rs. *Aéthes rutilàna* (Hübner) attacks juniper, tying the leaves together to form a tube in which the larva lives. The adult of this species has a wingspread of about 25 mm, and the front wings are orange marked with four brownish crossbands.

There are 110 North American species of Cochylìnae, and only three of the Clidanotìnae. The latter group is primarily tropical, and our species are in the genus *Thaumatógrapha* (= *Hilarógrapha*).

Family **Zygaènidae**—Smoky Moths and Burnets: The smoky moths are small, gray or black moths, usually with a reddish prothorax and often with other bright markings. Some exotic species, such as the European burnets and some large Chinese species, are often very colorful. The larvae have tufted hairs, and the more common North American species feed on grape or Virginia creeper. The grape leaf skeletonizer, *Harrisìna americàna* (Guérin), is a common species in this group. The adult is a small, narrow-winged, smoky moth with a reddish collar (Figure 34–39E), and the larvae are yellow with black spots. A number of these larvae will feed on the same leaf, lined up in a row and backing up as they skeletonize the leaf. There are 22 North American species of smoky moths.

Family **Megalopỳgidae**—Flannel Moths: These moths have a dense coat of scales mixed with fine curly hairs, which give the insects a somewhat woolly appearance. They are medium-sized to small and usually brownish in color. The larvae are also hairy, and in addition to the usual five pairs of prolegs, they have two pairs that are suckerlike and lack crochets. The larvae have stinging spines under the hairs and can cause even more irritation than the saddleback caterpillars. The cocoons are tough and are provided with a lid as in the Limacòdidae. They are usually formed on twigs. The crinkled flannel moth, *Lagòa crispàta* (Packard), is a common eastern species. It is a yellowish moth with brownish spots or bands on the wings and has a wingspread of a little over 25 mm. The larva feeds on blackberry, raspberry, apple, and other plants. This group is a small one, with only 11 North American species.

Family **Epipyrópidae**—Planthopper Parasites: These moths are unique in that the larvae are parasites of planthoppers (Fulgoròidea) and other Homóptera. The moth larva feeds on the dorsal surface of the abdomen of the planthopper, under the wings. These moths are relatively rare, and only a single species occurs in the United States. This is *Fulgoroècia exígua* (Edwards), a dark brownish purple moth with broad wings, pectinate antennae, and a wingspread of 8–13 mm.

Family **Dalcéridae**: This is a neotropical group, one species of which has been reported from Arizona: *Dalcérides ingénita* (Edwards). This moth is rather woolly and resembles a flannel moth. It has dark yellow front wings, orange hind wings, and a wingspread of 18–24 mm.

Family **Limacòdidae**—Slug Caterpillars: These insects are called slug caterpillars because the larvae are short, fleshy, and sluglike. The thoracic legs are small and there are no prolegs, and the larvae move with a creeping motion. Many of the larvae are curiously shaped or conspicuously marked. The cocoons are dense, brownish, and oval and have a lid at one end that is pushed out by the emerging adult. The adult moths (Figure 34–51A) are small to medium-sized, robust, and hairy and are usually brownish and marked with a large irregular spot of green, silver, or some other color.

A   B

L = 25 mm

Figure 34–51. Adult (**A**) and larva (**B**) of the saddleback caterpillar, *Sibìne stimùlea* (Clemens). **A,** 3×. (**B,** courtesy of Peterson; reprinted by permission.)

One of the most common species in this group is the saddleback caterpillar, *Sibìne stimùlea* (Clemens). The larva (Figure 34–51B) is green with a brown saddlelike mark on the back. These larvae have stinging hairs and can cause severe irritation to the skin. They feed principally on various trees.

Family **Pterophòridae**—Plume Moths: These moths are small, slender, and usually gray or brownish and have the wings split into two or three featherlike divisions (Figure 34–52). The genus *Agdístis* is unusual in having no wing splits. The front wing usually has two divisions, and the hind wing three. The legs are relatively long. When at rest, the front and hind wings are folded close together and are held horizontally, at right angles to the body. The larvae of plume moths are leaf rollers and stem borers, and some may occasionally do serious damage. The grape plume moth, *Geìna periscelidáctylus* (Fitch), is common on grape vines. The larvae tie together the terminal portions of the leaves and feed inside this shelter. Many plume moths have very spiny pupae. This is a fair-sized group, with 146 species in our area.

Family **Pyrálidae**—Snout and Grass Moths: This family is the third largest in the order, with more than 1375 species occurring in the United States and Canada. Most of the pyralids are small and rather delicate moths, and all have abdominal tympanal organs and a scaled proboscis. The front wings are elongate or triangular, with the cubitus appearing four-branched and the hind wings usually broad. Veins Sc and R in the hind wing are usually close together and parallel opposite the discal cell (the base of R is usually atrophied) and are fused or closely parallel for a short distance beyond the discal cell (Figure 34–15). Since the labial palps are often projecting, these moths are sometimes called snout moths.

The members of this family exhibit a great deal of variation in appearance, venation, and habits. The family is divided into a number of subfamilies, only a few of which can be mentioned here.

Subfamily **Nymphulìnae:** The larvae of most Nymphulìnae are aquatic, breathing by means of gills and feeding on aquatic plants. The water lily leaf cutter, *Sýnclita obliteràlis* (Walker), lives on

Figure 34–52. Plume moths (Pterophòridae). **A,** *Stenoptilòdes báueri* (Lange), female; **B,** *S. grándis* (Walsingham), female; 2×. (Courtesy of Lange and Hilgardia.)

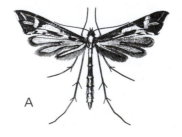
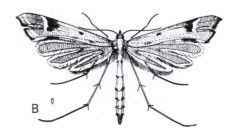

A   B

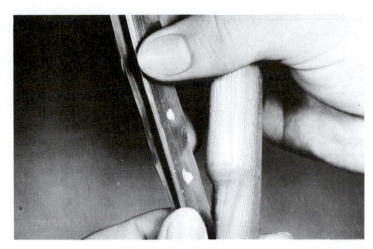

Figure 34–53.   The European corn borer, *Ostrínia nubilàlis* (Hübner). **A,** egg masses on corn; **B,** larva; **C,** adults (male at left, female at right); 2×. (Courtesy of the Illinois Natural History Survey.)

greenhouse water plants, in cases made of silk. Adult females dive underwater to lay eggs.

Subfamily **Pyraustinae:**   The subfamily is a large group (more than 375 North American species), and many of its members are relatively large and conspicuously marked. The most important species in this subfamily is the European corn borer, *Ostrínia nubilàlis* (Hübner), which was introduced into the United States about 1917 and has since spread over a large part of the central and eastern states. The larvae live in the stalks of corn and other plants and frequently do a great deal of damage. This species has one or two generations a year. It overwinters in the larval stage. The adult moths (Figure 34–53) have a wingspread of a little over 25 mm and are yellowish brown with darker markings. The grape leaf folder,

Désmia funeràlis (Hübner), is a black moth with two white spots in the front wing and one white spot in the hind wing. The larva feeds on grape leaves, folding the leaf over and fastening it with silk. The melonworm, *Diaphània hyalinàta* (L.), is a glistening white moth with the wings bordered with black (Figure 34–39A). The larva feeds on the foliage and burrows in the stems of melons and related plants. Other important species in this subfamily are the pickleworm, *Diaphània nitidàlis* (Stoll), and the garden webworm, *Achỳra rantàlis* (Guenée).

Subfamily **Pyralinae:**   This subfamily (27 North American species) is a group of small moths. The larvae of most species feed on dried vegetable matter. One of the most important species in this subfamily is the meal moth, *Pýralis farinàlis* L. The larva feeds on cereals, flour, and meal and makes silken tubes in these materials. The larvae of the clover hayworm, *Hypsopỳgia costàlis* (Fabricius), occur in old stacks of clover hay.

Subfamily **Crambìnae**—Close-Wings or Grass Moths: These are common moths in meadows, where the larvae (known as sod webworms) bore into the stems, crowns, or roots of grasses. Most of them feed about the base of grasses, where they construct silken webs. The moths are usually whitish or pale yellowish brown and, when at rest, hold the wings close about the body (hence the name "close-wing"). An important pest species in this subfamily is the sugarcane borer, *Diatraèa saccharàlis* (Fabricius) (Figure 34–54), the larva of which bores in the stalks of sugarcane. Most of the species in this group belong to the genus *Crámbus*.

Subfamily **Galleriìnae:** The best-known member of this subfamily is the bee moth or wax moth, *Gallèria mellonélla* (L.). The larva occurs in bee-hives, where it feeds on wax. It often does considerable damage. The adult has brownish front wings and a wingspread of about 25 mm.

Subfamily **Phycitìnae:** The subfamily is a large one (about 400 North American species), and most of the members have long narrow front wings and broad hind wings. The larvae vary considerably in habits. The best-known species in this subfamily are those that attack stored grain, the Indian meal moth, *Plòdia interpunctélla* (Hübner), and the Mediterranean flour moth, *Anagásta kuehniélla* (Zeller). The former is a gray moth with the apical two-thirds of the front wings dark brown, and the latter is uniformly gray (Figure 34–55). Both moths are rather small. The larvae of the Indian meal moth feed on cereals, dried fruits, meal, and nuts and spin webs over these materials. They often cause enormous losses in stored food supplies. The Mediterranean flour moth attacks all types of grain products and is an important pest in granaries, warehouses, markets, and homes.

Figure 34–54.   The sugarcane borer, *Diatraèa saccharális* (Fabricius) (Pyrálidae, Crambìnae), 2×. (Courtesy of USDA.)

Figure 34–55.   The Mediterranean flour moth, *Anagásta kuehniélla* (Zeller), 4×. (Courtesy of the Ohio Agricultural Research and Development Center.)

To this subfamily also belongs a moth from Argentina that has been used for the deliberate destruction of plants. The cactus moth, *Cactoblástis cactòrum* (Berg), has been introduced into Australia to control the prickly pear cactus. This moth has successfully destroyed the dense cactus growth over many square miles of territory in New South Wales and Queensland (see page 9).

Several species of *Diorýctria* bore into the cambium of the trunk, branches, and shoots and in the fresh cones of pines and other conifers. They are especially damaging to ornamentals and forest plantations, and the species attacking cones are probably the most damaging of the insect pests of forest tree seeds.

Another interesting species in this subfamily is the coccid-eating pyralid, *Laetília coccidívora* Comstock, the larva of which is predaceous on the eggs and young of various scale insects.

Family **Thyrídidae**—Window-Winged Moths: The thyridids are often small and dark-colored and have clear spaces in the wings (Figure 34–39F). All branches of the radius are present, and they arise from the usually open discal cell (Figure 34–23A). Some larvae burrow in twigs and stems and cause gall-like swellings. Others feed on flowers and seeds. The most common eastern species is probably *Dysòdia ocultàna* Clemens, which occurs in the Ohio Valley. Some tropical species are more colorful, and a few of these may occur in the Florida Keys.

Family **Hyblaèidae:** These moths are similar to the Noctùidae but differ in having two distinct anal veins in the front wing. This is a tropical group, one species of which occasionally occurs in the southern states. This species is *Hyblaèa pùera* (Cramer), which has the front wings brownish and the hind wings yellowish with two dark brown cross bands. It has a wingspread of about 26 mm.

Family **Hesperìidae**—Skippers: The skippers are for the most part small and stout-bodied, and they get their name from their fast and erratic flight. They differ from the butterflies (Papilionòidea) in having none of the five R branches in the front wings stalked, and all arise from the discal cell (Figure 34–8). The antennae are widely separated at the base, and the tips are usually recurved or hooked. Most skippers at rest hold the front and hind wings at a different angle. The larvae are smooth, with the head large and the neck constricted. They usually feed inside a leaf shelter, and pupation occurs in a cocoon made of leaves fastened together with silk. Most species overwinter as larvae, either in leaf shelters or in cocoons.

Nearly 300 species of skippers occur in North America. Most of these, including all the eastern species, belong to two subfamilies, the Pyrgìnae (Hesperiìnae of some authors) and the Hesperiìnae (Pamphilìnae of some authors). Three other subfamilies, the Pyrrhopygìnae, Heteropterìnae, and Megathymìnae occur in the South and Southwest.

Subfamily **Pyrrhopygìnae:** These skippers have the antennal club wholly reflexed; that is, the tip of the antenna is bent back before the club. This group is principally tropical, but one species, *Pyrrhopỳge aráxes* (Hewitson), occurs in southern Texas and Arizona. This is a large (wingspread 45–60 mm) dark-colored skipper with light spots in the front wings, and the wings are held horizontally when at rest. The larvae feed on oak.

Subfamily **Pyrgìnae:** In the front wings of the Pyrgìnae the discal cell is usually at least two-thirds as long as the wing. M_2 arises midway between M_1 and M_3 and is not curved at the base (Figure 34–8A). The middle tibiae lack spines. The males of some species have a costal fold, a long slitlike pocket near the costal margin of the front wing, which serves as a scent organ. Some species have scale tufts on the tibiae. Most of the skippers in this group are relatively large grayish or blackish insects (Figure 34–56A,E,F). The larvae feed principally on legumes.

One of the largest and most common species in this subfamily is the silver-spotted skipper, *Epargỳreus clàrus* (Cramer). It is dark brown with a large yellowish spot in the front wing and a silvery spot

Figure 34–56. Skippers (Hesperìidae). **A,** the silver-spotted skipper, *Epargỳreus clàrus* (Cramer) (Pyrgìnae), underside of wings, natural size; **B,** the least skipper, *Ancylóxipha nùmitor* (Fabricius) (Hesperiìnae), 1½×; **C,** the Hobomok skipper, *Poànes hóbomok* (Harris) (Hesperiìnae), 1½×; **D,** Peck's skipper, *Polìtes péckius* (Kirby) (Hesperiìnae); **E,** checkered skipper, *Pýrgus commùnis* (Grote) (Pyrgìnae), 1½×; **F,** the northern cloudy wing, *Thórybes pylàdes* (Scudder) (Pyrgìnae), slightly enlarged.

on the underside of the hind wing (Figure 34–56A). The larva feeds on black locust and related plants. The species overwinters as a pupa.

Subfamily **Heteropterinae**: This group is represented in North America by only five species (one in the genus *Carterocéphalus* and four in the genus *Pirùna*), and they are seldom encountered.

Subfamily **Hesperìinae**—Tawny Skippers: These skippers have the discal cell in the front wings less than two-thirds as long as the wing. M_2 in the front wings is usually curved at the base and arises nearer to M_3 than to M_1 (Figure 34–8B). The middle tibiae are often spined. The tawny skippers (Figure 34–56B–D) are usually brownish, with an oblique dark band (often called the stigma or brand) across the wing of the males. This dark band is composed of scales that serve as outlets for the scent glands. The larvae are chiefly grass feeders.

Subfamily **Megathyminae**—Giant Skippers: These skippers have a wingspread of 40 mm or more, and the antennal club is not recurved as in most other skippers. Giant skippers are stout-bodied and fast-flying. When at rest, they hold the wings vertically above the body. The larvae bore in the stems and roots of yucca and related plants. Maguey worms (Figure 2–4) are the larvae of a giant skipper.

Family **Papiliónidae**—Swallowtails and Parnasians: Two subfamilies of papilionids occur in our area, the Papilionìnae and the Parnassiìnae. These are sometimes given family rank. The Papilionìnae (swallowtails) are large, usually dark-colored butterflies that have the radius in the front wing five-branched and usually have one or more taillike prolongations on the rear side of the hind wing (Figure 34–57). The Parnassiìnae (parnassians) are medium-sized and usually white or gray with dark markings (Figure 34–58); the radius in the front wing is four-branched; and there are no taillike prolongations on the hind wings.

Subfamily **Papilionìnae**—Swallowtails: This group contains the largest and some of the most beautifully colored of our butterflies. In many species the two sexes are somewhat differently colored. This group contains the largest butterflies in the world, the giant birdwings of southeast Asia and Australia, some of which have a wingspread of about 255 mm. The larvae are usually smooth-bodied and possess an eversible scent gland or osmeterium (Figure 34–3, *osm*). This gland is everted from the upper part of the prothorax when the larva is disturbed and gives off a disagreeable odor. Some larvae have markings like eyespots at the anterior end and resemble the head of a small vertebrate. This resemblance, together with the "forked-tongue" appearance of the scent gland, makes them seem quite ferocious—though they are actually quite harmless. The chrysalis is attached to various objects by the cremaster and is held more or less upright by means of a silken girdle about the middle of the body (Figure 34–4A). The winter is passed in the chrysalis.

Swallowtails are widely distributed, but the following species are fairly common in the eastern states: The black swallowtail, *Papílio polýxenes astérius* Stoll (Figure 34–57C), is largely black, with two rows of yellow spots around the margin of the wings. The female has quite a bit of blue between the two rows of yellow spots in the hind wings. The larva feeds on carrot leaves, parsley, and related plants. The tiger swallowtail, *Papílio gláucus* L. (Figures 34–57B, 36–22), is a large yellow swallowtail

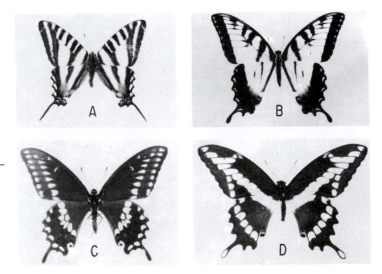

Figure 34–57. Swallowtail butterflies. **A,** the zebra swallowtail, *Eurydìtes marcéllus* (Cramer); **B,** the tiger swallowtail, *Papílio gláucus* L.; **C,** the black swallowtail, *Papílio polýxenes astérius* Stoll, male; **D,** the giant swallowtail, *Papílio cresphóntes* Cramer. About one-third natural size.

Figure 34–58. A parnassian, *Parnássius clòdius báldur* Edwards. About two-thirds natural size.

with black stripes in the front wings and black wing margins. In some individuals the wings are almost entirely black. The larva feeds on cherry, birch, poplar, and various other trees and shrubs. The spicebush swallowtail, *Papílio tròilus* L., is blackish, with a row of small yellowish spots along the margins of the front wings and extensive blue-gray areas in the rear half of the hind wings. The larva feeds on spicebush and sassafras. The zebra swallowtail, *Eurydìtes marcèllus* (Cramer) (Figure 34–57A), is striped with black and greenish white and has relatively long tails. The larva feeds on papaw. This species shows considerable variation, as the adults emerging in different seasons differ slightly in their markings. The pipe-vine swallowtail, *Báttus phílenor* (L.), is largely black, with the hind wings shading into metallic green posteriorly. The larva feeds on Dutchman's-pipe. The giant swallowtail or orangedog, *Papílio cresphóntes* Cramer (Figure 34–57D), is a large dark-colored butterfly with rows of large yellow spots on the wings. The larva feeds chiefly on citrus in the South and on prickly ash in the North.

Subfamily **Parnassiinae**—Parnassians: The parnassians are medium-sized butterflies that are usually white or gray with dark markings on the wings (Figure 34–58). Most of them have two small reddish spots in the hind wings. These butterflies pupate on the ground, among fallen leaves, in loose cocoonlike structures. After mating the male secretes a hard-drying substance over the genital opening of the female, thus preventing other males from inseminating the same female. The parnassians are principally montane and boreal in distribution.

Family **Piéridae**—Whites, Sulphurs, and Orange-tips: The pierids are medium-sized to small butterflies, usually white or yellowish in color with black marginal wing markings. The radius in the front wing is usually three- or four-branched (rarely five-branched in some orange-tips). The front legs are well developed, and the tarsal claws are bifid. The chrysalids are elongate and narrow and are attached by the cremaster and by a silken girdle around the middle of the body. Many pierids are very common and abundant butterflies and are sometimes seen in mass migrations.

The 63 North American species of pierids are arranged in four subfamilies, the Pierìnae (whites), Anthocharìnae (orange-tips), Coliadìnae (sulphurs or yellows), and Dismorphiìnae. The Dismorphiìnae is a tropical group, only one species of which occasionally gets into southern Texas.

Subfamily **Pierìnae**—Whites: These butterflies are usually white. There is usually a distinct humeral vein in the hind wing, and the third segment of the labial palps is long and tapering. One of the most common species in this group is the cabbage butterfly, *Pìeris ràpae* (L.) (Figure 34–59B), the larva of which often does considerable damage to cabbage and related plants. It has two or more generations a year and overwinters as a chrysalis. The pine butterfly, *Neophàsia menàpia* (Felder and Felder), is a white that is very destructive to ponderosa pine in the northwestern states.

Subfamily **Anthocharìnae**—Orange-tips: These are small white butterflies with dark markings (Figure 34–59A). The underside of the wings is mottled with green, and the front wings of many species are tipped with orange. These butterflies are mainly western. Only two species occur in the East, and they are relatively rare. The larvae feed on cruciferous plants.

Subfamily **Coliadìnae**—Sulphurs or Yellows: These pierids are yellow or orange and usually have the

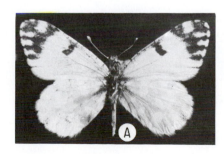

Figure 34–59. Pierid butterflies. **A,** an orange-tip, *Eùchloe creùsa lótta* (Beutenmüller); **B,** the cabbage butterfly, *Pìeris ràpae* (L.). **A,** slightly enlarged; **B,** slightly reduced.

wings margined with black. Rarely, they may be white with black wing margins. The humeral vein in the hind wing is lacking (Figure 34–13B) or represented by just a stub, and the third segment of the labial palps is short. Many species occur in two or more seasonal color forms. A common butterfly in this group is the orange sulphur or alfalfa butterfly, *Còlias eurýtheme* Boisduval. Most individuals of this species are orange with black wing margins, but some females are white. The larva feeds on clovers and related plants and often does serious damage to clover crops. The common or clouded sulphur, *C. philódice* Godart, is yellow with black margins. It often occurs in large numbers around muddy pools along roadsides. The larva feeds on clovers. The females of these sulphurs have the black marginal band on the wings broader than in the males, and there are light spots in this band, particularly in the front wings.

Family **Lycaènidae**—Coppers, Hairstreaks, Blues, Harvesters, and Metalmarks: These are small, delicate, and often brightly colored butterflies, and some are quite common. The body is slender, the antennae are usually ringed with white, and there is a line of white scales encircling the eyes. The radius in the front wing is three- or four-branched (three-branched in the Theclìnae, four-branched in the other subfamilies). M_1 in the front wing arises at or near the anterior apical angle of the discal cell (except in the Liphyrìnae; see Figure 34–60A), and there is no humeral vein in the hind wing (except in the Riodinìnae) (Figures 34–12B, 34–14, 34–60). The front legs are normal in the female, but are shorter and lack tarsal claws in the male. Lycaenid larvae are flattened and sluglike. Many secrete honeydew, which attracts ants, and some live in ant nests. The chrysalids are fairly smooth and are attached by the cremaster, with a silken girdle about the middle of the body. The adults are rapid fliers.

The approximately 160 North American species of Lycaènidae are arranged in six subfamilies, Liphyrìnae (Gerydìnae, Miletìnae), Lycaenìnae (Chrysophanìnae), Theclìnae, Eumaeìnae, Polyommatìnae (Plebeiìnae), and Riodinìnae.

Subfamily **Liphyrìnae**—Harvesters: The harvesters differ from the other lycaenids in having M_1 in the front wings stalked with a branch of R for a short distance beyond the discal cell (Figure 34–60A). The wanderer or harvester, *Feníseca tarquínius* (Fabricius), is the only member of this group occurring in the United States. It is a brownish butterfly with a wingspread of about 25 mm (Figure 34–61B). The larva is predaceous on aphids and is one of the few predaceous lepidopteran larvae. This species is

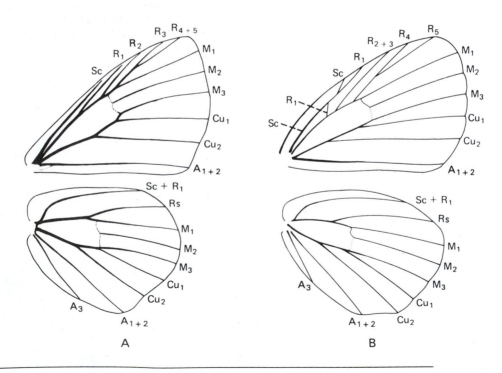

Figure 34–60.   Wings of Lycaènidae. **A,** harvester (Liphyrìnae); **B,** blue (Polyommatìnae).

Figure 34–61. **A**, the American copper, *Lycaèna phlaèas americàna* Harris (Lycaènidae, Lycaeninae); **B**, the harvester, *Feníseca tarquínius* (Fabricius) (Lycaènidae, Liphyrìnae); **C**, a snout butterfly, *Libytheàna bachmánii* (Kirtland) (Libythèidae); **D**, the northern metalmark, *Lephelísca boreàlis* (Grote and Robinson) (Riodinìnae). **A**, **B**, and **D**, slightly enlarged; **C**, about natural size.

rather local and uncommon and (in spite of its name) does very little wandering.

Subfamily **Lycaeninae**—Coppers: The coppers are small butterflies that are orange-red or brown (often with a coppery tinge) with black markings. The last anch of R in the front wings ($R_{3–5}$) is forked (with the branches R_3 and R_{4+5}) and arises at the anterior apical angle of the discal cell (Figure 34–14B). These butterflies generally occur in open areas such as marshes and meadows and along roadsides.

The American copper, *Lycaèna phlaèas americàna* Harris (Figure 34–61A), is one of the most common species in this group. The adults are quite pugnacious and often "buzz" other butterflies (and even collectors!). The larva feeds on dock (*Rùmex*).

Subfamilies **Theclinae** and **Eumaeinae**—Hairstreaks: The hairstreaks are usually dark gray or brownish, with delicate striping on the underside of the wings and usually with small reddish spots in the posterior part of the hind wings. There are usually two or three hairlike tails on the hind wings. There are only three branches of R in the front wing, and the last one is simple (Figure 34–12B). These butterflies have a swift, darting flight and are commonly found in meadows, along roadsides, and in other open areas.

One of the most common eastern species is the gray hairstreak, *Strỳmon mélinus* Hübner. The larva bores in the fruits and seeds of legumes, cotton, and other plants. The great purple hairstreak, *Átlides hálesus* (Cramer), is the largest eastern species, with a wingspread of a little over 25 mm. It is brilliantly

colored—blue, purple, and black—and quite iridescent. It occurs in the southern states. The elfins (*Incisàlia*) are small, brownish, early spring species that lack tails but have the edges of the hind wings scalloped. Most of our hairstreaks are in the subfamily Theclìnae; only two (in the genus *Eumaèus*, reported from Florida and Texas) are in the Eumaeìnae.

Subfamily **Polyommatinae**—Blues: The blues are small, delicate, slender-bodied butterflies with the upper surface of the wings blue. The females are usually darker than the males, and some species occur in two or more color forms. The last branch of R in the front wing is forked (as in the coppers), but arises a little proximad of the anterior apical angle of the discal cell (Figure 34–60B). Many larvae secrete honeydew, to which ants are attracted.

One of the most common and widespread species in this group is the spring azure, *Celastrìna làdon* (Cramer). This species exhibits considerable geographic and seasonal variation in size and coloring. The tailed blues (*Evères*) have delicate taillike prolongations on the hind wings.

Subfamily **Riodinìnae**—Metalmarks: The metalmarks are small, dark-colored butterflies that differ from other lycaenids in having the costa of the hind wing thickened out to the humeral angle and in having a short humeral vein in the hind wing (Figure 34–14A). Most species in this group are tropical or western, and only two occur in the East. The little metalmark, *Calephélis virginiénsis* (Guérin), with a wingspread of about 20 mm, occurs in the southern states, and the northern metalmark, *Lephelísca bo-*

reàlis (Grote and Robinson) (Figure 34–61D), with a wingspread of 25–30 mm, occurs as far north as New York and Ohio. The little metalmark is fairly common in the south, but the northern metalmark is quite rare. The larvae feed on ragwort, thistle, and other plants.

Family **Libythèidae**—Snout Butterflies: These are small brownish butterflies with long projecting palps. The males have the front legs reduced, with only the middle and hind legs used in walking, while the females have the front legs longer and use them in walking. One species, *Libytheàna bachmánii* (Kirtland), is common and widely distributed. This is a reddish brown butterfly with white spots in the apical part of the front wings and with the outer margin of the front wings rather deeply notched (Figure 34–61C). The larva feeds on hackberry.

Family **Nymphálidae**—Brush-Footed Butterflies: This is a fairly large group (about 140 North American species) and includes many common butterflies. The common name of the family refers to the fact that the front legs are much reduced and lack claws, and only the middle and hind legs are used in walking. This character occurs also in the Danàidae, Satýridae, and Libythèidae. The chrysalids are usually suspended by the cremaster (Figure 34–4B). This family is divided into nine subfamilies.

Subfamily **Heliconiìnae**—Heliconians: The heliconians differ from other nymphalids in having the humeral vein in the hind wing bent basad (Figure 34–12A) and the front wings relatively long and narrow (Figure 34–62). This group is largely tropical, and only five species occur in the United States. Our most common heliconian is the zebra butterfly, *Helicònius charitònius* (L.), a black butterfly striped with yellow (Figure 34–62A). This species occurs in the Gulf States, but it is most common in Florida. The chrysalis, when disturbed, wriggles about in a characteristic manner and produces a creaking sound. A heliconian that occurs over a large part of the southeastern United States, extending as far north as New Jersey and Iowa and with a southwestern subspecies extending into southern California, is the gulf fritillary, *Agràulis vaníllae* (L.). This butterfly is bright orange-brown with black markings (Figure 34–62B). The butterflies in this group appear to have distasteful body fluids and are avoided by predators. The larvae feed on various species of passion flowers.

Subfamily **Limenitidìnae**—Admirals, Viceroy, and Others: The members of this group are medium-sized butterflies in which the antennal club is long, and the humeral vein in the hind wing arises opposite the origin of Rs (Figure 34–11B). The viceroy, *Basilárchia archíppus* (Cramer), is a common species in this group that looks very much like the monarch. It differs in that it is slightly smaller, has a narrow black line across the hind wings, and has only a single row of white spots in the black marginal band of the wings (Figure 34–63A). The resemblance of the viceroy to the monarch is a good example of protective (or Batesian) mimicry. The monarch is "protected" by distasteful body fluids and is seldom attacked by predators, and the viceroy's resemblance to the monarch is believed to provide it with at least some protection from predators. The larva of the viceroy, a rather grotesque-looking caterpillar, feeds on willow, poplar, and related trees. It overwinters in a leaf shelter formed by tying a few leaves together with silk. The red-spotted purple, *B. árthemis astỳanax* (Fabricius), another common species in this group, is a blackish butterfly with pale bluish or

A

B

Figure 34–62. Heliconian butterflies (Nymphálidae, Heliconiìnae). **A,** the zebra butterfly, *Helicònius charitònius* (L.); **B,** the gulf fritillary, *Agráulis vaníllae* (L.). Slightly reduced.

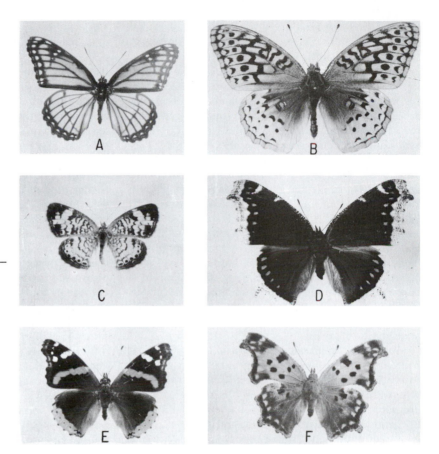

Figure 34–63. Brush-footed butterflies (Nymphálidae). **A,** the viceroy, *Basilárchia archíppus* (Cramer); **B,** the great spangled fritillary, *Speyéria cýbele* (Fabricius); **C,** the pearl crescentspot, *Phyciòdes thàros* (Drury); **D,** the mourning cloak, *Nýmphalis antìopa* (L.); **E,** the red admiral, *Vanéssa atalánta* (L.); **F,** the comma, *Polygònia cómma* (Harris). **C,** about natural size; the others slightly reduced.

greenish spots and with reddish spots on the underside of the wings. The larva, which is similar to that of the viceroy, feeds on willow, cherry, and other trees and overwinters in a leaf shelter. A similar butterfly, the banded purple, *B. árthemis árthemis* (Drury), occurs in the northern states. It has a broad white band across the wings.

Subfamily **Argynnìnae**—Fritillaries: The fritillaries are brownish butterflies with numerous black markings consisting principally of short wavy lines and dots. The underside of the wings is often marked with silvery spots. Most of the larger fritillaries belong to the genus *Speyéria* (Figure 34–63B). *Speyéria* larvae are nocturnal and feed on violets. The smaller fritillaries, 25–40 mm in wingspread, belong principally to the genus *Clossìnna* and *Bolòria*. Their larvae also feed on violets.

Subfamily **Melitaeìnae**—Crescentspots and Checkerspots: The members of this group are small butterflies (wingspread mostly 25–40 mm) in which the eyes are bare and the palps are densely hairy beneath. The crescentspots (*Phyciòdes*) are small brownish butterflies with black markings, and the wings (par-

ticularly the front wings) are margined with black (Figure 34–63C). They have a wingspread of about 25 mm. The larvae feed principally on asters. The checkerspots (*Euphydrỳas*) are similar to the crescentspots, but they are usually a little larger, and the darker areas on the wings are generally more extensive. The larvae feed on asters and related plants.

Subfamily **Nymphalìnae**—Anglewings, Tortoiseshells, Mourning Cloaks, and Others: These butterflies have the eyes hairy, and the hind wing is angled or tailed at the end of M_3. The anglewings (*Polygònia*) are small to medium-sized and brownish with black markings. The wings are irregularly notched and often bear taillike projections, and the distal half of the rear edge of the front wing is somewhat excavated (Figure 34–63F). The underside of the wings is darker and looks much like a dead leaf, and there is usually a small C-shaped silvery spot on the underside of the hind wing. The larvae feed principally on nettles, elm, hopvines, and other Urticàceae. The mourning cloak, *Nýmphalis antìopa* (L.), is a common butterfly that is brownish-black with yellowish wing margins (Figure 34–63D); the larvae are gregarious and feed chiefly on willow, elm, and poplar. This is one of the few butterflies that overwinters in the adult stage, and the adults appear early in the spring.

Another group of nymphalids (sometimes placed in the subfamily Vanessìnae) has the eyes hairy, but the margin of the hind wing is rounded, not angled or tailed at the end of M_3. This group includes the red admiral, *Vanéssa atalánta* (L.) (Figure 34–63E), a very common and widely distributed butterfly. The larva feeds principally on nettles, feeding in a shelter formed by tying a few leaves together. There are usually two generations a year. Two very similar and fairly common species in this group are the painted lady, *V. cárdui* (L.), and Hunter's butterfly, *V. virginiénsis* (Drury). These butterflies are orange-brown and brownish black above, with white spots in the front wings. The painted lady has four small eyespots on the underside of each hind wing, while Hunter's butterfly has two large eyespots on the underside of each hind wing. The larva of the painted lady feeds chiefly on thistles, while that of Hunter's butterfly feeds on everlastings.

Subfamily **Apaturìnae**—Hackberry Butterflies and Emperors: These butterflies are somewhat similar to the painted lady, but the dark areas in the front wings are brownish rather than black, and the eyes are bare. The larvae feed on hackberry, and adults are generally found around these trees.

Other nymphalid subfamilies in our area are the Charaxìnae (including the leaf-wings, *Anaèa*) and the Marpesiìnae. The Marpesiìnae include the purple-wings (*Eùnica*) and dagger-wings (*Marpèsia*).

These groups are principally tropical in distribution.

Family **Satýridae**—Satyrs, Wood Nymphs, and Arctics: These butterflies are small to medium-sized, usually grayish or brown, and they generally have eyelike spots in the wings. The radius of the front wings is five-branched, and some of the veins in the front wings (particularly Sc) are considerably swollen at the base (Figure 34–10B). The larvae feed on grasses. The chrysalis is usually attached by the cremaster to leaves and other objects.

One of the most common species in this group is the wood nymph, *Cercỳonis pégala* (Fabricius), a dark brown, medium-sized butterfly with a broad yellowish band across the apical part of the front wing. This band contains two black-and-white eyespots (Figure 34–64A). Another common species is the little wood satyr, *Megísta cỳmela* (Cramer), a brownish gray butterfly with prominent eyespots in the wings and with a wingspread of about 25 mm (Figure 34–64C). The pearly eye, *Enòdia portlándia* (Fabricius) (Figure 34–64D), a brownish butterfly with a row of black eyespots along the border of the hind wings, is a woodland species with a quick flight and a habit of alighting on tree trunks. Among the most interesting species in this group are the arctics or mountain butterflies (*Oenèis*), which are restricted to the arctic region and the tops of high mountains. A race of the melissa arctic, *O. melíssa semídes* (Say), is restricted to the summits of the White Mountains in New Hampshire, and a race of the polixenes arctic, *O. políxenes katáhdin* (Newcomb), occurs on Mount Katahdin in Maine. The

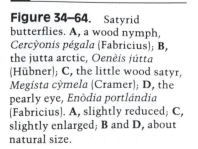

Figure 34–64. Satyrid butterflies. **A,** a wood nymph, *Cercỳonis pégala* (Fabricius); **B,** the jutta arctic, *Oenèis jútta* (Hübner); **C,** the little wood satyr, *Megísta cỳmela* (Cramer); **D,** the pearly eye, *Enòdia portlándia* (Fabricius). **A,** slightly reduced; **C,** slightly enlarged; **B** and **D,** about natural size.

jutta arctic, *O. jútta* (Hübner) (Figure 34–64B), is a wide-ranging circumpolar species that occurs farther south than do most other arctics. It may be found in the sphagnum bogs of Maine and New Hampshire.

Family **Danàidae**—Milkweed Butterflies: The danaids are large and brightly colored butterflies, usually brownish with black and white markings. The front legs are very small, without claws, and are not used in walking. The radius in the front wing is five-branched; the discal cell is closed by a well-developed vein; and there is a short third anal vein in the front wing (Figure 34–10A). The larvae feed on milkweed. The chrysalids are hung by the cremaster to leaves or other objects. The adults are "protected" by distasteful body fluids, and are seldom attacked by predators (see page 80).

The most common species in this group is the monarch butterfly, *Dánaus plexíppus* (L.), which occurs throughout the United States and a large part of the remainder of the world. The monarch is a reddish brown butterfly with the wings bordered by black. In most of the black marginal band there are two rows of small white spots (Figure 34–65A). The caterpillar is yellowish green banded with black, with two threadlike appendages at either end of the body (Figure 34–65B). The chrysalis is pale green spotted with gold.

The monarch is one of the few butterflies that migrates. Large numbers migrate south in the fall, and the species reappears in the North the following spring. The longest flight known for an adult monarch (based on a tagged individual) is more than 1800 miles (2900 km), from Ontario to Mexico (see page 81). The butterflies that migrate south in the fall overwinter in the south and usually start back north the following spring. They may reproduce in their wintering grounds or after a short northward flight in the spring. The butterflies that arrive in the northern United States in the summer are not the same individuals that left there the preceding fall but the offspring of individuals that reproduced in the wintering grounds or en route north (see Urquhart 1960). After two summer generations in the North, the fall generation returns to the same wintering grounds in Mexico, even though it is three generations removed from that of the previous winter. The principal wintering grounds for the monarch are in Mexico, but some winter in Florida (or Cuba) and in southern California.

The queen, *Dánaus gilíppus* (Cramer), a common species in the southeastern states, is similar to the monarch but is darker and lacks the dark lines along the veins. Its larva also feeds on milkweed. A subspecies of the queen occurs in the Southwest, to southern California.

Family **Thyatíridae**: The Thyatíridae are similar to the Noctùidae, but they have the cubitus appearing three-branched in the front wings and four-branched in the hind wings, and the veins $Sc + R_1$ and Rs in the hind wings are more or less parallel along the anterior margin of the discal cell. They have abdominal rather than thoracic tympanal organs. The larvae of this small group (16 North American species) feed on various trees and shrubs.

Family **Drepánidae**—Hook-Tip Moths: These moths are small, slender-bodied, and usually dull-colored and can generally be recognized by the sickle-shaped apex of the front wings. Abdominal tympanal organs are present. The cubitus in the front wings appears four-branched; in the hind wing $Sc + R_1$ and Rs are separated along the discal cell; and the frenulum is small or absent. The larvae feed on the foliage of various trees and shrubs. The most common species in this group is *Drépana arcuàta* Walker, a dirty white moth marked with dark brownish lines and with a wingspread of about 25 mm (Figure 34–66A). It occurs in the Atlantic states. This group is a small one, with only five species in North America.

Family **Geométridae**—Measuringworms, Geometers: This family is the second largest in the order, with some 1400 species occurring in the United States and Canada. The moths in this family are mostly small, delicate, and slender-bodied. The wings are usually broad and often marked with fine wavy lines. The two sexes are often different in color, and in a few species the females are wingless or have

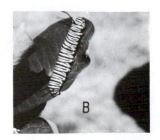

Figure 34–65. The monarch, *Dánaus plexíppus* (L.). **A,** adult male; **B,** larva. About one-half natural size.

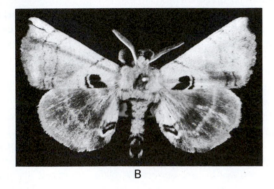

Figure 34–66. **A,** a hook-tip moth, *Drépana arcuàta* Walker, 2×; **B,** an apatelodid moth, *Apatelòdes torrefácta* Abbott and Smith, 1½×.

only rudimentary wings. The geometers are principally nocturnal and are often attracted to lights. The most characteristic feature of the wing venation is the form of the subcosta in the hind wing (Figure 34–20). The basal part of this vein makes an abrupt bend into the humeral angle and is usually connected by a brace vein to the humeral angle. The cubitus in the front wing appears three-branched. This family, like all the Geometròidea except the Sematùridae, has tympanal organs on the abdomen.

The larvae of geometers are the familiar caterpillars called inchworms or measuringworms (Figure 34–67). They have two or three pairs of prolegs at the posterior end of the body and none in the middle. Locomotion is accomplished by placing the posterior end of the body near the thoracic legs and then moving the anterior end of the body, thus progressing in a characteristic looping fashion. Many measuringworms, when disturbed, stand nearly erect on the posterior prolegs and remain motionless, resembling small twigs.

North American Geométridae are divided into six subfamilies: Archicarìnae, Oenochromìnae, Ennomìnae, Geometrìnae, Sterrhìnae, and Larentiìnae.

The largest of these is the Ennomìnae, which includes about half of the North American species. It differs from the other subfamilies in having M_2 in the hind wings weak or absent (Figure 34–20B).

This family contains the cankerworms, which feed on the foliage of various deciduous trees and often cause serious defoliation. The two common species are the spring cankerworm, *Paleácrita vernáta* (Peck) (Ennomìnae), and the fall cankerworm, *Alsóphila pometària* (Harris) (Oenochromìnae) (Figure 34–68). The spring cankerworm overwinters in the pupal stage, and the female lays its eggs in the spring. The fall cankerworm overwinters in the egg stage. The larvae of the spring cankerworm have two pairs of prolegs; the larvae of the fall cankerworm have three pairs. The adult females of both species are wingless.

Many of the geometers are common moths, but only a few can be mentioned here. The chickweed geometer, *Haemátopis gratària* (Fabricius) (Sterrhìnae), is a reddish yellow moth with the margins of the wings and two bands near the margins pink (Figure 34–69B). It has a wingspread of about 25 mm or less, and the larva feeds on chickweed. One of the largest moths in this family is the notch-wing geometer, *Énnomos magnàrius* Guenée (Ennomìnae). It has a wingspread of 35–50 mm. The wings are reddish yellow with small brown spots, and they shade to brown toward the outer margin (Figure 34–69A). The larvae feed on various trees. Many

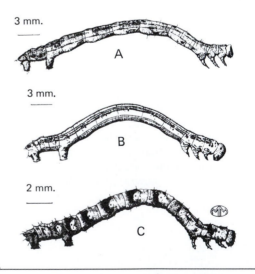

Figure 34–67. Larvae of Geométridae. **A,** *Pèro morrisonària* (H. Edwards); **B,** *Nepỳtia canosària* (Walker); **C,** *Protoboármia porcelària indicatòria* (Walker). (Courtesy of McGuffin and MacKay, and the Canadian Entomologist.)

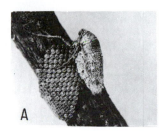
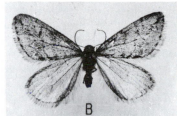

Figure 34–68. The fall cankerworm, *Alsóphila pometària* (Harris). **A,** adult female laying eggs; **B,** adult male. Natural size. (Courtesy of the Ohio Agricultural Research and Development Center.)

geometers are light green in color. One of the common species of this type is the bad-wing, *Dýspteris abortivària* (Herrich-Schäffer) (Larentiìnae) (Figure 34–69D). The front wings are large and triangular, and the hind wings are small and rounded. This moth has a wingspread of a little less than 25 mm. The larva rolls and feeds on the leaves of grape.

Several other members of this family are important forest pests. The hemlock looper, *Lambdìna fiscellària* (Guenée) (Ennomìnae), is a widely distributed species attacking hemlock and other conifers, and it has occurred in outbreak numbers. The adults resemble those of *Énnomos magnàrius* (Figure 34–69A). The mountain mahogany looper, *Anacamptòdes clivinària profanàta* (Barnes and McDunnough) (Ennomìnae), feeds on mountain mahogany (*Cercocárpus*) and bitterbrush (*Púrshia*) in the Northwest and is very destructive to both.

A European species in the subfamily Ennomìnae, *Bíston betulària* (L.), is an example of the phenomenon known as industrial melanism. In areas of Great Britain where there is heavy industry and the tree trunks become covered with soot, the light-colored individuals of this moth have been replaced by dark variants, which elsewhere are relatively rare. The dark forms have a better chance of escaping predation when alighting on soot-covered tree trunks than the light-colored form.

Family **Epiplèmidae:** Epiplèmidae are a small group of moths that are similar in size and general appearance to the Geométridae but differ in wing venation. They have Sc + R and Rs in the hind wing widely separated from near the base of the wing. The cubitus in the front wing appears three-branched, and the veins M_1 and R_5 are stalked and well separated from R_4. The larvae are sparsely hairy and have five pairs of prolegs. Eight species of this group occur in the United States. The moths are plain-colored and have a wingspread of about 20 mm.

Family **Sematùridae:** This family is represented in the United States by a single species, *Anuràpteryx crenulàta* Barnes and Lindsey, a Mexican species that ranges into Arizona. It is the only family of the Geometròidea that lacks abdominal tympana (but there are a few exotic families that also lack these structures).

Family **Uraniìdae:** This is a tropical group, most species of which are brightly colored and day-flying. A single species, *Urània fúlgens* (Walker), has been reported in Texas. This is a neotropical species that resembles a swallowtail butterfly. It is blackish with pale metallic greenish bands on the wings and the

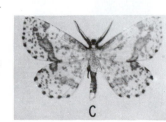
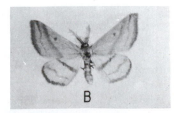

Figure 34–69. Geometer moths. **A,** the notch-wing geometer, *Énnomos magnàrius* Guenée; **B,** the chickweed geometer, *Haemátopis gratària* (Fabricius); **C,** the crocus geometer, *Xanthótype sóspeta* Drury; **D,** the bad-wing, *Dýspteris abortivària* Herrich-Schäffer. **A,** slightly reduced; **B** and **D,** slightly enlarged; **C,** about natural size.

tails of the hind wings whitish, and it has a wing-spread of 80–90 mm.

Family **Mimallónidae**—Sack-bearers: These insects are called sack-bearers because the larvae make cases from leaves and carry them about. The group is a small one, with four North American species in three genera (*Lacosòma, Nanitèta,* and *Cicínnus*). The moths in the genus *Lacosòma* are yellowish in color and about 25 mm in wingspread, with the distal margin of the front wings deeply scalloped (Figure 34–70A). Those in the genus *Cicínnus* are reddish gray peppered with small black dots and with a narrow dark line across the wings, a wingspread of about 32 mm, and the distal margin of the front wings evenly rounded (Figure 34–70B). The one species of *Nanitèta, N. elássa* Franclemont, occurs in the Southwest.

Family **Lasiocámpidae**—Tent Caterpillars, Lappet Moths, and Others: These moths are medium-sized and stout-bodied, with the body, legs, and eyes hairy. The antennae are somewhat feathery in both sexes, but the processes on the antennae are longer in the male. There is no frenulum, and the humeral angle of the hind wing is expanded and provided with humeral veins (Figure 34–23B). Most of these moths

Figure 34–71.   The eastern tent caterpillar, *Malacosòma americànum* (Fabricius). Left, egg mass; center, larvae; right, adult female. ½×. (Courtesy of the Ohio Agricultural Research and Development Center.)

A

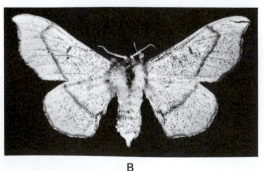

B

Figure 34–70.   Sack-bearer moths (Mimallónidae). **A,** *Lacosòma chiridòta* Grote, 2½× ; **B,** *Cicínnus melsheìmeri* Harris, 1½× .

are brown or gray in color. The larvae feed on the foliage of trees, often causing serious damage. Pupation occurs in a well-formed cocoon. Thirty-five species of lasiocampids occur in our area.

The eastern tent caterpillar, *Malacosòma americànum* (Fabricius) (Figure 34–71), is a common member of this group in eastern North America. The adults are yellowish brown. They appear in midsummer and lay their eggs in a bandlike cluster around a twig. The eggs hatch the following spring. The young that hatch from a given egg cluster are gregarious and construct a tentlike nest of silk near the eggs (Figure 34–72). This tent is used as a shelter, with the larvae feeding during the day in nearby branches. The larvae feed on a number of different trees but seem to prefer cherry. The larvae are black and somewhat hairy and have a yellow stripe down the middle of the back. When full-grown they wander off and spin their cocoons in sheltered places.

The forest tent caterpillar, *Malacosòma dísstria* Hübner, is widely distributed, but is probably more common in the South and Southwest, where it sometimes defoliates large areas. The larvae differ from those of the eastern tent caterpillar in that they have a row of keyhole-shaped spots (rather than a stripe) down the middle of the back. The adults are somewhat paler than those of the eastern tent caterpillar.

The lappet moths (*Tólype*) are bluish gray with white markings (Figure 34–73). The common name refers to the fact that the larvae have a small lobe or lappet on each side of each segment. The larvae of *T. véllida* (Stoll) feed on apple, poplar, and syringa, and

Figure 34–72. Tents of the eastern tent caterpillar. (Courtesy of the Ohio Agricultural Research and Development Center.)

those of *T. láricis* (Fitch) feed on larch. The two species of *Artàce* in North America are common in the South and Southwest. They are similar to *Tólype* but are white with black dots.

Our largest lasiocampids are species of *Glovéria*, some of which have a wingspread of 80 mm. They occur in the Southwest, and their larvae feed on the foliage of trees and shrubs, especially oaks and ceanothus.

Family **Apatelòdidae:** This family is represented in North America by five species (in two genera, *Apatelòdes* and *Olcecóstera*). These moths are similar to the Notodóntidae but usually have windowlike dots near the apex of the front wings. They have a wingspread of 40–50 mm (Figure 34–66B). The larvae feed on various shrubs and trees and pupate in the ground.

Family **Bombýcidae**—Silkworm Moths: Only a single species in this family occurs in North America, *Bómbyx mòri* (L.). This is a native of Asia that is occasionally reared in the United States. This insect has long been reared for its silk, and it is one of the most important beneficial insects. After centuries of domestication it is now a domestic species and probably does not exist in the wild. Many different varieties of silkworms have been developed by breeding. There are about a hundred species in this family, most of which occur in Asia.

The adult moth is creamy white with several faint brownish lines across the front wings, and it has a wingspread of about 50 mm. The body is heavy and very hairy. The adults do not feed, they rarely fly, and usually they live only a few days. Each female lays 300–400 eggs. The larvae are naked, have a short anal horn, and feed principally on the leaves of mulberry. They become full grown and spin their cocoons in about six weeks. When used for commercial purposes, the pupae are killed before they emerge, since the emergence of the moth breaks the fibers in the cocoon. Each cocoon is composed of a single thread about 914 meters long. About 3000 cocoons are required to make a pound of silk.

Sericulture is practiced in Japan, China, Spain, France, and Italy. It was introduced into the South Atlantic states in colonial times but did not succeed. The silk has a commercial value of $200 million to $500 million annually.

Family **Saturnìidae**—Giant Silkworm Moths and Royal Moths: This family includes the largest moths in our area, and it includes some of the largest lepidopterans in the world. The largest moths in North America (*Hyalóphora*) have a wingspread of about 150 mm or more, while some tropical species of *Áttacus* have a wingspread of about 250 mm. The smallest saturniids in our area have a wingspread of about 25 mm. Many members of this family are conspicuously or brightly colored, and many have transparent eyespots in the wings. The antennae are feathery (bipectinate or quadripectinate) for about half or more of their length and are larger in the male than in the female. The mouthparts are reduced, and the adults do not feed. The females produce a sex pheromone that males can detect from long distances downwind. Many species fly mostly during the daylight hours or at dusk.

Figure 34–73. A lappet moth, *Tólype véllida* (Stoll) (Lasiocámpidae). About natural size. (Courtesy of the Ohio Agricultural Research and Development Center.)

The larvae of saturniids (Figures 34–74, 34–75B) are large caterpillars, and many are armed with conspicuous tubercles or spines. Most of them (Saturniinae and most Hemileucìnae) pupate in silken cocoons that are attached to the twigs or leaves of trees and shrubs or that are formed among leaves on the ground. Some (Citheroniìnae and some Hemileucìnae) pupate in the ground without forming a cocoon. Most species overwinter in the pupal stage and have one generation a year. A few species in this group have been used for the production of commercial silk. Some of the Asiatic species have provided a silk that makes strong and long-wearing fabrics, but none of the North American species has proved satisfactory for commercial silk production.

The 68 North American species of saturniids are arranged in three subfamilies, the Citheroniìnae, the Hemileucìnae, and the Saturniìnae.

Subfamily **Citheroniìnae**—Royal Moths: The members of this group have two anal veins in the hind wing; the discal cell in the front wing is closed; and M_2 in the front wing is stalked with R for a short distance (Figure 34–22A). The antennae of the male are pectinate in the basal half only. The larvae are armed with horns or spines and pupate in the ground.

Our largest member of this group is the regal or royal walnut moth, *Citherònia regàlis* (Fabricius) (Figure 34–75A), which has a wingspread of 125–150 mm. The front wings are gray or olive-colored spotted with yellow, and with the veins reddish brown; the hind wings are orange-red, spotted with yellow; and the body is reddish brown with yellow bands. The larva (Figure 34–75B) is often called the hickory horned devil. When full grown it is 100–130 mm long and has curved spines on the anterior part of its body. Though very ferocious in appearance, this caterpillar is quite harmless. It feeds principally on walnut, hickory, and persimmon.

The imperial moth, *Èacles imperiàlis* (Drury), is a large yellowish moth with dark peppered spots. Each wing has a pinkish brown diagonal band near the margin (Figure 34–75C). The larva feeds on various trees and shrubs. A related species from Mexico, *E. óslari* Rothschild, enters our area in southern Arizona. The moths in the genus *Anisòta* are small, with wingspreads of 25–40 mm. Most of them are

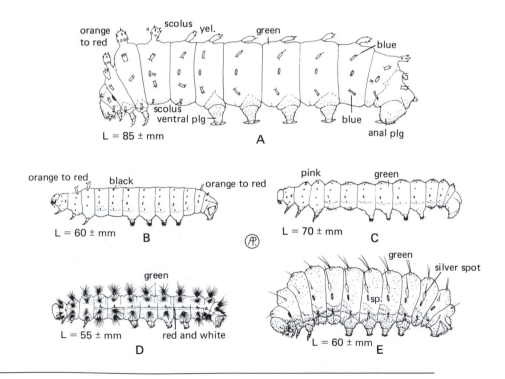

Figure 34–74.   Larvae of Saturnìidae. **A,** cecropia, *Hyalóphora cecròpia* (L.); **B,** promethea, *Callosàmia promèthea* (Drury); **C,** luna, *Áctias lùna* (L.); **D,** io, *Autómeris io* (Fabricius); **E,** polyphemus, *Antheraèa polyphèmus* (Cramer). *plg,* proleg. (Courtesy of Peterson; reprinted by permission.)

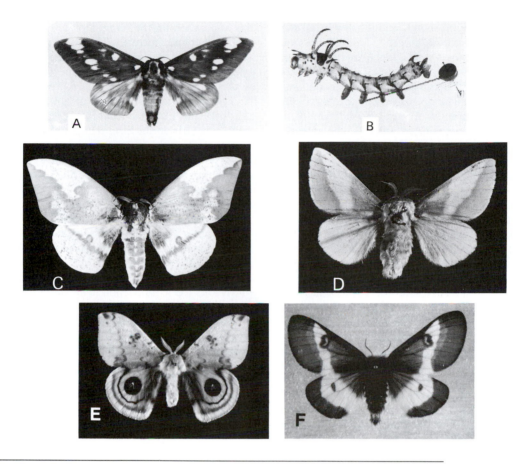

Figure 34–75.   Saturniid moths. **A,** adult, and **B,** larva of the regal moth, *Citherònia regàlis* (Fabricius), ½×; **C,** the imperial moth, *Èacles imperiàlis* (Drury), 1½×; **D,** the rosy maple moth, *Dryocámpa rubicúnda* (Fabricius), slightly enlarged; **E,** the io moth, *Autómeris ìo* (Fabricius), male, slightly reduced; **F,** the buck moth, *Hemileùca màia* (Drury), about natural size. **A–D,** Citheroniinae; **E–F,** Hemileucìnae.

brownish. The rosy maple moth, *Dryocámpa rubicúnda* (Fabricius), is pale yellow banded with pink (Figure 34–75D).

Subfamily **Hemileucìnae:** Some members of this group (*Autómeris*) have one anal vein in the hind wing, while others have two. The discal cell in the front wing is usually closed (Figure 34–22B); M₁ in the front wing is usually not stalked with R; and the antennae of the males are pectinate to the tip. Most moths in this group have wingspread of about 50 mm.

The io moth, *Autómeris ìo* (Fabricius), is one of the most common (and the largest) in this group. It has a wingspread of 50–75 mm and is yellow with a large eyespot in each hind wing (Figure 34–75E). The female is usually larger than the male, and its front wings are darker (reddish brown). The larva is

a spiny green caterpillar with a narrow reddish stripe, edged below with white, extending along each side of the body (Figure 34–74D). This larva should be handled with care, as the spines sting.

The buck moth, *Hemileùca màia* (Drury), is a little smaller than the io and is blackish with a narrow yellow band through the middle of each wing (Figure 34–75F). It occurs throughout the East, but it is not common. It is largely diurnal in habit, and its larva (which has stinging hairs) pupates in the ground. *Hemileùca nevadénsis* Stretch is a similar species occurring in the West. Its larva feeds on willow and poplar. Other species of *Hemileùca* feed on other trees or on grasses. Buck moths have a very rapid flight and are difficult to capture.

The pandora moth, *Colorádia pandòra* Blake, a western species, is a little smaller than the io. It is gray with lighter hind wings, and it has a small dark spot near the center of each wing. This species is an important defoliator of pines in the West.

Subfamily **Saturniinae**—Giant Silkworm Moths: The members of this subfamily have one anal vein in the hind wing; the discal cell of the front wing may be open (Figure 34–22C) or closed; and M_1 in the front wing is not stalked with R. The antennae of the male are pectinate to the tip.

The largest member of this subfamily in North America is the cecropia moth, *Hyalóphora cecròpia* (L.). Most individuals have a wingspread of 130–150 mm. The wings are reddish brown, crossed a little distad of the middle by a white band. In the middle of each wing is a crescent-shaped white spot bordered with red (Figure 34–76D). The larva (Figure 34–74A) is a greenish caterpillar that reaches a length of about 100 mm. It has two rows of yellow tubercles down the back and two pairs of large red tubercles on the thoracic segments. The cocoons are formed on twigs. Three related and very similar species of *Hyalóphora* occur in the West.

The promethea moth, *Callosàmia promèthea* (Drury), is sometimes called the spicebush silk moth because its larva feeds on spicebush, sassafras, and related plants. This moth is considerably smaller than the cecropia. The female is patterned a little like the cecropia, but the male (Figure 34–76B) is much darker, with a narrow marginal band of yellowish on the wings. Males often fly about during the day and, when on the wing, look a little like a large mourning cloak butterfly. The cocoon is formed in a leaf. The larva prevents the leaf from falling by securely fastening the petiole of the leaf to the twig with silk.

One of the most beautiful moths in this group is the luna moth, *Áctias lùna* (L.), a light green moth with long tails on the hind wings and with the costal border of the front wings narrowly bordered by dark brown (Figure 34–76C). The larva (Figure 34–74C) is greenish and feeds on walnut, hickory, and other trees, and its cocoon is formed in a leaf on the ground.

Another common moth in this group is the polyphemus moth, *Antheraèa polyphèmus* (Cramer), a large yellowish brown moth with a windowlike spot in each wing (Figure 34–76A). The larva (Figure 34–74E) is similar to that of the luna moth and feeds on various trees. Its cocoon is formed in a leaf on the ground.

Family **Sphíngidae**—Sphinx or Hawk Moths, Hornworms: The sphinx moths are medium-sized to large, heavy-bodied moths with long narrow front wings (Figure 34–77). Some have a wingspread of 160 mm or more. The body is somewhat spindle-shaped, tapering, and pointed both anteriorly and posteriorly. The antennae are slightly thickened in the middle or toward the tip. The subcosta and radius in the hind wing are connected by a cross vein (R_1) about opposite the middle of the discal cell (Figure 34–19B).

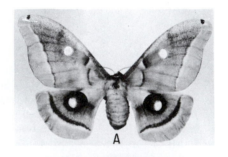

Figure 34–76. Giant silkworm moths (Saturniinae). **A,** the polyphemus, *Antheraèa polyphèmus* (Cramer); **B,** the promethea, *Callosàmia promèthea* (Drury); **C,** the luna, *Áctias lùna* (L.); **D,** the cecropia, *Hyalóphora cecròpia* (L.). **A** and **B,** ½×; **C** and **D,** ⅓×.

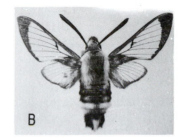

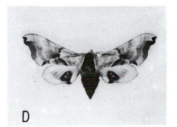

Figure 34–77.   Sphinx or hawk moths (Sphíngidae). **A,** the white-lined sphinx, *Hỳles lineàta* (Fabricius); **B,** a clear-winged sphinx, *Hémaris díffinis* (Boisduval); **C,** adult of the tobacco hornworm, *Mandùca séxta* (L.); **D,** the twin-spot sphinx, *Smerínthus jamaicénsis* (Drury). **A, C,** and **D,** ½×, **B,** about natural size.

The proboscis in many species is very long, sometimes as long as the body or longer. There are about 125 species of sphingids in North America.

These moths are strong fliers and fly with a very rapid wing beat. Some are day-fliers, but most of them are active at dusk or twilight. Most of them feed much like hummingbirds, hovering in front of a flower and extending their proboscis into it. These moths are sometimes called hummingbird moths, and in many species the body is about the size of a hummingbird. Some species (for example, *Hémaris*) have large areas in the wings devoid of scales and are called clear-wing sphinx moths. These are not to be confused with the clearwing moths of the family Sesìidae, which are smaller and more slender and have the front wings much more elongate (compare Figures 34–77B and 34–45).

The name "hornworm" is derived from the fact that the larvae of most species have a conspicuous horn or spinelike process on the dorsal surface of the eighth abdominal segment (Figure 34–78A). The name "sphinx" probably refers to the sphinxlike position that some of these larvae assume when disturbed. The larvae of most species pupate in the ground, in some cases forming pitcherlike pupae

(proboscis of the pupa looks like a handle). Some species form a sort of cocoon among leaves on the surface of the ground.

One of the most common species in this group is the tomato hornworm, *Mandùca quinquemaculàta* (Haworth). The larva (Figure 34–78A) is a large green caterpillar that feeds on tomato, tobacco, and potato. The larva of a similar species, *M. séxta* (L.), feeds on tobacco and other plants. The adults of these two species are large gray moths with a wingspread of about 100 mm. The hind wings are banded, and there are five (*quinquemaculàta*) or six (*séxta*) orange-yellow spots along each side of the abdomen (Figure 34–77C). These hornworms often do considerable damage to the plants on which they feed. Hornworms are often attacked by braconid parasites, which form small white silken cocoons on the outside of the caterpillar (Figure 34–78B).

The largest North American sphingids (in terms of wing surface area) are females of the southwestern *Páchysphinx occidentàlis* (H. Edwards), with a wingspread of up to 160 mm. A tropical species, *Cocỳtius antaèus* (Drury), which barely enters our area in southern Texas and Florida, can be even larger than *P. occidentàlis*. The smallest North American sphin-

Figure 34–78.   **A,** the tomato hornworm, *Mandùca quinquemaculàta* (Haworth); **B,** a parasitized hornworm; the white objects on the back of this larva are cocoons of braconid parasites. (**A,** courtesy of the Ohio Agricultural Research and Development Center.)

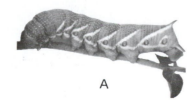

gid is probably *Cautèthia gròtei* H. Edwards, which has a wingspread of just over 30 mm.

Family **Notodóntidae**—Prominents: The prominents are usually brownish or yellowish moths that are similar to the Noctùidae in general appearance. The family and subfamily names (*not*, back; *odont*, tooth) refer to the fact that in some species there are backward-projecting tufts on the hind margin of the wings, which protrude when the wings are folded (they are usually folded rooflike over the body when at rest), and the larvae have conspicuous tubercles on the dorsal surface of the body. The prominents may be readily distinguished from the noctuids by the venation of the front wing (Figure 34–21B). In the Notodontidae, M_2 in the front wing arises from the middle of the apex of the discal cell, and the cubitus appears three-branched, whereas in the Noctùidae, M_2 in the front wing arises closer to M_3, and the cubitus appears four-branched (Figure 34–27). There are nearly 140 North American species in this family.

Notodontid larvae feed on various trees and shrubs and are usually gregarious. When disturbed, they often elevate the anterior and posterior ends of the body and "freeze" in this position, remaining attached by the four pairs of prolegs in the middle of the body. The anal pair of prolegs is often rudimentary or modified into spinelike structures.

In this group, most of the brownish moths that have narrow dark lines across the front wings belong to the genus *Datàna*. These are sometimes called handmaid moths (Figure 34–79A). The larvae are blackish with yellow longitudinal stripes. The yellow-necked caterpillar, *D. minístra* (Drury), feeds on apple and other trees. The walnut caterpillar, *D. integérrima* Grote and Robinson, feeds principally on walnut and hickory.

The red-humped caterpillar, *Schizùra concínna* (J. E. Smith), is a fairly common species in this group. The larva is black with yellow stripes, with the head and a hump on the first abdominal segment red (Figure 34–79B). The adult has a wingspread of a little over 25 mm. The front wings are gray with brown markings, and the hind wings are white with a small black spot along the rear edge. The larva feeds on apple and other orchard trees and on various shrubs.

Family **Dióptidae**—Oakworms: This is a New World group, most members of which occur in South America. Only two species occur in the United States. The only common species is the California oakworm, *Phryganídia califòrnica* Packard, which occurs in California. The adults are slender moths, pale translucent brown with dark veins, and have a wingspread of about 30 mm. The larvae feed on oak leaves and often do considerable damage.

Family **Lymantriidae**—Tussock Moths and Their Relatives: The lymantriids are medium-sized moths that are similar to the Noctùidae but differ in that they lack ocelli and have the basal areole in the hind wing larger (Figure 34–28). In most species (Figure 34–28A), M_1 in the hind wing is stalked with Rs for a short distance beyond the apex of the discal cell. The larvae are rather hairy and feed chiefly on trees. The tussock, gypsy, and browntail moths are serious pests of forest and shade trees. The tussock moths are native species, whereas the other two were introduced from Europe. There are 32 species of lymantriids in our area.

The white-marked tussock moth, *Òrgyia leucostígma* (J. E. Smith) (Figure 34–80), is a common species throughout most of North America. The males are gray, with lighter hind wings and plumose antennae, and the females are wingless. The eggs are laid on tree trunks or branches, usually near the cocoon from which the female emerged, and the species overwinters in the egg stage. The larva (Figure 34–80A) may be recognized by the characteristic tufts or brushes of hairs.

The gypsy moth, *Lymántria díspar* (L.), was introduced from Europe into Massachusetts about 1866. Since then, it has become widely distributed throughout New England and has caused widespread damage to forest trees. The females are white with black markings, and the males are gray (Figure 34–81). The females have a wingspread of about 40

Figure 34–79. Notodóntidae. **A,** *Datàna minístra* (Drury); **B,** the red-humped caterpillar, *Schizùra concínna* (J. E. Smith). Natural size. (**B,** courtesy of the Ohio Agricultural Research and Development Center.)

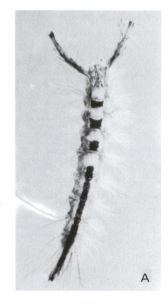

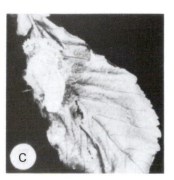

Figure 34–80.   The white-marked tussock moth, *Orgyia leucostígma* (J. E. Smith). **A**, larva; **B**, adult male; **C**, adult female. Slightly enlarged. (**A** and **C**, courtesy of the Ohio Agricultural Research and Development Center; **B**, photographed by Carl W. Albrecht.)

to 50 mm and the males are a little smaller. The eggs are laid on tree trunks or similar places, in a mass of the body hairs from the female. They overwinter and hatch the following spring. The females are very weak fliers and seldom travel very far from the cocoon from which they emerge. The dispersal of the species is accomplished largely by the young larvae.

The browntail moth, *Nýgmia phaeorrhoèa* (Donovan), is another serious pest of forest and shade trees that was introduced from Europe. It first appeared near Boston in the early 1890s and has since spread throughout New England. The adults are white, with a wingspread of 25–35 mm, and they have brownish hairs at the end of the abdomen. The males are a little smaller than the females. This species passes the winter as a larva in a leaf shelter. Both sexes are winged. The hairs of the larva, when blown onto human skin, cause an irritating rash.

The satin moth, *Leucòma sálicis* (L.), is a European species that appeared in the United States in 1920. It feeds on poplars and willows and is an occasional pest of poplars planted as shade trees or windbreaks. After its introduction it was considered an important pest, but the introduction of some European parasites has greatly reduced its numbers and importance.

Family **Arctiidae**—Tiger Moths, Footman Moths, Wasp Moths, and Others: This is a fairly large group (about 265 North American species), divided into four subfamilies (which are given family rank by some authorities): Pericopìnae, Lithosiìnae, Arctiìnae, and Ctenuchìnae.

Subfamily **Pericopìnae:**   The Pericopìnae are medium-sized moths that are usually black with large white areas in the wings. They occur in the South and West and are our most primitive arctiids. *Compòsia fidelíssima* Herrich-Schäffer, a day-flier, is a dark blue moth marked with red and white, found in southern Florida. Species in the genus *Gnophaèla* occur in the western and southwestern United States. Many tropical pericopines are among the most strikingly colored of all arctiids.

Subfamily **Lithosiìnae**—Footman Moths: The footman moths are small and slender-bodied, and most of our species are rather dull-colored. Some tropical species, however, are very colorful. The larvae of most species feed on lichens. The striped footman

Figure 34–81.   The gypsy moth, *Lymántria díspar* (L.), $\frac{2}{3} \times$. Male above, female below.

moth, *Hypoprèpia miniàta* (Kirby), is a beautiful insect. It has the front wings pinkish with three gray stripes, and the hind wings are yellow and broadly margined with gray. The lichen moth, *Lycomórpha phòlus* (Drury), is a small blackish moth with the base of the wings yellowish (Figure 34–82C). It looks a little like some of the lycid beetles. These moths occur in rocky places, and their larvae feed on lichens that grow on the rocks. Many species of the genus *Cisthène* are gray with various red markings or have other color combinations.

Subfamily **Arctiìnae**—Tiger Moths: This group contains the majority of the species in the family, and many of them are very common insects. A few are occasionally rather destructive to trees and shrubs. Many are very colorful and thus popular with collectors.

Most tiger moths are small to medium-sized and brightly spotted or banded. Some are white or rather uniformly brownish. The wing venation is very similar to that in the Noctuìdae, but Sc and Rs in the hind wing are usually fused to about the middle of the discal cell (Figure 34–26). These moths are principally nocturnal and, when at rest, hold the wings rooflike over the body. The larvae are usually hairy, sometimes very much so. The so-called woollybear caterpillars belong to this group. The cocoons are made largely from the body hairs of the larvae.

The tiger moths in the genus *Apántesis* have the front wings black with red or yellow stripes, and the hind wings are usually pinkish with black spots. One of the largest and most common species in the genus is *A. vírgo* (L.), which has a wingspread of about 50 mm (Figure 34–83A). The larva feeds on pigweed and other weeds and winters in the larval stage.

Estigmène acrèa (Drury) is another common tiger moth. The adults are white, with numerous small black spots on the wings, and the abdomen is pinkish with black spots (Figure 34–83B). The male's hind wings are yellowish. The larva feeds on various grasses and is sometimes called the salt-marsh caterpillar.

One of the best-known woollybear caterpillars is the banded woollybear, *Pyrrhárctia isabélla* (J. E. Smith). This caterpillar is brown in the middle and black at each end, and the adult is yellowish brown with three rows of small black spots on the abdomen. These caterpillars are often seen scurrying across the highways in the fall. They overwinter as larvae and pupate in the spring. The larva feeds on various weeds. The amount of black in the larva in the fall is thought by some to vary proportionately with the severity of the coming winter.

The larvae of some of the tiger moths feed on trees and shrubs and may often do serious damage. The fall webworm, *Hyphántria cùnea* (Drury), is a common species of this type. The larvae build large webs, often enclosing a limb of foliage, and feed within the web. These webs are common on many types of trees in late summer and fall. The adults are usually white with a few dark spots and have a wingspread of about 25 mm. Some are all white, or they may have varying amounts of black spotting. The larvae of the hickory tussock moth, *Lophocámpa càryae* (Harris) (Figure 34–84B), feed on hickory and other trees. The larva is somewhat similar to that of the tussock moths in the genus *Òrgyia*. The adults (Figure 34–84A) are light brown with white spots on the wings.

Subfamily **Ctenuchìnae**—Ctenuchas and Wasp Moths: These are small day-flying moths, some of which are wasplike in appearance (but not as wasplike as the Sesìidae). Most species are tropical and very colorful. They can be recognized by the vena-

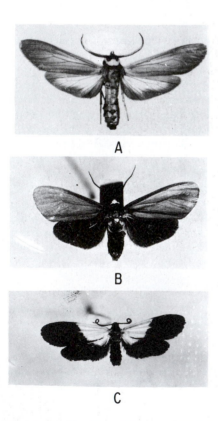

Figure 34–82. Arctiid moths. **A,** the yellow-collared scape moth, *Císseps fulvicóllis* (Hübner), 1½×; **B,** the Virginia ctenucha, *Ctenùcha virgínica* (Esper), natural size; **C,** the lichen moth, *Lycomórpha phòlus* (Drury), 1½×.

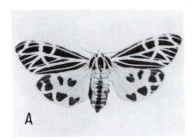

Figure 34–83.   Tiger moths (Arctiìnae). **A,** the virgin tiger moth, *Apántesis vírgo* (L.), ¾×; **B,** adult of the salt-marsh caterpillar, *Estígmene acrèa* (Drury), 1½×.

tion of the hind wing (Figure 34–25A): the subcosta is apparently absent. In the West, some species of ctenuchas are occasionally seen flying in large numbers, as if in migration.

Ctenùcha virgínica (Esper), a common species in the Northeast, has brownish black wings, a brilliant metallic bluish body, and an orange head (Figure 34–82B). The larva is a woolly yellowish caterpillar that feeds on grasses. The cocoon is formed largely of the body hairs of the caterpillar. The yellow-collared scape moth, *Císseps fulvicóllis* (Hübner), is somewhat smaller than the ctenucha, with narrower wings and with the central portion of the hind wings ligthter. Its prothorax is yellowish (Figure 34–82A). The larva of this species feeds on grasses, and the adults frequent goldenrod flowers.

Family **Noctùidae:**   This is the largest family in the order, with more than 2900 species in the United States and Canada. These moths are mostly nocturnal in habit, and the majority of the moths that are attracted to lights at night belong to this family.

The noctuids are mostly heavy-bodied moths with the front wings somewhat narrowed and the hind wings broadened (Figures 34–85, 34–86). The labial palps are usually long; the antennae are generally hairlike (sometimes brushlike in the males); and in some species there are tufts of scales on the dorsum of the thorax. The wing venation (Figures 34–24B, 34–27) is rather characteristic: M_2 in the front wing arises closer to M_3 than to M_1, and the cubitus appears four-branched; the subcosta and radius in the hind wing are separate at the base but fuse for a short distance at the base of the discal cell; and M_2 in the hind wing may be present or absent.

Figure 34–84.   The hickory tussock moth, *Lophocámpa càryae* (Harris) (Arctiìdae). **A,** adult, 1½×; **B,** larva. (Courtesy of Knull.)

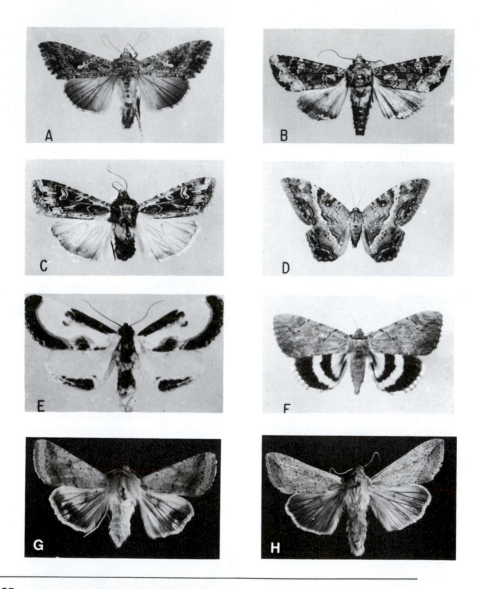

Figure 34–85. Noctuid moths. **A,** adult of the cabbage looper, *Trichoplùsia nì* (Hübner); **B,** adult of the yellow-headed cutworm, *Apàmea amputàtrix* (Fitch); **C,** *Eùxoa éxcellens* Grote (adult of one of the cutworms); **D,** the black witch, *Ascálapha odoràta* (L.); **E,** *Euthisanòtia gràta* Fabricius; **F,** the darling underwing, *Catócala càra* Guenée; **G,** adult of the corn earworm, *Heliòthis zèa* (Boddie); **H,** adult of the armyworm, *Pseudalètia unipúncta* (Haworth). **D,** $\frac{1}{3}\times$. **F,** slightly reduced; the other figures approximately natural size. (**G** and **H,** courtesy of the Ohio Agricultural Research and Development Center.)

Noctuid larvae are usually smooth and dull-colored (Figure 34–87), and most of them have five pairs of prolegs. The majority feed on foliage, but some are boring in habit and some feed on fruits. A number of species in this group are serious pests of various crops.

The family Noctùidae is divided into a number of subfamilies, some of which have been given family rank. No attempt will be made here to characterize all these subfamilies, and only a few of them will be mentioned.

Subfamilies **Herminìinae, Rivulìnae, Hypenodìnae,** *and* **Hypenìnae:** These moths are the most primitive noctuids and are commonly called quadrifids (M_2 in the hind wing is well developed, and the cubitus thus appears four-branched). Many of them

Figure 34–86. The eight-spotted forester, *Alýpia octomaculàta* (Fabricius), 1½×.

resemble pyralids, but they can be distinguished by their naked proboscis. *Nigètia formosàlis* Walker (Hypenodìnae) is a rather pretty mottled moth that is fairly common in the eastern United States.

Subfamily **Catocalìnae:** This group includes the underwings, relatively large and strikingly colored moths of the genus *Catócala*. They are forest or woodland species, and their larvae feed on the foliage of various trees. The hind wings are usually brightly colored with concentric bands of red, yellow, or orange (Figure 34–85F). At rest, the hind wings are concealed, and the front wings are colored much like the bark of the trees on which these moths usually rest. This group includes the largest noctuid in the United States, the black witch, *Ascálapha odoràta* (L.). This is a blackish species with a wingspread of 100–130 mm (Figure 34–85D). It breeds in the southern states, where the larvae feed on various leguminous trees. The adults sometimes appear in the northern states in late summer. *Ascálapha* and its relatives are sometimes placed in a separate subfamily, the Erebìnae. Other Catocalìnae include the large grass-feeding moths in the genus *Mòcis*, which occur in the Southeast and in the tropics.

Subfamily **Plusiìnae**—Loopers: These insects are called loopers because they have only three pairs of prolegs and move like measuringworms. The cabbage looper, *Trichoplùsia nì* (Hübner), is a serious pest of cabbage, and the celery looper, *Anágrapha falcífera* (Kirby), attacks celery. The adults of these loopers are dark brown, with a wingspread of about 35–40 mm, and have a small elongate silver spot in the middle of each front wing (Figure 34–85A). Many plusiines have golden or silver metallic markings in the front wings.

Subfamily **Nolìnae:** This group, which has been given family rank, contains small moths that have ridges and tufts of raised scales on the front wings. *Nòla ovílla* Grote is fairly common in Pennsylvania on the trunks of beeches and oaks. The larva feeds on the lichens growing on the trunks of these trees.

The larva of *N. triquetràna* (Fitch), a gray moth with a wingspread of 17–20 mm, feeds on apple, but it is seldom numerous enough to do much damage. The larva of the sorghum webworm, *N. sorghiélla* Riley, is a pest of sorghum.

Subfamily **Acontiìnae:** This group contains some of the most colorful noctuids. *Cydòsia nobilitélla* (Cramer) is a common species in the Southeast and is often confused with ermine moths in the genus *Átteva*. Species of *Spragueía* are also common in the East and are usually a mottled orange and black. The small moths of the genera *Tripùdia* and *Cobubàtha* of the Southeast are often confused with tortricids. They can be easily distinguished by their thoracic tympanal organs.

Subfamily **Agaristìnae**—Forester Moths: The foresters are usually black with two whitish or yellowish spots in each wing, and they have a wingspread of about 25 mm. The antennae are slightly clubbed. The eight-spotted forester, *Alýpia octomaculàta* (Fabricius), is a common species in this group (Figure 34–86). The larvae feed on grape and Virginia creeper and sometimes defoliate them. There are larger forester moths in the Southwest. The black and yellow *Gérra sevórsa* (Grote) of Arizona resembles some arctiids.

Subfamily **Amphipyrìnae:** This subfamily includes the genus *Spodóptera* (which contains several

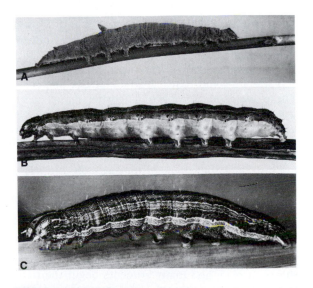

Figure 34–87. Larvae of Noctùidae. **A,** *Catocàla ultrònia* Hübner (an underwing); **B,** the fall armyworm, *Spodóptera frugipérda* (J. E. Smith); **C,** the armyworm, *Pseudalètia unipúncta* (Haworth). (Courtesy of the Ohio Agricultural Research and Development Center.)

species of armyworms) and such colorful diurnal moths as the western species of *Annáphila*.

Subfamilies **Noctuìnae** and **Hadenìnae:**   The larvae of many species in these groups (and in some other subfamilies as well) are called cutworms because they feed on the roots and shoots of various herbaceous plants, and the plant is often cut off at the surface of the ground. The cutworms are nocturnal in habit and hide under stones or in the soil during the day. The most important cutworms belong to the genera *Agròtis*, *Eùxoa*, *Féltia*, and *Perídroma* of the Noctuìnae and to *Lacinipòlia*, *Nephelòdes*, and *Scotográmma* of the Hadenìnae.

The corn earworm, *Heliòthis zèa* (Boddie) (Heliothìnae), is a serious pest. The larva feeds on a number of plants, including corn, tomato, and cotton, and is sometimes called the tomato fruitworm or the cotton bollworm. When feeding on corn (Figure 34–88), the larva enters the corn ear on the silks and eats the kernels from the tip of the cob. It burrows in the fruits of tomatoes and into the bolls of cotton. The adults are light yellowish in color and exhibit some variation in their markings (Figure 34–85G).

The armyworm, *Pseudalètia unipúncta* (Haworth) (Hadenìnae), feeds on various grasses and frequently does serious damage to wheat and corn. The common name of this insect refers to the fact that the larvae frequently migrate in large numbers to a new feeding area. The moths are light brown with a single white spot in the middle of each front wing (Figure 34–85H).

The noctuids have a pair of tympanal auditory organs located at the base of the metathorax. (Such organs are present in several other families of moths and are in some cases located on the abdomen.) These organs are capable of detecting frequencies of from 3 to more than 100 kHz,[3] and they appear to function in the detection and evasion of bats. Bats are able to detect prey (and obstacles) in complete darkness by means of a sort of sonar. They emit very high-pitched clicks (sometimes as high as 80 kHz) and locate objects from the echoes of these clicks.

Collecting and Preserving Lepidóptera

The order Lepidóptera contains many large and showy insects, and many students begin their collecting with these insects. Lepidóptera are generally fairly easy to collect, but they are more difficult to mount and preserve in good condition than insects in most other orders. Specimens must always be handled with great care because the scales, which give the specimens their color, are easily rubbed off, and in many species the wings are easily torn or broken.

Lepidóptera may be collected with a net, or they may be gotten directly into a killing jar without the use of a net. A net for collecting these insects should be of a fairly light mesh, light enough that the specimen can be seen through the net. Once netted, a specimen should be gotten into a killing jar or stunned as quickly as possible so that it will not damage its wings by fluttering and attempting to escape. Many collectors prefer to insert the killing jar into the net to get the specimen into the jar without handling the specimen directly. The killing jar should be of sufficient toxic strength to stun the insect quickly. If the specimen is removed to the killing jar by hand, it should be grasped carefully through the net by the body, pinched slightly to stun it, and then placed in the killing jar. It is not recommended that delicate species such as blues and hairstreaks be pinched. Large moths are most easily killed by the injection of alcohol into the thorax with a hypodermic needle (only a few drops are needed).

Many moths can be taken directly into a killing jar without the use of a net. A wide-mouthed jar is simply placed over the specimen when it is resting on some flat surface. The jar should be strong enough to stun the insect quickly, before it can flutter about too much inside the jar and damage its wings.

The best place to collect most Lepidóptera is on

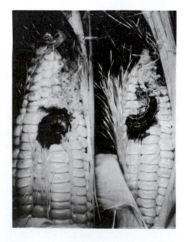

Figure 34–88.   Larva of the corn earworm, *Heliòthis zèa* (Boddie). (Courtesy of the Ohio Agricultural Research and Development Center.)

---

[3]Three kilohertz is in the top octave of the piano; the average upper limit of hearing in humans is about 15 or 16 kHz.

or near the plant on which the larva feeds. Many species, particularly butterflies, frequent flowers and may be collected while feeding. To obtain a large number of species, one must visit a variety of habitats and collect at all seasons. Many species occur only in certain habitats, and many have a short adult life and are on the wing only a short time each year.

Many moths are most easily collected at lights, especially ultraviolet ("black") lights. They may be collected by traps, but specimens collected in this way are often in poor condition unless special precautions are taken. Traps should have a screen of ⅜-inch mesh near the bottom to keep large specimens away from smaller ones, and there should be plenty of folded paper and the like to provide hiding places. A strong poison is needed, such as cyanide (usually calcium cyanide), and thus considerable care is needed in the operation of the trap. A stun trap could be made by using blocks of ice in the bottom, with ample provision for keeping the moisture down. The low temperatures in such a trap would immobilize the specimens, which could be removed in the morning or after a few hours of operation.

Specimens can be collected at lights if there is a flat white surface near the light for the insects to land on. The specimens can be taken directly from such a surface into a killing jar. Many interesting species can be obtained by sugaring (see Chapter 36).

One must take precautions to prevent specimens from becoming damaged after they are placed in the killing jar. The jar should be strong enough to stun a specimen quickly. Large and heavy-bodied specimens should not be placed in a jar along with small and delicate ones. The jar should not be allowed to become too crowded. It is advisable to remove the specimens soon after they have been stunned and then to place them in paper envelopes. Small moths are perhaps best killed in small cyanide vials (like that shown in Figure 36–4A), with pieces of cleansing tissue inside to prevent the insects from touching each other too much.

The best way to obtain good specimens of many species is to rear them, from either larvae or pupae. Suggestions for rearing are given in Chapter 36. By rearing, the collector not only obtains good specimens, but also can become acquainted with the larval stages of different species and the plants on which the larvae feed.

Specimens of Lepidóptera can be preserved in a collection in three ways: in paper envelopes (as in the case of Odonàta and some other groups), spread and pinned, and spread and mounted under glass (in Riker or glass mounts). Envelopes are used for temporary storage or in cases where the collection is large and space is not available for large numbers of spread specimens. If one desires to display his collection, the most useful type of mount is a Riker or glass mount. The best collections of Lepidóptera have the specimens pinned and spread. Many collectors find it best to field pin the smaller moths and spread them later. Moths with a wingspread of less than 10 mm should generally be pinned with a minuten pin and double-mounted as shown in Figure 36–14D.

All Lepidóptera that are pinned or mounted under glass should be spread. The beginning student or the person interested principally in displaying his collection is advised to spread his specimens in an upside-down position (Figure 36–13) and mount them in a glass or Riker mount. The advanced student or the person making a large collection should pin them or keep them in envelopes. Methods of spreading and mounting Lepidóptera are described in Chapter 36. It takes a little practice to become proficient in spreading these insects, and some of the smaller specimens will tax the skill and patience of the collector, but the resulting collection will be worth the effort. Even Microlepidóptera can be spread with the right equipment and practice. Some collectors spread micros in the field, or at least "puff" out their wings.

In a large collection of pinned Lepidóptera, space can be saved by putting the pins into the bottom of the box at an angle and overlapping the wings of adjacent specimens. A collection must be protected against museum pests by having naphthalene or some similar repellent in the boxes. It should be kept in the dark, for many specimens will fade if exposed to light for long periods.

References

Braun, A. F. 1948. Elachistidae of North America (Microlepidoptera). Mem. Amer. Entomol. Soc. 13:1–110; illus.

Braun, A. F. 1963. The genus *Bucculatrix* in America north of Mexico (Microlepidoptera). Mem. Amer. Entomol. Soc. 18:1–208; illus.

Braun, A. F. 1972. Tischeriidae of America north of Mexico (Microlepidoptera). Mem. Amer. Entomol. Soc. 28:1–148; illus.

Brewer, J. 1976. Butterflies. New York: Harry N. Abrams, 176 pp.; illus.

Brown, F. M., D. Eff, and B. Rotger. 1957. Colorado Butter-flies. Denver: Denver Mus. Nat. Hist., 368 pp.; illus.

Chapman, P. J., and S. E. Lienk. 1971. Tortricid Fauna of Apple in New York. Geneva: N.Y. State Agr. Expt. Sta., Cornell Univ., 122 pp.; illus. (Includes apple-feeding Gelechiidae and Oecophoridae.)

Clark, A. H., and L. F. Clark. 1951. The butterflies of Virginia. Smithson. Misc. Coll. 116(7):1–239; illus.

Collins, M. M., and R. D. Weast. 1981. Wild Silk Moths of the United States: Saturniinae. Cedar Rapids, Iowa: Collins Radio Company, 138 pp.; illus.

Common, I. F. B. 1970. Lepidoptera (moths and butterflies), pp. 765–866 in The Insects of Australia. Melbourne: Melbourne Univ. Press; illus.

Common, I. F. B. 1975. Evolution and classification of the Lepidoptera. Annu. Rev. Entomol. 20:183–203.

Covell, C. V., Jr. 1984. A Field Guide to the Moths of Eastern North America. Boston: Houghton Mifflin, 496 pp.; illus.

Davis, D. R. 1964. Bagworm moths of the western Hemisphere (Lepidoptera: Psychidae). U.S. Natl. Mus. Bull. 244:1–233; illus.

Davis, D. R. 1967. A revision of the moths of the subfamily Prodoxinae (Lepidoptera: Incurvariidae). U.S. Natl. Mus. Bull. 255:1–170; illus.

Davis, D. R. 1968. A revision of the American moths of the family Carposinidae (Lepidoptera: Carposinoidea). U.S. Natl. Mus. Bull. 289:1–105; illus.

Davis, D. R. 1975. A review of the Ochsenheimeriidae and the introduction of the cereal stem moth, *Ochsenheimeria vacculella* into the United States (Lepidoptera: Tineoidea). Smithson. Contrib. Zool. No. 192, 20 pp.; illus.

Davis, D. R. 1978a. A revision of the North American moths of the superfamily Eriocranioidea with the proposal of a new family, Acanthopteroctetidae (Lepidoptera). Smithson. Contrib. Zool. No. 251, 131 pp.; illus.

Davis, D. R. 1978b. The North American moths of the genera *Phaeoses*, *Opogona*, and *Oinophila*, with a discussion of the supergeneric affinities (Lepidoptera: Tineidae). Smithson. Contrib. Zool. No. 282, 39 pp.; illus.

Dominick, R. B. (Ed.). 1972—. The Moths of America North of Mexico. Oxford, England: E. W. Classey. (This is an ongoing series that, when complete, will consist of identification manuals for all species of moths occurring in North America north of Mexico. It will be published in about 150 parts, making 30 fascicles, written by selected specialists. The parts published to date are listed here under their respective authors.)

Dornfeld, F. J. 1980. The Butterflies of Oregon. Forest Grove: Timber Press, 275 pp.; illus.

Dos Passos, C. F. 1964. A synoptic list of Nearctic Rhopalocera. Lepidop. Soc. Mem. 1;145 pp.

Duckworth, W. D. 1964. North American Stenomidae (Lepidoptera: Gelechioidea). Proc. U.S. Natl. Mus. 116:23–72; illus.

Duckworth, W. D., and T. D. Eichlin. 1977. A classification of the Sesiidae of America north of Mexico. Occas. Pap. Entomol. (Calif. Dept. Agr.) 26:1–54.

Duckworth, W. D., and T. D. Eichlin. 1978. The clearwing moths of California (Lepidoptera: Sesiidae). Occas. Pap. Entomol. (Calif. Dept. Agr.) 27:1–80; illus.

Ebner, J. A. 1970. The butterflies of Wisconsin. Milwaukee Public Museum Popular Science Handbook No. 12, 205 pp.; illus.

Ehrlich, P. R. 1958. The comparative morphology, phylogeny, and higher classification of the butterflies (Lepidoptera: Papilionoidea). Univ. Kan. Sci. Bull. 39(8): 305–370; illus.

Ehrlich, P. R., and A. H. Ehrlich. 1961. How to Know the Butterflies. Dubuque, Iowa: Wm. C. Brown, 262 pp.; illus.

Eichlin, T. D., and H. B. Cunningham. 1978. The Plusiinae (Lepidoptera: Noctuidae) of America north of Mexico, emphasizing genitalic and larval morphology. USDA Tech. Bull. 1567, 122 pp.; illus.

Emmel, T. C. 1975. Butterflies. New York: Knopf, 260 pp.; illus.

Emmel, T. C., and J. F. Emmel. 1973. The butterflies of southern California. Nat. Hist. Mus. Los Angeles County Sci. Ser. 26:1–148; illus.

Evans, W. H. 1951–1955. Catalogue of American Hesperiidae. London: Brit. Mus. Nat. Hist., 3 vol., 521 pp.; illus.

Ferguson, D. C. 1972a. Saturniidae: Citheroniinae and Hemileucinae in part. The Moths of America North of Mexico, ed. R. B. Dominick, Fasc. 20, Part 2A, 153 pp.; illus.

Ferguson, D. C. 1972b. Bombycoidea: Saturniidae (conclusion: Hemileucinae in part, and Saturniinae). The Moths of America North of Mexico, ed. R. B. Dominick, Fasc. 20, Part 2B, pp. 11–275; illus.

Ferguson, D. C. 1978. Noctuoidea: Lymantriidae. The Moths of America North of Mexico, ed. R. B. Dominick, Fasc. 22.2, 110 pp.; illus.

Ferguson, D. C. 1985a. Geometroidea: Geometridae (part), subfamily Geometrinae. The Moths of America North of Mexico, ed. R. B. Dominick, Fasc. 18(1), 131 pp.; illus.

Ferguson, D. C. 1985b. Contributions toward reclassification of the world genera of the tribe Arctiini, Part 1: Introduction and a revision of the *Neoarctia-Grammia* group (Lepidoptera: Arctiidae; Arctiinae). Entomography 3:181–275.

Ferris, C. D., and F. M. Brown (Eds.). 1980. Butterflies of the Rocky Mountain States. Norman: University of Oklahoma Press, 442 pp.; illus.

Field, W. D. 1940. A manual of the butterflies and skippers of Kansas. Bull. Univ. Kan. Biol. Ser., Bull. Dept. Entomol. 12:1–328; illus.

Field, W. D. 1971. Butterflies of the genus *Vanessa* and of the resurrected genera *Basaris* and *Cynthia* (Lepidoptera: Nymphalidae). Smithson. Contrib. Zool. No. 84, 105 pp.; illus.

Fletcher, D. S. 1979. The Generic Names of the Moths of the World, Vol. 3: Geometroidea. London: British Museum (Natural History).

Fletcher, D. S., and I. W. B. Nye. 1982. The Generic Names of the Moths of the World, Vol. 4: Bombycoidea, Mimallonoidea, Sphingoidea, Castnioidea, Cossoidea, Zygaenoidea, Sesioidea. London: British Museum (Natural History).

Fletcher, D. S., and I. W. B. Nye. 1984. The Generic Names of the Moths of the World, Vol. 5: Pyraloidea. London: British Museum (Natural History).

Forbes, W. T. M. 1923–1960. Lepidoptera of New York and neighboring states. Part 1: Primitive forms, Microlepidoptera, Cornell Univ. Agr. Expt. Sta. Mem. 68, 729 pp.; illus. (1923). Part 2: Geometridae, Sphingidae, Notodontidae, Lymantriidae, Cornell Univ. Agr. Expt. Sta. Mem. 274, 263 pp.; illus. (1948). Part 3: Noctuidae, Cornell Univ. Agr. Expt. Sta. Mem. 329, 433 pp.; illus. (1954). Part 4: Agaristidae through Nymphalidae including butterflies, Cornell Univ. Agr. Expt. Sta. Mem. 371, 188 pp.; illus. (1960).

Ford, E. B. 1944. Moths. London: Collins, 266 pp.; illus.

Franclemont, J. C. 1973. Mimallonoidea and Bombycoidea: Apatelodidae, Bombycidae, Lasiocampidae. The Moths of America North of Mexico, ed. R. B. Dominick, Fasc. 20, Part 1; 86 pp.; illus.

Freeman, H. A. 1969. Systematic review of the Megathymidae. J. Lepidop. Soc. 23, Suppl. 1:1–59; illus.

Garth, J. S., and J. W. Tilden. 1986. California Butterflies. Berkeley: Univ. California Press, 208 pp.; illus.

Hardwick, D. F. 1965. The corn earworm complex. Mem. Entomol. Soc. Can. 40:1–245; illus.

Hardwick, D. F. 1970a. A generic revision of the North American Heliothidinae (Lepidoptera: Noctuidae). Mem. Entomol. Soc. Can. 73:1–59; illus.

Hardwick, D. F. 1970b. The genus *Euxoa* (Lepidoptera: Noctuidae) in North America. 1. Subgenera *Orosagrotis*, *Longivesica*, *Chorizagrotis*, *Pleonoctopoda*, and *Crassivesica*. Mem. Entomol. Soc. Can. 67:1–177; illus.

Harris, L., Jr. 1972. Butterflies of Georgia. Norman: Univ. Oklahoma Press, 326 pp.; illus.

Hasbrouck, F. F. 1964. Moths of the family Acrolepiidae in America north of Mexico (Microlepidoptera). Proc. U.S. Natl. Mus. 114:487–706.

Heinrich, C. 1923. Revision of the North American moths of the subfamily Eucosminae of the family Olethreutidae. U.S. Natl. Mus. Bull. 123:1–298; illus.

Heinrich, C. 1926. Revision of the North American moths of the subfamilies Laspyresiinae and Olethreutinae. U.S. Natl. Mus. Bull. 132:1–261; illus.

Heinrich, C. 1956. American moths of the subfamily Phycitinae. U.S. Natl. Mus. Bull. 207:1–581; illus.

Heppner, J. B. 1985. The Sedge Moths of North America (Lepidoptera: Glyphipterigidae). Gainesville, Fla.: Flora and Fauna, 254 pp.; illus.

Heppner, J. B., and W. D. Duckworth. 1981. Classification of the superfamily Sesioidea (Lepidoptera: Ditrysia). Smithson. Contrib. Zool. 314:1–144; illus.

Hodges, R. W. 1962. A revision of the Cosmopterygidae of America north of Mexico, with a definition of the Momphidae and Walshiidae (Lepidoptera). Entomol. Amer. 42:1–171; illus.

Hodges, R. W. 1964. A review of the North American moths in the family Walshiidae (Lepidoptera: Gelechioidea). Proc. U.S. Natl. Mus. 115(3485):289–330; illus.

Hodges, R. W. 1966. Revision of the nearctic Gelechiidae. I. The *Lita* group (Lepidoptera: Gelechioidea). Proc. U.S. Natl. Mus. 119:1–66; illus.

Hodges, R. W. 1971. Sphingoidea: Sphingidae. The Moths of America North of Mexico, ed. R. B. Dominick, Fasc. 21, 158 pp.; illus.

Hodges, R. W. 1974. Gelechioidea, Oecophoridae. The Moths of America North of Mexico, ed. R. B. Dominick, Fasc. 6.2, 142 pp.; illus.

Hodges, R. W. 1978. Gelechioidea, Cosmopterigidae. The Moths of America North of Mexico, ed. R. B. Dominick, Fasc. 6.1, 166 pp., illus.

Hodges, R. W. 1986. Gelechioidea: Gelechiidae (part), Dichomeridinae. The Moths of America North of Mexico, ed. R. B. Dominick, Fasc. 21, 178 pp.; illus.

Hodges, R. W., *et al.* 1983. Check List of the Lepidoptera of America North of Mexico. London: E. W. Classey and Wedge Entomol. Res. Found., 284 pp.

Holland, W. J. 1931 (rev. ed.). The Butterfly Book. New York: Doubleday, 424 pp.; illus.

Holland, W. J. 1968. The Moth Book. New York: Dover, 479 pp.; illus. (A reprinting of a book published in 1903 by Doubleday, Page.)

Hooper, R. R. 1973. The Butterflies of Saskatchewan. Regina, Canada: Mus. Nat. Hist., 216 pp.

Howe, W. H. (Ed.). 1975. The Butterflies of North America. New York: Doubleday, 632 pp.; illus.

Kimball, C. P. 1965. Lepidoptera of Florida. Arthropods of Florida and Neighboring Land Areas 1:1–363; illus.

Klots, A. B. 1951. A Field Guide to the Butterflies. Boston: Houghton Mifflin, 349 pp.; illus.

Klots, A. B. 1958. The World of Butterflies and Moths. New York: McGraw-Hill, 207 pp.; illus.

Lafontaine, J. D. 1987. Noctuoidea: Noctuidae, Noctuinae (part: *Euxoa*). The Moths of America North of Mexico, ed. R. B. Dominick, Fasc. 27.2, 234 pp.; illus.

Lindsey, A. W., E. L. Bell, and R. C. Williams. 1931. Hesperioidea of North America. J. Sci. Lab. Denison Univ., 26:1–142; illus.

MacKay, M. R. 1968. The North American Aegeriidae (Lepidoptera): A revision based on late-instar larvae. Mem. Entomol. Soc. Can. 58:1–112; illus.

MacKay, M. R. 1977. Larvae of the North American Tortricinae (Lepidoptera: Tortricidae). Can. Entomol. Suppl. 28:1–182; illus.

MacNeill, C. D. 1964. The skippers of the genus *Hesperia* in western North America, with special reference to California (Lepidoptera: Hesperiidae). Univ. Calif. Publ. Entomol. 35:1–230; illus.

McDunnough, J. 1938–1939. Check list of the Lepidoptera of Canada and the United States of America. So. Calif. Acad. Sci. Mem. Part 1: Macrolepidoptera, 274 pp. (1938). Part 2: Microlepidoptera, 171 pp. (1939).

McGuffin, W. C. 1967–1981. Guide to the Geometridae of Canada (Lepidoptera). Mem. Entomol. Soc. Can. 50 (1967), 86 (1970), 101 (1977), 117 (1981); illus.

Miller, L. D., and F. M. Brown. 1981. A catalogue/checklist of the butterflies of America north of Mexico. Mem. Lepidop. Soc. 2:1–280.

Miller, W. E. 1987. Guide to the olethreutine moths of midland North America (Tortricidae). USDA For. Serv. Agr. Handbook 660, 104 pp.; illus.

Morris, R. F. 1980. Butterflies and moths of Newfoundland and Labrador: the Macrolepidoptera. St. John's: Agric. Can. Publ. 1691, 407 pp.; illus.

Munroe, E. G. 1972a. Pyralidae: Scopariinae and Nymphulinae. The Moths of America North of Mexico, ed. R. B. Dominick, Fasc. 13, Part 1A; 134 pp.

Munroe, E. G. 1972b. Pyralidae: Odontiinae and Glaphyriinae. The Moths of America North of Mexico, ed. R. B. Dominick, Fasc. 13, Part 1B, pp. 135–250.

Munroe, E. G. 1973. Pyralidae: The subfamily Evergestinae. The Moths of America North of Mexico, ed. R. B. Dominick, Fasc. 13, Part 1C; pp. 253–304; illus.

Munroe, E. G. 1976a. Pyralidae: Pyraustinae. The Moths of America North of Mexico, ed. R. B. Dominick, Fasc. 13, Part 2A, 78 pp.; illus.

Munroe, E. G. 1976b. Pyralidae: Pyraustinae, Tribe Pyraustini. The Moths of America North of Mexico, ed. R. B. Dominick, Fasc. 13, Part 2B, pp. 81–150; illus.

Neunzig, H. H. 1986. Pyraloidea: Pyralidae (part), Phycitinae (part—*Acrobasis* and allies). The Moths of America North of Mexico, ed. R. B. Dominick, Fasc. 15.2, 82 pp.; illus.

Newton, P. J., and C. Wilkinson. 1982. A taxonomic revision of the North American species of *Stigmella* (Lepidoptera: Nepticulidae). Syst. Entomol. 7:367–463; illus.

Nye, I. W. B. 1975. The Generic Names of the Moths of the World, Vol. 1: Noctuoidea (part). London: British Museum (Natural History).

Nye, I. W. B, and D. S. Fletcher. 1986. The Generic Names of the Moths of the World, Vol. 6: Microlepidoptera. London: British Museum (Natural History).

Opler, P. A., and G. O. Krizek. 1984. Butterflies East of the Great Plains: An Illustrated Natural History. Baltimore: Johns Hopkins Univ., 294 pp.; illus.

Peterson, A. 1948. Larvae of Insects, Part 1: Lepidoptera and Plant-Infesting Hymenoptera. Ann Arbor, Mich: J. E. Edwards, 315 pp.; illus.

Powell, J. A. 1964. Biological and taxonomic studies on tortricine moths, with reference to the species in California. Univ. Calif. Publ. Entomol. 32:1–317; illus.

Powell, J. A. 1973. A systematic monograph of New World ethmiid moths (Lepidoptera: Gelechioidea). Smithson. Contrib. Zool. No. 120, 302 pp.; illus.

Powell, J. A., and W. E. Miller. 1978. Nearctic pine tip moths of the genus *Rhyacionia*; biosystematic review (Lepidoptera: Tortricidae, Olethreutinae). USDA For. Serv. Agr. Handbook. 514:1–51; illus.

Rings, R. W. 1977. A pictorial key to the armyworms and cutworms attacking vegetables in the north central states. Res. Circ. 231, Ohio Agr. Res. Develop. Center, 36 pp.; illus.

Rockburne, E. W., and J. D. Lafontaine. 1976. The cutworm moths of Ontario and Quebec. Can. Dept. Agr. Publ. 1593, 164 pp.; illus.

Sargent, T. D. 1976. Legion of Night: The Underwing Moths. Amherst: Univ. Massachusetts Press, 222 pp.; illus.

Selman, C. L. 1975. A pictorial key to the hawkmoths (Lepidoptera: Sphingidae) of eastern United States (except Florida). Ohio Biol. Surv., Biol. Notes No. 9, 21 pp.; illus.

Shaffer, J. C. 1968. A revision of the Peoriinae and Anerastiinae (auctorum) of America north of Mexico (Lepidoptera: Pyralidae). Bull. U.S. Natl. Mus. 280:1–124; illus.

Shull, E. M. 1987. The Butterflies of Indiana. Bloomington: Indiana Univ. Press, 272 pp.; illus.

Stehr, F. W. (Ed.). 1987. Immature insects. Dubuque, Iowa: Kendall/Hunt, 754 pp.; illus.

Stehr, F. W., and E. F. Cook. 1968. A revision of the genus *Malacosoma* Hübner in North America (Lepidoptera: Lasiocampidae): Systematics, biology, immatures, and parasites. Bull. U.S. Natl. Mus. 276:1–321; illus.

Tietz, H. M. 1973. An Index to the Described Life Histories, Early Stages and Hosts of the Macrolepidoptera of the Continental United States and Canada. Middlesex, England: E. W. Classey, 1042 pp. (2 vol.).

Tilden, J. W. 1965. Butterflies of the San Francisco Bay Region. Berkeley: Univ. California Press, 88 pp.; illus.

Tilden, J. W., and A. C. Smith. 1986. A Field Guide to Western Butterflies. Boston: Houghton Mifflin, 370 pp.; illus.

Tyler, H. A. 1975. The Swallowtail Butterflies of North America. Healdsburg, Calif.: Naturegraph, 192 pp.; illus.

Urquhart, F. A. 1960. The Monarch Butterfly. Toronto: Univ. Toronto Press, 361 pp.; illus.

Villiard, P. 1969. Moths and How to Rear Them. New York: Funk and Wagnalls, 242 pp.; illus. (Reprinted by Dover.)

Watson, A., D. S. Fletcher, and I. W. B. Nye. 1980. The Generic Names of the Moths of the World, Vol. 2: Noctuoidea (part). London: British Museum (Natural History).

Watson, A., and P. E. S. Walley. 1975. The Dictionary of Butterflies and Moths in Color. New York: McGraw-Hill, 296 pp.; illus.

Wilkinson, C. 1979. A taxonomic study of the microlepidopteran genera *Microcalyptris* Braun and *Fomoria* Beirne occurring in the United States of America (Lepidoptera: Nepticulidae). Tijds. Entomol. 122:59–90; illus.

Wilkinson, C., and P. J. Newton. 1981. The microlepidopteran genus *Ectoedemia* Busck (Nepticulidae) in North America. Tijds. Entomol. 124:27–92; illus.

Wilkinson, C., and M. J. Scobie. 1979. The Nepticulidae (Lepidoptera) of Canada. Mem. Entomol. Soc. Can. 107:1–129; illus.

Zimmerman, E. C. 1958a. Insects of Hawaii, Vol. 7: Macrolepidoptera. Honolulu: Univ. Hawaii Press, 542 pp.; illus.

Zimmerman, E. C. 1958b. Insects of Hawaii, Vol. 8: Pyraloidea. Honolulu: Univ. Hawaii Press, 456 pp.; illus.

Zimmerman, E. C. 1978. Insects of Hawaii, Vol. 9: Microlepidoptera (2 parts). Honolulu: Univ. Hawaii Press, 1903 pp.; illus.

Chapter 35

Order Hymenóptera[1]
Sawflies, Parasitic Wasps, Ants, Wasps, and Bees

From the human standpoint, this order is probably the most beneficial in the entire insect class. It contains a great many species that are of value as parasites or predators of insect pests, and it contains the most important pollinators of plants, the bees. The Hymenóptera are a very interesting group in terms of their biology, for they exhibit a great diversity of habits and complexity of behavior culminating in the eusocial organization of the wasps, bees, and ants.

The winged members of this order have four membranous wings. The hind wings are smaller than the front wings and have a row of tiny hooks (hamuli) on their anterior margin by which the hind wing attaches to a fold on the posterior edge of the front wing. The wings contain relatively few veins, and in some minute forms there are no veins at all. The mouthparts are mandibulate, but in many, especially the bees, the labium and maxillae form a tonguelike structure through which liquid food is taken (Figure 35–6). The antennae usually contain ten or more segments and are generally fairly long. The tarsi are usually five-segmented. The ovipositor is usually well developed. In some cases it is modified into a sting, which functions as an organ of offense and defense. Because the stinging organ

evolved from an egg-laying organ, only females can sting. The metamorphosis is complete, and in most of the order, the larvae are grublike or maggotlike. The larvae of most of the sawflies and related forms (suborder Sýmphyta) are eruciform and differ from those of the Lepidóptera in that they have more than five pairs of prolegs, lack crochets on these prolegs, and usually have only a single pair of stemmata. The pupae are exarate and may be formed in a cocoon, within the host (in the case of parasitic species), or in special cells.

Sex in most Hymenóptera is controlled by the fertilization of the egg. Fertilized eggs develop into females, and unfertilized eggs usually develop into males.

Classification of the Hymenóptera

The order Hymenóptera is divided into two suborders, each of which is further divided into superfamilies. In the suborder Sýmphyta the abdomen is broadly joined to the thorax, the trochanters are two-segmented, and there are nearly always at least three closed cells at the base of the hind wing (Figure 35–1). Nearly all the Sýmphyta are phytophagous. In the suborder Apócrita the basal segment of the abdomen is fused with the thorax and separated from the remainder of the abdomen by a constriction. The

[1]Hymenóptera: *hymeno*, god of marriage (referring to the union of front and hind wings by means of hamuli); *ptera*, wings.

665

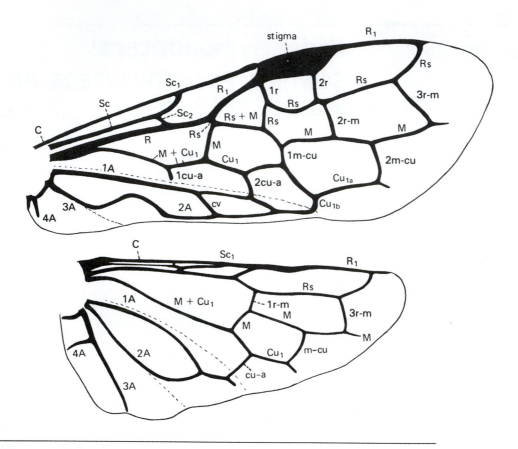

Figure 35–1. Wings of *Acanthólyda* (Pamphilìidae) showing the venational terminology of Richards (1977).

abdominal segment that is fused with the thorax is called the propodeum. The resulting four-segmented locomotory tagma is known as the *mesosoma* (or trunk). The posterior tagma is the *metasoma* (or gaster). The trochanters appear one- or two-segmented in the Apócrita, and there are not more than two closed cells at the base of the hind wing (Figure 35–2). The larvae of most species of Apócrita feed on other arthropods, although phytophagy has reevolved several times.

A synopsis of the order Hymenóptera is given in the following list. Alternate spellings, synonyms, and other arrangements are given in parentheses. The higher classification of the order is in a state of flux. The arrangement presented here follows in broad outline that of Brothers (1975), Krombein *et al.* (1979), and Rasnitsyn (1980). The groups marked with an asterisk are relatively rare or are unlikely to be taken by a general collector.

Suborder Sýmphyta (Chalastogástra)—sawflies and horntails

Superfamily Megalodontòidea
  *Xyèlidae
  *Pamphilìidae (Lỳdidae)—leaf-rolling and web-spinning sawflies
Superfamily Tenthredinòidea
  *Pérgidae (Acordulecéridae)
  Árgidae (Hylotómidae)
  Cimbícidae (Clavellarìidae)
  Dipriónidae (Lophýridae)—conifer sawflies
  Tenthredínidae—common sawflies
Superfamily Cephòidea
  Cèphidae—stem sawflies
Superfamily Siricòidea
  *Anaxyèlidae (Syntéxidae, Syntéctidae)—incense-cedar wood wasps
  Sirícidae (Urocéridae)—horntails
  *Xiphydrìidae—wood wasps
  *Orússidae (Orýssidae, Idiogástra)—parasitic wood wasps
Suborder Apócrita (Clistogástra, Petiolàta)
  Superfamily Stephanòidea
    *Stephánidae

Superfamily Ceraphronòidea
  Megaspìlidae (Ceraphrónidae in part, Callicer-
    átidae in part)
  Ceraphrónidae (Callicerátidae in part)
Superfamily Trigonalòidea
  *Trigonálidae
Superfamily Evaniòidea
  Evanìidae—ensign wasps
  Gasteruptìidae (Gasteruptiónidae)
  Aulácidae (Gasteruptìidae in part)
Superfamily Ichneumonòidea
  Bracónidae
  Ichneumónidae (including Paxylommátidae =
    Hybrizóntidae)
Superfamily Chalcidòidea
  *Mymarommátidae (Serphítidae)
  Mymàridae—fairyflies
  Trichogrammátidae
  Eulóphidae
  Elásmidae
  *Tetracámpidae
  Aphelìnidae (Eulóphidae in part, Encýrtidae in
    part)
  *Signiphòridae (Encýrtidae in part;
    Thysánidae)
  Encýrtidae
  *Tanaostigmátidae (Encýrtidae in part)
  Eupélmidae

Torýmidae (Callimómidae; including Poda-
    griónidae in part)
  *Agaónidae (Agaóntidae, Torýmidae in part)—
    fig wasps
  Ormýridae
  Pteromálidae (including Cleonýmidae in part,
    Chalcedéctidae, Eutrichosomátidae, and
    Miscogástridae)
  Eucharítidae (Eucharídidae, Euchàridae)
  Perilámpidae
  Eurytómidae—seed chalcids
  Chalcídidae (Chálcidae)
  Leucóspidae (Leucospídidae)
Superfamily Cynipòidea
  *Ibalìidae
  *Lioptéridae
  Figítidae
  Eucòilidae (Cynípidae in part)
  Cynípidae (including Alloxýstidae)—gall wasps
Superfamily Proctotrupòidea
  Pelecìnidae
  *Vanhornìidae (Proctotrùpidae in part, Sérphi-
    dae in part)
  * Prop_Ropronìidae
  *Helòridae
  Proctotrùpidae (Sérphidae)
  Diaprìidae (including Ambosítridae, Belýtidae,
    Cinétidae)

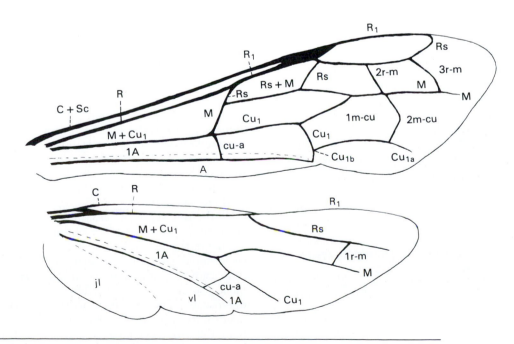

Figure 35–2. Wings of *Mỳzinum* (Tiphìidae), showing the venational terminology of Richards and the names of cells used in this book.

Sceliónidae
Platygástridae (Platygastéridae)
Superfamily Chrysidòidea (= Bethylòidea)
Chrysídidae (including Cléptidae)—cuckoo
wasps
Bethýlidae
Dryínidae
*Embolémidae (Dryínidae in part)
*Sclerogíbbidae
Superfamily Sphecòidea
Sphécidae (including Ampulícidae, Crabróni-
dae, Lárridae, Mellínidae, Nyssónidae,
Pemphredónidae, Philánthidae)
Superfamily Apòidea—bees
*Melíttidae
Collètidae (including Hylaèidae)—plasterer and
yellow-faced bees
Halíctidae—sweat bees
*Oxaèidae (Andrènidae in part)
Andrènidae
Megachìlidae—leafcutting bees
Anthophòridae (including Nomádidae, Eucéri-
dae, Ceratìnidae, Xylocòpidae)—cuckoo
bees, digger bees, and carpenter bees
Àpidae (including Bómbidae)—honey bees,
bumble bees, orchid bees
Superfamily Tiphiòidea
Tiphìidae (including Thýnnidae)
*Sierolomórphidae
*Sapýgidae
Mutíllidae (including Myrmosìnae)—velvet
ants
*Bradynobaènidae (Mutíllidae in part)
Superfamily Pompilòidea
Pompílidae (Psammochàridae)—spider wasps
*Rhopalosomátidae (Rhopalosòmidae)
Superfamily Scoliòidea
Scolìidae
Superfamily Vespòidea
Véspidae (including Euménidae, Masàridae)—
paper wasps, yellow jackets, hornets, ma-
son wasps, potter wasps
Superfamily Formicòidea
Formícidae—ants

Characters Used in the Identification of Hymenóptera

Wing Venation

Venational characters are used a great deal to separate the various groups of Hymenóptera. There are
not many veins or cells in the hymenopteran wings,
but homologizing this venation with that in other

orders has proved to be a problem. There are two
basic terminologies in use for the venation of the
Hymenóptera: a traditional system using terms specific for the order (Figure 35–3) and one developed by
Ross (1936) that attempted to homologize the venation with that of other insects. We generally will use
the modification of Ross's system by Richards (1977)
in this chapter to refer to veins (Figures 35–1, 35–2).
In those groups with highly reduced venation (Chalcidòidea and Proctotrupòidea especially), it is much
simpler to refer to the veins by their relative positions (see Figure 35–19B). We also follow Michener's
(1944) suggestions regarding the names of some cells
and use the positional terms marginal and submarginal cells (Figure 35–3, *MC, SM*).

Leg Characters

The leg characters used in identification are chiefly
the number of trochanter segments, the number and
form of the tibial spurs, and the form of the tarsal
segments. In the Sýmphyta and some superfamilies
of the Apócrita, there are two trochanter segments
(Figure 35–32A). In fact, the so-called second trochanter is actually a basal subdivision of the femur
and is never movably articulated distally. In the bees
(Apòidea) the first segment of the hind tarsus is
usually much enlarged and flattened and may in
some cases appear nearly as large as the tibia (Figure
35–15B,C). In some superfamilies the size and shape
of the hind coxae may help to separate families.

Antennal Characters

The antennae of Hymenóptera vary in form, number
of segments, and location on the face. In the Apócrita
the number of antennal segments and, in some cases,
the form of the antennae may differ in the two sexes.
In most aculeates the male has 13 antennal segments
and the female has 12. In the ants the antennae are
much more distinctly elbowed in the queens and
workers than in the males. In the Chalcidòidea the
antennal flagellum may be thought of as consisting
of three sections (Figure 35–25B): an apical clava
(*cva*), the ring segments basally (*rg*), and the funicle
between the two (*fun*). The clava is formed of 1–3
segments that are distinguished by their close association rather than necessarily any expansion. The
ring segments (or anneli) are minute, reduced segments, sometimes only visible under a compound
microscope. The key refers to the number of segments in the funicle. These are usually much longer
than the ring segments and easily distinguished
from them. In those few cases where it is unclear
whether a segment represents a large ring segment

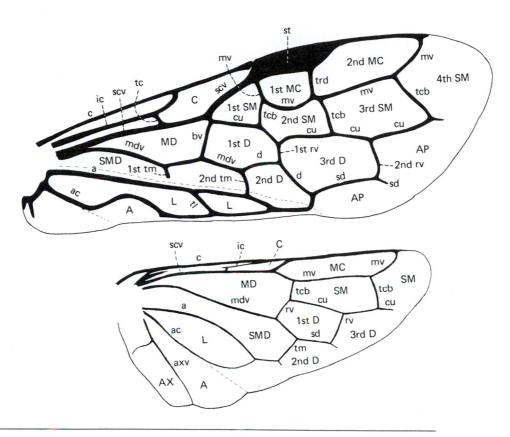

Figure 35–3. Wings of *Acanthólyda*, showing the old system of terminology (veins are shown by small letters, cells by capitals). Veins: *a*, anal; *ac*, accessory, lanceolate, or subanal; *axv*, axillary; *bv*, basal; *c*, costal; *cu*, cubital; *d*, discoidal; *ic*, intercostal; *mdv*, median; *mv*, marginal or radial; *rv*, recurrent; *scv*, subcostal; *sd*, subdiscal or subdiscoidal; *st*, stigma; *tc*, transverse costal; *tcb*, transverse cubitals; *tl*, transverse lanceolate; *tm*, transverse median; *trd*, transverse radial or transverse marginal. Cells: *A*, anal; *AP*, apical or posterior; *AX*, axillary; *C*, costal; *D*, discoidal; *L*, lanceolate; *MC*, marginal, *MD*, median; *SM*, submarginal; *SMD*, submedian. The basal cells (hind wing) are *MD*, *SMD*, and *L*.

or a small funicular segment, it should be included in the count of the latter.

Thoracic Characters

The thoracic characters used in identifying Hymen-óptera involve principally the form of the pronotum and of certain mesothoracic sclerites and sulci. The shape of the pronotum as seen from above (Figure 35–9A–D) serves to separate some families of Sým-phyta, and its shape as seen from the side serves to separate groups of superfamilies of Apócrita. The pronotum in the Apócrita may appear in profile more or less triangular and extending nearly or quite close to the tegulae (Figure 35–4C: Stephanòidea, Cera-phronòidea, Ichneumonòidea, Cynipòidea, Evaniòi-dea, Proctotrupòidea, and some Vespòidea), some-

what quadrate and not quite reaching the tegulae (Figure 35–4A,B: Trigonalòidea, Chrysidòidea, Chalcidòidea, some Vespòidea), or short and collar-like with a small rounded lobe on each side (Figures 35–4D, 35–12: Sphecòidea and Apòidea). Some Apó-crita (for example, the Chalcidòidea) have a distinct triangular prepectus in the lateral wall of the mes-othorax (Figure 35–4A, *pp*). The presence or absence of notauli (Figure 35–4A, *nt*, sometimes called par-apsidal furrows) and the form of the axillae (Figure 35–4A, *ax*) often serve to separate related families. In most Sýmphyta (all except Cèphidae) a pair of cenchri are found dorsally on or behind the metan-otum. These are rounded and roughened structures that come in contact with scaly patches on the pos-terior part of the fore wings and serve to hold the wings in place when they are folded over the body (Figure 35–7, *cen*).

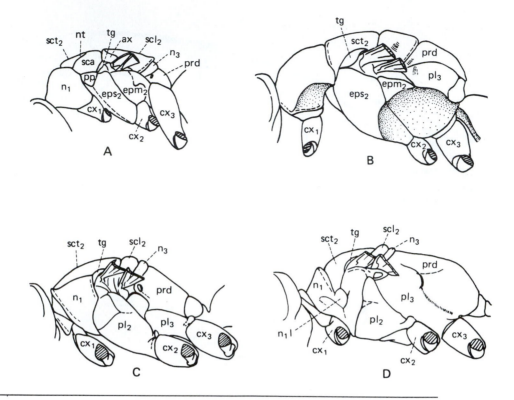

Figure 35–4. Mesosomatic structures in Hymenóptera, lateral view, **A,** chalcidoid (Torýmidae); **B,** cuckoo wasp (Chrysídidae); **C,** paper wasp (Véspidae); **D,** thread-waisted wasp (Sphécidae). *ax,* axilla; *cx,* coxa; *epm,* epimeron; *eps,* episternum; *n,* notum; n_1l, pronotal lobe; *nt,* notaulus; *pl,* pleuron; *pp,* prepectus; *prd,* propodeum; *sca,* scapula; *scl,* scutellum; *sct,* scutum; *tg,* tegula.

Abdominal Characters

In the superfamilies Ichneumonòidea, Stephanòidea, Cynipòidea, and Chalcidòidea, the ovipositor issues from the metasoma anterior to the apex, on the ventral side, and is not withdrawn into the body when not in use (Figure 35–5A). In most of the remaining Apócrita the ovipositor issues from the apex of the metasoma and is withdrawn into the body when not in use (Figure 35–5B). The shape of the metasoma or of the petiole may serve to separate related groups in some superfamilies.

Other Characters

In some of the wasps the shape of the compound eyes differs in different families, with the inner or mesal margins sometimes strongly emarginate. The mouthpart structures used to separate groups of Hymenóptera are chiefly the form of the mandibles and the structure of the tongue (see Figure 35–6). The

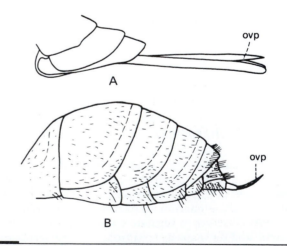

Figure 35–5. Position of the ovipositor in Hymenóptera. **A,** last sternite split ventrally, the ovipositor issuing from anterior to apex of abdomen (Ichneumónidae); **B,** last sternite not split ventrally, the ovipositor issuing from apex of abdomen (Sphécidae). *ovp,* ovipositor.

tongue provides some excellent characters for identification in the bees and should be extended when specimens are fresh and still flexible. The head and thoracic characters that involve the form of sclerites and sulci are usually easy to see except when the specimen is very small or very hairy. In the latter case, it may be necessary to separate or remove the hairs. Characters such as the size, shape, or color of the insect provide easy means of identification in many groups. "Minute" means 2 mm in length or less; small means 2–7 mm in length.

The principal difficulties likely to be encountered in keying out a specimen in this order are a result of the small size of some specimens. These are either difficult to see, or the specimens are weakly sclerotized and may collapse when air-dried. The larger specimens should not cause a great deal of difficulty. We have included here a key to all the families of Hymenóptera represented in the United States and Canada, though we realize that the student is likely to have some difficulty in keying out the smaller specimens. Counts of the number of antennomeres and tarsomeres are best done by shining the light below the specimen so that the structure is seen in silhouette. Groups that are relatively rare or are small in size and unlikely to be found and retained by the beginning student are marked with an asterisk.

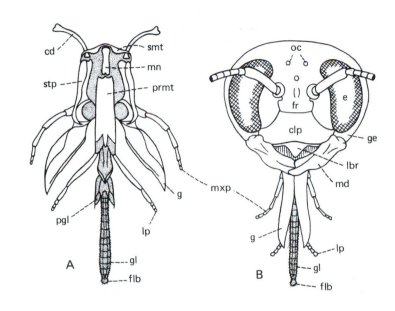

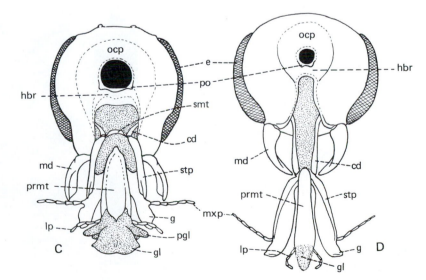

Figure 35–6. Head and mouthpart structure in bees. **A,** mouthparts of *Xylocòpa* (Anthophòridae, Xylocopìnae), posterior view; **B,** same, anterior view; **C,** mouthparts of *Hylaèus* (Collètidae, Hylaeìnae), posterior view; **D,** mouthparts of *Sphecòdes* (Halíctidae), posterior view. *cd,* cardo; *clp,* clypeus; *e,* compound eye; *flb,* flabellum; *fr,* frons; *g,* galea, *ge,* gena; *gl,* glossa; *hbr,* hypostomal bridge; *lbr,* labrum; *lp,* labial palp; *md,* mandible; *mn,* mentum; *mxp,* maxillary palp; *oc,* ocelli; *ocp,* occiput; *pgl,* paraglossa; *po,* postocciput; *prmt,* prementum; *smt,* submentum; *stp,* stipes.

Key to the Families of Hymenóptera[2]

The system of venational terminology used by Richards (1977; Figures 35–1, 35–2) is generally used in this key. Unless otherwise indicated, all venational characters refer to the front wing. For those species with highly reduced venation, the positional terms in Figure 35–19B are used. Cells are named according to the vein forming their anterior boundary; we continue to use the terms *submarginal* and *marginal* cells; cells used in the key are labeled in the accompanying figures. The number of marginal or submarginal cells refers to the number of *closed* cells. The groups marked with an asterisk are relatively rare or are unlikely to be taken by the general collector. No satisfactory keys to the family level or below are available that treat all Hymenóptera larvae, but Evans (1987) provides the most up-to-date keys for most groups. These are especially useful for sawfly larvae.

1. Base of abdomen broadly joined to thorax (Figures 35–7, 35–38 through 35–40), first abdominal tergum divided longitudinally (except Orússidae and rarely in Tenthredínidae), rarely these halves fused together, but fusion line visible; thorax with two pairs of spiracles, these located near wing bases and not visible dorsally; trochanters 2-segmented; hind wings nearly always with at least 3 closed basal cells (*B* in Figure 35–8); cenchri (Figure 35–7, *cen*) present (except Cèphidae); never less than 2 mm in length; (suborder Sýmphyta) **2**

1'. Base of apparent abdomen (the metasoma) constricted, more or less petiolate; first true abdominal tergum incorporated into functional thorax (the mesosoma), this therefore with three pairs of spiracles, the posterior pair clearly visible dorsally; trochanters 1- or 2-segmented; hind wings with 2 or

[2]We acknowledge here the generous and significant contributions to the chalcidoid portion of the key by G. A. P. Gibson, and to the bees by J. B. Whitfield.

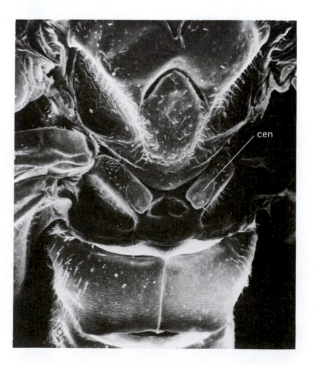

Figure 35–7.   Thorax and abdomen of Sýmphyta, dorsal view. *cen*, cenchri.

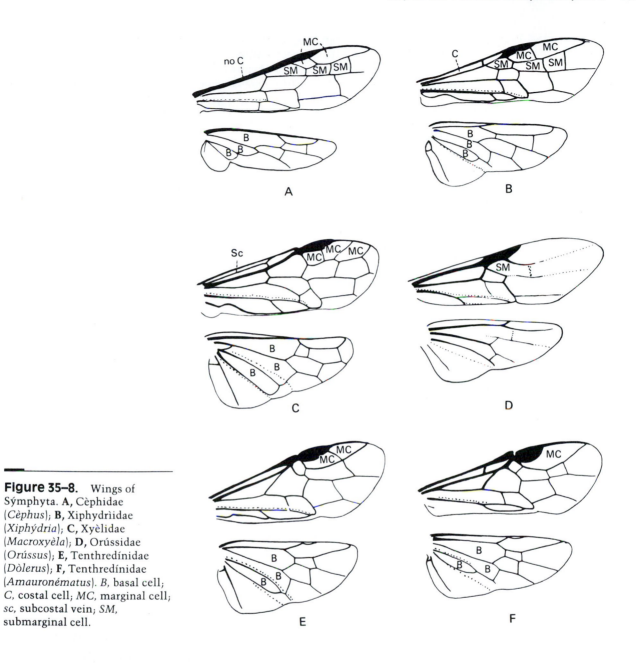

Figure 35–8. Wings of Sýmphyta. **A,** Cèphidae (*Cèphus*); **B,** Xiphydrìidae (*Xiphýdria*); **C,** Xyèlidae (*Macroxyèla*); **D,** Orússidae (*Orússus*); **E,** Tenthredínidae (*Dòlerus*); **F,** Tenthredínidae (*Amauronématus*). *B,* basal cell; *C,* costal cell; *MC,* marginal cell; *sc,* subcostal vein; *SM,* submarginal cell.

fewer closed basal cells (Figures 35–2, 35–13, 35–14, 35–19, 35–20, 35–31, 35–36A–C); cenchri absent; rarely metasoma broadly connected to mesosoma in minute species (suborder Apócrita) **13**

2(1).   Antennae inserted under a broad frontal ridge below eyes, just above mouth (Figure 35–9E); 1 submarginal cell (Figure 35–8D) ....**Orússidae***   p. 704

2′.   Antennae inserted above base of eyes, near middle of face; 1–3 submarginal cells **3**

3(2′).   Front tibia with 1 apical spur **4**

3′.   Front tibia with 2 apical spurs **7**

4(3).   Pronotum in dorsal view wider than long, shorter along midline than laterally (Figure 35–9D); mesonotum with 2 diagonal furrows extending antero-laterally from anterior margin of scutellum (Figure 35–9D); abdomen terminating in a dorsally located spearlike plate or spine ....**Sirícidae**   p. 703

4′.   Pronotum in dorsal view either U-shaped (Figure 35–9B) or more or less trapezoidal (Figure 35–9A,C); mesonotum without diagonal furrows; abdomen not terminating in a dorsally located spear or spine **5**

5(4′).   Pronotum in dorsal view U-shaped, posterior margin deeply curved, and very short along midline (Figure 35–9B); costal cell, and usually also vein Sc_2, present (Figure 35–8B); abdomen cylindrical ....**Xiphydrìidae***   p. 704

5′.   Pronotum in dorsal view not U-shaped, posterior margin straight or only slightly curved (Figure 35–9A,C); costal cell present or absent; vein Sc_2 absent; abdomen more or less flattened laterally **6**

6(5′).   Costal cell present and distinct; apical spur on front tibiae pectinate on inner margin; pronotum in dorsal view much wider than long (Figure 35–9C); California and Oregon ....**Anaxyèlidae***   p. 703

6′.   Costal cell absent or very narrow (Figure 35–8A); apical spur on front tibiae not pectinate on inner margin; pronotum in dorsal view about as long as or longer than wide (Figure 35–9A); widely distributed ....**Cèphidae**   p. 703

7(3′).   Antennae 3-segmented, third segment very long (Figure 35–10E), sometimes U-shaped ....**Árgidae**   p. 701

7′.   Antennae with more than 3 segments **8**

8(7′).   Third antennal segment very long, longer than following segments combined (Figure 35–10D); 3 (rarely 2) marginal cells and vein Sc present (Figure 35–8C) ....**Xyèlidae***   p. 701

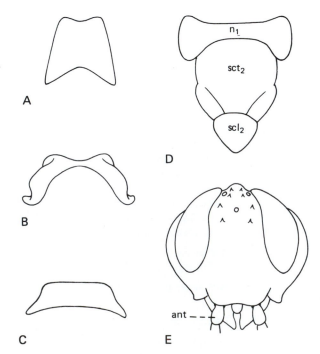

Figure 35–9. Head and thoracic characters of Sýmphyta. **A–D,** dorsal views; **E,** anterior view. **A,** pronotum of *Hartígia* (Cèphidae); **B,** pronotum of *Xiphýdria* (Xiphydrìidae); **C,** pronotum of *Syntéxis* (Anaxyèlidae); **D,** thorax of *Urócerus* (Sirícidae); **E,** head of *Orússus* (Orússidae). *ant,* base of antenna; $n_1,$ pronotum; $scl_2,$ mesoscutellum; $sct_2,$ mesoscutum. (**C,** redrawn from Ross.)

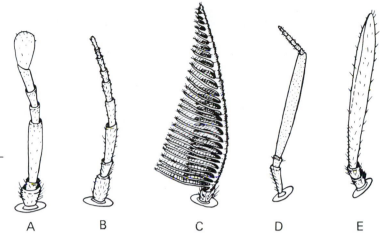

Figure 35–10. Antennae of Sýmphyta. **A,** Cimbícidae (*Címbex*); **B,** Tenthredínidae (*Leucopelmònus*); **C,** male Dipriónidae (*Neodíprion*); **D,** Xyèlidae (*Macroxyèla*); **E,** Árgidae (*Árge*).

A   B   C   D   E

8'.   Third antennal segment short (Figure 35–10A–C); 1 or 2 marginal cells (Figure 35–8E,F); vein Sc usually absent **9**

9(8').   Antennae clubbed, with 7 or fewer segments (Figure 35–10A); large, robust sawflies resembling bumble bees (Figure 35–38A) ....**Cimbícidae**   p. 702

9'.   Antennae filiform (Figure 35–10B), serrate, or pectinate (Figure 35–10C), rarely slightly clubbed **10**

10(9').   Antennae 6-segmented; anterior margin of scutellum more or less straight ....**Pérgidae***   p. 701

10'.   Antennae with more than 6 segments; anterior margin of scutellum V-shaped (Figure 35–38B,C) **11**

11(10').   Veins Sc and usually Cu$_1$ and cross vein cu-a present (Figure 35–1); antennae with 13 or more segments ....**Pamphiliidae***   p. 701

11'.   Veins Sc and Cu$_1$ absent and cross vein cu-a present (Figure 35–8E,F); antennae variable **12**

12(11').   Antennae 7- to 10-segmented and usually filiform (Figure 35–10B); 1 or 2 marginal cells (Figure 35–8E,F) ....**Tenthredínidae**   p. 702

12'.   Antennae with 13 or more segments and either serrate or pectinate (Figure 35–10C); 1 marginal cell ....**Dipriónidae**   p. 702

13(1').   First metasomatic segment (sometimes first 2 metasomatic segments) bearing a hump or node and strongly differentiated from rest of metasoma (Figures 35–11, 35–83); antennae usually elbowed, at least in female, with first segment long; pronotum more or less quadrate in lateral view, usually not reaching tegulae (Figures 35–11, 35–83); often wingless ....**Formícidae**   p. 737

13'.   First metasomatic segment not as above, or antennae not elbowed; pronotum variable **14**

14(13').   Wings well developed **15**

14'.   Wings vestigial or lacking **106**

15(14).   Pronotum with a rounded lobe on each side posteriorly that does not reach the tegula (Figures 35–4D, 35–12); venation usually complete or nearly so (Figures 35–13, 35–14) **16**

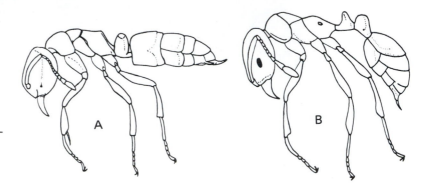

Figure 35–11. Ant workers. **A,** Ponerìnae (*Ponèra*); **B,** Myrmicìnae (*Solenópsis*).

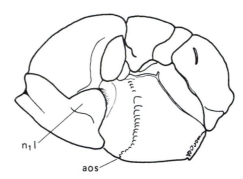

Figure 35–12. Mesosoma of *Hylaèus* (Collètidae, Hylaeìnae); lateral view. *aos,* anterior oblique sulcus on mesepisternum; n_1l, pronotal lobe.

15′.	Pronotum without a rounded lobe on each side posteriorly (Figure 35–4A–C), or if such a lobe is present (as in Figure 35–34), it reaches (or nearly reaches) the tegula; venation variable, sometimes much reduced **25**
16(15).	Body relatively bare, with all body hairs unbranched; first segment of hind tarsus similar in width and thickness to the remaining segments and not longer than the remaining segments combined (Figure 35–15A); metasoma often petiolate; posterior margin of pronotum (in dorsal view) nearly always straight ....**Sphécidae** p. 724
16′.	Body usually relatively hairy, with at least some body hairs (especially on mesosoma) branched or plumose (Figure 35–16); first segment of hind tarsus usually wider than the remaining segments and generally as long as or longer than the remaining segments combined (Figure 35–15B–D); metasoma not petiolate; posterior margin of pronotum (in dorsal view) usually more or less arcuate (Apòidea: bees) **17**
17(16′).	Jugal lobe in hind wing as long as or longer than M + Cu_1 cell (Figure 35–13A–E, *jl*); galeae and glossa short **18**
17′.	Jugal lobe in hind wing shorter than M + Cu_1 cell or lacking (Figures 35–13F, 35–14); galeae and glossa usually long **21**
18(17).	Glossa truncate, bilobed apically (Figure 35–6C); anterior oblique sulcus present on mesepisternum (Figure 35–12, *aos*); frons with one subantennal sulcus meeting inner side of antennal socket (as in Figure 35–17C, *sas*) ....**Collètidae** p. 729
18′.	Glossa pointed or somewhat rounded apically, not bilobed (Figure 35–6A,B,D); anterior oblique sulcus often absent from mesepisternum; frons with one or two subantennal sulci **19**

19(18').   Fore wing with first free segment of M strongly arched (Figure 35–13C); frons
               with one subantennal sulcus meeting inner side of antennal socket (as in
               Figure 35–17C); anterior oblique sulcus usually present on mesepisternum
               (as in Figure 35–12, *aos*); facial foveae absent ....**Halíctidae**   p. 729

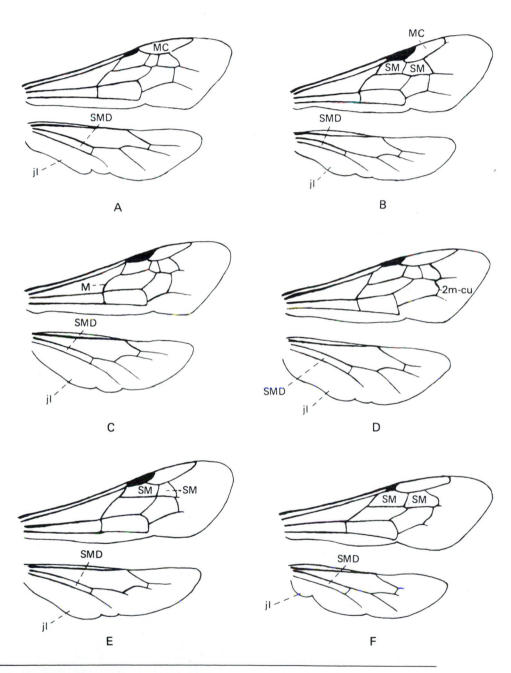

Figure 35–13.   Wings of Apòidea. **A,** *Andrèna* (Andrènidae, Andreninae); **B,** *Panùrga* (Andreñidae, Panurgìnae); **C,** *Sphecòdes* (Halíctidae, Halictìnae); **D,** *Collètes* (Collètidae, Colletìnae); **E,** *Hylaèus* (Collètidae, Hylaeìnae); **F,** *Coelióxys* (Megachìlidae, Megachilìnae). *jl,* jugal lobe; *MC,* marginal cell; *SM,* submarginal cells.

19'. Fore wing with first free segment of M straight or weakly arched (Figure 35–13A,B,D–F); frons with two subantennal sulci, one on each side of antennal socket (Figure 35–17A); anterior oblique sulcus almost always absent from mesepisternum; facial foveae, at least in females, present and distinct, often lined with dense feltlike pile (Figure 35–17A) **20**

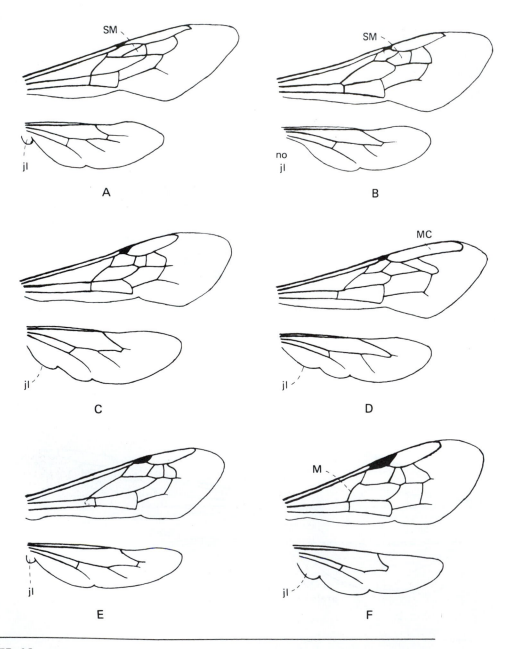

Figure 35–14. Wings of Apòidea. **A,** *Xylocòpa* (Anthophòridae, Xylocopìnae); **B,** *Bómbus* (Àpidae, Bombìnae); **C,** *Melissòdes* (Anthophòridae, Anthophorìnae); **D,** *Àpis* (Àpidae, Apìnae); **E,** *Nómada* (Anthophòridae, Nomadìnae); **F,** *Ceratìna* (Anthophòridae, Xylocopìnae). *jl,* jugal lobe; *MC,* marginal cell; *SM,* second submarginal cell.

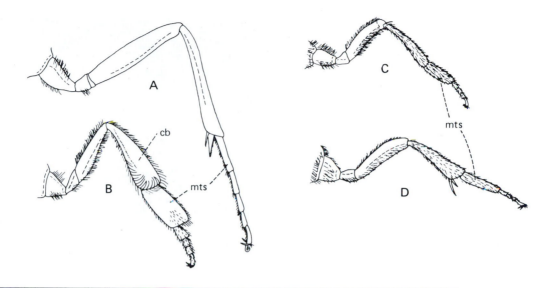

Figure 35–15. Hind legs of Sphecòidea (**A**) and Apòidea (**B–D**). **A**, *Sphéx* (Sphécidae); **B**, *Àpis* (Àpidae); **C**, *Andrèna* (Andrènidae); **D**, *Nómada* (Anthophòridae). *cb*, corbicula; *mts*, first tarsal segment.

20(19').	Stigma of fore wing very small, nearly absent; scopa of females present on hind tibiae and second metasomatic sternum (restricted to southwestern United States) ....**Oxaèidae**	p. 730
20'.	Stigma of fore wing of normal size (Figure 35–13A,B); females with scopa absent from second metasomatic sternum (large and widespread group) ....**Andrènidae**	p. 730
21(17').	Galeae and glossa short ("tongue" relatively short); segments of labial palpi similar and cylindrical (as in Figure 35–6D) ....**Melíttidae**	p. 728
21'.	Galeae and glossa elongate ("tongue" long); first two segments of labial palpi elongate and somewhat flattened to form a sheath for the "tongue" (Figure 35–6A,B) **22**	
22(21').	Fore wing with 2 submarginal cells (Figure 35–13F); labrum longer than wide, but with broad articulation with clypeus; subantennal sulci meeting outer side of antennal sockets (Figure 35–17B); scopa, when present, on metasoma (Figure 35–69) ....**Megachilidae**	p. 730
22'.	Fore wing with 3 submarginal cells (Figure 35–14A,B), rarely 2; if 2, then second submarginal cell much shorter than first; labrum usually wider than long or with narrow articulation with clypeus; subantennal sulci meeting inner sides of antennal sockets (Figure 35–17C); scopa, when present, usually on hind legs (rarely also on metasoma) **23**	
23(22').	Hind tibiae with apical spurs **24**	
23'.	Hind tibiae without apical spurs (Apìnae: *Àpis mellífera*) ....**Àpidae**	p. 732
24(23).	Hind wing with short jugal lobe present (Figure 35–14A,C,E,F) **Anthophòridae**	p. 731
24'.	Hind wing without jugal lobe (Figure 35–14B) (Bombìnae, Euglossìnae) ....**Àpidae**	p. 732

Figure 35–16. Scanning electron micrograph showing plumose body hairs of *Hylaèus* (Collètidae, Hylaeìnae).

25(15′).   Venation slightly to considerably reduced, front wings usually with 5 or fewer closed cells, and hind wings usually without closed cells (Figures 35–19, 35–20, 35–31 G) **26**

25′.   Venation complete or nearly so, front wings usually with 6 or more closed cells and hind wings with at least 1 closed cell (Figures 35–31 A–F,H, 35–33) ...**83**

26(25).   Pronotum in lateral view more or less triangular, and extending to tegulae or nearly so (Figure 35–4C); hind wings nearly always without a jugal lobe   **27**

26′.   Pronotum in lateral view more or less quadrate, and not quite reaching tegulae (Figure 35–4A,B); forms with 3 or more closed cells in front wings usually have a jugal lobe in hind wings **46**

27(26).   Metasoma arising on propodeum between bases of hind coxae or only slightly above them (as in Figure 35–18A–C); antennae variable **28**

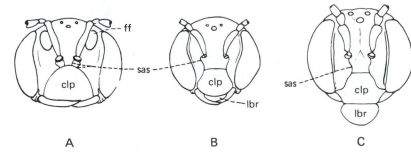

Figure 35–17. Heads of bees, anterior view. **A,** Andrènidae (*Andrèna*); **B,** Megachìlidae (*Ósmia*); **C,** Anthophòridae (*Triepèolus*, Nomadìnae), *clp*, clypeus; *ff*, facial fovea; *lbr*, labrum; *sas*, subantennal sulcus.

27'. Metasoma arising on propodeum far above bases of hind coxae (Figure 35–18D–F); antennae 13- or 14-segmented **84**

28(27). Fore wing with well-developed marginal cell and costal vein absent basally, without enlarged stigma (Figure 35–19A) **29**

28'. Fore wing either without marginal cell (as in Figure 35–19B–E, 35–20A,E) or costal vein present basally (Figure 35–20B–D,F–H); stigma often present...**33**

29(28). First segment of hind tarsus twice as long as the other segments combined, second segment with a long process on outer side extending to tip of fourth segment (Figure 35–21B); metasoma compressed, longer than head and mesosoma combined; antennae 13-segmented in female and 15-segmented in male; 7–16 mm in length ....**Ibalìidae***   p. 719

29'. First segment of hind tarsi much shorter, second segment without a long process on outer side; antennae variable, but usually 13-segmented in female and 14-segmented in male; generally 8 mm in length or less **30**

30(29', 110). Dorsal surface of scutellum with a rounded or oval elevation or keel in center (Figure 35–21D); first segment of Rs far longer than first free segment of M; second metasomatic tergum longer than third; antennae 11- to 16-segmented, usually 13-segmented in female and 15-segmented in male ....**Eucòilidae**   p. 719

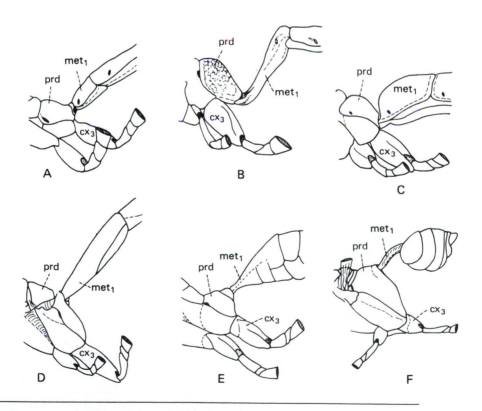

Figure 35–18. Base of the metasoma in parasitic Hymenóptera. **A**, Ichneumónidae; **B**, Ichneumónidae; **C**, Bracónidae; **D**, Gasteruptìidae; **E**, Aulácidae; **F**, Evanìidae. *met₁*, first metasomatic segment; *cx₃*, hind coxa; *prd*, propodeum.

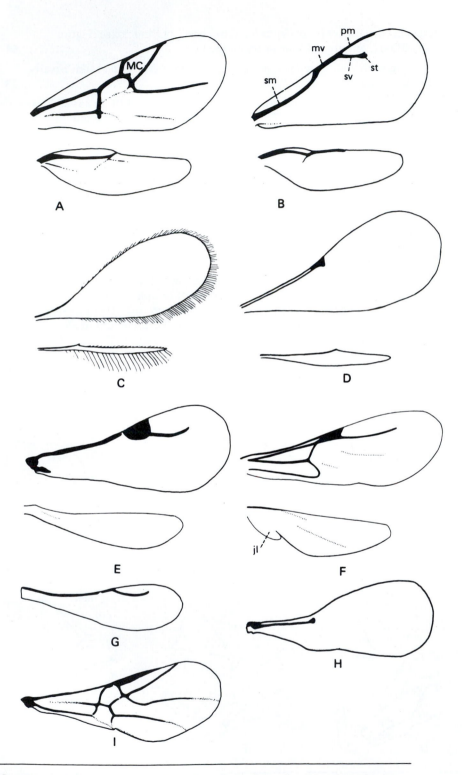

Figure 35–19. Wings of Hymenóptera. **A,** Cynípidae; **B,** Perilámpidae; **C,** Mymàridae; **D,** Diaprìidae (Diaprìinae); **E,** Megaspílidae; **F,** Bethýlidae; **G,** Ceraphrónidae; **H,** Platygástridae (Inostemmatìnae); **I,** Ichneumónidae (Paxyllomatìnae). *jl,* jugal lobe; *mv,* marginal vein; *pm,* postmarginal vein, *sm,* submarginal vein; *st,* stigma; *sv,* stigmal vein.

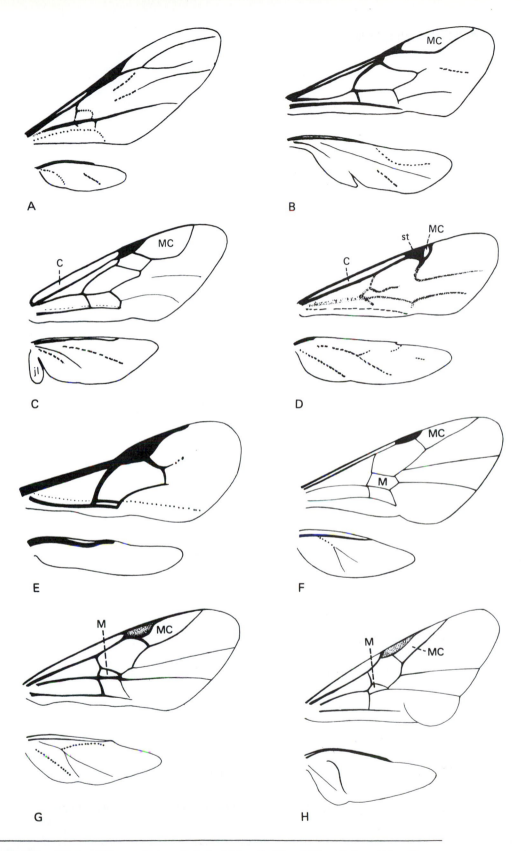

Figure 35–20. Wings of Hymenóptera. **A,** Pelecínidae; **B,** Chrysídidae; **C,** Evaniidae; **D,** Proctotrùpidae; **E,** Bracónidae (Aphidiìnae); **F,** Roproniidae; **G,** Vanhorniidae; **H,** Helòridae. *C,* costal cell; *jl,* jugal lobe; *M,* medial cell; *MC,* marginal cell; *st,* stigma.

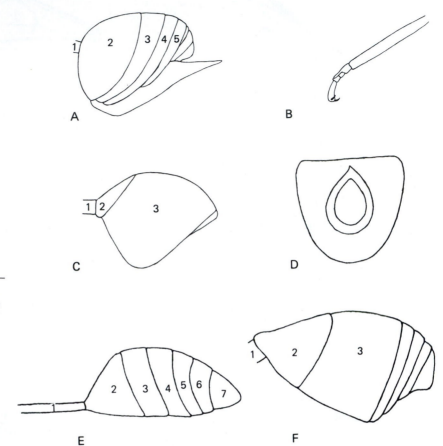

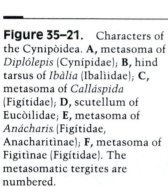

Figure 35–21.   Characters of the Cynipòidea. **A**, metasoma of *Diplólepis* (Cynípidae); **B**, hind tarsus of *Ibàlia* (Ibaliidae); **C**, metasoma of *Calláspida* (Figítidae); **D**, scutellum of Eucòilidae; **E**, metasoma of *Anácharis* (Figítidae, Anacharitìnae); **F**, metasoma of Figitìnae (Figítidae). The metasomatic tergites are numbered.

30′.   Dorsal surface of scutellum not as above; venation, metasomatic terga, and antennae variable **31**

31(30′). Second metasomatic tergum narrow, tongue-shaped, shorter than third (Figure 35–21C); first segment of Rs far longer than first free segment of M (Aspiceratìnae) ....**Figítidae*** .... p. 719

31′.   Second metasomatic tergum not tongue-shaped, or (some Cynipìnae) tongue-shaped, but much longer than third **32**

32(31′). Second metasomatic tergum at least half as long as metasoma (Figure 35–21A), or if shorter then first sector of Rs subequal in length to first free segment of M ....**Cynípidae** .... p. 719

32′.   Second metasomatic tergum less than half as long as metasoma (Figure 35–21E,F); first segment of Rs much longer than first free segment of M, or vein Rs + M lacking ....**Figítidae*** .... p. 719

33(28′). Costal vein present in basal portion of fore wing and costal cell absent (Figure 35–19I, 35–20E) **34**

33′.   Either costal vein absent basally or costal cell well developed **35**

34(33).   Metasomatic tergites 2 and 3 fused together; Rs and M separated basad of 2r (Figure 35–20E) ....**Bracónidae** .... p. 707

34'. Metasomatic tergites 2 and 3 separated and overlapping; veins Rs and M not separating until beyond 2r (Figure 35–19I) ....**Ichneumónidae***   p. 708

35(33', 110'). Fore tibia with 2 apical spurs; venation highly reduced: no closed cells in fore wing, stigmal vein distinctly arched toward costal margin, marginal vein extending from base of wing, submarginal vein absent (Figure 35–19E,G) (rarely veins absent entirely) (Ceraphronòidea) **36**

35'. Fore tibia with 1 apical spur; venation variable, submarginal vein usually present; in forms with reduced venation stigmal vein, if present, either straight or curved away from costal margin **37**

36(35). Middle tibia with 2 apical spurs; large apical spur on fore tibia forked apically; antennae 11-segmented in both sexes; stigma of fore wing usually large, semicircular (Figure 35–19E) (rarely linear or wings veinless in male Lagynodìnae) ....**Megaspilidae**   p. 705

36'. Middle tibia with 1 apical spur; large spur of fore tibia not forked apically; female antennae 9- or 10-segmented, male antennae 10- or 11-segmented; stigma of fore wing linear, appearing similar to marginal vein, but separated from it by a distinct break (Figure 35–19G) (stigma and stigmal vein rarely absent) ....**Ceraphrónidae**   p. 705

37(35',90). Antennal sockets separated from clypeal margin by distinctly more than 1 diameter of socket (Figure 35–22C, 35–59) **38**

37'. Antennal sockets contiguous with dorsal margin of clypeus or separated from it by less than 1 diameter of socket (Figure 35–22A,B) **43**

38(37). Antennae 10-segmented; hind wings with jugal lobe ....**Embolémidae***   p. 724

38'. Antennae 11- to 16-segmented; hind wings without a jugal lobe (Figures 35–19D, 35–31G) **39**

39(38'). Basitarsus of hind leg distinctly shorter than following segments; fore wing with Rs forked apically (Figure 35–20A) ....**Pelecinidae**   p. 722

39'. Basitarsus of hind leg distinctly longer than following segments; fore wing with Rs not forked or absent entirely **40**

40(39'). First antennal segment distinctly elongate, at least 2.5 times as long as wide; antennae usually arising from a distinct shelf (Figure 35–59); stigma absent or very small (Figures 35–19D, 35–31G) ....**Diapriidae**   p. 722

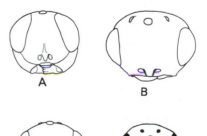

Figure 35–22. Head structure in the Proctotrupòidea, anterior view. **A**, Sceliónidae; **B**, Platygástridae; **C**, Proctotrùpidae; **D**, Vanhorniidae.

40′.   First antennal segment short, at most 2.2 times as long as wide; antennal shelf
            absent; stigma present (Figures 35–20D,F–H) **41**

41(40′).   Antenna 13-segmented; medial cell not defined; marginal cell very narrow
            (Figure 35–20D) ....**Proctotrùpidae**   p. 722

41′.   Antenna with 14 or 16 segments; medial cell defined (Figure 35–20F,H, *M*);
            marginal cell elongate (Figure 35–20F,H) **42**

42(41′).   Antenna 16-segmented (including 1 minute ring segment following pedicel);
            metasoma slightly wider than high, in lateral view tergites subequal in
            height to sternites; medial cell triangular (Figure 35–20H, *M*) .....**Helòridae**   p. 722

42′.   Antenna 14-segmented (without ring segment); metasoma strongly compressed
            laterally, in lateral view tergites much higher than sternites; medial cell
            polygonal (Figure 35–20F, *M*) ....**Roproniidae**   p. 722

43(37′).   First antennal segment short and stout, less than 2 times as long as wide;
            antenna 13-segmented; mandibles with tips pointing outward, and widely
            separated when closed (Figure 35–22D); fore wing with thick stigma, mar-
            ginal cell closed (Figure 35–20G) ....**Vanhorniidae**   p. 721

43′.   First antennal segment long and slender, distinctly more than 2.5 times as long
            as wide; antenna never with 13-segments; mandibles normal, touching or
            crossing when closed; fore wing with stigma absent, marginal cell never
            closed **44**

44(43′).   Second metasomatic tergite distinctly longer than all others, several times
            longer than tergite 3 ....**45**

44′.   Tergite 2 not distinctly longer than others, at most subequal in length to
            tergite 3 ....**Sceliónidae**   p. 722

45(44).   Fore wing with stigmal and usually postmarginal veins; antennae usually
            11- or 12-segmented, rarely 10-segmented ....**Sceliónidae**   p. 722

45′.   Fore wing without stigmal or postmarginal vein (Figure 35–19H), often
            entirely veinless; antenna with 10 or fewer segments ....**Platygástridae**   p. 723

46(26′).   Venation greatly reduced (as in Figure 35–19B), the hind wings without an
            incision setting off a jugal or vannal lobe; antennae elbowed; mesosoma
            usually with a distinct prepectus (Figure 35–4A, *pp*); trochanters generally
            2-segmented (Chalcidòidea) **47**

46′.   Wings with more veins, the hind wings usually with a lobe (jugal or vannal)
            set off by a distinct incision (Figures 35–19F, 35–20B); antennae usually not
            elbowed; trochanters usually 1-segmented (Chrysidòidea) **80**

47(46).   Hind femora greatly swollen and usually toothed or denticulate beneath (Fig-
            ure 35–23E); hind tibiae usually arcuate **48**

47′.   Hind femora not swollen or only slightly swollen, and either not toothed
            beneath or with only 1 or 2 teeth **51**

48(47).   Prepectus reduced and narrow, or almost entirely hidden; lateral angles of
            pronotum nearly reaching tegula; color black, brown, to yellow, never
            metallic **49**

48′.   Prepectus normal size, triangular, distinctly separating pronotum from tegula;
            color variable, often metallic **50**

49(48).   Fore wings usually folded longitudinally at rest; ovipositor curved up over
            dorsum of female; tegulae elongate ....**Leucóspidae**   p. 719

49′.   Fore wings not folded longitudinally; ovipositor directed posteriorly; tegula
            oval, not elongate ....**Chalcídidae**   p. 719

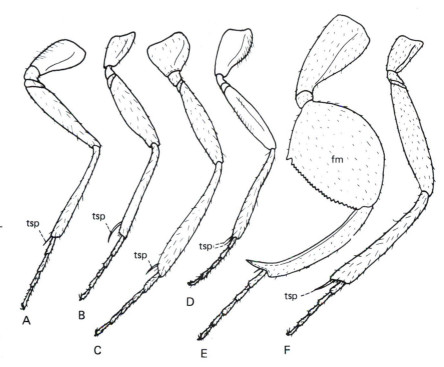

Figure 35–23. Legs of Chalcidòidea. **A,** front leg, Eulóphidae; **B,** front leg, Pteromálidae; **C,** hind leg, Pteromálidae; **D,** hind leg, Eurytómidae; **E,** hind leg, Chalcídidae; **F,** middle leg, Encýrtidae. *fm,* femur, *tsp,* tibial spur.

50(48′).	Inner margins of eyes diverging ventrally; antennae inserted distinctly below lower margins of eyes; body generally flattened ....**Pteromálidae**	p. 717
50′.	Inner margins of eyes parallel; antennae inserted near to or distinctly above lower margins of eyes; body convex (Podagrionìnae) ....**Torýmidae**	p. 717
51(47′, 112′).	Tarsi 3-segmented; wing pubescence often arranged in rows; minute insects ....**Trichogrammátidae**	p. 712
51′.	Tarsi 4- or 5-segmented; wing pubescence usually not arranged in rows; size variable **52**	
52(51′).	Petiole of metasoma 2-segmented, elongate; surface of fore wing with netlike reticulations; minute pale-colored species, less than 1 mm in length ....**Mymarommátidae***	p. 712
52′.	Either metasomatic petiole 1-segmented or metasoma sessile; fore wing normal, usually setose, without reticulations; size and color variable **53**	
53(52′).	Bases of antennae widely separated, inserted closer to eyes than to each other; frons with a distinct transverse sulcus above antennal insertions, and with a pair of longitudinal sulci along mesal margins of eyes (Figure 35–24); small to minute species, usually less than 1 mm in length ....**Mymáridae**	p. 712

Figure 35–24. Head structure in Mymàridae.

53'.   Antennal insertions closer to each other than to eyes; frons without such sulci; size variable **54**

54(53').   Tarsi 4-segmented **55**

54'.   Tarsi 5-segmented **60**

55(54).   Antennal funicle with 4 or fewer segments (Figure 35–25A,C) **56**

55'.   Antennal funicle with 5 or more segments (Figure 35–25B) **59**

56(55).   Hind coxa greatly enlarged and flattened; outer surface of hind tibiae with short dark bristles arranged in zigzag lines or otherwise forming a distinctive pattern (Figure 35–26); fore wings narrow; male antennae branched ....**Elásmidae**   p. 712

56'.   Hind coxa subequal in size to middle coxa; outer surface of hind tibia without bristles forming a pattern; fore wings and male antennae variable **57**

57(56').   Mesopleuron convex (as in Figure 35–27A); antennal clava long and unsegmented (and flagellum appearing to be 1-segmented) or body minute (<1 mm) **58**

57'.   Mesopleuron with well-developed groove for reception of middle femur; antennal clava usually short and divided into 2 or 3 segments; body rarely < 1 mm ....**Eulóphidae**   p. 712

58(57).   Axillae meeting along dorsal midline of mesothorax; notauli absent; small, but >1 mm in length ....**Encýrtidae***   p. 714

58'.   Axillae separated medially; notauli present; minute (<1 mm) ....**Aphelínidae***   p. 713

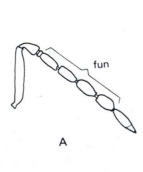

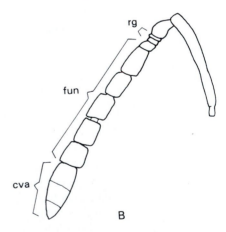

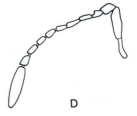

Figure 35–25.   Antennae of Chalcidòidea. **A**, Eulóphidae; **B**, Pteromálidae; **C**, Trichogrammátidae; **D**, Mymàridae. *cva*, clava; *fun*, funicle; *rg*, ring segments.

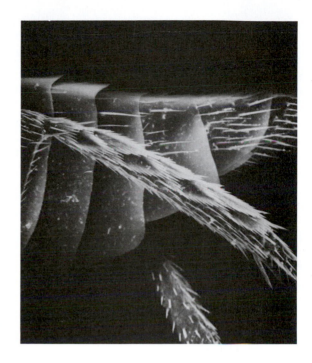

Figure 35–26.   Hind tibia of *Elásmus* sp. (Elásmidae).

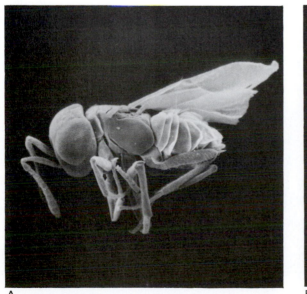

A

B

Figure 35–27.   Encýrtidae. **A,** lateral habitus; **B,** tarsus and apex of tibia of middle leg.

59(55').   Notauli usually absent; mesopleuron convex (Figure 35–27A); midtibial spur
            long, thick (Figure 35–27B); middle basitarsal segment usually densely se-
            tose beneath; males and females; large, very common group ......**Encýrtidae**   p. 714

59'.   Notauli complete; mesopleuron with groove for reception of middle femur;
            midtibial spur short, thin; basitarsus "normal"; males only
            ....**Tetracámpidae***   p. 713

60(54').   Head long, oblong, with a deep longitudinal groove above (Figure 35–52A);
            front and hind legs stout, tibiae much shorter than femora, middle legs slen-
            der (females; Florida, California, Arizona) ....**Agaónidae***   p. 717

60'.   Head and legs not as above **61**

61(60').   Antennal funicle with 4 or fewer segments **62**

61'.   Antennal funicle with 5 or more segments **64**

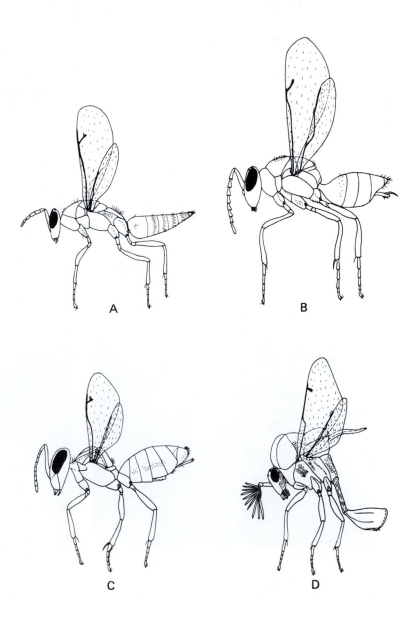

Figure 35–28. Chalcidòidea. **A,**
Eulóphidae; **B,** Encýrtidae; **C,**
Eupélmidae; **D,** Eucharítidae.

62(61).   Axillae not separated from scutellum, together the two forming a narrow transverse band across mesosoma; propodeum with a median triangular area; middle tibia with lateral spurs ....**Signiphòridae**   p. 714

62'.   Axillae distinctly separated from scutellum; propodeum without a distinct triangular area; middle tibia with apical spurs only **63**

63(62').   Axillae contiguous medially; notauli absent ....**Encýrtidae**   p. 714

63'.   Axillae widely separated medially; notauli present ....**Aphelìnidae**   p. 713

64(61').   Mesopleura large and convex, usually without a femoral groove (Figure 35–27A); apical spur of middle tibia generally very large and stout (Figure 35–27B) **65**

64'.   Mesopleura with a groove for reception of the femora (Figures 35–28D, 35–29); apical spur of middle tibia not enlarged **67**

65(64).   Middle coxae inserted in front of midline of length of mesopleuron and nearly contiguous with fore coxae; prepectus flat; axillae wider than long and meeting medially.. **Encýrtidae**   p. 714

65'.   Middle coxae usually inserted distinctly behind midline of length of mesopleuron and widely separated from fore coxae; rarely with middle coxae inserted near midline of length of mesopleuron, in these cases prepectus strongly protuberant, covering posterior margin of mesopleuron; axillae either not meeting medially or longer than wide **66**

66(65').   Prepectus inflated and covering posterior portion of pronotum (especially apparent viewed from below); mesosoma compact; Florida, California, Arizona ....**Tanaostigmátidae***   p. 716

66'.   Prepectus flat, not protruding over pronotum; mesosoma usually elongate; widely distributed ....**Eupélmidae**   p. 716

67(64').   Mandibles sickle-shaped, with 1 or 2 teeth on inner side; mesosoma strongly elevated (Figure 35–28D); axillae contiguous and sometimes forming a transverse band anterior to scutellum; scutellum sometimes large and produced posteriorly; metasoma compressed, the second segment very large ....**Eucharítidae***   p. 718

67'.   Mandibles stout, not sickle-shaped, and with 3 or 4 teeth at apex; mesosoma not elevated; axillae usually separated, and triangular; scutellum and metasoma variable in shape **68**

68(67').   Metasoma dorsally with transverse rows of deep pits or with strongly developed transverse crenulae; metasoma of female conical and elongate, of male oblong; cerci short, sessile; hind tibia with two apical spurs, either with inner spur distinctly longer than outer and usually curved, or both very long ....**Ormýridae**   p. 717

68'.   Metasoma without such sculpture; hind tibiae with one or two spurs, these relatively straight and short, often difficult to see **69**

69(68').   Prepectus fused with pronotum or rigidly attached to it and anterior portion of mesepisternum; metasoma with petiole often very small and inconspicuous, first two large terga fused dorsally and covering at least half the metasoma, metasoma often appearing short and triangular in lateral view; mesosoma usually coarsely punctate, robust ....**Perilámpidae**   p. 718

69'.   Prepectus present as an independent sclerite, not fused with pronotum; metasoma usually with terga 2 and 3 independent (except some Pteromálidae); mesosoma usually with fine sculpture dorsally, if coarsely punctate, then usually longer than high **70**

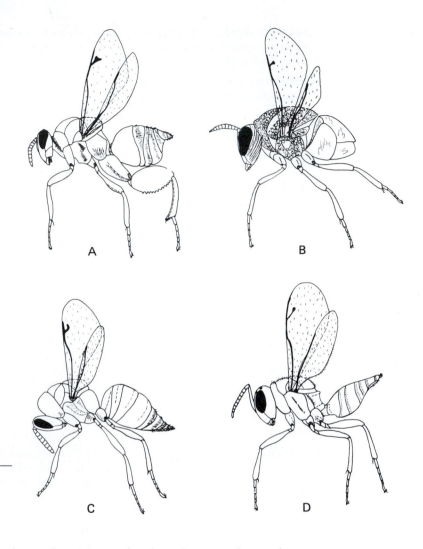

Figure 35–29. Chalcidòidea. **A,**
Chalcídidae; **B,** Perilámpidae; **C,**
Eurytómidae; **D,** Pteromálidae.

70(69').   Females; metasoma either with ovipositor sheaths as long as or longer than
            mesosoma and metasoma combined, or metasoma with ovipositor sheaths
            and apical terga greatly elongated to form a distinctive "tail" .....**Torýmidae**   p. 717

70'.   Males and females; apical metasomatic terga not elongated, ovipositor sheaths
            distinctly shorter than combined length of mesosoma and metasoma **71**

71(70').   Females; ovipositor sheaths at least one-third length of hind tibiae, often
            longer; cerci elongate, peglike; hind coxa much larger than fore coxa, more
            or less triangular in cross section ....**Torýmidae**   p. 717

71'.   Both males and females; ovipositor sheaths usually shorter; cerci very short,
            barely raised above surface of metasoma; hind coxa subequal in size to fore
            coxa, more or less circular in cross section **72**

72(71').   Males; fore wing with postmarginal vein much shorter than marginal vein,
            subequal in length to stigmal vein; hind coxa much larger than fore coxa,
            more or less triangular in cross section; inner margins of eyes parallel in
            frontal view ....**Torýmidae**   p. 717

72'.   Males and females; fore wing venation not as above; hind coxae variable, if
            large and triangular in cross section, then inner margins of eyes diverging
            ventrally **73**

73(72').   Collar of pronotum (the posterior portion, excluding the narrowed, necklike anterior part) at least half as long as mesoscutum, elongate or rectangular in dorsal view **74**

73'.   Pronotal collar less than half length of mesoscutum, or pronotum with sides converging, bell-shaped **78**

74(73).   Stigma of fore wing with conspicuous knoblike expansion; funicle 7-segmented; prepectus large, triangular ....**Torýmidae**   p. 717

74'.   Stigma usually not greatly enlarged; if so, then funicle with 6 or fewer large segments and prepectus small and inconspicuous **75**

75(74').   Head or body partly metallic in color **76**

75'.   Head and body entirely nonmetallic **77**

76(75).   Funicle 5-segmented; propodeum depressed or with longitudinal furrow medially ....**Eurytómidae**   p. 719

76'.   Funicle with more than 5 segments or propodeum evenly convex or flattened ....**Pteromálidae**   p. 717

77(75').   Antennae inserted at or above lower margins of eyes; funicle usually with 6 or fewer segments, if with more then propodeum with longitudinal furrow medially ....**Eurytómidae**   p. 719

77'.   Antennae inserted below lower margins of eyes; funicle either with 7 segments or propodeum flattened or convex, often with longitudinal carina medially ....**Pteromálidae**   p. 717

78(73').   Fore tibial spur short, straight, about one-fourth length of basitarsus; propodeum distinctly setose medially; pronotum as long as or longer than mesoscutum ....**Tetracámpidae***   p. 713

78'.   Fore tibial spur usually distinctly curved, if not, then more than one-fourth length of basitarsus; propodeum bare; pronotum usually distinctly shorter than mesoscutum **79**

Figure 35–30.   Opened chela of foreleg of female dryinid.

79(78').   Males; apical spur of middle tibiae long, slender; apex of fore tibia with 1 or more short, stout spines on side opposite tibial spur; femoral groove on mesopleuron with minute netlike sculpture; mesopleuron often with light line extending anteriorly from middle coxa ....**Eupélmidae**   p. 716

79'.   Males and females; apical spur of middle tibia short and apex of fore tibia without spines; if otherwise, then femoral groove of mesopleuron with coarse netlike sculpture or punctured and light lines absent ...**Pteromálidae**   p. 717

80(46').   Antennae with 22 or more segments and arising low on face; Arizona (males) ....**Sclerogíbbidae***   p. 724

80'.   Antennae with 10–13 segments **81**

81(80').   Antennae 10-segmented; front tarsi of female usually pincerlike (Figure 35–30) ....**Dryínidae***   p. 724

81'.   Antennae 12- or 13-segmented; front tarsi not pincerlike **82**

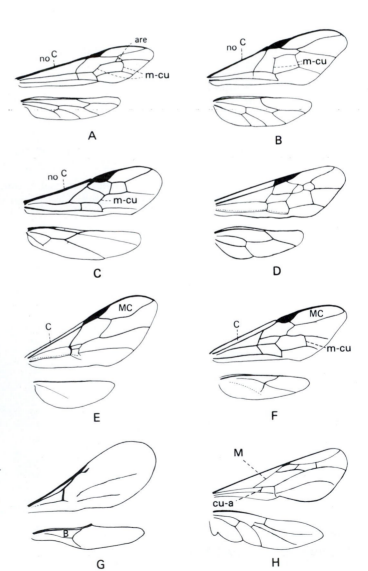

Figure 35–31. Wings of Hymenóptera. **A,** Ichneumónidae (*Megarhýssa*); **B,** Ichneumónidae (*Òphion*); **C,** Bracónidae; **D,** Trigonálidae; **E,** Gasteruptìidae; **F,** Aulácidae; **G,** Diapriidae (Belytìnae); **H,** Rhopalosomátidae (*Rhopalosòma*). *are,* areolet; *B,* basal cell; *C,* costal cell; *MC,* marginal cell.

82(81′).   Metasoma with 3–5 visible terga, the last one often dentate apically; head not elongate; body usually metallic blue or green and coarsely sculptured ....**Chrysídidae**   p. 723

82′.   Metasoma with 6 or 7 visible terga; head usually oblong and elongate; body black ....**Bethýlidae**   p. 724

83(25′).   Metasoma arising on propodeum far above bases of hind coxae (Figure 35–18D–F) **84**

83′.   Metasoma arising on propodeum between bases of hind coxae or only slightly above them (as in Figure 35–18A–C) **87**

84(27′,83).   Hind wings with a distinct jugal lobe (Figure 35–20C); metasoma short, oval to circular and compressed, with a cylindrical petiole (Figure 35–18F, 35–43) ....**Evaniidae**   p. 706

84′.   Hind wings without a distinct jugal lobe (Figure 35–31 E,F); metasoma elongate **85**

85(84′).   Prothorax long and necklike; venation usually complete, the front wings with a stigma (Figure 35–31 E,F); antennae 14-segmented; length over 8 mm; widely distributed **86**

85′.   Prothorax not long and necklike; venation reduced, much as in Figure 35–19A, the front wings without a stigma; antennae 13-segmented in female and 14-segmented in male; length less than 8 mm; Texas ....**Lioptéridae***   p. 719

86(85).   One m-cu cross vein or none, and 1 submarginal cell or none (Figure 35–31E); usually black, with relatively short antennae ....**Gasteruptiidae**   p. 707

86′.   Two m-cu cross veins and 1 or 2 submarginal cells (Figure 35–31F); usually black with a reddish metasoma, and the antennae relatively long ....**Aulácidae**   p. 707

87(83′).   Hind trochanters 2-segmented (Figure 35–32A), the distal segment sometimes poorly defined, rarely the trochanters 1-segmented; antennae with 14 or

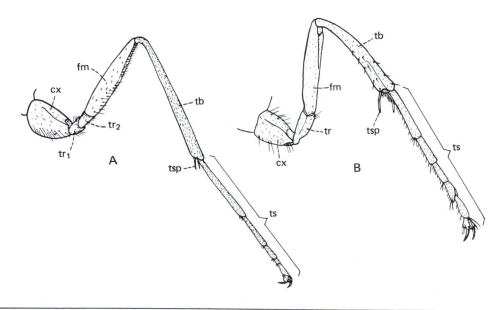

Figure 35–32. Legs of Hymenóptera. **A,** Ichneumónidae; **B,** Sphécidae. *cx,* coxa; *fm,* femur; *tb,* tibia; *tr,* trochanter; *ts,* tarsus; *tsp,* tibial spurs.

more segments; hind wings usually without a jugal lobe (Figure 35–31 A–D); ovipositor variable, but sometimes long, half as long as metasoma or longer, and permanently exserted (Figure 35–5A) **88**

87'.   Hind trochanters 1-segmented (Figure 35–32B); antennae usually 12-segmented in females and 13-segmented in males; hind wings usually with a jugal lobe (Figure 35–33); ovipositor short, issuing from apex of metasoma (usually as a sting), and usually withdrawn into metasoma when not in use (Figure 35–5B) **92**

88(87).   Head somewhat spherical, set out on a long neck, and bearing a crown of teeth; costal cell usually present but narrow; 1 submarginal cell or none; female with a long ovipositor; length usually over 10 mm ....**Stephánidae***   p. 705

88'.   Head not as above; venation, size, and ovipositor variable **89**

89(88').   Costal cell present (Figure 35–31 D); ovipositor very short **90**

89'.   Costal cell absent (Figure 35–31 A–C); ovipositor often long **91**

90(89).   Venation somewhat reduced, with not more than 1 submarginal cell; antennae 14- or 15-segmented **37***

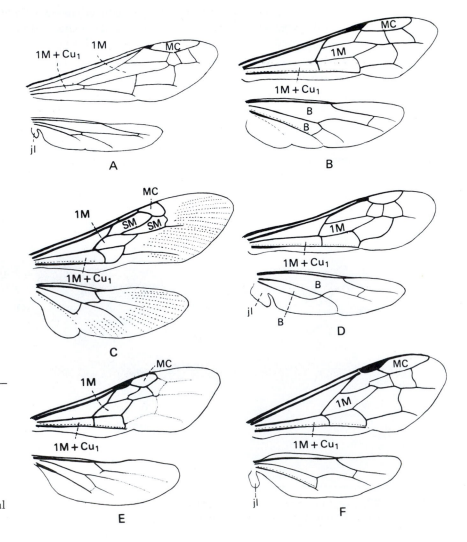

Figure 35–33. Wings of Hymenóptera. **A,** Véspidae (*Polístes*); **B,** Tiphìidae (*Mỳzinum*); **C,** Scolìidae (*Scòlia*); **D,** Pompílidae; **E,** Mutíllidae (*Dasymutílla*); **F,** Mutíllidae (Myrmosìnae). *B,* basal cell; *jl,* jugal lobe; *MC,* marginal cell; *SM,* submarginal cell.

90′.   Venation not reduced, with 2 or 3 submarginal cells; antennae with 16 or more
            segments ....**Trigonálidae***   p. 706

91(89′).   Two m-cu cross veins (Figure 35–31 A,B), or if with only 1, then the metasoma
            3 times as long as rest of body and with tip of propodeum prolonged behind
            hind coxae; metasomatic tergites 2 and 3 independent, overlapping; vein Rs
            + M absent, first submarginal and 1M cells confluent; size variable, from a
            few mm up to 40 mm or more in length (excluding ovipositor)
            ....**Ichneumónidae**   p. 708

91′.   One m-cu cross vein (Figure 35–31 C) or none; first submarginal and 1M cells
            usually separated by vein Rs + M; metasoma not greatly elongate, tergites 2
            and 3 (at least) fused; propodeum not prolonged behind hind coxae; mostly
            small insects, rarely over 15 mm in length ....**Bracónidae**   p. 707

92(87′).   1M cell long, much longer than 1M + Cu₁ cell, and usually about half as
            long as wing (Figure 35–33A); wings usually folded lengthwise at rest; 3
            submarginal cells; posterior margin of pronotum (in dorsal view)
            U-shaped ....**Véspidae**   p. 736

92′.   1M cell usually shorter than 1M + Cu₁ cell and no more than one-third as
            long as wing (Figure 35–33B–F); wings usually not folded longitudinally at
            rest; 2 or 3 submarginal cells; posterior margin of pronotum (in dorsal view)
            usually straight or slightly arcuate **93**

93(92′).   Mesopleuron with a transverse sulcus (Figure 35–34, *su*); hind legs long, the
            hind femora usually extending to or beyond apex of metasoma; body
            bare ....**Pompílidae**   p. 735

93′.   Mesopleuron without a transverse sulcus; legs shorter, the hind femora usually
            not extending to apex of metasoma; body often somewhat hairy **94**

94(93′).   Mesosternum and metasternum together forming a plate divided by a trans-
            verse sulcus, and overlapping bases of middle and hind coxae, the hind coxae
            well separated (Figure 35–35A); wing membrane beyond closed cells with
            fine longitudinal wrinkles (Figure 35–33C); apex of metasoma of male with
            3 retractile spines; large, often brightly colored wasps ....**Scoliidae**   p. 735

94′.   Mesosternum and metasternum not forming such a plate, though there may be
            a pair of plates overlying bases of middle coxae (Figure 35–35B); hind coxae

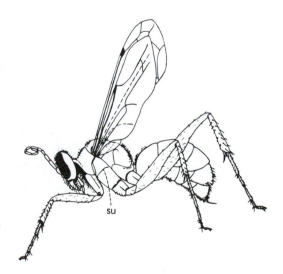

Figure 35–34.   A spider wasp (Pompílidae), showing
the transverse sulcus (*su*) across the mesopleuron.

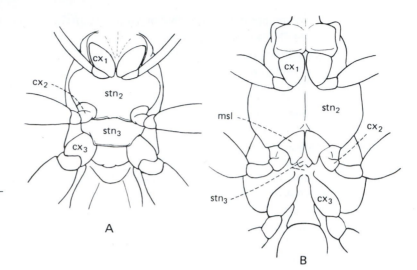

Figure 35–35. Mesosoma, ventral view. **A,** *Scòlia* (Scolìidae); **B,** *Típhia* (Tiphìidae). *cx,* coxa; *msl,* mesosternal lobe; *stn₂,* mesosternum; *stn₃,* metasternum.

contiguous or nearly so; wing membrane beyond closed cells usually not wrinkled; apex of metasoma of male without 3 retractile spines; size and color variable **95**

95(94′).   Antennae clavate (Figure 35–36D); 2 submarginal cells (Figure 35–36A); length 10–20 mm; color usually black and yellow; western United States (Masarìnae) ....**Véspidae**   p. 736

95′.   Antennae not clavate; other characters variable **96**

96(95′).   Cross vein cu-a more than two-thirds its length distad of first free segment of M (between M + Cu₁ and Rs, Figure 35–31H); hind tarsi very long; flagellar segments of antennae long and slender, each with 2 apical spines; light brown wasps, 14–20 mm in length ....**Rhopalosomátidae***   p. 735

96′.   Cross vein cu-a opposite first free segment of M or nearly so (Figure 35–33E,F); tarsi not as above; flagellar segments of antennae without apical spines; size and color variable **97**

97(96′).   Mesosternum with 2 lobelike extensions behind, which project between and partly cover bases of middle coxae (Figure 35–35B); hind wings with a jugal lobe (Figure 35–2) (Brachycistidìnae, Tiphiìnae, Myzinìnae, Anthoboscìnae) ....**Tiphìidae**   p. 734

97′.   Mesosternum without such lobes, at most a pair of minute toothlike projections behind; hind wings with or without a jugal lobe **98**

98(97′).   Apex of 2M + Cu₁ cell produced above, and jugal lobe in hind wing about half as long as 1M + Cu₁ cell (Figure 35–36C); length 6–7 mm; western United States (Euparagiìnae) ....**Véspidae***   p. 736

98′.   Not exactly fitting above description **99**

99(98′).   Hind wings with a distinct jugal lobe (Figure 35–33F) **100***

99′.   Hind wings without a distinct jugal lobe (Figure 35–33E) **104**

100(99).   Metasomatic segments separated by strong constrictions; eyes usually not emarginate **101**

100′.   Metasoma without such constrictions; eyes sometimes emarginate **102***

101(100).   Apex of abdomen with an upcurved spine; jugal lobe of hind wing at least half as long as cell M + Cu₁ (Methochìnae) ....**Tiphìidae**   p. 734

101'.   Apex of abdomen without an upcurved spine; jugal lobe in hind wing less than
           one-third as long as cell M + Cu₁ (Myrmosìnae) ....**Mutíllidae**   p. 734

102(100'). Body bare, marked with yellow or white; eyes deeply emarginate; widely dis-
           tributed (Sapygìnae) ....**Sapýgidae***   p. 734

102'.   Body usually very hairy; color and eyes variable; western United States ...**103***

103(102'). Second metasomatic tergum with lateral submarginal felt lines (narrow
           longitudinal bands of relatively dense, closely appressed hairs); usually very
           pubescent (males) ....**Bradynobaènidae***   p. 734

103'.   Second metasomatic tergum without lateral felt lines; body and legs clothed
           with long erect hairs; males and females (*Fedtschénkia*, California)
           ....**Sapýgidae***   p. 734

104(99').   Shining black, 4.5–6.0 mm in length; second metasomatic tergum without
           lateral felt lines (see 103); males without spines at apex of metasoma; eyes
           not emarginate mesally; males and females ....**Sierolomórphidae***   p. 734

104'.   Not shining black, but very hairy and often brightly colored; size variable but
           usually over 6 mm in length; second metasomatic tergum usually with
           lateral submarginal felt lines; usually with 1 or 2 spines at apex of
           metasoma **105**

105(104'). Middle tibia with 1 apical spur; antennal sockets not produced into tubercles
           (western United States) ....**Bradynobaènidae***   p. 734

105'.   Middle tibia with 2 apical spurs; antennal sockets produced dorsally into large
           tubercles (widespread) ....**Mutíllidae**   p. 734

106(14').   Antennae with 16 or more segments **107**

106'.   Antennae with fewer than 16 segments **109**

107(106).   Hind trochanters 1-segmented (rarely 2-segmented); ovipositor issuing from
           apex of metasoma and usually withdrawn into metasoma when not in use;
           females; Arizona ....**Sclerogíbbidae***   p. 724

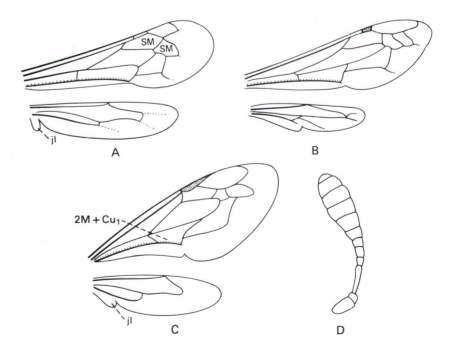

Figure 35–36. Characters
of Véspidae. **A,** wings of
Pseudomaśaris (Masarìnae); **B,**
wings of *Véspa* (Vespìnae); **C,**
wings of *Euparágia*
(Euparagiìnae); **D,** antenna of
Pseudomásaris (Masarìnae). *jl*,
jugal lobe; *SM,* submarginal
cell.

107'.   Hind trochanters 2-segmented; ovipositor issuing from anterior to apex of me-
             tasoma and permanently exserted; widely distributed **108***

108(107').   Metasoma petiolate, petiole curved and expanded apically ....**Ichneumónidae***   p. 708

108'.   Metasoma not petiolate, or if petiolate, then petiole is not curved or expanded
             apically ....**Bracónidae***   p. 707

109(106').   Pronotum triangular in lateral view, reaching tegula posteriorly **110**

109'.   Pronotum more or less quadrate in lateral view, distinctly separated from
             tegula...**111**

110(109).   Metasoma laterally compressed; ovipositor issuing from anterior to apex of
             metasoma and permanently exserted (wingless Cynipòidea) **30**

110'.   Metasoma cylindrical or depressed dorsoventrally, rarely laterally compressed;
             ovipositor issuing from apex of metasoma and usually withdrawn when not
             in use (wingless Embolémidae, Proctotrupòidea, Ceraphronòidea) **35**

111(109').   First antennal segment elongate, antennae elbowed; prepectus well developed
             and triangular (Figure 35–4A, *pp*); ovipositor issuing from anterior to apex of
             metasoma and permanently exserted (wingless Chalcidòidea) **112**

111'.   Antennae filiform; ovipositor issuing from apex of metasoma, usually as a
             sting, and usually withdrawn into metasoma when not in use (Figure 35–5B)
             ....**114**

112(111).   Males; associated with figs; head prognathous, heavily sclerotized, often very
             large; ocelli absent **113**

112'.   Males and females; head hypognathous, of more normal size; ocelli
             present **51**

113(112).   Metasoma much drawn out to a point apically or broadened at tip; antennae
             short and stout, 3- to 9-segmented (see also 60) ....**Agaónidae***   p. 717

113'.   Metasoma not pointed or enlarged apically ....**Torýmidae***   p. 717

114(111').   Second metasomatic segment with lateral felt lines (see 103); body usually
             very pubescent; antennae usually 12-segmented, rarely 11- or 13-segmented;
             females **115**

114'.   Second metasomatic segment without lateral felt lines **116***

115(114).   Pronotum immovably fused to mesoscutum; lateral felt lines on tergum 2,
             sternum 2 or both; thoracic pleura flattened ....**Mutíllidae**   p. 734

115'.   Pronotum separated from rest of mesosoma by distinct, flexible articulation;
             lateral felt lines present only on tergum 2; thoracic pleura
             protuberant ....**Bradynobaènidae***   p. 734

116(114').   Antennae 10-segmented ....**Dryínidae***   p. 724

116'.   Antennae 12- or 13-segmented **117***

117(116').   Antennae arising in middle of face; hind tarsi very long, nearly as long as tibiae
             and femora combined; first metasomatic segment long and slender; wings
             present but very short (*Olíxon*) ....**Rhopalosomátidae***   p. 735

117'.   Antennae arising low on face, near margin of clypeus; tarsi and metasoma not
             as above **118**

118(117').   Head elongate, usually longer than wide; front femora usually thickened in
             middle; females ....**Bethýlidae***   p. 724

118'.   Head not elongate, usually oval and wider than high **119**

119(118').   Mesosternum with two lobelike extensions behind covering bases of mid coxae
             (Brachycistidìnae)..**Tiphíidae**   p. 734

119′.	Mesosternum without such lobes, at most with a pair of minute toothlike projections posteriorly **120**	
120(119′).	Mesosoma divided into 3 parts (Methochìnae) ....**Tiphìidae**	p. 734
120′.	Mesosoma divided into 2 parts, the prothorax being well separated from the remaining fused segments (Myrmosìnae) ....**Mutíllidae**	p. 734

SUBORDER **Sýmphyta:** The members of this suborder, except for the family Orússidae, are phytophagous or xylophagous, and most are external feeders on foliage. The larvae of the external feeders are eruciform (Figure 35–37) and differ from the larvae of the Lepidóptera in that they have more than five pairs of prolegs that lack crochets and usually have only one pair of stemmata. The larvae of a few species bore in stems, fruits, wood, or leaves (leaf miners). These larvae usually have the prolegs reduced or absent. All the Sýmphyta have a well-developed ovipositor, which is used in inserting the eggs into the tissues of the host plant. In the Tenthredinòidea and Megalodontòidea the ovipositor is somewhat sawlike, hence the common name "sawflies" for the members of this group.

Most of the Sýmphyta have a single generation a year and overwinter as a full-grown larva or as a pupa, either in a cocoon or in some sort of protected place. Most of the external feeders overwinter in a cocoon or cell in the soil, while boring species usually overwinter in their tunnels in the host plant. Some of the larger species may require more than one year to complete their development.

Family **Xyèlidae:** The Xyèlidae are medium-sized to small sawflies, mostly less than 10 mm in length, that differ from other sawflies in having three marginal cells (Figure 35–8C) and the third antennal segment very long (longer than the remaining segments combined) (Figure 35–10D). Unlike all other sawflies except the Pamphilìidae, the costal cell of xyelids is divided by a longitudinal vein, the subcosta. The larva feed on various trees. *Xyèla* larvae feed on the staminate cones of pine; those of *Pleroneùra* and *Xyèlecia* bore in the buds and developing shoots of firs; and other species attack hickory and elm. Adults may be collected in the early spring feeding on the catkins of willows and birches. This group is a small one (29 North American species), and none of its members is of very great economic importance.

Family **Pamphilìidae**—Web-Spinning and Leaf-Rolling Sawflies: These sawflies are stout-bodied and usually less than 15 mm in length. Seventy-two species occur in North America. Some larvae are gregarious, and some feed singly. The gregarious ones live in silken nests formed by tying several leaves together, and the solitary ones live in a shelter formed by rolling up a leaf. Members of this group are uncommon, and only a few of them are of much economic importance. Some species of *Acanthólyda* and *Cephálcia* are pests of conifers; *Neurótoma inconspícua* (Norton) (a web-spinning species) feeds on plum; and *Pamphílius pérsicum* MacGillivray (a leaf-rolling species) feeds on peach.

Family **Pérgidae:** The sawflies in this group (four North American species) are fairly small and occur from the eastern states west to Arizona, but they are uncommon. Their larvae feed on the foliage of oak and hickory. Our species belong to the genus *Acordulécera.*

Family **Árgidae:** The Árgidae are a small group (59 North American species) of medium-sized to small, stout-bodied sawflies, easily recognized by

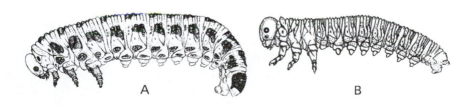

Figure 35–37. Sawfly larvae. **A,** *Neodíprion lecóntei* (Fitch) (Dipriónidae); **B,** *Allántus cínctus* (L.) (Tenthredínidae). (Courtesy of USDA.)

the characteristic antennae (Figure 35–10E). Males of a few species have the last antennal segment U-shaped or Y-shaped. Most of the argids are black or dark-colored. The larvae feed chiefly on various kinds of trees, but *Árge humeràlis* (Beauvois) feeds on poison ivy, *Sphacóphilus cellulàris* (Say) feeds on sweet potato, and *Schizocerélla pilicórnis* (Holmgren) mines leaves of *Portuláca*.

Family **Cimbícidae:**   The Cimbícidae are large, robust sawflies with clubbed antennae. Only 12 species are found in the United States and Canada. Some resemble bumble bees. The most common species is the elm sawfly, *Címbex americàna* Leach, a dark blue insect 18–25 mm in length (Figure 35–38A). The female has four yellow spots on each side of the abdomen. The full-grown larva of this species is about 40 mm long, with the diameter of a pencil, and is greenish yellow with black spiracles and a black stripe down the back. When at rest or when disturbed, it assumes a spiral position. Often, when disturbed, it will eject a fluid, sometimes for a distance of several centimeters, from glands just above the spiracles. This species has one generation a year and overwinters as a full-grown larva in a cocoon in the ground. It pupates in the spring, and the adults appear in early summer. The larvae feed chiefly on

elm and willow. Other species are commonly found feeding on honeysuckle.

Family **Dipriónidae**—Conifer Sawflies: These are medium-sized sawflies with 13 or more antennal segments. The antennae are serrate in the female and pectinate or bipectinate in the male (Figures 35–10C, 35–38B,C). The larvae (Figure 35–37A) feed on conifers. They may sometimes do serious damage, and species of *Díprion* and *Neodíprion* have been important forest pests especially in Canada and the northern United States. Forty-four species occur in this area.

Family **Tenthredínidae**—Common Sawflies: This is a very large group (about 790 North American species), and probably nine out of ten of the sawflies the general collector is likely to encounter will belong to this family. The adults are wasplike insects, often brightly colored, and are usually found on foliage or flowers searching for host plants, mates, or prey (many of the adults are predaceous). They are medium-sized to small, rarely over 20 mm in length (Figure 35–39). The larvae (Figure 35–37B) are eruciform, and most of them are external feeders on foliage. When feeding, they usually have the body (or the posterior part of it) coiled over the edge of a leaf. There is usually a single generation a year, and the

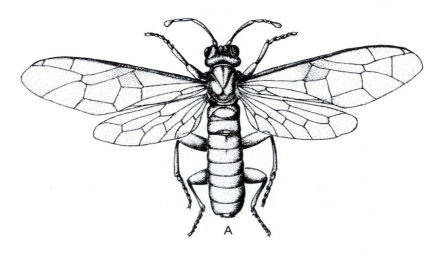

A

Figure 35–38.   Sawflies. **A,** the elm sawfly, *Címbex americàna* Leach, male (Cimbícidae); **B,** the red-headed pine sawfly, *Neodíprion lecóntei* (Fitch), male (Dipriónidae); **C,** same, female. (**B** and **C,** redrawn from USDA.)

B

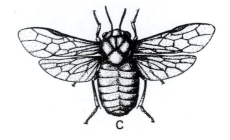

C

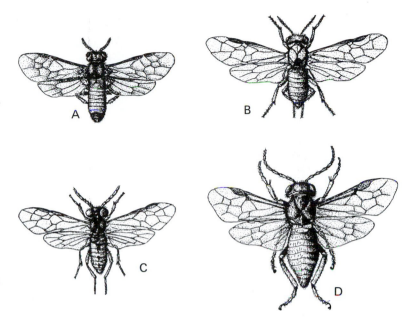

Figure 35–39. Common sawflies (Tenthredínidae). **A,** the birch leaf miner, *Fenùsa pusílla* (Lepeletier), male; **B,** the cherry and hawthorn sawfly, *Profenùsa canadénsis* (Marlatt), female; **C,** same, male; **D,** the raspberry leaf sawfly, *Prióphorus mòrio* (Lepeletier), female. (**A,** redrawn from Friend and the Bulletin of the Connecticut Agricultural Experiment Station; **B** and **C,** redrawn from Parrot and Fulton and the Bulletin of the Geneva, N.Y., Agricultural Experiment Station; **D,** redrawn from Smith and Kido and Hilgardia.)

insect overwinters in a pupal cell or cocoon, either in the ground or in a protected situation.

Sawfly larvae feed chiefly on various trees and shrubs, and some of them are very destructive. The larch sawfly, *Pristíphora erichsònii* (Hartig), is a very destructive pest of larch and, when numerous, may cause extensive defoliation over large areas. The imported currant-worm, *Némanus ríbesii* (Scopoli), is a serious pest of currants and gooseberries.

A few species in this group are gall makers, and a few are leaf miners. Species of the genus *Euùra* form galls on willow, one of the most common being a small oval gall on the stem. The birch leaf miner (Figure 35–39A), *Fenùsa pusílla* (Lepeletier), which makes blotch mines in birch, is a serious pest in the northeastern states. It has two or three generations a year and pupates in the ground. The elm leaf miner, *Fenùsa úlmi* Sundevall, mines in elm leaves and frequently does quite a bit of damage.

The family Tenthredínidae is divided into eight subfamilies, separated chiefly on the basis of wing venation. The two sexes are differently colored in many species.

Family **Cèphidae**—Stem Sawflies: These are slender, laterally compressed sawflies (Figure 35–40). The larvae bore in the stems of grasses, willows, and berry plants. *Cèphus cínctus* Norton bores in the stems of wheat and is often called the wheat stem sawfly (Figure 35–40C). The adult is about 9 mm in length, shining black, and banded and spotted with yellow. *Cèphus cínctus* is an important wheat pest in the western states. A similar species, *C. pygmaèus*

(L.), occurs in the east. *Jànus ínteger* (Norton) bores in the stems of currants. The adult is shining black and about 13 mm in length. There is a single generation a year, and the insect overwinters in a silken cocoon inside the plant in which the larva feeds. Twelve species are found in Canada and the United States.

Family **Anaxyèlidae**—Incense-Cedar Wood Wasps: This family is represented by only a single species, *Syntéxis libocèdrii* Rohwer, which occurs in northern California and Oregon. The adult female is black and 8 mm in length. The larva bores in the wood of the incense cedar, often in trees that have been weakened, for example, by fires.

Family **Sirícidae**—Horntails: Horntails are fairly large insects, usually 25 mm or more in length, and the larvae are wood-boring. Both sexes have a horny spearlike plate on the last abdominal segment, and the female has a long ovipositor. Most of the 19 North American species attack conifers, but the most common eastern species, *Trèmex colúmba* (L.), attacks maple, beech, and other hardwoods. *Trèmex* is a brown and black insect about 40 mm in length (Figure 35–41A). The larvae are seldom sufficiently numerous to do a great deal of damage, and the trees that are attacked are usually old, weakened, or diseased. Pupation occurs in the burrow made by the larva, which ends near the surface of the wood (Figure 35–41B). Species of siricids are sometimes accidentally transported in wood for fuel, construction, or furniture and can occasionally be found well outside their normal geographic range.

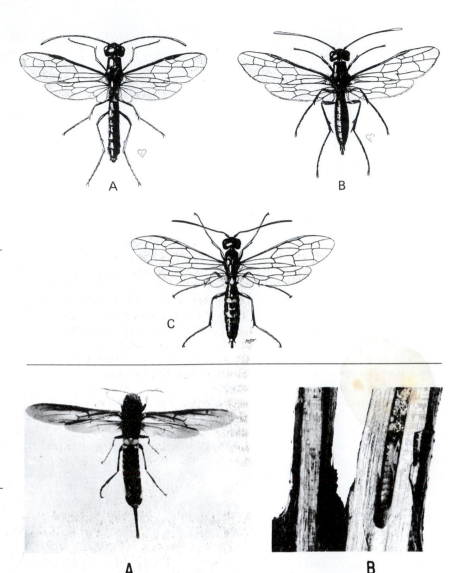

Figure 35–40. Stem sawflies (Cèphidae). **A,** *Tráchelus tábidus* (Fabricius), male; **B,** same, female; **C,** the wheat stem sawfly, *Cèphus cínctus* Norton, female. (Courtesy of USDA.)

Figure 35–41. **A,** an adult horntail, *Trèmex colúmba* (L.); **B,** horntail pupa in the larval gallery. (**A,** courtesy of the Ohio Agricultural Research and Development Center.)

A **B**

Family **Xiphydrìidae**—Wood Wasps: The wood wasps are small to moderate-sized (5–23 mm in length) cylindrical insects somewhat similar to the horntails, but they lack the horny plate at the apex of the abdomen. The larvae bore in small dead limbs and branches of deciduous trees. There are only six North American species, all in the genus *Xiphýdria*, and none is very common.

Family **Orússidae**—Parasitic Wood Wasps: This is a small group of rare insects (ten North American species), the adults of which are somewhat similar to horntails but considerably smaller (8–14 mm in length). The larvae as far as known are parasites of the larvae of metallic wood-boring beetles (Bupréstidae), and possibly other wood-boring Coleóptera

and Hymenóptera. These wasps seem to be related to the Apócrita and some authorities have classified them there or in their own suborder, the Idiogástra. The adults are on the wing from early spring to early summer and can be found searching the trunks of dead and dying trees.

SUBORDER **Apócrita:** The Apócrita differ from the Sýmphyta in having the first abdominal tergum (the propodeum) intimately associated with the thorax and separated by a distinct constriction from the rest of the abdomen. The middle tagma of the body (the mesosoma) is thus four-segmented. In addition, the hind wings have no more than two basal cells, and the fore tibiae have a single apical spur (except the Ceraphronòidea). Apocritan larvae are usually grublike or maggotlike and vary in feeding habits. Most are parasitic or predaceous on other insects, and others are plant feeders. The adults feed chiefly on flowers, sap, other plant materials, and honeydew. Some of the parasitic species occasionally feed on the body fluids of the host (Figure 35–49B).

A great many species in this suborder are parasitic in the larval stage on other insects or other arthropods and, because of their abundance, are very important in keeping the populations of other insects in check. The term *parasitoid* is often used for these insects. Both true parasites and parasitoids live in or on the body of another living animal (the host) during at least part of the life cycle. A parasite usually does not kill its host or consume a large part of the host tissues, but the immature stages of a parasitoid consume all or most of the host's tissues and eventually kill it. In this sense, parasitoids are similar to predators. Most of the parasitic Apócrita lay their eggs on or in the body of the host, and many have a long ovipositor with which hosts in cocoons, burrows, or other protected situations may be reached. In some cases only a single egg may be laid on the host (solitary parasitism, except in the case of polyembryony, see below); in others several to many eggs may be laid on the same host (gregarious parasitism). Pupation may occur on, in, or near the host, or some distance from it. Some species are thelytokous; that is, females develop from unfertilized eggs, and males are rare or absent altogether. Polyembryony occurs in a few species: a single egg develops into many larvae. Some of the parasitic species are hyperparasites; that is, they attack an insect that is a parasite of another insect.

The superfamilies of Apócrita differ in the form of the pronotum, the character of the ovipositor and antennae, the number of trochanter segments, and the wing venation. All the members of the Stephánidae, Ceraphronòidea, Trigonálidae, Evaniòidea, Ichneumonòidea, Proctotrupòidea, Chrysidòidea, Tiphiòidea, Scoliìdae, and Rhopalosomátidae and most of the Chalcidòidea and Cynipòidea are parasites of insects or other arthropods. The Apócrita evolved from forms with a piercing ovipositor similar to that of siricoids, but as a rule the females of most parasitic and phytophagous species cannot sting people. In the Chrysidòidea, Sphecòidea, Apòidea, Tiphiòidea, Pompilòidea, Scoliòidea, Vespòidea, and some of the Formícidae, the ovipositor is modified into a sting, whose primary function is to inject venom, either to paralyze its host or prey, or as a defensive mechanism. Females of these groups can often inflict painful wounds. In these species (grouped together as the Aculeàta) the egg does not pass through the ovipositor during oviposition, but emerges from its base.

The remaining Apócrita are grouped by some authorities in a taxon called either Parasítica or Terebrántes, but many consider this to be a heterogeneous and unnatural grouping.

The Apócrita is by far the larger of the two suborders of Hymenóptera, with about 16,000 of the approximately 17,100 North American species.

Family **Stephánidae:** The stephanids are a small group (six North American species) of rare insects that are parasites of the larvae of wood-boring beetles. The adults are 5–19 mm in length, slender, and superficially similar in appearance to the more common ichneumonids (Figure 35–42A). The head is somewhat spherical, is set out on a neck, and bears a crown of about five teeth around the median ocellus. The hind coxae are long, and the hind femora are swollen and toothed beneath. This group is much more common in the tropics, and most of our six species occur in the West. Stephanids have long been classified in the Ichneumonòidea, but they retain many features considered to be ancestral for the Apócrita as a whole and are now classified in their own superfamily.

Family **Megaspilidae:** Both this family and the next are unique among the Apócrita in having two fore tibial spurs. Together they form the superfamily Ceraphronòidea. Winged megaspilids can usually be recognized by the large semicircular or ellipsoidal stigma in the fore wing from which arises the curved stigmal vein (Figure 35–19E). A similar venation is found in some dryinids, but megaspilids can be distinguished from them by the triangular shape of the pronotum in lateral view (Figure 35–42B). Some species are wingless or brachypterous; these may be distinguished from ceraphronids by the presence of two middle tibial spurs. There are two subfamilies, the Megaspilìnae and the much rarer Lagynodìnae. Very little is known of the habits of these wasps; they have been reared from Homóptera Sternorrhýncha as hyperparasites of other Hymenóptera, from the larvae of Neuróptera and Díptera, and from the puparia of flies. Some *Lagynòdes* have been collected in ant nests. One common species, *Dendrócerus cárpenteri* (Curtis), is a hyperparasite of the braconid parasites of aphids.

Family **Ceraphrónidae:** Ceraphronids (Figure 35–42C) are distinguished from other Apócrita by the presence of two spurs on the apex of the fore tibia and, usually more easily, by their distinctive wing venation (Figure 35–19G). The veins are highly reduced with a long marginal vein, a linear stigma (separated from the marginal vein by a break), and the curved stigmal vein. Wingless forms are fairly common and can be distinguished from megaspilids by the single spur on the middle tibia. Very little is

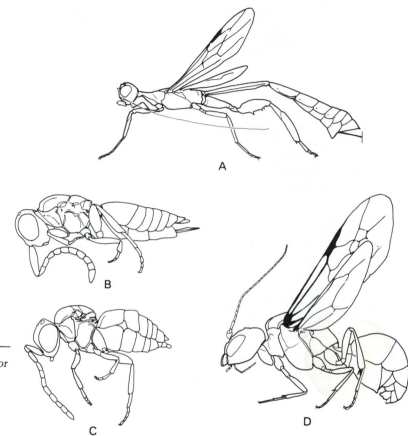

Figure 35–42. **A,** *Megíschus bicolor* (Westwood) (Stephánidae), ovipositor truncated; **B,** Megaspílidae; **C,** Ceraphrónidae; **D,** *Poecilogonálos costális* (Cresson) (Trigonálidae). (**A** and **D,** redrawn from Townes.)

known of the hosts of ceraphronids, but species have been reared both as primary parasites of Díptera, Neuróptera, and Homóptera and as hyperparasites of Díptera and Hymenóptera. Some have been collected in ant nests, but their precise hosts are unknown. These creatures are fairly common, but because of their small size they are rarely retained by collectors. Specimens can be easily found by sweeping or by sifting soil and leaf litter.

Family **Trigonálidae:** The trigonalids are a small group (four North American species) of rather rare insects. They are medium-sized, usually brightly colored, and rather stout-bodied. They look much like wasps (Figure 35–42D), but their antennae are very long and with 16 or more segments.

The trigonalids are parasites of Véspidae or of the parasites of caterpillars. Some exotic species are primary parasites of sawfly larvae. Females lay large numbers of very minute eggs on foliage. In the case of the species attacking caterpillar parasites, the eggs hatch when eaten by a caterpillar, and the trigonalid larva attacks the ichneumonid, tachinid, or other parasite larva present within the caterpillar.

In the species that attack vespid larvae, it is thought that the eggs are eaten by a caterpillar, which is in turn eaten by a vespid wasp, which in regurgitating the caterpillar and feeding it to its young, transfers the trigonalid larvae from the caterpillar to the wasp larvae.

SUPERFAMILY **Evanioidea:** The members of this group have the metasoma attached high above the hind coxae (Figure 35–18D–F), the antennae filiform and 13- or 14-segmented, the trochanters 2-segmented, and the venation generally fairly complete in the front wings (front wings with a costal cell). Some (Gasteruptiidae and Aulácidae) superficially resemble ichneumonids.

Family **Evaniidae**—Ensign Wasps: The ensign wasps are black or black and red, somewhat spiderlike insects, 10–25 mm in length (Figure 35–43). The metasoma is very small and oval and is attached by a slender petiole to the propodeum considerably above the base of the hind coxae (Figure 35–18F); it is carried almost like a flag (hence the common name for this family). The ensign wasps are parasites of the egg capsules of cockroaches and are likely to be found in buildings or on the forest floor where cockroaches occur.

Family **Gasteruptiidae:** These insects resemble ichneumonids, but they have short antennae and a costal cell in the front wings, and the head is set out on a slender neck. They have one submarginal cell or none and one m-cu cross vein or none (Figure 35–31E). They are generally dark in color with brown or orange markings. Adults are fairly common and can be found on flowers, particularly wild parsnip, wild carrot, and related species. The larvae are parasites of solitary wasps and bees, and females are often found flying around nesting sites of these hosts, such as dead logs.

Family **Aulácidae:** The aulacids resemble the gasteruptiids, but they are usually black with a reddish metasoma, the antennae are longer, and there are two m-cu cross veins in the front wings (Figure 35–31F). These insects are parasites of the larvae of wood-boring beetles and xiphydriid wood wasps, and adults may be found around logs in which the hosts occur.

SUPERFAMILY **Ichneumonòidea:** This is a very large and important group, and its members are parasites of other insects or other invertebrate animals. These insects are wasplike in appearance, but (with few exceptions) cannot sting humans. The ichneumonoids are very common insects and may be recognized by the following characters: (1) the antennae are filiform, usually with 16 or more segments; (2) the hind trochanters are two-segmented; (3) the costal cell is absent; (4) the ovipositor arises anterior to the tip of the metasoma and is permanently exserted (Figure 35–5A; sometimes the ovipositor is very short and does not protrude far beyond the apex of the metasoma); and (5) the pronotum in lateral view is somewhat triangular.

Family **Bracónidae:** This is a large (more than 1900 North American species) and beneficial group of parasitic Hymenóptera. The adults are usually relatively small (Nearctic species are rarely over 15 mm in length). They resemble ichneumonids in lacking a costal cell but differ in that they have no more than one m-cu cross vein (Figure 35–31C), and the second and third metasomatic tergites are fused together. Braconid biology is very diverse (Figures 35–44, 35–45). The family contains both ectoparasites and endoparasites, solitary and gregarious species, and primary and secondary parasites. All life stages of host, from egg to adult may be attacked (in the case of species attacking eggs, the adult wasp emerges from the host larva or prepupa). Many species in this family have been of considerable value in the control of insect pests.

The classification of the Bracónidae is presently the subject of revision. Van Achterberg (1984) recognized 35 subfamilies, of which 25 occur in North America. The Macrocentrìnae, Agathidìnae, Chelonìnae, Microgastrìnae, and most Rogadìnae (Rhogadìnae), Gnaptodontìnae, Dirrhopìnae, Miracìnae, Acaeliìnae, Homolobìnae, Sigalphìnae, Orgilìnae, and Cardiochilìnae are parasites of lepidopteran larvae. The gregarious forms of the Macrocentrìnae all appear to be polyembryonic. The Chelonìnae are egg-larval parasites: the female oviposits into the host egg, and the parasite matures and emerges from the late larva or pupa. Species of *Apánteles* and related genera (Microgastrìnae) (Figure 35–45C–E) are very common and often familiar because the gregarious larvae of some species emerge in large numbers and spin their cocoons in a large mass on the body of the host (Figure 34–78B). The Helconìnae, Histeromerìnae, Cenocoeliìnae, and Doryctìnae are parasites of beetle larvae, attacking chiefly wood-boring beetles. The Ichneutìnae attack larvae of sawflies and lepidopteran leaf miners; the Alysiìnae and Opiìnae attack Díptera. Braconìnae have been reared from concealed larvae of several orders of Holometábola. The Euphorìnae are very diverse biologically: they attack hosts in the orders Lepidóptera, Hemíptera, Hymenóptera, Coleóptera, Neuróptera, and Psocóptera. This subfamily includes species that are parasites

Figure 35–43. An ensign wasp, *Prosevània fúscipes* (Illiger). **A,** male; **B,** female. (Courtesy of Edmunds.)

A   B

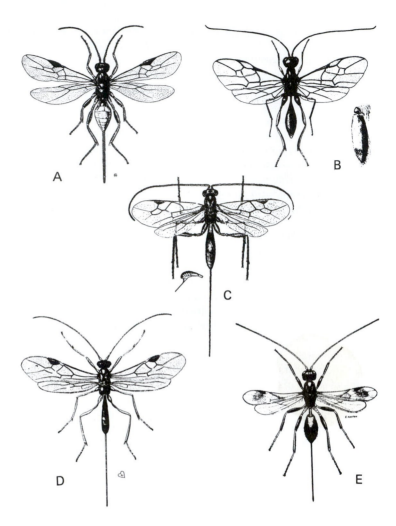

Figure 35–44. Bracónidae. **A,** *Coelìòdes dendróctoni* Cushman, female (Braconìnae), a parasite of bark beetles (Scolýtidae); **B,** *Metèorus nigricóllis* Thomson, male (Euphorìnae), a parasite of the European corn borer (insert shows cocoon); **C,** *Macrocéntrus ancylívorus* Rohwer, female (Macrocentrìnae) (insert, lateral view of metasoma), a parasite of various tortricid moths; **D,** *Macrocéntrus grándii* Goidanich, female, a parasite of the European corn borer; **E,** *Spàthius canadénsis* Ashmead, female, a parasite of bark beetles (Scolýtidae). (**A,** courtesy of DeLeon and the New York Entomological Society; **B,** courtesy of Parker and the Entomological Society of Washington; **C** and **D,** courtesy of USDA; **E,** courtesy of Kaston and the Connecticut Agricultural Experiment Station.)

of adult insects, as well as hyperparasites. The Aphidìinae is a well-known group that is exclusively endoparasitic in the nymphs and adults of aphids. The Neoneurìnae are endoparasites of worker ants. The Blacìnae attack primarily the larvae of Coleóptera, but species of one tribe have been reared from boreid larvae (Mecóptera).

  Family **Ichneumónidae**—Ichneumonids: This family is one of the largest in the entire Insécta, with more than 3300 described species occurring in North America, and its members are to be found almost everywhere. The adults vary considerably in size, form, and coloration, but the majority resemble slender wasps (Figures 35–46, 35–47). They differ from aculeates in that they have the antennae longer and with more segments (usually 16 or more antennal segments in ichneumonids and 12 or 13 in most aculeates), and they lack a costal cell in the front wings. In many ichneumonids the ovipositor is quite

long (Figure 35–46A), often longer than the body, and it arises anterior to the tip of the metasoma and is permanently extruded. In the aculeates the ovipositor issues from the tip of the metasoma and is withdrawn when not in use. In ichneumonids the 1M and 1R$_1$ (first discoidal and first submarginal) cells in the front wing are confluent, owing to the loss of vein Rs + M, and the second submarginal cell (the 1Rs cell), lying opposite the 2m-cu cross vein, is often quite small (Figure 35–31A, *are*). This small cell (called the areolet) is lacking in some ichneumonids (Figure 35–31B). The ichneumonids (with very few exceptions) differ from the braconids in having two m-cu crossveins, the braconids having only one or none (Figures 35–20E, 35–31C). In many species the two sexes may differ considerably in color, size, body form, or even the presence of wings.

  Most ichneumonids are parasitoids; that is, the larva feeds and develops on a single host that it eventually kills. A few species, however, are better described as mobile predators in that they feed upon a number of individual "hosts" before completing development—for example, eggs within a spider egg sac or a line of small carpenter bee larvae within a nest. The hosts of ichneumonids include species in the insect orders Lepidóptera, Hymenóptera, Díptera, Coleóptera, Neuróptera, and Mecóptera, as well as spiders and spider egg sacs. The host range of individual species is, however, quite variable, some attacking a wide variety and others being highly specialized to one or a few host species. The adult female must locate the host and then may oviposit on, in, or near it (the last in confined situations such as galleries within wood), and the larva may feed upon the host from the outside through its cuticle (as an ectoparasite), or it may live within the hemocoel of the host (as an endoparasite). Most ichneumonids are solitary, a single individual developing

from a single host, although some are gregarious. Many species are hyperparasitic; that is, they are parasitoids of other parasitoids, usually ichneumonids, braconids, or tachinids.

The family Ichneumónidae is divided into 24 subfamilies. There is disagreement among workers as to the nomenclature to be used, but, in general, the concepts on ichneumonid systematics developed by Townes (1969–1971) are widely followed. We use here the family group names outlined by Fitton and Gauld (1976, 1978).

The largest ichneumonids in the United States and Canada belong to the subfamily Pimplinae. Some of these may be 40 mm or more in body length, and the ovipositor may be twice as long as the body. These insects attack the larvae of horntails, wood wasps, and wood-boring Coleóptera. The long ovipositor is used in getting the eggs of the ichneumonid into the tunnels of the host, and the ovipositor

Figure 35–45. Bracónidae. **A,** *Microgáster tibiàlis* Nees, female (Microgastrìnae), a parasite of the European corn borer; **B,** *Chélonus texànus* Cresson (Chelonìnae), a parasite of various noctuid moth larvae; **C,** *Apánteles diatraèae* Muesebeck, male (Microgastrìnae), a parasite of the southwestern corn borer, *Diatraèa grandiosélla* Dyar; **D,** same, female; **E,** *Apánteles thómpsoni* Lyle, female, a parasite of the European corn borer; **F,** *Phanómeris phyllótomae* Muesebeck, female (Rogadìnae), a parasite of birch leaf-mining sawflies. (**A,** courtesy of Vance and the Entomological Society of America; **B–F,** courtesy of the USDA.)

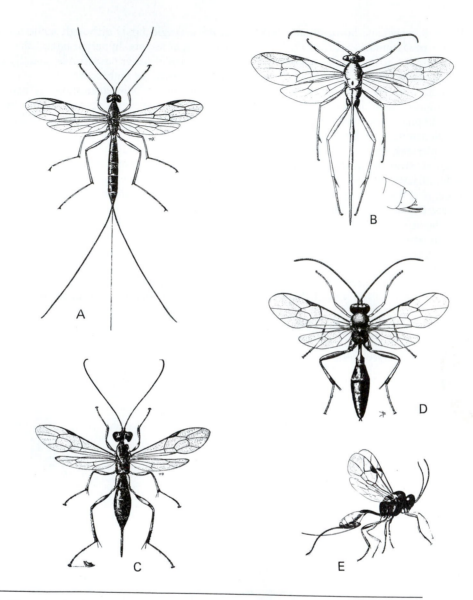

Figure 35–46. Ichneumónidae. **A,** *Rhysélla nítida* (Cresson), female (Pimplìnae); **B,** *Casinària texàna* (Ashmead), female (Campopleginae) (insert shows tip of metasoma in lateral view); **C,** *Phytodiètus vulgàris* Cresson, female (Tryphonìnae); **D,** *Phobocámpe dísparis* (Viereck), female (Porizontìnae); **E,** *Tersílochus conotràcheli* (Riley), female (Tersilochìnae). (**A** and **C,** courtesy of Rohwer; **B,** courtesy of Walley; **D** and **E,** courtesy of the U.S. National Museum.)

may sometimes penetrate 13 mm or more of wood. The laborious process of plunging the ovipositor deep within the wood takes several minutes. The egg is greatly deformed as it passes through the valvulae but regains its shape after emerging from the other end. Retraction of the ovipositor is also relatively slow. It is not uncommon to find what look like thin black needles protruding from the wood of

a dead tree. These are the ovipositors of females that either were unable to free themselves or were eaten while in the process of oviposition. The genus *Megarhýssa* contains several very large species that attack horntails. *Rhysélla nítida* (Cresson) (Figure 35–46A) attacks wood wasps (Xiphydrìidae). Some of the other Pimplìnae are parasites of Lepidopterous larvae; some (especially those in the tribe Polysphinctìni) attack spiders; and some attack wood-boring Coleóptera.

Most of the ichneumonids in the subfamily Tryphonìnae are parasites of sawflies. *Phytodiètus vulgàris* Cresson (Figure 35–46C) attacks tortricid moths. Some members of this subfamily carry their eggs on the ovipositor, attached by short stalks. When a suitable host is found, the eggs are attached to the skin of the host by a stalk, and if no host is found, the eggs may be discarded. The parasite larvae usually complete their development in the cocoon of the host.

The members of the subfamily Phygadeuontìnae are mostly external parasites of pupae in cocoons. A few attack wood-boring beetle larvae, a few attack dipterous larvae, some attack spider egg sacs, and a few are hyperparasites of braconids or other ichneumonids (Figure 35–47). The members of the subfamily Ichneumonìnae are internal parasites of Lepidóptera. They oviposit in either the host larva or the host pupa, but always emerge from the host pupa. Most species in this subfamily have the two sexes quite different in appearance, and many are bright and colorful mimics of vespids or pompilids. The Banchìnae are internal parasites of caterpillars; the Ctenopelmatìnae are chiefly parasites of sawflies, ovipositing in the host larva and emerging from its cocoon; the Oxytorìnae attack fungus gnats (Mycetophílidae and Sciàridae); and the Diplazontìnae attack Sýrphidae, laying their eggs in the egg or young larva of the host and emerging from the puparium of the host. The Campoplegìnae are parasites of lepidopterous larvae: *Casinària texàna* (Ashmead) (Figure 35–46B) is a parasite of the saddleback caterpillar, and *Phobocámpe dísparis* (Viereck) (Figure 35–46D) is a parasite of the gypsy moth. The Tersilochìnae are parasites of beetles: *Tersílochus conotràcheli* (Riley) (Figure 35–46E) is a parasite of the plum curculio.

Females of Ophionìnae (which are parasites of caterpillars) have a very compressed metasoma and a short, very sharp ovipositor. Most ichneumonids when handled will attempt to sting by poking at one's fingers with their ovipositor, but in most cases this can scarcely be felt. The ovipositor of the Ophionìnae, on the other hand, can actually penetrate the skin, and the effect is much like a sharp pinprick. Most of these ichneumonids are yellowish to brownish in color and about 25 mm in length. They often come to lights at night.

SUPERFAMILY **Chalcidòidea:**   The chalcidoids constitute a large and important group of insects, with about 2200 described North American species. Nearly all are very small, and some are quite minute. Some of the Mymàridae, for example, are less than 0.5 mm in length. Chalcidoids are to be found almost everywhere, but because of their small size they are frequently overlooked—or worse, discarded—by the beginning student. Most are only about 2 or 3 mm in length, although a few (for example, some of the Leucóspidae) may reach a length of 10 or 15 mm. The members of this group occur in a wide variety of

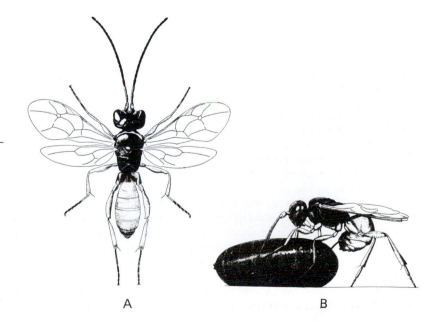

Figure 35–47.   A hyperparasitic ichneumonid, *Phygadeùon subfúscus* Cresson (Phygadeuontìnae). **A,** adult male; **B,** female ovipositing in puparium of the host. The host of this ichneumonid is a tachinid fly, *Aplomyiópsis epiláchnae* (Aldrich), which is a parasite of the Mexican bean beetle, *Epiláchna varivéstis* Mulsant (see Figure 32–83). (Courtesy of USDA.)

A   B

habitats, and it is seldom that one can sweep through vegetation without coming up with a few of them.

The chalcidoids can generally be recognized by the reduced wing venation (Figure 35–19B); the antennae are usually elbowed and never contain more than 13 segments; the pronotum is somewhat quadrate and does not reach the tegulae; and there is usually a large, exposed prepectus present in the side of the mesosoma (Figure 35–4A). Most of the chalcidoids are dark-colored, and many are metallic blue or green in color. There is a great deal of variation in body shape in this group (Figures 35–28, 35–29, 35–48 through 35–53), and some have rather peculiar, even marvelous, shapes. The wings are reduced or lacking in many species.

Most chalcidoids are parasites of other insects, attacking chiefly the egg or larval stage of the host. Most hosts are in the orders Lepidóptera, Díptera, Coleóptera, and Homóptera. Since these orders contain most of the crop pests, the chalcidoids are a very beneficial group, helping to keep pest populations in check. Many species have been imported into the United States to act as a means of controlling insect pests. A few chalcidoids are phytophagous, their larvae feeding inside seeds, stems, or galls.

This superfamily is divided into a number of families. Some families consist of distinctive-looking insects and are easily recognized, but in some cases the separation of families is rather difficult. To complicate matters for the student, there are differences of opinion among entomologists about the limits of some families.

Family **Mymarommátidae:**   This is a small group of rare species that have only recently been discovered in North America. Their hosts are unknown, but specimens have been collected in moist woodlands. They appear similar to the mymarids in having the base of the fore wing constricted and the venation highly reduced (even for a chalcidoid). The hind wing is greatly reduced to a slender strip bearing hamuli on its apex. Some authors place the mymarommatids outside the Chalcidòidea, although it is recognized that the two taxa are closely related.

Family **Mymàridae**—Fairyflies: Mymarids are all parasites of the eggs of other insects. Their hosts include species in the orders Odonàta, Orthóptera, Psocóptera, Thysanóptera, Hemíptera, Homóptera, Coleóptera, Lepidóptera, and Díptera. They are distinguished from all other chalcidoids by a series of unique sulci on the head (Figure 35–24): a set parallel to the inner edges of the compound eyes on the frons and vertex, and a distinctive transverse sulcus running between the eyes above the antennal insertions. In addition, most species are characterized by

the stalked, parallel-sided hind wings and the narrow base of the fore wings (Figure 35–19C). These insects are all minute, usually less than 1 mm in size. Consequently, they are poorly known, but they are a common and diverse component of most insect faunas.

Family **Trichogrammátidae:**   The trichogrammatids are also insect egg parasites. They are very small creatures. For example, adults of the genus *Megaphrágma*, parasites of the eggs of thrips, are no more than 0.18 mm in total length. Trichogrammatids may be most easily recognized by their three-segmented tarsi. In addition, the metasoma is broadly attached to the mesosoma, and the second phragma projects far within it (visible in specimens in alcohol); the antennae are short, with seven or fewer segments (including ring segments); and the fore wing often has setae arranged in lines (these last three characters are also found in some other chalcidoids). The genus *Trichográmma* is the best known group and has been widely used as a biological control agent. It is, however, not as abundant, either in species or total numbers, as those in the genera *Oligóseta*, *Paracentròbia*, and *Aphelinòidea*. As with most other microhymenoptera, even though this family is very common, it is often overlooked or missed by collectors and is therefore relatively poorly known.

Family **Eulóphidae:**   The Eulóphidae are a large group (more than 500 described North American species) of rather small insects (1–3 mm in length). They are parasites of a wide variety of hosts, including a number of major crop pests (Figures 35–48B,D, 35–49E). Their biology is extremely varied, but most species parasitize either the egg or larva of their host. Eulophids may be recognized by the four-segmented tarsi (Figure 35–23A) and the axillae extending forward beyond the tegulae. Some species of Aphelìnidae and Encýrtidae and all Elásmidae also have four-segmented tarsi. Characters to distinguish these are included in the key and in the discussions of these families. Many eulophids are brilliantly metallic in color, and the males of many species have pectinate antennae. These wasps are, in general, rather weakly sclerotized, and the bodies of specimens often collapse when dried.

Family **Elásmidae:**   Sixteen species of elasmids have been recorded in North America, all belonging to the genus *Elásmus*. The members of this group have the tarsi of all legs four-segmented, and they are sometimes classified as a subfamily of the Eulóphidae. Elasmids may be distinguished from eulophids by their grossly enlarged and flattened hind coxae and the peculiar dark bristles on their hind tibiae (Figure 35–26). These bristles form unique patterns that are used for identifying species. Elas-

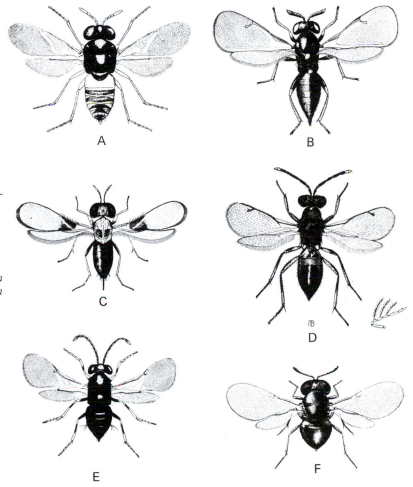

Figure 35–48. Chalcidòidea. **A,** *Aphelìnus jucúndus* Gahan, female (Aphelìnidae), a parasite of aphids; **B,** *Tetrástichus bruchóphagi* Gahan (Eulóphidae), a parasite of the clover seed chalcid, *Bruchóphagus platýptera* (Walker); **C,** *Centródora speciosíssima* (Girault), female (Aphelìnidae), a parasite of cecidomyiids and chalcidoids that attack wheat; **D,** *Hemiptársenus aneméntus* (Walker), female (Eulóphidae), a parasite of leaf-mining sawflies; **E,** *Zarhópalus inquísitor* (Howard), male (Encýrtidae), a parasite of aphids and mealybugs; **F,** *Ooencýrtus kuvánae* (Howard), female (Encýrtidae), an imported egg parasite of the gypsy moth. (**A** and **E,** courtesy of Griswold and the Entomological Society of America; others, courtesy of USDA.)

mids attack the larvae of small Lepidóptera or their hymenopteran parasites (Bracónidae and Ichneumónidae), and one species has been reared from paper wasps (*Polístes*, Véspidae).

Family **Tetracámpidae:**   This is a rare family that seems to combine features of the larger Eulóphidae and Pteromálidae. Some male tetracampids have four-segmented tarsi, but both males and females may be distinguished from other North American eulophids and pteromalids by the dense pilosity on the propodeum. Only two species have been recognized in North America. *Dipriocámpe díprioni* (Ferrière), an egg parasite, was introduced into Canada to control the European pine sawfly, *Neodíprion sértifer* (Geoffroy) (Dipriónidae). *Epiclèrus neárcticus* Yoshimoto occurs in the eastern United States and Canada.

Family **Aphelìnidae:**   This is a group of very common but small parasites, usually about 1 mm in total length. They have been classified at various

times in the Eulóphidae and Encýrtidae, but it now seems clear that they should be recognized as an independent family. The number of antennal segments is reduced to eight or fewer (not counting the minute ring segments) as in the Eulóphidae, but most species have the tarsi five-segmented, the metasoma appears broadly attached to the propodeum (in many cases the second phragma is visible and extends well into the metasoma), the marginal vein is elongate, and the postmarginal and stigmal veins are reduced. A few encyrtids have four-segmented tarsi and reduced antennal segmentation; aphelinids may be distinguished from these by their elongate marginal vein. Those species of aphelinids with five-segmented tarsi (the majority) may be distinguished from encyrtids by the reduction in the number of antennal segments, their small size, reduced stigmal and postmarginal veins, and the presence of a groove on the mesopleuron for reception of the middle femur.

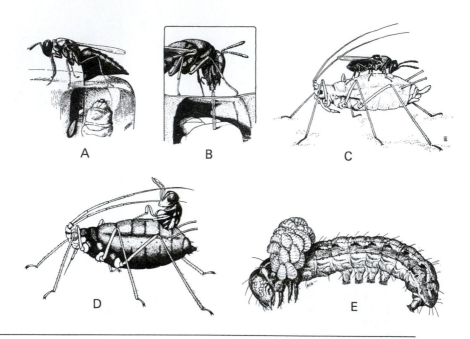

Figure 35–49.   Feeding and emerging chalcidoids. **A,** *Habrócytus* (Pteromálidae) ovipositing; **B,** *Habrócytus* feeding at the tube made by the ovipositor; **C,** *Zarhópalus inquísitor* (Howard) (Encýrtidae) feeding at an oviposition puncture made in the abdomen of an aphid; **D,** adult of *Aphelìnus jucúndus* Gahan (Aphelìnidae) emerging from an aphid; **E,** a colony of *Epuléctrus* larvae (Eulóphidae) feeding on a caterpillar. (**A** and **B,** courtesy of Fulton and the Entomological Society of America; **C** and **D,** courtesy of Griswold and the Entomological Society of America; **E,** courtesy of USDA).

Aphelinids attack a broad range of hosts, the common factor seeming to be that they are sessile. The best known species are those that attack scale insects (Homóptera). A number of species have been very important as biological control agents of these hosts. Other species have been reared from aphids; whiteflies; eggs of Homóptera, Orthóptera, and Lepidóptera; cecidomyiid pupae; and as hyperparasites of other Hymenóptera attacking Homóptera. The curious phenomenon of adelphoparasitism is found in some groups: the females develop as parasites of scale insects, while the males develop as hyperparasites attacking parasites of scale insects, often females of their own species! This is a fairly common group of parasites, but they are generally not represented in collections because of their small size and the fact that the bodies of specimens usually collapse when dried.

Family **Signiphòridae:**   The signiphorids are small, stout-bodied chalcidoids that attack scale insects, whiteflies, and other Homóptera or are hyperparasites of the chalcidoids attacking Homóptera. They are rather uncommon, but very distinct creatures because of the broad attachment of the meta-

soma, the elongate, unsegmented antennal club, the lateral spurs on the middle tibia, and the triangular area on the propodeum.

Family **Encýrtidae:**   The Encýrtidae are a large and widespread group, with some 345 described North American species. They are usually 1–2 mm in length and can be distinguished from most other chalcidoids by the broad convex mesopleura (Figure 35–27A). In most of the chalcidoids the mesopleura have a groove for the femora, but this groove is lacking in the encyrtids (also lacking in the signiphorids, tanaostigmatids, some aphelinids, and some eupelmids). The encyrtids differ from the eupelmids in that they have the fore and middle coxae closely approximated, the mesonotum is convex, and they lack notauli or have them incomplete. Most of the encyrtids are parasites of Homóptera—aphids (Figure 35–49C), scale insects, mealybugs, and whiteflies—and they are very important as biological control agents of these insects. The group also contains species attacking insects in the orders Hemíptera, Neuróptera, Díptera, Lepidóptera, Coleóptera, and Hymenóptera. All life stages, including eggs, larvae, nymphs, and adults are hosts of various species. Two genera in particular, *Hunteréllus* and *Ixodíphagus*, are remarkable, for they parasitize the nymphal stage of ticks. The genus *Ooencýrtus* is commonly encountered; its species are parasites of the eggs of some Hemíptera, Neuróptera, and Lepidóptera. *Ooencýrtus kuvánae* (Howard) (Figure 35–48F; also known in the literature as *kuwánai*), for example, has been introduced as a parasite of the eggs of the gypsy moth. A few encyrtids are hyperparasites. Polyembryony occurs in a number of species, with from 10 to more than 1000 young developing from a single egg.

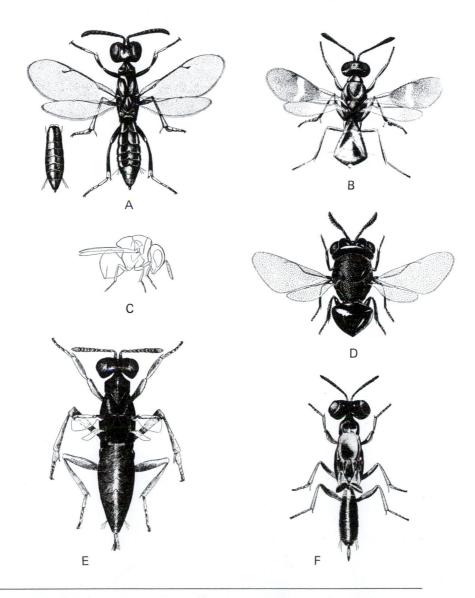

Figure 35–50. Chalcidòidea. **A, B, E, F,** Eupélmidae; **C, D,** Perilámpidae. **A,** *Eupélmus allýnii* (French), female (insert is metasoma of male), a parasite of the Hessian fly; **B,** *Anastàtus dísparis* Ruschka, an imported egg parasite of the gypsy moth; **C,** *Perilámpus platygáster* Say, a hyperparasite attacking *Metèorus dimidàtus* (Cresson), a braconid parasite of the grape leaf folder, *Dèsmia funeràlis* (Hübner) (Pyrálidae), lateral view; **D,** same, dorsal view; **E,** *Eupélmus atropurpùreus* Dalman, female, a parasite of the Hessian fly; **F,** *Eupelmélla vesiculàris* (Retzius), female, which attacks insects in the orders Coleóptera, Lepidóptera, and Hymenóptera. (Courtesy of USDA.)

Family **Tanaostigmátidae:** Four species in this rare group have been recorded from Florida, Arizona, and California. The larvae appear to be gall makers.

Family **Eupélmidae:** The Eupélmidae are a large group (88 North American species), and some species are fairly common. They are similar to the encyrtids, but they have the mesonotum flatter, and notauli are present (Figure 35–50A,B,E,F). Some of them are wingless or have very short wings (Figure 35–50E,F). Males of many species are very similar to, if not indistinguishable from, male pteromalids.

Many of the eupelmids are good jumpers and often tumble about after jumping, before gaining a foothold. Their jumping is accomplished by greatly enlarged leg muscles that insert on the mesopleuron. The enlargement of the area of attachment of these muscles accounts for the characteristic convex mesopleuron of both encyrtids and eupelmids. When eupelmids jump, the middle legs are literally thrown out of their sockets and the mesonotum is contorted so strongly that the head and tip of the metasoma may actually touch. Many specimens retain this position when killed, with the body in a U shape and the middle legs thrown forward in front of the head. The species of this group attack a wide variety of hosts, and a number are known to attack hosts in several different orders. Species of the most common subfamily, the Eupelmìnae, can be collected in a

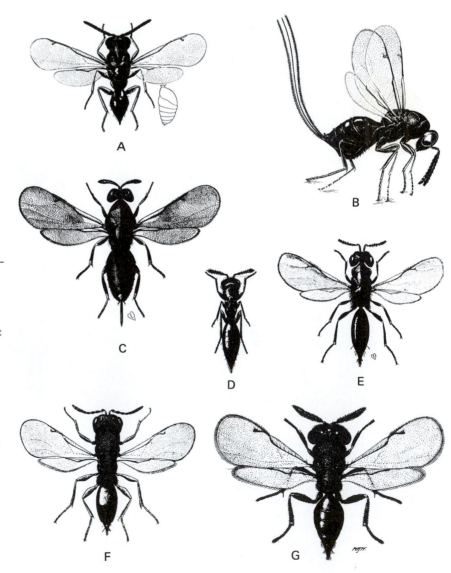

Figure 35–51. Chalcidòidea. **A–C,** Torýmidae; **D–G,** Eurytómidae. **A,** *Torýmus vàrians* (Walker), the apple seed chalcid, male (insert is a lateral view of the metasoma); **B,** same, female; **C,** *Liodontómerus perpléxus* Gahan, female, a parasite of the clover seed chalcid (**G** in this figure); **D,** *Harmólita grándis* (Riley), the wheat strawworm, a wingless female; **E,** *Harmólita trítici* (Fitch), female, the wheat jointworm; **F,** *Eurýtoma pachyneùron* Girault, female, a parasite of the Hessian fly and the wheat jointworm (**E** in this figure); **G,** *Bruchóphagus platýptera* (Walker), the clover seed chalcid. (Courtesy of USDA.)

wide variety of habitats. The less common subfamilies are often seen on dead wood, presumably searching for wood-boring Coleóptera as hosts.

Family **Torýmidae:**   The torymids are somewhat elongate insects, 2–4 mm in length, generally with a long ovipositor. The hind coxae are usually very large, and there are distinct notauli on the mesoscutum (Figure 35–51A–C). This group includes both parasitic and phytophagous species: the Torymìnae, Erimerìnae, and Monodontomerìnae attack gall insects and caterpillars; the Podagrionìnae attack mantid eggs; and the Idarnìnae and Megastigmìnae attack seeds.

Family **Agaónidae**—Fig Wasps: This group is represented in the United States by two species, *Blastóphaga psènes* (L.) and *Secundeisènia mexicàna* (Ashmead). The former occurs in California and Arizona, and the latter in Florida. *Blastóphaga psènes* (Figure 35–52) was introduced into the United States to make possible the production of certain varieties of figs. The Smyrna fig, which is grown extensively in California, produces fruits only when it is pollinated with pollen from the wild fig, or caprifig, and the pollination is done entirely by fig wasps. The fig wasp develops in a gall in flowers of the caprifig. The blind and flightless males (Figure 35–52B) emerge first and may mate with females still in their galls. The female, on emerging from the gall, collects pollen from male flowers of the caprifig and stores it in special baskets (corbiculae). The female pollinates figs of both types (Smyrna fig and caprifig), but oviposits successfully only in the shorter flowers of the caprifig. Fig growers usually aid in the process of Smyrna fig pollination by placing in their fig trees branches of the wild fig. When the fig wasps emerge from the wild fig, they are almost certain to visit flowers of the Smyrna fig and thus pollinate them.

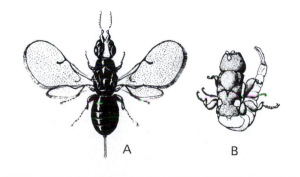

Figure 35–52.   The fig wasp *Blastóphaga psènes* (L.). **A,** female; **B,** male. (Courtesy of Condit and the California Agricultural Experiment Station.)

Family **Ormýridae:**   The Ormýridae are similar to the Torýmidae, but have the notauli indistinct or lacking and have a very short ovipositor. Most species are metallic blue or green and have distinctive large pits on the metasomatic segments. They are parasites of gall insects.

Family **Pteromálidae:**   The Pteromálidae is a huge group of parasitic wasps (about 340 described North American species). The bulk of the species are placed in two large and poorly defined subfamilies, the Miscogastrìnae and Pteromalìnae. In addition to these there are a large number of small but distinctive groups that are usually given subfamily status (e.g., the Spalangiìnae, common parasites of the puparia of flies associated with dung). Other groups, such as the Perilámpidae and Eucharítidae, are commonly accorded familial status, but these are recognized as being closely related to subgroups within pteromalids. The classification of these wasps is in a very immature stage, and a fair amount of shuffling of taxa should be expected as the species and their relationships become better known.

The pteromalids are both morphologically and biologically diverse. It is probably easier to identify them by eliminating the other possibilities than to try to characterize the family. In general, the tarsi are five-segmented, the antennal funicle has five or more segments, and the pronotum, seen in dorsal view, is constricted anteriorly (thus giving it the shape of a bell, often referred to as campanulate). While the females of some families such as Eupélmidae and Torýmidae are often quite distinctive, it may sometimes be difficult, if not impossible, to distinguish the males from "typical" pteromalids. The best strategy for identification is to first run specimens through the key and then check the descriptions and key characters of the other chalcidoid taxa. The others with five-segmented tarsi are the Perilámpidae, Eupélmidae, Encýrtidae, Tanaostigmátidae, Chalcídidae, Leucóspidae, Eurytómidae, Eucharítidae, Agaónidae, Torýmidae, Ormýridae, and Aphelinidae.

Most of these insects are parasitic and attack a wide variety of hosts. Many are very valuable in the control of crop pests. Species are known that attack eggs, larvae, nymphs, and pupae. Both solitary and gregarious parasites are found, and some species are hyperparasitic. Hosts include species in the orders Lepidóptera, Hymenóptera, Homóptera, Díptera, and Coleóptera, and spiders and their egg sacs. A few species are gall formers.

The adults of some species of pteromalids (and some other chalcidoids, e.g., some eulophids) feed on the body fluids of the host, which exude from the puncture made by the parasite's ovipositor (as in

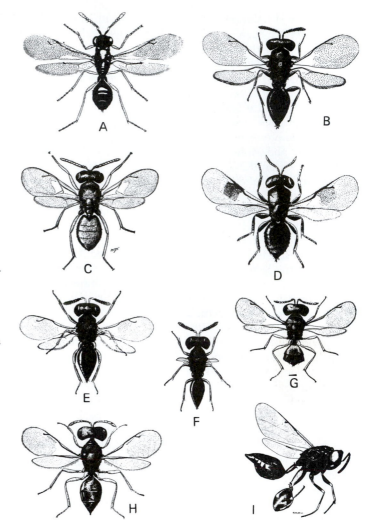

Figure 35–53. Chalcidòidea. A–H, Pteromálidae; I, Chalcídidae. **A,** *Ásaphes lùcens* (Provancher), male, a parasite of aphids; **B,** *Bubékia fállax* Gahan, female, a parasite of the Hessian fly; **C,** *Pterómalus eùrymi* Gahan, a parasite of the alfalfa caterpillar, *Còlias eurýtheme* Boisduval; **D,** *Merisóporus chalcidóphagus* (Walsh and Riley), female, a parasite of the Hessian fly; **E,** *Eupterómalus subápterus* (Riley), female, a parasite of the Hessian fly; **F,** same, a subapterous female; **G,** *Callítula bicolor* Spinola, male, a parasite of various flies and platygastrids; **H,** same, female; **I,** *Spilochálcis flavopícta* (Cresson), a parasite of various Coleóptera, Lepidóptera, and Hymenóptera. (**A,** courtesy of Griswold and the Entomological Society of America; **B–I,** courtesy of USDA.)

Figure 35–49C). In the case of *Habrócytus cerealéllae* (Ashmead), which attacks larvae of the angoumois grain moth and in which the larvae are out of reach of the adult pteromalid (in the seed), a viscous fluid is secreted from the ovipositor and is formed into a tube extending down to the host larva. The body fluids of the host are sucked up through this tube by the adult (Figure 35–49A,B).

Family **Eucharítidae:** Eucharítidae are rather distinctive-looking insects with very interesting habits. They are fair-sized (at least for a chalcidoid), black or metallic blue or green in color, with the metasoma petiolate and the scutellum often spined. The mesosoma often appears somewhat humpbacked (Figure 35–28D). These chalcidoids are parasites of the pupae of ants. The eggs are laid, usually in large numbers, on leaves or buds, and hatch into tiny flattened larvae called planidia. These planidia

lie in wait on the vegetation or on the ground and attach to passing ants, which carry them to the ant nest. Once in the ant nest, the planidia leave the worker ant that brought them there and attach to ant larvae. They do little or no feeding on the larvae of the ant, but feed after the larva has pupated. This family is especially diverse in species and in elaborate structure in the tropics (where ants are most diverse).

Family **Perilámpidae:** The Perilámpidae are stout-bodied chalcidoids with the mesosoma large and coarsely punctate and the metasoma small, shining, and triangular (Figures 35–29B, 35–50C,D). Some species, including the common *Perilámpus hyalìnus* Say, are brilliantly metallic in color and superficially resemble cuckoo wasps (Chrysídidae); most others are black. Perilampids are frequently found on flowers. Some species are hyperparasites, attacking the Díptera and Hymenóptera that are parasites of caterpillars and grasshoppers. Others attack free-living insects in the orders Neuróptera, Coleóptera, and Hymenóptera (Sýmphyta). The perilampids, like the eucharitids, lay their eggs on foliage, and the eggs hatch into planidial larvae (small, flattened, able to go without feeding for a considerable time). These planidia remain on the foliage, attach to a passing host (usually a caterpillar), and penetrate into its body cavity. If a hyperparasite enters a caterpillar that is not parasitized, it usually does not develop. If the caterpillar is parasitized, then the perilampid larva usually remains inactive in the caterpillar until the caterpillar parasite has pupated, and then attacks the parasite.

Family **Eurytómidae**—Seed Chalcidoids: The eurytomids are similar to the perilampids in having the pronotum and mesoscutum coarsely punctate, but differ in that they have the metasoma rounded or oval and more or less compressed (Figures 35–29C, 35–51D–G). The metasoma of males is often strongly petiolate. They may be distinguished from pteromalids by the quadrate shape of the pronotum in dorsal view and the coarsely punctate mesosoma. They are usually black, but may be yellow or even metallic in color. They are generally more slender in build than the perilampids. Eurytomids vary in habits. Many are parasitic, but some are phytophagous. The larvae of species in the genus *Harmólita* (Figure 35–51D,E) feed in the stems of grasses, sometimes producing galls on the stems. Some of these insects are often serious pests of wheat. The clover seed chalcid, *Bruchóphagus platýptera* (Walker) (Figure 35–51G), infests the seeds of clover and other legumes. A few species in this group are hyperparasitic.

Family **Chalcídidae**: The Chalcídidae are fair-sized chalcidoids (2–7 mm in length) with the hind femora greatly swollen and toothed (Figures 35–23E, 35–29A, 35–53I). They differ from the leucospids in having the ovipositor short and the wings not folded longitudinally when at rest. Pteromalids in the subfamily Chalcedectìnae also have enlarged hind femora, but these species are metallic in color. Chalcidids are usually black or yellow with various markings, but never metallic. Similarly, Podagrionìnae (Torýmidae) have enlarged hind femora, but like most other chalcidoids, these have a large and exposed prepectus. The prepectus of chalcidids is quite small and mostly hidden internally.

The chalcidids are parasites of Lepidóptera, Díptera, and Coleóptera. Some are hyperparasitic, attacking tachinids or ichneumonids.

Family **Leucóspidae**: The Leucóspidae are usually black- or brown-and-yellow insects, and they are parasites of bees and wasps. They are rather uncommon but may occasionally be found on flowers. They are stout-bodied; many have the wings folded longitudinally at rest; and they look a little like a small vespid. The ovipositor in most species is long and curves upward and forward over the metasoma, ending over the posterior part of the mesosoma. Like the chalcidids, the leucospids have the hind femora greatly swollen and toothed on the ventral side.

SUPERFAMILY **Cynipòidea**: The members of this group are mostly small or minute insects with distinctively reduced wing venation (Figure 35–19A). Most species are black, and the metasoma is usually somewhat laterally compressed. The antennae are filiform, the pronotum extends back to the tegulae, and the ovipositor issues from the anterior to the apex of the metasoma. In the fore wing the marginal cell (cell R₁) is usually well developed. Of the more than 800 species in this group in the United States, some 640 (all in the subfamily Cynipìnae) are gall makers or gall inquilines. The others, as far as is known, are parasites.

Family **Ibaliidae**: The ibaliids are relatively large (7–16 mm in length) yellow and black insects. They have the metasoma somewhat elongate, and the marginal cell in the fore wing is distinctively elongate. They are parasites of horntails (Sirícidae) and can most easily be found on or about logs containing these hosts.

Family **Lioptéridae**: These insects have the metasoma petiolate and attached far above the bases of the hind coxae. Three rare species occur in Texas and California. Their immature stages are unknown.

Family **Figítidae**: The members of this group are parasites of the pupae of lacewings and Díptera. The family is divided into three subfamilies, primarily on the basis of the structure of the metasoma. The Anacharitìnae, which have the metasoma distinctly petiolate and the second tergum longer than the third (Figure 35–21E), attack the cocoons of lacewings (Chrysòpidae). The Aspiceratìnae, in which the second metasomatic tergum is narrow and much shorter than the third (Figure 35–21C), attack the pupae of syrphid flies. The Figitìnae, in which the second tergum is only slightly shorter than the third (Figure 35–21F), attack the pupae of Díptera.

Family **Eucòilidae**: The Eucòilidae can be recognized by the rounded cuplike elevation on the scutellum (Figure 35–21D). This structure is at times quite elaborate, and the scutellum may also be developed in a posterior spine. Eucoilids are parasites of the pupae of flies.

Family **Cynípidae**—Gall Wasps and Others: This family is divided into three subfamilies, Alloxystìnae, Charipìnae, and Cynipìnae. The Alloxystìnae are hyperparasites, attacking Bracónidae and Aphelìnidae (Hymenóptera) that are parasitic in aphids; 31 species are known in North America. Only a single species of Charipìnae has so far been recorded in North America; the species of this subfamily are parasites of psyllids (Homóptera).

The Cynipìnae, or gall wasps (Figure 35–54), are a large group, and many species are quite common. Within the subfamily are species that are either gall makers or gall inquilines (in rare cases possibly either). Most species of gall makers attack oaks (*Quércus*) or members of the rose family (Rosàceae) (Figure 35–55). The female wasp oviposits into meristematic tissue that is actively growing or will be the next spring—for example, buds of twigs, flowers, or leaves. The feeding of the wasp larva somehow causes a growth reaction on the part of the host plant that results in the formation of a gall. The wasp larva feeds upon the elaborated gall tissue, pupates within this enclosure, and chews an exit hole to emerge. The galls themselves come in a wide variety of forms, the shape being determined by the species of gall wasp that is feeding within. Many galls are quite large and apparent, as in the various types of oak leaf galls, but some are formed within stems or twigs or even underground on the roots (some wasp species burrow down more than 1 meter to oviposit on oak roots), and these are not apparent to a casual observer. Many galls are dehiscent; that is, they fall off the host plant to the ground with the gall maker still within. Some galls even continue to grow after falling!

The life cycles of many gall makers are very complex. Some species are very similar to other Hymenóptera: they are bisexual, males and females emerge from their galls and mate, mated females then seek out hosts in which to oviposit; fertilized

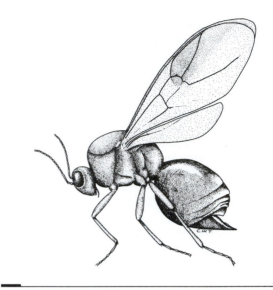

Figure 35–54. A gall wasp, *Diplólepis ròsae* (L.). This species develops in the mossy rose gall (Figure 35–55D).

eggs develop into females, unfertilized eggs into males (arrhenotokous parthenogenesis). Cynipids with this type of life cycle are typically univoltine and attack a wide variety of plants other than oaks and roses. Some species with this general type of life cycle have abandoned the production of males and reproduce by means of thelytokous parthenogenesis. In these the eggs fail to complete meiosis and develop into diploid females; males are rare or entirely absent.

From this point further complications are found. Some species alternate sexual and asexual genera-

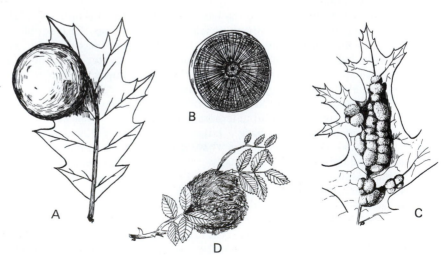

Figure 35–55. Galls of Cynípidae. **A,** an oak-apple gall, caused by *Amphíbolips* sp.; **B,** another oak-apple gall, cut open to show the interior and the central capsule in which the gall wasp larva develops; **C,** the woolly oak gall, caused by *Callirhỳtis lanàta* (Gillette); **D,** the mossy rose gall, caused by *Diplólepis ròsae* (L.). (Redrawn from Felt.)

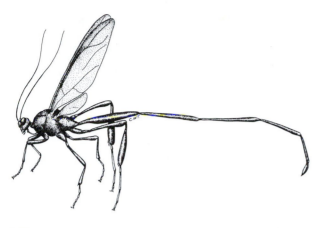

Figure 35–56. A pelecinid, *Pelecìnus polyturàtor* (Drury), female, 1½×.

tions. The sexual generation consists of males and females. These emerge and mate, and the females search out a host in which to oviposit. However, all of her progeny develop into females (the so-called agamic generation). After the agamic generation completes its larval development, the adult wasps emerge, find a host, and oviposit. Some of these unfertilized eggs develop into males of the sexual generation, some into females. In some species the offspring of a given agamic female will all be males, another's will all develop into females. The genetic mechanisms by which the sex of the larvae of the sexual generation is determined are very poorly understood. The adult wasps of the sexual and agamic generations are usually very different in morphology and produce different types of galls on different parts of the host plant. In some cases the two generations must reproduce on different species of hosts. As a result, the sexual and agamic generations have typically been described as separate species of gall wasps, sometimes even in different genera.

The inquiline species have somehow lost the ability to induce the host plant to produce galls. These wasps oviposit into galls produced by other species, and their larvae feed upon the elaborated gall tissue. The inquiline larvae do not normally seem to feed directly on the original gall-making larva, but the latter often does not survive to emerge.

SUPERFAMILY **Proctotrupòidea:** All the members of this superfamily are parasites, attacking the immature stages of other insects. Most of them are small or minute and black, and they may be confused with cynipids, chalcidoids, or some of the aculeates. The smaller members of this group have a much reduced wing venation, but they may be distin-

guished from chalcidoids by the structure of the mesosoma and ovipositor. The pronotum in the proctotrupoids appears triangular in lateral view and extends to the tegulae, and the ovipositor issues from the tip of the metasoma rather than from anterior to the tip.

Family **Pelecìnidae:** The only North American species in this group is *Pelecìnus polyturàtor* (Drury), a large and striking insect. The female is 50 mm or more in length and shining black, with the metasoma very long and slender (Figure 35–56). The male, which is extremely rare, is about 25 mm long and has the posterior part of the metasoma swollen. When captured the females will swivel the metasomatic segments and thrust with the ovipositor, but they rarely penetrate the skin. This insect is a parasite of the larvae of june beetles, and the adults emerge in middle to late summer.

Family **Vanhorniidae:** This family is closely related to the Proctotrùpidae and contains only two species worldwide, one known from Scandinavia and one eastern North American species, *Vanhòrnia eucnemídarum* Crawford, which is a parasite of the larvae of eucnemid beetles. *Vanhòrnia* is characterized by its exodont mandibles—that is, the apical teeth point laterally rather than mesally (Figure 35–22D)—and a long ovipositor that is curved forward beneath the body of the female.

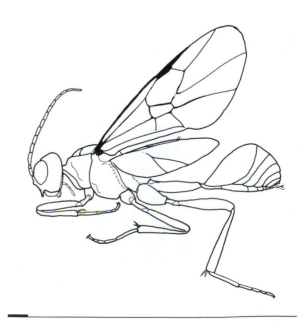

Figure 35–57. *Roprònia gármani* Ashmead. (Redrawn from Townes.)

Family **Roproniidae:** This family contains three rare North American species of *Roprònia*. The adults are 8–10 mm in length and have a laterally flattened, somewhat triangular and petiolate metasoma and a fairly complete venation in the front wing (Figures 35–20F, 35–57). The immature stages are parasites of sawflies.

Family **Helòridae:** This family contains two species in North America, *Helòrus anomálipes* Panzer and *H. ruficórnis* Foerster. These are black insects about 4 mm long with a fairly complete venation in the front wings (Figures 35–20H, 35–58). Both are parasites of the larvae of lacewings (Chrysòpidae), and the adult helorid emerges from the host cocoon.

Family **Proctotrùpidae:** Most of the Proctotrù-pidae range in length from 3 to 6 mm (some are larger). The Nearctic species may be recognized by the large stigma in the front wing, beyond which is a very narrow marginal cell (Figure 35–20D). As far as is known, they are solitary and gregarious parasites of the larvae of Coleóptera and Díptera. The wasp larvae consume their host and then pupate with the end of the metasoma still inside the remains of the host (this also occurs in Pelecìnidae).

Family **Diapriidae:** The diapriids are small to minute insects, most of which are parasites of immature Díptera. They can usually be recognized by the shelflike protuberance in about the middle of the face from which the antennae arise (Figure 35–59). The family contains four subfamilies. The Ambosi-trìnae are most diverse in the southern continents of Australia (and New Zealand), South America, and

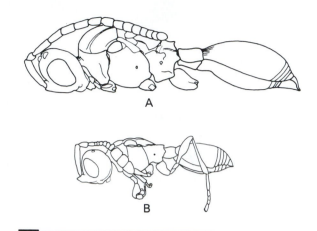

Figure 35–59. Diapriidae. **A,** Belytìnae; **B,** Diapriìnae.

southern Africa (and Madagascar). Only a single species extends its range into the Nearctic: *Propsillòma columbiànum* (Ashmead) is found as far north as southern Canada. The Ismarìnae are recognized by the absence of the typical diapriid frontal shelf; 11 species occur in the United States and Canada and, as far as is now known, these are hyperparasites of dryinids. Most of the approximately 300 North American species in the family belong to just two subfamilies, the Diapriìnae and the Belytìnae. The Diapriìnae are small to minute and have a very much reduced wing venation with no closed cells in the hind wings (Figure 35–19D). Most are parasites of Díptera, but some are associated with ants (in a few cases, parasitic on the ants; in many cases it is unknown whether they parasitize the ants or other ant associates). The Belytìnae are usually larger and have a closed cell in the hind wings (Figure 35–31 G). Diapriids are easily collected by sweeping. The Belytìnae are very common in moist wooded areas, for they attack fungus gnats (Mycetophílidae) and other flies breeding in fungi.

Family **Sceliónidae:** The Sceliónidae are small insects that are parasites of the eggs of spiders and insects in the orders Orthóptera, Mantòdea (in the Old World and Australia), Hemíptera, Homóptera, Embiidìna, Coleóptera, Díptera, Lepidóptera, and Neuróptera. Some of them have been successfully used in the control of crop pests.

The eggs of the hosts of scelionids come in a variety of shapes and sizes, and the wasps themselves are quite diverse in body form (Figure 35–60). For example, the genus *Macroteleia* parasitizes the eggs of Tettigonìidae (Orthóptera) and the wasps are relatively large and elongate. *Baèus,* in contrast, attacks

Figure 35–58. *Helòrus anomálipes* Panzer, female (Helòridae). (Courtesy of Clancy and the University of California.)

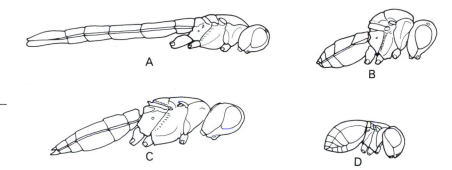

Figure 35–60. Sceliónidae, illustrating variation in body form. **A,** *Macrotèleia;* **B,** *Grỳon;* **C,** *Barycònus;* **D,** *Baèus.*

the spherical eggs of spiders, and the wingless females are almost spherical themselves. Most scelionids have the metasomatic segments divided into a large median sclerite and narrow laterotergites or laterosternites. These latter structures interlock to form a sharply angled margin on the metasoma. However, several genera of scelionines and the entire subfamily Telenomìnae have the laterosternites reduced or absent and the laterotergites greatly enlarged. As a consequence, the metasoma of these species is rounded laterally. In most species the antennae are 12-segmented in both sexes, but varying degrees of reduction in the number of segments is common. Telenominc females have either 11- or 10-segmented antennae. As an extreme, the females of *Ídris, Baèus,* and related genera have seven-segmented antennae with a large unsegmented club. The females of a number of genera have the first metasomatic tergum more or less enlarged into a hornlike protuberance which houses the ovipositor when it is not in use. The species of this family are very common, and the greatest diversity of adults may be collected in spring and late summer when the eggs of their hosts are available.

Family **Platygástridae:** The Platygástridae are minute, shining black insects with a highly reduced wing venation (Figure 35–19H). In most cases the wings are completely veinless. The antennae are usually ten-segmented and are attached very low on the face, next to the clypeus (Figure 35–22B). Most of the platygastrids are parasites of the larvae of Cecidomyìidae. *Platygáster hiemàlis* Forbes is an important agent in the control of the Hessian fly. Others attack mealybugs and other Homóptera Sternorrhýncha. Polyembryony occurs in several species in this family, with as many as 18 young developing from a single egg. Several groups of the subfamily Inostemmatìnae have a horn formed from the first metasomatic tergum as in scelionids (Figure 35–61B). In some species this horn extends far over the mesosoma and its apex fits into a notch in the posterior part of the head. Others, such as the genus

Synòpeas, have the second metasomatic sternum enlarged into a pouch or hornlike structure within which the elongate ovipositor is withdrawn when not in use (Figure 35–61A).

Family **Chrysídidae**—Cuckoo Wasps: The cuckoo wasps are small insects, rarely over 12 mm in length, that are metallic blue or green in color. The body is usually coarsely sculptured. Some of the chalcidoids and bees are similar in size and color, but the cuckoo

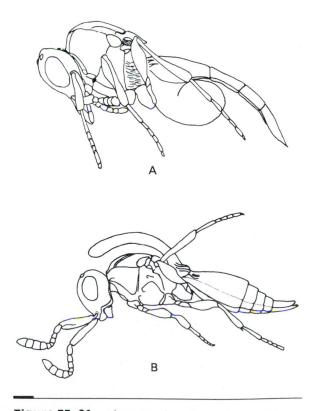

Figure 35–61. Platygástridae, illustrating some metasomatic modifications to accommodate the elongate ovipositor. **A,** *Synòpeas* (Platygastrìnae); **B,** *Inostémma* (Inostemmatìnae).

wasps can be recognized by the wing venation (Figure 35–20B)—a fairly complete venation in the front wing but no closed cells in the hind wing—and the structure of the metasoma. In most species the metasoma consists of only three of four visible segments and is hollowed out ventrally. When a cuckoo wasp is disturbed, it usually curls up in a ball. Most of the cuckoo wasps are external parasites of full-grown wasp or bee larvae. The species in the genus *Cléptes* attack sawfly larvae, and those in *Mesitiópterus* attack the eggs of walkingsticks.

Family **Bethýlidae:** The Bethýlidae are small to medium-sized, usually dark-colored wasps. The females of many species are wingless and antlike in appearance. In a few species, both winged and wingless forms occur in each sex. These wasps are parasites of the larvae of Lepidóptera and Coleóptera. Several species attack moths or beetles that infest grain or flour. A few species will sting people.

Family **Dryínidae:** The Dryínidae is a fairly small group (111 species in the Nearctic) of parasitoids of Homóptera Auchenorrhýncha. The two sexes are often quite different in appearance and can be associated only by rearing. Both males and females have ten-segmented antennae and are often characterized by their large heads and broad, strongly toothed mandibles. Most females are remarkable in that the fore tarsi are developed into chelae used for grasping and holding the hoppers used as hosts (Figure 35–30). Female dryinids catch a host adult or nymph with their chelae, sting and temporarily paralyze it, and lay an egg between two thoracic or abdominal segments. The parasitoid larva feeds internally on the host, although during most of its development a part of the body of the larva protrudes in a saclike structure. The parasite, when full-grown, leaves the host and spins a silken cocoon nearby. Polyembryony occurs in *Aphelòpus thèliae* Gahan, which attacks the treehopper *Thèlia bimaculàta* (Fabricius), with 40 to 60 young developing from a single egg. Many adult females are also predaceous on leafhoppers. Some dryinid females are remarkable ant mimics and may be associated with myrmecophilic hoppers.

Family **Embolémidae:** This small rare family is sometimes classified with the dryinids. Both have the antennae ten-segmented in both sexes. The antennae of embolemids arise from a frontal shelf similar to that in the family Diapriídae. Males are winged, females wingless. Two species of embolemids are known from North America. *Ampulicomórpha confùsa* Ashmead has been reared from nymphs of Achìlidae (Homóptera) feeding on fungi beneath the bark of fallen logs. Species of *Embolémus* (outside of North America) have been collected from ant nests that contain aphids or scale insects.

Family **Sclerogíbbidae:** This family is represented in North America by a single, very rare species occurring in Arizona, *Probéthylus schwárzi* Ashmead. A few sclerogibbids (occurring in other parts of the world) are known to be parasites of Embiidína.

SUPERFAMILY **Sphecòidea**—Sphecoid Wasps: There are differences of opinion regarding the taxonomic arrangement of the sphecoid wasps and some of the names used for them. We follow here the arrangement of Bohart and Menke (1976), who put the sphecoids in a single family, the Sphécidae.

Family **Sphécidae:** Sphecids can be distinguished from other wasps by the structure of the pronotum: in dorsal view the posterior margin is straight, and there is usually a constriction between it and the mesoscutum (forming a collar); laterally the pronotum terminates in a rounded lobe that does not reach the tegulae. Most sphecids have a more or less vertical sulcus on the mesopleuron, the episternal sulcus. Such a sulcus is present in most vespoids, but the mesopleural sulcus in pompilids is transverse (Figure 35–34). The inner margins of the eyes are not notched in most sphecids. This is also the case with the pompilids, but most vespoids do have the inner margins of the eyes notched.

Sphecid wasps differ from the bees, which have a similar pronotal structure, in several ways: (1) all the body hairs are simple (some are branched or plumose in bees); (2) the basal segment of the hind tarsus is not particularly widened or flattened (as it is in most bees) and has at its base, on the inner side, a brush of hairs in a slight depression, opposed by a pectinate tibial spur; (3) sphecids are relatively bare, while many bees are quite hairy; and (4) the posterior margin of the pronotum in dorsal view is straight (usually slightly arcuate in bees). Most Sphécidae are moderate-sized to large, with a complete wing venation, but a few are quite small. Body length in this family varies from about 2 to more than 40 mm. Some of the very small sphecids have a much reduced wing venation, with only four or five closed cells in the front wing. Nine subfamilies are found in North America.

The members of this large family (more than 1100 North American species) are solitary wasps, though large numbers of some of them may sometimes nest in a small area, and a few show the beginnings of social organization (a small number of tropical species are eusocial). They nest in a variety of situations. Most of them nest in burrows in the ground, but some nest in various kinds of natural cavities (hollow plant stems, cavities in wood, and the like), and some construct nests of mud. Females hunt for arthropod prey that serves as food for their offspring.

The prey is stung and paralyzed and then placed within the nest. In most cases the nest is completely provisioned before the egg is laid, but in some cases the female wasp continues to provide new prey items as her offspring grow (known as progressive provisioning). Some groups of sphecids are restricted to a particular type of prey as larval food, but a few groups vary considerably in their selection. A wide variety of arthropods are used, including Orthóptera, Blattària, Hemíptera, Homóptera, Coleóptera, Díptera, Lepidóptera, Hymenóptera, and spiders. A few are cleptoparasitic, building no nest but laying their eggs in the nests of other wasps, their larvae feeding on the food stored for the host larvae.

The subfamily Spheciñae, or thread-waisted wasps, are very common insects, and most of them are 25 mm or more in length. Some of our largest sphecids are in this subfamily. The common name refers to the very slender petiole of the metasoma. The two genera *Scéliphron* and *Chalýbion* are commonly called mud daubers. They construct nests of mud and provision them with spiders. These nests usually consist of a number of cells, each about 25 mm long, placed side by side. They are common on ceilings or walls of old buildings. Two species in each of these genera occur in the Nearctic, the most common being *S. caementàrium* (Drury) and *C. califòrnicum* (Saussure). The former is blackish brown with yellow spots, yellow legs, and clear wings, and the latter is metallic blue with bluish wings. Another common ground-nesting species of Spheciñae is *Sphéx ichneumòneus* (L.), which is reddish brown with the tip of the metasoma black (Figure 35–62C).

The genus *Trypóxylon* (Larrìnae) includes the organ-pipe mud daubers (some of which reach a length of 25 mm or more), which make nests of mud (Figure

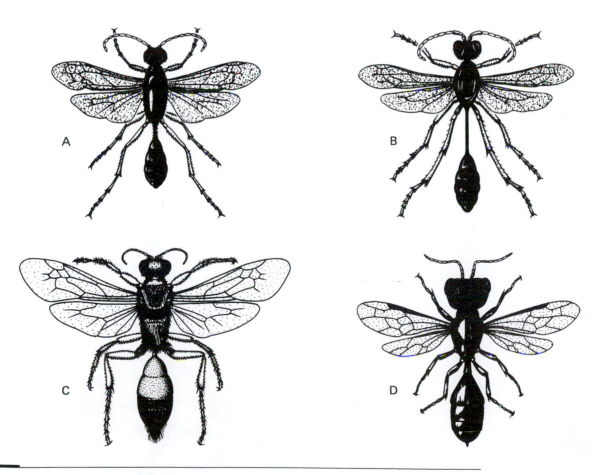

Figure 35–62.   Sphecid wasps. **A,** *Chlorìon aeràrium* Patton; **B,** *Ammóphila nígricans* Dahlbom; **C,** *Sphéx ichneumòneus* (L.); **D,** *Pémphredon inornàtus* Say.

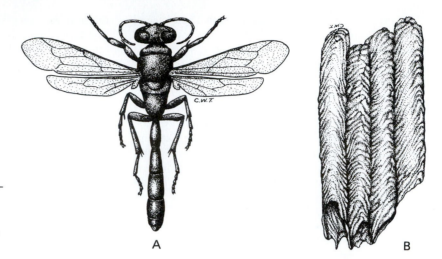

Figure 35–63.   An organ-pipe mud dauber. **A,** adult of *Trypóxylon clavàtum* Say, $3\frac{1}{2}\times$; **B,** nest of *T. polítum* Say.

35–63). Other species of this common genus nest in the ground or in various natural cavities. These wasps provision their nests with spiders.

The members of the Crabronìnae (Figure 35–64) are small to medium-sized rather stocky wasps. They are fairly common insects, and most are either black with yellow markings or entirely black. They can usually be recognized by the large quadrate head, with the inner margins of the eyes straight and converging below, and the single submarginal cell. These wasps vary in their nesting habits. Most nest in the ground, but some nest in natural cavities such as hollow stems or cavities in wood. The principal prey is flies, but some take other insects such as beetles, bugs, hoppers, or small Hymenóptera.

The cicada killers (Nyssonìnae: *Sphècius*) are large insects (up to 40 mm in length) that provision their nests with cicadas. One common species, *S. speciòsus* (Drury), is black or rusty, with yellow bands on the metasoma (Figure 35–65A).

The sand wasps (Nyssonìnae) are rather stout-bodied wasps of moderate size (Figure 35–65B). This is a fairly large group (about 75 North American species), and its members are common around beaches, sand dunes, and other sandy areas. They nest in burrows, and a great many may nest in a

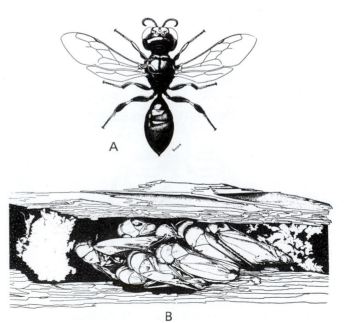

Figure 35–64.   A square-headed wasp, *Crossócerus annùlipes* (Lepeletier and Brullé) (Sphécidae, Crabronìnae). **A,** adult, $2\times$; **B,** a section of a rotting log in which this wasp has stored leafhoppers. (Courtesy of Davidson and Landis and the Entomological Society of America.)

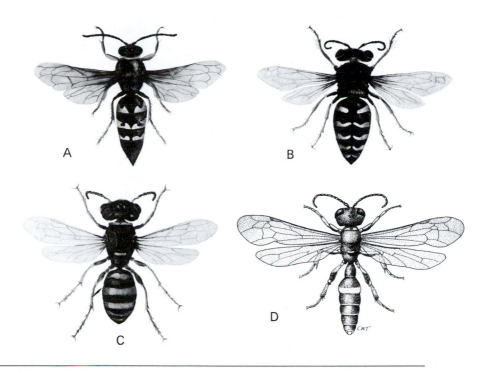

Figure 35–65.   Sphecid wasps. **A,** the cicada killer, *Sphècius speciòsus* (Drury), about natural size; **B,** a sand wasp, *Bémbix americànus spinòlae* Lepeletier, slightly enlarged; **C,** a bee-killer wasp, *Philánthus ventílabris* Fabricius, 2×; **D,** weevil wasp, *Cérceris clypeàta* Dahlbom, 2×.

small area. In some species the adults continue to feed the larvae during their growth. The adults are very agile and rapid fliers, and although they can sting, one can walk through a colony—with the wasps dashing all about—without being stung. *Stíctia carolìna* (Fabricius), an insect about 25 mm long and black with yellow markings, is fairly common in the South. Because it often hunts for flies (mostly Tabánidae) near horses, it is called the horse guard. Other sand wasps are black with yellow, white, or pale green markings.

The species of the tribe Philanthìni (Philanthìnae; Figure 35–65C) provision their nests with bees, principally halictids, and are usually called bee-killer wasps or bee wolves. They are common insects (29 North American species). The Cercerìni (Philanthìnae) (Figure 35–65D) may be called weevil wasps, as they provision with beetles (Curculiónidae, Chrysomélidae, and Bupréstidae). They are common insects, and a little over a hundred species occur in our area.

SUPERFAMILY **Apòidea**—Bees: Bees are common insects and are to be found almost everywhere, particularly on flowers. About 3500 species occur in North America. Many other species of Hymenóptera may be collected at flowers feeding upon nectar. Bees are unusual in that they visit the flowers not only for the carbohydrates provided by the nectar, but also to collect the pollen produced by the plant with which to provision their nests. In most species the larvae feed and develop upon a mass of pollen stored in the cell by the female bee, in contrast to other aculeates in which the cells are provisioned with arthropod prey (the Masarìnae in the family Véspidae also provision their nests with pollen). Nests are typically constructed in the soil, but a wide variety of natural cavities may be used, such as abandoned rodent nests, tree hollows, the emergence holes of wood-boring beetles, or the hollow stems of plants. Some species of bees collect pollen from only a very narrow range of hosts; others may visit practically any plant in bloom. Most species are solitary; that is, each female is capable of constructing a nest and reproducing. These species construct a cell, completely provision it with pollen (mass provisioning), oviposit on or near the pollen, then close the cell and begin construction of another. The eusocial bees typically progressively provision the cells in their nest, bringing more pollen to the larvae as they grow or providing them with honey (collected in the form of nectar from flowers and concentrated by evaporation).

The bees are closely related to the Sphécidae, and together they form a distinctive group within the Hymenóptera. The two superfamilies have the pronotum terminating laterally in rounded lobes that do not reach the tegulae. The distinctive features of the nonparasitic bees have to do largely with the transport of pollen (Figures 35–15B, 35–66). Most bees are quite hairy, and as they visit flowers, a certain amount of pollen sticks to their body hairs. This pollen is periodically combed off with the legs and transported on brushes of hairs called scopae (located on the ventral side of the metasoma in Megachìlidae) or on corbiculae (the broad, shiny, slightly convex outer surfaces of the hind tibiae [Figure 35–15B, *cb*], as in the social Àpidae). A few species transport pollen in their crop. The bees that are cleptoparasites, that is, those that live as "cuckoos" in the nests of other bees, are usually wasplike in appearance, with relatively little body hair and without a pollen-transporting apparatus. These can be recognized as bees by their more flattened hind basitarsi and the plumose body hairs.

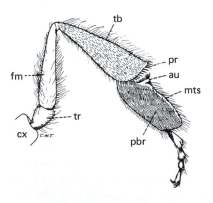

Figure 35–66. Hind leg of a honey bee, inner surface, showing the pollen-transporting apparatus. *au*, auricle; *cx*, coxa; *fm*, femur; *mts*, first tarsal segment; *pbr*, pollen brush; *pr*, pollen rake or pecten; *tb*, tibia; *tr*, trochanter. The pollen is collected off the body hairs by the front and middle legs and deposited on the pollen brushes (*pbr*) of the hind legs. The pollen on the pollen brush of one leg is raked off by the rake (*pr*) on the other, the pollen falling on the surface of the auricle (*au*); the closing of the tarsus on the tibia forces the pollen upward, where it adheres to the floor of the pollen basket or corbicula (which is on the outer surface of the tibia). As this process is repeated, first on one side and then on the other, the pollen is packed into the lower ends of the pollen baskets until both are filled (see Figure 2–1).

The maxillae and labium of bees form a tongue-like structure through which the insect sucks up nectar. There is some development of such a tongue in other Hymenóptera, but in many bees the tongue is elongate, and the bee is thus able to reach the nectar in flowers with a deep corolla. The structure of the tongue differs considerably in different bees and provides characters that are used in classification.

The two sexes of bees differ in the number of antennal segments and metasomatic tergites. The males have 13 antennal segments and 7 visible metasomatic tergites. The females have only 12 antennal segments and 6 visible metasomatic tergites.

The pollen-collecting bees play an important role in the pollination of plants. Some of the higher plants are self-pollinating, but a great many are cross-pollinated; that is, the pollen of one flower must be transferred to the stigma of another. Cross-pollination is brought about by two principal agencies, the wind and insects. Wind-pollinated plants include the grasses (such as the cereal grains, timothy, and the like), many trees (such as the willows, oaks, hickories, elms, poplars, and conifers), and many wild plants. The insect-pollinated plants include most orchard fruits, berries, many vegetables (particularly the cucurbits), field crops (such as the clovers, cotton, and tobacco), and flowers. Most of the pollination is done by bees, often chiefly honey bees and bumble bees, but a great deal of pollinating is done by solitary bees. Many growers, by bringing in hives of honey bees when the plants are in bloom, have been able to get greatly increased yields of orchard fruits, clover seed, and other crops that are dependent on bees for pollination. When it is realized that the annual value of insect-pollinated crops in the United States is about $19 billion, it will be apparent that the bees are extremely valuable insects.

There are differences of opinion about the classification of bees. The arrangement followed here is that of Michener (1974), in which the North American bees are classified in eight families. Identification of bees to family is sometimes difficult because the characters are hidden beneath the dense body hairs or the tongue is folded beneath the head. The hairs may be carefully scraped off or pushed aside with an insect pin, and the tongue can be extended while the specimen is still fresh and flexible.

Family **Melíttidae:** The melittids are small, dark-colored, rather rare bees, similar in nesting habits to the Andrènidae. They differ from other short-tongued bees (Collétidae, Halíctidae, and Andrènidae) in that they have the jugal lobe of the hind wing shorter than the M + Cu$_1$ cell. They differ from the

Megachìlidae, Anthophòridae, and Àpidae (the long-tongued bees) in that they have the segments of the labial palps similar in size and cylindrical (the labial palps of the Megachìlidae, Anthophòridae, and Àpidae have the first two segments elongate and flattened). Our species nest in burrows on the soil.

Three subfamilies and 31 species of Melíttidae occur in North America: the Macropidìnae (with two submarginal cells and very broad stigma), the Dasypodìnae (with two submarginal cells and a narrow stigma), and the Melittìnae (with three submarginal cells).

Family **Collètidae**—Plasterer Bees and Yellow-Faced Bees: These bees have the tongue short and either truncate or bilobed at the apex (Figure 35–6C). The family is divided into three subfamilies, the Colletìnae, Diphaglossìnae, and Hylaeìnae, and more than 150 species are known from North America.

The Colletìnae, or plasterer bees, burrow into the ground to nest and line their burrows with a thin translucent substance. They are of moderate size and are quite hairy, with bands of pale pubescence on the metasoma. There are three submarginal cells, and the second m-cu cross vein is sigmoid (Figure 35–13D). Ninety-seven species of these bees have been recorded from North America. The Hylaeìnae, or yellow-faced bees, are small, black, very sparsely hairy bees, usually with yellow markings on the face (Figure 35–67) and with only two submarginal cells (Figure 35–13E). They are very wasplike in appearance, and the hind legs of the female do not have pollen brushes. Pollen for larval food is carried to their nests in the crop, mixed with nectar, instead of on the body or legs. These bees nest in various sorts of cavities and crevices, in plant stems, or in burrows in the ground. North American species belong to the genus *Hylaèus*, and many are very common bees.

Family **Halíctidae**: The halictids are small to moderate-sized bees, often metallic, and can usually be recognized by the strongly arched first free segment of the medial vein (Figure 35–13C). Most of them nest in burrows in the ground, either on level ground or in banks. The main tunnel is usually vertical, with lateral tunnels branching off from it and each terminating in a single cell. Large numbers of these bees often nest close together, and many bees may use the same passageway to the outside. More than 500 species of halictids occur in our area.

Three subfamilies of halictids occur in the United States: the Halictìnae (the largest and most common of the three subfamilies), the Nomiìnae, and the Dufoureìnae. The Dufoureìnae differ from the other two subfamilies in that they have only two submarginal cells and have the clypeus short, usu-

Figure 35–67.   A yellow-faced bee, *Hylaèus modéstus* Say, 10×.

ally not longer than the labrum, and in profile strongly convex and protruding. The Nomiìnae, represented by the genus *Nòmia*, have the first and third submarginal cells about the same size. These bees are often of considerable importance in the pollination of plants.

In the Halictìnae the third submarginal cell is shorter than the first. This group contains several genera of fairly common bees. In *Agapóstemon* (Figure 35–68B), *Augochlorópsis*, *Augochlorélla*, and *Augochlòra*, the head and mesosoma are a brilliant metallic green. These bees are small, 14 mm in length or less, and some of the bees in the genus *Augochlòra* are only a few millimeters in length. The other fairly common genera are *Dialíctus*, *Lasioglóssum*, and *Sphecòdes*. These usually have the head and mesosoma black or dull green. Some members of the genus *Lasioglóssum* are frequently attracted to people who are perspiring, and are called sweat bees. The bees in the genus *Sphecòdes* are rather wasplike in appearance, and the entire metasoma is red. These are parasites (cleptoparasites) of other bees.

Halictids are extremely diverse in terms of their social biology, spanning the spectrum from solitary species, either nesting alone or in congregations, to primitively eusocial species. The level of social "development" seems to be intertwined with poorly understood environmental constraints: some species show great differences in social behavior in different parts of their range or at different times of the year. Eusociality, per se, is clearly not an evolutionary goal toward which these bees are inevitably moving, but most likely represents an adaptive strategy for a particular time and place. Michener (1974), in fact, argues that it is quite likely that in addition to

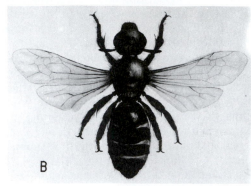

Figure 35–68.   Solitary bees. **A,** *Andrèna wilkélla* (Kirby) (Andrènidae); **B,** *Agapóstemon viréscens* (Fabricius) (Halíctidae).

having evolved many times, eusociality may have been lost just as often by different species.

Family **Oxaèidae:**   This group is chiefly tropical and is represented in the United States by two species each in the genera *Protoxaèa* and *Mesoxaèa* that occur in the Southwest. These solitary bees are large and fast-flying and nest in deep burrows in the soil.

Family **Andrènidae:**   The andrenids are small to medium-sized bees that can be recognized by the two subantennal sulci below each antennal socket (Figure 35–17A). They nest in burrows in the ground, and their burrows are similar to those of halictids. Sometimes large numbers of these bees will nest close together, usually in areas where the vegetation is sparse.

The approximately 1200 species of andrenids in North America are arranged in two subfamilies, the Andrenìnae and the Panurgìnae. The Andrenìnae have the apex of the marginal cell pointed or narrowly rounded and on the costal margin of the wing, and they usually have three submarginal cells (Figure 35–13A). The Panurgìnae have the apex of the marginal cell truncate and usually have only two submarginal cells (Figure 35–13B). The vast majority of species of Andrenìnae belong to the genus *Andrèna* (Figure 35–68A), and these are very common springtime bees. Most Panurgìnae belong to the genus *Pérdita*. The Panurgìnae are moderate-sized to minute, and many have yellow or other bright markings.

Family **Megachìlidae**—Leafcutting Bees: The leafcutting bees are mostly moderate-sized, fairly stout-bodied bees (Figure 35–69). They differ from most other bees in having two submarginal cells of about equal length (Figure 35–13F), and the females of the pollen-collecting species carry the pollen by means

of a scopa on the ventral side of the metasoma rather than on the hind legs. The common name of these bees is derived from the fact that in many species the nest cells are lined with pieces cut from leaves. These pieces are usually very neatly cut out, and it is not uncommon to find plants from which circular pieces have been cut by these bees. A few species in this family are parasitic. The nests are made in various places, occasionally in the ground but more often in some natural cavity, frequently in wood. The vast majority of nonparasitic species are solitary.

Figure 35–69.   A leaf-cutting bee, *Megachìle latimànus* Say, 3×.

Figure 35–70. A cuckoo bee, *Triepèolus lunàtus* (Say) (Anthophòridae), 3×.

This family is divided into two subfamilies, the Lithurgìnae and the Megachilìnae. The former is represented in our area by a single genus, *Lithúrge* (with five species), which occurs chiefly in the South, and its members feed largely on cactus flowers. The Megachilìnae form a large group (more than 600 North American species) of widespread distribution. Some of the more common genera of Megachilìnae are *Anthídium, Dianthídium, Stèlis, Herìades, Hóplitis, Ósmia, Megachìle,* and *Coelióxys.* The bees in the genera *Stèlis* and *Coelióxys* are parasitic. One introduced species of *Megachìle* is an important pollinator of alfalfa in the West.

Family **Anthophòridae**—Cuckoo Bees, Digger Bees, and Carpenter Bees: This family differs from the Àpidae in having the hind tibiae with apical spurs, a jugal lobe in the hind wing, the genae very narrow, and the maxillary palps well developed. It is divided into three subfamilies: the Nomadìnae, the Anthophorìnae, and the Xylocopìnae.

Subfamily **Nomadìnae**—Cuckoo Bees: All the bees in this group are parasites in the nests of other bees. They are usually wasplike in appearance and have relatively few hairs on the body. They lack a pollen-transporting apparatus; the clypeus is somewhat protuberant; the front coxae are a little broader than long; and the last metasomatic tergite usually (at least in females) has a triangular platelike area. Some of these bees (for example, members of the large genus *Nómada*) are reddish and of medium or small size. Others (for example, *Epèolus* and *Triepèolus;* Figure 35–70) are fair-sized (13–19 mm) and dark-colored with small patches of pale pubescence.

Subfamily **Anthophorìnae**—Digger Bees: The digger bees resemble the Nomadìnae in the form of the clypeus, front coxae, and the tergal plate on the last metasomatic segment, but are robust and hairy (Figure 35–71A). The subfamily includes both parasitic and nonparasitic species. Most of the latter are solitary, but some nest communally. Digger bees nest in burrows in the ground or in banks, and the cells are lined with a thin wax or varnishlike substance.

Subfamily **Xylocopìnae**—Carpenter Bees: These bees do not have the clypeus protuberant; the front coxae are transverse; and the last metasomatic segment lacks a triangular platelike area. These bees make their nests in wood or plant stems. The two North American genera in this group, *Ceratìna* and

Figure 35–71.   Anthophorine bees. **A,** a digger bee, *Anthóphora occidentàlis* Cresson, 2×; **B,** a cuckoo bee, *Melécta califórnica miránda* Fox, 2×, an inquiline of *A. occidentàlis.* (Courtesy of Porter.)

Xylocòpa, differ somewhat in habits and differ considerably in size. The small carpenter bees (*Ceratìna*) are dark bluish green and about 6 mm in length. They are superficially similar to some of the halictids, particularly since the first free segment of the medial vein is noticeably arched, but they may be distinguished from halictids by the much smaller jugal lobe in the hind wings (compare Figures 35–13C and 35–14F). These bees excavate the pith from the stems of various bushes and nest in the tunnels so produced (Figure 35–72). The large carpenter bees (*Xylocòpa*) are robust bees about 25 mm in length, similar in appearance to bumble bees, but they have the dorsum of the metasoma largely bare (Figure 35–73A), and the second submarginal cell is triangular (Figure 35–14A). These bees excavate galleries in solid wood.

Family **Àpidae**—Bumble Bees, Honey Bees, and Orchid Bees: The Àpidae differ from the Anthophòridae in that the maxillary palps are vestigial, the genal area is broad, corbiculae are present on the hind legs, and there is no pygidial plate. Most Àpidae are eusocial.

Subfamily **Bombìnae**—Bumble Bees: Bumble bees can usually be recognized by their robust shape and black and yellow coloration (Figure 35–73B); a few are marked with orange. They are relatively large bees, most of them being 20 mm or more in length. The hind wings lack a jugal lobe (Figure 35–14B). Bumble bees are very common insects, and they are important pollinators of certain kinds of clover because of their very long tongues.

Most bumble bees nest in the ground, usually in a deserted mouse nest or bird nest or similar situation. The colonies are annual (at least in temperate regions), and only the fertilized queens overwinter. Nests are initiated by solitary, fertilized queens that have overwintered. These queens are often very con-

Figure 35–73. **A,** a large carpenter bee, *Xylocòpa virgínica* (L.) (Xylocopìnae); **B,** a bumble bee, *Bómbus pennsylvánicus* (De Geer) (Bombìnae). 1½×.

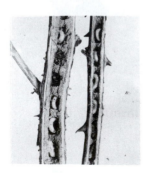

Figure 35–72. Nest of the small carpenter bee, *Ceratìna dùpla* Say.

spicuous in the spring as they search for a nest site. The first brood raised by the queen consists entirely of workers. Once the workers appear, they take over all the duties of the colony except egg laying. They enlarge the nest, collect food and store it in saclike "honey pots" built from wax and pollen, and care for the larvae. Later in the summer, males and queens are produced, and in the fall all but these queens die.

Species in the genus *Psíthyrus* are parasites of other bumble bees (*Bómbus*). *Psíthyrus* females differ from those of *Bómbus* in having the outer surface of the hind tibiae convex and hairy (flat or concave and largely bare in *Bómbus*). These bees have no worker caste. The females invade the nests of other bumble bees and lay their eggs, leaving their young to be reared by the workers of the host nest.

Subfamily **Euglossìnae**—Orchid Bees: The euglossine bees are brilliant metallic, often brightly colored bees that are tropical in distribution. They have a very long tongue; they have apical spurs on the hind tibiae; they lack a jugal lobe in the hind wings; and the scutellum is produced backward over the metasoma. The common name of orchid bees arises because the males are attracted to orchid flowers and are important in their pollination. The males do not feed on this pollen and the orchids do not produce nectar; it is thought that the males may derive precursor chemicals for a sex pheromone from the flowers. Females are not attracted to orchids. Both parasitic and nonparasitic species are found in the subfamily. The latter include solitary and parasocial species. One species in this group, *Eulaèma polychròma* (Mocsary) has been recorded from Brownsville, Texas.

Subfamily **Apinae**—Honey Bees: Honey bees may be recognized by their golden brown coloration and characteristic shape (Figure 35–74), the form of the marginal and submarginal cells in the front wing (Figure 35–14D), and the absence of spurs on the hind tibiae. These bees are common and well-known insects, and they are the most important bees in the pollination of plants. They are extremely valuable insects, as they produce some $300 million worth of honey and beeswax annually, and their pollinating activities are worth 130–140 times this amount.

Only a single species of honey bee occurs in North America, *Àpis mellífera* L. This is an introduced species, and most of its colonies are in man-made hives. Escaped swarms usually nest in a hollow tree. The cells in the nest are in vertical combs, two cell layers thick. Honey bee colonies are perennial, with the queen and workers overwintering in the hive. A queen may live several years. Unlike the bumble bee queen, a honey bee queen is unable to start a colony by herself. As in most of the Hymenóptera, the sex of a bee is in large part controlled by the fertilization of the egg: fertilized eggs develop into females, and unfertilized eggs develop into males. Whether a larval honey bee destined to become a female becomes a worker or queen depends on the sort of food it is fed. There is normally only one queen in a honey bee colony. When a new one is produced, it may be killed by the old queen, or one of the queens (usually the old queen) may leave the hive in a swarm, along with a group of workers, and build a nest elsewhere. The new queen mates during a mating flight and thereafter never leaves the nest except to swarm. The males serve only to fertilize the queen and die in the act of mating. They do not remain in the colony long, as they are eventually killed by the workers.

Our honey bees, which have been introduced into this continent from Europe, are not particularly aggressive and are easy to manage. In 1956 an African strain of the honey bee was brought into southern Brazil with the intention of interbreeding them with the European strain. Mated queens and workers accidentally escaped and established wild colonies. This strain of the bee has become known as the "killer bee." Since its introduction this strain has spread over a large part of South and Central America, and it will in all likelihood soon reach the United States. These bees produce more honey than the European strain, but they are very aggressive. At the slightest disturbance they will attack people or animals with great ferocity, often chasing them 100–200 meters (sometimes as far as a kilometer). Both livestock and people have been killed by these bees. Beekeeping practices in South America have changed somewhat as a result of the introduction of this strain: colonies are now generally removed from settlements and livestock. Attempts are being made to reduce the aggressiveness of these bees by crossbreeding and selection.

Honey bees have a very interesting "language," a means of communicating with one another (see von Frisch 1967, 1971). When a worker goes out and discovers a flower with a good nectar flow, she returns to the hive and "tells" the other workers about it—the type of flower, its direction from the hive, and how far it is. The type of flower involved is communicated by means of its odor, either on the body hairs of the returning bee or in the nectar it

Figure 35–74.   The honey bee, *Àpis mellífera* L. 5×.

brings back from the flower. The distance and direction of the flower from the hive are "told" by means of a dance put on by the returning worker. Many social insects have a "language" or a means of communication, but its exact nature is known in relatively few species.

Family **Tiphìidae:**   Most tiphiids are easily recognized by the platelike lamellae that extend over the bases of the middle coxae. The Tiphìinae is the largest subfamily, with about 140 North American species, and its members are fairly common and widely distributed. They are black, mostly medium-sized, and somewhat hairy, with short, spiny legs (Figure 35–75A). The larvae are parasites of scarab beetle larvae. One species, *Típhia popilliávora* Rohwer (Figure 35–75A), has been introduced into the United States to aid in the control of the Japanese beetle. The Myzinìnae are generally a little larger (length up to about 25 mm) and more slender than the Tiphìinae and are black with yellow markings. The upcurved spine at the end of the male metasoma looks like a vicious sting, but is not dangerous. Fourteen species occur in the United States and Canada, and some are fairly common. These wasps are parasites of the larvae of scarab beetles. The Brachycistidìnae are medium-sized, brownish, somewhat hairy wasps that are common throughout the West. The females are wingless and are not seen as often as the males. About 70 species occur in our area, but little is known of their immature stages. The Anthoboscìnae is represented by a single species, *Lálapa lùsa* Pate, which occurs in Idaho and California. Nothing is known of its immature stages. The Methochìnae are small, usually black wasps, in which the females are wingless and generally much smaller than the males. Five species occur in the United States and Canada, and they are widely distributed but uncommon. The Methochìnae are parasites of the larvae of tiger beetles.

Family **Sierolomórphidae:**   The Sierolomórphidae are a small (six North American species) but widely distributed group of shining black wasps 4.5–6.0 mm in length. They are quite rare, and nothing is known of their immature stages.

Family **Sapýgidae:**   The Sapýgidae are a small (17 North American species) and rare group. The adults are of moderate size, usually black spotted or banded with yellow, and with short legs. They are parasites of leaf-cutting bees (Megachìlidae) and wasps.

Family **Mutíllidae**—Velvet Ants: These wasps are called velvet ants because the females are wingless and antlike and are covered with a dense pubescence (Figure 35–76). In most mutillid females the mesosomatic segments are completely fused to form an immovable boxlike structure (the pronotal and mesonotal suture is movable in the subfamily Myrmosìnae). The males are winged and usually larger than the females and are also densely pubescent. Most species have "felt lines" laterally on the second metasomatic tergum. Felt lines are narrow longitudinal bands of relatively dense, closely appressed hairs. The females have a very painful sting. Some species can stridulate, and they produce a squeaking sound when disturbed. Most of the mutillids whose life histories are known are external parasites of the larvae and pupae of various wasps and bees. A few attack certain beetles and flies. Mutillids are generally found in open areas. This group is a large one (about 435 North American species), and most species occur in the South and West, especially in arid areas.

Family **Bradynobaènidae:**   The bradynobaenids were formerly classified in the family Mutíllidae because many of them have the lateral felt lines on

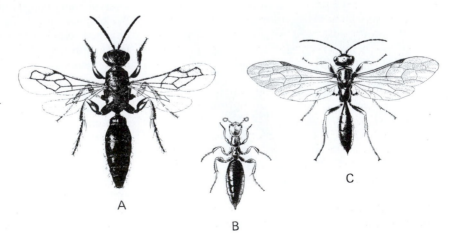

Figure 35–75.   Tiphiid wasps. **A,** *Típhia popilliávora* Rohwer, male (Tiphìinae); **B,** *Neozelobòria próximus* Turner, female (Brachycistidìnae); **C,** same, male. (**A,** courtesy of USDA; **B** and **C,** courtesy of Burrell and the New York Entomological Society.)

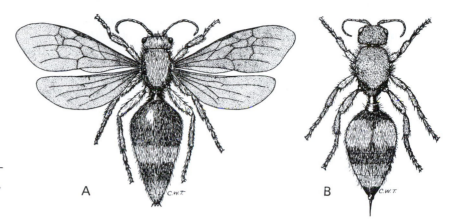

Figure 35–76.   A velvet ant, *Dasymutílla occidentàlis* (L.). **A,** male; **B,** female.

the second metasomatic tergum. The males are winged and the females apterous. The males are distinguished from the mutillids by the presence of a jugal lobe in the hind wing. In the females there is a flexible articulation between the pronotum and mesonotum. Forty-eight species are found in western North America. The subfamily Typhoctìnae is nocturnal; the Chyphotìnae are diurnal. Their hosts and larval biology are unknown.

Family **Pompílidae**—Spider Wasps: The pompilids are slender wasps with long spiny legs, a pronotum that is somewhat quadrate in lateral view, and a characteristic transverse sulcus across the mesopleuron (Figures 35–34, 35–77). The more common members of this group are 15–25 mm in length, but some western species are 35–40 mm in length. Most spider wasps are dark-colored, with smoky or yellowish wings. A few are brightly colored. They are often recognizable because of their habit of nervously flitting the wings while searching on foot. (There are a number of pompilid mimics, for example in the Sphécidae and Ichneumónidae, that also have this habit.) The adults are usually found on flowers or on the ground in search of prey. The larvae of most species feed on spiders (hence the common name), although these are not the only wasps that attack spiders. The spider wasps generally capture and paralyze a spider and then prepare a cell for it in the ground, in rotten wood, or in a suitable crevice in rocks. Some spider wasps construct a cell first, then hunt for a spider to store in the cell. A few species attack the spider in its own cell or burrow and do not move it after stinging and ovipositing on it. A few species oviposit on spiders that have been stung by another wasp. The spider wasps are fairly common (290 North American species), and the females have a very painful sting.

Family **Rhopalosomátidae**: This group includes three rare species that occur in the East, *Rhopalo-*

sòma neárcticum Brues, *Lìosphex vàrius* Townes, and *Olíxon bánksii* (Brues). *Rhopalosòma neárcticum* is 14–20 mm or more in length, is light brown in color, and superficially resembles ichneumonids in the genus *Òphion*, but it does not have the metasoma compressed, the antennae contain only 12 (female) or 13 (male) segments, and there is only one m-cu cross vein in the front wing (Figure 35–31 H). *Olíxon bánksii* is about 6 mm long and has greatly reduced wings that extend only to the tip of the propodeum. The larvae of these wasps attack crickets.

Family **Scolìidae**: The Scolìidae are large, hairy, and usually black with a yellow band (or bands) on the metasoma (Figure 35–78). Larvae of these wasps are external parasites of the larvae of scarabaeid beetles. The adults are commonly found on flowers. The females burrow into the ground to locate a host. When they find a grub, they sting it and paralyze it, then burrow deeper into the soil and construct a cell

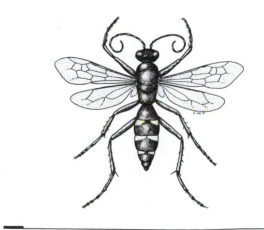

Figure 35–77.   A spider wasp, *Episỳron quinquenotàtus* (Say), 2½×.

Figure 35–78.   *Scòlia dùbia* Say (Scolìidae), a parasite of the green June beetle. (Courtesy of Davis and Luginbill and the North Carolina Agricultural Experiment Station.)

around the grub. Many grubs may be stung without the wasp ovipositing. Such grubs usually do not recover. Twenty-three species have been recorded in North America.

SUPERFAMILY **Vespòidea:**   The vespoid wasps differ from the Sphecòidea in the form of the pronotum (Figure 35–4C,D) and from the Pompílidae in lacking a transverse sulcus on the mesopleuron. Most of the vespoids have the posterior margin of the pronotum strongly U-shaped in dorsal view, and all but the Masarìnae have the 1M cell very long. These wasps usually fold their wings longitudinally at rest.

The vespoid wasps have been classified in from one to several families. We follow here the arrangement of Carpenter (1982) and put them in a single family.

Family **Véspidae**—Paper Wasps, Yellow Jackets, Hornets, Mason Wasps, Potter Wasps: This is a relatively large group (325 North American species), and its members are very common and well-known insects. Most are black with yellow or whitish markings (Figure 35–80) or brownish (Figure 35–82A). Some species are eusocial, and the individuals in a colony are of three castes: queens, workers, and males. The queens and workers have a very effective sting. In some species there is very little difference between the queens and workers, but usually the queen is larger.

The social vespids construct a nest out of a papery material that consists of wood or foliage chewed up and elaborated by the insect. The colonies in temperate regions exist for just a single season. Only the queens overwinter, and in the spring each queen starts a new colony. The queen begins construction of a nest (or she may use a nest built in a previous year) and raises her first brood, which consists of workers. The workers then assume the duties of the colony, and thenceforth the queen does little more

than lay eggs. The larvae are fed chiefly on insects and other animals.

Subfamily **Euparagiìnae:**   This small and rare group of vespids is found only in the western United States. The subfamily contains only one genus, *Euparágia*, with six described Nearctic species. This is the sister group of all other species in the Véspidae, and it is unique among them in that these insects do not fold the wings longitudinally at rest. One species, *E. scutellàris* Cresson, builds a shallow nest in the soil and provisions its cells with weevil larvae.

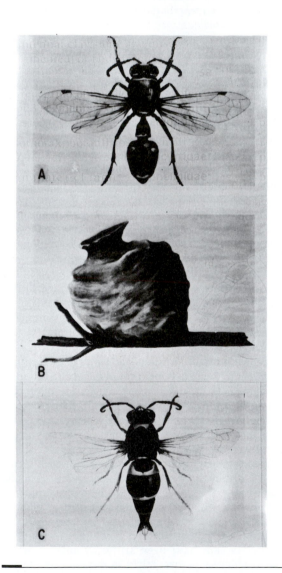

Figure 35–79.   **A,** adult, and **B,** nest, of a potter wasp, *Eùmenes fratérnus* Say; **C,** a mason wasp, *Rýgchium dorsàle* (Fabricius); this species nests in small colonies in vertical burrows in the ground.

Subfamily **Masarìnae:** The members of this subfamily are limited to the western United States. Most of the members of this group are black and yellow wasps, 10–20 mm in length. They differ from other vespids in having only two submarginal cells and in having the antennae clubbed. They make nests of mud or sand attached to rocks or twigs and provision their nests with pollen and nectar. This group is a small one, with only 21 species (14 in the genus *Pseudomasàris*) in North America.

Subfamily **Eumenìnae**—Mason and Potter Wasps: These are solitary wasps and, in terms of numbers of species, the most abundant vespids (260 species in North America). They vary considerably in their nesting habits, but most of them provision their nests with caterpillars. Some species use cavities in twigs or logs for a nest, others burrow in the ground, and others make a nest of mud or clay (Figure 35–79B). Most of them are black marked with yellow or white, or entirely black, and they vary in length from about 10 to 25 mm.

Subfamily **Vespìnae**—Yellow Jackets and Hornets: Most of our 18 North American species of Vespìnae belong to the genus *Véspula* (Figure 35–80B). These wasps are eusocial, and their nests consist of several to many tiers of hexagonal paper cells, all enclosed in a papery envelope (Figure 35–81). Some species build their nests in the open, attached to branches, under a porch, or beneath any projecting surface. Other species build their nests in the ground. The most common exposed nests, some of which may be nearly 0.3 meter in diameter, are made by the bald-faced hornet, *Dolichovéspula maculàta* (L.), an insect that is largely black with yellowish white markings (Figure 35–80A). Most yellow jackets (Figure 35–80B) nest in the ground.

Subfamily **Polistìnae**—Paper Wasps: The Polistìnae are elongate and slender, with a spindle-shaped metasoma, and are usually reddish or brown in color marked with yellow (Figure 35–82). They are primitively eusocial: colonies may be started by individuals or by a small group of females. Their nests (Figure 35–82B) consist of a single, more or less circular, horizontal comb of paper cells, suspended from a support by a slender stalk. The cells are open on the lower side while the larvae are growing, and are sealed when the larvae pupate. The most common North American species in this subfamily belong to the genus *Polístes* (17 species). In addition to these, two species of *Mischocýttarus* occur in the southern and western United States, one species of *Brachygástra* occurs in southern Texas and southern Arizona, and two species of *Polýbia* have been recorded from Nogales, Arizona.

Family **Formícidae**—Ants: This is a very common and widespread group, well known to everyone. The ants are probably the most successful of all the insect groups. They occur practically everywhere in terrestrial habitats and outnumber in individuals most other terrestrial animals. The habits of ants are often very elaborate, and a great many studies have been made of ant behavior.

Though most ants are easily recognized, there are a few other insects that strongly resemble and mimic ants, and some of the winged forms of ants resemble wasps (from which they are derived). One of the distinctive structural features of ants is the form of the pedicel of the metasoma, which is one- or two-segmented and bears an upright lobe (Figures 35–11, 35–83). The antennae are usually elbowed (the males may have the antennae filiform), and the first segment is often very long.

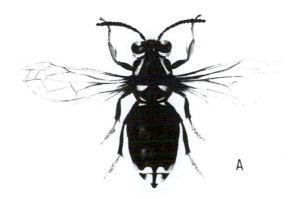
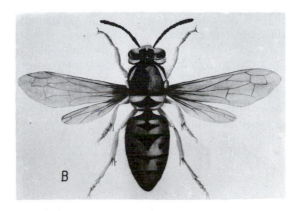

Figure 35–80.   Vespìnae. **A,** the bald-faced hornet, *Dolichovéspula maculàta* (L.); **B,** a yellow jacket, *Véspula macùlifrons* (Buysson).

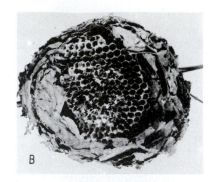

Figure 35–81. Nests of the bald-faced hornet, *Dolichovéspula maculàta* (L.). **A,** a nest as seen from below, showing entrance opening; **B,** a nest with the lower part of the outer envelope removed to show a tier of cells.

Figure 35–82. A paper wasp, *Polístes fuscàtus pállipes* Lepeletier. **A,** adult female; **B,** adult on nest. (**B,** courtesy of USDA.)

All ants are basically eusocial insects (some parasitic species occur), and most colonies contain at least three castes: queens, males, and workers (Figure 35–83). The queens are larger then the members of the other castes and are usually winged, though the wings are shed after the mating flight. The queen usually starts a colony and does most of the egg laying in the colony. The males are winged and usually considerably smaller than the queens. They are short-lived and die soon after mating. The workers are sterile wingless females that make up the bulk of the colony. In the smaller ant colonies there are usually just the three types of individuals, but in many of the larger colonies there may be two or three types within the worker caste. These may vary in size, shape, or behavior.

Ant colonies vary greatly in size, from a dozen or more up to many thousands of individuals. Ants nest in all sorts of places. Some nest in cavities in plants (in stems, in nuts or acorns, in galls, and so on); some (for example, the carpenter ants) excavate galleries in wood; but perhaps the majority of ants in North America nest in the ground. The ground nests of ants may be small and relatively simple, or they may be quite large and elaborate, consisting of a maze of tunnels and galleries. The galleries of some of the larger ground nests may extend several feet

underground. Certain chambers in such underground nests may serve as brood chambers, others as chambers for the storage of food. Most ants will shift their brood from one part of the nest to another as environmental conditions change.

Males and queens in most ant colonies are produced in large numbers only at one time of the year, when they emerge and engage in mating flights. Shortly after mating, the males die. The queen sheds her wings immediately after the mating flight, locates a suitable nesting site, makes a small excavation, and produces her first brood. This first brood, consisting of workers, is fed and cared for by the queen. Once the first workers appear, they take over the work of the colony—nest construction, caring for the young, gathering food, and the like—and henceforth the queen does little more than lay eggs. The queens of some species may live for several years. There may be more than one queen in some colonies. In some species of ants, certain castes or types of individuals may not be produced until the colony is several years old. In some species the queen goes into an already established colony. This established colony may be of her own or of an alien species. In the latter case her offspring may be spoken of as temporary or permanent social parasites, as the case may be.

The feeding habits of ants are rather varied. Many are carnivorous, feeding on the flesh of other animals (living or dead); some feed on plants; some feed on fungi; and many feed on sap, nectar, honeydew, and similar substances. Ants in the nest often feed on the secretions of other individuals, and the exchange of food between individuals (trophallaxis) is a common occurrence.

Ants produce a number of exocrine secretions that function in offense, defense, and communication. These are emitted to the outside chiefly through the openings on the head or at the apex of the metasoma. The sting serves as the chief means of offense and defense (Dolichoderìnae and Formicìnae lack a sting). All ants may bite, and some can do so rather severely. Some ants give off or eject from the anus a foul-smelling substance that serves as a means of defense. Many ant secretions act as alarm substances, some stimulate group activity, and many (laid down by a foraging individual) serve as an odor trail that other individuals can follow. Some of these secretions appear to play a role in caste determination.

Subfamily **Dorylinae:**   The Dorylinae are the legionary ants or army ants. They are mostly tropical, but one genus (*Éciton*) occurs in the southern and southwestern sections of the United States. These ants are nomadic and often travel in distinct files or "armies." They are highly predaceous. The queens in this group are wingless.

Subfamily **Cerapachyinae:**   This subfamily is represented in North America by three very rare species

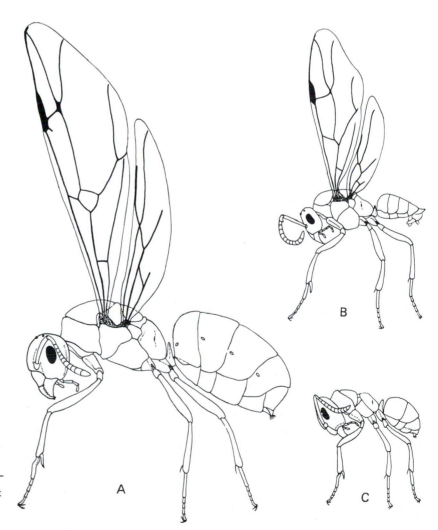

Figure 35–83.   Castes of an ant (*Formìca* sp.). **A,** queen; **B,** male; **C,** worker.

occurring in Arizona and Texas. The colonies are usually small, consisting of a few dozen individuals or less. These ants are predaceous.

Subfamily **Ponerinae:** In this subfamily the pedicel of the metasoma is only one-segmented, but there is a distinct constriction between the next two segments posterior to the pedicel (Figure 35–11A). The only common genus in the East is *Ponèra*. The workers are 2–4 mm in length, and the queens are only a little larger. These ants form small colonies and nest in rotten logs or stumps or in the soil beneath various objects. They feed on other insects. In the tropics ponerines are important predators.

Subfamily **Pseudomyrmicinae:** These ants are very slender and nest in hollow twigs, galls, and other cavities in plants. They are largely arboreal in habit. Our five species are restricted to the southern United States.

Subfamily **Myrmicinae:** This is the largest subfamily of ants (300 North American species), and its members can usually be recognized by the fact that the pedicel of the metasoma is two-segmented (Figure 35–11B). The members of this group are widely distributed and vary considerably in habits. The ants in the genera *Pogonomýrmex* and *Pheidòle* are often called harvester ants. They feed on seeds and store seeds in their nests. The fungus ants of the genus *Trachymýrmex* feed on fungi that they cultivate in their nests. The leaf-cutting ants (*Átta*) cut pieces of leaves, carry them to their nests, and feed on a fungus grown on these leaves. *Átta texàna* (Buckley) is common in some parts of the South and Southwest, and sometimes does considerable damage by its leaf-cutting activities.

The imported fire ants, *Solenópsis invícta* Buren and *S. ríchteri* Forel, are important pests in the Southeast. They were introduced into Alabama from South America in 1918 and have since spread over much of the Southeast from the Carolinas to Texas. The red imported fire ant, *S. invícta*, is the more common form. The black imported fire ant, *S. ríchteri*, has a rather limited distribution in a few of the southeastern states. These ants are aggressive insects with a painful sting and, when disturbed, are quick to attack both people and animals. The workers are 3–6 mm in length and reddish brown in color. A mature nest may contain up to 100,000 or more individuals. The nests are hard-crusted mounds that may sometimes be as large as a meter high and a meter across and may be constructed on agricultural land, homesites, school yards, and recreational areas, where they are not only an eyesore but a hazard to people and animals. On farms the mounds may cause damage to agricultural machinery, and many workers are reluctant to work in areas where the ants occur because of their painful stings. A related native species, *S. molésta* Say, the thief ant, is a common house-infesting species in the South and West. Ants of the genus *Solenópsis* may be distinguished from other myrmicine ants by the fact that the antennae are ten-segmented with a two-segmented club.

Subfamily **Dolichoderinae:** In this subfamily and the following one, the pedicel of the metasoma consists of a single segment, and there is no constriction between the next two segments (as in Figure 35–83). This is a small group (19 North American species), and most of its members occur in the southern part of the United States. Most of them are rather small, the workers being less than 5 mm in length. These ants possess anal glands that secrete a foul-smelling fluid, which can sometimes be forcibly ejected from the anus for a distance of several centimeters. One species, the Argentine ant, *Iridomýrmex hùmilis* (Mayr), was a common household pest in the southern states before the imported fire ants appeared.

Subfamily **Formicinae:** This is the second-largest subfamily of ants (200 North American species), and it is widespread in distribution. There is considerable variation in habits in this group. The genus *Camponòtus* includes the carpenter ants, some of which are the largest ants in North America; *C. pennsylvánicus* (De Geer) is a large black ant that excavates a series of anastomosing galleries in wood for its nests. Unlike termites, the carpenter ants do not feed on the wood.

The ants in the genus *Polyérgus* are slave makers and are entirely dependent on slaves. When a *Polyérgus* queen starts a new colony, she raids a nest of another species, usually a *Formìca*, and kills the queen in that colony. The *Formìca* workers then usually adopt the *Polyérgus* queen. To maintain the colony, the *Polyérgus* ants make raids on *Formìca* colonies, killing the workers and carrying off the pupae.

The worker caste of *Polyérgus* is given to fighting, whereas the slaves take over the activities of nest building, brood rearing, foraging, and the like. The *Polyérgus* ants are often called Amazons. *Polyérgus lùcidus* Mayr, a brilliant red species, is fairly common in the eastern United States. The genus *Làsius* contains a number of small field ants that make small mound nests and feed largely on honeydew. Many of them tend aphids, storing the aphid eggs through the winter and placing the young aphids on their food plant in the spring.

Formìca is a very large genus, containing about 70 North American species. Many are mound-building species. The mounds of *F. exsectòides* Forel, a common species in the eastern United States, are sometimes 0.6–0.9 meter high and two or more meters across. The United States varieties of *F. sanguínea* Latreille are slave makers, somewhat similar in habits to the Amazon ants. They periodically raid the nests of other species of *Formìca* and carry off worker pupae. Some of these are eaten, but others are reared and take their place in the *sanguínea* colony. The honey ants of the genus *Myrmecocýstus*, which occur in the southwestern United States, are of interest in that some of the individuals (termed "repletes") serve as reservoirs for the honeydew collected by other workers.

Collecting and Preserving Hymenóptera

Most of the general collecting methods described in Chapter 36 will apply to the insects in this order. Species of Hymenóptera are to be found almost everywhere, and to secure a large variety of species, one should examine all available habitats and use all available methods of collecting. Many of the larger and more showy Hymenóptera are common on flowers. The parasitic species may be reared from parasitized hosts, or they may be taken by sweeping. Passive trapping techniques, such as Malaise traps, flight-intercept traps, and pan traps are extremely effective in capturing a wide diversity of species that would otherwise go unnoticed. A number of species search for hosts or prey underground and are best collected by using Berlese funnels.

Since many of the Hymenóptera sting, it is well to exercise care in removing them from the net. One way is to get the insect into a fold in the net and then put this fold into the killing jar until the insect is stunned. Another effective method is to get the insect confined in the end of the net (almost all winged aculeates will fly upward toward the light), grasp the end of the net from the outside just below the insect, then reach inside with the killing jar and evert the end of the net into the jar, put the top on over the net, and slide the net out between the jar and lid. Some of the larger ichneumonids are able to "sting" by jabbing with their short sharp ovipositor. Any large Hymenóptera should be handled with care. Aside from the pain normally associated with a sting, some people have severe allergic reactions to the venom that can be life-threatening. Many stinging Hymenóptera feeding on flowers can be collected directly into a killing jar without the use of a net. Most Hymenóptera can be easily killed using a jar charged with ethyl acetate. In addition, because they are generally sturdier than Díptera, for example, Hymenóptera can be killed and stored in alcohol and then later dried and mounted. Often, sweeping vegetation and dumping the contents into alcohol is the most time-efficient method for capturing microhymenoptera (see Chapter 36).

The smaller Hymenóptera should be mounted on a point, or if they are extremely minute, they should be preserved in liquid or mounted on a microscope slide. It is usually necessary to mount the more minute forms on microscope slides for detailed study. Some of the best characters for the identification of bees are in the mouthparts; therefore, the mouthparts of these insects should be extended if possible. All specimens, whether pinned or mounted on points, should be oriented so that the leg and thoracic characters and venation can be easily seen.

References

Ananthakrishnan, T. N. 1984. The biology of gall insects. London: Edward Arnold, 362 pp.; illus.

Andrews, F. G. 1978. Taxonomy and host specificity of Nearctic Alloxystinae with a catalog of the world species (Hymenoptera: Cynipidae). Occasional Papers on Entomology, California Department of Food and Agriculture, No. 25, 128 pp.; illus.

Askew, R. R. 1971. Parasitic Insects. New York: American Elsevier, 316 pp.; illus.

Bohart, R. M., and L. S. Kimsey. 1982. A synopsis of the Chrysididae in America north of Mexico. Mem. Amer. Entomol. Inst. No. 33, 266 pp.; illus.

Bohart, R. M., and A. S. Menke. 1976. Sphecid Wasps of the World: A Generic Revision. Berkeley: University of California Press, 695 pp.; illus.

Bouček, Z. 1974. The pteromalid subfamily Eutrichosomatinae (Hymenoptera: Chalcidoidea). J. Entomol. (B) 43:129–138; illus.

Bouček, Z. 1974. A revision of the Leucospidae (Hymenoptera: Chalcidoidea) of the world. Bull. Brit. Mus. Nat. Hist. (Entomol). Suppl. 23, 241 pp.; illus.

Bouček, Z. 1978. A generic key to Perilampinae (Hymenoptera, Chalcidoidea), with a revision of *Krombeinius* n. gen. and *Euperilampus* Walker. Entomol. Scand. 9:299–307; illus.

Brothers, D. J. 1975. Phylogeny and classification of the aculeate Hymenoptera, with special reference to Mutillidae. Univ. Kan. Sci. Bull. 50(11):483–648; illus.

Burks, B. D. 1940. Revision of the chalcid-flies of the tribe Chalcidini in America north of Mexico. Proc. U.S. Natl. Mus. 88:237–354; illus.

Burks, B. D. 1971. A synopsis of the genera of the family Eurytomidae (Hymenoptera: Chalcidoidea). Trans. Amer. Entomol. Soc. 97:1–89; illus.

Carpenter, J. M. 1982. The phylogenetic relationships and

natural classification of the Vespoidea (Hymenoptera). Syst. Entomol. 7:11–38.

Carpenter, J. M. 1986. Cladistics of the Chrysidoidea (Hymenoptera). J. N. Y. Entomol. Soc. 94:303–330; illus.

Carpenter, J. M. 1987. Phylogenetic relationships and classification of the Vespinae (Hymenoptera: Vespidae). Syst. Entomol. 12:413–431; illus.

Clausen, C. P. 1940. Entomophagous Insects. New York: McGraw-Hill, 688 pp.; illus.

Cole, A. C. 1968. *Pogonomyrmex* Harvester Ants: A Study of the Genus in North America. Knoxville: University of Tennessee Press, 222 pp.; illus.

Creighton, W. S. 1950. The ants of North America. Bull. Mus. Comp. Zool. Harvard, 104, 585 pp.; illus.

Crozier, R. H. 1975. Animal Cytogenetics, 3: Insecta, 7: Hymenoptera. Berlin: Gebrüder Borntraeger, 95 pp.; illus.

Darling, D. C. 1978. Revision of the New World Chrysolampinae (Hymenoptera: Chalcidoidea). Can. Entomol. 118:913–940; illus.

Dasch, C. E. 1964. Ichneumon-flies of America north of Mexico. 5. Subfamily Diplazontinae. Mem. Amer. Entomol. Inst. No. 3:1–304; illus.

Dasch, C. E. 1971. Ichneumon-flies of America north of Mexico. 6. Subfamily Mesochorinae. Mem. Amer. Entomol. Inst. No. 16, 376 pp.; illus.

Dasch, C. E. 1979. Ichneumon-flies of America north of Mexico. 8. Subfamily Cremastinae. Mem. Amer. Entomol. Inst. No. 29, 702 pp.; illus.

Dasch, C. E. 1984. Ichneumon-flies of America north of Mexico. 9. Subfamilies Theriinae and Anomaloninae. Mem. Amer. Entomol. Inst. No. 36, 610 pp.; illus.

Doutt, R. L., and G. Viggiani. 1968. The classification of the Trichogrammatidae (Hymenoptera: Chalcidoidea). Proc. Calif. Acad. Sci. 20:477–586; illus.

Duncan, C. D. 1939. A contribution to the biology of North American vespine wasps. Stanford Univ. Publ. Biol. Ser. 8(1):1–272; illus.

Eberhard, M. J. W. 1969. The social biology of the polistine wasps. Misc. Publ. Mus. Zool. Univ. Mich. No. 140, 101 pp.; illus.

Eickwort, G. C. 1969. A comparative morphological study and generic revision of the augochlorine bees (Hymenoptera: Halictidae). Univ. Kan. Sci. Bull. 48:325–524; illus.

Evans, H. E. 1963. Wasp Farm. Garden City, N.Y.: Natural History Press, 178 pp.; illus.

Evans, H. E. 1978. The Bethylidae of America north of Mexico. Mem. Amer. Entomol. Inst. No. 27, 332 pp.; illus.

Evans, H. E. 1987. Order Hymenoptera, pp. 597–710 *in* F. Stehr (Ed.), Immature Insects. Dubuque, Iowa: Kendall/Hunt, 754 pp.; illus.

Evans, H. E., and M. J. W. Eberhard. 1970. The Wasps. Ann Arbor: University of Michigan Press, 265 pp.; illus.

Evans, H. E., and C. M. Yoshimoto. 1962. The ecology and nesting behavior of the Pompilidae (Hymenoptera) of the northeastern United States. Misc. Publ. Entomol. Soc. Amer. 3:65–120.

Felt, E. P. 1940. Plant Galls and Gall Makers. Ithaca, N.Y.: Comstock, 364 pp.; illus.

Fitton, M. G., and I. D. Gauld. 1976. The family-group names of the Ichneumonidae (excluding Ichneumoninae). Syst. Entomol. 1:247–258.

Fitton, M. G., and I. D. Gauld. 1978. Further notes on family-group names of Ichneumonidae (Hymenoptera). Syst. Entomol. 3:245–247.

Frisch, K. von. 1967. The Dance Language and Orientation of Bees. Cambridge, Mass.: Belknap Press of Harvard University Press, 566 pp.; illus.

Frisch, K. von. 1971 (rev. ed.). Bees, Their Vision, Chemical Senses, and Language. Ithaca, N.Y.: Cornell University Press, 157 pp.; illus.

Gibson, G. A. P. 1985. Some pro- and mesothoracic characters important for phylogenetic analysis of Hymenoptera, with a review of terms used for the structures. Can. Entomol. 117:1395–1443; illus.

Gibson, G. A. P. 1986. Evidence for monophyly and relationships of Chalcidoidea, Mymaridae, and Mymarommatidae (Hymenoptera: Terebrantes). Can Entomol. 118:205–240.

Graham, M. W. R. de V. 1969. The Pteromalidae of northwestern Europe (Hymenoptera: Chalcidoidea). Bull. Brit. Mus. (Nat. Hist.) Entomol. Suppl. No. 16, 908 pp.; illus.

Gregg, R. E. 1963. The Ants of Colorado, Their Taxonomy, Ecology, and Geographic Distribution. Boulder: University of Colorado Press, 792 pp.; illus.

Heinrich, G. H. 1977. Ichneumoninae of Florida and neighboring states (Hymenoptera: Ichneumonidae, subfamily Ichneumoninae). Arthropods of Florida and Neighboring Land Areas 9:1–350; illus.

Hurd, P. D., Jr., and E. G. Linsley. 1976. The bee family Oxaeidae with a revision of the North American species (Hymenoptera: Apoidea). Smithson. Contrib. Zool. No. 220, 75 pp.; illus.

Kimsey, L. S. 1984. A re-evaluation of the phylogenetic relationships in the Apidae (Hymenoptera). Syst. Entomol. 9:435–441.

Krombein, K. V. 1967. Trap-Nesting Wasps and Bees. Washington, D.C.: Smithsonian Press, 576 pp.; illus.

Krombein, K. V., P. D. Hurd, Jr., D. R. Smith, and B. D. Burks. 1979. Catalog of Hymenoptera in America North of Mexico, 3 vols. Washington, D.C.: Smithsonian Press, 2735 pp.

LaBerge, W. E., *et al.* 1967–1985. A revision of the bees in the genus *Andrena* of the western hemisphere. Part 1 (1967): *Callandrena*, Bull. Univ. Nebr. State Mus. 7:1–316; illus. Part 2 (1969): *Plastandrena, Aporandrena, Charitandrena*, Trans. Amer. Entomol. Soc. 95:1–47; illus. Part 3 (by W. E. LaBerge, and J. K. Bousman) (1970): *Tylandrena*, Trans. Amer. Entomol. Soc. 96:543–605; illus. Part 4 (1971): *Scraptopsis, Xiphandrena*, and *Rhaphandrena*, Trans. Amer. Entomol. Soc. 97:441–520; illus. Part 5 (by W. E. LaBerge and D. W. Ribble) (1972): *Gonandrena, Geissandrena, Parandrena, Pelicandrena*, Trans. Amer. Entomol. Soc. 98:271–358; illus. Part 6 (1973): Subgenus *Trachandrena*, Trans. Amer. Entomol. Soc. 99:235–371; illus. Part 7 (by W. E. LaBerge and D. W. Ribble) (1975): Subgenus *Euandrena*, Trans. Amer. Entomol. Soc. 101:371–446; illus. Part 8

(1977): Subgenera *Thysandrena, Dasyandrena, Psammandrena, Rhacandrena, Euandrena, Oxyandrena*, Trans. Amer. Entomol. Soc. 103:1–143; illus. Part 9 (by J. K. Bousman and W. E. LaBerge) (1979): Subgenus *Melandrena*, Trans. Amer. Entomol. Soc. 104:275–389; illus. Part 10 (1980): Subgenus *Andrena*, Trans. Amer. Entomol. Soc. 106:395–525; illus. Part 11(1985): Minor subgenera and generic key, Trans. Amer. Entomol. Soc. 111:441–567; illus.

Lanham, U. N. 1951. Review of the wing venation of the higher Hymenoptera (suborder Clistogastra), and speculations of the phylogeny of the Hymenoptera. Ann. Entomol. Soc. Amer. 44:614–628; illus.

Lindauer, M. 1977. Communication Among Social Bees. Cambridge, Mass.: Harvard University Press, 161 pp.; illus.

Lofgren, C. S., W. A. Banks, and B. M. Glancey. 1975. Biology and control of imported fire ants. Annu. Rev. Entomol. 20:1–30; illus.

Marsh, P. M., S. R. Shaw, and R. A. Wharton. 1987. An identification manual for the North American genera of the family Braconidae (Hymenoptera). Mem. Entomol. Soc. Wash. No. 13, 98 pp.; illus.

Masner, L. 1976. A revision of the Ismarinae of the New World (Hymenoptera, Proctotrupoidea, Diapriidae). Can. Entomol. 108:1243–1266; illus.

Masner, L. 1980. Key to genera of Scelionidae of the Holarctic region, with descriptions of new genera and species (Hymenoptera: Proctotrupoidea). Mem. Entomol. Soc. Can. 113, 54 pp.; illus.

Masner, L., and P. Dessart. 1967. La classification des categories superieures des Ceraphronoidea (Hymenoptera). Bull. Inst. R. Sci. Nat. Belge 43(22), 33 pp.; illus.

Michener, C. D. 1944. Comparative external morphology, phylogeny, and a classification of the bees (Hymenoptera). Bull. Amer. Mus. Nat. Hist. 82:151–326; illus.

Michener, C. D. 1974. The Social Behavior of Bees: A Comparative Study. Cambridge, Mass.: Belknap Press of Harvard University Press, 404 pp.; illus.

Michener, C. D. 1975. The Brazilian bee problem. Annu. Rev. Entomol. 30:399–416; illus.

Michener, C. D. 1981. Classification of the bee family Melittidae, with a review of species of Meganomiinae. Contrib. Amer. Entomol. Inst. 18(3), 135 pp.; illus.

Michener, C. D., and R. W. Brooks. 1984. Comparative study of the glossae of bees. Contrib. Amer. Entomol. Inst. 22(1), 73 pp.; illus.

Michener, C. D., and M. H. Michener. 1951. American Social Insects. New York: Van Nostrand, 267 pp.; illus.

Middlekauff, W. W. 1969. The cephid stem borers of California (Hymenoptera: Cephidae). Bull. Calif. Insect Surv. 11:1–19; illus.

Middlekauff, W. W. 1983. A revision of the sawfly family Orussidae for North and Central America (Hymenoptera: Symphyta, Orussidae). Univ. Calif. Publ. Entomol. 101, 46 pp.

Mitchell, T. B. 1960–1962. Bees of Eastern United States. Vol. 1, N.C. Agr. Expt. Sta. Tech. Bull. 141 (1960), 538 pp.; illus. Vol. 2, N.C. Agr. Expt. Sta. Tech. Bull. 152 (1962), 557 pp.; illus.

Morse, R. A. 1975. Bees and Beekeeping. Ithaca, N.Y.: Cornell University Press, 296 pp.; illus.

Moure, J. S., and P. D. Hurd, Jr. 1987. An annotated catalog of the halictid bees of the Western Hemisphere (Hymenoptera: Halictidae). Washington, D. C.: Smithsonian Press, 405 pp.

Naumann, I. D., and L. Masner. 1985. Parasitic wasps of the proctotrupoid complex: A new family from Australia and a key to world families (Hymenoptera: Proctotrupoidea *sensu lato*). Austral. J. Zool. 33:761–783; illus.

Oeser, R. 1961. Vergleichend-morphologische Untersuchungen über den Ovipositor der Hymenopteren. Mitt. Zool. Mus. Berlin 37:3–119.

Olmi, M. 1984. A revision of the Dryinidae (Hymenoptera). Mem. Amer. Entomol. Inst. No. 37 (2 vols.), 1913 pp.; illus.

Piek, T. (Ed.). 1986. Venoms of the Hymenoptera: Biochemical, Pharmacological and Behavioural Aspects. New York: Academic Press, 576 pp.

Quinlan, J. 1979. A revisionary classification of the Cynipoidea (Hymenoptera) of the Ethiopian zoogeographical region: Aspicerinae (Figitidae) and Oberthuerellinae (Liopteridae). Bull. Brit. Mus. (Nat. Hist.) Entomol. 39:85–133.

Rasnitsyn, A. P. 1969. Origin and evolution of the lower Hymenoptera (in Russian). Tr. Paleontol. Inst. 123:1–196; illus.

Rasnitsyn, A. P. 1975. Early evolution of the higher Hymenoptera (Apocrita) (in Russian). Zool. Zh. 54:848–859; illus.

Rasnitsyn, A. P. 1980. Origin and evolution of the Hymenoptera (in Russian). Tr. Paleontol. Inst. 174:1–190; illus.

Rasnitsyn, A. P. 1988. An outline of evolution of the hymenopterous insects (Order Vespida). Oriental Insects 22:115–145; illus.

Richards, O. W. 1962. A Revisional Study of the Masarid Wasps (Hymenoptera, Vespoidea). London: British Museum, 294 pp.; illus.

Richards, O. W. 1977 (2nd ed.) Hymenoptera: Introduction and Key to Families. Handbooks for the Identification of British Insects, vol. 6(1), 100 pp.; illus. (Other papers in this series, by various authors, cover groups within Hymenoptera.)

Richards, O. W. 1978. The social wasps of the Americas, excluding the Vespinae. London: British Museum (Natural History), 580 pp.; illus.

Ross, H. H. 1936. The ancestry and wing venation of the Hymenoptera. Ann. Entomol. Soc. Amer. 29:99–111; illus.

Ross, H. H. 1937. A generic classification of Nearctic sawflies (Hymenoptera, Symphyta). Ill. Biol. Monogr. No. 15:1–172; illus.

Schauff, M. E. 1984. The Holarctic genera of Mymaridae (Hymenoptera: Chalcidoidea). Mem. Entomol. Soc. Wash. No. 12, 67 pp.; illus.

Schneirla, T. C. 1971. Army Ants: A study in Social Organization. San Francisco: Freeman, 350 pp.; illus.

Seeley, T. D. 1985. Honeybee ecology: A study of adaptation

in social life. Princeton, N.J.: Princeton University Press, 201 pp.; illus.

Short, J. R. T. 1978. The final larval instars of the Ichneumonidae. Mem. Amer. Entomol. Inst. No. 25, 508 pp.; illus.

Smith, D. R. 1969. Key to genera of Nearctic Argidae (Hymenoptera) with revisions of the genera *Atomacera* Say and *Sterictiphora* Billberg. Trans. Amer. Entomol. Soc. 95:439–457; illus.

Smith, D. R. 1969. Nearctic sawflies. I. Blennocampinae: Adults and larvae. USDA Tech. Bull. No. 1397, 179 pp.; illus.

Smith, D. R. 1969. Nearctic sawflies. II. Selandriinae: Adults. USDA Tech. Bull. No. 1398, 48 pp.; illus.

Smith, D. R. 1971. Nearctic sawflies. III. Heterarthrinae: Adults and larvae. USDA Tech. Bull. No. 1429, 84 pp.; illus.

Smith, D. R. 1974. Conifer sawflies, Diprionidae: Key to North American genera, checklist of world species, and new species from Mexico. Proc. Entomol. Soc. Wash. 76:409–418; illus.

Smith, D. R. 1976. The xiphydriid woodwasps of North America. Trans. Entomol. Soc. Amer. 102:101–131; illus.

Smith, D. R. 1979. Nearctic sawflies. IV. Allantinae: Adults and larvae. USDA Tech. Bull. No. 1595, 172 pp.; illus.

Smith, E. L. 1970. Evolutionary morphology of the external genitalia. 2. Hymenoptera. Ann. Entomol. Soc. Amer. 63:1–27; illus.

Smith, M. R. 1943. A generic and subgeneric synopsis of the male ants of the United States. Amer. Midl. Nat. 30:273–321; illus.

Spradbery, J. P. 1973. Wasps: An Account of the Biology and Natural History of Social and Solitary Wasps. Seattle: University of Washington Press, 416 pp.; illus.

Townes, H. 1948. The serphoid Hymenoptera of the family Roproniidae. Proc. U.S. Natl. Mus. 98:85–89; illus.

Townes, H. 1949. The Nearctic species of the family Stephanidae (Hymenoptera). Proc. U.S. Natl. Mus. 99: 361–370; illus.

Townes, H. 1949. The Nearctic species of Evaniidae (Hymenoptera). Proc. U.S. Natl. Mus. 99:525–539; illus.

Townes, H. 1950. The Nearctic species of Gasteruptiidae (Hymenoptera). Proc. U.S. Natl. Mus. 100:85–145; illus.

Townes, H. 1956. The Nearctic species of trigonalid wasps. Proc. U.S. Natl. Mus. 106:295–304; illus.

Townes, H. 1969–1971. The genera of Ichneumonidae. Part 1 (1969), Mem. Amer. Entomol. Inst. No. 11, 300 pp.; illus. Part 2 (1969), Mem. Amer. Entomol. Inst. No. 12, 537 pp.; illus. Part 3 (1969), Mem. Amer. Entomol. Inst. No. 13, 307 pp.; illus. Part 4 (1971), Mem. Amer. Entomol. Inst. No. 17, 372 pp.; illus.

Townes, H. 1977. A revision of the Rhopalosomatidae (Hymenoptera). Contrib. Amer. Entomol. Inst. 15(1), 34 pp.; illus.

Townes, H. 1977. A revision of the Heloridae (Hymenoptera). Contrib. Amer. Entomol. Inst. 15(2), 12 pp.; illus.

Townes, H., and V. K. Gupta. 1962. Ichneumon-flies of America north of Mexico. 4. Subfamily Gelinae, tribe Hemigasterini. Mem. Amer. Entomol. Inst. No. 2, 305 pp.; illus.

Townes, H., and M. Townes. 1978. Ichneumon-flies of America north of Mexico. 7. Subfamily Banchinae, tribes Lissonotini and Banchini. Mem. Amer. Entomol. Inst. No. 26, 614 pp.; illus.

Townes, H., and M. Townes. 1981. A revision of the Serphidae (Hymenoptera). Mem. Amer. Entomol. Inst. No. 32, 541 pp.; illus. (Includes both Proctotrupidae and Vanhorniidae.)

van Achterberg, C. 1984. Essay on the phylogeny of Braconidae (Hymenoptera: Ichneumonoidea). Entomol. Tidskr. 105:41–58.

Waage, J., and D. Greathead (Eds.). 1987. Insect Parasitoids. New York: Academic Press, 389 pp.; illus.

Weber, N. A. 1972. Gardening ants, the attines. Mem. Amer. Philos. Soc. 92:1–146; illus.

Wheeler, G. C., and J. Wheeler. 1972. The subfamilies of Formicidae. Proc. Entomol. Soc. Wash. 74:35–45; illus.

Wheeler, G. C., and J. Wheeler. 1976. Ant larvae: Review and synthesis. Mem. Entomol. Soc. Wash. No. 7, 108 pp.; illus.

Wilson, E. O. 1971. The Insect Societies. Cambridge, Mass.: Harvard University Press, 548 pp.; illus.

Chapter 36

Collecting, Preserving, and Studying Insects

One of the best ways to learn about insects is to go out and collect them. Handling them and preparing collections will reveal to the student many things that he or she will not get from the textbooks. Many people find the collecting of insects an extremely interesting hobby, for it provides not only the satisfaction that comes from being in the field, but also the satisfaction of learning at first hand. The student will develop much more interest in insects by collecting and handling them than he will merely looking at pictures or preserved specimens. He will see the specimens alive and thus gain an insight as to their habitats, habits, and behavior—information often as valuable as morphological characters in determining their taxonomic position.

When and Where to Collect

In collecting insects—as with hunting, fishing, bird-watching, or almost any activity—there is a direct correlation between time and effort expended and proficiency gained. The uninitiated person can go through habitats literally swarming with insects and be totally unaware of their presence unless bitten or stung by them. There are few outdoor activities that will sharpen one's powers of observation and perception, test one's patience and skill, and

provide a never-ending source of wonderment and pleasure like collecting insects.

Insects can be found practically everywhere and usually in considerable numbers. The more kinds of places in which one looks for them, the greater the variety one will be able to collect. The best time to collect is in summer, but insects are active from early spring until late fall, and many can be found in hibernation during the winter. Many insects are active the year round in southern areas of the United States. The adults of many species have a short seasonal range; therefore, anyone who wishes to get the greatest variety should collect throughout the year. Since different species are active at different times of the day, at least some kinds of insects can be collected at any hour. Bad weather conditions, such as rain or low temperature, will reduce the activity of many insects, thus making it more difficult to find or collect them, but others are little affected and can be collected in any kind of weather. A person who knows where to look can find insects in the average community at any hour of the day, any day of the year.

Because many kinds of insects feed upon or frequent plants, plants provide one of the best places for collecting. Insects can be picked, shaken, or swept off the plant with a net. Different species feed on different kinds of plants, and one should therefore examine all sorts of plants. Every part of the plant may harbor insects. The majority will probably be on the foliage or flowers, but others may be on or in the stem, bark, wood, fruits, or roots.

Various types of debris often harbor many kinds of insects. Some species can be found in the leaf mold and litter on the surface of the soil, particularly in woods or areas where the vegetation is dense. Others can be found under stones, boards, bark, and similar objects. Still others can be found in rotting or decaying material of all sorts, such as fungi, decaying plants, the bodies of dead animals, rotting fruits, and dung. Many of the insects in these situations can be picked up with the fingers or forceps. Others can be obtained by sifting debris.

Many insects can be found in or around buildings or on animals or humans. Many use buildings, cavities under buildings, culverts, and similar places as a shelter, and some species are most easily collected in such situations. Other insects found in buildings feed on clothing, furniture, grain, food, and other materials. Insects that attack animals are usually to be found around those animals, and a person interested in collecting species that attack humans can often get them with little effort—by letting the insects come to the collector.

On warm evenings, insects from various sources are attracted to lights and can be collected at street or porch lights, on windows or screens of lighted rooms, or at lights put up especially to attract them. This is one of the easiest ways of collecting many types of insects. Blue lights seem to be more attractive than red or yellow ones.

A great many insects—only the immature stages in some cases, and all stages in others—are found in aquatic situations. Different types of aquatic habitats harbor different species, and different insects can be found in different parts of any particular pond or stream. Some are to be found on the surface; others occur on aquatic vegetation; others are attached to or are under stones or other objects in the water; and still others burrow in the sand or muck of the bottom. Many aquatic insects can be collected by hand or by means of forceps. Others are most easily collected by various types of aquatic collecting equipment.

The adults of a great many species are best obtained by collecting the immature stages and rearing them. This process involves collecting cocoons, larvae, or nymphs and maintaining them in some sort of container until the adults appear. It is often possible to get better specimens by this method than by collecting adults in the field.

Many nocturnal insects are not attracted to lights. The collector must search for them at night and capture them by hand. Examination of tree trunks, leaves and other vegetation, fallen logs, rock faces, and other habitats at night will reveal a sizable arthropod fauna, one unsuspected by those who confine their collecting to the daylight hours. Flashlights and lanterns of various sorts are useful for night collecting, but the best sort of light is a headlamp. Not only does such a light leave both hands free (insect collectors often wish they had three or four extra arms and hands), but its beam focuses the wearer's attention on smaller areas and sharpens his or her perception; the lamp illuminates only the area where the collector is looking. Excellent results may be obtained with a headlamp having an elastic headband and operated by a 6-volt battery attached to the wearer's belt.

Collecting Equipment

The minimum equipment necessary to collect insects is one's hands and some sort of container for the specimens collected. However, one can do much better with a net and killing jar, or better yet with some sort of shoulder bag containing some additional equipment. For general collecting it is best to have at least the following items:

1. Insect net
2. Killing jars
3. Pillboxes containing cleansing tissue
4. Envelopes, or paper for making envelopes
5. Vials of preservative
6. Forceps
7. Hand lens
8. Sheet of plain white paper

Some of these items, particularly the killing jars, pillboxes, envelopes, and vials of preservative, are most easily carried in a shoulder bag. Forceps and hand lens can be attached to a string around one's neck and carried in a shirt pocket. Strictly speaking, a hand lens is not a means of collecting, but it is useful for examining insects in the field.

Other items of value for some types of collecting are as follows:

9. Aspirator
10. Beating umbrella or sheet
11. Sifter
12. Traps
13. Aquatic collecting equipment
14. Headlamp (for night collecting)
15. Sheath knife
16. Camel's-hair brush

Insect Net

Insect nets can be purchased from a supply house or can be homemade. Homemade nets are fairly easy to make and are much less expensive than supply-house nets. A method of constructing an insect net is shown in Figure 36–1. The handle should be light and strong, and about 1 meter long. The rim should be about 0.3 to 0.4 meter in diameter and made of fairly heavy wire (No. 6 to No. 8 gauge). Grooves and holes are cut in one end of the handle (Figure 36–1A). The wire for the rim is bent as shown in Figure 36–1B, fitted into these holes and grooves, and fastened in place with heavy cord, fine wire, or friction tape, or a 50-mm length of metal tubing may be slipped over it.

The ideal shape for the bag is shown in Figure 36–1D. The material for the bag can be made from a single piece of cloth cut as shown in Figure 36–1E, and if the edges are sewed together with French seams, the net can be used with either side out. The bag should be made of two types of cloth, a heavy band (muslin or canvas) around the rim and a lighter material for the main part of the bag. The choice of the latter material will depend on the type of collecting for which the net will be used. A net for general collecting should have a sufficiently open mesh that an insect can be seen through it. The best material is probably marquisette or scrim (cheese-cloth is unsatisfactory because it snags too easily). With a more open mesh (for example, bobbinet), many smaller insects will escape through the meshes. A net used primarily for beating or sweeping should be made of muslin or fine-mesh bolting cloth, through which even the smallest insects cannot escape. The metal rim and handle of these nets are usually made of stronger material than an aerial net used for general collecting.

Some people prefer an insect net that can be taken apart and carried compactly or inconspicu-

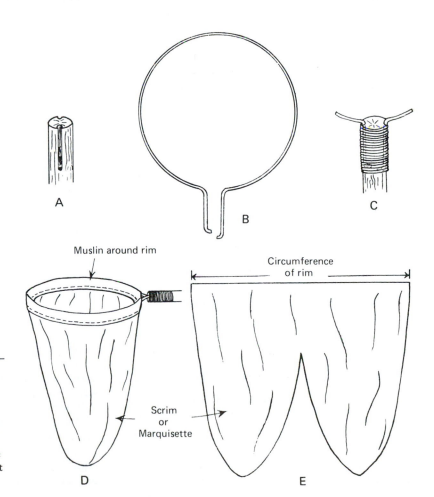

Figure 36–1. A homemade insect net. Grooves and holes are cut in the end of the handle, as in **A;** the wire for the rim is bent as shown in **B,** fitted into the holes and grooves, and held there with heavy cord, wire, or friction tape (**C**). The material for the bag is cut as in **E,** and the finished net is shown in **D.**

Muslin around rim

Circumference of rim

Scrim or Marquisette

ously. Such a net can be made from a collapsible frame known as a landing net, which can be bought in a sporting-goods store (Figure 36–2).

A net used with care will last a long time. It should be kept away from stout thorns and barbed wire (to avoid tearing), and it should be kept dry. Insects caught in a wet net are seldom fit for a collection, and moisture eventually rots the net fabric.

One may operate in either of two general ways when collecting insects with a net: he or she may look for particular insects and then swing at them, or the collector may sweep (simply swing the net back and forth, usually through vegetation). The former method is usually used for collecting the larger insects and often demands a certain amount of speed and skill. The latter method will produce the greater quantity and variety of insects, though it may occasionally damage some delicate specimens.

When a particularly active insect is caught, one must use certain precautions to prevent the insect from escaping before it can be transferred to the killing jar. The safest method is to fold the net over with the insect in the bottom of the net (Figure 36–3). The insect is then grasped through the net (provided it is not one that stings) and transferred to the killing bottle. If the insect is one that stings (when in doubt it is better to assume that it *does* sting), there are three methods of transferring it to the killing bottle. (1) The fold of the net containing the insect can be put into the killing bottle until the insect is stunned, then the insect can be picked out of the net and put into the bottle. (2) The insect can be grasped through the net with forceps, rather than with the fingers, and transferred to the bottle. (3) The insect can be gotten into a fold of the net, stunned by pinching (the *thorax*), and then transferred to the killing bottle.

Sweeping is the best way for the general collector to obtain the greatest number and variety of insects. After sweeping, one may wish to save the entire catch or only certain specimens. It is preferable to transfer the entire catch to the killing jar and *later* discard any specimens the collector does not wish to save. The best way to save the entire catch is to shake the insects into the bottom of the net and then place this part of the net in the killing jar (a wide-mouthed jar is best for this), which is covered until the insects are stunned. Then the net contents are dumped onto a sheet of paper (in a protected area out of the wind), the larger pieces of vegetation or other debris are removed by hand, and the paper contents are dumped into the killing jar. Once the results of sweeping have been dumped onto the sheet of paper, the collector may pick out the specimens (in the field) that he or she wishes to save, but it is better to save the entire catch and do the sorting after returning from the field. If the results of sweeping are examined under a binocular microscope, many interesting insects may be found (and can be saved) that would otherwise be overlooked.

Another method of getting the results of sweeping (or an individual insect) from the net to the killing jar is to insert the killing jar into the net. This procedure may save time compared with the method described in the preceding paragraph, but it seldom gets *all* the material taken in sweeping, and sometimes individual insects may escape. The insect(s) may be worked into the bottom of the net with a few swings, and the net pinched off just above them. Then hold the tip of the net up (many insects tend to move upward to escape), insert the killing jar into the net (with the lid removed), quickly move it past the pinched-off point, and work the specimens into the jar. The jar may be capped from the outside long enough to stun the insects, or one may work it to the open end of the net (with the lid over the jar outside the net), then remove the lid from the outside and cap the jar. Some insects may escape with this method, but with a little experience, losses will be minimized.

Sweeping is often the only practical method of capturing small or minute insects. Because of their size, however, these specimens tend to dry out very rapidly, and the appendages, particularly the antennae, are subject to extensive breakage. One means

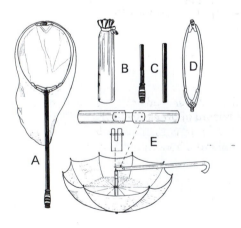

Figure 36–2. A collapsible net and beating umbrella. The net (**A**) may be collapsed (**D**), the handle removed and unjointed (**C**), and all these parts placed in a carrying bag (**B**). The beating umbrella (**E**) has a hinged joint in the handle and is held in the position illustrated when in use. (From DeLong and Davidson, courtesy of the Ohio State University Press.)

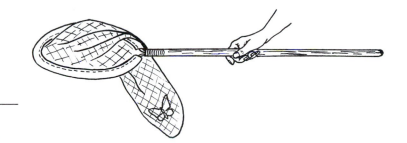

Figure 36–3. An insect net turned to prevent the escape of captured specimens.

to avoid this problem is to dump the entire contents of the net into a plastic bag (a 1-gallon food storage bag works well) filled about a quarter to a third full of water and with one or two drops of liquid detergent (or any other surfactant) added. The detergent reduces the surface tension of the water so that the insects are quickly wetted and drown. Specimens may be kept in the water for periods up to several hours. As soon as possible, however, they should be transferred to 70% alcohol. This transfer may be made as the specimens are sorted (the same day they are caught). If time for this procedure is not immediately available, the catch may be poured from the plastic bag into small mesh bags (made of the same fine material as the sweeping net). The mesh bag is then closed with a twist tie and placed in a container of alcohol. After 24 hours the bag is drained and placed in fresh alcohol. Specimens can then be sorted at the collector's leisure. This method works well for collecting minute parasitic Hymenoptera and small beetles, for example, but it may not be appropriate for some other groups. Small flies may have the taxonomically important bristles broken off, and many mirids lose their hind legs when placed in alcohol.

Killing Bottles

If the insect is to be preserved after it is captured, it must be killed in such a way that it is not injured or broken. Some sort of killing bottle is required for this purpose. Bottles of various sizes and shapes may be used, depending on the type of insects involved, and various materials may be used as the killing agent. It is desirable when in the field to have two or three bottles of different sizes for insects of different types. A separate bottle should always be used for Lepidóptera, because their delicate wings may be damaged by other insects (especially beetles) and because their wing scales will come off and adhere to other insects (making them look dusty). It is desirable to have one or more small bottles (perhaps 25 mm in diameter and 100–150 mm in length) for small insects and one or more larger bottles for larger

insects. Corked bottles are preferable to screw-capped bottles, but either type will do. Wide-mouthed bottles or jars are better than narrow-necked ones. All killing bottles, regardless of the killing agent used, should be conspicuously labeled "POISON," and all glass bottles should be reinforced with tape to prevent shattering in case of breakage.

Several materials can be used as the toxic agent in a killing bottle, but we prefer cyanide. Such bottles kill quickly and last a long time, while most other materials kill more slowly and do not last as long. Cyanide is extremely poisonous, but with certain precautions, bottles made with it can be just as safe as bottles made with some other killing agent.

Cyanide bottles can be made in two general ways (Figure 36–4). Those made with small vials have a plug of cotton and a piece of cardboard to hold the cyanide in the bottle, while those made with larger jars have plaster of paris holding the cyanide in the bottle. Sodium or potassium cyanide is the cyanide used in most cyanide bottles. Calcium cyanide is sometimes used in killing bottles made with small vials.

A calcium cyanide killing bottle is made as shown in Figure 36–4A. The cotton and cardboard should be packed down tightly, and the cardboard should have some pinholes in it. The bottom and rim of the bottle should be reinforced with tape to reduce the hazard of breakage. If the killing bottle is capped with a large cork, it may be convenient to put the cyanide in a hole in the bottom of the cork and keep it there with a plug of cotton and a covering of cloth. Calcium cyanide is a dark gray powder that is often used as a fumigant. It is extremely poisonous. It should be handled with great care, and only persons familiar with its properties should use it. This type of bottle is ready for use as soon as it is prepared.

A cyanide bottle made with plaster of paris takes longer to prepare but will last longer. A bottle made with calcium cyanide will last a month or two, whereas one made with sodium or potassium cyanide and plaster will last a year or two. The potassium (or sodium) cyanide should be in a finely granular or powdered form, and the bottle is made as

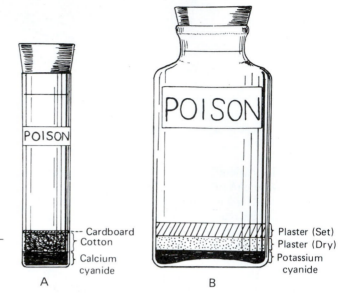

Figure 36–4.   Cyanide bottles. **A,** a small bottle made up with calcium cyanide; **B,** a large bottle made up with plaster of paris.

shown in Figure 36–4B. After the wet plaster has been poured in, the bottle should be left uncorked, preferably outdoors, until the plaster has thoroughly set and dried (a day or two). Then it is corked, the bottom is taped, a poison label is put on, and after another day or so it is ready for use.

Other materials that can be used as killing agents in insect bottles are ethyl acetate, carbon tetrachloride, and chloroform. Ethyl acetate is the least dangerous of the three to use. Bottles using these materials are made by putting some sort of absorbing material in the bottle and soaking it with the agent. Cotton makes a good absorbent material, but if it is used it should be covered with a piece of cardboard or screen; otherwise, the insects become entangled in the cotton and are difficult or impossible to remove without damage. If ethyl acetate or carbon tetrachloride is used, the absorbent material can be plaster of paris that has been mixed with water, poured into the bottom of the bottle, and allowed to set and thoroughly dry. Killing bottles made with these materials do not last very long and must be recharged frequently. Carbon tetrachloride and chloroform are poisonous, and one should avoid breathing the fumes. Ethyl acetate is relatively nontoxic to humans (it is an ingredient of nail polish).

The efficiency of a killing bottle depends to a large extent on how it is used. It should never be left uncorked any longer than is necessary to put insects in or take them out. The escaping gas reduces its strength, and an uncorked bottle (particularly one made up with cyanide) is a hazard. The inside of the bottle should be kept dry. Bottles sometimes "sweat"; that is, moisture from the insects (and sometimes from the plaster) condenses on the inside of the bottle, particularly if it is exposed to bright sunlight. Such moisture will ruin delicate specimens. It is a good idea to keep a few pieces of cleansing tissue or other absorbent material in the bottle at all times, to absorb moisture and to prevent the insects from getting badly tangled up with one another. This material should be changed frequently, and the bottle wiped out periodically. A bottle that has been used for Lepidóptera should not be used for other insects unless it is first cleaned to remove scales that would get on new insects put into the bottle.

Other Types of Collecting Apparatus

Aerial nets such as those already described are standard collecting equipment for most work, but many other devices are useful in certain situations or for collecting certain types of insects. Some of the more important of these are described here. The collector who has a little ingenuity will be able to devise many others.

Aspirator.   This is a very useful device for capturing small insects, particularly if one wishes to catch them alive. Two types of aspirators are shown in Figure 36–5. Sucking through the mouthpiece will draw small insects into the vial (A) or tube (B), and a cloth over the inner end of the mouthpiece tube prevents the insects from being sucked into the mouth. If one has a series of these vials or tubes, an

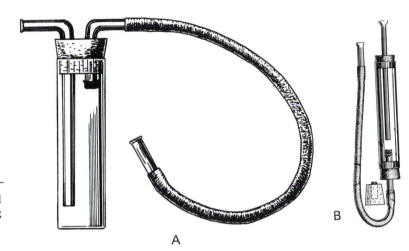

Figure 36–5.   Aspirators. **A**, the vial type; **B**, the tube type. (**B**, from DeLong and Davidson, courtesy of the Ohio State University Press.)

insect-filled one can be removed and replaced with an empty one.

Beating Umbrella.   Many insects that occur on vegetation feign death by dropping off the plant when it is jarred slightly. The collector can take advantage of this habit by placing a collecting device underneath a plant and then jarring the plant with a stick. The insects that fall onto the collecting device beneath may be easily picked up. The best device for this sort of collecting is a beating umbrella (Figure 36–2E), an umbrella frame covered with white muslin or light canvas. A white sheet, or even an open insect net, may also be used to catch insects jarred off a plant.

Sifters.   Many small and unusual insects that occur in trash and leaf litter are most easily collected in no other way. The simplest collecting procedure is to take a handful of material and sift it slowly onto a large piece of white cloth, plastic, or cardboard. The tiny animals falling onto the white surface will reveal themselves by their movement and can be picked up with an aspirator or a wet brush. The material may also be sifted onto a white cloth from a small box with a screen bottom.

Perhaps the simplest way of getting the insects and other animals out of soil, debris, or leaf litter is to use a Berlese funnel (Figure 36–6). A Berlese funnel is an ordinary (usually large) funnel containing a piece of screen or hardware cloth, with a killing jar or container of alcohol below it, and the material to be sifted placed on the screen. An electric light bulb is placed above the funnel, and as the upper part of the material in the funnel dries, the insects and other animals move downward and eventually

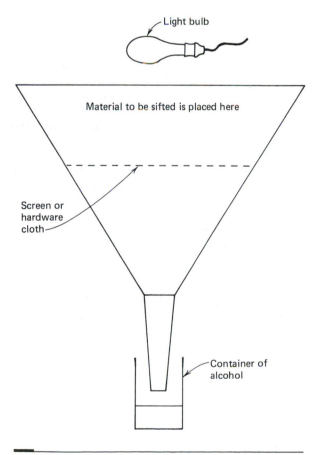

Figure 36–6.   A Berlese funnel. The funnel can be supported by a ringstand, or by three or four legs attached near the middle of the funnel. The light bulb can be that of an ordinary gooseneck lamp, or it can be in a metal cylinder placed over the top of the funnel. The material to be sifted is placed on the screen.

fall into the container below the funnel, where they are killed. A Berlese funnel is the best device for collecting debris-inhabiting insects, mites, pseudoscorpions, and small spiders.

Anyone using a Berlese funnel will notice that many of the animals collected (for example, the springtails and many of the mites) remain on the surface of the alcohol. The fact that many soil- and debris-inhabiting animals will float on alcohol or water makes it possible to get many of these animals out of such materials by putting the material in water. Many animals come to the surface of the water, where they can be removed and placed in alcohol.

Traps.   Traps are an easy and often very effective method of collecting many types of insects. A trap is any device, usually containing something to which the insects are attracted, that is so arranged that once the insects get into it, they cannot get out. The attractant used and the general form of the trap will be determined by the type of insects one wants to collect. Space does not permit a description here of many types of traps, but a few can be mentioned. The ingenious collector should be able to devise any that are not described (see Peterson 1953).

A trap or other device using light as the attractant frequently yields insects in a quantity and quality not obtained by any other type of collecting. Many types of bulbs may be used, some of which are more attractive to insects (or at least to certain types of insects) than ordinary incandescent bulbs. Blacklight, ultraviolet, and mercury-vapor bulbs often attract more insects than ordinary light bulbs.

A light trap for insects may be made in such a way that insects coming to the trap are diverted, by a series of baffles, into a cyanide jar or container of alcohol (Figure 36–7D). Such a trap will catch a lot of insects, but the specimens taken may not always be in very good shape. One can get specimens in better condition by simply waiting at a light and getting desired insects directly into a killing bottle or aspirator as they settle on something near the light (for example, a wall, screen, or sheet).

Walk-in light traps are sometimes used at more or less permanent locations. Such a trap is simply a screened chamber with a light mounted at the top. Insects attracted to this light, instead of falling into a jar of cyanide or alcohol, settle on the floor or walls of the chamber where they can be picked up by the operator.

A rather elaborate device which is gaining popularity among insect collectors is the Malaise trap, named for Dr. René Malaise of Sweden (Figure 36–7C). Many modifications of this trap have been developed, but they are all essentially tentlike struc-

tures of fine netting into which flying insects wander. The underlying principle of this type of trap is that insects usually move upward in attempting to escape, and in the Malaise trap they eventually move into a collecting apparatus at the top of the trap and are killed in a jar of alcohol or one charged with cyanide or ethyl acetate. Such traps often turn up rare, unusual, or elusive insects not taken by collectors using conventional methods. Directions for building Malaise traps are given by Townes (1962, 1972).

Traps of the type shown in Figure 36–7B are useful for catching flies that are attracted to decaying materials such as meat and fruits. If the trap is visited frequently, the specimens it catches can be retrieved in good condition. Varying the bait will produce a more varied catch.

Pitfall traps of the type shown in Figure 36–7A are useful for catching carrion beetles and other insects that do not fly readily. Such a trap may be made of a large tin can, preferably with a few holes punched in the bottom to prevent water from accumulating in it, and with some sort of screen over the bait to permit easy removal of the insects caught. The can is sunk in the ground with its top at ground level. Most of the insects attracted by the bait will fall into the can and be unable to get out. The bait may be a dead animal, a piece of meat that will eventually decay, fruit, molasses, or some similar material. Here again, varying the bait will yield a more varied catch.

Pan traps are similar in some respects to shallow pitfall traps. The pan (or bowl or any type of shallow container) is sunk in the ground and half filled with water to which a few drops of a liquid detergent have been added to reduce the surface tension. Pans painted yellow are especially attractive to many species. The insects are either attracted to or inadvertently stumble into the trap, are wetted, and drown. The catch is removed from the pan with a small aquarium dip net. Traps containing only water must be tended every day to remove the insects before they decompose. Various preservatives can be added to the water to significantly delay the process of decomposition. Filling the trap with water saturated with salt is an economical but somewhat bulky alternative (a great deal of salt is required). A 50/50 solution of ethylene glycol and water also works well. Traps that will not be tended for several days generally require some sort of roof over them (e.g., a suspended sheet of plastic) to keep the killing/preservative solution from being diluted by rainwater. Specimens caught in such traps should be carefully rinsed in water before being placed in alcohol. Pan traps are especially effective in catching minute insects that are found close to the ground where it is difficult to sweep.

Flight-intercept traps are in some ways a combination of Malaise and pan traps. Some insects, especially small ones, never reach the collecting apparatus at the top of a Malaise. They may crawl through the netting, fly off it before reaching the top, or fall off the trap to the ground. To catch these, a trough, pan, or similar device filled with a killing/preservative fluid (such as those described above) is placed beneath a single panel of fine netting spread across the flight path of the insects. A knock-down insecticide may be ''painted'' onto the fabric to capture specimens that may land on the netting. Designs for this type of trap may be found in Peck and Davies (1980) and Masner and Goulet (1981).

Household insects that do not fly, such as silverfish and cockroaches, can be trapped by means of an

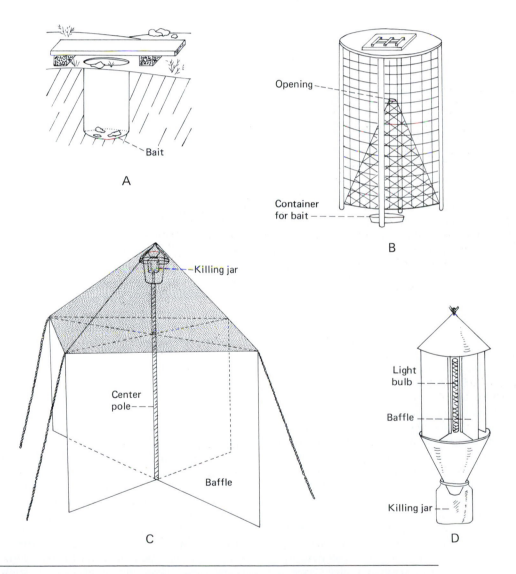

Figure 36–7. Insect traps. **A,** a pitfall trap, consisting of a can sunk in the ground; **B,** a fly trap, a cylindrical screen cage with a screen cone at the bottom; the bait is placed in a container below the center of the cone, and flies attracted to the bait eventually go through the opening at the top of the cone into the main part of the trap, from which they can be removed through the door at the top; **C,** a Malaise trap, a square tentlike structure supported by a central pole, with screen or cloth baffles across the diagonals, and a killing jar at the top; **D,** a light trap; specimens attracted to the light are funneled into the killing jar at the bottom.

open-topped baited box: a box 100 or 125 mm deep is placed on the floor, provided with a ramp from the floor to the top of the box, and baited with dog biscuits, crackers, or some similar materials. If the upper 50 to 75 mm of the box is coated on the inside with petroleum jelly, the insects that get into the box will not be able to crawl out.

Many insects can be caught by "sugaring," that is, preparing a sugary mixture and spreading it on tree trunks, stumps, or fence posts. Various mixtures may be used, but one containing something that is fermenting is probably the best. It may be made with molasses or fruit juices and a little stale beer or rum.

Aquatic Collecting Equipment.   Many aquatic insects can be collected with one's fingers or with forceps when one is examining plants, stones, or other objects in the water, but many more can be collected by using a dip net, strainer, dipper, or other device. A dip net can be made like an aerial net, but should be shallower (no deeper than the diameter of the rim) and much stronger. The handle should be heavy, and the rim should be made of 6- or 9-mm metal rod and securely fastened to the handle. The part of the bag that is attached to the rim should be of canvas, and it is desirable to have an apron of the same material extending down over the front of the bag. The rim need not be circular. Many collectors prefer to have the rim bent in the form of the letter D. The bag may be made of heavy marquisette or bolting cloth. Strainers of the tea type, with a rim from 50 to 150 mm in diameter, are useful for aquatic collecting if they are not subjected to hard use. Dip nets or strainers can be used to collect free-swimming forms, forms on vegetation, and forms burrowing in the sand or muck of the bottom. A good catch can often be obtained in streams by placing the net or strainer at a narrow place in the current and then turning over stones or disturbing the bottom upstream from the net. Retrieving insects from the muck and debris collected in a net or strainer is not always easy, for most of them are not noticed until they move. A good way to locate them is to dump the contents of the net into a large white pan with some water. Against the white background, the insects can be more easily located and picked out. The best device for collecting small free-swimming forms such as mosquito larvae or midge larvae is a long-handled white enameled dipper. Small larvae are easily seen against the white background of the dipper and can be removed with an eye dropper.

Other Equipment.   The collector should have a sheet of plain white paper for transferring the results of sweeping from the net to the killing jar (as noted previously). This is as important a part of the collector's equipment as the net itself. A large heavy knife will be useful for prying up bark, cutting open galls, or digging into various materials. A vial of insect pins is useful for pinning together mating pairs before they are put into the killing jar. A notebook and pencil should always be a part of the collector's gear. The collecting of certain types of insects often requires special items of equipment. The amount and type of equipment a collector uses will depend entirely on the sort of collecting he or she expects to do.

Handling the Catch

The collector must learn by experience how long it takes for the killing bottles to kill an insect. He or she will learn that some insects are killed quickly, while others are very resistant to the killing agent. A mosquito in a strong cyanide bottle will be killed in a few minutes, whereas some of the snout-nosed beetles may remain alive in the same bottle for an hour or two. The catch should be kept in the killing bottle until the specimens are killed but not much longer. Many insects will become discolored if left in too long, particularly in a bottle containing cyanide. It is advisable to remove insects within an hour or two after they are killed.

Specimens removed from the killing bottle in the field may be placed in pillboxes or paper envelopes for temporary storage. The pillboxes should contain some sort of absorbent material, such as cleansing tissue, that will reduce the bouncing around of the specimens during transportation and will absorb excess moisture. Paper envelopes, either ordinary letter envelopes or triangular envelopes like that shown in Figure 36–8, are excellent for temporary storage of large-winged insects such as butterflies, moths, or dragonflies. These triangular envelopes can be made quickly from a sheet of notebook paper, and specimens will remain in good condition in them. Data on the collection can be written on the outside.

Many insects may be killed by dropping them directly into 70–90% ethyl or isopropyl alcohol, where they can be stored indefinitely. This method is used exclusively for many insects, such as very minute forms that are to be mounted on microscope slides for detailed study (springtails, lice, fleas, and some Coleóptera, Hymenóptera, and Díptera) and many soft-bodied insects that may shrivel when mounted dry (camel crickets, termites, mayflies, stoneflies, caddisflies, and others). On the other

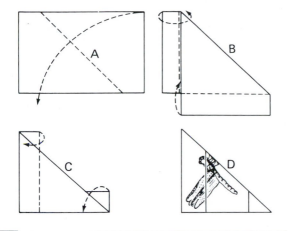

Figure 36–8. A method of folding triangular paper envelopes for insect specimens. The paper is folded as illustrated in **A**, **B**, and **C**, to form the completed envelope, **D**. (From DeLong and Davidson, courtesy of the Ohio State University Press.)

hand, adult Lepidóptera and Odonàta, as well as most Díptera, should not be placed in alcohol. If the facilities are available, the field catch can be stored temporarily in a refrigerator, or it can be frozen and kept for an extended period. Any collector will soon learn the best way to kill and preserve the various kinds of insects.

Each day's catch should be processed as soon as possible. If specimens are to be pinned in the field, the pinning should be done before they become too stiff to handle without breaking off appendages. Many small insects dry very quickly. Specimens to be preserved in alcohol should be put into alcohol as soon as possible after they are killed (or killed directly in alcohol) and after a day transferred to fresh 70–80% alcohol (to counteract the diluting effect of the insects' body fluids). Insects that are to be stored in paper envelopes (such as Odonàta and Lepidóptera) should be processed while they are still soft enough to be folded (with the wings above the body).

It is extremely important to associate each lot of insects collected with a data slip indicating at least the place and date of the collection. A specimen without data may perhaps be better than no specimen at all—but not much! A specimen with incorrect data is even worse and will create problems for later workers, especially taxonomists who place considerable importance on the data accompanying specimens. In most instances, such data can be supplied only by the collector, and the longer he or she waits to label the catch, the greater the chance for errors in the labeling.

Mounting and Preserving Insects

Insects can be mounted and preserved in various ways. Most specimens are pinned, and, once dried, these will keep indefinitely. Specimens too small to pin can be mounted on "points," on tiny "minuten" pins, or on microscopes slides. Large and showy insects, such as butterflies, moths, grasshoppers, dragonflies, and others, may be mounted in various types of glass-topped display boxes. Soft-bodied forms (nymphs, larvae, and many adults) should be preserved in fluids.

Relaxing

All insects should be mounted as soon as possible after they have been collected. If they are allowed to dry, they become brittle and may be broken in the process of being mounted. Specimens stored in pillboxes or envelopes for a long time must be relaxed before they are mounted. Relaxing may be accomplished by means of a relaxing chamber or a special relaxing fluid, or sometimes hard-bodied insects such as beetles can be relaxed enough to pin by dropping them in hot water for a few minutes.

A relaxing chamber can be made of any wide-mouthed can or jar that can be made airtight. The bottom of the jar is covered with wet sand or cloth (preferably with a little carbolic acid added to prevent mold); the insects are put in the jar in open shallow boxes; and the jar is tightly closed. Special jars for this purpose can also be obtained from supply houses. One must learn by experience how long it takes to relax an insect, but specimens are usually sufficiently relaxed to mount after a day or two in such a chamber.

Entire specimens, or parts thereof, can often be relaxed by dipping them in a relaxing fluid for several minutes. The formula for this fluid (sometimes known as Barber's fluid) is as follows:

95% ethyl alcohol	50 cm^3
Water	50 cm^3
Ethyl acetate	20 cm^3
Benzene	7 cm^3

Another method of relaxing a specimen is to inject tap water into it with a hypodermic syringe (with a 20- or 25-gauge needle). The needle is inserted into the thorax under the wings, and the thorax is completely filled with water. This method is particularly useful for Lepidóptera (except perhaps the very small ones) that have been kept in paper envelopes. After injection the specimen is returned to the envelope for 5–20 minutes, after which it should be relaxed enough to mount.

Cleaning Specimens

It is seldom necessary to clean specimens, and it is often better not to do so. A little dirt is preferable to a damaged specimen. Cleaning specimens is most likely to be desirable when they have been collected from mud, dung, or a similar material, some of which has adhered to the specimens. The easiest way to remove this material is to put the specimens in alcohol or in water to which a detergent has been added. If the material to be removed is greasy, cleaning fluid can be used.

Dust, lint, Lepidóptera scales, and the like may be removed by means of a camel's-hair brush dipped in ether, chloroform, acetone, or other cleaning fluid. This method will also remove films of oil or grease that sometimes exude from pinned specimens. Recently ultrasonic cleaners have become available that clean specimens quickly and thoroughly.

Pinning

Pinning is the best way to preserve hard-bodied insects. Pinned specimens keep well, retain their normal appearance, and are easily handled and studied. The colors often fade when the insect dries, but this fading is difficult to avoid. Bright colors are generally better preserved if the specimens are dried rapidly.

Common pins are undesirable for pinning insects. They are usually too thick and too short, and they rust. Insects should be pinned with a special type of steel pin known as an insect pin. These pins are longer than common pins; they can be obtained in various sizes (thicknesses); and they do not rust. Insect-pin sizes range from 00 to 7. The smaller sizes (that is, smaller in diameter) are too slender for general use, for which sizes 2 and 3 are best. Size 7 pins are longer than the other sizes (and will not fit in some insect boxes or drawers); these pins are used in pinning very large insects, such as some tropical beetles. Insect pins may be obtained from various supply houses (see list on page 787).

Insects are usually pinned vertically through the body as shown in Figures 36–9 and 36–10. Forms such as bees, wasps, flies, butterflies, and moths are pinned through the thorax between the bases of the front wings. With flies and wasps it is desirable to insert the pin a little to the right of the midline. Bugs are pinned through the scutellum (Figure 36–9C), a little to the right of the midline if the scutellum is large. Grasshoppers are usually pinned through the posterior part of the pronotum, just to

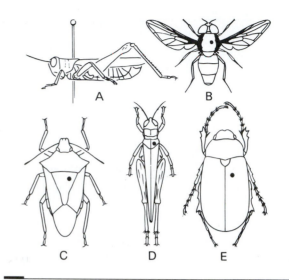

Figure 36–9.   Methods of pinning insects. **A,** lateral view of a pinned grasshopper; the black spots in the other figures show the location of the pin in the case of flies (**B**), bugs (**C**), grasshoppers (**D**), and beetles (**E**). (Courtesy of the Illinois Natural History Survey.)

the right of the midline (Figure 36–9D). Beetles, earwigs, and large hoppers should be pinned through the right fore wing, about halfway between the two ends of the body (Figure 36–9E). The pin should go through the metathorax and emerge through the metasternum (see Figure 28–4) so as not to damage the bases of the legs. Dragonflies and damselflies are best pinned horizontally through the thorax, with the left side uppermost. This method reduces the space necessary to house the collection, and a specimen so pinned can be studied just as easily as one pinned vertically. If the specimen does not have wings together above its back when it dies, the wings

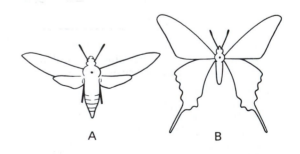

Figure 36–10.   Pinning Lepidóptera. These insects are pinned through the center of the thorax, in both moths (**A**) and butterflies (**B**). (Courtesy of the Illinois Natural History Survey.)

should be so placed and the specimen put into an envelope for a day or so until it has dried enough for the wings to remain in this position. Then it is carefully pinned through the upper part of the thorax, below the base of the wings.

The easiest way to pin an insect is to hold it between the thumb and forefinger of one hand and insert the pin with the other. All specimens should be mounted at a uniform height on the pin, about 25 mm above the point, but there should be enough of the pin above the insect (for example, with heavy-bodied insects) to permit a comfortable finger hold. Uniformity (and this applies to the position of the insect) can be obtained with a pinning block. Pinning blocks are of various types (Figure 36–11), but a common type (Figure 36–11A) consists of a block of wood in which three small holes have been drilled to different depths, usually 25, 16, and 9.5 mm.

If the abdomen sags when the insect is pinned, as it sometimes does, the pinned specimen may be stuck on a vertical surface with the abdomen hanging down and left there until it dries. If the insect is pinned on a horizontal surface, a piece of stiff paper or cardboard may be placed on the pin beneath the insect to support it until it dries.

It is not necessary that the appendages of a pinned insect be in a lifelike position (though the appearance of the collection will be greatly improved if they are), but it is desirable to have them projecting out from the body slightly so that they can be easily examined. The legs should be extended enough so that all parts are easily visible, and the wings should be extended out from the body so that the venation can be seen. Pinned bees that have the tongue extended will be easier to identify than those with the tongue folded tightly against the underside of the head.

Various types of mounting boards are used by entomologists to position the appendages of insects while they dry. These may be made of balsa wood, cork, styrofoam, cardboard, or any soft material that allows a pin to be inserted deeply enough for the lower surface of the specimen to rest on a flat surface. Pins can then be used to arrange the legs, antennae, or other parts in any position desired and hold them there until the specimen dries. Once the student becomes familiar with the characters used in identification in various groups, he can arrange and prepare his specimens accordingly.

A sheet of cork, balsa wood, or other soft material is very useful for the temporary storage of pinned insects until they can be sorted and put into boxes.

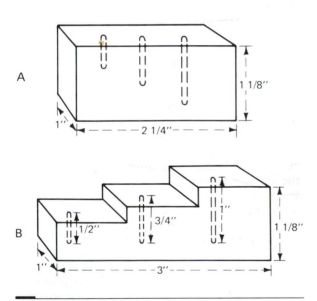

Figure 36–11. Pinning blocks. These may be a rectangular piece of wood containing holes drilled to different depths (**A**), or a block shaped like stair steps, with holes drilled to the bottom (**B**). The block of the type shown in **A** usually has the holes drilled to depths of 25, 16, and 9.5 mm. After a specimen or label is placed on the pin, the pin is inserted into the appropriate hole until it touches bottom—into the deepest hole for the specimen, the middle hole for the label bearing the locality and date, and the last hole for any additional label. For thick-bodied insects, one should leave enough room above the insect to grasp the pin. (From DeLong and Davidson, courtesy of the Ohio State University Press.)

Spreading Insects

When a specimen is pinned, the position of the legs or wings of most insects does not greatly matter, as long as all parts can be easily seen and studied. With moths, butterflies, and possibly some other insects, and in the case of insects mounted in display boxes (see the following), the wings should be spread before the insect is put into the collection. The method of spreading depends on whether the specimen is mounted pinned or unpinned, and the position into which the wings should be put depends on the type of insects.

An insect that is to be part of a pinned collection is spread on a spreading board (Figure 36–12). Spreading boards can be obtained from a supply house or made at home. An insect to be mounted under glass, as in a Riker or glass mount, may be spread on any flat surface such as a piece of corrugated cardboard or a sheet of cork or balsa wood. An insect spread on a spreading board is ordinarily spread dorsal side up, and the pin is left in the insect. One spread on a flat

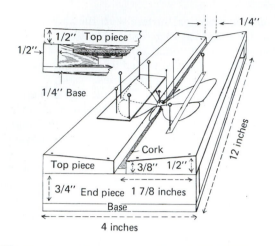

Figure 36–12. The spreading board, showing dimensions, details of construction (inset), and a spread specimen. The wings of the specimen may be held in place by a single broad strip of paper as shown on the left wings, or by a narrower strip and pins as shown on the right wings. (Courtesy of the Illinois Natural History Survey.)

surface for a Riker mount is spread in an upside down position, and the pin is *not* left in the body of the insect.

There are certain standard positions for the wings of a spread insect. In the case of butterflies and moths (many figures in Chapter 34) and mayflies (Figure 10–1), the rear margins of the front wings should be far enough forward so that there is no large gap at the side between the front and hind wings. With grasshoppers, dragonflies, damselflies, and most other insects, the front margins of the hind wings should be straight across, with the front wings far enough forward that they just clear the hind wings. The front and hind wings of a butterfly or moth are always overlapped, with the front edge of the hind wing *under* the rear edge of the front wings. With other insects the wings are usually not overlapped.

The actual process of spreading an insect is relatively simple, though it requires a little practice to acquire any degree of proficiency. One must be very careful not to damage the specimen in the spreading process. Butterflies and moths must be handled with particular care in order to avoid rubbing off the scales on the wings; these insects should be handled with forceps. If the specimen is to be mounted on a spreading board, it is first pinned (like any other pinned insect), with the pin inserted in the groove of the spreading board until the wings are flush with the

surface of the board. If the specimen is to be upside down on a flat surface, the pin is inserted into the thorax from underneath, and the insect is pinned on its back on some flat surface. It is often advisable to place a pin along each side of the body to prevent it from swinging out of line.

The steps in spreading a butterfly are shown in Figure 36–13. The wings are moved into position by pins and held there by strips of paper or other material pinned to the board, and the antennae are oriented and held in position by means of pins. The wings should be maneuvered by pins from near the base of the wing, along the front margin. The veins are heavier at this point and there is less likelihood of tearing the wing. Do not put the pin through the wing if it can be avoided, because doing so leaves a hole. The specimen should be fastened down securely, and it may sometimes be necessary to use more strips of paper than are shown in Figure 36–13. This figure illustrates a method of spreading an insect upside down on any flat surface, and the final step in this process is to hold the body down with forceps and carefully remove the pin (G). If the specimen is spread on a spreading board, the steps are similar, but the pin is left in the specimen.

The length of time it takes a spread specimen to dry will depend on the size of the specimen and such other factors as temperature and humidity. No general statement of time required can be made. The student will have to learn this by experience. To determine whether the specimen is ready to be removed from the spreading board, touch the abdomen gently with a needle: if the abdomen can be moved independently of the wings the specimen is not yet dry; if the body is stiff, the specimen can be removed. Some of the larger moths may take a week or more to dry thoroughly. In every case, care should be taken that the data on the specimen not be lost. These data can be noted alongside the specimen when it is spread.

In camp work or in the lower school grades, for example, mounting in a Riker or similar mount is preferable to spreading the specimen pinned. Such specimens are more easily displayed and are less subject to breakage. On the other hand, spread specimens in good scientific collections are nearly always pinned. Circumstances will determine what type of spreading method is to be used.

Mounting Small Insects

Insects too small to pin may be mounted on a card point (Figures 36–14A–C, 36–15), on a "minuten" pin (Figure 36–14D), or on a microscope slide, or

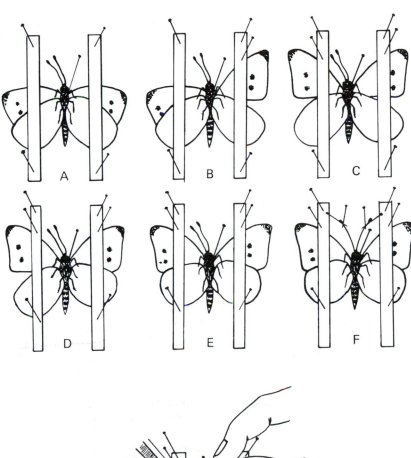

Figure 36–13.   Steps in spreading a butterfly upside down on a flat surface. **A**, position before starting to raise the wings; **B**, the front wing on one side raised; **C**, the front wing on the other side raised, with the hind margins of the front wings in a straight line; **D**, the hind wing on one side raised; **E**, the hind wing on the other side raised; **F**, the antennae oriented and held in position by pins; **G**, removing the pin from the body of the butterfly.

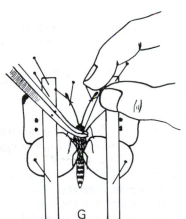

they may be preserved in liquid. Most small specimens are mounted on points.

Points are elongated triangular pieces of light cardboard or heavy paper, about 8 or 10 mm long and 3 or 4 mm wide at the base. The point is pinned through the base, and the insect is glued to the tip of the point. Points can be cut with scissors or, preferably, they can be cut with a special type of punch (obtainable from supply houses).

Putting an insect on a point is a very simple process. The point is put on the pin, the pin is grasped by the pointed end, and the upper side of the

tip is touched to the glue and then touched to the insect. One should use as little glue as possible (so that body parts are not covered by it), and the specimen should be correctly oriented on the point. The standard positions of an insect mounted on a point are shown in Figure 36–14A–C. If the insect is put on the point dorsal side up (A), the point should not extend beyond the middle of the body. It is important that body parts to be examined for identification should not be embedded in glue. Beetles mounted on points should always have the ventral side of the body visible.

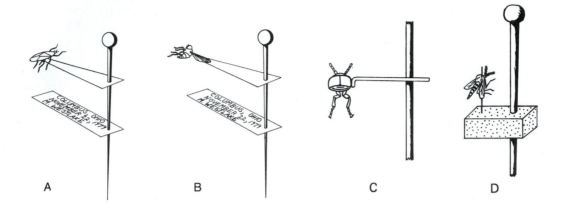

Figure 36–14. Methods of mounting minute insects. **A,** a bug on a point, dorsal side up; **B,** a fly on a point, left side up; **C,** a beetle mounted dorsal side up, attached by its side to the bent-down tip of the point; **D,** a mosquito mounted on a minuten pin.

The glue used in mounting insects on points should be quick-drying and should be quite hard when it sets. Preferably, it should be soluble in water or alcohol so that specimens can be easily removed if necessary (e.g., for dissection or slide mounting.) Glue, used with care, is also useful in repairing broken specimens and replacing broken-off wings and legs.

Drying Specimens

Small specimens will dry quickly in the open air, but it may sometimes be desirable to hasten the drying of larger insects artificially. Large specimens will eventually dry in the open air, but it is not advisable to leave them exposed for very long because of the possibility of damage by dermestids, ants, or other pests. A chamber with one or more light bulbs can be used for rapid drying. A simple drying chamber can be made from a wooden box with a door on one side. Slats may be placed on the sides of the box to allow mounting or spreading boards to be arranged at various distances from the heat source (the light bulbs). Such boxes should be vented with a few small holes in the side or top to allow moisture to escape.

Many soft-bodied arthropods (insect larvae, spiders, and others) can be dehydrated by critical-point drying, freeze-drying, or vacuum drying. These techniques yield specimens that are not particularly fragile, show no distortion and very little color loss, and subsequently show no indication of reabsorption of water or decomposition. After dehydration they are pinned and stored like any other pinned insect.

The equipment and procedures used in critical-point drying are discussed by Gordh and Hall (1979); freeze-drying methods are described by Woodring and Blum (1963) and by Roe and Clifford (1976); and those for vacuum drying are described by Blum and Woodring (1963).

Another method of preserving larvae, which is often used for caterpillars, is inflation. Inflated lar-

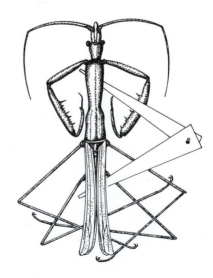

Figure 36–15. A method of mounting long slender insects that are too small to pin; such insects are mounted on two points.

vae are very fragile, but they show excellent color preservation and little or no distortion. The equipment and procedures used in inflating larvae are described by Peterson (1948).

Preservation of Insects in Fluids

Any type of insect can be preserved in fluid. Insects may be preserved in fluid temporarily until one has an opportunity to pin them, and many collectors prefer to store their collections in fluid rather than dried in envelopes or pillboxes. However, specimens preserved in fluids are usually not so easily examined as those on pins or points, and in general any insect that *can* be preserved dry should be mounted on a pin or point.

The forms for which preservation in fluids is the standard means of preservation are the following: (1) soft-bodied insects (for example, mayflies, caddisflies, stoneflies, midges, and others), which would shrivel and become distorted if pinned and allowed to air-dry; (2) many very small insects, which are best studied in detail when mounted on a microscope slide (for example, lice, fleas, thrips, Collémbola, and others; (3) insect larvae and most insect nymphs; and (4) arthropods other than insects.

The fluid generally used for the preservation of insects and other arthropods is ethyl alcohol (70–80%). The preservation or fixation of tissues is better for many forms if certain other substances are added to the alcohol. The most commonly used modifications of ethyl alcohol are the following:

Hood's solution:

70–80% ethyl alcohol	95 cm³
Glycerine	5 cm³

Kahle's solution:

95% ethyl alcohol	30 cm³
Formaldehyde	12 cm³
Glacial acetic acid	4 cm³
Water	60 cm³

Alcoholic Bouin's solution:

80% ethyl alcohol	150 cm³
Formaldehyde	60 cm³
Glacial acetic acid	15 cm³
Picric acid	1 g

Ethyl alcohol (and the modifications of it just mentioned) can also be used as a killing agent for many insects and other arthropods, but it is unsatisfactory as a killing agent for insect larvae. The killing agents commonly used for larvae are the following:

KAAD mixture:

95% ethyl alcohol	70–100 cm³
Kerosene	10 cm³
Glacial acetic acid	20 cm³
Dioxane	10 cm³

XA mixture:

95% ethyl alcohol	50 cm³
Xylene	50 cm³

If KAAD is used, the amount of kerosene should be reduced for soft-bodied larvae such as maggots. Larvae killed in either of these mixtures are ready for transfer to alcohol for storage after $\frac{1}{2}$ to 4 hours. In the transfer to alcohol, the alcohol should be changed after the first few days, as it becomes diluted by the body fluids of the animal put in it. Any of these killing agents are likely to remove the bright colors of larvae, especially greens, yellows, and reds. All known killing and preserving fluids are likely to destroy some colors.

A problem always encountered when specimens are preserved in fluids is the evaporation of the fluid. The vials should be stoppered with rubber, neoprene, or polyethylene (not cork stoppers), and it is advisable to use oversize stoppers that do not extend very far into the bottle. Screw-cap vials are satisfactory if the cap is tight-fitting. Procaine vials or tubes (usually available free from any dentist) make ideal temporary containers for many small forms. All containers should be well filled with fluid and should be examined at least once or twice a year so that evaporated fluid can be replaced. Evaporation may be retarded by covering the stoppers with some sort of sealing material such as paraffin. Another method is to place a number of small stoppered vials in a large jar with a rubber gasket.

Mounting on Microscope Slides

Many small arthropods (lice, fleas, thrips, midges, mites, and others), and often such isolated body parts as legs or genitalia, are best studied when mounted on microscope slides. Material so mounted is generally transferred to a slide from preserving fluid, and the mount may be temporary or permanent. Temporary mounts are used for material that is to be returned to the preserving fluid after study. Such mounts may last anywhere from a few minutes to many months, depending on the mounting medium used. Permanent mounts are used for material that is not to be returned to the preserving fluid after study. Such mounts do not last indefinitely, but may last for many years. Specimens mounted on microscope slides for class use are usually mounted as permanent mounts. Specimens of particular taxonomic value, which one would like to keep indefinitely, should be kept in fluids and mounted for study only in temporary mounts.

Many small or soft-bodied specimens may be mounted directly in a mounting medium, but others (especially dark-colored or thick-bodied specimens or such structures as genitalia) must be cleared before mounting. Some mounting media have a clearing action. Several substances may be used as clearing agents, but the most commonly used are probably potassium hydroxide (KOH) and Nesbitt's solution. KOH can be used for almost any arthropod or arthropod structure. Nesbitt's solution is often used for clearing such small arthropods as mites, lice, and Collémbola. After clearing in KOH, the specimen should be washed in water (preferably with a little acetic acid added) to remove any excess of the KOH. Its subsequent treatment will depend on the type of medium in which it is mounted. Specimens cleared in Nesbitt's solution can be transferred directly to some mounting media, but with other media, they must be run through certain reagents first.

KOH used for clearing is a 10–15% solution. The formula for Nesbitt's solution is as follows:

Chloral hydrate	40 g
Concentrated HCl	2.5 cm³
Distilled water	25–50 cm³
(more for lightly sclerotized specimens)	

KOH can be used cold or warm, or the specimen may be boiled in it. Boiling is faster but may sometimes distort the specimen. Clearing in cold KOH requires from several hours to a day or more. The same specimen may be cleared in a few minutes by boiling. Nesbitt's solution is usually used cold, and the clearing may require from a few hours to a few days.

Small specimens mounted on microscope slides can be mounted on a regular slide without any special support for the glass other than the mounting medium itself. Larger or thicker specimens should be mounted on a depression slide or with some sort of support for the cover glass, to keep it level and to prevent the specimen from being flattened. The support for a cover glass on an ordinary microscope slide may consist of small pieces of glass or a piece of fine wire bent into a loop. Some specimens are best studied in a depression slide or a small dish without a

cover glass so that the specimen can be maneuvered and examined from different angles. If a cover glass is added, most specimens are mounted dorsal side up. Fleas are usually mounted with the left side up, and many mites are commonly mounted ventral side up.

The media most often used for temporary slide mounts are water or alcohol, glycerine, and glycerine jelly. Water and alcohol evaporate rapidly, and mounts with these materials generally last only a few minutes unless more of the medium is added. Temporary slides made with glycerine or glycerine jelly are much better and last a relatively long time. They can be made semipermanent by "ringing" (putting a ring of asphaltum, nail polish, or a similar material around the edge of the cover glass). With glycerine jelly, a bit of the jelly is put on the slide and liquefied by heat. Then the specimen is added and oriented, and a cover glass is put on. This material cools to a solid jelly. Specimens mounted in glycerine jelly can be unmounted by reversing the process. Specimens can be put into glycerine or glycerine jelly directly from water or alcohol.

The media used for permanent slide mounts are of two general types; those with a water base, and resins. Specimens can be mounted in water-base media directly from water or alcohol. Such mounts are somewhat less permanent than resin mounts, but their life can be prolonged by ringing. Specimens mounted in a resin (natural or synthetic) must first be dehydrated (by running through successively increasing concentrations of alcohol: 70, 95, and 100%), and then through xylol and into the resin. The most commonly used resin is balsam. There are many water-base media, but the following is one of the best:

Hoyer's chloral hydrate (Berlese's fluid):

Water	50 cm³
Gum arabic	30 g
Chloral hydrate	200 g
Glycerine	20 cm³

The gum arabic should be ground-up crystals or powder, not flakes. This mixture should be filtered through glass wool before use.

All permanent slide mounts take some time to dry. They should be kept horizontal (cover glass up) during drying and are best stored in slide boxes in this same position.

It is sometimes desirable to stain an insect before it is mounted. A number of different stains are suitable for this purpose, but one very commonly used is acid fuchsin. The procedure to be followed in using this stain on scale insects is outlined on page 347.

Studies of Insect Genitalia

Many taxonomic studies of insects involve a detailed study of the external genitalia (see page 59), particularly those of the male. The genitalia are sclerotized structures that can sometimes be studied in the dried insect without any special treatment of the specimen, but in most cases they are partly or largely internal and must be removed and cleared for detailed study.

The procedures followed in removing and clearing genitalia will vary depending on the type of insect. In some cases the insect (if mounted dry) can be relaxed, either by the use of a relaxing fluid (see page 755) or by placing the specimen in a relaxing chamber for a time, and genitalia may be removed with a small dissecting needle and then cleared in KOH. In other cases the abdomen (or the apical part of it) is removed and cleared in KOH, and the genitalia are dissected out after clearing. Clearing may be accomplished in a few minutes by boiling, or it may be accomplished by leaving the genitalia in the KOH for a longer period at room temperature. In the latter case, clearing may require from a few hours to a few days, depending on how heavily sclerotized these structures are. Overclearing renders the genitalia transparent and difficult to study. Such genitalia are more easily studied if stained with borax carmine after clearing.

After the genitalia are cleared, they are washed in water with a little acetic acid added (about 1 drop per 50 cm³ of water) and placed in small dishes of glycerine for study. They can be mounted on microscope slides, but this approach permits a study from only one angle. In small dishes they can be turned and studied from any angle desired.

After the study is completed, the genitalia are stored in microvials of glycerine (vials about 10–12 mm in length), and these vials are kept with the specimens from which the genitalia were removed. If the genitalia came from a pinned specimen, the vial is put on the pin (the pin going through the cork of the vial) below the specimen. Genitalia removed from a specimen must be handled in such a way that they can always be associated with the specimen from which they came.

Labeling

The scientific value of an insect specimen depends to a large extent on the information regarding the date and locality of its capture and also on such additional information as the name of the collector and the habitat or food plant in or on which the specimen was collected. The beginning student may look upon such labeling as an unnecessary chore, but the time will always come when data on a specimen are indispensable. An insect collector should *always* label his specimens with date[1] and locality: this is the minimum amount of data for a specimen. Additional data are desirable, but optional.

The appearance of a collection of pinned insects is greatly influenced by the nature of the labels. Small, neat, and properly oriented labels add much to the collection. They should be on fairly stiff white paper and preferably not larger than 6 by 19 mm in size. They should be at a uniform height on the pin, parallel to and underneath the insect. If only one label is used, it is placed about 16 mm above the point of the pin. If more than one label is used, the uppermost one should be at this distance above the point. The labels should be oriented so that all are read from the same side. We prefer that they be read from the left side (Figure 36–16), but some people

[1]Most entomologists abbreviate the date as day–month (in Roman numerals)–year; 6 May 1988, would be abbreviated 6–V–1988.

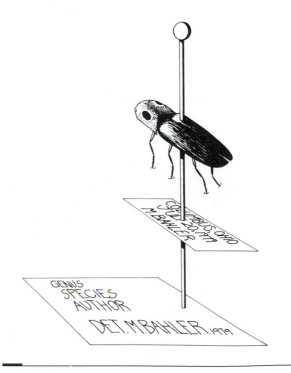

Figure 36–16. The identification label, giving the scientific name of the insect and the name of the person identifying the specimen.

prefer that they be read from the right side. In the case of specimens mounted on points, the label should extend parallel to the point (Figure 36–14A,B) and be offset like the point. If the pinned specimens in the collection have the labels read from the right, specimens on points placed with them should have the point directed downward. If the pinned specimens have the labels read from the left, specimens on points placed with them should have the point directed upward (so that all labels can be read from the same side). If there are two or more labels on the pin (for example, one for the locality, date, and collector, as in Figure 36–17, and another for the host plant), the labels should be parallel and arranged to be read from the same side.

Labels indicating locality, date, and collector may be printed by hand with a fine-pointed pen, or they may be obtained partly printed from a supply house (Figure 36–17). A number of labels may be typed on a sheet of plain paper and reduced by a photocopier. This process will usually require more than one reduction from the original, and care must be taken that the labels remain legible.

The preceding discussion applies to labels containing data concerning the locality, date, and collector, and not to labels identifying the insects. Identifying labels are discussed next, under "Housing, Arrangement, and Care of the Collection."

Labels for specimens preserved in fluids should be written on a good grade of rag paper with India or other waterproof ink and placed inside the container with the specimen(s). Labels for specimens mounted on microscope slides are attached to the upper surface of the slide, on one or both sides of the cover glass.

Housing, Arrangement, and Care of the Collection

The basic considerations in housing, arrangement, and care of an insect collection are the same whether the collection consists of a few cigar boxes of specimens or thousands of museum drawers containing millions of specimens. The specimens in a collection must be systematically arranged and protected from museum pests, light, and moisture. The general arrangement of a collection will depend principally on its size, the purpose for which it is intended, and the method used in preserving the specimens (whether they are pinned, in envelopes, in liquid, on slides, and so on).

Pinned insects should be kept in dustproof boxes having a soft bottom that will permit easy pinning. Several types of insect boxes may be purchased from supply houses. The most commonly used type is made of wood, about 230 by 330 by 60 mm in size, with a tight-fitting lid and an inner bottom of sheet cork, composition board, or foam plastic. Such boxes usually cost from $10.00 to $25.00. The better boxes of this type are called Schmitt boxes.

Satisfactory low-cost pinning boxes may be made of cigar boxes or heavy cardboard boxes by lining the bottoms with sheet cork, balsa wood, foam plastic, or soft corrugated cardboard. This bottom material should be glued in place or cut so that it fits very tightly into the box. The enthusiastic beginner will soon find that he requires more than one box. He will initially wish to arrange his specimens by orders and will probably have a separate box (or more than one box) for each order. As the collection grows he can add more boxes, so that he can expand with a minimum of rearranging or transferring specimens from box to box.

For a small collection that is housed in one or a few boxes, an arrangement similar to that shown in Figure 36–18 is suggested. It is unlikely that anyone except the specialist will have the specimens in his collection identified further than to family, and for many collectors, particularly the beginner, it will be difficult enough to carry the identification that far. The simplest arrangement, therefore, is to have the specimens arranged by order and family, with the order label (containing the order name and common name) on a separate pin and the family label (containing family and common names) either on a sep-

Columbus Columbus Columbus Columbus Columbus Columbus
    O.   O.   O.   O.   O.   O.
Columbus Columbus Columbus Columbus Columbus Columbus
    O.   O.   O.   O.   O.   O.
Columbus Columbus Columbus Columbus Columbus Columbus
    O.   O.   O.   O.   O.   O.
Columbus Columbus Columbus Columbus Columbus Columbus
    O.   O.   O.   O.   O.   O.
Columbus Columbus Columbus Columbus Columbus Columbus
    O.   O.   O.   O.   O.   O.

Lincoln Co., Lincoln Co., Lincoln Co., Lincoln Co., Lincoln Co.,
    Me.   Me.   Me.   Me.   Me.
D.J. Borror D.J. Borror D.J. Borror D.J. Borror D.J. Borror
Lincoln Co., Lincoln Co., Lincoln Co., Lincoln Co., Lincoln Co.,
    Me.   Me.   Me.   Me.   Me.
D.J. Borror D.J. Borror D.J. Borror D.J. Borror D.J. Borror
Lincoln Co., Lincoln Co., Lincoln Co., Lincoln Co., Lincoln Co.,
    Me.   Me.   Me.   Me.   Me.
D.J. Borror D.J. Borror D.J. Borror D.J. Borror D.J. Borror

Figure 36–17. Two sheets of printed locality labels (actual size), each label with a space for writing in the date. Labels containing the name of a town are often preferable to those containing only the name of a county, especially in sections of the United States where the counties are large.

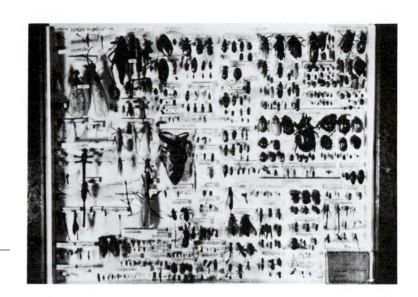

Figure 36–18. A synoptic insect collection.

arate pin or on the pin of the first insect in a row of specimens in that family. There are various ways of arranging the specimens in a small collection, but the arrangement should be neat and systematic, and the labels should be easily seen.

Most large institutions and many private collectors house their collections in uniform glass-topped museum drawers that fit into steel cabinets. Specimens may be pinned directly into the cork or foam plastic bottoms in such drawers, but usually they are pinned in small unit trays of various sizes that fit snugly in the drawers (Figure 36–19). The unit tray system facilitates rapid expansion and rear-rangement of the collection without the need to handle individual specimens, which is time-consuming and hazardous to the specimens. The unit trays are of a convenient size to fit under a dissecting microscope, so that unless it is necessary to examine the ventral surface of a specimen, the specimen can be examined without removing it from the tray, thus reducing the chance of breakage.

In larger collections, such as those of specialists or those in museums, where the specimens are identified to species, the species determination is usually put on a plain white or bordered label placed low on the pin against the bottom of the box. This label

Figure 36–19. A drawer of a large insect collection.

contains the complete scientific name (genus, species, subspecies if any), the name of the describer, the name of the person making the determination, and the date (usually the year only) the determination was made (Figure 36–16). In large collections where each drawer contains a series of unit trays (Figure 36–19), each tray usually contains specimens of just one species.

Many insect collectors eventually become interested in and concentrate their efforts on a particular order, family, or genus. By contacts and exchanges with other collectors interested in that group, a collector may build up a sizable collection and be in a position to contribute to our knowledge of that group by his publications. Some collectors prefer to specialize on insects from a particular habitat (aquatic insects, wood borers, flower-frequenting insects, gall insects, leaf miners, and so on), medically important insects, insect pests of particular types of plants (Figure 36–20), beneficial insects, or those with particular habits (predators, parasites, scavengers, and so on). The possibilities are many.

We believe that everyone interested in entomology, regardless of the field in which he or she is primarily interested, should concentrate on a particular taxonomic group. A certain satisfaction comes with a thorough knowledge of even a small group of animals, and such study can prove to be a very interesting hobby for a person whose major interest or occupation is in another field.

Display Mounting

Many collectors may wish to keep their collection in containers where the insects can be easily displayed. Several types of mounts are useful for this purpose. A pinned collection may be easily displayed if it is mounted in glass-topped boxes or in glass-doored wall cabinets. In the latter case the back of the cabinet should be covered with a material that will permit easy pinning. Butterflies, moths, and many other insects may be displayed in Riker mounts—boxes in which the insects are directly under the glass top on cotton (Figure 36–21). Cases somewhat similar to Riker mounts, but without the cotton and with glass on the top and bottom (Figures 36–22A, 36–23A), are useful for displaying one or a few specimens (that is, one or a few in each mount). It is also possible to enclose specimens between sheets of plastic or to embed specimens in plastic.

Riker Mounts.   A Riker mount (Figure 36–21) is a cotton-filled cardboard box with most of the lid removed and replaced with glass, and with the glass top holding the insects in place on the cotton. Riker mounts may be of almost any size (0.3 by 0.4 meter is about the largest size that is practical) and are about 19 to 25 mm deep. They can be purchased from supply houses, but they are easily made at home. All that is required is a box, glass, cotton, and binding. Almost any sort of cardboard box may be used. If it is too deep, it can be cut down. Cardboard

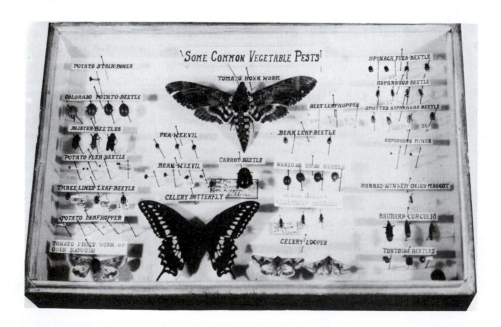

Figure 36–20.   An illustrative collection, showing some common pests of vegetables.

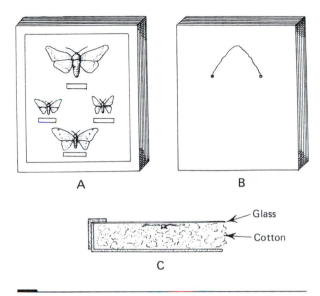

Figure 36–21. The Riker mount. **A,** front view; **B,** back view; **C,** sectional view showing a specimen in place under the glass on the cotton.

is most easily cut with a razor blade held in a holder; such holders can be purchased from any hardware store or "five-and-dime." A section of the lid is cut out, leaving a margin around the edge of the lid about 6 to 9 mm. A piece of glass (windowpane thickness will do) is then cut to fit on the inside of the lid. Anyone who can use a glass cutter can cut the glass himself, often from discarded pieces. Otherwise, one can buy the glass and have it cut at the hardware store. Before the glass is put into the lid, it is well to cover the lid with binding tape. This will greatly improve the appearance of the box, particularly if the box originally had printing on it. Black tape makes the best-looking boxes. A little practice will enable one to cover a homemade box neatly. The glass is held in the lid with strips of gummed paper or masking tape on the four sides, each strip as long as that side of the glass. The cotton used should be of a good grade, with a smooth surface. It should be thick enough to extend a little way above the sides of the box before the lid is put on, and should be cut a little small and stretched to fit the box. If one wishes to hang up this sort of mount, two brass fasteners can be put into the bottom (from the underside, and reinforced on the inside with gummed paper) and a piece of string or wire tied between the two fasteners (Figure 36–21B). One should be careful to place the insects in the box so that they will be right side up when the box is hung. When large-bodied insects are placed in a Riker mount, a little hole should be teased

in the cotton with forceps for the body of the insect. After the specimens are in the box, the lid is put back on and fastened with pins or tape.

It is sometimes desirable to mount individual insects in small Riker mounts. Such mounts may be made in any small box (for example, a pillbox), and if the box is not more than 50 or 75 mm wide, a sheet of plastic (which can be cut with scissors) can be used in place of the glass.

Glass Mounts. Mounts similar to Riker mounts, but without the cotton and with glass on the top and bottom (Figure 36–22A, 36–23A) are excellent for displaying individual moths, butterflies, or other insects. They are made in two general ways: all glass (Figure 36–22) or with a cardboard frame (Figure 36–23). The size will depend on the size of the specimen(s) to be mounted. One should allow a margin on all four sides of the mount, and the mount should be deep enough to accommodate the body and legs of the specimen. Mounts for large-bodied insects such as sphinx moths will be fairly heavy if made entirely of glass, and for such insects a mount with a cardboard frame may be preferable because they are easier to make.

The only materials needed to make an all-glass mount are glass, a transparent cement, and binding tape. One can obtain scrap window glass free at most hardware stores and cut it himself. A commercial household cement, which is fast-drying and easily applied, is a suitable cement. Many tapes are suitable, but the best is probably an electrical tape (black, 19 mm wide).

Glass cutting is easy to learn, safe, and much cheaper than having the glass cut professionally. One needs a glass cutter, a perfectly flat surface, a straightedge (for example, a yardstick or ruler), and some way of holding the straightedge firmly against the glass when using the cutter. The glass is scratched *with a single stroke* of the cutter; with practice, one can learn the pressure necessary to make this scratch. The glass is broken by pressing *away from* the scratch. Pieces can be broken in the hands or at the edge of the table; narrow pieces should be turned over and tapped firmly (with the reverse end of the cutter) along the scratch line until the glass breaks. The narrower the piece to be cut off, the more skill necessary to cut it evenly.

A glass cutter keeps its edges longer if the wheel is immersed in a light oil (for example, kerosene) when not in use. For a better cut, the cutter wheel should be oiled during use. If one measures the glass accurately and marks it with ink before each cut, he should be able to cut glass to within 0.5 mm of the desired size.

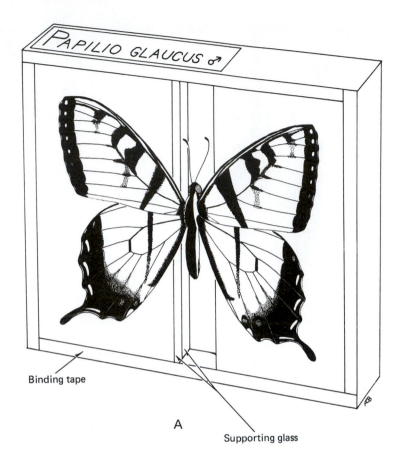

A

Supporting glass

Binding tape

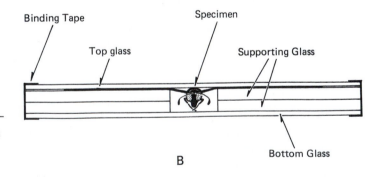

B

Binding Tape

Top glass

Specimen

Supporting Glass

Bottom Glass

Figure 36–22.   The all-glass mount. **A,** a completed mount; **B,** sectional view of the mount.

To make an all-glass mount, proceed as follows:

1. Specimens to be displayed in glass mounts must first be spread upside down on a piece of sheet cork, balsa wood, corrugated cardboard, or other flat surface, with the wings and antennae in a standard position (see pages 758–759 and Figure 36–13). The legs should be pressed close to the body of the specimen to minimize its thickness.

2. Cut two identical pieces of single-weight window glass for the top and bottom of the mount, allowing at least 6 mm margin on all four sides of the spread specimen(s).

3. Cut enough support pieces of glass (single weight or double weight) to provide room for the body of the insect (Figure 36–22B). These supporting pieces should equal one dimension (usually the shorter) of the top and bottom pieces, and they should be separated in the

center of the mount by a distance two or three times the width of the insect's body.

4. Clean all glass thoroughly, preferably with a commercial glass cleaner.

5. Place the bottom piece of glass on a clean flat surface and remove the lint from it with a camel's-hair brush. Place a small drop of cement on the corners of one end. After removing the lint from one of the supporting pieces, press the piece down in place with the end of the brush handle, line it up with the edges of the bottom piece, and remove any excess cement that oozes out.

6. Continue building up needed thicknesses of supporting glass on each side, aligning each piece carefully and allowing time for each to set before adding the next. Place the cement only on the outer corners of the glass, and use only a small drop. Some cement may spread inward and be visible in the completed mount, but this will not be objectionable.

7. When the supporting pieces are cemented in position, place the specimen on the supporting pieces and center it. Put a small drop of cement on the four corners, and place the top piece of glass in position, being careful not to move the specimen. Press the top down hard, and place a small weight on it. Leave this weight in place until the cement sets (15 minutes to an hour or more).

8. Tape the sides of the mount. The tape covers the sharp edges of the glass, seals the mount, and gives it a finished look.

9. Cement a label on the top edge, if desired (Figure 36–22A).

10. Store in a dry place to discourage mold.

A glass mount with a cardboard frame (Figure 36–23) is very similar to the all-glass mount but contains only one pair of supporting pieces of glass. The remaining thickness of the mount is made up by the frame. The sides of the mount are of two layers of cardboard. The outer layer may be thin, but the inner layer should be of very heavy cardboard such as that used in certain types of packing case (*not* corrugated cardboard). The inner cardboard should be at least as thick as the glass. If such cardboard is not available, it can be made by cementing two or more thicknesses of ordinary cardboard together. The width of the cardboard strips forming the inner layer of the sides will determine the depth of the mount and the amount of space available for the body and legs of the insect. A good mount of this type requires considerable care in cutting and fitting the parts. The glass and cardboard must be measured and cut very exactly. Figure 36–23 shows how this type of glass mount is made.

If large numbers of glass mounts are to be made, the use of standard sizes will simplify glass cutting, displaying, and storing. Two or more specimens can be put in a mount by placing them in a vertical column (with two series or pieces of supporting glass) or side by side (with at least three series or pieces of supporting glass, the lateral ones being narrower than the middle ones). Specimens mounted in a vertical row should be about the same thickness. If one is thicker, the thinner one may slip. Because the specimens are held in position by the top piece of glass, it is important that this piece be pressed down tightly against the specimen.

Plastic Mounts.   Butterflies, moths, and other insects may be mounted for display between two

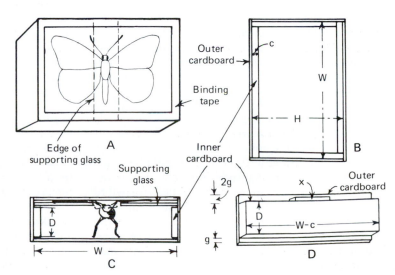

Figure 36–23.   Construction of a glass mount. **A,** completed mount; **B,** top view of the frame, showing the construction of the corners; **C,** sectional view; **D,** view from inside of one side of the frame, showing how the two layers of cardboard are put together. c, thickness of inner cardboard; D, width of inner strip of cardboard; g, thickness of glass; H, height of case; W, width of case, x, a cardboard wedge to prevent the supporting glass from slipping sideways.

sheets of a fairly thick transparent plastic. Each sheet is bulged out where the body of the insect will be (the plastic can be so shaped when it is heated). The two sheets are put together, with the insect between, and sealed around the edges with acetone or some other sealing material. Such sheets can be obtained, all ready for use, from some supply houses.

Many types of insects may be embedded in Bioplastic. This is a rather involved process, and space does not permit describing it in detail here. The materials needed, together with instruction for their use, can be obtained from supply houses. Ward's Natural Science Establishment has prepared a booklet entitled *How to Embed in Bioplastic*, which is a complete manual on the subject. The mountings described here are only a few of the possible types useful for displaying insects. An ingenious collector should be able to devise many additional types.

Protecting the Collection

All insect collections are subject to attack by dermestid beetles, ants, and other museum pests, and if the collection is to last any length of time, certain precautions must be taken to protect it from these pests. Various materials may be used for this purpose, but one material commonly used is naphthalene (in flake or ball form). Naphthalene flakes can be put into a small cardboard pillbox that is firmly attached to the bottom of the insect box (usually in one corner) and has a few pin holes in it. Paradichlorobenzene can also be used, but it volatilizes more rapidly than naphthalene and must be renewed at more frequent intervals. A combination of equal parts of naphthalene and paradichlorobenzene will protect the specimens for a considerable time. To protect specimens in Riker mounts, naphthalene flakes should be sprinkled under the cotton when the mount is being made. A collection should be checked periodically to make sure that plenty of repellent is present. If boxes or drawers are stored in tight cabinets that are not opened frequently, the repellent should last a long time.

It should be emphasized that paradichlorobenzene and naphthalene are only repellents, and while they will keep out potential pests, they will not kill pests already in the collection. If a box or drawer is found to be infested with pests, it should be fumigated (with carbon disulfide, ethylene dichloride, methyl bromide, or Vapona strips) or heat-treated to destroy these pests. Heating boxes, cases, or mounts to 150°F (66°C) or higher for several hours (if the boxes are such that the heat will not damage them) will destroy any dermestids or other pests they may

contain. Many good collections have been ruined by pests because the collector failed to protect them.

Packing and Shipping Insects

A dried insect on a pin is such a fragile object that it would seem almost impossible to ship a box of pinned insects through the mails and have it arrive at its destination with the specimens intact. It can be done if a few simple rules are followed. The preparation of specimens for shipment is based largely on the treatment they are likely to receive in transit. They will be turned upside down and sideways and subjected to severe and repeated jarring. Therefore, the two most important considerations are to make certain that all pins are firmly anchored, so that they cannot work loose and bounce around and break specimens, and that the box in which they are pinned is placed in a larger box, surrounded by packing material to cushion the blows the package will invariably receive.

We are concerned here with the transporting or shipping of *dead* insects. Before transporting or shipping living insects, one should check with quarantine officials and the postal authorities.

Pinned specimens should be inserted firmly into the bottom of the insect box, preferably with pinning forceps. The bottom of the box should be of a material that will hold the pins firmly. Large specimens should be braced with extra pins to prevent them from swinging around and damaging other specimens. Long appendages, or a long abdomen, should be braced and supported by extra pins. A sheet of cardboard cut to fit the inside of the box (with a slot cut out along one side to facilitate removal) should be placed over the top of the pinned specimens, and the space between this and the lid of the box should be filled with cotton, Cellucotton, or a similar material. This arrangement prevents the pins from being dislodged during shipment. One should *never* include in a box of pinned specimens vials of insects preserved in fluid, regardless of how firmly the vials may appear to be fastened in the box. The rough handling the average box gets when going through the mail may dislodge even the most "firmly" attached vial and ruin the specimens.

If a box of pinned insects contains specimens from which the genitalia (or other parts) have been removed and stored in a microvial on the pin below the insect (see page 763), special precautions must be taken to make sure these vials do not come loose and damage specimens in the box. Pins containing such vials should be inserted far enough so that the vial rests on the bottom of the box. The vial is then held in a fixed position by insect pins, one placed at the end of the vial and two other crossed over the middle of the vial.

When specimens preserved in fluids are to be shipped, measures should be taken to protect the specimens in the containers. The containers should be completely filled with fluid, and it is sometimes desirable to add cotton or some similar material in the container to prevent the specimen from bouncing about. Small and delicate larvae, such as mosquito larvae, should be in vials so completely filled with fluid that there is not even an air bubble in the vial. An air bubble in a vial can have the same effect on a specimen as a solid object in the vial would have. One method of removing all air bubbles is to use glass tubes stoppered with rubber stoppers, filling the vial containing the specimens to the brim and then carefully inserting the stopper with a pin alongside it (to allow excess fluid to escape). When the stopper is in place, the pin is removed. Another way of getting the vial completely filled with liquid (without any air bubbles) is to fill the vial to the brim and insert the stopper with a hypodermic needle through it. The excess fluid comes out through the needle, and when the needle is removed, the stopper seals (if the process is carefully done) and there is no air bubble inside the vial.

If two or more containers of insects in fluid are packed in the same box, they should be wrapped in wide strips of Cellucotton or some similar soft material so that no two vials are in contact.

Insects in glass or Riker mounts can ordinarily withstand considerable jolting without damage, but care should be taken that the glass of these mounts does not get broken. Such mounts should be packed in an abundance of soft packing material, and no two of them should touch each other in the box.

Insect material mounted on microscope slides should be shipped in wooden or heavy cardboard slide boxes, preferably boxes in which the slides are inserted into grooves and are on edge in the box. Strips of a soft material should be placed between the slides and the lid of the box, so that the slides do not bounce about.

Dried specimens in envelopes or pillboxes should be packed in such a way that the specimens do not bounce around inside the box. Pillboxes should be padded inside with Cellucotton to immobilize the specimens, and boxes containing envelopes should be filled with cotton or Cellucotton.

Boxes containing pinned insects, insects in fluids, microscope slides, or dried insects in envelopes or pillboxes that are to be sent through the mail should be wrapped in paper to keep out fragments of packing material and packed inside a larger box. The outer box should be selected so as to allow at least 50 mm of packing material (excelsior, shredded paper, cotton, styrofoam chips, and so forth) on all sides of the smaller box. This packing material should not be so loose as to allow the inner box to rattle around or so tight that the cushion effect is lost.

Whenever material is shipped through the mail, an accompanying letter should be sent to the addressee, notifying him of the shipment. Packages of dead insects sent through the mail are usually marked "Dried (or Preserved) Insects for Scientific Study" and are sent by parcel post. It is well to mark such packages for gentle handling in transit, though such marking does not always insure that they will not get rough treatment. Material shipped to points inside the United States should be insured, though it may be difficult to place an evaluation on some material. The statement "No Commercial Value" on a box shipped from one country to another will facilitate the box getting through customs.

Work with Living Insects

Anyone studying insects who does nothing but collect, kill, and mount these animals and study the dead specimens will miss the most interesting part of insect study. The student who takes time to study *living* insects will find that they are fascinating and often amazing little animals. Living insects can be studied in the field or in captivity. Many are very easy to keep in captivity, where they can be studied more easily, and often at closer range, than in the field.

Keeping Living Insects in Captivity

Relatively little equipment or attention is required to keep an insect alive in captivity for a short period. Insects can be brought in from the field, kept in a cage of some sort for a day or so, and then released. On the other hand, rearing adult insects from their immature stages or maintaining cultures of insects through one or more generations usually requires more equipment and attention. However, there are many types of insects that are fairly easy to rear or culture.

Rearing adult insects from immature stages is an excellent way to learn about their habits and life histories. The activities of insects in cages can generally be more easily observed, and certainly observed to a greater extent, than insects in the field.

Many insects collected as immatures and reared will be found to be parasitized, and the parasites will emerge rather than the host insect, particularly in the case of caterpillars.

Cages for Insects.   Almost anything will serve as a suitable cage for keeping insects in captivity for a short time or for rearing some types of insects. The simplest type of cage is a glass (or clear plastic) jar of some sort covered with gauze held in place with a string or rubber band (Figure 36–24A). The jar may vary in size from a small vial up to a large (4-liter or larger) jar, depending on the size and numbers of the insects. In some cases food, water, or other materials necessary to the well-being of the insects can simply be placed in the bottom of the jar. Such containers are also suitable for aquaria. Mosquitoes, for example, can be reared in vials that hold only a few cubic centimeters of water.

Cages suitable for rearing some types of insects or for display can be made of cardboard, gauze, and clear plastic. Any small cardboard box can be used. Its size will depend on the size of the insect it is to contain. Holes cut in the ends and covered with gauze will provide ventilation; clear plastic or glass in the front will provide visibility; and the top may be covered with either glass, clear plastic, or an opaque lid.

A more permanent type of cage can be made of window screen with a wood or metal framework. The bottom 25 mm or so of a large tin can with a cylinder of screen inserted in it (Figure 36–24B) makes a good cage. Cages of wood and screen can be made with the opening at the top, like a lid, or with a door on one side. If the cage is to be used for fairly active insects and it is necessary to get into the cage frequently, it should be provided with a sleeve (Figure 36–25A).

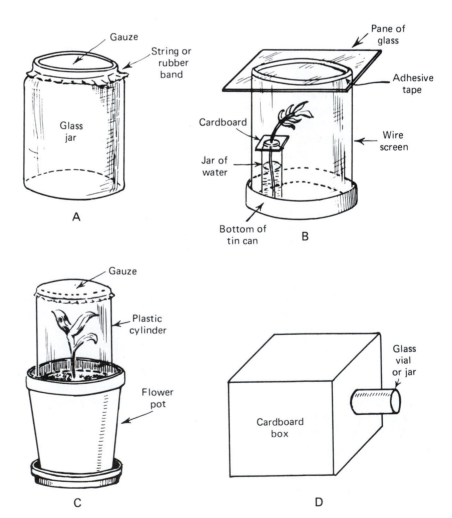

Figure 36–24.   Some types of insect cages. **A,** jar cage; **B,** cylindrical screen cage; **C,** "flowerpot" cage; **D,** an emergence box.

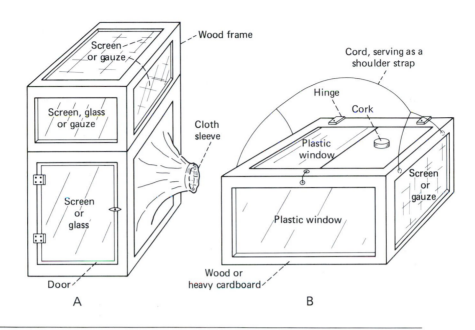

Figure 36–25. Insect cages. **A,** sleeve cage; **B,** a field carrying cage.

When one is rearing a plant-feeding insect, and the plant upon which it feeds is not too large, the insect can be reared in a "flowerpot" cage (Figure 36–24C). The plant is planted in a flowerpot or a large tin can, and a cylinder of glass, plastic, or screen is placed around the plant and covered at the top with gauze.

An emergence box such as that shown in Figure 36–24D works well for rearing adults from larvae living in debris, soil, excrement, and other materials. The material containing the larvae is placed in the box, which is then closed tightly. When the adults

emerge, they are attracted by the light coming into the box through the vial and go into the vial.

The best way to rear some insects is to leave them in their habitat in the field and cage them there. Many types of cages can be constructed around an insect in the field. In the case of a plant-feeding insect, a cage consisting of a roll of clear plastic or fine screen, with gauze at each end, may be placed around that part of the plant containing the insect (Figure 36–26B), or a cage made of window screen on a wooden framework may be built about part of the plant. Many plant-feeding insects can be

Figure 36–26. Methods of caging insects in the field. **A,** a tanglefoot barrier on a leaf, for small nonflying insects; **B,** a cage of plastic and gauze for caging insects on their food plant. (**A,** courtesy of Davidson.)

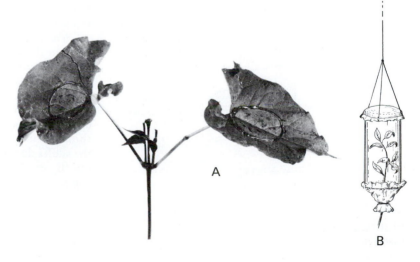
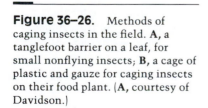

confined on a certain part of a plant by means of barriers of some sort, such as Tanglefoot bands (Figure 36–26A). Aquatic insects can be reared in cages of screen submerged in their habitat. The screen should be fine enough to prevent the escape of the insect but coarse enough to allow food material to enter.

Cages made of heavy cardboard or wood, gauze, and plastic can easily be fitted with a shoulder strap and used to bring living material from the field into the laboratory or classroom. With a carrying cage such as the one shown in Figure 36–25B, large materials can be put into the cage by lifting the lid, or single insects may be put into the box through the hole in the lid.

When one is rearing insects indoors, he must usually make sure that the conditions of temperature and humidity are satisfactory and that sufficient food and water are provided. Many insects, such as leaf-eating caterpillars, must be regularly provided with fresh food. Fresh leaves must be added every day or so, or there must be some way of keeping large amounts of foliage fresh in the cage for several days at a time. If the insect requires water, the water may be provided by means of a beaker inverted in a petri dish (Figure 36–27); by a vial full of water, plugged with cotton, and lying on its side in the cage; by a sponge soaked with water; or by some similar means.

Peterson (1953) describes a great variety of cages and other devices for rearing insects, both in the laboratory and in the field.

Some Insects Easily Reared. Some of the easiest insects to rear indoors are those that normally live indoors, for example, the insects that attack flour, meal, or other stored food products. They may be kept and reared in the original container of the food material or in a glass jar covered with fine gauze. It is usually not necessary to provide these insects with moisture. The various stages of the insect can be obtained by sifting the meal, and some of these can be added to fresh meal to keep the culture going.

Cockroaches are excellent insects for rearing, since they are fairly large and active, most people are familiar with them, and in most places they are abundant and easily obtained. A culture may be started by trapping some adults (page 753). Cockroaches can be reared in various types of containers, a large glass or plastic jar covered with gauze, or even an open box, provided the box is several centimeters deep and the upper 50 or 75 mm of the sides is smeared with petroleum jelly so that the cockroaches cannot climb out. These insects are practically omnivorous, and many different types of material will serve as suitable food. Dog biscuits make a good food. Plenty of water should be provided.

Many types of insects that have aquatic immature stages can be reared easily from the immature to the adult stage. The type of aquarium needed will depend on the type of insect being reared. Small forms feeding on organic debris or microorganisms can be reared in containers as small as vials. Larger ones, particularly predaceous forms, require larger containers. Larvae or pupae of mosquitoes, for example, can be kept in small containers in some of the same water in which they were found, with a cover over the container to prevent the escape of the adults. When vials are used, the simplest cover is a plug of cotton. In many cases it is necessary to simulate the insect's habitat in the aquarium (for example, have sand or mud in the bottom and have some aquatic plants present), and in the case of predaceous insects, such as dragonfly nymphs, smaller animals must be provided as food. The water must be aerated for some aquatic types. In maintaining an aquarium, one should strive to keep all the conditions in the aquarium as close as possible to conditions in the animal's normal habitat.

When one is attempting to maintain aquatic insects in the laboratory generation after generation, special provision must be made for the different life-history stages that frequently require special food, space, or other conditions. Some mosquitoes are relatively easy to maintain in culture in the laboratory, especially species that normally breed continuously through the warmer parts of the year, and in which the adults do not require a large space for their mating flights. The yellow fever mosquito, *Aèdes aegýpti*, is easily cultured in the laboratory.[2] At a tem-

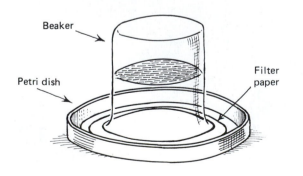

Beaker
Petri dish
Filter paper

Figure 36–27. A method of providing water for caged insects.

[2]Since this species is an important disease vector, special precautions should be taken to prevent the escape of any individuals reared.

perature of 85°F (30°C) the development from egg to adult requires only 9–11 days. The females must obtain a blood meal before they will produce eggs. A person's arm can provide this meal, but a laboratory animal such as a rabbit (with the hair shaved from a portion of its body) is better. The adults are allowed to emerge in cages with a capacity of about 0.028 m³ (1 ft³). A solution of honey in the cage will provide food for the males (which do not feed on blood) and for the females before their blood meal.

A small dish of water is placed in the cage for egg laying. If paper or wooden blocks are placed in this water, the eggs will be deposited on these at the margin of the water as it recedes. These eggs will usually hatch within 10 to 20 minutes after they are placed in water at room temperature, even after months of desiccation. If the larvae are reared in large numbers, they are best reared in battery jars. As many as 250 larvae can be reared in a 150 mm battery jar half-filled with water. The larvae can be fed ground dog biscuit, which is sprinkled on the surface of the water daily. For the first-instar larvae, 30–35 milligrams should be used daily. This amount should be increased for successive instars up to 140–150 milligrams daily for fourth-instar larvae. Pupation of the fourth-instar larvae takes place 7–9 days after the eggs hatch, and adults emerge about 24 hours later.

It is usually fairly easy to rear adult insects from galls. The important thing in rearing most gall insects is to keep the gall alive and fresh until the adults emerge. The plant containing the gall can be kept fresh by putting it in water, or the gall may be caged in the field. If the gall is not collected until the adults are nearly ready to emerge (as determined by opening a few), it can simply be placed inside a glass jar, in a vial of water, and the jar covered with gauze. This same procedure can be used to rear out adults of leaf miners that pupate in the leaf. If the leaf miner pupates in the soil (for example, certain sawflies), the plant containing the insect should be grown in a flowerpot cage.

Adults of some wood-boring insects are easily reared out. If the insect bores into drying or dried wood, the wood containing the larvae can be placed in an emergence box like that shown in Figure 36–24D. If it bores only in living wood, the adults can be obtained by placing some sort of cage over the emergence holes (in the field).

Termite cultures are easily maintained in the laboratory and are of value in demonstrating the social behavior and the wood-eating and fungus-cultivating habits of these insects. Various types of containers can be used for termite culture, but the best for demonstration purposes is either a battery jar or a glass-plate type of container (Figure 36–28). A termite colony will last quite a while without queens in either type of container, but will prove more interesting if queens or supplemental queens are present.

If a battery jar is used, 6 mm or so of earth is placed in the bottom of the jar and a sheet of wood is placed on either side of the jar. Balsa wood is the best because the termites become established in it quickly. Thin, narrow strips of a harder wood are placed on each side between the balsa wood and the glass, and pieces are placed between the sheets of balsa wood to hold them in place. Termites placed in such a container become established in a few hours. They tunnel through the earth and the wood and build fungus "gardens" (which are apparently an important source of nitrogen and vitamins) between the wood and the glass. The wood will be destroyed in a few weeks and must be replaced. Water must be added every few days. A pad of cotton can be thoroughly moistened and placed between the glass and the wood at the top of each side.

A glass-plate type of container is somewhat similar to the ant nest described later, but has a metal rather than a wood frame (Figure 36–28). The container should be about 0.3 m wide, 0.3 m high, and 13 mm thick, and it should have a pan at the base to hold it upright. No earth need be used in this type of container. A piece of balsa wood is placed in the container with narrow strips inserted between it and the two glass plates (front and rear). The termites are placed in the space between the wood and glass. A thin pad of cotton batting is placed over the top of the wood, between the two glass plates, and this is

Figure 36–28. A glass-plate type of container for rearing termites.

thoroughly soaked with water about twice a week. The fungus gardens are maintained here as in the battery-jar culture.

The chief problem encountered in rearing caterpillars is that of providing suitable food. Because many caterpillars feed only on certain species of plants, it is necessary to know the food plant of a caterpillar one wishes to rear. Caterpillars may be reared in almost any sort of cage, provided the cage is cleaned and fresh food is provided regularly. Plant food can be kept fresh longer if it is put in a small jar of water inside the cage. A cover on the top of the water jar, around the stem of the plant, will prevent the caterpillars from falling into the water (Figure 36–24B). If the caterpillar is one that requires special conditions for pupation, the conditions must be provided. Butterfly larvae will usually pupate on the leaves or on the sides or top of the cage. Most moth larvae will pupate in the corner of the cage or under debris of some sort. Moth larvae that pupate in the ground (for example, the larvae of sphinx moths) should be reared in a cage containing several centimeters of soil.

Many of the larger moths pupate in the fall and emerge as adults in the spring, and their cocoons can be collected in the fall. If these cocoons are brought indoors in the fall, they may dry out or the adults may emerge in the middle of the winter (though the second possibility may not be objectionable). The drying-out can be prevented by putting the cocoons in a jar that has 25 mm or so of soil in the bottom and sprinkling the soil and cocoon with water about once a week. To keep the moths from emerging in the middle of winter, they may be kept in screen cages (preferably cages containing some dirt or debris) outdoors (for example, on the outside windowsill of a room). If an emerging moth kept in an outdoor cage is a female, and if it emerges at a time when other moths of its kind are on the wing, it will often attract male moths from a considerable distance.

Because of their social behavior, ants make very interesting animals to maintain in indoor cages. The simplest type of ant cage, particularly for display, is a narrow vertical cage with a wooden framework and glass sides (Figure 36–29). This is filled with an ant-soil mixture obtained by digging up an ant hill, preferably a small one under a stone or board. This mixture should contain all stages and castes if possible. The queen can usually be recognized by her

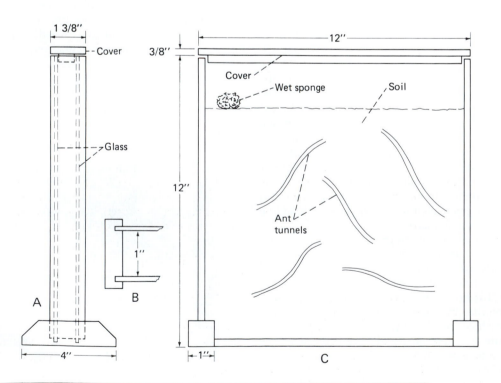

Figure 36–29. Vertical type of ant cage. **A,** end view; **B,** top view of one end showing cage construction; **C,** front view.

Figure 36–30.   An observation bee hive.

larger size. The glass sides of the cage should be darkened by covering them with some opaque material; otherwise, all the tunnels the ants make will be away from the glass and not visible. Food and moisture must be provided. Food can be provided by putting a few insects into the cage from time to time or by putting a few drops of diluted molasses or honey on a small sponge or wad of cotton in the cage. Moisture can be provided by keeping a wet sponge or wad of cotton on the underside of the lid or on top of the dirt.

An observation beehive makes an excellent class demonstration. It can be set up inside a classroom window, and the bees can come and go at will, yet all that goes on inside the hive can be observed. Space does not permit a detailed description of how an observation beehive is constructed, but Figure 36–30 shows what it is like. One who wishes to set up an observation beehive should get in touch with a local beekeeper and ask for help and suggestions.

There are a number of insects that will prove interesting to rear or maintain for a short time in captivity. Singing insects such as crickets, katydids, or cicadas may be kept caged for a time with rela-

tively little difficulty. If case-making insects are caged, it will often be possible to observe how the cases are made, and perhaps special materials (such as colored bits of glass for caddisfly larvae usually using sand grains) may be provided for the case. Caging predaceous insects with their prey (particularly mantids), and parasitic insects with their hosts, will demonstrate these interrelationships. With a little knowledge of a species' food habits and habitat requirements, the ingenious student can usually devise methods of rearing almost any type of insect.

Marking Insects

The practice of marking animals so that individuals or groups can be subsequently recognized has been used in studies of many kinds of animals and has yielded a great deal of information about the animals marked, in some cases information that could not have been obtained by any other method. With larger animals such as birds (by banding), mammals (by tagging, tattooing, ear marking, and other methods), and fish (by gill tagging), each animal is marked differently and can be individually recognized. With insects, some methods involve the marking of mass lots of individuals; others involve the marking of insects individually.

The small size of most insects makes it impractical to mark them with any sort of numbered tag. Consequently most of the marking of insects, especially small insects, consists of marking mass lots of individuals. Flies that are live-trapped may be sprayed with various dyes (acid fuchsin, eosin, methylene green, and others) and released. The use of different colors serves to mark lots released from different points or at different times. Some insects can be marked with radioactive materials by feeding the adults or larvae with these materials. The marked individuals are identified by means of special instruments designed to detect radioactivity.

Some types of insects can be marked so that individuals can be recognized. Numbered tags have been used to mark Lepidóptera, and the largest program of marking Lepidóptera has been with the monarch butterfly (Urquhart 1960). Many thousands of monarchs have been marked, using paper tags 17 by 7 mm in size (made of specially treated paper and using a special adhesive) folded over the leading edge of the front wing near the body. The most distant

recovery of a marked monarch was an individual marked in Ontario and recovered 3010 km (1870 miles) away, in Mexico, about four months after it was marked.

Insects such as bees can be marked on the thorax with dots of different-colored enamel, the color and positions of each dot representing a particular digit. Insects such as dragonflies and damselflies can be marked with dots on the wing (Figure 36–31). The dots, of a fast-drying material like nail polish or India ink, are put on with a fine brush or pointed stick. Individual insects can also be marked by cutting off certain sections of certain legs or by cutting characteristic notches in the wings.

A great deal can be learned about the habits and behavior of an insect by the use of marking techniques, for example, length of life, mating habits, territorial behavior, movements and flight range, and changes in color or habits with increasing age of the adult. With adequate data on the recaptures of marked individuals, it is sometimes possible to estimate populations and the rate of population turnover resulting from emergence and deaths or from movements of individuals into or out of a given study area.

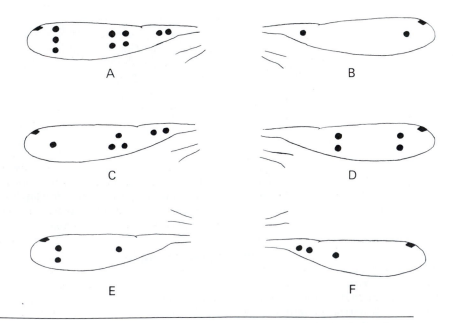

Figure 36–31. A method of marking damselfly wings. Dots may be placed at three locations on the wing: proximal to the nodus (one or two dots), just distal to the nodus (one to four dots), and just proximal to the stigma (one to three dots). Each insect marked has an identifying number consisting of two letters (indicating which wing is marked) and three digits (indicating the number of dots in each of the three locations on the wing). The specimens shown here are identified as follows: **A,** LF243; **B,** RF101; **C,** LF231; **D,** RF022; **E,** LH012; **F,** RH210. (From Borror 1934).

The basic formula for calculating populations from the recaptures of marked individuals is relatively simple. If a given sample consisting of M individuals is collected in a given area, marked, and released, then M/P of the population is marked (where P is the total population of the area). If this population is sampled again later, assuming that none of the marked individuals has died, that no new individuals have emerged, and that the marked individuals have become uniformly dispersed over the sampling area, then the proportion of the second sample that is marked is the same as it was when the marked individuals were first released. If the total number in the second sample is represented by C, and the number of marked individuals in this sample is represented by M', then the proportion of the second sample that is marked is M'/C. Thus,

$$\frac{M}{P} = \frac{M'}{C}$$

Therefore,

$$P = \frac{M \times C}{M'}$$

or

total population

$$= \frac{\text{(number marked) (total recaptured)}}{\text{number of marked individuals recaptured}}$$

In most ecological studies of a particular insect, some technique of marking can be used to advantage. A high school biology class, camp nature-study class, or similar group might undertake a study involving marking as a group project. There are many insects in every neighborhood that could be marked either in mass lots or individually. Not only would such a project arouse considerable interest, since many people would be on the lookout for the marked insects, but a great deal of information about the insect might be obtained from the study.

Censuses of Insect Populations

It is seldom practical to make a census of an insect population in a field by counting every insect. Most field studies involve some method of estimating the population from samples. Sampling techniques can be designed to estimate the total population in a given area, or they can be designed to indicate comparative populations. The former involves making accurate counts on sample areas that are representative of the entire area studied, and the latter involves using some standard sampling procedure that, when used at different times or in different places,

gives information on population trends or differences. The particular method used in any case will depend on the nature of the area chosen for census and the species in which the investigator is interested.

In cases where the total population in an area such as a field is to be estimated, the insects in a number of small sample areas are collected and counted. A cylinder covering an area of about 0.093 m² (1 ft²) is put down over the vegetation, and a fumigant is introduced into the cylinder to stun or kill the insects caught there. Then all the material inside the cylinder, together with the soil below it to some standard depth, is taken to the laboratory and examined, and the insects (and perhaps other animals as well) are carefully counted. The total population of the area is calculated from several such samples. The accuracy of this method depends on the number and the representativeness of the samples. The number of samples taken will usually depend on the amount of time the investigator has for this study.

Most of the methods used to estimate field populations, particularly in cases where the investigator is interested in only one or a few species, involve procedures designed to count a standard percentage of the population. This percentage may be unknown, but it is possible to determine population trends or to compare the populations of different areas by this method. The sampling techniques used will depend largely on the habits of the species concerned. A common method of sampling the populations on low vegetation is to take a given number of standard sweeps with an insect net and count the catch. For other insects the investigator may count the insects (or points of insect injury) on a certain number of plants, fruits, or leaves. Traps may be used in some cases to determine population trends or differences. Many different sorts of counting techniques may be used in studies of this sort, and in any given study the techniques must be adapted to the characteristics of the species being studied. The aim in each case is to count a uniform percentage of the population.

In some cases it may be possible to obtain a fairly accurate estimate of total population of a given species in a given area by means of marking. This technique was discussed in the preceding section.

Photographing Insects

Photographing insects, especially in color, has become a common practice of both the professional entomologist and the layman. Insect photographs are used extensively to illustrate books, bulletins, or journal articles, for class use, and for illustrating public lectures. Many books (for example, Ross 1953) have been written about the photography of insects and other natural history subjects, so we need not go into this subject in detail here.

A large assortment of lenses, filters, adapters, and synchronized flash and other lighting equipment is currently available, so that the photographer can select almost anything needed to photograph either the entire insect or a small part of it. Lenses are available for almost any size of magnification that may be desired.

Pictures of dead or mounted insects may be useful for some purposes, but pictures of living insects, or at least insects that *look* alive and are in a natural pose, are far better. Taking such pictures is often a difficult problem, but it may be solved in one of two general ways: (1) by using equipment permitting a very short exposure time, and getting as close as possible without disturbing the insect; and (2) by stupefying the insect temporarily so that more time is available for taking the photograph. Using various chemicals (for example, CO_2) or chilling the insect, may serve to condition it for this type of photographic exposure. It is often possible to get a good picture by training the camera on a spot where the insect will eventually alight and then waiting for the insect to alight there. Many insects may be photographed by aiming the camera at a flower and photographing the insects when they come to the flower.

Photomicrographic equipment (camera, lighting, and so on) has been developed that can be attached to (or built into) a microscope. Such equipment enables one to photograph very minute insects, or parts of insects, at high magnification. The scanning electron microscope (SEM) is another piece of equipment that produces pictures of very high magnification, often showing details that cannot be seen with an ordinary microscope.

One can get pictures of considerable entomological interest without photographing any insects at all. Insect nests or cocoons, damaged leaves or other objects, wood-borer tunnels, and similar objects make excellent photographic material and are usually much easier to photograph than living insects.

Photographing insects has become a hobby with many naturalists and camera enthusiasts, who choose insects as well as flowers and birds because of their color patterns or because they are intrigued by the habits and biology of these animals.

Drawing Insects

The student will sooner or later have occasion to make drawings of insects or insect structures, either for personal notes, as a part of a laboratory exercise, or as part of a research report prepared for publication. One need not be a natural artist to prepare good drawings of insects. The first aim of entomological drawing is accuracy rather than artistry, and simple line drawings often serve better than elaborately shaded or wash drawings.

The student should strive primarily for accuracy in drawings of insects or insect structures. A gifted artist can make a freehand drawing that is fairly accurate, but most people require some sort of mechanical aid to obtain accuracy. There are several devices and techniques by which one can turn out an accurately proportioned drawing with a minimum of effort. These include the use of a camera lucida, a projection apparatus, cross-hatching, and careful measurements of the specimen to be drawn. A camera lucida (Figure 36–32) is a device that fits over the eyepiece of a microscope. It contains a system of prisms and mirrors so arranged that, by looking through it, the observer sees both the object under the microscope and the paper on which the drawing is to be made, and can draw exactly what he or she sees through the microscope. It takes a little practice to learn how to use a camera lucida, but a person who has gotten the knack of it can turn out accurate drawings rather rapidly. A camera lucida is a rather expensive piece of equipment and is likely to be available only in well-equipped university research laboratories.

Any insect or insect structure that is fairly flat and translucent can be drawn by projection. The object to be drawn is projected by means of a photographic enlarger, projection lantern, or other projec-

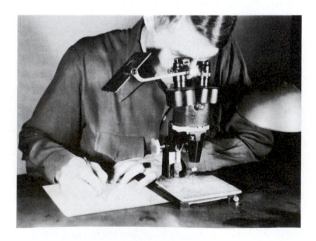

Figure 36–32.   The camera lucida in use.

tion apparatus onto a sheet of paper, and the drawing is traced over the projected image. This is the ideal method of making drawings of insect wings, which can be mounted between two glass slides. Elaborate projectors can be obtained that will give magnifications of from four to five up to several hundred, but they are rather expensive. Photographic enlargers, slide projectors, or microprojectors can be used if one does not want too much magnification.

The cross-hatching principle can be used for making drawings at a different scale. The object to be drawn is observed through a grid of crossed lines and drawn on coordinate paper, the detail of the object being put in one square at a time. For drawing a macroscopic object, a grid made of crossed threads can be set up in front of the object. For microscopic objects, a transparent disk on which fine cross-lines are scratched is put into the eyepiece of the microscope. For copying a drawing at a different scale, a grid of one scale is put over the drawing to be copied, and the details of the drawing are copied one square at a time on coordinate paper that has a different scale. With a good photocopier reductions or enlargments can also be easily made.

A wall chart or any greatly enlarged drawing can be made from a text figure either by projection or by the cross-hatching method. Text drawings can be projected by an opaque projector and traced, or they can be enlarged on a chart by using the grid principle described in the preceding paragraph.

A person who does not have any of these mechanical aids can achieve a considerable degree of accuracy by carefully measuring the specimen to be drawn and then making the drawing agree with these measurements. Measurements of small objects should be made with dividers.

The simplest way to obtain a symmetrical drawing, when one is drawing an animal (or part of an animal) that is bilaterally symmetrical, is to make only the right or left half of the drawing from the specimen and then to trace the other half from the first side.

Whether or not a drawing should contain some sort of shading depends on what one wishes to show. Many drawings of insect structures (for example, most of the drawings in this book showing anatomical characters) will show what they are intended to show without any shading, or perhaps with a few well-placed lines. If one wishes to show contour or surface texture, as would be shown in a photograph, more elaborate shading will be necessary. This shading may be done by stippling (a series of dots, as in Figure 6–30), parallel or crossed lines (for example, the eyes in Figure 14–10), a series of dots and lines (for example, Figure 25–12), or the use of a special

type of drawing paper containing tiny raised areas (stipple board, coquille board, Ross board, and so on, which were used in preparing such drawings as those in Figures 28–57 and 28–69). There are press-on sheets of various types of shading, stippling, lines, cross-hatching, and other patterns, which provide a quick yet satisfactory method of obtaining shading and texture in drawings.

One who is preparing a drawing for publication should keep in mind the method by which the drawing will be reproduced and the character of the publication in which it will appear. Most printed illustrations are reproduced by either a zinc etching, a halftone, or photo-offset. The zinc process is used for line drawings. It reproduces only black and white, and the original must be made with India ink. Photographs are reproduced by means of halftones. A halftone plate is made by photographing through a screen the picture to be reproduced, and the printed illustration is made up of a series of tiny dots. In the photo-offset process black-and-white drawings and photographs are reproduced about equally well. Fine lines in a black-and-white drawing are usually reproduced better by photo-offset than by a zinc etching. Drawings prepared for publication are ordinarily made about twice the size at which they will be reproduced, sometimes larger. The subsequent reduction tends to eliminate minor irregularities in the original drawing. If the reduction is very great, particularly in a zinc reproduction, the fine lines will disappear, or lines close together on the original drawing will appear run together in the printed drawing.

The student who wishes to learn how to prepare good drawings should study the better drawings in textbooks and research papers. By studying carefully the details of such drawings, he will learn some of the tricks of giving an effect of contour with a minimum of shading, and he will learn the methods of shading that best produce the desired effects. He will also learn something of the preferred style of arranging and labeling drawings.

The Projection of Insect Materials

Any insect or insect part that is not too big or too opaque can be projected by means of an ordinary slide projector or microprojector. All that is necessary is to have the material on a slide or in some form that can be put into the projector. Projected materials are very useful teaching devices, and while many slides for projection can be obtained from supply houses, many can be made by the student or teacher.

Wing Slides

The wings are the insect parts that are the easiest to prepare for projection and that often give a better projection than one made by photography. Most insect wings are transparent or nearly so, and, when projected, show the venation beautifully. Most colored wings, when the coloring is in the wing membrane, show this color upon projection as well as or better than a colored photographic transparency. Wings that are thick and opaque, such as the elytra of beetles, do not project very well unless they are first cleared (see page 762). Wings of Lepidóptera must be cleared or bleached before they are mounted if the projection is designed to show venation. The procedures involved in this process have been discussed previously (page 595).

Most insect wings mounted for projection can be broken off a dried insect and mounted (dry) between two 50-by-50-mm glass slides. This process generally takes only a few minutes, and the mounted wings will last indefinitely. If the wings removed from a dried insect are folded (for example, as in Orthóptera, Plecóptera, and some other insects), they must be unfolded and flattened before being mounted. However, they must first be softened or relaxed, or attempts to unfold them will only tear the wings. Such wings can usually be relaxed with a few drops of alcohol or relaxing fluid (see page 755). After the wing is flattened out (on one 50-by-50-mm slide), it should be allowed to dry before the cover slide is added and the slide bound.

Wings mounted for projection between 50-by-50-mm slides should be oriented in a standard fashion, as shown in the wing drawings in this book. The slide is labeled on the outside, generally on the binding tape.

Slides of Other Insect Parts

Almost any insect part that is more or less flattened and not too opaque can be mounted between 50-by-50-mm slides or on a microscope slide and projected—for example, mouthparts, legs, antennae, genitalia, or other parts. Structures that are particularly opaque should be cleared (in KOH) before they are mounted.

Insects or insect parts that are mounted on microscope slides can be projected with a microprojector, or by means of a 50-by-50-mm slide projector if a special carriage is made for the slide (Figure 36–33). The projection of a microscope slide with a 50-by-50-mm slide projector is generally not very satisfactory unless the specimen on the slide is at least 6 mm long.

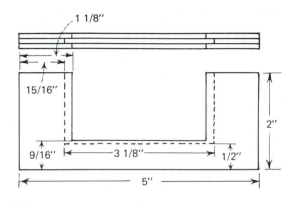

Figure 36–33. A carriage for microscope slides, for projection in a slide projector.

Elaborate and expensive microprojectors for projecting minute organisms on microscope slides are available from supply houses handling optical equipment, but a fairly satisfactory microprojector can be made with a microscope, a slide projector with a strong bulb (300–500 watts), some opaque cloth, and a mirror. A diagram of such a microprojector is shown in Figure 36–34. The cloth is used over the space between the projector and the substage of the microscope and around the substage, to prevent the escape of light. Such a setup will give a fairly clear field up to 0.9 meter or more in diameter, and in a well-darkened room magnifications of up to 100 times can be used. A somewhat more elaborate homemade microprojector is described by H. S. Seifert in *Turtox News* 29(1):30–33 (1951).

Projection of Living Insects

Small aquatic insects can be placed in a slide-sized water cell (Figure 36–35) and projected with almost any slide projector. The result is like a motion picture. The materials for making such a cell cost less than 10 cents.

Such a cell can be made with two 50-by-50-mm slides, which can be purchased at any photographic supply store, and narrow strips of single-weight window glass. These strips are cut 8 mm ($\frac{5}{16}$ inch) wide, with the strips at the bottom 50 mm ($1\frac{15}{16}$ inches) long and those at the sides 42 mm ($1\frac{5}{8}$ inches) long. The sides and bottom of the cell are made of two thicknesses of this glass, making the inside of the cell 4.8 mm ($\frac{3}{16}$ inch) thick. Any good waterproof cement (for example, household cement) may be used in putting the cell together. The trick in making a cell of this sort is to make it watertight, and pieces

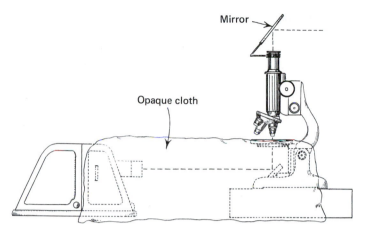

Mirror

Opaque cloth

Figure 36–34. Diagram of a homemade microprojector. The opaque cloth is fastened tightly around the projector and around the base of the microscope to prevent the escape of light.

should be cemented together carefully. A strip of wood could be used in place of the strips of glass, or the entire cell could be made of plastic instead of glass, but glass is the preferred material.

If the slide carriage of the projector will not take this cell (and it probably won't, remove the carriage and insert a narrow strip of thin wood or heavy cardboard into the bottom of the slide carriage aperture, in such a way that the cell will rest on this strip. The cell is filled to about 6 mm from the top with water, the organisms to be projected are added, and the cell is inserted into the projector. In some

projectors this cell will heat up after 10 or 15 minutes of use; hence it is advisable to have one or two extra cells that can be used alternately to avoid overheating. The image on the screen will be upside down, but this is a minor detail. If one desires it right side up, it can be inverted by means of mirrors.

Sources of Information

Information on insects is available in the form of literature published by various federal and state organizations, from various private organizations such as supply houses, museums, and societies, and from a great mass of books and periodicals. Much of this literature will be available in a good library, and a good bit of it can be obtained at little or no cost to the student or teacher. Information is also available from contacts with other people who are interested in insects—amateurs and workers in universities, museums, and experiment stations. Materials such as slides, movies, and exhibits are available from supply houses, museums, and often various state or private agencies.

Government Publications

Many government publications are available to the public free of charge, and others can frequently be obtained free through a senator or congressman. Publications for sale are available at a nominal cost. There is a wealth of literature on insects available from the government.

Information on the publications of various governmental agencies can be obtained from the Divi-

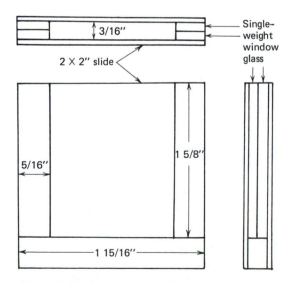

3/16″

2 X 2″ slide

Single-weight window glass

5/16″

1 5/8″

1 15/16″

Figure 36–35. A water cell for the projection of small living insects by means of a slide projector.

sion of Public Documents, Government Printing Office, Washington, D.C. 20402. This office publishes a number of lists of publications (one is on insects), which are available without cost. Most government publications on insects are published by the U.S. Department of Agriculture, and information on the publications of this department may be obtained from the following sources: (1) List 11, *List of the Available Publications of the U.S. Department of Agriculture* (revised every year or so), available from the U.S. Department of Agriculture, Washington, D.C. 20250; (2) various indexes published by the USDA; (3) indexing journals, such as the *Agricultural Index* and *Bibliography of Agriculture*; and (4) the *Monthly List of Publications and Motion Pictures*, formerly published monthly but now published every two months (available free from the USDA).

The federal government has many publications dealing wholly or in part with insects. These include several serial publications, such as the *Journal of Agricultural Research* (semimonthly, discontinued since 1949), *The Experiment Station Record* (monthly, discontinued since 1946), and *Bibliography of Agriculture* (monthly). Some publications, such as the USDA yearbooks and various annual reports, appear once a year. Publications of a great many series appear irregularly. Among those that frequently deal with insects are the bulletins, farmers' bulletins, technical bulletins, circulars, and miscellaneous publications of the USDA and the publications of the Smithsonian Institution and the U.S. National Museum.

State Publications

Many of the publications of state agencies are available free to residents of that state. In some states there are several agencies whose publications would be of interest to the student or teacher of entomology, particularly the state agricultural experiment station, the state extension service, the state departments of education and conservation, the state biological or natural history survey, and the state museum. Information on the publications available from these agencies can usually be obtained by writing to the agencies directly. The publications of various state agencies are listed in the *Monthly Check List of State Publications*, which is published by the Library of Congress.

Many state agricultural experiment stations are closely associated with the state agricultural college and are located in the same town. The state extension service is nearly always a part of the state agricultural college. State departments of education or conservation are usually located in the state capital.

State museums are usually located in the state capital or in the same town as the state university. Most state universities have museums that contain insect collections and that often publish papers on insects. State biological surveys are usually associated with the state university or the state agricultural college.

The locations of the state agricultural experiment stations and the state agricultural extension services in the 50 states are given in Table 36–1, with zip codes given in parentheses. Many states have one or more branch stations in addition to the principal experiment station, but only the principal station is listed. The agricultural extension services in the various states are associated with the state university or state agricultural college.

Miscellaneous Agencies

Biological supply houses are useful sources of equipment, material, and often publications of interest to an entomologist. All supply houses publish catalogs, which are sent free or at a nominal cost to teachers and schools. These catalogs are of value in indicating what can be obtained from the supply houses, and many of their illustrations will suggest things that ingenious students or teachers can prepare themselves.

A list of the supply houses handling entomological equipment and supplies is given on page 787. Some of these (for example, General Biological and Carolina Biological Supply House) put out a monthly publication that is sent free to teachers. These publications often contain articles of a technical nature as well as suggestions for the teacher. General Biological Supply House also publishes a series of leaflets called Turtox Service Leaflets, which cover a variety of subjects, and many of them are of value to the student or teacher of entomology.

Many societies, museums, and research institutions publish material that is useful to entomologists. Entomological societies (see the following), state biological survey organizations, and organizations such as the National Audubon Society (950 Third Ave., New York, N.Y. 10022) will send lists of their publications on request.

Directories of Entomologists

Anyone interested in insects will find it profitable to become acquainted with others who have similar interests. A person who is located near a university, museum, or experiment station should become acquainted with the workers there who are interested in insects. Persons throughout the country who are interested in various phases of entomology can often be located by consulting the membership lists of the various entomological societies, which are usually published at intervals in the societies' journals or various directories. Some of the most useful directories of people working in entomology and other biological fields are mentioned here. They are usually available in a good public or university library.

Directory of Zoological Taxonomists of the World: This was published by the Society of Systematic Zoology in 1961. It contains (1) a detailed classifica-

Table 36–1
Locations of the State Agricultural Experiment Stations and the State Extension Services

State	Experiment Station	Extension Service
Alabama	Auburn (36830)	Auburn Univ., Auburn (36830)
Alaska	College (99735)	Univ. Alaska, College (99735)
Arizona	Tucson (85721)	Univ. Arizona, Tucson (85721)
Arkansas	Fayetteville (72701)	Univ. Arkansas, Fayetteville (72701)
California	Berkeley (94720)	Univ. California, Berkeley (94720)
Colorado	Fort Collins (80521)	Colorado State Univ., Fort Collins (80521)
Connecticut	New Haven (06504)	Univ. Connecticut, Storrs (06268)
Delaware	Newark (19711)	Univ. Delaware, Newark (19711)
Florida	Gainesville (32603)	Univ. Florida, Gainesville (32603)
Georgia	Experiment (30212)	Univ. Georgia, Athens (30601)
Hawaii	Honolulu (96822)	Univ. Hawaii, Honolulu (96822)
Idaho	Moscow (83843)	Univ. Idaho, Moscow (83843)
Illinois	Urbana (61801)	Univ. Illinois, Urbana (61801)
Indiana	Lafayette (47907)	Purdue Univ., Lafayette (47907)
Iowa	Ames (50010)	Iowa State Univ., Ames (50010)
Kansas	Manhattan (66504)	Kansas State Univ., Manhattan (66504)
Kentucky	Lexington (40506)	Univ. Kentucky, Lexington (40506)
Louisiana	Baton Rouge (70803)	Louisiana State Univ., Baton Rouge (70803)
Maine	Orono (04473)	Univ. Maine, Orono (04473)
Maryland	College Park (20742)	Univ. Maryland, College Park (20742)
Massachusetts	Amherst (01003)	Univ. Massachusetts, Amherst (01003)
Michigan	East Lansing (48823)	Michigan State Univ., East Lansing (48823)
Minnesota	St. Paul (55101)	Univ. Minnesota, St. Paul (55101)
Mississippi	State College (39762)	Mississippi State Univ., State College (39762)
Missouri	Columbia (65202)	Univ. Missouri, Columbia (65202)
Montana	Bozeman (59715)	Montana State Univ., Bozeman (59715)
Nebraska	Lincoln (68503)	Univ. Nebraska, Lincoln (68503)
Nevada	Reno (89507)	Univ. Nevada, Reno (89507)
New Hampshire	Durham (03824)	Univ. New Hampshire, Durham (03824)
New Jersey	New Brunswick (08903)	Rutgers Univ., New Brunswick (08903)
New Mexico	University Park (88070)	New Mexico State Univ., University Park (88070)
New York	Ithaca (14850)	Cornell Univ., Ithaca (14850)
North Carolina	Raleigh (27607)	North Carolina State Univ., Raleigh (27607)
North Dakota	Fargo (58103)	North Dakota State Univ., Fargo (58103)
Ohio	Wooster (44691)	Ohio State Univ., Columbus (43210)
Oklahoma	Stillwater (74075)	Oklahoma State Univ., Stillwater (74075)
Oregon	Corvallis (97331)	Oregon State Univ., Corvallis (97331)
Pennsylvania	University Park (16802)	Pennsylvania State Univ., University Park (16802)
Rhode Island	Kingston (02881)	Univ. Rhode Island, Kingston (02881)
South Carolina	Clemson (29631)	Clemson Univ., Clemson (29631)
South Dakota	Brookings (57007)	South Dakota State Univ., Brookings (57007)
Tennessee	Knoxville (37901)	Univ. Tennessee, Knoxville (37901)
Texas	College Station (77843)	Texas A&M Univ., College Station (77843)
Utah	Logan (84321)	Utah State Univ., Logan (84321)
Vermont	Burlington (05401)	Univ. Vermont, Burlington (05401)
Virginia	Blacksburg (24061)	Virginia Polytechnic Inst., Blacksburg (24061)
Washington	Pullman (99163)	Washington State Univ., Pullman (99163)
West Virginia	Morgantown (26506)	West Virginia Univ., Morgantown (26506)
Wisconsin	Madison (53706)	Univ. Wisconsin, Madison (53706)
Wyoming	Laramie (82071)	Univ. Wyoming, Laramie (82071)

tion of the animal kingdom, with a list of the specialists working on each group, and (2) an alphabetical list of the specialists, with their addresses. It is particularly valuable in locating someone who is an authority on a particular group of animals.

Naturalists' Directory: This is published every few years by World Natural History Publications, 1330 Dillon Heights Ave., Baltimore, Md. 21228. The entries include the name, address, and special interests and are arranged alphabetically under the various states, Canadian provinces, and many foreign countries.

Directories of the U.S. Department of Agriculture: *Directory of Organization and Field Activities of the U.S. Department of Agriculture,* USDA Agricultural Handbook No. 76; *Professional Workers in State Agricultural Experiment Stations and Other Cooperating State Institutions,* USDA Agricultural Handbook No. 305. These directories are revised every year or two and are particularly useful for determining who is located at a particular university or experiment station.

American Men and Women of Science, 16th edition (1986): The entries are listed alphabetically and include a biographical sketch.

Entomological Societies

There are a great many entomological societies in the United States, membership in which is generally open to anyone interested in entomology. The dues vary but are generally $10 or more per year. Members receive the publications of the society, notices of meetings, and newsletters. The national societies usually have meetings only once a year. Smaller local societies may have meetings at more frequent intervals.

A list of the entomological societies in the United States and Canada may be found in *Entomol. News* 42(4):126–130 (1931), and a list of the entomological societies of the world may be found in *Bull. Entomol. Soc. Amer.* 2(4):1–22 (1956). Some of the better-known entomological societies in the United States and Canada, with their addresses and principal publications, are as follows:

American Entomological Society, Academy of Natural Sciences, Philadelphia, Pa. *Transactions of the American Entomological Society,* quarterly. *Entomological News,* monthly except July and August.

Cambridge Entomological Club, Harvard University, Cambridge, Mass. *Psyche,* quarterly.

Entomological Society of America, 9301 Annapolis Road, Lanham, MD 20706 *Annals of the Ento-mological Society of America,* bimonthly. *Environmental Entomology,* bimonthly. *Journal of Economic Entomology,* bimonthly. *Bulletin of the Entomological Society of America,* quarterly.

Entomological Society of Canada, Ottawa, Ontario. *Canadian Entomologist,* monthly. This journal was begun in 1868 by the old Entomological Society of Canada; from 1871 to 1951 it was published by the Entomological Society of Ontario; from 1951 to 1960 it was published jointly by the Entomological Society of Ontario and the new Entomological Society of Canada; the latter society has published this journal since 1960.

Entomological Society of Washington, Washington, D.C. *Proceedings of the Entomological Society of Washington,* quarterly.

Florida Entomological Society, Gainesville, Fla. *The Florida Entomologist,* quarterly.

Kansas (Central States) Entomological Society, Manhattan, Kan. *Journal of the Kansas Entomological Society,* quarterly.

Michigan Entomological Society, East Lansing, Mich. *Great Lakes Entomologist* (before 1971 called *Michigan Entomologist*), published quarterly since July 1966.

New York Entomological Society, New York, N.Y. *Journal of the New York Entomological Society,* quarterly.

Pacific Coast Entomological Society, San Francisco, Calif. *The Pan-Pacific Entomologist,* quarterly.

General References

The following is a list of the more important general references, usually available in a large library, that will help one locate a particular book, periodical, or other reference on a zoological or entomological subject. Anyone planning to do a substantial amount of work in a large library should become familiar with the method of cataloging the library's holdings, and the general layout of the library (including the location of the materials one is likely to use).

Zoological Record: This is a bibliography of the world literature on zoology that has been published annually since 1864. It contains titles of papers, books, and the like, arranged alphabetically under some 19 major sections. Each of the 19 sections contains a subject index and a systematic index (to order, families, and so forth).

Biological Abstracts: This is an abstracting journal, published monthly, with the papers arranged in each issue under a number of major subject matter headings. Each volume is fully indexed. This is a very useful reference in all fields of biology.

Union List of Serials in the Libraries of the United States and Canada: This volume, with its supplements, contains a list of periodicals, with an indication of the libraries in the United States and Canada that have each periodical, and the volumes that each library has. Supplements since 1950 are under the title *New Serial Titles.* These references are useful in determining where a particular periodical may be obtained (for example, through an interlibrary loan) if it is not present in one's local library.

Index to the Literature of American Economic Entomology: This was published from 1917 to 1962, the first several volumes about every five years and the more recent volumes yearly. Volume 18 (1962), which covers the literature of 1959, is the last in this series. This is a very valuable index for entomologists. The entries in each volume are arranged alphabetically by author and subject, and the subject classification is quite detailed. The more recent volumes cover the literature from North America, Hawaii, and the West Indies.

Review of Applied Entomology: This is published monthly in two series: A, agricultural entomology; and B, medical and veterinary entomology. It is an abstracting journal of the world literature on applied entomology. The entries are not arranged in any special sequence, but each volume contains an author and a detailed subject index.

Bibliography of Agriculture: This is published monthly. It lists references, alphabetically by subject, on subjects pertaining to agriculture from all over the world. It contains a section on entomology.

Agricultural Index: This index is published monthly. It is a detailed index, alphabetically arranged by subject, to some 150 American and English periodicals and to government publications.

Bibliography of the More Important Contributions to American Economic Entomology: Parts 1 to 5 are by S. Henshaw, 1890–1896, and Parts 6 to 8 are by N. Banks, 1898–1905.

Entomological Abstracts: This is published monthly, and each yearly volume contains about 9000 abstracts. The abstracts in each issue are arranged under a variety of headings, and each volume contains a subject index.

Apiculture Abstracts: This is published quarterly. The abstracts are arranged under a variety of headings in each issue, and each volume contains a subject and an author index.

The following references, usually available in a large library, are of a more general nature than those just listed, but they are often of value to a zoologist or entomologist:

Document Catalogue: This journal is published monthly. It lists all government publications, alphabetically by author and subject, and is a comprehensive list of all government publications.

Monthly Checklist of State Publications: Publications are listed in this journal by states and departments, with an annual index by author, title, and subject. This reference is useful as a source of information on the publications of such state agencies as experiment stations, universities, wildlife departments, and the like.

The United States Catalogue and the Cumulative Book Index: This is published monthly, with cumulations at intervals. All books and pamphlets printed in English are listed alphabetically by author, title, and subject. This reference is a useful source of information on current or recent books.

Bibliographic Index: This is a journal, published quarterly. It is a bibliography of bibliographies classified by subjects arranged alphabetically.

A World Bibliography of Bibliographies: Four editions are now out, 1939–1940, 1947–1949, 1955, and 1956. This covers most separate bibliographic works published in European languages since 1740. It is general in scope and stronger in the humanities than in technical fields.

Sources of Entomological Supplies

Many of the materials needed for making an insect collection or working with insects can be home-made, but some must be obtained from a supply house. The following are some of the leading biological supply houses in the United States:

American Biological Supply Company, 1330 Dillon Heights Ave., P.O. Box 3149, Baltimore, Md. 21228.

Arthropod Specialties Co., P.O. Box 1973, Sacramento, Calif. 95809. (This company is a good source of the plastic microvials used in genitalia studies.)

Bio Metal Associates, 316 Washington St., El Segundo, Calif. 90245. Eastern Office: BioQuip East, 115 Rolling Rd., Baltimore, Md. 21228. Western Office: BioQuip West, P.O. Box 61, Santa Monica, Calif. 90406.

Carolina Biological Supply Co., (1) Burlington, N.C. 27215; (2) Powell Laboratories Division, Gladstone, Ore. 97027.

Entomological Research Institute, Lake City, Minn. 55041.

Entomological Supplies, Inc., 5655 Oregon Ave., Baltimore, Md. 21227.

General Biological Supply House, Inc., 8200 S. Hoyne Ave., Chicago, Ill. 60620.

Ward's Natural Science Establishment, Inc., P.O. Box 1712, Rochester, N.Y. 14603. Ward's of California, P.O. Box 1749, Monterey, Calif. 93942.

A great many concerns throughout the country handle optical equipment such as microscopes, laboratory supplies, and scientific instruments. Each year (usually in the fall) the American Association for the Advancement of Science, in a special issue of *Science,* publishes a "Guide to Scientific Instruments." This guide gives information on where instruments and apparatuses of various sorts can be obtained. A few of the leading suppliers of laboratory equipment (many of whom also handle entomological supplies) are as follows:

Aloe Scientific, 1831 Olive St., St. Louis, Mo. 63103.

AO Instrument Company, Eggert & Sugar Rd., Buffalo, N.Y. 14215.

Bausch and Lomb Optical Company, 77466 Bausch St., Rochester, N.Y. 14602.

Central Scientific Company, 1700 Irving Park Rd., Chicago, Ill. 60613.

The Chemical Rubber Company, 18901 Cranwood Pkwy., Cleveland, Ohio 44128.

Clay-Adams Company, 141 E. 25th St., New York, N.Y. 10010.

Cole-Parmer Instrument Company, 7330 N. Clark St., Chicago, Ill. 60626.

Dennoyer-Geppert Company, 5235 Ravenswood Ave., Chicago, Ill. 60640.

Fisher Scientific Company, 711 Forbes Ave., Pittsburgh, Pa. 15219.

General Scientific Equipment Company, Limekiln Pike and Williams Ave., Philadelphia, Pa. 19150

E. Leitz, Inc., 468 Park Ave., New York, N.Y. 10016.

Matheson Scientific, Inc., 1735 N. Ashland Ave., Chicago, Ill. 60622.

Welch Scientific Co., 7300 Linder Ave., Skokie, Ill. 60076.

Will Scientific, Inc., Box 1050, Rochester, N.Y. 14603.

References

Beirne, B. P. 1955. Collecting, preparing and preserving insects. Can. Dept. Agr. Entomol. Div. Publ. 932, 133 pp.; illus.

Blaker, A. A. 1965. Photography for Scientific Publication: A Handbook. San Francisco: Freeman, 159 pp.; illus.

Blum, M. S., and J. P. Woodring. 1963. Preservation of insect larvae by vacuum dehydration. J. Kan. Entomol. Soc. 36:96–101; illus.

Borror, D. J. 1934. Ecological studies of *Argia moesta* Hagen (Odonata) by means of marking. Ohio J. Sci. 34(2):97–108; illus.

Borror, D. J. 1948. Analysis of repeat records of banded white-throated sparrows. Ecol. Mongr. 18(3):411–430; illus.

Borror, D. J. 1958. A projection cell for small aquatic organisms. Turtox News 36(2):50–51; illus.

Borror, D. J., and A. C. Borror. 1961. Glass mounts for displaying Lepidoptera. Turtox News 39(12):298–300; illus.

Byers, G. W. 1958. Individual identification labels for pinned insect specimens. Entomol. News 69:113–116.

Byers, G. W. 1959. A rapid method for making temporary insect labels in the field. J. Lepidop. Soc. 13(2):96–98.

Cruickshank, A. D. (ed.). 1957. Hunting with the Camera. New York: Harper and Row, 215 pp.; illus. (Chap. 4, Insects, by E. S. Ross, pp. 108–134; illus.).

Delong, D. M., and R. H. Davidson. 1936. Methods of Collecting and Preserving Insects. Columbus: Ohio State University Press, 20 pp.; illus.

Edwards, J. G. 1963. Spreading blocks for butterfly wings. Turtox News 41(1):16–19; illus.

Gordh, G., and J. C. Hall. 1979. A critical point drier used as a method of mounting insects from alcohol. Entomol. News 90:57–59.

Hillcourt, W. 1950. Field Book of Nature Activities. New York: Putnam, Sons, 320 pp.; illus.

Kalmus, H. 1960. 101 Simple Experiments with Insects. Garden City, N.Y.: Doubleday, 194 pp.; illus.

Kinne, R. 1962. The Complete Book of Nature Photography. New York: A. S. Barnes, 191 pp.; illus.

Knudson, J. W. 1972. Collecting and Preserving Plants and Animals. New York: Harper and Row, 320 pp.

Levi, H. W. 1966. The care of alcoholic collections of small invertebrates. Syst. Zool. 16:183–188.

Mansuy, M. C. 1929. Collection and preservation of insects for use in the study of agriculture. USDA Farmers' Bull. 1601, 19 pp.; illus.

Martin, J. E. H. 1977. Collecting, preparing, and preserving insects, mites, and spiders. The Insects and Arachnids of Canada, Part 1, 182 pp.; illus.

Masner, L., and H. Goulet. 1981. A new model of flight-interception trap for some hymenopterous insects. Entomol. News 92:199–202; illus.

Miller, D. F., and G. W. Blaydes. 1962 (2nd ed.). Methods and Materials for Teaching Biological Sciences. New York: McGraw-Hill, 453 pp.; illus.

Needham, J. G., P. A. Galtsoff, F. E. Lutz, and P. S. Welch. 1937. Culture Methods for Invertebrate Animals. Ithaca, N.Y.: Comstock, 590 pp.; illus.

Oldroyd, H. 1958. Collecting, Preserving, and Studying Insects. New York: Macmillan, 327 pp.; illus.

Oman, P. W., and A. D. Cushman, 1948. Collection and

preservation of insects. USDA Misc. Publ. 601, 42 pp.; illus.

Orlans, F. B. 1977. Animal Care from Protozoa to Small Mammals. Reading, Mass.: Addison Wesley, 374 pp.; illus.

Papp, C. S. 1968. Scientific Illustration: Theory and Practice. Dubuque, Iowa: William C. Brown, 318 pp.; illus.

Peck, S. B., and A. E. Davies. 1980. Collecting small beetles with large-area "window" traps. Coleop. Bull. 34:237–239; illus.

Peterson, A. 1948. Larvae of Insects, Part 1: Lepidoptera and Plant-Infesting Hymenoptera. Ann Arbor, Mich.: Edwards Bros., 315 pp.; illus.

Peterson, A. 1953 (7th ed.). A Manual of Entomological Techniques. Ann Arbor, Mich.: J. W. Edwards, 367 pp.; illus.

Post, R. L., D. G. Aahus, H. F. Perkins, and G. L. Thomasson. 1969. Insect collecting manual. Dept. Entomol., N. Dak. State Univ., N. Dak. Insect Ser. Publ. 8, 36 pp.; illus.

Roe, R. M., and C. W. Clifford. 1976. Freeze-drying of spiders and immature insects using commercial equipment. Ann. Entomol. Soc. Amer. 69:497–499; illus.

Ross, E. S. 1953. Insects Close Up. Berkeley: University of California Press, 79 pp.; illus.

Sabrosky, C. W. 1937. On mounting micro-Diptera. Entomol. News 48:102–107.

Sabrosky, C. W. 1971. Packing and shipping pinned insects. Bull. Entomol. Soc. Amer. 17(1):6–8.

Smith, R. C., and R. H. Painter. 1966 (7th ed.). Guide to the Literature of the Zoological Sciences. Minneapolis: Burgess, 238 pp.

Southwood, T. R.E. 1966. Ecological Methods, with Particular Reference to the Study of Insect Populations. London: Methuen, 391 pp.; illus.

Townes, H. 1962. Design for a Malaise trap. Proc. Entomol. Soc. Wash. 64:253–262; illus.

Townes, H. 1972. A light-weight Malaise trap. Entomol. News 83:239–247; illus.

Urquhart, F. A. 1960. The Monarch Butterfly. Toronto: University of Toronto Press, 361 pp.; illus.

Valentine, J. M. 1942. On the preparation and preservation of insects with particular reference to Coleoptera. Smithson. Inst. Misc. Coll. 103(6):1–15; illus.

Wagstaffe, R., and J. H. Fidler (Eds.). 1955. The Preservation of Natural History Specimens, Vol. 1: Invertebrates. New York: Philosophical Library, 205 pp.; illus.

Woodring, J. P., and M. Blum. 1963. Freeze-drying of spiders and immature insects. Ann. Entomol. Soc. Amer. 56:138–141; illus.

Zweifel, F. W. 1961. A Handbook of Biological Illustration. Chicago: University of Chicago Press, 131 pp.; illus.

Glossary

The definitions given here apply primarily to the use of these terms in this book; elsewhere some terms may have additional or different meanings. Some terms not listed here may be found in the Index.

abdomen   The posterior of the three body divisions (Figure 3–1, *ab*).

accessory cell   A closed cell in the front wing of Lepidóptera formed by the fusion of two branches of the radius, usually the R₂ cell (Figure 34–17, *acc*).

accessory gland   A secretory organ associated with the reproductive system.

accessory pulsatile organ   Contractile organs that function to move hemolymph into and out of appendages.

accessory vein   An extra branch of a longitudinal vein (indicated by a subscript *a*; for example, an accessory of M_1 is designated M_{1a}).

acrostichal bristles   One or more longitudinal rows of small bristles along the center of the mesonotum (Díptera; Figure 32–6, *acr*).

acrosternite   The portion of a sternum anterior to the antecostal suture.

acrotergite   The portion of a tergum anterior to the antecostal suture.

aculea (pl., *aculeae*)   Minute spines on the wing membrane (Lepidóptera).

aculeate   With aculeae (Lepidóptera); with a sting (Hymenóptera).

acuminate   Tapering to a long point.

acute   Pointed; forming an angle of less than 90°.

adecticous   A type of pupa in which the mandibles are immovable and nonfunctional.

adfrontal areas   A pair of narrow oblique sclerites on the head of a lepidopterous larva (Figure 34–3, *adf*).

adventitious vein   A secondary vein, neither accessory nor intercalary, usually the result of cross veins lined up to form a continuous vein.

aedeagus   The male intromittent organ; the distal part of the phallus; penis plus parameres.

aestivation   Dormancy during a warm or dry season.

agamic   Reproducing parthenogenetically, that is, without mating.

alinotum   The notal plate of the mesothorax or metathorax of a pterygote insect (Figure 3–6, *AN*).

alula (pl., *alulae*)   A lobe at the base of the wing (Díptera; Figure 32–4, *alu*); see *calypter.*

ametabolous   Without metamorphosis.

anal   Pertaining to the last abdominal segment (which bears the anus); the posterior basal part (for example, of the wing).

anal area of the wing   The posterior portion of the wing, usually including the anal veins.

anal cell   A cell in the anal area of the wing; cell 1A (Díptera; Figure 32–4B, *A*).

anal crossing   Where A branches posteriorly from Cu + A (Odonàta; Figure 11–5, *Ac*).

anal lobe   A lobe in the posterior basal part of the wing.

anal loop   A group of cells in the hind wing of dragonflies, between Cu_2, 1A, and, 2A, which may be rounded

(Figure 11–7B), elongate (Figure 11–7C), or foot-shaped (Figure 11–5, *alp*).

anapleurite The upper and outer of the two incomplete subcoxal rings that form the thoracic pleurites.

anepimeron The portion of the anapleurite posterior to the pleural suture.

anepisternum The portion of the anapleurite anterior to the pleural suture.

annulated With ringlike segments or divisions.

anteapical Just proximad of the apex.

anteapical cell A cell in the distal part of the wing (leafhoppers; Figure 25–1, table).

anteclypeus An anterior division of the clypeus (Figure 11–8, *aclp*).

antecosta (pl., *antecostae*) An internal ridge on the anterior portion of a tergum or sternum that serves as the site of attachment of the longitudinal muscles.

antecostal suture An external groove that marks the position of the internal antecosta.

antecoxal sclerite A sclerite of the metasternum, just anterior to the hind coxae.

antenna (pl., *antennae*) A pair of segmented appendages located on the head above the mouthparts and usually sensory in function (Figure 3–15).

antennal club The enlarged distal segments of a clubbed antenna (Figure 28–3, *acl*).

antennal fossa A cavity or depression in which the antennae are located: (Figure 32–5, *af*).

antennal groove A groove in the head capsule into which the basal segment of the antenna fits (Figure 28–3, *agr*).

antennule The first antennae of Crustàcea (Figure 6–24, *antl*).

antenodal cross veins Cross veins along the costal border of the wing, between the base of the wing and the nodus, extending from the costa to the radius (Odonàta; Figure 11–5, *an*).

antepenultimate The third from the last.

antepygidial bristle One or more large bristles on the apical margin of the seventh (next to the last) tergum (Siphonáptera).

anterior Front; in front of.

anterior cross vein The r-m cross vein (Díptera; Figure 32–4B, *acv*).

anterodorsal In the front and at the top or upper side.

anteromesal In the front and along the midline of the body.

anteroventral In the front and underneath or on the lower side.

anus The posterior opening of the alimentary tract (Figure 3–22, *ans*).

aorta The anterior nonpulsatile portion of the dorsal blood vessel.

apical At the end, tip, or outermost part.

apical cell A cell near the wing tip (Figure 25–1, table; Figure 32–4B, *SM*; Figure 35–3, *AP*).

apical cross vein A cross vein near the apex of the wing (Plecóptera, Figure 20–7D, *apc*; Homóptera, Figure 25–1, table).

apodeme An invagination of the body wall forming a rigid process that serves for muscle attachment and for the strengthening of the body wall.

apolysis The separation of the epidermis from the cuticle (part of the process of molting).

apophysis (pl., *apophyses*) A tubercular or elongate process of the body wall, either external or internal (Figure 3–4, *apo*).

appendix A supplementary or additional piece or part (of the homopteran wing, see Figure 25–1, *ap*).

apterous Wingless.

apterygote A primitively wingless hexapod.

aquatic Living in water.

arcuate Bent like a bow, or arched.

arculus A basal cross vein between the radius and the cubitus (Odonàta; Figures 11–5 through 11–7, *arc*).

areole An accessory cell (see also *basal areole*).

areolet A small cell in the wing; in the Ichneumónidae, the small submarginal cell opposite the second m-cu cross vein (Figure 35–31, *are*).

arista A large bristle, usually dorsally located, on the apical antennal segment (Díptera; Figure 32–5, *ar*).

aristate Bristlelike; with an arista; aristate antenna (Figures 3–15J, 32–14A,B).

arolium (pl., *arolia*) A padlike structure at the apex of the last tarsal segment, between the claws (Orthóptera; Figure 14–4D, *aro*); a padlike structure at the base of each tarsal claw (Hemíptera; Figures 24–1, 24–3A, *aro*).

arrhenotoky A form of parthenogenesis in which females are produced from fertilized eggs, males from unfertilized eggs.

articulation A joint as between two segments or structures.

aspirator A device with which insects may be picked up by suction (Figure 36–5).

asymmetrical Not alike on the two sides.

asynchronous muscle A rapidly contracting muscle in which the individual contractions are not initiated by a neuronal impulse (compare *synchronous* or *neurogenic* muscle).

atrium (pl., *atria*) A chamber; a chamber just inside a body opening.

atrophied Reduced in size, rudimentary.

attenuated Very slender and gradually tapering distally.

auricle A small lobe or earlike structure (Hymenóptera; Figure 35–66, *au*).

auxiliary vein The subcosta (Díptera; Figure 32–4, *av*).

axilla (pl., *axillae*) A triangular or rounded sclerite laterad of the scutellum and usually just caudad of the base of the front wing (Hymenóptera; Figure 35–4, *ax*).

axillary cell A cell in the anal area of the wing (Díptera, Figure 32–4, *axc*; Hymenóptera, Figure 35–3, *AX*).

axillary sclerites The small sclerites at the base of the wing that translate deformations of the thorax into wing movements (Figure 3–11, *axs*).

band A transverse marking broader than a line.

basad Toward the base.

basal anal cell An anal cell near the wing base; a cell at the base of the wing between 1A and 2A (Plecóptera; Figure 20–1, *BA*).

basal areole A small cell at the base of the wing; the cell at the base of the wing between Sc and R (Lepidóptera; Figures 34–26 through 34–28, *BA*).

basal cell A cell near the base of the wing, bordered at least in part by the unbranched portions of the longitudinal veins; in the Díptera, one of the two cells proximad of the anterior cross vein and the discal cell (Díptera, Figure 32–4B, *B*; Hymenóptera, see Figure 35–8, *B*).

basal vein A vein in about the middle of the front wing, extending from the median vein to the subcostal or cubital vein; the first free segment of M (Hymenóptera; Figure 35–3, *bv*).

basalare (or basalar sclerite) An epipleurite located anterior to the pleural wing process.

basement membrane A noncellular membrane underlying the epidermal cells of the body wall (Figures 3–2, 3–4, *bm*).

basisternum That part of a thoracic sternum anterior to the sternacostal suture.

beak The protruding mouthpart structures of a sucking insect; proboscis (Figures 3–17 through 3–20, *bk*).

bifid Forked, or divided into two parts.

bilateral symmetry See *symmetry*.

bilobed Divided into two lobes.

bipectinate Having branches on two sides like teeth of a comb.

biramous With two branches; consisting of an endopodite and an exopodite (Crustàcea).

bisexual With males and females.

bituberculate With two tubercles or swellings.

bivalved With two valves or parts, clamlike.

blastoderm The peripheral cell layer in the insect egg following cleavage (Figure 3–37C, *bl*).

book gills The leaflike gills of a horseshoe crab (Figure 6–2, *bg*).

book lung A respiratory cavity containing a series of leaflike folds (spiders).

borrow pit A pit formed by an excavation, where earth has been "borrowed" for use elsewhere.

boss A smooth lateral prominence at the base of a chelicera (spiders).

brace vein A slanting cross vein; in Odonàta, a slanting cross vein just behind the proximal end of the stigma (Figure 11–7E, *bvn*).

brachypterous With short wings that do not cover the abdomen.

brain The anterior ganglion of the nervous system, located above the esophagus; in insects composed of the protocerebrum, deutocerebrum, and tritocerebrum.

brain hormone A chemical messenger produced by neurosecretory cells in the brain that activates the prothoracic glands to produce ecdysone (also known as PTTH or prothoracicotropic hormone).

bridge cross vein A cross vein anterior to the bridge vein (Odonàta; Figure 11–5, *bcv*).

bridge vein The vein that appears as the basal part of the radial sector, between M_{1+2} and the oblique vein (Odonàta; Figure 11–5, *brv*).

brood The individuals that hatch from the eggs laid by one mother; individuals that hatch at about the same time and normally mature at about the same time.

bucca (pl., *buccae*) A sclerite on the head below the compound eye and just above the mouth opening (Díptera; Figure 32–5, *buc*).

buccula (pl., *bucculae*) One of two ridges on the underside of the head, on each side of the beak (Hemíptera; Figures 3–17, 24–1, *buc*).

bursa copulatrix A pouch of the female reproductive system that receives the male genitalia during copulation.

bursicon A hormone involved in the process of sclerotization.

caecum (pl., *caeca*) A saclike or tubelike structure, open at only one end.

calamistrum One or two rows of curved spines on the metatarsus of the hind legs (spiders; Figure 6–7, *clm*).

calcaria Movable spurs at the apex of the tibia (Figure 14–4J,K, *clc*).

callus (pl., *calli*) A rounded swelling.

calypter (pl., *calypteres*) One or two small lobes at the base of the wing, located just above the haltere (Díptera; Figure 32–4, *cal*) (also called *squama*).

camera lucida A device enabling one to make accurate drawings of objects seen through a microscope; when it is attached to the eyepiece of a microscope (Figure 36–32), the observer can see the object under the microscope and his or her drawing paper at the same time.

campaniform sensillum A sense organ consisting of a dome-shaped cuticular area into which the sensory cell process is inserted like the clapper of a bell (Figure 3–27B).

campodeiform larva A larva shaped like the dipluran *Campòdea* (Figure 8–3), that is, elongate and flattened, with well-developed legs and antennae, and usually active.

capitate With an apical knoblike enlargement; capitate antenna (Figure 3–15F).

carapace A hard dorsal covering consisting of fused dorsal sclerites (Crustàcea; Figure 6–24, *crp*).

cardo (pl., *cardines*) The basal segment or division of a maxilla (Figure 3–16A, *cd*); one of two small laterobasal sclerites in the millipede gnathochilarium (Figure 6–32B, *cd*).

carina (pl., *carinae*) A ridge or keel.

carinate Ridged or keeled.

carnivorous Feeding on the flesh of other animals.

caste A form or type of adult in a social insect (termites, see Figure 17–2; ants, see Figure 35–83).

catapleurite The lower and inner of the two incomplete subcoxal rings that form the thoracic pleurites (also called the catepleurite, katepleurite, and coxopleurite).

catepimeron The portion of the catapleurite posterior to the pleural suture.

catepisternum The portion of the catapleurite anterior to the pleural sulcus.

caterpillar An eruciform larva; the larva of a butterfly (Figure 34–3), moth, sawfly, or scorpionfly.

caudad Toward the tail, or toward the posterior end of the body.

caudal Pertaining to the tail or posterior end of the body.

caudal filament A threadlike process at the posterior end of the abdomen.

cell A space in the wing membrane partly (an open cell) or completely (a closed cell) surrounded by veins.

cenchrus (pl., *cenchri*) Roughened pad on the metanotum of sawflies (Sýmphyta) serving to hold the wings in place when folded over the dorsum.

cephalad Toward the head or anterior end.

cephalic On or attached to the head; anterior.

cephalothorax A body region consisting of head and thoracic segments (Crustàcea and Aráchnida; Figure 6–5, *cph*).

cercus (pl., *cerci*) One of a pair of appendages at the posterior end of the abdomen (Figure 3–1, *cr*).

cervical Pertaining to the neck or cervix.

cervical sclerite A sclerite located in the lateral part of the cervix, between the head and the prothorax (Figure 3–6, *cvs*).

cervix The neck, a membranous region between the head and prothorax (Figure 3–6, *cvx*).

chaetotaxy The arrangement and nomenclature of the bristles on the exoskeleton (Díptera; Figures 32–5, 32–6).

cheek The lateral part of the head between the compound eye and the mouth (see *gena*).

chelate Pincerlike, having two opposable claws.

chelicera (pl., *chelicerae*) One of the anterior pair of appendages in arachnids (Figure 6–5, *ch*).

cheliped A leg terminating in an enlarged pincerlike structure (Crustàcea; Figure 6–24, *chp*).

chemoreceptor A sensillum capable of detecting chemicals (by olfaction and/or gustation).

chitin A nitrogenous polysaccharide formed primarily of units of N-acetyl glucosamine, occurring in the cuticle of arthropods.

chordotonal organ A sense organ, the cellular elements of which form an elongate structure attached at both ends to the body wall.

chorion The outer shell of an arthropod egg.

chrysalis (pl., *chrysalids* or *chrysalides*) The pupa of a butterfly (Figure 34–4A,B).

cibarium A preoral cavity enclosed by the labrum anterior, the hypopharynx or labium posteriorly, and the mandibles and maxillae laterally.

circumesophageal connective A nerve connecting the tritocerebral lobes of the brain with the subesophageal ganglion (Figure 3–22, *cec*).

class A subdivision of a phylum or subphylum, containing a group of related orders.

claval suture The suture of the front wing separating the clavus from the corium (Hemíptera; Figure 24–1, *cls*).

claval vein A vein in the clavus (Hemíptera, Homóptera; Figure 25–3, *clv*).

clavate Clublike, or enlarged at the tip; clavate antennae (Figure 3–15D,E).

clavus The oblong or triangular anal portion of the front wing (Hemíptera and Homóptera; Figures 24–1, 24–4, *cl*).

claw tuft A dense tuft of hairs below the claws (spiders; Figure 6–7D, *clt*).

cleft Split or forked.

cleptoparasite A parasite that feeds on food stored for the host larvae.

closed cell A wing cell bounded on all sides by veins.

closed coxal cavity One bounded posteriorly by a sclerite of the same thoracic segment (front coxal cavities, Coleóptera; Figure 28–7B), or one completely surrounded by sternal sclerites and not touched by any pleural sclerites (middle coxal cavities, Coleóptera; Figure 28–7D).

clubbed With the distal part (or segments) enlarged; clubbed antennae (Figure 3–15D–F,L,M).

clypeus A sclerite on the lower part of the face, between the frons and the labium (Figure 3–13, *clp*).

coarctate larva A larva somewhat similar to a dipterous puparium, in which the skin of the preceding instar is not completely shed but remains attached to the caudal end of the body; the sixth instar of a blister beetle, also called a pseudopupa (Figure 28–71H).

coarctate pupa A pupa enclosed in a hardened shell formed by the last larval skin (Díptera; Figure 3–44F).

cocoon A silken case inside which the pupa is formed.

collophore A tubelike structure located on the ventral side of the first abdominal segment of Collémbola.

collum The tergite of the first segment (Diplópoda; Figure 6–32A, *colm*).

colon The large intestine; that part of the hindgut between the ileum and the rectum (Figure 3–22, *cn*).

colulus A slender pointed structure lying just anterior to the spinnerets (spiders).

commensalism A living together of two or more species, none of which is injured thereby, and at least one of which is benefited.

commissure A structure (trachea or nerve) that connects the left and right sides of a segment.

common oviduct The median tube of the female internal genitalia leading from the lateral oviducts to the gonopore.

compound eye An eye composed of many individual elements or ommatidia, each of which is represented externally by a facet; the external surface of such an eye consists of circular facets that are very close together or of facets that are in contact and more or less hexagonal in shape (Figure 3–1, *e*, Figure 3–29C,D).

compressed Flattened from side to side.

concave vein A vein protruding from the lower surface of the wing.

condyle A knoblike process forming an articulation.

connate Fused together or immovably united.

connective A structure (such as a trachea or nerve) that runs from one segment to another.

constricted Narrowed.

contiguous Touching each other.

convergent Becoming closer distally.

convex vein A vein protruding from the upper surface of the wing.

corbicula (pl., *corbiculae*) A smooth area on the outer surface of the hind tibia, bordered on each side by a fringe of long curved hairs, which serves as a pollen basket (bees).

corium The elongate, usually thickened, basal portion of the front wing (Hemíptera; Figure 24–4, *cor*).

cornea The cuticular part of an eye (Figure 3–29, *cna*).

cornicle One of a pair of dorsal tubular structures on the posterior part of the abdomen (aphids; Figure 25–6C, *crn*).

corniculi (sing., *corniculus*) see *urogomphi*.

coronal suture A longitudinal suture along the midline of the vertex, between the compound eyes (Figure 3–13, *cs*).

corpus allatum (pl., *corpora allata*) One of a pair of small structures immediately behind the brain, involved in secretion of juvenile hormone (Figure 3–26, *ca*).

costa A longitudinal wing vein usually forming the anterior margin of the wing (Figure 3–10, C); a sclerotized ridge in the cuticle.

costal area The portion of the wing immediately behind the anterior margin.

costal break A point on the costa where the sclerotization is weak or lacking or the vein appears to be broken (Díptera; Figures 32–19A,B, 32–20 C–E, *cbr*).

costal cell The wing space between the costa and the subcosta.

coxa (pl., *coxae*) The basal segment of the leg (Figure 3–8, *cx*).

coxopleurite See *catapleurite*.

coxopodite The basal segment of an arthropod appendage.

coxosternum A sclerite representing the fusion of the sternum and the coxopodites of a segment.

crawler The active first instar of a scale insect (Figure 25–29B).

cremaster A spinelike or hooked process at the posterior end of the pupa, often used for attachment (Lepidóptera; Figure 34–4, *cre*).

crenulate Wavy, or with small scallops.

cribellum A sievelike structure lying just anterior to the spinnerets (spiders; Figure 6–8B, *crb*).

crochets (pronounced *croshays*) Hooked spines at the tip of the prolegs of lepidopterous larvae (Figure 34–3, *cro*).

crop The dilated posterior portion of the foregut, just behind the esophagus (Figure 3–22, *cp*).

cross vein A vein connecting adjacent longitudinal veins.

cruciate Crossing; shaped like a cross.

cryptonephridia Malpighian tubules that are closely associated with the hind gut and surrounded by a membrane, thus separating this complex from the rest of the hemocoel.

ctenidium (pl., *ctenidia*) A row of stout bristles like the teeth of a comb.

cubito-anal cross vein A cross vein between the cubitus and an anal vein (Figure 3–10, cu-a).

cubitus The longitudinal vein immediately posterior to the media (Figure 3–10, Cu).

cuneus A more or less triangular apical piece of the corium, set off from the rest of the corium by a suture (Hemíptera; Figure 24–4, *cun*).

cursorial Fitted for running; running in habit.

cuticle (or *cuticula*) The noncellular outer layer of the body wall of an arthropod (Figures 3–2, 3–4, *cut*).

cyst A sac, vesicle, or bladderlike structure.

deciduous Having a part or parts that may fall off or be shed.

decticous A type of pupa with movable, functional mandibles.

decumbent Bent downward.

deflexed Bent downward.

dentate Toothed, or with toothlike projections.

denticulate With minute toothlike projections.

depress To lower an appendage (e.g., leg or wing).

depressed Flattened dorsoventrally.

desmosome One form of subcellular attachment between the plasma membranes of two adjacent cells.

deutocerebrum The middle pair of lobes of the brain, innervating the antennae.

deutonymph The third instar of a mite (Figure 6–19D).

diapause A period of arrested development and reduced metabolic rate, during which growth, differentiation, and metamorphosis cease; a period of dormancy not immediately referable to adverse environmental conditions.

dichoptic The eyes separated above (Díptera).

dicondylic A joint with two points of articulation.

diecious Having the male and female organs in different individuals, any one individual being either male or female.

dilated Expanded or widened.

direct flight mechanism Generation of wing movements by means of muscles pulling on the base of the wings.

disc The central dorsal portion of the pronotum (Hemíptera).

discal cell A more or less enlarged cell in the basal or central part of the wing (Homóptera, the R cell, Figure 25–1; Lepidóptera, Figure 34–6, *D*; Díptera, Figure 32–4B, *D*).

discal cross vein A cross vein behind the discal cell (Díptera; Figure 32–4B, *dcv*).

distad Away from the body, toward the end farthest from the body.

distal Near or toward the free end of an appendage; that part of a segment or appendage farthest from the body.

diurnal Active during the daytime.

divaricate Extending outward and then curving inward toward each other distally (divaricate tarsal claws; Figure 28–10A).

divergent Becoming more separated distally.

dormancy A state of quiescence or inactivity.

dorsad Toward the back or top.

dorsal Top or uppermost; pertaining to the back or upper side.

dorsal blood vessel Median upper tube that forms the primary portion of the circulatory system of arthropods.

dorsal diaphragm An incomplete wall of muscle separating the area around the dorsal blood vessel (the pericardial sinus) from the rest of the hemocoel.

dorsocentral bristles A longitudinal row of bristles on the mesonotum, just laterad of the acrostichal bristles (Díptera; Figure 32–6, *dc*).

dorsolateral At the top and to the side.

dorsomesal At the top and along the midline.

dorsoscutellar bristles A pair of bristles on the dorsal portion of the scutellum, one on each side of the midline (Díptera).

dorsoventral From top to bottom, or from the upper to the lower side.

dorsum The back or top (dorsal) side.

Dyar's rule The increase in width of the larval head capsule by a factor of 1.2–1.4 from one molt to the next.

ecdysis (pl., *ecdyses*) Molting; the process of shedding the exoskeleton.

ecdysone (or *ecdysteroid*) Hormone produced by the prothoracic glands that initiates apolysis.

eclosion Hatching from the egg.

ectoparasite A parasite that lives on the outside of its host.

ejaculatory duct The terminal portion of the male sperm duct (Figure 3–31B, *ejd*).

elateriform larva A larva resembling a wireworm, that is, slender, heavily sclerotized, with short thoracic legs, and with few body hairs (Figure 28–49B).

elbowed antenna An antenna with the first segment elongated and the remaining segments coming off the first segment at an angle (Figure 3–15N).

elevate To raise an appendage (e..g, leg or wing).

elytron (pl., *elytra*) A thickened, leathery, or horny front wing (Coleóptera, Dermáptera, some Homóptera; Coleóptera, Figure 28–1, *el*).

emarginate Notched or indented.

embolium A narrow piece of the corium, along the costal margin, separated from the rest of the corium by a suture (Hemíptera; Figure 24–4C, *emb*).

emergence The act of the adult insect leaving the pupal case or the last nymphal skin.

empodium (pl., *empodia*) A padlike or bristlelike structure at the apex of the last tarsal segment, between the claws (Díptera; Figure 32–2, *emp*).

endite The basal segment of the spider pedipalp, which is enlarged and functions as a crushing jaw (Figure 6–5B, *cx*).

endocuticle (or *endocuticula*) The innermost and unsclerotized layer of the cuticle (Figure 3–2, *end*).

endoparasite A parasite that lives inside its host (for example, Figure 32–83B).

endophallus The inner eversible lining of the male aedeagus.

endopodite The mesal branch of a biramous appendage (Figure 6–1, *enp*).

endopterygote Having the wings developing internally; with complete metamorphosis.

endoskeleton A skeleton or supporting structure on the inside of the body.

entire Without teeth or notches, with a smooth outline.

entomophagous Feeding on insects.

epicranium The upper part of the head, from the face to the neck (Lepidóptera; Figure 34–3, *epcr*).

epicuticle (or *epicuticula*) The very thin, nonchitinous, external layer of the cuticle (Figure 3–2, *epi*).

epidermis The cellular layer of the body wall, which secretes the cuticle (Figure 3–2, 3–4, *ep*).

epigastric furrow A transverse ventral suture near the anterior end of the abdomen, along which lie the openings of the book lungs and the reproductive organs (spiders; Figure 6–5B, *ef*).

epigynum The external female genitalia of spiders (Figure 6–5B, *epg*).

epimeron (pl., *epimera*) The area of a thoracic pleuron posterior to the pleural suture (Figure 3–6, *epm*).

epipharynx A mouthpart structure on the inner surface of the labrum or clypeus; in chewing insects, a median lobe on the posterior (ventral) surface of the labrum.

epiphysis (pl., *epiphyses*) A movable pad or lobelike process on the inner surface of the front tibia (Lepidóptera).

epiphyte An air plant, one growing nonparasitically upon another plant or upon a nonliving object.

epipleura (pl., *epipleurae*) The bent-down lateral edge of an elytron (Coleóptera).

epipleurite A small sclerite in the membranous area between the thoracic pleura and the wing bases (Figure 3–6, *epp*).

epiproct A process or appendage situated above the anus and appearing to arise from the tenth abdominal segment; actually, the dorsal part of the eleventh abdominal segment (Figure 3–1, *ept*).

episternum (pl., *episterna*) The area of a thoracic pleuron anterior to the pleural suture (Figure 3–6, *eps*).

epistomal suture (or *sulcus*) The sulcus between the frons and the clypeus (Figure 3–13, *es*), connecting the anterior tentorial pits.

epistome The part of the face just above the mouth; the oral margin (Díptera).

eruciform larva A caterpillar; a larva with a more or less cylindrical body, a well-developed head, and thoracic legs and abdominal prolegs (Figure 34–3).

esophagus The narrow portion of the alimentary tract immediately posterior to the pharynx (Figure 3–22, *eso*).

estivation see *aestivation*.

eusocial A condition of group living in which there is cooperation among members in rearing young, reproductive division of labor, and overlap of generations.

eusternum The ventral plate of a thoracic segment exclusive of the spinasternum.

evagination An outpocketing, or saclike structure on the outside.

eversible Capable of being everted or turned outward.

exarate pupa A pupa in which the appendages are free and not glued to the body (Figure 3–44C–E).

excavated Hollowed out.

excretion The elimination of metabolic wastes from the body.

exocuticle (or *exocuticula*) The layer of sclerotized cuticle just outside the endocuticle, between the endocuticle and the epicuticle (Figure 3–2, *exo*).

exopodite   The outer branch of a biramous appendage (Figure 6–1, *exp*).

exopterygote   With the wings developing on the outside of the body, as in insects with simple metamorphosis.

exoskeleton   A skeleton or supporting structure on the outside of the body.

exserted   Protruding or projecting from the body.

external   The outside; that part away from the center (midline) of the body.

exuvium (pl., *exuvia*)   The cast skin of an arthropod.

eye, compound   See *compound eye.*

eye, simple   See *ocellus.*

eye cap   A structure overhanging or capping the compound eye (Lepidóptera; Figure 34–29B, *ec*).

face   The front of the head, below the frontal suture (Díptera; Figure 32–5, *fa*).

facet   The external surface of an individual compound-eye unit or ommatidium.

falx   An interantennal suture with internal sclerotized margins connecting the upper ends of the antennal fossae (Siphonàptera).

family   A subdivision of an order, suborder, or superfamily, containing a group of related genera, tribes, or subfamilies. Family names of animals end in *-idae.*

fastigium   The anterior dorsal surface of the vertex (grasshoppers).

fat body   An amorphous organ involved in intermediate metabolism, storage, and storage excretion.

feces   Excrement, the material passed from the alimentary tract through the anus.

felt line   A narrow longitudinal band of relatively dense, closely appressed hairs (Mutíllidae).

femur (pl., *femora*)   The third leg segment, located between the trochanter and the tibia (Figure 3–8, *fm*).

fibula   A more or less triangular jugal lobe in the front wing that serves as a means of uniting the front and hind wings (Lepidóptera; Figure 34–34, *fib*).

filament   A slender threadlike structure.

file   A filelike ridge on the ventral side of the tegmen, near the base; a part of the stridulating mechanism in crickets and long-horned grasshoppers (Figure 14–2).

filiform   Hairlike or threadlike, filiform antenna (Figure 3–15B).

filter chamber   A modification of the alimentary canal in Homóptera in which the anterior portion of the midgut is closely associated with the hindgut (Figure 3–23).

flabellate   With fanlike processes or projections; flabellate antenna (Figure 3–15L).

flabellum (pl., *flabella*)   A fanlike or leaflike process (Hymenóptera; Figure 35–6, *flb*).

flagellomere   One of the subsegments of the flagellum.

flagellum (pl., *flagella*)   A whiplike structure; that part of the antenna beyond the second segment (Figure 3–15N, *fl*).

flexor muscle   A muscle that decreases the angle between two segments of an appendage.

foliaceous   Leaflike.

follicle   A minute cavity, sac, or tube.

follicular epithelium   Layer of epithelial cells surrounding the oocyte.

fontanelle   A small, depressed, pale spot on the front of the head between the eyes (Isóptera; Figure 17–3, *fon*).

foramen magnum   The opening on the posterior side of the head, through which pass the internal structures that extend from the head to the thorax (Figure 3–13, *for*); also occipital foramen.

foregut   The anterior portion of the alimentary tract, from the mouth to the midgut.

fossorial   Fitted for or with the habit of digging.

frass   Plant fragments made by a wood-boring insect, usually mixed with excrement.

frenulum   A bristle or group of bristles arising at the humeral angle of the hind wing (Lepidóptera; Figure 34–6, *f*).

frons   The head sclerite bounded by the frontal (or frontogenal) and epistomal sulci and including the median ocellus (Figure 3–13, *fr*).

front   That portion of the head between the antennae, eyes, and ocelli; the frons.

frontal bristles   Bristles above the antennae, away from the edge of the compound eye (Díptera; Figure 32–24B, *fb*).

frontal lunule   A small crescent-shaped sclerite located just above the base of the antennae and below the frontal suture (Díptera; Figure 32–5, *frl*).

frontal suture   One of two sutures arising at the anterior end of the coronal suture and extending ventrad toward the epistomal sulcus (Figure 3–13, *fs*); a suture shaped like an inverted U, with the base of the U crossing the face above the bases of the antennae and the arms of the U extending downward on each side of the face (Díptera, Figure 32–5, *fs*; actually a ptilinal suture).

frontal vitta   An area on the head between the antennae and the ocelli (Díptera; Figure 32–5; *fv*).

frontogenal suture (or *sulcus*)   A more or less vertical suture on the front of the head, between the frons and the gena.

fronto-orbital bristles   Bristles on the front next to the compound eyes (Díptera; Figure 32–5, *fob*).

funiculus (or *funicle*)   The antennal segments between the scape and the club (Coleóptera), or between the pedicel and club (Hymenóptera).

furca   A fork or forked structure; a forked apodeme arising from a thoracic sternum (Figure 3–7, *fu*).

furcula   The forked springing apparatus of the Collémbola.

galea   The outer lobe of the maxilla, borne by the stipes (Figure 3–16A, *g*).

gall   An abnormal growth of plant tissues, caused by the stimulus of an animal or another plant.

ganglion (pl., *ganglia*)   A knotlike enlargement of a nerve, containing a coordinating mass of nerve cells (Figure 3–22, *gn*).

gaster   The rounded part of the abdomen posterior to the nodelike segment or segments (Hymenóptera Apócrita).

gastric caecum Caecum located at the anterior portion of the midgut.

gena (pl., *genae*) The part of the head on each side below and behind the compound eyes, between the frontal and occipital sulci (Figure 3–13, *ge*).

genal comb A row of strong spines borne on the antero-ventral border of the head (Siphonáptera; Figure 31–1).

generation From any given stage in the life cycle to the same stage in the offspring.

geniculate Elbowed, or abruptly bent; geniculate antenna (Figure 3–15N).

genital chamber See *bursa copulatrix*.

genitalia The sexual organs and associated structures; the external sexual organs (Figures 3–32, 3–33).

genovertical plate An area on the head above the antenna and next to the compound eye (Díptera; Figure 32–5, *gvp*), also called orbital plate.

genus (pl., *genera*) A group of closely related species; the first name in a binomial or trinomial scientific name. Names of genera are latinized, capitalized, and when printed are italicized.

germarium Apical portion of the ovariole or sperm follicle.

gill Evagination of the body wall or hindgut, functioning in gaseous exchanges in an aquatic animal.

glabrous Smooth, without hairs.

globose, globular Spherical or nearly so.

glossa (pl., *glossae*) One of a pair of lobes at the apex of the labium between the paraglossae (Figure 3–16C, *gl*); in bees, see Figure 35–6.

gnathochilarium A platelike mouthpart structure in the Diplópoda, representing the fused maxillae and labium.

gonangulum A sclerite of the female external genitalia derived from the second gonocoxa, connecting the second gonocoxa, ninth tergum, and first gonapophysis.

gonapophysis (pl., *gonapophyses*) A mesal posterior process of a gonopod, in the female forming the ovipositor (see Figures 3–32, *gap*; 9–1); first or second valvula.

gonocoxa A modified coxa that forms a part of the external genitalia (= valvifer).

gonoplacs Lateral sheaths enveloping the ovipositor in pterygotes (= third valvulae).

gonopod A modified leg that forms a part of the external genitalia.

gonopore The external opening of the reproductive organs.

gonostylus Stylus of a genital segment (abdominal segment 8 or 9).

gregarious Living in groups.

grub A scarabaeiform larva; a thick-bodied larva with a well-developed head and thoracic legs, without abdominal prolegs, and usually sluggish (Figures 3–43B, 28–37).

gula A sclerite on the ventral side of the head between the labium and the foramen magnum (Figure 28–4, *gu*).

gular sutures Longitudinal sutures, one on each side of the gula (Figure 28–4, *gs*).

gustation Taste, detection of chemicals in liquid.

gynandromorph An abnormal individual containing structure characteristics of both sexes (usually male on one side and female on the other).

haltere (pl., *halteres*) A small knobbed structure on each side of the metathorax, formed from a modified hind wing (Díptera; Figure 7–4, *hal*).

hamuli (sing., *hamulus*) Minute hooks; a series of minute hooks on the anterior margin of the hind wing, with which the front and hind wings are attached together (Hymenóptera).

haustellate Formed for sucking, the mandibles not fitted for chewing (or absent).

haustellum A part of the beak (Díptera; Figures 3–19, 3–20, *hst*).

head The anterior body region, which bears the eyes, antennae, and mouthparts (Figure 3–1, *hd*).

heart The posterior pulsatile portion of the dorsal blood vessel.

hemelytron (pl., *hemelytra*) The front wing of Hemíptera (Figure 24–4).

hemimetabolous Having simple metamorphosis, like that in the Odonàta, Ephemeróptera, and Plecóptera (with the nymphs aquatic).

hemocoel A body cavity filled with blood.

hemocyte A blood cell.

hemolymph The blood of arthropods.

herbivorous Feeding on plants.

hermaphroditic Possessing both male and female sex organs.

hertz Cycles per second (Hz).

heterodynamic life cycle A life cycle in which there is a period of dormancy.

heterogamy Alternation of bisexual with parthenogenetic reproduction.

heteromerous The three pairs of tarsi differing in the number of segments (Coleóptera, for example, with a tarsal formula of 5–5–4).

hibernation Dormancy during the winter.

hindgut The posterior portion of the alimentary tract, between the midgut and the anus.

holocrine secretion Release of enzymes by disruption of the entire cell.

holometabolous With complete metamorphosis.

holoptic The eyes contiguous above (Díptera).

homodynamic life cycle A life cycle in which there is continuous development, without a period of dormancy.

homonym One and the same name for two or more different things (taxa).

honeydew Liquid discharged from the anus of certain Homóptera.

hornworm A caterpillar (larva of Sphíngidae) with a dorsal spine or horn on the last abdominal segment (Figure 34–78).

horny Thickened or hardened.

host The organism in or on which a parasite lives; the plant on which an insect feeds.

humeral Pertaining to the shoulder; located in the anterior basal portion of the wing.

humeral angle The basal anterior angle or portion of the wing.

humeral bristles   The bristles on the humeral callus (Díptera; Figure 32–6, *hb*).

humeral callus   One of the anterior lateral angles of the thoracic notum, usually more or less rounded (Díptera; Figure 32–6, *hc*).

humeral cross vein   A cross vein in the humeral portion of the wing, between the costa and subcosta (Figure 3–10, h).

humeral suture   The mesopleural suture (Odonàta; Figure 11–4, *pls*₂).

humeral vein   A branch of the subcosta that serves to strengthen the humeral angle of the wing (Neuróptera, Figure 27–2C, *hv*; Lepidóptera, Figure 34–23B, *hv*).

humerus (pl., *humeri*)   The shoulder; the posterolateral angles of the pronotum (Hemíptera).

hyaline   Like glass, transparent, colorless.

hypermetamorphosis   A type of complete metamorphosis in which the different larval instars represent two or more different types of larvae (Figure 28–71).

hyperparasite   A parasite whose host is another parasite.

hypodermis   See *epidermis*.

hypognathous   With the head and the mouthparts located ventrally (for example, as in Figure 3–13).

hypopharynx   A median mouthpart structure anterior to the labium (Figures 3–16, 3–18 through 3–20, *hyp*); the ducts from the salivary glands are usually associated with the hypopharynx, and in some sucking insects the hypopharynx is the mouthpart structure containing the salivary channel.

hypopleural bristles   A more or less vertical row of bristles on the hypopleuron, usually directly above the hind coxae (Díptera; Figure 32–6, *hyb*).

hypopleuron (pl., *hypopleura*)   The lower part of the mesepimeron; a sclerite on the thorax located just above the hind coxae (Díptera; Figure 32–6, *hypl*).

hypostigmatic cell   The cell immediately behind the point of fusion of Sc and R (Neuróptera, Myrmeleontòidea; Figure 27–4, *hcl*).

hypostomal bridge   Mesal extension of the hypostomae on each side to meet below the foramen magnum.

Hz   Hertz (cycles per second).

ileum   The anterior part of the hindgut (Figure 3–22, *il*).

imago (pl., *imagoes* or *imagines*)   The adult or reproductive stage of an insect.

inclinate   Bent toward the midline of the body.

indirect flight mechanism   Generation of wing movements by means of muscles producing distortions in the shape of the thorax.

inferior appendage   The lower one (Anisóptera) or two (Zygóptera) of the terminal abdominal appendages, used in grasping the female at the time of copulation (male Odonàta; Figure 11–4A, *ept*; 11–4C, *iap*).

infraepisternum   A ventral subdivision of an episternum (Figure 11–4, *iep*).

inner vertical bristles   The more mesally located of the large bristles on the vertex, between the ocelli and the compound eyes (Díptera; Figure 32–5, *ivb*).

inquiline   An animal that lives in the nest or abode of another species.

instar   The insect between successive molts, the first instar being between hatching and the first molt.

instinctive behavior   Unlearned stereotyped behavior, in which the nerve pathways involved are hereditary.

integument   The outer covering of the body.

intelligence   The capacity to modify behavior as a result of experience.

interantennal suture   A suture extending between the bases of the two antennae (Siphonáptera; Figure 31–5, *ias*).

intercalary vein   An extra longitudinal vein that develops from a thickened fold in the wing, more or less midway between two preexisting veins (Ephemeróptera; Figures 10–3, 10–4, 10–6, ICuA).

internuncial neuron (or *interneuron*)   A neuron that connects with two (or more) other neurons.

intersternite   An intersegmental sclerite on the ventral side of the thorax; the spinasternum.

interstitial   Situated between two segments (interstitial trochanter of Coleóptera; Figure 28–9D, *tr*).

intima   The cuticular lining of the foregut, hindgut, and tracheae.

intra-alar bristles   A row of two or three bristles situated on the mesonotum above the wing base, between the dorsocentral and the supra-alar bristles (Díptera; Figure 32–6, *iab*).

invagination   An infolding or inpocketing.

isosomotic   With an equal concentration of solutes.

iteroparous   A type of life history in which the animal reproduces two or more times during its lifetime.

Johnston's organ   A sense organ similar to a chordotonal organ, located in the second antennal segment of most insects; this organ functions in sound perception in some Díptera.

joint   An articulation of two successive segments or parts.

jugal lobe   A lobe at the base of the wing, on the posterior side, proximad of the vannal lobe (Hymenóptera; Figures 35–13, 35–14, *jl*).

jugal vein   The most posterior of the major longitudinal vein systems according to Kukalová-Peck.

jugum   A lobelike process at the base of the front wing, which overlaps the hind wing (Lepidóptera; Figure 34–5, *j*); a sclerite in the head (Hemíptera and Homóptera; Figures 3–17, 24–1, *j*).

katepleurite   See *catapleurite*.

keeled   With an elevated ridge or carina.

kHz   Kilohertz (kilocycles per second).

labellum   The expanded tip of the labium (Díptera; Figures 3–19, 3–20, *lbl*).

labial   Of or pertaining to the labium.

labial gland   Exocrine organ opening on or at the base of the labium, usually functioning as salivary or silk gland.

labial palp   One of a pair of small feelerlike structures arising from the labium (Figure 3–16C, *lp*).

labial suture   The suture on the labium between the postmentum and prementum (Figure 3–16C, *ls*).

labium One of the mouthpart structures, the lower lip (Figures 3–13, *lbm*, 3–16C).

labrum The upper lip, lying just below the clypeus (Figure 3–13, *lbr*).

labrum-epipharynx A mouthpart representing the labrum and epipharynx.

lacinia (pl., *laciniae*) The inner lobe of the maxilla, borne by the stipes (Figure 3–16A, *lc*).

lamella (pl., *lamellae*) A leaflike plate.

lamellate With platelike structures or segments; lamellate antennae (Figures 3–15M, 28–6C,D).

lamina In the cuticle, a layer of cuticle with chitin microfibrils oriented in the same direction.

lamina lingualis (pl., *laminae linguales*) One of two median distal plates in the millipede gnathochilarium (Figure 6–32B, *ll*).

lanceolate Spear-shaped, tapering at each end.

larva (pl., *larvae*) The immature stage, between egg and pupa, of an insect having complete metamorphosis; the six-legged first instar of Àcari (Figures 6–19B, 6–22A); an immature stage differing radically from the adult.

larviform Shaped like a larva.

laterad Toward the side, away from the midline of the body.

lateral Of or pertaining to the side (that is, the right or left side).

lateral oviduct A tube in the female internal genitalia connecting the ovaries and the common oviduct.

laterotergite A tergal sclerite located laterally or dorsolaterally.

lateroventral To the side (away from the midline of the body) and below.

leaf miner An insect that lives in and feeds upon the leaf cells between the upper and lower surfaces of a leaf.

ligula The terminal lobe (or lobe) of the labium, the glossae and paraglossae.

linear Linelike, long and very narrow.

longitudinal Lengthwise of the body or of an appendage.

looper A caterpillar that moves by looping its body, that is by placing the posterior part of the abdomen next to the thorax and then extending the anterior part of the body forward; a measuringworm.

lorum (pl., *lora*) The cheek; a sclerite on the side of the head (Hemíptera and Homóptera; Figures 24–1, 25–1, *lo*); the submentum in bees (Figure 35–6, *smt*).

luminescent Producing light.

lunule, frontal See *frontal lunule*.

maggot A vermiform larva; a legless larva without a well-developed head capsule (Díptera; Figure 3–43A).

Malpighian tubules Excretory tubes that arise near the anterior end of the hindgut and extend into the body cavity (Figure 3–22, *mt*).

mandible Jaw; one of the anterior pair of paired mouthpart structures (Figure 3–16, *md*).

mandibulate With jaws fitted for chewing.

marginal cell A cell in the distal part of the wing bordering the costal margin (Díptera, Figure 32–4B, *MC*; Hymenóptera, Figure 35–3, *MC*).

marginal vein A vein on or just within the wing margin; the vein forming the posterior side of the marginal cell (Hymenóptera; Figures 35–3, 35–19B, *mv*).

margined With a sharp or keellike lateral edge.

maxilla (pl., *maxillae*) One of the paired mouthpart structures immediately posterior to the mandibles (Figure 3–16, *mx*).

maxillary Of or pertaining to the maxilla.

maxillary palp A small feelerlike structure arising from the maxilla (Figure 3–16A, *mxp*).

maxilliped One of the appendages in Crustàcea immediately posterior to the second maxillae.

mechanoreceptor A sensillum sensitive to physical displacement.

media The longitudinal vein between the radius and cubitus (Figure 3–10, M).

medial cross vein A cross vein connecting two branches of the media (Figure 3–10, m).

median In the middle; along the midline of the body.

medio-cubital cross vein A cross vein connecting the media and cubitus (Figure 3–10, m-cu).

membrane A thin film of tissue, usually transparent; that part of the wing surface between the veins; the thin apical part of a hemelytron (Hemíptera; Figure 24–4, *mem*).

membranous Like a membrane; thin and more or less transparent (wings); thin and pliable (cuticle).

mental setae Setae on the mentum (Odonàta; Figure 11–3, *mst*).

mentum The distal part of the labium, which bears the palps and the ligula (Figure 3–16C, *mn*); a median, more or less triangular piece in the millipede gnathochilarium (Figure 6–32B, *mn*).

merocrine secretion Release of enzymes across the cell membrane, without destruction of the entire cell.

meroistic ovariole Ovariole with nurse cells.

meropleuron (pl., *meropleura*) A sclerite consisting of the meron (basal part) of the coxa and the lower part of the epimeron.

mesad Toward the midline of the body.

mesal At or near the midline of the body.

mesenteron The midgut, or middle portion of the alimentary tract (Figure 3–22, *mg*).

mesepimeron (pl., *mesepimera*) The epimeron of the mesothorax (Figures 3–6, 28–4, epm_2).

mesepisternum (pl., *mesepisterna*) The episternum of the mesothorax (Figures 3–6, 28–4, eps_2).

mesinfraepisternum A ventral subdivision of the mesepisternum (Odonàta; Figure 11–4, iep_2).

meson The midline of the body, or an imaginary plane dividing the body into right and left halves.

mesonotum The dorsal sclerite of the mesothorax (Figure 3–1, n_2).

mesopleural bristles Bristles on the mesopleuron (Díptera; Figure 32–6, *mpb*).

mesopleuron (pl., *mesopleura*) The lateral sclerite(s) of the mesothorax; the upper part of the episternum of the mesothorax (Díptera; Figure 32–6, pl_2).

mesoscutellum The scutellum of the mesothorax (Figure 3–6, scl_2), usually simply called the scutellum.

mesoscutum The scutum of the mesothorax (Figure 3–6, sct_2).

mesosoma In Apócrita (Hymenóptera) the middle tagma of the body, composed of the three thoracic segments and the first true abdominal segment (the propodeum).

mesosternum The sternum, or ventral sclerite, of the mesothorax.

mesothorax The middle or second segment of the thorax (Figure 3–1, th_2).

metamere A primary body segment (usually referring to the embryo).

metamorphosis A change in form during development.

metanotum The dorsal sclerite of the metathorax (Figure 3–1, n_3).

metascutellum The scutellum of the metathorax (Figure 3–6, scl_3).

metasoma In Apócrita (Hymenóptera) the posterior tagma of the body, comprised of all segments posterior to the propodeum.

metasternum The sternum, or ventral sclerite, of the metathorax.

metatarsus (pl., *metatarsi*) The basal segment of the tarsus (Figure 6–5, *mts*).

metathorax The third or posterior segment of the thorax (Figure 3–1, th_3).

metazonite The posterior portion of a millipede tergum when the tergum is divided by a transverse groove.

metepimeron (pl., *metepimera*) The epimeron of the metathorax (Figure 3–6, epm_3).

metepisternum (pl., *metepisterna*) The episternum of the metathorax (Figure 3–6, eps_3).

metinfraepisternum A ventral subdivision of the metepisternum (Odonàta; Figure 11–4, iep_3).

micropyle A minute opening (or openings) in the chorion of an insect egg, through which sperm enter the egg (Figure 3–37, *mcp*).

midgut The mesenteron, or middle portion of the alimentary tract (Figure 3–22, *mg*).

millimeter 0.001 meter, or 0.03937 inch (about $\frac{1}{25}$ inch).

minute Very small; an insect a few millimeters in length or less would be considered minute.

molt A process of shedding the exoskeleton; ecdysis; to shed the exoskeleton.

molting gland See *prothoracic glands*.

monecious Possessing both male and female sex organs, hermaphroditic.

moniliform Beadlike, with rounded segments; moniliform antenna (Figure 3–15C).

monocondylic A joint with a single point of articulation.

morphology The science of form or structure.

motor neuron A neuron that forms a synapse with a muscle.

mutualism A living together of two species of organisms, with both species being benefited by the association.

myiasis A disease caused by the invasion of dipterous larvae.

myogenic Produced by muscle; contraction of a muscle generated by that muscle itself, without neuronal stimulus.

myriapod A many-legged arthropod; a centipede, millipede, pauropod, or symphylan.

naiad An aquatic, gill-breathing nymph.

nasute soldier (or *nasutus*) An individual of a termite caste in which the head narrows anteriorly into a snout-like projection (Figure 17–2B).

neurogenic Produced by a neuron; contractions of muscle stimulated by a neuronal impulse.

nidi In the midgut, clusters of regenerative epithelial cells.

nocturnal Active at night.

node A knoblike or knotlike swelling.

nodiform In the form of a knob or knot.

nodus A strong cross vein near the middle of the costal border of the wing (Odonàta; Figures 11–5 through 11–7, *nod*).

notal wing process Point at which the notum articulates with the wing (or axillary sclerites at the base of the wing).

notaulus (pl., *notauli*) A longitudinal line on the mesoscutum of Hymenóptera, marking the separation of the dorsal longitudinal and dorsoventral flight muscles (Figure 35–4A, *nt*); also sometimes called notaulix (notaulices), parapsidal furrow, or parapsidal suture.

notopleural bristles Bristles on the notopleuron (Díptera; Figure 32–6, *nb*).

notopleural suture A suture between the notum and the pleural sclerites (Figure 28–4, *npls*).

notopleuron (pl., *notopleura*) An area on the thoracic dorsum, at the lateral end of the transverse suture (Díptera; Figure 32–6, *npl*).

notum (pl., *nota*) The dorsal sclerite of a thoracic segment; the fused second gonapophyses of the ovipositor.

nurse cells Nutritive cells associated with the developing oocyte.

nymph An immature stage (following hatching) of an insect that does not have a pupal stage; the immature stage of Àcari that has eight legs.

oblique vein A slanting cross vein; in Odonàta, where Rs crosses M_{1+2} (Figure 11–5, *obv*).

obtect pupa A pupa in which the appendages are more or less glued to the body surface, as in the Lepidóptera (Figure 3–44A,B, 34–4).

occipital foramen See *foramen magnum*.

occipital suture (or *sulcus*) A transverse suture in the posterior part of the head that separates the vertex from the occiput dorsally and the genae from the postgenae laterally (Figure 3–13, *os*).

occiput The dorsal posterior part of the head, between the occipital and postoccipital sutures (Figure 3–13, *ocp*).

ocellar bristles Bristles arising close to the ocelli (Díptera; Figure 32–5, *ob*).

ocellar triangle A slightly raised triangular area in which the ocelli are located (Díptera; Figure 32–5, *ot*).

ocellus (pl., *ocelli*) A simple eye of an insect or other arthropod (Figure 3–13, *oc*).

olfaction The sense of smell; the ability to detect chemicals in a gas.

olistheter A tongue-in-groove mechanism connecting the first and second gonapophyses of the ovipositor.

ommatidium (pl., *ommatidia*) A single unit or visual section of a compound eye (Figure 3–29D).

onisciform larva See *platyform larva.*

oocyte Egg.

oogenesis The production of eggs.

oogonium (pl., *oogonia*) The primary germ cells of the female.

ootheca (pl., *oothecae*) The covering or case of an egg mass (Mantòdea, Blattària).

open cell A wing cell extending to the wing margin, not entirely surrounded by veins.

open coxal cavity One bounded posteriorly by a sclerite of the next segment (front coxal cavities, Coleóptera; Figure 28–7A), or one touched by one or more pleural sclerites (middle coxal cavities, Coleóptera; Figure 28–7C).

operculum (pl., *opercula*) A lid or cover.

opisthognathous With the mouthparts directed backward.

opisthorhynchous With the beak directed backward.

oral Pertaining to the mouth.

oral vibrissae A pair of stout bristles, one on each side of the face near or just above the oral margin, and larger than the other bristles on the vibrissal ridge (Díptera; Figure 32–5, *ov*).

orbital plate An area on the head above the antenna and next to the compound eye (Díptera; Figure 32–21 C, *orp*); also called genovertical plate.

order A subdivision of a class or subclass, containing a group of related superfamilies or families.

osmeterium (pl., *osmeteria*) A fleshy, tubular, eversible, usually Y-shaped gland at the anterior end of certain caterpillars (Papiliónidae; Figure 34–3, *osm*).

ostiole A small opening.

ostium (pl., *ostia*) A slitlike opening in the insect heart.

outer vertical bristles The more laterally located of the large bristles on the vertex, between the ocelli and the compound eyes (Díptera; Figure 32–5, *ovb*).

ovariole A more or less tubular division of an ovary (Figure 3–31, *ovl*).

ovary The egg-producing organ of the female (Figures 3–22, 3–31A, *ovy*).

oviduct The tube leading away from the ovary through which the eggs pass (Figures 3–22, 3–31A, *ovd*).

oviparous Laying eggs.

ovipore The external opening of the female reproductive system through which the eggs pass during oviposition.

oviposit To lay or deposit eggs.

ovipositor The egg-laying apparatus; the external genitalia of the female (Figures 3–1, 3–32, 11–4E, and 35–5, *ovp*).

oviscapt Modification of the terminal abdominal segments of a female to serve as an egg-laying organ.

paedogenesis The production of eggs or young by an immature or larval stage of an animal.

palp A segmented process born by the maxillae or labium (Figure 3–16, *lp, mxp*).

palpifer The lobe of the maxillary stipes that bears the palp (Figure 3–16A, *plf*).

palpiger The lobe of the mentum of the labium that bears the palp (Figure 3–16C, *plg*).

panoistic ovariole Ovariole without nurse cells.

papilla A small nipplelike elevation.

paraglossa (pl., *paraglossae*) One of a pair of lobes at the apex of the labium, laterad of the glossae (Figure 3–16C, *pgl*).

paramere A structure in the male genitalia of insects, usually a lobe or process at the base of the aedeagus.

paranotum Lateral expansion of the notum.

paraproct One of a pair of lobes bordering the anus lateroventrally (Figures 3–1, and 11–4A, *ppt*).

parasite An animal that lives in or on the body of another living animal (its host), at least during a part of its life cycle, feeding on the tissues of its host; most entomophagous insect parasites kill their host (see *parasitoid*).

parasitic Living as a parasite.

parasitoid An animal that feeds in or on another living animal for a relatively long time, consuming all or most of its tissues and eventually killing it (also used as an adjective, describing this mode of life). Parasitoid insects in this book are referred to as parasites.

parthenogenesis Development of the egg without fertilization.

patella A leg segment between the femur and tibia (arachnids; Figure 6–5, *ptl*).

paurometabolous With simple metamorphosis, the young and adults living in the same habitat, and the adults winged.

pecten A comblike or rakelike structure.

pectinate With branches or processes like the teeth of a comb; pectinate antenna (Figure 3–15H); pectinate tarsal claw (Figure 28–11B).

pedicel The second segment of the antenna (Figure 3–15N, *ped*); the stem of the abdomen, between the thorax and the gaster (ants).

pedipalps The second pair of appendages of an arachnid (Figure 6–5, 6–14, *pdp*).

pelagic Inhabiting the open sea; ocean-dwelling.

penultimate Next to the last.

pericardial sinus The body cavity surrounding the dorsal blood vessel, limited ventrally by the dorsal diaphragm.

perineural sinus The body cavity surrounding the ventral nerve cord, limited dorsally by the ventral diaphragm.

peristome The ventral margin of the head, bordering the mouth.

peristalsis Waves of contraction.

peritrophic membrane A membrane in insects secreted by the cells lining the midgut; this membrane is secreted when food is present and forms an envelope around the food; it usually pulls loose from the midgut, remains around the food, and passes out with the feces.

perivisceral sinus The body cavity surrounding the digestive system, reproductive system, etc., between the dorsal and ventral diaphragms.

petiolate Attached by a narrow stalk or stem.

petiole A stalk or stem; the narrow stalk or stem by which the abdomen is attached to the thorax (Hymenóptera); in ants, the nodelike first segment of the abdomen.

pH A measure of the acidity or alkalinity of a medium. A pH value of 7.0 indicates neutral; lower values indicate acid, and higher values alkaline. Defined as $-\log[H^+]$.

phallotreme External opening of the male reproductive system on the aedeagus.

phallus The male copulatory organ, including any processes that may be present at its base.

pharynx The anterior part of the foregut, between the mouth and the esophagus (Figure 3–22, *phx*).

pheromone A substance given off by one individual that causes a specific reaction by other individuals of the same species, such as sex attractants, alarm substances, etc.

photoperiod The relative amount of time during the day in which it is light (or dark).

phragma (pl., *phragmata*) A platelike apodeme or invagination of the dorsal wall of the thorax (Figure 3–7, *ph*).

phylum (pl., *phyla*) One of the dozen or so major divisions of the animal kingdom.

phytophagous Feeding on plants.

pictured With spots or bands (pictured wings; Figure 32–67).

pilifer One of a pair of lateral projections on the labrum (Lepidóptera; Figure 34–2, *pf*).

pilose Covered with hair.

planidium larva A type of first-instar larva in certain Díptera and Hymenóptera that undergoes hypermetamorphosis; a larva that is legless and somewhat flattened.

plastron A bed of very dense and very fine hairs used to hold an air bubble close to the body and across which gas exchange takes place.

platyform larva A larva that is extremely flattened, as the larva of Psephènidae (Figure 28–48) (also called onisciform larva).

pleural Pertaining to the pleura, or lateral sclerites of the body; lateral.

pleural apophysis (or *arm*) Internal process extending from the pleural suture to the sternal apophyses.

pleural suture (or *sulcus*) A suture of a thoracic pleuron extending from the base of the wing to the base of the coxa, which separates the episternum and epimeron (Figures 3–1, 3–6, *pls*).

pleural wing process The structure articulating with the wing (specifically with the second axillary sclerite).

pleurite A lateral or pleural sclerite.

pleuron (pl., *pleura*) The lateral area of a segment.

pleurotergite A sclerite containing both pleural and tergal elements.

pleuropodium Embryonic appendages of the first abdominal segment.

plumose Featherlike; plumose antenna (Figure 3–15I).

poikilothermous Cold-blooded, the body temperature rising or falling with the environmental temperature.

point A small triangle of stiff paper, using in mounting small insects (Figure 36–14).

pollen basket See *corbicula*.

pollen rake A comblike row of bristles at the apex of the hind tibia of a bee (Figure 35–66, *pr*).

polyembryony An egg developing into two or more embryos.

polytrophic ovariole Meroistic ovariole in which trophocytes pass into the vitellarium with the oocyte.

porrect Extending forward horizontally; porrect antennae (Figure 32–21G,I).

postabdomen The modified posterior segments of the abdomen, which are usually more slender than the anterior segments (Crustácea, Figure 6–26A, *pa*; see also the postabdomen in a scorpion, Figure 6–3).

postalar callus A rounded swelling on each side of the mesonotum, between the base of the wing and the scutellum (Díptera; Figure 32–6, *pc*).

posterior Hind or rear.

posterior cell One of the cells extending to the hind margin of the wing, between the third and sixth longitudinal veins (Díptera; Figure 32–4B, *P*).

posterior cross vein A cross vein at the apex of the discal cell (Díptera; Figure 32–4B, *pcv*).

postgena (pl., *postgenae*) A sclerite on the posterior lateral surface of the head, posterior to the gena (Figure 3–13, *pg*).

postgenal bridge Mesal extension of the postgenae on each side to meet below the foramen magnum.

posthumeral bristles Bristles on the anterolateral surface of the mesonotum, just posterior to the humeral callus (Díptera; Figure 32–6, *pb*).

postmarginal vein The vein along the anterior margin of the front wing, beyond the point where the stigmal vein arises (Hymenóptera; Figure 35–19B, *pm*).

postmentum The basal portion of the labium, proximad of the labial suture (Figure 3–16C, *pmt*).

postnodal cross veins A series of cross veins just behind the costal margin of the wing, between the nodus and stigma, and extending from the costal margin of the wing to R_1 (Odonàta; Figures 11–5, 11–6, *pn*).

postnotum (pl., *postnota*) A notal plate behind the scutellum bearing a phragma, often present in wing-bearing segments (Figure 3–6, *PN*).

postoccipital suture The transverse suture on the head immediately posterior to the occipital suture (Figure 3–13, *pos*).

postocciput The extreme posterior rim of the head, between the postoccipital suture and the foramen magnum (Figure 3–13, *po*).

postpetiole The second segment of a two-segmented pedicel (ants).

postscutellum A small transverse piece of a thoracic notum immediately behind the scutellum; in Díptera, an area immediately behind or below the mesoscutellum (Figure 32–15B, *pscl*).

postvertical bristles A pair of bristles behind the ocelli, usually situated on the posterior surface of the head (Díptera; Figure 32–5, *pv*).

preapical Situated just before the apex; preapical tibial bristles of Díptera (Figure 32–23B, *ptbr*).

prebasilare A narrow transverse sclerite, just basal to the mentum in the gnathochilarium of some millipedes (Figure 6–32B, *pbs*).

precosta The most anterior of the major longitudinal wing veins (according to Kukalová-Peck).

predaceous Feeding as a predator.

predator An animal that attacks and feeds on other animals (its prey), usually animals smaller or less powerful than itself. The prey is usually killed and mostly or entirely eaten; many prey individuals are eaten by each predator.

prefemur The second trochanter segment of the leg.

pregenital Anterior to the genital segments of the abdomen.

prementum The distal part of the labium, distad of the labial suture, on which all the labial muscles have their insertions (Figure 3–16C, prmt).

preoral Anterior to or in front of the mouth.

prepectus An area along the anteroventral margin of the mesepisternum, set off by a suture (Hymenóptera; Figure 35–4, pp).

prepupa A quiescent stage between the larval period and the pupal period; the third instar of a thrips (Figure 26–2B).

presutural bristles Bristles on the mesonotum immediately anterior to the transverse suture and adjacent to the notopleuron (Díptera; Figure 32–6, psb).

pretarsus (pl., *pretarsi*) The terminal segment of the leg, typically consisting of a pair of claws and one or more padlike structures (Figure 3–8B,D, ptar).

proboscis The extended beaklike mouthparts (Figure 32–37, prb).

proclinate Inclined forward or downward.

proctodaeum The hindgut, or the hindmost of the three major divisions of the alimentary tract, from the Malpighian tubules to the anus.

procuticle The form in which the cuticle is initially secreted by the epidermis, before sclerotization takes place.

produced Extended, prolonged, or projecting.

proepimeron (pl., *proepimera*) The epimeron of the prothorax (Figure 28–4, epm₁).

proepisternum (pl., *proepisterna*) The episternum of the prothorax (Figure 28–4, eps₁).

profile The outline as seen from the side or in lateral view.

prognathous Having the head horizontal and the mouthparts projecting forward.

proleg One of the fleshy abdominal legs of certain insect larvae (Figure 34–3, prl).

prominence A raised, produced, or projecting portion.

prominent Raised, produced, or projecting.

promote To move anteriorly.

pronate To turn the leading edge of the wing downward.

pronotal comb A row of strong spines borne on the posterior margin of the pronotum (Siphonáptera; Figures 31–1, 31–2).

pronotum The dorsal sclerite of the prothorax (Figures 3–1, 3–6, n₁).

propleural bristles Bristles located on the propleuron (Díptera; Figure 32–6, ppb).

propleuron (pl., *propleura*) The lateral portion, or pleuron, of the prothorax (Figure 32–6, pl₁).

propodeum The posterior portion of the thorax, which is actually the first abdominal segment united with the thorax (Hymenóptera, suborder Apócrita; Figure 35–4, prd).

proprioception Detection by an animal of the position of parts of its own body.

prosoma A term referring to the anterior part of the body, usually applied to the cephalothorax; the anterior part of the head or cephalothorax.

prosternum The sternum, or ventral sclerite, of the prothorax.

prothoracic glands Endocrine glands located in the prothorax (generally) that secrete ecdysone.

prothoracicotropic hormone See *brain hormone*.

prothorax The anterior of the three thoracic segments (Figure 3–1, th₁).

protocerebrum The dorsal lobes of the brain, innervating (*inter alia*) the compound eyes and ocelli.

protonymph The second instar of a mite (Figure 6–19C).

proventriculus The valve between the foregut and midgut.

proximad Toward the end or portion nearest the body.

proximal Nearer to the body or to the base of an appendage.

prozonite The anterior portion of a millipede tergum when the tergum is divided by a transverse groove.

pruinose Covered with a whitish waxy powder.

pseudarolium (pl., *pseudarolia*) A pad at the apex of the tarsus resembling an arolium.

pseudocercus (pl., *pseudocerci*) See *urogomphi*.

pseudocubitus A vein appearing as the cubitus, but actually formed by the fusion of the branches of M and Cu₁ (Neuróptera; Figure 27–3B, pscu).

pseudomedia A vein appearing as the media, but actually formed by the fusion of branches of Rs (Neuróptera; Figure 27–3B, psm).

pseudopupa A coarctate larva; a larva in a quiescent pupalike condition, one or two instars before the true pupal stage (Coleóptera, Melòidae; Figure 28–71H).

pseudovipositor See *oviscapt*.

pteralia See *axillary sclerites*.

pteropleural bristles Bristles on the pteropleuron (Díptera; Figure 32–6, ptb).

pteropleuron (pl., *pteropleura*) A sclerite on the side of the thorax, just below the base of the wing, and consisting of the upper part of the mesepimeron (Díptera; Figure 32–6, pt).

pterostigma A thickened opaque spot along the costal margin of the wing, near the wing tip (also called the stigma) (Odonàta; Figures 11–5, 11–6, st).

pterothorax The wing-bearing segments of the thorax (mesothorax and metathorax).

pterygote Winged; a member of the subclass Pterygòta.

ptilinum A temporary bladderlike structure that can be inflated and thrust out through the frontal (or ptilinal) suture, just above the bases of the antennae, at the time of emergence from the puparium (Díptera).

PTTH See *brain hormone*.

pubescent Downy, covered with short fine hairs.

pulvilliform Lobelike or padlike; shaped like a pulvillus; pulvilliform empodium (Figure 32–2B, emp).

pulvillus (pl., *pulvilli*) A pad or lobe beneath each tarsal claw (Díptera; Figure 32–2, pul.)

punctate Pitted or beset with punctures.

puncture A tiny pit or depression.

pupa (pl., *pupae*) The stage between the larva and the adult in insects with complete metamorphosis, a nonfeeding and usually an inactive stage (Figure 3–44).

puparium (pl., *puparia*) A case formed by the hardening of the last larval skin, in which the pupa is formed (Díptera; Figure 3–44F).

pupate To transform to a pupa.

pupiparous Giving birth to larvae that are full grown and ready to pupate.

pygidium The last dorsal segment of the abdomen.

pyloric valve The valve between the midgut and hindgut.

quadrangle A cell immediately beyond the arculus (Odonàta, Zygóptera; Figure 11–6, *q*).

quadrate Four-sided.

radial cell A cell bordered anteriorly by a branch of the radius; the marginal cell (Hymenóptera; Figure 35–3, *MC*).

radial cross vein A cross vein connecting R₁ and the branch of the radius immediately behind it (Figure 3–10, r).

radial sector The posterior of the two main branches of the radius (Figure 3–10, Rs).

radius The longitudinal vein between the subcosta and the media (Figure 3–10, R).

raptorial Fitted for grasping prey; raptorial front legs (Figure 24–2).

reclinate Inclined backward or upward.

rectum The posterior region of the hindgut (Figure 3–22, *rec*).

recurrent vein One of two transverse veins immediately posterior to the cubital vein (Hymenóptera; Figure 35–3, *rv*); a vein at the base of the wing between the costa and the subcosta, extending obliquely from the subcosta to the costa (Neuróptera; Figure 27–2C, *hv*).

recurved Curved upward or backward.

remote To move posteriorly.

reniform Kidney-shaped.

reticulate Like a network.

retina The receptive apparatus of an eye.

retractile Capable of being pushed out and drawn back in.

rhabdom A rodlike light-sensitive structure formed of the inner surfaces of adjacent sensory cells in the ommatidium of a compound eye (Figure 3–29, *rh*).

Riker mount A thin glass-topped exhibition case filled with cotton (Figure 36–21).

rostrum Beak or snout.

rudimentary Reduced in size, poorly developed, embryonic.

rugose Wrinkled.

saprophagous Feeding on dead or decaying plant or animal materials, such as carrion, dung, dead logs, etc.

scape The basal segment of an antenna (Figure 3–15N, *scp*).

scapula (pl., *scapulae*) One of two sclerites on the mesonotum immediately lateral of the notauli (Hymenóptera; Figure 35–4, *sca*); also called parapsis.

scarabaeiform larva A grublike larva, that is, one with the body thickened and cylindrical, with a well-developed head and thoracic legs, without prolegs, and usually sluggish (Figures 3–43B, 28–37).

scavenger An animal that feeds on dead plants or animals, or decaying materials, or on animal wastes.

scent gland A gland producing an odorous substance.

scientific name A latinized name, internationally recognized, of a species or subspecies. The scientific name of a species consists of the generic and specific names, and that of a subspecies consists of the generic, specific, and subspecific names. Scientific names are always printed in italics.

sclerite A hardened body-wall plate bounded by sutures or membranous areas.

sclerotized Hardened.

sclerotization The process of becoming hardened.

scolopophorous organ See *campaniform sensillum*.

scolytoid larva A fleshy larva resembling the larva of a scolytid beetle.

scopa (pl., *scopae*) A small, dense tuft of hair.

scraper The sharpened anal angle of the front wing (tegmen) of a cricket or long-horned grasshopper, a part of the stridulating mechanism.

scrobe A groove or furrow; antennal scrobe (Figures 28–3, 28–92, *agr*).

scutellum A sclerite of the thoracic notum (Figure 3–6, *scl*); the mesoscutellum, appearing as a more or less triangular sclerite behind the pronotum (Hemíptera, Homóptera, Coleóptera).

scutum The middle division of a thoracic notum, just anterior to the scutellum (Figure 3–6, *sct*).

sebaceous glands Glands secreting fatty or oily material.

sectorial cross vein A cross vein connecting two branches of the radial sector (Figure 3–10, s).

segment A subdivision of the body or of an appendage, between joints or articulations.

semiaquatic Living in wet places or partially in water.

seminal vesicle A structure, usually saclike, in which the seminal fluid of the male is stored before being discharged; usually an enlargement of the vas deferens (Figure 3–31B, *smv*).

sense cone or **sense peg** A minute cone or peg, sensory in function (Figures 3–27, 26–5, *scn*).

sensillum (pl., *sensilla*) An organ capable of detecting external stimuli.

sensory neuron A neuron capable of generating an action potential in response to an external stimulus (such as physical displacement, temperature, humidity, chemicals, etc.).

serrate Toothed along the edge like a saw; serrate antenna (Figure 3–15G).

sessile Attached or fastened, incapable of moving from place to place; attached directly, without a stem or petiole.

seta (pl., *setae*) A bristle.

setaceous Bristlelike; setaceous antenna (Figure 3–15A).

setate Provided with bristles.

setulose Bearing short, blunt bristles.

sigmoid Shaped like the letter S.

simple Unmodified, not complicated; not forked, toothed, branched, or divided.

spatulate Spoon-shaped; broad apically and narrowed basally, and flattened.

species A group of individuals or populations that are similar in structure and physiology and are capable of interbreeding and producing fertile offspring, and that are different in structure and/or physiology from other such groups and normally do not interbreed with them.

spermatheca (pl., *spermathecae*) A saclike structure in the female in which sperm from the male are received and often stored (Figure 3–31 A, *spth*).

spermatogenesis The production of sperm cells.

spermatogonium A primary germ cell of the male.

spermatophore A capsule containing sperm, produced by the males of some insects.

spermatozoon (pl., *spermatozoa*) A functional, usually motile, sperm cell.

sperm duct A tube connecting the bursa copulatrix of ditrysian Lepidóptera to the vagina.

sperm follicle A tubelike subdivision of the testis in which spermatogenesis occurs.

spinasternum An intersegmental sclerite of the thoracic venter that bears a median apodeme or spina, associated with or united with the sclerite immediately anterior to it; also called the intersternite.

spindle-shaped Elongate and cylindrical, thickened in the middle and tapering at the ends.

spine A thornlike outgrowth of the cuticle.

spinneret A structure with which silk is spun, usually fingerlike in shape (Figures 6–5B, 6–8B–E, *spn*).

spinose Beset with spines; spinose costa in Díptera (Figure 32–19H).

spiracle An external opening of the tracheal system; a breathing pore (Figures 3–1, 3–25, *spr*).

spiracular bristles Bristles very close to a spiracle (Díptera; Figure 32–22, *spbr*).

spiracular plate A platelike sclerite next to or surrounding the spiracle.

spur A movable spine (when on a leg segment, usually located at the apex of the segment).

spurious claw A false claw; a stout bristle that looks like a claw (spiders).

spurious vein A veinlike thickening of the wing membrane between two true veins; an adventitious longitudinal vein between the radius and the media, crossing the r-m cross vein (Díptera, Sýrphidae; Figure 32–11A–C, *spv*).

squama (pl., *squamae*) A scalelike structure; a calypter; the palpiger (Odonàta; Figure 11–9, *plg*).

stadium (pl., *stadia*) The period between molts in a developing arthropod.

stalked With a stalk or stem; with a narrow stemlike base; of veins, fused together to form a single vein.

stemmata (sing., *stemma*) The lateral eyes of insect larvae.

sternacostal suture (or *sulcus*) A suture of the thoracic sternum, the external mark of the sternal apophysis or furca, separating the basisternum from the sternellum.

sternal apophysis (or *sternal arm*) See *furca*.

sternellum The part of the eusternum posterior to the sternacostal suture (sulcus).

sternite A subdivision of a sternum; the ventral plate of an abdominal segment.

sternopleural bristles Bristles on the sternopleuron (Díptera; Figure 32–6, *stb*).

sternopleuron (pl., *sternopleura*) A sclerite in the lateral wall of the thorax, just above the base of the middle leg (Díptera; Figure 32–6, *stpl*).

sternum (pl., *sterna*) A sclerite on the ventral side of the body; the ventral sclerite of an abdominal segment (Figure 3–1, *stn*).

stigma (pl., *stigmata*) A thickening of the wing membrane along the costal border near the apex (Figures 11–5, 11–6, 35–1, *st*).

stigmal vein A short vein extending posteriorly from the costal margin of the wing, usually a little beyond the middle of the wing (Hymenóptera; Figure 35–19B, *sv*).

stipes (pl., *stipites*) The second segment or division of a maxilla, which bears the palp, the galea, and the lacinia (Figure 3–16A, *stp*); lateral lobes of the millipede gnathochilarium (Figure 6–32B, *stp*).

stomodaeum The foregut.

storage excretion The removal of metabolic wastes by isolation within certain tissues or cells.

stria (pl., *striae*) A groove or depressed line.

striate With grooves or depressed lines.

stridulate To make a noise by rubbing two structures or surfaces together.

stripe A longitudinal color marking.

stylate With a style; stylelike; stylate antenna (Figure 3–15K).

style A bristlelike process at the apex of an antenna (Figure 3–15K, *sty*); a short slender, fingerlike process (Figure 9–1, *sty*).

stylet A needlelike structure; one of the piercing structures in sucking mouthparts.

stylus (pl. *styli*) A short, slender, fingerlike process (Figure 9–1, *sty*).

subalare (or *subalar sclerite*) An epipleurite located posterior to the pleural wing process.

subantennal sulcus A groove on the face extending ventrally from the base of the antenna (Figures 3–13, 35–17, *sas*).

subapical Located just proximad of the apex.

subbasal Located just distad of the base.

subclass A major subdivision of a class, containing a group of related orders.

subcosta The longitudinal vein between the costa and the radius (Figure 3–10, Sc).

subcoxa Leg segment of primitive arthropods basad of the coxa, hypothesized to be incorporated into the thoracic wall to form the thoracic pleurites (see *anapleurite*, *catapleurite*).

subequal Approximately, or almost, equal in size or length.

subesophageal ganglion The knotlike swelling at the anterior end of the ventral nerve cord, usually just below the esophagus (Figures 3–22, 3–26, *segn*).

subfamily A major division of a family, containing a group

of related tribes or genera. Subfamily names end in
-*inae*.

subgenal suture (or *sulcus*) The horizontal suture below
the gena, just above the bases of the mandibles and
maxillae, a lateral extension of the epistomal suture
(Figure 3–13, *sgs*).

subgenital plate A platelike sternite that underlies the
genitalia.

subgenus (pl., *subgenera*) A major subdivision of a genus,
containing a group of related species. In scientific
names, subgeneric names are capitalized and placed in
parentheses following the genus name.

subimago The first of two winged instars of a mayfly after
it emerges from the water.

submarginal cell One or more cells lying immediately
behind the marginal cell (Hymenóptera; Figure 35–3,
SM).

submarginal vein A vein immediately behind and paral-
leling the costal margin of the wing (Hymenóptera;
Figure 35–19B, *sm*).

submentum The basal part of the labium (Figure 3–16C,
smt).

subocular suture (or *sulcus*) A suture extending ventrally
from the compound eye (Figure 3–13, *sos*).

suborder A major subdivision of an order, containing a
group of related superfamilies or families.

subquadrangle A cell immediately behind the quadrangle
(Odonàta, Zygóptera; Figure 11–6, *sq*).

subspecies A subdivision of a species, usually a geographic race. The different subspecies of a species ordinarily are not sharply differentiated. They intergrade
with one another and are capable of interbreeding. (For
names of subspecies, see *scientific name.*)

subtriangle A cell or group of cells proximad of the triangle (Odonàta, Anisóptera; Figure 11–5, *str*).

successions Groups of species that successively occupy a
given habitat as the conditions of the habitat change.

sulcate With a groove or furrow.

sulcus (pl., *sulci*) A groove formed by an infolding of the
body wall (Figure 3–4); a groove or furrow.

superfamily A group of closely related families. Superfamily names end in *-òidea.*

superior appendage One of the two upper appendages at
the end of the abdomen, a cercus (Odonàta; Figure
11–4, *sap*).

supinate To turn the trailing edge of the wing downward.

supplement An adventitious vein formed by a number of
cross veins being lined up to form a continuous vein,
located behind and more or less parallel to one of the
main longitudinal veins (Odonàta; Figure 11–5, *mspl*,
rspl).

supra-alar bristles A longitudinal row of bristles on the
lateral portion of the mesonotum, immediately above
the wing base (Díptera; Figure 32–6, *spb*).

suture An external linelike groove in the body wall, or a
narrow membranous area between sclerites (Figure
3–4, *su*); the boundary between two fused sclerites;
the line of juncture of the elytra (Coleóptera).

swimmeret An abdominal appendage that functions as a
swimming organ (Crustàcea; Figure 6–24, *sw*).

symbiont An organism living in symbiosis with another
organism.

symbiosis A living together, in a more or less intimate
association, of two species, which benefits both.

symmetry A definite pattern of body organization; bilateral symmetry, a type of body organization in which
the various parts are arranged more or less symmetri-
cally on either side of a median vertical plane, that is,
where the right and left sides of the body are essentially
similar.

synchronous muscle A muscle in which each contraction
is initiated by the reception of a neuronal impulse.

synonyms Two or more names for the same thing (taxon).

systematics The study of the relationships among
organisms.

taenidium (pl., *taenidia*) A circular or spiral thickening
in the inner wall of a trachea.

tagma (pl., *tagmata*) A group of segments of the body
specialized for a given function, e.g., the head, thorax,
and abdomen of insects.

tandem One behind the other, the two connected or attached together.

tarsal claw A claw at the apex of the tarsus, derived from
the pretarsal segment of the leg (Figure 3–8, *tcl*).

tarsal formula The number of tarsal segments on the
front, middle, and hind tarsi, respectively.

tarsomere A subdivision, or "segment," of the tarsus.

tarsus (pl., *tarsi*) The leg segment immediately beyond
the tibia, sometimes consisting of one or more "segments" or subdivisions (Figure 3–8, *ts*).

taxon (pl., *taxa*) A group of organisms classified together.

taxonomy The science of classification into categories of
varying rank, and the describing and naming of these
categories.

tegmen (pl., *tegmina*) The thickened or leathery front
wing of an orthopteran.

tegula (pl., *tegulae*) A small scalelike structure overlying
the base of the front wing (Figure 35–4, *tg*).

telopod (telopodite) The portion of the leg beyond the
coxopodite.

telotrophic ovariole Meroistic ovariole in which the nurse
cells remain in the germarium.

telson The posterior part of the last abdominal segment
(Crustàcea); the posterior spinelike tail of the Xiphosùra; the posterior nonmetameric portion of the body.

tenaculum A minute structure on the ventral side of the
third abdominal segment that serves as a clasp for the
furcula (Collémbola).

teneral A term applied to recently molted, pale, soft-bodied individuals.

tentorial pits Pitlike depressions on the surface of the
head that mark the points of union of the arms of the
tentorium with the outer wall of the head. There are
usually two tentorial pits in the epistomal suture (Figure 3–13, 3–14, *atp*) and one at the lower end of each
postoccipital suture (Figure 3–13, 3–14, *ptp*).

tentorium The endoskeleton of the head, usually consisting of two pairs of apodemes (Figure 3–14).

tergite A subdivision of the tergum.

tergum (pl., *terga*)   A sclerite on the dorsal side of the body; the dorsal sclerite of an abdominal segment (Figure 3–1, *t*).

terminal   At the end; at the posterior end (of the abdomen); the last of a series.

terrestrial   Living on land.

testis (pl., *testes*)   The sex organ in the male that produces sperm (Figure 3–31B, *tst*).

thelytoky   A form of parthenogenesis in which only females are produced from unfertilized eggs, males being very rare or absent.

thorax   The body region behind the head, which bears the legs and wings (Figure 3–1, *th*).

tibia (pl., *tibiae*)   The fourth segment of the leg, between the femur and the tarsus (Figure 3–8, *tb*).

tibial spur   A large spine on the tibia, usually located at the distal end of the tibia.

tormogen cell   An epidermal cell associated with a seta, which forms the setal membrane or socket (Figure 3–2, *tmg*).

toxicognath   A poison jaw (centipedes, Figure 6–34, *pj*; a modified leg).

trachea (pl., *tracheae*)   A tube of the respiratory system, lined with taenidia, ending externally at a spiracle, and terminating internally in the tracheoles (Figure 3–25).

tracheole   The fine terminal branch of the respiratory tubes.

translucent   Allowing light to pass through, but not necessarily transparent.

transverse   Across, at right angles to the longitudinal axis.

transverse suture   A suture across the mesonotum (Díptera; Figure 32–6, *trs*).

triangle   A small triangular cell or group of cells near the base of the wing (Odonàta, Anisóptera; Figures 11–5, 11–7, *tri*).

tribe   A subdivision of a subfamily, containing a group of related genera. Names of tribes end in *-ini*.

trichobothria   Minute sensory hairs on the tarsi (spiders; Figure 6–7B, *trb*).

trichogen cell   The epidermal cell from which a seta develops (Figure 3–27, *trg*).

tripectinate   Having three rows of comblike branches.

tritocerebrum   The ventral lobes of the brain.

triungulin larva   The active first-instar larva of the Strepsíptera and certain beetles that undergo hypermetamorphosis (Figure 28–71A, 29–1F).

trochanter   The second segment of the leg, between the coxa and the femur (Figure 3–8, *tr*).

trochantin   A small sclerite in the thoracic wall immediately anterior to the base of the coxa (Figure 28–9B, *tn*).

trophallaxis   The exchange of alimentary canal liquid among colony members of social insects and guest organisms, either mutually or unilaterally; trophallaxis may be stomodeal (from the mouth) or proctodeal (from the anus).

trophocyte   See *nurse cells*.

tropism   The orientation of an animal with respect to a stimulus, either positive (turning toward the stimulus) or negative (turning away from the stimulus).

truncate   Cut off square at the end.

truss cell   See *hypostigmatic cell*.

tubercle   A small knotlike or rounded protuberance.

tylus   The clypeal region of the head (Hemíptera; Figure 24–1, *ty*).

tymbal   A sclerotized plate in the sound-producing organ of a cicada (Figure 25–11, *tmb*).

tympanal hood   One of a pair of tubercles or rounded prominences on the dorsal surface of the first abdominal segment (Lepidóptera).

tympanum (pl., *tympana*)   A vibrating membrane; an auditory membrane or eardrum (Figures 3–8D, 25–11, *tym*).

types   Specimens designated when a species or group is described to serve as the reference if there is any question about what that species or group includes. The type of a species or subspecies (the holotype) is a specimen; the type of a genus or subgenus is a species; and the type of a tribe, subfamily, family, or superfamily is a genus.

unisexual   Consisting of or involving only females.

uric acid   Chemical commonly used by terrestrial insects for excretion of nitrogenous wastes.

urine   Fluid containing excreted wastes.

urogomphi (sing., *urogomphus*)   Fixed or movable cercuslike processes on the last segment of a beetle larva (also called pseudocerci or corniculi).

uropod   One of the terminal pair of abdominal appendages, usually lobelike (Crustàcea; Figure 6–24, *ur*).

vagina   The terminal portion of the female reproductive system, which opens to the outside (Figures 3–22, 3–31A, *vag*).

valvifers   The basal plates of the ovipositor, derived from the basal segment of the gonopods.

valvulae   The three pairs of processes forming the sheath and piercing structures of the ovipositor.

vas deferens (pl., *vasa deferentia*)   The sperm duct leading away from a testis (Figure 3–31B, *vd*).

vas efferens (pl., *vasa efferentia*)   A short duct connecting a sperm tube in the testis with the vas deferens (Figure 3–31B, *ve*).

vein   A thickened line in the wing.

venter   The ventral side.

ventrad   Toward the ventral side or underside of the body; downward.

ventral   Lower or underneath; pertaining to the underside of the body.

ventriculus   Midgut.

vermiform larva   A legless wormlike larva, without a well-developed head (Figure 3–43A).

ventral nerve cord   Paired nerve lying along the lower surface of the hemocoel, containing segmentally arranged ganglia.

vermiform   Wormlike.

vertex   The top of the head, between the eyes and anterior to the occipital suture (Figure 3–13, *ver*).

vesicle   A sac, bladder, or cyst, often extensible.

vestigial Small, poorly developed, degenerate, nonfunctional.

vibrissae, oral See *oral vibrissae*.

vitellarium Portion of the ovariole in which vitellogenesis takes place.

vitelline membrane The cell wall of the insect egg; a thin membrane lying beneath the chorion (Figure 3–37, *vm*).

vitellogenesis Transfer of vitellogenins to the developing oocyte with consequent increase in size of the oocyte.

vitellogenin Yolk precursor molecule.

vulva Opening of the vagina (= ovipore).

vulvar lamina The posterior margin (usually prolonged posteriorly) of the eighth abdominal sternite (female Anisóptera).

wireworm An elateriform larva; a larva that is slender, heavily sclerotized, with few hairs on the body, and with thoracic legs but without prolegs; the larva of a click beetle (Figure 28–49B).

Y-vein Two adjacent veins fusing distally, forming a Y-shaped figure (for example, the anal veins in the front wing, Figure 34–32).

zoöphagous Feeding on animals.

References

Borror, D. J. 1960. Dictionary of Word Roots and Combining Forms. Palo Alto, Calif.: Mayfield, 134 pp.

Brown, R. W. 1954. Composition of Scientific Words. Washington, D.C.: published by the author, 882 pp.

Carpenter, J. R. 1938. An Ecological Glossary. London: Kegan, Paul, Trench, Trubner, 306 pp.; illus.

Dorland, W. A. N. 1932 (16th ed.). The American Illustrated Medical Dictionary. Philadelphia: W. B. Saunders, 1493 pp.; illus.

Hanson, D. R. 1959. A Short Glossary of Entomology with Derivations. Los Angeles: published by the author, 83 pp.

Henderson, I. F., and W. D. Henderson. 1939 (3rd ed., revised by J. H. Kenneth). A Dictionary of Scientific Terms. London: Oliver and Boyd, 383 pp.

Jaeger, E. C. 1955. A Source Book of Biological Names and Terms. Springfield, Ill.: C. C. Thomas, 317 pp.

Jardine, N. K. 1913. The Dictionary of Entomology. London: West, Newman, 259 pp.

Pennak, R. W. 1964. Collegiate Dictionary of Zoology. New York: Ronald Press, 583 pp.

Smith, J. B. 1906. Explanation of Terms Used in Entomology. Brooklyn, N.Y.: Brooklyn Entomol. Soc., 154 pp., illus.

Snodgrass, R. E. 1935. Principles of Insect Morphology. New York: McGraw-Hill, 667 pp.; illus.

Torre-Bueno, J. R. de la. 1937. A Glossary of Entomology. Lancaster, Pa.: Science Press, 336 pp.; illus.

Tuxen, S. L. (Ed.). 1970 (rev. ed.). Taxonomists Glossary of Genitalia of Insects. Copenhagen: Enjar Munksgaard, 359 pp.; illus.

Tweney, C. F., and L. E. C. Hughes (Eds.). 1940. Chambers' Technical Dictionary. New York: Macmillan, 957 pp.

Index

Numbers in italics refer to pages bearing illustrations only; numbers in boldface indicate the most important page references. Common names of species and subspecies are listed in the singular; those of more inclusive groups are listed as plurals. Many items not in this index may be found in the Glossary.

α-glycerophosphate, 43
aaroni, Neoneura, 199
Aaroniella, 268
    eertmoedi, 272
abbreviatus, Phlegyas, 304
Abdomen, 24, *25,* 26, 104, *108, 111,* 132
    segmentation of, 26
Abdullah, M., 479
Abedus, 294
abietis, Adelges, 339, *341*
abortivaria, Dyspteris, 647
Acaeliinae, 707
Acalymma vittata, 14, 459
Acalypta lillianis, 299
Acalyptratae, 501, 559
Acalyptrate muscoid flies, 501, 503, 508,
    519, *523–525,* 531, 563, 565
Acanalonia bivittata, 334
Acanaloniidae, 314, 315, *334,* **335**
Acanthametropus, 178
Acanthocephala femorata, 306
Acanthoceridae, 373
Acanthocerus aeneus, 423
Acanthoclisinae, 366, 367
Acantholyda, 666, 669, 701
Acanthopteroctetidae, 591, 597, **622**
Acanthoscelidae, 374
Acanthoscelides obtectus, 454, 455
Acanthosomatid stink bugs, 286
Acanthosomatidae, 286, 293, **308**

Acarapis, 129
    woodi, 129
Acari, 105, **124**
    classification of, 125
Acarida, 105
Acaridida, 125
Acariformes, 125, **127**
Acarina, 105
Acaroidea, **129**
Acartophthalmidae, 501, 528, **562**
Acartophthalmus nigrinus, 562
Accent
    acute, 95
    grave, 95
    rules of, 96
Accessory glands, 58
Acentropus, 621
Aceratagallia, 328, 332
    curvata, 13
    longula, 13
    obscura, 13
    sanguinolenta, 13, *330*
Acerentomidae, 164, **165**
Acerentulus barberi barberi, 165
acerifoliella, Paraclemensia, 623
Acerpenna, 178
Acetate, ethyl, 750
Acetylglucosamine, 25
Achaearanea, 120
    tepidariorum, 120

Acherontia, 83
    atropos, 83
Acheta domesticus, 224
Achilidae, 314, 316, **334**
    parasites of, 724
Achyra rantalis, 635
Acicnemidinae, 464
Acid
    tannic, 8
    uric, 47
Acidogona melanura, 562
Acinopterus, 329
    angulatus, 14
Aclerdidae, 314, 319, **342**
Acleris gloverana, 632
Acmaeodera
    prorsa, 429
    pulchella, 428
Acoma, 421, 423
Acontiinae, **659**
Acordulecera, 701
Acorduleceridae, 666
Acorn moth, 625, 626
Acorn weevils, **472,** 626
Acorns, 626
Acoustic behavior, 82
    sound production, 82
Acragidae, 592
acrea, Estigmene, 656, 657
Acrididae, 10, 53, 211, 213, **214**

Cedar, incense, 703
Cedar beetles, *38*, 373, **418**
Cedars, 629
Cediopsylla, 492, 496
Celastrina ladon, 641
Celery, 14, 560, 625, 659
Celery looper, 659
Celithemis, 198
　elisa, 198
Cell, 32
　discal, 32
　gland, *25*
　neurosecretory, 55, 57
　nurse, 56
　tormogen, *25*
　trichogen, *25*
Cellar spiders, 112, **120**
cellularis, *Sphacophilus*, 702
Cellulose, 46
celtidismamma, *Pachypsylla*, 336
Cement layer, 26
Cenocoeliinae, 707
Cenozoic era, 148
Censuses of insect populations, 779
Centipede, common house, *141*, 143
Centipedes, 16, 80, 102, *141*, **142**
　soil, **143**
　stone, **143**
Centrodora speciosissima, 713
Centroptilum, 178
Centrotinae, 325
Centruroides, 106
　sculpturatus, 106
Cephalcia, 701
Cephalocarida, 102, **134**
Cephaloidae, 374, 398, **446**
Cephalothorax, 104, *108*, 132
Cephenemyia, 570, 571
Cephidae, 666, 669, 672, 673, 674, **703**, 704
Cephoidea, 666
Cephus, 673
　cinctus, 703, *704*
　pygmaeus, 703
Cerambycidae, 75, 371, 374, *380*, 383, 400, 405, 432, 446, **449**, *450*, *451*, 455, 461
　Aseminae, 451, **452**
　Cerambycinae, 76–78, 451, **454**
　key to the subfamilies of, 450
　Lamiinae, 450, *451*, **452**, *453*
　Lepturinae, 76–78, 451, **454**
　Parandrinae, 450, **451**, *452*
　parasites of, 440
　Prioninae, 450, **452**, *453*
　Spondylinae, 450, **451**
Cerambycinae, 76–78, 451, **454**
Cerapachyinae, 739
Ceraphronidae, 667, *682*, 685, **705**, *706*
Ceraphronoidea, 667, 669, 685, 700, 704, 705
Cerastipsocus venosus, 273
Ceratina, 678, 731
　dupla, 732
Ceratinidae, 668
Ceratitis capitata, 561
Ceratocanthidae, 373

Ceratocanthinae, 419, **423**
Ceratocombidae, 286
Ceratocystus ulmi, 15
Ceratophyllidae, *491*, 492, 493, *494*, **496**
　Amphipsyllinae, 492, 494, **496**
　Ceratophyllinae, 492, 494, **496**
　Leptopsyllinae, 492, 494, **496**
Ceratophyllinae, 492, 494, **496**
Ceratophylloidea, 492
Ceratophyllus, 492, 496
　gallinae, 496
Ceratopogonidae, 77, 500, *511*, 512, 513, **545**, *547*
Cercerini, 727
Cerceris clypeata, 727
cercerisella, *Gelechia*, 625
Cercocarpus, 626, 647
Cercopidae, 314, 318, **325**
Cercus, *25*, 28
Cercyonis, 599
　pegala, 644
Cereal leaf beetle, 458, *459*
Cereal stem moth, 592, 629
cerealella, *Sitotroga*, 627
cerealellae, *Habrocytus*, 718
Cereals, 355, 425, 431, 436, 446, 566, 636
cerealum, *Limothrips*, 355
ceriferus, *Ceroplastes*, 342
Cernotina, 582
Cerobasis, 270
Cerococcidae, 314, 320, **343**
Cerococcus, 343
　kalmiae, 343
　quercus, 343
Cerodontha dorsalis, 563
Cerophytidae, 374, 403, **429**
Cerophytum, 429
Ceroplastes, 342
　ceriferus, 342
Cerostoma, 617
Cerotoma variegata, 13
Ceruridae, 592
Cervical sclerite, 28, *29*
Cervidae, parasites of, 571
cervinus, *Pantomorus*, 470
Cervix, 28, *29*, 35
cervula, *Ischnura*, *188*, 200
Cerylon, 392, 441
　castaneum, 441
Cerylonidae, 374, 392, **441**
Cetoniinae, 421, *424*, **425**, 426
Ceuthophilinae, 211
Ceuthophilus, 222
　maculatus, *222*
Ceutorhynchinae, 466, **473**
Ceutorhynchus rapae, 473
Chaetocnema pulicaria, 14, 460
Chaetopsylla, 492, 496
Chaetosema, 589
Chaetosiphon fragaefolii, 67
Chaetotaxy, **506**, *507*
Chafer, rose, 16, 424
Chafers, **423**, 424
　shining leaf, **424**
Chagas disease, 20, 303

Chalarus, 519
Chalastogastra, 666
Chalcedectidae, 667
Chalcedectinae, 719
Chalcid
　apple seed, *716*
　clover seed, 69, *713*, *716*, 719
Chalcidae, 667
Chalcididae, 667, 686, 687, 692, 717, *718*, **719**
Chalcidoidea, 9, 37, *38*, 75, 77, 148, 153, 303, 667–670, 672, 686, 687, 688, 690, 692, 700, 705, **711**, 712, *713–716*, *718*, 720, 723
　parasites of, *713*, 714
Chalcidoids, seed, 667, **719**
chalcidophagus, *Merisoporus*, 718
Chalcophora fortis, 427
chalybea, *Altica*, 460
Chalybion californicum, 725
Chamaemyia, *524*, *525*
Chamaemyidae, 502
Chamaemyiidae, 502, *524*, *525*, 529, 530, **565**
Chamber
　filter, 46
　genital, 57
Chamberlin, R. V., 139
champlaini, *Agrilus*, 426, *429*
Channel
　food, *40–42*
　salivary, *40–42*
Chaoboridae, 500, 513, **541**
Chaoborus, 50, 541
　flavicans, *541*
Chapman, R. F., 43
Charaxinae, 644
Charidotella bicolor, 460
Charipinae, 719
charitonius, *Heliconius*, 642
Chauliodes, 363, 364
Chauliodidae, 592
Chauliognathidae, 374
Chauliognathus, *402*, 433
　pennsylvanicus, 433
Checkered beetles, 374, **437**, *438*
Checkered skipper, 637
Checkerspots, 592, **643**
Cheese skipper, 15, 561, *563*
Cheimophila salicella, 626
Cheleutoptera, 148
Chelicera, 103, *108*, *109*
Chelicerata, 102, **103**
　collecting and preserving, 131
　references on, 144
Chelisoches morio, 245
Chelisochidae, 244, **245**
Chelonariidae, 373, 402, **427**
Chelonarium lecontei, 427
Chelonethida, 105
Cheloninae, 707, 709
Chelonus texanus, 709
Chelopistes meleagridis, 278, 281
Chelymorpha, 456
　cassidea, 460, *461*
Chemical communication, 85
Chemical defenses of insects, 4, 79